UNIVERSAL TERRORS, 1951–1955

Interview Books by Tom Weaver

A Sci-Fi Swarm and Horror Horde: Interviews with 62 Filmmakers (2010)

I Talked with a Zombie: Interviews with 23 Veterans of Horror and Sci-Fi Films and Television (2009; paperback 2014)

Earth vs. the Sci-Fi Filmmakers: 20 Interviews (2005; paperback 2014)

Double Feature Creature Attack: A Monster Merger of Two More Volumes of Classic Interviews (2003)

(A combined edition of the two earlier Weaver titles *Attack of the Monster Movie Makers* and *They Fought in the Creature Features*)

Eye on Science Fiction: 20 Interviews with Classic SF and Horror Filmmakers (2003; paperback 2007)

Science Fiction Confidential: Interviews with 23 Monster Stars and Filmmakers (2002; paperback 2010)

I Was a Monster Movie Maker: Conversations with 22 SF and Horror Filmmakers (2001; paperback 2011)

Return of the B Science Fiction and Horror Heroes: The Mutant Melding of Two Volumes of Classic Interviews (2000)

(A combined edition of the two earlier Weaver titles *Interviews with B Science Fiction and Horror Movie Makers* and *Science Fiction Stars and Horror Heroes*)

Science Fiction and Fantasy Film Flashbacks: Conversations with 24 Actors, Writers, Producers and Directors from the Golden Age (1998; paperback 2004)

It Came from Horrorwood: Interviews with Moviemakers in the SF and Horror Tradition (1996; paperback 2004)

They Fought in the Creature Features: Interviews with 23 Classic Horror, Science Fiction and Serial Stars (1995; paperback 2014)

Attack of the Monster Movie Makers: Interviews with 20 Genre Giants (1994; paperback 2014)

Science Fiction Stars and Horror Heroes: Interviews with Actors, Directors, Producers and Writers of the 1940s through 1960s (1991; paperback 2006)

Interviews with B Science Fiction and Horror Movie Makers: Writers, Producers, Directors, Actors, Moguls and Makeup (1988; paperback 2006)

Other Books by Tom Weaver

John Carradine: The Films (1999; paperback 2008)

Poverty Row HORRORS! Monogram, PRC and Republic Horror Films of the Forties (1993; paperback 1999)

By Tom Weaver with Michael Brunas and John Brunas

Universal Horrors: The Studio's Classic Films, 1931–1946, 2d ed. (1990; illustrated casebound 2007)

By Tom Weaver with David Schecter and Steve Kronenberg

The Creature Chronicles: Exploring the Black Lagoon Trilogy (2014)

All from McFarland

Universal Terrors, 1951–1955

Eight Classic Horror and Science Fiction Films

Tom Weaver *with* David Schecter,
Robert J. Kiss *and* Steve Kronenberg

McFarland & Company, Inc., Publishers
Jefferson, North Carolina

The chapters on *Creature from the Black Lagoon* and *Revenge of the Creature* are abridged from chapters in *The Creature Chronicles: Exploring the Black Lagoon Trilogy* by Tom Weaver, David Schecter and Steve Kronenberg (McFarland, 2014).

LIBRARY OF CONGRESS CATALOGUING-IN-PUBLICATION DATA

Names: Weaver, Tom, 1958– author. | Schecter, David- author. | Kiss, Robert J., 1973– author. | Kronenberg, Steve, 1950– author.
Title: Universal terrors, 1951–1955 : eight classic horror and science fiction films / Tom Weaver with David Schecter, Robert J. Kiss and Steve Kronenberg.
Description: Jefferson, N.C. : McFarland & Company, Inc., Publishers, 2017. | Includes bibliographical references and index.
Identifiers: LCCN 2017019920 | ISBN 9780786436149 (softcover : acid free paper) ♾
Subjects: LCSH: Horror films—United States—History and criticism. | Universal Pictures Corporation.
Classification: LCC PN1995.9.H6 W393 2017 | DDC 791.43/617—dc23
LC record available at https://lccn.loc.gov/2017019920

BRITISH LIBRARY CATALOGUING DATA ARE AVAILABLE

ISBN (print) 978-0-7864-3614-9
ISBN (ebook) 978-1-4766-2776-2

Front cover artwork by Kerry Gammill

Printed in the United States of America

McFarland & Company, Inc., Publishers
Box 611, Jefferson, North Carolina 28640
www.mcfarlandpub.com

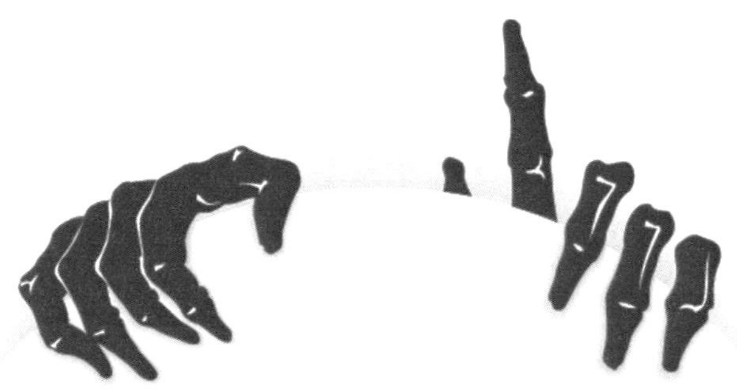

To the memory of producer William Alland,

the workhorse of the Universal lot in the 1950s, responsible for the starting lineup of new Universal monsters: the Xenomorphs, the Gill Man, the Metaluna Mutant, Tarantula and more;

And to Ned Comstock,

the workhorse of the USC Cinematic Arts Library. Nobody whose name isn't on the cover worked on this book more than Ned did.

Table of Contents

Introduction	1
The Strange Door (1951)	3
The Black Castle (1952)	52
It Came from Outer Space (1953)	88
Creature from the Black Lagoon (1954)	164
This Island Earth (1955)	209
Revenge of the Creature (1955)	279
Cult of the Cobra (1955)	309
Tarantula (1955)	359
Notes	411
Index	423

Opposite, clockwise from top left: Leo G. Carroll in *Tarantula*; the Glob look of *It Came from Outer Space*; *Creature from the Black Lagoon*; *This Island Earth*; Boris Karloff in *The Strange Door*; the spaceship from *It Came from Outer Space*.

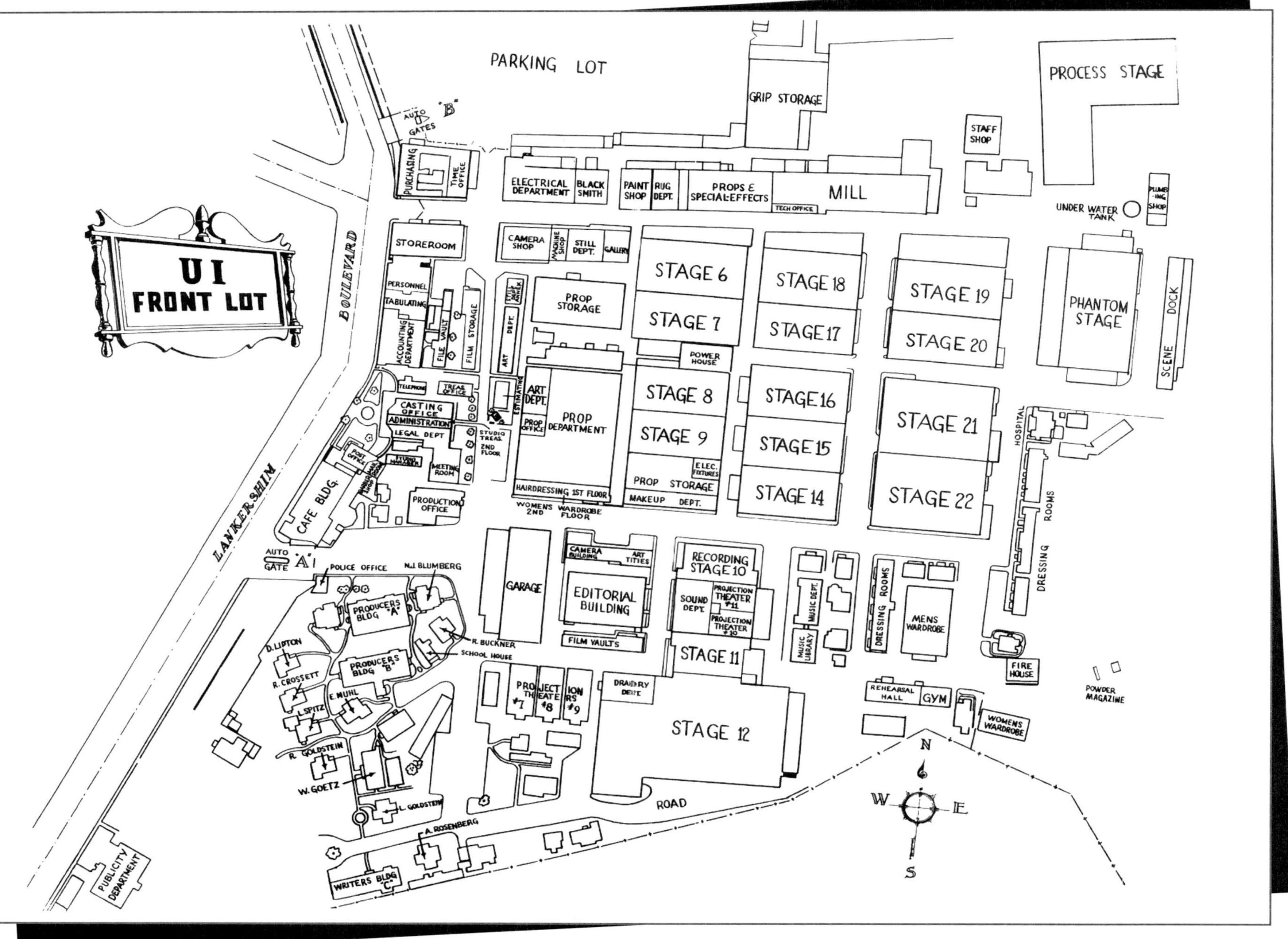

In 1951, a 24-page booklet titled "Eyeing UI" was created for visiting sales executives. In the introduction, interestingly, Universal was called "the plant" where its moviemakers work. The centerfold was this map of the layout of the front lot. Many of the stages and other buildings will be mentioned throughout this book.

Introduction

When a Hollywood movie becomes a big success, you don't have to wait 27 years for a sequel. But that's how long the world has had to wait for this book, a follow-up to 1990's *Universal Horrors: The Studio's Classic Films, 1931–1946* by Michael Brunas, John Brunas and Tom Weaver (me). The long national nightmare is over, you now hold it in your hands. Or maybe somebody's holding it *for* you. For a gaggle of folks who call themselves Monster **Kids**, we're sure startin' to look a little geriatric. We lucky ones who are still on this side of the grass. (McFarland sent me a contract to write this book in June 1997, with a deadline of June 1, 1999. As I sheepishly submitted the manuscript in 2016, one of the McFarland poobahs tried to assuage my guilt—or, more likely, to make me feel worse—by pointing out, "You're only one millennium late!" A second McFarland McWisenheimer chimed in, "We're excited to have the manuscript in house; our correspondence dates back to '96. That's 1896, I believe.")

Fortunately/unfortunately (choose one), this book is like a movie sequel whose creators hope you have only a vague recall of the original movie, because the follow-up isn't consistent with it. For the convenience, and the sanity, of this book's authors, the ground rules this time are very different.

When the Bruni and I wrote *Universal Horrors*, we tossed in everything plus the Carpathian sink: We included every Universal horror movie made between 1931 and 1946 *and*, as long as we were at it, we figured, why not cover the quasi-horror movies? Soon we also found ourselves writing about movies that weren't horror by any stretch of the imagination but were *advertised* as horror (*Secret of the Chateau, The Man Who Reclaimed His Head*, more). Several of Universal's 12 Sherlock Holmes movies were horror, and we figured, "Why write about half of them, why not write about *all* of them?," which led to the inclusion of *Sherlock Holmes in Washington, Pursuit to Algiers, Dressed to Kill* and others that are horror movies like Rondo Hatton was a bobby-soxer. We included *Night Key* only because it had a horror star (Boris Karloff) *in* it. How we missed covering *Postal Inspector* with Bela Lugosi, I cannot explain. Oh, wait a minute: In the second edition, we wrote about that one too!

We could (and did) do this for the *1931–1946* book *becauuuuuse* ... each entry was just a few pages, no great effort, so where was the harm?

Well, the Universal fright flicks of the 1950s are (*duh!*) newer, some as much as 30 years, and therefore much more production paperwork exists and, for a while anyway, many more of the moviemakers still dwelt in the land of the interview-able living. This book's average chapter came to 135 manuscript pages—so lengthy that our coverage of these movies is being split into *three* books: the Gill Man monograph *The Creature Chronicles* (published in 2014); this book; and the eventual sequel (1956–1960). Do you think the Bruni and I would have included *Secret of the Chateau* in *Universal Horrors* if the chapter had to be 135 pages long? And would you have read it? Did you even read the three-page *Secret of the Chateau* chapter John Brunas did write? I thought not!

So for better or worse, *Universal Terrors, 1951–1955* brings you only the gen-yoo-wine Universal horror and monster movies of that era. To stray off into horror-comedies like the Abbott and Costellos might have been okay, and that possibility was considered, but ... *Meet the Invisible Man, ... Meet the Mummy*, etc., would have opened the door to the sci-fi *Abbott and Costello Go to Mars*, which has no horror or monsters. And then we would have been obliged to write about the sci-fi *Ma and Pa Kettle Back on the Farm* (1951). No fantasy films, because that would necessitate chapters on *You Never Can Tell* (1951), about a poisoned German Shepherd reincarnated as a man; *It Grows on Trees* (1952), about a Connecticut housewife whose backyard tree sprouts $5 bills; *Harvey* (1950), *Bonzo Goes to College* (1952), the whole Francis the Talking Mule series, Arabian Nights movies where "magicky" stuff happens, *ad nauseam.* Can you imagine reading 135 pages about each of these? Thirty-five pages? Would you believe … *five* pages? I thought not! We could have written *Universal Horrors*-length chapters about these tangential movies and intermingled them with the 135-page chapters, but how ridiculous and lopsided would that have looked?

All those other movies will be covered in an appendix at the end of the follow-up book, if by a miracle McFarland remembers the insincere promise I've just made and forces me to do it. In the meantime, *Universal Terrors* will laser-focus on the studio's straight-up chillers and monster movies, with as much information as my co-authors and I could find and as many interesting (we hope) observations as we could make. From a galaxy of friends old and new, we got a lot of help in the "information" and "interesting observations" departments, and also the "rare photos" department and a dozen other departments. Their noble ranks include:

Everett Aaker, Julie Adams, Ron Adams, John Agar, Susan Alland, William Alland, John Antosiewicz, Brad Arrington, Buddy Barnett, Mike Barnum, Sally Baskin, Marty Baumann, Wayne Berwick, Judeena Blackmer, Michael F. Blake, Ted Bohus, Steve Boone, Margaret Borst, Ronald V. Borst, Robert Boyle, Ray Bradbury, Gibby Brand, Patrick Briggs, Pat H. Broeske, Ricou Browning, John Brunas, Mike Brunas, Jon Burlingame, Bob Burns, Kathy Burns, John Carpenter, Sandy King Carpenter, Elspeth Carroll, Ben Chapman, Lissa Morrow Christian, all the great folks on the Classic Horror Film Board, Jim Clatterbaugh, Marian Clatterbaugh, John Clymer, Richard Collins, David Colton, Ned Comstock, Heidi Conley, Deborah Corday, Mara Corday, Henry Corden, William Cottrell, Ann Cullen, Richard E. Cunha, Joe Dante, Dee Denning, Richard Denning, Bruce Dettman, Faith Domergue, Ross Elliott, Sue Elliott, Glenn Erickson, Henry Escalante, Harry Essex, Julian Fant, Michael Fitzgerald, Sally Forrest, Judy Fresco, Robert M. Fresco, Jody Frisch, Bob Furmanek, Scott Gallinghouse, Kerry Gammill, Ramona Garcia, Dorothy Gertz, Irving Gertz, Bruce Goldstein, R.W. Goodwin, Alex Gordon, Richard Gordon, Daniel Griffith, Harald Gruenberger, John Guth, Brett Halsey, Susan Hart, Richard Heft, Tom Hennesy, John Herbert, D.J. Hoek, Roy Hofheinz, Joyce Holden, Robert Hoy, Kathleen Hughes, Marsha Hunt, Gordon Hunter, Joe Indusi, Jeff Janeczko, Russell Johnson, Joe Kane, Larry Kartiganer, Dr. Annette Kaufman, Douglas Kennedy, Jack Kevan, Bob King, Greg Kintz, Hal Lane, Renee Le Feuvre, Harris Lentz, Donna Lucas, Tim Lucas, Greg MacAyeal, Adie Grey Mackenzie, Boyd Magers, William Malone, Ginny Mancini, Henry Mancini, Greg Mank, Kevin Marrazzo, Mark Martucci, Dr. Carl Mason, Elizabeth Maury, Kathleen Mayne, Dave McDonnell, Charles McNabb, Kenny Miller, John Morgan, Jeff Morrow, Bruce Mozert, Edward Mussallem, Dave Narz, John Narz, MaryLou Narz, Robert Neill, Lori Nelson, Ted Newsom, Debra Paget, Kit Parker, Michael Pate, Carol Peterson, Joseph Pevney, William Phipps, Tao Porchon, Larry Powell, Fred Olen Ray, Rex Reason, Shirley Ann Reason, Joe Reiner, William Reynolds, Gary Rhodes, Alan K. Rode, Allan Rosen, Arthur Ross, Ethmer Roten, Alexander Rotter, C. Robert Rotter, Angie Rubin, Eduardo Rubio, Mary Runser, Barbara Rush, Hans J. Salter, Jay Sayer, Dan Scapperotti, David Schow, Rich Scrivani, Gloria Selph, Robert Skotak, Chris Soldo, Ginger Stanley, Richard Stapley, Herman Stein, Bonnie Stevenson, Stephen Strimpell, Tony Timpone, Mamie Van Doren, Kate Vukovich, Laura Wagner, Ray Walston, Michelle Weis, Dawn Wells, June Wilkinson, Lucy Chase Williams, Wade Williams, Annie Wollock, Tom Woodruff, Jim Wynorski and John Zacherle.

This book includes chapters on *Creature from the Black Lagoon* and *Revenge of the Creature* even though they were covered in *The Creature Chronicles*, which you already own (right??). That's because *this* book needed to be "complete" in its coverage of horror and monster flicks, 1951–55. The *Black Lagoon* and *Revenge* chapters herein are *vastly* abridged versions of their *Creature Chronicles* chapters.

There are more introductory comments that I could make, but seeing as how my deadline was 1999 and it's now 2017, I should get going. See you again in 2033!

—**Tom Weaver**

The Strange Door (1951)

A note on this book's lists of crew members: Universal's Daily Production Reports list uncredited workers by last name only ("Still Photographer: Walling," "Best Boy: Burnette," etc.). I've included them anyway, and in many cases I have parenthetically made safe guesses as to who the people might be; for instance, there was at that time a script clerk named Connie Earle, so you'll see on the following crew list "Script Clerk: Earle (Connie Earle?)." Perhaps some future researcher will dig deeper and improve upon these lists.

Full Credit Information

CREDITS: Produced by Ted Richmond; Directed by Joseph Pevney; Screenplay: Jerry Sackheim; Based on the Short Story "The Sire de Malétroit's Door" by Robert Louis Stevenson; Photography: Irving Glassberg; Editor: Edward Curtiss; Art Directors: Bernard Herzbrun and Eric Orbom; Set Decorators: Russell A. Gausman and Julia Heron; Sound:

Leslie I. Carey and Glenn E. Anderson; Music Director: Joseph Gershenson; Costumes: Rosemary Odell; Makeup: Bud Westmore; Hair Stylist: Joan St. Oegger; UNCREDITED: Music Conductor: Joseph Gershenson; Tracked Music Composers: Hans J. Salter, Frank Skinner, Charles Previn, Paul Dessau, William Lava, Paul Sawtell, Edward Ward and Miklós Rózsa; Musicians: Emo Neufeld, George Kast, Manuel Compinsky, Louis Pressman, Ambrose Russo, Lou Klass, Sam Fordis, Leon Goldwasser, Samuel Cytron, Sarah Kreindler (Violin), Joseph Reilich, Cecil Bonvalot, Harriet Payne (Viola), Joseph Ullstein, Stephen De'ak, Lajos Shuk (Cello), Harold E. Brown (Bass), Arthur C. Smith, Ethmer Roten, Jr. (Flute), Arthur Gault (Oboe), Blake Reynolds, Alan Harding, Karl Leaf (Clarinet), Lloyd Hildebrand (Bassoon), Willard Culley, Jr., Alfred Williams (Horn), Gene LaFreniere, Don Linder, Robert Goodrich (Trumpet), John Stanley, Bruce Squires, H.L. Menge (Trombone), Harold McDonald, Ralph Collier (Drums), Lyman Gandee, Al Mack (Piano), Joseph Quintile (Harp), Chauncey Haines (Novachord), Edwin C. Miller (Guitar); Production Manager: James Pratt; Unit Production Manager: Edward Dodds; Assistant Director: Jesse Hibbs; Second Assistant Director: Les Warner; Dialogue Director: Irvin Berwick; Special Effects: David S. Horsley; Camera Operator: Kyme Meade; Assistant Cameraman: Haddow (Ledge Haddow?); Still Photographer: Walling (William Walling?); First Grip: Brown (Everett Brown?); Second Grip: Losey (Art Losey?); Gaffer: Kurland (Norton Kurland?); Best Boy: Burnette (Lester Burnette?); First Prop Man: Robert Laszlo; Assistant Prop Man: Lawrence (Carl Lawrence?); Wardrobe Men: Eli (Truman Eli?) and Martin; Makeup: Armstrong (Del Armstrong?) and Perell (Sid Perell?); Hair Stylist: Forman (Ray Forman?); Sound Recordist: Rixey (John W. Rixey?); Mike Man: Mitchell; Cable Man: Healey; Script Clerk: Earle (Connie Earle?); Stand-in: Douglas Wall; 81 minutes.

CAST: Charles Laughton (*Sire Alan de Maletroit*), Boris Karloff (*Voltan*), Sally Forrest (*Blanche de Maletroit*), Richard Stapley (*Denis de Beaulieu*), William Cottrell (*Corbeau*), Alan Napier (*Count Grassin*), Morgan Farley (*Rinville*), Paul Cavanagh (*Edmond de Maletroit*), Michael Pate (*Talon*); UNCREDITED: Claudia Jordon (*Singer*), Monique Chantel, Tao Porchon, Chantal De Leca (*Barmaids*), Jack Chefe, Albert Petit, Barry Norton (*Townsmen*), Charles Horvath (*Turec*), Eddie Parker (*Moret*), Jennings Miles (*Denis' Coachman*), Sol Gorss, Don Turner (*Guards*), Keith McConnell (*Second Courier*), Patrick Whyte (*Butcher*), George Kirby (*Cook*), Michael Hadlow (*Wine Steward*), Herbert Evans (*Clergyman*), Stanley Mann (*Servant*), Harry Cording (*Sleeping Barracks Room Guard*), Bruce Riley (*Footman*), Sailor Vincent (*Stunt Double for Charles Laughton*), Don Turner (*Stunt Double for Boris Karloff*), Paul Baxley, Sol Gorss, Tom Steele (*Stunt Doubles for Richard Stapley*), Carey Loftin (*Stunt Double for William Cottrell*), Wes Hopper.

Production History

By Tom Weaver

Could someone at Universal have had a "thing" for doors? Right from 1931, the kickoff of the studio's first and greatest horror cycle, some of the movies' most unforgettable moments involved doors, doorways and dramatic entrances.

Remember the Monster's (Boris Karloff) first appearance in the 1931 *Frankenstein*, backing through a doorway into Henry Frankenstein's laboratory and then, still framed in the entrance, turning to face Arthur Edeson's camera in that haunting close-closer-closest sequence of shots. In Karloff's next Universal horror *The Old Dark House* (1932), audiences get their initial glimpse at the actor as the butler Morgan in a shot in which we watch from outside as he

Even after science fiction films became the rage in the 1950s, Universal stuck to their Gothic guns with movies like "Robert Louis Stevenson's *THE STRANGE DOOR*" (that's the on-screen title) with Boris Karloff.

opens the Old Dark Front Door a crack, more and more of his scarred ugliness revealed in tight close-up as the door opens wider. Next, in *The Mummy* (1932), Boris' Ardath Bey is first seen in an inside-looking-out set-up, through the slats of the louver door of the expedition's hut-headquarters; once he opens it, he remains regally rooted in the entryway for a "Take a good look" moment. In *The Invisible Man* (1933), the bundled-up, bandaged, black-goggled Invisible One (Claude Rains) positions himself in the Lion's Head Inn doorway, high-and-mightily surveying the roomful of frightened yokels while the fierce winter storm bites at his back. Even in *Dracula* (1931), the terror really begins when the front door of Count Dracula's Transylvanian castle lair opens without human agency, to the astonishment of the newly arrived "unwary fly" Renfield (Dwight Frye).

Then in 1951, Universal re-entered the horror arena with a combination chiller-costume melodrama in which the ornate door of a centuried chateau plays the title role (the name of the movie during production was, in fact, simply *The Door*) and actually assumes a pivotal part in the proceedings.

The Strange Door was based on "The Sire de Malétroit's Door" by Robert Louis Stevenson, one of Scotland's masters of prose, from the adventure yarns *Treasure Island* and *The Master of Ballantrae* to the terror tales "The Body-Snatcher" and *The Strange Case of Dr. Jekyll and Mr. Hyde.* One of the twentysomething writer's first ventures into fiction, the short story was initially published in *Temple Bar* magazine in 1878.

In the story "The Sire de Malétroit's Door" by Robert Louis Stevenson (pictured), Denis de Beaulieu is a sobersided 21-year-old soldier; *Strange Door* screenwriter Jerry Sackheim made Denis the bad apple on a proud parental tree. Could Sackheim have derived inspiration from RLS's own life? Stevenson went through a phase where he was such a habitué of low dives and brothels that his parents were ready to disown him.

"The Sire de Malétroit's Door": Synopsis

Denis de Beaulieu, a cavalier "not yet two-and-twenty," visits the town of Château Landon in September 1429, "a rough, warfaring epoch." After calling on a friend and remaining long past midnight, the young Frenchman tries to find his way back to his inn through the moonless, starless night, but is soon lost in the near-total blackness. On a quiet by-street, fleeing a party of presumably drunken men-at-arms ("It was as like as not that they would kill [Denis] like a dog and leave him where he fell"), Denis leans against the oak door of an elaborate house. It unexpectedly opens on noiseless hinges, Denis stumbles inside, and the door swings shut with a sound like the falling of an automatic bar: "The inner surface [of the door] was quite smooth, not a handle, not a moulding, not a projection of any sort. He got his finger-nails round the edges and pulled, but the mass was immovable."

Denis has fallen into a trap set by the house's owner Alain, Sire de Malétroit, a white-haired, pink-bearded old gent. De Malétroit's orphaned niece Blanche has, in the old man's eyes, dishonored the family by catching the fancy of a young captain and accepting letters he silently passed to her in church. One day after Mass, de Malétroit took from her hand a new letter which contained the captain's request that she leave the door of her home open some evening so that they might finally have a few words. Denis having entered the house in the dead of night, de Malétroit is convinced that he is the smitten captain. Backed by armed men, de Malétroit announces to Denis that he has two hours to agree to marry Blanche, or he will be hanged from a rope dangling from an iron ring outside one of the house's great windows.

Denis is left alone with the young and beautiful Blanche, who is already dressed as a bride. Sobbing, she tells him the above-described background story, and Denis is sympathetic to her plight (and attracted to her). As the deadline looms and the sun begins to rise, Denis tells her,

"I would as gladly leap out of that window into the empty air as lay a finger on you without your free and full consent. But if you care for me at all do not let me lose my life in a misapprehension; for I love you better than the whole world! and though I will die for you blithely, it would be like all the joys of Paradise to live on and spend my life in your service."

"After all that you have heard?" she whispered, leaning towards him with her lips and eyes.

"I have heard nothing," he replied.

"The captain's name was Florimond de Champdivers," she said in his ear.

"I did not hear it," he answered, taking her supple body in his arms and covering her wet face with kisses.

A melodious chirping was audible behind, followed by a beautiful chuckle, and the voice of Messire de Malétroit wished his new nephew a good morning.

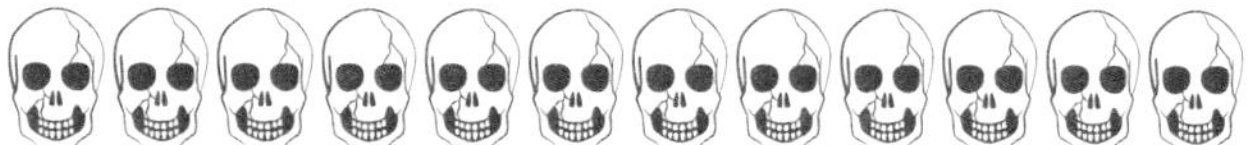

Filled with courtly, perfumed dialogue of the type above, this quaintly romantic tale of a medieval shotgun wedding was hardly the stuff of nightmares. So to *Strange Door* screenwriter Jerry Sackheim (1904–79) fell the task of providing the additional elements expected in a movie from Screen Horror's cathedral, Universal. Beginning in the mid–1930s, Sackheim's writing résumé is a long list of now-unremembered programmers; one of them, Republic's *The Fatal Witness* (1945), was highlighted by the climactic appearance of a ghost. With the coming of television, Sackheim branched out into that new medium, penning *Science Fiction Theatre*s, *Highway Patrols*, *Lassie*s *et al.* The fantasy-adventure *The Boy and the Pirates* (1960), which Sackheim co-wrote with wife Lillie Hayward, was one of his last credits prior to his 1961 retirement; he thereafter devoted himself to his two hobbies, American antiques and dog breeding. Leaving no survivors upon his death at age 74, he willed his estate to Actors and Others for Animals.

Dragging "The Sire de Malétroit's Door" into the horror realm was accomplished by adding such great Gothic desirerata as an architectural maelstrom of a chateau, peepholes a-plenty (every one comes complete with an eye), ghostly wailing, torture chamber, etc. The final product is, in fact, a well-disguised remake of Universal's *The Raven* (1935): A man (Bela Lugosi's Dr. Vollin in *The Raven*, Charles Laughton's de Maletroit in *The Strange Door*) wants to "tear torture out of himself" by taking it out on others. In both movies, Karloff plays the villain's unwilling henchman and has a loyalty to the girl which makes his creepy character more audience-friendly. The respective arch-villains first imprison the girl's father below their homes, then put the girl *and* her man in a room with crushing walls. Karloff, coming to their rescue, fights with the villain. The innocents are freed by Karloff, who succumbs to injuries sustained in battle, and the villain is crushed to death by his own torture device.[1]

The film was first announced as *The Door,* which remained its title throughout production. Assigned to direct: 39-year-old Joseph Pevney, who began his show biz career in 1924 as a boy soprano on the vaudeville circuit in his native New York City. Roles on Broadway followed, then marriage to former child star Mitzi Green. His 1946 movie debut was in *Nocturne*, a whodunnit in which it turns out that Pevney dunnit. The following year he was excellent in the prizefight classic *Body and Soul* as up-and-coming boxer John Garfield's best friend and manager (he fatally runs afoul of Garfield's ruthless new "owner," gambler Lloyd Gough).

In the Stevenson story, the sire was a little old gentleman whose countenance "had a strongly masculine cast; not properly human, but such as we see in the bull, the goat, or the domestic boar; something equivocal and wheedling, something greedy, brutal, and dangerous. ... [T]he smile, the peaked eyebrows, and the small, strong eyes were quaintly and almost comically evil in expression. Beautiful white hair hung straight all round his head, like a saint's." In the movie, Charles Laughton just looks like a "Peer of Sneer"—which is what the pressbook called him! (Photograph courtesy Ronald V. Borst/Hollywood Movie Posters.)

In 1950, Pevney made his directing bow via Universal's crime melodrama *Shakedown*. Early in his Universal directing career he specialized in action pictures, including the highly successful *Iron Man* (1951), another boxing story, which makes him seem an offbeat choice for *The Strange Door*. "I don't know *why* I did *The Strange Door*," he admitted to me. "I was a new director and I was *assigned* movies in those days, and they told me, 'This is what you're gonna do.' I'd do three or four pictures a year, when I started. But as I stayed with the studio and people got to know me (I was there for nine years, which I think was unheard-of in those days), I was able to turn things down."[2]

The sire (Charles Laughton, standing) and the boys in his band, Rinville (Morgan Farley, left) and Corbeau (William Cottrell). Surely Universal didn't intend for members of the movie's rogues gallery to come across as gay; but as Laughton once famously said, "They can't censor the gleam in my eye." (Photograph courtesy John Antosiewicz.)

It may be amusing to note that Laughton reported to Universal to play *The Strange Door*'s sadistic sicko Alan de Maletroit immediately following the wind-up of a ten-performance Bible-reading tour. His $25,000 payday for *Strange Door* ($8333.33 a week for three weeks) was less than the $100,000-per-picture he earned in better days, but a huge improvement over the pittances he had been recently receiving for his labors in the "little theater" vineyards. On May 14, the day prior to the start of shooting *The Strange Door*, Laughton, Karloff, romantic leads Richard Stapley and Sally Forrest, supporting player William Cottrell and director Pevney were medically examined at the studio for insurance purposes and all were found to be fit except Karloff, who because of his age, 63, was accepted for accident-only. A studio memo pointed out that "sickness insurance may be provided at an additional rate."

Synopsis

The Strange Door opens in a village in France in the 18th century (as opposed to the Stevenson story's 1429). As in the second paragraph of the Stevenson story, night winds sweep the wet cobblestone streets and dead leaves run riot. A horse-drawn coach (complete with footman) stops in front of a tavern, Le Lion Rouge, and Alan, the Sire de Maletroit (Charles Laughton), disembarks. Inside, the aristocrat shoots a disdainful look at a girl singer and ignores a barmaid (subtext!) as he crosses the room to sit at a table where he holds darkly ominous council with his confederates Corbeau (William Cottrell) and Rinville (Morgan Farley). At the bar across the room is Denis de Beaulieu (Richard Stapley), a young wastrel with his long dark hair gathered in a ribbon at the back of his head. He is admiring a pretty barmaid's (Tao Porchon) contours Braille style; when she tries to get away, he roughly crushes her against himself and kisses her. Observing the scene, the animated Rinville babbles, "Believe me, sire, he is all that you could ask for. A drunken, brawling, cheating villain!"

"His sins would make the Devil blush," adds the blasé Corbeau.

After de Maletroit expresses satisfaction with the blackguard who has been pointed out to him, he and his two cronies exit. Now, as they've pre-arranged, a burly patron, Turec (Charles Horvath), antagonizes and attacks Denis and a brawl begins. Another de Maletroit henchman, Moret (Eddie Parker), conspicuously places a pistol on the bar; Denis, pushed against the bar, picks it up. Turec pulls his own pistol from his belt and shoots. Denis fires a reply. Turec crumples to the floor.

"Murderer! He's killed Turec! *Get* him!" Moret shouts to the onlookers, and Denis finds himself battling assorted attackers who apparently object to a self-defense killing. Making a swashbuckling swinging-chandelier escape, Denis climbs into a public coach *very* conveniently stationed just outside, ordering the driver (Jennings Miles) to take him to Paris. The driver (yet *another* de Maletroit minion) whips up the horses—but then, just outside town, stops, climbs down from his perch and tells Denis to pay in advance. With the now-mounted, torch-carrying tavern mob riding into view, Denis is forced to flee on foot into the nearby woods. He soon finds himself outside a chateau; it's environed by dead-looking trees and the ground around it is covered in fog on this otherwise fogless night, just like in a horror movie. When he leans against its huge, iron-studded door, it yields behind his weight so that he topples inside, and then closes with a noise like the falling of an automatic bar. Reaching for a knob and seeing that there *is* none, Denis realizes he is trapped.

Sitting placidly in a library wing chair is de Maletroit, who knows Denis' name and calls him "nephew." (Denis: "'Nephew'? What gibberish is this? I'd as soon a baboon were my uncle!") De Maletroit, sly and unctuous, playing with a key on the end of a chain, mystifies Denis by knowing all about the tavern fracas, and says that Denis must marry his (de Maletroit's) niece Blanche. Obviously the sire is nuts so Denis bolts, rushing out of the room through a draped doorway—but then there's the sound of a struggle, and moments later he is hauled back in by two of the sire's guards. Talon (Michael Pate), another de Maletroit toady, accompanies the guards as they drag Denis through the hallways, which eerily echo with the sound of a man's wailing.

The movie's most put-upon character, beyond a "chateau" of a doubt: Paul Cavanagh's Edmond, imprisoned in what a *Strange Door* poster calls "The Dungeon of the Doomed!" (Photograph courtesy John Antosiewicz.)

Back in the library, de Maletroit is visited by Corbeau, Rinville, Moret—and the "murdered" Turec. Moret's pistol, used by Denis, was loaded with a blank; the sire's intricate plan to frame Denis and engineer his arrival at the chateau has succeeded. Voltan (Boris Karloff), the lackey in charge of the unseen wailing man, is caught eavesdropping, thrown to the floor and kicked by the sire. Blanche (Sally Forrest) makes a late-night entrance into Denis' tower room through a secret panel and implores him not to be a party to any scheme of her evil uncle's.

The next day, de Maletroit tells Denis and Blanche that, because Blanche entered Denis' room during the night, they must marry promptly. (De Maletroit to Blanche: "You're 20, well past the age when maidenhood is fashionable.") In the story's next nod to the Stevenson tale, Blanche reminds de Maletroit of her love for Armand, a young captain who has been conspicuous by his absence of late. Her uncle is unmoved. Some of the dialogue in this scene gives the impression of having been written to appeal to the comic in Laughton:

BLANCHE: Please, give me a little time.
DE MALETROIT [*suddenly sounding quite reasonable*]: Most assuredly. I wouldn't have you rush headlong into this [marriage], it takes *time* to kindle the fires of love. [*Delivered like a punchline:*] You shall have, uh, 24 hours!

The comedy, such as it is, continues when de Maletroit exits the scene and finds Corbeau waiting around a corner for him:

DE MALETROIT [*flushed with boyish excitement*]: They've begun by disliking each other; hatred will come later!

In the dankness of the dungeon, de Maletroit torments the occupant of a small cell, a wild-eyed, hairy wretch (a hard-to-recognize Paul Cavanagh). Dressed in tattered rags, gazing aimlessly, making baby-like noises and softly scratching at a stone wall with his fingernails, this madman is the sire's brother Edmond, who years ago married Helene, the sire's beloved; Helene died giving birth to their daughter Blanche. Losing Helene infuriated de Maletroit (and apparently turned him off on women in general), so he has kept Edmond in this cell for 20 years; decades in this "living grave" have destroyed Edmond's mind. De Maletroit is now about to exact further revenge upon him by ruining the life of Blanche via forced marriage to Denis, whom he describes to Edmond as "a scoundrel chosen with infinite care ... to destroy her." (The key which de Maletroit always keeps with him is the key to Edmond's cell.) Just moments after playing two scenes for comedy, Laughton here is quite effective as he madly imitates Edmond's hysterical laughter and announces with devilish glee, "To hear you beg for mercy, that would be my supreme pleasure!"

The joke, however, is on de Maletroit: Edmond has actually been able to endure the years of imprisonment and retain his sanity thanks to the dog-like devotion and kindnesses of Voltan. (By pretending to be mad, Edmond has stayed his brother's murderous hand.) Now aware of his daughter's impending nuptials and the character of the bridegroom, Edmond instructs the loyal Voltan to kill Denis.

Entering Denis' bedchamber, Voltan hovers over the sleeping man with deadly intent until Blanche unexpectedly re-enters through the secret door. (In one of the movie's funnier moments, Denis, awakened, gives the dilapidated Voltan the once-over and then talks about him like he's not there, disdainfully asking Blanche, "Who is this … *nightmare*?") When Blanche asks Voltan to help Denis escape, the simple-minded lackey is conflicted; Karloff gets this across by frowning and waving his hands in the air in a very Monster-like way. Voltan leads Denis down into a barracks room where Moret and Turec spot them and a brawl begins, Denis going toe to toe with Turec (for the second time) and Voltan battling Moret. Voltan stabs Moret and then moves toward the grappling Denis and Turec, taking aim at Denis' back. But the battlers unexpectedly switch positions and Voltan perforates Turec instead. Denis doesn't realize what really happened despite the look of "Didn't mean to do *that*!" plastered all over Voltan's kisser.

Mystified by the reappearance of Turec, the man he supposedly killed in the tavern rumble, Denis now realizes that some evil grand plan is in operation and decides to stay and protect Blanche. Amongst the guests at the wedding reception, Denis finds Count Grassin of Normandy (Alan Napier), a friend of his family's, and appeals to him for help. Grassin says his coach will make a two a.m. appearance outside the chateau's south wing.

After the marriage ceremony is performed (off-camera) and the guests have minuet-ed off into the night, de Maletroit urges dead-drunk bridegroom Denis to head upstairs to consummate his marriage. But Denis is only feigning inebriation and, in Blanche's bedroom, is quite the gentleman, assuring her that, following their escape, they can soon get this "mockery of a marriage" annulled. Blanche looks disappointed by Denis' comment, which leads to further palaver, and soon the two are expressing their love for each other. Exiting through a secret passage, they make their way past slumbering guards to an exterior door. Grassin is dead in the waiting coach, knifed in the back for his attempted interference. You almost need a scorecard for the ensuing melee, which is punctuated by lightning flashes and rumbles of thunder: Denis fights with Corbeau, Voltan strangles a footman (Bruce Riley), Rinville pistol-whips Denis, Voltan throws a knife into the back of Rinville, and Corbeau shoots Voltan in the arm. Voltan topples into the river.

The Strange Door with Sally Forrest and Charles Laughton (top) was descended from the Golden Age Horror *The Black Room* (1935) where Boris Karloff was the peer who preyed on the peasantry—not to mention Marian Marsh. (Photographs courtesy Ronald V. Borst/Hollywood Movie Posters.)

Displeased that Blanche and Denis are happy in their new altared state, de Maletroit and Corbeau take them at pistol-point to the dungeon, where Blanche meets the father she has always believed to be dead. She and Denis are locked in his cell with him. The chateau has a waterwheel which is turned by river currents; de Maletroit pulls an iron lever to engage its huge rotating gears with other apparatus, making the stone walls of the cell begin to press inward. Like a worse-for-wear *deus ex machina*, Voltan appears on the scene bullet-wounded and nearly drowned but still sufficiently sturdy to attack Corbeau on the parapet above the waterwheel. We don't see what Voltan does to Corbeau but, after we hear a scream and a splash, we consider Corbeau well disposed of. De Maletroit puts his knife in Voltan's back and yet the unstoppable servant engages him hand to hand and pushes him through a wooden railing into the river. Voltan is exultant when he finds that de Maletroit's chain and cell door key are in his hand but—shot once, perhaps twice, and now stabbed—he soon collapses.

As de Maletroit attempts to climb out of the river, he gets pulled into the giant gears and jams them, and the cell walls stop moving. But soon the force of the current dislodges his corpse, the gears again begin moving and the Rube Goldberg operation re-commences. Voltan arrives in the nick of cinema time: His life ebbing out, he crawls close enough to the cell to push the key within reach of Denis. After some anxious fumbling, Denis unlocks and slides open the door. He, Blanche and Edmond quit the cell just seconds before the walls crush a table and come together completely.

Later, in the chateau entrance hall, a workman finishes the job of adding a handle to the Strange Door. With Blanche standing by, Edmond (now shaven, clean as a new dime and dressed in regal finery) tells Denis, "My boy, this door brought you into our lives. It stands open now. You're free to leave as you came, or stay, if you wish." Denis indicates that "stay" is his wish, cuing a swell of romantic music. We watch from outside, through the doorway, as the lovers clinch and Edmond closes the now not-so-strange door.

Cast Biographies

Charles Laughton as Sire Alan de Maletroit

The son of hotel proprietors, Charles Laughton was born in Scarborough, England, at the turn of the 20th century. After World War I service, he turned his attention to the stage, appearing in productions at the Royal Academy of Dramatic Art where he was a top student, and making his West End debut in 1926. His stage successes brought him to the attention of Hollywood, but he resisted the studios' overtures until Paramount proffered a three-year, two-film-a-year, select-your-own-roles contract. Relocating to California with his actress-wife Elsa Lanchester, Laughton found that his kickoff Paramount assignment *Devil and the Deep* (1932), written by old friend Benn Levy, had been delayed and that in the interim, the studio was loaning him to Universal. Thus the 32-year-old actor had his Hollywood unveiling in *The Old Dark House*, coincidentally also written by Levy, and co-starring Karloff.

TOM WEAVER: Did "the public" know that Laughton was gay in the '40s and '50s?

WILLIAM PHIPPS: *No*! Laughton and Elsa and I had many conversations, the three of us, about that, and Laughton said that he suffered greatly because he was born a *criminal*. Being born a homosexual in those days was criminal, and I think especially so in England. So to him, he was born a criminal. It must have been terrible to live with that.

Charles Laughton and Elsa Lanchester, in the early years of what was for Laughton (and maybe her, too) a happy marriage. After about ten years, things took a turn.

Actor Phipps first met Laughton in 1941 and became a close friend to Laughton and Lanchester several years later (and to the ends of their lives). According to Phipps, Laughton told him privately that marriage to Lanchester was "wonderful" for the first ten years or so, "sex and everything." But then things changed: "Elsa was open about her dislike for children," Phipps continued, "and Laughton resented the fact that she denied him children [refused to become a mother]. *He* wanted children. He loved children, he really did, and he got along so great with them. Like he directed the two kids in *The Night of the Hunter* [1955], and he loved Margaret O'Brien when they did *The Canterville Ghost* [1944]—they adored each other. He was a kid at heart, he *was* a child!"[3]

Fast-forward two decades through Laughton's career, past his Oscar win for *The Private Life of Henry VIII* (1933), his Oscar nomination for *Mutiny on the Bounty* (1935), past two more Hall of Fame genre films, *Island of Lost Souls* (1932) and *The Hunchback of Notre Dame* (1939), and we find his star in decline: Hitting the half-century mark, the actor was now keeping the wolf from his Curson Avenue door by doing "little theater" productions at places like The Stage on La Cienega Boulevard, and working as an acting teacher. (The teaching, Laughton's agent Paul Gregory later told an interviewer, "was just an ego trip for Laughton. He fancied himself with people following him around adoring him.") Simon Callow, author of *Charles Laughton: A Difficult Actor*, revealed that at The Stage, "[Laughton], like everyone else, was on an Equity 'little theaters' minimum salary of $10 a week."

Laughton also toured the country, at each one-night stand doing a whole evening of readings. (His readings started during World War II, as entertainment for hospitalized servicemen, and later became public performances.) In her autobiography *Elsa Lanchester Herself*, the actress wrote that Laughton was pressured by Gregory to do a film in order to publicize his name as a reader—and the film turned out to be *The Strange Door*.

"You know, you seem to fit so well everywhere," Tennessee Ernie Ford told Laughton during a TV variety show skit. It was just scripted schtick but when it came to the Laughton of the 1950s, truer words were never spoken. It was impossible to say where you'd next find the portly performer, whether crossing the country on a Bible-reading tour, or doing slapstick with Abbott and Costello in a kiddie matinee stinkbomb movie, or giving another Oscar-nominated performance in Billy Wilder's *Witness for the Prosecution* (1957), or introducing Elvis Presley on *The Ed Sullivan Show*, or directing *The Night of the Hunter*, a four-star suspense classic which makes you want to cry that he didn't direct more.

When Charles Laughton died, Kirk Douglas, star and executive producer of 1960's *Spartacus* (with Laughton as a Roman senator, pictured), told the press, "Laughton was an actor who dared. The modern trend in acting is to underplay and, as a result, many actors come up doing nothing. But when Laughton was on the stage or screen, you knew it."

Hollywood trade papers announced in mid–1962 that Billy Wilder's upcoming *Irma La Douce* would star Jack Lemmon, Shirley MacLaine and Laughton, the latter as a commentator telling the story as it unfolds. But cancer had been afflicting the chain-smoking actor since January (in his arm and back); he underwent surgery at New York's Memorial Hospital for Cancer and Allied Disease, then months of cobalt treatment. He was confined to Cedars of Lebanon for three months (he smoked even in his hospital bed) and then was granted his last wish, to be sent home to die. On December 15, a few days after signing his will with an X, Laughton died in his sleep, with Elsa and his brother Frank at his bedside. "He was not only powerful, but a vehicle of power," said eulogist Christopher Isherwood. The novelist, who saw Laughton play Lear at Stratford-on-Avon, recalled, "You felt you were in touch with something which was the very inspiration of Shakespeare himself."

Boris Karloff as Voltan

> I'd like to see [some of the new sci-fi films]. I understand they now have monsters who are vegetables [*The Thing from Another World*, 1951]. Fascinating!
>
> —Boris Karloff, 1951 interview with Bob Thomas

Born William Henry Pratt…

In 2017, what four written words fill a Monster Kid's heart with dread more than "Born William Henry Pratt"?—especially when they're followed by dozens of paragraphs (or dozens of pages) of biographical and career information we've all known by heart since the days when Grandma played the gramophone in the parlor? This book will not subject you to the 11,000th recitation. The future Boris Karloff was born in England in 1887, began his acting career on the stage and went Hollywood in 1919. His breakthrough role as the Monster in 1931's *Frankenstein* made him *the* top horror star of his era. He died with his boots on in 1969. Fini. You're welcome.

Sally Forrest as Blanche de Maletroit

Strange Door supporting player Michael Pate's impression of Sally Forrest was that she was "a wonderful girl and a really hard-working young actress [who] sort of went through her paces wondering how in God's name she'd finished up in a picture like that!" In the 21st century, Forrest herself still didn't know. "Don't ask *me*! I guess I went out on an interview and got it," she told me. She admitted that horror pictures were not her favorites, but quickly added that in 1951 she hadn't *seen* many—or any *other* types of pictures, for that matter. "I had not seen many movies growing up. We were very *poor*."

Born in San Diego in 1928, Forrest (real name: Katherine Sally Feeney) was the daughter of a Navy man and picked up her schooling at his various naval bases (San Francisco; Bremerton, Washington; Seattle, etc.) where he was stationed. By the time she was 12, the family had moved 13 times. She wanted to be a ballet dancer and studied with a San Diego teacher. On the side, she did some photographic modeling during her high school days. In the mid–1940s, while still a high schooler, she landed an MGM contract as a dancer. Even though she danced in the background of production numbers and was always uncredited, "it was very exciting, it was quite a plum to get that. I stayed there for several years." She also stepped out of the chorus to work as a dancing coach.

After leaving MGM, Forrest received special "introducing" billing for her first starring film: She played an unwed waitress expected a baby in *Not Wanted* (1949), one of the budget pictures on socially important themes which Ida Lupino and her producer husband Collier Young made in the late 1940s and early '50s. "I don't know if this was just publicity," she told *Films of the Golden Age* interviewer Jerry De Bono, "but the press reported that anywhere from 200 to 300 actresses had read for the part before it was my turn." She added that she auditioned at the Youngs' Mulholland Drive home: "When I finished, Ida said, 'You're the one we've been looking for. You've got the part.'" When Forrest later called her mother with the incredible news, Mom's reaction was, "That's nice, dear. Come home now. Dinner's ready." Forrest next played a polio victim in Lupino's *Never Fear* (1950), then returned to MGM, this time as an actress rather than a dancer.

According to director Joseph Pevney, Charles Laughton (left) was fond of Sally Forrest (right). Richard Stapley (center) thought "she was a little bit too American" to play the movie's frightened French maiden.

It was on loan-out from MGM that Forrest made *The Strange Door*, turning 26 during production. In the summer between *Strange Door* production and release, she wed her agent Milo Frank. Her last two movies were for Howard Hughes' RKO: the 1956 manhunt melodrama *While the City Sleeps* ("I didn't like [director] Fritz Lang, he was a cranky old bear," she told me) and, her most notorious credit, the tongue-in-cheek 1955 swashbuckler *Son of Sinbad*, with Forrest second-billed as a handmaiden. Forrest's sensual dance was one of its highlights; on *Sinbad*'s original release, it was cut in the U.S. but seen in Europe. One of her favorite *Son of Sinbad* memories was of a very hot day when, at lunchtime, stars Dale Robertson (Sinbad) and Vincent Price (Omar Khayyam)—"I don't know *what* possessed them!"—climbed up into the catwalks and began throwing down bags of water! In 1954, between these two RKOs, Forrest took over from Vanessa Brown in the role of the cuddlesome Girl Upstairs in Broadway's hit comedy *The Seven Year Itch*.

After *While the City Sleeps*, Forrest was ready to fly to New York to reunite with husband Milo, now working there for CBS. But Howard Hughes offered her a long-term contract, then put her in a Beverly Wilshire Hotel suite to await the finalization of the contract. She soon found out that, like others before her, she'd been promised big things by Hughes and stashed away as some sort of "crazy game" on his part. She told interviewer De Bono that, after two thumb-twiddling months, she booked a flight to New York and...

One of Hughes' right-hand men met me at the L.A. airport to plead with me not to leave. I kept asking the usual, "Where's my first picture?" As we waited, my flight was "held up," and "held up" again, and then again. Hughes' assistant would say about each delay in departure, "See, that's an omen. You're not meant to go back to New York. I know about these things." Well, the airline was TWA, which Hughes owned, so you can guess why my flight out was being mysteriously "held up." Finally, after eight hours at the terminal, they saw I was determined, and they let me go.

Forrest also trod the boards in stock productions (*Damn Yankees, Remains to Be Seen, Bus Stop, No No Nanette*) and did TV work. She and her husband eventually moved into the one-time Beverly Hills residence of Jean Harlow and MGM executive Paul Bern. They said in 1956 that

The Case of the Disappearing Costume: According to Sally Forrest, on the first day of shooting her *Son of Sinbad* dance scene, her costume looked decent enough; on the second day it was skimpier, and on the third day it was "down to practically nothing." Welcome to Howard Hughes' RKO, Sally! (Photograph courtesy C. Robert Rotter, *Glamour Girls of the Silver Screen* website.)

they'd swear it was haunted by Jean, but decades later she admitted to me that they'd actually seen no sign of her. "No, of course not," she laughed. "We were just *hoping*. It would be lovely to see a ghost, wouldn't it?"

According to her publicity, she announced in 1956 that she wanted to do nude underwater photos (she confirmed for me in the 2000s that she was serious about that); that she collaborated with A.E. van Vogt on a science fiction novel ("No, I didn't really do that, but A.E. was a friend of ours all of my professional life"); and that *Star Trek* was her husband's idea. "Milo wrote this, and we had a deal, and then we went on a vacation, and when we came back, the deal was not there and something called *Star Trek* came out. That happens in Hollywood, you know."

In 2008, Forrest told me, "I live a very pleasant life, actually. Unhappily, my husband is dead [as of 2004], *that's* not very pleasant, but I still live in our lovely house, I have a beautiful garden, I have many, many friends. It's a good life." In 2015, after a long bout with cancer, Forrest, 86, died in her Beverly Hills home.

Richard Stapley as Denis de Beaulieu

"I was *really* in love with America—I mean, it was an unbelievable experience for me," English-born Richard Stapley told me about his early years in the U.S. "My sort-of 'best' years in England had been interrupted by the war, and suddenly to come to this lotus land.... I was very lucky. The places I was introduced to and the people I met ... really very, very worthwhile, wonderful people."

Hailing from Westcliff, Essex, England, Stapley attended all the right schools and dreamed of being a concert pianist, then later decided on shooting for a stage career. Gossip columnist Prunella Hall wrote in 1951 that he "achieved the rather enviable record in his own country of being kept so busy that he never had a day off between the end of one show and the beginning of another." Not too long out of his teens, he wrote a satirical novel entitled *I'll Wear It on My Head* which was published in Blighty; when he came to New York with hopes of getting it published here, he also carried a letter of introduction to acting legends Lunt and Fontanne. According to Stapley, Lynn Fontanne said she could offer him a job as the understudy to juvenile lead Montgomery Clift in their production *O Mistress Mine*, "and I was very, very stupid. I'd been with the Old Vic in London and I'd done some fairly important things. One's in a new country and one should have eaten humble pie. I *should* have done that, because Clift left to go to Hollywood in about like two months after that ... and who knows what my story might have been."

After playing some stage roles in the East, Stapley made his first trek to Hollywood and appeared in the Bulldog Drummond mystery *The Challenge* (1948) and in MGM's *The Three Musketeers* (1948) and *Little Women* (1949). Louis B. Mayer told Stapley they were going to try to make him a star, beginning with an Andy Hardy–type series, in which he would appear with Peter Lawford, June Allyson and Janet Leigh, and *The Running of the Tide*, in which he would play Montgomery Clift's brother.

When these productions did not materialize and Stapley found himself "mostly sitting," he returned to New York, but then made a second sojourn to the movie capital, this time under a contract shared by Universal and independent producer Hal B. Wallis. During Hollywood Adventure Version 2.0, *The Strange Door* was the first movie he made. According to Stapley, at one point during production its producer Ted Richmond

> **came to the gates at Universal and said to my wife [former professional figure skater Susan Strong], 'We're gonna dust off a lot of Douglas Fairbanks, Jr., films and revise them for Richard, because he's coming across very much like Douglas Fairbanks, Jr.' So I was in seventh heaven, I**

thought, 'God, that's marvelous'—even though, actually, I don't really *like* costume dramas. I don't like them particularly to watch, and I *really* don't like playing in them. The ridiculous thing is, when I came to America, what I wanted to do was play a *cowboy*, really [*laughs*]!

There were no "Fairbanks Jr. movies" in Stapley's Universal future (in fact, no further Universals at *all*); his subsequent Hollywood jobs included a supporting role in Fox's *King of the Khyber Rifles* (1953), several Sam Katzman movies (one of them a Johnny Weissmuller Jungle Jim) and episodic TV. Decades before Andrew Lloyd Webber's Broadway hit *Sunset Blvd.*, he collaborated with his songwriting partner Dickson Hughes and actress Gloria Swanson on *Starring Norma Desmond*, a musical adaptation of the 1950 hall-of-famer *Sunset Blvd.* in which Swanson had starred. "She said she thought she could get the rights [to turn the movie into a stage musical] and she took me down to Paramount very much the same way she took William Holden down to Paramount in the movie. In an old car, and the gates were opened, and we went in, and she *did* get the rights. Then we spent quite a lot of time together, the three of us, and wrote the whole score. It was going to be done on Broadway by Robert Fryer and Lawrence Carr, and she did one of the big numbers ['The Wonderful People Out There in the Dark'] on TV's *The Steve Allen Show*." All their work came to naught.[4]

Again changing his address (and now his name, to Richard Wyler), he returned to Europe, where he starred in the U.K. series *Man from Interpol*. He also appeared in a number of Italian spy pictures and Spaghetti Westerns, the latter scratching his "cowboy" itch. Other activities included motorcycle racing and landing another wife, Elizabeth Emerson. Circa 1978 he wrote a script called *Future Tense*,

which was going to be done with Jon Voight. He was gonna do it, definitely, and it was gonna have a huge international cast. It was the kind of thing where you thought, "It *can't* not go," but it ended in three years of commuting across the Atlantic and coming to Hollywood and losing this person and that person. After three years of that, I got fed up with the business for awhile. I became involved with a motorcycle courier company in London, because I had raced motorcycles.

Stapley, 86, died of kidney failure at a Palm Springs hospital in March 2010. According to his obituary in the English newspaper *The Independent*, "Some unfortunate [latter-day] business deals meant that Stapley's finances were not good and the last decade of his life was dependent on the generosity of acquaintances"; however, let's take that with a grain of salt because the same writer calls Billy Wilder's 1950 film *Sunset Blvd.* a musical. Nearly all of Stapley's published obituaries make a point of mentioning the 2004 publication of his novel *Naked Legacy*, but try finding a mention of it anywhere *but* his obits.

Production

Scheduled to be made in 18 days, *The Door* began production on Stage 7 on Tuesday, May 15, with the shooting of the Lion Rouge tavern scene. It was a full day bringing together stars Laughton and Richard Stapley, supporting players William Cottrell and Morgan Farley, uncredited actors Charles Horvath and Eddie Parker, eight bit players, stuntmen Paul Baxley, Carey Loftin, Don Turner, Sol Gorss and Wes Hopper, two dozen extras, coach horses, saddle horses and more. The shooting call was for nine a.m., and by 9:40 they had their first shot (bit player Claudia Jordon, in long shot, singing part of "Je N'en Connais Pas La Fin"). Next they got a close shot of Jordon doing the complete number, footage destined to land on the cutting room floor; in the movie we hear just the very end of the song. Musicologists might smile at the inclusion of "Je N'en Connais Pas La Fin" in this drama of the 1700s, as it was just 12 years old in 1951! Read more about it in David Schecter's essay on the music of *The Strange Door* below.

The perks of stardom: Charles Laughton's set call was an hour or two later than everyone else's. In his first on-camera work, Laughton as the sire made his entrance into Le Lion Rouge and, lingering just inside the door, gave the place the once-over. Once the camera pulled back and panned with the

A wastrel who has sailed far from his noble family on a sea of license, Denis (Richard Stapley, left) is put in a wife-or-death situation by the insidious sire (Charles Laughton, right).

sire as he joined tablemates Corbeau and Rinville, the rest of the morning was spent filming their discussion of the dissolute Denis.

First considered for the role of Corbeau was Robert Douglas, then in the process of playing villainous roles in several Universal movies, most memorably the Douglas Sirk-directed *Mystery Submarine* (1950) in which he gave an excellent performance as the scar-faced renegade commander of a German sub. According to *The Strange Door*'s pre-production Tentative Cast Report, Douglas was slated to work three weeks for $3000, with the notation "[Douglas' agent] thinks he can deliver him for this price."

William Cottrell, with his haughty manner and "George Arliss face," was a good (and no doubt more affordable) substitute for Douglas. In the opening tavern scene, with the sire sneering with indifference at the girl singer and a barmaid during his beeline to the table of his associates, we get the insinuation of an all-gay confab. Later in the movie, during the planning-the-wedding scene, we see that Corbeau, when not doing the sire's dirty work, handles domestic duties at the chateau. There's more than a touch of the lily about him as he addresses the help (butcher, cook, wine steward, etc.), foppish and prim in his housekeeper-ly role. (Corbeau to cook: "I would suggest also a pie of venison ... flavored with truffles and spices ... and eels, of course ... and snails ... *lots* of snails...") "Cottrell, daringly, plays his role as if he has a huge crush on the baddie," Kim Newman wrote in his *Video Watchdog* #130 review of Universal's 2006 DVD *The Boris Karloff Collection*.

After lunch, Stapley as Denis went into action, pawing and kissing a resistant barmaid who spits, "*Non mais dit donc, espece de brute*!" The actress, Tao Porchon, may be the last survivor of *The Strange Door*: She's still going strong, not as an actress but as a yoga instructor (the world's oldest). Having practiced the art since age eight in India, she has taught in India, France and the U.S. In September 2005, when she traveled to Washington, D.C., to teach a yoga class at a Capitol Hill gym, a *Washington Post* article on her amazing career was illustrated with a shot of the lithe octogenarian doing the gravity-defying yoga power move "the peacock pose," balancing her body's weight on her hands while suspending her torso and legs above the floor. At age 96, she and a 26-year-old male dance partner made an appearance on a 2015 episode of the TV reality show *America's Got Talent*; Porchon, in sparkling silver dress and cherry red high heels, got wild cheers from the audience and a standing ovation from judges Howard Stern, Heidi Klum, Mel B and Howie Mandel. The recipient of three hip replacements, she told the judges, "I don't let anything get the better of me."

Denis' lip-lock with another barmaid is interrupted by Charles Horvath's Turec. Photographing their brawl took up most of the rest of the afternoon, along with shots of Denis in his Fairbanks-like fight with other tavern men. After dinner, cast and crew moved to European Street for some night-for-night shooting. The first order of business was the movie's opening shot: the sire arriving by coach at Le Lion Rouge. The tavern signboard is swinging and dead leaves blowing along the street courtesy of wind machines. For the rest of the night, they photographed the scene in which Denis frantically exits the tavern, climbs aboard the public coach and rides away—with ten angry horsemen in pursuit. Stapley recalled for me the first day of *Strange Door* production: "I was there like at seven o'clock in the morning and I finished in the last shot [at 11:35 p.m.], so it was a long day. My first day at the studio and I had to do that scene where I fight [Horvath] in the tavern and leap up and catch the chandelier and swing right across the room. It wasn't an easy scene, particularly for a first day."

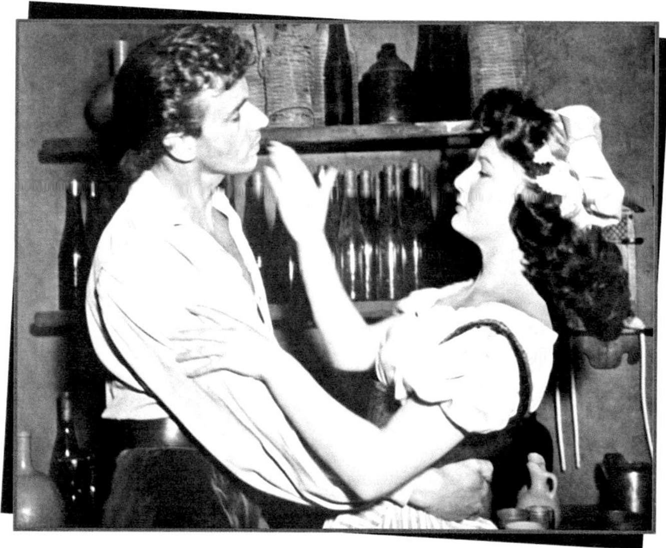

The minders of Hollywood's manners, the Breen Office, told Universal that the Lion Rouge tavern women must not be suggestive of prostitutes; objected to a scene of men slapping a girl on the rump; and advised the moviemakers to be careful with the scene in which Denis fondles the barmaid: "His action in 'apparently approaching a sensitive zone' is unacceptable." Pictured: Richard Stapley, Tao Porchon.

His most vivid memory of that May 15 was of his initial encounter with the movie's star:

Charles Laughton came onto the set and was introduced to me, and just sort of grunted. And was really... I'd almost call him *obnoxious*. A couple of people said, "My God, he's difficult..." He probably sort of felt that *The Strange Door* was a little bit beneath him. "He wants to see you prove yourself," somebody said. Anyway, I wasn't very comfortable. But he was very impressed with what I did, so he sort of became more friendly gradually.

Also adding to Stapley's first-day blues: Joseph Pevney. "For the part I played," Stapley told me, "the director wanted to have another actor, I forget his name. It wasn't until probably the third, fourth day that he really became happy with me. And that's a horrible way to begin a picture. What with Laughton as well, it probably was the worst first day I've ever had on a film!" Decades later, talking to me, Pevney sounded like he *still* wasn't "happy" with his movie's romantic lead: "Richard Stapley? Not very pleasant memories. He was kind of stuffy. And not a very good actor, as I recall." Michael Pate told me that his memory of Stapley was that he was "a little nervous in the service."

Activity on May 16 was less strenuous. On Stage 18's Entrance Hall set, Stapley began the day with the movie's "title character," the Strange Door itself: Denis unintentionally stumbles through the chateau doorway into the "House of Evil.... Lair of Nameless HORRORS!" (poster ad line). In the afternoon, on the Library set, they shot the first part of the scene where de Maletroit and Denis meet. There's a tense cat-and-mouse quality to the back-and-forth between the effete, enigmatic sire and the smooth-talking ruffian Denis, perhaps partly due to the fact that Laughton had seen to it, the day before, that their association began badly. On the 17th, more of the library scene was shot, starting with Denis darting out of the room through a draped doorway and being dragged back *in* by two guards. The guard on the left is Sol Gorss, one of Stapley's stunt doubles on this movie, the other Don Turner, Karloff's stunt double. With Denis tightly held by the guards, and with de Maletroit henchman Talon (Michael Pate) observing, the sire takes a white-hot toddy iron out of the fireplace flames and menacingly holds it up to Denis' face. But then he dips it into his cup of wine, takes a sip and pours the rest over Denis' helpless head.

"I seem to remember that Richard Stapley, the young leading man, was given a really hard time," Pate told me. "Laughton simply delighted in pouring that malmsey wine all over his head in the film!"

Scenes involving eating turn up with such regularity in Laughton movies that either screenwriters knew he made the most of them and included them on their own initiative, or Laughton requested them. It began with his first feature-length film, the English silent *Piccadilly* (1929), where Laughton has a bizarre, self-indulgently acted cameo: At the posh Piccadilly Club, the actor, looking very blasé, and sometimes acting as though he's in a trance, is oblivious to everything but the meal in front of him; when he notices a mysterious smudge on a plate, he goes ballistic, harassing his servers and the club owner, furiously pounding the table. Laughton's *Strange Door* dining hall scene, shot on the afternoon of the 17th, is a takeoff on *The Private Life of Henry VIII*'s (1933) comical banquet scene in which Laughton as the 16th-century monarch belches as he tears into a capon with his hands, talks with his mouth full (as food falls out), throws half-eaten pieces over his shoulder, and then goes into an angry tirade ("Refinement's a thing of the past ... manners are *dead*!").

In *The Strange Door*, Laughton dominates the dining hall scene opposite Cottrell, Farley and Pate, and again enjoys a ham holiday: "This mutton is *good*!" he practically shouts at the outset, giving audiences a heads-up as to what to expect. He proceeds to talk with his mouth full, point with his knife, shake his head so hard his double-chins flap, rock with laughter, make faces, throw a chop end over end to Pate—and then, just as in *Henry VIII*, have an abrupt mood swing into self-pity ("I can't trust anyone, I'm surrounded by rogues!"). For *Henry VIII*, in which Laughton occasionally went over the top in a loud, bawdy, look-at-me way identical to his sire in *The Strange Door*, he got an Oscar; for *The Strange Door*, Laughton got people like his biographer Callow calling his performance "a nightmarish display of an acting machine out of control."

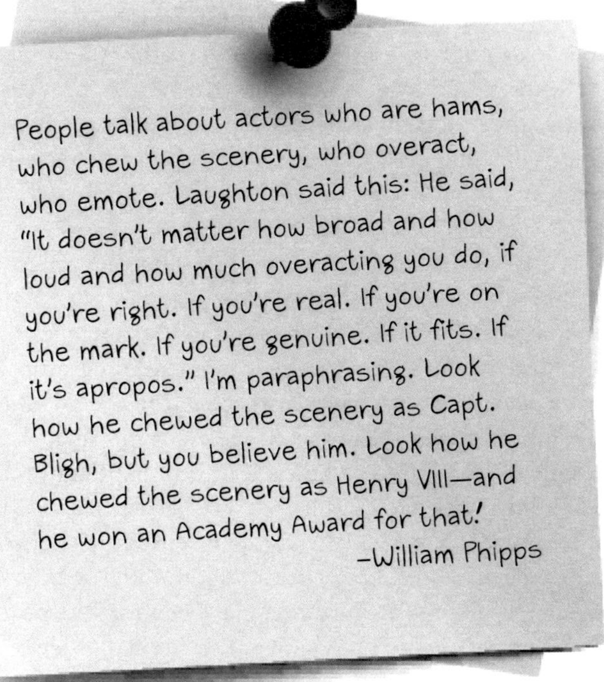

"We copied the *Henry VIII* thing; maybe I asked him to do it," director Pevney recalled for me. "If you're gonna put a big helping on Charles Laughton's plate, you better let him do Henry VIII or the audience is going to be disappointed [*laughs*]! That one sequence in *Henry VIII* made him a motion picture star, that throwing-the-bones-over-his-shoulder, hitting-the-liveried-servants-with-the-bones, slobbering-all-over-the-place routine, and it stood out in people's memory."

Sits and Giggles: Charles Laughton, seen here yukking it up in the dining hall scene, once said, "On the screen, I generally have been cast, mostly by my choice, as a wicked, blustering or untidy character. Now I am ready to admit that in real life Charles Laughton is all of those things." From left, Michael Pate, Laughton, William Cottrell, Morgan Farley. (Photograph courtesy John Antosiewicz.)

Also on the 17th, Stapley reported a bit of news that he'd withheld for two days, that he had sustained several slight injuries in the tavern fight. He was treated in the studio hospital for a wrenched right foot and bruises on his lower back and thigh.

May 18, Sally Forrest's first day on the movie, was devoted entirely to Stage 18 filming of the drawing room scene in which the sire tells Blanche she must marry Denis. In Forrest's follow-up scene with Stapley, perhaps her best moment in the movie, Blanche movingly tells Denis her sad life story: "If I've held anything really dear to me, it's been snatched away, destroyed..." and citing as examples a maid-companion and a little spaniel. Viewers, of course, know at once that the sire has sent them off into the next world. When she speaks of Armand, the now mysteriously missing young captain she loves, the audience instantly senses that he's shared the

After William Cottrell's years in Hollywood, he returned to his native Oregon, where circa 1980 Greg Luce, future founder of Sinister Cinema, worked with him at an Ashland community playhouse presenting Noël Coward's *Nude with Violin* (Cottrell directing, Luce in a small part). The two struck up a friendship, and on one occasion watched *The Strange Door* together at Luce's. Cottrell told Luce that he and Laughton wanted to make *Strange Door* tongue-in-cheek and that they were dismayed when Pevney wanted it straight. It goes without saying that, despite his director's preference, Laughton frequently did play for laughs.[5]

Cottrell also revealed that, in the abovementioned dining hall scene, Laughton would not swallow the meat he was putting in his mouth, instead spitting it out after every take; Laughton said that eating food under the hot lights, and under the stress of enacting a movie scene, would induce vomiting. A few minutes later, said Cottrell, one of the other actors in the scene *did* vomit. (Using the process of elimination, that would be Morgan Farley.) I talked 20 years later to a 20-years-older Cottrell, who could no longer recall the dining hall incidents—but you often notice, after you've interviewed enough oldtimers, that some of the stories they tell you one year are gone from their memory banks the next.[6]

Universal's first horror heroine of the 1950s, Sally Forrest, poses with the Strange Door.

fate of maid and mutt.[7] Prominently featured in this scene, balusters suggest bars and remind us that the sire has clipped the wings of (imprisoned) these two lovebirds.

Pevney told me how Forrest got her *Strange* role: "Sally Forrest was a 'find' of Ida Lupino, and Ida insisted that I see her and use her in the picture. She was a beautiful girl, structurally her facial structure was wonderful, but her skin was not very good. Laughton liked her." Richard Stapley liked doing the film with her and thought she was "a very sweet person," but not really suited for the role of Blanche because "she was a little bit too American." (Because Stapley was nice to me, I won't mention that for the role of Denis, *he* was a little bit too English!) Forrest told me that she considered the movie "a frivolous little thing" but stressed that she enjoyed doing a period picture and wearing the costumes of the era.

The rest of this Blanche-Denis drawing room scene was shot on the 19th, plus a corridor scene between the sire and Corbeau which Laughton unabashedly plays for laughs. "Charles could not take the gothic tale seriously and made a delicious mockery of it—a horror put-on," Lanchester wrote in *Elsa Lanchester Herself*. "He was so villainous and he shook his jowls with such relish and rolled his tongue around his mouth and spat out, and what with the rattling chains and creaking doors—well, it was exactly right for the story." Movie critics, Laughton biographers and horror fans may question the suitability of that approach, but there can be no denying that Laughton at times *is* burlesquing his material, perhaps most egregiously in the de Maletroit-Corbeau corridor scene mentioned above, with the sire exclaiming, "I'm in the mood for relaxation, let's visit the dungeon!" He then marches out of the frame with a happy grin, a crazy light in his eyes and a Groucho-like forward-leaning posture, as though he were on TV playing a loutish lord for big yuks in a *Red Skelton Show* skit.

"If I had known Laughton a little bit better, I think I'd have played my part completely differently," said Stapley. "I'd have played it much more as a sort of satire of the thing. But I didn't have the film experience then to come out with what I'd call an 'original' performance. I don't think you *can* in a film that's going that quickly, with that budget and everything."

Pevney told me,

> **The truth of the matter is that Laughton enjoyed doing this film *immensely*, because he didn't want to play it like a straight piece of theatrics. Laughton had to find some kind of a gimmick to make it work for *him* and, by golly, he found the gimmick: Laughton played it for the *humor* of the situation! The both of us laughed our way through the entire production! We previewed it in downtown L.A., and the top studio brass was surprised and shocked to hear audiences *laughing*! Well, that's what it was *played* for.**

Lanchester remembered things differently: In *Elsa Lanchester Herself*, she wrote that during the *Strange Door* shooting, Pevney did not know that Laughton was being funny. "[W]hen the film was shown at a preview, the audience rocked with laughter at Charles' every movement and spit. Afterward, its director came and said, 'Charles, they laughed at you! Isn't it terrible?'" She continued,

> **Charles secretly felt a personal triumph. He had been paid only $25,000 [to star in *Strange Door*], but it didn't seem to matter. I remember *Time* magazine giving Charles a marvelous review, saying the whole thing was very corny but it was a great evening to see Charles Laughton once more come back and ham it up and enjoy it so much, along with the audience. Charles was often criticized for being a ham, but his hamming in this case was an art and it was fun.**

The 19th had begun with the drawing room scene where Blanche and Denis tell de Maletroit they shouldn't marry, and it ended with the library scene in which the two characters, now married, tell the nobleman they want to *stay* married. In the latter scene, Laughton does a good bit of his acting looking directly into the camera.

Did Sally Forrest end up with the portrait of Helene (actually a portrait of Forrest) seen in the movie? No; in fact, she scoffed at the question, saying that while it may have looked all right on-screen, it looked pretty funny up close. "It was not the kind of thing you put up [in your house]," she said laughing. Left to right, Richard Stapley, Forrest, Charles Laughton.

On the set, in response to Sally Forrest's line, "Uncle, what's back of your hatred?" Laughton gave a hard yank on a drawstring, in order to open a curtain and suddenly reveal a life-sized portrait of Blanche's mother. It *had* to have been a laugh-out-loud moment when just at this dramatic juncture, the drawstring broke. This created a half-hour delay.

In scenes shot on this fifth day of production, Laughton does seem to be more into the spirit of fun—and Richard Stapley, talking to me, guessed that it was "about the fifth day" that the actor began to thaw. He told me that, by then, Laughton had become friendly

> **to the point that he said, "Why don't you and your wife come into the dressing room and have a martini?" We talked about literature. I had never read Thomas Wolfe, and so over these martinis he would recite marvelous passages from *Look Homeward, Angel* and *You Can't Go Home Again*, two of Wolfe's greatest books. Those were really some wonderful moments, because I was being introduced to an author I was very, very aware of but I hadn't read. This was very exciting to me—I mean, how many people would be poured a martini by Charles Laughton himself and listen to readings from Thomas Wolfe? That, and Ted Richmond's statement [about starring Stapley in old Fairbanks Jr. vehicles], made the film a little bit more to me than a quickie at Universal.**

"Laughton was a great charmer and a great raconteur," said Pevney. He continued,

> **There was one point during the shooting when he asked *me* to come into his dressing room and listen to something and give him my honest opinion. It was something that he was preparing to do on tour; it was *Don Juan in Hell* [a one-act play excerpted from George Bernard Shaw's *Man and Superman*, done in lecture-reading style]. Well, sir, he read me this thing in the dressing room and I said, "My God, that's *beautiful*. Of *course*, you've *got* to do it!" Now, I don't attribute to my liking it the fact that he went ahead and *did* it [*laughs*]; he just wanted to get my opinion, and I was spellbound. He read magnificently.**

Pevney later caught *Don Juan in Hell* in a packed house in Pasadena.

May 21, the first day of a new week, began impressively: On the drawing room set, bustling with extras, there was an 80-second take in which the camera

- dollies in on Rinville, seated at a table, putting sealing wax on an envelope containing a wedding invitation, and handing envelopes out to couriers;
- gives us a long look at an invitation on the table;
- follows a departing courier to a different part of the room where Corbeau gives instructions to a butcher and a cook;
- and then follows Corbeau and a wine steward across the room until a staircase appears in the background; an agitated Talon rushes down it to talk to Corbeau...

A long rehearsal preceded the filming of this action. Notice that, toward the end, it came close to being spoiled: As Talon hotfoots it into the scene, his stiff-looking cravat is bouncing and finally sticks upside-down to the lower half of his face; he has to swat it down in order to begin talking. In the lineup of servants you'll notice *The Hideous Sun Demon*'s (1959) Patrick Whyte as the butcher and *The Ape Man*'s (1943) George Kirby as the cook.

Cast and crew convened on Stage 14 on May 22 and, on the Denis' Tower Room set, filmed the scene of Denis and Blanche's first meeting, plus the scene of Denis and Talon, the latter revealing that in the Middle Ages, Cabrissade the legendary torturer "used this chateau for some of his favorite experiments." Pate, with a makeup scar bisecting one eyebrow, makes Talon the sire's one "likable" henchman with

Michael Pate (seen struggling with Sally Forrest) is a *very* subordinate *Strange Door* bad guy—ninth-billed, he *just* made it onto the on-screen cast list. But three members of the movie's preview audience called him the actor they liked best. "Michael Pate was a wonderful, terrific guy, *good* actor," director Joseph Pevney recalled.

just a few smiles, a few glib bits of self-deprecation and a couple of sarcastic lines. Pate was the one baddie carried over from *Strange Door* to its 1952 follow-up *The Black Castle* but, alas, there he played a more stereotypical, "Central Casting" baddie, not a "likable" one.

May 23 commenced with the photographing of the second half of the *loooong* library scene (almost ten minutes from start to finish), begun days before. De Maletroit exchanges dialogue with Corbeau and Rinville, taunts Turec—and then catches Voltan (Boris Karloff) spying on them behind a panel. Turec and Moret seize Voltan and cast him to the floor, and the noble ignobly kicks him in the knee. Karloff's Voltan is a woebegone-looking soul (and a Crime of Fashion in his shabby blouse), and being thrown to the floor and kicked was rather an inglorious way for the actor to start work on the movie. But, genre-wise, he had entered an inglorious period.[8]

What Universal had done to Poor Bela in the 1940s—reduced him to supporting roles in horror movies—they were now doing with Poor Boris. The studio's Lugosification of Karloff began in 1949 with his casting as a red herring in *Abbott and Costello Meet the Killer, Boris Karloff* and continued with *The Strange Door* and *The Black Castle*, where again he played a member of the villain's household retinue who goes on to become a reluctant hero. There was then a return to Universal stardom for Boris in *Abbott and Costello Meet Dr. Jekyll and Mr. Hyde* (1953), but that was his last feature there. One wonders which Karloffilm had Robert Louis Stevenson spinning faster in his Samoan grave, *The Strange Door* or *Abbott and Costello Meet Dr. Jekyll and Mr. Hyde.*

Universal paid second-billed Boris $6000 a week ($2,333.33 a week less than Laughton); back in the days of the six-day Hollywood work week, the studio's May 4, 1951, Tentative Cast Report called for him to work one and five-sixths weeks for a total of $12,000. And by the way, in case you didn't know, Boris Karloff was a wonderful guy:

"Karloff? **Wonderful** guy," Pevney told me. He continued,

> He shocked the hell out of me. First of all, from seeing him in *Frankenstein*, I thought he would be huge. All of the angles in *Frankenstein* were fairly low when he was alone, and when he was with other people he was always on [lifts] of some sort, I guess. Anyway, he was a very short guy, which surprised me. And *all* he cared about was gardening, that's *all* he wanted to talk about, he loved his garden. Now, this was such a strange combination of talents—an actor who was known for his murderous roles, loving to be a gardener! Strange and wonderful! Very charming guy, very, very sweet, warm, wonderful fellow. In *The Strange Door*, he looked for the humor in the thing; he took the tip from Charles and he played it with a little humor, too, as I recall.

Richard Stapley described Karloff to me as "a beautiful guy, a gentle, **wonderful** person, approachable and friendly." Sally Forrest told me, "[Laughton and Karloff] were ***wonderful***, they were so amusing, and it was fun working with 'em. Laughton with his funny, fat tum and his wig and his curlicues! He would stand around and he would *pose* in doorways—not say a thing, but wait for everybody to giggle. And of course we had to. Karloff was more serious. They were both very intelligent people."

Laughton's last shot of the day again involved the portrait of Helene: The sire draws up a chair, pulls the drapery drawstring to reveal it, sits, stretches like a cat and shows himself to be a card-carrying nutcase with his breathy rant "I have waited 20 years for this night, Helene. Twenty years…! Twenty years…! Twenty years…!" Again, as with his previous scene with the portrait where the drawstring broke, one take of this intense close-up shot was comically ruined, this time by a fly that either buzzed him or used him as a landing pad while he was in mid-rant. (What *wouldn't* we Monster Kids give for a Universal Horrors blooper reel?) After that, Karloff appeared in a not-in-the-movie shot of Voltan, sent on a mission of murder by Edmond, ducking a guard and then climbing a spiral staircase to Denis' tower room. Meanwhile, Sally Forrest was on a one-day break from the making of this gloomy flick: She was hundreds of miles north, in San Francisco, glamorizing the premiere of her newest Ida Lupino movie *Hard, Fast and Beautiful*, with Sally as a young tennis champ.

On Michael Pate's final day on the picture, May 24, he and Stapley did the Tower Room scene where Denis looks down from the window at the spinning waterwheel ("The Millwheel of Death!," one *Strange Door* poster calls it). Next, and last for Pate, was the scene in which Talon, snoozing in a chair outside Denis' door, is clobbered by Voltan. For a couple of reasons, Pate probably didn't mind coming to the end of his term of *Strange Door* employment. One was that he was less than happy to be around Charles Laughton. He told me,

> I think everyone [in the business] loved Elsa Lanchester without reservation, but some found Charles a difficult kind of person to get on with. *The Strange Door* had kind of a strange cast where I think Charles had them all a little bit enthralled. You know, everyone *professionally* pays respects to whoever's the don, whoever's the Kahuna—that's the pecking order. And one must accept that, that's the rightful thing to do. But Charles was inclined to *expect* a little bit of that, and yet at the same time equally quick to reject it.
>
> One day he asked me, "Are you English, or what?" I said, "No, no, I'm just ordinary common Australian. In any case," I added, "I don't care for the English."
>
> "Ohhhhh," he said, and all of a sudden became an Anglophile and got up a bit on his high horse about the noble English and all of that kind of thing. I said we [Australians] didn't have any lack of respect for [the English] for what

Let's hope that Talon (Michael Pate, right) is hungry because Voltan (Boris Karloff) is fixin' to serve him up a knuckle sandwich. For Karloff, *The Strange Door* was the end of the road as far as playing physical heavies.

they did about getting out of Dunkirk or for the Blitz or for what they did in the desert or for the campaigns that they fought from the start of D-Day and all of that. But I felt that the people concerned, from Churchill on down, had rather "let down" the Australian troops who were involved in Malaya, in Singapore. Friends of mine had spent a long time as prisoners of war, and one or two I know had a *terrible* time of it. And of course we lost a considerable number of men. So *I* wasn't very happy about the English, I never cared that much for the English in *that* area of the war, and so I said this to him. So he and I were sort of just a little bit standoffish. He also gave me just a little bit of a pain, pontificating and having his little cronies laugh and giggle at his jokes and what he *thought* were in-jokes and all that kind of thing. So it wasn't a great atmosphere there. ... [I]t could have been a rollicking kind of a fun picture and it turned out to be a little like treading on eggshells. But I was enjoying the other side of it, Karloff and Sally Forrest and Joe Pevney, and the whole atmosphere of doing this kind of a show.

The actor was more frank with interviewers Tom and Jim Goldrup in the 2006 volume of their book series *Feature Players: The Stories Behind the Faces*:

[Laughton] could be miserable to people. I don't know why he did it, but he had kind of a thing about himself toward other young men, and was very cruel to them. He tried it on me later on in the picture and I said to him, "Please don't try that kind of shit on me. It won't work with me. I'm not one of your boys.[9] ... Don't try to put me down—because I don't give a shit about whether I ever work with you again or not!" ... I was not going to take any guff from anyone. ... Hollywood meant a lot to me, but every man has got to be his own man or your life's not worth living.

In addition to dealing with Laughton, Pate had to contend with too-tight thigh-high boots and an even more uncomfortable wig. He told me,

I'd just come from doing a film with Burt Lancaster [*Ten Tall Men*, 1951] for which I'd cropped my hair, like a G.I. cut. It had grown out a bit by the time I was starting *The Strange Door*, but still it was tough for the hairdresser to fix a wig or a three-quarter wig onto those little half-inches (or less) of hair. I've blanked my memory out on her name 'cause I cheerfully would have killed her during that period. She used to just *adore* screwing little bits of my hair with elastic bands and punching them through with bobby pins and other hairpins to hold the wig on me. Really, I've never had headaches in my *life*, except during that film. By four o'clock in the afternoon, the pull on the hairs to hold that wig on my head gave me some of the best headaches that anyone could have *ever* had![10] So it wasn't an enjoyable film physically, it was physically a very disconcerting film for me, that required me keeping a very, very firm discipline on myself, or otherwise I might have told Mr. Charles Laughton what he could *do* with himself!

Another hapless heroine falling into the clutches of diabolical de Maletroit (Charles Laughton)? No, it's *Strange Door* set visitor Peggy Dow, perhaps on a break from her simultaneously shot movie *Reunion in Reno*.

Pate's aversion to Laughton's on-set antics did not alter his view of Laughton as one of *the* acting greats:

> **Over a period of time, Laughton possibly was the *preeminent* English actor of that kind, I would say from early days most certainly. There's a person of great eminence who possibly should have been knighted for his work in the English theater and in English and American films—I see no reason why he *shouldn't* have been. So maybe it was disappointments that caused Charles to be a difficult person. It seemed a shame to me that such a gigantic talent as he wasn't utilized more.**

Pate has yet more to say about Laughton in our interview in the book *It Came from Weaver Five* (McFarland, 1996), reprinted as *It Came from Horrorwood* in 2004.

Shooting on May 24 continued with the Voltan-Blanche-Denis Tower Room scene. On May 25 they shot the scene of Blanche and Denis in Blanche's room (Stage 14), which begins with Denis entering, pretending to be drunk. Maybe Richard Stapley *was* drunk: In the afternoon, take after take after take is listed on production paperwork as "NG [no good] Stapley." At the end of this day, and the start of the 26th, the moviemakers alternated between scenes of Voltan guiding Denis through the bowels of the chateau, and of Blanche and Denis making their escape on those same sets. Before and after lunch on the 26th, the movie's best action scene was shot: Voltan and Denis as tag team partners in the elaborate armor room fight with Turec and Moret. Sol Gorss and Don Turner, the guards who overpowered Denis in the library, here double for Stapley and Karloff respectively, while Charles Horvath and Eddie Parker as Turec and Moret do their own fighting. With knives, swords, a mace and a suit of armor used as weapons, and with two one-on-one fights simultaneously raging on two levels (the armor room and the stairs and balcony above), it has the feel of a Republic serial donnybrook. The loud, exciting musical accompaniment (familiar to Monster Kids from *Creature from the Black Lagoon*) quickens the pulse. For diehard Universaholics, there's also the geeky joy of seeing Karloff, king of Universal Horrors, locking horns with Eddie Parker, dean of the Universal Horrors stuntmen! The last shot of the day featured Harry Cording, Lugosi's hulking manservant Thamal in the 1934 *The Black Cat*, as a sleeping barracks room guard who, awakened by a cat, almost spoils Blanche and Denis' whisper-quiet getaway.

Fifty-seven extras turned out for the wedding of Blanche and Denis, shot on the Stage 18 Drawing Room set on Monday, May 28. In the midst of the festivities, there's an odd moment where we see, in close-up, the sire looking around casually, with "THE DOOR" (as it's called on the Daily Production Report) in the blurry background. The sire turns to stare at it, the Door comes into focus and the sire becomes blurry, and then the sire turns away and comes into focus again. It's as if the moviemakers felt that, in a movie called *The Door*, it ought to be featured somewhere other than the beginning and the end and gave it a prominent but pointless mid-movie cameo.

Alan Napier, who had his first good-sized Hollywood movie role in *The Invisible Man Returns* (1940), returned this day to the Universal Horrors fold as the flowery, snuff-sniffing Count Grassin, one of the sire's wedding guests. The sky-high (6'5") Napier first set eyes on Laughton in the 1920s, in the basement Common Room at the Royal Academy of Dramatic Art; according to Napier's posthumously published autobiography *Not Just Batman's Butler*, he and Reginald Gardiner were flirting with a pretty girl when she noticed "a fat and not very prepossessing young man" coming down the stairs and she exclaimed, "If it's a new student, it's a shame to take the money!" Napier and Gardiner had to make inquiries to learn that his name was Charles Laughton; a few years later, Laughton and Napier were sharing the Old Vic stage in a revival of *The Cherry Orchard*.[11]

In the original Stevenson story, one conversation between Denis and Blanche leads to the altar. In *The Strange Door*, it leads to altar-cation: Richard Stapley (top left) vs. Charles Horvath, Boris Karloff (top right) vs. Eddie Parker. (Photograph courtesy John Antosiewicz.)

It's in this wedding party scene that we learn for the first time that Denis comes from a good background: "the Normandy de Beaulieus," as Count Grassin puts it. This is not hard for viewers to accept, as throughout much of the movie Denis has spoken and carried himself in an upper-crust way. He's miles above the only other men we see outside the chateau, which would be the tavern goons, who don't appear to have evolved much from apes. Poor de Maletroit: He waits 20 years to put the cherry atop his Revenge Sundae and then, out of all the wretched refuse of France's peasant class, he selects a lapsed blue-blood who needs just one small nudge to go from Goofus to Gallant (or, to say it in a more Stevenson-ian way, from Hyde into Jekyll). Denis' transition from lout to Lochinvar is a bit abrupt but, with an 81-minute running time and the heavy hand of Breen Office-enforced respectability pressing down, a more gradual (or less complete) reformation was perhaps not possible.

After filming ended for the day, Pevney and others went to the Phantom Stage to inspect the newly prepared tunnel and cell sets. May 29 started with a scene begun at the end of the day before, the post-wedding dining hall sequence where the sire lewdly savors the moment as he whispers to the drunken, singing Denis that it's time to go to Blanche: "*Arouuuuse* yourself ... it's time you joined your *briiiide*...!" It's surprising that this interlude, which plays like a detour into Tod Slaughter territory, was apparently okay with the censor, since what we're seeing is the sire taking diabolical pleasure in getting Denis revved-up to rape the girl. The sleepy-eyed sire watches with a smug smile as his guards lead Denis toward Blanche's bedchamber, then luxuriously stretches (*à la* Laughton's Emperor Nero in 1932's *The Sign of the Cross*) and yawns in a shot that grotesquely caps the scene.

Driven mad by the lust for revenge, the sire (Charles Laughton) forces Blanche (Sally Forrest) into what he thinks will be a three-ring marriage: engagement ring, wedding ring, suffering. *The New York Times* categorized Laughton's performance as "more farcical than evil."

Next came the end-of-movie scene where Blanche, Denis and the now well-groomed and resplendent revenant Edmond (Paul Cavanagh) stand by as a workman adds a handle to the Strange Door, and Denis says that he'll henceforth be "a willing prisoner" in the chateau if Blanche will have him (which of course she will). For the closing shot, an "exterior" where we see into the chateau from the "outside," a tree branch shadow was cast upon the door to enhance the illusion of outdoor shooting. Filmed but not included in this feel-good finale: footage of Blanche and Denis again looking at the portrait of Blanche's mother, before joining Edmond and the workman in the entrance hall.

At 3:20 in the afternoon there was a move from Stage 18 to the Phantom Stage, where they got a start on the scene of Voltan hurrying to Edmond's cell as the sire torments the prisoner. A day off (Wednesday, May 30, Memorial Day) and then back to the bowels of the chateau for the rest of the scene. There were two takes of the shot where the sire taunts Edmond, one with Edmond screaming intermittently, the other with him screaming throughout. Just before noon they got the screen-filling, dimly lit close-up of the sire, gripping and pressing his face against the cell bars, mocking Edmond's laughter and shouting, "That's right, *sssscream*!!"—the moment when viewers realize that while Edmond is more conspicuously mad, the sire is madder. After lunch, the moviemakers tackled a number of shots for various parts of the finale, including de Maletroit's passageway walk as he's tormented by Corbeau's voice in his mind's ear ("She *is* like her mother, like her mother, like her mother..."). Late in the day, Karloff added to the unintentional(?) humorousness of the movie: Voltan, injured in his battles with Corbeau and the sire, enters the dungeon, holds the cell door key high and, radiant with triumph, announces to the cell prisoners, "Master ... the key ... *the key*!"—and then his eyes get all Krispy Kreme (glazed over) and he flops to the floor like a dead mackerel! In the early evening, after rehearsing part of the final cell scene, director Pevney decided not to shoot it until the next day, citing the importance of the scene and the lateness of the hour.

On May 31, with *The Strange Door* nearing the end of production, one Universal producer was already pushing for the studio to make its next horror movie. The producer, Albert J. Cohen; the horror movie he wanted to see produced:

The Werewolf of Paris, based on Guy Endore's 1933 novel. That day, he wrote in a memo,

> **Not only is the title of this a natural, in my opinion, but in keeping with the "unusual and exploitation horror pictures" that seem to be doing business at the box office, I think this one has excellent possibilities. There are some elements in there that will require both elimination and careful handling—but the final result can be a very exciting picture. If I remember correctly, the book has been around for quite awhile and I dare say can be purchased at a reasonable price. As a matter of fact, I think if we are interested enough, that a complete flat deal for both the book and a screenplay to be written by Endore can be made.**

Cohen ends the memo with an added thought: "[It] occurs to me that if quick action is taken on this subject, many of the sets now being used in *The Door* can be used for this story." Raymond Crossett, head of Universal's story department, was another fan of the idea of making *Werewolf*, calling it "the ultimate in horror stories—a well-written, imaginative and fascinating tale. It has a compelling box office title; and a screen treatment could easily delete the most unpleasant aspects." Universal did not bite on the idea of making Endore's tale of werewolf attacks and rapes and cannibalism and sado-masochism (and and and), but a decade later they released Hammer's cleaned-up adaptation *The Curse of the Werewolf*. Monster Kids may find it fun to speculate what a 1951 Universal *Werewolf of Paris* would have been like, and wonder if the studio's go-to guy for horror flicks, Karloff (*Abbott and Costello Meet the Killer, Boris Karloff, A&C Meet Dr. Jekyll and Mr. Hyde, The Strange Door, The Black Castle*) would have been part of the cast.

The *Strange Door* cast and crew had a nine a.m. shooting call on Friday the first of June, and after a bit more rehearsal, the filming of the cell scene recommenced. On screen, these dark, dank subterranean scenes, complete with the sound of river water garrulously gurgling past, do create a persuasively medieval mood, so it's fun to spot on the production paperwork a notation about a delay caused by the noise of a passing airplane. After lunch, they got shots of cellmates Blanche, Denis and Edmond reacting to the moving walls and trying to stop their progress with Edmond's cot, which instantly buckles upward and breaks into pieces. *Strange Door*'s walls-coming-together scene is much more suspenseful than the equivalent footage in the movie that presumably inspired it, the 1935 *The Raven*—and according to Stapley, more suspenseful on the set than in the movie!

"It was far more frightening experiencing that in person than it came over in the film," he told me. "I had to call out and say 'Stop!' at one point when the walls were coming together. I thought I was really gonna be crushed, and they had to stop it. Once the mechanics of [the moving walls] started, it was very difficult to *stop* 'em—and we all knew this. There couldn't be any hold-up. I had to get that key [from Voltan]!" When I laughed, he interjected, "No, I'm not kidding! My arm was bruised and everything else!" Stapley also recalls that at one point while reaching through the cell bars for the key, "the gate began to give!" Last shot of the day: the inside-the-cell shot of the prisoners exiting as the walls, in the foreground, crush a table and then close together. The way Blanche runs to the fallen Voltan, then instantly leaves his side to sadly embrace her father, makes us realize that Voltan's a goner.

Laughton's last day on the movie, June 2 found cast and crew on the Process Stage for Exterior Parapet and Waterwheel Scenes. June 2 footage included the sire using the lever to mesh the waterwheel gears, Corbeau shooting Voltan, Voltan choking Corbeau, the sire stabbing Voltan, Voltan pushing the sire off the parapet into the water, the sire climbing out of the water too close to the cogs, etc. Needless to say, in these action vignettes, with players Laughton and Karloff a bit past their freshness date, we see a good bit of their stuntmen, Don Turner again substituting for Karloff and Sailor Vincent for Laughton. Vincent, a welterweight boxer turned stuntman and bit player, had previously

For the soggy sire, comeuppance is about to arrive via the crushing cogs of his own elaborate torture device. Charles Laughton could have gotten away with using a double in this scene but wanted to do it himself. (Photograph courtesy Ronald V. Borst/Hollywood Movie Posters.)

doubled Laughton in *The Hunchback of Notre Dame,* swinging on a rope to rescue Esmeralda from the gallows platform. No longer a welterweight (or even close), Vincent handled the action for plus-sized players like Laughton, Edward G. Robinson, W.C. Fields, Alan Hale and Barton MacLane.

Regarding the waterwheel and parapet, Pevney told me,

> On the Process Stage the carpenters came in and built a 20 × 40 or 30 × 40 foot [enclosure] on the stage cement floor. It was made of wood, glued or nailed together, and then waterproofed as best they could in those days. Then canvas was laid inside it and the water was poured in. Of course, water began to leak out the side [*laughs*]. I remember sandbags, allll around this thing, absorbing the water so it wouldn't get on the rest of the stage.
>
> Well, wouldn't you know, as soon as Laughton saw that huge waterwheel turning, he said, "Joe, I wanna do this" [the scene of the sire in the water]. Well, I was scared to death! Now, Laughton had a *very* good stuntman-double, the guy looked exactly like Laughton in long shots, no problem, so I could have put the stuntman in there in the long shot, turned the wheel, and then cut in and done a close-up of Laughton after we'd wet him down with off-stage water. Well, no, Laughton wanted to do it, so I had him put on the waterwheel, strapped in tight. And there wasn't too much clearance [between the bottom of the waterwheel and the stage floor], because I think the "tank" was only about four foot deep. But enough to clear his belly, in any event. They had to make sure that he didn't get hung up on the bottom, because he not only could have gotten hurt, but he could have gotten *worse* than hurt, who knows? There were lots of people standing by to make sure the darn thing worked.
>
> I started in a long shot, showed the entire wheel, then I moved in slowly, as I remember the shot, and sure enough up came Laughton, blubbering and spitting and spewing water as only he could do it! Well, nobody was deeply impressed; *he* was [*laughs*], but nobody else was terribly impressed with that stunt!

Pevney's story of strapping Laughton to the waterwheel doesn't pass the smell test; in the movie, he gets nowhere near it. But we do see just enough of the actor in the water—despite fog lying atop the water, and posts that block our view—to know that it's him, so Pevney's account of Laughton *wanting* to do the wet and wild scene rings true. Pevney continued, "Laughton and I respected each other. He was a terrific guy, a true professional, wonderfully warm, sensitive. Loved fun. *Loved fun.* And he had a heck of a good time. Now, I don't know what *he* said about the picture, but I can assure you, he had a heck of a good time doing this movie!" For Laughton, the role of de Maletroit, tyrant-master of the chateau (and, apparently, much of the country around), was a return to the tyrannical types which he had essayed in the 1930s, on land (*The Sign of the Cross,* 1932, *White Woman,* 1933, *The Barretts of Wimpole Street,* 1934), sea (*Mutiny on the Bounty*), island (*Island of Lost Souls*) and more.

Also shot that day: Corbeau on the parapet, dramatically confronting de Maletroit after the latter has set the cell's crushing walls in motion. Pointing out that Blanche is very much like the beloved Helene, Corbeau obviously wants to see if he can shake the sire's resolve to carry this murderous plot through to the finish; Corbeau must feel the need to know if he (Corbeau) is still the Beta sadist to de Maletroit's Alpha. (Corbeau's insubordination here might be payback for the sire calling him squeamish in an earlier exchange.) For a moment it looks as though de Maletroit may crack ("You go too *far*, Corbeau!" he shouts as he sinks to his knees and buries his face in his crossed arms). But then the sire pulls the lever out of its slot, throws it into the river, crosses his arms and makes a face that's half defiance, half Droopy Dog. Story-wise, this flare-up is completely dispensable but it's appealingly macabre to find one of the movie's resident sadists doing a gut check on the other. When de Maletroit discards the lever, proving that he *is* willing to carry on, Corbeau is so impressed by his passion for "both love and hate" that there's a quiver in his voice as he humbly declares, "I'm *still* your servant." This kinky face-off is Cottrell's stand-out scene in the movie.

A shot of the sire floundering in the water below the parapet was Laughton's last shot of the day, and he left the studio that night finished with the movie. Four nights later, he was on an airplane, headed for England for a month-long tour of *Don Juan in Hell* with Charles Boyer, Cedric Hardwicke[12] and Agnes Moorehead.

In addition to Laughton and Karloff providing a link to horror flicks of yore, much of the music in *Strange Door* came from the archives (as musicologist David Schecter will explain at length below). For fans who grew up watching the Universal franchise monster movies of the 1930s and '40s, *Strange Door*'s reuse of some of "their" music gives it a huge lift. But the above-described dungeon scenes are *devoid* of music. The sounds of the rushing river, the creaking and groaning of the waterwheel apparatus and the grinding noise of the cell's moving stone walls combine in a sinister symphony that helps create what *Harrison's Reports* called "considerable suspense."

On Monday, June 4, the next-to-last day of shooting, the filmmakers again met on the Process Stage for the burial grounds scene. The first shot of the day: a high shot of the entrance to this boneyard, a strictly off-the-cob, only-in-the-movies Grislyland of grave markers, religious statues, dead trees, low-lying fog (it looks more like a blanket of snow) and intermittently lightning flashes. Throughout the day, various acts of mayhem were put on film: Denis wrestling with Corbeau, Voltan strangling a footman (Bruce Riley),

On Universal's Process Stage, Charles Laughton (top left) shows off his waterwheel as William Cottrell keeps Sally Forrest and Richard Stapley at gunpoint. The waterwheel scenes were so obviously done on an interior set that it's hard to keep in mind that it's *supposed* to be outside. (Photograph courtesy John Antosiewicz.)

Rinville getting a knife in his back (and directing a "*Why*? Why *me*?" look into the camera before he falls), Corbeau shooting Voltan, and Voltan (in a nice dolly shot) toppling from the bank into the fast-moving, fog-covered river. Don Turner, Tom Steele and Carey Loftin were the stuntmen on hand for this action-filled scene. Making money for doing nothing: In his second and last day on the movie, Alan Napier sat in the coach playing the dead (knife in the back) Count Grassin.

After 61 hot dinners were served, actors and crew members moved to the spot where seemingly *all* Universal horror moviemakers inevitably find themselves, the back lot Tower of London. In "exterior" scenes shot on the Process Stage, the ground fog had stayed put but now, outdoors, the wind kept blowing it away. Shot that night, beginning at about 8:40: Blanche and Denis running down that oh-so-familiar exterior staircase to Count Grassin's coach; then, after a change of clothes for Richard Stapley, Denis, pursued by townsmen from the tavern, approaching the Door; the Door opening so that Denis stumbles inside; and townsmen searching near the Door for Denis. As the clock neared midnight, the movie's title character was ready for its close-up: The cameraman shot a minute and 15 seconds of footage of the Door, to be seen behind the main titles.

The Door, scheduled for 18 days of shooting, did indeed wrap on its 18th day, June 5, yet another long day for Stapley. There was a crew call of 12:42 in the afternoon and then, both on the Process Stage and the Phantom Stage, they did some filming, most notably a high shot (photographed from the soundstage catwalk) of the spinning waterwheel, a guard pacing the platform above it. This would be integrated into a matte shot incorporating the chateau wall and the running sweep of the river (Denis' dizzying p.o.v. from his tower room). Also shot: gears rising out of the river and engaging with the waterwheel gears; the sire (a dummy) crushed in the gears; and Denis in the public coach, with rear-projected backgrounds. After dinner they moved outdoors to the Hershey Property for shots of the speeding public coach, the mounted townsmen in pursuit, Denis making a dash for freedom, the torch-carrying townsmen on his trail, etc. One take was spoiled when Stapley fell; he changed shoes to avoid a second slip. At 2:10 on the morning of June 6, the company was dismissed and the final day of principal photography came to an end.

> Fat Boy [Laughton] was terrific. He looked like Gorgeous George.
>
> —a sneak preview audience member's *Strange Door* "Preview Comment Card" remark

On Tuesday, August 7, 1951, the movie's first (and perhaps only) sneak preview took place at L.A.'s United Artists Theatre following the showing of the Joel McCrea Western *Cattle Drive*. At that point, it was still titled *The Door* and presumably the print shown had that on-screen title. Preview Comment Cards were filled out by 95 audience members, most between the ages of 18 and 30. The results were encouraging:

How Would You Rate The Picture

Outstanding	19
Excellent	24
Very Good	26
Good	17
Fair	5
Poor	2

Responding to the question, "Whom did you like best in the picture?," 44 chose Charles Laughton, with Boris Karloff and Richard Stapley sharing a very distant second place (14 each), Michael Pate receiving three votes—and Sally Forrest and Paul Cavanagh tied at 0. The question "Which scenes did you like most?" found many in agreement that the climactic "closing walls" scene was the best in the picture; others opted for "Love scenes," and two cited Laughton's dining hall antics. The "closing walls" scene also scored high in the "Which Scenes, If Any, Did You Dislike?" category, with commenters complaining that it was too dragged-out. A whopping 64 said that the picture held their interest throughout, with only two dissenting. Seventy-eight people said they would recommend the movie to their friends; nine said they wouldn't.

Any Added Comment?

Excellent acting—interesting plot without being too gruesome.
Maybe a little too much on the gory side.
Kept you on the edge of your seat.
Suspense very thrilling.
Best picture I have seen in many months.
All were excellent.
Whew!
Keep track of Richard Stapley.
Did not like Richard Stapley.
Sally Forrest stinks.
This is the first picture attended in year since bought television. Pictures will have to be more exceptional before I come again.
Good for hair-raising thrills.
Wall scene stolen from Edgar Allan Poe.
Too unreal. Corny in parts. Hysteria too overdone.
A waste of film and talent.
It stinks.

In that same month, Universal made the decision to change the title of their Gothic horror-adventure from *The Door* to the infinitesimally more interesting *The Strange Door*. On October 25, many promotional ideas were discussed in a meeting at Seattle's Olympic Hotel. The contribution of Herb Sobottka of the Hamrick Theatre was to point out that Laughton by himself was box office poison. Fred Danz of Sterling Theatres, perhaps with Disney's recent (1950) *Treasure Island* in mind, said that he was of the opinion that Robert Louis Stevenson's name *not* be connected to the advertisements, Danz believing that the Stevenson name would suggest "kid stuff" rather than horror. The ads do mention Stevenson but, possibly as a result of Danz's objection, only as part of the line "Robert Louis Stevenson's Masterpiece of Terror." The trailer too uses the "Masterpiece of Terror" line, following it up with, "Only the Pen of a Master Could Create Such Horror and Suspense."

Marginalia

• The May 24, 1934, installment of radio's *The Fleischmann's Yeast Hour* featured Rudy Vallee singing, some banjo player banjo-ing and, as if that weren't enough, a "Sire de Maletroit's Door" adaptation with Helen Chandler and Melvyn Douglas. In August 1947, the radio series *Escape*, a showcase for tales of adventure and intrigue, dramatized Stevenson's story with Ramsey Hill, Elliott Lewis and Peggy Webber. There were also TV versions in the late 1940s and early '50s, including a *Your Show Time* episode with Dan O'Herlihy and a *Lux Video Theatre* with future Universal Horrors stars Richard Greene (*The Black Castle*) and Coleen Gray (*The Leech Woman*).

• Also shooting at Universal in May 1951 when *The Strange Door* was made: one of their "Westerns in the sand," *Flame of Araby*, with Lon Chaney, Jr., fourth-billed as a Corsair lord. A too-good-to-be-true Howard Heffernan-bylined news story had Chaney visiting the *Strange Door* set as Laughton and Karloff were rehearsing their gruesome fight scene: "It was with apparent nostalgia that Lon observed the two in their final death struggle. He nodded his head and smiled approvingly. 'The old man would have loved being in this one,' he said."

• Charles Higham, writing about *The Old Dark House* in *Charles Laughton: An Intimate Biography,* claims that Karloff didn't appeal to Laughton. Per Higham, *Old Dark House* director James Whale was "a cool, elegant and terrible snob [who] spoke contemptuously of Boris, calling him 'a coal-heaver, a truck driver.' While Charles hated that kind of class consciousness, he still didn't warm to Karloff." Laughton biographer Simon Callow also reported that Laughton "never cared for Karloff." Talking to interviewer James Bawden, Raymond Massey laid it on the line: "[Laughton] positively loathed Boris Karloff who was rumored to be part Indian—Charles was a white supremacist."

Standing up for his old pal Laughton, William Phipps hotly contested the Massey statement:

> That's the most absurd thing I ever heard of. It's ridiculous! When you read that to me, the first thing that came to my mind was the

fact that Laughton came to see me in a play [*Forward the Heart*, 1961] that I did at the Circle Theater where I played a blind man who falls in love with his caretaker [Kim Hamilton], who was black. And when my character found out that she was black, his prejudice showed and he ended up committing suicide. Laughton, after seeing the play, said that it was absurd because, as he put it, "Love is love. What *difference* does it make that she's black?" He did not have any bias or prejudice that way; in fact, of everybody I've ever known, he was the furthest from being prejudiced or a white supremacist. It was just completely beyond him!

• Except for the bit players seen as the Lion Rouge singer and the barmaids, no one in *The Strange Door* speaks French or even bothers with a French accent. Once Denis runs out of the tavern, the character names de Maletroit and Corbeau are all that's "French" about the movie.

• On the Friday of the film's first week in production, *The Hollywood Reporter*'s run-down of pictures in progress listed Nathan Juran as its art director, but on-screen in the finished film, only Bernard Herzbrun and Eric Orbom are credited; I don't know whether the Oscar-winning art director of John Ford's *How Green Was My Valley* (1941) actually worked on the movie at all. Juran certainly worked on Universal's *next* horror film: The following year, he made his directorial bow at the helm of *The Black Castle*.

• Laughton's screen-hogging in *Strange Door* occasionally calls to mind his Squire Pengallan in Alfred Hitchcock's *Jamaica Inn* (1939): more head-of-the-dinner-table pigging-out and holding court, stretching like a cat, jabbing a finger at listeners to make an angry point, bombastically shouting to summon underlings, etc. In both movies, Laughton's characters show themselves to be men of bottomless rudeness and to be clueless about their own crudity. Of course, both were preceded by Laughton's Henry VIII, who with food falling out of his mouth decries "coarse brutes. There's no *delicacy* nowadays."

• Perhaps some body padding would have made Boris Karloff more suitable to the role of the uber-tenacious Voltan, who doesn't break a sweat out-wrestling Moret in the barracks; strangling the footman in the cemetery; dispatching Corbeau after he (Voltan) has been shot once or twice; and opening a can of whoop-ass on de Maletroit despite the bullets *and* a knife driven in his back up to the hilt! Dear Boris was a fine actor but in *Strange Door*, looking his age and *then* some, and probably tipping the Toledos at a buck-fifty soaking wet, he looks decidedly out of place laying the smackdown on all and sundry. Karloff, in his last "physical heavy" role, is a bust.

• Karloff came close to acting in a movie adaptation of a Robert Louis Stevenson tale in the 1930s, when Universal kept announcing their intention to make the author's "The Suicide Club" a vehicle for him. (When their plans fell through, Universal sold the "Suicide Club" screen rights to MGM, where in 1936 it became the Robert Montgomery-starring *Trouble for Two.*) The first and by far the best of Karloff's three Stevenson-derived movies was Lewton's 1945 *The Body Snatcher*, based on RLS's 1885 short story; he gave an Oscar-caliber performance as Gray, the cabman who spends his midnights despoiling graves in 18th-century Edinburgh kirkyards in order to supply cadavers to Dr. MacFarlane's (Henry Daniell) anatomical chop-shop. Next for Karloff came *The Strange Door* and then, two years later *Abbott and Costello Meet Dr. Jekyll and Mr. Hyde*, such a far cry from Stevenson's novella that RLS receives no screen credit. It's funny that, in *Strange Door* publicity, Universal called Stevenson's innocuous "The Sire de Malétroit's Door" a "Masterpiece of Terror"; and then two years later, with *A&C Meet J&H*, took the author's "masterpiece of terror" *Strange Case of Dr. Jekyll and Mr. Hyde* and turned it into something innocuous! Karloff's last brush with Stevenson was on the small screen in 1960, when "Special Guest Star" Boris played Capt. Billy Bones in the *DuPont Show of the Month* episode "Treasure Island."

• Apparently Karloff wouldn't or couldn't do his own stunts so he's doubled now and then. It appears to me that at least twice, the moviemakers try to camouflage his use of a double. In the armor room fight, I believe we're seeing Karloff's double high on the stairs as Stapley and

Boris Karloff as Voltan the "sad sack" dungeon keeper, in the half-lit chateau catacombs. Gotta love the piled-up human bones in the hanging cage!

Horvath grapple in the foreground; the double starts hustling down the winding staircase, exits out the right side of the frame, and then on ground level Karloff enters from the right. Later, when Voltan climbs out of the river and up the side of the waterwheel platform, it appears to be the double until he momentarily passes out of sight, and then Dear Boris lifts his head into view at the top. Colorado-born Don Turner, Karloff's *Strange Door* double, had gone from cowboy and lumberjack to one of the movie business' best-known stuntmen, doubling for Errol Flynn in perhaps all of his most famous Warner Brothers pictures.

• Voltan is gaunt, gray-haired, gray-faced, and looks as though he's never been young—and yet the character proves throughout the movie to be the toughest customer in the de Maletroit stable. William Cottrell told me about an occasion when he and other actors "were all sitting around, waiting to be called on the set. Boris was in complete makeup, and while we were sitting there, out came one of the assistants and he said, 'Mr. Karloff, would you mind getting into makeup now? We're about ready to start.' Boris talked about that for several days, saying, 'What is the *matter* with them? Do I look so bad?' Of course it was an accident, because Boris was a very charming-looking man in real life."

• In 1951, after a years-long Hollywood horror movie drought, *three* were released at practically the same time, *The Son of Dr. Jekyll*, *Bride of the Gorilla* and *The Strange Door*—and Paul Cavanagh was in all three of 'em. His *Strange Door* role as Edmond could be considered a dry run for his appearance in a later Universal, *The Purple Mask* (1955), where again he played a noble, Duc de Latour; where again he's a dungeon prisoner; and where again he's reunited with his daughter (Colleen Miller) when *she's* imprisoned *with* him!

• Another small but noticeable link between *The Strange Door* and the 1935 *Raven*: What Monster Kid, growing up with Lugosi's pronouncement of how long it will take for the pendulum to descend upon Judge Thatcher ("*Fif-teeen minnn-nnnutes!*"), doesn't flash back to it when de Maletroit tells his cell prisoners how much time divides them from death-by-crushing-walls: "You have at most ... *fif-teeen minutes!*"

• "I don't know really why Laughton ever said yes [to doing *The Strange Door*], except he was quite keen to just pull money in," said Richard Stapley. "Karloff, I thought, gave quite a nice performance, and it was thrilling to work with him because when I was a kid at school he was the original Frankenstein and all those [other monsters]. That was kind of exciting."

• In the *Strange Door* pressbook, the thoroughly fishy-sounding item "Karloff Salutes Monster Role" contends that one day during production, Karloff observed the 20th anniversary of the 1931 *Frankenstein* "by donning the Frankenstein makeup and wardrobe and going through several scenes from the Frankenstein series for the pleasure of cast and crew members of his newest film.... It took the veteran actor an entire morning to change himself into the gruesome character" from the 1931 shocker, which was shot (says the pressbook) on the same soundstage as *Strange Door*.

• *The Strange Door*'s radio spots laid the emphasis not on the horror elements but on "thrilling adventure" and "strange romance," even fibbing that the movie is "brilliant in swordplay" despite the fact there really *is* no swordplay. Laughton and Karloff are called "your favorite supermen of suspense" in the 60-second radio spot, the 30-second one adding that in this movie they "face each other for the first time," the copywriters unaware of (or choosing to ignore) *The Old Dark House*. The way these radio

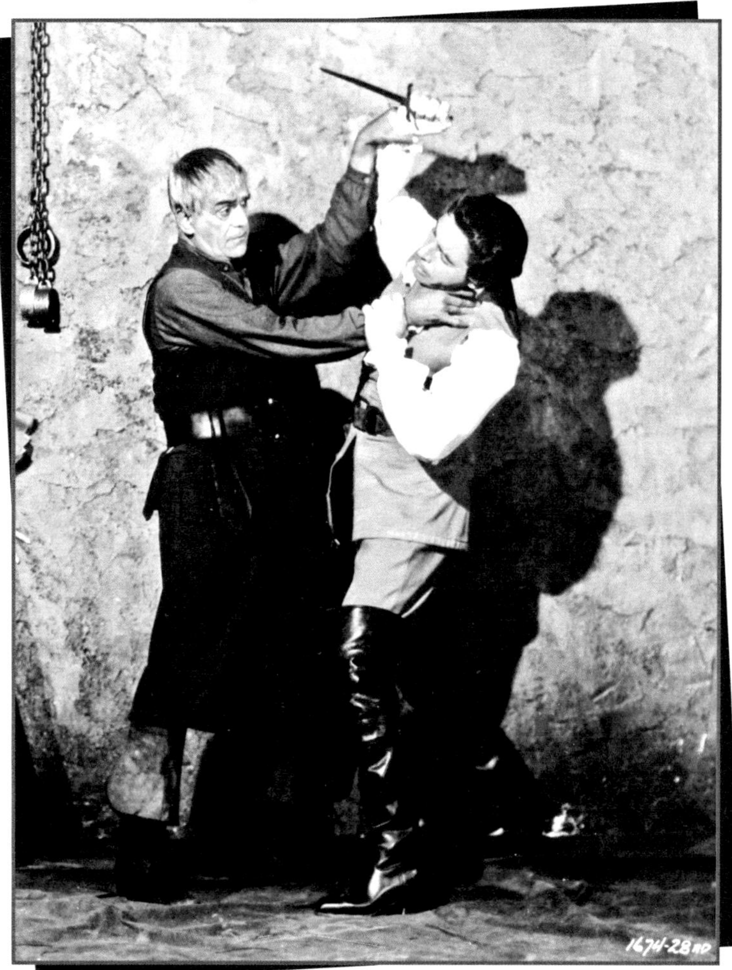

Once you notice that a good bit of the *Strange Door* plot was derived from the 1935 *The Raven*, it's fun to also pick up on the fact that two of the sire's birds of prey are named Talon (a bird's claw) and Corbeau (French for raven). In this posed photograph with no basis in the movie, Michael Pate's Talon (with knife) tangles with Boris Karloff.

spots for Universal's first 1950s horror movie put the accent on the story's "strange romance" ("the most sensational courtship in fiction"), and downplay the horror, is reminiscent of Universal's soft-pedaling of *Dracula* (1931), the first movie in their '30s horror cycle ("The story of the strangest passion the world has ever known!").

Even the pressbook's tips for exhibitors were "horror-lite," to put it mildly: Run ads praising the doors of fine restaurants and other local establishments, encourage the local library to setup a special table display of Robert Louis Stevenson books, paint a large question mark on the door of a vacant store, etc. (Yawn.) The loopiest suggestion was to get a department store to build three doors in one of their larger windows and put a valuable piece of merchandise behind one of the doors—then ask locals to try to guess which door *and* to attempt to *describe* the unseen merchandise!

• According to *Elsa Lanchester Herself*, for some 1952 productions of *Don Juan in Hell*, Laughton and Paul Gregory signed Karloff to take over the role of the Devil, which Laughton was relinquishing. They then changed their minds and had Vincent Price play the part. Lanchester added, "Charles, however, often had other people do his dirty work—so the stage manager notified Karloff of the change."

From what William Phipps knew of Laughton and Lanchester, he didn't think the "Charles had others do his dirty work" anecdote rang true.

> I don't believe that. *I* saw Laughton dismiss people, *he* did it himself. Remember [actor] James Anderson? I got him into Laughton's group; on my recommendation, Laughton took him. Well, he misbehaved, and Laughton told him to leave, never come back. Then the next day while we were rehearsing—I think we were working on *Twelfth Night*—Anderson came in and sat down, uninvited. Laughton went over to him and said, "No, Jimmy. No. No." He just kept saying, "*No*, Jimmy," and Jimmy just kept looking at him, and Laughton kept saying, "No, Jimmy," and finally Jim got up and left. That was a tense scene. So Laughton was no coward, believe me. He was in the fuckin' *war*, God damn it, he was a soldier in World War I, he put his life on the line. He could have copped out on his homosexuality there, but he didn't. That tells you somethin', doesn't it?
>
> Elsa made up a lot of stories. Right after Laughton died, she went on a few talk shows and started bellyaching about his being a homosexual, and she didn't know it, and it ruined her life, and "the sacrifices [she] made," and blah blah blah, and *that* was a bunch of bullshit. She knew all along, and she stayed with him because she basked in the glory, she rode the tail of the comet. So I don't think that Karloff situation ever happened. I think she just wanted to make that dig about Laughton having other people do his dirty work.

• Universal's "Summary of Production Budget" for the movie, compiled on December 19, 1951, shows that it had total direct charges of $284,100; the addition of studio overhead charges raised the tally to $368,620.

The Release

By Robert J. Kiss

Theatrical First Run, Halloween 1951 to August 1952

Lined up by Universal-International as a November 1951 release, *The Strange Door* was started early as a stand-alone attraction at a handful of "special pre-release Halloween shows" at Shea's circuit theaters east of the Mississippi on the night of October 31. Since this was a Wednesday, with most potential patrons needing to be at work or college the next morning, the majority of venues kicked off their "midnight screenings" well before the witching hour. Shea's Theater in Jamestown, New York, opening its doors at 10:30 p.m., while the Weller Theater in Zanesville, Ohio, held out until 11:30 p.m.

Ads for the Zanesville opening implored, "First Showing! Not a Repeater!," and were thus the first to highlight a concern that remained tangible throughout *The Strange Door*'s first run: namely, that it might be mistaken for a reissue of an old pre–1945 title. With the dearth of (serious) horror movie production since that time, cinemagoers had grown accustomed to virtually all horror titles being reruns, and the Laughton and Karloff names offered no guarantee that this was a new picture.

In fact, the Shea's circuit Halloween screenings in the east had been beaten to the projector by the 550-seat Granada Theater in Spokane, Washington, where *The Strange Door* had opened for a week of regular business on October 30, as the top half of a double-bill with Republic's 56-minute Roy Rogers cheapie *Heart of the Rockies*. In addition to constituting the *de facto* premiere of *The Strange Door*, this also inaugurated the widespread presentation of the picture with a distinctly low-rent supporting feature, as outlined in detail in the section on double-bills below.

From the first week of November, Universal started to release *The Strange Door* around the nation in decidedly piecemeal fashion, with the majority of early playdates limited to California, the Northwest, the Midwest and the East Coast. By May 1952, the movie was already playing second-run engagements in numerous towns and cities, while other parts of the nation had yet to see it at all. For example, it would not open at the downtown LaPlaza Theatre in the 97,000-strong city of St. Petersburg, Florida, until as late as August 12. Consequently, the first run of *The Strange*

Door may be considered to have extended from Halloween 1951 through to roughly the end of August 1952.

The picture's box office performance appears to have been as erratic as its release schedule, with San Francisco reporting grosses that were 65 percent above normal for a first-run picture, many other major cities claiming average to slightly below-average trade (referred to in *Variety* with such underwhelmed adjectives as "okay," "fairish" and "so-so"), while first-run theater owners in Pittsburgh announced dismal takings amounting to *less than one-third* of the norm throughout the month of February 1952. These extreme fluctuations can be attributed to an array of different factors, including the quantity and effectiveness of ballyhoo undertaken by individual venues; the overall quality of the bill relative to the establishment in which it was being shown; the extent to which local advertising reassured patrons that *The Strange Door* was indeed a new movie; and prevailing weather conditions (with the Pittsburgh opening coinciding with temperatures having plunged to five degrees).

Stand-Alone Presentation

Within a sample of 1200 first-run movie theaters across the U.S. which showed *The Strange Door* between Halloween 1951 and August 1952, 22 percent presented the picture as a stand-alone attraction. This type of presentation was most common at small-town and rural venues where single bills were already the established norm. However, it was also attested at special openings of the movie for Halloween or New Year, as well as at a limited number of engagements at upscale city houses. The latter tend to have underperformed, with the run commencing on November 22 (Thanksgiving Day) at Philadelphia's Midtown Theatre generating grosses that were ten percent below average, indicating that *The Strange Door* was not quite strong enough to carry the bill at premier establishments.

Double-Bills

Absolutely the most usual way to have originally encountered *The Strange Door* was on a double-bill, with this form of presentation accounting for 75 percent of screenings within the sample of 1200 first-run theaters nationwide. Since no regular co-feature had been assigned (adding to the general impression that Universal lacked a cohesive marketing strategy for the picture), it ended up playing alongside a seemingly endless array of different movies; the two lists below attest a ludicrous 142 co-features from within the sample. Although a few theater owners opted to create an all-horror bill by pairing *The Strange Door* with a reissued 1940s title or with one of the other two horror features released during the fall of 1951—Realart's *Bride of the Gorilla* and Columbia's *The Son of Dr. Jekyll*—the overwhelming majority continued to embrace the familiar concept of a "balanced" program that aimed at securing broader appeal by presenting works from two distinct genres.

The Strange Door was almost equally likely to play as the top or bottom half of the bill, with a slim majority of 53 percent of venues electing to show it as the lower-billed sup-

King Karloff looks a good bit more presentable, making a December 1951 *Strange Door* promotional appearance at New York's Criterion Theatre, than he does in the movie itself. The shot above was snapped in the lobby by teenager Richard Bojarski, 23 years later the author of the book *The Films of Boris Karloff.* (Photographs courtesy John Antosiewicz.)

porting feature. This should not, however, be taken to mean that patrons who saw the movie as a top-billed "main attraction" experienced it in the same way as those who encountered it on the lower half of a bill, as the two distinct lists of co-features below seek to demonstrate.

As the Top Half of a Double-Bill

Theaters which presented *The Strange Door* as the top half of a double-bill were predominantly lower-rung suburban, neighborhood and small-town venues offering low ticket prices and a large number of daily screenings. Eighty-eight percent of the supporting co-features on the list below are in black-and-white, and one in four is a reissue rather than a new release. Monogram, Republic and Lippert product abounds, with short running times the order of the day: the average length of these co-features is 73 minutes, with 21 of the titles running 60 minutes or less. Universal releases account for a scant five percent of the total, with the studio having made no discernible effort to control both halves of the bill at these venues.

If one considers this list in terms of representing those titles to which *The Strange Door* was perceived to be of superior caliber and quality, and alongside which it was therefore suited for play as a top-billed attraction, then it places the picture in an altogether lowly position within the hierarchy of theatrical features in circulation during 1951 and 1952.

All of the second-billed co-features within the sample of 1200 theaters nationwide are arranged alphabetically below. The month mentioned in each case is the earliest in which the pairing was attested. Engagements with *The Son of Dr. Jekyll* made for a double dose of (loose) Robert Louis Stevenson adaptations, though theater owners had more sense than to point this out to patrons.

(*) signifies a slightly more substantial number of playdates for the double-bill.
bold titles are Universal releases.

February 1952 *Along the Navajo Trail* (Roy Rogers; Republic reissue)
February 1952 *As You Were* (William Tracy)
August 1952 *Bad Man from Big Bend* (Cal Shrum; Astor reissue of *Swing, Cowboy, Swing*)
March 1952 *Bandit Queen* (Barbara Britton)
May 1952 *Barber of Seville* (Ferruccio Tagliavini)
January 1952 *The Basketball Fix* (John Ireland)
May 1952 *The Black Lash* (Buster Crabbe)
December 1951 (*) *Bride of the Gorilla* (Barbara Payton)
February 1952 *Calling Bulldog Drummond* (Walter Pidgeon)
January 1952 (*) *Captain Blood* (Errol Flynn; Warner Bros. reissue)
May 1952 *Captive of Billy the Kid* (Rocky Lane)
April 1952 *The Catman of Paris* (Carl Esmond; Republic reissue)
March 1952 *Cherokee Uprising* (Whip Wilson)
February 1952 *Colorado Sundown* (Rex Allen)
November 1951 *Corky of Gasoline Alley* (Scotty Beckett)
December 1951 *Crazy Over Horses* (The Bowery Boys)
May 1952 *Criminal Lawyer* (Pat O'Brien)
May 1952 *Dangerous Venture* (William Boyd; United Artists reissue)
February 1952 *Darling, How Could You!* (Joan Fontaine)
May 1952 *Desert Pursuit* (Wayne Morris)
December 1951 *East Side Kids* (Vince Barnett; Savoy Films reissue)
January 1952 *Finders Keepers* (Tom Ewell)
April 1952 *The First Legion* (Charles Boyer)
April 1952 *The Golden Horde* (Ann Blyth)
November 1951 *The Great Mike* (Stuart Erwin; independent reissue)
November 1951 *The Green Finger* (Anthony Hulme)
January 1952 *Hard, Fast and Beautiful* (Sally Forrest)
January 1952 (*) *Havana Rose* (Estelita Rodriguez)
October 1951 *Heart of the Rockies* (Roy Rogers)
July 1952 *The Hills of Utah* (Gene Autry)
May 1952 *Honeychile* (Judy Canova)
June 1952 *Insurance Investigator* (Richard Denning)
April 1952 *Journey into Light* (Sterling Hayden)
January 1952 *Jungle Headhunters* (exploitation)
December 1951 *Jungle of Chang* (exploitation)
February 1952 *Kentucky Jubilee* (Jerry Colonna)
August 1952 *The Longhorn* (Wild Bill Elliott)
January 1952 *The Magic Carpet* (Lucille Ball)
February 1952 *The Man from Tumbleweeds* (Wild Bill Elliott; Astor reissue)
March 1952 *Man of the Forest* (Randolph Scott; Favorite Films reissue)
December 1951 *Maniacs on Wheels* (Dirk Bogarde)
June 1952 *Marked for Murder* (Tex Ritter; Madison Pictures reissue)
February 1952 *Mask of the Dragon* (Richard Travis)
March 1952 *Mr. Muggs Rides Again* (East Side Kids; Favorite Films reissue)
February 1952 *Nightmare Alley* (Tyrone Power; 20th Century-Fox reissue)
January 1952 *Northwest Territory* (Kirby Grant)
December 1951 *Odette* (Anna Neagle)
February 1952 *The Old West* (Gene Autry)
January 1952 *One Woman's Story* (Ann Todd)
March 1952 *The Petty Girl* (Joan Caulfield)
January 1952 *Purple Heart Diary* (Frances Langford)
February 1952 *The Raging Tide* (Shelley Winters)

March 1952 *Return of the Texan* (Dale Robertson)
April 1952 *Rodeo* (Jane Nigh)
May 1952 *The Sellout* (Walter Pidgeon)
January 1952 *Silver City* (Edmond O'Brien)
May 1952 *Six-Gun Trail* (Tim McCoy; independent reissue)
May 1952 *Sky High* (Sid Melton)
May 1952 *Slaughter Trail* (Brian Donlevy)
April 1952 *Smoky Canyon* (Charles Starrett)
December 1951 (*) *The Son of Dr. Jekyll* (Louis Hayward)
March 1952 *The Soul of a Monster* (George Macready; Columbia reissue)
March 1952 *Spooks Run Wild* (Bela Lugosi; Astor reissue)
April 1952 *Stage to Blue River* (Whip Wilson)
February 1952 *Sudan* (Maria Montez; independent reissue)
May 1952 *Sunset Pass* (James Warren; RKO reissue)
January 1952 *Superman and the Mole-Men* (George Reeves)
February 1952 *Tale of the Navajos* (documentary)
February 1952 *Tales of Robin Hood* (Robert Clarke)
November 1951 *The Taming of Dorothy* (Jean Kent)
January 1952 *Tars and Spars* (Alfred Drake; Columbia reissue)
May 1952 *Three Husbands* (Eve Arden)
November 1951 *Tokyo File 212* (Florence Marley)
May 1952 *Try and Get Me!* (Frank Lovejoy; United Artists reissue of *The Sound of Fury*)
December 1951 *Two Dollar Bettor* (John Litel)
April 1952 *Wanted: Dead or Alive* (Whip Wilson)
January 1952 *Wells Fargo Gunmaster* (Rocky Lane)
April 1952 *The Wild Blue Yonder* (Wendell Corey)
February 1952 *Woman in the Dark* (Penny Edwards)
April 1952 *Yellow Canary* (Anna Neagle; RKO reissue)

As the Bottom Half of a Double-Bill

By contrast, theaters which presented *The Strange Door* as the bottom half of a double-bill were chiefly upper-tier metropolitan and small-town venues with opulent decor, a limited number of daily screenings, and ticket prices to match. On *this* list, one-third of all co-features are in color, major studio product predominates, and only two reissue titles are evidenced. While the average length of co-features at theaters employing *The Strange Door* as the top half of the bill was 73 minutes, here just two titles have a running time shorter than this (*Fort Osage* and *The Red Badge of Courage*, at 72 minutes and 69 minutes respectively) and the average length is a fulsome 89 minutes.

Perhaps more significantly, 27 percent of the titles on this list are Universal releases, several of which represent the most widely employed top-billed co-features. This implies that, while the studio was unable to readily supply any "lesser" movies that could play in support of *The Strange Door*, it had no problem coming up with "better" pictures for it to play in support of. In other words: Universal treated *The Strange Door* essentially as "supporting feature" fare, and accordingly as one of the lesser wares among its inventory of new releases at this time.

All of the top-billed co-features within the sample of 1200 theaters nationwide are arranged alphabetically below; the month mentioned in each case is the earliest in which the pairing was attested. Two of the more widespread couplings pair *The Strange Door* with a second Joseph Pevney-directed Universal feature, in the shape of *The Lady from Texas* and *Meet Danny Wilson*. Just as in the case of venues employing *The Son of Dr. Jekyll* as a supporting picture, those playing *The Strange Door* in support of Universal's *The Treasure of Lost Canyon* made nothing whatsoever of the fact that this constituted a double bill of Robert Louis Stevenson-inspired fare.

(*) signifies a slightly more substantial number of playdates for the double-bill
(**) signifies a regular affiliation of the titles (at between 5% and 7% of theaters)
bold titles are Universal releases

February 1952 *An American in Paris* (Gene Kelly)
May 1952 *At Sword's Point* (Cornel Wilde)
June 1952 *The Battle at Apache Pass* (Jeff Chandler)
May 1952 *The Big Carnival* (Kirk Douglas)
April 1952 *The Big Trees* (Kirk Douglas)
March 1952 *Boots Malone* (William Holden)
Aug. 1952 *Brave Warrior* (Jon Hall)
April 1952 *Bright Victory* (Arthur Kennedy)
June 1952 *Bugles in the Afternoon* (Ray Milland)
February 1952 *Cattle Drive* (Joel McCrea)
December 1951 (*) *Cave of Outlaws* (Macdonald Carey)
March 1952 (*) *The Cimarron Kid* (Audie Murphy)
January 1952 *Close to My Heart* (Ray Milland)
February 1952 *Crosswinds* (John Payne)
February 1952 *Darling, How Could You!* (Joan Fontaine)
May 1952 *Deadly Enemies* (Rod Cameron; Realart reissue of *The Runaround*)
February 1952 *Detective Story* (Kirk Douglas)
February 1952 *Distant Drums* (Gary Cooper)
February 1952 *Double Dynamite* (Frank Sinatra)
February 1952 (**) *Elopement* (Clifton Webb)
May 1952 *Father of the Bride* (Spencer Tracy)
December 1951 *Finders Keepers* (Tom Ewell)
January 1952 *Fixed Bayonets!* (Richard Basehart)
January 1952 (**) *Flame of Araby* (Maureen O'Hara)
June 1952 *Flaming Feather* (Sterling Hayden)
July 1952 *Fort Osage* (Rod Cameron)

April 1952 *Francis Goes to the Races* (Donald O'Connor)
April 1952 *A Girl in Every Port* (Groucho Marx)
December 1951 *High Sierra* (Humphrey Bogart; Warner Bros reissue)
March 1952 *His Kind of Woman* (Robert Mitchum)
March 1952 *Hotel Sahara* (Yvonne De Carlo)
February 1952 *I'll See You in My Dreams* (Doris Day)
April 1952 *Jack and the Beanstalk* (Abbott and Costello)
March 1952 *Japanese War Bride* (Shirley Yamaguchi)
December 1951 (*) *The Lady from Texas* (Mona Freeman)
December 1951 (*) *The Lady Pays Off* (Linda Darnell)
February 1952 *Little Egypt* (Rhonda Fleming)
March 1952 *Lone Star* (Clark Gable)
May 1952 *Love Is Better than Ever* (Elizabeth Taylor)
July 1952 *Ma and Pa Kettle at the Fair* (Percy Kilbride and Marjorie Main)
December 1951 *The Magic Carpet* (Lucille Ball)
March 1952 *The Man with a Cloak* (Joseph Cotten)
March 1952 (*) *Meet Danny Wilson* (Frank Sinatra)
January 1952 *The Mob* (Broderick Crawford)
January 1952 *My Favorite Spy* (Bob Hope)
April 1952 *On the Loose* (Joan Evans)
December 1951 *Pardon My French* (Paul Henreid)
March 1952 *Purple Heart Diary* (Frances Langford)
March 1952 (*) *The Raging Tide* (Shelley Winters)
May 1952 *Rawhide* (Tyrone Power)
March 1952 *The Red Badge of Courage* (Audie Murphy)
April 1952 *Return of the Texan* (Dale Robertson)
November 1951 (*) *Reunion in Reno* (Mark Stevens)
January 1952 *Rhubarb* (Ray Milland)
April 1952 *Sailor Beware* (Martin and Lewis)
January 1952 *Saturday's Hero* (John Derek)
July 1952 *Scandal Sheet* (Broderick Crawford)
March 1952 *The Sellout* (Walter Pidgeon)
May 1952 *Silver City* (Edmond O'Brien)
Aug. 1952 *Steel Town* (Ann Sheridan)
January 1952 (*) *Submarine Command* (William Holden)
May 1952 *The Tanks are Coming* (Steve Cochran)
January 1952 *Texas Carnival* (Esther Williams)
December 1951 *Thunder on the Hill* (Claudette Colbert)
May 1952 *The Treasure of Lost Canyon* (William Powell)
January 1952 *Two Tickets to Broadway* (Tony Martin)
April 1952 *Viva Zapata!* (Marlon Brando)
February 1952 *Week-end with Father* (Van Heflin)
February 1952 *The Well* (Gwendolyn Laster)
January 1952 *The Whip Hand* (Elliott Reid)
March 1952 *The Wild Blue Yonder* (Wendell Corey)

With Live Stage Accompaniment

Further indicative of the *carte blanche* extended to theater owners to pair *The Strange Door* with almost anything they could come up with, roughly two percent of venues within the sample of 1200 first-run theaters nationwide employed a live stage performance as accompaniment to the feature. The earliest and most notable example of this took place at the 2800-seat RKO Orpheum in Minneapolis from November 24, 1951, in the form of a magic show by the legendary Harry Blackstone, Sr. As irresistible as this may sound to modern ears, *Variety* reported that trade was "disappointing." Subsequent live stage accompaniments to *The Strange Door* were restricted to smaller venues and comprised lower-echelon spook shows and performances by local bands.

Triple-Bills

Finally within the sample of 1200 first-run venues, around one percent screened *The Strange Door* on a triple-bill. This unusual way of encountering the movie was attested solely in heavily populated areas of Northern California and Texas where low-priced triple- and quadruple-bills were already an established norm thanks to the presence of multiple theaters and/or drive-ins in direct competition with each other.

All of the triple-bills attested within the sample are arranged alphabetically below. The month mentioned in each case is the earliest in which the usage was attested.

Mar 1952 *Bride of the Gorilla* (Barbara Payton) + *The Mummy's Tomb* (Lon Chaney, Jr.)
May 1952 *Five* (William Phipps) + *M* (David Wayne)
May 1952 *Jungle Woman* (Acquanetta) + *Last of the Wild Horses* (James Ellison)

Beyond the First Run

In second run between 1952 and 1954, *The Strange Door* was employed primarily as a supporting feature on non-genre-matched double-bills, although it made a small-scale horror-based comeback when chosen to accompany first-run screenings of *The Black Castle* at a limited number of venues. From 1955, it turned up almost exclusively at one-off midnight engagements for Halloween and Friday the 13th, prior to being further relegated to three- and four-feature bills at $1-per-carload drive-ins. Even within this context, bookings had become few and far between by 1959, and the movie wouldn't be widely seen again until it went to television. *The Strange Door* made its small-screen debut as a special Halloween feature on CBS-affiliated WTOP-TV (now WUSA-TV) in Washington, D.C., with the broadcast commencing at 11:27 p.m. on October 30, 1964, 13 years to the day since its theatrical debut. The movie swiftly aired on other stations, so that it had reached televiewers from coast to coast by the end of February 1965. It thereafter showed up regularly on TV schedules throughout the late 1960s and the 1970s.

The Critics' Corner

Harrison's Reports: The story … is completely fantastic. This unreality, however, should make little difference to the avid horror-picture fans, for it offers more than a fair share of spine-chilling thrills, as well as some fast and exciting action.

Variety (October 30, 1951, review): Despite there being no grotesquely made-up central character, [it] emerges a horror-shocker, in many ways reminiscent of same studio's Frankenstein-Wolf Man-Dracula successes. Well-done film should fare well at the b.o., especially in the hypoed exploitation play-dates, inasmuch as similar-veined pictures have been conspicuously absent of late.

Variety (October 31, 1951, review): [I]ts b.o. potential appears to be limited to bookings as supporting fare for subsequent-runs. … Producer Ted Richmond appears to have wrung maximum values out of a modest budget.

Universal changed Robert Louis Stevenson's Denis from a brave cavalier to a prominent family's disinherited scion (Richard Stapley). Stapley's appraisal of the film: "I didn't think an awful lot of it. I thought the script was careless and the characters weren't really well-defined. The direction was … sort of economical. Really, the whole thing turned out to be little more than a B movie." (Photograph courtesy John Antosiewicz.)

The Hollywood Reporter: It is only a matter of half the running time before the narrative becomes monotonous and obvious. What chills the piece possesses are contained in the final minutes.… Laughton does the best possible with the sadistic character, playing with no holds barred and no subtlety. Boris Karloff seems rather wasted in a sympathetic role.

Motion Picture Herald: A surprisingly strong cast is given a weak and illogical story to work with.… Charles Laughton, still suffering from a bad case of *Mutiny on the Bounty*, satirizes himself in the character he has made so famous. He plays the evil nobleman to the hilt, including a couple of scenes that are outright tasteless in their brutality of spirit.

Motion Picture Daily: The dialogue becomes at times comic in its Shakespearean eloquence but this may not bother the adventure-loving.…

Kinematograph Weekly: The picture has a Fairbanks-like opening, but during the middle stages it is hard going. Charles Laughton unconsciously mimics [English comedian] Robb Wilton as de Maletroit.…

Boxoffice: Producer Ted Richmond mounted the proceedings with a shrewd eye to period and aura.

Time: The film itself is puerile stuff [but Laughton] makes it fun to watch whenever he looms into sight.

Cue: [An] outrageously overacted desecration of Robert Louis Stevenson's short story thriller.

Newsweek: Direction, writing and acting are all of a piece, and Laughton seems to be having a grand time even when he ends up bubbling and screaming in the maw of a churning waterwheel.

Hollywood Citizen-News: As melodramas go, it has its moments—but, too, it has some it could do without.

The New Yorker: [A] picture that isn't long in clarity.… All the acting is deplorable, but none more awkward than that of Sally Forrest and Richard Stapley, the young romantic leads. Their manner of reading lines almost justifies Mr. Laughton's atrocious giggling and snorting.

Elsa Lanchester (in *Elsa Lanchester Herself*): I saw the film and enjoyed it very much.

Fangoria magazine (1996): [Laughton] makes a mockery of the portentous proceedings with an effete, indulgent performance in which he minces, preens, pouts and makes himself at all times the center of attention.… Your personal tolerance level for fruity, over-the-top acting will determine which side of *The Strange Door* you're on.

David Colton, burgomeister of the Classic Horror Film Board (2006): As crazy a film as it is—and it *is* crazy, ranking up there with *The Black Cat* and *The Raven* in its celebration of torture and incestuous psychologies—the film is eminently watchable.

The Universal Music Factory

By David Schecter

From the 1930s through the '50s, many of Universal's motion picture scores received shorter shrift than those created by other studios and production companies. It's not that Universal didn't have the necessary musical talent to draw from, but because it was a cheaper studio, its music budgets often couldn't allow the same resources that other studios could. To surmount this problem, quite a few of their scores reused music written for prior Universal films.

This penchant for recycling music from earlier pictures wasn't unique to Universal, but whereas the larger studios would occasionally reuse themes or a few cues (individual pieces of film music) in subsequent movies, they did this less frequently, including in trailers. As trailers sometimes needed to be completed before the films themselves were scored, previously written compositions were often employed. Republic and Columbia serials extensively reused music the same way Universal did with its *Flash Gordon* serials, as many of these low-budget productions used almost non-stop music over their multi-hour presentations.

Universal's approach to scoring their movies was in stark contrast to how the majority of Hollywood film scores were created, where a studio contract composer or a freelancer would be enlisted to write an original background score, and he'd be credited with writing the music in the motion picture. Although Columbia tended to treat its music scores in a similar fashion as Universal, they could probably be given more of a pass on this, as Universal had a superior staff of in-house composers who could easily have provided original music much more than Columbia did.

Music from many Universal pictures had multiple lives because it was "tracked" (reused) in subsequent studio productions. In the 1940s and early '50s, the source movies that provided these cues covered practically every genre, including swashbucklers, romances, melodramas, comedies, Westerns and horror movies. Some of the titles providing old music for their new productions included *Arizona Cyclone, Bombay Mail, Buck Privates Come Home, Curtain Call at Cactus Creek, Enter Arsene Lupin, Family Honeymoon, The Fighting O'Flynn, For the Love of Mary, The Ghost of Frankenstein, House of Dracula, The Invisible Man Returns, The Killers, Letter from an Unknown Woman, Pillow of Death, River Lady, The Saxon Charm, Sherlock Holmes and the Voice of Terror, Son of Frankenstein, South Sea Sinner, Up in Central Park, The Web, The Wolf Man, Wyoming Mail, You Gotta Stay Happy* and countless others. This music was written by staff and freelance composers such as Daniele Amfitheatrof, Johnny Green, Karl Hajos, Miklós Rózsa, Hans J. Salter, Paul Sawtell, Walter Scharf, Frank Skinner, Edward Ward and Eric Zeisl.

There were certainly a fair share of Universal motion pictures in the 1950s that sported complete original scores composed by a single composer, including Hans Salter's *Bend of the River* and *Finders Keepers* and Frank Skinner's *The World in His Arms* and *The Man from the Alamo*, but there were many more films whose scores were at least partly filled with previously written cues by more than one composer. Sometimes, entire scores would be fashioned together from prior sources, whereas other times these concoctions were freshened up with the addition of some new material. These jerry-rigged scores often combined older music written by multiple composers with some original material,

Universal-International's contract orchestra. (Photograph courtesy Ethmer Roten.)

also often composed by more than one writer. But because all the music would usually be recorded by Universal's contract orchestra, it helped create a more unified musical whole. However, the main reason the music was re-recorded was because the Musicians Union didn't allow previously recorded tracks to be used in subsequent motion pictures.

The same exact cues were often reused time and again, but this was probably done more out of familiarity than laziness, as the composers in charge of assembling these scores knew which cues had worked in the past and which would likely be suitable in the future. The music manuscripts for these pieces were bound in books that were alphabetized by film title and kept in the studio's music library. They were in the form of conductor's scores, which were shorthand versions of the bulkier full orchestral scores. These abbreviated scores allowed the conductor to lead the orchestra without having to flip pages every few seconds, which could be both noisy and also lead to conducting or performance mistakes. The music library also contained loose cues that were catalogued in folders bearing titles like "chase," "fight," "pretty" and "suspense." One category was called "neutral," which supposedly meant that the music didn't really do much of anything. Although such a piece might have been the perfect musical solution for an important dialogue scene that needed to be clearly heard, "neutral" wasn't a term most composers enjoyed having their music associated with! These folders contained some of the most frequently used cues that the music department would return to through the years. Need something fun and playful? Just grab a cue from the "light and lively" folder and you were good to go. The studio's music librarian Nick Nuzzi was held in high regard by the composers and everyone else in the department.

Universal didn't reuse music because their composers couldn't think of anything new to write. On the contrary, these gifted artists always preferred to compose their own music rather than tweak somebody else's from an earlier project. Although Universal's composers usually selected which library cues would be tracked into the pictures they were working on, as hired guns they weren't allowed to choose whether an assignment would require original or reused material. That would have been dictated by Joseph Gershenson, the head of the music department, or his assistant Milton Rosen. And when working within tight budgets, as Universal almost always was, it was quicker and cheaper to complete a score when it didn't have to be composed from scratch. Adjusting a few measures here and having the orchestra record already written pieces was a breeze compared to composing entirely new cues, which would then need to be orchestrated and their parts copied so the studio musicians could perform them.

The music that was reused had less to do with the composer who wrote it or the genre of film it was written for. Even film noirs had gentle or romantic music that could be purloined, and costume dramas and comedies had action music that could fit many chase situations. A particular library cue was chosen simply because it seemed to fit with the mood or action of the scene it was being considered for. While Frank Skinner's brilliant horror score for *Abbott and Costello Meet Frankenstein* was dusted off for subsequent Abbott and Costello "Meet the Monster" films, the music didn't suit the comedy team's non-monster movies. And Milton Rosen and Arthur Lange's superb score for Abbott and Costello's *The Time of Their Lives* didn't have many additional lives simply because the style of that singular score didn't lend itself to a lot of other motion pictures.

Music from many forgotten or should-be-forgotten films was endlessly recycled if it could serve as generic fight, love or atmospheric music, while music from more

Left to right: Max Rapp's secretary, contractor Max Rapp, unidentified woman, Milton Rosen, Joseph Gershenson, orchestrator David Tamkin, Louis Gershenson (Joseph's father, a Universal security officer), Henry Mancini, music librarian Nick Nuzzi, unidentified man. (Photograph courtesy Henry Mancini Estate.)

highly regarded or famous films was skipped over if it didn't match the dramatic needs of the newer pictures. If music was too closely associated with the film for which it was originally written, it was less likely to be reused. However, as most moviegoers could only recognize a popular song rather than a film music theme, that didn't happen very often. Even as famous a theme as Herman Stein's *Creature from the Black Lagoon* monster motif would occasionally get reused in non–Creature settings, but at least this was handled with relative restraint. That it was used so infrequently is rather surprising, because movies were not yet being aired on television or sold in video formats, so audiences weren't as familiar with the music as they are today; therefore, they were less likely to have been pulled out of the drama by something they recognized hearing in a previous movie.

However, even given most theatergoers' ignorance of film music, over time the constant reuse of the same old cues resulted in a staleness in many of Universal's scores. Even when tracked music seemed to suit a new use fairly well, small mismatches in the melody, structure or orchestration could make it an imperfect fit, calling attention to itself in an unintended and undesirable way. By the early 1950s, some library cues had been called back into service so many times that it's hard to believe the manuscripts didn't disintegrate due to overuse, but the studio kept multiple copies of them, and they were printed on extremely heavy-duty stock.

The most obvious means of spicing up these hash-like scores was to have a new main title composed for it, but there were also a lot of main titles that were used more than once. One was Herman Stein's opening musical statement from the 1952 Western *The Lawless Breed*, which was later reused in *Tarantula, Showdown at Abilene* and in a bastardized fashion in *Monster on the Campus*. If there was enough post-production time or dramatic motivation, a few newly composed pieces could be added elsewhere to a picture, perhaps serving as a theme for a particular character or incident that needed special emphasis. An example of this was Jack Arnold's *Girls in the Night* (1953), which was almost entirely tracked except for a new "Main Title," "End Title" and "End Cast" by Henry Mancini, and a three-part climactic chase by Stein called "Interrupted Murder," which lasted for six and a half minutes. The long pursuit required something unique and intricately tied to the visuals, something only an original composition could accomplish as expertly as Stein's creation did.

The difference between the music budget of an average film and an expensive one was usually rather insignificant, so there wasn't always much logic or creative sense as to why one movie was blessed with an original score while another wasn't. Although many prestigious films were given the royal musical treatment with a new score by Salter or Skinner, the days of bringing in an outside composer like Miklós Rózsa to score and conduct films such as *Kiss the Blood Off My Hands* or *The Naked City* had pretty much ended. Many of Universal's larger-budgeted films used much more library music than one would have expected, but this probably happened because the extra money went to more famous actors and directors, more involved sets, flashier costumes and almost anything but music. Just as baffling, some of Universal's lower-budgeted programmers—while often being excuses to trot out the same tired library cues from a decade or more in the past—would occasionally have completely or nearly complete original scores composed for them. The 1956 throwaway *The Mole People* would seem to be one of the last pictures to deserve superlative musical enhancement, but it boasts a marvelously evocative pseudo-ethnic score by Heinz Roemheld and Salter, with a few additional cues by Stein. And the 1955 comedies *Abbott and Costello Meet the Keystone Kops* and *Abbott and Costello Meet the Mummy*, made long after the duo's financial and artistic peak, contained a total of over 100 minutes of original compositions, and only 11 seconds of tracked music. They followed the comedy team's *Abbott and Costello Meet the Invisible Man, Abbott and Costello Go to Mars, Lost in Alaska* and *Abbott and Costello Meet Dr. Jekyll and Mr. Hyde*, all of which contained a wealth of reused cues.

Although a film's music budget occasionally entered into whether a new score could be written, a more important determining factor was the production schedule at the time the movie needed to be scored. Universal had a number of composers under contract, and they weren't going to be allowed to sit around on the payroll smoking and drinking on the lot, so they'd be working on at least one picture—if not more—at all times. A composer might spend three days on one project, then a week on a second, and then help out on a cue or two for another production as deadlines dictated. These deadlines were probably the reason that a major film like *Creature from the Black Lagoon*—which you'd think would have deserved an original score—instead contained a wealth of borrowed music, while *Cult of the Cobra*—definitely a lesser monster thriller—was fortunate enough to receive an all-new score courtesy of four composers.

For the most part, it wasn't always easy finding a totally original score in a Universal motion picture, so given the studio's propensity to reuse music so often, fantastic film lovers should be grateful that Universal treated this genre as well as it did. Of the studio's 18 sci-fi-horror films of the 1950s, nine were blessed with original or nearly original scores: *It Came from Outer Space, This Island Earth, Cult of the Cobra, The Mole People, The Incredible Shrinking Man, The Deadly Mantis, The Land Unknown, Curse of the Undead* and *The Leech Woman*. Another three contained a healthy portion of original music: *Creature from the Black Lagoon*, *The Creature Walks Among Us* and *The Monolith Monsters*. The remaining six were mostly cobbled together from previous sources: *The Strange Door*, *The Black Castle*, *Revenge of the Creature*, *Tarantula*, *The Thing That Couldn't Die* and *Monster on the Campus*. In this last category, the first two movies were made before the studio hit its '50s stride with its new assemblage of composers, the middle pair came when Universal was cranking these titles out so fast that they might have been overextending themselves musically, and the final two were released when the music situation in Hollywood was changing in major ways. By this time, the quality of the films was heading toward rock-bottom, and the scores were following suit.

Each composer had his specialty at the studio and was pigeonholed to some extent, so certain composers would find more or less work within certain film genres. And even within a given movie, either Gershenson or Rosen would sometimes assign specific types of scenes to particular writers. For instance, Mancini was asked to score more than his share of "lighter" cues at the beginning of his career, some serving as instrumental source music (music heard over a record player, radio or TV, or as background music in a restaurant or nightclub). There were certainly numerous exceptions to this, and sometimes individual composers would work on specific reels, or handle scenes pertaining to particular story threads. Every composer could and did write every imaginable type of cue, but over time you can detect certain composers' outputs skewed in particular directions. Within the confines of 1950s science fiction and horror, the number of these movies each composer contributed to—including the four Abbott and Costello sci-fi/horror-related pictures—was: Henry Mancini (15), Hans J. Salter (15), Herman Stein (15), Irving Gertz (11), William Lava (7) and Heinz Roemheld (4), with Frank Skinner (8), Milton Rosen (6), and Paul Sawtell (4) being represented mainly or entirely by tracked music.

Musical accompaniment benefits science fiction, fantasy and horror films because it helps suspend the audience's pronounced disbelief, as a good score has a way of drawing you into the drama and emotions of a picture despite implausible plots or visuals. Some of Universal's 1940s and '50s horror films contained copious amounts of music, with 70 percent of *The Incredible Shrinking Man*'s running time featuring underscore, 72 percent of *Revenge of the Creature*'s, and the 60 percent neighborhood for a number of others.

While film music from a wide variety of genres made its way into some of Universal's sci-fi and horror movies, on the other side of the coin, music specifically written for these fantastic films managed to reappear in decidedly non-science fiction settings. The 1956 Jack Arnold-directed crime drama *Outside the Law*, starring Ray Danton and Leigh Snowden, reused 12 cues originally composed for *Creature from the Black Lagoon* and *The Creature Walks Among Us*. Herman Stein's "Visitors from Space" from *It Came from Outer Space* appeared in a flashback life raft scene at the beginning of the 1959 Jeff Chandler tearjerker *A Stranger in My Arms*.

Songs were also reused from picture to picture, usually as source music, because music used in this fashion didn't serve the same dramatic purpose as underscore, songs were often chosen more for business reasons than artistic ones. The composers and the music publishers who owned the songs would benefit from the reuse of their tunes in movies, which is why song pluggers hung around the studios trying to get their old and new compositions placed in the

Irving Gertz, left, and Herman Stein in 1996. (Photograph courtesy Monstrous Movie Music.)

productions. Although Universal and other studios usually preferred to use songs owned by their own publishing arms, sometimes a specific composition they didn't own was necessary to the plot. In those cases, they'd have to license the song for the picture, and the writers and the music publisher of that tune would receive royalties throughout the duration of the film's copyright, which continues to this day for many movies made after the 1920s.

Universal depended upon a few songwriters when they needed a catchy tune—as the composers who wrote their orchestral film music were seldom given this assignment. Stein always regretted that he almost never got to write a "tune" that had the potential of becoming a hit, something his melodic gifts were certainly capable of providing. But even Mancini, who received more song assignments than most of the other staff composers, didn't get many record releases or publicity for his film songs, as there seemed to be a major disconnect between Universal's songwriters and the studio's music publishing company that should have been promoting their works.

While tracking orchestral music from older films into new ones doesn't sound very creative, it was both a musical challenge and an exacting technical job. The particular cues being considered for reuse were usually selected from the music library by one or more of Universal's composers. The pieces usually needed to be reworked in terms of orchestration, tempo and dynamics, and they sometimes required compositional alterations. A composer would decide which measures to borrow from each older piece, and then he'd often stitch the disparate sections together by adding a newly written measure or two so one cue fragment would flow into the next, as contiguous cues were often written by different composers who had diverse styles. After a composer sketched out a blueprint of the musical amalgamation, the studio's copyist would create new conductor's scores so the music could be performed with the orchestra. The musician's parts would either be written out, or if there were only slight adjustments made to the earlier versions, those older parts might be marked to reflect the changes. But regardless of all the alterations, a definite attempt was made by the music department to keep track of the components that were assembled into this new creation. This allowed the composers and publishers of the original pieces to continue to get paid for their music, because even when these earlier compositions were reworked, they were rearrangements rather than being brand-new compositions, and arrangers didn't get paid royalties the way composers did. After a movie was edited, any new cues needed would be composed and then recorded along with the tracked pieces and added to the soundtrack. Then cue sheets would be prepared, these legal documents serving to keep track of the name and duration of every cue in the picture, along with who wrote them, what music publishing companies controlled their rights, the type of music it was (underscore, a song performed on camera, a song performed in the background, etc.), and sometimes it would be noted whether the music was newly composed or a reuse of an earlier creation. But cue sheets were far from being completely accurate, and sometimes cues credited with being newly written were not. The composers, often under a time crunch, or finding their Muse on a temporary vacation, would occasionally borrow from pieces they had written for previous movies. Sometimes they even adapted the works of others (either consciously or unconsciously) without any mention of that being notated on the cue sheets, although it's likely that these omissions were accidental or merely clerical errors.

The composer and the person who adapted it for a future use would occasionally end up being listed as co-writers, creating the false impression that composers sometimes collaborated on individual cues, which they almost never did. Other times, reuses or adaptations were given new cue names, breaking their links to the past regarding the true authorship of the pieces. Because of this, there are times when it's difficult knowing exactly who came up with a particular musical theme, especially since the composers couldn't always remember whether they were the primary authors or not. These altered credits affected who received income for the use of this music, because the composers and their publishers are paid royalties by performing rights societies based on cue sheet information.

Although there didn't seem to be any ghostwriting going on at Universal, there were many backroom deals in the film music industry for purely financial reasons. That's something to be aware of when you're looking at cue sheets, contracts, credits and other legal documents purporting to state who actually wrote what music. Because truth is often a lot stranger than copyright registrations! So, while cue sheets are a great source to try to understand certain aspects about the music used in a movie, they should not be considered inerrant sources.

By the beginning of the 1950s, a sea change had already begun at Universal-International. During the previous decade, there had been a litany of musical directors (a.k.a. music supervisors), whose job was to run the music department and sometimes conduct the scores. These included Edgar Fairchild, Charles Previn, Hans Salter, Paul Sawtell, Milton Schwarzwald, Frank Skinner and Edward Ward, but by the start of the '50s there was only Joseph Gershenson. Although 1940s holdovers Salter and Skinner would get their share of sole or joint music credits on their new movies, for the most part, Gershenson's name as music supervisor would be the only music credit to appear on the vast majority of Universal's films from 1949 until 1969. Newcomers Stein and Mancini had been signed to contracts and were handling more of the writing, while freelancers Irving Gertz, William Lava, Heinz Roemheld and others found recurring employment with the studio. Around this time, Universal's music library was also freshened up a bit, with cues from more recent melodramas, Westerns, swashbucklers and other genres being added to the older pieces.

The Russian-born Gershenson began his show business career in 1920 conducting pit orchestras in movie theaters to accompany silent films. His earliest work for Universal was as an associate producer, producer or executive producer on films such as *Dark Streets of Cairo, House of Dracula* and *Little Giant,* sometimes under the name Joseph G. Sanford. He resumed this aspect of his career in the late 1950s, producing *Step Down to Terror, Monster on the Campus, Curse of the Undead* and *The Leech Woman.* Gershenson was not a film composer, but he is remembered for being an excellent administrator and a very solid conductor, having a good sense of timing and understanding the nuances of drama.

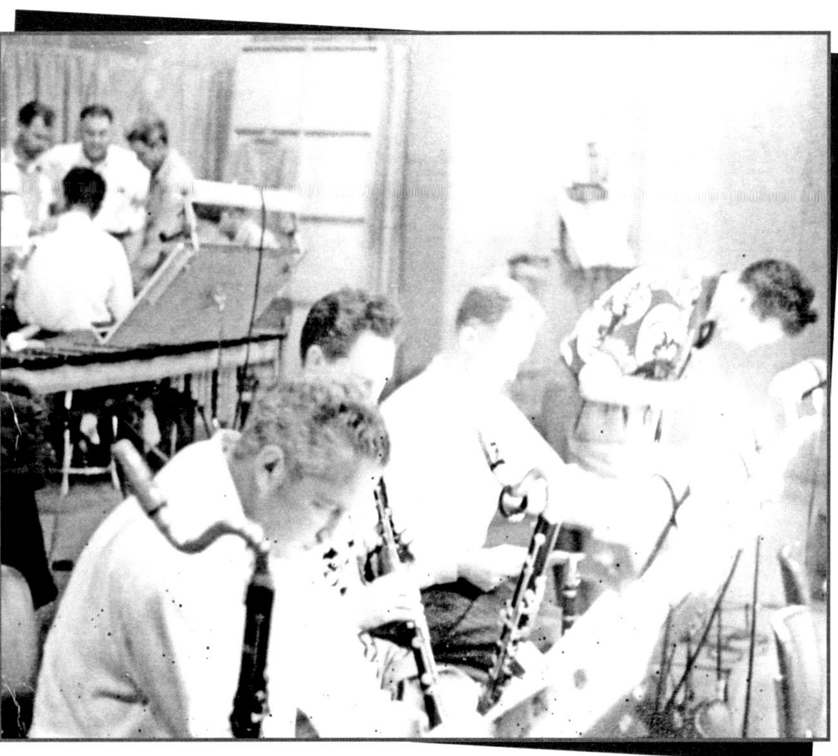

The musicians between takes at a Universal recording session. (Photograph courtesy Ethmer Roten.)

Gershenson was also a superb judge of talent, giving aspiring composers like Stein and Mancini the opportunities they deserved, and he put together a team of staff and freelancers that would be split into various groupings and assigned to specific pictures. He sometimes moved a composer off one film and onto another with seemingly little regard to logic, but the composers were talented enough to mesh their talents with the others to create musical tapestries that sounded a lot less disjointed than anyone had a right to expect. While it would be easy to blame Gershenson for allowing too many Universal movies to be dependent upon the constant reuse of older music, the studio had very tight budgets in every aspect of production, and it's doubtful that the amount of money allotted to the music department would have allowed entirely original scores for most of its pictures.

Because the music was usually orchestrated by the gifted David Tamkin (and occasionally Charles Maxwell), conducted by Gershenson, and performed by the same contract musicians on Universal's Stage 10 recording stage, that further coalesced these disparate elements into what seemed—without paying too much attention—to be the work of a single author, albeit one with an extremely wide range of compositional abilities. In later years, Gershenson claimed that he would audition the composers' themes to decide which would be used, but that wasn't how it happened. All the composers were very talented musicians and craftsmen whose knowledge and dramatic instincts allowed them to function together without outside "guidance." They alone were able to create the best scores possible, whether from contributing original material or by weaving together pre-existing pieces. However, because Gershenson usually received the only music credit on a picture, that created the false impression that he was some sort of compositional genius on the order of Mozart or Beethoven. In fact, he didn't write a note of film music, although he was occasionally credited with contributing lyrics to a song that appeared in a Universal movie.

Around the time Gershenson took over Universal's music department, some of his composers began receiving music publishing rights for their new compositions. This meant that although the studio was permitted to use the music synchronously in the motion pictures they were producing, they didn't own other publishing rights that they had when Universal Music Corporation owned the music. What's important about this change was that now certain publishers and other parties had a larger financial interest in having their own music used, as royalties would be paid when the films played in overseas venues, and eventually on television, or if records or sheet music were sold. How and why this occurred is beyond the scope of this book, but it helps to keep this in mind because business matters were often more responsible than anything else as to why certain music was used in Universal's motion pictures. Because in Hollywood, financial considerations always trump artistic ones.

While it's often been stated that composers and other creative artists have little business sense, most of the composers who made their way through the Hollywood ranks were well aware that they needed good business advisors. Although composing was their line of work, they were definitely doing it for the money, too, so the smart ones hired business managers, agents, accountants and attorneys to help them get work, to maximize their income, and to protect their assets from all the crooks lurking in Tinseltown. Unfortunately for some of them, their business managers, agents, accountants and attorneys occasionally turned out to be among the biggest crooks they would ever encounter!

The business aspect of film music went hand in hand with the creative aspect of a Hollywood composer's life. While Henry Mancini was undeniably an incredibly talented composer and arranger, he also knew how to play the game. Whether it was hosting parties and knowing whom to invite or saying the right things to those above you in the industry, a successful composer needed to know a lot more than just how to write memorable themes and melodies.

This short detour into the business side of Universal's film music should not make anyone think that any particular studio's music department was more or less honest than another's. Nor does the fact that few of Universal's composers received credit for their work mean that Universal was a second-tier studio in terms of quality. Although they didn't have anyone in their stable as famous as Bernard Herrmann, Alfred Newman, Miklós Rózsa, Max Steiner, Franz Waxman or others of their illustrious ilk, the quality of Universal's musical output compared favorably with more musically renowned studios like 20th Century-Fox, MGM and Warner Brothers. True, Universal's smaller orchestra couldn't provide the same instrumental density that the larger studios could, but the Universal team was every bit as capable and creative as those of the other studios' music departments. Whether it was for a glossy Rock Hudson soap opera, an Audie Murphy or Rory Calhoun Western, or a pulp sci-fi thriller with rubber-faced monsters, Universal's composers consistently churned out high-quality background music regardless of the quality of the films it was written for. The scores usually elevated the pictures to a higher level, at times being the best parts of the productions.

Dooratorio: The Music of The Strange Door

By David Schecter

The Strange Door followed the same path taken by many of Universal's 1940s horror pictures, in that it contained an all-tracked score, pieced together from sections of cues written for prior Universal productions. It's not known who handled this particular assignment. It's doubtful that staff composers Hans Salter or Frank Skinner did, as they were probably busy composing original cues or scores for more important films. But in the wacky world of Universal music, one never knows! The duty of deciding which music library cues would be appropriated for this new picture might have been done by Herman Stein, who had just been hired as an arranger. Or perhaps the job fell to Joseph Gershenson's assistant Milton Rosen. Although the score was a compendium of unrelated fragments—and an original score certainly would have served the picture better—at least some good music choices were made that enhanced the scenes in the proper dramatic fashion. Gershenson received the only music credit in the movie: "Musical Direction."

The Strange Door's music budget was a meager $15,500, a small percentage of the overall budget, and there were many expenses that ate up that budget beyond the cost of the composers and musicians. Some of those were song clearances for previously written tunes ($400), song arrangers ($100), music copyists ($1000), a music contractor who was in charge of hiring musicians and looking after them ($170), and the pre-score musicians and singers ($230). Other costs involved the technical end of things, including hiring a stenographer, synch man, music cutters (editors) and assistant cutters, setting up equipment, recording the music and, of course, there were always catch-all costs to further eat away at the budget, including "miscellaneous," "miscellaneous labor" and providing for an "operating staff." The members of Universal's 36-piece orchestra received $7171 for 40 minutes of underscore, with some of the players doubling (playing two instruments) and being paid at a 50 percent higher rate so the studio wouldn't have to hire extra musicians. After all these expenses, that left the conductor and composers $2000 for their work on the picture. Considering that a music score is one of the most important aspects of a production and can help a film overcome many flaws, the small music budget reveals that the value of a good score was underappreciated by Universal and Hollywood in general. In many senses, that situation continues to this day.

The Universal-International orchestra on Stage 10. (Photograph courtesy Ethmer Roten.)

Recording sessions under the working title *The Door* were held on July 20, 1951, with Gershenson conducting, and the six hours of recording time would have been just about long enough to record the entire 35-minute score. It appears that this was a legitimate session where the stitched-together score was recorded anew, as opposed to a "dummy session" where the musicians basically went through the motions of playing, but then actual original recordings from earlier films would be spliced together to form the soundtrack. Such a fake performance was sometimes done when library music was being reused in a score, and even though the musicians were paid, it was much easier to get a good performance because you already had the old one recorded! You can hear some edit points in the soundtrack that could imply that at least some of the music might have derived from previously recorded tracks, but imprecise music editing or last-minute editing changes made to the picture can also create the same spotty results.

For this film, Universal's contract orchestra was supplemented by organist Chauncey Haines, who was hired to play Novachord, a role he would fill for Universal throughout much of the decade. Haines' songwriting and arranging career went back to the turn of the 20th century; due to his expertise on the Wurlitzer organ, he was generally considered the greatest silent movie accompanist in Los Angeles during the 1920s. The Novachord was a polyphonic synthesizer invented in 1939 by Laurens Hammond (who also created the Hammond organ). The 72-key instrument (most pianos have 88) had long been employed in Hollywood to help bolster the meager string sections of studio orchestras, but by the 1940s and '50s Novachords were being used to create spooky or out-of-the-ordinary atmospheres. Both the Novachord and Hammond organ contributed mightily to many of Universal's horror and science fiction soundtracks.

There were two other recording sessions held for *The Door*, but both were for a single player. The first session lasted two hours on May 14, 1951, where guitarist Edwin Miller, who's heard in the film's opening tavern scene doing just over a minute of "Guitar Improvising," received just under $40 for his work. The tavern scene was filmed the following day, with the recording being played back so the action could be matched to the music. The unknown singer who performed the song "Je N'en Connais Pas La Fin" was paid $150 for her day's work, but it's unclear whether she recorded it at the same session or added her vocal later. The song was a slightly anachronistic addition to the movie, as it was written by the French songwriting team of lyricist Raymond Asso and composer Marguerite Monnot. The pair wrote many songs for chanteuse Édith Piaf, and she had a hit with it in 1939. Asso was a French lyricist who was involved with Piaf both romantically and musically, and Monnot was one of the first popular female songwriters.

The second recording session (three hours on May 28, 1951) featured pianist Al Mack, who also earned about $40 for his efforts. This recording occurred the same day the wedding scene was shot, and although the session paperwork doesn't mention that the recording was for "rehearsal," "coaching" or "sideline," it's possible that he was playing off-screen so the musicians and the dancers in the scene could perform to the music, which would eventually be replaced by the orchestral recording done almost two months later.

The *Strange Door* score borrows from a wide range of films, with many, but not all, being horror pictures. The source movies are: *House of Frankenstein* (Hans Salter, Frank Skinner, Charles Previn and Paul Dessau); *House of Dracula* (Salter and Skinner); *Frankenstein Meets the Wolf Man, Frenchie, Invisible Agent, The Invisible Man's Revenge, Scarlet Street, This Love of Ours, Thunder on the Hill* and *The Web* (Salter); *She-Wolf of London* (William Lava); *The Pearl of Death* (Lava, Salter and Paul Sawtell); *House of Horrors* (Lava, Salter and Skinner); *Jungle Woman* and *The Scarlet Claw* (Sawtell); *The Climax* (Edward Ward); *Arabian Nights, Back Street* and *Pillow of Death* (Skinner); and *The Killers, Lady on a Train* and *Secret Beyond the Door* ... (Miklós Rózsa). Salter was strongly represented in the soundtrack, with 32 of the 55 cues being written or co-written by him, including 14 of the last 15 pieces in the film. To get a sense of the "impersonal" nature of a score such as this, consider that Universal's 1951 Macdonald Carey Western *Cave of Outlaws* paradoxically uses many of the same horror music sources as *The Strange Door*, including *Frankenstein Meets the Wolf Man, House of Dracula, House of Frankenstein, House of Horrors* and *Pillow of Death.*

Composer Hans Salter. (Photograph courtesy Bob Burns.)

The Strange Door's 35 minutes of music only covers about 43 percent of the film's 81-minute running time. This percentage was below that of many 1940s and '50s horror movies, where substantial amounts of music were used to help suspend disbelief. Perhaps because *The Strange Door* didn't have a lot of disbelief to be suspended—unless you consider the incredibly far-fetched sequence of events required to somehow get Denis from the tavern to the sire's house so the plot could unwind—this thinly scored approach fit the type of picture it was, with much talk and few extended action sequences. The other main reason for the score's brevity is because the last 13 minutes of the film before the End Title are devoid of music. This was a surprising approach, as a movie's climax is usually action-packed, as this one is, and action is almost always scored.

The cues in *The Strange Door* have an average length of about 38 seconds, so there was obviously not a lot of musical continuity in the stitched creation. Most tracked pictures are cobbled together from shorter excerpts of many pieces of music. This is because longer representations of cues written for previous pictures aren't likely to fit new scenes accurately, so shorter moments are chosen that can more easily be matched to each particular action or mood. Very few cues were published by non-Universal companies—the majority being controlled by Universal Music Corporation—meaning that in addition to not having to pay any composers to write new music for the movie, the studio's music publishing arm earns performance royalties to this day whenever the film airs around the world.

The Strange Door opens with William Lava's "Main Title" fanfare from *She-Wolf of London*

Composer William Lava and Lee Lava at their wedding. (Photograph courtesy William Lava family.)

(1946), followed by the Lava-Salter-Skinner-credited "Main Title" from *House of Horrors* (1946). The *House of Horrors* piece was adapted—probably by Lava—from the Salter-composed "Main Title" from *The Invisible Man's Revenge* (1944). This installment in the "Invisible" series featured music by Salter, Lava and Eric Zeisl, but whether this cue had even earlier incarnations, who's to say? But it shows how writers credited with a specific piece are not necessarily the ones who first composed it.

You can get a sense of why a specific piece might have been selected for reuse in a subsequent film by watching the sequence in *The Strange Door* when Denis thinks he has killed a man at the tavern. The music chosen was Salter's "Kroner Dies," composed for the 1947 Edmond O'Brien-Ella Raines-Vincent Price thriller *The Web*. Whoever selected this music for *The Strange Door* was either already familiar with *The Web*'s score, or the music manuscript for "Kroner Dies" was catalogued along with similar compositions having to do with violence or death. Along with cues from *House of Frankenstein* and *Pillow of Death*, music from *The Web* was represented more than other films lending music to *The Strange Door*. Salter's "Murder of Corpse" plays for almost a minute and a half when Denis awakens and finds Blanche in his room; queasy strings and other devices effectively enhance the mysterious atmosphere. In *The Web*, this cue covers a scene where Vincent Price's character plans to murder a man he thought he'd *already* killed. Also from *The Web*, Salter's "The Idea" is heard when Denis bids farewell to Blanche and follows Voltan down to the door leading to the armor room. Other *Web* cues punctuate dramatic moments in *The Strange Door*, such as when Rinville gets a knife in the back.

Orchestrator David Tamkin. (Photograph by Louis Kaufman, courtesy Annette Kaufman.)

Orchestrator David Tamkin received a screen credit for his work on *The Web*, but he seldom received movie credits, a fate suffered by other orchestrators working during this era. Tamkin did manage to get credits on *Abbott and Costello Meet Frankenstein, Ivy, Ride the Pink Horse, River Lady* and a few others, all before Universal's new musical era of the 1950s began and his credits vanished into the ether. Tamkin was born August 28, 1906, in Chernigov, the Ukraine, and his family emigrated to Portland, Oregon, shortly after his birth. He played violin as a youth, and studied composition with Francis Richter and others, also studying at the University of Oregon. He worked briefly with Ottorino Respighi and Ernest Bloch, and began his tenure with Universal in the late 1940s, orchestrating for a variety of movies. He also orchestrated many scores by Dimitri Tiomkin, Jerry Goldsmith and others. Tamkin's best-known composition was his 1933 Jewish opera *The Dybbuk*, with a libretto by his brother Alex. Although it had to wait 18 years for its first performance (by the New York City Opera), it received excellent notices. Tamkin was the main orchestrator on most of Universal's films of the 1950s, and he was held in extremely high esteem by his industry colleagues. Both Henry Mancini and Herman Stein revered his talent, and they learned much from watching him flesh out their compositions. Tamkin died on June 21, 1975.

Another example of why a particular library cue might have been chosen occurs just over an hour into *The Strange Door* when Denis believes that Count Grassin is a traitor (he's not—he's merely dead). The Salter piece "Double Crossed" from Fritz Lang's brilliant *Scarlet Street* is used here, the logic probably being that what's good for one traitorous act is good for another. In *Scarlet Street*, "Double Crossed" is heard when Christopher Cross (Edward G. Robinson) arranges a surprise meeting between his harridan wife and her first husband, whom she had believed was dead. Of course, there's also the possibility that the music was chosen because one scene dealt with a supposedly living person who is actually dead, while the other dealt with a supposedly dead person who is actually alive. But it's doubtful anyone other than Salter would have been able to figure out that particular "connection." This was a popular library cue, also being used in *Hollywood Story* (1951), an enjoyable William Castle-directed crime film starring Richard Conte and Julie Adams. When Voltan leads a suspicious Denis into the armor room in *The Strange Door*, Frank Skinner's "Torture Chamber" from the 1942 Jon Hall-Maria Montez adventure *Arabian Nights* covers the action, the thinking probably being that both rooms contained weapons of some kind, so similar music would be effective.

Salter's "Dr. Nieman Attacked," one of many *House of Frankenstein* cues in *The Strange Door*, is used in Reel One when Denis, believing that he's killed a man, flees the tavern. From the same source film, "Dracula Destroyed," credited to Salter and Paul Dessau, plays for 1:21 when Denis fears that de Maletroit will brand him with the toddy iron, the weird touches on Novachord, vibraphone and xylophone adding to the potential horror of the sequence. "Dr. Nieman Attacked" soon makes a return visit when de Maletroit tells his men to take Denis to his chamber. Because the two cues share thematic material from *House of Frankenstein*, they fit together without anyone being the wiser. "Elonka Whipped" by Salter and Dessau plays for a mere five seconds when de Maletroit kicks Voltan, who's been caught eavesdropping. Obviously it was felt that whipping and kicking made for close musical relatives. Another *House of Frankenstein* composition, Salter and Dessau's "Dracula's Ring," was chosen for Voltan's first visit to Edmond, as the servant promises to kill Denis. Salter and Dessau's "The Pentagram" plays for almost a minute and a half when de Maletroit and Corbeau take Denis and Blanche down to the dungeon just before the climax. As with many of the tracked music uses, suitable underscore could have been found in hundreds of sources, so why this last particular cue was chosen over others isn't known, but it's likely that the person selecting the music was already familiar with the cue and was confident it would fit the new scene. It's also possible that somebody decided to use as many cues as possible from *House of Frankenstein* to make the quest for tracks a little simpler. Again, Salter might be a good candidate here, but it's likely many people working in Universal's music department were already pretty familiar with this score.

Another *House of Frankenstein* piece, Salter and Dessau's "Dan's Love" serves as the Denis and Blanche love theme throughout the movie. It's first heard about 31 minutes "in" when she discusses her previous love, and again about 23 minutes later—shortly after their marriage—when Denis tells Blanche that she can have it annulled. Although it's a pretty melody, it has a gypsy tinge not appropriate for this picture, and if you already associate it with the amorous feelings of hunchback Daniel for Ilonka the gypsy girl in *House of Frankenstein*, its dramatic-cinematic baggage can be a little disconcerting. It's possible that *House of Frankenstein*'s score was reused so much in *The Strange Door* because of the Karloff connection, but it was more likely because nearly every horror or vaguely horrific Universal film seemed to borrow from that particular score, a superb work that contained a wide range of thematic material.

Another vintage Salter cue that appears in *The Strange Door* (although co-credited to Sawtell and Lava) is "Alias the Doctor," heard when Denis enters the chateau and finds himself trapped by the knobless door that closes behind him. "Alias the Doctor" was written for the Sherlock Holmes movie *The Pearl of Death* for the sequence when Giles Conover and the Creeper enter the doctor's house, where Holmes awaits them, disguised as a physician. Obviously, the person in Universal's music department who chose this music for *The Strange Door* knew it was suitable for enhancing a scene when somebody enters a house under abnormal circumstances. *The Pearl of Death* had a spare but colorful score, with snippets of its Sawtell cue "Curtains for the Creeper" appearing on two occasions in *The Strange Door*, both when Voltan attempts to knife the sleeping Denis, only to be interrupted by Blanche. More Salter music can be heard courtesy of "In a Stupor" from *The Invisible Man's Revenge*. It plays right before Denis first encounters de Maletroit, this cue probably being chosen

A 2016 photograph of Ethmer Roten, Universal's flutist from 1946 until 1989. He played on all their 1950s monster and science fiction films. (Photograph courtesy Monstrous Movie Music.)

because the music's tone fits the confusion the intruder is experiencing. Almost two minutes of "Suicide," taken from Salter's Academy Award-nominated score for the 1945 Merle Oberon-Claude Rains movie *This Love of Ours*, covers the sequence when de Maletroit clears the room of Voltan and his men so he can look at the hidden painting of Blanche's mother.

Miklós Rózsa had an incredibly distinctive writing style, and because of that, his tracked cues usually jump out from other non–Rózsa pieces around it. His Hungarian-influenced music from *The Killers'* cue "Full House" can be heard after Blanche flees Denis' room following their initial meeting. After de Maletroit smashes a jug of water in front of the imprisoned Edmond, about half a minute of "Locked Door" from Rózsa's *Secret Beyond the Door ...* offers more of his unique musical strains. "Slippers Found" from the Deanna Durbin mystery *Lady on a Train* contributes a mere 11 seconds when Voltan gets ready to knife Denis amidst the suits of armor. Although it would have only taken about a half-hour for a composer to write enough new music to fill up this time slot, there was obviously no interest whatsoever in providing any original underscore for this movie.

Universal's woodwind section. Back row: Karl Leaf, Al Harding, Blake Reynolds, Lloyd Hildebrand; front row: Ethmer Roten, Art Smith, Norman Benno. (Photograph courtesy Ethmer Roten.)

Because of all the creepy creeping-around music found in the *Inner Sanctum* entry *Pillow of Death* (1945), many of its Frank Skinner cues were appropriated for *Strange Door*, which had a lot of creeping-around action needing musical enhancement. "Amelia's Trick" occurs when Talon awakens Denis by tossing a chair across the room. After this piece, there's an 8:36 gap with no musical accompaniment, the result of a lot of talk and no action in this part of the picture. "Amelia's Trick" reappears after the armor room fight, as Denis tells Voltan that the tavern "killing" was a frame-up. Two excerpts from *Pillow of Death*'s "The Attic" play when Voltan leaves Edmond's cell and sneaks up to Denis' room to try to kill him, and the same movie's "Linen Closet" is heard for over two minutes about 57 minutes into *The Strange Door* when Denis and Blanche enter a secret passage and wind up in the armor room. *Pillow of Death* is a prime example of a relatively minor Universal film that was superbly enhanced by plenty of original music that provided much of the atmosphere found in that contrived thriller. If you happen to be a Novachord fan (and who isn't?), you're in for a treat, because many of Skinner's cues prominently feature that electronic keyboard.

One can catch a smidgen of some future, famous Universal "monster music" in *The Strange Door* just before their armor room battle with the baddies, the fight being embellished by 43 seconds of Salter's "Attempted Murder" from *Thunder on the Hill*. This Douglas Sirk-directed thriller, made the same year as *The Strange Door*, features a beauteous 23-year-old Ann Blyth, with the climactic cue accompanying the maniacal Dr. Jeffries (Robert Douglas) attacking Sister Mary (Claudette Colbert) in the church bell tower. *Thunder on the Hill*'s Salter-composed score provided cues for many movies throughout the 1950s, and the section of "Attempted Murder" chosen for *The Strange Door* also appears prominently in *Creature from the Black Lagoon*. In the Gill Man film, it is heard as part of a Salter cue called "Doping the Monster," used when David sprays the Gill Man with rotenone while he wraps a cable around the Creature-built barricade.

Although most people who are familiar with this music probably know it from the Creature movie, the same music also turned up in Salter's 1952 adventure score for *Against All Flags*, where it's titled "Rescue, Part 2" and used during the climactic swordfight between Errol Flynn and Anthony Quinn. Salter obviously liked this music a lot, because it's also found in two different cues in his score for the 1952 Jeff Chandler Western *The Battle at Apache Pass*: "Cochise Fights Neegam" and "Geronimo Vanquished." In the mostly tracked 1952 Jeff Chandler swashbuckler *Yankee Buccaneer*, the same music reappears, also under the title "Geronimo Vanquished," and it turns up in *The Black Castle* as "Attempted Murder." *Thunder on the Hill* provided a number of other cues to Universal movies of the 1950s, but "Attempted Murder" stands out in terms of the frequency with which it was reused. Whether or not this particular music had even earlier incarnations than *Thunder on the Hill* under additional titles isn't known, but it wouldn't be surprising to learn that Salter composed it the sixth grade, and based his high school alma mater on it.

The total avoidance of music during *The Strange Door*'s dungeon climax was a curious choice. Although the creaking and roaring sound effects contribute to the sequence, highly dramatic moments like Blanche reuniting with her father, the deaths of lead characters Voltan and de Maletroit, and the collapsing prison that threatens to crush the young lovers are accompanied by a lot of noise but precious little dramatic energy. Even given that another two dozen unrelated bits and pieces of already familiar library cues probably would have been selected if music had been used here, the absence of underscore—whether by design or because there wasn't enough time to track this part of the movie—results in an unemotional and unsatisfying climax.

The Strange Door closes with Frank Skinner's "End Title" from *Back Street*, and while the tone of the piece fits the drama (and offers a smidgen of Mendelssohn's "Wedding March"), the rest of the cue's melody is unrelated to anything previously heard in *The Strange Door*, and therefore, along with some of the other music in the picture, it sounds like it doesn't belong. (On November 2, 1951, *Variety* columnist Viola Swisher wrote, "Don't ask us howintheworld [*sic*] he remembered, but seeing UI's *Strange Door*, a smart kid we know noticed the fade-out music is the same theme used by the studio for *Back Street* about 10 years ago.") While the individual pieces chosen for *The Strange Door*'s soundtrack almost always fit the mood or action of the picture, because they were written by multiple composers using different themes from a wide variety of films and genres, all the creative juggling and editing in the world can't hide the slapdash nature of the score. Although the technical job of piecing everything together was well-done, an original score by a single composer like Salter, Skinner, Lava or a freelancer would have better served the film, perhaps adding to the claustrophobic feeling of the picture or helping to improve various aspects of the drama through unifying themes.

The Strange Door contains a small musical contribution from Herman Stein, whose music would play as big a role as anyone's in Universal's 1950s science fiction films, but who was just beginning his tenure with the studio. In *The Strange Door*, Stein hadn't yet been permitted to compose, but he arranged "March of the Priests" (from Mozart's opera *The Magic Flute*) for chamber orchestra, which is heard during the movie's wedding scene as de Maletroit escorts Blanche down the stairs. The source music cue that plays right before it was not orchestrated by Stein, that being the well-known minuet from Luigi Boccherini's "String Quintet in E." Even if you aren't familiar with the name of the piece, it's quite possible you've heard the music before. The six musicians appearing in these musical sequences are performing (from memory—not using sheet music) on two violins, cello, flute, clarinet and harp. It's likely that a piano was playing while the scene was filmed to allow the musicians and dancers to try to have their actions match the music that would be added two months later during the main recording session. By having the piano play at a predetermined tempo, the orchestra could later match that pace so that recording would fit the sequences perfectly. The musicians in the wedding scene were paid more than the other extras in that scene, presumably because they were actual musicians as well as acting the part of musicians.

Analysis
By Steve Kronenberg

Somehow, horror fans in 1948 had to know that, with *Abbott and Costello Meet Frankenstein*, the beloved Universal monsters had breathed their last gasp. There were simply no other plots in which to pigeonhole the classic creatures of yore. But the echoes of the classics died hard. Thus, it's fitting that Universal would open the 1950s with two consecutive monster-less Gothic melodramas, *The Strange Door* (1951) and *The Black Castle* (1952). The texture and mood of the studio's Golden and Silver Age horror films were as indestructible as its monsters: Both pictures contain indelible echoes of their predecessors.

Like Robert Louis Stevenson's story (and like many Universal horrors of the 1940s), *The Strange Door* begins atmospherically: A howling night wind signals the arrival of a coach to the Le Lion Rouge, and out of the coach comes the corpulent Charles Laughton as Alan de Maletroit. Laughton glides through the smoky, moody ambiance of the tavern with ease—and we immediately know that his delightfully decadent persona will rule the film. Indeed, despite the pres-

On left: The sire talks a good game of revenge but he must not be very good at it because, even after a lifetime under his roof, Blanche (Sally Forrest) has an angel face, appears well-educated and still has spunk. You'd think that by now she'd be more like the invalid, crying-herself-to-sleep Elizabeth Browning (Norma Shearer in photograph on right) after a lifetime under the London townhouse roof of *her* pitiless papa (Laughton again) in the 1934 *The Barretts of Wimpole Street.*

ence of Boris Karloff, *The Strange Door* is Laughton's show from start to finish. The former Dr. Moreau gives what may be an unprecedented ham-fisted, scenery-chewing performance dominated by smirking facial expressions and richly delivered dialogue. His deliciously flamboyant performance drives the film and helps us ignore the sire's bizarre plot motive.

Laughton immediately establishes de Maletroit's effete, sarcastic style as he traps and confronts Richard Stapley's Denis for the first time. As he explains his nefarious marriage plan to the young rogue, Laughton runs his pinky finger over his mouth and plays with a mysterious key. Laughton's effeminate, taunting hand movements meld beautifully with the cruel persona he has created in de Maletroit. As he sits before a painting of his beloved Helene—the engine of the sire's revenge—our eyes go to the actor's wringing, nearly spasmodic hands, which best express his pent-up rage. And when he presents Sally Forrest's Blanche at the wedding ceremony, Laughton delicately escorts her through the throng of guests with an upraised left hand and silken, graceful body language. In another scene, Laughton threatens Stapley with a hot toddy iron, then displays a wide grin, delicately dips the iron into a cup of wine and delightedly toasts: "Your good health, nephew!"

In addition, Laughton's decadent performance is reminiscent of his Dr. Moreau from *Island of Lost Souls* (1932), one of several classic echoes that resonate through *The Strange Door*. In one scene, Laughton's de Maletroit reclines on a table, giggling over his vengeful scheme in a manner identical to the one his Moreau displays in *Island of Lost Souls*. When two of de Maletroit's henchmen dawdle in the doorway of the library, Laughton bellows at them as if he were Moreau addressing one of his Beast-Men: "Don't stand there like clods, come on *in* here!"

Moreau's cruelty also bleeds into Laughton's portrayal of de Maletroit. Watch him deliver a wheezing laugh and shake his mangy head as he sits at the dining hall table and insists that the imprisoned Denis be given "every consideration." Then, in an echo of his Oscar-winning 1933 performance as Henry VIII, Laughton's de Maletroit proceeds to devour a lamb chop with gusto, then tosses another to his servant Talon (Michael Pate) and mutters, "Here, dog!" Laughton extends his cruelty to Voltan (Karloff), brother Edmond's loyal servant, by threatening to feed the man's liver to the swine. Another significant residue of Moreau is Laughton's ability to feign disgust or wounded feelings—when he possesses neither emotion. After ordering the murder of Count Grassin, Laughton says, in mock disgust, "But it *did* upset me. I'm, I'm averse to bloodshed. Besides, knives—so untidy!"; regarding Stapley and Forrest's unsuccessful escape attempt, Laughton cruelly pretends to be hurt: "Wh-wh-wh-why do you want to desert me so soon? You dissatisfied with your surroundings? Why, you never even said goodbye to me!"

Laughton's physical idiosyncrasies, his twitching face and delicate hand movements, are superbly augmented by his dialogue delivery. Particularly striking is his ability to string together several lines while enunciating each word perfectly and accentuating key words in each scene. This talent is especially displayed when Laughton forces Stapley to sign the Articles of Marriage. Stapley reminds Laughton that he's not allowed sufficient time for the publishing of the Banns. Laughton's cadenced reply: "Examine the date on this document, nephew, the fourteenth day of September. That is the night on which you honored me by walking through my door, it is *also* the date of the publishing of the Banns!"

Later, a dismayed de Maletroit is told by Blanche and Denis that they have fallen in love and there is nothing he

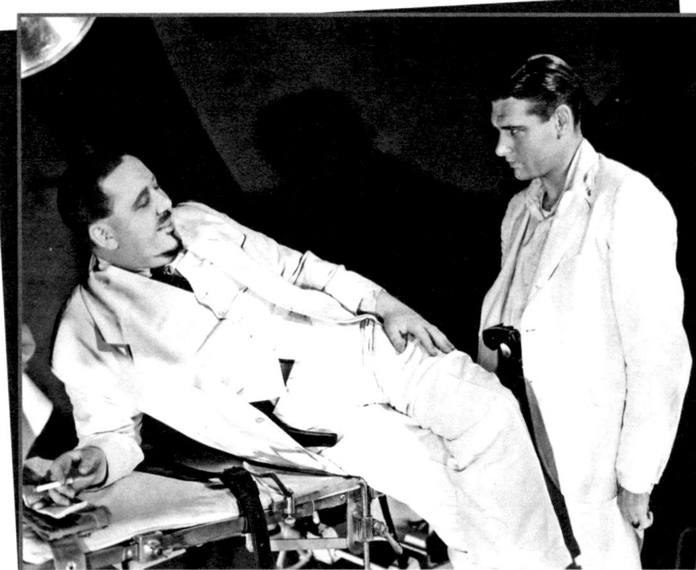

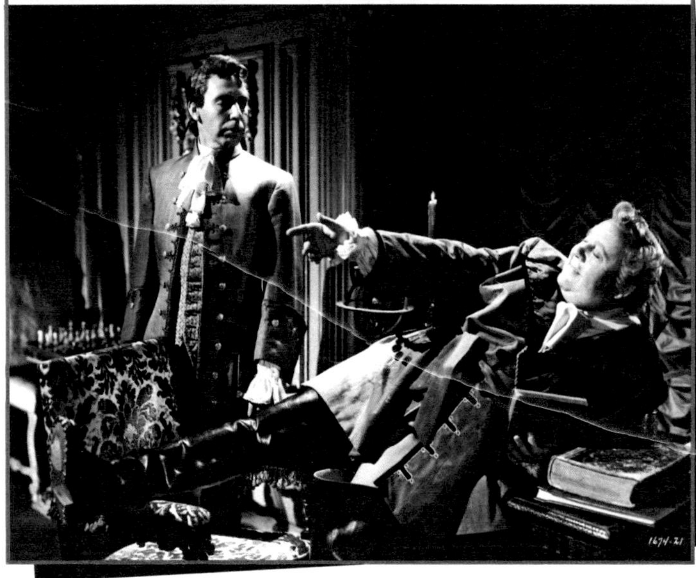

Whether discussing the Beast-Men with Richard Arlen in *Island of Lost Souls'* House of Pain (top), or conferring with his *Strange Door* sidekick William Cottrell (bottom), Charles Laughton would add to the grotesqueness of the moment by plopping his hulk on a table. (Photographs courtesy Ronald V. Borst/ Hollywood Movie Posters.)

can do about it. Laughton's beautifully delivered reply, as he casually rubs his cheek with his forefinger: "How *wrong* you *are*. There are *many* things I can *doooo*. But I'm afraid you'd find them rather disagreeable..."

The Strange Door is one of the best examples of Laughton's superbly timed latter-day style of dialogue delivery: robust, enthusiastic pronunciation with added emphasis on select words. It was a style that characterized subsequent memorable performances in *Witness for the Prosecution* (1957), *Spartacus* (1960) and *Advise and Consent* (1962). Likewise, Laughton's penchant for smooth, sardonic cruelty, coated in gossamer vocal tones and delicate hand gestures, marks *The Strange Door* as a personal triumph for him.

But Laughton is not the film's only attraction. Despite his secondary role, Karloff ably augments Laughton's blustery Gothic persona. Paul Cavanagh's imprisoned Edmond, who pretends to be insane to placate mad brother Laughton, depends on Karloff's Voltan to thwart Laughton's vengeful plans. As Cavanagh languishes in his cell, Karloff, in a manner reminiscent of Janos Rukh in *The Invisible Ray* (1936), rolls his eyes and purses his lips as he professes his fear of Laughton's de Maletroit. But he still agrees to help destroy Laughton as he coldly pledges his loyalty to Cavanagh: "It was my wish to serve you, master." The scene calls to mind Karloff's initial confrontation with John Carradine's Dracula in *House of Frankenstein* (1944), as Dr. Niemann promises to serve the count in exchange for the vampire's help in dispatching former enemies. When Cavanagh tells Karloff to prevent the wedding by disposing of Stapley, Karloff intones, "It will be done." When Karloff delivers the line with his characteristically deep, ominous voice and evil smile, we flash back to Niemann, *The Mummy*'s Ardath Bey and the mad title character in the memorable 1962 *Thriller* episode "The Incredible Doktor Markesan." We also note Karloff's appropriately menacing side as he coldly (and eagerly) strangles and knifes the sire's henchmen during Blanche and Denis' escape attempt. In fact, Karloff's facial expressions in these scenes are reminiscent of those of his beloved Monster during the murder scenes in *Frankenstein* and *Son of Frankenstein*.

Significantly, *The Strange Door* makes a hero of Karloff—one of the few times the actor found himself in such a film role. Yet, while Karloff is clearly on the side of right, he still cuts a menacing figure. He seems more subdued than Laughton (*everyone* in the film does), but his eye-rolling, jaw-jutting, sinister performance defies critics who felt that he walked through the film.

The remainder of *The Strange Door*'s supporting cast is competent, if unexciting. Richard Stapley's semi-heroic Denis is an appropriately swaggering, womanizing swashbuckler. But it's a stock performance that's missing the kind of carefree bravado that made Errol Flynn such a memorable star. Sally Forrest, as Blanche, looks luminous and virginal in a competent but all-too-familiar turn as the damsel distressed by the sire. One exception is Michael Pate as the scarred, insidious Talon, another henchman. Pate's brief contribution is characterized by steely eyes and a cold grin—a good prelude to his later, vampiric role in Universal's *Curse of the Undead* (1959).

The Golden Age resonance of the Laughton and Karloff performances are complemented by *Strange Door*'s Gothic set design (courtesy of art directors Bernard Herzbrun and

Charles Laughton tears into the role of the wicked nobleman like Henry VIII demolishing a pheasant. There are moments in *Strange Door* when Laughton has a bad case of the cutes, but it *is* a novelty to see a legit Universal Horror where the villain sometimes plays for laughs.

Eric Orbom). The chateau interiors are a crazy quilt of angles and overhanging arches, augmented by an illusion of vast depth—all of which are reminiscent of Charles D. Hall's memorable *Bride of Frankenstein* (1935) interiors. In our first look at Laughton's manse, foregrounded by dead, bare trees, the ground around it is covered in mist, making it look like something out of the Borgo Pass. D.p. Irving Glassberg keeps the lighting effectively low-key and treats us to an occasional subjective shot, and his use of shadow imagery is a nice homage to the great Golden Age cinematographers. In addition, much of the *Strange Door* music is lifted from scores from 1940s Universal Horrors; for example, the romantic byplay between Forrest and Stapley is punctuated by the sad gypsy theme that characterized the Larry Talbot-Ilonka scenes in *House of Frankenstein.*

Some cranky critics continue to carp that *The Strange Door* is mediocre pseudo-horror, a last gasp by Universal to recapture the "old days." But in 1951, where was Universal to take the great monsters of the "old days"? Rather than a last gasp, better to call *The Strange Door* an unsuccessful "first gasp": the look of Gothic horror without the monsters, but with the ripe performances, moody sets and borrowed music that characterized Old World Horror.

The Black Castle (1952)

Full Credit Information

CREDITS: Produced by William Alland; Directed by Nathan Juran; Story and Screenplay: Jerry Sackheim; Photography: Irving Glassberg; Editor: Russell Schoengarth; Art Directors: Bernard Herzbrun and Alfred Sweeney; Set Decorators: Russell A. Gausman and Oliver Emert; Sound: Leslie I. Carey and Joe Lapis; Music Director: Joseph Gershenson; Costumes: Bill Thomas; Makeup: Bud Westmore; Hair Stylist: Joan St. Oegger; Dance Director: Hal Belfer; Special Photography: David S. Horsley; Assistant Director: William Holland; UNCREDITED: Original Music Composer: Milton Rosen; Conductor: Joseph Gershenson; Tracked Music Composers: Hans J. Salter, Frank Skinner, Charles Previn, Paul Dessau, Miklos Rozsa, Daniele Amfitheatrof, Frederick Herbert, William Lava, Paul Sawtell and Milton Rosen; Musicians: Emo Neufeld, George Kast, Manuel Compinsky, Louis Pressman, Ambrose Russo, Lou Klass, Sam Fordis, Leon Goldwasser, Samuel Cytron, Sarah Kreindler (Violin), Joseph Reilich, Cecil Bonvalot, Harriet Payne (Viola), Joseph Ullstein, Stephen De'ak, Lajos Shuk (Cello), Harold E. Brown (Bass), Arthur C. Smith, Ethmer Roten, Jr. (Flute), Arthur Gault (Oboe), Blake Reynolds, Alan Harding, Karl Leaf

(Clarinet), Lloyd Hildebrand (Bassoon), Willard Culley, Jr., Alfred Williams (Horn), Gene LaFreniere, Don Linder, Robert Goodrich (Trumpet), John Stanley, Bruce Squires, H.L. Menge (Trombone), Harold McDonald, Ralph Collier (Drums), Lyman Gandee (Piano), Joseph Quintile (Harp); Production Manager: James Pratt; Unit Production Managers: Art Siteman and Dodds (Edward Dodds?); Second Assistant Directors: Ronnie Rondell, Murphy and McLain (Gordon McLean?); Camera Operators: Kyme Meade, Dodds (William Dodds?) and Davis (Harry Davis?); Assistant Cameramen: Sam Rosen, Muchmore, Moore, Haddow (Ledger Haddow?) and Swartz (Lou Swartz?); Still Photographers: Schoenbaum and Lacy (Madison S. Lacy?); First Grip: Everett Brown; Second Grip: Losey (Art Losey?); Gaffer: Norton Kurland; Best Boys: Burnette (Lester Burnette?), Damion and Harris; First Prop Man: Julius "Blackie" Rosenkrantz; Assistant Prop Man: Carl Lawrence; Wardrobe Man: Roger Weinberg; Wardrobe Woman: Bernice Pontrelli; Makeup: Ray Romero; Hair Stylists: Ann Locker and Beth Langston; Sound Mixer: Harry Moran; Sound Recordists: Brown (Ralph Brown?) and Richard/Richards?; Mike Men: Butler, Franklin, Bolger (Jack Bolger, Jr.?) and Robert (Augustus Robert?); Cable Men: Lewis, Dill and Healy; Script Clerk: Winnie Gibson; Dialogue Director: Daniels (Jack Daniels?); Stand-ins: Edward Scarpa and Milton Freibrun; Publicist: Niemeyer (Harry Niemeyer?); SECOND UNIT (March 26, 1952): Director: Frank Shaw; Unit Manager: Siteman (Art Siteman?); Assistant Director: McLean (Gordon McLean?); Script Clerk: Abbott (Betty Abbott?); Cameraman: Williams; Camera Operator: Lathrop (Philip Lathrop?); Assistant Cameraman: Haddow (Ledger Haddow?); Grips: Hawkins (Benny Hawkins?) and Roffredo; PER NATHAN JURAN: Set Designer and Production Sketch Artist: Nathan Juran; 81 minutes.

CAST: Richard Greene (*Sir Ronald Burton*), Boris Karloff (*Dr. Meissen*), Stephen McNally (*Count Karl Von Bruno*), Paula Corday (*Countess Elga Von Bruno*), Lon Chaney (*Gargon*), John Hoyt (*Count Stieken*), Michael Pate (*Count Ernst Von Melcher*), Nancy Valentine (*Therese*), Tudor Owen (*Romley*), Henry Corden (*Fender*), Otto Waldis (*Krantz*); UNCREDITED: Bernard Szold (*Koppich*), Bruce Riley (*Sir David's Secretary*), Leslie Denison (*Sir David Latham*), John Roy (*Guardhouse Guard*), Paul Maxey (*Reimer*), Roy Engel (*Franz Graber*), Chuck Hamilton (*Guard*), William H. O'Brien (*Servant*), Mel Koontz, Allen Pinson (*Stunt Doubles for Richard Greene*), Polly Burson (*Stunt Double for Paula Corday*), Bob Bryant (*Stunt Double for Lon Chaney*), Frank Inn (*Stunt Double for Tudor Owen*), Fred Cavens, Albert Cavens (*Doubles in Green Man Fencing Scene*), UNCONFIRMED: Wheaton Chambers (*Farmer*), Clyde McLeod [Hazardous Day Player], Frieda Stoll [extra].

Production History

By Tom Weaver

In these days of interplanetary drama, *The Black Castle* is something different—an old-fashioned horror film without the aid of an atomic pistol or a monster from Mars.
—George E. Phair, "Retakes," *Variety*, October 23, 1952

The initial box office returns for *The Strange Door* must have been quite encouraging: Just weeks after the *Door* opened, a nearly identical movie was already being prepared at Universal, whose motto should have been "All things being sequel..." Like *Strange Door*, this follow-up was a Jerry Sackheim-scripted thriller harking back to the studio's old style, with threads of mystery, revenge and swashbuckling, and again set in a medieval Europe where genteel sadism could flourish unembarrassed by law enforcement agencies. (In democracy, it's your vote that counts; in feudalism, it's your count that votes.) Sackheim made this new movie's good guy good-er and its bad guy badder—and eye-patched and scarred to boot. And the castle stronghold where the villain has established his dominion features a water-filled pit boiling with thrashing, rumbling alligators!

THIS IS THE NIGHT THAT *HORROR* WALKS ON TWO FEET!

***The Black Castle* ... lair of a human monster and his beast-like minions. Few have entered its dark walls and none lived to tell its sinister secret.**

Yet, one man dared defy the Master of Evil—to steal his most beautiful prey.—*Black Castle* poster text

This effort to "up" the horror ante also extended into the casting process with *both* of Universal's *auld lang syne* monster men now on hand: Boris Karloff playing the same sort of sympathetic-somber castle rat as in *Strange Door*, and Lon Chaney as a physically imposing, half-mad brute (the closest thing to the "beast-like minions" promised on the poster). Horror movie-wise it was Chaney's first such character, but for the rest of the decade, it was his scare-film specialty: *Indestructible Man* (1956), *The Black Sleep* (1956), *The Alligator People* (1959).

The difference between 1952 and days gone by, however, was that Karloff, the face of Universal Horror in the 1930s, and Lon, the face of the franchise in the '40s, were now just faces in the crowd.

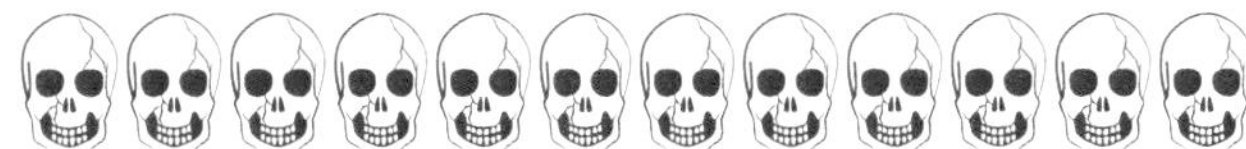

In the 1950s, the center of the Universal Monsterverse was William Alland, formerly one of Orson Welles' Mercury Players, a World War II combat pilot in the Asiatic-Pacific theater, and an award-winning radio producer. At Universal he began as an assistant to producer Leonard Goldstein but around the beginning of 1952 he was upped to full producer on the Valley lot and drew his first several assignments. The Western *The Raiders* with Richard Conte and *The Black Castle*, his first two productions, began within days of each other in March.

"At a studio, they have hundreds of projects—scripts that never got made, stories that they bought and never shot," Alland told me. "Going through that material, I came upon [*The Black Castle*] and it looked like something that could be made relatively cheaply."

Boris Karloff was suffering arthritic pain when he made *The Black Castle*, according to leading lady Paula Corday—but she added, "[He] was as courteous and professional as always." (Photograph courtesy John Antosiewicz.)

In the early stages of preparation, the movie briefly bore (and we *do* mean bore) the title *The Sign of the Green Man*, an unexciting moniker referencing an inn, the Green Man, visited in two scenes. A *Hollywood Reporter* squib announcing the signing of Richard Greene over the February 23–24, 1952, weekend also contained the tidbit that the coming chiller would take place in 1850 France, the same country as *The Strange Door*. Instead the movie became a terror tale from the Vienna woods (well, Austria woods). The year isn't specified, but protagonist Ronald Burton's narration mentions Emperor Charles VI, which places the action between 1711 and 1740.

Strange Door director Joseph Pevney was originally slated to direct *The Black Castle*, but according to the March 5, 1952, *Variety*, he asked to be relieved of the assignment, "stating he felt he didn't have enough time to prep the pic properly." What happened next? Depends on who you believe. In a *Starlog* interview conducted by Steve Swires, Nathan Juran—an art director in 1952, with an Oscar for John Ford's *How Green Was My Valley* (1941) under his belt—claimed that he was initially assigned to the fright flick as art director and dutifully designed the sets and drew production sketches. When Universal wouldn't allow Pevney to make several significant script changes, Pevney bowed out, and studio publicity chief William Gordon and director Douglas Sirk recommended that Juran take the helm. With the production start date just two weeks away, Juran nervously agreed. Alland remembered the situation differently, telling me, "Nathan Juran was an art director—an *excellent* art director—and he *begged* me to let him direct that film. So I asked for Juran, I gave him his chance, and he did an excellent job on that one."

However he got the job, Juran soon became aware that he had a problem. He told *Starlog*:

I suddenly realized how *little* I knew. I had been in the picture business for so many years, trying to understand what

According to *Black Castle* director Nathan Juran (middle, between Richard Greene, left, and Boris Karloff), "Boris was a *joy*, and he did his work beautifully. He put so much into the picture that wasn't in the script." (Photograph courtesy Ronald V. Borst/ Hollywood Movie Posters.)

was going on. But when I was at the point of delivery, I had to learn *everything* all over again. Fortunately, I had a wonderful assistant director named Bill Holland, who kept me on the straight and narrow, and made sure I got the necessary coverage. All the actors did an outstanding job, without *any* help from their rookie director.

Born Naftuli Hertz Juran in Romania, Juran was the fourth of six children of a shoemaker. At age six, he relocated to America with his parents and siblings, settling in Minneapolis where his father built them a one-room house with no electricity or running water. Following schooling here and abroad, Juran worked as an architect. During a vacation to California, he began to land jobs at various studios. At RKO, he was given the nickname "Jerry" by art director Perry Ferguson; at MGM, he designed Juliet's (Norma Shearer) bedroom for the 1936 *Romeo and Juliet*; and at 20th Century-Fox, he and art department head Richard Day shared the *How Green Was My Valley* Oscar. During World War II, Juran was assigned to the Field Photographic Unit of the O.S.S., under the supervision of Commander John Ford; after his discharge, he resumed his art director career and received another Oscar nomination for 1946's *The Razor's Edge*. A succession of Universal assignments (*Kiss the Blood Off My Hands, Harvey, Winchester '73, Bright Victory, Bend of the River*, more) helped pave the road to his promotion to director.

In late May 1951, while still working on *The Strange Door*, Boris Karloff told columnist Bob Thomas that he was selling his Hollywood home in anticipation of relocating to New York. According to Thomas, this decision by Karloff "is partly due to the heavy-footed monster which catapulted him to fame exactly 20 years ago": Karloff told Thomas that in recent years he had been concentrating on stage work in order to shed the label of movie menace.[1] The actor added,

I think the first love of any actor is the stage. And actually, I have been away from Hollywood more than I have been here in the past ten years. I spent three and a half years in *Arsenic and Old Lace*, another six months with it overseas and two years in *Peter Pan*.

Also, there are more things to keep an actor busy in New York. You have the stage, television and radio. Out here [Hollywood], it's mostly pictures. If you're not working, there's not much else to do but garden. I like gardening but not as a full-time job.

Ending his 32-year residence of Hollywood, Karloff became a Manhattanite, moving with his wife, Evelyn, to the gabled, fortress-like Dakota, 72nd Street and Central Park West, fashionable home to many prominent theater people. The first movie to subsequently bring him back to Tinseltown was *The Black Castle*, the third and last step in Universal's Lugosification of their former terror flick topliner. While Karloff was making *The Black Castle*, he stayed at the stately Chateau Marmont. Appropriately, since he was there because he was making *Black Castle*, it was a hotel modeled after an infamous royal residence in France.

In addition to *Black Castle* stars Richard Greene and Karloff, both paid $5000 a week with a three-week guarantee, other outside talent included Lon Chaney at $2000 a week for two weeks and Paula Corday at $500 a week for three weeks. Production was slated to begin on Wednesday, March

12, on the Phantom Stage, the huge, tin-roofed structure where, according to "studio oldtimers" cited in the *Black Castle* pressbook, "more than five hundred film players have met violent cinematic deaths." Silent screen horror maestro Lon Chaney inaugurated the reign of mayhem in the 1925 *The Phantom of the Opera* "when he hacked loose the chains which supported the chandelier of the replica of the Paris Opera House and sent it crashing onto the heads of Parisian opera lovers." The pressbook writer continued,

> **Since that fateful day, the stage has been used for some of the most pretentious massacre scenes this side of Custer's Last Stand. More stars than you can shake a well-tempered battle-axe at have been mutilated, electrocuted, hung, guillotined and dismembered on the famous stage during its lengthy history as a sound-proofed atelier of horrors.**

Synopsis

Right off the proverbial bat, we know we are in the terrain of terror: Outside a fortress-like edifice in Austria's Black Forest, a wolf howls, night winds whip up dead leaves, lightning flashes and the thunder doesn't come in mere claps but in standing ovations. This is the home of Count Karl Von Bruno. Inside a nearby mausoleum, servants Fender (Henry Corden) and Koppich (Bernard Szold) ruefully prepare to seal the wooden coffins of Sir Ronald Burton (Richard Greene) and Countess Elga Von Bruno (Paula Corday). "It's almost as if he were alive," Fender says of Burton, whose eyes are open and seem to be staring. An extreme close-up of Burton's frozen face is accompanied on the soundtrack by his echoey voice: "Alive! Of *course* I'm alive! Fender! *Fender*! ... Can't you see what he's doing to us? He's *burying us alive*!"

Following this lapel-grabber of an opening, a Burton-narrated flashback takes us back several weeks, to the day when he came to Vienna to see Sir David (Leslie Denison), English minister at the court of Emperor Charles VI. Burton is distressed over the disappearance of Sterling and Brown, close friends not heard from since they stopped at the Green Man, an inn in Von Bruno's Black Forest province. Five years earlier, during a West African expedition, Burton, Sterling and Brown discovered that Von Bruno, posing as a white god, had taken control of a local tribe and its ivory riches. In a battle between the Englishmen's forces and Von Bruno's followers, the latter were routed and the count himself was wounded, proving to the natives that he was mortal; the natives then rose up against him and drove him out of the country. Burton's suspicions of foul play are running high, so Sir David has arranged for him to pose as "Richard Beckett" and to receive an invitation to do a spot of hunting on the Von Bruno estate. There, "undercover," he will seek proof that the count has done ill to Sterling and Brown.

Photoplay's Black Castle reviewer wrote, "Boris Karloff [above] is on hand, but since he's gone soft and can no longer be depended upon for fiendish behavior, Lon Chaney [top] looms up at intervals for extra menace."

Burton and his doting valet Romley (Tudor Owen) are soon en route through the murk of a cold, windy night to the castle, first bumping and jolting along in their own hired coach, then making a Renfield-like transfer to a Von Bruno coach driven by Fender. At the noisy, crowded Green Man, Burton is dining with Romley and Fender when no-account counts Stieken (John Hoyt) and Von Melcher (Michael Pate) arrive and can't find an empty table. They arrogantly demand Burton's and a two-on-one swordfight ensues, the counts vs. Burton. Burton jabs Stieken in the arm and then not only defeats but embarrasses Von Melcher. The two nasty nobles beat a hasty retreat. Attending to Burton's injured hand, Romley points out that Burton is wearing his silver ring with a small black stone African idol face mounted in it. Burton, Sterling and Brown each got one from the African natives who turned on

Who at Universal thought that horror movies and *rings* went together? *Strange Door* makes a big deal out of the ring the sire took from Armand; in *Black Castle* we hear about rings almost from beginning to end; and in *Abbott and Costello Meet Dr. Jekyll and Mr. Hyde,* Tubby obsesses over London physician Henry Jekyll's ring. Stranger still: Jekyll wears one of the Little Black Sambo rings left over from *The Black Castle*! Pictured: Tudor Owen (left), Richard Greene. (Photograph courtesy John Antosiewicz.)

Von Bruno; if Burton had worn it into the Black Castle, it would have given him away.

Burton arrives at Von Bruno's castle as Stieken's injured arm is being treated by Dr. Meissen (Boris Karloff). Posing as "Beckett," Burton formally meets Von Bruno (Stephen McNally), Stieken and Von Melcher, and reacts with surprise when he learns that the animal to be hunted is an imported African leopard. Entering the room to fetch Burton's trunk, Von Bruno's mute bodyguard Gargon (Lon Chaney) knits his brow when he sees the Englishman, giving the impression that he half-remembers him. The implication is that Gargon—one of Von Bruno's men in Africa, his tongue torn out by the natives whom the Englishmen set upon him—saw Burton there and will blow his cover if and when he remembers.

We now reach the point, inevitable in these movies, where the characters repair to the drenched-in-atmosphere catacomb sets: Von Bruno escorts Burton through the drip and damp of winding passageways to the leopard's cage. And the count makes his wife, Elga, accompany them, primarily because she doesn't *want* to; his sadistic side obviously calls for a regular routine of mental cruelty toward the demure young blonde. Six months earlier, Elga, the daughter of a teacher, was forced by fate, melodrama and marriage contract to wed Von Bruno; "No one here can defy the count," she tells Burton. Anxious to search the dungeon for clues, Burton gets Elga to accompany him. As they approach a door, a heavy spiked gate falls from above, nearly crushing them. The door leads to a cavernous room with a water-filled pit alive with alligators "no doubt imported to the Black Forest from Florida" (*New York Herald Tribune*). The 'gators are stock footage, the actors in the foreground added via SFX chicanery.

In the Black Castle's Great Hall, congregated around a breakfast table groaning with food, are all the lumps in the cream of Black Forest society; they feed themselves as leopard hunt host Von Bruno gives them final instructions. One hunter, beautiful blonde Therese (Nancy Valentine), has eyes for no one but Von Bruno and he has eye (single) for no one but her. On horseback, the hunters venture out into the gray, misty forest, Von Bruno pairing with Burton. Closing in on their prey, the two men dismount and take separate trails. Burton topples into a large pit where the black leopard is already trapped. Despite his hunting knife, Burton is moments from death when a shot rings out, killing the big cat. Unbeknownst to Burton, the fight has been observed by the other hunters, standing at the pit's edge; Von Bruno fired the fatal shot.

Burton is given credit for the kill and that night, at a party, he is awarded the prize, a pair of dueling pistols. (Von Bruno: "May these weapons never fail you.") As Burton and Elga dance the quadrille, it looks as though affection is blooming. Burton then notices that she wears as a pendant a stone African idol face identical to the one in his ring. Later, in the privacy of her bedroom, he tells her his whole story; takes the pendant in order to present it to the emperor as proof that the count murdered Sterling and Brown; and promises to come back for her. They are overheard by an unseen Stieken. Later, while drunk, Stieken tries to tell Von Bruno what he has learned. In the clichéd movie manner, he gets as far as "Beckett.... Beckett is..." when he collapses to the floor. Meissen pronounces him dead, omitting the small detail that he, Meissen, poisoned Stieken to prevent him from spilling the beans. Like Karloff's Voltan in *The Strange Door*, this new Karloff character feels a fatherly affection for the damsel in distress and wants to see her freed from the count's cruel clutches.

Von Bruno suspects that what Stieken was *going* to tell him was that Elga and Burton had become lovers, so he consigns her to a dungeon cell. Unaware of this new development, Burton cites "pressing business matters in London" as the reason for his sudden departure the next morning. Meissen follows and catches up with him that night at the Green Man, describing Elga's danger and convincing him to come back to the castle. In the meantime, Von Bruno has learned the true identity of "Richard Beckett" and is furious that he has departed. When the focus of his rage (Burton) returns, Von Bruno puts him in the dungeon with Elga. Von Bruno stands outside their cell and, in an extreme close-up, lets rip with a demented rant:

> **For five years I lived in a nightmare of hate, reliving the agony I suffered because of *this* [*tears off the eye patch to reveal his pale, dead right eye*]. I found only one relief for that agony: the hope that someday, somehow I'd find you!**

That night, Romley sneaks into the dungeon to attempt to free his master and Elga. A guard rings an alarm bell and Von Bruno, his men and their dogs hot-foot it onto the scene. Romley dies valiantly, trying to hold them off, while Burton and Elga escape through the alligator pit room (inching their way along a narrow ledge above the water). But in the mausoleum on the far side, they are intercepted by Von Bruno and Gargon. Burton jabs a torch into the face of Gargon, then battles the strongman and pushes him backward into the alligator pit.

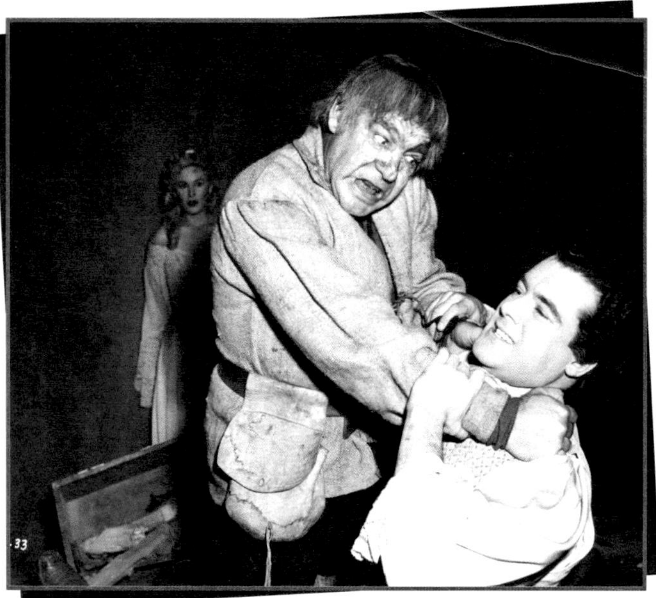

The mausoleum fight between Richard Greene and Lon Chaney was the last thing Chaney did on his last day on *The Black Castle*—his final Universal Horror. How marvelously appropriate that his "last hurrah" was as a monster (of sorts), in the kind of fight scene that Chaney enjoyed doing ... and on his father's legendary Phantom Stage. (Photograph courtesy John Antosiewicz.)

Clubbed into unconsciousness by Von Bruno, Burton soon finds himself back in the dungeon cell with Elga. Meissen tells them about a drug which for ten hours will retard their heart action and breathing to the point that they will appear lifeless. He says that if they take it, Von Bruno will immediately inter them in the mausoleum and then he (Meissen) will rescue them ... if he can. Despite the dreadful danger, the lovers take the drug. Infuriated by their "deaths" (i.e., robbed of the pleasure of torturing them), Von Bruno seizes a sword and is about to take it out on Meissen. His lips loosened by fear, the old doctor reveals that Burton and Elga are actually in a death-like state. This gives the count the devil of an idea: He's thrilled and upborne by the opportunity to bury them alive, a fate more horrible than anything he could have devised. Later, as Meissen stands over the coffins apologizing to Burton and Elga, Von Bruno overhears and fatally stabs him in the back.

The flashbacks end and, in a continuation of the scene that opened the movie, Fender and Koppich are seen nailing the lid onto Burton's coffin. Burton moans, and the two startled servants begin prying up their nails. Arriving with Von Melcher to oversee the interment, Von Bruno is outraged to see the nails being yanked. He angrily shoves the lid aside to reveal Burton with his dueling pistols in his hands; Meissen had secretly placed them in his coffin! Living up to Von Bruno's toast at the post-hunt celebration, Burton's weapons do not fail him: He shoots Von Bruno with one and Von Melcher with the other.

In a "feel-good" postscript in the castle courtyard, Burton and Elga board a coach and lock lips as a jubilant Fender, their newly hired servant, drives it out through the gateway of the Black Castle.

Cast Biographies

Richard Greene as Sir Ronald Burton

It can take an actor years, even decades, to become a leading player in Hollywood, but it took Richard Greene only a few days. When Greene played the juvenile lead in a touring version of Terence Rattigan's *French Without Tears* at the Royal Theatre in Birmingham, England, he was seen by a 20th Century-Fox talent scout who wired his boss Darryl F. Zanuck about the young actor with the Tyrone Power look. Zanuck felt that Greene would be right for the romantic lead in the adventure film *Four Men and a Prayer*

(1938), which was already shooting, and offered him a Fox contract. Greene signed on the dotted line and, with the ink probably still wet, was on his way to Southampton to catch a steamer to New York. From there he hurried to Newark Airport, flew to California and, five days and 21 hours after stepping off English soil, was at Fox preparing to co-star in a John Ford movie.

Greene was born in Plymouth, England, the son of stage character actors (and the grandson of motion picture pioneer William Friese-Greene). He was still a teenager when he stage-debuted in a 1933 Old Vic production of *Julius Caesar*. Between subsequent stage acting assignments, he earned £1 a sitting modeling hats and shirts. *French Without Tears* was the break that enabled him to make the leap to Lotus Land, where his dimples and Tyrone Power-Robert Taylor-style good looks had some in the industry scoffing "just another pretty boy." "Pretty boy," yes, but quite a popular one: In 1940, when 56 newspapers in key cities representing 22 million readers asked them to elect a king and queen of Hollywood, the screen heartthrob took an early lead before being overtaken by Power. In 1938, when he went missing while on a hunting trip in Kaibab National Forest on the wild Utah-Arizona border, the story of the search parties' efforts made headlines for days, including the front page of the *New York Daily News*.

In 1940, reacting to the war in Europe, Greene returned home and joined His Majesty's 27th Lancers as a private, attaining the rank of captain before being invalided out in the summer of 1945; in the interim, he married actress Patricia Medina. The interruption in his career robbed it of its momentum but he continued appearing in leading roles on both sides of the Atlantic. His marriage to Medina ended in Splitsville around the time of *Black Castle*, Medina telling the divorce court judge that Greene was "moody, cold, indifferent, humiliating and insulting." (Sounds like Count Von Bruno!) Greene starred in a *Lux Video Theatre* TV version of "The Sire de Malétroit's Door" the same year as Universal's *The Strange Door*.

In *The Black Castle*, our first look at Greene's Sir Ronald includes tight, count-the-pores close-ups as he lies cataleptic in the coffin, his disembodied voice crying out the attention-getting line, "He's *burying us alive*!" Now, for the benefit of intrigued audience members, the tone of his voice goes from frantic to businesslike as the immobilized Englishman packs up his worries about his imminent premature burial in order to give the movie audience the backstory on his dilemma. (As usual in movies told in flashbacks, we see scenes in which the flashback-storyteller was not involved and can't have known about.) Burton is a too-good-to-be-true hero, putting Honor with a capital H above his own safety, and doting on his manservant Romley (Donald Crisp lookalike Tudor

Richard Greene in his Fox heyday, with Wendy Barrie in *The Hound of the Baskervilles* (1939), where he got top billing over Basil Rathbone and Nigel Bruce in their debut Holmes-and-Watson vehicle. In that film, Greene nearly falls victim to the Baskerville family curse—a curse brought on by the depredations of his *very* Count Von Bruno-like ancestor Sir Hugo, "The Beast of the Baskervilles."

Owen) as much as Romley dotes on *him*. Whether being charming with Elga on the dance floor or dashing in his sword- and fistfights with Von Bruno's servants and sycophants, Burton keeps his wits about him at all times and is the epitome of foursquare, stiff-upper-lip gallantry. He's the perfect hero for *The Black Castle*, a rollicking "dime novel" of an adventure story.

From a bankbook standpoint, Greene's big break came in 1955 when he began starring in the half-hour TV series *The Adventures of Robin Hood* as the storied 12th-century outlaw in forest green. Shot at Nettlefold Studio at Walton-on-Thomas, it was the first commercial show to be seen in three countries (England, the U.S. and Canada) and had 32 million viewers a week; Ring Lardner, Jr., and other blacklistees wrote episodes under assumed names. Greene continued to steal from the rich and give to the poor in Hammer's *Sword of Sherwood Forest* (1960), which he also produced.

Greene's earnings from 143 *Robin Hood* episodes having made him the equivalent of a millionaire, he bought a 400-

acre stud farm in Ireland and became a leading breeder. He also continued acting, playing Nayland Smith in two of Christopher Lee's Fu Manchu movies, and climbing into a second coffin in the Amicus horror anthology *Tales from the Crypt* (1972), where his fate was even worse than what Count Von Bruno intended for him.

According to Patricia Medina's autobiography *Laid Back in Hollywood: Remembering*, one day in the early '80s she received a phone call from a friend of Greene's, telling her that Greene had invested very badly trying to start a new TV series; that he'd also lost a lot of money training horses; that his wife had separated from him and kept the house; that he was living in a tiny cottage in the north of England; and that he'd had a serious accident and couldn't work. Medina's husband Joseph Cotten overheard her half of the conversation and, after the end of the call, handed her an envelope with a generous check inside. Cotten said, "You have always remained friends with him. Write him a note from both of us. That check should help him. I certainly hope it does."

Richard Greene, the former "glamour boy of the movies," died in 1985 at his Norfolk, England, home.

Boris Karloff as Dr. Meissen

See the Karloff bio in the *Strange Door* chapter.

Stephen McNally as Count Karl Von Bruno

> Stephen McNally was a blunt, macho type of fellow, wondering what in hell's name he was doing playing in a period film, but I thought he was terribly good in it...
>
> —Michael Pate

The actor playing the Black Castle's resident sadist was actually a native of "da Bronx" (real name: Horace McNally), the son of a professor; one brother became a Jesuit priest, the other a school principal. A graduate of Fordham Law School, he once worked for a year and a half as a $20-a-week lawyer. Horace then decided to take down his law shingle, becoming an actor in hopes of making enough money to marry and have a family. He enrolled in the American Academy of Dramatic Arts to study acting; six months later, he landed a stock job in Woodstock; next he was on Broadway in 1940's *The Man Who Killed Lincoln*, which lasted all of five performances. Late that year he began co-starring in Broadway's *Johnny Belinda*, which got such a drubbing from drama reviewers that it *should* have lasted only five performances, but instead had a prosperous 40-week run. McNally played a Nova Scotia doctor who teaches deaf-mute farm girl Belinda (Helen Craig) sign language and lip-reading.

Heeding the advice of another Horace, McNally opted to go west in 1942 and was soon appearing in MGM features and shorts. When *Johnny Belinda* came to the screen in 1948, Jane Wyman played the deaf-mute part (and won an Oscar), Lew Ayres got the role of the doctor (and was Oscar-nominated), and McNally was in the supporting cast as the drunken ruffian who rapes and impregnates Wyman. McNally's attitude about his switch from doctor to dastard: "I decided if they wanted me to be a heavy, I'd give them the meanest characterization this side of a grave robber. I went into that picture with a burning determination to make people hate me." The movie's director Jean Negulesco told him, "Horace is the wrong name for you" and he agreed, changing it to Stephen.

Tall, black-haired, stalwart Stephen McNally may look like the meanest man on earth when you see him [as movie villains] but in real life he is just the opposite.

Stephen is my neighbor. It is a usual thing to see him with his five children packed in the car, or romping, or walking with them.

My first acquaintance with Stephen McNally was when I saw him passing the plate in church [Louella O. Parsons, 1949].

In his early days at Universal, McNally alternated between double-tough bad guys and good guys. He played one of his rottenest Western rogues, complete with Von Bruno–like scar over his right eye, in director Anthony Mann's *Winchester '73* (1950) and a reluctant Western hero in producer Val Lewton's *Apache Drums* (1951). After a number of successive "good guy" roles, McNally's "sneer-driven perf" (*VideoScope* magazine) as *Black Castle*'s 18th-century archfiend was an about-face for the actor, who threw himself into the tyrant role whole-hog and gave his hambone free rein.

According to Alex Gordon, producer of 1965's *Requiem for a Gunfighter*, for McNally the paycheck, not the play, was the thing: Ultimate movie fan Gordon hoped that, between takes on *Requiem*, McNally would reminisce for him about past Hollywood experiences, and was disappointed to find that the actor was completely disinclined. "He was practically impossible to work with. ... He was only concerned about the money," Gordon told *Western Clippings* magazine. Well, McNally *was* the father of eight by that time, which had to have been expensive. (In 1953, when he "only" had six, he already had more kids than any other leading actor in Hollywood.)

In addition to dozens of movie roles, McNally also guested on umpteen TV series and had one of his own, *Target: The Corruptors* (1961–62), a newspaper drama with McNally as a "rackets reporter" who each week exposed a different type of underworld corruption. He died of heart failure in June 1994, at age 82.

Black Castle producer William Alland thought Stephen McNally was excellent in the picture but added, "He was a very strange man, very difficult to know—rather taciturn. He was relegated pretty much to Westerns and to playing heavies throughout most of his career, but I thought he was a very good actor." (Photograph courtesy John Antosiewicz.)

Paula Corday as Countess Elga Von Bruno

Paula Corday led a globetrotting existence as a child, living in different countries with her family in the pre–World War II years. "I am so glad that I have seen the world as it was," she said in her first interview (1943), "because it will not be the same after the war."

She was born in Papeete, Tahiti, in 1920, the daughter of an attaché at the Swiss embassy; her real name was Jeanne Paule Teipo-Ite-Marama Croset, which is actually a boy's name and means "Ball of Light." Her father was French-Swiss, her mother British-Spanish-Italian, and during her youth, just *some* of the places where she, her parents and her brother Gaston lived were Australia, France, Switzerland, India and the U.S. Their home in 1937 was a ten-room house in Shanghai (with four house servants); the family was in Korea on a family vacation when the Japanese attacked Shanghai that August. "We returned in the fall and for two years lived through the bomb raids. No, it is not too frightening to be bombed. Not after the first two or three. You become accustomed to it. It is just annoying."

In 1939 her father brought his family to America, leaving them here the following year when he returned to his Shanghai headquarters. She went to drama school and was spotted by a movie talent scout; even though workplaces didn't like to employ foreigners during the war years, RKO was permitted to engage her. (According to a Colin Briggs article in *Films of the Golden Age* magazine, Orson Welles was instrumental in getting her hired at RKO. Welles also suggested a name change to Rita Corday because of her resemblance to Rita Hayworth.) The gal who had been sent halfway around the world to escape the war soon found herself appearing in a war movie: a bit in RKO's *Hitler's Children*, her debut.

Under the name Rita Corday, she acted in a number of RKO series movies: Gildersleeve, Mexican Spitfire, eerie entries in the Dick Tracy and Falcon series. Her one stand-out screen assignment during those years was the role of Mrs. Marsh, distraught mother of the crippled girl (Sharyn Moffett) in Val Lewton's Karloff starrer *The Body Snatcher* (1945). After leaving RKO, she studied acting in New York, then returned to California and made her Universal debut (under the new name Paule Croset) in director Max Ophüls' *The Exile* (1947). Corday received special "introducing" billing for her role as a farm owner in 1660 Holland who falls

Russell Wade and Paula Corday in *The Body Snatcher* (1945), one of Boris Karloff's best. Corday and Karloff reunited in *The Black Castle*.

Black Castle villain and victim Stephen McNally and Paula Corday reunited on "Gun Molls and Floozies" night at the Hollywood Roosevelt Hotel on Hollywood Boulevard in the late 1980s. (Photograph courtesy Gordon Hunter.)

in love with a dashing farmhand she doesn't know is actually exiled British monarch Charles Stuart (Douglas Fairbanks, Jr., who also scripted and produced).[2] Fairbanks dubbed her "The Tyrolean Blonde" and got the credit for re-discovering her. That same year, she married Harold Nebenzal (the son of Seymour Nebenzal, producer of such German film classics as 1931's *M*). During her marriage, husband Harold produced the 1951 *M* remake with David Wayne. It was in her next incarnation, as Paula Corday in the 1950s, that she appeared in *The Black Castle,* made on a one-picture deal with Universal. With a touch of an accent reminiscent of Simone (*Cat People*) Simon's Irena, she played the long-suffering Elga, forced into marriage in a land where beauty is a girl's misfortune, and had a reunion with *Body Snatcher* star Karloff.

A few more film roles followed, plus some TV work, but by the early 1960s Corday was the mother of two and had dropped both the acting and the husband. Briggs wrote in *Films of the Golden Age* that once the kids left the nest, she found her life lonely but enjoyed swimming. Her daughter Deborah told me, "I remember my mother saying over and over again that if she were to do it all over again, she would have been a forest ranger as she loved the outdoors." Paula lost a leg to diabetes in 1991.

"Ball of Light" flickered out on November 21, 1992, in Century City of complications following a gall bladder operation.

Lon Chaney as Gargon

The son of the silent screen's Man of a Thousand Faces Lon Chaney was Lon Chaney, Jr.—all of us horror movie fans call him that, even though he was billed Lon Chaney, Jr., in only one horror movie. He was Universal's go-to guy for monster roles during the war years: the Wolf Man, Frankenstein, Mummy and Dracula. Then in 1946 he refused to sign a new deal, and left the studio a few weeks later (the discord was a matter of money).

In 1952, the hard-boiled egg in the Universal Horror salad was back on his old stomping grounds playing the mute Gargon in *The Black Castle.* In the four years since *Abbott and Costello Meet Frankenstein* (Chaney's previous Universal Horror), there'd been a lot of Jim Beam under the bridge; in the same way that Universal Lugosified Karloff, they (and other moviemakers) "Rondo Hatton-ized" the perpetually lubed-up Chaney, giving him menace roles with little or no dialogue. At the time ('52), the actor and his missus were still in the same small, modest house they'd occupied throughout his days of playing Universal's flagship monsters, 12750 Hortense Street in Studio City, just five or six miles from the studio's gates.

Michael Pate, who shared several *Black Castle* scenes with Chaney, told me,

> **I've read all kinds of things about him being disadvantaged by a famous father, being a bit of a drunk (to say the least!), being occasionally obnoxious, etc., etc., but I found him to be a very warm, agreeable fellow. We talked about other films that he'd been in, especially *Of Mice and Men* [1939]. If all his films had been of that quality, he'd have probably been more highly thought of. He was very stereotyped at that time in the horror roles that he was doing, but he just simply went about his job; he wasn't really living in the shadow of his famous father, if ever he had. He was a very nice, gentle person and I particularly liked him.**

In the months leading up to *Black Castle,* Chaney was part of a vaudeville show appearing in different parts of the country. When he began playing Gargon on March 20, he hadn't worked in a movie since September or October of the year before, when he sported old age makeup in both *The Bushwhackers* and *High Noon,* two Westerns made simultaneously.[3]

The hard drinking took a toll on Chaney's face and physique; if his father had lived into his seventies, which of them would have looked fitter in the 1960s? "Junior" kept busy on TV and in movies for the first half of that decade, but then he became the exclusive property of rock-bottom indie movie producers. By the '70s he appears to have become completely unemployed, probably unemploy*able.* Chaney, 67, died in 1973; local TV station KCBS wanted to

Universal's Phantom Stage housed *Black Castle*'s sets for the Green Man inn, the mausoleum, dungeon cell and more. It also provided a backdrop for a silly publicity picture of Lon Chaney and Paula Corday. (Photograph courtesy John Antosiewicz.)

include in their news report an interview with an old acting colleague, speaking fondly of him, but Lon had burned all his bridges and they could find no one. At last a cancer-stricken Glenn Strange, exactly ten weeks from Death's Door himself, crawled out of his bed of pain to say a few kind on-camera words.

Chaney's body was donated to the USC School of Medicine. There, supposedly, his liver and lungs were put on display because a chance to examine organs *that* ravaged by booze and cigarettes was a once-in-a-deathtime opportunity.

Production

On March 12, 1952, *Black Castle* principal photography began on the Phantom Stage with a shot of Green Man innkeeper Krantz (Otto Waldis) lighting a hanging lantern in the window; the camera then pulls back across the room to precede him (and give viewers a look at the place) as he totes a tray of food to the table of Burton and Romley (Richard Greene and Tudor Owen). The inn is abuzz with activity courtesy of 30 extras. As Burton converses with Krantz, there's a cute, easy to miss bit of business in the foreground that establishes that Romley is forever looking out for his master: He eyeballs the empty plate brought for Burton's use, picks it up and begins rubbing at one spot with his cloth napkin.

Henry Corden, the future voice of cartoondom's Fred Flintstone, next came on camera as Von Bruno's overworked drudge Fender, who makes it a threesome at Burton's table just in time for the entrance of John Hoyt and Michael Pate as Stieken and Von Melcher. The latter slaps a roast chicken from Fender's hands, presumably making this Just Another Day in the Life of Fender; we get the impression that for this Black Castle serf, kicks and blows are his bed and breakfast.

After some dueling rehearsing, the two-on-one Burton vs. Stieken and Von Melcher swordfight began. Father-and-son movie swordsmen Fred and Albert Cavens were on hand that day (and the next) to work as doubles; Fred, a Belgian-born fencing legend, began his career in the days of silent swashbucklers when he helped choreograph the action in Douglas Fairbanks movies. Michael Pate told me that he did his own *Black Castle* swordfighting and that, in the course of his career, "I got to be quite adept with a foil and also with the epee and even with a scimitar":

You had to learn the routines perfectly and *do* them immaculately; you couldn't flip around when you were using such weapons. The points were blunted just a little so that they wouldn't get into you if you got jabbed, but many a time you got nicked if you were careless. I remember Basil Rathbone having his whole wig cut right up the middle by Danny Kaye on *The Court Jester* [1956]; Danny did a couple of leaps forward unexpectedly and bounced the epee right off Basil's forehead, right through to the back of his head. It cut straight through his wig and into his pate, as a matter of fact! I don't remember whether there were stitches but there was quite a lot of blood where the epee grazed the top of his head.

The Black Castle marked a return to Universal Horror for Pate, previously seen as Talon, one of the smaller snakes in the *Strange Door* vipers' nest. Here he plays a quite similar role, although promoted from lowly retainer to count. At decade's end (1959), in his third Universal chiller, Pate had the starring role of a vampire out west in *Curse of the Undead*.

The Green Man set was again packed with extras the next morning as the sword battle continued. In the scene's most memorable moment, Burton sidesteps a Von Melcher lunge and the villain's sword gets stuck in a pig on a fireplace spit, provoking raucous laughter from bibulous onlookers. It's nice to have this action scene in the opening reel, just as it was nice to have Denis' barroom brawl and the subsequent chase at the beginning of *The Strange Door*; otherwise the first halves of both movies would be nothing but talk and "planting the plot."

After this scene was finished around five p.m., the shooting of the second Green Man scene began with Boris Karloff's Dr. Meissen, out of breath and in the throes of anxiety, making his entrance ("The countess' life is in great danger!"). Meissen makes the attention-getting admission that he poisoned Stieken—dialogue which had met with the disapproval of the Breen Office. The censor wrote Universal, "In order to overcome any suggestion that Dr. Meissen has committed an heroic act in murdering Count Stieken, and so as not to glorify the same, we believe it would be well to insert a line by [Burton] on the order of, 'You, a murderer! Why?'" Universal got away with *not* including any such extra line.

In *The Strange Door,* Boris was a dull-witted servant in a madman's medieval chateau of horrors whereas here, in the same sort of hostile work environment, he's a house physician; the *dis*similarities end there, since Dr. Meissen is simply Voltan with a medical black bag. Scripter Sackheim re-gifts *Black Castle* audiences with a Karloff character who serves all the same plot purposes as in *Strange Door*: He's devoted to the put-upon lady of the castle, risking his life to help her; gets a knife in the back from the villain as his reward; but in his dying moments he gives the lady and her gentleman the means to escape grisly death (the cell door key in *The Strange Door*, the dueling pistols here). Universal did not wholly Lugosify Karloff: Whereas some of the minor characters played by Bela in Universal Horrors meant little or absolutely nothing to the plot (Marnay in 1940's *Black Friday*, Eduardo in the 1941 *Black Cat*, Rolf in 1942's *Night Monster*), Boris' are pivotal in his 1950s Horrors as he saves the day in both.

A new day: March 14. A new set: the Black Castle's Great Hall and Entrance Hall on Stage 7. A new hyper-villain for the Classic Horror catalogue: forty-one-year-old Stephen McNally as the eye patch-wearing scourge of the Black Forest, Karl Von Bruno. Von Bruno's black patch was producer William Alland's idea.

Strange Door and *Black Castle* have much in common but the main thing that sets them apart is their villains. Their embrace of evil makes the Sire de Maletroit and Count Von Bruno shirt-tail kin but personally they couldn't be more different: The macho, masculine Von Bruno is a far cry from the effete, abdominous sire. First and foremost, Von Bruno does not leave the dirty work to others while keeping his own hands clean. In fact, "Countzilla" has difficulty keeping his hands to him*self*, digging his finger into Stieken's sword wound (and later giving him a backhand slap), surprising Fender with a backhand uppercut, roughing up Elga, giving Dr. Meissen a backhand *and* a bitch slap—*plus* beating the leopard's cage with a whip, shooting Romley and clubbing Burton. And all this in just the little window of time we spend with the gentleman in this story, which we suspect comes at the end of a lifetime of volcanic violence. In a contemporary interview, McNally called Von Bruno

a part that I can really sink my teeth into. I slap women around physically, drive them into insanity mentally, poison some of my best friends and order a couple of young lovers buried alive.

(McNally probably *didn't* say that, it sounds a lot more like something a publicist wrote, but it's still a great quote.) McNally, Lon Chaney, John Hoyt and Michael Pate are a far more formidable, red-blooded bunch of baddies than the assortment of fruits and nuts in *The Strange Door*, part of why *The Black Castle* is the more satisfying film.

March 14 filming began on the Great

A horror-costume adventure hybrid in the *Strange Door* style, *The Black Castle* dished up a fistfight, gun deaths and even swordplay: the Green Man encounter between Burton (Richard Greene, right) and Von Melcher (Michael Pate). (Photograph courtesy John Antosiewicz.)

Hall set with Dr. Meissen treating Stieken's sword wound. This is the scene where audiences first see Karloff, who wears glasses here for the only time in the movie. John Hoyt, playing the scene shirtless, displays a great physique which the actor also showed off in other movies—and even in a nude calendar called "The Bare Grays"![14] In another take not seen in the movie, an obviously jumpy Stieken drops his glass and draws his sword when he's startled by the noisy entrance of an off-camera Gargon. The actor set to play Gargon, Lon Chaney, wasn't on the set; his first day was almost a week away.

Stage 7 was where all shooting took place from March 14 to 20 and then part of the 21st. On the 15th, they got a start on the post-leopard hunt party and dance. For one brief but impressive shot, the camera was brought up to some high point, shooting down past a candle chandelier at the dancers in their fancy party dress, the musicians, guests chatting by the giant fireplace, etc.

> Nancy Valentine, who left the screen to become the wife of the Maharajah of Cooch Behar, will make her return in a feature role in Universal-International's *The Black Castle*.
>
> —*The Hollywood Reporter*, March 18, 1952

Beauty is sin-deep: Therese (Nancy Valentine) sets her sights on the wife-weary Count Von Bruno (Stephen McNally), baiting him with everything she can get on the hook. And he's more than ready to trade in the countess for a newer model. (Photograph courtesy John Antosiewicz.)

In the party scene, Von Bruno memorably introduces Valentine's Therese as a woman "who can out-ride, out-shoot, yes, and out-*drink* most of the men in this room." (After delivering this encomium, he makes it a point to acidulously add, "My peasant wife can do nothing.") Valentine was more often mentioned in gossip columns of the day than seen on movie and TV screens; the model turned starlet was frequently linked, professionally and/or socially, with Hollywood heavyweights Howard Hughes, Orson Welles, David O. Selznick *et al.* Then there was her courtship and (possible) marriage to the maharajah, whom she met while dancing the rumba at New York's El Morocco. After a week she was calling him "Coochie" and soon she was announcing that she'd be the next maharani. For several years the gossip columnists (and their readers) weren't quite sure whether the two had secretly married, or (if they had) if the marriage was legal, or why the Indian government refused to recognize the marriage, *ad infinitum* well beyond the point of "Who *cares*?"; in the meantime, the yes/no maharani was beating the Hollywood bricks for acting gigs on such low-level teleseries as *Racket Squad* and *Sky King*. In 1952, perhaps the height of this tempest in a turban, it must have been amusing for audience members aware of the Nancy Valentine Saga to see this royal wannabe in the *Black Castle* cast, aggressively putting out the lure for the titled Von Bruno. Her other genre credits are the Karloff-hosted *Thriller* episode "Yours Truly, Jack the Ripper" (as a victim of the still-loose-in-the-1960s Ripper) and the very *It Came from Outer Space–like* TV movie *Night Slaves*. The latter aired in 1970, the same year that Coochie died as a result of injuries sustained in a fall from a horse while playing polo in Jaipur.

On Monday the 17th, more of the party sequence was shot, plus the scene of the leopard hunters forgathered prior to the hunt. March 18 found Von Bruno and Von Melcher collecting taxes from tenants, and learning from Krantz that departed guest "Beckett" was actually their old enemy Burton. On hand that day, according to production paperwork, were actor Wheaton Chambers (playing a farmer) plus 12 chickens, 12 ducks and one small pig. The pig can be seen and heard but none of the birds, and neither hide nor hair of Chambers. Next on the agenda: the mid-movie scene of Burton making his goodbyes and leaving the castle, and the next-day scene where he apologetically returns. Shot on the 19th was the Upstairs Alcove scene of Burton and Elga kissing—and Burton filching her pendant.

There's very little that's (intentionally) funny about the Count Von Bruno or McNally's performance. The one exception: a black-comic scene in which Von Bruno, sitting at the head of the Great Hall dining table ravenously

Isn't it bad enough that Count Von Bruno (Stephen McNally, right) is a tyrant, an ogre and a murderer? Did the movie also have to make him a *tax collector*? Leaning over the table is Otto Waldis; first in line behind him, playing a cloth merchant, is Roy Engel, President Grant on TV's *The Wild Wild West.* (Photograph courtesy John Antosiewicz.)

digging into his breakfast, amuses his tablemate Von Melcher (and himself) by doing some straight-faced "Mr. Innocent" schtick. In an out-of-character, low-key way, he talks about dungeon prisoner Elga in the past tense, as though she's already dead and as though he had nothing to do with it, and then refers back to the *first* countess, whom he *did* kill:

> **Could anyone have been closer to me than my first wife? Yet when she died ... [*can't think of anything to say next*] ... ummm ... [*Loses interest in doing schtick, drops it*:] Pass the sausage!**

Watching this exchange, Universal Horror-holics can't help but think back to Laughton's *Henry VIII* scene in *The Strange Door*: It's the same sort of room (including a fireplace in the background), the same sort of situation (the main heavy at the head of the table, stuffing his face and trying to be funny), and the "straight man" in *both* movies, occupying the same spot on the baddie's right, is Michael Pate. Since both scenes were shot on Stage 7, it's probably partly (or mostly) the same set!

Comparing the performances of Laughton and McNally is a hard-to-resist impulse. McNally's Von Bruno has a streak of cruelty that spills over into his humor, the same as Laughton's sire; but McNally's humor includes a vulpine, honey-tongued brand of verbal abuse. In his case, the overarching impression is of a one-note sadist with anger management issues. Laughton as de Maletroit, on the other hand, slices his ham with stylish zest and is often an amusing counterpoise to *The Strange Door*'s atmosphere of gloom. Probably no fan would opine that McNally was more fun to watch than the scenery-chewing Laughton, but on the other hand, probably no one has ever said (as some fans *do* about Laughton and *The Strange Door*) that McNally did his picture more harm than good.

Starting in the late afternoon, cast and crew shot the trophy room scene in which the poisoned Stieken turns up his toes. Leading up to this scene in the movie, the audience senses that Karloff's Dr. Meissen, although a Von Bruno lackey, is naughty but nice, but we can't be sure. After all, we initially saw this medical man amusing himself by being purposely un-gentle with Stieken's sword wound, even grinning with anticipation when he knew Stieken was about to yelp in pain. But in the party scene, the looks that pass between Elga and Meissen tip us off that, odd duck though he may be, he's her one lifeline in this house of horrors, and this gives us a better opinion of him.

The half-lit trophy room scene where Meissen examines Stieken features one of Karloff's best *Black Castle* moments: The audience has a worm's-eye view as Meissen looks for a sign of life in Stieken. The physician smiles broadly at the realization that Stieken is dead; then, as he begins to turn his head to look up and behind him at Von Bruno and Von Melcher, the smile morphs into a look of feigned horror. Karloff times it so that the last trace of smile disappears at the last split-second before they can see his face.[5]

"I thought Boris was one of the loveliest people that I'd ever come across. We had many a chat on the set over a cup of coffee, a cigarette or a pipe," Michael Pate told me. He went on:

> **He turned out to be such a charming, laid-back, relaxed Englishman, just a marvelous person. He was always considerate, always charming; he had a nice attitude toward "being Boris Karloff." I think, generally speaking, he was just a little tired of playing "the Boris Karloff part," but he never showed it all that very much. He just went about his work, did his business as it was expected of him, in the style that people had become accustomed to. ... He was in a situation where you take the money and run, and I guess somewhere in the back of his mind he figured that that was the most secure way to do his work, and continue to live as comfortably as he'd always liked to.**

"[Karloff] had a funny little expression, that looked as though the most tremendous thinking was going on behind his eyes," Juran told *Starlog* magazine's Steve Swires. "One time I asked him: 'How do you know to do that? It's so good for the film.' Karloff gave me a sly smile, and said, 'It's just an old trick of the trade. I'm not thinking *a thing*'"

On March 20, Lon Chaney was examined for insurance purposes and stepped into *The Black Castle*. In the pressbook, the item "Young Chaney Turns Down Father's Roles" claims that the actor had had dozens of offers to reprise characters made famous by his silent-star dad and unhesitatingly nixed them all; Chaney is quoted as saying, "My theory is that actors shouldn't be imitators of other actors, even in the case of their own parents." But in June 1952, on the set of the Gary Cooper Western *Springfield Rifle*, Chaney told reporter Erskine Johnson that he had recently been approached by an indie producer expressing an interest in making a movie biography of the Man of a Thousand Faces, and volunteered, "I wouldn't insist on playing it myself, I couldn't do it unless they'd let me act like my old man did instead of directing me."[6]

If these quotes are legit, it's an interesting turnaround; could Chaney have been sufficiently pleased with his own pantomime performance as *Black Castle*'s moptop mute that it changed his attitude toward playing some of Dear Old Dad's characters? Although most of his *Black Castle* screen time is spent glowering in the backgrounds, he does get the benefit of an impressive intro: As Von Bruno, Stieken and Von Melcher greet the newly arrived Burton in the Great Hall, Gargon makes an equally great entrance. Accompanied by an ominous *House of Frankenstein* music cue, he lopes into the room and into a close-up which provides us a good look at his "Tell me about the rabbits!" simpleton smile and blond Buster Brown wig. (The sight of a blond Lon also stirs memories of his Lennie in *Of Mice and Men*, the 1939 Best Picture nominee and Chaney's one brush with The Big Time.) When Gargon sets eyes on Burton, the movie's best non-action scene commences: Chaney pantomimes surprise, then inquisitiveness (as he gets right up in the Englishman's face), then torment and frustration (as only Chaney could do it) as he strains his simple brain to place the man. Could his famous father have played that scene any more effectively? In fact, given the elder Chaney's penchant for playing to the back row, could he have done it as *well* as his son does here?

In the afternoon, parts of the movie's finale were filmed: guests and servants paying their respects at the coffins of Burton and Elga; Dr. Meissen speaking to the catatonic Burton ("I—I beg you ... do not think too badly of me...") and getting a knife in the back from Von Bruno ("I forgive you, Meissen!"); and the through-the-fireplace-flames shot of a stolid Von Bruno and an antsy Von Melcher, anticipating their visit to the mausoleum. You *know* that Von Bruno has nothing to fear from local law enforcement when he apparently can put forth without explanation that his young wife *and* a young visitor died on the same day and no one cries foul.

March 21: more Entrance Hall and Great Hall shots for various parts of the movie, the Burton-Elga balcony scene and then, after an afternoon move to Stage 8, the Von Bruno-Elga bedroom scene where he roughs her up and she says she despises him. Proving that she's right to do so, Von Bruno calls Gargon into the room and gives him a thrill by telling him, "The countess is in your care." Last shot of the day: a close-up of Elga reacting to the approach of the stupidly grinning Gargon.

Stage 8 was again the center of activity on Saturday, March 22, and Monday the 24th. Another *Strange Door*-inspired scene was the first thing shot on the 22nd: Gargon entering Burton's room via secret panel and standing over the sleeping man, *à la* Voltan and Denis in *Door*. Other sets used that day: Elga's room, Von Bruno's sitting room and Burton's room. On the latter set they did the scene of Von Bruno slapping Fender and accusing him of stealing the dueling pistols. Henry Corden, who played Fender, was being mistreated on-camera as well as off-:

Hits and missus: The marriage made in Horror Heaven is coming to an end as the bad-to-the-bone Von Bruno (Stephen McNally) gets tough with his defiant bride (Paula Corday).

The Black Castle was [Nathan Juran's] first directorial job and he was very nervous, and he used a couple of people as whipping boys. I was one of them, because I was not famous or any of that. So it was difficult. I would do something and he wouldn't like it, and instead of just saying, "No, try it another way" or "Let's do it this way," he would sort of be *angry* with me for having done it the way I did. He did that with others too. On *The Black Castle*, he was a little nervous. Understandable. But he didn't have to take it out on the other people—including me.

The company was dismissed at 5:50 on Saturday the 22nd. On Monday the 24th, cast and crew might have read in *Variety*:

"Art Is Long; Time Fleeting"

Hurry-up call for a fig leaf was made on UI's *The Black Castle* set over the weekend when members of Irving Glassberg's camera crew suddenly discovered that a bronze statue of a youth serving as a background prop for Stephen McNally was strictly *au naturel* material.

Statue had remained unnoticed in the background, and the Grecian youth's total nudity wasn't discovered until Glassberg and crew moved in for a tight close-up of McNally. Having been established in the long shot, it was necessary to keep the statue in for the close-up and only solution was to fall back on the method used by more conservative museums and a few private collectors around the country and resort to the conventional fig leaf.

There wasn't a stock leaf anywhere in the prop department, but technicians in the studio plaster shop came to the rescue and turned out an artistic plaster job within 20 minutes after the emergency call.

The Daily Production Reports of March 21 and 22 do not confirm this "news" story.

On Monday, after getting more footage on the Sitting Room set, there was an after-lunch move to the Phantom Stage and its dusky dungeon passage set where Von Bruno, Burton, Elga and Gargon visit the caged leopard. They began shooting the scene that afternoon and finished the next morning. A nice low-angle, through-the-cage-bars shot gives us the leopard in the foreground, Von Bruno, Burton and Elga beyond. When the half-witted Gargon pounds on the top of the small cage with a whip, Von Bruno envisions a Gargon-leopard hand-to-claw struggle, a mental image that fills him with Zaroff-like giddiness: "Can you picture such a struggle? An unarmed man against the king of the jungle!"

Next came the filming of other subterranean passage scenes: Burton and Elga exploring; Von Bruno and Von Melcher escorting Burton to the dungeon cell; Romley creeping up on the sleeping guard. (*Photoplay*'s *Black Castle* reviewer called the movie's corridors "as labyrinthine as the plot.") The next day, March 26, this work continued: Burton being tossed in the cell with Elga; Von Bruno's no-eye-patch "I lived in a nightmare of hate" tirade; Meissen giving the lovers his death-in-life drug. As Von Bruno rants at the imprisoned Burton and Elga, you can't help but remember the equivalent *Strange Door* scenes of de Maletroit taunting *his* dungeon prisoners. When Von Bruno pulls off his eye patch to reveal his dead eye (in close-up), the movie's horror quotient goes up a notch.

Contact lenses which fit over the cornea of the eye to simulate blindness are fast becoming a standard "prop" for the Hollywood movie makers.

Arthur Kennedy started it last year when he wore a pair of the lenses in his eyes to simulate total blindness in the film *Bright Victory*.

Now Stephen McNally is using similar lenses for his starring role in Universal-International's horror-thriller, *The Black Castle* [Universal publicity release, 1952].

Changing the appearance of movie actors' eyes started a lot earlier than *Bright Victory*. In silent days, Lon Chaney wore what was called a glass shield over one eye in *The Road to Mandalay* (1926). John Barrymore had white eyeballs as the title character in *Svengali* (1931), Joseph Cotten had milky-looking eyes as the elder Jed Leland in *Citizen Kane* (1941), Howard Da Silva had a Von Bruno–type eye in *They Live by Night* (1948), Debra Paget wore contact lenses to change her eye color from blue-green to brown for *Broken Arrow* (1950), etc. Incidentally, the none-too-

Paula Corday, preparing to drink the death-in-life drug, considered Richard Greene (right) "her favorite leading man" and Boris Karloff (center) "a very nice, gentlemanly person—very gentle, very quiet, and soft-spoken."

accurate publicity item quoted above also mentions that McNally's Viennese nobleman "is supposed to have had an eye gouged out by fellow actor Boris Karloff."

It was back to the Phantom Stage on March 27, starting with the dungeon cell scene in which Meissen, afraid for his life, tells Von Bruno that Burton and Elga are not dead but in a death-like state. Production paperwork makes it appear as though Stephen McNally blew quite a few takes this morning. Next came the scene where Romley springs Burton and Elga from their cell; just prior to shooting, a ceiling was put on the set, one of several seen in the movie. Then it was time for Romley's heroic last stand, stool in hand, at the base of a staircase as Von Bruno, Gargon, guards and dogs swarm toward him. When Romley is attacked by the dog, Tudor Owen was doubled by Frank Inn, the well-known Hollywood animal trainer and future owner-trainer of Benji.[7] The police dog used in the scene, perhaps the property of Inn, did not hurt him but *did* bite a Hazardous Day Player, Clyde McLeod, on the posterior. McLeod was taken to the hospital but returned to work, so he was all right in the end. Notice that the dog, upset by the firing of a gun, turns tail and ad libs a hasty retreat, against the tide of Burton and Elga's pursuers. Chaney twisted his knee on the 27th, but didn't report it until the next day.

Another bogus news item, "*Black Castle* Stand-ins Balk at Playing Dead," ran in the March 28 *Variety*:

> **Dummies were substituted for live stand-ins yesterday on UI's *The Black Castle* set, following reluctance of the bona-fide stand-ins to spend better part of the day stretched out in oak coffins while the technical crew lined up on them for lighting effects.**
>
> **Scene in the horror-thriller calls for stars Richard Greene and Paula Corday to be shown lying stiffly in the coffins.... When the two stand-ins for Greene and Miss Corday expressed distinct apprehension about spending the day wrapped in wooden kimonos, director Nathan Juran came to their rescue and ordered the prop department to furnish the dummy workers.**

Work started late on March 28 (a ten a.m. shooting call) because they'd be working into the night. The place: the black heart of the Studio of Horrors, the back lot's exterior Tower of London sets. Henry Corden reminds us that those imposing sets were also used "in the old tits-and-sand pictures [Universal's Arabian Nights-style adventures]. If you wanted to show the castle of the high muckymuck in a tits-and-sand picture, *those* were the sets. They were *very* well made and they were constantly being taken care of."

"I used a lot of leftovers—I was the Leftover King!" producer Alland laughingly told me about all the recycled sets (and and and) seen in *The Black Castle*. "That was true of Universal in general: They were very, very cost-conscious, and anything that could be reused *was* reused."

The morning began with Burton and Romley's arrival at the Black Castle, the coach rumbling into the courtyard with three huge, barking dogs positioned in the foreground, alertly observing the action. Then they filmed the fade-out shot of Burton and Elga's coach's departure from the castle, happy, grateful servants lined up and down the distant background castle staircase waving their goodbyes as (*à la* Errol Flynn's *The Adventures of Robin Hood*) the giant entranceway doors close behind them. Later, in a very high shot from a crane, the moviemakers filmed (for the middle section of the movie) footage of Burton and Romley's coach coming and going from the courtyard. There was another mishap this day, off-camera: Extra Frieda Stoll was toted off to the hospital because of a leg injury sustained when a bench collapsed during the lunch break.

In the afternoon, with fires lit in a few braziers, wind machines in operation and "lightning" flashing, Von Bruno and Von Melcher walked amidst a throng of mourners as the coffins of Burton and Elga were carried down the castle staircase and through an archway into the cemetery. After dinner, when it was dark, the moviemakers shot the scene of Fender emerging from the mausoleum and throwing a rock at the howling wolf (played by a dog). A bit after nine, with "rain" pouring down and additional "lightning," Von Bruno and Von Melcher, their expressions matching the weather, descended the castle steps and marched across the courtyard and through the cemetery to the mausoleum door.

For some reason, there was a Saturday the 29th retake of Dr. Meissen's coffin-side death scene. It was filmed on Stage 9, not the Stage 7 Great Hall set where it was done the first time, which is why the shot seems out of place in the movie; in this retake, we see only a blank wall behind Meissen, and it looks like they didn't even bother to give him a coffin (or *any*thing) to lean on as he addresses the off-camera body of Burton. Later they also reshot part of the dungeon cell scene in which Meissen blabs to a livid Von Bruno that Burton and Elga drank poison from his bag. Again the Stage 9 retake looks noticeably different than the rest of the scene which was shot on the Phantom Stage. This was Karloff's last shot on his last day on his last "straight" Universal horror movie (he did later appear in *Abbott and Costello Meet Dr. Jekyll and Mr. Hyde*).[8] Also filmed on Stage 9 that day: Burton's visit to Sir David at the British Ministry.

After dinner, and after sunset, players and crew reconverged on an area of the back lot above Nursery Ranch for the scene of Burton, Romley and their luggage transferring from their hired coach to Von Bruno's. Wind machines, the dubbed-in sound of heavy wind, actors acting cold and talking about the cold add up to a teeth-chattering experience for the viewer, unless you happen to know that March 29 was a mostly sunny 72-degree day and therefore probably a lovely spring evening.

The coffins of Burton and Elga are carried from the castle to the mausoleum—the pallbearers unaware that the Englishman and the countess are not dead but sleepeth. That's Henry Corden (center) leading a pack of extras down Universal's Tower of London staircase. (Photograph courtesy John Antosiewicz.)

Koppich (Bernard Szold) talking about Burton and Elga, nailing shut Burton's coffin and then—*Dead Man Squawking*?—reacting to Burton's groans and pulling the nails with prybars. There was a bit of action just before lunch: a medium shot of Von Bruno and Von Melcher entering, and Burton dispatching both with dueling pistols bullets. Von Bruno is shot in cold blood, Von Melcher in self-defense (he draws his sword, but it happens too fast for viewers to see without resorting to slow motion). Near the end of the day they filmed (from inside the coffin) the seen-in-the-movie shot of the lid sliding off and Von Bruno getting blasted.

The mausoleum fight (Burton vs. Von Bruno and Gargon) was started late on April 1 and finished on the 2nd. For the shots where Burton shoves a torch into the faces of Von Bruno and Gargon, there was glass between the actors and the flames. Slo-mo the shot of Chaney getting the torch in the face and notice that you can see the reflection of the ap-

The bundled-up players, huddled around a fiercely burning coal brazier, were likely sweating bullets.

Monday, March 31, the start of the last week of production, was spent on the Phantom Stage, where they got shots of the alligator pit room's giant spiked gate falling: the first time when Burton and Elga pass, the second time to cut off the pursuit of Von Bruno, Gargon and the guards. Presumably the falling gate posed some danger: Allen Pinson and Polly Burson, stunt doubles for Richard Greene and Paula Corday, were there all day, no doubt substituting for the stars in some of the several takes. (Burson, a former Wild West show trick rider, was one of Julie Adams' *Creature from the Black Lagoon* doubles the following year.) In the late afternoon, part of the scene where Romley clubs the sleeping guard was re-shot.

All of the April 1 filming was done on the Phantom Stage's Mausoleum set, mostly getting shots of Fender and

Paula Corday with the skeleton of Sterling ... or is it Brown? According to the movie's publicist, this was a genuine human skeleton of undetermined origin, housed in the prop department storeroom for the previous 25 years. (Photograph courtesy John Antosiewicz.)

proaching torch on the glass; and that he appears to be wearing burn makeup even before he's "burned." Elga gets shoved against a coffin that's standing on end nearby; it topples and opens and, for about one second, we see through a lot of flying dust a skeleton. In order for the audience to know that the skeleton is that of Sterling or Brown, the moviemakers put an African ring on its finger, but the shot is so fleeting and there's so much dust that the ring is impossible to spot. Again on hand as doubles for Burton and Elga were stunt performers Pinson and Burson. Chaney's *Black Castle* stuntman was Bob Bryant, later the ash-encrusted title character Quintillus in 1958's *Curse of the Faceless Man*. A close-up of Burton rising up from below the frame line with a bloody head wound wasn't used in the movie. For the rest of the day, they photographed Burton and Elga inching their way along the narrow ledge on the walls of the alligator pit room. Toward the end of this scene, male audience members had the fun of seeing Corday's shapely legs clearly silhouetted in a shot lit so that the lower half of her filmy gown becomes see-through.

The next-to-last day of principal photography, April 3, was the end of the road (last day of employment) for McNally and Pate as they took part in the leopard hunt. Fog swathes the characters in its dense gauze, perhaps partly to set a mood and partly to make it harder to tell that the scene was actually shot indoors, on Stage 19. The dead stag and the half-eaten boar were presumably dummies. Again we get Zaroff-like dialogue from Von Bruno: "They kill without emotion," he says of the other hunters; "I kill with my *heart*."

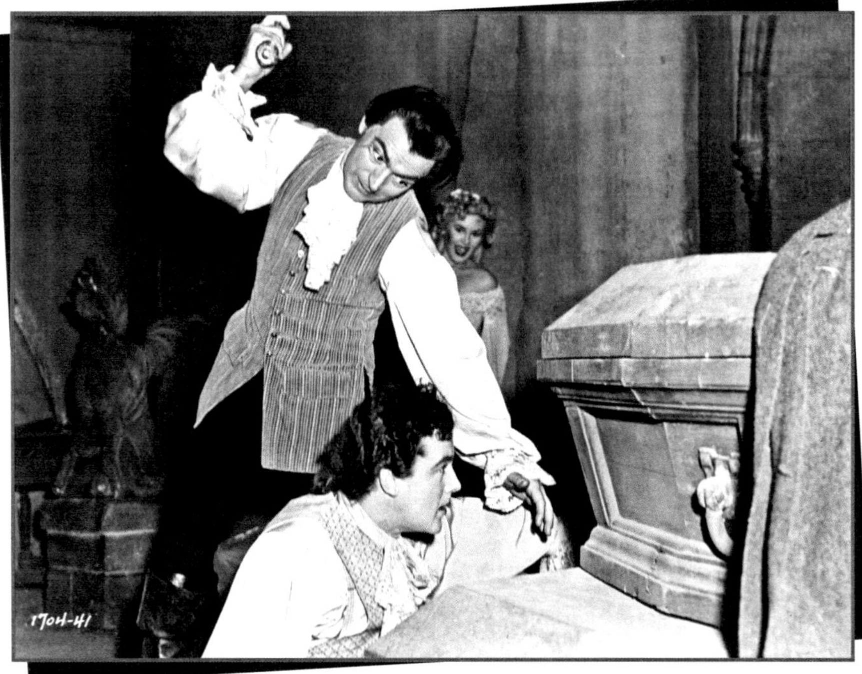

The too-bad-to-be-true Von Bruno (Stephen McNally, *sans* eye patch *and* contact lens) is about to pistol-whip Burton (Richard Greene). The Breen Office tsk-tsked that the movie's story "seems to lack a sufficient voice for morality."

On April 4 the bottom-of-the-pit battle between Burton and the leopard was shot. There were two leopards on hand (on paw?) plus, to double Richard Greene's Burton, veteran animal trainer and lion "rassler" Mel Koontz. The latter worked in 600+ movies, on-camera in approximately half of them, battling a lion (for Elmo Lincoln), a tiger (for Clark Gable), lions *and* tigers (for Victor Mature) and even putting his head in a lion's mouth (for Mae West!). He was in charge of the big cats on *Cat People* (1942).

The day's work ended after a few short scenes were photographed in front of a process screen, including Burton and Romley inside the hired coach on their bumpy way to the dead-of-night rendezvous with Von Bruno's coach. Viewers learn everything they need to know about Burton from a bit of business in this early scene: He and Romley are seated side by side sharing a lap robe, and when the sleeping Romley reacts to the biting cold by gathering the entire thing onto himself, Burton resigns himself to being blanketless. (Just minutes later in the movie, Burton's kindnesses toward Fender, including an invitation to share his Green Man dinner table, reinforce our impression of Burton as "friend to the common man.")

At the end of this 21st day of principal photography, the movie was finished, one day over schedule. This was offset by cancelling a planned post-production day of animal shots. For a movie made that quickly by a first-time director (working for a first-time full producer), it contains a remarkable number of unusual, often striking shots: We see lots of ceilings, get an up-from-the-floor look at Dr. Meissen's examination of the dead Stieken, and watch action from vantage points inside a cupboard, inside the leopard's cage, behind burning fireplace logs, inside Burton's coffin, etc.

Tyro director Juran moves the camera and his players with chess match strategy, prompting *Kinematograph Weekly*'s reviewer to call the photography "brilliant." According to Michael Pate, who was directed by Juran in "The Walls of Jericho," a 1967 episode of Irwin Allen's teleseries *The Time Tunnel*, "Nathan was still trying to shoot television as he would a feature, and of course Irwin came down on the set and rapidly changed *that* idea!"

Universal's exploitation tips for *The Strange Door* had been almost laughably bland (starting with a *Let's Make a Deal*–type department-store window setup of three doors and hidden merchandise), but for *Black Castle* they urged exhibitors to

Toothy smiles behind the scenes on *The Black Castle*: Paula Corday and friend. (Photograph courtesy John Antosiewicz.)

play up the spooky angles: "false fronts" for theaters with fake stone archways and giant waist-up shots of the stars (the latter lit by night by baby spots masked with red or green gelatin), doormen and/or ticket takers with black eye patches, ushers roaming the streets wearing eye patches and with "teaser copy" on their backs ("WATCH FOR THE MAN WITH *THE BLACK EYE PATCH*"), etc.

The *Strange Door* live radio spots were also weak tea, minimizing the horror, while the ones written for *The Black Castle* laid it on thick, even promising terrors way beyond what is found in the movie!:

ANNOUNCER: (THUNDER) "THE BLACK CASTLE! ... Above ghostly wreaths of fog it rises, like a stone monster in a sea of mist! Behind its moldering walls the hour draws near! For this is the night that horror walks on two feet! (Gong) ... THE BLACK CASTLE ... Beneath its battlements are tombs of the living dead, catacombs of fanged horror! In its medieval halls tonight, a gathering of lovely women, of men who hunt in a strange game ... (Thunder) THE BLACK CASTLE brings you Richard Greene on a mission of vengeance ... Boris Karloff, master of metaphysics and poison ... Stephen McNally, the devil's advocate ... Paula Corday, the lady in the crypt ... Lon Chaney, keeper of catacombs! ... These, the characters! And this, the hour dedicated to strange vengeance! ... An eerie wind screams through skeletal trees ... a gaunt black panther slinks among the gravestones on a violent errand of death! Somewhere among the shadows a paw scratches on the damp stones ... Somewhere in the darkness a whimper ends in a scream of terror as the unforgettable climax in THE BLACK CASTLE brings you Hollywood's new high in thrills, chills and extraordinary adventure!"

Marginalia

• In the interim between *Strange Door* and *Black Castle*, Boris Karloff was the recipient of a special tribute at the annual membership meeting of the Screen Actors Guild. At the November 11, 1951, confab, held in the Hollywood Legion Stadium, a gold life membership card was given to Boris, "who was a founder in 1933 of the union and for many years active in its affairs as a director and officer" (*The New York Times*).

• Composer-lyricist Frederick Herbert wrote a two-stanza song, "Steal a Kiss," for use in the film, but only a few lines of it are heard (during the post-leopard hunt party scene).

• As I wrote extensively about *The Black Castle*, making repeated references to Ronald Burton posing as Richard Beckett, I kept getting confused by the knowledge that Richard Burton played Becket (in 1964's *Becket*). I felt a little better about this minor mental block when I noticed that *Time* magazine's *Black Castle* review (December 8, 1952, long before there *was* a *Becket*) calls the movie's hero Sir Richard Burton.

• John Hoyt's Stieken moans and groans in pain as Dr. Meissen attends to his injured arm, prompting Von Bruno to mention that the ancient Romans were pain worshippers. Stieken loudly and petulantly pouts, "I'm *not* an ancient Roman!" It's an ironic line if you remember Hoyt as ancient Romans in *Androcles and the Lion* (1952), *Julius Caesar* (1953), *Spartacus* (1960), *Cleopatra* (1963) and probably more.

• Second-billed Karloff and fifth-billed Chaney play members of the Von Bruno household but the movie never puts them in the same scene. The two actors specialized in horror movies and in the '40s and '50s worked numerous times at Universal and yet *Black Castle* and *House of Frankenstein* are the only two movies in which both appear. This makes *House of Frankenstein* the only movie where fans can see them together.

Karloff was a gent so I assume this was inadvertent but, interviewed in the early 1960s by Colin Edwards, he called Lon Chaney, Jr., the son of "the *great* Lon Chaney"—putting the emphasis on "great" in a way that made it sound like he was stressing that Jr. *wasn't*. Later in the interview, when Edwards asked him to talk about Jr., Karloff ignored the question and instead talked more about Sr. The seasoned

Monster Kid can't help but consider the possibility that Boris may have gotten a bellyfull of the Lonster on *House of Frankenstein* and put him on his "If you can't say something nice…" list.

• Boris Karloff was the Sceptred Isle's gift to Hollywood Horror and, because he plays supporting, non-villainous roles in *Strange Door* and *Black Castle*, his fans invariably give Von Bruno-worthy sneers at the mention of those titles and fault Universal for casting him in them. But Karloff said in the 1951 interview quoted above that he *wanted* to "shed the label of movie menace," so the Karloff-lovers are actually sneering at a career decision made by the Great Man himself. I wonder if they'd have done it to his face, and/or if they'd have told Universal in 1951 and '52, "I'm Karloff's biggest fan but if he isnt going to play the villain in these movies, then you shouldn't use him at all." With fans like this, Karloff doesn't need enemies.

• Kudos to the editor who timed it so that one of the stock footage alligators begins a series of death rolls, as if it's ripping apart a victim, at the very moment we hear the screaming Gargon hit the water. (Can a mute scream?)

• Hollywood censors … who can figure them out? Apparently *Black Castle*'s scenes of violence (Burton mauled by the leopard, Gargon hit in the face with a torch, Gargon eaten by alligators, Von Bruno and Von Melcher shot point-blank, characters about to be buried alive, lots more) were okay with them, but they drew the line and called it unacceptable for Von Bruno to kick Dr. Meissen! (In *The Strange Door*, the sire does kick Voltan, but off-camera.)

• *The Black Castle* begins as *Strange Door* did, with the hero embroiled in a fight in a crowded inn. Both movies end with hero and heroine facing Edgar Allan Poe-inspired death, crushing walls in *Door*, premature burial in his-and-hearse coffins in *Castle*. At least the middles are different.

• There's a rich cinematic tradition of evil nobles putting themselves beyond the pale of human laws and holding the local populace tight in the grip of terror, but with all due respect to Count Von Bruno and *The Strange Door*'s Sire de Maletroit, both appear to be busts in that department. When the sire saunters into Le Lion Rouge (a cobblestone's throw from his chateau), no one cares; maybe no one knows who he *is*. We don't get to see Von Bruno rub elbows with the rabble, but dozens of Green Man patrons rock with laughter at the public humiliation of his number two man, Von Melcher. These featherweight fiends could take lessons from such memorable menace-to-the-community types as *The Black Room*'s (1935) wicked baron (Boris Karloff), *Mr. Sardonicus*' (1961) masked baron (Guy Rolfe)—even from non-horror movie aristocrats like the marquis (Basil Rathbone) in *A Tale of Two Cities* (1935).

You know *The Black Castle* is going to be delightfully old-fashioned and unrestrained in its melodramatic action the first time we see the inside of the mausoleum, with skulls displayed on a shelf and a gargoyle with a torch in its mouth. Pictured: Paula Corday. (Photograph courtesy Ronald V. Borst/ Hollywood Movie Posters.)

• A dungeon guard, clubbed by Romley, soon awakens and tugs on a rope; next we see an insert shot of a large tower bell swinging and clanging. Universal Horror know-it-alls will recognize it as a shot from *Secret of the Chateau* (1934), where the bell sounds in the wee hours of the night and one character whispers, "There's an old legend that its ringing is always followed … by a *death*." In *The Black Castle*, its ringing is followed by *two* deaths: Romley and Gargon.

• Dr. Meissen gives Burton and Elga a death-in-life drug to get them out of Von Bruno's dungeon. Death simulation drugs were a standby of romantic fiction and in many movies; perhaps the *Black Castle* screenwriter recalled the 1941 Douglas Fairbanks Jr. swashbuckler *The Corsican Brothers* in which Dr. Paoli (H.B. Warner) performed that same strange service for dungeon prisoner Fairbanks.

• *The Black Castle* did not get a sneak preview; however, at 8:30 on the evening of July 17, there was an on-the-lot screening for the cast and company.

Presumably because Elga was *forced* to marry Von Bruno, the Breen Office insisted that the two have "as little physical contact as possible." But a wife is a wife, so the Breen Office requested that scenes between Elga and Burton *also* be as hands-off as possible! Away from the cameras, Richard Greene, Paula Corday and Stephen McNally were under no such restrictions. (Photograph courtesy John Antosiewicz.)

• One movie regularly co-featured with *The Black Castle* was *Bela Lugosi Meets a Brooklyn Gorilla*, a pairing that gave Monster Kids a Karloff-Lugosi double-bill of *new* titles, and put on a single screen all three of horror's MVPs: Karloff, Chaney and Lugosi). Lugosi was then, of course, weathering the mother of all film career meltdowns—but any casual movie fan catching the *Brooklyn Gorilla-Black Castle* combo would have to be forgiven for thinking that Bela (top-billed in his movie, his name in the title, lots of screen time) was still flying high, and that Karloff and Chaney, minor players in *Black Castle*, were the ones on the fast track to Palookaville.

• Westerns and other types of high-testosterone pictures were *Black Castle*'s usual companion feature, but not at Schine's Eckel Theatre in Syracuse, New York, where the bloodthirsty horror flick shared the screen with the "Bring the Sunday School kids" comedy *Sally and Saint Anne* with Ann Blyth!

• According to *Black Castle*'s "Summary of Detail and Cost Report," it had total direct charges of $309,100 (about $24,000 more than *The Strange Door*). Studio overhead charges brought the grand total to $401,830.

• The players' reactions to the movie:

Michael Pate told me, "*Black Castle* was an infinitely better picture than *Strange Door* all around; it had a more interesting story and it was a more vigorous type of film. There were a lot of good things in it."

John Hoyt to Tony Timpone in *Fangoria* #51: "It was not a film I particularly admired. ... I didn't like what I had to do, and it was ridiculous with alligators in the cellars."

Henry Corden told me, "It was fun watching your tape of *The Black Castle* with my wife, who of course hadn't seen it—we've only been married five years. Angelina loved it because she loves *me* and she loves to see me. But the movie itself was very slow-moving, and it didn't quite hit its points when it should have. The heroes were *he*-roes and the villains were *vil*-lains ... you know, *that* kind of thing, very simplistic. But it was fun seeing *me*, I must say! I never *looked* so good! Nice and thin, and lotsa hair—and the hair was *dark* [*laughs*]!"

• After *Strange Door* and *Black Castle*, Universal could easily have stayed "old school" rather than gone the sci-fi route. In fact, more horror movies *were* contemplated, post–*Black Castle*. One was producer Ross Hunter's *Carmilla*, based on the Sheridan Le Fanu novel. Val Lewton

Richard Greene as the dauntless Sir Ronald Burton, British determination personified, grappling with guards in the bowels of the Black Castle. (Photograph courtesy John Antosiewicz.)

screenwriter DeWitt Bodeen (*Cat People, The Curse of the Cat People, The Seventh Victim*) was engaged by Hunter to script it; "The Le Fanu novel is so old it's in public domain and it deals with women who are vampires. It's just as creepy as it sounds," Louella O. Parsons wrote in February 1953. "[T]hey are very high on it at U I. Well, I can tell them De-Witt will do a good job." *Picturegoer* magazine even reported, "Marlene Dietrich may make a horror-film comeback [*sic*]. She is reading the script of *Carmilla*, a *Dracula*-style story about human vampires. U-I plans to shoot it in 3-D." Bodeen's 16-page treatment is one of the appendices in Gary D. Rhodes' *Dracula's Daughter* (2017), part of BearManor Media's "Scripts from the Crypt" series. (Read more about *Carmilla* in the *It Came from Outer Space* chapter.)

Ace researcher Bob Furmanek says that Universal, at around this same time, was also considering a color 3-D *Frankenstein*. Furmanek has read Universal paperwork indicating that some executives asked to screen the 1931 Karloff original in order to evaluate a remake's potential.

The Release

By Robert J. Kiss

Theatrical First Run, Halloween 1952 to August 1953

The release history of *The Black Castle* bears considerable similarity to that of *The Strange Door* the previous year, albeit with a few noteworthy nuances dangling over the battlements.

For starters, Universal launched both movies as "special pre-release shows" on Halloween night, before placing them in general release from the first week of November. However, *The Black Castle*'s pre-release opening proved substantially larger than that of *The Strange Door*. For one thing, this was because Halloween 1952 fell on a Friday, meaning that theater owners were far more inclined to book a midnight show than they had been in 1951, when Halloween had fallen rather inconveniently on a Wednesday, right in the middle of the work and school week. For another, Halloween screenings of *The Strange Door* had been limited to a single circuit of theaters east of the Mississippi, whereas *The Black Castle* was made available to venues throughout the 48 states. Concern that patrons might mistake the first-run feature for a reissue remained as pronounced in local advertising for *The Black Castle* as it had been in regard of *The Strange Door*, with the Campus Theatre in Denton, Texas, for example stressing "It is Entirely New" in all publicity during the days leading up to October 31, 1952.

Both movies were then released nationwide in decidedly piecemeal fashion from the beginning of November, with major cities including Philadelphia and Los Angeles among the first to see *The Black Castle*. It circulated most widely between January and April 1953, but not until August 1953 did it reach a number of midwestern, southeastern and southern towns with populations ranging from 5000 to 50,000. Thus, the theatrical first runs of *The Strange Door* and *The Black Castle* alike may be considered to have extended over a ten-month period from Halloween to the end of August. In both instances, this meant that the feature was already playing at second-run venues in some localities before other parts of the nation had the chance to see it at all. One extremely early second-run booking of *The Black Castle* in the Greater Los Angeles area took place at the 1362-seat Strand Theatre in Long Beach's The Pike amusement zone, where sandy-toed patrons could catch the movie on a double-bill with Lippert's noirish crime drama *Loan Shark*, starring George Raft, for the bargain price of 29¢ (or 9¢ for under-12s) on January 13 and 14, 1953.

Within two samples of 1200 first-run movie theaters across the U.S., stand-alone showings accounted for 22 percent of *Strange Door* engagements and 24 percent of *Black Castle* engagements. The most common way to have first experienced either feature

The Black Castle features lots of 1940s Universal Horrors music and that decade's top star Lon Chaney, *plus* Boris Karloff, and much better production values than the studio's B horror flicks of the '40s; consider it the best of both worlds. From left: Chaney, Richard Greene, Stephen McNally, Paula Corday.

was on a double-bill, which accounted for 75 percent of screenings in both cases. With no fixed companion picture, *The Strange Door* played opposite 142 different co-features and *The Black Castle* alongside 137. Both Universal horror movies occupied a similarly lowly position within the hierarchy of theatrical features in circulation between 1951 and 1953, generally topping the bill only when paired with cheapie Westerns or reissues, and otherwise serving as B-feature support to major studio releases. However, as highlighted by the two sections on double-bills below, *The Black Castle* was deployed in a more strategic manner aimed at optimizing profits. Specifically, this meant that a far greater percentage of its first-run bookings took the form of support for major releases at upscale theaters with higher ticket prices, and that these major releases were more frequently Universal product, allowing the studio to control the entire bill at these "better" establishments.

Stand-Alone Presentation

The overwhelming majority of *The Black Castle*'s Halloween pre-release screenings were a stand-alone show. The next morning, the picture also opened in this manner for seven days of regular play at Philadelphia's 1457-seat Stanton Theatre. Just as with the stand-alone presentation of *The Strange Door* at the city's Midtown Theatre the previous November, the movie underperformed, with *Variety* reporting "slow trade," effectively confirming that it wasn't suited to carrying such lengthy bookings at big city houses. All subsequent stand-alone engagements within the sample of 1200 first-run movie theaters across the U.S. lasted for one, two or three days only, and took place either at slightly less prestigious city theaters, or in small towns where single bills were already the established norm. *The Black Castle* additionally racked up a substantial number of one-day stand-alone bookings as a Friday the 13th attraction in both February and March 1953. (The date proved far from unlucky for horror film distributors that year, since it fell for yet a third time in November.)

Perhaps more significantly, *The Black Castle* was also the first of a string of 1950s Universal-International horror and sci-fi features to be accorded distinct treatment in Texas. While stand-alone presentations represent 24 percent of showings nationwide within the sample of 1200 first-run movie theaters, this figure rises to a staggering 72 percent at Texas hardtops and drive-ins, suggesting that a special distribution deal was almost certainly in place for the territory.

As the Top Half of a Double-Bill

Although double-bill screenings account for three out of every four first-run engagements of both *Strange Door* and *Black Castle*, the latter was employed far less frequently as a top-billed feature at lower-rung suburban, neighborhood and small-town venues. Indeed, such bookings make up just 28 percent of its double-bill showings, compared with 47 percent of those for *Strange Door* the previous year. This represents a significant shift, with trade at higher-ticket theaters showcasing major studio A-pictures apparently being actively targeted over the (s)lower revenues to be made at downmarket establishments.

In the following list of 55 titles that played in support of *The Black Castle*, just three are Universal releases, indicating that the studio made next to no effort to control both halves of the bill at these types of venues. The lone Universal title to have received any substantial degree of play in this context—and then only at four percent of theaters employing *The Black Castle* as a top-billed feature—was *The Strange Door*, making a decidedly low-key "comeback" at theaters keen to present an all-horror bill. Though balanced programs comprising movies of two distinct genres account for the majority of pairings below, the array of genre-matched bills coupling *Black Castle* with a horror reissue title nevertheless stands out, including *All That Money Can Buy*, *Calling Dr. Death*, *The Cat Creeps*, *The Curse of the Cat People*, *The Leopard Man*, *The Soul of a Monster* and even the mighty *King Kong*. At seven percent of venues, the imported British thriller *The Hour of 13* was also, rather misleadingly, marketed as a horror co-feature. While Realart's horror-sci-fi-comedy *Bela Lugosi Meets a Brooklyn Gorilla* supported *The Black Castle* at some 13 percent of such engagements—though only in the Midwest, and for so long as Jack Broder was able to get away with using his "NO—It's Not JERRY LEWIS" tagline!

In all other regards, the fare on these bills was much as it had been when *The Strange Door* was released. Eighty-five percent of co-features were in black-and-white, and roughly one in four was a reissue. Short running times remained the order of the day, with the average length of the supporting pictures on the list below just 69 minutes, and 16 of the titles running 60 minutes or less.

The second-billed co-features within the sample of 1200 theaters nationwide are arranged alphabetically below. The month mentioned in each case is the earliest in which the pairing was attested.

(*) signifies a more substantial number of playdates for the double-bill (at between four and seven percent of venues).
(**) signifies regular use of the double bill (at 13 percent of venues).
bold titles are Universal releases.

August 1953 *Abilene Town* (Randolph Scott, Realart reissue)
February 1953 *Barbed Wire* (Gene Autry)
December 1952 *Battles of Chief Pontiac* (Lex Barker)

May 1953 *Beauty and the Bandit* (Gilbert Roland)
December 1952 (**) *Bela Lugosi Meets a Brooklyn Gorilla* (Bela Lugosi)
February 1953 *Bells of San Angelo* (Roy Rogers, Republic black-and-white reissue)
April 1953 *Beyond the Border* (Tito Guízar, Republic reissue)
April 1953 *Border Saddlemates* (Rex Allen)
March 1953 *Bugs Bunny Cartoon Revue* (animated compilation)
December 1952 *Calling Dr. Death* (Lon Chaney, Realart reissue)
February 1953 *The Cat Creeps* (Lois Collier, Realart reissue)
February 1953 *Comin' Round the Mountain* (Abbott and Costello)
March 1953 *The Curse of the Cat People* (Simone Simon, RKO reissue)
February 1953 *Daniel and the Devil* (Edward Arnold, Astor reissue of *All That Money Can Buy*)
January 1953 *Desperadoes' Outpost* (Rocky Lane)
March 1953 *Fargo* (Wild Bill Elliott)
December 1952 *Flat Top* (Sterling Hayden)
April 1953 *Ghost Chasers* (Bowery Boys)
February 1953 *Gypsy Wildcat* (Maria Montez, Realart reissue)
December 1952 *Hangman's Holiday* (Ann Todd, retitling of *Daybreak*)
December 1952 *Hellgate* (Sterling Hayden)
March 1953 *Holiday Rhythm* (Mary Beth Hughes)
December 1952 (*) *The Hour of 13* (Peter Lawford)
July 1953 *Iron Mountain Trail* (Rex Allen)
July 1953 *Ivory Hunter* (Anthony Steel)
February 1953 *Junction City* (Charles Starrett)
February 1953 *Kansas Territory* (Wild Bill Elliott)
June 1953 *King Kong* (Fay Wray, RKO reissue)
January 1953 *Ladies of the Chorus* (Marilyn Monroe, Columbia reissue)
February 1953 *Lawless Cowboys* (Whip Wilson)
February 1953 *The Leopard Man* (Dennis O'Keefe, RKO reissue)
May 1953 *Man from the Black Hills* (Johnny Mack Brown)
July 1953 *The Marksman* (Wayne Morris)
February 1953 *The Maverick* (Wild Bill Elliott)
June 1953 *Mr. Walkie Talkie* (William Tracy)
December 1952 *Models Inc.* (Howard Duff)
February 1953 *Montana Territory* (Lon McCallister)
April 1953 *Pecos River* (Charles Starrett)
June 1953 *Rebel City* (Wild Bill Elliott)
May 1953 *Riders of the Range* (Tim Holt)
December 1952 *Road Agent* (Tim Holt)
July 1953 *Rodeo* (Jane Nigh)
March 1953 *The Sinners* (Serge Reggiani, Commander Pictures dubbed reissue)
May 1953 *Son of the Renegade* (Johnny Carpenter)
Oct. 1952 *The Soul of a Monster* (Rose Hobart, Columbia reissue)
January 1953 (*) *The Strange Door* (Charles Laughton)
February 1953 *Stronghold* (Veronica Lake)
February 1953 *Tales of Robin Hood* (Robert Clarke)
December 1952 *Target Hong Kong* (Richard Denning)
December 1952 *Tromba: The Tiger Man* (René Deltgen)
February 1953 *Voodoo Tiger* (Johnny Weissmuller)
June 1953 *Wagons West* (Rod Cameron)
December 1952 *Wells Fargo Gunmaster* (Rocky Lane)
December 1952 *When Worlds Collide* (Richard Derr)
May 1953 *Winning of the West* (Gene Autry)

As the Bottom Half of a Double-Bill

By contrast, the 72 percent of double-bill engagements at which *The Black Castle* played at more prestigious theaters in support of a new major studio release, include only a single reissue title and *no* all-horror

You *know* there's room for improvement in your marriage when your reproof "Nothing but evil ever comes to this castle—*nothing*!" is one of your *lesser* gripes: Paula Corday as the mistress of the Black Castle.

bills (perhaps because these establishments considered such fare to be "beneath them"). Here, the majority of co-features (56 percent) were in color, with the average running time a hearty 90 minutes. Moreover, 29 percent of titles (corresponding to 42 percent of engagements) on the list below are Universal releases, indicating the studio's eagerness to control both halves of the bill in these instances, with *The Black Castle* pegged even more squarely as "ideal supporting feature fare" than *The Strange Door* had been.

One Universal title, the Technicolor Western *The Raiders* starring Richard Conte, constituted something of a regular co-feature for *The Black Castle*, heading the bill at fully 21 percent of engagements of this type across a wide array of states between November 1952 and May 1953. A second Technicolor Western with a nineteenth-century setting, 20th Century-Fox's *Pony Soldier* with Tyrone Power, accounted for a further 18 percent of bookings, although its use was limited to certain sections of the East Coast, including New York State.

All of the top-billed co-features within the sample of 1200 theaters nationwide are arranged alphabetically below. The month mentioned in each case is the earliest in which the pairing was attested.

(*) signifies a more substantial number of playdates for the double-bill (at between four and ten percent of venues).
(**) signifies regular use of the double-bill (at between 18 percent and 21 percent of venues).
bold titles are Universal releases.

July 1953 *Abbott and Costello Go To Mars* (Abbott and Costello)
March 1953 *Abbott and Costello Meet Captain Kidd* (Abbott and Costello)
December 1952 (*) *Against All Flags* (Errol Flynn)
July 1953 *Angel Face* (Robert Mitchum)
April 1953 *Apache War Smoke* (Gilbert Roland)
June 1953 *Babes in Bagdad* (Paulette Goddard)
December 1952 (*) *Back at the Front* (Tom Ewell and Harvey Lembeck)
March 1953 *The Battle at Apache Pass* (John Lund)
December 1952 *Battle Zone* (John Hodiak)
February 1953 *Because of You* (Loretta Young)
August 1953 *Big Jim McLain* (John Wayne)
December 1952 *The Big Sky* (Kirk Douglas)
February 1953 *Blackbeard, the Pirate* (Robert Newton)
November 1952 *The Blazing Forest* (John Payne)
January 1953 *Bloodhounds of Broadway* (Mitzi Gaynor)
December 1952 *Bonzo Goes to College* (Maureen O'Sullivan)
May 1953 *Brave Warrior* (Jon Hall)
January 1953 *The Brigand* (Anthony Dexter)
March 1953 *The Browning Version* (Michael Redgrave)
May 1953 *Cattle Town* (Dennis Morgan)
March 1953 *City Beneath the Sea* (Robert Ryan)
February 1953 *Cleopatra* (Claudette Colbert, Paramount reissue)
May 1953 *Confidentially Connie* (Van Johnson)
March 1953 *Cripple Creek* (George Montgomery)
December 1952 *Death of a Salesman* (Fredric March)
March 1953 *The Duel at Silver Creek* (Audie Murphy)
November 1952 *Eight Iron Men* (Bonar Colleano)
January 1953 *Everything I Have is Yours* (Marge and Gower Champion)
January 1953 *Fearless Fagan* (Janet Leigh)
July 1953 *Has Anybody Seen My Gal* (Piper Laurie)
November 1952 (*) *Horizons West* (Robert Ryan)
August 1953 *Houdini* (Tony Curtis)
January 1953 *Hurricane Smith* (Yvonne De Carlo)
February 1953 *Invasion USA* (Gerald Mohr)
April 1953 *Ivanhoe* (Robert Taylor)
January 1953 (*) *The Lawless Breed* (Rock Hudson)
May 1953 *The Lone Hand* (Joel McCrea)
May 1953 *Lost in Alaska* (Abbott and Costello)
December 1952 *Lure of the Wilderness* (Jean Peters)
December 1952 *The Lusty Men* (Susan Hayward)
January 1953 (*) *Meet Me at the Fair* (Dan Dailey)
January 1953 *Million Dollar Mermaid* (Esther Williams)
April 1953 *The Mississippi Gambler* (Tyrone Power)
April 1953 *Montana Belle* (Jane Russell)
December 1952 *Night Without Sleep* (Linda Darnell)
August 1953 *Off Limits* (Bob Hope)
January 1953 *Operation Secret* (Cornel Wilde)
February 1953 *Outpost in Malaya* (Claudette Colbert)
February 1953 *The Pathfinder* (George Montgomery)
March 1953 *Phone Call from a Stranger* (Shelley Winters)
January 1953 (**) *Pony Soldier* (Tyrone Power)
January 1953 *The Prisoner of Zenda* (Stewart Granger)
December 1952 *The Quiet Man* (John Wayne)
November 1952 (**) *The Raiders* (Richard Conte)
February 1953 (*) *The Redhead from Wyoming* (Maureen O'Hara)
January 1953 *Ride the Man Down* (Brian Donlevy)
January 1953 *Road to Bali* (Bing Crosby and Bob Hope)
March 1953 *Rogue's March* (Peter Lawford)
January 1953 *Ruby Gentry* (Jennifer Jones)
May 1953 *Saddle Tramp* (Joel McCrea)
November 1952 *Sally and Saint Anne* (Ann Blyth)
July 1953 *San Antone* (Rod Cameron)
December 1952 (*) *The Savage* (Charlton Heston)
May 1953 *Seminole* (Rock Hudson)
March 1953 *The Silver Whip* (Dale Robertson)
December 1952 *Somebody Loves Me* (Betty Hutton)

January 1953 *Something for the Birds* (Victor Mature)
January 1953 *Stars and Stripes Forever* (Clifton Webb)
January 1953 *Stop, You're Killing Me* (Broderick Crawford)
April 1953 *The Thief* (Ray Milland)
March 1953 *Thunderbirds* (John Derek)
December 1952 (*) *Toughest Man in Arizona* (Vaughn Monroe)
April 1953 *Treasure of the Golden Condor* (Cornel Wilde)
August 1953 *Trouble Along the Way* (John Wayne)
March 1953 *The Turning Point* (William Holden)
May 1953 *Untamed Frontier* (Joseph Cotten)
December 1952 *Way of a Gaucho* (Rory Calhoun)
May 1953 *The Winning Team* (Doris Day)
February 1953 *With a Song in My Heart* (Susan Hayward)
July 1953 *The World in His Arms* (Gregory Peck)
November 1952 *Yankee Buccaneer* (Jeff Chandler)

With Live Stage Accompaniment

Within the sample of 1200 first-run movie theaters across the U.S. between Halloween 1952 and August 1953, just under one percent elected to pair *The Black Castle* with live stage accompaniment. The most significant example of this uncommon form of exhibition took place at New York City's celebrated 1733-seat Palace Theater on Broadway, where the feature was presented over the week of New Year 1953 alongside an eight-act vaudeville bill, scoring—as *Variety* reported—a "socko $30,000" in eight days. Other live stage accompaniments to *The Black Castle* were restricted to smaller venues and comprised spook shows and performances by local bands (just as had been the case a year earlier with *The Strange Door*).

Beyond the First Run

The Black Castle perhaps suffered slightly from overexposure following its extensive deployment as a special horror attraction at Halloween 1952 and on Friday the 13th in both February and March 1953; by the time Halloween rolled around anew in 1953, it was already relegated to playing on three-movie bills at discount theaters and drive-ins. It continued to receive a fairly meager number of bookings of this type through to 1957, after which it all but disappeared from view. Then Universal revived the movie to serve as supporting fare one final time, at a limited number of first-run engagements of its Hammer imports *The Phantom of the Opera* and *Paranoiac* during 1962 and 1963. Adverts for these double-bills made no mention of the fact that the picture was a decade old, and for the youthful generation of horror fans attending these shows, it may well have been the first time that they'd heard of *The Black Castle*, with everything old having become new (box office fodder) again.

A scant six weeks ahead of *The Strange Door*, *The Black Castle* made its small-screen debut during September 1964, being shown in a 2:30 p.m. slot on Sacramento, California's, KCRA TV on September 11, and in a 9:30 p.m. slot on Las Vegas' KSHO-TV (now KTNV-TV) on September 30. The movie reached stations in the rest of the nation by late spring 1965, after which it appeared regularly in television schedules throughout the second half of the 1960s and the 1970s.

The Critics' Corner

New York Times: Parents are specifically warned that an inordinate amount of needlessly sadistic action is to be seen in this aberration. ... To open [this movie] at any time is a mistake: to tender it to the public on Christmas Day is remarkably indiscreet.

New York Herald Tribune: I'm afraid I've outgrown this kind of thing, but one feels some sympathy for the tastes of one's childhood—it would have delighted me once, I'm sure.

Hollywood Reporter: This lively melodrama of the Edgar Allan Poe school has all the required ingredients.... As handsomely produced by William Alland and directed by Nathan Juran, who injects plenty of action and suspense while drawing engagingly earnest performances from a good cast, *The Black Castle* stacks up as excellent program fare.

Harrison's Reports: A good program horror melodrama, the kind that gives one the chills. ... The three principals do good work, and so does Boris Karloff.

Cue: [A] horrendous little melodrama ... that seems a sort of comic book celluloid thriller.

Time: *The Black Castle* tries hard to chill the moviegoer's spine. Most of the time, however, this boy-meets-ghoul melodrama is only tepid theatrics.

Boxoffice: A feature designed to curdle the blood and chill the spine that succeeds in its purpose with the aid of a good story, striking backgrounds and expert characterizations by a name cast.

Motion Picture Exhibitor: [I]t is just a programmer, with the names not too potent for the marquee.

Photoplay: Verdict: Not very horrible horror film.

TV Guide: Lurid costume horror-melodrama, nicely dished up.

Fangoria magazine (1996): *Black Castle* not only features all the necessary equipage for this type of full-bodied Gothic..., it also has admirable atmosphere, an agreeably adventuresome flavor and some genuinely fine art direction and photography.... The last of the old-fashioned Universal horror costumers, *The Black Castle* dishes up action and chills with ghoulish gusto....

Tracks in the Castle: The Music of *The Black Castle*

By David Schecter

The Black Castle arrived a year after *The Strange Door*, continuing the trend of Universal not treating its horror-related movies with the musical respect they deserved. The prior year's *Abbott and Costello Meet the Invisible Man* (1951), which provided ample opportunities for original music and new themes, instead contained tracked music courtesy of Daniele Amfitheatrof, Johnny Green, William Lava, Miklós Rózsa, Hans Salter, Paul Sawtell, Frank Skinner, Walter Scharf, Eric Zeisl and others. Some of the cues came from obvious sources such as *The Invisible Man Returns* and *The Invisible Man's Revenge*, along with other typical horror sources like *Abbott and Costello Meet Frankenstein, House of Dracula* and *Pillow of Death*. Some less-likely suspects included the recent Universal productions *Curtain Call at Cactus Creek, Deported, Harvey, I'll Be Yours, River Lady, Up in Central Park, The Saxon Charm, South Sea Sinner* and *Wyoming Mail*. While Universal wasn't freshening up their approach to scoring films, at least they were freshening up their music library a bit.

Not being in the horror genre, the comedy team's previous movie, *Abbott and Costello in the Foreign Legion*, was another all-tracked affair, using many of the same composers. The music was gathered from seemingly unrelated films like *Abbott and Costello Meet Frankenstein, Buck Privates Come Home, Cobra Woman, Francis, Mexican Hayride, The Senator Was Indiscreet, White Savage, White Tie and Tails* and *You Gotta Stay Happy*, although cues from *The Desert Hawk, Slave Girl* and *Sudan* seemed to make a little more sense.

And going back even further to 1949, Bud and Lou's *Abbott and Costello Meet the Killer, Boris Karloff* was another musical disappointment. Although following on the heels of the very successful ... *Meet Frankenstein* with its brilliant and mostly original Frank Skinner score, the Karloff-themed picture was again a tracked mishmash. Over 70 percent of the cues came from ... *Meet Frankenstein*, with the rest originating in *Arizona Cyclone, Buck Privates Come Home, Family Honeymoon, Feudin,' Fussin' and A-Fightin,' The Fighting O'Flynn, Letter from an Unknown Woman, River Lady, Who Done It?, You Gotta Stay Happy* and even three Deanna Durbin pictures (*For the Love of Mary, I'll Be Yours, Up in Central Park*).

Perhaps Universal felt at this point that horror pictures were strictly second-rate productions, because plenty of non-horror films up to the time of *The Black Castle* had received original scores (*The Battle at Apache Pass, Bend of the River, The Prince Who Was a Thief, Untamed Frontier*), or at least partly original scores (*The Duel at Silver Creek, Has Anybody Seen My Gal, Here Come the Nelsons, Horizons West, Just Across the Street, Lost in Alaska, Son of Ali Baba, Yankee Buccaneer*). If that was the case, it's a shame that *The Black Castle* didn't get an original score, because the studio's 1950s Boris Karloff pictures weren't really horror movies anyway—they were period pieces with Karloff thrown in to attract monster fans that Universal wasn't providing product for. The cheapness of the production probably prevented them from affording the luxury of newly composed music, and therefore, just as with *The Strange Door, The Black Castle* was the recipient of less-than-courteous musical support.

The Black Castle's music budget was about $14,500, similar to *The Strange Door*, which was to be expected considering they were both scored in a comparable fashion. Money was budgeted for song arrangers and orchestral arrangers, but because there weren't any songs in the movie, it's not known whether anyone got paid for work they didn't do, or if at one time there were plans to include songs. Four days of rehearsal pianists were also part of the budget, probably needed to serve as a guide to allow the on-screen musicians and actors to perform in the party scene.

There were some minor differences between the approaches taken in *The Strange Door* and *The Black Castle*. Although a lot of music from *House of Frankenstein* was again reused, *The Black Castle*'s score borrowed primarily from a different set of sources, and a new composer was thrown into the mix. Another distinction was that, of the 86 cues in *The Black Castle*, not all of them came from earlier motion pictures—only 85 pieces were recycled! So it was not technically an all-tracked picture ... just 98.84 percent tracked. *The Black Castle* contained a solitary cue written specifically for the movie, although it must be admitted that those behind that decision were being cautious, as the piece was only seven seconds long.

There are 31 more cues in *The Black Castle* than there were in *The Strange Door*, and 86 cues in an 82-minute movie is a large number of individual pieces. Only 11 cues are longer than one minute—and most of them are only barely longer—with just a single piece reaching the two-minute mark. One might think it would have been easier having a composer write a new 45-minute score rather than stitching together so many fragments that average out to 31 seconds a cue. But orchestrating new music and creating new parts for the players would have definitely taken a lot of additional time (and therefore, money). Instead, movie fans get to play *Name That*

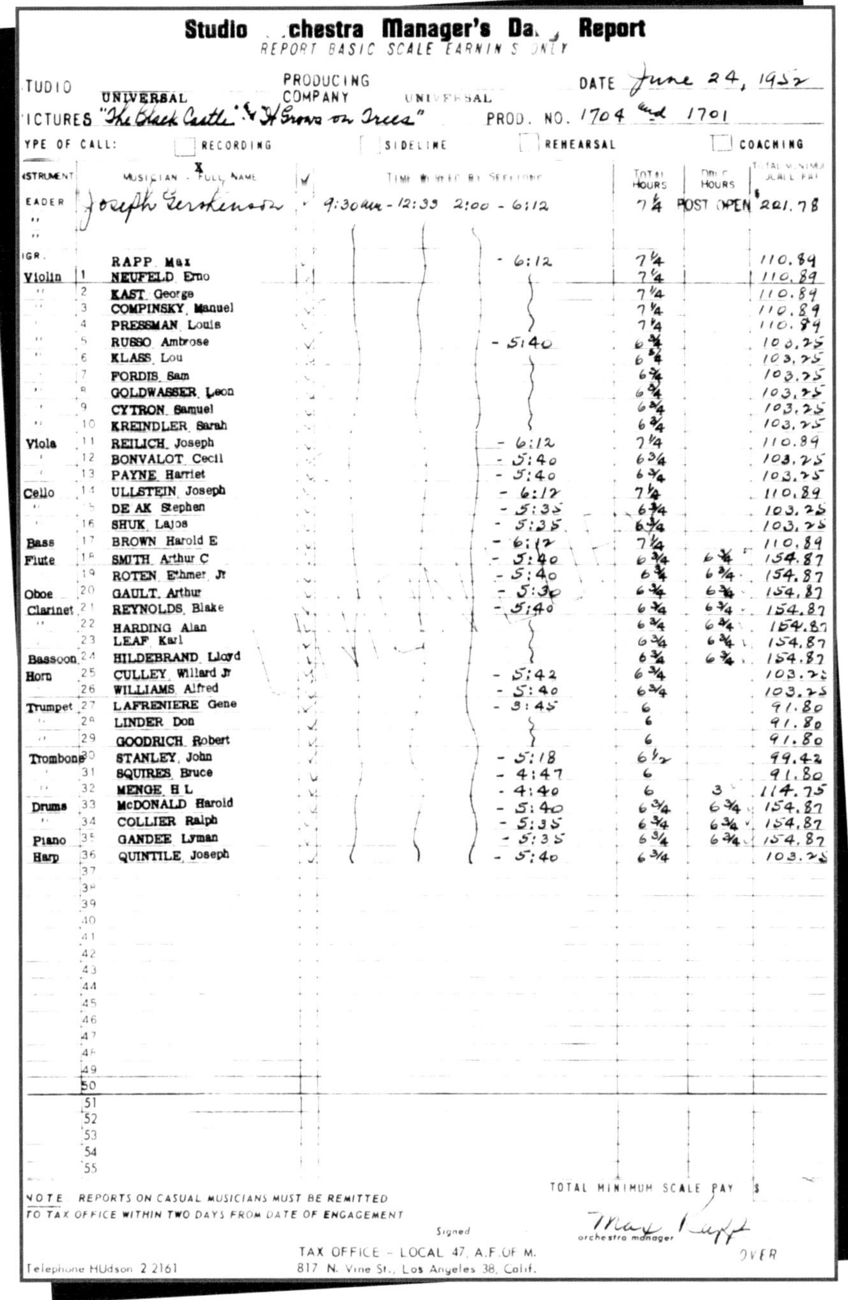

Studio .chestra Manager's Da., Report

REPORT BASIC SCALE EARNIN S ONLY

TUDIO UNIVERSAL PRODUCING COMPANY UNIVERSAL DATE June 24, 1952

ICTURES "The Black Castle" & "It Grows on Trees" PROD. NO. 1704 and 1701

YPE OF CALL: RECORDING SIDELINE REHEARSAL COACHING

STRUMENT		MUSICIAN - FULL NAME	TIME WORKED BY SECTIONS	TOTAL HOURS	DBL. HOURS	TOTAL MINIMUM SCALE PAY
EADER		Joseph Gershenson	9:30am - 12:33 2:00 - 6:12	7¼	POST OPEN	$221.78
"						
"						
IGR.		RAPP, Max	- 6:12	7¼		110.89
Violin	1	NEUFELD, Erno		7¼		110.89
"	2	KAST, George		7¼		110.89
"	3	COMPINSKY, Manuel		7¼		110.89
"	4	PRESSMAN, Louis		7¼		110.89
"	5	RUSSO, Ambrose	- 5:40	6¾		103.75
"	6	KLASS, Lou		6¾		103.75
"	7	FORDIS, Sam		6¾		103.75
"	8	GOLDWASSER, Leon		6¾		103.75
"	9	CYTRON, Samuel		6¾		103.75
"	10	KREINDLER, Sarah		6¾		103.75
Viola	11	REILICH, Joseph	- 6:12	7¼		110.89
"	12	BONVALOT, Cecil	- 5:40	6¾		103.75
"	13	PAYNE, Harriet	- 5:40	6¾		103.75
Cello	14	ULLSTEIN, Joseph	- 6:12	7¼		110.89
"	15	DE AK, Stephen	- 5:35	6¾		103.75
"	16	SHUK, Lajos	- 5:35	6¾		103.75
Bass	17	BROWN, Harold E	- 6:12	7¼		110.89
Flute	18	SMITH, Arthur C	- 5:40	6¾	6¾	154.87
	19	ROTEN, Ethmer, Jr	- 5:40	6¾	6¾	154.87
Oboe	20	GAULT, Arthur	- 5:30	6¾	6¾	154.87
Clarinet	21	REYNOLDS, Blake	- 5:40	6¾	6¾	154.87
"	22	HARDING, Alan		6¾	6¾	154.87
	23	LEAF, Karl		6¾	6¾	154.87
Bassoon	24	HILDEBRAND, Lloyd		6¾	6¾	154.87
Horn	25	CULLEY, Willard Jr	- 5:42	6¾		103.75
	26	WILLIAMS, Alfred	- 5:40	6¾		103.75
Trumpet	27	LAFRENIERE, Gene	- 3:45	6		91.80
"	28	LINDER, Don		6		91.80
"	29	GOODRICH, Robert		6		91.80
Trombone	30	STANLEY, John	- 5:18	6½		99.42
"	31	SQUIRES, Bruce	- 4:47	6		91.80
"	32	MENGE, H L	- 4:40	6	3	114.75
Drums	33	McDONALD, Harold	- 5:40	6¾	6¾	154.87
"	34	COLLIER, Ralph	- 5:35	6¾	6¾	154.87
Piano	35	GANDEE, Lyman	- 5:35	6¾	6¾	154.87
Harp	36	QUINTILE, Joseph	- 5:40	6¾		103.75
	37					
	38					
	39					
	40					
	41					
	42					
	43					
	44					
	45					
	46					
	47					
	48					
	49					
	50					
	51					
	52					
	53					
	54					
	55					

TOTAL MINIMUM SCALE PAY $

NOTE: REPORTS ON CASUAL MUSICIANS MUST BE REMITTED TO TAX OFFICE WITHIN TWO DAYS FROM DATE OF ENGAGEMENT

Signed Max Rapp orchestra manager

TAX OFFICE – LOCAL 47, A.F. OF M.
817 N. Vine St., Los Angeles 38, Calif.

Telephone HUdson 2 2161

OVER

A union report listing the musicians who performed on *The Black Castle*. (Courtesy Monstrous Movie Music.)

Tune when they listen to *The Black Castle*'s soundtrack, trying to guess where all but one of those cues originated.

A recording session conducted by Joseph Gershenson was held on June 24, 1952, for both *The Black Castle* and *It Grows on Trees*. Most of the players were there for under seven hours, which doesn't seem like enough time to record all the music. However, it's certainly possible that all or most of *The Black Castle*'s music was newly recorded, as there might have been another recording session for either *The Black Castle* or *It Grows on Trees*, whose records the Musicians Union couldn't locate, an unfortunate fate shared by many sessions from that era. The music editing in *The Black Castle* isn't always as well-done as it was in *The Strange Door*, with the score displaying an inconsistency in how some cues lead into the following ones. Rather than each cue musically flowing to the next, a few pieces sound faded-in and faded-out, which shouldn't have happened if the music had been freshly performed by Universal's orchestra. This provides some evidence that the score might have used at least some previously existing tracks rather than only newly recorded music. Erno Neufeld was Universal's concertmaster (leader of the orchestra and first violinist) at the *Black Castle* recording session and throughout the 1950s. He was a well-respected musician who also taught violin, and his work can be heard on countless records, in addition to Universal's soundtracks. Max Rapp, a gospel songwriter (and Milton Rosen's co-writer of *House of Frankenstein*'s "Gypsy Tantrums"), was the studio's orchestra manager for this session, serving in that same capacity during the decade.

The Black Castle's soundtrack was strongly represented by Hans Salter's music, with 27 cues being written or co-written by him. In addition to his pieces being lifted from some of the same films contributing to *The Strange Door*, such as *Frankenstein Meets the Wolf Man*, *House of Frankenstein* and *The Web*, other cues came from *The Ghost of Frankenstein*, *Son of Dracula* and the 1945 Merle Oberon drama *This Love of Ours*. The first two-and-a-half minutes of *The Black Castle* sound more like "Salter's Greatest Monster Hits" than a cohesive film score. The opening fanfare comes from Salter, Skinner and Charles Previn's "Main Title" from *The Wolf Man*, followed on its heels by Salter's "Main Title" from *Son of Dracula*. After the credits, Salter and Paul Dessau's memorable "Dracula Destroyed" from *House of Frankenstein* is heard, and after a wolf howls, Salter's "Main Title" from *Frankenstein Meets the Wolf Man* briefly sounds. Before our brains can even process all this musical information, the scene moves indoors to the tune of "Brain Transfer" from Salter's *The Ghost of Frankenstein*.

House of Frankenstein provides 14 cues to *The Black Castle*, with eight of them being Paul Dessau and Hans

Salter's "Dan's Love." As in *The Strange Door*, the piece serves as the movie's love theme, this time highlighting the romance between Sir Ronald Burton and Countess Elga. It's first heard about 25 minutes into *The Black Castle* when the countess explains how she and the count wound up together, then reappears about 13 minutes later when she and Burton break away from the dance. As Burton discusses the stolen pendant with her, two excerpts of the piece are separated by "The Business," a Salter cue from *The Web*. By this time in Universal's history, it was beginning to seem as if *anyone* could fall in love with "Dan's Love" playing in the background. Dessau and Salter's "The Burgermeister Murdered" from *House of Frankenstein* lends over a minute of musical support to the scene that introduces Lon Chaney as Gargon. Similarly predictable, Salter's *Thunder on the Hill* cue "Attempted Murder" makes an appearance—albeit a brief one—in yet another Universal motion picture when Gargon enters Burton's room through a secret panel and observes him sleeping.

Frank Skinner wrote or co-wrote 19 cues that were included in *The Black Castle*, with source films that weren't used in *The Strange Door* being *Black Friday, The Exile, Hollywood Story, The House of the Seven Gables, The Mummy's Hand, The Raging Tide* and *The Sleeping City*. "The Duel" from *The Exile* is used in *The Black Castle* during—what else?—the duel at the inn. The music sounds suspiciously as if it had been dialed in and out of the soundtrack rather than being newly recorded for the movie. *Hollywood Story* provides the flashback music just under four minutes into *The Black Castle*, with the vibraphone shimmers in "Hollywood Theme" helping to transport the viewer back in time. Skinner's "More White Stuff" from *The Sleeping City* plays quietly after Dr. Meissen tells Burton that he poisoned Count Stieken in order to silence him.

The music manuscripts from Skinner's *Pillow of Death*—used to great effect in *The Strange Door*—must have been getting pretty dog-eared in Universal's music library by now, but they still figured prominently in the last 20 minutes of *The Black Castle*. "Vivian's Body" is heard about an hour into the picture when Fender warns Romley that his master is in trouble, and when Burton and the countess are locked in the dungeon together and Romley attempts to rescue them, "Vivian's Body," "Linen Closet," "Fletcher Crypt" and "Evergreen Cemetery" are all heard one after another. "Vivian's Voice" is used for over a minute when Burton, drugged in his coffin, tries to alert the men who are sealing it, with Novachord making the eerie sequence as creepy as possible. It seems likely from all this usage that the person who pieced together the score was flipping through the conductor's book of *Pillow of Death* when he was trying to find music to include in *The Black Castle*, as opposed to just finding loose scores just lying around in various folders.

This time around, Miklós Rózsa's music came via the 1949 film noir *Criss Cross*, his distinctive Hungarian style being heard during Burton's opening carriage journey to the castle, courtesy of the cue "Steve Pleads," excerpts of which play on four different occasions for a total of two minutes. Rózsa was a good personal friend of Universal's orchestrator David Tamkin, making certain to give Tamkin autographed copies of his classical compositions even decades after the two worked together at Universal.

Daniele Amfitheatrof's music did not figure in *The Strange Door*, but *The Black Castle* employed 21 of his cues, previously written for *An Act of Murder, Ivy* and *Rogues' Regiment*, all fairly recent Universal productions. Which makes one wonder whether he might have played a hand in assembling the score. A number of Amfitheatrof's cues were used one after another, but it's doubtful that any consistency of compositional style was noticed by anyone in the audience. And even film music experts would have had a hard time noting any such compositional "flow," as Amfitheatrof's writing style could be quite circuitous even when presented all by itself. You can hear 44 seconds of the composer's "Hotel Bedroom" from *An Act of Murder* near the beginning of *The Black Castle* when Burton tries to call out that he's been buried alive, with the cue's string tremolos and vibraphone helping to evoke the weirdness of the situation. The vibra-

Daniele Amfitheatrof, whose 1940s Universal music was reused in *The Black Castle*. (Photograph courtesy Daniele Amfitheatrof family.)

phone is related to the xylophone, but it contains resonating tubes with a motor-driven propeller in each tube that allows the player to sustain notes and change the vibrato. Because it can create "blurry" notes, it is an exceptional instrument for producing ethereal effects, and that's why it figured prominently in the scores of many SF and horror films.

Amfitheatrof's "Platinum Tool" from *Rogues' Regiment*, a 1948 Dick Powell Foreign Legion adventure, serves to underscore the first-reel sequence when Burton's hired coach stops and the baggage is switched to the count's coach for the remainder of the journey to the castle. Another *Rogues' Regiment* cue, "Come and Get Me," accompanies the countess leaving her room and observing a number of doors mysteriously closing. Low woodwinds keep the sequence eerie, with faster figures as she becomes more worried. After this scene, there's a short vocalization of the song "Steal a Kiss" at the post-leopard hunt party scene. Although the cue sheets claim this tune is public domain and the author was unknown—meaning Universal didn't have to pay any licensing fees to use it in the picture—the song was actually composed by Frederick Herbert, who was one of Universal's primary lyricists as well as the studio's head music editor. Only a few lines of "Steal a Kiss" are heard in the movie, whereas Herbert wrote more than that. Since he was uncredited on the cue sheets, Herbert never received performance royalties when the film played.

Songwriter Frederick Herbert (standing) with colleague Arnold Hughes in 1949. (Photograph courtesy John Herbert.)

Two more Amfitheatrof cues from *Rogues' Regiment* and one from the same composer's *An Act of Murder* color the sequence when Count Stieken is poisoned and the countess is interrogated by her husband, before Skinner, Salter, Dessau and Lava contribute a few short cues to the end of the sequence as the count angrily leaves his wife at the mercy of Gargon. As Burton departs the castle about 52 minutes into the picture, two excerpts from "Heindorf Dies" (yet another *Rogues' Regiment* cue) add a little thematic unity to the picture by using related music to cover similar action. The previously mentioned "Platinum Tool" is reprised near the picture's end when Fender and Koppich reopen the groaning Burton's coffin. An attempt was made to provide some consistency to the score by using multiple cues from the same pictures; but because so many different movie sources were pillaged, that tended to dilute the success of this approach.

Two usages of Amfitheatrof's "Jervis Dead" from the 1947 Joan Fontaine melodrama *Ivy* cover the sequence when Burton snoops around the castle and the countess runs into him. Pizzicato (plucked) strings add suspense to this low-key but effective composition. Those same pizzicatos can be heard courtesy of *Ivy*'s "Final Investigation" when Gargon leaves Burton's room through the secret panel about 28 minutes into the picture. "Roger Arrested," also from *Ivy*, plays when the countess announces that she will not be going on the leopard (a.k.a. panther) hunt, whereupon the count sarcastically tells her not to worry about his safety. The "Reel 3-DD Bugle Call" that resounds to initiate the hunt was overdubbed onto "Roger Arrested" and was not credited to any composer. Further cues from *Ivy* ("Roger Waits," "The Inspector" and "Interruption") provide the subdued musical background at the inn when Meissen informs Burton that the countess is in danger, as well as in the following scene when innkeeper Krantz tells the count that Burton has been asking embarrassing questions. "The Plea, Part 2" was chosen to musically illustrate the count knifing Meissen as he talks to Burton in his coffin.

At the party following the leopard hunt, two excerpts from Wolfgang Amadeus Mozart's "Eine Kleine Nachtmusik" ("Menuetto" and a very slow "Serenade in G Major") play in the background. Universal used both the "Romance" and "Menuetto" movements from this same composition three years later in *This Island Earth*. Four musicians were among the extras on the two days the party scene was filmed, and they appear in *The Black Castle* as a string quartet (two violins, a viola and a cello) playing without sheet music. A "dance record" was used during the first day's shooting, while a piano "for direct recording" was employed the second day. It's doubtful that the scene would have been filmed with a record playing on the set, but if it was, another recording of the music would have been added after the fact. It's more likely that both the record and the piano were used to provide musical guidance for the on-screen musicians and the actors. Perhaps the record didn't work out properly and they decided to try the piano the second day? Regardless, Universal's orchestra would have played the actual music heard in the movie at the eventual orchestral recording session, unless a previously recorded track was added to the soundtrack during post-production.

For horror music fans, there are lots of pieces in *The Black Castle* beyond *House of Frankenstein* and *Pillow of Death* that might evoke monster memories. "Experiment Successful," credited to William Lava and Salter from *The Invisible Man's Revenge*, plays when Burton stalks the leopard in the foggy woods, with pizzicato strings, vibraphone, woodwind trills and celesta contributing to the atmosphere. A brief snatch of Skinner's "Peggy Kidnapped" from *The Mummy's Hand* is heard while Burton and Romley journey by carriage from the castle. Lava's "Dracula's Theme #2" from *House of Dracula* applies somewhat inappropriate spookiness when the count looks out the castle window and is pleasantly surprised to notice that Burton has returned. Salter's "Graveyard" from *Frankenstein Meets the Wolf Man* covers the action as Burton is led to the dungeon where the countess has been imprisoned, this music definitely conjuring images of Universal monsterfests, followed by another snippet of "Dan's Love" that keeps the monstrous mood going. The familiar "Monster Talks" from Salter's *Ghost of Frankenstein* plays twice as Romley frees Burton and the countess from their cell, and Sawtell's "Curtains for the Creeper" from *The Pearl of Death* is used when Burton is knocked out in the mausoleum. Perhaps Universal figured since there weren't any monsters in this Boris Karloff picture, the music might make people *think* there were.

At about the 70-minute mark, more monsterish sounds are provided via Lava's "Transfusion" from *House of Dracula*, which accompanies the discussion about the drug that will make Burton and the countess appear to be dead. While it seems obvious why "Transfusion" would be considered for this plot point, the actual ingestion of the drug uses another instance of Skinner's "Fletcher Crypt" from *Pillow of Death*. "Second Transformation" conjures images of Lon Chaney, as this *Frankenstein Meets the Wolf Man* cue plays while Dr. Meissen apologizes to Burton, who lies drugged in his coffin. Lava's "Dracula's Theme #3" from *House of Dracula* augments the count looking at Burton and the countess and ordering their coffins sealed, while Salter, Skinner and Charles Previn's "Queen's Hospital" from *Frankenstein Meets the Wolf Man* lends sadness as the coffins are nailed shut as the count stands before a fireplace. Lava's "Dracula's Theme #4" (there were obviously no shortage of Dracula themes lying around) from *House of Dracula* propels the sequence where the count and Von Melcher head to the mausoleum, the energy of the music increasing the suspense that the leisurely

Conductor's score of Milton Rosen's "Killer Coke #2" from *Iron Man*, used in *The Black Castle*. (Photograph courtesy Monstrous Movie Music.)

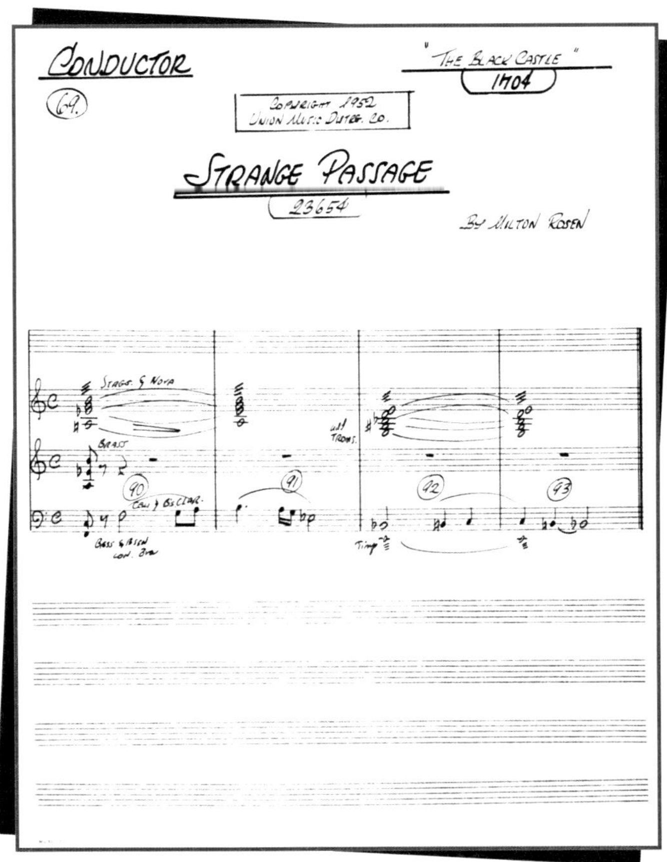

Conductor's score of Milton Rosen's "Strange Passage," the only original cue written for *The Black Castle*. (Photograph courtesy Monstrous Movie Music.)

visuals don't provide. When Burton lies in his coffin and shoots the count and Von Melcher, then lifts the countess to safety, Sawtell's "Dave's Delirium" from *Dead Man's Eyes* highlights the event. All of these cues are appropriate in their new uses from an action standpoint, but they do little more than that, and there's nothing to thematically tie them to characters or ideas in the picture—always an unfortunate result when using tracked music from a wide variety of movies.

Milton Rosen makes five brief appearances in *The Black Castle* via cues from *Smuggler's Island, Tangier* and *Iron Man*, with the frenzied "Killer Coke" and "Killer Coke #2" from the last picture being heard twice, once when the count angrily whips the leopard cage. These two nearly identical pieces appeared a total of seven times in *Iron Man*. However, the real surprise is the seven-second Rosen cue "Strange Passage." This piece was written specifically for *The Black Castle*, barely being heard between the two previously mentioned excerpts of Salter's "Monster Talks." It plays during the escape sequence when Burton and the countess prepare to enter the "horrible room" (the room with the alligator pool). All of Rosen's cues are very short and, for the most part, either unnecessary or barely heard in the soundtrack mix, but there's a good possibility that "Strange Passage" might have been incorporated into the score in order to help inaugurate an independent publishing company that had recently been formed.

Born in Yonkers, New York, on August 2, 1906, Milton Sonnett Rosen attended Damrosch's Institute of Musical Art, and two of his early concert works were performed at Carnegie Hall and by the Boston Symphony Orchestra under Arthur Fiedler. After working as a violinist, composer, arranger and conductor for radio and theaters, he became a composer and conductor for Universal in 1939. From 1950 through 1973, Rosen was assistant to the head of the studio's music department, occasionally taking on the role of musical director, and he conducted many of the studio's shorts. He supervised, arranged, composed and conducted for more than 300 features, shorts and TV commercials, contributing songs or scores to pictures including *The Challenge, City Beneath the Sea, Enter Arsene Lupin, Lost in Alaska, Pirates of Monterey, Ride Clear of Diablo, Shady Lady, Slave Girl, The Spider Woman Strikes Back, Sudan, Tangier, Target Unknown* and *The Time of Their Lives*. He passed away on December 28, 1994, in Kailua, Hawaii.

The Black Castle's soundtrack comes to a close with Skinner's "End Title" from *The House of the Seven Gables* (1940), which received an Oscar nomination for Original Score, and of course, there's one final appearance of "Dan's Love" from *House of Frankenstein* to let us know that Burton and the countess will live happily ever after. As with *The Strange Door*, while *The Black Castle*'s unoriginal musical aggregation is handled professionally enough, a new score from the pen of one or two composers probably would have resulted in an improved motion picture, even for viewers who weren't focused on the music.

When the words "monsters" and "money" became interchangeable at Universal, the studio began to seize on subthemes to its classic horror films: the Kharis Mummy series, the "monster rallies" of the mid–1940s, the Ape Woman trilogy. Regardless of the merits of any of those films, Universal was running out of ideas for its horror cycle.

It took the studio only two films to burn out the "madman in the dark castle" theme that ushered in the 1950s with *The Strange Door*. The second and final nail in the coffin was

The Black Castle, a marginally interesting variation of *The Strange Door*'s plot and style. Indeed, *The Black Castle*, at first blush, seems a near-carbon copy of *The Strange Door*. What's missing is a sustained sense of style, an enthusiastic Boris Karloff and, most importantly, a flamboyant, Charles Laughton–like villain.

The Black Castle begins promisingly as the opening titles are superimposed over a "spooky castle" illuminated by occasional lightning flashes. (The superb castle miniature was made a decade earlier for *The Ghost of Frankenstein*; look closely and see the name FRANKENSTEIN carved into the stone above the archway.) The soundtrack is marked by those reliable and familiar Universal "thunder" effects that date back to the creation scene in the 1931 *Frankenstein*. Art directors Bernard Herzbrun and Alfred Sweeney dress the castle courtyard and cemetery in classically moody attire: windblown leaves, bare trees, twisted terrain. The film's opening moments are reminiscent of the memorable introduction to 1943's *Frankenstein Meets the Wolf Man*, 1944's *House of Frankenstein* and 1945's *House of Dracula*. (Not a big surprise, since set decorator Russell A. Gausman also helped design the sets for those films.) Another alumnus of *The Strange Door*, Irving Glassberg glides his camera through the setting in a style reminiscent of Karl Freund.

Karloff is back, but even more restrained than in *The Strange Door*. Paula Corday plays Stephen McNally's beautiful wife, Countess Elga Von Bruno, whose convenient hatred for her sadistic husband sets up the romantic entanglement with Greene's heroic Burton. But Corday establishes herself as a stronger heroine than Sally Forrest's demure Blanche in *The Strange Door*; she chides Von Bruno for his cold, sadistic ways.

For any classic horror fan, *The Black Castle*'s main attraction would be Boris Karloff. Like Voltan in *The Strange Door*, Karloff's Dr. Meissen initially seems sinister but turns out to be a benign character who, in the end, rides to the rescue of the romantic leads. One of Karloff's best *Black Castle* scenes comes when he confronts Richard Greene's Burton at the Green Man. Karloff's Meissen, ever-loyal to his countess, begs Greene to return to the castle and rescue her from McNally's murderous Von Bruno. Karloff's always-expressive eyes are wide with emotion and his voice modulates from deep, mellifluous phrasing to a crescendo of frenzy as he implores Greene to save the countess. But this scene is the best that Karloff has to offer in the film. Karloff has been faulted, sometimes unfairly, for "sleepwalking" through roles he felt beneath him. However, in *The Black Castle*, the criticism applies. Karloff goes through the film smiling mysteriously and half-heartedly feigning menace. Even in *The Strange Door* we were given touches of the classic Karloff—and some unexpected heroics to boot. In *The Black Castle*, he barely makes a difference. The same goes for the film's other horror icon, Lon Chaney. He plays Gargon, one of McNally's servants, as a hulking, mute brute—a kind of "beginning of the end" for Chaney. He shambles through *The Black Castle* looking alternately confused and baleful, before being pushed into the alligator pit by Richard Greene.

McNally's Count Von Bruno is a weak substitute for Charles Laughton's delectable hamming. McNally is a competent but stock villain who knows how to effect a cruel leer and laugh but little else. Instead of a moustache to twirl, McNally's veneer of evil is provided by a black eye patch. Yet, his blustery, smirking, eye-rolling menace may remind classic horror fans of a poor man's Lionel Atwill. The resemblance is enhanced by McNally's penchant for occasionally speaking out of the left side of his mouth, an affectation which Atwill also displayed. Atwill fans will want to fast-forward to the scene in which McNally has both Greene and Corday imprisoned and taunts Greene with his murderous plans. McNally's voice and facial expressions gradually build to a mad rage—the kind of "slow burn" which Atwill practically patented.

Australian Michael Pate began his Hollywood movie career with *Strange Door* and *Black Castle* weasels and seemed perfect for horror movies—but soon veered into Westerns, including many Indian roles! At one point during *Black Castle* production, he took time off to apply for his American citizenship papers.

Paula Corday's Countess Von Bruno (a far more interesting heroine than *The Strange Door*'s Blanche) has the film's best line: McNally is showing off (and cuddling up to) the buxom Nancy Valentine, and also singing her praises: "Therese won third prize today for shooting the biggest boar. Quite a feat for a woman, don't you think?" Corday's reply: "I don't know. I seem to have got one without even firing a shot!"

Richard Greene's Sir Ronald Burton is a better, more believable hero than *The Strange Door*'s Richard Stapley. Yet Greene provides no more than stolid, stock support. He spends less time acting and more time reacting to McNally's menace and Corday's comeliness.

Two of *The Black Castle*'s saving graces are John Hoyt and Michael Pate. Both men are dependably despicable as Von Bruno's best friends. Pate looks even more sinister than McNally—and might have delivered a better performance as Von Bruno. Hoyt's face had the kind of wan, oddly ascetic quality that lends additional spookery to any genre work. (The same could be said for Peter Cushing's looks.) Hoyt provided some effective evil in many other genre and non-genre films of the era, and also as the sourpuss who turns out to be the title menace in the classic *Twilight Zone* episode "Will the Real Martian Please Stand Up?"

Black Castle's shots of Von Bruno (Stephen McNally, right, with Michael Pate) taken from inside the giant fireplace, through the leaping flames, give him that "Infernal Majesty" look.

The Black Castle's art direction and photography provide limited reminders of Universal Horror's glory days. In addition to the atmospheric opening, there is Burton's night journey to Von Bruno's castle, augmented by howling winds and Irving Glassberg's balanced photography, which illuminates the windblown faces of Von Bruno's servants and coachmen with flickering firelight. And while the castle interiors are not nearly as evocative as those in *The Strange Door*, Glassberg maintains low-key lighting throughout the film, giving the sets a dark, cavernous ambiance.

In the end, *The Black Castle* is, like *The Strange Door*, a Gothic costume melodrama. But *Castle* is more costume than Gothic. Perhaps the film was most noteworthy as the last "straight" Universal Horror for Karloff and Chaney and as the *first* genre effort of producer William Alland, who went on to produce the three Gill Man movies and other sci-fi shockers. Summing up *The Black Castle* for Tom Weaver, Alland recalled, "I was fascinated with the material, and it looked to me like a real easy shoot. So I slapped it together and did it. I didn't see it as a great work of art or anything like that, it was just another movie for me—one that I felt would have its audience. I'm sure it made money, but I have no idea how much."

The Strange Door and *The Black Castle* were both efficient entries in a somewhat old-fashioned vein of melodrama, and certainly better production- and acting-wise than many of the throwaway Universal horror B-movies of the 1940s, but in the Atom Age their time had passed. Universal retained their imposing Tower of London exteriors and torchlit dungeon sets but they were not used again for horror purposes in the '50s with the last-gasp exception of *Francis in the Haunted House* (1956), in which they represented a medieval castle reconstructed in the American Midwest (and reportedly haunted by an armor-wearing ghost on horseback). The rest of the 1950s saw Universal return to making monsters—of a newer and bigger sort.

It Came from Outer Space (1953)

Full Credit Information

CREDITS: Produced by William Alland; Directed by Jack Arnold; Screenplay: Harry Essex; Story: Ray Bradbury; Photography: Clifford Stine; Special Photography: David S. Horsley; Editor: Paul Weatherwax; Art Directors: Bernard Herzbrun and Robert Boyle; Set Decorators: Russell A. Gausman and Ruby R. Levitt; Sound: Leslie I. Carey and Glenn E. Anderson; Music Director: Joseph Gershenson; Gowns: Rosemary Odell; Makeup: Bud Westmore; Hair Stylist: Joan St. Oegger; Assistant Director: Joseph E. Kenny; UNCREDITED: Screenplay Contributor: Ernest Nims; Original Music Composers: Herman Stein, Irving Gertz and Henry Mancini; Conductor: Joseph Gershenson; Orchestrator: David Tamkin; Tracked Music Composer: Henry Mancini; Musicians: Emo Neufeld, Manuel Compinsky, Louis Pressman, Ambrose Russo, Lou Klass, Sam Fordis, Samuel

Cytron, Sarah Kreindler, Leon Goldwasser, Howard Colf (Violin), Joseph Reilich, Cecil Bonvalot, Harriet Payne (Viola), Joseph Ullstein, Stephen De'ak, Alec Compinsky (Cello), Harold E. Brown (Bass), Arthur C. Smith, Ethmer Roten, Jr. (Flute), Arthur Gault (Oboe), Blake Reynolds, Alan Harding, Karl Leaf (Clarinet), Lloyd Hildebrand (Bassoon), Willard Culley, Jr., Alfred Williams (Horn), Gene LaFreniere, Don Linder, Robert Goodrich (Trumpet), John Stanley, Bruce Squires, H.L. Menge (Trombone), Harold McDonald, Ralph Collier (Drums), Lyman Gandee, Ignace Hilsberg (Piano), Joseph Quintile (Harp), Jack Barsby (Tuba), Dr. Samuel Hoffman (Theremin); Assistant Directors: George Lollier and Frank (Fred Frank?); Second Assistant Directors: T. Nelson (Terence Nelson?), Green (Marshall Green?), George Lollier and Bowles (Phil Bowles?); Dialogue Director: Irvin Berwick; Production Manager: Gilbert Kurland; Unit Production Manager: Mack D'Agostino; Camera Operators: Harvey Gould and James King; Assistant Cameramen: Lew Swartz, Haddow (Ledge Haddow?), Egan, Polito (Gene Polito?), Marlatt (Mark Marlatt?), Pierce, Vaughn (Roy Vaughn?) and Reisbord (William Reisbord?); Camera Technicians: Polito (Gene Polito?), Swartz/Schwartz? (Lou Swartz?) and Haddow (Ledge Haddow?); Still Photographers: Bert Anderson and Jones; Gaffers: Tom Ouellette, Monroe (Warren Monroe?) and Smith (Irving Smith?); First Grips: Walter Woodworth and Paup (Dean Paup?); Second Grip: Carl Johnston; Best Boy: Everett Lehman; Electrician: Lloyd Hill; Camera Mechanics: F. McConihay and Jones; First Prop Man: Robert Laszlo; Assistant Prop Men: Carl Lawrence, Johnson, Gunstrom (Harry Grundstrom?), Case (Edward Case?) and Nunley (Bill Nunley?); Makeup: John Holden, Grimwood (Burris Grimwood?) and Hadley (Joe Hadley?); Hair Stylist: Sue Kirkpatrick; Sound Recorders: Cunliffe (Donald Cunliffe?), James Swartz and Buffinger; Mike Man: Frank Wilkinson; Sound Mixers: Andy Anderson and Moran (Harry Moran?); Sound Maintenance: Sheehan; Cable Men: Smith and Janssen; Set Dresser: Joseph Kish; Editor: Bill Moore; Script Clerk: Jack Herzberg; Cashier: Koehler; Timekeeper: Arthur; Coordinators: Charles Baqueta and Gockel (Ray Gockel?); Publicist: Niemeyer (Harry Niemeyer?); Wardrobe Men: Rydo Loshak; Wardrobe Women: Nevada Penn and Prior (Rose Pryor?); Radio Man: Buffinger; Stand-ins: Bob Lawson, Virginia Eubank, Harold Lockwood; SECOND UNIT—APPLE VALLEY **(February 4–7, 9–11, 16, 1953)**: Director: Joseph E. Kenny; Production Manager: Gilbert Kurland; Unit Manager: Mack D'Agostino; Assistant Director: P. Bowles (Phil Bowles?); Second Assistant Director: B. Sheehan (Bill Sheehan?); Cameraman: David S. Horsley; Camera Operators: Meade (Kyme Meade?), Lathrop (Philip Lathrop?) and King (James King?); Assistant Cameraman: Polito (Gene Polito?), Mark Marlatt, Haddow (Ledge Haddow?) and Sharp; Camera Technician: Mark Marlatt; Camera Mechanic: F. McConihay; Still Photographers: Jones (Eddie Jones?); Makeup: Grimwood (Burris Grimwood?) and Hadley (Joe Hadley?); Hair Stylist: Sue Kirkpatrick; Wardrobe Man: Velcoff (Alexander Velcoff?); First Grip: Thompson (Wes Thompson?); Second Grip: Gulliver (Stanley Gulliver?); First Prop Man: Keyes (Ed Keyes?); Assistant Prop Man: Lawrence (Carl Lawrence?); Electricians: Tracy/Tracey? and Meehan; Battery Man: Meehan; Best Boy: Peets; Script Clerk: Otto; Cashier: Koehler; Timekeeper: Arthur; Prop Shop Man: Baker; First Aid; R.A. Guyer; Stuntman: Joe Walls; SECOND UNIT—SIERRA CANYON **(February 19, 1953)**: Unit Manager: Mack D'Agostino; Assistant Director: George Lollier; Script Clerk: Abbott (Betty Abbott?); Cameraman: David S. Horsley; Camera Operator: King (James King?); Assistant Cameraman: Mark Marlatt; First Grip: Thompson (Wes Thompson?); Second Grip: Smith; First Prop Man: Rosenkrantz (Julius Rosenkrantz?); Technician: Haddow (Ledge Haddow?); SECOND UNIT—UNIVERSAL BACK LOT, **Stage 12 and Stage 21 (March 5–7, 1953)**: Director: Joseph E. Kenny; Unit Manager: Mack D'Agostino; Assistant Director: Holland (William Holland?); Script Clerks: Hughes (Dorothy Hughes?) and Cannon (Adele Cannon?); Cameraman: David S. Horsley; Camera Operator: King (James King?); Assistant Cameramen: Vaughn (Roy Vaughn?) and Pierce; Technician: Marlatt; First Grip: Thompson (Wes Thompson?) and Smith; Second Grip: Gulliver (Stanley Gulliver?); Gaffers: Tracey and Harmon; Best Boy: Kaufman; First Prop Man: Carl Lawrence and Martino (Sol Martino?); Coordinator: Gockel (Roy Gockel?); ADDED SCENES AND RETAKES **(April 15, 16, 17 and 23, 1953)**: Director: Jack Arnold; Cameraman: Glassberg (Irving Glassberg?); Art Director: Robert Boyle; Assistant Director: George Lollier; Production Manager: Gilbert Kurland; Makeup: Jack Kevan; Hair Stylist: Sue Kirkpatrick; Camera Operator: Drought; Assistant Cameramen: Kenny, Hager (Robert Hager?), Vaughn (Roy Vaughn?) and Haddow (Ledge Haddow?); First Grip: Brown; Second Grip: Jones; Gaffer: Kurland (Norton Kurland?); Best Boy: Burdette; First Prop Man: Rosenkrantz (Julius Rosenkrantz?); Wardrobe Woman: Nevada Penn; Sound Mixer: Neal; Sound Recorder: James Swartz; Mike Man: Muchmore (John Muchmore?); Cable Man: Carroll; Script Clerk: Forrest (Bob Forrest?); Coordinator: Baqueta (Charles Baqueta?); PER WILLIAM ALLAND: Story Idea: William Alland; 80 minutes.

CAST: Richard Carlson (*John Putnam/Glob Putnam*), Barbara Rush (*Ellen Fields/Glob Ellen*), Charles Drake (*Sheriff Matt Warren*), Joe Sawyer (*Frank Daylon/Glob Frank*), Russell Johnson (*George/Glob George*), Kathleen Hughes (*Jane Dean*); UNCREDITED: Dave Willock (*Pete Davis*), Alan Dexter (*Dave Loring*), Robert Carson (*Dugan—*

American Press), Dick Pinner (*Lober—Press Dispatch*), George Eldredge (*Dr. Snell/Glob Snell*), Brad Jackson (*Bob/Glob Bob*), Richard Cutting (*Radio Announcer Voice*), Warren MacGregor (*Toby/Glob Toby*), Edgar Dearing (*Sam/Glob Sam*), George Selk (*Tom/Glob Tom*), Whitey Haupt (*Perry*), Virginia Mullen (*Mrs. Daylon*), William Pullen (*Deputy Reed*), Ned Davenport (*Man Outside Newspaper Office*); IN UNUSED FOOTAGE: Dale Van Sickel, Al Wyatt (*Stunt Doubles—Sheriff's Office Fistfight*); UNCONFIRMED: Shep Menken (*Monster Voice*).

Production History
By Tom Weaver

> If there is any life on other planets, it is doubtful if it has developed into human form. Even if these creatures are intellectually developed beyond humans so that they have abolished war and conflict, there will be a shock when they meet Earth people.
>
> The two races will be so dissimilar that conflict is bound to result.
>
> —*It Came from Outer Space* writer Ray Bradbury to columnist Bob Thomas, March 1953

From silent days right through the end of the 1950s, *the* place to watch monster movie history in the making was the Universal lot, where change was in the air in February 1953. Among the several films in production: *Abbott and Costello Meet Dr. Jekyll and Mr. Hyde*, one of the last gasps for the type of "old school" horror movie (Frankenstein, the Wolf Man, etc.) in which Universal had specialized for nearly a quarter century. The slapstick comedy, which reduces the werewolf-like Mr. Hyde to a figure of kiddie-matinee fun, was also the final Universal feature for horror megastar Boris Karloff, and as such marked the end of an amazing era of macabre moviemaking at the "Studio of the Monsters."

But this of course was not the end of Universal monsters. Beginning on February 10, the *A&C Meet J&H* company's neighbors on the lot now included the cast and crew of producer William Alland's 3-D alien visitation tale *It Came from Outer Space*, a new type of monster movie for a new, Atom Age, ready-for-sci-fi generation of moviegoers. On the 16th, as a goofy *A&C Meet J&H* free-for-all was being staged (Bud and Lou vs. the suffragettes), the low point of this "last gasp" flick, *It Came from Outer Space* director Jack Arnold and his crew were in nearby Sierra Canyon, filming part of one of *the* seminal scenes of '50s sci-fi: astronomer John Putnam, descending into what he believes to be a meteorite impact crater, and finding himself standing outside the open portway of a crash-landed alien spaceship. At Universal, the end of the old was overlapping with the start of the new: As one "door" (traditional, literature-based monsters played by stars like Karloff) closed, another door—a spaceship portway—began to open.

> Once upon a time Dracula and Frankenstein were considered major league monsters, but not now. Coming up at Universal is the winnah and new champeen—*The Atomic Monster* [later retitled *It Came from Outer Space*].
>
> —George E. Phair, "Retakes," *Variety*, September 30, 1952

The first time the public had its hair raised by the arrival of outer space monsters was on Halloween (well, October 30) 1938 when Orson Welles' *The Mercury Theater on the Air*'s radio adaptation of H.G. Wells' novel *The War of the Worlds* innovatively took the form of simulated news flashes, including a description of the crash landing of a "huge, flaming object" (initially mistaken for a meteor) on a Grovers Mill, New Jersey, farm; its identification as a rocket cylinder; the emergence of Martian monsters; and the invaders' deadly heat ray attacks upon onlookers. Many listeners didn't hear much past that point: Terror-stricken, they took to the streets. One woman, hysterical, was prevented by her husband from taking poison. The unprecedented stunt resulted in a wave of lawsuits, the complainants citing everything from broken legs and miscarriages to an inability to speak without stuttering. Several years later, in a Kansas City hotel lobby, Welles was pummeled by a stranger who later claimed that he had vowed to murder Welles because the Martian broadcast was responsible for his wife's suicide.[1] (Yes, I know that most of these stories were "fake news." But what great stories!)

In the late 1940s and early '50s, the public was very UFO-conscious, with the Air Force finally admitting that mysterious objects in the sky could indeed be the flying saucers of an advanced civilization, surveilling our planet. In this climate, it isn't surprising that the ball was hit out of the box office park by 1951's *The Man from Planet X*, *The Thing from Another World* and *The Day the Earth Stood Still*, a triple-header followed by Universal's first 3-D production (and the first-ever 3-D science fiction film), *It Came from Outer Space*.

The one man common to Welles' "War of the Worlds" broadcast and *It Came from Outer Space* was William Alland. He was an actor in the former, providing the voices of over a dozen background characters, and the producer of the latter.

"Many of my films were based on one- or two-page ideas that I would submit to the studio, and they would say, 'Yeah, go ahead, work on it,'" Alland told me. "In fact, I don't think I even had to show [Universal executive] Bill Goetz my outline for *It Came from Outer Space*, I just told him about it and he said *go*." He continued:

I had an idea to make a science fiction film, and the very simple idea was this: A spaceship accidentally crashes on Earth, and the beings in it take one look around at this place and say, "Jesus Christ, let's get the hell out of *here*." Because they sense that we're an inferior breed—savage, brutal, stupid, beastly. They understand that we are a species that destroys anything that frightens us, that destroys anything we don't understand. I wrote this up in a couple of pages with the idea that they crash here, they want to get out, they realize that the Earth beings want only to destroy them, and *they* have the power to destroy *us* if they have to. (But they don't want to do that, they just want to get out.) And, ultimately, cooler heads prevail and they are allowed to leave. That's basically what I had.

The studio said, "Get a writer and see what you can come up with." They had such confidence in me—I'm serious!—that I got permission to do four pictures a year for seven years, for God's sake. That's an incredible accomplishment. One of the reasons was that they gave me *carte blanche*—they knew that I would always come in under budget, they knew that my pictures always had a beginning, a middle and an end, and that they *worked*, see? As a matter of fact, that began to work to my *detriment*; one of the reasons that I got out is because I couldn't get them to buy a decent property for me. They wanted me to come up with my own ideas all the time.

Now faced with the chore of choosing a writer, Alland thought immediately of Ray Bradbury, then known for his short story collections *The Martian Chronicles* and *The Illustrated Man* and for his work in magazines ranging from the pulps (*Weird Tales*) to the slicks (*Collier's*, *The Saturday Evening Post* and *Esquire*). According to Alland, "Over lunch, I told him the very simple idea, and he said, 'Fine, I think I can do this for you'—we didn't even discuss it that much. And he went off, and came back about two weeks later with an absolutely, *incredibly* beautiful treatment. Actually, you could have *shot* it, it was so photographic, so complete. It was almost like a silent movie—there was very little dialogue in it."

Ray Bradbury *sans* eyeglasses, and rocking a Mickey Spillane haircut, in a late 1950s shot. Looking back on his first film-writing assignment *It Came from Outer Space,* he told Tom Weaver it was "a very nice small film. Nothing to be ashamed of. Plenty of credit for everyone."

In late August 1952, Bradbury's work began. The 32-year-old commuted by bus from his West Los Angeles home to Universal and did his writing in a two-office bungalow he shared with Sam Rolfe, who was writing a Western. Sixty years later, Bradbury told *Monsters from the Vault* interviewer Terry Pace,

I was so thrilled to be working at the same studio that had made *The Hunchback of Notre Dame, The Phantom of the Opera, Dracula, The Mummy* and *The Invisible Man*—movies that changed my life in the 1920s and '30s. As soon as I moved into the studio bungalow and started work, I went over to the *Phantom of the Opera* stage and stood in the middle of the theater where they had filmed the opera house scenes. It was so glorious to be there in person, standing at long last with the ghost of Lon Chaney, my childhood hero. I felt like I was five years old all over again.

At noon each day, according to Sam Weller's book *The Bradbury Chronicles*, the studio's new $300-a-week employee took his sack lunch to the "Main Street, America" set on the back lot, where the "quaint, charming houses conjured warm memories of his Illinois childhood." Bradbury told Weller, "There was an entire street, just like the street in Waukegan [Illinois] where I was born. And there was a house very much like my grandparents' house, and I sat on the front steps of the porch and had my lunch."

According to a *Starlog* interview with Bradbury, Universal was initially leery about hiring him, because at that point he'd never written a screenplay. "[Universal was] not sure I could do it, and I, of course, knew I could," he told the magazine's Jeff Szalay. Bradbury told me that, during his time at Universal, he actually wrote *two* treatments:

I told them that their idea [for the movie] was okay but that I had a better one. I offered to write *two* versions, one for them, one for me. They thought I was crazy. They said, "But won't you do better work on *your* idea?" "Yes," I said, "because it is a better concept. Okay? And if you choose the wrong one of my versions, I'll leave. If you choose the right one, I'll stay and finish a longer version." I wrote the two versions, turned them in and the studio had enough sense to see that, indeed, my version was better than theirs.

Bradbury related the tale of his first screenwriting assignment more colorfully in "The Turkey That Attacked New

York," his introduction to the 1981 anthology *They Came from Outer Space: 12 Classic Science Fiction Tales That Became Major Motion Pictures*. He began by saying that the story of his experiences "might shed a little light on why fiction is so often excellent and films so often shoddy," and continued:

> **All [Universal] knew was that they wanted Something to arrive from Outer Space: a grisly monster, a proper fright that the Westmore brothers could have fun with in the makeup department. In my preliminary talks with the producer and director, I could see we were light years apart. I wanted a more subtle approach, something with a real idea in it. They saw only the obvious—and the vulgar obvious at that.**

He went on to describe doing the best job he could, writing a treatment using "their mildewed idea," "using their creaking machinery as center," and then having some good fun writing the second one, "my own just for me." Within 48 hours of submitting both, Bradbury was told that Universal was going to go with *his* version; "Frankly, I was stunned."

A little bird sent "Turkey" to Alland, sensing it might ruffle his feathers—and it did: "I read that cockamamie thing, and it just *outraged* me," he told me. "[Bradbury] denigrated us [Alland and Arnold], didn't mention our names, and wrote with contempt about the whole experience—outrageous!" By the time of our 1995 interview, Alland had no memory of Bradbury's two-treatments approach, and in fact was adamant that it did not happen that way. Boiling over, he told me, "I'm too old and too tired to call him up and say, 'You fuckin' liar, what's the matter with you?' but if *you* ever meet him, you can tell him that I told you he's a god-damn liar."

Wellll.... Bradbury wasn't a liar, there *were* two treatments. *But* (a huge "but"), as far as story points go, the two treatments are more or less identical up until just the last few pages.[2] It'd be a lot more accurate to say that Bradbury wrote *one* story and gave Universal two endings to choose from. For years, sloppy photocopies were available "under the table" to diehard fans, and then in 2004 Gauntlet Publications came out with an entire book on *It Came from Outer Space* which featured *four* treatments: three nearly word-for-word-identical ones and then a much longer fourth one based on his "better concept" (i.e., the same story as the others but with a different ending).

Ground Zero (The Atomic Monster)

This 38-page Bradbury treatment was first seen by fans in the Gauntlet book; perhaps it was originally meant for Bradbury's eyes only and never submitted to Universal, as it's undated, filled with cross-outs and handwritten scribbles, and gives every evidence of having been written in extreme haste. (For example, he alternately calls Putnam "the astronomer" and "the reporter" and alternately calls Ellen the "woman assistant" of Putnam and the fiancée of Putnam.) Two titles, *Ground Zero* and *The Atomic Monster*, are typed on the top page of this treatment, which in later years Bradbury classed as his attempt to fill the Alland-Arnold directive for something "vulgar obvious."

A meteor streaks across the desert night sky and crashes as the inhabitants of a small town watch in awe. Next, via "a camera helicopter," we (the audience) descend into the crater and find a huge space rocket under one rim of the pit. The camera continues through an open hatchway where now there is "a hint, a suggestion of black moving against black. A faint whirling of sparks, like fireflies, a glitter, a whisper of steam, a soft breathing."

Young astronomer John Putnam and fiancée Ellen have seen the crash from his house. Hiring a helicopter and pilot, they fly to and land in the smoldering crater, where the soles of their shoes smoke as they explore until they find the spaceship. The helicopter pilot enters through the hatchway and doesn't come back; Putnam is about to follow when an avalanche covers the ship. When officials, newsmen and excavators converge on the scene the next day, Putnam's report of "a hollow ship" is dismissed. Putnam and Ellen are driving back to town that night when something flashes across the road; Putnam: "[It was] a man! ... No, no, not a man, I don't know, a coyote perhaps, or a shadow, or something. A bird, yes, maybe only a bird."[3] As they drive off, "the camera 'walks' mind you to the center of the road, and watches the car vanish off into the night. The wind blows. The stars shine."

A few days later, while driving around searching for the Something they saw on the road, Putnam and Ellen come upon telephone linesmen Frank and George. Frank has Putnam join him atop a pole and listen, via headphones, to "the darnedest [sound] you ever heard" coming over the wires. After the linesmen drive away, they skid to a stop in their truck when they see an oncoming 50-foot-high whirlwind of dust. "Camera moves from thirty feet away, rapidly, toward truck, as if it was a person walking, beginning to run, as if it was the whirlwind." As it comes right up to the truck, the men's expressions change from awe to fear.

Putnam and Ellen discover the truck with doors open and blood on the seat and running board. George comes up behind them and, staring off into space, unconvincingly claims that Frank is chasing a line tapper they caught in the act. His face subtly quivers and shape-shifts as he talks. Putnam spots Frank's bloody body lying nearby. Certain that George killed him, he and Ellen fetch the sheriff, but on their return to the spot, they find nothing. That night, when Frank and George

Jack Arnold said that to make an effective sci-fi movie, "you have to create tension, create the right mood, atmosphere. ...If you're asking an audience to believe something that does not correspond to reality, and if you want this audience to ignore reality ... you need to create an atmosphere in which anything can happen." The Richard Carlson-Joe Sawyer "wind in the wires" scene is nothing if not an atmosphere-builder.

are seen standing outside a bar, the sheriff dismisses the affair. Out on the desert near a ghost town, an old prospector and his mule are confronted by *some*thing that makes both man and animal scream. The next morning, three gold miners have the same experience in the lower level of their mine.

Putnam tells the sheriff that space creatures have arrived and are in the process of repairing their ship; when seen by Earthlings, they use hypnosis to make onlookers think they're seeing familiar human faces. The two men agree to call in the government for help. Meanwhile, out on a desert road, motorist Ellen sees Frank and gets him into her car. With a cream-white moon in each of his staring eyes, he talks about being afraid and alone and wanting to go home—and tells her to drive him in the direction of the mine. When Ellen resists, his face becomes mirror-like and reflects thousands of stars, as he clasps her wrist with a lizard's hand. When Ellen glances quickly at his face, "[w]e get the merest glimmer, a suggestion only, of something from a nightmare, something that suggests a spider, a lizard, a tiger, something dark and terrible, something that glistens softly...."

Searching for the missing Ellen, Putnam, the sheriff and his deputies take to the night sky in two helicopters and chase Ellen's car, driven at high speed by Frank. The sheriff unsuccessfully tries to shoot the car's gas tank. Frank stops the car and carries Ellen into the nearby mine. On foot, Putnam races to the mine entrance and there finds *an* Ellen whom he senses is really an alien. She asks him for his gun but he points it at her, and despite her pleas ("Oh, please, don't, don't!") he shoots her four times. She *is* an alien (luckily for Putnam!): "Closeup of Ellen's face. It almost splinters, like glass. It almost sparkles, like luminescent fire." Putnam enters the mine, where he finds the real Ellen in the clutches of an alien version of himself. "Get out," says the invader. "We don't want trouble. We just want to leave. The girl will be our hostage. When we are ready to go, she'll be released." Putnam shoots his duplicate and then, after a fight, throws him down a mine shaft.

Exiting the mine, Putnam and Ellen encounter the sheriff. Putnam finds some dynamite and suggests using it to seal the entrance. The sheriff lights a stick but, instead of tossing it into the mine, he throws it up at the deputies' hovering helicopter and blows it out of the sky. The alien-turned-"sheriff" lights a second stick and is preparing to throw it at Putnam and Ellen when Putnam shoots him; the dynamite goes off in his hand, killing him. Putnam and Ellen then blow up the mine entrance. They find the real sheriff and revive him as state police helicopters and cars arrive.

Putnam points out that the spaceship in which the creatures are now trapped underground must have enough oxygen to keep them alive for years, so the government can take its time ("One week, one month, a year, five years from now") deciding whether to reopen Pandora's Box. In the meantime, he adds, we have to make sure that one of the creatures isn't still on the loose. "You never know. It could be one of us. Behind one of our faces the enemy could be hiding. The Government will have to make a thorough check all the way down the line."

Looking at the crater from a departing helicopter, Putnam says, "God forgive us for leaving them buried this way. God help them to rest in peace and wake some other day, maybe, and finally go all the way home, wherever that may be, across the universe, if necessary, or across a thousand universes of stars."

Atomic Monster (Treatment dated September 3, 1952)

This is merely a more professionally typed version of the above, undated one, identical except for corrections (e.g., Putnam is no longer repeatedly mislabeled a reporter) and a few nearly invisible changes (for instance, following the crater avalanche that buries the spaceship and traps the helicopter pilot inside it, Putnam and Ellen hitchhike back to town instead of flying back in the copter).

Atomic Monster (Treatment dated September 4, 1952)

This is a *second*, one-day-later retyping of the same "vulgar obvious" yarn, this one augmented by a midpoint scene in which Ellen and an agitated Putnam walk the night streets of the town, looking at wax figures in a store window, eyeing rings in a jewelry shop window, etc. The linesmen appear, walking in the shadows across the street, but "Putnam and his woman do not turn to see them pass. They only listen to them pass."

It Came from Outer Space (September 1952)

Over 100 pages long, this deluxe treatment is quite an elaborate blueprint for the movie that eventuated. It's full of dialogue (much of which was eventually used), suggestions for shot compositions, camera placement and camera moves, tips to help set the mood of particular scenes, ideas for the composers and more. ("It was my first experience in a studio and I let my enthusiasm run rampant, giving them more than they expected," Bradbury told me. "Like a fool, I gave them 80 or 90 pages of treatment, which was, in effect, a screenplay.") The extant copy of this treatment (dated September 1952) is filled with many October pages of changes.

In a succession of shots, the denizens of the desert town of Sand Rock, Arizona, population 20,000, are seen "rolling up the sidewalks" for the night (store owners turning off lights, doors and windows being locked, etc.). As the courthouse clock strikes nine, each chime takes us further out of the town and up a hill to the small house of John Putnam, "part-time astronomer, part-time naturalist, part-time everything that it pleases him to be." He is having an outdoor candlelight dinner with schoolteacher girlfriend Ellen, a vigorous, practical woman who "in another day, might have come across the plains in a Conestoga wagon." While standing by Putnam's telescope, their faces are lit by a bright glare as the UFO zooms across the sky. Putnam excitedly insists that he wants to be the first to see the crash-landed meteor: "Lord, Lord, what a break this could be! I feel *wonderful*!"

At the bottom of the crater, an immense spaceship is rammed into the west wall amidst steaming rocks; we watch as a panel moves inward, creating a hatchway. "The CAMERA GLIDES INTO [the] darkness inside the ship" and we get the suggestion of a shape moving in the blackness, along with a faint "chiming and ringing" sound (which will subsequently accompany every appearance of a creature, in original *and* "human" form).

Putnam convinces crop duster Bill Stevens to fly him and Ellen to the crater by saying that a chunk of the meteor will be "worth plenty." As the helicopter hovers over the crater, Stevens says, "It's something," prompting the overcome-with-joy Putnam to cry out, "*Some*thing! *Every*thing! Nothing like this has happened in the history of mankind! And we *saw* it! We're the luckiest people in the world!"

"It's nice," says Stevens.

Stevens stays with his helicopter while Putnam and Ellen hike down to the bottom of the crater. There they find the spaceship and look in through a huge oval-shaped doorway—as *something* inside looks *out* at *them*. Putnam is about to enter when the door suddenly slams shut, creating an avalanche that covers over the ship. Up on the crater rim, Stevens scoffs at their account. When the cars of Desert Rock townsfolk begin to arrive, Stevens advises Putnam and Ellen not to retell the story "if you want to go on walking around out in the open." As the area fills with gawkers, a Desert Rock radio station announcer, recording a program for next-morning transmission, offers the microphone to Putnam, who draws a skeptical crowd as he describes the discovery of the spaceship. By the time he finishes, the onlookers are laughing. "You just tore yourself right up the middle," says Stevens. Heading away from the helicopter hangar by car, Putnam and Ellen have a close encounter with an unidentifiable thing on the road.

At Putnam's house the next morning, reporters become so annoying that he grabs one by the scruff of the neck and seat of his pants and heaves him out the door. His next bit of aggravation is a phone call from his university professor, the elderly Dr. Snell, a semi-comic relief character who keeps pooh-poohing Putnam's sighting claims ("[N]ow all that silly business to one side, that joke about the rocket ship, the space ship, John...") and changing the subject. The crater, meanwhile, swarms with Lookie Loos and radio and TV representatives describing the scene *à la* the character of commentator Carl Phillips in Orson Welles' *War of the Worlds* broadcast.

Putnam walks into the Board of Education as Ellen is being told by the "very prim" board president that if she continues to be seen with him, she'll lose her job. In front

At a deadly pace, It Came from Outer Space: In the movie's pre-credits sequence, a hollow spaceship prop, lit from within by a burning can of magnesium powder, slides down a wire toward the camera.

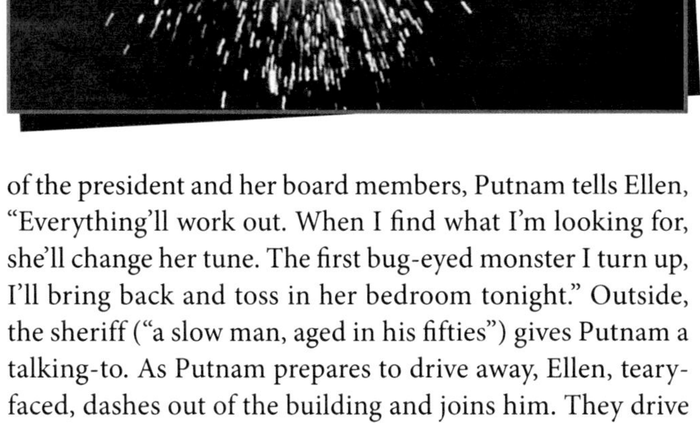

of the president and her board members, Putnam tells Ellen, "Everything'll work out. When I find what I'm looking for, she'll change her tune. The first bug-eyed monster I turn up, I'll bring back and toss in her bedroom tonight." Outside, the sheriff ("a slow man, aged in his fifties") gives Putnam a talking-to. As Putnam prepares to drive away, Ellen, teary-faced, dashes out of the building and joins him. They drive past the crater where the state's blowhard governor is giving a speech.

Putnam and Ellen have a brief make-out session in the moving car and then come upon linesmen Frank and George, the former letting Putnam listen to the mysterious sound on the wires. Frank and George go off in search of a line tapper and instead are caught in the whirlwind. Putnam and Ellen later find their bloody truck, meet a subtly shape-shifting George, and see the outflung hand of a presumably dead Frank—but no body can be found when they return with the sheriff. In town, Putnam spots and chases after Frank and George, who take refuge inside the tunnel-like entrance to an empty store. They whisper to him to keep away and promise that the real linesmen are alive.

That night, three prospectors are accosted by the aliens, one in the middle of a ghost town street as his mule neighs in terror, the other two in the lower level of their mine. Putnam and Ellen are in a café where the jukebox is too loud for us to hear their conversation. We can tell that Putnam is angry and worried, almost shouting, and buries his face in his hands. This is followed by a nearly no-dialogue scene in which the lovers, arm in arm, walk the empty streets: Putnam is agitated by staring wax dummies in a store window; a man in a newspaper office makes a monster-like face at the passing Putnam as other men in the office laugh; outside a jewelry store window, Putnam and Ellen look at a display of rings and Ellen holds up her hand to show that it has no ring on it; and they pass a store window with a wax figure in a wedding dress. The sheriff comes up behind them, asking them to come with him to his office, where the wives of the linesmen are reporting them missing. This coupled with a hardware store robbery and missing person reports (a mineralogist, a mechanical engineer and an electrical engineer) has forced the sheriff to come over to Putnam's side ... although he raises the possibility that Putnam robbed the store and kidnapped the three men himself, "to give yourself a big publicity boost." After driving the linesmen's wives home, Ellen has her desert road run-in with Frank.

An alien's phone call to the sheriff's office alerts Putnam and the sheriff to the abduction of Ellen. At dawn on the desert, Putnam (on foot) follows an alien version of Ellen to a mine shaft entrance, where a voice from out of the darkness within tells Putnam that they (the creatures) accidentally crash-landed on Earth but have built a machine that will enable them to dig their way back to their ship, and once it's repaired, they can take off. Putnam asks the creature to come out into the sun and be seen, but it refuses:

Get a load of the Kong-plus-sized alien arm reaching behind the miners to scoop them in; it's visible on the left (with arrow added), mostly hidden by white smoke on the right. An arm that big makes you wonder about the size of the whole. Pictured: Edgar Dearing, Warren MacGregor.

We dared not show ourselves in our true guise, or, like the octopus from your teeming ocean, or the maggot that you find upon meat that has lain for hours in the sun, you would kill us. The God that made us made us different.

Putnam continues to insist. Now the camera gives us a creature's p.o.v. shot, moving out into the daylight. Putnam's reaction: "CLOSEUP, sweat bubbling his face, screaming, Putnam, eyes shut! Raving, raving, raving! … [R]unning, staggering, falling, running, staggering, falling, finally lying and crying, crying, crying it all out of himself." (It's hard to conceive of any configuration of matter that could produce this over-the-top reaction in a *scientist,* of all people—someone no doubt familiar with the appearance of this world's most outlandish-looking specimens; who had several minutes to brace himself; and who just found the alien to be unfailingly polite, even giving a shout-out to the Almighty!) In a dry wash nearby, the sheriff listens to Putnam's description of the creature and comes out with a crazy-sounding rant:

Nothing like this has ever happened to me. I can't get hold of it. All I want to do is start firing off guns. Only that makes any sense to me now. … [W]hat I don't understand I hate, and what I hate I want to put away or kill. That's the way I've always lived.

The two continue to talk and talk and talk, with the sheriff leaning toward forming a posse to find the creatures' hiding place and rescuing Ellen, and Putnam countering, "If you go in there, they'll kill her. And then there's only one thing I'll ever want in my life, Sheriff, so help me God, and that'll be to find you off guard some day and kill you!"

There are more mountains of dialogue to surmount once the two men get back to the sheriff's office, where the lawman (obviously a disaster waiting to happen) looks out the window at the faces of passersby and gets worked up wondering aloud which might be space creatures in human form. ("Sheriff," murmurs Putnam, "take it easy.") The sheriff also talks about an article he read ("Did you know, Putnam, more murders are committed at 92° than at any other temperature?") as a shot of a thermometer shows that it's (you guessed it) 92°. The alien version of Frank picks *now* of all times to walk up to the window and smile in at the lawman (probably not the wisest move in this or any other galaxy), and a moment later, inside the office, a tiny spider drops down on its thread and dances between the two men's faces. "The disaster" happens: The sheriff screams, punches his fist through the window, pulls his gun and shoots alien Frank six times. Alien Frank's face begins to melt and run, blood runs from the bullet holes in his shirt and what looks like a melting jellyfish protrudes from one sleeve; then, looking human again, he wanders away. The sheriff comes outside, vomits in the street and cries. As he composes himself and starts to assemble a posse from the crowd of onlookers, Putnam drives off, blinking away tears and apologizing out loud to the desert [*sic*].

The injured Alien Frank drives out into the desert, stops and stands swaying next to the truck. The sheriff and his posse arrive at the spot in their cars, get out and shoot him at least 20 times. Putnam arrives via rented helicopter at the mine, where Alien Ellen nearly succeeds in tricking him into falling into a chasm. When she asks for his gun and throws herself at him to get it, he shoots her three times. In another part of the mine, Putnam finds an alien clone of himself who bitterly complains that his people's dream of visiting other planets is now about to end "with a mob of idiots and fools at our throats. Our harvest is fear." (Hey. Don't do the crime—kidnap eight people—if you can't do the time, dawg!) Alien Putnam shoots a fiery ray at Putnam, a struggle ensues, and Putnam throws Alien Putnam down a nearby shaft.

Another space creature, the face not visible in the darkness, appears, and Putnam promises it that he will keep the posse away while they continue to dig for their crippled ship. The creature nods agreement and allows Putnam to leave with the hostages. After all are outside, Putnam shoots into a pile of dynamite. The explosion destroys the mine entrance.

As the sun sets and the first stars appear, Putnam, the rescued hostages, the sheriff and the posse members are preparing to leave the scene when the spaceship rises out of the crater and vanishes into the sky. "God help them, they didn't want to hurt us," says Putnam. "All they wanted was to get out before they were discovered. What a shame I ever became suspicious. What a shame I pried around. It all would have gone better if I'd kept my mouth shut." Putnam and Ellen leave in the helicopter and two words move quietly up out of the steaming crater toward us: **THE END**.

Producer Alland assumed that he could have Bradbury follow up on his preliminary work and write the screenplay—a suggestion instantly vetoed by his boss. Alland told me,

> **Bill Goetz said, "What do you mean? Are you crazy? You're not going to let Bradbury do the screenplay, are you? You need a screenwriter to do that. *He's* not a screenwriter." It was amazing! But in those days, my guts were in my butt—I rarely stood up and fought for anything. If Goetz didn't want him, he didn't want him. So then, the next question was, what do I do to preserve this beautiful piece of writing?**

Enter Harry Essex (1910–1997), a New Yorker whose first jobs in young adulthood had included stints in the offices of the local newspapers *The Daily Mirror* and *The Brooklyn Eagle*. In the mid-1930s, while employed at the *Mirror* and dreaming of a Hollywood career, the twentysomething Essex and co-worker Sid Schwartz wrote a treatment which years later (1941) became Universal's *Man Made Monster*; they also wrote the Broadway play *Something for Nothing*, which lasted two performances (*The Hollywood Reporter*: "crudely constructed"; *New York Daily News*: "incredibly stupid"). All 128 lbs. of Essex enlisted in the Signal Corps during World War II; just a few days after his discharge, he ran into an acquaintance whose current assignment was finding playwrights to turn into screenwriters for Columbia Pictures. During his first several years in movieland, Essex was among the writers on well-done detective procedurals like *He Walked by Night* (1948) and *The Killer That Stalked New York* (1950) but mostly he toiled in the marshes of the B picture. He and Bradbury first crossed paths during the making of *Outer Space*.

"My meetings with Harry Essex were very pleasant," Bradbury said in an interview in the *It Came from Outer Space* book:

> **When I first had lunch with him, the film was in production. The first thing he said to me was, "What a fool you were to let your long treatment go through because the studio hired me and mainly what I did was re-type your treatment and turn it into a screenplay. You gave them 80 or 90 pages [actually, 100-plus] and a treatment is only supposed to be 30 or 40. But thank you for the gift." He was very kind about it and very generous.**

Not behind Bradbury's back, he wasn't. In my interview with Essex, he shockingly tried to glom practically *all* the *Outer Space* credit, insisting that a three-page story was all that Bradbury ever wrote—and that the Bradbury treatments I owned were actually his (Essex's) despite Bradbury's name on the covers! (He did allow that Bradbury had "attempted" to write a screenplay, but "it was just no good. He's not a screenplay writer.") Giving him more rope with which to hang himself, I asked if it bothered him that Bradbury is so often credited for the movie's success. "Well, it disturbed me for a while, yeah," continued the pants-on-fire screen scribe. "All my friends and all the people 'in the know' knew what the facts were, but I doubted that the public knew. When Bernard Shaw and Joe Blow write something, they're going to give all the credit to Shaw!"

In 1995, when I told Alland of Essex's reality-lite contentions, he quite understandably let out a gasp of "Oh, my God!":

> **Isn't that *sad*, that he needs to do that? What would a man want to do that for? I've told Ray several times he ought to publish that treatment. It was marvelous, it was just *beautiful*. As I said, you could actually *shoot* it, almost! Oh, for God's sake, Harry Essex is trying to take the credit?! Isn't that terrible! Oh, that's an outrage! Harry called me maybe a year ago ... and if I knew this *then*, I would have chewed his ass out! That's sad, that's really sad. ... Harry must be 80 years old by now, so, who the hell knows?, maybe by this time, he's talked himself into that.**

Arthur Ross, who worked on the screenplay of *Creature from the Black Lagoon* (1954) before Essex came aboard, was even more blunt about this situation, telling me that *It Came from Outer Space* "was Ray Bradbury's story and his dialogue and his picture. I think Harry Essex was psychotic!"

Essex most certainly was not the author of *It Came from Outer Space* to the extent that he wanted me to believe. But if indeed he told Bradbury that pretty much all he did was re-type Bradbury's final treatment, he was hugely *minimizing* his contributions. (There was just no in-between with this guy!) *Assuming* that most of the differences between Bradbury's

September-October 1952 treatment and the finished film are Essex's doing, it was he who wrote Putnam's opening narration, and made a real character out of the sheriff, instead of the Bradbury-conceived slow, aged, Stetson-wearing madman who makes a cartoon-strip speech about hating and wanting to kill anything he doesn't understand (and who lives up to it by blasting Alien Frank for smiling). Essex also gives the sheriff more screen time, introducing him in the first crater scene rather than a third of the way into the story as Bradbury does.

Other changes between Bradbury's treatment and the movie: Ellen does not accompany Putnam to the bottom of the crater and does not see the spaceship; Putnam is mocked by reporters at the crater rather than in his house; Dr. Snell is a sensible-looking scientist who visits the crater instead of being a kooky character on the other end of a phone chat; Putnam kills Alien Ellen less cold-bloodedly; and Putnam has an uplifting climactic speech ("There'll be other nights, other stars for us to watch ... they'll be back...") rather than the glum, pessimistic one in the treatment: "It's all over. They've gone home. ... For good. Forever. And they won't come back."

Just as good for the movie was the *deletion* of unpromising-sounding Bradbury material: a narratively useless scene of a pouting major at the Pentagon fielding a phone call from *The New York Post*; the silent movie-ish comic-romantic window-shopping scene; Ellen's squabble with the Board of Education; Putnam's exaggerated-and-*then*-some reaction to a glimpse of the creature in the mine; and Putnam's killing of the alien Putnam. Essex (or *some*one) also eliminated reams of unnecessary dialogue (including a heated argument about the spaceship's shock absorbers) and rewrote a lot of the dialogue that was retained—even improving Bradbury's "92° speech" with some pruning. (From Bradbury's version: "But 92°, Fahrenheit, people get itchy, itchy. People get itchy, irritable, hot, cranky. Mean." Apparently at 92° they also don't know when to stop talking!)

In Ray Bradbury's treatment, Putnam and Ellen see the spaceship in the crater; in the movie, only Putnam sees it. This makes him even more of "a man alone," compelled to plead his case to Ellen too. Pictured: Barbara Rush, Richard Carlson. (Photograph courtesy Alexander Rotter.)

Universal-International has started preparations on an exploitation film tentatively titled *From Out of This World*, an original by science-fiction writer Ray Bradberry [sic], author of *Martian Chronicle* [sic] and *Illustrated Man*.

The studio, which collaborated on the idea, has assigned the property to William Alland, who will put it into production about mid-January.—*The Hollywood Reporter*, November 3, 1952

This book's companion volume *The Creature Chronicles* revealed that Universal editorial department head Ernest Nims made a number of excellent story suggestions that found their way into *Creature from the Black Lagoon*. Nims was also involved on *It Came from Outer Space*, sitting down with Alland to discuss Essex's script on January 10, 1953, and then putting his list of cuts and suggestions in an eight-page memo to Alland. Keep in mind as you read them that initially, the moviemakers' plan was for the strangers from outer space to remain off-camera throughout the movie. Nims' modifications:

- [*To indicate that an alien is leaving its just-crashed spaceship:*] Use a shadow effect in the crater of a "glob" gliding along. We could then cut to—a lizard as it scuttles out of sight—a rabbit running—cut back to shadow effect of "glob" moving—cut to birds shrieking, flapping their wings. [The scared animals can be found in Bradbury's treatment; perhaps Essex omitted them, and Nims was putting them back.]
- [*For the highway night scene where Putnam and Ellen leave the car after glimpsing a Glob on the road ahead:*] Have camera glide out from behind the giant cactus as if the camera itself were a person. It glides to the center of the road as if it were watching the car vanish down the road. The camera would then turn and glide from the highway. As it moves off into the desert we pan down disclosing that it leaves a mica trail and fade out.
- [*For the desert scene where Putnam and Ellen search for the mysteriously missing Frank and George:*] Show Ellen and Putnam approaching the foliage from the "glob's" point of view. They stop, slowly turn their backs toward camera, looking off in a different direction. The

camera would then glide from behind the bushes and approach the two figures. As the camera moves in close, a gelatin-like hand comes from behind camera and touches Ellen's shoulder.

• [*For the conversation between Putnam, in the mine entrance, and the Glob in the darkness within:*] The voice of the monster: "If I did, you'd be so terribly hurt by the sight of me that you would want to kill me. You and I are so dissimilar as to horrify one another."

• [*For the Putnam-Glob Putnam confrontation:*] I feel that it is most important that we show that the pulsating machine, which Putnam's double controls by a lever, can do something. Perhaps the double could pull the lever slightly and the machine and everything around could start shaking. At this point Putnam could say—"Stop! Stop it!" This effect could be obtained by shaking the camera and we could use a tremendous sound effect over this bit of action.

Nims advised that they should drop "the entire schoolhouse sequence." (Perhaps the scene in question resembled the one described in the September 1952 *It Came from Outer Space* synopsis above.) He also wrote that in the mine entrance confrontation scene between Putnam and a Glob, "I feel the audience must see a quick, shocking, horrible flash of the 'glob' as it moves out of the shadow."

You've noticed that Nims calls the aliens "globs." The movie's Daily Production Reports also call them globs and designates the aliens-in-human-form as Glob Frank, Glob George, etc. The movie's composers used "Glob" in several cue titles. So this book will also call them globs, even though the movie's publicists wanted fans to call them Xenomorphs.

Alland's movie went by a slew of titles during the run-up to the start date. According to one Bradbury interview, Universal initially had the title *The Meteor* in mind. His "vulgar obvious" treatments were variously titled *Ground Zero, The Atomic Monster* and *Atomic Monster* and his "better concept" treatment was titled *It Came from Outer Space*. In an early press release, Universal announced that the picture was tentatively being called *From Out of This World*. In November 1952, a Universal memo read, "Please be advised that the working title for the movie presently called *The Atomic Monster* is now *The Man from Outer Space*." Next it became *The Strangers from Outer Space*.

In addition to titles coming and going, so did one female lead: On January 19, 1953, Universal contractee Julie Adams, just finishing work on the Western *The Stand at Apache River*, was assigned to the sci-fi thriller. But a day later, *Variety* announced that brand-new contract player Barbara Rush, initially assigned *Back to God's Country* (1953) as her first picture there, was instead going into *The Strangers from Outer Space*. Columnist Edwin Schallert told his readers that for Rush, *Strangers* was "a reportedly better assignment" than *Back to God's Country* (which wound up with Marcia Henderson) and he pointed out that its sci-fi theme "keeps her on the route she previously traveled in *When Worlds Collide*."[4]

Over the January 17–18 weekend, Universal exercised its option on Jack Arnold and at the same time assigned him to his first sci-fi film. Talking about the genesis of *It Came from Outer Space*, Arnold told interviewer John Landis:

> **At that time, Warner Bros. happened to have made *House of Wax* [1953]. So Universal said, "We have got to do something, too," and for some reason they came to me. They gave me a story by Ray Bradbury, and I loved it. And they said, "You're going to make it in 3-D. You know how to do that, don't you?" I said, "Sure." I wasn't going to tell them no.**

Jack Arnold (real name: John Arnold Waks) was born on the kitchen table of the family home in New Haven, Connecticut, the son of 16-year-old Russian immigrant Matthew Waks, a streetcar conductor, and his 15-year-old wife Edith. He was raised in New York and began acting on Broadway in the 1930s. Using a 16mm camera, he made money on the side by filming highlights of plays and selling the footage to the actors.[5] Come World War II, the underweight

Jack Arnold's *With These Hands* was Oscar-nominated for Best Documentary. Here's New York City's Gotham Theater on the night of its 1950 premiere. (Photograph courtesy Kheel Center, Cornell University.)

Arnold wanted to serve in the Air Force, and sewed a three-pound weight in his shorts in order to pass the physical. Before becoming a pilot, he worked for about eight months as a cameraman for documentarian Robert J. Flaherty's unit.

After his discharge, Arnold formed a company and made educational and promotional films (i.e., 1948's *The Chicken of Tomorrow* for the Agriculture Department). His last assignment of this type was a public relations film for the International Ladies' Garment Workers' Union, *With These Hands* (1950), made in New York with Broadway actors Sam Levene, Arlene Francis and Joseph Wiseman. The story of a cloakmaker (Levene), from the sweatshop days of 1910 to his pensioned retirement, this feature-length documentary received an Academy Award nomination.

Director Jack Arnold (middle) with the stars of *Girls in the Night* (1953), his first Universal movie. From left: Glen Roberts (aka Leonard Freeman), Patricia Hardy, Joyce Holden and Harvey Lembeck. (Photograph courtesy Joyce Holden.)

"That film about the horrific garment factory fire [*With These Hands*]—*that* was his big claim to fame," a Universal contractee (who wished to remain anonymous) told me. She continued:

> **I believe it was because of that film that Universal signed him. We were all given such a big buildup about him when he was signed, we were told, "We've got a new director coming on the lot, and he made an Oscar-nominated movie" and so on and so forth. We were all anticipating a man who practically walked on water. And [*laughs*] ... and then I walked into his office and he unzipped his fly! But then, *half* of the producers and directors did that, and I got kind of used to it...! He was a dirty old man.**

Since she did eventually have Arnold as a director, I asked, "So, was he a genius, or just another director?" and she replied, "Oh, just another director. But he was very easy to work with, *that* I *will* say. And very pleasant to work with. As long as I wasn't *alone* with him!"[6]

Russell Johnson told me, "Long before we did *It Came from Outer Space*, I had seen something that Jack Arnold had directed in New York, a terrific piece about the Garment Workers Union called *With These Hands*. So I knew who he was before we ever started to work." Concerning the man who directed him in *Outer Space, The Space Children* (1958) and dozens of *Gilligan's Island* TV episodes, Johnson continued, "You can work with a lot of directors who really can't make up their minds about things, but Jack always knew what he was doing. He was always there, always ready. He was a terrific guy, and very good. I was very happy to work with Jack, any time."

Arnold had been signed by Universal in February 1952 but not until September did he draw his first assignment, *Girls in the Night*, a drama about the New York slums' switchblade-and-zip gun set, partly shot on Manhattan's Lower East Side. *Girls* was reviewed by *Variety* while *Outer Space* was in pre-production, the paper's Chan describing Mr. Walk-on-Water's direction as "listless" and calling the movie itself a "trite, dullish dualer."

On January 20, 1953, Hollywood censor Joseph I. Breen notified Universal that the first-draft screenplay *The Strangers from Outer Space*, dated January 15 and submitted for his approval, conformed to the basic provisions of the Production Code. One of his few admonitions was his usual comment "kindly avoid excessive gruesomeness throughout," drawing specific attention to the mine scene where Putnam zigs and zags to avoid the ray being fired by Glob Ellen. (From the script: "If it finds him it cuts him in two.")

That same day, January 20, Barbara Rush and Charles Drake, joined by Hugh O'Brian, met on a Stage 14 sheriff's office set for "Rehearsals for Test." There was no camera, no crew, just the three players, Arnold, unit manager Mack D'Agostino and assistant director Joseph E. Kenny. On the 21st, again on that set, there were all-day 3-D camera tests in which Rush, Drake and the movie's $2500-a-week star, 39-year-old Richard Carlson, enacted some of the movie's scenes. While doing the "92° fight scene," Carlson "punched" Drake, who reeled out of the shot as Carlson's "fist comes out into audience" (a shot description from that day's Production Report). Other action shots staged to test the stereoscopic process included O'Brian throwing a tin can at the camera; O'Brian vaulting over a rail toward the camera; and Carlson throwing a chair through a window toward the camera and firing a gun at the camera.

On January 30, there were makeup and wardrobe tests for Carlson, Rush, Drake, Johnson and Joe Sawyer. *Outer Space*'s Summary of Production Budget was prepared on January 31, 1953; its compilers predicted total direct charges of $452,700 and a grand total of $588,510.

While *It Came from Outer Space* was in the works, Universal surrounded it with as much secrecy as they could—partly in an attempt to whet the curiosity of the press and the public, but perhaps also out of genuine concern that some other outfit might get wind of what they were doing and beat them to the punch with a similar picture (*à la Rocketship X-M* getting into theaters ahead of *Destination Moon* in 1950 and *The Man from Planet X* line-jumping in front of *The Thing from Another World* in '51). Although the mantle of "hush-hush" was for publicity purposes, actual precautions were taken: In a January 1953 memo, Universal's assistant publicity director Sam Israel said that it was going to be a "top secret" production:

> **We are now making rather elaborate plans to accomplish this. It will involve special police, special badges for the crew and players working on the picture, a general order to all studio personnel against discussing the picture or attempting to get on the set, etc., etc. I am confident that all this will get us a great deal more publicity and certainly more provocative publicity than would otherwise be the case. We will also put all scripts under lock and key and presumably the director and the players will receive the pages they are to cover daily, in order to assure secrecy. All this is set down by way of making sure that there are no leaks except those that we deliberately arrange.... This should be fun.**

Barbara Rush and Richard Carlson looking very domestic in an *Outer Space* publicity shot. In his *Photon* magazine interview, Carlson called the movie an experiment and added, "[Universal] didn't think it would go big, or they wouldn't have put *me* in it, you know!"

And *all* Universal studio employees received this memo: "It is requested that all studio personnel, unless properly authorized, refrain from visiting the sets where the production of *It Came from Outer Space* is being filmed. There will be no exceptions to the order and our police department has been instructed to prevent anyone from visiting the set. To avoid embarrassment to yourself, please adhere to these instructions." As the writer of the *Outer Space* pressbook put it, "[S]tudio executives ordered the sound stage closed tighter than a fat girl's girdle." Bob Thomas wrote in March, after the veil of secrecy had been lifted, that *Outer Space*

> **was filmed in its entirety with a "no visitors" sign on the stage door. Usually the sign is merely to keep the riffraff out, but this time it was for real. Even the studio's press agent was not allowed on the set, and that is being drastic.**

Universal also tried to withhold the fact that *It* was going to be in 3-D. The first announcements of the movie, in mid–1952, don't mention 3-D but of course there'd have been no thought of it at that time; *Bwana Devil*, the movie that started the 3-D craze, didn't premiere until Thanksgiving. But even after Universal decided to make it a depthie, they didn't publicize that fact, as far as I can tell. (It looks like they even kept it from cast members for as long as they could. In the '70s, Richard Carlson told *Photon* magazine interviewer Mark McGee that he didn't know until the first day on the set that it was going to be in 3-D.) In late January 1953, while Universal was doing 3-D camera tests with Carlson, Barbara Rush *et al.*, *Film Bulletin*, presumably misled by Universal, reported,

> **Very hush-hush. Universal-International has been working on a third dimension camera which company executives hope to have in operation by early Spring. Sources close to William Goetz say he expects to employ the new gimmick on at least three productions this year.**

But like "A LION in your lap!," the cat was soon out of the bag: In the February 2 *Variety* story "10 Studios Prepping Variations of 3-D," *Outer Space* is one of the many current or upcoming titles mentioned. *The Hollywood Reporter*'s every-Friday feature "Hollywood Production.... Pictures Now Shooting" didn't call *Outer Space* 3-D on February 6 but did every week thereafter. And on February 9, *Film Bulletin* reported that Universal "has been secretly filming a trio of musical shorts, as well as the feature *It Came from Outer Space*, in 3-D…"

Synopsis

Universal-International's logo, a rapidly rotating Earth against a backdrop of flashing stars, was never more appropriate. An ominous Herman Stein-composed music cue, played on a Theremin, accompanies the image. After a fade to black comes a fast-tracking shot of a fireball streaking comet-like across the starless night sky over a desert landscape—or, as Bradbury described it in his treatment, "a bright blazing stream of fire, like a gush of molten metal from the stars, races from horizon to horizon!" In the following shot, we get a gopher's-eye view of the UFO—a glowing sphere covered with soccer ball-like hexagons—as it grows larger, plummeting directly into the camera and exploding. The title **It Came from Outer Space** is superimposed in dimensional letters over the flames and flying rocks.

This pre-credits sequence is actually an advance peek at a coming event: The story proper begins with an aerial view of Sand Rock, Arizona, as narrator John Putnam calls it "a nice town … knowing its past, and sure of its future." At writer-astronomer Putnam's small house outside of town, a clock is chiming midnight as Putnam, a Sand Rock newcomer, and his schoolteacher girlfriend Ellen (Barbara Rush) finish a candlelight dinner and step outside to look at the stars through a telescope. Suddenly the UFO streaks across the sky with a blinding flash and a supersonic roar. For a second time we see it plunging toward us, and the screen-filling explosion.

Next comes a sequence with a building sense of dread as atmospheric and effective as anything found in the previous decades' forays into vampire's castles, mad labs and werewolves' woods: With more Theremin music (Stein's cue "Visitors from Space") on the soundtrack, the camera enters the impact crater, moving through great clouds of smoke and dust in this giant wound in the earth, and ultimately finds the spaceship, still incandescent, imbedded in a crater wall; it's a first-rate miniature. Most of the smoke around the ship is rising while elsewhere on the screen, other smoke (actually probably mist from dry ice) is running *down* the crater wall, adding to the other-worldly weirdness of the image. In the middle of one of the spaceship's hexagon shapes, a hexagon-shaped portion moves inward and aside, and through this portway we can see and hear a far-out piece of machinery winding down as its lights dim. We begin to hear heavy breathing. Then, just six minutes into the movie, a Glob—"nothing more than a large, hairy eye surrounded by an outer coat of Jell-O" (reviewer Al Ricketts, *Pacific Stars and Stripes*)—looms out of the darkness. A Glob point-of-view shot, with a shimmering bubble (resembling a twitching fish eye) superimposed over it, takes us out the portway and into the crater. The creature leaves a glittering trail and scares some critters, including an owl. (Notice, on the bottom right side of the screen, the wire yanked to make the poor bird flip upside down.)

Putnam and Ellen are soon in the helicopter of Pete Davis (Dave Willock), a crop duster they've roused from sleep to take them to the impact crater. They land near the crater and, over Ellen's objections, Putnam descends by foot into it; in a striking shot, he walks up to, and disappears *into*, a fast-blowing cloud of smoke. Over a great musical stinger courtesy of Henry Mancini, we see the unforgettable long shot of Putnam on a ledge, frozen at his first sight of the luminous spaceship. In a Glob p.o.v. shot, this one from inside the ship, the camera looks out at Putnam through the opening, then backs away as he approaches. The door closes with an enormous clang which sets the entire crater rumbling. Putnam runs for his life as rocks begin to tumble from above and an entire crater wall collapses, completely covering the spaceship. One of the shots of 3-D rocks flying toward and past the camera is seen twice.

Putnam gets a taste of things to come when his claim of seeing some kind of a ship gets a

One of *the* iconic images of '50s sci-fi, too good *not* to include in this book even though you've seen it published 100 times: Putnam is the first to learn of the arrival of Strangers from Outer Space. This is actually a miniature crater set complete with half-a-spaceship (probably about eight feet across) and a Putnam doll (perhaps ten inches tall).

"Somethin' musta hit this guy in the head!" reaction from Pete and, as cars from town approach, an "Oh, please, don't tell them what you told *us*" from Ellen. On the crater rim, Sheriff Warren (Charles Drake) and *Sand Rock Star* publisher-editor Loring (Alan Dexter) listen to Putnam's yarn with extreme skepticism. Pete copters Putnam and Ellen back to the airfield. As the couple drives along a telephone pole-lined road, the camera tracks them (in a helicopter shot) as the Glob's musical motif is played, indicating that they are being followed and being overtaken. Oozing vapor, one of the bulbous brutes glides out into the road ahead of them, prompting Putnam to swerve and brake, but by the time they get out of the car and look around, it's gone. Putnam and Ellen aren't sure what, if anything, they saw (which is strange, because it was illuminated in their headlights on the road right in front of them for a full seven seconds).

With Putnam's absurd-sounding account the headline story in the next morning's *Sand Rock Star*, he receives a zero's welcome at the impact crater, which is now a beehive of activity. (Even though the crater is only a few hours old, it already looks like something that's been there for 50,000 years.) Putnam expects a more sympathetic hearing from his colleague Dr. Snell (George Eldredge), who is making tests on the crater floor, but even this man of science can't swallow Putnam's yarn. Sheriff Warren, who used to be Ellen's father's deputy and has a protective attitude toward her, warns Putnam, "If you want to destroy yourself, that's *your* lookout. But leave Ellen alone."

On the road, Putnam and Ellen meet up with telephone company linesmen Frank (Joe Sawyer) and George (Russell Johnson), the former atop a phone pole using his headphones to listen to the "darnedest noise ever" on the wires. In a mood-evoking scene, Putnam climbs the telephone truck ladder and gives a listen as Frank, suddenly sounding rather mystical, talks softly about the strangeness of the desert and of the wind that "gets in the wires and hums and listens and talks." Between the evocative Bradbury dialogue, Sawyer's *sotto voce* delivery and the Henry Mancini music cue "Talking Wires," this unpromising-sounding (on paper) scene hits a homer.

In search of a possible line tapper, Frank and George drive past phone poles as, again, a helicopter tracking shot of the truck (past the phone wires) and the unearthly music create the impression that the men are being pursued and outpaced by a living force that travels *along* the wires. A Glob moseys into the road ahead of the truck, forcing it to screech to a stop; we get a monster's-eye view of George climbing out and being enveloped in white smoke and scooped into a giant Glob arm. Putnam and Ellen come upon the empty truck and find blood on the door, then follow a glittering Glob trail off-road. In a subjective shot, the camera comes up behind Ellen, a human hand materializing out of mist on the right side, and it touches her shoulder, startling her. It's an alien duplicate of George, strangely pale (not to mention a bad case of morning face!) and speaking in a hollow, robotic voice. At one point, he looks into the sun without blinking. After Putnam and Ellen leave, Glob George walks over to the *real* Frank and George, lying on the ground half-conscious nearby. He tells them that it is within their (the aliens') power to look like any human; "For a time, it will be necessary."

Certain that George has killed Frank, Putnam and Ellen drag Sheriff Warren back to the scene, where they find nothing but a dead coyote. Later, back in town, Warren gets a private, derisive laugh at Putnam's expense when he sees Glob Frank and Glob George walking down the street. (Or maybe he's laughing at their robotic shoulder-to-shoulder walk!) Putnam hurries after them into an alley and finds them standing in the half-light just inside a building's side doorway. When Putnam asks about the real Frank and George, Glob Frank says they're alive and will not be harmed if Putnam does as he's told. Glob Frank: "Give us time. Time, or terrible things will happen. Things so terrible, you have yet to dream of them."

That night, out on the desert, prospector Tom (George Selk) gets the Glob treatment, and then, near the entrance to the Excelsior Mine, so do his pals Toby (Warren

The *Outer Space* script calls for Putnam to see nothing in the dark hallway but "the two sets of glowing eyes" (Globs Frank and George). Their eyes don't glow in the movie but the effect was added to this still. The script also indicated that Glob Frank's eyes should be "fiery" when he blocks the road in front of Ellen's car, and that Glob Ellen, standing in the desert, should have "[t]he fire in her eyes." (Photograph courtesy Ronald V. Borst/Hollywood Movie Posters.)

MacGregor) and Sam (Edgar Dearing). The mine must be quite near the crater because, as we later see, a lower-level tunnel now leads up to a section of the spaceship exterior with an open portway.

George's girlfriend (Kathleen Hughes) and Frank's wife (Virginia Mullen) report the men's disappearance to Sheriff Warren. When the lawman learns that Dr. Snell and his assistant have also gone missing, he begins to put some credence in Putnam's claims of shape-shifting alien visitors. Ellen, driving alone on the desert, brakes when Glob Frank appears in the road ahead of her (a particularly terrible rear-projection shot). He climbs into the passenger seat and, in a Glob Frank's-eye shot, transforms into a Glob before the screaming Ellen.

Back at the sheriff's office (where the sheriff answers the phone "Hello?"), Putnam receives a call from one of the Globs, alerting him to the fact that they now have Ellen. Obeying the Glob's order, Putnam spends the night in a designated spot in the desert and, as a cold night turns to day, he sees Glob Ellen on a windy nearby hilltop, chicly clad in black chiffon. Glob Ellen runs, Putnam hightails it after her, and he soon finds that he has been lured to the Excelsior Mine entrance. From the thick dark of the tunnel comes an echoey alien voice, explaining that the Globs have inadvertently landed on Earth, are now repairing their ship, and will be leaving by nightfall. Ignoring the alien's claim that "you would be horrified at the sight of us," Putnam insists that it come out so he can see it (apparently forgetting that he already *has*). The cyclopean creature ponderously galumphs into full view as Putnam covers his face with his hands and turns.

Later, *again* at the sheriff's office, the pressure in this cooker rises steadily; tensions between Putnam and the steamed-up lawman hit critical mass when the temperature reaches 92° (the thermo-equivalent of "Susquehanna!") as Glob Frank walks right past the large street-front window. Warren tries to charge after him, Putnam intervenes and a fistfight ensues. Putnam prevails, and holds Warren at gunpoint with the sheriff's gun while Glob Frank makes his getaway.

Enraged, Warren organizes a posse that goes out into the desert, sets up a roadblock and waits for Glob Frank's truck. As it approaches, they open fire, causing the truck to plow into a rock wall and burn with Glob Frank inside. Intent on warning the Globs about the posse, Putnam returns to the mine, where Glob Ellen appears in the semi-darkness and nearly succeeds in tricking him into walking off the edge of an unseen chasm. She points at Putnam with a wand-like length of pipe that emits a cartoony ray, missing Putnam but blasting long, deep gashes out of the rock wall behind him. Putnam starts slinging lead and Glob Ellen stops at least one of his bullets. A Glob Ellen p.o.v. shot conveys that she teeters and reverts to a Glob before toppling into the chasm.

Forging ahead, Putnam enters a basin where Globs Frank, Snell, Bob and the miners, supervised by a Glob Putnam, are working near an open spaceship portway. Glob Putnam is aware of the posse's approach and, preferring mass destruction to death by mob violence, revs up an annihilative "power machine." Putnam implores Glob Putnam to free the prisoners as a show of good faith and, indicating the power machine, reminds him, "You can always reach out, destroy us, with that." Glob Putnam releases Ellen, Frank, George, Snell, Bob and the miners; led by Putnam, they hurry outside. Putnam throws a lit dynamite bundle back into the mine, blowing up the entrance so that the approaching posse cannot enter.

As Putnam, the former captives, Warren and his posse congregate near the smashed mine entrance, the earth beneath their feet begins to shake. Amidst shooting sparks and an explosion, the spaceship erupts out of the crater and streaks back into space.

Cast Biographies

Richard Carlson as John Putnam/Glob Putnam

Columnist Bob Thomas began an August 1953 write-up on Richard Carlson with:

> **A joke making the Hollywood rounds:**
>
> **"How come that Richard Carlson appears in so many science fiction movies?"**
>
> **"Oh, he's part Martian!"**
>
> **The person who is most amused by the gag is Richard Carlson. He can afford to laugh—he's the busiest actor in Hollywood.**
>
> **Carlson has been working like a beaver in such pseudo-science epics as *The Magnetic Monster, It Came from Outer Space, Riders to the Stars* and *The Maze*....**
>
> **Why is he so much in demand for such films?**

The answer, according to Carlson, was that in every science fiction story, "there has to be a scientist. I'm one of the few actors who look the academic type. People believe that I might have just stepped out of a laboratory." In *It Came from Outer Space*, visual shorthand (elbow patches on his coat, a pipe) is also used to convey that Carlson's John Putnam is an intellectual.

A Minnesotan, Carlson went from college plays to the Broadway stage to Hollywood, making his first movie in 1938. He was in his late twenties when he began playing movie professors and doctors, not to mention Thomas Jef-

Richard Carlson looks understandably wary in this *Outer Space* pose. He was in five sci-fi and/or monster movies in 1953–54, and also directed one of them, prompting *Variety* to write that his name "is becoming almost synonymous with science fiction films." (Photograph courtesy John Antosiewicz.)

ferson (first as a glib young prankster, then as the pensive governor of Virginia) in 1940's *The Howards of Virginia*. Amidst a number of movies nobody ever heard of, he had good supporting roles in *Back Street, The Little Foxes* (both 1941) and *White Cargo* (1942). The latter, set on a West African rubber plantation, found him enamored of the half-caste African jungle temptress Tondelayo (a cocoa-butter-smeared Hedy Lamarr), teaching her cheek-to-cheek dancing and ultimately marrying her, with dire consequences.

After World War II Naval service, Carlson abandoned Hollywood for more than a year to play legit engagements, including a Chicago run in the title role in *Mister Roberts*. Years after his stint as an MGM contractee, he got to work for the studio again but he had to travel to Darkest Africa to do it: Starting in December 1949, he spent months there playing the very dull role of Deborah Kerr's brother in *King Solomon's Mines*.

It probably *was* Carlson's "bright boy" image that started him in sci-fi, first as the A-Man protagonist of the pseudo-scientific *The Magnetic Monster* (1953). In McGee's *Photon* interview, Carlson said that Universal was hopeful that their 3-D *It Came from Outer Space* would debut ahead of Warners' 3-D *House of Wax*, which was shooting at the same time. "We didn't," Carlson said, "but [*Outer Space*] was a tremendous success for Universal. So naturally, when they started another picture, *Creature from the Black Lagoon*, they wanted me, just because I was in something that was a hit. You make *Planet of the Apes* and you want the same cast next time. It doesn't mean *you're* a 'big shot.'"

Carlson never *was* much of a Hollywood big shot. The closest he came was, as Bob Thomas reported above, in the 1950s when he hopped from one SF feature to another *and* toplined TV's *I Led 3 Lives* in which he played Herbert A. Philbrick, a high-level member of the Communist party who's actually an FBI counterspy. (In Season One episodes, the Philbrick house is actually Carlson's house, inside and out.) Carlson had a piece of the series, and it made him a mint. In Hedda Hopper's January 3, 1954, column, she predicted stardom in the futures of 18 actors and actresses, some of them newcomers and others veterans, and on the list, amidst names like Grace Kelly, Audrey Hepburn and Anthony Quinn, was Carlson, who, she wrote, "came into his own last year for a very peculiar reason—the sudden interest in science fiction pictures.... On the screen he's become the prototype of the young professor who's forever discovering new mysteries of life."

Then, just as abruptly as Carlson began dominating the sci-fi movie scene, he was done with them (or vice versa); after *Black Lagoon*, Hollywood's go-to guy for monster flicks never starred in another. He went back into the supporting player ranks and also began writing and directing for both movies and TV. His directing résumé was highlighted by *Riders to the Stars* (1954); the Westerns *Four Guns to the Border* (1954) and *Kid Rodelo* (1966), both based on Louis L'Amour novels; and TV episodes of *The Man and the Challenge, Men Into Space, Thriller, Letter to Loretta et al.* Carlson's one sci-fi script *Island of the Lost* (1967), set on an uncharted South Pacific island inhabited by prehistoric critters, carnivorous ostriches, etc., was bland and Disney-esque, probably just the way producer Ivan Tors (*Flipper, Gentle Ben*) wanted it.

Baby Boomers who didn't see Carlson in sci-fi movies probably first found him in some of the Bell Laboratory Science Series TV specials which later became inescapable classroom time-fillers in the days of 16mm projectors and pull-down screens; USC professor and Shakespearean scholar Dr. Frank C. Baxter (as Dr. Research) and Carlson played eggheads bantering about scientific principles with cartoon characters and marionettes. Then, years before *Mission: Impossible*, TV Western star Carlson led *Mackenzie's*

Richard Carlson's youthful looks receded ... along with his hairline ... and he went from playing heroes to heels. *Tormented* (1960), in which he played a composer haunted by the ghost of the woman he murdered, was his first top-billed role in years, and his last-ever.

Raiders in a fact-based 39-episode Ziv series: Carlson's Ranald Mackenzie, under secret orders from President Grant, cleaned up the U.S.-Mexico border, sometimes using extra-legal tactics, and knowing that if he's caught, Uncle Sam will disavow any knowledge of his actions.

Perhaps Carlson's career as a big-screen leading man got tripped up by the stuck-out foot of John Barleycorn (he was well-known as a tippler); in the mid–1950s, he started getting old fast. By the 1960s he was more than a bit seedy-looking, and now seemed to be cast more often than not as baddies. This husband and father of two was also quite the big dame hunter, according to actress Marsha Hunt. Starting in the late 1930s, Hunt and her husband and Carlson and *his* wife, Mona (1918–90), were close friends, but Hunt's warm feelings for Carlson cooled when she learned whose skirts he was chasing: "He went after Mona's best friends," Hunt told me. "He left no stone unturned, I'm afraid. At least by all accounts. It was so far from the person I had first known, the bridegroom, still in the honeymoon state and the excitement of making a home and starting a family and all of that wholesome tradition that along the way has been *so* changed and *so* lost." She went on:

Never a word from Mona. It was everyone *else* who seemed to know. And Mona lived for Richard. I sensed at her funeral that their boys [Christopher and Richard Henry], who dutifully gathered from San Francisco and one other place where they lived.... I sensed that they were there out of respect for tradition more than actual love of Mona. I'm just guessing, but I think she may have been ... not *neglectful* of the boys, but I *know* that for her, they always came *after* Richard. This is someone who lived for her husband, and she was so devoted, so proud of him. She was *so* impressed with his intelligence, his knowledge, his charm, Richard was her whole world, and that's why it was so awful to learn again and again, from here and there and everywhere, about Richard's [philandering].

In the 1962 *Thriller* episode "Kill My Love," Carlson plays the close-to-home role of a hard-drinking horndog of a husband; this cad strangles one "spare rib" (Kasey Rogers) with her own stocking and, when wifey (K.T. Stevens) finds out, takes the sensible "They can only hang me once" attitude and disposes of her as well.

On November 15, 1977, Carlson was admitted to Encino Hospital after suffering a cerebral hemorrhage. He never regained consciousness, and died on the 25th at age 65. Read more about him in the *Creature from the Black Lagoon* chapter of this book's companion volume *The Creature Chronicles.*

Barbara Rush as Ellen Fields/Glob Ellen

Barbara Rush's parents Roy and Marguerite met when Marguerite was superintendent of a Kansas City hospital and Roy, wounded by shrapnel in the First World War, was confined there. Barbara was born in Denver and spent her first ten years traveling around the Midwest with her family; Roy was now a mining company attorney whose work took him from one mining town to another. Once the Rushes settled in Santa Barbara, young Barbara got involved with little theater groups. A member of the University of California Players, she won the best actress of the year award for her performance as Birdie in *The Little Foxes.* A scholarship at the Pasadena Playhouse led to her participation in many plays there; her plan was to graduate, go to New York, wait tables and do theater. She told me,

I was in a [Pasadena Playhouse] class where I think there were 12 men, they were there on the G.I. Bill, and *me.* Because I was in a class with all these boys, I got to do all the parts of the girl in all the scenes that we had to do. I got to do *all* those scenes, and each of those guys only had *one* scene, with me [*laughs*]. Tom Browne Henry ran the Pasadena Playhouse (and was a wonderful actor himself), and he liked my work, I guess, so he called Milton Lewis, a very well-known Paramount talent scout. Milt discovered *so* many people [including William Holden, again at the Pasadena Playhouse]. He came over, and I ended up with a screen test at Paramount.

With Jerry Hopper directing, Rush did her test (opposite contractee Paul Lees) on the studio's Stage 15. Paramount signed the 23-year-old and loaned her out to make

A Study in Starlet: Barbara Rush doing the kinds of things that many young actresses *did*, early in their careers. "If there's one thing a starlet hated, it was being called a starlet, because it was so diminishing," she said, laughing, in 2016. "Like we weren't *big* enough to be a star!" (Photographs courtesy C. Robert Rotter, *Glamour Girls of the Silver Screen* website.)

her screen bow in director Douglas Sirk's *The First Legion*, a drama set in a house of the Jesuit Order. (It was based on a play that had an all-male cast, mainly Jesuit priests. To give the movie "femme appeal," the moviemakers broke years of precedent by casting Rush as the cripple who is miraculously healed.) Then, for Paramount, she went to Canada for the historical actioner *Quebec*; joined the cast of TV's *The Goldbergs* in a movie adaptation (it was the first teleseries to receive theatrical film treatment); and replaced Gail Russell in the Arizona-made Western *Flaming Feather*. Her busy 1950 was capped by a December 3 Boulder City, Colorado, marriage to Jeffrey Hunter, a UCLA post-grad student newly embarked on a 20th Century-Fox film career.

A source of frustration at Paramount, for Rush and no doubt other screen newbies, was their inclusion in the Golden Circle, a group described by *Variety* as "young talent just out of college or drama schools who have been signed for a pre-stardom buildup.... [The contingent] is used for various junkets and introduced at exhib meetings." Rush told me,

There were quite a few of us and we were all under contract. And instead of putting us into film, lots of times they sent us to New York and to various functions and so forth. We all wanted to be in movies, we didn't want to be interviewed, didn't want to make personal appearances. When you're very young and you're under contract to a studio, you're just trying to get the best film you can, and feel lucky when you *get* it. What you really want is to *work*. You want the work, you want the movie.

Nineteen fifty-one began promisingly with Rush co-starring in George Pal's science fiction *When Worlds Collide*. A few months after the August 1952 birth of son Christopher Hunter, Rush was signed at Universal, where they played musical chairs with her: assigning her to *Back to God's Country* and then shifting her to *It Came from Outer Space*, assigning her to *The Glass Web* before giving her *Taza, Son of Cochise*. A well-received performance as Jane Wyman's stepdaughter in director Sirk's *Magnificent Obsession* raised her stock at the studio. While continuing at Universal (*The Black Shield of Falworth, Captain Lightfoot*, more), she also started doing TV, including a one-hour *Lux Video Theatre* remake of Hitchcock's *Shadow of a Doubt* with Rush as the devoted niece of Uncle Charlie. "[A] harrowing, chilling tale of suspense ... very fine performances by Frank Lovejoy [as Uncle Charlie] and Barbara Rush," *Variety* raved.

Moving to Fox led to parts in more substantial movies with brighter stars: James Mason (*Bigger Than Life*, 1956), Marlon Brando and Montgomery Clift (*The Young Lions*, 1958), etc. Working with people who "raised the bar," Rush became a more impressive actress herself: "I was somebody who was just *bent* on being better," she told me. "I studied, I took classes, I worked with voice teachers, I did everything I could to improve." Taking a tip from Joan Crawford, she even became conscious of how she was lit and photographed and began expressing her wishes to the cameramen—"and they *appreciated* the fact that I had taken the time to learn what they were doing!"

Starting in the 1960s, her cool beauty was more often on display on TV (most notably *Peyton Place*) than on movie screens; sci-fi and horror fans will remember her poised performances on the genre shows *The Outer Limits* ("The Forms of Things Unknown") and *Night Gallery* (H.P. Lovecraft's

"Cool Air"). On *Batman,* Rush's diabolical Nora Clavicle uses her wiles to become Gotham City police commissioner, calls Batman on the Batphone to tell him his services are no longer required (then snips the phone cord)—and implements her plan to blow up Gotham City, which she's insured for $10 million. By this time, Rush had shed husband Hunter and was the wife of uber-publicist Warren Cowan, half of Rogers & Cowan, the world's biggest entertainment PR firm. They lived with three sets of children, his, hers (Christopher) and theirs: daughter Claudia Cowan. "We traveled a lot as a family," Claudia (now the Fox News Channel's San Francisco correspondent) said in 1997, "and my mom still has this habit of exploring cities on foot. My earliest memories were trying to keep pace with her as she took me on walking adventures, sometimes to really depressing parts of whatever town we happened to be visiting."

Rush's latter-day TV credits have included *Flamingo Road, Fantasy Island, Magnum, P.I., All My Children, 7th Heaven* and the new *Outer Limits.* Here she is in a recent shot with composer Kathleen Mayne (left) and furry pals.

After an eight-month Chicago run in the play *Forty Carats,* Rush was named actress of the 1969–70 season by the Sarah Siddons Society. ("I just appreciated that Sarah Siddons award so much," she told me, "'cause I'd never been awarded for ... *any*thing!") Soon thereafter, she was on to Husband #3, Jim Gruzalski, a sculptor she met at an Engelbert Humperdinck concert; that marital knot unraveled rather more quickly than the others. *Peege* (1973), a short (28-minute) student film, wowed reviewers, with *Variety*'s Murf singling out co-star Rush as "magnificent" and calling her performance "one more reminder that Rush has far more abilities than the screen has yet to utilize. There are major starring roles which should be written for her, and some in recent years which she should have played." (*Peege* was named to the Library of Congress' National Film Registry in 2007.) Rush's other stage credits include the one-woman show *A Woman of Independent Means* which she performed first at the Back Alley in Van Nuys and then on Broadway.[7]

One of the best things about her profession, Rush told me, was the opportunity

> **to work with *great* actors, like Marlon, like James Mason, like Kirk Douglas. Even women—Jane Wyman, for instance, I was just so impressed with her. [Actors like these] know all their lines and they're right there and they know what they're doing. I don't think I ever had an actor, an *important* actor I worked with, who wasn't very kind to me. And to everybody else. The thing that you're just so thrilled about is how they treat you. And how they help make your performance better. Little by little you learn a lot and *you* kind of graduate into being better. They were wonderful people. And that's when it becomes very special. You just feel, "I am lucky. I got to work with Kirk. I got to work with James Mason. I was very, very lucky to work with Sinatra..."**

I interrupted to ask her what it was like to reach the point in her career where some young co-star might say, "I got to work with Barbara Rush."

She didn't answer, she just laughed: "I don't know if anybody's ever said that!"

Charles Drake as Sheriff Matt Warren

Charles Drake (real name: Charles Ruppert) was born in Bayside, Long Island, New York, and two years later moved with his mother to New London, Connecticut. According to his Hollywood publicity, he was "the sole son of a renowned chemical engineer, now dead"; was "over-educated" at Bulkeley School, Bordentown Military Academy, Nichols College and Jennings School; and was listed on the New York Social Register. He left college with a commercial advertising degree and went to work in New York department stores.

The author of *Unmasked: A Memoir* (Vantage Press, 2003), Jolene DeLisa, had a fling with Drake from the mid- to late 1960s, and devoted a section of her book to him. Their first date

> **was at the Bel Air Hotel. He told me his life story, starting with his lonely childhood. He had had a life of privilege as far as material things were concerned, but he was an only child raised by a domineering mother.**

On Drake's first trip to Hollywood, while supporting himself by working in a parking lot and living at a YMCA, he got the ice treatment from the various studios. After five months, he saw no future in it and hitchhiked back to New York. There he was a runner-up on the radio contest show *Gateway to Hollywood* and his prize was an RKO contract. Redubbed Charles Drake, he was shipped *back* to movieland and debuted in the studio's *Career*.[8]

Newly married to his high school sweetheart Rosamond, the handsome blond 21-year-old Drake landed additional roles at RKO (including the 1939 *The Hunchback of Notre Dame*, in which he reportedly plays *three* small parts), and then worked at Paramount and Warners. At the latter studio, he signed a term contract in 1941 and played a score of minor characters, mostly uncredited. Fifty-five years before *Titanic*'s (1997) Leonardo DiCaprio and Kate Winslet steamed up the windows of the touring car, Bette Davis and her beau Drake got caught kissy-facing in the back seat of a limousine on an ocean liner's freight deck in 1942's *Now, Voyager*.

During World War II, Drake served with the U.S. Army Combat Engineers Corps; then he went back to acting if not to Rosamond (they divorced not long after his discharge). Columnist Eleanor Harris called him "a giant edition of an Arrow Collar ad: he towers six feet three-and-one-fourth inches tall.... His best friends [include] actor Tom Neal.... He goes through books at the rate of one a night because he can't sleep until 2 a.m., and while he reads he gnaws on—of all things—sardines and candied yams!"

Better roles began coming his way postwar, including a tag team pairing with Albert Dekker as *Tarzan's Magic Fountain*'s (1949) heavies, determined to exploit a lost tribe's fountain of youth. (Drake's overkill comeuppance: a flaming arrow goes into his back and out the front—and then he falls off a cliff!) In the spring of 1949, he drew a term acting ticket at Universal, where the second male lead in *The Story of Molly X* was to be his inaugural assignment. But *Molly X* came and went without Drake, the actor instead making his Universal bow in an unbilled bit as a hotel clerk in *Johnny Stool Pigeon* (1949).

At the Valley lot, Drake alternated between now-forgotten bread-and-butter pictures and some of the studio's biggest 1950s hits, including *It Came from Outer Space, Winchester '73* (1950), *The Glenn Miller Story* (1954) and *To Hell and Back* (1955). In the whimsical comedy-fantasy *Harvey* (1950), Drake plays Elwood P. Dowd's (James Stewart) psychiatrist, one of several characters mellowed by their association with rumpot Dowd and Dowd's "pooka" companion, the invisible 6'3¾" white rabbit Harvey. Just as farout, *You Never Can Tell* (1951) features Drake as a ruthless fortune-hunter whose plan involves poisoning a German Shepherd; the dog is reincarnated as a human (Dick Powell) looking to settle the score. At Universal, Drake was evenly divided between good guy and bad guy assignments; as columnist Jimmie Fidler pointed out, "The man who can play heavy as well as hero works twice as much in Hollywood. [Drake] is equally at home whispering sweet nothings in the heroine's ear or planning to annihilate her boyfriend." He left Universal in 1954, about the same time he split from second wife Ruth, the mother of their two daughters. His '50s movie résumé also included such notable (if only to us) titles as *Tobor the Great* (1954), a sci-fi adventure for kids, and *Step Down to Terror* (1958), a programmer-level remake of Hitchcock's 1943 *Shadow of a Doubt* with Drake in the psychopathic killer role.

Drake also had small-screen genre credits: *The Dick Powell Show*'s eerie "The Clocks," episodes of *The Man from U.N.C.L.E., Star Trek, Land of the Giants* and, amusingly for *It Came from Outer Space* fans, the 1967 *The Invaders* episode "The Saucer" in which he plays a scientist-type who stumbles upon one of the Invaders' spaceships in the desert (where else?) and, unlike John Putnam, is quite determined to alert the authorities. Also amusing was a *Theatre '59* episode in which he played a murderer, but stepped out of character to do the middle commercial pitch. As one reviewer noted, "[He] then returned with the mood lost forever to his slight case of murder." In the disasterpiece *Valley of the Dolls* (1967), Drake played the beauty products manufacturer who makes secretary Barbara Parkins a model and the face of his company, "The Gillian Girl"—and then makes her *his* girl.

Maybe Drake's psycho performances weren't as

In *Outer Space*, Charles Drake's workaday sheriff is scornful of astronomer Putnam, who's forever "squintin' up at the stars." A year later, Drake—top-billed in a movie for the first and only time—played a Civil Interplanetary Flight Commission higher-up in *Tobor the Great* (pictured).

much of a stretch as one might assume. In 1964, It Came from Out ... of the Bushes: Drake, that is. He waited in the shrubbery in front of 40-year-old Jane Wilcoxson's house as she came home after a date, then jumped out and beat her with his fists and knocked her down several stairs. Police summoned to the scene found the tough-guy actor hiding nearby. While Wilcoxson was treated at UCLA Medical Center, Drake was booked on a charge of assault with a deadly weapon. Then in 1966, a newspaper item revealed that Drake was trying to revive his career—and "if publicity can do it, Chuck is well on his way." The article went on to relate that his current love, a stunning brunette socialite, "told him to take a walk. Mr. Drake did. He walked right into her house, made a terrible scene and shoved her all over the place until gendarmes, called by a neighbor, arrived to put him out."

After his first night with Jolene DeLisa, the two were inseparable. She wrote,

> **[F]rom there it was first class restaurants, flowers, and lovely thoughtful gifts. The way I had always dreamed of being treated. ... And he was a sensational lover.**
>
> **He invited me to dinner at his home on a hill overlooking Beverly Hills. The street was even named after him—Drake Lane. Much bigger Hollywood stars had never had a Beverly Hills street named after them!**
>
> **We drove up a driveway lined with palm trees and parked by an oval-shaped swimming pool. From the outside, the California ranch house was charming. I expected it to be just as lovely inside, but was shocked at the disorder within his walls.**
>
> **The setting was like Charles would turn out to be: beautiful on the outside and a shambles on the inside. Objects were broken and cracked, and there were burnt holes in the sofa. Even his maid had stopped coming, so he was the housekeeper, something he was hopeless at. The story of his life was in that house. A broken marriage, rage, and drunken scenes.**
>
> **But he was a gourmet chef and had gone to a great deal of trouble to prepare a lovely meal with wine, flowers, candlelight, and a roaring fire in an old stone fireplace. He had even written out a menu on beautiful stationery, ending with "lovemaking begins promptly at 10 p.m."**
>
> **As I looked out the huge glass windows overlooking Beverly Hills, I thought all of my dreams had come true. But I would soon learn there would be three of us in the relationship: Charles, me, and the bottle.**

Drake's mid–1940s publicity claimed that his wish was to be a screen actor always, but apparently there was a change of heart (or an inability to get work), because he played his last roles in the mid–1970s. In Richard Lamparski's 1986 edition of *Whatever Became of...?*, the Drake entry revealed that "[h]e declines to give any details about his present life." Right from my start as an interviewer, I'd have liked to talk with him, but back then I had no way to find a long-retired actor with such a common name. Imagine my chagrin to learn, once it was too late, that in 1981, he'd made a public appearance in Tarrytown, New York, at the Warner Library—visible from my house! Drake, now (1981) a resident of East Lyme, Connecticut, had found amidst his own clutter a kinescope of his live *Robert Montgomery Presents* TV episode "Catch a Falling Star," in which he starred as a washed-up actor, and mentioned this discovery to its director James Beach, a Tarrytown resident. (*Motion Picture Daily* had called it the best TV episode of 1956.) Beach suggested that there be a benefit showing at the library ($7.50 a ticket), which Beach, Drake and fellow cast member Anthony Messuri attended. I was at home a couple blocks away, possibly wondering whatever became of Charles Drake.

In 1994, following a lengthy illness, 76-year-old Drake died at his East Lyme home.

Russell Johnson as George/Glob George

Russell Johnson's movie career might have begun years earlier than it did, had he not drawn the short straw.

While Johnson was studying at the Actors' Lab in Hollywood in 1946, a student production of Sidney Kingsley's Pulitzer Prize-winning play *Men in White* was planned. It would be performed just twice, a same-day matinee and evening performance; Johnson was tapped to star in one and his fellow student Bill Phipps would star in the other. The two young actors drew straws to determine who'd do what, and Phipps lucked out: He got the long straw and the chance to perform in the evening, when studio scouts, casting directors, agents *et al.*—busy during the day—would attend. Sure enough, Charles Laughton saw and liked Phipps' work and, that very night, took him aside to talk to him about a part in his upcoming stage presentation *Galileo*; Phipps' association with Laughton led to an RKO screen test and a contract at that studio. As a result of *Men in White*, Phipps began climbing the ladder of success while Short Straw Johnson's matinee performance slipped into the unremembered past.[9] (In 1952, Johnson got even: In the movie *Loan Shark*, he killed Phipps!)

Lady Luck and Russell Johnson appear to have been strangers throughout much of his young life. He was born in 1924 in Ashley, Pennsylvania, coal mine country. The oldest of seven, he was eight when his dad, a railroad detective, died of pneumonia. This being the time of the Great Depression, his mother was unable to support the entire family so she sent Russell and two brothers to Girard College, a Philadelphia school for poor white orphan boys. A ward of the state, he received some military training there, and also four years of drama study. With World War II raging, Johnson enlisted on his 18th birthday. He was a 20-year-old navigator-bombardier, flying his forty-fourth mission, when his B-25 was shot down by the Japanese in the Philippines. Johnson was sprayed with shrapnel that broke his ankles and killed the radio operator next to him. In his 1993 book *Here on Gilligan's Isle*, he wrote that he was in a New Guinea hospital when he received a Purple Heart:

> **Two men came up to my bed, one carrying a stack of black boxes. The officer read the routine orders with no emotion at all: "For wounds received in action.... Second Lt. Russell Johnson, 0765497, is hereby awarded the Purple Heart by order of Colonel Smith." Or *some* colonel.**
>
> **When the officer finished his speech, the sergeant with him put a little spin on the box as he tossed it at me. It slid across my chest and stopped at my throat. It was an interesting way to be awarded the Purple Heart.**

At the Actors' Lab, Russell picked up a lot of experience and even a young actress wife, Kay Cousins. (According to a 1952 Universal studio bio of Johnson, "Like her husband she is best at 'meanie' roles.") He played important parts at the Circle Theater while at the same time working a variety of jobs to pay the grocery bills. In 1951, the actor made his movie debut (unbilled) in a flashback scene in *Rancho Notorious,* running an Old West saloon's crooked Chuck-a-Luck game. Paul Henreid, producer-director-star of the upcoming *For Men Only* (1952), was impressed by one of Johnson's little theater performances and cast him in this indictment of fraternity hazing on college campuses. Playing the school's star footballer and sadistic pledgemaster, Johnson was a standout in the cast of unknown faces, "getting a lot of punch into a mean, warped character" (*Variety*) who, just as his warm-up act, compels a student to shoot a puppy on Hell Night!

Russell Johnson: "I was very taken with *It Came from Outer Space* because it was one of the first 3-D films ever made. The cameras and all that stuff were built on the studio lot by the camera guys, and there were all kinds of camera problems and so forth that had to be solved in the midst of shooting." (Photograph courtesy Ronald V. Borst/Hollywood Movie Posters.)

Universal executives, interested in Kathleen Hughes, screened *For Men Only*, liked what they saw and signed her; then, a few weeks later, again on the strength of *For Men Only*, they signed Johnson, the first Purple Heart World War II vet signed to a long-term deal there since Audie Murphy. Johnson's procession of "meanie" movie roles continued when he made his Universal bow as a kidnapper in *Ma and Pa Kettle at Waikiki*, shot early in 1952. Amidst several Westerns where Johnson was a lout or a lawbreaker, Universal announced he'd be playing the romantic lead in *Law and Order* (1953), but this was misleading: Yes, he does play kissy-face with beauty contest winner turned actress Ruth Hampton, but he was sixth-billed (not the lead) and was mostly annoying in the role of the hotheaded kid brother of town-taming sheriff Ronald Reagan. He sacrificed himself to save the leads in both *This Island Earth* and *Attack of the Crab Monsters* (1957) but generally the movie casting folks confined him to playing polecats. He was nicer on TV, and even co-starred as a marshal on the Western series *Black Saddle*; by this time he was the father of young David and Kimberly. His small-screen genre credits included *Thriller*, *Twilight Zone* and *The Outer Limits*. A Trekkie, he *wanted* to be on *Star Trek*, and a couple times was up for a role, but didn't make it.

In 1964, "a three-hour tour" turned into the start of a three-year run for Johnson on *Gilligan's Island,* the legendarily lowbrow sitcom about dingalings shipwrecked on an uncharted isle. There were seven regulars—Bob Denver, Alan Hale, Jim Backus, Natalie Schafer, Tina Louise, Dawn Wells, Johnson—and Johnson found himself playing seventh banana as the Professor, a high school science teacher with more degrees than a thermometer. The Professor could MacGyver *any*thing together (for instance, a battery charger out of coconut shells, seawater, pennies and hairpins) but, as the series' fans liked to quip, he couldn't fix the small hole in the bottom of their beached boat. Johnson's *New York Times* obituary described the Professor as "a good-looking but nerdy academic, an exaggerated stereotype of the man of capacious intelligence with little or no social awareness. Occasionally approached romantically by [Tina Louise's Ginger,] he remained chaste and unaffected." *Gilligan's Island* was #1 in its time period for three seasons. "Russ was a gentleman through and through with a fabulous sense of humor," Dawn Wells told me. "Handsome, too, with his smile and the twinkle in his eyes!"

Gilligan's Island was a ratings hit but reviewers were unkind and Johnson, who thought of himself as a Serious Actor, let himself be plagued to the point of misery for being part of it. Surely it didn't help that, after the show's cancellation, it looked as though his career was still stranded on that island. Probably hating himself every day other than payday, he rejoined other *Gilligan* regulars in "reunion" TV movies and even voiced the Professor on *Gilligan* cartoon series. When visiting Westminster Abbey in 1979, he and wife Kay were surrounded by a score of American tourists who recognized him as the Professor, asking for autographs and taking pictures. "I was embarrassed, and I was annoyed, because I did not want to do this kind of thing in what I considered a hallowed place," he wrote in *Here on Gilligan's Isle*. "I kept asking the people, 'Please, please, not in Westminster Abbey. This is a church.'" He wrote elsewhere in the book, probably without much exaggeration, "That series has affected my life every day since."

Kay died in 1980; Russell married again a few years later, and moved with his family to Seattle in 1988. In 1993 when I interviewed him on stage at a Towson, Maryland, convention called Nostalgia Vision, he said he was currently doing voiceover work in radio and TV commercials, narrating industrial films, and preparing for a ten-city tour to promote *Here on Gilligan's Isle*. Near the back of that book, he revealed that son David was L.A.'s first AIDS services coordinator until leaving that job because "[he] has the very disease he fought so diligently against." Johnson ended his part of the book a few lines later with:

> **I would simply like you to know about the strength and bravery of my son. He's an extraordinary fellow who doesn't deserve this illness. There isn't a person on this earth who deserves AIDS.**

After 39-year-old David's 1994 death, Johnson was quoted in *The National Enquirer*, "It's up to me to continue to fight for understanding and acceptance of people with AIDS."

In the last years of *his* life, Russell Johnson lived on an island (ha!) in Washington's Puget Sound. A victim of kidney failure, he died at home in 2014.

Production

As you read the following day-by-day rundown of the February 4–March 9 shooting of *It Came from Outer Space*, you'll notice that almost none of the descriptions of Glob scenes match what's in the finished film. That's because the plan at the start was for the Globs never to be seen. If the movie had been made to the exact specifications of the final script draft, Glob-wise we would have seen only (on Putnam's windshield and on the phone truck windshield) the reflection of a phosphorescent, elongated eye; then, when Putnam stands at the Excelsior Mine entrance and demands that a Glob show It-self, we would have gotten a

> **FLASH SHOT—WHAT HE SEES**
> **An instant's sight of the horrific creature, enveloped in smoke. (NOTE: EXACT DESCRIPTION OF THE CREATURE TO BE PROVIDED)—then CAMERA SWINGS UPWARD....**

On Tuesday, February 3, 1953, Jack Arnold headed the list of crew members making the trip to Apple Valley, a Mojave Desert community 100 miles northeast of Universal; it was there that many of the exteriors for the movie, now officially called *It Came from Outer Space*, were shot. The Mojave Desert reportedly has the best air in California, the kind of air that denizens of Smog Angeles, an hour and a half away, never get to taste. In the 1990s, U.S. troops preparing to be sent overseas as part of Operation Desert Storm were first trained in the High Desert because its wintertime temperatures are very much the same as in the Mideast: You can have frostbite before breakfast and sunstroke by noon.

That winter day, February 3, Arnold and some of the key personnel scouted locations. Wednesday, February 4, was the first day of shooting, and also the day that Universal Studio manager M.W. Weiner wrote a memo to cast and crew members, reinforcing the memos that had come before:

> **In view of the unusual nature of this production and the newly developed techniques which are being employed in its filming, it is requested that you refrain from any discussion of this picture. The studio has taken precautionary measures to keep unauthorized personnel from visiting the set for this reason. We are counting on your cooperation to maintain this necessary secrecy in order that the processes used in the production may not be copied by others before this picture is released.**

Also on that date, *Variety* reported that the thesps working in the "top-secret *It Came from Outer Space*" were being required to sign a loyalty pledge that they would not divulge the nature of its plot or dialogue. A few weeks later, gossip maven Hedda Hopper wrote in her column, "Universal-International is keeping [*It Came from Outer Space*] so tightly under wraps that Dick [Carlson] tells me even he has to wear an identification badge to get on the sound stage where it's being shot."

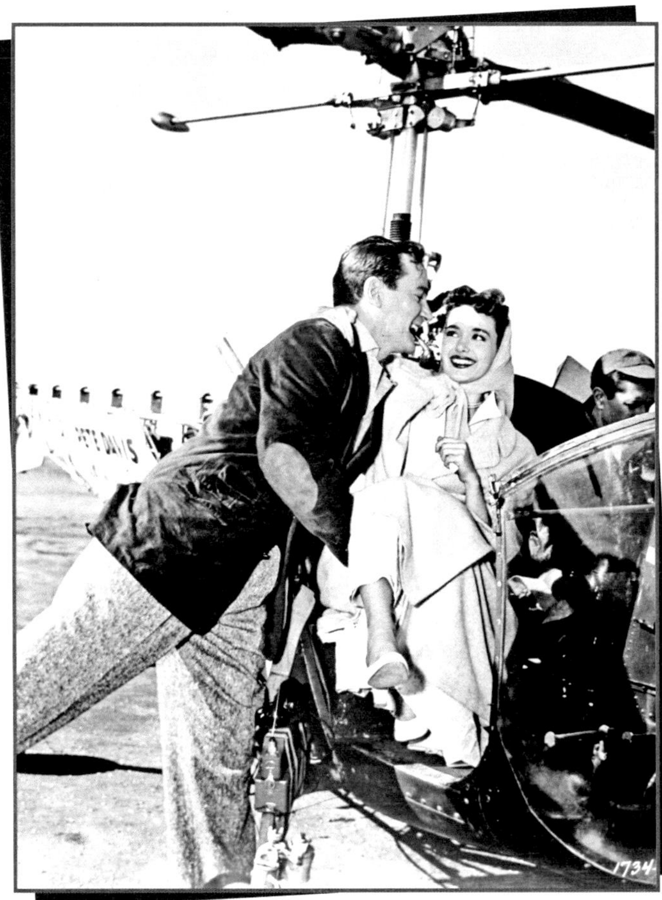

Copters were fairly new to the movies in 1953, and *Outer Space* was the second sci-fi feature in which one was seen. The first was *When Worlds Collide*—coincidentally also starring Barbara Rush, pictured here with Richard Carlson.

If industry spies *were* trying to catch a glimpse of the *Outer Space* troupe on opening day, Wednesday, February 4 would have brought them to the Apple Valley Airport and to the nearby crater location; at both spots, Carlson, Barbara Rush and Dave Willock (as pilot Pete Davis) enacted day-for-night helicopter scenes. Second unit director Joseph E. Kenny spent that afternoon on desert roads shooting drive-bys of Putnam's convertible and the sheriff's car, plus some background plates.

On the 5th, a day when Arnold's work was intermittently interrupted by sunlight fluctuations, he directed more scenes at the lip of the crater, among them: Putnam, Ellen and Pete's arrival; Putnam, post-landslide, insisting that there's a ship in the crater; and, shot from a high parallel, the arrival of Sheriff Warren (Charles Drake) and newspaper publisher Loring (Alan Dexter). Dexter had recently made a good showing as a no-nonsense homicide detective in Arnold's *Girls in the Night*.

Kenny and his crew had the same-day job of getting m.o.s. footage of the posse men in their cars and afoot. Drake and Dexter appeared in some of these scenes, along with the 17 extras. Arnold took over the direction of the posse men the following day, supervising the scene in which they level their guns and fire at Glob Frank's approaching truck and the subsequent shot of a vehicle on its side, engulfed in flames. The burning vehicle doesn't look like a truck, it looks like a car, with perhaps a piece of scaffolding laid across it to suggest the truck ladder. If this item from *Variety*'s "Hollywood Inside" column (March 11) is to be believed, we're seeing the immolation of a classic car:

> **TOLL THE BELLS FOR poor old Gertrude, a 1918-model Pierce Arrow sedan which had been around the UI lot as long as most of the oldtimers can remember. Lon Chaney had ridden in her for scenes, and so had Norman Kerry and Mary Philbin and other stars of yesteryear. Earlier this week she was run over a cliff on the studio back lot for a sequence in *It Came from Outer Space*. Her demise was not total, however, for before she went over the embankment her motor was removed by a studio mechanic.**
>
> **And what's left of her now will run the pumps that supply a back lot lake with water.**

On the Apple Valley crater location, *Outer Space* crew members have built scaffolding for the high shot of the sheriff and Loring joining Putnam, Ellen and Pete on the lip formation. Jack Arnold's first unit spent seven days in the Mojave, second unit director Joseph E. Kenny a bit longer. (Photograph courtesy Robert Skotak.)

Whatever is burning, burned in early February, not early March, and on the Apple Valley location, not on the Universal back lot, and it didn't go over any cliff. There might be a germ of truth *some*where in that item, but don't ask me where it is. (To make everyone's confusion complete, Universal's official *Outer Space* still set includes a shot of the burning whatever-it-is and it's captioned, "A Scientist's automobile destroyed by invisible forces.") This roadblock scene was shot at Dead Man's Point, a location seen again in Alland-Arnold's *Tarantula* (1955).

Arnold then made another pilgrimage to the crater and got the day-for-night shot of the sheriff and Loring arriving in their cars ("There's Ellen and Putnam!" "There's Pete's copter!"). Kenny's second unit spent part of the day working with Arnold's unit, the rest getting shots of his own, starting with a tracking shot (from a helicopter) of Putnam's car zipping along the highway with telephone poles and their rising and falling wires in the foreground. Also shot: Glob Frank stepping out into the road in front of motorist Ellen, the KLTV truck and Putnam's car arriving at the crater, and a helicopter shot of Victorville, California, the first thing seen in the movie after the title ("This is Sand Rock, Arizona, of a late evening in early spring…").

The weekend brought no rest for the troupe: On Saturday, Arnold began shooting the morning-after-the-crash scene of crater activity involving soldiers, newsreel men, reporters, etc.—a total of 11 extras. Seen in the roles of taunting reporters Dugan and Lober were day players Robert Carson (the brother of actor Jack Carson) and Dick Pinner; a year later, the latter co-starred in Roger Corman's first movie as producer, *Monster from the Ocean Floor*. Among the items on the second unit's to-do list were helicopter shots of Putnam's convertible (being driven by Ellen) and the phone truck.

On Sunday the 8th, Arnold & Co. again worked at the crater location shooting scenes for various parts of the movie: more with the pushy reporters, day-for-night footage of Putnam and the sheriff looking for Dr. Snell; etc. During the latter scene, Putnam stupidly adds to the sheriff's worries by ominously saying, "Wouldn't it be a fine trick if I weren't really John Putnam at all … something from another world come here to give you a lot of false leads…," one of several times Putnam lives up to his rep as Public Putz #1.

On the main unit's last day on location, Monday, February 9, they shot part of the scene in which Putnam and Ellen encounter linesmen Frank and George, the former atop a pole listening to "the wind in the wires." While on the phone truck ladder, actor Joe Sawyer ran the linesman's spike on one shoe into the other leg. He was treated on the set by the first aid man and then brought to nearby Victorville where a Dr. Dorain closed the wound with four stitches. Dramatizing the minor incident as only a movie studio can, Universal prepared a news item that doubled the number of stitches, called it a severe laceration and claimed that Sawyer had to recuperate for a week; by the time *Variety* reported the incident, the detail that Sawyer fell from the pole had been added. The truth is that, after his visit to Dr. Dorain, Sawyer went right back to the set and back to work.

Toward the end of the "wind in the wires" scene, George removes his coveralls and we see that he's fully dressed underneath, including a long-sleeved shirt. A few scenes later, when Glob George addresses Frank and George, both George and Glob George are dressed, George in his regular clothes and Glob George in the coveralls; Glob George's coverall sleeves are rolled up to show us his bare arms, an indication that coveralls are all he has on. See *Outer Space* enough times and you'll realize that these small touches, plus frequent dialogue references to clothes, are there to let us know that the Glob replicants are initially naked. There's the business of George showing us that he has two full layers of clothes (so that he and Glob George can both be dressed when they share a scene minutes later); in a sheriff's office scene, Jane mentions that Frank and George (actually Glob Frank and Glob George) came home for clothes before they disappeared; Putnam goes home to find that his clothes closet has been emptied.

There is one exception to this "rule": the Glob p.o.v. shot (complete with superimposed alien eye) of Putnam and Ellen walking in the desert in search of Frank and George. As the camera dollies in toward their backs, we see the ever-present Glob mist, we see some of that mist coalesce into a hand and touch Ellen's shoulder—and when she and Putnam whirl around, they see Glob George fully dressed, which he shouldn't be. (But I'm not complaining!) It's wonderful that in this Glob p.o.v. shot, the moving camera starts out high, to remind us of the colossal size of these extraterrestrial abominations, then comes down to "our size" during the unseen metamorphosis. The idea that a towering Glob is noiselessly creeping up behind two hapless humans in the middle-of-desert-nowhere is darn scary, and the scene features darn-scary Henry Mancini music to boot; it adds up to perhaps the best moment in the movie.

Interviewed for German TV about *It Came from Outer Space*, Jack Arnold commended his "Glob actors" (Carlson, Rush, Sawyer, Johnson):

I just had good actors. I said, "Look, you're an alien. Everything seems somehow stilted. You do not know so exactly how to walk or greet or talk to someone, although you can of course speak. But this culture is completely alien to you."

I showed that in quite different ways. For example, when [Glob George] took an unblinking look into the sun, or when one appeared in the form of Barbara Rush. She then

stands up on a hill, and suddenly somewhere else. The actors played as if they were really aliens. I wanted the aliens to assume as much as possible of the personality and the physical characteristics of the people in whose shape they slipped—for their own safety, so that they were not discovered.

For the actors, it was a difficult task, because they had to act almost like zombies. We discussed the detail on the set before we filmed, and tried various ways. Some things were simply bizarre, and I did not accept them. Every effort had to be very subtle, and I think that worked well then. Exaggerations would have made the movie into a comedy.[10]

The *Variety* story "UI's *Outer Space* Invaders Jar Serenity of Apple Valley" (February 12, 1953) is obviously based on exaggerations and just plain lies provided by Universal. After an opening paragraph establishing that *Outer Space*'s cast and technicians are under orders *not* to reveal anything about the movie until after its release, it asks readers to believe that the Apple Valley location shooting sites bristled with lawmen with shotguns to keep away the curious! It continued:

Jack Arnold "did a fine job" directing *Outer Space*, according to Richard Carlson in his *Photon* magazine interview; "He always had his eye on performances." Barbara Rush said in 2016, "I liked Jack Arnold a lot, I really did. He was on his way up, so this was an important film for him. So we all tried our best to please him." (Photograph courtesy Ronald V. Borst/Hollywood Movie Posters.)

Citizens of Apple Valley ... were the first to report that a platoon of armed deputy sheriffs was surrounding actors and film technicians....

"At first I thought they were guarding a new type jet plane that had landed accidentally," said the owner of an Apple Valley drinking emporium who attempted to see what was going on. "Then I got a look at some people with arms, legs, torso, but no heads, and I got out of there as quick as I could."

The story ended by identifying producer Alland as a man who "helped produce [*sic*] that panic-provoking Orson Welles 'War of the Worlds' CBS broadcast." (Alland was hardly its producer.)

Leaving second unit director Kenny and his crew behind, Arnold, his actors and other first unit crew members returned to Universal that night. Tuesday, February 10, was their first day of shooting on the lot: On Stage 19 they got a start on the highly charged Sheriff's Office scene in which the stressed-out Warren argues with Putnam (including the 92° speech) and then fights with him. First, stuntmen Dale Van Sickel and Al Wyatt went through the fight motions and then the principals, Carlson and Drake, gave it a go. (None of this footage is in the movie; Carlson and Drake later did the fight a second time on a different Sheriff's Office set.) At one point there was a nine-minute break for "first aid for actor," but the paperwork doesn't say which.

Meanwhile, Kenny's second unit was still in the Mojave, in a dry lake shooting in long shots (with doubles) the macabre interlude where Glob Ellen appears like a modern version of some mythological temptress, and Putnam runs up and down rocky slopes after her. "The scene is masterful, on a level with Welles or Hitchcock," Dana M. Reemes wrote in *Directed by Jack Arnold*, probably unaware that it was directed by Kenny, not Arnold. (That said, perhaps Arnold gave Kenny sketches and/or to-the-last-detail instructions how to shoot it. Weeks later, Arnold *did* shoot, on a Universal stage, the close-ups of Carlson and Rush that were inserted into the scene.) Kenny ended the workday with the striking shot of Putnam, in the stolen sheriff's car, speeding right up to and *under* the camera (which was on a crane).

February 11 found Arnold & Co. getting various shots on Universal's Courthouse Square, including one of Putnam and Ellen in the convertible, an unnerved Putnam reliving the experience of encountering Glob George: "The pallor of that face!" (Russell Johnson told me, "The only thing I didn't like about making that movie was, they put gray makeup on Joe Sawyer and me [for their scenes as Globs], and when we would walk into the commissary, everybody moved away from us!") In shots that wound up on the cutting room floor, Glob Frank and Glob George, noticing that Putnam is following them, *run* from him.

Barbara Rush recalls the filming of the scene of Globs

Frank and George "casually" strolling down the street and told me:

Russ and that darling man Joe Sawyer, they were made up to look kind of chalky. And in the scene where they walk down the main street, they were playing aliens trying to look like what they thought a human being *might* look like ... but they hadn't quite learned yet. So they were just staring straight ahead like robots. They were trying to look natural and of course they looked just the opposite. If you saw them walking down the street, looking neither right nor left but straight ahead, you'd know right away, "Here come the aliens!" You could spot 'em a mile away [*laughs*]!

Late in the afternoon, the staff killed approximately a half-hour (waiting for darkness) by looking at dailies, then got a few more shots that ultimately wouldn't be used, one of them a night-for-night of Putnam standing on the sidewalk outside the sheriff's office, and stepping inside when the telephone rings (the Glob calling to say they've got Ellen). In the movie, as Putnam talks on the sheriff's candlestick phone with the Glob, he's in close-up and we hear only his side of the conversation and Henry Mancini's eerie composition "Telephone Message," but the script called for viewers to also be able to hear part of the Glob's message, including the words "dirt road," "main highway" and "wait for us."

Among the shots taken by Kenny in Apple Valley that day were a Glob Frank p.o.v. shot of the truck crash into the rock wall and, for the opening reel, a Glob p.o.v. shot as it climbs up toward and then gains the raised rim of the crater and eyeballs the surrounding flatlands and distant mountains. With the camera in an "extension cradle," the latter was shot a variety of ways: with a walking effect, with*out* one, slow and fast.

On February 12, the first unit returned to Courthouse Square to shoot more Sand Rock street scenes. On a new Sheriff's Office set, this one behind the SHERIFF'S OFFICE—SAND ROCK COUNTY window on the Square, Richard Carlson and Charles Drake again went fist to fist, with car and foot traffic visible out the large window behind them. Notice that, as they fight, the camera bobs and weaves, as if it was hand-held; this may have been a bit ahead of its time in a 1953 movie. Then the moviemakers got shots of Sheriff Warren hustling across the street and forming a posse. The display case in front of the *Sand Rock Star* newspaper office contains the **STAR GAZER SEES MARTIANS** paper from the day before so apparently it's not a daily.

There was a return to the Stage 19 Sheriff's Office set on.... Friday the 13th. *Un*true to its portentous reputation, this was a *lucky* day for Kathleen Hughes: The Universal contractee had implored her bosses to let her strut her sexy stuff in the small role of Jane, George's buxom girlfriend who reports his disappearance to the sheriff, and she got her way. Notice that as the scene starts, she's passing the time by doing a little light reading: the sheriff's wanted posters!

In our 2000 interview, Hughes said,

I heard that Universal was going to do their first 3-D movie, *It Came from Outer Space*, so I got hold of the script. I'd already heard that Barbara Rush and Richard Carlson were doing the leads, and so I looked through the script to see if there was anything *I* could play and I found this little part. I thought that would be fun. So I went to the front office and I said, "*I* want to play that part"—and *they* said, "This role is much too small. You just played a second lead in *Sally and Saint Anne* [1952]. You need to do bigger parts." I said, "It's in *3-D*. How can it be too small? It's in *3-D*. Please, please, pleeeease!" I just begged and begged and begged. And then they used me to test the 3-D cameras—because I was so three-dimensional [*laughs*]! They had me in a bathing suit, parading up and down on a little platform—that's how they tested their cameras. And that's why there's a clip of me [in the end credits] of *It Came from Outer Space* in a bathing suit—that was from the camera test. So I was glad that I had done that, because it gave me some extra footage!

In 1953, Hughes told Hollywood columnist Emily Belser:

I had played so many small parts as sweet nothings and gotten nowhere that even my uncle [F. Hugh Herbert] told me to get out of the business. Then I landed this sexy bit,

Outer Space's Sheriff's Office scenes were shot on two sets, one on Stage 19 and the other (pictured) behind a façade on Courthouse Square, with outdoor extras and cars visible through the window as they pass. In 1958, producer-director Bert I. Gordon used this set, again as a sheriff's office, in *Earth vs the Spider*. (Photograph courtesy Ronald V. Borst/Hollywood Movie Posters.)

and convinced 'em I could sizzle as well as simmer. ... I never knew I had it in me until Paul Henreid said he thought I could do it [in his movie *For Men Only*, 1952] if I'd bleach my hair. I did and started studying the cats and there you are!

Interviewed in 1953, sexy Kathleen Hughes (front and center) said of her *Outer Space* role, "It's difficult to say exactly how I found out how to play a role like this, but I have four cats—alley cats—all of which I observe closely." From left: Virginia Mullen, Hughes, Charles Drake, Richard Carlson, Barbara Rush. (Photograph courtesy Ronald V. Borst/Hollywood Movie Posters.)

Hughes told me that the only downside to landing the role was finding out that Richard Carlson, on whom she'd had a crush since she was a little girl,

was *not* a very nice person! No, he wasn't! Although we didn't work together, I kind of hung around the set of *It Came from Outer Space* to get to know him, because I *had* admired him so much. But the more I got to know him [*sigh*] ... the less I *liked* him! ... Oh, he just told terrible stories. I don't want to go into it, but in talking to him, the things that he told I just didn't *like*. They were stories that a not-very-nice person would tell [about] other actors ... stuff that I would have just as soon *not* heard.

Read more about her experiences with Carlson in this book's companion volume *The Creature Chronicles*.

Tall (5'9"), slender Hughes in her form-fitting skirt and blouse "drew a lot of attention with her outstanding charms in *It Came from Outer Space*" (columnist Bob Thomas). *Variety*'s Brog surmised that she was cast "to show that sticks and stones are not the only things that can be projected into the auditorium." After a May 4 sneak preview, an audience member filling out his preview card put it less coyly: "Man, is that Kathleen stacked!!" According to *The Hollywood Reporter*, Hughes was given a co-starring role in *The Glass Web* (1953), another Jack Arnold-directed 3-D, on the strength of her *Outer Space* performance. The *Glass Web* poster called her "That 3-D sensation of *It Came from Outer Space*."

Also featured in this scene is actress Virginia Mullen as Frank's wife, reporting *her* man missing. In the history of *It Came from Outer Space* screenings, Mullen, weepy and misery-worn, has never taken a single male eye off of Hughes. Soon Mullen would have more to weep about: Two months after shooting this scene, she was one of the 13 movie-related people questioned by the House Un-American Activities Committee during their latest whistle stop visit to La-La Land. She told them that since age six, acting was her chosen profession: "It has been a rather sporadic career. For the last 15 years, I have been both mother and father to two very fine sons and this has necessitated my taking numerous jobs that I don't think you would want to be bored with all the details of. For the last five years, however, I have worked as an actress in motion pictures, a character actress, a very unimportant one." Asked to name a few of her movies, she said she wouldn't, for fear that the American Legion would picket them. After failing to respond to a second question, she spoke of watching a recent TV program in which

a gentleman spoke of people like myself as hiding behind all the hogwash of the Constitution. To me it is not hogwash. That is a document that guarantees to me the freedom to worship where I please, to read what I please, and to think what I please, and it is my understanding that Congress may make no laws abridging those freedoms. Then there is that other amendment that says you cannot force me by rack or thumbscrew, or any other method, to bear witness against myself, the right to silence. Sir, gentlemen, I do choose to remain silent.

More questions from the investigators, more dummying-up by Mullen, with the actress at one point adding,

I am going to decline to answer the question. I am fully aware of the consequences of my declination. But Christ said that man cannot live by bread alone; and I hope that this will be a strength to me in the coming period when I am not permitted to earn the bread for my sons.

Mullen was a close associate, presumably a friend of William Alland; they worked together on the Peabody Award-winning radio series *Doorway to Life*, a child psychology show, and co-wrote at least one teleplay; also, she's in Alland's *Outer Space* and his 1952 films *The Treasure of Lost Canyon* and *The Raiders*. And according to Alland, it was she who got him to become a Communist Party member.

True to Mullen's prediction, 1953 appears to have been the end of the road (and the end of the bread) for her as an actress. Alland appeared before HUAC in a November 23, 1953, executive hearing and talked about his days as a member of the Communist Party. When he named names, Virginia Mullen was one of them, but she was already yesteryear's news to the HUAC folks so presumably no harm was done. I'd like to think *all* the names he gave them had already been named, i.e., he tried to give HUAC the impression he wanted to be fully compliant while at the same time giving them no (pardon the pun) Red meat. Another person he fingered was actor and radio writer Stanley Waxman, the treacherous Dr. Harding of *Zombies of the Stratosphere* (1952). Like Mullen, Waxman had long ago been sought out and interrogated by the committee.

Alland told me that he testified because Universal head of production Edward Muhl summoned him into his office and said, "Bill, we *love* you, but I have to tell you, if you don't cooperate with that committee, you're through!" Describing his testimony to me as "not very revealing," Alland encouraged me to get a transcript through the Freedom of Information act because he wanted me to *know* he hadn't done any singing; I never did seek out a transcript.[11] Because Alland spoke before the committee, he is nowadays vilified by a few Monster Kid fanboys who know in their heart of lion's hearts that if they'd been in that situation, they'd have told the committee where to get off, and so powerfully that committee members' heads would have hung low in contrition, so why didn't Alland (*et al.*) do the same? Some people must find self-delusion to be a lovely path to contentment.

After Hughes and Mullen were dismissed from the Sheriff's Office set at 4:10 p.m., shooting continued with the scene of Putnam struggling to convince Warren that space visitors are taking the form of abducted locals. Here Putnam is breaking his promise to Glob Frank ("I want to *help* you"), endangering the captives (Glob Frank: "Your friends are alive; they will not be harmed if you do as we say") and perhaps the whole Earth. And he blabs to the sheriff for no reason other than, like a child, he's busting with the news. By impulsively spilling the beans to Warren, who'd never have suspected the truth on his own, Putnam puts the law enforcer in an impossible situation; we can "thank" Loose Lips Putnam for all the climactic chaos. In the finale, as Putnam makes his all-wise speech with The Girl hanging on his arm and his every word, it's easy to forget that by betraying the Globs, he was responsible for the destruction of Glob Frank and Glob Ellen—in fact, killing the latter himself.[12]

On Valentine's Day, Saturday the 14th, the moviemakers worked at the lot's Gausman Gulch, shooting scenes in and around the Excelsior Mine (miners Sam and Toby investigating a noise, Putnam approaching the entrance in pursuit of Glob Ellen, Putnam running out of the mine along with the alien abductees and then dynamiting the entrance, the sheriff and his posse arriving on the scene, etc.). Monday brought the troupe to Sierra Canyon to shoot part of the suspenseful scene in which Putnam explores the smoldering crater. It's like a descent into Hell as he warily makes his way down the slope; burns his hand by touching a boulder; is riveted with awe as clearing smoke reveals the open spaceship hatch; examines the Glob trail; and runs for his life as falling earth indicates the imminent crater wall collapse. All the rocks dropping and bouncing toward Richard Carlson were no doubt made of cork or some other light material.

Sierra Canyon shooting continued on the 17th, starting with day-for-night footage of Putnam, perched on the crater lip formation, describing the now-buried spaceship to Ellen and Pete. Next came the crater scene with Putnam, Dr. Snell (George Eldredge) and Snell's young assistant Bob (Brad Jackson). According to *Los*

At the finale, when Putnam says, "It wasn't the right time for [Earthmen and the aliens] to meet," one hopes that he's sufficiently self-aware to know that *this* time, *he* was the whole problem. The only reason things ever got ugly was that, on the night of the spaceship crash, the Globs had their Close Encounter of the Nerd Kind with Putnam. From left: Barbara Rush, Richard Carlson, Charles Drake.

Angeles Times columnist Edwin Schallert (February 6, 1953), Jackson—future star of Roger Corman's *The Saga of the Viking Women and Their Voyage to the Waters of the Great Sea Serpent* (1957)—had been brought to Universal's attention by Shelley Winters and was making his debut in *Outer Space*. In the movie, Jackson's character calls John Putnam "odd," but his *Viking Women* co-star Jay Sayer told me that in real life, Jackson was the odd one. "He thought he was the reincarnation of Rudolph Valentino, and he talked about himself in the third person: 'Brad Jackson can't do this because it would interfere with his career,' 'Brad Jackson can't eat this food because it's not healthy for his body' and so on."

"He was *really* into reincarnation—he was into *all* that really occult stuff," said Kenny Miller, who appeared with Jackson in the supernatural drama *The Search for Bridey Murphy* (1956). "In fact, he was so spooky about it, that's one of the reasons people wouldn't *hire* him. He was a great-lookin' guy and a good actor, but he was so involved in that kind of stuff." Jackson died in 2009 at age 80.

Putnam (Richard Carlson) holds the Globs at gunpoint in the mine basin. Standing next to him is Glob Putnam, played in the movie by Carlson (via split screen) but in this photograph by ... who knows? Probably Carlson's stand-in. Also pictured, going counterclockwise: George Selk in overalls, Warren MacGregor, George Eldredge, Brad Jackson, Russell Johnson, Edgar Dearing. (Photograph courtesy John Antosiewicz.)

According to *Variety*, Richard Carlson, dismissed that day at 4:55, planned to then fly to San Diego to make four radio and TV appearances to plug *The Magnetic Monster* (opening in that area the next day) and fly home that same night. He was on the *Outer Space* set at 8:30 the next morning.

On the 18th, the company went back to Stage 19, work beginning with the filming of the alley confrontation between Putnam and Globs Frank and George. The alley is pretty obviously an interior set, which blunts the scene's effectiveness. Then back onto the Sheriff's Office set for shots for two different parts of the movie, one of them the scene where a Glob phones with news of Ellen's abduction. Notice that as the sheriff answers the phone, onlooker Putnam has his pipe upside down in his mouth; it's also upside down when Pete's helicopter brings Putnam and Ellen back to the airport. Surely there's a good reason for pipe smokers to do this, but that doesn't make Putnam look any less ridiculous at these moments.

That night, Arnold and key personnel inspected two important Stage 12 sets, the elaborate Exterior Desert and the mine basin where Glob Putnam supervises last-minute spaceship repairs. The latter set was utilized the very next day, with Arnold and his crew contending with the task of shooting split-screen 3-D shots of Putnam arguing with Glob Putnam, the latter activating the power machine with an eye toward mass destruction. While in *reel* life Putnam talks Glob Putnam out of it, in real life there *was* a "detonation" on the set: As electrician Lloyd Hill made a connection, a short circuit burned spots in his shirt and jacket and chipped a lens in his eyeglasses.

For this mine basin scene, footage of Carlson as Putnam was shot first and then, in the tail end of the afternoon, the footage of Carlson as Glob Putnam. (The script differentiates between the two by calling Glob Putnam "Putnam's Figure.") In between, Carlson underwent a "makeup change" that took 26 minutes—no doubt the gray Glob makeup mentioned earlier by Russell Johnson. I don't know about you but to me Putnam, Frank, George, etc., look about the same, makeup-wise, as their Glob replicants. Glob Putnam's power machine was previously seen as Queen Allura's Visor Screen in the same-year *Abbott and Costello Go to Mars*.

A second unit crew equipped with a fog machine and a wind machine started the day in Sierra Canyon filming odds and ends: Putnam p.o.v. shots of a Glob trail, a shot from Ellen and Pete's p.o.v. as Putnam descends into the crater through fast-blowing smoke, etc. The latter was photographed during the first unit's lunch break so it might be Carlson in this shot ... but probably not. The second unit crew then moved to a "Sepulveda location" for a variety of shots of a girl (presumably Barbara Rush) driving a car. Scene numbers on the production report indicate that these shots were to be featured at the very start of the movie (Ellen en route to Putnam's house, perhaps?); they were not used.

As mentioned above, Richard Carlson said in *Photon*

that Universal wanted to get *Outer Space* into release ahead of *House of Wax*—but on February 20 the Vincent Price movie wrapped, and *Outer Space* still had a ways to go. On the 20th, the filmmakers continued with the mine basin scene *and* began the climactic mine exterior scene, which meant that pretty much the whole cast, top to bottom, worked, not to mention stand-ins and extras. The day began with the basin scene, including Glob Putnam's activation of the power machine. Photographed but not used: a shot of Putnam and the released hostages, in the tunnel and headed for the egress, joining hands after Putnam's flashlight dies.

Then came the Stage 12 "exterior" in which the characters react to the "earthquake" and the spaceship blast-off, with Putnam prophesizing that the strangers from outer space will return. It's an uplifting soliloquy, and much better without the tag called for in the script: There, when Putnam finishes his feel-good speech ("But there'll be other nights, and other stars to watch. They'll be back…"), newspaperman Loring shrugs and walks up to the camera, blotting out the others behind him. Looking right into the camera and talking to *us*, he delivers the *non sequitur* line, "Whatever it is, you'll read about it … tomorrow." With that, he moves aside, revealing Putnam and Ellen locked in an embrace. Now the script calls for this final shot, superimposed over Putnam and Ellen:

[The crater,] steaming as in the beginning … a mist-like smoke rising from the pit of it.… Ellen and Putnam are off now.… The wind blows.… We hear the faint playing of the harp … a whisper … then out of the crater something starts upward and at us.… It becomes:

THE END

The February 21, 1953, *Harrison's Reports* cited "the phenomenal grosses" currently being piled up by the first commercial 3-D feature *Bwana Devil* and said that it was almost impossible to keep up with the announcements of pictures to be produced in the 3-D process, guesstimating the number at about 30. On that date, Arnold's company was back on Stage 12, shooting on the Exterior Desert set. Stage 12 was not only the largest soundstage on the Universal lot but one of the largest in the world, then and now. Keep in mind as you watch the *Outer Space* desert-exteriors-that-are-really-*in*teriors that if you were on that "desert" in 1953 in the Time Machine, you could travel back 12 years and be in *The Wolf Man*'s foggy forest. Go back another six years to visit the *Bride of Frankenstein* laboratory, or another four to see *Frankenstein*'s. Then one more year to soak up the atmosphere in Castle Dracula and Carfax Abbey. Go back two more years and watch the stage being constructed for the 1929 film *Broadway*.

The scenes shot on that set on Saturday the 21st: Putnam and Ellen discovering the abandoned phone company truck (with blood on the door) and following a Glob trail into the desert; a Glob George p.o.v. shot as he creeps up behind them and touches Ellen's shoulder (in one take, Barbara Rush was draped in black velvet); the conversation between Putnam, Ellen and Glob George; and Putnam spotting an arm and hand, extending from behind a large rock. On Monday, more of the Putnam-Ellen-Glob George scene was filmed, plus the scene of Glob George addressing the just-waking, dumbfounded Frank and George (which included split-screen shots). To go from Glob George to George, Russell Johnson underwent a late morning makeup change (17 minutes). In the afternoon, Charles Drake's sheriff joined Putnam and Ellen in searching for Frank's body.

That same day, the entire width of the country away, *The New York Times*' Thomas M. Pryor told readers:

Universal-International is in the market for an actress who would like to play a vampire, perhaps in three dimensions. The studio has a suitable story property

A great shot of the Stage 12 desert set (notice the mountains painted on the backdrop on the right). The set builders installed telephone poles that were full-size (or close) and then, to make the set look even more vast, smaller and smaller ones down the road, the last pole six feet or less. Then, painted on the backdrop, there were still more dwindling-in-size poles. William Alland called this set "remarkable, it worked like a charm, and it was very cheap to do." (Photograph courtesy Robert Skotak.)

in *Carmilla*, a novel by Sheridan Le Fanu, in which the heroine, if such she may be called, comes out of her grave in the dark of night, kills a couple of unsuspecting persons and then sets out to get revenge on a few of her one-time lovers. ... [Producer Ross Hunter] is on the hunt for an actress to take over where Bela Lugosi left off some time ago in the Dracula type high jinks. [Read more about *Carmilla* in the *Black Castle* chapter.]

Needless to say to readers of this book, Universal did not make *Carmilla*. With the success of *Outer Space* and *Creature from the Black Lagoon*, it was time for Universal Horror standbys Dracula, Frankenstein and all their kith and kin to get their gold watches and retirement dinners. On the Phantom Stage, one would like to think.

> Gone are the monsters known of yore, the strange old-fashioned creatures
> Like Dracula and Frankenstein with fierce and ugly features.
> With interstellar films on tap, a change has taken place—
> The monster on the screen today must come from outer space.
>
> —George E. Phair, "Retakes," *Variety*, September 16, 1953

Director Arnold used three Stage 12 sets on February 24:

• the Exterior Mine Entrance and Interior Mine Shaft sets, where (among other shots) he got "Glob's Point of View" shots of miners Toby and Sam reacting in terror;

• the mine basin set, with Ellen stepping out of the ship and giving Glob Putnam a leery look;

• and Exterior Desert shots a-plenty: miner Tom and his balking mule; various Glob's-eye-view shots of Tom reacting and getting Globbed; Putnam (again) doing his movie-ending "They'll be back..." spiel; and Frank on the phone pole, talking about hearing strange sounds over the wires.

No fan could be faulted for finding the abovementioned "wind in the wires" scene the best in the movie. It's certainly Joe Sawyer's best scene as his linesman Frank, with "a mystic expression in his eyes" (script description), muses about the mysteries of the desert. "Phantom of the Movies" Joe Kane wrote that *Outer Space* "relies more on atmosphere and mood than on cheap thrills to weave its cinematic spell," and Sawyer's expertly delivered speech could be used as Exhibit A.

"Joe Sawyer was the *best*," Russell Johnson told me with much enthusiasm. He continued:

He started in films in the late '20s or the very early '30s, he was in films for years and, God, he was a real fine film actor. *And*, a great influence on people on the set: He was a happy guy, and that showed, and he could tell stories starting in the morning and never repeat himself all day, about his experiences in the film industry. After we made [*It Came from Outer Space*], I used to watch for him in the old movies on television, and I'd see him a lot. He was a great character actor and he was wonderful and I had great admiration for him.

Joe Sawyer, seen here as Frank (or is it Glob Frank?), was a footballer, well-paid to play for various colleges, before he gravitated to Hollywood and studied drama at the Pasadena Playhouse. He then tackled a couple hundred movie roles big and small. (Photograph courtesy Ronald V. Borst/Hollywood Movie Posters.)

Sawyer (real surname: Sauers) was born in Ontario in 1901 but raised from childhood in the U.S. There are only two genre movies on his entire film list but they're both "cherce": *It Came from Outer Space*, one of the best sci-fi pictures of the '50s, and Boris Karloff's *The Walking Dead* (1936), one of the best horror pictures of the '30s. In 1954, he landed a regular part on *The Adventures of Rin-Tin-Tin*, a boy-and-his-dog Western TV series. (Early in that show's run, *Variety* reported that Sawyer had a sideline job "building a sub-division at Santa Paula, has 18 homes up"—and that *Rin-Tin-Tin* star James Brown, who had a redwood fence company, was putting up the fences!) Sawyer's first wife was actress Jeane Wood (which made him the son-in-law of director Sam Wood); after this brief union, he married June Golden, the love of his life. Her 1960 leukemia death rocked him, and he turned his back on the biz. He eventually retired to Ashland, Oregon, and died at Ashland Community Hospital from liver cancer at 81. He had three sons and a daughter, Patty Sauers, who played a few small movie parts in the '70s.

Work ended on the 24th with shots of Frank and George in the cab of their truck, Glob smoke enveloping them. In at least one of the takes, Frank got out of the truck, raised a wrench and reacted to being hit. On the 25th, there were more Exterior Desert shots of Putnam, Ellen and the sheriff looking for Frank's body, and then the night scene where Putnam and Ellen (in their car) see the Glob, skid to a stop, turn on the car's spotlight, and mistake a Joshua tree for the monster. The last shot of that scene, as described on the Daily Production Report:

> **Glob's Point of View to car—John & Ellen get in car drive out [camera left] as [camera pans left] to see car in far [background]...**

If the movie had been made as the final draft script specified, black mist would have begun to fill Frank and George's (Joe Sawyer, left, Russell Johnson) truck as the prelude to their abduction.

By the time the camera pans left, the real car is no longer on the road. The "car" we see in the distance is actually a miniature, probably right up against the backdrop. The use of a miniature car makes the set look bigger than it is.

More Exterior Desert shooting the next day, the 26th: the middle-of-the-night scene of Putnam and Warren arriving at the spot designated by the Glob phone caller; the early morning scene of Putnam returning by foot to that spot ("I *saw* them, Matt! I saw them as they really are!"); and the scene where Putnam and Ellen return to the Joshua tree by daylight to search for clues. "[The desert is] alive and waiting for you," Putnam menacingly murmurs to Ellen, a smug, half-mad look on his face. "Ready to *kill* ya if ya go too far. The sun'll get ya, or the cold at night. A thousand ways the desert can kill..." Putnam delivers this speech in his spookiest "Halloween story" voice, acting like a 14-karat kook to the point where the scariest thing in the desert, at that particular moment, is *him*. No wonder Sand Rock thinks of him as a weirdo ... and Monster Kid Fandumb embraces him!

Carlson looks a little peaked and drawn in his "A thousand ways the desert can kill..." scene (don't you think?), and that might be because he was getting sick. Viruses, germs, etc.—"the littlest things, which God, in His wisdom, had put upon this Earth"—began to strike the *Outer Space* set, affecting ... no, not the Globs with no resistance to our bacteria, but crew and cast members. The Daily Production Reports don't specifically say it was influenza, but it must have been; in the first quarter of 1953, some states were seeing outbreaks of virus influenza and other respiratory infections nearing epidemic proportions. The Far East and Europe were also in its grip; just for starters, the pope, the king of Belgium and about a third of the people of France were laid low in late January.

> **Hollywood's glamor citizens began to find themselves in new roles—they're being cast in "The Great Flu Epidemic" along with the rest of the nation.**
>
> **...City health officials say the epidemic probably will hit this area in full force next month. But already cameras were grinding to a stop as stars, moviemakers and technicians wobbled home with the flu.**
>
> **The 20th Century-Fox studio was hardest hit with three pictures closed because of illness [Aline Mosby, United Press, January 27, 1953].**

The hospitalization of Jack Benny was a front-page *Los Angeles Times* story on February 23; it was announced that his pre-recorded radio show would be heard as scheduled that weekend, but the plug was pulled on that weekend's episode of his live TV show (an episode that would have spoofed *Dr. Jekyll and Mr. Hyde*). Carlson may have been the first *Outer Space* participant to feel the bite of the flu bug: On the morning of February 27, on Stage 12, after he and Charles Drake resumed shooting the desert scene where they argue about the Globs holding Ellen, there was a 40-minute-plus interruption as Carlson went to the studio hospital. He was examined and treated by an insurance doctor, returned to the set and shot a bit more of the scene but then, on the doctor's advice, he was sent home. Rearranging the schedule, the company moved to the Process Stage where they shot the night car scene of Ellen forced to brake for Glob Frank in the middle of the desert road. After Glob Frank is in the car, he takes Ellen's hand (those shots were not used).

Carlson returned to Stage 12 the next day, Saturday the 28th, but stand-in Bob Lawson, camera operator Harvey Gould and grip William Woodworth were all M.I.A. due to illness, and sound mixer Andy Anderson, also stricken, went home in mid-morning. The company forged ahead, shooting the scene in Putnam's yard (Putnam and Ellen at the telescope and reacting to the passing meteor) and shots of Putnam, framed in the mine entrance, having his powwow with the unseen Glob in the black-as-blindness tunnel.

Barbara Rush told me,

> **In so many of the films about outer space and the aliens coming, the aliens came to *kill* us. For some reason, they made them killers. And Ray Bradbury thought, as I thought, if these aliens were bright enough to *get* to our planet, they wouldn't want to kill us. They'd be smart people! I had great admiration for Ray Bradbury because he was a wonderful writer.**
>
> **Another movie where the creature doesn't come to kill us is *E.T.* [1982], which I particularly loved. Sweet little Martian [*laughs*]! I thought that was one of the most touching pictures.... I was just weeping at the end! I loved them having the sense to make E.T. welcome. If aliens ever *came*, *I* would welcome them! "How'd you *get* here?" [*Laughs*] "Teach me how you *got* here!"**

On Monday morning, March 2, cast and crew continued shooting the Putnam-Glob mine entrance scene, including the close-up of Putnam reacting with extreme horror to the sight of the space cyclops. A short time later, a section of the mine set collapsed, requiring a half-hour repair job. The Glob voice heard in this scene is Russell Johnson with a bit of reverb.

The rest of the day was devoted to the final-reel mine interior of Putnam and Glob Ellen talking to each other across the chasm; she shoots at him with the ray pipe, and pistol-packing Putnam fires a reply. Well, five replies. Carlson, still sick, was then sent home early.

Joe Sawyer and Russell Johnson worked on the Process Stage on March 3, climbing into a phone truck mock-up for scenes of the two linesmen screeching to a stop after a Glob glides into the road ahead of them. One of the shots taken that day, according to the Daily Production Report:

> **George & Frank in truck as it finishes swerve to side of road—they look around to os [off-screen] Glob—Frank gets out of car with wrench—starts to swing at Glob—is hit—falls out below frame—George cringes back as os Glob starts toward him.**

At the end of the day, they shot Glob Frank's death scene: Joe Sawyer seen through the truck windshield, which was rigged so that it appears that bullets are striking it. On March 4 it was back to Stage 12's Mine Shaft set, completing Putnam and Ellen's cross-chasm handgun vs. ray pipe showdown, and then a move to Stage 9 and the Putnam home interior for the scene of Putnam listening to the radio as a mocking announcer calls him "a young publicity-seeking astronomer." When Ellen opens the door and screams, we see a boy (Whitey Haupt) with an Official *Tom Corbett, Space Cadet* Cosmic Vision Helmet, a Buck Rogers Sonic Ray (a signal flashlight in the shape of a gun) and an annoying high voice. In a *Take One* interview, a scornful Ray Bradbury scoffed that no one would scream that way at a kid in a spaceman outfit: "That's bad direction. Jack Arnold is responsible for that. He should be paddled. I'm sure he's embarrassed whenever he recalls that scene." It turns out that the kid was sent by the sheriff to summon Putnam to his office; doesn't Putnam have a phone?

On a busy March 5, the moviemakers continued with the boy-at-the-door scene, then shot the opening reel's Putnam-Ellen candlelight dinner interlude. Part of that scene was shot through the fireplace, another part with three lit candles in the foreground; according to several sneak preview Comment Cards, this was some of

Putnam (Richard Carlson) is protective of the Globs even after they've abducted seven locals—and then his fiancée (Barbara Rush). As one wisenheimer blogger quipped, "Note to self: If I'm ever elected president, don't appoint Johnny as Head of Homeland Security!" (Photograph courtesy John Antosiewicz.)

Some members of *Outer Space*'s sneak preview audience thought the telescope scene was the 3-D movie's (pardon the pun) *stand-out* moment. Pictured: Richard Carlson, Barbara Rush. (Photograph courtesy John Antosiewicz)

the best 3-D in the movie. Then on Stage 21 they got shots of Putnam, Ellen and Pete in the helicopter plus shots of these three characters, *and* Sheriff Warren and Loring, congregated on the crater rim (Putnam: "There's some kind of a *ship* down there.").

That same day, there was a ghastly accident on the front lot, where second unit director Kenny was shooting day-for-night scenes of helicopter takeoffs and landings. The helicopter had landed and the motor was shut off when property man Carl Lawrence walked into its still-spinning stabilizer rotor. After being treated by the studio hospital's Dr. Gourson, he was taken by ambulance to St. Joseph's Hospital. His jaw and skull were fractured and he lost his right eye. "I *do* remember that, it was a terrible accident," Barbara Rush (who did not witness it) told me. "Oh, gosh, that was awful, awful!"[13] The show must go on: After lunch, Kenny and his crew adjourned to Stage 12 for high shots of Putnam (played by a double) looking down into the mine chasm.

On March 6, Charles Drake's last day on the picture, *Outer Space* continued moving toward completion with the filming of bits and pieces of several scenes on various sets and various stages: Putnam and Ellen rushing into the sheriff's office and trying to enlist his help (Ellen: "You wanted some proof, Matt? Well, maybe we've *got* something for ya now!"); a close-up of Putnam after his alley run-in with Globs Frank and George; Putnam at home listening to the sarcastic radio commentator ("No one has yet turned up any bug-eyed monsters threatening Earth..."); Ellen answering the door at Putnam's and screaming; Putnam coming home to find a Glob trail and an empty clothes closet, etc. Kenny's second unit was doing the same sort of thing on Stage 21: With Joe Sawyer in a truck mock-up in front of a process screen, he filmed Glob George at the wheel of the truck, including footage where projectiles fired from an air gun shatter the candy glass windshield. In the last shot of the day, the camera was stationary as the spaceship hatch opened, then moved forward through blowing smoke and into the opening, panning left onto black velvet.

On Saturday, March 7, Richard Carlson worked with both the first and second units as directors Arnold and Kenny filmed a number of "outdoor" shots on Stages 14 and 21: Putnam and Ellen in his convertible and at the crater; Putnam, Dr. Snell and Bob in the crater; the inside-the-spaceship-looking-out shot of Putnam cautiously approaching as the hatch begins to close; Putnam reacting to the hail of small rocks as the crater avalanche begins.

Principal photography was completed on Monday, March 9.

If you've read these paraphrases of the Daily Production Reports closely, you know that *Outer Space was* made the way the script called for it to be made: with no on-camera monsters. In the movie as we know it today, there are seven sightings:

- Sighting #1: We first see a Glob looming out of the interior darkness of the spaceship (approximately 6:10 on the DVD). The script instead indicated that *in* that darkness we were supposed to see

> the suggestion of moving ... black against black ... whispers ... soft breathing...
>
> Now we hear faintly a strange music, as though the delicate tinkling made by something dropped across the strings of a harp ... (THESE SOUNDS TO BECOME THE IDENTIFYING THEME HEREAFTER.) ... Always, while we do not see specifics, we sense some presence ... a mist, a series of whispering sounds.

- Sighting #2: A Glob drifts onto the dark road ahead of Putnam and Ellen's convertible (18:10). But in the script, Putnam swerves the car and we get a close shot of its windshield "as a 'light'—like an eye through a cloud of mist, grotesque and elongated, stretches across the mirrored glass, then is gone."
- Sighting #3: A Glob drifts onto the road ahead of Frank and George's truck (32:55). But in the script, they gape through the windshield of the moving truck as a thick cloud forms ahead of them, then spirals around like a whirlwind.

"The whirlwind growing taller, larger ... as it moves head on against the truck." Now in a shot of the windshield of the moving truck, we see "the eye—phosphorescent and elongated, mirrored against the glass..." The truck skids to a stop on the soft shoulder, black mist surrounding the vehicle so that to the men inside, it looks like night. After the men sit for a few moments in "terrible silence" in the dark truck, Frank picks up a wrench and George opens the door, black mist rolling into the cab. From the monster's p.o.v. we see Frank get out of the truck and raise the wrench at the camera—but then there's the sound of a thud and he falls.

- Sightings #4 and #5: A Glob (well, actually, just its "arms") engulfs the miners (Tom at 44:20, Sam and Toby a minute later). In the script, there's no "arm," just the black mist creeping at them.
- Sighting #6: A Glob lumbers out of the darkness of the mine shaft toward Putnam (59:10). Viewers get to eyeball the extraterrestrial eyeball for more than ten seconds whereas the script wanted us to have merely a "flash shot" of it.
- Sighting #7: Glob Putnam changes into a Glob (76:30), amidst a Captain Marvel-"Shazam!"-like cloud of white smoke. There's no mention of this shot in the script.

It's almost surprising that the making of *It Came from Outer Space* got *this* far along, at the Studio of Monsters, without a physical monster as part of the proceedings. Inevitably, the decision-makers decreed that it probably should have one: On March 27, 18 days after the movie wrapped, the brass instructed some of their art directors to screen the picture and prepare sketches of their conception of the creatures. According to the minutes of a March 30 executive meeting: "If the art directors come up with something better than the test scenes now in the picture, we will reshoot the footage in which the creatures appear."

"It was my feeling that we should never see the people from outer space," art director Robert Boyle told me. He continued,

> **The studio said, "Well, we *have* to see them because the audience will *expect* to see them," and I said, "No, *never* show these people, just show the effect they have on the characters who *do* see them." I struggled against making it at all, but my arguments were to no avail and I finally gave in because the studio insisted on having scenes in which we saw the creatures from outer space, which I always hated. We did it, and it wasn't very good.**

When I asked Boyle about the attitudes of Alland and Arnold, he admitted, "That was another disappointment. They sort of buckled under the studio's request."

Yes, Alland buckled, but to hear *him* tell it, not right away. He told me it was William Goetz who insisted on a monster, and described how he (Alland) objected to the idea:

> ***I*** **never wanted [audiences] to see what these creatures look like. What I wanted to show was our people taking a look at 'em and they're absolutely appalled and dismayed and they scream and faint—but we don't show the creatures to the audience. What I wanted to convey is that what they look like is *so* beyond anything we can accept that we couldn't have achieved it. But the studio insisted on making [a Glob]. ... I felt that *It Came from Outer Space* was such a good movie, the *concept*, the thematic *idea* was so good, and the special effects in general were so good, that the monster scenes just cheapened it for me.**
>
> **What I did when Universal insisted on a monster was go to a lab and shoot some pictures of amoebas, using an electronic microscope—I wanted it to be a kind of an amoeba creature. Well, Universal didn't want that, so I said, "To hell with it. *You* guys figure out what you want."**

The art directors submitted their sketches and the execs selected two for manufacture and screen-testing.

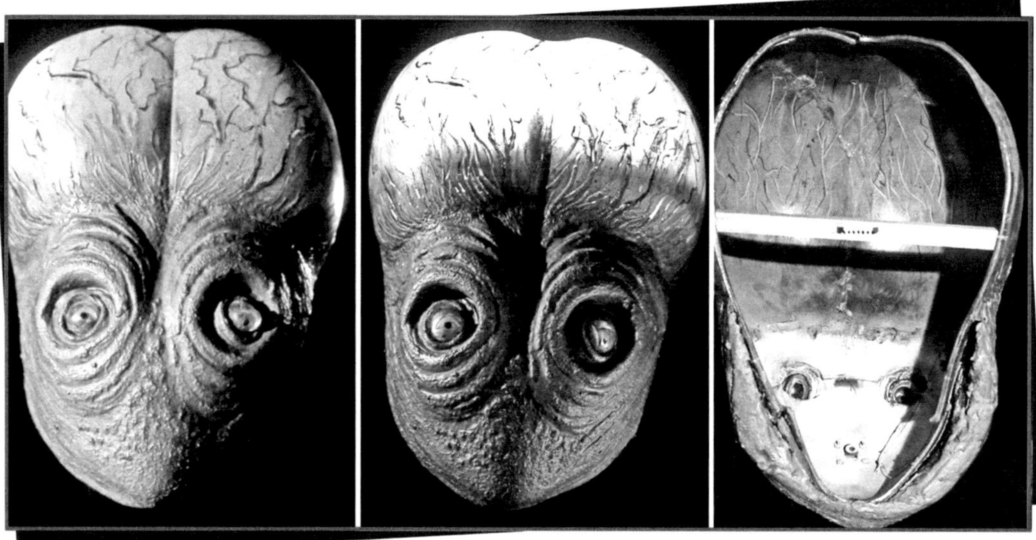

Three shots of Glob #2, taken by Bob Burns once it was part of Monster Kid Bill Malone's collection. Left: Glob #2 "at rest." Middle: The top of the head, resembling an exposed brain, was translucent so that a built-in light would make it glow (as it does in this photo). Also inside the top part was a small fan with colored silk ribbons attached; the fan breeze would make them flutter, and from the outside, this would look like "brain wave activity." Right: Looking into the head from the back.

The two monsters created to "compete" in screen tests were Glob #1, the one-eyed, embryo-like creature eventually seen in the movie, and Glob #2, a large alien head. (Envision the head of *This Island Earth*'s Metaluna Mutant and you'll have a very good idea what Glob #2 looked like: Universal being a studio where *nothing* went to waste, the Metaluna Mutant head was a months-later spin-off of Glob #2.) Boyle told me that, "unfortunately," he worked on Glob #1. (He injected "unfortunately" because, as mentioned above, he was opposed to the movie *having* an on-screen monster.) "We made it out of all kinds of stuff, spun glass, spun sugar, all kinds of odd things, anything to make it look not-human. It was not very big, maybe the size of a big basketball. I've forgotten exactly how it was manipulated, but I think it was suspended by filaments [too fine to show up on film]."

Even before the two monsters were screen-tested, there was an April 6 morning meeting where Alland, Arnold, editorial department head Richard Cahoon and editor Paul Weatherwax discussed the proposed extra scenes and retakes. Below are most of the additions and changes recommended for shooting, as listed on a same-day memo from Ernest Nims, who presumably also attended and contributed:

For the interior spaceship scene:

> Camera starts in the black—dollies past new section interior space ship (to be constructed) onto full shot of the monster, vaguely seen in black background.
>
> An eye effect (through circular lines or white smoke and spun glass around edge of screen) will be used on all scenes throughout the picture from the monster's point of view.

For the scene where a Glob explores the crater:

> A new dolly shot will be photographed—shooting down and following the monster as mica flakes drop to the ground.
>
> NOTE: We will also photograph the same shot, using railroad ties, as the background to be used later as the monster moves out from the darkness of the mine shaft.

To be projected on a process screen for the interior car scene where Putnam and Ellen first see a Glob:

> The camera shooting from behind Putnam and Ellen. We see the monster glide from the desert onto the road.
>
> Full shot of monster from Putnam and Ellen's point of view as it looms into the camera with its eye protruding.

For the Glob George p.o.v. shot where he comes up behind Ellen and touches her shoulder:

> Glob George's (Russ Johnson) hand appears as spun glass and dissolves into human hand as it reaches out to touch Ellen.

To be projected on a process screen for the interior truck scene where Frank and George first see a Glob:

> The camera shooting from behind George and Frank. The monster glides from the desert onto the road.
>
> Full shot of monster from George and Frank's point of view as it looms into the camera with its eye protruding.
>
> George and Frank react to monster off-scene. George opens door from driver's side and is immediately enveloped in spun glass.

For the scene of Glob George talking to the lying-on-the-ground Frank and George:

> Close shot of Glob George speaking new dialogue to other George off-scene.

For the Glob p.o.v. footage where the miners are Globbed:

> Prospector reacting to monster and being enveloped by spun glass.
>
> Two miners reacting to monster and being enveloped by spun glass.

For the scene where Glob Frank gets into the car with Ellen:

> Interior Ellen's car—close angle. Frank's hand dissolving into spun glass.
>
> Frank's face dissolving into spun glass.

For the scene where the phone truck—and Glob Frank—burn:

> Frank's face dissolving into spun glass.

For the mine scene where Glob Ellen is shot by Putnam:

> Ellen's face dissolving into spun glass.

For the mine scene where Putnam calls upon the Glob to come out into the daylight:

> Monster appears from darkness of the mine and we see his face for the first time.

Jack Arnold said in the German TV interview:

> I wanted no monster at all. I don't think that one can invent anything that comes close to the imagination of the audience, especially in a film like I envisioned it. At the entrance of the mine when [Putnam] says, "Come out! I want to see you!," I did not want the monster to really come out. It should remain vague, shadowy. And I wanted to give him a different voice than the one in which they speak when they assume human form. The gist of the story is this: If something is different from us, then we hate it immediately. And that's still true. That's what was important to me, and not how the alien looks. But [Universal] said, "No, we need something for advertising."
>
> "All right," I said, "then let the special effects people do a few drafts, and I'll decide on one. But I will make a maximum of two cuts, and none longer than a few seconds. I will not dwell on it, I do not want to see how this works, I just want a glimpse."
>
> "Well, let's see."
>
> "That you will," I said. "But you get from me only what I am shooting."
>
> So that was it. Then they came with this great eye that I did not really want. I think in the film you can see it only twice very briefly. [Actually, we see the Globs quite a number of times, as

listed above.] That was for the box office. This allowed them to advertise, with this eye on the posters.[14]

On April 14, the two monsters—Glob #1, the eventual winner, and Glob #2, the Metaluna Mutant-esque head, were the subject of Silent Photographic Effects Tests with Arnold as director. As Boyle mentioned above, Glob #1 was the size of a big basketball; according to Bob Burns, Glob #2 was almost two feet tall and about a foot wide (and greenish in color). The crew included a cameraman named Glassberg, probably Irving Glassberg (*The Strange Door, The Black Castle*, Francis the Talking Mule movies, dozens more). From this point until the end of the last day of production, April 23, all the shooting I will describe took place on Stage 12.

First Glob #1 was featured in a series of shots in which it emerged from the mine darkness. This footage was shot in various ways: double-speed and normal speed, with and without smoke, etc. Late in the afternoon, "life-sized" Glob arms were tested: Russell Johnson was there to climb out of a pickup truck and react to an off-camera Glob before Glob arms encircled him and smoke filled the screen. Bob Burns says that the Glob arms "always reminded me of Sally Rand, who was famous for doing her 'feather fan dance' in the nude." He added that he thought the heavy blasts of white smoke, featured in every "arms scene," were to help hide how the arms were manipulated.

After dinner, Arnold & Co. resumed work with Glob #2 now the focus of attention: In a series of takes, it emerged from the darkness "eyes glowing ... smoking" as the camera filmed it at normal speed and double speed. The company was dismissed at 8:50 that evening.

There was a noon crew call on April 15, the first day of "Retakes." These are some of the extra shots that were filmed:

- A medium close shot of Glob George telling an off-screen George not to be afraid.
- Process plate shots of Glob #1 moving right to left across the roadway amidst smoke. In some shots, its eye protruded; in one shot, it stayed in its socket.
- Shots of Glob #1 for use in the just-after-the-crash spaceship scene. In some takes, its eye protruded.
- Process plate shots of Glob #2 making its smoky right-to-left roadway crossing. In one take, its eyes protruded.
- Shots of Glob #2 for use in the just-after-the-spaceship-crash scene. In one take, its eyes protruded.

The Globs and the human cast and crew worked until 11:26 p.m. At some point overnight or the next morning, it was decided that Glob #2 would get its walking papers and Glob #1 would stay on the payroll: The one-eyed prop was selected to play the title "It." (Or does the title "It" refer to the spaceship?) On the 16th, Glob #1 worked all day: emerging from the mine darkness (in one shot, its eye protruded, in other shots it stayed in), shots where the camera dollies into a close-up of the protruding eye, etc. The workday ended with a trucking insert shot of the Glob's mica trail on the crater floor.

April 17 was "3-D Day" in Los Angeles, the L.A. City Council having unanimously adopted a resolution to proclaim it so, to recognize the "significance of the premiere of *House of Wax*." At Universal, that date marked the return of *Outer Space* cast members Carlson, Rush, Joe Sawyer, Russell Johnson and the three actors who played the miners. Bright and early, the crew got over-the-shoulders shots of Putnam and Ellen in the car as the process plate shot of Glob #1, shot less than 48 hours earlier, was projected onto a screen in front of them. Then the moviemakers did the same for Frank and George in a truck mock-up. The same shot of Glob #1 gliding out onto the road was used both times; notice the identical blast of white vapor from its right side.

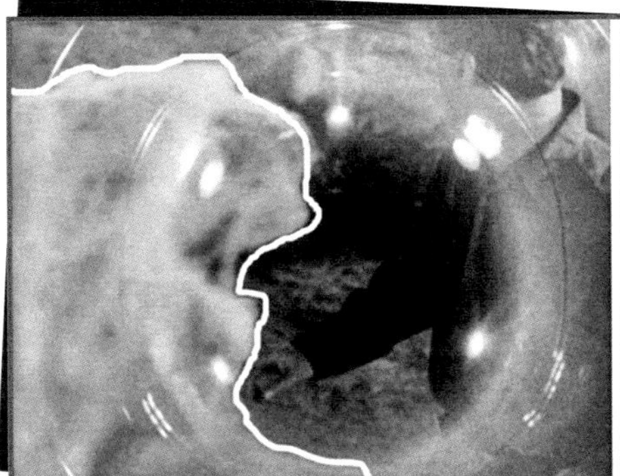

Here, side by side, are two *Outer Space* shots where you see the Glob arms. Kinda. They're outlined in these frame grabs. The Glob eye superimposition and the clouds of white smoke make it very hard to spot arms that almost *look* like white smoke. Russell Johnson is in the image on the left, Edgar Dearing and Warren MacGregor on the right. (Frame grabs and outlining courtesy of Bob Burns.)

The first shot after lunch was a Glob p.o.v. of George climbing out of the truck and reacting with horror to the monster, before Glob arms and smoke envelop him. The next victim of the Glob p.o.v. camera was miner Tom, falling to the ground and getting the Glob-arms-and-smoke treatment; then, in the mine entrance, Toby and Sam.

"ADDED SCENES & RETAKES FINISHED THIS DAY" was typed on the April 17 Daily Production Report—but Carlson and Rush were brought back on April 23 for "Tests and Retakes." This Daily Production Report is missing its

In a 1953 interview, Richard Carlson said that on the *Outer Space* set, the Glob was called Junior. Harry Essex claimed that they called it the Fried Egg. Maybe William Alland (in 1995) came up with the best descriptor: "[That] stupid, furry, whatever-the-hell-it-was." (Photograph courtesy Robert Skotak.)

page or pages of scenes, slates and descriptions (if it ever *had* one) so the only clue as to what was filmed are scene numbers that make it a safe guess that Rush appeared in a retake of the shot of Glob Ellen on the receiving end of Putnam's bullets, and Carlson played Glob Putnam in the mine basin shot where thick white mist rises around him, as he begins to revert to Glob form. On this April 23 production report are the typed words "FINISHED THIS DATE" after 30 days of first unit, 12 days of second unit and four days of retakes.

On May 4, just 11 days after Carlson and Rush appeared in the last of the retakes, *It Came from Outer Space* was sneak-previewed at the Leimart Theatre in Leimart, California. The Leimart was chosen, according to *Variety*, "due to fact it's one of the very few houses in Southern California equipped with four projectors and is thus able to show 3-D pix without an intermission." The "q.t. showing," Hollywood's first 3-D sneak preview, followed the exhibition of Columbia's *The Glass Wall*. According to the preview cards, 53 audience members found the movie Outstanding, 36 Excellent, 55 Very Good, 26 Good and 14 Fair. Carlson was liked best by 159 responders, Rush by 32. Despite having practically no screen time at all, Kathleen Hughes made a healthy showing, tying for third place (with Charles Drake) with 18 votes.

What Scenes Did You Like Most?

I liked the scenes in the mine. When Barbara Rush fires the gun. When they went to see the ship after it struck earth and seeing the open door.

They were all very exciting and held your interest. The meteor flying through space was my favorite. (Beginning picture.)

Love scene at 1st of feature. (Good acting.) Landslide for 3-D aspect was terrific.

When the alien beings showed their true selfs.

When we saw the terrible man from space.

When I saw the monster.

The showing of the Mars Men.

On the patio with the telescope.

The ones where the eye lens engulfs the "victims."

I thought all scenes were outstanding, especially since it was my first 3-D picture. It was quite a thrilling experience for me. I enjoyed it thoroughly.

Got a thrill when a rock flew at me, and also when Ellen Fields shot the light at me.

Scene with telescope coming over audience (seemed to).

When Barbara Rush fired the ray gun I felt as tho it hit my left eye and I felt it for quite awhile afterwards.

Looking through the fireplace at John and Ellen in the first part of the picture....

The scene in the sheriff's office when Kathleen Hughes comes in.

Which Scenes, If Any, Did You Dislike?

None. [Scores of respondents answered "None."]

Only one, when you showed "it" coming out of the mine, it could have been more scary.

None—but the weird music could be softened.

Could have shown the visitors more [longer]. I wanted to see clearly what they looked like.

The scene where Joe [sic] gets shot and the truck burns.

The scene where the candles appear to be in the audience.

The comment cards give the impression that Ellen's screaming (at the Joshua tree, at Glob George's hand on her shoulder, at the space-helmeted boy, at the transformation of Glob Frank) was a source of general irritation. (The first time she *should* have screamed—when the Glob drifted out onto the highway ahead of Putnam's car—she didn't!) Other complaints:

Weird music was too loud and long.

Too much looking thru the eye of monster.

Office scene where George's girl is introduced. George's girl friend too sexy for this type picture.

Constant bickering. Thought C. Drake was no good.

I thought the costume inappropriate for Ellen's double.
The middle got boring.

The question, "Did the picture hold your interest?" brought forth other quibbles, including, "John Putnam as a man of science seemed lacking in ordinary ability to contact any understanding people. He must have been known as a screwball before." In answer to "Were all the story points clear to you?," one respondent wrote, "I was not sure if Putnam sealed the tunnel to trap the Outer Space men or to keep the sheriff from entering." Perhaps as a result of this individual's confusion, release prints included the post-dubbed Putnam line "Hurry up! We've *got* to keep that posse away from 'em!" as miner Sam runs to fetch the bundle of dynamite.

Any Added Comment?

Yes, one. Only ages of 16 and up to see it.
It's the best picture I have ever seen.
It was great. Never saw anything like it.
Terrific. Should make more of these kind of movies—especially Bradbury's.
It was too scarey [sic].
Make your monster clearer next time, please.
The thing could have looked weirder.
I think I personally would of enjoyed it much more if there had been some well-known stars in the picture but it was very good.
In places it could give a person heart failure.

For Barbara Rush, playing Ellen entailed a lot of standing behind Richard Carlson and letting rip with several screams too many. Rush's star rose once she began co-starring in *much* bigger movies (*The Young Lions, The Young Philadelphians, Come Blow Your Horn*, more), so that her presence in *Outer Space* now gives it an extra touch of class.

It was a big night for Jack Arnold all around: His movie was well-received, *and* he left the preview upon getting word that his pregnant wife Betty had been rushed to Cedars of Lebanon hospital. The first of their two daughters, Susan Edith, seven pounds, two ounces, was born on May 5. Susan Arnold went on to work in various capacities in the movies, from actress to casting director to producer of a handful of films, including *Benny & Joon, Grosse Pointe Blank* and the too-terrible-for-words 1999 remake of *The Haunting*.

Variety reviewer Brog got to see *It Came from Outer Space* on May 18 at Universal, "on [the studio's] huge screen in an aspect ratio of 1.85 to 1," and he reported that it "proves one thing. Three-D has been waiting for, and needing, widescreen projection. The big treatment gives it added excitement and completely eliminates the dimishing effect so noticeable in picture size with standard projection." By the time Brog's review ran, a "widescreen" signboard had been installed at Universal to ballyhoo *It Came from Outer Space*; it consisted of five 24-sheet panels, each bearing a single word of the title. Universal also made up, for the first time in its history according to *Variety*, four separate and distinct trailers to plug *Outer Space. Variety* said that there was "a 3-D one to bally the 3-D version; a 2-D plug announcing the 3-D version; a 2-D heralding the 3-D version on a widescreen with stereophonic sound, and a 2-D teaser announcing the 3-D version. P.S.—There will be no trailer exploiting the 2-D version which will also be available."

Outer Space's May 26 "world premiere" was actually a *dual* premiere held at two Hollywood theaters, the Pantages and the RKO Hillstreet. As the date loomed, it took on a feeling of "event" as it would mark the first time 3-D played on a widevision screen, and in stereo to boot. (From various advertisements: "Plus amazing STEREOPHONIC SOUND (3 TIMES MORE REALISTIC)"; "HEAR THE NEW MOVIE MIRACLE OF DIRECTIONAL STEREOPHONIC SOUND (3 times more realistic)"; "AMAZING NEW STEREOPHONIC SOUND ... The Sound Follows the Action.") Wider screens had to be installed at both theaters to accommodate the movie; the Pantages screen was expanded to 23 × 39 and the Hillstreet screen became 22 × 37, both theaters losing about 50 seats on the sides of the screen because of the new set-up. (According to a May 18 *Hollywood Reporter* item, the screen, developed by the studio, was "curved on a 90-degree radius" and coated with aluminum paint "for a light-magnifying factor of 4–1." Whatever that means.) To ballyhoo the coming movie, various people connected with it (Richard Carlson, Barbara Rush, Kathleen Hughes, William Alland, Harry Essex, Jack Arnold) appeared on dozens of television and radio shows; at the time, this local TV-radio campaign was *the* most extensive ever given a Universal feature.

In his German TV interview, Arnold described the premiere as "a typical Hollywood gala, with all the trimmings." There were as many as 60 celebrities at the Pantages, among them Ray Bradbury, Dana Andrews, Rory Calhoun, Yvonne De Carlo, Joel McCrea and his wife Frances Dee, Richard Denning, Anne Francis, Rhonda Fleming, Mitzi Gaynor, Art Linkletter, Marjorie Main, Maureen O'Hara, Edward G. Robinson, Donna Reed, Mickey Rooney, Robert Stack and Shelley Winters. At the RKO Hillstreet, among many others, were Kathleen Hughes, Mr. and Mrs. Russell Johnson, Julie Adams, Susan Cabot, Leslie Caron, Piper Laurie, Lori Nelson, Richard Long, Hugh O'Brian, Mamie Van Doren and Barbara Rush's husband Jeffrey Hunter. According to a *Hollywood Reporter* item from three days before, Universal wanted Carlson and Rush to attend both premieres and had chartered a helicopter (presumably *not* Pete Davis') to carry them from the Pantages roof to the roof of the Hillstreet, an approximately six-minute trip. Rush told me that she did *not* fly from one theater to the next. The Pantages was where Bob Burns saw it for the first time, and in the 2002 David J. Skal documentary *The Universe According to Universal* (a bonus feature on the *Outer Space* DVD) he recalled the experience:

At the *Outer Space* premiere, Edward G. Robinson and wife Gladys prepare for an out-of-this-world 3-D experience. A month later, the actor was in front of Universal's 3-D cameras in director Jack Arnold's *The Glass Web*.

> **It was a perfect 3-D vehicle, 'cause you had *so* many things happening, so many eerie things, and smoke and stuff that could almost come right out of the screen at you. ... It was wonderful.**

More information about the Pantages and Hillstreet world premiere(s), including the fact that the movie had already world-premiered elsewhere, can be found in Dr. Robert J. Kiss' write-up "The Release" below.

Jack Arnold devised a plan to give the Pantages audience even more 3-D than they'd bargained for: He told the German TV interviewer,

> **It occurred to me that we should have some fun. I took my property manager and some people from the team into my confidence. My plan was to build a catapult in the premiere cinema and load it with boulders made of Styrofoam. "We shoot them off when the avalanche comes down," I said. In the film there is the scene where [Putnam] discovers the spaceship and then a rock avalanche comes down that almost buries him. And at the point where the boulders are flying—in 3-D, mind you—I gave the command for the catapult. You could hear the screams, as the spectators were hit by the Styrofoam stones. They believed the rocks came directly from the screen. This gave the film some publicity, and there was a lot of talk about it. People flocked to the cinemas and were very disappointed when no rocks were flying around their ears. We could not set this up every time as we had at the premiere.**

In another telling of the story, Arnold said there were *two* catapults, one on each side of the screen; "You should have heard the screams," he laughed. David S. Horsley also enjoyed himself at a New York showing of *Outer Space*: In an interview conducted by Paul Mandell for the June 1982 *Starlog*, he recalled showing the movie

> **to a press audience, by invitation only, at ten o'clock in the morning. I worked all night long, getting the projectors superimposed, getting the screen in place for the showing the next day. I stood in back of the house [and] what a kick I got out of watching the critics—these sophisticates, you know—ducking and weaving and dodging the flying cork rocks! It was some experience!**

Reviewer Philip K. Scheuer cited the "super-realistic landslide during which—thanks to the Polaroid illusion—the impulse to dodge falling rocks becomes practically irresistible."

The premiere made Universal the first company to have

pictures playing in widescreen on both coasts (their *Thunder Bay* with James Stewart was running in New York). All the hype paid off: *It Came from Outer Space*'s opening day business at the two theaters was approximately $7400, the highest gross for any Universal picture *in* those theaters. A *Hollywood Citizen News* reviewer was impressed with the double premiere but not with *Outer Space* itself, calling its story "the least of the film's assets. … The picture is not nearly so suspenseful as it sounds, and some of the dialogue is incredible even for a weird story." But this was a voice in the wilderness: On July 6, a *Los Angeles Times* article with a New York dateline reported that the thriller had "[l]ines several blocks long of paying customers" and called it "Universal-International's biggest money-maker in many years"—which doesn't sound like it could possibly be correct, but what do I know? Erskine Johnson made the same claim on the movie's behalf, and pointed out, "Hollywood's 3-D boom keeps getting dire, 'it-can't-last' predictions from film industry leaders. But every new depthie hits the box office jackpot."

> It seems as if Universal has succeeded in doing what it set out to do—inspire fear in the hearts, and stomachs, of those who will see *It Came from Outer Space.*
>
> —*Harrison's Reports*, May 23, 1953

A full-page ad in the June 10 *Variety* proclaimed *It Came from Outer Space* "BIG AS 3-D'S BIGGEST" and rolled out the proof:

> **BIGGEST** week in 7 years at Hillstreet and Pantages in Los Angeles!
>
> **BIGGEST** business of any U-I picture in 7 years, Hippodrome in Cleveland!
>
> **BIGGEST** opening in 3 years, Orpheum in Kansas City!
>
> **BIGGEST** business in 2 years, Lafayette in Buffalo!
>
> Third **BIGGEST** business in entire history of Paramount, Syracuse!

In the summer of 1953, columnist Harold Heffernan wrote about the new crop of sci-fi movie monsters:

> **Boris Karloff, Peter Lorre and Bela Lugosi are cute Wampas Baby stars compared to these newly conceived denizens of the film factories. At Universal-International, their newest star is all head, six feet tall and four feet wide. One giant eye centers his vein-networked forehead and ectoplasm oozes out with his every move.**[15]

"*It Came from Outer Space* has got to be one of the top three or four 3-D movies of all time," 3-D historian Bob Furmanek said in *The Universe According to Universal.* "The photography, the story, the performances, the music—everything works together to make it a great film, even flat."

Outer Space's November 25, 1953, Summary of Production Budget reveals that it had total direct charges of $532,400, with studio overhead charges boosting the grand total to $703,570. According to David S. Horsley, who did the special photography for *Outer Space* (and got an on-screen full-card credit as a mark of Universal's appreciation), it made $6.5 million on its original run; who knows if that's true or not. The $1,600,000 it made domestically (U.S. and Canada) earned it a spot on *Variety*'s list of 1953's top grossers, where it was more or less tied with another Universal, the Errol Flynn vehicle *Against All Flags* (an end-of-1952 release). Other movies that made $1,600,000 in 1953: *Mr. Scoutmaster, Never Wave at a WAC, The Stars Are Singing* and *The Stranger Wore a Gun.*

The top-grossers list was headed by Fox's Biblical epic *The Robe* which made between 20 and 30 million domestically. Universal releases topping *Outer Space* were *The Mississippi Gambler* with Tyrone Power ($3,000,000), *Thunder Bay* ($2,400,000), *Ma and Pa Kettle on Vacation* ($2,200,000), *Francis Covers the Big Town* ($1,800,000) and *Desert Legion* with Alan Ladd ($1,650,000).

As an audience-grabber, 3-D went to the dogs fairly quickly, but it was still hot in early 1953 and helped *It Came from Outer Space* land on *Variety*'s list of the year's biggest moneymakers. Other sci-fis on that list: *The Beast from 20,000 Fathoms, The War of the Worlds* and *Abbott and Costello Go to Mars*. Pictured: Barbara Rush and friend.

"*It Came from Outer Space* made a *tremendous* amount of money," Alland told me. "First of all, in spite of the fact that it was in 3-D (which it didn't start out to be!), it did very well. It was then re-released with*out* 3-D, and did even greater. It made a lot of money, considering the thing only cost four or five hundred thousand dollars." (Apparently the movie made Alland a fan of pithy pronouns in his titles: When he was prepping his next sci-fi *Creature from the Black Lagoon*, two of the titles he suggested were *It Came from Out of the Sea* and *It Walks the Sea*.)

"I *always* tried to have an underlying thematic idea in my films," Alland added. He continued,

> **Most of my films, if you'll examine them, have a plea for humanity, for decency. For being *human*, so to speak. ... [*It Came from Outer Space*] certainly did talk about hysteria, paranoia, all these things—that was the whole point. The point was that human beings destroy when they don't understand what the hell they're confronting. Human beings are *so* terrified of the unknown that, instead of facing it, they deny its existence, as we do about what's going on on Earth right now. We're destroying the Earth so fast, it's pathetic, but we won't stand still long enough to face it. We *don't know*—and we don't *want* to know.**
>
> **In a sense, that's what *It Came from Outer Space* is about. The moral of *It Came from Outer Space* is: Don't destroy things just because you don't understand them. Don't try to read evil into what is not understandable. And don't be afraid of the unknown. Those were the points the story was supposed to get across.**

Other Script-to-Screen Changes

• In the movie, after the crash, the spaceship portway opens to reveal the dark interior; all we see is a king-sized apparatus whose flashing lights dim and then go out, leaving the screen black. But in the *script*, "WHAT WE SEE—SHOOTING THROUGH OPEN DOOR—AS DOOR OPENS" is a

> vast expanse of metallic floor space, stretching some two hundred feet in diameter. ... [The floor is] smooth and shiny, almost the texture and characteristics of aluminum. From the ceiling of this massive ship down to the floor, it's almost five stories in height.

The script next describes a gravity-defying "globular mechanism suspended in air by no apparent structural brace." It whirs and pulses irregularly like a giant heart in trouble, "and with every pulsation it emits a glowing light which reveals the high rounded sides of the spaceship." When it stops pulsing, the interior is plunged into darkness—and a Glob starts making its unseen presence felt.

• In the script, as Putnam descends into the crater, a mist-like haze "hugs the ground as though he were walking on clouds..."

• For better or worse, the movie eliminated a number of extremely minor, completely unnecessary characters from the script. After Putnam climbs out of the crater babbling about the spaceship, other townsmen begin to arrive: Sheriff Warren and Loring, as in the movie, *plus* a workman ("I seen it and I heard it ... like splashin' a ball of liquid fire ... then down it goes, BANG!") and a gas station attendant and his customer. Making his first daytime visit to the crater in the movie, Putnam is accosted by reporters Dugan and Lober; in the script, there's a third newsman, Jerriman. Also at the crater is a minister, looking into the pit; "in his eyes a gentleness, a wonderment at 'God's work.'" When he hears a photographer say, "A miracle I tell you! ... That's what it is, a miracle," the minister smiles.

• In the movie, every Glob's-eye-view shot is seen through a superimposure of what looks like a large, perfectly round, watery, twitching eye. If the moviemakers had stuck to the script, every one of the space visitors' p.o.v. shots would have been made recognizable as such by "mist in front of lens" (sometimes accompanied by the visitors' identifying music).

• You get the impression, watching the movie, that Sheriff Warren might have wanted, at some point in his life, maybe even now, to pitch a little woo at Ellen. The script makes his interest in Ellen 100 percent fatherly: He tells Putnam that he knew Ellen's father, before she was born: "He was still a deputy working for me." Charles Drake would have looked too young for the sheriff role if that line had been retained.

• Putnam and Warren seem less friendly in the script, where Putnam calls him "sheriff" instead of "Matt."

• In the movie, Frank's "wind in the wires" speech seems to be just the right length, but in the script the speech (and spooky Frank) wear out their welcome a bit: He *does* sound like he's been out in the sun too long when he goes on to wonder "if some of the snakes and the coyotes and tumbleweeds don't just climb the telephone poles at noon, far off where you can't see them, and listen in on us human beings." Time for another ice-cold wet sponge and your sports drink, Frank!

• After driving around searching for a line tapper, Putnam and Ellen pull over and decide to start looking instead for Frank and George; Putnam makes a U-turn. At this point, the script called for two shots not found in the movie: first, a shooting-through-the-wires helicopter shot of Putnam's car, the copter camera riding along with it as phone poles race by (denoting that a Glob is tailing them). Next there was to have been an insert shot of the speedometer ("jumping—50, 55, 60, 65, 70... The roar of the engine intensified..."). These shots would have added a bit of eeriness *and* excitement to the scene. The copter shot of Putnam's car was not filmed because the car broke down.

• In the Essex screenplay, Glob Tom is a witness to the Globbing of Toby and Sam. As he looks on, we were to have seen him in a medium close shot with stars in the background: "It's a lonely face. It seems lost, the eyes gentle yet frightening."

• Okay, what the heck is the deal with Putnam and Ellen? In the movie's first scene, she's at his house at midnight (the very *idea*!) and they talk about what things will be like when they're married. But then, outside by the telescope, when she obviously wants him to kiss her, he looks like he *wants* to—and then he chickens out. Ellen has a line that indicates that he's a chronic chickener-outer, and the moment passes. This is our "hero," a guy who backs off when his fiancée wants a kiss?

Putnam never does kiss her in the movie, but he does in the script. In the second Putnam's House scene, just before the space-helmeted kid arrives, there's a "moment of enchantment" where, after a lot of buildup, "he grabs her close to him and kisses her. When they break, the two stand there, eyes locked, deeply affected by the impulsive act." The script description of this action creates the impression that these two characters have at last had their first-ever kiss.

• The poor Globs! All they *are* is eyes, and yet they apparently can't see well. The script calls for a Glob p.o.v. shot as the Glob in the mine shaft talks to Putnam, and indicates that Putnam should be seen in extreme close-up, "his features horribly distorted ... the way the [Glob] sees him."

Poor Globs Part Deux: They can travel through outer space, they know how to take the form of Earthlings, they manage to repair their spaceship with stuff stolen from a phone truck and a Nowheresville USA hardware store—these one-eyed marvels can do everything except see their own movie in 3-D!

• There's an upset finish to the Sheriff's Office fistfight when Putnam the egghead astronomer, brainy and "soft" and not brave enough to kiss his own girl, comes out on top over the hard-case lawman. If you think the sheriff's a sore loser in the movie, get a load of what he does in the script: After Putnam hands him back his gun, Warren "slashes out with it, catching Putnam across the face and knocking him to the ground." The Breen Office called this "excessively brutal" and recommended a change, and the action was eliminated.

• For fans of People Getting Burned Alive scenes, there coulda been a doozy in *It Came from Outer Space*: Through Glob Frank's truck's shot-up windshield, and through flames, we might have seen him,

> head back, sprawled grotesquely.... We hear the strange music ... then the SHIMMERING SCREEN ... and through it the change to its original form.... First the features blot out the face taking on the form of something gelatinous ... transparent ... then a hand reaches up into shot as though to cover its face. The hand opens and closes once ... a reaction to its death as the flames cover over the sight of it and cremate it.

• Dodging deadly ray beams, Putnam shoots Glob Ellen right in the mine shaft. As his bullets find their mark, the script wanted us to "hear the sound of something like a delicate mirror being shattered. Then a burst of the strange music as though a cry coming from the creature in Ellen's clothes." She topples into the abyss and into the water. In the movie, Putnam looks down and sees a section of the surface frothing; in the script, he sees only Ellen's dress "floating in the water; then it goes down."

• In the movie, Putnam seals the mine entrance by lighting the fuse on a bundle of dynamite sticks and slinging it into the mine. The script describes different action—and describes it confusingly, as though it was written in haste. As Putnam and the hostages run out of the mine, Putnam grabs a-hold of Sam (whom he calls Tom!) and asks for his help sealing the entrance. Putnam and Sam drag a heavy box out of the mine and empty its contents (dynamite sticks) across the entrance. Then they go outside, where Putnam draws his gun (as if he intends to detonate the dynamite with a bullet) and tells Sam to run for it. Now the script calls for a shot of the hostages running into the arms of the approaching posse men—and by the time we see Putnam again, he's setting off the dynamite with a plunger.

Unlike the actors playing the movie's other "Globbed" characters, Barbara Rush wasn't required to wear the creepy gray Glob makeup: "No, I was made to look quite glamorous, with chiffon and so forth." Pictured: Richard Carlson, Rush.

Script-to-Screen Non-Changes

As mentioned above, Ernest Nims made a number of pre-production script suggestions, many of which were incorporated into the movie. But some of them were not; for example:

• After the scene of Putnam and Ellen, outside Putnam's house, reacting to the "meteor" crash, Nims suggested that they

> cut back to an added scene of Putnam and Ellen. He tells Ellen to get the car ready as he rushes toward the house. Cut to interior of house as Putnam enters to telephone, dials operator and asks to be connected with Dr. Snell at the observatory and dissolve out.

• Nims objected to the script's omission of some of Putnam's night-of-the-crash dialogue (from page 19 of Bradbury's treatment):

> "I thought that I saw some sort of footsteps leading away from the ship. I think it is the most important thing in our lives tonight and tomorrow that this section of Arizona be designated a Sealed Zone by the government until such time as we are certain that no hostile being from another world is free among us."

• He also wanted Bradbury's capper to the wind-in-the-wires scene included in the movie:

> PUTNAM
>
> It's true.
>
> FRANK
>
> What?
>
> PUTNAM
>
> I never thought it was true, never thought it could really happen. The hair on the back of my neck. Just then. It stood up. I felt it move.

• When Putnam searches the alley for Globs Frank and George, Nims wanted a Globs p.o.v. shot:

> Shooting from a dark hallway toward the street. As we see Putnam running into the scene from distance, camera glides back deeper into the hallway, giving the effect of trying to hide from Putnam.

• And in the alley confab between Putnam and Globs Frank and George:

> During this scene cut to a point of view shot from Putnam's angle, showing light beams coming from the eyes of Frank and George in the darkness.

• Nims called for Glob Ellen to die as Bradbury described in his treatment:

> CLOSEUP of Ellen's face. Her mouth opens to scream. The scream changes terribly, from high to a choking, low sound. The face almost splinters. It looks like a smashed windshield, a spiderweb of cracks and shards. It sparkles like luminescent fire. The eyes glow red-hot. The face begins to melt. Her voice melts. "Ah … ah…" she moans….

Marginalia

• *The Man from Planet X, The Day the Earth Stood Still,* etc., depicted men from space as anything but war-like—and at the same time, so did the bush pilot whose 1947 report of sighting a formation of flying saucers sparked the whole craze. In a 1952 interview, 37-year-old Kenneth Arnold of Boise, Idaho, presented his new contention that flying saucers are actually "a living, thinking creature" that inhabits the stratosphere, and no menace at all. "They are some kind of living force," he told his interviewer, columnist Inez Robb. "They can more or less change their density at will." Given that this interview was published in August 1952, right at the time when *It Came from Outer Space* was first being proposed, one has to wonder if William Alland read it and was intrigued by its assertion that we have nothing to fear from extraterrestrials but fear itself.

• In the 1950s, Alland was the first Universal producer to make a (straight, non-comedic) sci-fi movie—but he came this close to being the second. In the spring of 1952, as Paramount's George Pal put finishing touches on *The War of the Worlds*, Pal announced his plan to produce *Conquest of Space*, about the construction of a satellite in outer space. At the same time, Universal producer Aaron Rosenberg had the idea for an identical picture, *Space Island*, and according to *Variety* was having William D. Powell (the son of actor William Powell) develop the storyline. Rosenberg planned to shoot it later that year (1952), but it never happened.

• Ray Bradbury may have been a little bit of a big deal in some literary circles in 1952 but apparently he wasn't on Hollywood's radar: In the trade papers, enough *Outer Space* announcements misspell his name Bradberry that it seems likely the error began in a Universal press release. One has to assume that his name was new to the trade paper editors who didn't correct it.

• Gauntlet Publications' 2004 book *It Came from Outer Space* includes Bradbury's previously unpublished 1952 short story "A Matter of Taste," set on a "rain and jungle world" of wise and peaceful seven-foot-tall spiders. Told in first person (first spider?), the yarn is spun by an arachnid who welcomes Earthmen arriving by spaceship, and is perplexed and dismayed by the fear the Earthmen exhibit despite all the spider's reassurances and kindnesses. A number of the ideas that Bradbury cooked up for that story, he reused in *It Came from Outer Space*.

• While Bradbury was turning Alland's story idea into a treatment, Alland was himself putting pen (or typewriter keys) to paper: His three-page document "THE SEA MONSTER" A Story Idea By WILLIAM L. ALLAND is dated October 2, 1952. Over the course of many script drafts, it evolved into *Creature from the Black Lagoon*.

• Someone at Universal floated the notion that *Outer Space* should kick off with a prologue featuring some real-life egghead with a top name in the scientific community. The idea was adopted—but not until three years later, when USC English professor Dr. Frank Baxter dished up a lecture for the kiddie matinee audiences who came to see *The Mole People*.

• *It Came from Outer Space* was in production 30 days. Richard Carlson worked all 30, even when sick. From the time we first hear narrator Putnam's voice right after the main title, he's in almost every scene, with a few obvious exceptions (our visit inside the spaceship, the Globbing of the linesmen and Ellen, a couple more).

After two decades of horror and science fiction movies featuring half-mad and mad-mad scientists, villainous as often as not, Carlson's A-Man in *The Magnetic Monster* and Putnam in *Outer Space* represented a new'n'improved type of monster movie scientist: an intellectual, yes, but also clean-cut, could-be-athletic, a pleasing, "just folks" personality, and sufficiently good-looking that you can see why the leading lady might be interested (and usually is). Putnam was the model for subsequent Universal sci-fi heroes, most of whom would look more natural holding a golf club than a test tube.

Barbara Rush made two '50s sci-fis, one each for the era's top two producers, George Pal (*When Worlds Collide*) and William Alland (*It Came from Outer Space*). For her work in the latter, she was one of the winners of that year's "Most Promising Newcomer—Female" Golden Globe.

• Joking dialogue in the opening scene (Putnam and Ellen at Putnam's house) gives the impression that Putnam doesn't have a lot of money. Or maybe he just poormouths himself to give Ellen that wrong impression: His ride is a hot-off-the-assembly-line Ford Crestline Sunliner, "newest and smartest car under the sun!" and "a 'top-downer's delight'" (vintage car ad).

• I gave an *It Came from Outer Space* DVD to Eduardo Rubio, head tour guide at Arizona's world-famous Meteor Crater, so he could determine the size of the spaceship (from the shot of Putnam outside it) and the size of the crater (one crater visitor describes it as "about 1000 yards around"). I then asked him to tell me what the real effect of the spaceship crash would have been. According to Rubio, extreme heat would have prevented the Glob from leaving its spaceship minutes after the crash; even Putnam couldn't have made a same-night descent into the crater. The dust cloud should have taken weeks or months to lie back down. There'd have been nothing left of the prospectors' Ground Zero mine. And nothing left of the prospectors—in fact, for several miles around, all life—from vegetation on up—would have been wiped out. That would include Sand Rock, just a couple minutes away. And yet in the movie, the surrounding area is completely unaffected; we see a dog (coyote? whatever), a rabbit and an owl lazing at the crater's edge, and later learn that helicopter pilot Pete slept through it all. Lesson learned: In 1952, Ray Bradbury may have been a big fish in the small pond of science fictioneers but, when it came to meteors and impact craters, he didn't know his asteroid from a hole in the ground.

More proof that Bradbury was embarrassingly beyond clueless on the subject: In his *Ground Zero* (*The Atomic Monster*) treatment, Putnam calls the crash-landed spaceship "the biggest meteor that ever hit earth ... a small planet almost." Even the dimmest schoolkid knows that if something that size hit us, it'd be curtains for the whole planet.

• Like 3-D movie directors Andre de Toth and Herbert L. Strock, I don't see in 3-D, so I needed to rely on 3-D restoration expert Greg Kintz to tell me that in the close-up insert shots of the Glob "face" as seen by Putnam and Ellen in his car, and by Frank and George in their truck, its eye very much "pops out" of the screen. And even in long shots of Globs, said Kintz, "in 3-D, especially when viewed in projected 3-D where the 3-D layering is more pronounced on a large screen, it is very clear that the eye protrudes from the body."

• One hopes for the sake of Putnam's wallet that helicopter pilot Pete didn't charge him much for the ride, as they arrive at the crater only five minutes ahead of people from town in their cars.

• *Outer Space* has a few stretches of dialogue that are poetic ... and a few that are pathetic. Exhibit A: As Putnam ducks the avalanche and clambers uphill toward Pete:

PUTNAM: I'm **all right**, Pete! Down here!
PETE: Are ya **all right**?
PUTNAM: Yeah, I'm **all right**.
ELLEN (running into the scene): John! John! Are ya **all right**?

• When Putnam thinks a meteor has crashed, he proclaims, "It's the biggest thing that's ever happened in our time." Dr. Snell isn't quite as impressed. In the crater on the morning after the crash, Snell tells the just-arrived Putnam he's been snooping around for about an hour and Putnam says, "Oh, you've just gotten started then." Snell practically yawns, "Wellll, hardly. *I've* seen enough," like a tourist itching to leave some tired museum. And when we see that day's *Sand Rock Star*, the banner headline **STAR GAZER SEES MARTIANS** and front page story aren't about the "meteor," they're about local loon Putnam's claim that he saw a spaceship! "The biggest thing that's ever happened in our time"—*not*. Even in the Nowheresville town where the crash took place, it wasn't the most newsworthy thing that happened *that day*!

• Bradbury may have drawn on family history in creating some of his *Outer Space* characters. In 1906, his Illinois-based grandfather got gold fever and began investing in mining companies and spending months at a time in the Nevada desert, hoping to strike it rich; he was briefly joined by his teenage son Leonard. Leonard—eventually Ray's father—later became a Power and Light company linesman. Five of the nine Globbed characters in Outer Space are linesmen and miners.

• Just before a Glob slides out into the road in front of Putnam and Ellen's car, and just before a Glob slides in front of Frank and George's truck, and just before Glob Frank steps in front of Ellen in the convertible, there are tracking helicopter shots of each vehicle. These shots, always accompanied by eerie music, give viewers the idea that dematerialized Globs are traveling through the roadside phone lines to catch up with, and overtake, the motorists. This adds a bit more grotesqueness to Frank's "wind in the wires" speech: The implication may be that the strange sounds that come and go on Frank's headphones are dematerialized Globs zipping along the wires, whizzing past that very pole and then disappearing into the distance.

• Speaking of the "wind in the wires" scene: The notion of "Keep *listening to* the skies!" dates back to the end of the 19th century when radio pioneers, assuming that civilizations on other worlds had mastered broadcast technology, tried to intercept their transmissions. At his Colorado radio facility, inventor Nikola Tesla listened for signs of intelligent life in outer space; for years he and others, including Guglielmo Marconi, used to hear sounds that they assumed were from space when actually they were sound waves created by lightning, thousands of miles away. In 1931, Bell Telephone had one of their workers try to figure out what was interfering with trans-Atlantic phone calls. At a New Jersey observation post, the worker turned a large antenna every which way to determine where the noises were emanating from, and couldn't locate them until he turned the antenna *up*—and he came to the conclusion that the strange transmissions were originating in the center of the Milky Way. It turned out that *those* noises had also been produced naturally, but it's interesting that the idea of telephone employees hearing sounds from space over their wires was a real-life occurrence that Bradbury, a kid at the time, may have heard about.

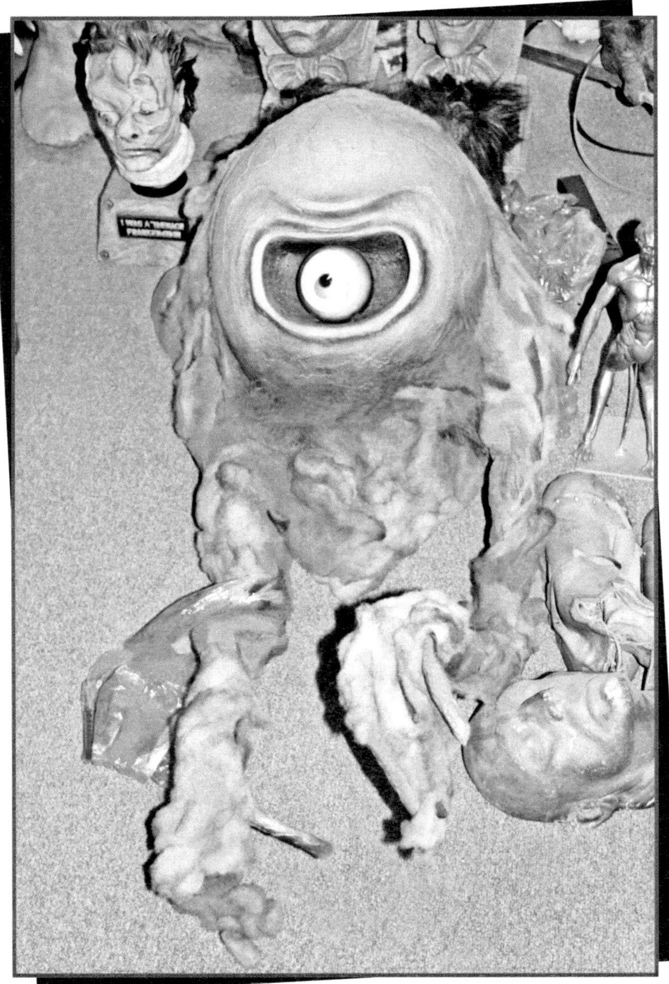

Just for fun, special effects maven Robert Skotak made this Glob replica for Bob Burns' collection. The egg-shaped body was carved out of Styrofoam. The glossy-looking stuff is cellophane, the fluffy stuff is fiberfill (cotton). Skotak didn't want to use angel hair (finely spun glass) as Universal did for the film Glob, since it can give handlers bad cuts. (Photograph courtesy Bob Burns.)

Talk about "identity theft": The Globs, shipwrecked on this island Earth, can replicate humans, starting with Glob George (Russell Johnson, right). Frank (Joe Sawyer) doesn't know it yet but he's next.

• After the first crater scene, why does a Glob pursue and overtake Putnam and Ellen's speeding car? To get a good look at homo sapiens? To eliminate somebody (Putnam) who saw too much? To replicate them? And why, after stopping their car, does It do *nothing?* Maybe Putnam's traveling companions Smith & Wesson had something to do with it.

• John Putnam is a bridge between the men of science in Universal's monster oldies (creepy and/or obsessed) and their boy-next-door, "Tennis, anyone?" scientists of the 1950s (personable, heroic, on the side of the angels). Putnam falls into the second category, but there are traces of the old: He *is* quite single-minded, and considered a kook by his neighbors, and he "loses it" a bit as he rants long and loud at Dr. Snell. Then in his "A thousand ways the desert can kill..." scene, he comes across like a real creep. In that scene he even *looks* creepy, or at least sleep-deprived, as Richard Carlson in real life was ill when he played it.

But after a while, Putnam *should* look a little sleep-deprived. Presumably he was up-and-at-'em all day prior to the movie's opening scene (Putnam and Ellen in his house at midnight); Putnam spends half the night getting to the crater and exploring it; presumably he never gets to bed, because by the time he arrives at the crater the next morning, he's already written the article "Report on the Arrival of Strangers from Outer Space" for Dr. Snell. Then he's up all *that* day, and that night, *and* the whole of the next day. We never once see him yawn when by the end he should be hallucinating, having spasms and starting to lose the power to walk.

• For the benefit of Putnam and Ellen, Glob George explains away the blood on the phone truck by saying, "I cut my hand," and showing them the back of his left hand. A few minutes later, when we see the real George lying on the ground, notice that there's blood on the back of *his* left hand. The Glob duplicate of George is exact right down to George's fresh wound.

• In the alley scene, when Globs Frank and George are in the building talking through the doorway to Putnam outside, notice that the Globs aren't really in a room but (if I'm not mistaken) standing in front of a wall with the upper edges and corners of a room drawn on it. And, adding another subliminal layer of strangeness, their shadows are cast on the wall to the right of them, on the wall to the left of them, and even on the ceiling.

• When Universal makeup department sketch artist and Gill Man designer Milicent Patrick did a *Creature from the Black Lagoon* publicity tour, several of the resultant articles reported that *Outer Space*'s ectoplasmic Globs were partly or solely her creation. In all the articles I've seen, it's the writer who contributes that factoid, it's never part of a Patrick quote, so I don't know if the writers got that from her or from Universal press material. I also don't know if it's true.

• If *Outer Space* viewers know what to look for, they can see the Globs' arms in the Glob p.o.v. shots, as they come in from the sides to scoop in a victim, but they're hard to spot in long shots of the Globs themselves. According to Bob Burns and Greg Kintz, only when watching a 3-D print, and only in the mine entrance scene, do you notice (for a split-second) its arms jutting out at you at the bottom of the frame. Even in head-on photographs of the Glob that feature the arms, you cannot tell that they *are* arms without the third dimension, because they blend in with the rest of the Glob behind them.

• Shed a tear for Glob Frank: In Bradbury's deluxe treatment, he climbs into Ellen's car accompanied by "the cool clear sound of soft bells, and the harp in the wind" (which Ellen hears) and, in response to Ellen's "Where've you been?" he whispers:

> A long ways off, a long ways. And I'm so afraid. And I'm very much alone. And the most important thing now is to go home, just to go home, that's all I want now, to go all the way home away from here.

Thinking he is Frank, Ellen doesn't get his drift, and wants to take him into town. When she continues not getting his drift, he puts his hand on her wrist and she watches it shimmer, watches it change to what looks like a lizard's claw, watches it change to a gelatinous mass (etc.), and surely now realizes that this isn't Frank and that she's in Trouble with a capital T.

In Harry Essex's script, Glob Frank touches Ellen's hand on the steering wheel and we see "a metamorphosis to an icy gelatinous mass, a mist coming out of it—then the clear form of Frank's hand again." This didn't make it to the screen.

• The dimensions of the "average" Glob are hard to gauge—although, since they can take any shape, perhaps they can also take any size. In the final-reel shot where Glob Putnam reverts to its true form, the space creature seems to be nearly double the man's height, which would make it a formidable ten-footer. The mine entrance looks to be nine or ten feet high, and the Glob (barely) gets through it, so *that's* consistent. But Glob p.o.v. shots, looking way down at the terrified George and the miners, create the impression that the Glob's eye is ten feet (or more) in the air, which would make the height of the Glob ... perhaps 20 feet? This larger size is confirmed by our backseat's-eye-view of Globs on the road ahead of Putnam's car and the linesmen's truck, where they look to be two storeys tall. Whether they're ten feet tall or 20, shed a *second* tear for poor Glob Frank, who reassumes Glob form in the passenger seat of Ellen's car where leg room would certainly be a comfort issue!

• First let's acknowledge that the Globs gave telephone linesmen Frank and George a real rough day, day and a half. But would Frank and George have traded places with the linesmen in *The Black Scorpion* (1957)? I think not!

• The Glob replicants of Frank and George aren't very good at acting "human"—on the Sand Rock street, they look like a couple of walking ghosts—but the Glob replicant of Ellen is lithe and lively and is second-to-none in the "haughty looks" department. Glob Ellen somehow also knows what a man wants: To lure Putnam, she wears makeup and earrings and rocks a strapless, low-cut black evening gown with flowing scarf, rather than one of Ellen's usual prim outfits which make her look like *Guys and Dolls*' buttoned-up Sarah Brown of the Save-a-Soul Mission. One wonders if Glob Ellen is a he or a she or if all Globs are Its.

• The dream-like interlude where, by dawn's early light, Putnam chases Glob Ellen over hill and desert dale coulda-shoulda been one of the movie's eerier scenes but it's slightly spoiled by the way it alternates between a real exterior (the Mojave) and Stage 12, with four different players (doubles in the desert, Carlson and Rush on Stage 12). It's easy to tell the difference between the exteriors and the "exterior," and even in long shots it's obvious that the woman in the real desert isn't Rush.

• While watching the Glob lolloping out of the mine, it's difficult not to be reminded of the first Martian's emergence from the rocket cylinder in the *Mercury Theatre* "War of the Worlds" broadcast: With revulsion in his voice, commentator Carl Phillips (played by Frank Readick) attempts a word picture of the loathsome creature, calling it "large as a bear," but ultimately words fail him and he is reduced to describing it as "indescribable."

• Throughout this chapter, I've been painting Putnam as a jerk whose inability to keep secrets causes all the final-reel ruckus. But let's save a little blame for the Globs, too. A Glob makes a **phone call** (keep that in mind) to the sheriff's office, talks to Putnam and tells him to go to a certain spot in the desert; and from there, Glob Ellen leads him to the Excelsior Mine, the Globs' "hideout." *Why* did the Globs allow Putnam to learn the location of their hideout (which he later blabs to the sheriff)? So that a Glob can tell Putnam something it could have told him on the phone!

• Now that we know that the original plan for *Outer Space* was for the Globs to go all but unseen, this begs the *Curse of the Demon*-style question, "Would the movie be more effective if we hadn't seen them?" I think it would have been more effective if *one* Glob had been seen *once*: the Glob in the Excelsior Mine, Humpty Dumpty-ing out into the light at Putnam's insistence, after nearly a full hour of suspenseful build-up. The fact that we see Globs time and again, starting at the six-minute mark, does smack of juvenility.

But to now take the opposite stand, the sight of a 20-foot Glob slithering out of the desert darkness to loom over and scoop up the miners mighta been a highlight of '50s horror, *à la* equivalent scenes in *Tarantula*.

• Who invades Putnam's house and steals his clothes, a Glob or Glob Putnam? Presumably a Glob, since it leaves a Glob trail; but it's hard to picture one of those gents poking around inside a house, exiting with arms full of clothes, and getting them back to the mine. Then again, it's also hard to picture a buck-naked Glob Putnam doing the dirty work.

• Sheriff Warren's "92° speech" was reprised in Bradbury's "Touched with Fire," a short story about two elderly, retired insurance salesmen spying on a hot-tempered, aggressive tenement woman, determined to save her before she provokes her own murder. It was published in 1955, the same year that Bradbury adapted it for *Alfred Hitchcock Presents*' "Shopping for Death," made at Universal. In that episode, Robert H. Harris as one of the salesmen harps on the ramifications of 92°. For this half-hour *Hitchcock* episode, Bradbury was paid $2250, just $750 less than he made on *It Came from Outer Space*.

• The sheriff starts rounding up a posse, and less than two minutes later the posse men are at their roadblock, leveling their guns at Glob Frank's approaching truck. You have to wonder what the sheriff could have told these men in those two minutes (which includes travel time!) about their friend and neighbor Frank that would prompt them to unhesitatingly obey his order to fill the unarmed fellow full of lead.

• Glob Frank is consumed in the burning truck and Glob Ellen drops into the water at the bottom of the mine chasm and dissolves like a year's supply of Bromo-Seltzer. In both cases, no trace is left of the Glob. The movie also makes sure to show us that the their glittering trails disappear without residue. Nothing in the crater backed up Putnam's story of a spaceship crash; probably nothing will back up a report of a spaceship take-off. In months and years to come after the departure of the strangers from outer space, Sand Rock citizens will have some mighty tall tales to tell the world, but not one iota of physical evidence.

• When Glob Ellen points her ray pipe at the camera and fires, a series of balls of light come at the audience in 3-D. But in the next shot, her target, Putnam, is ducking and weaving to avoid being hit by an unbroken line of bright light.

• The most trivial item (by far) in a book packed with trivia: *It Came from Outer Space* takes place over the space of 43 hours. The story starts in Putnam's house as a clock chimes midnight ("Twelve sharp," he tells Ellen). The spaceship flies past and crashes two minutes later, 12:02 a.m. The next-morning scene of Putnam and Ellen arriving at the buzzing-with-activity crater is the start of a day and a half of strange doings, and the spaceship takes off just as it's getting dark. Putnam's opening narration lets us know that the story takes place in early spring. In early spring, the Arizona sun sets at about seven p.m. Voila, 43 hours.

• But if the movie takes place in early spring, why does the sheriff's big page-a-day wall calendar show February 11? Possible answer: An in-use calendar must have been used to dress this set a day or two in advance of the February 13 shooting of this scene.

Twice in the movie, the Globs' glitter trails seem to wait for Putnam (Richard Carlson) to see them, and then immediately vanish.

• A number of members of the sneak preview audience who filled out cards couldn't understand how there could be a Glob Putnam when Putnam wasn't Globducted. My geeky guess is that the Glob hidden in the shadows of the mine later became Glob Putnam, having gotten a good long look at Putnam during their conversation.

• *Outer Space* fans often cite the "fact" that its story was unusual and original for its time in that the aliens don't arrive to take over. Actually, when *Outer Space* premiered, the only previous 1950s E.T. that was antisocial was the Thing from Another World; all the others (X in *The Man from Planet X*, Klaatu in *The Day the Earth Stood Still*, even the Phantom in the nothingburger movie *Phantom from Space* [1953]) were non-hostile. In the 1953 United Press article "Writer Never Rode in Airplane But Spins Tales of Rocket Ships," Ray Bradbury said he was averse to the usual sci-fi movies in which the alien visitors are villains, but as he elaborates upon this point, of course he can name-drop only one (The Thing) because at that time, there was only one. (Could he have been thinking of serials?)

Wise in his or her generation, one member of the *Outer Space* sneak preview audience yawned on a Comment Card, "Story too much like any other Martian picture."

• How big a bang was Glob Putnam fixing to set off with the power machine? It's not specified but Glob Frank's threat "[T]errible things will happen. Things so terrible, you have yet to dream of them" makes us think one-less-planet-in-our-solar-system big. Incidentally, one wonders why the Globs are taking the drastic step of mass suicide and planetary destruction when all they have to do to protect themselves from the posse is re-enter their ship and close the impregnable door. A better question: Why worry about the posse *at all* when it's still quite a ways away and, as we soon see, the spaceship is already repaired and about a minute away from blast-off?

• Starting with Putnam and the sheriff in *It Came from Outer Space*, a succession of Universal sci-fi movies featured two male leads in conflict: Reed and Williams in *Creature from the Black Lagoon*, Exeter and Cal in *This Island Earth*, Matt and Prof. Deemer in *Tarantula*, Barton and Morgan in *The Creature Walks Among Us*. None of the other twosomes is as "chalk and cheese" as Putnam and the sheriff, and yet only in *It Came from Outer Space* are both still alive at the end of the movie.

• The message that most Monster Kids take away from *It Came from Outer Space* is that when a bunch of friendly E.T.s need to pull over on our little shoulder of the intergalactic highway to repair their ride, we fear them only because they don't look like us, and we try to kill them, and the moral is that we'd better clean up our barbarous act. But are we really so bad? In one day, the Globs abduct eight people; there's blood on the phone company truck which, even to Putnam, looks bad. (Putnam to the Glob in the mine: "You've kidnapped and stolen! For all I know, even murdered!") When local law enforcement gets after the perpetrators, nearly a full day after the eighth abduction (hardly a knee-jerk reaction), they're men who have never seen the Globs and therefore are not judging them on their looks; in fact, all but Sheriff Warren are unaware that they might be going after aliens. If the situation was reversed, if eight Globs disappeared in one day on Planet Glob, isn't this what the Globs would do? What's "barbarous" about it?

And the Globs—are they really so friendly? They unnecessarily abduct Ellen; break into Putnam's house and steal his clothes, needlessly sowing the seeds of doubt in the mind of their one protector; the mine entrance Glob says they'll destroy the hostages if they don't get their way; an unprovoked Glob Ellen tries to cut Putnam in half with a ray beam, and Glob Putnam wants to destroy the whole county or the whole state or maybe our whole planet, because *he* resents that *Earthmen* resent eight of our neighbors kidnapped or killed. What's "friendly" about this? Glob Frank says, "We don't want to hurt anyone," and the mine entrance Glob says, "We have souls and minds and we are good," but Glob actions speak louder than Glob words.

• To get a look at Glob #2 (the Metaluna Mutant–like alien head), catch the 1964 *Alfred Hitchcock Hour* episode "The Sign of Satan." It opens with host Hitch standing on a bright, bare, misty set, saying he's doing a "remote broadcast" from Mars and expressing disappointment that the planet has turned out to be uninhabited. At the end, as he does his outro, he is approached from behind by a tall figure wearing a Glob #2 head. In "The Night of the Glowing Corpse," a 1965 *Wild Wild West* episode, Jim West (Robert Conrad) is tailing a femme fatale through the blackness of an amusement park spookhouse when a figure with a Glob #2 head suddenly lights up and lets out a piercing cry, startling him.

Universal picked the correct Glob (the cyclopean Glob #1) for use in *It Came from Outer Space*. When seen on *Hitchcock* and *Wild Wild West*, Glob #2 is supposed to look funny—and it does.

• William Malone, director of *Creature* (1985), *House on Haunted Hill* (1999), *FeardotCom* (2002) and others, told me that he came into possession of Glob #2 around 1970. "A friend of mine came over with it, not knowing what it was and saying that he got it from a guy at the studio—it was being tossed. When I first got it, the eyes were able to protrude or withdraw and there were remnants of color silk ribbon glued to the inside of the dome and a mount for a fan to blow the ribbons around. The head was made of vacuum-formed clear acetate with the lower portion covered in green foam rubber. It was very nicely made." Malone has since sold it to another collector.

• A May 11, 1953, *Los Angeles Daily News* article revealed that, after Glob #1 was photographed for the movie, it was immediately destroyed. According to writer Howard McClay's account, the Glob scenes were shot behind locked doors over the space of ten hours and then the entire crew, "sworn to secrecy about [its] physical appearance" until the movie's debut, were on hand for its cremation in the studio's backlot incinerator. The idea that Universal held an actual

THE NIGHT THE EARTH WILL NEVER FORGET!

Above, a 24 x 82 paper banner for placement over theater entrance doors. The snipe above it (THE NIGHT THE EARTH WILL NEVER FORGET!) came on a separate piece of paper; if the theater was showing *Outer Space* flat, the snipe could be affixed to the banner over the words 3-DIMENSION. (Photograph courtesy 3-D Film Archive.)

ceremony (with the on-the-payroll crew in attendance) sounds silly, and the report of the prop's immediate destruction is hard to believe; what if the film didn't come out or if one more shot was later needed? But the fact remains that Glob #1 has never resurfaced.

• Universal got their money's worth out of the short shot of the spaceship making its flaming arc across the night sky over desert trees and hills. It's used twice at the beginning of the movie, the spaceship going right to left, and twice at the end, the footage flipped to make it go left to right.

• There's no list of cast and crew members at the beginning of *Outer Space*; in an unusual touch for 1953, they appear at the end. The Screen Writers Guild objected to the placement of the writers' credit at the end but must have eventually relented (or Universal ignored their complaint) because that's where they are. Other contemporaneous sci-fis that also saved their credits for the finish: Richard Carlson's *The Magnetic Monster* and W. Lee Wilder's Tedium Trifecta of *Phantom from Space* (1953), *Killers from Space* and *The Snow Creature* (both 1954).

The galling thing about *Outer Space*'s writing credits isn't that they're at the end but that Harry Essex's name on-screen is large, with a small "Story by Ray Bradbury" cowering underneath. Not only *that*, but it appears that Bradbury made $3000 to Essex's $7875.

• *À la* the on-screen credits of *The Black Cat* (1934) and *The Wolf Man* (1941), the names of the *Outer Space* actors are superimposed over shots of each. Some of these shots are flipped, putting the part in Carlson's hair on the other side, putting Charles Drake's badge on the wrong side of his shirt, etc.

• In early April 1953, many weeks before the release of *Outer Space*, Universal placed an ad in the Hollywood trades that included the line, "Filmed in scientifically perfected eye-resting FULL-SEPIA Mono-Color!" But soon afterwards, somebody or other connected with the movie got a look at Columbia's new sepia-and-3-D crime drama *Man in the Dark* in a downtown L.A. theater "and they cancelled their sepia plans for *Outer Space*," said 3-D expert Bob Furmanek. "There was too much loss of light with the polarizing filters and glasses."

• Ray Bradbury was surely thinking back to his short story "A Matter of Taste" when he wrote in a Universal-commissioned *It Came from Outer Space*-related essay,

> Until such time as we can differentiate between outward appearances and the creature in action, we will not be in a position to live peacefully on this world, or be prepared to accept visitors from Mars or any other planet. Before we start looking around to find a large 1000-pound boot with which to step on a nine-foot-tall spider-like arrival from Mars, I think we should ready ourselves to consider whether this is really a spider or an intellect with an I.Q. of 180, peace-loving, and all in all a good-thinking creation of the Lord. We have stepped on too many spiders in the last 2000 years without stopping to look if we were not also stepping on our dreams.

• The shadow of death hangs over the average monster movie, with characters regularly falling victim to the monster(s) or to each other. But except for two of *Outer Space*'s "monsters" (the Globs), no one dies in this movie. Four years later, there'd be no casualties in *The Land Unknown* and *The Incredible Shrinking Man*.

• In his review of *Outer Space*, Philip K. Scheuer irreverently but not inaccurately boiled the picture's premise down to, "Like Abbott and Costello recently, these stellar visitors have landed on the wrong planet."

• On June 2, 1953, with *Outer Space* in release and raking in the dough, Army Archerd wrote in *Variety*, "Bill Goetz is the fair-haired boy at UI. It was he who ordered

Universal went to the trouble of creating the most alien-looking of all Hollywood aliens ... but on the poster it's mundanely represented by what looks exactly like a human eye squirting a giant tear. (Photograph courtesy Bob Furmanek.)

Outer Space into outer dimensions." And on July 2, Archerd made the funny observation, "Jack Arnold is the only director in town who's directed twice as many 3-D's as flatties." (*Girls in the Night* was flat, *It Came from Outer Space* and *The Glass Web* 3-D.)

• After co-writing *Outer Space* and *Creature from the Black Lagoon*, Harry Essex was assigned to write the treatment for yet another Universal "scientification" story, one with the working title *1980*. The October 30, 1953, *Variety* reported that Aaron Rosenberg would produce and that the movie would have as its theme "what the world will be like 30 years hence." Around this same time, an Essex ad in industry trades said he was writing *Electric Man* (perhaps a remake of *Man Made Monster*?) for Universal.

• Universal's *The Monolith Monsters* (1957) may have reused *Outer Space*'s spaceship prop, blurring the image so that the soccer ball pattern isn't visible (in *Monolith*, it *is* supposed to be a meteor). You *can* still kinda-sorta see the tail fin. More likely what we see in *Monolith* is an unused *Outer Space* shot of the plummeting spaceship. *Monolith* does reuse the *Outer Space* shots of the fiery impact.

• In January 1958, the Crest Theatre in Wichita, Kansas, double-billed *It Came from Outer Space* (in 3-D) and *This Island Earth* for a week and grossed over $4000, a very satisfactory take for that house. Universal garnered other dates for the twin-bill in the territory and also prepared *Creature from the Black Lagoon* for a 3-D reissue there (many theaters still had the 3-D projection equipment and glasses). *Variety* quoted a Kansas City Universal exchange manager as saying that many of the patrons were teenagers, "likely a strong factor in the new success of 3-D because many of them did not see it the first time around or were too young to remember it."

• Over the March 29–30, 1958, weekend, Universal protested World Films' registration of the title *It! The Terror from Beyond Space* with the MPAA, insisting that the title of that soon-to-be-released sci-fi actioner was too similar to *It Came from Outer Space*. Universal was particularly concerned as their film was being reissued.

• The *Voyage to the Bottom of the Sea* TV series went all-ahead-flank into Rip-Off Waters with the *It*-derived first-season (black-and-white) episode "The Sky Is Falling." A flying saucer causes worldwide panic (via *The Day the Earth Stood Still* stock footage of Klaatu's spaceship and running crowds) and then purposely plunges into the sea. Once the *Seaview* tracks it down, Admiral Nelson (Richard Basehart) is allowed to board the saucer, where he is confronted by an alien with the face of (yes) Admiral Nelson. "Glob Nelson" says that he has assumed Nelson's form because his real appearance would "offend" Earthmen, and explains that a fuel line rupture has forced this emergency pit stop on our little island in space. Meanwhile, the Sheriff Warren counterpart is aboard *Seaview*; to insure that no audience member fails to discern from Rear Admiral Tobin's (Charles McGraw) attitude and dialogue that he's trigger-happy, his nickname is "Trigger-Happy"! The episode ends with the saucer heading back into space and Nelson expressing the hope that we (mankind) will be wise enough to treat them as friends should they ever return.

• Bradbury's story "The Burning Man" may also prompt readers to recall the Universal movie: On a desert-like patch of road on a broiling mid–July day, a woman and her young

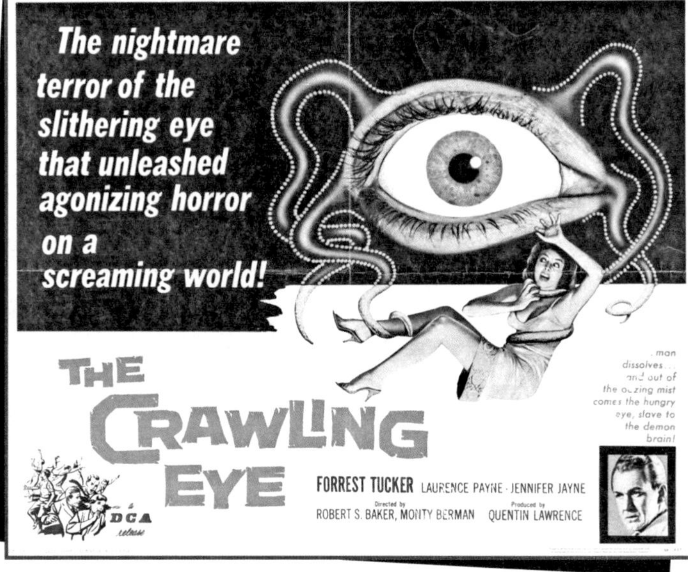

The English sci-fi thriller *The Crawling Eye* (1958) may have been guilty of "borrowing" the Glob look for its monsters. And its poster artist mighta "derived inspiration" from a piece of *Outer Space* art. (*Outer Space* art courtesy Robert Skotak.)

nephew pick up an unkempt hitchhiker who soon begins raving about this'n'that and at one point glares "right up [at the sun] without blinking," *à la* Glob George.

• Based on a 1965 novel by Jerry Sohl, the telemovie *Night Slaves* (1970) also brings back (too many) memories of *It Came from Outer Space*. Husband-and-wife travelers James Franciscus and Lee Grant begin a short stay in a small town where, in the wee hours, Franciscus notices that many of the locals and even Grant have silent, zombie-like get-togethers in the street, climb into open trucks and leave town. It turns out that a spaceship has made our planet the stopover for needed repairs, with the alien in charge each night taking control of the townspeople's minds and making them work on the ship for four hours. Franciscus, unaffected because of a metal plate in his head, infiltrates the group but is confronted by the alien, who is using the body of a local simpleton (Andrew Prine) as a shell. He entreats Franciscus, "I ask you reasonably, stop trying to make others aware of our presence." Leslie Nielsen co-stars as the uniformed local sheriff, understandably hard to convince (*à la* Sheriff Warren) and unaware that he himself is part of the nightly work force.

Sucked into *It Came from Outer Space II*'s crashed spaceship, a boy (Jonathan Carrasco) swims around its interior. Two days before this Sci-Fi Channel movie's "Planetary Premiere," its *New York Daily News* review was titled "Its 2d coming is from hunger."

• Funnily enough, ripoffs like *Night Slaves* were more recognizably based on *Outer Space* than the 1996 Sci-Fi Channel remake *It Came from Outer Space II*. Brian Kerwin stars as a famous still photographer who returns to his desert hometown to find it run-down, populated with geeks, riffraff and dysfunctional types—and now the site of a spacecraft's crash landing. Alternately represented by blue rocks and a bright blue, Jell-O-like goo, the aliens replicate humans, cause the temperature to rise dangerously and create a panic, and it becomes Kerwin's job to save the day. The plot features bits and pieces from many '50s SF flicks, and is perhaps more reminiscent of *Quatermass 2* (1957) and *I Married a Monster from Outer Space* (1958) than of William Alland's 1953 movie. Bradbury and Essex get a story credit; Tony (*Leave It to Beaver*) Dow produced; and the supporting cast includes Howard (*Your Show of Shows*) Morris as a prospector and Lauren (*The Love Boat*) Tewes as a TV-addicted housewife. "The fact that this is a remake not sequel, yet carries the suffix *II* anyway, is a clue about how clearly the makers of this new version were thinking when they made it. In other words, not very"—David Bianculli, *New York Daily News*.

• Much more recognizably derived from *Outer Space*, 2009's *Alien Trespass* (shooting title: *It Came from Beyond Space*) is another on the list of recent movies that pay homage to, and spoof, but mostly spoof, 1950s monster flicks. With glasses and pipe, Eric McCormack stars as a Handsome, Earnest Astronomer who rushes to the Mojave Desert site of what he thinks is a meteor crash, and instead finds a spaceship. Returning home in his stead is a duplicate McCormack; he's actually the extraterrestrial law enforcement marshal Urp, who's taken on McCormack's form in order to recapture a prisoner: the Ghota, a phallic-looking one-eyed creature that escaped by disabling Urp's ship in flight and forcing the Earth landing. The plot is most like *The Brain from Planet Arous* (1957) but *It Came from Outer Space* will remain front and center in oldies fans' minds because of the imitation *Outer Space* score (complete with Theremin) and the recreation of several *Outer Space* scenes: the "meteor" observed by an astronomer and his wife (McCormack and Jody Thompson) on an imitation *Outer Space* set (backyard candlelight dinner table and telescope), a first-look at the Ghota through the spaceship portway, McCormack's crash site visit and spaceship discovery, the Ghota halting a truck on a desert road, a kid with space helmet and ray gun, and a collection of characters watching the spaceship's climactic departure in an *Outer Space–like* lineup. The movie was shot mostly in and around Vancouver and the interior of British Columbia; the desert scenery (Ashcroft, B.C.) looks very much like the locales seen in *Outer Space*, *Tarantula*, etc., and gives us an idea how these '50s faves might have looked in color. In the movie's press materials, co-star Jenni Baird said she watched *Outer Space* many times and was influenced by Barbara Rush and other actors in that film.

One *Outer Space* actor came close to appearing in *Alien Trespass*: Producer-director R.W. Goodwin, a Washington state resident, told me that he originally intended for his friend and neighbor Russell Johnson to play the comic relief character Wilson, a nutty boozer who lives with his dog in a small shack (reminiscent of the Old Man's shack in the 1958 *The Blob*). Wilson is eventually absorbed by the Ghota, leaving behind a muddy-looking puddle. "I was not feeling well at the time, I have a bad back, and I couldn't have played the part," Johnson told me. "These guys were working on a shoestring up there in Canada, and I didn't want to be messing up a production. I was sorry I couldn't do it."

• Ray Bradbury met Steven Spielberg for the first time in 1977, on the morning after Bradbury saw a preview of *Close Encounters of the Third Kind*. As they shook hands, Spielberg asked, "How did you like *your* film?" To the confused Bradbury he then explained, "*Close Encounters* wouldn't have been born if I hadn't seen *It Came from Outer Space* six times when I was a kid. Thanks." (Spielberg had even made the main character Richard Dreyfuss a linesman like Joe Sawyer and Russell Johnson in *Outer Space*.) After Bradbury's June 2012 passing, Spielberg said, "He was my muse for the better part of my sci-fi career."

• Dana M. Reemes wrote in *Directed by Jack Arnold* that, "in terms of narrative architecture and point of view," *It Came from Outer Space* is superior to *Close Encounters*. "If one subtracted the elaborate and costly special effects from *Close Encounters*, what remained would be much like an improvised film school project."

"I didn't like [*Close Encounters*]," Arnold told *Cinefantastique*'s Stephen Rebello:

> It had no point of view. I don't know what he's saying. To spend as much money as he did and to have no story except that there are some beings who are going to come down and play some crazy music and that's *it*? It hurts me to see that kind of money being spent because it only means there's *less* money available for everything else. Why, I could have made *ten* films with that!

• *It Came from Outer Space* also influenced another major genre MVP: According to director John Carpenter,

> I had a tremendously important experience happen to me when I was four years old. I went into the movie theater with my mother and I saw a film called *It Came from Outer Space* in 3-D. I put on the glasses and the opening sequence has this meteor streaking across the sky. It came directly at the camera, came out of the screen, and blew up right in my face. I shrieked as a young kid and ran up the aisle in terror; I had never experienced anything like that. Then I stopped and I realized, "This is incredible, what a feeling, I want to be able to do that, how can I get that kind of reaction?" It suddenly made me feel completely alive and terrified, but there was nothing to be terrified of, I was in a movie theater. From that moment on, movies thrilled me. They took me away from my real life.

His wife Sandy told me as a side note that one of her earliest gifts to him was a complete set of *It Came from Outer Space* lobby cards, framed, which currently hang in his office.

• This chapter's long enough already, agreed? Agreed. But for fans who want to get even *deeper* into the weeds (learn more about the spaceship prop, the shot where it plummets into the camera, how the Glob was manipulated, *ad nauseam*), there's my audio commentary on Universal's *It Came from Outer Space* DVD and Blu-ray.

The Release

By Robert J. Kiss

The World Premiere(s)

It Came from Outer Space opened simultaneously at two RKO theaters, the Pantages on Hollywood Boulevard and the Hillstreet in downtown Los Angeles, on the evening of May 26, 1953, with the event specifically billed as the world premiere. Ads promised a cavalcade of "firsts"—the first Universal-International 3-D feature, the first widescreen 3-D picture, the first 3-D science fiction story, the first all-3-D program—in addition to listing the names of 33 A-list movie stars who would be in attendance that evening, with emcee duties being conducted by U-I leading man Jeff Chandler at the Hillstreet and by radio-television luminary Larry Finley at the Pantages. Although *Outer Space* would go on to achieve heavy grosses in major cities across the U.S., its box office success in Los Angeles proved exceptional, with *Boxoffice* reporting trade that was three and a half times the average. The two RKO theaters listed a gross of $163,000 at the end of the picture's four-week stay on their (newly widened) screens.

However, the first public showing of *It Came from Outer Space* had in fact already taken place as a one-off midnight screening during the night of May 22–23 at Schine's Paramount Theater in Syracuse, New York, where it had been billed as the "world premiere prevue." The movie then opened for regular business at Schine's Paramount at 10:45 a.m. on May 26, referred to in all publicity—*just as the double-opening in Los Angeles that night would be*—as the "world premiere." What the Syracuse premiere lacked in star power, it made up for in ballyhoo, with a costumed "space man" parading outside the 1500-seat theater, balloons (some containing free passes) being dropped from high buildings, the local Walgreens serving a special *It Came from Outer Space* sundae, and three other big stores putting up "lavish" tie-in window displays and running competitions that included a beauty contest to find "Miss 3-D," with the lucky winner receiving an all-expenses-paid four-day trip to New York City. There was also a steady stream of multimedia advertising for the Syracuse opening in local newspapers and on radio and television.

3-D vs. Flat Screenings

As unusual as it may sound, *It Came from Outer Space* effectively had *two* first runs at theaters; the first as a 3-D picture between late May and November 1953, and the second as a new 2-D release between late November 1953 and February 1954.

When initially released, *Outer Space* was made available solely in 3-D, and venues in major towns and cities proved swift to book the "depthie" between May and July 1953. Indeed, in his syndicated column of July 29, Walter Winchell singled out *Outer Space* and *The Beast from 20,000 Fathoms* as "the current box office champs." However, although new 3-D openings continued to take place in mid-sized and smaller towns between August and November, these were considerably fewer in number, with bookings entirely dependent on the willingness of theater owners in these communities to convert their premises for 3-D. With a much smaller local customer base available to them to help amortize the costs of conversion, the reticence of many small-town theater owners in this regard is readily understandable.

When *It Came from Outer Space* opened simultaneously at two L.A. theaters, it was (according to this *Los Angeles Times* ad) the "1st time anywhere!" ... if by "anywhere" you mean "anywhere except Syracuse, New York," where the movie had bowed several days earlier.

At the end of September, full-page ads in the trade press announced that "[i]n line with Universal-International's policy of serving all of its pictures to all of its customers," the recently released 3-D feature *Wings of the Hawk* would also be made available in 2-D with immediate effect, while the "firmly established 3-D boxoffice hit" *It Came from Outer Space* could be "booked for 2-D exhibition starting November 29." In fact, Universal brought this date forward to November 21, with many small-town and rural theaters eagerly booking the flat version as a special attraction for the week around Thanksgiving Day, which fell on November 26. Just as the 3-D first run of *Outer Space* wound to an end, so its 2-D first run commenced, with bookings remaining strong throughout December, and the picture's "second" first run continuing on with many tens of new openings during January and February 1954.

Within a sample of 1200 first-run movie theaters across the U.S. between May 1953 and February 1954, some 77 percent showed *Outer Space* in 3-D, with the remaining 23 percent playing it in 2-D. The 3-D screenings took place almost without exception in major towns and cities between May and November 1953, while 2-D screenings were limited to smaller communities between late November 1953 and February 1954. Amid all the financial success of its first 3-D feature, Universal surely also became keenly aware of the scale and importance of an "unconvertible" small-town and rural sector for whom a shift to 3-D remained financially unrealistic. All of the company's subsequent 3-D features were released simultaneously in deep and flat versions.

3-D First Run with Nat King Cole, May to November 1953

From its "world premiere prevue" screening onwards, the 3-D *Outer Space* played on a fixed bill with Universal's 18-minute 3-D musical short *Nat "King" Cole and Russ Morgan and His Orchestra*. Studio publicists dubbed this pairing "the first all-3-D program." Within the sample of 1200 first-run movie theaters across the U.S., fully 99 percent of those that screened *Outer Space* in 3-D employed *Nat "King" Cole* as accompaniment, making this absolutely the most common way to have originally experienced the sci-fi feature during its first run.

This does not quite represent the full picture, though, since a limited number of theaters within the above 99 percent elected to "augment" the two-unit bill with a *third* component.

For one in every 100 theaters, this meant adding another 3-D short to the line-up. At Chicago's B & K United Artists Theatre, for example, the list of "firsts" associated with the Universal bill was further extended through the addition of (what ads described as) "Hollywood's first comedy featurette in 3-D"—in the form of Columbia's Three Stooges haunted house short *Spooks!*—to create the "first 3-D combination program." Once again, however, Schine's Paramount in Syracuse had beaten all others to the punch: Fifteen days prior to the opening of Chicago's ostensible "first 3-D combination program" on June 10, it had already added the 3-D boxing newsreel *Rocky Marciano, Champion vs. Jersey Joe Walcott, Challenger* to the bill during its first week of regular screenings of *Outer Space* and *Nat "King" Cole*. Beginning in August, a small number of midwestern venues also made use of Norman McLaren's three-minute 3-D abstract animated short *Now Is the Time* to create a distinct (though not exactly substantially longer) three-unit "All in 3-Dimension" bill.

One in every ten theaters, meanwhile, supplemented Universal's 3-D *It Came from Outer Space-Nat "King" Cole* combo with a 2-D supporting feature, resulting in something that approximated a "balanced" double-bill. This behavior was attested exclusively in large towns and cities where multiple first-run movie houses were showing *Outer Space*, making it quite understandable that individual local theater owners should attempt to stand out from their immediate competitors by offering a "bigger" program. By early September 1953, the number of directly competing first-run venues exhibiting *Outer Space* in densely populated areas had diminished drastically, and so the use of 2-D supporting features correspondingly all but disappeared at this point as well.

All of the 2-D supporting features employed on 3-D bills within the sample of 1200 first-run movie theaters are arranged alphabetically below. The month mentioned in each case is the earliest in which the usage was attested. No individual titles stood out as receiving particularly widespread employment within the sample.

June 1953 *All Ashore* (Mickey Rooney)
July 1953 *Ambush at Tomahawk Gap* (John Hodiak)
June 1953 *Code Two* (Ralph Meeker)
August 1953 *Jamaica Run* (Ray Milland)
August 1953 *Johnny the Giant Killer* (animated)
June 1953 *Law and Order* (Ronald Reagan)
August 1953 *The Lone Hand* (Joel McCrea)
September 1953 *Sky Commando* (Dan Duryea)
July 1953 *A Slight Case of Larceny* (Mickey Rooney)
August 1953 *Sombrero* (Ricardo Montalban)
August 1953 *Star of Texas* (Wayne Morris)
July 1953 *Take Me to Town* (Ann Sheridan)
August 1953 *Terror on a Train* (Glenn Ford)
July 1953 *Torpedo Alley* (Mark Stevens)
August 1953 *Tropic Zone* (Ronald Reagan)

This still leaves one percent of 3-D screenings of *It Came from Outer Space* that were *not* accompanied by *Nat "King" Cole and Russ Morgan and His Orchestra*. All such screenings within the sample took place solely at theaters that opened *Outer Space* as a special Halloween attraction on the weekend of October 31, which fell on a Saturday in 1953. Seemingly this was the only time during the movie's first run in 3-D that Universal supplied it as a stand-alone, having no doubt rightly surmised just how out-of-place the smooth, upbeat tones and rhythms of its usual accompanying short might sound in the context of a spooky holiday entertainment.

2-D First Run, November 1953 to February 1954

Outer Space and *Nat "King" Cole*'s connection had its basis solely in the fact that both were in 3-D. Universal evidently saw no need to release the musical short in a flat version, and so the two broke off their association for the 2-D first-run release of *Outer Space* commencing on November 21.

Within the sample of 1200 U.S. first-run movie theaters between May 1953 and February 1954, 47 percent of *Outer Space*'s 2-D engagements took the form of a stand-alone presentation supported by unspecified "selected shorts." The overwhelming majority of such screenings took place in what might be termed "one-theater towns," where stand-alone presentations were already the long-established norm, since theater owners had no direct competition and consequently seem to have felt no compulsion to invest in a second feature.

The remaining 53 percent of 2-D first-run engagements were as part of a balanced (i.e., non-genre-matched) double-bill in small towns that had more than a single movie theater and, accordingly, a degree of healthy competition. Perhaps indicating that *Outer Space* was no longer quite the newest sci-fi monster on the block—or even that its effect had been significantly diminished through the loss of 3-D—this was the only first-run screening context within which *Outer Space* sometimes represented the *lower* half of the bill, in particular when screened alongside other (more recent) Universal releases, as was the case at over one-third of such screenings nationwide.

All of the co-features employed on 2-D bills within the sample of 1200 first-run movie theaters are arranged alphabetically below. The month mentioned in each case is the earliest in which the usage was attested. Although Universal titles (**bold** in the list below) account collectively for 36 percent of these engagements, there was no single title whose employment stood out as particularly widespread within the sample.

November 1953 *Abbott and Costello Go to Mars* (Abbott and Costello)
February 1954 *Abbott and Costello Meet Dr. Jekyll and Mr. Hyde* (Abbott and Costello)
November 1953 *The All American* (Tony Curtis)
December 1953 *Arrowhead* (Charlton Heston)
November 1953 *Bandits of Corsica* (Richard Greene)
November 1953 *Conquest of Cochise* (John Hodiak)
December 1953 *Devil's Canyon* (Virginia Mayo)
February 1954 *Forbidden* (Tony Curtis)
November 1953 *Fort Algiers* (Yvonne De Carlo)
December 1953 *The Golden Blade* (Rock Hudson)
December 1953 *The Great Sioux Uprising* (Jeff Chandler)
February 1954 *Gun Fury* (Rock Hudson)
December 1953 *Kansas Territory* (Wild Bill Elliott)
December 1953 *The Kid from Gower Gulch* (Spade Cooley)
December 1953 *Miss Robin Crusoe* (Amanda Blake)
December 1953 *Perils of the Jungle* (Clyde Beatty)
December 1953 *Roar of the Crowd* (Howard Duff)
December 1953 *The Stand at Apache River* (Stephen McNally)
December 1953 *Take Me to Town* (Ann Sheridan)
January 1954 *Take the High Ground!* (Richard Widmark)
December 1953 *Terror on a Train* (Glenn Ford)
January 1954 *Those Redheads from Seattle* (Rhonda Fleming)
February 1954 *Thundering Caravans* (Allan "Rocky" Lane)
December 1953 *Valley of Head Hunters* (Johnny Weissmuller)
January 1954 *The Veils of Bagdad* (Victor Mature)

Beyond the First Run

Once *Outer Space*'s theatrical first-run had concluded, the feature's 2-D version went on to circulate at repertory and discount theaters and drive-ins during the latter half of the 1950s and the early '60s. It turned up initially during 1955 and 1956 double-billed with other distributors' sci-fi features of comparable vintage, including the Lippert release of *Spaceways* and United Artists' *Phantom from Space*. Universal subsequently deployed the movie in a more strategic way that allowed it to take control of the entire bill, pairing it with such titles as *The Deadly Mantis, The Incredible Shrinking Man* or any of the features in the Black Lagoon trilogy. By 1960, however, *Outer Space* was being served up strictly as multiple-bill fare at low-end venues, for example playing drive-ins in the southwest as part of a four-feature "All Outer Space Show" that also offered car-bound space jockeys the opportunity to gaze upon the varied (or "mixed," if you prefer) delights of *It Conquered the World* (1956), *From the Earth to the Moon* and *Plan 9 from Outer Space* (both 1958).

Triple-dimensions and double the fun: In 1972, *It Came from Outer Space* was re-released in tandem with *Creature from the Black Lagoon*.

The 2-D version of *Outer Space* was sold to television in 1964. Further removed from its original presentational format after having been panned-and-scanned for the small screen, the picture made its West Coast debut in late March, prior to reaching the rest of the nation during October and November of that year.

The Critics' Corner

Time: [*It Came from Outer Space*] is a crisp combination of shocker and sociological comment. ... Director Jack Arnold has made good use of the barren brooding desert expanses with their lonely, unreal look of another world, and the picture is well acted, particularly by Richard Carlson.

Movie Spotlight: [I]f 3-D pictures no longer thrill you, you may become bored by this unbelievable story.

Photoplay: Despite an earnest lead performance by Richard Carlson and some striking trick effects, movie science fiction isn't given much of a lift here.

The New York Times: To paraphrase T.S. Eliot, *It Came from Outer Space* burst into Loew's State yesterday with a bang and went out with a whimper.

Los Angeles Daily News: [T]he film cuts the buck as far as being top entertainment is concerned without resorting to tricks. Rather, scenes that make maximum use of the 3-D photography are presented in a logical manner, have a definite place in the telling of the story and are not merely put there to take advantage of the stereo process.

Los Angeles Times (Philip K. Scheuer): [T]he tremolo effects have been hopped up to such an extent—by means of a caterwauling Theremin, female screams and a camera which keeps going "boo!" at us—and these effects assault us from so many unexpected and unreasonable quarters that the inevitable reaction sets in. with sanity restored, we find ourselves caught in a downdraft of suspicion that what we succumbed to was little more than the pretension of a glorified "B."

By such high-handed methods, too, the picture all but invalidates its message—which is, as I gathered it, "Love thy interspacial neighbor."

Columnist Frank Morriss, "Here, There and Hollywood": The basic idea that mankind, afraid of the unknown, is not yet ready to receive a friendly visitor from another planet is an excellent one. The story only weakens itself by a lot of nonsensical hocus-pocus about the Martians being able to assume the guise of any one they wished. Barbara Rush ... is also asked to skip about the desert in an evening gown, for no reason at all, other than it contributes *décolleté*.

The Hollywood Reporter: *It Came from Outer Space* should prove a gold mine for Universal-International. It is also a solid piece of eerie entertainment, replete with wild screams and bug-eyed monsters guaranteed to send scared customers out of this world. Stereophonic sound gets its best usage to date ... the screams seeming to come from the next seat, the directional sound also being very effective during the dialogue. ... The Bradbury name should also help swell the returns on this film. Bradbury rates as one of the three top science-fiction writers of today and will serve as a draw with the millions of rabid s-f fans. ... Director Jack Arnold and photographer Cliff Stine share honors in achieving the weird, tense mood. Stine gets some scalp-tingling effects in lensing the non-physical space beings....

Films in Review (the article "Horror Films" by William K Everson, 1954): ... *It Came from Outer Space* shows that these new technics [3-D, stereophonic sound] can change the face of the horror film but not its form. All the stock characters are there, all the familiar situations. The scientist (Richard Carlson) explains early in the proceedings that he is compelled to work alone in the desert because the townspeople distrust him—later they also believe him mad. The sudden close-up of the "thing" with the huge eye isn't much different from the shock close-up in *The Most Dangerous Game* of a pickled human head floating in a jar of alcohol. Like the Frankenstein monster, the "thing" is basically sympathetic, for all its hideous appearance, for, let alone, it will harm nobody. The old-time interfering and bumbling burgomaster of Lionel Belmore or E.E. Clive is reincarnated in the hot-headed and unreasonable sheriff of Charles Drake. And when, in the final reel, the townspeople riot through the countryside bent on destroying the invaders, one can't help but recall the mobs of villagers with flaming torches raging to kill the Frankenstein monster.

Harrison's Reports: [*Outer Space*] is very fine, for it has been produced and directed with great skill. The spectator is held in tense suspense by the fear of the unknown.

Oakland (California) *Tribune*: I saw my first three-dimensional movie last week, and got the bargain package—large screen, 3-D and stereophonic sound all rolled into one.

It Came from Outer Space was the title of this technical melange, and I must say I wasn't bored. Trying to keep those ill-fitting cardboard-framed glasses over my ears, ducking a rock avalanche which seemed to be landing in my lap, and looking around to see where the sound was coming from left me completely exhausted.

Variety columnist Frank Scully ("Scully's Scrapbook," July 1, 1953): What I liked best about [*Outer Space*] is that Bradbury clothed his hero in civilized trappings. His hero was a scientist instead of a trigger-happy member of the military arm. He believed the visitors from outer space meant no more harm to the emigrant or native-born Americans than Columbus meant to the native-born Americans he first met 462 years ago. So Brad's [*sic*] hero tried to brief his fellow-townsmen in hospitality instead of hate, and in courage and confidence instead of fear and distrust.

This is right down my alley in international and interplanetary relations and I was glad to see that Bradbury gave his hero the mind and the means to help the visitors, who seemingly were grounded by accident, to get back on their course and kiss this dizzy planet goodbye.

Interview with 3-D Restoration Wizards

In 2016, Bob Furmanek of the 3-D Film Archive and his colleague Greg Kintz did a major *It Came from Outer Space* fix-up for Universal during the lead-up to the movie's 3-D Blu-ray release. These **D**edicated **D**evotees of the **D**epthies made the stereophonic track sound like it did in theaters in 1953, and made the 3-D *better* than it was in 1953. Unlike past preparers of home video versions of *It Came from Outer Space*, Furmanek and Kintz **D**id their **D**ue **D**iligence and gave the movie the kind of above-and-beyond enhancement that may permanently affect the way it's historically ranked. With work like this, they not only preserved 3-D movie history; they *made* it.

It Came from Outer Space "rescuers" Greg Kintz, left, and Bob Furmanek of the 3-D Film Archive.

As the October 4 release date of the Blu-ray neared, I interviewed Furmanek and Kintz for issue #32 of *Screem* magazine, partially reprinted below.

Q: *Every* It Came from Outer Space *fan knows that we have you guys to thank for the fact that the 3-D in this movie will be as good or better than ever. Do we have you to thank for* It Came *coming out on Blu-ray in 3-D at all? In other words, did you approach Universal and get the ball rolling?*

Bob Furmanek: Basically what happened was that we worked with a company in Scotland called Panamint on a 3-D Blu-ray release of the 20th Century-Fox classic *Inferno* [1953]. It did very well. Panamint has a deal where they're able to secure licenses for Region 2 release [Europe, Africa, the Middle East, French territories, etc.] of Universal films, and *It Came* was available to license. They went ahead and secured it, and we knew that we could work with existing transfers to create a 3-D master.

News of this upcoming 3-D Blu-ray release leaked in a strange way: Panamint had a test page on their website announcing the 3-D Blu-ray. But it was not marked private, and someone found it by chance when doing a Google search. The news spread like wildfire across the Internet—all the home theater groups and others shared it. The head of Universal's home video division saw this and said, "Wait a minute. We don't *have* a 3-D master. How are they *doing* this?" He contacted Panamint, and to make a very long story short, we wound up doing the work *for Universal*. Panamint decided to pull out of the project because they would not have made much if they had to limit their release to just Region 2, and they would effectively be competing with Universal's release. It became a 100 percent Universal Home Video project for all regions.

Greg Kintz: Once we went with Universal, they were able to supply us with additional elements. The work involved a number of steps. We were working with existing transfers but these were not done with a 3-D master in mind so there were quite a few variations between the left and right sides. The timing of one transfer for one eye and overall framing of one transfer vs. the next one can be different. So I had to compensate for that. Adding to that was the fact that in 1953 when the movie was made, it was Universal's first 3-D feature and the camera rig often was misaligned. In addition to the baked-in vertical alignment issues, there were shots when the movie would go out of sync by one frame and it was originally edited that way; in other cases, it would actually flip-flop, where the left eye sees the right eye view and vice versa. It was definitely a learning process for the studio to both photograph and edit a film for 3-D presentation. But, all that being said, *It Came from Outer Space* is *easily* in the top five of the "golden age" 3-D features of the 1950s.

Q: *In the top five out of … how many?*

Furmanek: There were 50 domestic 3-D features. This may sound like a sales pitch or a cliché, but it's true: People will now see *It Came from Outer Space* on 3-D Blu-ray looking *better* than it did in theaters in 1953, *because* of all the fixes and corrections that Greg has done to the film.

In 1953, the film was really rushed through production, and especially through editing, because Universal was trying to get it into theaters very, very quickly. I have on audio tape an interview that Richard Carlson did to promote the film in 1953, and in between questions, when they were just sorta talking "off mike," the tape was still rolling, and the interviewer asked, "Why was there so much secrecy surrounding the making of this film?" The interviewer knew that the set was closed to visitors, and that everyone in the cast had to sign a pledge of secrecy about the film. And Richard Carlson said, "Do you want to know the truth? We were trying to beat *House of Wax* into theaters." That was also why the film was put through so quickly. In light of that, it's quite amazing how well they did with the 3-D staging. It's absolutely sensational. You've really got to credit director Jack Arnold, and the cinematographer Clifford Stine, and … well, *all* the people who worked on it need to be recognized for putting such a great 3-D production through so quickly. And, as Greg said, they learned, because their next 3-D film *Wings of the Hawk* [1953] didn't have a lot of the technical issues that plagued *It Came from Outer Space.*

In addition to all the fixes that Greg has done visually to the film, people are going to hear the original three-channel stereophonic sound for the first time in 63 years. He restored an *amazing* track.

Kintz: *It Came from Outer Space* was one of the first mag [magnetic] tracks, and we often associate mags with multi-channel sound. And indeed, *It Came* has a very directional three-channel mix, left, center and right. It's a very dynamic soundtrack. In previous releases, the center channel had been slightly raised; now for the first time on home video, this track is being presented with all three tracks at correct levels, confirmed with the original tones, and the three-channel sound field sounds *so* much better, so much more balanced. You notice the left and right channels much more in this mix, as it was originally heard in '53.

Furmanek: The laserdisc had the stereo track, *but* it was very compressed, very modified from what the original audio contained. This will be the first time for people at home to hear it as it was originally mixed. I just had some people over to my home the other day for a screening in 3-D, and one of my guests brought his seven-year-old son. This kid is a big Universal monster fan; in fact, his favorite movie of all time is *Frankenstein Meets the Wolf Man.* He knows this stuff, but he had never seen *It Came from Outer Space*. And, you know what? He got really spooked in the first reel. His father told me later, "It wasn't the 3-D or the visuals, it wasn't what his eyes were showing him. It was the *sound*." The explosion, the avalanche, when Barbara Rush screams out of the right channel when they see the silhouette of the Joshua tree—the sound was so enveloping that *that* spooked his son more than what he was watching. It's a real big part of the film that people haven't had a chance to experience, and I think it's going to help re-establish the film as one of the great science fiction films of that time.

Kintz: Regarding the sound, we have an article up on the 3-D Film Archive website that goes into this in even more detail. [Editor's note: Google up Greg's 3-D Film Archive article "It's in the Mix."]

Q: *The spaceship plunging toward the camera, Glob Ellen firing her "ray gun" toward the camera – you can tell, even in 2D, what some of the movie's 3-D highlights were. What are some of the scenes that'll surprise us in 3-D?*

Furmanek: Kathleen Hughes [*laughs*]! She lent herself well to stereo photography. In fact, she made such a great impression with her appearance in this film that it led to a prominent role in Jack Arnold's 3-D production of *The Glass Web* [1953] with Edward G. Robinson. Getting back to *It Came*: Another highlight in 3-D is the famous scene in the sheriff's office with the sheriff, Charles Drake, talking about the temperature, 92 degrees. Well, there's a shot that places his gun in the foreground, hanging up in its holster, and it really adds an extra punch to the whole layout of that sequence.

Kintz: There are subtleties that you might not have noticed in previous video versions, even previous 3-D versions that were in the inferior anaglyph. Something as subtle as mist and fog has a very nice dimensional layering that now can finally be seen.

Furmanek: A common myth for decades now has been that *It Came* and *Creature from the Black Lagoon* and some of the others were originally shown with the red-and-cyan glasses. That's not true, they were all shown originally with polarized light, very similar to the 3-D that is seen in presentations today. *It Came* and *Creature* were both reissued in the 1970s in a single-strip red-and-blue system, anaglyphic

3-D, which was a heckuva lot easier to present in theaters because you didn't have to interlock two 35mm projectors and you didn't need a silver screen. But it *severely* degraded the image. Those reissues and the Universal 8 [Super 8mm] release of the film in anaglyph presented a very inferior version of the 3-D.

Kintz: In 1980, MCA Home Video released anaglyphic versions of *Creature from the Black Lagoon* and *It Came*, and they were so bad, they actually did a recall.

Q: *The Globs—on the Blu-ray, when you see one in 3-D in a long shot, will we be able to tell that its eye is protruding?*

Furmanek and Kintz [*stereophonically*]: Oh, yes!

Q: *And will we finally we able to make out its arms in 3-D? A lot of fans who've seen this movie umpteen times still don't know they* have *arms.*

Furmanek: Yeah, they're certainly there. There's a lot to "take in" with that character, because you only see it for a few seconds at a time, but the arms *do* extend from the body. It was definitely a character design done for 3-D impact.

Q: *When this is a hit, what do you push Universal to do next?*

Furmanek: Well, we have to say *Revenge of the Creature* [1955]. I think at this point, everybody involved with the Blu-ray release of *It Came* is very encouraged and enthusiastic with the response that it's gotten. In fact, Best Buy had so much interest, they had to upload a second webpage in order to accommodate the pre-orders. And that doesn't happen very often. So the interest in this title, and the pre-sales, have been very strong, and I've already been told that if this does well, it'll make it that much easier to green-light another 3-D restoration. Very likely *Revenge of the Creature* would be next on the drawing board.

Q: *Of the remaining Universal 3-Ds—*Wings of the Hawk, The Glass Web *and* Taza, Son of Cochise *[1954]—which one has the best 3-D?*

Furmanek: *Glass Web* is probably the strongest of the three, because of the cast and story—

Q: *No, no! Just 3-D-wise.*

Kintz: Well, Kathleen Hughes + *Glass Web* + 3-D = what more do you want? [*Laughs*]

Furmanek: The Westerns [*Wings* and *Taza*] benefit from two great directors, Budd Boetticher and Douglas Sirk respectively, and for *Taza,* they went out to Utah and did some amazing location scenes. It's very hard to select one from the group because each has special qualities that make it unique. Rest assured, we don't give up easily and are doing our very best to get as many vintage 3-D films onto Blu-ray as possible!

Kintz: Unfortunately, the only ones who *won't* be able to view these films in 3-D, of course, are the Globs, because they only have one eye [*laughs*]!

It Came from Stein, Gertz and Mancini: The Music of It Came from Outer Space

By David Schecter

In 1953, Universal-International made a quantum leap in how they scored their science fiction-horror movies compared to how they'd previously approached them. The stellar original score composed for *It Came from Outer Space* was a major musical improvement over the soundtrack heard in the studio's recently released science fiction-comedy, *Abbott and Costello Go to Mars*. This mostly unfunny outing mixed original music by Herman Stein, Henry Mancini and Milton Rosen with a slew of tracked cues from the likes of *Francis Goes to the Races, Ma and Pa Kettle at Waikiki,* and even going as far back as 1942 (*Pittsburgh*) and 1943 (*We've Never Been Licked*).

Stein wrote the main thematic material for *Abbott and Costello Go to Mars*, and his music covered many sequences where Universal had nothing suitable in their music library. These included the film's bouncy "Main Title"—a composition that was one of the composer's personal favorites—as well as some sequences in the rocket, in New Orleans and in outer space. Mancini handled most of the original music after the ship lands on Venus, as Universal's composers would occasionally be assigned entirely different reels in a picture. Unfortunately, the writers were forced to use more than their share of "*wah-wahs*" on muted trumpet and other brass for comedic effect. Even though Stein's themes were used throughout a good portion of the movie, the music that ended the show was the "End Title" from *Lost in Alaska* (1952) and the "End Cast" from *Enter Arsene Lupin* (1944). This absence of one of Stein's themes as the curtain closer speaks volumes for the lack of artistic consideration taken in this and many other 1950s Universal films.

Born in Philadelphia, Pennsylvania, on August 19, 1915, Herman Stein taught himself orchestration by studying scores at the library. He was working professionally by age 15, and was soon arranging for radio programs and jazz orchestras, including work during the 1930s and '40s for Count

Basie, Blanche Calloway, Red Norvo and others. After moving to Los Angeles in 1948, he studied composition with the esteemed Mario Castelnuovo-Tedesco, but after only one lesson, Castelnuovo-Tedesco realized he had nothing to teach his newest pupil, so the two instead became lifelong friends. In 1950, Stein sent Joseph Gershenson a recording containing his first movie score, written for *Career for Two,* an industrial film about the banking industry. Gershenson hired him immediately as an arranger for Universal, and Stein became a staff composer the following year, his first composing job for the studio being *Here Come the Nelsons* (1952).

Along with Henry Mancini, Stein's muscular, jazz-influenced style of American writing would help define the sound of Universal in the 1950s, and science fiction music in particular, as he created some of the most memorable themes for the studio's horror films of this era. The composer's writing graced close to 200 films and shorts, among them *Abbott and Costello Meet the Keystone Kops, All I Desire, Creature from the Black Lagoon, Dawn at Socorro, Destry, The Far Country, Francis in the Haunted House, The Great Man, Horizons West, The Intruder, I've Lived Before, The Lady Takes a Flyer, Naked Alibi, Tarantula, This Island Earth, Tumbleweed* and *The Unguarded Moment.* Stein also wrote music for commercials and television, including *Daniel Boone, Lost in Space* and *Wagon Train.* He passed away at his home in Los Angeles on March 15, 2007, after finally receiving some recognition for the years he spent in relative obscurity, due to his lack of screen credit on many of his motion pictures.

Abbott and Costello Go to Mars was able to reuse music from a number of Universal comedies, but because *It Came from Outer Space* was the studio's first serious venture into science fiction in a long time, as well as their first invaders-from-space picture, there was really nothing very appropriate in the music library that could be tracked into the movie. Wisely, the music department decided to avoid using library cues for this particular picture, so Putnam and Ellen's romance in this Jack Arnold production was not augmented by "Dan's Love" from *House of Frankenstein.* Nor did Universal decide to use the comedic *Abbott and Costello Go to Mars* music to accompany the crash landing of the Globs' spaceship, which would have definitely altered the tone of the picture!

Because *It Came from Outer Space* was a much more important production than Universal's recent science fiction or horror-related films, any remaining possibility of employing tracked music would probably have been nixed by musical director Gershenson. During the last few years, he had begun assembling a talented group of staff writers and freelancers, many with a decidedly modern American sound, and three of them would provide *It Came from Outer Space* with its brilliant original score. Even so, it's to the studio's credit that they refused to use library cues in certain romantic, action and atmospheric sequences, since at least some of those non-science fiction scenes could have been scored via older compositions. Although to be completely accurate, it should be mentioned that the movie does contain a two-second excerpt of a tracked pop song heard over a radio.

It Came from Outer Space's modernistic 36-minute musical conglomeration was divided fairly evenly among freelancer Irving Gertz and staff composers Mancini and Stein, with Stein responsible for writing much of the picture's thematic material. Gershenson trusted the 37-year-old composer a lot, which is why Stein was often chosen to write main titles. Stein described these pieces as being "naked," with no dialogue or sound effects for the music to hide behind, and because of that, he considered these cues to be the scariest pieces he had to compose. Some of Stein's work in the main title arena can be heard in *A Day of Fury, The Glass Web, The Great Man, Horizons West, Johnny Dark, The Lady Takes a Flyer, No Name on the Bullet* and *Quantez.* His music would figure in ten of the studio's 1950s science fiction main titles, including *Creature from the Black Lagoon, It Came from Outer Space, This Island Earth* and *The Land Unknown.*

Not even a newly written orchestral score was deemed sufficient to create the necessary alien ambience for *It Came from Outer Space*, so the three composers together decided to add a Theremin to the mix. Sounding like a mentally unbalanced wailing woman, this bizarre electronic instrument had already been used in a number of 1940s psychological film scores like Miklós Rózsa's *Spellbound, The Lost Weekend* and *The Red House.* It had also appeared in recent outer space-themed scores such as Ferde Grofé's *Rocketship X-M,* Dimitri Tiomkin's *The Thing from Another World* and Bernard Herrmann's *The Day the Earth Stood Still.* However, as these latest pictures had come in such rapid succession, the Theremin wasn't yet considered the science fiction cliché it would soon become. It would also be heard in other 1953 scores like Herschel Burke Gilbert's *Project Moon Base* and William Lava's *Phantom from Space.* In *It Came from Outer Space*, the Theremin was mainly used to make viewers aware of the mostly unseen Globs' presence, as well as to add a shock layer over the orchestra during alien "attack" sequences.

The Theremin was played by Dr. Samuel Hoffman, a podiatrist who was pretty much the only game in town for that instrument. Due to the extreme difficulty of anyone getting the right notes out of the contraption, perhaps it's more accurate to say that it was actually the Theremin that played Dr. Hoffman. The composers were probably already aware of the troublesome nature of the instrument, which is played by moving your hands in its general vicinity without actually touching it. Therefore, the orchestral score was recorded first, and when those final takes were accepted and "locked," only then was Hoffman brought in to do his best to hit the right notes, which were overdubbed onto the orchestral recording. This approach meant that the studio didn't have to pay the musicians in the orchestra the overtime that surely would have resulted from trying to record the Theremin along with the other 38 players, all of whom could play their instruments nearly flawlessly.

Universal's contract orchestra of about three dozen instrumentalists would vary slightly from film to film, but it primarily consisted of two flutes (also playing alto flute and piccolo), one oboe-English horn, one bassoon, four clarinets (some doubling bass clarinet), two French horns, three trumpets, three trombones, one keyboard (on piano, celesta and organ), harp, percussion, ten violins, two violas, four cellos and one bass. The make-up of a typical classical or studio orchestra's string section usually has more violas than cellos, but Universal frequently reversed the balance, probably because cellos have a more powerful sound, which would give additional weight to this part of the orchestra. For *It Came from Outer Space*, tuba player Jack Barsby was added to provide some extra *oomph* to the brass, and Ignace Hilsberg served as an additional keyboard player. Hilsberg had doubled for actor Laird Cregar during the piano-playing scenes in the 1945 film *Hangover Square*. The *It Came from Outer Space* score was recorded in seven hours and 15 minutes on April 23, 1953, and Samuel Hoffman was brought in for six hours the following day, earning $91.80 for his efforts, which was part of Universal's $200 Theremin budget. That it took six hours to record all the right notes speaks volumes about the difficulty of playing that instrument, as it wasn't a Theremin-heavy score.

Even with the careful approach taken with the Theremin, the recording sessions still didn't work out exactly the way the composers had envisioned, and a number of passages that should have featured that instrument ended up without it, or else different notes were played from what was written in the scores. The film's "Main Title" enters rather timidly, as it's possible the opening Theremin notes weren't quite what were hoped for; the middle of that same cue was similarly diminished on the soundtrack, again obscuring the electronic howl. But somehow, Hoffman and his pet Theremin managed to produce enough usable notes that helped contribute to a truly marvelous score that greatly enhanced the picture's drama.

Partly because several projects had similar problems recording the feisty electronic doodad, trombonist Paul Tanner and inventor Bob Whitsell later created the Electro-Theremin, a much more practical version of the instrument that a player could physically touch, thereby resulting in note-wise accuracy. That's the instrument heard in everything from *The Giant Gila Monster, Lost in Space* and *My Favorite Martian* to the Beach Boys' songs "Good Vibrations," "I Just Wasn't Made for These Times" and "Wild Honey."

Adding to the difficulties of creating *It Came from Outer Space*'s soundtrack was that the script initially called for the aliens to be pretty much unseen except for a single eye and some smoke—and then when Universal decided that a more visual Glob would replace this subtler approach, a number of scenes whose music had already been recorded needed to be reshot. But instead of having the composers rewrite those compositions and the orchestra re-record them, those additional expenses were avoided by editing the already recorded music tracks to make them fit the altered visuals as well as possible. If you have nothing better to do, you can try hearing some of those ragged music splices during Stein's "The Thing Follows" and "Prospector Globbed," Gertz's "Kidnapping Ellen" and "Killing Glob Ellen," and Mancini's "Rescued."

Although Universal's collaborative scores could occasionally sound non-uniform, because the composers' contributions are spread equally throughout the films, and also because all the writers used some of the same musical themes (which didn't always happen in the studio's pictures), *It Came from Outer Space*'s score comes across as very cohesive. While Stein still sounds like Stein, Gertz sounds like Gertz, and Mancini sounds like Mancini, one composer's cue follows naturally into the next composer's contribution. An added benefit to the soundtrack is that the three different writing styles add some density that a score written by a solitary composer probably wouldn't have. The orchestrations, conducting and sound of the recording hall further cement the different elements into a seamless whole, resulting in a moody and unearthly aural atmosphere tinged with jolts that augment many of the picture's 3-D thrills.

There are many musical treats in the score, and even though it's difficult hearing Stein's "Main Title" in the movie, it's different from almost every opening musical statement of that era. Rather than featuring a hummable melody, it introduces Stein's four-note Glob theme that serves as the centerpiece of the score. Solo Theremin plays portions of the theme before offering the complete version (*ooooo-wooooo-ooooo-wooooo*), and then a full-

Herman Stein's main theme from *It Came from Outer Space*. (© 1953 Gilead Music Co.)

orchestral variation of the motif follows. It's one of the shortest main titles ever, clocking in at a mere 28 seconds, and its purpose is to get you into the drama as quickly as possible, as Universal saved the credits for the end of the show, which is where that hummable melody can be found.

This was the first time in many Universal sci-fi-horror pictures where a memorable theme was offered that colored the entire score. While it never achieved the status of Stein's *BAH-BAH-BAHHH!* Gill Man theme from the following year's *Creature from the Black Lagoon*, it did set the tone for many—but not all—of the 1950s Universal sci-fi thrillers by offering a musical motif that was relied on throughout the bulk of the picture (*This Island Earth, Cult of the Cobra, The Mole People, The Incredible Shrinking Man, The Monolith Monsters* and all three Creature movies). Although it might be claimed that some of these pictures were harmed when a memorable theme wasn't employed in them, such as *The Land Unknown* and *The Leech Woman*, that was merely one of the problems. While the Glob theme was an excellent one, it didn't permeate filmgoers' brains because the aliens weren't seen very frequently, and therefore their motif wasn't used too much. In addition, the theme was orchestrated in many different ways—an appropriate film scoring approach—but one that prevented listeners from being exposed to the same exact music again and again, as would happen with the blaring trumpet version that hammered home the Creature theme.

Stein's "Sand Rock" is the lovely piece of Americana that plays under John Putnam's opening narration, and it's the only purely tonal and melodic piece heard until the "End Title." This was a sophisticated dramatic approach taken by the composers, whose writing lets us know that something is awry from the moment the aliens arrive, and the score remains that way until they depart at the end. Written for upper woodwinds, harp and cantabile (singable) strings, the evocative "Sand Rock" also turns up in romantic settings in *Revenge of the Creature* and *Tarantula,* during the happy ending of the Audie Murphy Western *Drums Across the River* (1954) and in the Jock Mahoney Western *Money, Women and Guns* (1958), where it highlights a gorgeous ranch.

You can hear hints of musical unpredictability in Gertz's romantic "Star Gazing," which underscores Ellen's conversation with Putnam as he peers through his telescope. The bittersweet music is tinged with uncertainty and describes their stagnant relationship as well as the events that are about to unfold. At the end of the composition, a frenzied orchestral explosion was unfortunately dialed out of the film's soundtrack in favor of the sound effects of the spaceship approaching. The composer requested the piece be played "very light and celestial," and the music manages to divert attention from Ellen's silly astrological pronunciations, as her scientifically minded beau probably wouldn't have had much in common with a woman possessing such medieval notions about the stars. However, Putnam's own astronomical knowledge is called into question when he refers to the crashed object as a meteor rather than a meteorite, the latter being a meteor that has reached Earth.

Freelancer Irving Gertz had already done much work for Columbia and independent production companies before he was first called on by Joseph Gershenson, and the composer's unique talents would be required at Universal many times up until 1960. Born in Providence, Rhode Island, on May 19, 1915, he studied with Wassili Leps at the Providence College of Music. Upon arriving in California before World War II, he began work in Columbia's music department, including orchestrating for Paul Sawtell and other composers. After serving in the war in the U.S. Army Signal Corps, Gertz began composing for films for Columbia, during which time he studied with both Mario Castelnuovo-Tedesco and Ernst Toch. Gertz served as composer and music director for many independent features during the 1940s and 1950s, with some of his work at Universal being for *Abbott and Costello Meet the Mummy, Bullet for a Badman, Cult of the Cobra, The Deadly Mantis, Fluffy, Four Girls in Town, He Rides Tall, Hell Bent for Leather, The Incredible Shrinking Man, Istanbul, Smoke Signal, To Hell and Back* and *Wild Heritage.* A few of his other pictures include *The Alligator People,*

This Irving Gertz sketch shows meteor-crashing music deleted from "Star Gazing." (© 1953 Accolade Music Publishing Co.)

Bandits of Corsica, The First Traveling Saleslady, Hell on Devil's Island, Jungle Goddess, Last of the Redmen, Overland Pacific and *The Wizard of Baghdad*. In 1960, he was hired by 20th Century-Fox, where he worked as a composer and music director for over 12 years. Some of his TV work was done for *Daniel Boone, The Invaders, Land of the Giants, Peyton Place* and *Voyage to the Bottom of the Sea*. After his film career ended, Gertz concentrated on writing concert works, which included "Liberty! Liberté!" and "Salute to All Nations." A sweet, gentle, funny and erudite man, his contributions to the art of film scoring were considerable. He passed away in Los Angeles on November 14, 2008, at age 93.

"Visitors from Space" is probably the most familiar *It Came from Outer Space* cue due to a bastardized, abbreviated version being re-recorded for the 1959 Coral Records album "Themes from Horror Movies," conducted by Dick Jacobs. The beautifully thought-out Herman Stein composition (as heard in the film, not as butchered on the album) begins as the camera tracks down to the smoky crater where the spaceship has crash-landed, with the deliberate composition meshing perfectly with the moving shot. A brassy fanfare accompanies the opening of the ship's hatch, and then a moodily quiet section for alto flute and bassoon was unfortunately somewhat obscured in the film by the sound of the alien breathing. (It should be pointed out that although the Globs look nothing like us, they sure do breathe similarly.)

When we first come eyes to eye with one of the creatures, the Theremin cries out, and then groaning brass and pounding timpani lend a sense of power to the undulating eyeball alien. If anyone was going to laugh at its bizarre appearance, the seriousness of the music prevents that. Wind chimes tinkle and Novachord plays a four-note theme to create a motif associated with the aliens' glittering trails. "Visitors from Space" is a truly stunning composition that exhibits Stein's ability to push some of his music towards modernism without going over the edge and creating something dissonant and unpleasant. The complete piece can be heard as part of a 20-minute *It Came from Outer Space* suite released in 1996 by the *Monstrous Movie Music* label, founded by this author and his wife.

Mancini's "John's Discovery, Part 1" and "John's Discovery, Part 2" (recorded as separate cues to avoid an edit that would have occurred during the reel change in the middle of the music) highlight the scene where Putnam descends into the crater and finds himself staring at the crashed ship in that singular cinematic science fiction moment. Novachord, harp and piatti (cymbals) contribute to his sense of isolation, and French horns and trombones provide low brass, which adds to the ominous musical accompaniment. The composer uses similar voicings in the brass that Stein's did in "Visitors from Space," which helps the cues mesh so well. Mancini's writing in this sequence shows that even at this early stage of his film music career, his dramatic instincts were already well-developed. In his later, more famous years, he would downplay some of the work he did during this part of his musical life, probably because the projects weren't always highly regarded. Adding to that was the important fact that he shared compositional duties with other writers and wasn't credited on most of these 1950s Universal contract assignments, so the pictures didn't have the same importance to him. Regardless, some of Mancini's most striking dramatic compositions came during his staff years at Universal. When Mancini arrived at Universal the year before *It Came from Outer Space*, Stein was given the job of showing him the ropes. Hank (as he was known to his friends) was already an extremely capable writer, so he needed little coaching or assistance.

Born in Cleveland, Ohio, on April 16, 1924, and raised in West Aliquippa, Pennsylvania, Henry Mancini studied at New York's Juilliard School of Music. After World War II, he was hired as a pianist-arranger for Tex Beneke's Glenn Miller Orchestra, and he studied in Hollywood with Ernst Krenek and Mario Castelnuovo-Tedesco. Mancini wrote music for clubs and radio shows, including work for Bob Crosby, Buddy Rich and David Rose. In 1952, he was hired by Universal and for the next seven years he wrote at least partial scores for more than 100 of the studio's films, among them *Border River, Creature from the Black Lagoon, The Creature Walks Among Us, Damn Citizen, Flood Tide, The Golden Blade, The Great Impostor, Man Afraid, So This Is Paris, The Tattered Dress, Touch of Evil* and *Walking My Baby Back Home*. Mancini then went on to compose a long line of classic film scores, including *Breakfast at Tiffany's, Experiment in Terror, Hatari!* and *The Pink Panther*, and he wrote for TV series such as *Peter Gunn, Newhart* and *Remington Steele*. Just a few of his well-known songs are "Days of Wine and Roses," "Dear Heart" and "Moon River." Mancini won many Grammy Awards and Academy Awards, and released numerous popular record albums. He wrote a book on orchestration entitled *Sounds and Scores* and an autobiography, *Did They Mention the Music?* in which he reminisces about his years at Universal. He was a much-loved member of the Hollywood community, and was often eager to help and give his time to others. He passed away on June 14, 1994, while still actively composing excellent film music and recording some of it for posterity.

Stein's "The Thing Follows" augments the nighttime scene when Putnam and Ellen drive from the airport and just miss hitting a jaywalking Glob. In the film, the Theremin bookends at the beginning and end of this cue duplicate material that derived from "Visitors from Space." Quotes like this were seldom done because the composer couldn't think of anything original. Rather, they were likely due to time constraints as well as because most film scores have thematic elements to them, and occasional repetitions are conducive to helping tie various cues together so the score becomes an overarching creation. As Putnam shines his spotlight on a three-dimensionally threatening Joshua tree, part of "The Thing Follows" was "dialed out" of the soundtrack, as it was probably felt that musical silence would heighten the shot's effectiveness. You can get a sense of Stein's subtle approach to much of his writing when he only gently accentuates Ellen surprising Putnam with a touch from behind, rather than trying to create a full-blown musical stinger. The music that remains in the picture is an effective way of reminding the viewer that the aliens are nearby, even if they are unseen. The final Theremin passage that accompanies the glitter trail sounds a little "off," perhaps not one of Dr. Hoffman's finest moments. Some of the music in "The Thing Follows" that was deleted from *It Came from Outer Space* is audible in *Creature from the Black Lagoon*, when two instances of the cue play before the Gill Man escapes from his wooden cage on the *Rita* deck. The piece made further appearances in the all-tracked films *Running Wild* and *Monster on the Campus*.

After the end of "The Thing Follows," there isn't any music in *It Came from Outer Space* for over seven minutes, but that absence doesn't hurt the movie, as the desert scenes during this span are dialogue-heavy, and the musical silence in the remote environment actually lends a realistic touch to the proceedings.

Gertz's "Mysterious Desert," heard when Putnam looks through his binoculars and ponders where the aliens might be hiding, contains a misterioso in the form of a four-note ostinato (repeated musical phrase). This theme further signifies the enigmatic aliens; it's later used by Mancini and Stein in some of their own cues, which adds to the cohesion of the multi-composered score. The motif seems to hint that the Globs are thinking creatures, as opposed to merely being horrific monsters, and that plays a significant role in the theme of the picture. It's not known which writer came up with this particular motif, but it does have that Mancini "feel" to it. "Mysterious Desert" creates much of its mysteriousness due to extensive use of harp and vibraphone, with Novachord and celesta adding further color. The brass is quiet and muted, befitting the desert while not intruding upon the dialogue. Quite a bit of this piece was reused in uncredited fashion four years down the line in *The Monolith Monsters*' cue "Simpson's Place, Part 2." It occurs in that picture when Dave comes across Ginny's parents, turned to stone by the extraterrestrial crystals.

A measure from Henry Mancini's "Talking Wires." (© 1953 Northridge Music Co.)

Irving Gertz's slime-trail music from "Mysterious Desert." (© 1953 Accolade Music Publishing Co.)

Mancini's unearthly "Talking Wires" might have been mixed a bit too quietly in *Outer Space*'s soundtrack, one of the few musical mistakes in the movie, but even so, it's spookily effective when Putnam eavesdrops on the aliens through the phone lines. Created with string harmonics, Novachord, vibraphone and harp, it's a sound effects-type piece that remains indelibly with the viewer long after the scene is over. You can hear the same basic creation much more clearly during Mancini's "Telephone Message," which plays 23 minutes later when Putnam takes a call from an alien at the sheriff's office; the music accomplishes much more than any words could. Mancini was probably given both of these scenes due to their connection regarding the telephone. He would later use a nearly identical effect in his "Water Witch Theme" for *The Thing That Couldn't Die* (1958), a film that also included multiple reuses of "Talking Wires."

When George and Frank are Globbed, Mancini's "The Thing Strikes" begins with an evocative pair of upward piano runs to accentuate the telephone line, then Theremin and Novachord join in before the full-orchestral attack, which is a variation of material Stein wrote for "Visitors from Space." Excerpts of "The Thing Strikes" were reused six times in *Tarantula* action sequences to great effect, unless you already associated them with *It Came from Outer Space*, in which case you probably wondered why so many Universal monsters sounded the same. Mancini offered a re-orchestrated version of "The Thing Strikes" (along with "Desert Rendezvous," another *Outer Space* cue) in his enjoyable 1990 *Mancini in Surround* CD. This was around the same time he began playing some of his "monster music" during his concert tours.

"Zombie George," a three-minute Mancini composition, is heard when Putnam and Ellen drive back to find the telephone workers, the piece effectively using Theremin (playing the alien theme), Novachord and shimmering harp and vibraphone to accentuate Glob George staring into the sun without blinking. The cue also contains Mancini's rendition of the four-note ostinato Gertz employed in "Mysterious Desert." ("Zombie George" makes a brief appearance in *Monster on the Campus* when the giant dragonfly first appears at the window.) After Putnam and Ellen drive away, we hear the Mancini-composed "George's Double," with violins and violas teeming with Novachord to create weird-sounding chords that enhance the strangeness of the situation. The piece was rather oddly chosen to serve as the only tracked orchestral cue in *The Deadly Mantis*, where it accompanies an image of an aircraft carrier searching for the big bug. "George's Double" also made a nearly two-minute appearance in the opening scene of *The Thing That Couldn't Die*.

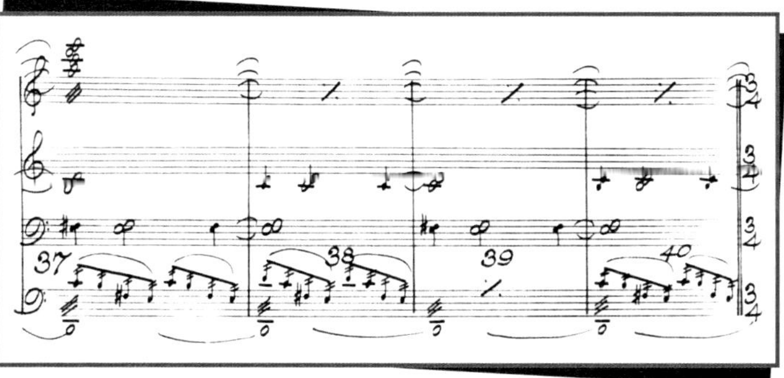

Henry Mancini's ostinato. (© 1953 Northridge Music Co.)

Conductor's score of Henry Mancini's "Zombie George." (© 1953 Northridge Music Co.)

Stein's "Globs Give Instructions" is heard as Putnam spots Globs Frank and Glob George in town and follows them into an alley. A harp pluck alerts Putnam to the aliens' presence, with Novachord and vibraphone applying an extraterrestrial sheen to the piece. The four-note alien theme reinforces the idea that things aren't as they seem, and a second harp pluck signals the invaders' sudden disappearance from the alley. When Putnam confronts them inside a building, Stein copied eight bars of the ostinato Mancini wrote for "Zombie George," which, due to its repetitive nature, provides atmosphere without interfering with the dialogue. It's not known why Stein didn't provide his own version of this motif, as Gertz did in "Mysterious Desert." The powerful timpani-laden music that plays as the aliens walk past Putnam adds a sense of power completely missing from the mundane visual. "Prospector Globbed," another Stein composition, segues from the previous cue and highlights the sequence when three scruffy-faced prospectors (including Edgar Dearing, who plays a scruffy-faced miner in *Tarantula*) are taken over by the shape-changing aliens at the Excelsior mine shaft. The piece, which combines original Stein material with two five-bar phrases written for Mancini's "The Thing Strikes," was mutilated in the movie after images of the Glob

Herman Stein sketch showing copied bars from "Globs Give Instructions." (© 1953 Gilead Music Co.)

were subsequently added. This resulted in some of Stein's music being excised, with other music repeated or included out-of-context, leaving behind some audible edits in the picture. Because of the amount of music that was deleted, it's likely the scene itself was also substantially reduced.

The only use of previously written music in *It Came from Outer Space* is a two-second excerpt of Mancini's "Jitterbug Routine," an instrumental song that plays over the radio. Originally composed for the 1952 Ann Blyth comedy *Sally and Saint Anne*, it was a very popular source music cue: It's heard via a record player in Jack Arnold's *Girls in the Night*, and in the Audie Murphy biopic *To Hell and Back*, Audie dances to it in a restaurant. Although this need not be mentioned, the dance scene in *Sally and Saint Anne* that featured this music was the favorite acting experience in the entire career of Robert Nichols (*The Thing from Another World*, *This Island Earth*). If you watch *Sally and Saint Anne*, you will understand why.

Gertz's "Dr. Snell Disappears" quietly augments the sheriff informing Putnam that the Wayne Observatory astronomer has been reported missing. There's a curious sadness to the music, which uses two flutes in the melody, and as the scene switches to the desert at night, tremolo strings and foreboding woodwinds, then celesta and Novachord, stress the ominous implications of the disappearance. "Kidnapping Ellen" augments Glob Frank stopping Ellen's car, with Gertz employing thunderous timpani and Theremin to heighten the impact of the abduction. This scene was edited after it was scored, and five measures near the beginning of the piece wound up containing solo Theremin rather than the orchestral music that Gertz wrote. It almost sounds as if the orchestra was dialed down on the soundtrack to allow the Theremin to creep through. This was an odd alteration because the Glob doesn't appear until the cue's end, and it's possible that during the orchestral recording session it was decided that solo Theremin would accomplish what they wanted without the rest of the players, so that Theremin part was recorded the next day. The alien eye special effect in this scene and elsewhere in the movie was referred to as an "'amoeba' effect" on Gertz's music sketch.

Mancini contributed the moody "Desert Rendezvous," which begins as Putnam waits out in the desert cold to hear from the aliens. A melody on G flute telegraphs that something strange is in the wind, while piano and Novachord accentuate the appearance of one of the extraterrestrials posing as Ellen. Orchestral trills cry out as Glob Ellen looks around one final time while Putnam calls out for her to wait, the music helping to build the dramatic impact right before she vanishes. Mancini applies some leeway to the four-note alien theme by playing variations of it mostly on strings, a fitting approach for a beautiful female alien. Barbara Rush was amused that she had to wear an elegant black evening dress for this scene, as if the mere appearance of her in something more casual wouldn't have been enough to entice her beau to follow her.

The 31-second Stein cue "The Thing" plays when a Glob reveals itself to Putnam at the opening of the mine shaft, the piece being thematically related to Stein's earlier "Visitors from Space." Mancini's "Visitors" covers the scene when Putnam returns to his home, only to discover that he's been visited by aliens, whose glittering trail motif sounds. Unless the music wasn't synched exactly as intended, Mancini slightly telegraphs the event in a subtle yet effective way, as the music begins when Putnam—but not the audience—sees that his front door is not locked. An orchestral crescendo signals that something important is about to be revealed, but which merely turns out to be his clothes having been removed from the closet. Still, it gets the viewers on the edge of their seats for the 3-D effect of the empty hangers. A vibraphone shimmer is added when the trail disappears from the floor. This cue is a good example of how Mancini used motifs that the other composers also employed, but gave them his own voice.

Conductor's score of Herman Stein's "The Thing." (© 1953 Gilead Music Co.)

"Glob Frank Killed," an electrifying cue by Gertz, highlights the action sequence when Putnam drives out to the mine to warn the aliens, while the angry townsfolk race to setup a barricade to stop Glob Frank's truck. The cue ebbs and flows to match the back-and-forth cuts between the car, the townsfolk and the blockade, and prominent timpani near the end musically punctuates the bullets being fired at the alien. Gertz was a master at creating cues of a serpentine nature, and the way this part of the film goes back and forth between different subjects made this the perfect type of piece for him to score. A few measures of "Glob Frank Killed," with piccolo accompanying the image of Glob Frank driving, were repeated by Gertz 18 seconds apart, which saved him a bit of composing time. If you love this cue, you'll have a good excuse to watch *Monster on the Campus*, where portions of it are tracked in seven times for a total of over six minutes.

"Killing Glob Ellen" segues from the prior composition, right after Frank's truck explodes. Muted brass, woodwinds, vibe and Novachord color the opening of the piece, and then Gertz offers a slightly re-orchestrated version of "Mysterious Desert" when Putnam enters the mine. As he encounters Glob Ellen, a lengthy Theremin solo occurs, and after he is almost lured to his death down a chasm, marimba, vibraphone and upper strings "on the fingerboard" lead to a second Theremin appearance just before Glob Ellen falls to her doom. Probably due to the additional film editing done after the score was recorded, part of "Killing Glob Ellen" was replaced with some of Gertz's "Kidnapping Ellen," with Theremin being added to the mix. A bit of Theremin solo from "Killing Glob Ellen" was also used 14 minutes earlier in *Outer Space*, when Putnam gets an eyeful of the Glob in the mine tunnel.

Mancini's "Rescued" enlists vibraphone, Novachord, harp and other colorings as it depicts the human hostages leaving the mine. Around the time Glob Putnam resumes his extraterrestrial appearance, further musical edits can be heard due to both the film and its soundtrack being altered to accommodate the added Glob footage. Theremin was also overdubbed onto this part of the music, even though Mancini specifically requested that it remain "tacet" (unplayed) during the composition. His "End Title" is heard as the spaceship blasts off to continue its journey, with ascending woodwinds accompanying the departure, and triumphant brass letting us know that a noble event has just occurred. The moment the sheriff says, "Well, they've

Conductor's score of Irving Gertz's "Glob Frank Killed." (© 1953 Accolade Music Publishing Co.)

gone," Mancini brings us back to the world of normalcy as he writes in melodic tonalities as Stein did in "Sand Rock" at the beginning of the picture, and which he'd reprise in the next cue. It's details like this that separate superior film scoring from lesser writing, and it's extremely likely that the three composers mapped out this approach in advance. Mancini's music ends after Putnam's optimistic comment "They'll be back" when the time is right for our two worlds to meet again. This cue had further uses in Universal motion pictures, and it ably opened the trailer for *Tarantula*.

Stein's gorgeous "End Cast," a full-orchestral rendition of "Sand Rock," plays during the end credits. Beginning with a chime, this composition is probably the loveliest end cue in any of Universal's sci-fi thrillers, as the film itself was one of the most positive and upbeat. As the melody is thematically, orchestrationally and harmonically linked to the picture's opening, it provides the perfect closure for the film both musically and dramatically. Unfortunately, this was something Universal failed to do on too many other occasions when they should have known better. In countless pictures, they would lug out an End Cast that was a chestnut from the music library, but which had nothing to do with the rest of the score, or they would add a happy-ending End Cast when the movie had a less-than-happy ending. Maybe they figured that a perky, upbeat musical closure would make audiences forget that they had just watched a 90-minute downer and they'd be more likely to go see the next Universal motion picture.

To be fair, other studios were equally guilty of taking this rose-colored approach. "Always leave 'em laughing," or at least smiling, seemed to be Hollywood's *modus operandi* regarding their closing musical statements. Fortunately, Stein's *Outer Space* ending matched the optimistic sentiment of the movie's climax. His "End Cast" appeared in other Universal films, including an abbreviated version that ended *Running Wild*. Stein's music played an important role in a dozen of Jack Arnold's pictures, and in the director's *Man in the Shadow* (1957), the "End Cast" was, intriguingly, the only tracked cue in an otherwise entirely original orchestral score. Could it be that Arnold had an affection for the piece and requested that it be used at the end of this picture?

From beginning to end, *It Came from Outer Space*'s score proved that when it came to classic science fiction film music, Universal could deliver the goods as well as any other studio. Unfortunately, and par for the course, the only music credit in the picture went to Joseph Gershenson for musical direction, perpetuating the misconception that the head of the music department was Universal's main musical talent. The studio's policy was to omit a composing credit when more than one composer worked on the same picture, unless the main writer contributed 80 percent of the music, in which case that single composer would receive an on-screen credit along with Gershenson. According to Herman Stein, the department didn't want multiple composers credited because it would seem as if the film was scored "by committee." But as will be explained later, that probably wasn't the only reason the composers didn't receive screen recognition.

The lack of a composer's credit is the main reason so many of Universal's scores aren't treated with the same musical respect that other soundtracks have received, going all the way back to the late 1930s. Other genre classics like Akira Ifukube's *Godzilla*, Max Steiner's *King Kong* and Bronislau Kaper's *Them!* could easily be discussed and rhapsodized by film critics and cineastes because there was a composer's *name* to heap the praise on. Employees who toiled in other Universal departments, including makeup and special effects, were also denied screen credit, as this was an era when credit sequences only lasted for about 75 seconds, and a very limited number of people could be listed. (As opposed to today, when credits seem to take up half the picture's running time.) While the practice of short-shrifting music credits occurred at other studios, Universal's composers were probably affected the most because their studio used multiple composers more often than anywhere else.

Despite the obvious luster the original score added to *It Came from Outer Space*, from a musical standpoint, Universal wasn't going to instantly start acting like a major

In *The Universe According to Universal*, Irving Gertz said that composing *Outer Space* music was "a wonderful challenge.... I loved every bit of it. [Far-out movies] give the composer a lot of elbow room to write freely, and unconfined." Pictured: Gertz and wife Dorothy in the legendary Bob Burns Basement, flanking a Stranger from Outer Space (held by David Schecter). (Photograph courtesy Monstrous Movie Music and Bob Burns.)

studio. Shortly after the film's release, the next Abbott and Costello horror-related movie appeared, and musically speaking, it was another sorry affair. *Abbott and Costello Meet Dr. Jekyll and Mr. Hyde* contained almost no original music, instead tracking in cues from *Abbott and Costello Meet Frankenstein, Buck Privates Come Home, Curtain Call at Cactus Creek, Double Crossbones, Family Honeymoon, Feudin,' Fussin' and A-Fightin,' The Fighting O'Flynn, Francis Goes to the Races, I'll Be Yours, The Invisible Man's Revenge, Ivy, Katie, Kiss the Blood off My Hands, The Life of Riley, Ma and Pa Kettle at Waikiki, Ride 'Em Cowboy, River Lady, Rogues' Regiment, The Senator Was Indiscreet, Swell Guy, Take One False Step, The Time of Their Lives, Up in Central Park, The Web, The Wistful Widow of Wagon Gap* and *You Gotta Stay Happy.* There were a couple of new songs by Frederick Herbert and Arnold Hughes, and two newly composed source music cues, one each by Mancini and Stein. But they weren't enough to add any sense of freshness to the musical sensibilities of that picture, as many of the source movies were the same ones used to create the scores for *The Strange Door* and *The Black Castle.*

Analysis
By Steve Kronenberg

It Came from Outer Space was Universal's opening salvo in the Atomic Age. Its two predecessors *The Strange Door* and *The Black Castle* merely hearkened back to the Gothic horrors of yore, and the 100-percent-guaranteed laugh-free *Abbott and Costello Go to Mars* misfired on all cylinders. *It Came from Outer Space* was the company's first full-bore science fiction film of the 1950s, and one of its best. It was a watershed film in other ways as well: the first to employ the human-alien doppelganger concept, a full three years before *Invasion of the Body Snatchers* (1956); the first 3-D science fiction film; the first 3-D film in widescreen; and the first of several SF forays of the team of producer William Alland and director Jack Arnold.

Initially, what grabs and holds our attention is the superb cinematography. The film practically burns its way onto the screen with the wondrous opening shot of the alien spaceship: The camera tracks the craft as it blazes across the desert sky; then the ship heads directly for the audience before the massive explosive and the "reveal" of the film's title in bold dimensional letters. This startling introductory vision is somewhat reminiscent of the opening to the earlier *The Thing from Another World*, which opens with its title literally *burning* its way through the screen.

The camera then takes us into the crater created by the crashed ship—a menacing tableau first seen in a moody long shot. We are drawn *into* the crater in a spooky tracking shot reminiscent of Karl Freund's initial journey into Castle Dracula in the 1931 Bela Lugosi classic, and ever closer to its otherworldly contents. Amidst a smoky mist, the camera lingers on the ship's hatch, which slowly opens. We then get a 1930s-style tracking shot into the blackness of the ship—another delightful throwback to Freund's photographic style in *Dracula*. Finally, the spooky buildup results in a fine close-up of the amorphous alien preparing to emerge.

There are excellent shots of the crater (actually, a miniature) as seen from Pete's helicopter as Putnam, Ellen and Pete approach it, and the camera captures the sheer vastness of the crater as the curious Putnam ventures down into it, enveloped in smoke. We get a jolting, realistic view of the landslide that obliterates the ship from view and then threatens to obliterate Putnam. The camera captures some of the latter action from below as the stones cascade down one side of the crater.

Throughout the film, the camera lingers on the sheer *isolation* of the desert—reminiscent of the chilly Arctic mood of *The Thing* and, more significantly, the malevolent loneliness of Borgo Pass and Henry Frankenstein's watchtower laboratory. The night shots of the desert are especially unnerving: The camera glides along its dark expanse, yet another homage to Freund's ethereal tracking work in *Dracula*. The sinister visions of the desert by night add a scare quotient to the scene in which the three grizzled miners are waylaid by a Glob.

Some of the movie's finest moments are provided by point-of-view shots of various cast members during their

Meteorite? Pfffft. Meteor-*wrong*! With shock and awe, Putnam (Richard Carlson) finds that the UFO is actually a spaceship.

encounters with the alien. We get a haunting, beautiful shot of Ellen's alien double standing atop a hill, her dress, scarf and hair billowing in the desert wind. *This* Ellen is a seductive, malevolent banshee—a striking contrast to the prim, perky Barbara Rush we see throughout the film. (Dana Wynter's alien transformation in *Invasion of the Body Snatchers* seems virtually *inspired* by this vision of Ellen.) The camera's focus on her windblown clothes and hair—augmenting her unearthly quality—is nearly identical to the way Alfred Hitchcock photographed Kim Novak in the hilltop scene in *Vertigo* (1958). Putnam's confrontation with Glob Ellen occurs in the mine, highlighted by Clifford Stine's shadowy, atmospheric camerawork.

In addition, Stine shines in the alley scene in which Richard Carlson opens the door to reveal the Glob doubles of Joe Sawyer and Russell Johnson. At first, Stine shows us only the Globs' dark, oversized shadows on the inside of the door—a technique again reminiscent of Freund and his Golden Age peers. Stine then delivers a memorable view of both doubles—pallid, cadaverous and swathed in darkness. Our haunting view of these ghostly doppelgangers concludes as Glob Frank tells Putnam to give them time, "or terrible things will happen."

Despite helicopter pilot Pete's "Oh, brother!" reaction to Putnam's spaceship-in-the-crater story, the star-gazer (sitting) tries it out on a larger audience—with the same result. The middle-of-the-night scene was actually shot in broad daylight, as this photograph reveals. From left: Charles Drake, Barbara Rush, Alan Dexter, Dave Willock, Richard Carlson. (Photograph courtesy Ronald V. Borst/ Hollywood Movie Posters.)

It Came from Outer Space is infused with a sense of dread and horror largely due to the moody camerawork and the various cinematographers' absorption of the expressionist techniques of their forebears. The film's thematic obsession with fear of the unknown is beautifully captured by their aptitude for the shadowy, desolate imagery of Gothic horror.

Equally significant—and jarring—is the use of subjective camera angles. *Outer Space* is perhaps the first science fiction film to employ the subjective camera as a lens for the *monster's* point of view. Whenever the alien is viewing its desert environs or an Earthling, we see what It sees through a large, superimposed orb symbolic of the creature's eye. Through this device, *we* see what It sees: an amazed and frightened Putnam and Ellen; the landscape on which the creature is stranded; a terrified George as It advances on him.

In one particularly memorable scene, Glob Frank encounters Ellen in the desert. As the alien orb engulfs the screen, a horrified Ellen sees the duplicate Frank for what he *really* is—but we see her terror through the *alien's eye*. Even when the creature *isn't* on screen, the ominous p.o.v. lens reminds us that the alien is everpresent. The subjective technique is consistently fascinating, and perfectly in keeping with the film's empathy for the alien.

No less interesting than the camerawork is Richard Carlson's excellent performance as amateur astronomer John Putnam. Carlson's rational, credible approach is a highlight of *It Came from Outer Space* and it blends with Barbara Rush's equally believable performance as Ellen. Carlson's facial expressions, in particular, augment his sense of wonder and amazement as he first encounters the alien and attempts to convince Ellen and Charles Drake's Sheriff Matt Warren. Watch Carlson's hands shake with fear and excitement as he exclaims to Pete, "I tell you I *saw this thing*!" (the spaceship).

Throughout the film, Carlson emotes believably and rationally as he seeks to prove the alien's existence. Carlson's Putnam, like the mad doctors we have come to know and love, is a "true believer" convinced of science's wondrous possibilities. Yet he never lets his enthusiasm build to a manic crescendo: His performance is modulated and controlled, an homage to such predecessors as Robert Cornthwaite in *The Thing from Another World* and William Schallert in *The Man from Planet X*. Cornthwaite and Schallert, like Carlson, downplayed their performances as scientists attempting to reach out to extraterrestrials. And, like Schallert and Cornthwaite, Carlson's Putnam is misunderstood as an intellectual renegade. In one scene, Putnam's mentor Dr. Snell describes Putnam as "individual and lonely, a man who thinks for himself."

Carlson also uses his eyes and mouth to convey the frustration he feels. At one point, he beams a look of genuine gratitude at Barbara Rush as she stands by him and tries to understand his conviction that the alien exists. In another scene, he stands in the desert and, murmuring to himself, nearly begs the alien to show itself: "Maybe I'm looking right *at* you and don't even *see* you. Come on *out*!" It's a scene again reminiscent of Cornthwaite's efforts to reason with James Arness' creature at the end of *The Thing*.

Putnam's burden later shifts from convincing his neighbors of the aliens' existence to convincing the sheriff not to destroy them. There's palpable horror and astonishment in his face as he sees an alien for the first time after coaxing one out of the darkness of the mine. But his desperation to save the alien is also superbly conveyed as he confronts the angry and frightened sheriff. In one memorable scene, Putnam desperately tries to bring Warren face to face with his fear by comparing the sheriff's attitude about the aliens to his attitude about a spider: "Why are you afraid of it? Because it has eight legs? Because its mouth moves from side to side instead of up and down?" Carlson's superbly modulated performance carries the film and conveys its essential moral theme: the danger of fearing and refusing to understand that which is ugly, different or unknown. It's a classic horror film theme pioneered by *Frankenstein* (1931), but it also resonates through three other Jack Arnold-Universal films of the 1950s, *Creature from the Black Lagoon*, *Revenge of the Creature* and *The Incredible Shrinking Man*.

Carlson is given fine support by Barbara Rush, whose Ellen subtly goes from non-believer to true believer under Putnam's influence. Charles Drake's portrayal of Sheriff Warren is marked by the same reasoned, temperate approach adopted by Carlson. Instead of delivering a flinty, cold-hearted stereotype, Drake's Warren listens intently to Carlson and makes every effort to believe before his fear overcomes him and he begins thinking with his fists.

We are also treated to the appearance of two B-movie and television stalwarts, Russell Johnson and Joe Sawyer. Both actors affect an affable likability, but when they are duplicated, their faces take on a cold, menacing, zombie-like quality. In fact, their empty, cruel and unfeeling visages as alien doubles predate identical characterizations in *Invasion of the Body Snatchers*.

The sense of eeriness and mystery that permeates *It Came from Outer Space* is accentuated by the music of Herman Stein, Henry Mancini and Irving Gertz. Stein's use of the Theremin is especially evocative, setting a spooky tone from the very beginning, and augmenting the creepiness of the desolate desert scenes. Stein obviously took a cue from Bernard Herrmann and Dimitri Tiomkin, both of whom used the Theremin to startling effect in, respectively, *The Day The Earth Stood Still* and *The Thing from Another World*. Mancini and Gertz ably abetted Stein with loud crescendos during the scenes in which the alien is revealed and begins duplicating Earthlings.

It Came from Outer Space, like many of its contemporaries, was a product of its time. The fear engendered by Communism and McCarthyism envelops the film, just as paranoia drove *The Thing from Another World*, *The War of the Worlds*, *Invasion of the Body Snatchers* and *It Conquered the World*. But *Outer Space* is more akin to *The Man from Planet X* and *The Day the Earth Stood Still*, preaching moderation over mass hysteria, an effort to understand the unknown before the trigger is pulled. In fact, Glob George tells Frank: "We cannot—we would not—take your souls or minds or bodies." With its plea for reason over fear and hatred, *It Came from Outer Space* helped buck the paranoid trend of the 1950s and paved the way for the benevolent views conveyed by the more modern films *Close Encounters of the Third Kind* (1977) and *E.T. the Extra-Terrestrial* (1982). The final-reel scene, in which the kidnapped locals emerging unharmed from the spaceship into the mine basin, seems a direct influence on the conclusion of *Close Encounters*.

It Came from Outer Space has an intelligent, moderate approach to science fiction, while still delivering the wonder and the horror that grace the finest and most frightening genre films.

Creature from the Black Lagoon (1954)

Full Credit Information

CREDITS: Produced by William Alland; Directed by Jack Arnold; Underwater Sequences Directed by James C. Havens; Screenplay: Harry Essex and Arthur Ross; Story: Maurice Zimm; Photography: William E. Snyder; Special Photography: Charles S. Welbourne [a.k.a. "Scotty" Welbourne]; Editor: Ted J. Kent; Art Directors: Bernard Herzbrun and Hilyard Brown; Set Decorators: Russell A. Gausman and Ray Jeffers; Sound: Leslie I. Carey and Joe Lapis; Music Director: Joseph Gershenson; Julie Adams' Wardrobe: Rosemary Odell; Hair Stylist: Joan St. Oegger; Makeup: Bud Westmore; Assistant Director: Fred Frank; UNCREDITED: Story Idea: William Alland; Contributors to Screenplay: Ernest Nims and Leo Lieberman; Original Music Composers: Hans J. Salter, Herman Stein and

Henry Mancini; Tracked Music Composers: Robert Emmett Dolan, Milton Rosen, Herman Stein, Henry Mancini and Hans J. Salter; Orchestrator: David Tamkin; Conductor: Joseph Gershenson; Musicians: Emo Neufeld, Manuel Compinsky, Louis Pressman, Ambrose Russo, Lou Klass, Sam Fordis, Samuel Cytron, Sarah Kreindler, Leon Goldwasser, Howard Colf (Violin), Joseph Reilich, Cecil Bonvalot, Harriet Payne (Viola), Joseph Ullstein, Stephen De'ak, Alec Compinsky (Cello), Harold E. Brown (Bass), Arthur C. Smith, Ethmer Roten, Jr. (Flute), Arthur Gault (Oboe), Blake Reynolds, Alan Harding, Karl Leaf (Clarinet), Lloyd Hildebrand (Bassoon), Willard Culley, Jr., Alfred Williams (Horn), Gene LaFreniere, Don Linder, Robert Goodrich (Trumpet), John Stanley, Bruce Squires, H.L. Menge (Trombone), Harold McDonald, Ralph Collier (Drums), Lyman Gandee (Piano), Joseph Quintile (Harp), Jack Barsby (Tuba); Creature Costume Designer: Milicent Patrick; Creature Costume Makers: Jack Kevan, Chris Mueller, Jr., Milicent Patrick, Tom Case, Rudolph Parducci, John Kraus, Elmer Balogh, John Phiefer and Frank Acuna; Production Manager: Gilbert Kurland; Assistant Directors: Russ Haverick and Kenny (Joseph E. Kenny?); Sound Editors: Ray Craddock and Al Kennedy; Unit Manager: Foster Thompson; Camera Operators: Kyme Meade and Lathrop (Philip Lathrop?); Assistant Cameramen: Charles Alder, Robert Hager and King (James King?); Optical Department Supervisor: Roswell Hoffman; Cameraman ("Nebula & Explosion" sequence, "Gill Man on Fire" trick shots *et al.*): David S. "Stan" Horsley; Mechanical-Visual-Special Effects Supervisor ("Nebula & Explosion" sequence): Charlie Baker; Pyrotechnic Supervisor ("Nebula & Explosion" sequence): Eddie Stein; Still Photographer: Bert Anderson; Script Clerks: Luanna Sherman and Hughes (Dorothy Hughes?); First Grips: Everett Brown and Wes Thompson; Second Grips: Les Neal and Cowie (Charles Cowie?); Gaffer: Norton Kurland; Best Boy: Lester Burnette; First Prop Man: Harry Grundstrum; Assistant Prop Men: Burke (Ross Burke?), Barrett (Hoyle Barrett?), Murdock (Robert Murdock?), Martino (Solly Martino?) and Neel (Roy Neel?); Wardrobe Woman: Rosamonde Prior; Wardrobe Man: Roger J. Weinberg; Makeup: Frank Westmore, Bob Dawn, Perrell (Sidney Perell?), Hadley (Joe Hadley?) and Marcellino (Nick Marcellino?); Hair Stylists: Lillian Burkhart and Kirkpatrick (Sue Kirkpatrick?); Sound Recorder: Donald Cunliffe; Mike Men: Jack Bolger and Strong; Sound Mixer: Freericks; Cable Men: Frank Artman, Marks and Healey; Dialogue Director: Irvin Berwick; Coordinator: Ray Gockel; Lily Boy: Egan (William Egan?); Stand-ins: Sue Curtis, Joe Walls, Harold Lockwood and Otto Malde; Propmaker: Fred Knoth; UNCONFIRMED: Production Coordinator: Ellis Coleman; FLORIDA CREW: Assistant Director: George Lollier; Unit Manager: James T. Vaughn; Script Clerk: Jack Herzberg; Assistant Cameraman: Walter Bluemel; Camera Crew Member: Clifford Poland; Still Photographer: Harry Walsh; Underwater Still Photographer: Bruce Mozert; Camera Mechanic: F. McConihay; First Grip: Fletcher; Makeup: Tom Case and Mark Reedall; Propmaker: Frank Brendel; First Aid Man: R.A. Guyer; Diving Trainer for Jack Betz and Stanley Crews: Fred Zendar; Safety Divers: Fred Zendar, Charles McNabb, Patsy Boyette, Robert Lee Tinney, Frank Den Bleyker; UNCONFIRMED FLORIDA CREW: Underwater Cameraman: Bruce Mozert; INSERTS CREW: Cameraman: Robinson (George Robinson?); Camera Operator: Coopersmith (William Coopersmith?); Assistant Cameraman: Wyckoff (Robert Wyckoff?); First Grip: Hawkins (Ben Hawkins?); Technician: Schwartz; Battery Man: McCathy; 79 minutes.

CAST: Richard Carlson (*Dr. David Reed*), Julia Adams [Julie Adams] (*Kay Lawrence*), Richard Denning (*Dr. Mark Williams*), Antonio Moreno (*Dr. Carl Maia*), Nestor Paiva (*Lucas*), Whit Bissell (*Dr. Edwin Thompson*), Bernie Gozier (*Zee*), Henry Escalante (*Chico*), UNCREDITED: Ben Chapman, Ricou Browning (*The Gill Man*), Al Wyatt (*The Gill Man on Fire*), Rodd Redwing (*Luis*), Julio Lopez [Perry Lopez] (*Tomas*), Sydney Mason (*Dr. Matos*), Stanley Crews (*Richard Carlson's Underwater Double*), Ginger Stanley (*Julie Adams' Swimming Double*), Helen Morgan, Polly Burson (*Julie Adams' Stunt Doubles*), Jack Betz, Frank Den Bleyker (*Richard Denning's Underwater Doubles*); UNCONFIRMED: Richard Cutting (*Narrator*); IN UNUSED FOOTAGE: Cliff Lyons (*Richard Carlson's Stunt Double*), Allen Pinson (*Richard Denning's Stunt Double*).

Production History

By Tom Weaver

After his expedition to an Amazon tributary in Brazil, a scientist brings back to civilization what looks like the forearm of a creature thought to be long-extinct. Now, with new expedition members, he returns to the Amazon, traveling by boat back into the primordial jungleland where he and his colleagues encounter monsters from the prehistoric past.

Yes, monsters, plural, because the above is not a recap of the plot of *Creature from the Black Lagoon* but of the 1912 novel *The Lost World*. That Arthur Conan Doyle tale first came to the movies as a silent in 1925. Eight years later, its basic plot was transplanted to the Indian Ocean for *King Kong* (1933).

In 1954, the *Lost World* storyline resurfaced again in *Creature from the Black Lagoon* which, like the novel and the silent movie, is set in Brazil, on the Amazon. But *Black La-*

goon producer William Alland wasn't thinking of *The Lost World* when he started devising his monster movie; he was thinking back, believe it or not, to an Orson Welles dinner party.

The year was 1940 and the place was the home of stage and radio wunderkind turned Hollywood picturemaker Welles, then in the midst of crafting his movie masterpiece *Citizen Kane*. Present at the gathering were Welles; his girlfriend, Mexican actress Dolores del Rio; Mexican cinematographer Gabriel Figueroa; and actor William Alland, a member of Welles' renowned Mercury Theatre. Then 24, Alland was playing in *Kane* the small but pivotal part of the shadow-shrouded *News on the March* newsreel reporter Thompson. In 1995, Alland recalled for me:

> **In idle conversation, Figueroa told the story about the fact that there is this creature that lives up in the Amazon who is half-man, half-fish. Once a year he comes up and claims a maiden, and after that, he leaves, and the village is then safe for *another* year. We just looked at him. He said, "You people think I'm joking, don't you?" and he then *insisted* that this was absolutely true, that he could produce *photos* and this and that…! He went on and on and on and on and we said, "Yeah, yeah, yeah, yeah…" [*laughs*], and we went on to other things. But he, for about five *minutes* there, held forth about how this was *not* a myth, that there really was such a creature, that the Amazonian people talked about him all the time, etc.**

Gabriel Figueroa (1907–97), the award-nominated cinematographer of *The Pearl, Los Olvidados, The Night of the Iguana et al.* ... and a guy who truly believed that a man-fish haunted the Amazon. (Photograph courtesy Film Forum.)

Possible? Well, who can say? As Sir John Roxton states in *The Lost World*, the more you know of South America, "the more you would understand that anythin' was possible—*anythin'*." He continued,

> **[T]here are 50,000 miles of waterway runnin' through a forest that is very near the size of Europe. You and I could be as far apart from each other as Scotland is from Constantinople, and yet each of us be in the same great Brazilian forest. Man has just made a track here and a scrape there in the maze. Why, the river rises and falls the best part of 40 feet, and half the country is a morass that you can't pass over. Why shouldn't somethin' new and wonderful lie in such a country?**

Fast-forward to 1952, past Alland's war service as a combat pilot (56 South Pacific missions) and award-winning radio career, and we find his shingle hanging at Universal-International. Forever trying to dream up new screen tales, his mind flashed back to the Welles dinner party and Figueroa's strange account. With a few clever embellishments, he put it down on paper as

"THE SEA MONSTER"
A Story Idea By WILLIAM L. ALLAND

Alland's three-page "Sea Monster" memo, dated October 2, 1952, begins by describing the night of the Welles party. Figueroa's already tall tale reaches new heights in the retelling: Alland wrote that he had once had dinner with a South American movie director [*sic*] who revealed that, living underwater and on the banks of the Amazon River, there exists a race of beings that resemble humans in shape but have gills in place of ears; webbed hands and feet; and fishlike skin:

> **[A] friend of my informant organized a small expedition and proceeded up the Amazon to find these creatures. He was never heard from again. However, many months later some natives found and brought back to civilization a camera which was identified as belonging to the explorer. There was some film in this camera and when developed—there it was, big as life, a seven-foot creature with gills, webbed hands and feet, and a scaly skin. My informant swore he has been shown this photograph and promised me that some day he would send me a print.**

Alland went on to write that he complimented the storyteller on his "fine imagination" and yet continued to wonder if such creatures could actually exist. At this point in the memo, he proposes a film called *The Sea Monster*, which would open with a scene of just such an after-dinner conversation and one character regaling his listeners with the story of the Amazon fish-men. Another expedition ("with a beautiful girl along, of course") sets out in a small boat, their arrival in the fish-men's Amazon waters watched by "a strange pair of eyes glistening under water." The beautiful blonde sees the eyes ("filled with lust and desire") and screams. Shots are fired but nothing is found.

The scientist of the expedition turns heavy, sends the blonde's boyfriend off on a wild goose chase, then "overpowers the girl, chloroforms her, ties her, semi-nude, onto a raft, [and] sets a snare-trap around the raft." As he watches, the webbed hand of the monster reaches up and drags the unconscious girl into the water. From here, Alland suggested two possible story directions: (1) The boyfriend succeeds in rescuing her, and the monster is killed, or (2) the monster is captured and brought to a small South American seaport, but it escapes and terrorizes the area. "Needless to say," Alland concludes, "the monster's end is brought about by his desire for the blonde-haired girl of the expedition."

The second proposed ending instantly calls to mind *King Kong*, and in fact indicates that "The Sea Monster"'s *whole plot* is lifted from *Kong*. When I asked the always forthright Alland about the similarities, he made no effort to deny it: "Absolutely! As a matter of fact, [reusing *Kong*'s basic plot] was the whole idea. Oh, sure, that was my idea!" he laughed. Surely not coincidentally, RKO's summer 1952 theatrical reissue of *King Kong* had just racked up gross profits of $2,500,000.

The job of turning Alland's idea into a treatment went to 43-year-old Maurice Zimm, a longtime writer but a newcomer to the movies: His submission *Black Lagoon*, dated November 8, 1952, was his first written-for-the-movies story to reach the screen.

Black Lagoon

(treatment by Maurice Zimm)

A winch cable lowers a bathysphere from a trawler into ocean waters, a TV camera covering the activity. An on-camera announcer says into his hand-mike that famed undersea explorer Dr. Lyman Reed has reached a depth of 4000 feet—well on his way to establishing a one-mile record for underwater descent. Kay Lawrence, a blonde heiress, reaches Reed via radio and warns the man she loves that the seas are getting too rough, and that she's about to order that the bathysphere be brought back up. Over a speaker comes Reed's retort: "*I* give the orders, Kay. And if you even try, this will be the last time I ever let you talk me into bringing you along." Another sudden lurch of the ship cuts off communication and prompts Reed's assistant Donovan to order that the winch be reversed. The crane hoists the bathysphere back aboard the trawler and a groggy, shaken Reed emerges. He's thankful to have been rescued and vows that tomorrow he'll make another attempt at breaking the record.

That night, Reed explains to Kay the reason for his recent, reckless behavior: He needs to break the record in order to get money from the TV network, and from product endorsements, in order to finance a South American expedition. He shows her a letter from his explorer-friend Carl Sloan who insists that there exists in the Amazon "a species which Sloan has named 'Pisces Man.' … Like the human race. Except for such things as gills." Reed needs $64,000 to organize an expedition to come to Sloan's aid with special equipment that will enable them to capture a specimen. Kay offers to foot the bill but Reed refuses with a smile. Later, out on the deck, she uses a chisel to damage the portable generator that powers the bathysphere equipment. Reed groans, "You wrecked the Field Coils."

"Which means, Lyman, that you'll have to take my money—for the Expedition."

At the office of Kay's estate handler Miles Faraday, she asks for a $64,000 check to finance the expedition. Faraday offers to write the check on the condition that she stay behind, but she wraps him around her finger. Faraday later phones Ted Clayton, the Lawrence Oil Company troubleshooter, and offers him a substantial bonus to infiltrate the Reed expedition and keep an eye on Kay.

Clayton makes his way to the docks of the South American town of Leticia and locates the *Pongo*, the sternwheeler chartered by the Reed expedition. In the pilot house he encounters a barefoot man in T-shirt and dungarees: Tasha, the captain of what he calls the "old wessel." Clayton offers his services as mate (or engineer or steward), but Tasha has one man, Joe, filling all those positions. Behind Tasha's back, Clayton bribes Joe to quit without notice.

At the Leticia airfield, Tasha and his new mate-engineer-steward Clayton meet the just-arrived Reed, Kay, Kay's secretary Winifred "Winnie" Adams ("considerably past the bloom of youth") and Donovan and take them to the *Pongo*. That night, a man in torn clothes shuffles weakly up the boat's gangplank and demands to see Reed. Clayton escorts the stranger to the salon, where Reed recognizes him as Carl Sloan. Sloan says that the other two members of his expedition are dead; they'd tried to capture the Pisces Man alive, without traps and nets. To prove what he's saying, the half-mad scientist produces the petrified forearm and webbed, taloned hand of a monster, unearthed by his men before they died.

Soon the *Pongo* is en route to the Black Lagoon; in the galley, comedy relief rears its ugly head as Tasha and Winnie clash, with Winnie eventually showing him who's boss. The

Pongo arrives at its destination, a point five miles from the Black Lagoon. In a series of trips aboard an outboard motor–powered dugout canoe, Reed, Sloan and Donovan bring traps and special nets of spun steel to the Lagoon via a water trail. After a week of nothing but empty nets and traps, Reed is becoming frustrated. One day he is convinced to let Kay accompany them to the Lagoon. Determined to get her man (Reed), she is at her most enticing as she sits in the bow of the canoe, "her stunning figure arrayed in an abbreviated sunsuit." A pair of human-and-yet-not-human eyes peer at her from below the surface of the water but only Sloan notices them. During their next trip to the Lagoon, a webbed hand silently breaks the surface and reaches for Kay, but it disappears when Clayton shouts a warning cry from the bank. The fact that Clayton surreptitiously followed them makes him a suspicious character to the others.

For the next two weeks, Sloan haunts the lagoon watching for some further sign of the Pisces Man. Romance blooms as Tasha is served kugel by an increasingly giggly and girlish Winnie. Reed, sick with fever, wonders if Kay can not only overlook the difference in their ages but also the fact that his first love will always be science. Consumed by his hatred for Clayton, Sloan throws a spear from ambush, knocking him into the water. He's saved from the piranha by Tasha and Donovan.

The next day, Sloan asks a hesitant Kay to accompany him to the Lagoon. There he chloroforms her, places her on a raft, and conceals himself in the branches of an overhanging tree. When the Pisces Man climbs onto the raft and caresses her blonde hair, Sloan drops a net over him and jumps down. The monster tears the net apart like it was gossamer thread and then crushes Sloan to death. Clayton arrives to see the Pisces Man drop into the water with Kay in his arms. He swims after them, to the floor of the Lagoon ("like an underwater fairyland") and then into a tunnel which leads up into a grotto "as enchanting as a child's dream. It's bathed in the soft glow of luminous, multi-colored rocks which decorate the walls in designs reminiscent of the first artistic strivings of the human race. ... [A]t the far end is a shadowy recess in which can be seen decorated mounds resembling graves."

The Gill Man places Kay on the "floral carpet" and then backs into the shadows, his gaze still fixed on her. When she wakes and is startled by the sight of the Gill Man, he approaches slowly, making a crooning sound that is almost human, a look of pleading in his eyes. Clayton attacks the Gill Man with a machete, but the creature knocks it from his hand and the fight is on. Clayton applies a headlock, closing off the creature's gills until he drops unconscious.

Kay and Clayton bring the news of the Pisces Man's lair to Reed. Kay's pleas to leave the Pisces Man in peace fall on deaf ears; under Reed's supervision, the grotto's underwater tunnel entrance is dynamited, forcing a weakened, gasping-for-air Pisces Man to crawl to a surface entrance. He is seized by the men and placed in an enormous water-filled tank on the *Pongo* afterdeck. On the third night of the voyage back to Leticia, Kay is drawn to the prison-tank and looks in at the Pisces Man, whose eyes are "so human, so tortured, so pleading."

Crowds swarm on the Leticia docks trying to get a look at the creature; to Kay, it's all as "tawdry and revolting" as a freak sideshow. That night, in the airfield hangar where a cargo carrier (with the tank aboard) is stored, she again looks in at the Pisces Man, whose eyes seem to say, "It's now or never ... now or never." She unbolts the tank door and stands unafraid as the grateful creature gently touches her as he deplanes. Reed sees the Pisces Man entering the jungle and shouts orders that he be recaptured. At military headquarters, Col. Harbus organizes lines of defense throughout the eight miles of jungle between the airfield and the river. On a shadowy Leticia side street, the Pisces Man realizes that the soldiers are getting too close and climbs through the unlocked window of a house into the room of a sleeping blonde child. On his way out, he adjusts the coverlet over the child.

Wielding a rifle, the obsessed Reed is waiting on the Amazon shore as the Pisces Man, weak after four hours on land, staggers out of the jungle. Reed realizes that no one is close enough to stop him from getting to the water and begins firing. Riddled with bullets, the Pisces Man crawls into the water, which begins to churn as piranha converge. Clayton must prevent the frenzied Reed from jumping into the river after him.

The next morning, Kay is seated aboard the cargo carrier, waving out the window at Tasha ("He looks like he'd just stepped out of a Mail Order Catalog, his civilian wardrobe is so completely and uncomfortably new") and Winnie (who now sports a ring on her third finger, left hand). Kay turns to Reed, seated beside her, and he promises that what happened last night won't stand between them. But she knows it will. And when she sees Clayton boarding a passenger plane across the field, she bolts from her seat and runs to him.

•••••••••••••••••••••••••

Among the writing contributors to *Black Lagoon* (Alland, Arthur Ross, Harry Essex), Zimm has always received short shrift in the fan press. And, judging from his 72-page treatment, perhaps deservedly so! If filmed, his would been a very different type of movie from the monster-rific, kiddie-thrill-packed *Creature from the Black Lagoon*; Zimm's treatment is as much about the Reed-Kay-Clayton triangle (plus the comic-relief Tasha-Winnie romance) as the sea monster. Although violent when provoked, Zimm's Pisces Man is in his own way civilized and, with Kay, almost courtly. Zimm mentions his scalloped gills which at a distance "resemble the bobbed hair of a knight of old"; if he'd looked like that in the movie, it might have added to the subliminal impression that this horror hails from the royal family of movie monsters. In short, Zimm's descriptions and depiction of the Pisces Man make him seem more human than monster. And this appears to be exactly the type of "monster" that Zimm's boss Alland wanted. Alland told me,

> **I had an idea of how this creature should look—I wanted him to look much more human. I had a marvelous sculptor create [a small statue of] a very sad, beautiful monster—in fact, it *wasn't* a monster, it was far more "attractive," more "romantic-looking" than the beast we ended up with. While it had fish lips and this, that and the other, *my* creature was all done as a sort of an aquatic development of a *man*. And I was so pleased with it! It would still frighten you, but it would frighten you because of how human it was, not the other way around.**

Zimm's treatment gave Alland the aquatic variant on *King Kong* he wanted: Dr. Reed, a Carl Denham–like adventurer and publicity hound, organizes a shipboard expedition to search unexplored territory for a prehistoric monster, and allows a beautiful blonde to accompany them. The girl is abducted by a heavy and delivered into the clutches of the monster, but rescued by the virile male lead. Later, the monster itself is captured and brought to civilization, but manages to escape. Even *Kong*'s "Beauty and the Beast" angles are intact, with Zimm overdoing it almost shamelessly, as in the scene where the Pisces Man adjusts the blanket of the sleeping child. In the entire Zimm treatment, the Pisces Man only kills two people (Sloan and a sentry in Leticia—the latter "off-camera") even though there are extraneous characters galore.

The Zimm treatment was critiqued in a one-page December 11 memo. "This treatment seems to hold promise of becoming an excellent horror-suspense film," the memo writer began. "The handling of the monster and his surroundings is first-rate." Then came the Howevers: the stage-setting goes on too long, the leading man is not introduced "until considerably too late," there's just too much of Tasha and Winnie, etc. The writer closes by saying that he discussed his ideas with Alland, who was in "general agreement" about them. He continues, "[Alland] further indicated that he would change the ending to provide a means of possibly continuing this into sequels by keeping the monster alive, or at least leaving his fate in doubt at the end of the picture." It's interesting to learn that, right from the project's earliest stages, Alland could see far enough ahead to sense that his fantastic man-fish might deserve its own Dracula-Frankenstein-Mummy (etc.)-type *series*.

Alland and director Jack Arnold spent part of the next ten months making the 3-D *It Came from Outer Space*, adapted by writer Harry Essex from treatments by Ray Bradbury. During that time, tinkering continued on the *Black Lagoon* script. In that era of six-day work weeks, Zimm labored over his treatment from October 23 to December 2, 1952. Leo Lieberman worked over the course of the following two months. Arthur Ross left his mark between March 2 and April 30, 1953; his second-draft screenplay, dated March 19, is a veritable "Missing Link" script, partially spanning the gap between the Zimm treatment and the final Harry Essex screenplay in *Black Lagoon*'s "evolution." According to Ross, Alland came to him claiming to be "in terrible trouble" with *Black Lagoon*. Ross told me,

> **[Alland] had a draft, and it was just impossible—the front office turned it down, they weren't gonna do the picture. Bill said, "Would you look at it?" and I said, "Let me read it and see." At that same time, I had just finished reading Jacques Cousteau's *The Silent World*, his first really big important book, and it occurred to me that what was wrong with [the script] was that it was an imitation of films that had been made in that genre at Universal for 25 years. The only difference was that it was an underwater creature instead of a mummy or Frankenstein or Dracula. I said, "Bill, you've got a mad scientist in your story, and that's passé.... It seems to me that what should be at work here is the fact that it is a scientist curious about the forces of nature, and how nature evolves, and nature's relationship to Man. What he is trying to demonstrate is that nature can be *examined*, but it cannot be *troubled*, it cannot be *dislocated*. The more you attack what is natural in the world, the more likely it will do something to protect itself." That, I thought, should be the essential viewpoint: the scientist warning others not to make a freak out of the Creature. The conflict was that, when they *did*, the Creature became something dangerous to all of them. ... *The Silent World* gave me the most *profound* idea for *Creature*, the idea that the scientist is the hero, not the villain. The scientist is a humanist who *inquires* of nature rather than dictating to it or exploiting it. He's the one who holds out for not harming the Creature.**
>
> **... [Alland] was very nice, and he understood what I was trying to do. He knew that the first approach had failed terribly, the old-fashioned script that he had. Universal had a history of that kind of story—Frankenstein attacks, the Mummy attacks, the *dummy* attacks [*laughs*], any number of things like that, and there was always a mad scientist doing something crazy that provoked it. But I said, "No, we're living in another era, we're living in another time." That was the giant step that I took, and it made *Creature* something quite different.**

Black Lagoon

(second-draft screenplay by Arthur Ross)

This screenplay is a lot closer to the eventual movie than the Zimm treatment, but I'm not in a position to credit all (or *any*) of the changes to Ross, since Leo Lieberman worked on the project for two months during the interim between Zimm and Ross, and I don't know what his contributions were. According to Ross, quoted above, he changed the tenor of the whole script, but until Lieberman's pages come to light, we're taking Ross' word for that. Another elusive item is Ross' earlier (April 17) stab at an acceptable screenplay.

Ross' second-draft screenplay opens with a scene of a speedboat roaring across the waters of a Southern California cove and stopping beside the empty motorboat of David Reed, a Pacific Institute of Marine Life ichthyologist who, clad in lung-diver gear, is working 40 feet below. The speedboat driver is Kay Lawrence, a lovely young woman who gives the impression of "great assurity … especially with men," and her passenger is Reed's colleague Edwin Hempstead. Summoned to the surface, Reed is introduced to Kay; a daughter of privilege, she is proposing to make a $50,000 endowment to the Institute. (This is the only version of the script I've found where the male and female leads are initially strangers to each other.) At the Institute, Reed talks about the Brazilian trip that Kay's money will finance. He and fellow scientists intend to study a particular species of lungfish, and many other fish, to learn how life evolved.

On a wharf in Manaus, Brazil, we meet two more expedition members, zoologist Dr. Sansoni and geologist Dr. Mark, as well as the slovenly Tasha, captain of the *Pongo* (still a weather-beaten sternwheeler). Accompanying the group is Kurt Dreier, a hunter who will take them to the native Indian village where they can examine a pointy-headed skeleton that recently washed up from the river. The skeleton lives up to the hype; the script describes it as "a large skeletal form of the torso, neck and head of an animal. Except for the large size, the rib-cage and spinal column and pelvis bone look almost human. The head, however, is like the skull of [a] prehistoric thing. It is tapered, has a mouth more like a beak."

On the deck of the *Pongo*, Reed and Kay discuss Dreier, who is constantly living up to his German name with talk of the survival of the fittest and the mindset of kill-or-be-killed. As they converse, we vaguely discern underwater the face of a fish looking up; when it moves closer to the surface, the outline of the Gill Man's face is seen. Kay spots it and throws herself into Reed's arms. Reed is leaning out over the side, trying to get a look, when "with a terrible churning of water," the amphibian rears out of the water and knocks the burning lantern from his hand.

The next day, Reed and Dreier don aqualungs and descend in search of the humanoid. In the dark water, they dimly spot the monster and Reed takes pictures, the camera flashes giving them split-second glimpses of him. Dreier fires his harpoon gun, and gets the Gill Man in the side, before Reed yanks the weapon from his hands. Later, below decks on the *Pongo*, Reed puts the negative of one of his photos in a slide projector and shines the image on a white wall: "[There,] in clear sight, is the Gill Man. The structure, his webbed feet, his head, the gills, the webbed hands—all clear and sharp."

Rotenone, a drug that paralyzes fish, is put into the lagoon in an effort to catch the amphibian man. Finally he emerges from the water near the shore and disappears into the jungle growth. Some of the men chase him into a densely overgrown area. The Gill Man fights and mangles a jaguar and then runs like a trapped animal, "throwing aside trees." When he reappears on the shore, he stumbles after a hysterical Kay before collapsing. When the men appear out of the jungle, Reed has to hit Dreier to stop him from shooting the Gill Man.

The beast is loaded into a steel tank on the *Pongo* stern. That night, peering at him through a viewing porthole, Kay observes, "It seems to look at us with a kind of sullen accusation because it's imprisoned." Reed and Kay talk, the latter beating herself up over a failed marriage, and then they have their first kiss. Suddenly the Gill Man pushes the tank apart. Grabbing one of Tasha's native boat hands, the monster raises him overhead and fatally smashes him to the deck. He then dives into the lagoon.

The expedition members' planned getaway lasts only as long as it takes them to get to the lagoon entrance, which is now blocked by a log barricade below the surface. (Kay: "This was built by '*him*'—wasn't it?") Putting on their diving gear, Reed and Dreier make a series of attempts to fasten a winch chain to the logs, so that the *Pongo* can pull them away, but the Gill Man thwarts them. On the next attempt, Reed can't stop Dreier from chasing after the Gill Man. Reed quickly returns to the boat to get a harpoon gun, but Kay talks him out of going back into the water. Realizing that she's right, Reed merely stands on the deck looking out at the water while, below, Dreier and the Gill Man play a subaquatic cat-and-mouse game. It ends when they go *mano a claw-o*, the Gill Man tearing out Dreier's air hose and mouthpiece and continuing to hold him while he drowns.

Reed decides that they must force the Gill Man aboard the *Pongo* in order to kill him. Rotenone is mixed with water, and then with radium compound, and put in an air tank so that it can be fired under pressure; armed with this unusual weapon, Reed again descends into the deeps. More subaquatic encounters with the Gill Man ensue, with Reed warding him off with the luminous rotenone. The Gill Man finally retreats onto the shore but that night climbs silently onto the *Pongo*. Sansoni wanders into his clutches and is grabbed, lifted overhead and lethally thrown down onto the deck. There's now some round-and-round-the-deck hide-and-seek–style suspense but eventually "the numbers game" catches up to the Gill Man as our heroes come at him from all directions: Tasha and Mark put many bullets into him, and Reed shoots a harpoon at him. Finally, as the badly wounded, faltering monster is closing in on Mark, Reed comes up behind him with a fire axe and delivers a fatal blow.

The last scene is set on the foredeck of the *Pongo* as it makes its way back to civilization. Reed says he wishes they could have taken the Gill Man alive and blames Dreier for all that happened; Kay keeps telling him it isn't nice to talk about Dreier like that but Reed still badmouths him, calling him "as much a dead end of nature as the animal he fought." He finally changes the subject, mentioning how "very affectionate" Kay has gotten a few times over the last 24 hours, and the movie fades out as he takes her in his arms and kisses her.

•••••••••••••••••••••••••

This script is a step in the right direction but still not what the ichthyologist ordered. First and foremost, the Beauty and the Beast touches, introduced on Day One in Alland's "The Sea Monster," have all gone missing: In their brief encounters, the Gill Man doesn't react to Kay any differently than he does to any of the men—or, for that matter, to the jaguar! And aside from Kay's comment that the Gill Man, imprisoned inside the *Pongo*'s steel tank, wears an accusing look, she obviously regards him as nothing more than a monster and an object of terror. Without the Beauty and the Beast angle, the story might as well be about an expedition or safari encountering any powerful *real-life* wild animal.

Discussing the movie with me, Ross said that Alland

wanted to put in *more* of the woman. Here comes this big Creature with his cock four feet long, he's going to fuck her, and she gets away just in time—but she *does* think about him [*laughs*]! ... I had done as much [Beauty and the Beast] as I thought it was correct to do, because essentially that wasn't the story. The fact that the Creature was attracted to the woman was not the reason he fought back.... But Bill wanted more of the *King Kong* element in *Creature*, so [Harry Essex came in]. Really, all he did was add more of the girl. Underwater shots, the Creature sees her, the Creature gets an erection [*laughs*].... I rather felt that the nature of the Creature's relationship to the woman in the picture was quite simplistic.

Also M.I.A. is the Kay of the movie-to-come. Once the Gill Man turns up in this draft, *this* Kay becomes a bundle of nerves, alternating from a frightened and defeatist attitude to complete hysteria. Kay's fear of the Gill Man is so strong and so sustained, she becomes pitiable.

Black Lagoon

(step outline of proposed changes by Harry Essex)

In the pool of *Black Lagoon* writers, "the last one in" was Harry Essex, who in the months since working on *It Came from Outer Space* had conspicuously kept his wagon hitched to the tri-dimensional star: He co-wrote the 3-D *Devil's Canyon* (1953), *Southwest Passage* (1954) and *I, the Jury* (1953), also directing the latter. The earliest Essex contribution to *Black Lagoon* that I have seen is a 17-page June 8, 1953, composition titled "Step Outline—Proposed Changes for *Black Lagoon*," which reads like a synopsis. I am not in a position to ascribe everything (or *anything*) new or different in the following synopsis to Essex, without knowing what writing (if any) Ross and/or others did in the interim. Common sense dictates that *some* of the changes are Ross', since his second-draft script was dated March 19 and he was employed on the picture until April 30; one assumes he did a good bit of additional writing in all those weeks.

Essex's step outline opens (like the movie) with a lookback at the formation of the Earth, with narration complete with Genesis quote. From here we fast-forward to modern times and an Amazon beach where geologist Jose Malona and his native guides are examining the skeleton of what appears to be a prehistoric fish five feet in length. Malona snaps a photograph which, in an insert shot, we see published in *Life* magazine; and then through the insert whips a speedboat, racing across a Southern California bay. Driver Kay Lawrence has a copy of *Life* in her hands as she arrives at the spot where David Reed and an assistant are diving for fish specimens. She brought Reed the magazine because the article supports some of Reed's thoughts on evolution, and his theory that an even more completely developed human form of marine life could conceivably still exist.

Reed and Kay return to the Marine Institute where both are employed by Mark Williams, Kay's fiancé. Businesslike and humorless, Williams appreciates Reed's excitement over the fossil find and says that he has persuaded the Institute to finance a trip to South America so that Reed can get a first-hand look at it.

Reed, Kay, Williams and Williams' physician Dr. Sansoni are soon in Brazil, heading up the Amazon aboard a beat-up fishing boat, the *Pongo*, captained by Tasha. En route, Williams senses that Reed and Kay are attracted to one another. In Malona's tent, the geologist shows the expedition members the bones of the fish, a coelacanth. Reed drops the bombshell that the bones are not prehistoric but contemporary; this marine animal had been alive as recently as a year ago. On the beach where the coelacanth bones were found, there's agreement that it came from somewhere up the river, probably some inland stream. As they talk, the camera pans over the water until we get a quick glimpse, just the impression, of the Gill Man beneath the surface.

That night, back in the tent, there's a discussion as to whether to continue the search or return home. Williams is against proceeding; he believes it's a wild goose chase but his real reason is that he doesn't want Reed and Kay to continue to be together. Malona says he suspects that the coelacanth came from "a lost lagoon" several hundred miles upriver; if Williams won't join them, then Malona would like to go there with Reed. When Kay volunteers to accompany them, Williams is forced to go along (to keep tabs on Kay).

At the lagoon, Reed dons an aqualung and goes underwater to pick up some sample bits of rock; we now get our second semi-glimpse of the Gill Man, who is watching from concealment. When Kay goes for a swim, the Gill Man reaches up and touches her, causing her to scream and make a hasty return to the *Pongo*. The Gill Man follows and gets caught in a *Pongo* net, tearing a giant hole in it in order to escape.

Later, on deck, Kay tells Reed that she met Williams when she was a university student and he was an instructor; he aided her financially, helped her carve out a career in zoology and even gave her her present job. As they talk, the Gill Man swims close to the boat to get a look at Kay. She sees him and lets out a scream. The next morning, Reed is preparing to dive down to try to take pictures of the creature in his natural habitat; Williams, who has decided to accompany him, arms himself with a harpoon gun. Underwater, Reed manages to snap only one photo before the panicked Williams fires a harpoon into the man-fish. Topside, Reed takes him to task for his hostile behavior. In the developed photograph, we get our first good, complete look at the Gill Man: seven feet tall, earless, with arms and legs "and a tail not unlike the shark."

Set on capturing the Creature, Reed drops rotenone into the lagoon. By that night, the Gill Man is forced to come to the surface in shallow water; in this scene, his aversion to light is established when he flees from the spotlight. In pursuit, Reed and Williams swim down to the spot where he disappeared and come up through a submerged entrance into an air-filled grotto described as an "an under-world fairy-land" that "offers the feeling of a cathedral" and even "gives off music"(?!). In the grotto, the creature and "some animal" [*sic*] have a struggle to the death (the animal's), after which the Gill Man darts through an opening and emerges from a cave entrance onto the beach where Kay is sitting. Desperate to get back to the water, he staggers to the edge and collapses inches from Kay. Williams is all for killing the helpless creature, aiming his rifle between the Gill Man's "pleading eyes." Reed knocks him down to stop him.

The creature is put in a tank on the *Pongo* deck. As Sansoni keeps vigil, Kay comes along and they have a long talk about her strained relationship with Williams. With the harpoon head still embedded in his side, the Gill Man lets out a moan; Kay asks Sansoni to help her get it out. Sansoni draws the bolt to open the tank cover and the creature leaps out. Sansoni blocks his path and tries to reason with him(!), and gets himself knocked down. The creature is starting toward the screaming Kay as Reed and others appear on deck. Repelled by Reed's flashlight, the merman hurdles the rail and drops back into the drink.

Reed comes up with a plan to go to the nearest native village for more rotenone. As they attempt to leave the lagoon, they see that the Gill Man has set up a barricade (a huge log) across its narrow entrance. The Gill Man thwarts their attempt to pull the log away with a cable, and Reed and Williams must descend into the water to re-attach it. As Reed is working, Williams looks at Reed's back, tempted to send a harpoon through his rival—and then takes aim and lets one fly. Reed hears it and moves clear. The Gill Man watches as Reed and Williams proceed to stalk one another in a harpoon duel. When the Gill Man feels threatened, he grabs and kills Williams.

On Reed's next dive, he's armed with a solution of rotenone (to paralyze the Gill Man) and radium (its light will frighten him). A few squirts buy him enough time to secure the cable around the log, which now can be pulled away. The Gill Man, dazed, climbs aboard the *Pongo*, heading toward Reed until he sees Kay and changes course. Reed fires several bullets point blank into the monster but cannot prevent him from grabbing Kay and going over the rail. Armed with a knife, Reed follows them down through the water to the grotto, where Kay is unconscious and the Gill Man is lying in wait in the darkness for Reed. Kay wakes and screams, alerting Reed to the monster's presence. Reed throws rocks and a knife to hold off the Gill Man but he continues to advance, backing Reed up against a wall. Death seems imminent until Tasha and Sansoni come in through the beach entrance and fire a barrage of shots into the Gill Man. The monster now moves toward them but they stand their ground, firing away and "literally tearing [the Gill Man] apart." The Gill Man drops into a well-like pool of water, sinking into it as the expedition members stand in hushed silence.

Aboard the homeward-bound *Pongo,* Kay mentions Williams' death while Reed remains silent, unwilling to reveal Williams' murderous attack. From the bottom of the 17th and final page: "In some ways the fish has it all over man. No memory of the past. All future—and as she goes into [Reed's] arms, Sansoni sees them and nods approvingly."

• •

Interesting variations from previous drafts, and from the movie, are found in this version. The fossil bones which provide the story's takeoff point are those of a coelacanth rather than those of a merman. Reed and Kay are back to knowing each other prior to the start of the story, but Kay now has as a fiancé her boss Mark Williams, whose obsession in this draft is not capturing or killing the Gill Man (as in the movie) but separating Reed and Kay—or, if all else fails, killing Reed. The movie's centerpiece, the Black Lagoon swim with Kay above and the Creech below, is now penciled in, but in preliminary, perfunctory form: When Kay unknowingly happens to swim to the spot where he's submerged, his webbed hand (all we see of him) reaches out and touches her, prompting her to frantically return to the boat. An on-deck discussion between Reed and Kay provides us with a bit of Kay–Mark Williams backstory (he was her university instructor and benefactor, and guided her career) that, truth be told, the movie could have used.

Kay's desire to remove the harpoon head from the captured Gill Man makes the reader think that an "Androcles and the Lion"-type moment is in the offing, but the beastie is up and out of the tank as soon as Sansoni draws the bolt, before the Gill Man can know *why* he opened it. (The Beauty and the Beast moments have begun to creep back into the storyline, but they're minor and inconsequential until the final pages and the Creature's abduction of Kay.) Williams' underwater attempt to harpoon Reed was another plot embellishment wisely smothered at birth; for one thing, the ensuing harpoon duel, with the divers stalking each other in and out of shadowy water, sounds like a blueprint for sheer boredom because after a while, few audience members would know who was who—the downfall of nearly all such multi-character sub-aquatic action scenes.

On Saturday, July 25, 1953, William Alland and Universal's editorial department head Ernest Nims got together to discuss the latest version of the *Black Lagoon* script (presumably one by Harry Essex, since he had been assigned to the movie since June 1). Nims subsequently sent Alland a six-page list of the changes discussed in that meeting. *The* major proposal in this memo was a buildup of the scene in which Kay's lagoon dip is disrupted by the Gill Man below. To the best of my knowledge, in all pre–July 25 scripts, the scene had entailed nothing more than Kay coincidentally swimming to the spot directly above the submerged Gill Man, who has observed her from this fixed position and now touches her leg; in a fright, she immediately returns to the boat. The memo advised "[dramatizing] to a greater extent this section of the script where Kay is swimming toward the boat" with an underwater shot of a "shadow effect of [the] creature following Kay" and a "down-shot" into the water of the creature approaching her. These may be the first-ever suggestions to beef up the scene that would become the movie's undisputed highlight.

Essex's August 7 revised second-draft screenplay reflects Nims and Alland's changes and additions and therefore greatly resembles the coming movie. A synopsis follows:

On the banks of the Amazon, geologist Carl (changed from Jose) Malona has found in a limestone wall the fossilized skeleton of a prehistoric hand and forearm. Nearby, a green, mossy hand with webbed talons pokes up out of the water and rests on the bank. In this draft, the action starts early: Up next is the night scene of Malona's native worker Luis, alone in a camp tent, being accosted by the Gill Man. Luis tries to chop at him with his machete, but the monster grabs and drags him off. (Again in this draft, we don't get a real look at the man-fish until late in the game.)

After the aquarium "Let's put on an expedition!" scene, we find its members Reed, Kay, Williams and Sansoni aboard Tasha's boat. Reed's movie soliloquy about the area's oversized critters ("The Amazonian rat is as big as a sheep," etc.) is now divvied up between Reed, Malona and Sansoni, and interspersed with stock footage of Indian natives paddling a canoe, a giant anteater, a foot-long centipede, etc. When they get to the geological camp, Malona's two native guides are missing. In the tent is found an ouanga—several twigs bound together by hairs. "It's a tribal charm to ward off—demons," says Malona. "Apparently something frightened my boys."

Following an unsuccessful attempt to find more of the fossil, Reed advances the theory that part of the limestone wall may have long-ago dropped into the water and been carried up river. As the boat heads in that direction, just under the surface a long, shark-like shadow can be seen in its wake; a hand reaches out of the water so that we recognize it as the green, taloned thing we saw at Malona's camp.

At the Black Lagoon, Reed and Williams put on aqualungs and go down for rock samples. From a forest of ribbon weeds, the Gill Man watches them. After Reed and Williams return to the boat, Kay takes her swim, and this time (per Nims and Alland) the Gill Man—seen as a shadow effect in an underwater shot and as a silhouette in a down-shot—follows her back to the *Pongo*. The incident with the torn trawling net is capped by the discovery of a finger with web portion attached. Reed and Williams descend again, the former toting a camera, the latter a harpoon gun, and when the Gill Man appears, both take a shot. The Creature later comes up onto the boat and kills Tasha's Indian guide Mala.

An attempt to drug the Creature with rotenone leads to the discovery of his grotto; as in earlier drafts, it's still the type of "enchanting" spot where a Disney-cartoon princess might hang her tiara. As they search it, Reed and Williams find a portion of the shirt of Malona's native worker and an ouanga, proof that *both* of Malona's men are dead. In a nearby section of the grotto is the Creature, who we in the audience were now to clearly see for the first time: "He's some seven feet tall, a giant, his webbed hands reaching ahead of him." Rotenone-drugged, he staggers out onto the beach and makes a beeline for Kay. Also on the beach is Garu, Mala's brother, who gets between the monster and the girl and pays with his life. The Gill Man picks up Kay, carrying her with his taloned fingers open so he doesn't hurt her, when the rotenone at last takes effect.

The captured Creature has a brief stay in a makeshift tank on the *Pongo* deck before busting out and going after Kay. Sansoni steps in with a kerosene lantern while Kay, now behind the Creature, picks up a rifle, aims and pulls the trigger; we hear a click but no explosion. Again she pulls the trigger, with no result. The ammo is wet. (One wonders how the Beast would have felt about his Beauty if he'd observed this display of un-affection.) Though mauled by the Creature, Sansoni manages to drive him off by shattering the lantern against him and setting him afire.

The single-minded Williams is all for trying to recapture the man-fish but he's overruled, and soon the *Pongo* is headed for the lagoon entrance. But a huge dead-tree barricade now lies horizontally across the narrow opening. Reed goes below to attach a winch cable to the tree, and Williams joins him to stand watch. When the Creature appears, Williams takes off after him, bent on taking him single-handedly. The Creature catches him and won't let go, tearing the air hose from his mouthpiece. Reed is too late to prevent Williams' drowning.

From here to the end, the script mirrors the movie almost exactly: the Gill Man vs. Reed and his rotenone spray gun, the abduction of Kay, Reed's attempt at a rescue in the grotto, and the last-second arrival of Malona and Tasha, their automatic rifles firing a deadly barrage.

Again we get a few steps closer to the movie-as-produced, especially with Kay's lagoon swim starting to build toward what it eventually became, and with Williams now hard-driving and possessed by the need to capture the Creature. There's also the usual attempt to create suspense by giving us nothing but partial glimpses of the merman for most of the movie.

The evolutionary chain of *Black Lagoon* scripts appears to have reached its dead end with a *revised* revised version of Essex's second draft; my copy has August 28, 1953, handwritten on the bottom of the title page, and it's filled with many pages of "Changes" dated September 22 and 23. The most notable "Changes" pages add to the Kay–Creature swimming scene, calling for an "almost playful" Gill Man to swim upside-down beneath her in the lagoon as he follows her back to the boat.

The Beauty and the Beast touches, which Alland included from the get-go but which went AWOL in several of the scripts, were now all in place; in fact, the Gill Man's infatuation with Kay was now *too* obvious for the MPAA's Joseph Breen, who had a September 1, 1953, confab with Universal's William Gordon to stress that care be exercised in the Kay–Gill Man scenes, "to avoid any sexual emphasis that might suggest bestiality."

Some Early Casting Ideas

Through these months of script evolution, the casting process was also underway. The earliest casting-related paperwork I've found, dated May 22, 1953, gives the movie's title as *The Black Lagoon* and it indicates that three Universal contractees were under consideration for the top role of Dr. David Reed: Gregg Palmer, Bart Roberts (a.k.a. Rex Reason) and Richard Long. Julie Adams is already listed as playing Kay, and Richard Denning has the role of Dr. Mark Williams earmarked for him. The part of Dr. Sansoni (a character name later changed to Dr. Thompson) was up for grabs between Donald Randolph and Paul Cavanagh. Confusingly, on this paper, Ramon Novarro seems to be up for either the part of Reed's mentor Carl Malona or the villainous Kurt Dreier. Novarro in the cast *would* have been a mark of distinction for *Black Lagoon*; the singing waiter-turned-silent movie headliner played the title role in Metro's 1925 superproduction *Ben-Hur* and was second only to Rudolph Valentino as a Hollywood "Latin Lover" in the pre-talkie era.

August 4 is the date on the next casting memo I've seen, and there's now a semi-major name in the *Black Lagoon* lead: For the role of Reed, Universal had lined up Frank Lovejoy, the Bronx-born actor then finishing a good run of starring and co-starring roles at Warner Brothers. Five thousand dollars a week for five weeks was set aside for Lovejoy salary-wise. This August 4 memo has Julie Adams, Richard Denning and Nestor Paiva listed for their eventual screen roles. Randolph and Cavanagh are both still in the running for the job of playing Dr. Sansoni, and Novarro is now listed only for the role of Carl Malona. Evidently *someone* involved on the movie had their sights set on a silent-era romantic star in this role, as Antonio Moreno wound up with the gig. Moreno was a heartthrob right up to the rise of the talkie era; in Clara Bow's *It* (1927), she's a department store shopgirl who has a lust-at-first-sight reaction to the entrance of store owner Moreno: "Sweet Santa Claus, give me *him*."

> Script of *The Black Lagoon* calls for an amphibious man. How about Johnny Weissmuller?
>
> —George E. Phair, "Retakes," *Variety*, September 16, 1953

In late July 1953, a *Black Lagoon* location scouting crew prepared to leave for Florida to find a body of water where the underwater scenes—nearly a quarter of the film—could be shot. Among the spots under consideration: Wakulla Springs, one of the world's largest and deepest freshwater springs, located in Wakulla County cypress swamps several miles south of the state capital Tallahassee. Its waters were perfect for their purposes. Vodka-clear and anesthetizingly cold, they come gushing up from an underwater cave, hundreds of thousands of gallons a minute.

The Wakulla Springs area had remained primitive right up into the mid-1930s when it was purchased by Edward Ball, brother-in-law of industrialist Alfred I. du Pont. Developing it became a passion for Ball, who promptly began construction on Wakulla Springs Lodge, a two-story marble-and-masonry hotel. In 1941, Ball hired Newton Perry (1908–1987) to manage Wakulla Springs. A product of southern Georgia, Perry had come to Florida as a kid; nearly every day he would walk the six miles from his Ocala home to Silver Springs, where he was as much at home in the water as on land. He went from giving 25-cent swimming lessons at Silver Springs, to Ocala High School's 16-year-old swim coach, to the state's top collegiate diver. In a 1982 *Ocala Star-Banner* article, Ray Washington wrote about the way Perry hitched himself to Florida's burgeoning tourist industry:

> **At springs around the state he performed what were to become the first underwater tourist shows. The idea of breathing through underwater tubes was his. Riding bicycles, foot racing, teaching class—anything that could be done on land, he proved it could be done underwater too.**
>
> **Newt Perry was in demand across the state. He shuttled back and forth between the springs as they developed—Silver Springs, Wakulla Springs, Cypress Gardens, Weeki Wachee. He was the king of the springs. He loved Rainbow Springs. He discovered Hart Springs. He seemed to be everywhere there was a spring that needed swimming.**

But prior to that tourist show activity, Perry was the manager of Wakulla Springs, luring MGM moviemakers there to shoot above- and below-the-water scenes for 1941's *Tarzan's Secret Treasure*. He became the go-to guy for studios needing to shoot water scenes.

During this era, someone who got to know Perry, and to know Wakulla Springs, was a Tallahassee kid named Ricou Browning—soon to achieve movie immortality as the Creature from the Black Lagoon.

When Ricou Browning was a kid, he wanted to be Tarzan or a cowboy. As a young adult, he considered becoming a doctor and even took classes, "but I wasn't too bright in some of 'em," he recalled, laughing. In between, Browning (right) was a teenage private at Lackland Air Force Base in San Antonio, Texas; he left the service a corporal.

In November 2003, 73-year-old Browning gave an extensive interview to Wakulla Springs State Park Ranger Mike Nash, describing his nearly lifelong "history" with the place. He began by talking about one of his first-ever visits to Wakulla:

> **I think we were on the back of a truck, maybe 15 or 20 kids out of Tallahassee's Leon High School.... We came to the springs and I fell in love with it. It was just beautiful. As it is right now, it was full of squirrels, full of fish, full of eelgrass, and the water was freezing. We spent, I think, the entire day here and from then on I came every weekend. And I got to know Newt Perry very well. His wife ... trained all of us in diving. He taught us in swimming, and at that time he had an air compressor and a pump right next to the diving tower and an air hose that ran out from that. He taught us all how to hose-breathe [while underwater]. It's kinda like drinking water out of a hose. You drink the water you want, and you let the rest spill on the ground. Well, breathing from a hose is the same way. You take what air you want and let the rest just spill out.**

Browning told me about his boyhood experience of working for the first time as a "performer" at Wakulla:

One of the glass bottom boats would go from a dock area out over the spring, hand-rowed by a boat captain—they were all colored guys in those days. Today the boats have electric outboard motors, but in those days they rowed with oars. The boat captain had a speech that came out kinda like a song, about the spring and things that were done there, movies that were made there, Henry the Pole-Vaulting Fish and all of those various things.

Then he'd row over near the diving tower, where the other kids and I would be waiting, and tell his passengers, "I can get one of those boys to swim underwater with an air hose, and you folks can watch him." He would yell out to one of us and we'd go in the water with an air hose, swim down … the deepest would be about 80 feet. We'd swim around and then work our way all the way back up to the boat. And the captain would say, "Give him applause" and "If you want to give this boy some money, just throw it on the glass," and then *he* would throw a quarter onto the glass bottom of the boat so that it'd make a sound. The passengers didn't know that *he* threw that first coin, 'cause they'd be looking out of the boat at the kid in the water. They'd hear the clink of the quarter and *they'd* take out money and throw it onto the glass. The captain would collect the money, and at the end of the day he'd split it with us. Some of us kids would earn 30, 40 dollars a day, and that was big, big money.

Sportswriter-movie producer Grantland Rice shot some of his short subjects below the surface of Wakulla's waters. The documentary *The Wonders of Wakulla Springs* features clips from Rice shorts, among them the comedic *What a Picnic!*: In that 1945 release, the driver of a filled-with-teens Model T convertible (Ricou Browning's brother Clement Walker "Buddy" Browning Jr., with high schooler Ricou sitting right behind him) drives into the water until it, and *they*, are completely submerged. The kids then bail out and, at the bottom of the spring, begin to roast frankfurters, have a picnic, smoke a cigarette, dance, etc. This is just one of several Rice shorts in which Browning can be seen.

Perry's promotional skills made the picnic and recreational areas of Wakulla Springs a real "hot spot" in the '40s. All day long, kids from Tallahassee, soldiers from Dale Mabry Field and gals from Florida State College for Women, wall-to-wall people, would swim, dance to jukebox music, etc. "Buddy" and Ricou worked there: In the summer, they were lifeguards, soda jerks, ticket sellers, grass mowers, whatever needed to be done. In cooler weather, when business was slow, they went underwater with air hoses and, in shallow areas where eelgrass interfered with swimmers, they pulled it up until the chilliness of the water forced them to retreat inside the Lodge and warm up beside its big fireplace.

In 1947, 17-year-old Browning enlisted in the Air Force, rising to the rank of corporal before leaving in 1950. At 20, while attending Florida State University, he worked in his first "Hollywood movie": The Pine-Thomas adventure *Crosswinds* (1951) was made in Florida and Browning got the job of underwater double for Forrest Tucker, fighting with star John Payne in scenes shot at the bottom of Weeki Wachee Springs. A few months later, he married; son Ricky was born at the end of 1952. During this period Ricou supported himself by producing and performing in Newt Perry's underwater "mermaid shows" at Weeki Wachee. Browning also worked at a Tampa state fair, acted as chief lifeguard of a pool in a Tallahassee park, etc., and resumed his FSU studies.

Then, in July 1953, came The Phone Call. He told me that Newt Perry

phoned me and said that he had received a call about showing some Hollywood people [*Black Lagoon* location scouts] Wakulla Springs. He couldn't make it, he was busy in Miami doing *some*thing, so he asked me if I wouldn't mind showing it to them. I said fine. So these people called me and told me when they were coming into town, and I met 'em at the airport in Tallahassee. It was Jack Arnold and the cameraman, "Scotty" Welbourne, and a couple other people, I just don't remember who they were. I took them to Wakulla Springs and showed 'em the area, and they loved it. "Scotty" had his underwater camera and he asked me if

Ricou Browning (kneeling) in a photograph taken at Weeki Wachee Springs. He's flanked by his sister Shirley, left, a member of his *Black Lagoon* and *Revenge of the Creature* underwater safety teams, and Ginger Stanley, who doubled for Julie Adams in *Black Lagoon* and Lori Nelson in *Revenge*.

> I would get in the water with him and swim in front of the camera so they could get some perspective. [With a person in the shot, viewers would have some idea of the size of the fish, eelgrass, logs, etc., they were also seeing.] I said sure, so I did. They saw the spring and the river and loved 'em. We had dinner that night, talked a little bit about the Springs, and they left. The kind of movie they were planning to make—not once did the subject come up. Just that there was going to be a lot of underwater.

The moviemakers did decide to utilize Wakulla Springs for *Black Lagoon*'s underwater scenes; it was picturesque, its water was transparent and, at its bottom, caves and cliffs offered ideal crannies for a Gill Man to lurk. Wakulla shooting would be done by a second unit working at the same time that the main unit was busy at Universal, which meant that underwater doubles would be needed for Reed, Kay, Williams—and the Gill Man. Some time after the location scouts' departure, Ricou's phone rang once again, and it was Jack Arnold on the other end. The director asked, "How would you like to be the Creature?"

"Creature? *What* creature?"

"We're doing a film about an underwater monster," Arnold explained. "We've tested a lot of people for this part, but I'd like to have you play the Creature—I like your swimming. Do you want to do it?" Browning said, "Sure!"

According to the minutes of an August 5, 1953, Studio Operating Committee meeting, "The swimmer will arrive at the studio next Monday to be outfitted for the part." Twenty-three-year-old Browning, FSU physical education major, husband and father of an eight-month-old, indeed was on a Sunday, August 7, flight to the movie capital, and the makeup department's work on the Creature costumes to be worn by Browning and the "on-land" Gill Man Ben Chapman went into high gear.

Many hands and minds were involved in the ideation and fabrication of the eventual Gill Man outfit. The paper trail extends all the way back to its sketchy description in William Alland's 1952 memo "The Sea Monster," itself possibly based on Gabriel Figueroa's "word picture" ("painted" at the 1940 Orson Welles party) of the supposedly true-life fish-men of the Amazon. Various screenwriters starting with Maurice Zimm added their own details. But the foam rubber didn't hit the road until the process of building a costume actually began.

Bud Westmore's brother Frank was one of many makeup men who worked on *Black Lagoon*: Wardrobe man Roger J. Weinberg had the job of drying out the actual perspiration on the wardrobe of various players, and Frank's job was to then apply *synthetic* perspiration to the dried-out clothes, to match the perspiration stains in previous and following shots! Two decades later, Frank wrote the "warts and all" book *The Westmores of Hollywood* which looked back at his family's movieland history. He devotes several pages to *Black Lagoon*, mentioning that Alland initially

> assigned the special effects department and the staff shop (which makes statues and other props) to develop his concept of what the sea creature should look like. The movie had a budget of only $650,000, and Alland was trying to circumvent the makeup department to save both time and money. For two months they wrestled with the problem. When they finished, [Ricou Browning] put on their handiwork and got into the Underwater Tank on the back lot. Instead of projecting menace, he looked like a man swimming around in long rubber underwear with black hair stuck to it.

The "black hair" part notwithstanding, Frank is obviously describing the fish-faced, mostly smooth-skinned outfit matching Alland's mental picture of what the Creature should look like: "much more human" than the eventual Gill Man, "very sad, beautiful," "far more 'attractive,' more 'romantic-looking' than the beast we ended up with." For years, Monster Kid Numero Uno Bob Burns was friends with Universal makeup department sculptor Chris Mueller, Jr., who worked on *Black Lagoon*; Burns has a memory of Mueller dismissively calling that incarnation of

Ricou Browning in what makeup department sculptor Chris Mueller called the Pollywog suit, atop the studio tank. Co-star Julie Adams is on the right. (Photograph courtesy Bob Burns.)

the Creature "The Pollywog," a nickname that Burns assumes Mueller concocted himself. If "The Pollywog" was good enough for Mueller, that's good enough for this book; hereinafter, that's what we'll call it too.

In an August 22 memo, unit manager James T. Vaughn wrote that the Pollywog suit was estimated to be ready for testing on September 2. He continued:

> **Tests should include underwater shots in a suitable location such as Catalina where foliage and underwater growth can be found to determine the 3-D effect upon the spectator. ... The monster should be photographed both under water and on land. Mr. Arnold is afraid that on land the absence of live eyes will give the mask a Mardi Gras feeling. ... Re the monster double for land work, an extra outfit has been ok'd. Mr. Alland wants a man as tall as possible and is looking at athletes for this purpose. It is my opinion that a professional stuntman should be employed, since certain of the work requires the knowledge and timing of a professional. He should also have acting ability in other scenes not of a stunt nature. Arnold is in agreement on this. The Makeup Department estimates they will require ten days with the new monster to develop the outfit, and the cost consideration of employing a stuntman for this purpose enters into the decision.**

Say "cheesy!": Wearing the Pollywog head and hands, Ricou Browning cavorts at the bottom of the Underwater Tank. (Photograph courtesy Bob Burns.)

The Pollywog suit, with Browning inside, got its first and probably last on-camera workout on September 5, when a test was shot—not at Catalina, as Vaughn suggested, but in the Underwater Tank. There was a 12:36 p.m. crew call (director Arnold, 3-D underwater cameraman Welbourne, the makeup department's Jack Kevan, more) and a 1:00 set call for actors Julie Adams and Ricou Browning. Adams showed up on time, wearing *a* bathing suit but not *the* hubba-hubba bathing suit she wears in the movie. (She was there for publicity photo purposes.) Browning and Welbourne got in the water, the latter shooting approximately 1400 feet of film as Browning gracefully swam. Intrigued, Adams asked to be allowed to put on an aqualung and swim a bit; Welbourne, concerned for her safety and initially hesitant, finally agreed. With Browning standing by in case anything went wrong, the actress got into the tank and loved the experience. She and Browning were dismissed at 3:45, the crew sticking around to shoot "tests on air gun and spears."

According to Adams, Universal exec Edward Muhl said he "hated" the look of the Pollywog suit on film. Browning was there when it happened: He told me,

> **We all went into the screening room, people sat down and started watching the test footage they had filmed. I was there watching, along with the makeup guys and—well, *every*body was in there who had anything to do with the suit. Then when the thing was over, there was kinda silence until [James] Pratt and Muhl, two guys that I guess were the heads of the studio, spoke up and said, "That *sucked*!" Then everybody chimed in and said about the same thing.**

Alland told me that when studio brass insisted that "his" non-monstrous monster, the Pollywog, wasn't sufficiently scary (and/or that it "sucked"), he stepped back and allowed Westmore and Co. to take over completely. "I just turned that over to them," Alland recalled, adding:

> **I cannot take credit or blame for how the Creature's appearance turned out. To me, it was a cartoon, but apparently all of *you* people [adult-olescent Monster Kids] thought it was great. As I said, my concept originally was of a much more poetic and strangely beautiful—although frightening—kind of a being, who could become angry, who could become friendly, who could love. [The eventual costume] was just beyond my pale. But I'm wrong, everybody else loved it.**

So who designed the "classic Creature"? Its creators began to die before most monster-movie fact-finders were born, so the complete story is lost to time. A still-existing Universal memo shows that Jack Kevan got a one-week's-pay bonus for the outstanding job he did "designing and working extremely long hours" on the Gill Man, so obviously he had no small hand in the matter. Bob Burns picked the brain of Gill Man sculptor Mueller, and according to Mueller, the humanoid we know and loved was designed by artist-actress Milicent Patrick.

On her résumé from the late 1960s (or later), she gives her name as

BARONESSA di POLOMBARA
Milicent Patrick
Formerly
Mildred Elizabeth Fulvia di Rossi

and claimed to have been born an Italian baroness. She was raised in South America and in San Simeon, California, where her father C.C. Rossi spent ten years "building the William Randolph Hearst Estate, as engineer, architect and superintendent of construction." Patrick won "three scholarships in Art at Madam Chouinard's Art Institute" and claims to have been the first woman animator at Walt Disney Studios. She also worked as a model and, in the late 1940s, began acting in movies.

Claws celeb: the massive mitts of Universal's newest monster movie star, in the process of being fabricated. (Photograph courtesy Bob Burns.)

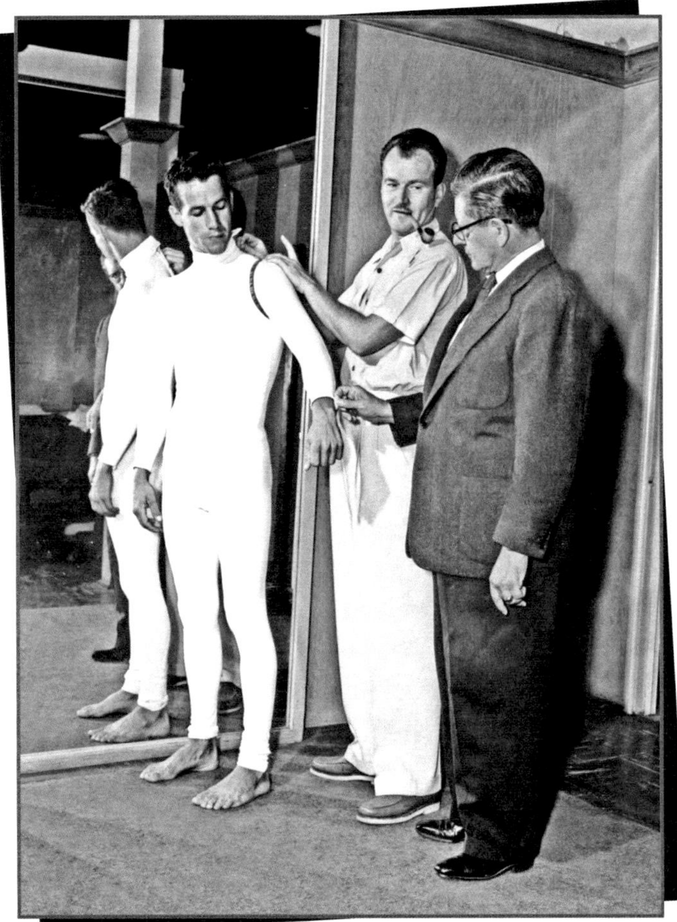

Ricou Browning wears the white leotard onto which the foam rubber Gill Man pieces will be glued. (Photograph courtesy Bob Burns.)

According to a *Creature* publicity story on Patrick, she was playing a small and uncredited role in Universal's *The World in His Arms* (1952) when, anxious to resume her artist career, she showed some of her drawings to Bud Westmore. As a result, she won the assignment of creating the "pirate faces" for actors who would be appearing opposite Errol Flynn in the studio's upcoming *Against All Flags* (1952). Subsequent subjects for "makeup illustrator" Patrick included Jack Palance (and all the character parts) in *Sign of the Pagan* (1954); she also contributed to the creation of the *It Came from Outer Space* Globs and, according to *Mirror* magazine, to the look of Mr. Hyde in 1953's *Abbott and Costello Meet Dr. Jekyll and Mr. Hyde*.

Burns didn't think to ask Mueller if Patrick had any input on the Pollywog but he, Burns, feels she probably did. "Chris Mueller said that Milicent was the sweetest lady in the world and that she was in [on *Black Lagoon*] from the very beginning," said Burns, "and as far as he was concerned, *she* designed the whole thing. I got that right from Chris, and he wasn't the kind of guy to lie. Chris said that Bud Westmore had nothing to do with the design of the Creature. The way Chris put it was, 'Westmore signed the checks and got in the pictures [the still photographs of the makeup men at work]. That's about it.'"

In a September 21 inter-office memo, unit manager Sergei Petschnikoff wrote to production manager Gilbert Kurland:

Westmore and Kevan *hope* to have one suit for the monster and the two heads ready to test about October 3rd. Should this suit be o.k., it will take three or four more days to make

another underwater suit to take to Florida. They are also making bits and pieces for the land monster, which they hope to have ready about a week after the water monster is o.k'd.

The original plan, according to a July 2, 1953, *Hollywood Reporter* item, was for *Black Lagoon* to roll in late August or early September, but the need for the design and fabrication of an all-new monster suit delayed the start of filming for weeks. Julie Adams called Welbourne and said that, because there was nothing to do during this unexpected hiatus, she'd like to use the aqualung in the ocean. To her delight she found herself, a few days later, en route with Welbourne and Browning to Catalina, where they met friends of Welbourne's who had a boat, and she had a few days of underwater adventure, including a descent to a sunken yacht.

Finally, on October 5, *the* Creature suit we all know and love was ready for its 3-D close-ups: Back at the Underwater Tank, director James Havens was scheduled to shoot "Photo Water Tests" of Ricou Browning in his new "Water Gill Man" suit, plus footage of Julie in her bathing suit. The Daily Production Report shows that work began smoothly with a full shot of Adams "as she dives into water. Shooting up from in water. She comes f.g. toward camera and swims away to exit b.g."; next they got a shot of Browning's Gill Man "in water shooting up as he swims around." But Welbourne's underwater camera stripped a gear and landed in the studio's machine shop from 11:30 a.m. to 1:30 p.m. Later in the day, it stripped another gear. In defeat, one of the production people wrote on the Report, "Unable to finish scheduled tests due to loss of light and fatigue of Rico [*sic*] Browning."

One problem that needed to be resolved quickly: The costume for this underwater beast was made of foam rubber ... and foam rubber *floats*. Jack Kevan told me, "We found out that he couldn't get underwater because the sponge had so much air in it, so we developed a system of weights and so on. We used lead weights to counter-balance

At Universal's Underwater Tank (round, 30 feet deep, 20 feet in diameter), Ricou Browning is about to perform for the cameras in his "Water Gill Man" outfit. At ground level outside the tank, cameramen could direct their cameras through the windows (one is to the left of the door) and photograph underwater action. Notice the three Gill Man heads atop the tank.

Brooklyn Eagle reporter Jane Corby, who interviewed Creature costume designer Milicent Patrick at Toots Shor's 51st Street (New York) restaurant, wrote that the Gill Man "is encased in scaly armor, like a turtle's, has fins on his legs, suction cups on his feet, webbed paws with talons, and a face like that of an angry codfish." Patrick mused, "He would probably create a sensation if he walked in here and ordered a drink." (Photograph courtesy Bob Burns.)

the sponge; also, the suit would absorb a lot of water, which also lent weight to it."

"I wore a chest plate that was thin lead," Browning told me. "It had straps permanently attached to the lead on one side, and the loose ends of those straps went around my back and over my shoulders and hooked to the *other* side of the chest plate and held it in place. The same thing with thigh weights. Same thing with ankle weights."

The "hose-breathing" technique Ricou Browning learned as a kid helped him make the Gill Man the 1950s' coolest movie monster.

Also on October 5, wardrobe tests were made on Stage 9. Among the six players modeling their threads was the movie's star: no, not Frank Lovejoy, but Richard Carlson, leading man in Universal's still-in-theaters *It Came from Outer Space*. Lovejoy was "out" because, according to a September 8 Hedda Hopper column, he got his wires crossed and committed himself to two pictures whose shooting schedules overlapped, *Black Lagoon* and MGM's *Men of the Fighting Lady* (1954). Lovejoy ended up in *Fighting Lady* while Carlson took over in *Black Lagoon*.

On October 6, Havens and Welbourne again shot Gill Man test footage: First they photographed Browning on land, then coming out of the U-I back lot's Park Lake and finally in the Underwater Tank. The actor wore as many as three different Creature heads that day, the one he sported in the tank designated in paperwork as the "#3-Head."

Vision was a problem for Browning. Inside his Gill Man head he tried wearing goggles, the type that pearl divers wear, but water would get into them and then there was no way to get it out. A face-mask made the Gill Man face bulge too much. Ultimately it was just his naked eyes seeing out through the eyeholes in the Gill Man helmet. "It was kind of like looking through a keyhole," he told me. "And looking through an underwater keyhole without a mask on, your vision is blurred—*very* blurred. It was very awkward seeing, and a lot of it was kind of hit and miss."

Synopsis

The action begins in outer space with a crash course on the formation of the Earth and the creation of life in its oceans. After some aerial stock footage of a jungle, we cut to the river's-edge camp of Brazilian geologist Dr. Carl Maia (Antonio Moreno), where there's excitement in the air: Extending out of a limestone wall is a just-unearthed, claw-like skeleton hand and forearm, with webbed fingers suggesting a prehistoric amphibian. Maia tells his native helpers Luis and Tomas (Rodd Redwing and Perry Lopez) that he is leaving for the Instituto de Biología Marítima in Morajo Bay to get help for the job of digging out the rest of the skeleton. Unnoticed by Maia and the natives, bubbles are surging to the surface of the water just a few feet off-shore, and then a web-taloned hand—the live counterpart of the fossil—reaches out of the water and rakes its claws along the bank.

The scene switches to Manaus in Northern Brazil, where Dr. Maia and ichthyologist Kay Lawrence (Julie Adams) race in a speedboat from the Instituto's Morajo Bay pier to an anchored barge: Kay's boyfriend David Reed (Richard Carlson) has descended from the barge via aqualung to look for specimens of lungfish. Summoned to the surface, Reed is happy to see his old teacher Maia, who asks, "Are you two married yet?"

"No, no," Kay says wearily. "David says we're together all the time anyway. Might as well save expenses." Maia shows Reed a photo of the petrified hand, which fascinates him. Later, in a combination office-aquarium at the Instituto, the fossil (now mounted on a stand) is the center of attention as Reed, Kay, their boss Mark Williams (Richard Denning), Maia and Dr. Thompson (Whit Bissell) decide to comprise an expedition and recover more of the skeleton. Reed is especially keen on learning more about this "missing link" between land and marine life, as it may lead to a means for modern-day man to adapt to the rigors of future life on other planets with different atmospheres and pressures.

Meanwhile, back at Maia's camp, the webbed hand again reaches out of the water; the camera now "becomes" the Gill Man and approaches the tent occupied by Luis and Tomas. Antagonized when Luis throws a lantern, the monster pie-faces the quailing, whimpering native with his baseball mitt-sized hand, then turns his attention to Tomas. From outside, we watch the tent shake as the Gill Man's boar-like roars and his victims' screams fill the air.

A ramshackle fish-hauling boat, the *Rita*, chugs up the Amazon; its captain is the grizzled, greasy Lucas (Nestor Paiva) and his crewmen are brothers Zee and Chico (Bernie Gozier, Henry Escalante). The weather is hot, Williams is hotter ("Couldn't Maia find anything better than this *barge*?!") and we get a foretaste of the way the very different Reed and Williams tend to squabble and how Kay tries to act as peacemaker. We also get the idea that part of the reason for Williams' irritability is the fact that longtime colleague Kay has gone for Reed rather than for him.

The party arrives at Maia's camp and discovers the natives' bodies, their ripped-up condition giving Lucas probable claws to suggest they fell victim to a jaguar. Yet again the webbed hand reaches out of the water, this time for the unsuspecting Kay's ankle, but she walks away in the proverbial nick of time. A montage of pickaxe, shovel and sift box activity indicates the passage of eight sweltering, sweat-stained days of excavation into the limestone wall; Williams is angry and disappointed over their failure to find the skeleton and makes no bones about it. Reed suggests that in the distant past, part of the bank may have fallen into the river, with the current breaking it up and carrying it away. According to Lucas, this tributary dead-ends at a lagoon. "My boys call it 'the Black Lagoon,' the paradise," he says, adding with a laugh, "Only, they say, nobody has ever come back to *prrrrove* it!"

The Black Lagoon, accessible through a narrow inlet, is eerie and otherworldly. Reed and Williams don aqualungs and descend in quest of rocks to compare to those in the limestone wall. ***BAH-BAH-BAHHH!***: Our first look at the Gill Man comes when Williams swims over his hiding place and the monster unexpectedly rises up into the shot. He's got a man's body, a fishy face, scales and fearsome claws. Unaware of his presence, the two men return to the *Rita* where Reed's description of the lagoon depths ("Like another *world*") gives Kay ideas. Unobserved, she sheds her shirt to reveal a snug-fitting one-piece white bathing suit and dives in for a swim. In an amazing scene that probably elicited oohs'n'aahs and squeals of terror in equal number in 1954, the captivated Creature backstrokes through the water directly beneath her, "obviously as taken up with her figure as any mere man might be" (to quote a sneak preview audience

Fossil hunters (from left) Antonio Moreno, Richard Denning, Richard Carlson, Nestor Paiva, Julie Adams and Whit Bissell will find only horror, first at Dr. Maia's camp, then in the Black Lagoon.

member's preview card). Kay is unaware that anything is below, and even does some Esther Williams–like underwater rolls, until the Creature mischievously pokes at her ankles. When she returns to the *Rita*, the Gill Man follows and gets tangled in a trawling net hanging over its side. His efforts to escape rock the boat and crack the boom. When the ruckus subsides and the net is brought up, the onlookers see a Gill Man–sized hole in it plus a torn-off claw. Kay, examining the claw and remembering being touched during her swim, lets out a gasp.

On their next dive, Reed is packing a camera and Williams a speargun. The Creature watches and semi-playfully tries to avoid them, but Williams finally catches sight of the fish-man and puts a spear in him. In the *Rita*'s bunk room, as Reed develops a photo he hopes will feature the Creature, Lucas mentions that an old native woman once told him the legend of a man who lives underwater. Meanwhile, up on deck, the Creature pounces upon the screaming Chico (the monster's one unprovoked killing in the movie).

A plan is hatched to capture the Creature by dropping into the lagoon sacks of rotenone, a drug that native fishermen make from roots to paralyze and catch fish. Throughout the day and that night, as the motionless bodies of small fish dot the water's surface, a watch is kept for a similarly smashed Creature. The marine monster attempts to climb aboard the *Rita* but is scared off by a hanging lantern. Hoping to catch him while he's still groggy, Reed and Williams hit the water in pursuit, trailing him down to the underwater entrance to an air-filled grotto. The Creature exits the grotto through a beach entrance and begins walking toward an unsuspecting Kay who is sitting nearby. His machete raised high, Zee races to her rescue, but the Creature fatally throttles him. As the Creature attempts to carry off the yelping Kay, the rotenone kicks in and he collapses. Williams, arriving on the scene, becomes maniacal and beats the kayoed Creature with a rifle until Reed intercedes. After sealing the unconscious Creature in a water-filled tank on the *Rita* deck, Reed insists on revisiting and photographing the grotto. *Everyone* goes with him except Kay and Thompson, the latter left to stand guard over the Creature. The Creature awakens and (off-camera) smashes his way free, mauling Thompson before diving off the boat.

Our Heroes try to make their getaway the next day but the Creature prevents their departure by placing a dead tree horizontally across the lagoon inlet's narrow entrance. Reed realizes he must go into the water and wrap a cable around the half-submerged tree so that it can be winched aside; Williams, consumed by the thought of killing the Creature, tries to get Reed to let him tag along. A bunk room fistfight ensues, with Williams coming out on the losing end.

Reed descends into the water and Williams follows, again going after the Gill Man. This time the hunter becomes the hunted, the Creature and his tormentor fighting until the Creature uses his teeth to tear out Williams' air hose. Williams' air tanks pull his lifeless body to the surface.

For his next descent, Reed arms himself with a jerry-rigged rotenone "spray gun" to keep the Creature at bay; this time his attempt to attach a cable to the tree barricade is successful. The Devonian Don Juan creeps aboard the *Rita*, seizes Kay and dives overboard, swimming with her down to his grotto entrance. Reed makes the same descent, enters the grotto and finds the unconscious Kay in a partially flooded cave chamber, ceremoniously draped across a slab of rock. Lying in wait for Reed's arrival, the Creature moves in on him. Reed is about to lose a knife-to-claw battle with the beastie when Maia and Lucas enter the grotto via the beach entrance, their rifles blazing. Bleeding from multiple bullet holes, the gurgling Gill Man staggers out of the cave and toward the water's edge. Maia is taking careful aim at his back, about to go for the kill, when Reed reaches out and pushes down his rifle. The Creature wades into the water, swims through some weeds and, in the final shot, limply drifts down into inky darkness.

Cast Biographies

Richard Carlson as Dr. David Reed

See the Carlson bio in the *It Came from Outer Space* chapter and in this book's companion volume *The Creature Chronicles*.

Julie Adams as Kay Lawrence

The only child of alcoholic parents, she was born Betty May Adams in Waterloo, Iowa. In her self-published 2011 autobiography *The Lucky Southern Star: Reflections from the Black Lagoon* she wrote in a humorous way about the fact that she was conceived out of wedlock, her parents rushing to the altar, fibbing about her birth date, etc., back in the days when such things mattered greatly. Just days after her third birthday, what little money the family had went "poof" in the 1929 stock market crash. In *Southern Star* she wrote that, as a result, her mismatched parents "moved from town to town as my father earned a living as a cotton buyer for a large textile company. Our transient lifestyle and the brutal economics of those trying times meant that we never owned a house. Rather, we lived in a series of rented houses or apartments."

Her father died when she was 15 (cirrhosis of the liver), leaving Adams and her mother with very little. As a consequence of the mother's heavy drinking, the two ended up living apart from each other, Mom moving in with her own sister in Iowa, Julie living in Arkansas with an aunt (her father's sister) and uncle who treated her like a daughter. After being crowned Miss Little Rock, and coming *thisclose* to becoming Miss Arkansas, she got the idea that she might have the looks needed to make it in the movies. Flying to California was the 19-year-old's first-ever time on an airplane.

While waiting for studio doors to swing open for her, Adams worked as a secretary and lost her Southern accent with the help of a speech and acting coach. B-movie stardom came suddenly, and in spades, when she landed the female lead in a cheapie Western, *The Dalton Gang* (1949) with Don "Red" Barry, and the producers then asked her if she'd star in their next *six* Westerns—which were all to be made simultaneously!

Universal's *Bright Victory* (1951) was the story of a World War II veteran (Arthur Kennedy), permanently blinded by a sniper's bullet, returning home to adapt to a new type of life; Adams, third-billed, plays the fiancée he left behind—who now can't see spending her life with him. At a sneak preview where audience members filled out Comment Cards, enough of them praised Adams that Universal put her under contract at $150 a week. In *Bright Victory* she used the screen name Julia Adams, and retained it for several years (even in *Black Lagoon*) before it was changed to Julie Adams.

For over six years Adams "had a place where I felt like I belonged" (Universal), playing in movies with stars ranging from James Stewart, Tyrone Power, Charlton Heston and fellow Hollywood newbie Rock Hudson to Francis the Talking Mule and, yes, the Gill Man. She told *Psychotronic Video* magazine interviewer Dennis Daniel that, when assigned to *Black Lagoon*, she thought, "I don't know if I really want to be in a monster picture," but she *also* didn't want to go on suspension so she forged ahead with it, swimsuit scene and all. So many of her other Universals were Westerns and other period pieces that *The Hollywood Reporter*'s Milton Luban wrote in his *Creature* review, "Lovely Julia Adams, finally out of crinoline costumes, reveals a gorgeous pair of gams." In 1953, for publicity purposes, Universal had her legs insured for $125,000 by Lloyds of London.

In 1954, Adams and Ray Danton acted together in *The Looters,* shot in the Colorado Rocky Mountains; by the time it hit theaters in the spring of '55, she was Mrs. Danton. After *Slim Carter* (1957), Adams' run at Universal came to an end. In the years that followed, she made a handful of additional movies, but spent much more time working in TV. Son #1, Steven Danton, is now a busy assistant director and Son #2 Mitchell Danton, named after Robert "Mitch" Mitchum, is an editor; the latter co-wrote her autobiography.

Before her marriage to Danton ended in divorce, they acted together several more times, including a *Night Gallery* episode; he also directed her both pre- and post-split, mostly in TV episodes but also in the horror flick *Psychic Killer* (1975). For more upscale audiences, "guest artist" Adams played leading roles in more than a dozen stage productions throughout the country, some in conventional theaters, others in dinner theaters and one in a theater-in-the-round dinner theater: *The Prime of Miss Jean Brodie*, *The Glass Menagerie*, *Butterflies Are Free*, *Auntie Mame*, *Long Day's Journey into Night* and more.

After years of ducking the celebrity autograph scene, Adams finally dipped a toe into those dark waters in the 2000s at the behest of Ben Chapman. It began with an appearance at 2002's Creaturefest, an event held at the Wakulla Springs State Park and Lodge with Adams, Chapman and Adams' underwater double Ginger Stanley in attendance. After Chapman died in 2008, she continued down the autograph show road, always accompanied by a relative or friend. In 2011 her book *The Lucky Southern Star* debuted at the Egyptian Theatre on Hollywood Boulevard; Adams was in attendance, and the appropriately all–Julie

Julie Adams and Ricou Browning pose with Marian Clatterbaugh, center, of *Monsters from the Vault* magazine at the 2012 Monster Bash in Butler, Pennsylvania.

double-bill that night was *Black Lagoon* (in 3-D) and her James Stewart Western *Bend of the River* (1952). Sons Steven and Mitch both have two kids, making her the grandmother of four.

This book's companion volume The Creature Chronicles *includes biographies for* Black Lagoon *co-stars Richard Denning, Antonio Moreno, Nestor Paiva and Ben Chapman.*

Production

Black Lagoon's pre-production shooting phase began one year, almost to the day, after William Alland wrote "The Sea Monster." On the morning of Wednesday, September 30, 1953, director Jack Arnold, Julie Adams and a small crew shot at the Hermosa Beach Aquarium, then one of the largest and best attractions of its type in the world. For the camera's looking-out-of-the-aquarium shot of Kay (Adams), there were multiple takes on one slate. Members of the camera unit remained at the aquarium to photograph plates and other fish footage while Arnold *et al.* headed off to Portuguese Bend for the shooting of Morajo Bay speedboat scenes.

On October 3, a budget meeting was held and a *Black Lagoon* budget of $595,000 was set. On October 5, a small crew returned to Portuguese Bend to shoot process plates of the area. Cameras also rolled at Universal: As mentioned previously, at the Underwater Tank "Photo Water Tests" were made of Browning in the new'n'improved Gill Man outfit plus, on Stage 9, wardrobe and makeup shots of Carlson, Adams, Denning, Moreno, Paiva and Bissell.

October 6 was the last day of second unit tests, with Havens and Welbourne shooting Gill Man Browning in a dry suit on land and then coming out of Park Lake. At the Underwater Tank, they photographed him wearing his #3-Head (whichever one *that* was) and made tests of the rotenone.

The sixth was also Day One of Arnold's first unit production. The work was scheduled to take 21 days, rather a long time considering the fact that he was making, in effect, a one-hour movie. (The Florida unit's footage, plus opening and closing credits, etc., would bring the running time up to 79 minutes.) On this first day, there was a crew of 65 and a company shooting call of 8:45 a.m.; all the players were there early (Julie Adams the earliest, at 6:45). The first shot of principal photography: a "full moving shot" (the camera on the deck of the *Rita*, shooting past the smoking funnel and cast members standing in the forward section) as the boat squeezes through the narrow passage and into the lagoon. Throughout pre-production shooting, it seemed as though nothing had gone exactly right, and that went for this first shot also: There was supposed to be a fog effect but they couldn't make it happen, and apparently the cable towing the boat came loose, necessitating repairs.

Various *Rita* deck scenes were shot throughout the day: the lowering of the trawling net, Reed climbing aboard and presenting Kay with the bottom-of-the-lagoon "bouquet," etc. "Bad light" put an end to things at 4:55. Most of the next two days were spent on the same location photographing Adams cavorting in the water for the topside half of the Kay–Gill Man swim scene and footage of the *Rita* rocking as the Gill Man attempts to escape the submerged net. On the 8th, *Black Lagoon*'s second unit, headed by director James Havens, planed out for the Florida Panhandle for two weeks of filming underwater footage.

Among the scenes put on film on October 9: the Creature's legs and feet as he walks the *Rita* deck, and the Creature descending upon the screaming Chico. Ben Chapman did *not* work, according to the

Kay (Julie Adams) climbs back aboard the *Rita* after her ill-advised swim. Notice on the left the big block "gobo" (a piece of grip equipment) and, at the top, the hands of the crew member holding it. Also pictured, from left: Antonio Moreno, Whit Bissell, Richard Denning, Richard Carlson, Nestor Paiva.

Daily Production Report, so it's anybody's guess as to who wore the Creature costume in those two shots. The doomed Chico was played by Henry "Blackie" Escalante, a Mexican actor-stuntman hailing from a family of circus trapeze artists. Escalante once told me that he was the Gill Man in scenes shot at Universal; nothing in the production paperwork backs up his claim but *some*body was in the monster suit (or parts of the suit) on days when production paperwork indicates the *absence* of Ben Chapman, so why not him? The scenes in question also include the Gill Man's arm reaching out of the water at Maia's camp, his arm coming through the bunk room porthole, and more. So with a big question mark and an even bigger grain of salt, put the name of "Blackie" Escalante on the list of people who might have played Blackie LaGoon in some of those shots. Although certainly not the shot where the Gill Man kills Chico—because Chico *was* Escalante!

On the morning of Saturday, October 10, the first unit moviemakers were in Sierra Canyon, which here represented Dr. Maia's camp. The day began with delays (waiting for light, repairing the camera) but then proceeded smoothly: The scene depicting the discovery of the fossilized hand was shot, plus part of the later scene where the expedition members arrive and find the bodies of Luis and Tomas. On the morning of Monday, October 12, overcast skies and poor light meant that additional electricians and artificial light were needed. The "Interior Cabin and Dark Room" fistfight between Reed and Williams was shot on Stage 21 on the 13th. Stunt doubles Cliff Lyons and Allen Pinson were on hand, but the brawl as seen on film is all Carlson and Denning. The company went on to shoot more cabin scenes, including the memorable vignette when the Gill Man's hand reaches through the open porthole and hovers over the bandaged and bedridden Dr. Thompson.

Meanwhile, 2260 miles away (give or take), the *Black Lagoon* second unit was arriving at their home for the next few weeks, the Wakulla Springs Lodge, 80 or 100 yards from the edge of the body of water where they'd be shooting. Some of the guest rooms, plus the dining room and terrace, had (and *have*) a view of the Spring and River. They grabbed a noon-to-one lunch and then, typical of this problem-plagued production, found themselves unable to get the 3-D camera to operate. They then set up a process camera on a boat, in order to shoot plates of river and jungle backgrounds—and had trouble with the camera's batteries! By 5:12, less than an hour after they'd finally started shooting, they called it quits. The next morning, Gill Man Ricou Browning officially started working, but only appeared on-camera for a few minutes at the very end of the day. In order to play an aquatic monster without the use of air tanks, he used the amazing "hose-breathing" techniques he'd been taught during his teen years. What this involved, Browning told me, was:

Coming down from a compressor on the surface, I'd have an air hose, the air coming out of it with some force. I'd stick the air hose in my mouth and breathe from it, like you would drink water from a hose in your backyard. There's kind of a little knack to it, but I learned it when I was very young, at Wakulla Springs.... It was something I did very naturally, and so it came easy for me. I could insert the hose in the mouth of the Creature, then I'd have to go a couple of inches further, to get to my own mouth, and then breathe.

Let's say we were ready to do a scene: With me, I would have a safety man with an air hose and I'd be breathing, and when I was ready to go, I'd give the cameraman "Scotty" Welbourne the okay sign—hand signals—and I'd keep breathing. When he would give me the signal he was rolling the camera, I would release the air hose, giving it back to the safety man, and then (if it was just a swim-through) I would swim by camera. On the other side, there'd be another safety man who'd give me a different air hose. So I had safety men in various places in order to get air. The compressor on the surface supplied air to my safety men's multiple hoses ... sometimes more than one compressor. If I got to where I was really desperate for air, I would just stop everything and go limp, and the safety man would swim in to me and give me an air hose. Or if I was in a fight scene, I would just stop fighting and not do any-

In the weeks leading up to Ben Chapman's first day on the *Black Lagoon* set, the moviemakers got a number of shots that included partial glimpses of the Gill Man (just his legs, just an arm, etc.) plus the split-second shot where he attacks Chico. Presumably this unidentified actor or extra is the "placeholder" Gill Man. On the right are observers Julie Adams and Richard Carlson. (Photograph courtesy Bob Burns.)

thing, and then they would come in and give me an air hose. I had people that I had worked with underwater for years prior to this, so I had a lot of confidence in them. They were very good and it worked fairly well.

Browning got to pick the members of his safety team; some were co-workers from water shows (like Patsy Boyette, a Weeki Wachee "mermaid") and others were people with whom he'd gone cave-diving. One safety man, his longtime friend Charles McNabb, took part in all three Gill Man movies.

The second unit crew's "workplace" was a boat-and-raft set-up; the raft was held up by six air-filled 55-gallon drums. An upcoming shot would be discussed and rehearsed on the raft, and then the cast and underwater crew would go down and shoot. The compressors pumping out the air for Browning's underwater hose-breathing use were noisy and would have interfered with rehearsals, so they were kept on a second boat and/or raft.

Also shot underwater in Wakulla on October 14 was the footage where Reed (played by FSU student Stanley Crews), working at the bottom of Morajo Bay, notices the jiggling 40-foot marker. It's not hard, in the new millennium, to take some of the underwater scenes in *Black Lagoon* and the other Gill Man movies for granted, but in the mid–1950s they were real attention-getters: Scuba-diving was a newish phenomenon and public interest was at its peak. Truth be told, these scenes were movie history-makers: It was the first time that a 3-D camera had gone underwater *and*, as William Alland pointed out to me, it was a *free-floating underwater camera in a natural environment*, practically unheard-of prior to *Black Lagoon*. "Scotty" Welbourne, *Black Lagoon*'s second unit d.p., was its inventor. Alland told me that Welbourne

developed an underwater camera to use with scuba gear. He had a little inner tube that was tied to the bottom of the camera, and with a CO_2 cartridge he could inflate or deflate that, and get neutral buoyancy with it and swim all over the place and take movies. "Scotty" had already done some free-swimming movie photography in the ocean—nobody had ever done that before.

A *Revenge of the Creature* publicity item pointed out that the filming of pictures underwater, which had been going on for 40 years, was revolutionized by "lens artist" Welbourne when he did *Creature from the Black Lagoon*. In 1954 when *Revenge* was made, there were only three of Welbourne's tri-dimensional cameras in existence: The first was built by Welbourne in his shop, the second was built in a Universal shop from Welbourne's specifications, and the third was built at Disney, again from his specifications. Powered by a battery unit inside it, it weighed 200 pounds but it could be pushed or pulled through water, always floating on an even keel. It rose or sank in the water, still always on an even keel, by responding to either of two buttons pressed by the operator. The speed of its ascent or descent was regulated by the amount of pressure on the buttons. "It was a big monster of a camera," Browning told interviewer Mike Nash. "And to handle that camera, 'Scotty' did a magnificent job."

"'Scotty' was an absolute artist, he was tremendous," Alland said in *The Man Who Pursued Rosebud*. "All the underwater stuff in [*Black Lagoon*]—hey, I've seen nothing done since that's any more artistically beautiful than the stuff in that."

At Universal, the 14th began with the usual difficulties (a heavily overcast sky, poor light and a camera in need of repair) and then several scenes were shot at a variety of locations. The entire morning was spent at Park Lake shooting rowboaters Reed and Williams dropping rotenone sacks into the lagoon and discussing the Gill Man. Then in the afternoon, on Stage 21, parts of two cabin scenes were shot, starting with the tail end of the developing-the-photo sequence. Put on film but not used in the movie: a shot of Williams talking, with the camera dollying in to show us, through a porthole behind him, the legs of the Gill Man going past the opening. (Chapman again is *not* on the list of actors present.)

On the 15th, more Park Lake scenes were committed to film, including the drugged fish floating on the lagoon surface and the flareup between Williams and Lucas, who holds a knife beneath Williams' chin. In North Florida, the morning's work was lost due to yet more camera problems. There was an addition to the small Wakulla cast that day: 27-year-old Jack Betz, yet another FSU student, who had the job of doubling Richard Denning's character Mark Williams. There was more aggravation for the *Black Lagoon* crew on the 16th, with *two* camera breakdowns and then heavy rain making the waters too dark.

On the morning of October 16, the cast and crew at Universal tried to get the shot in which the *Rita* runs into the Gill Man's tree barricade. On the first attempt, the *Rita* was being towed by cables attached to a winch, but the winch couldn't pull the boat fast enough for the action to look realistic. As most of the company members had lunch, prop shop men re-rigged things so that the *Rita* would now be pulled by an off-screen, on-shore truck. Again things went awry. In order *not* to have to wait as the boat was *re*-rerigged, Arnold and Co. jumped ahead in the script and shot an on-deck discussion *of* the tree barricade plus the reaction to the Gill Man's smashing of the rowboat.

Saturday, October 17, 1953, began with grief: According to the minutes of a subsequent Studio Operating Committee meeting, "The company had an exterior call, but the boat had been pulled on shore to rig the underwater cable for

Watched by Richard Denning, Nestor Paiva, Julie Adams and Antonio Moreno, Richard Carlson tries to get a cable around the Gill Man's tree barricade.

positive stopping of the boat [as it hit the barricade, I assume]. While on shore the water in the boat sank the stern and more water rushed in and the boat tipped over." Hastening to a Stage 21 cover set, the moviemakers photographed a variety of silent shots of the Gill Man's hand coming through the porthole. (Is it Chapman's hand? Who knows? He signed his contract to join the picture's cast that day, but apparently had not yet been fitted for his Creature costume.) Then they tackled the Instituto de Biología Marítima office-aquarium scene where, with rear-projected fish as a backdrop, the movie's leading characters examine the skeleton hand. Not surprisingly, given all the unexpected snags, *Black Lagoon* was now two days behind schedule and approximately $6000 over budget.

As mentioned above, October 17 was the date on Ben Chapman's "Screen Actors Guild Inc. Minimum Free Lance Contract" which called for him to play the role of "Gill Man" at a salary of $300 a week; "The terms of employment hereafter shall begin on the 17th day of October 1953, and shall continue thereafter until the completion of the photography and recordation of said role." Needless to say, the contract's seventh clause—that the player agrees to furnish all "wearing apparel reasonably necessary for the portrayal of said role"—wasn't applicable in Chapman's case!

In Florida the cameras worked well that day, but on Sunday, October 18, there were more breakdowns, and yet again "The Sunshine State" failed to live up to its nickname as heavy rain caused blackness underwater. Mechanical defects and bad weather weren't the only on-location difficulties: According to William Alland, second unit director James C. Havens didn't turn out to be much of a second unit director. Alland told me,

After we picked the locations in Florida and everything, we sent "Scotty" Welbourne down there to shoot second unit stuff, underwater. And we sent down a very famous second unit director named James Havens to direct it. Well, after they were there a few days, I got a call from the production manager: "You'd better come down here, there's all hell breaking loose. Havens and Welbourne are not getting along." So I went down, and what I found out was that Havens was scared to go underwater! What he did was, he would swim on the surface with a snorkel, and look *down* 50 feet to see what was going on [*laughs*]! That's the God's truth! Havens had sketched out how he wanted the thing to be shot and everything, and Welbourne was saying, "Hey, I can't do it that way. He can't see what's down there, and I can't do things based on a sketch that he might show me. I gotta take advantage of what's there." Havens' position was, "Look, he won't do the scenes as I instruct him." But Havens wouldn't put on scuba and go down!

Now I'm there, see, so what I did was, I tried to *shame* Havens into doing it. I put on scuba gear and went down there with "Scotty" and watched him doing his stuff and so forth, then came out and said to Havens, "Listen, either you go down and see what he's doing and work with him, or you've just got to get out of the way." And he said, "Well, I'll just get out of the way, that's all." He *stayed* there, but he did not have a damn thing to do with any of the stuff that went on underwater.

Considering the fact that almost one-fourth of the movie takes place underwater, I asked Alland if fans talking about the direction of *Black Lagoon* should say that it was directed by Jack Arnold and "Scotty" Welbourne. His emphatic reply was, "Absolutely. 'Scotty' Welbourne directed the underwater stuff."

Wanting more than one take on this situation, I also put the question to Ricou Browning, who looked at things differently. He disputed Alland's memory that Havens was "scared" to go underwater, saying that Havens simply "wasn't

Ben Chapman liked to call himself "an entertainer" rather than an actor, and considered dancing and singing his forte. In his early days, his dancing partner was Tani Marsh, who in 1957 played the skinny-dipping, cat-fighting Naomi in *From Hell It Came*.

capable, in other words, he wasn't *trained* to go underwater. He was topside on an inner tube, looking down wearing a facemask, watching as much as he could what was going on. And that was *it*. He depended a great deal on 'Scotty' Welbourne, and 'Scotty' was a pretty sharp character. [Havens] kind of just left it to him and us to do our thing. And he would watch, and comment now and then." More recently I put the question to him again, and he added a few more particulars:

> **We would stand on the raft with Havens and we would talk about and rehearse the scene that we were about to do, "Creature swims after girl" or whatever. Then when the rest of us [without Havens] got underwater, we'd have to figure out *how* to swim after the girl, or *how* to do whatever it was we had to do. "Scotty" and I would figure that out. If it looked good, "Scotty" and I would come up and say "It was great!" and Havens would say "Fine!," and then we'd go on to the *next* sequence.**

On the question of who should receive credit for the direction of the underwater scenes, Browning replied, "I would just say a combination of people. I would give Havens credit."

On Monday, October 19, the long arm of the law—Murphy's Law—again reached out for the Florida company: At a depth of 60 feet they were shooting Reed and Williams' second dive when water pressure cracked the glass in the camera's watertight housing, creating a hour-long setback. The gang at Universal again attempted to get the jinxed shot of the *Rita* ramming the tree barricade; they also shot subsequent scenes of Our Heroes trying to move the tree with cable and winch. Chapman is listed on production paperwork for showing up on the lot that day to be "fitted in Makeup." "Fitting in Makeup" is written next to Chapman's name on the Production Report for October 20, and then he did work on-camera that night: Standing in knee-deep waters near the jungle-like edge of Park Lake, he played the scene where the Gill Man is blinded by the *Rita*'s spotlight, snatching at the empty air in front of him, and

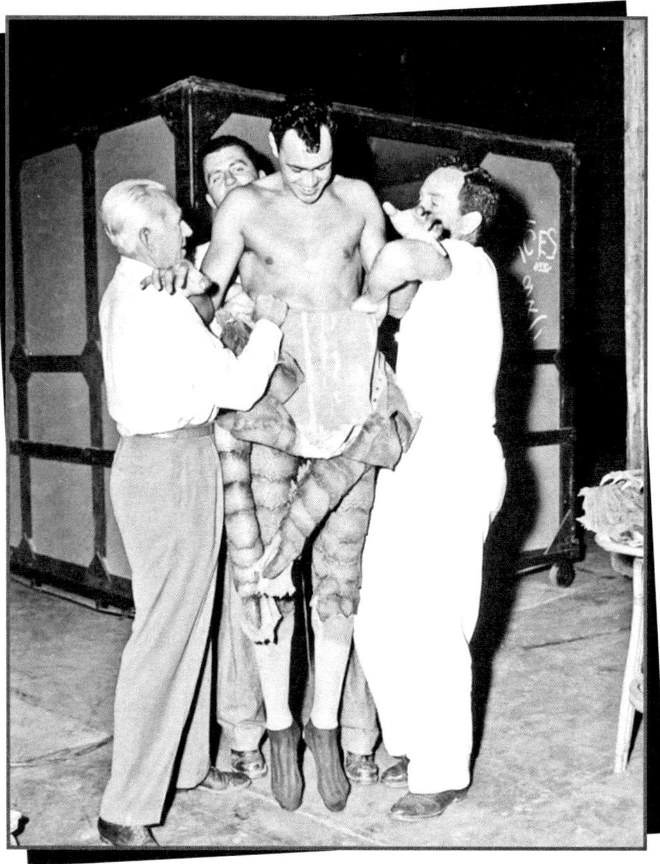

Creature (dis)comforts: "Land Gill Man" Ben Chapman on tiptoes as the suit is pulled up tight on him. Part of the challenge of playing the man-beast was to stay the same weight throughout production: "If I lost weight, the suit would crinkle all over, and if I gained, of course, I'd have had trouble getting into it."

then sinking into the water to exit. This scene was then shot two more times, the third and last time with tubes hooked up to the Creature gills to produce the breathing effect.

Bob Burns agrees that this was probably the first time Chapman was in front of the camera and that in all previously shot footage of the Creature, someone else was inside the world's weirdest onesie. "By the time Ben finally came on, they *had* to have demos of his suit already, they had to have pieces put together just to see what it was going to look like. So in those other scenes [the Creature's arm reaching out of water and through the porthole, the Creature's legs and feet as he walks the *Rita* deck, etc.], we're probably seeing some extra that they hired. I don't think it was even a stuntman, they wouldn't *need* a stuntman, I'm sure it was just an extra they got and said, 'Okay, we want you to put your hand through here' or 'Walk over here, we need to see your feet walkin' by,' stuff like that." Chapman did claim to have done *ev-er-y* topside Gill Man shot but the Production Reports contradict him. For example, on the October 9 Production Report's list of actors, his is one of several names scratched out (meaning that none of them worked on that date)—and that was the day the Gill Man attacked Chico. A $25 extra *did* work that day, from 9 a.m. until 11:50, departing minutes after the completion of the attack scene.

In their scuba-diving gear, Richards Carlson and Denning were also in Park Lake on the night of the 20th. (Reed: "That's where [the Gill Man] went under." Williams: "I'm going to take a look. You wait here.") Denning recalled the ordeal for me, admitting that he and Carlson were able to stay in the water until 8:00 partly thanks to some potent potables:

It was October and it was freezing cold. We were out in the water and we were tired and it was late, and the prop man kept bringing us brandy to keep us from freezing to death. It worked great, and we were going just fine. And then we finally wrapped it up and we went to the dressing rooms—they were nice and warm. All of a sudden [*slurring his words*], that brandy just hit like a sledgehammer! But out in the cold and the wet and wind, it didn't bother us at all!

October 21 began at Park Lake the way *many* days began ("8:40: Camera breakdown discovered; 8:40–9:15: Camera being repaired"), and then the troupe got down to the business of shooting a day's worth of scenes and individual shots for various parts of the picture. In North Florida, however, Monster Movie History was being made: Ginger Stanley, Julie Adams' 21-year-old double, was now part of the unit as they began shooting "the underwater ballet" with Ricou and Ginger becoming the *Fred* and Ginger of sci-fi.

The first shot committed to film that day was shortened for inclusion in the movie: "[Medium shot] Shooting up to bottom of boat ladder and net—Kay dives in to make big underwater arc—[Camera tilts down] with her dive to big [close-up] of Gill Man watching—he swims out over [camera]." In the edited version, the camera does begin to tilt down after her entrance into the water, but the shot ends before it gets to the Gill Man. Then more of this unforgettable, hypnotic Kay–Creature swim sequence was filmed. It's impressive that the Florida-made "synchronized swimming" part of the scene (the Gill Man directly below Kay) came out as well as it did considering the challenges faced by Browning, who was required to swim upside-down, holding his breath, hoping water didn't go up his nose, swimming the same speed as Stanley and maintaining the same short distance from her without ever touching her—all while being unable to properly see!

A lot has been written about *Black Lagoon*'s water ballet, some of it kinda hifalutin. In Universal's made-for-DVD documentary *Back to the Black Lagoon* (2000), Adams said all that really needs to be said in just three words: According to Julie, it's "a love scene." In *The Lucky Southern Star* she wrote about seeing that footage for the first time:

For me, one of the more exciting moments during [*Black Lagoon*] production was when we all went to see the Florida unit dailies, with Ricou and Ginger doing their beautiful "water ballet." The way he mimicked her every move was mesmerizing, and even more amazing when it was cut together with the first unit shots of me swimming on the surface. I still love seeing it.

On October 22, the Florida unit wrapped up the Gill Man–Kay swimming scene, while at Universal there was more Park Lake activity, including the scene of the Gill Man climbing aboard the *Rita*, grabbing Kay and jumping overboard with her in his clutches. Chapman did the "stunt" himself but Adams was replaced by stuntwoman Polly Burson the two times it was photographed: The first time was the shot we see in the movie, the second time (after Burson's hair dried) a reverse full shot of the boat, the camera panning down with them to the water.

Most of the actors were dismissed between 4:00 and 4:25. The actors playing Maia's native helpers Luis and Tomas, Rodd Redwing and Perry Lopez, stuck around a few more hours for Sierra Canyon shooting of the Creature's-eye-view scene of the man-fish advancing on their tent, and the full shot of the tent quaking as the unseen Gill Man wreaks havoc inside. On October 23, they shot day-for-night beach footage of the Gill Man making a beeline for Kay, scuffling with Zee, picking up and carrying Kay, collapsing and being beaten by the rifle-swinging Williams, etc.

Meanwhile, in the Florida Panhandle, swimming scenes featuring Reed, Williams and the Gill Man were photographed,

Screecher from the Black Lagoon. The way Julie Adams' Kay maintains perfect makeup and hair throughout pretty much the whole movie may not be credible but who'd have it any other way? Pictured: Adams, Ben Chapman.

plus *out*-of-the-water shots of Wakulla's primeval-looking banks and various critters. The good news: The 23rd was very productive for *Black Lagoon* units on both coasts. The bad news: The movie was now *three* days behind schedule and approximately $12,500 over budget.

It was a "gang's all here" day at Universal on Saturday the 24th with the entire screen-credited cast (plus Chapman, Rodd Redwing and Perry Lopez) on the Park Lake set. There was *of course* a hold-up in getting started: Chapman was late because the makeup department was repairing his damaged Gill Man suit (the second one wasn't yet ready). On the beach, the first order of business was to get a shot of the Gill Man lifting Zee (Gozier) and flinging him into the camera. Apparently Gozier was going to do the stunt himself, as no stuntman's name appears on the day's paperwork. Gozier was supposed to hang from a wire strung from the up-out-of-camera-range arm of a crane, but the wire broke in a rehearsal. Due to the length of time needed to fix the problem, a decision was made to get that shot later. But the moviemakers must have known that there was a possibility that they'd never get around to it, because later that morning they shot a less spectacular death scene for Zee (the Gill Man choking and dropping him). Ultimately the lifting-and-throwing shot *was* never filmed. Before and after lunch, they filmed part of the movie's final scene: the shot of the bullet-riddled Gill Man staggering into the water, followed and watched by David, Kay, Maia and Lucas.

In Florida, October 24 began with the shooting of various point-of-view shots of Wakulla plus a few more "wildlife shots" (a bird or two, baby alligators on a log). Then the camera was changed over for underwater and the below-the-waterline brawl between Williams and the Gill Man was filmed: Browning and Jack Betz fought and rolled, battled at the top of a cliff and raised a mud cloud as they tussled in weeds. The muddiness of the water necessitated a halt in shooting at 4:12.

On Sunday, October 25, the moviemakers finished the underwater Gill Man–Williams fight scene. On Monday they put on film a shot of the "dead" Gill Man floating down toward the camera; another version of that scene in which he swims feebly down to a ledge and then dies, floating off the ledge and into the depths; and the shot of the Gill Man, with Kay under his arm, making his lengthy swim down to the submerged entrance to his cave. According to Browning, it was an 80-foot dive,

Richard Denning, whaling away at the prostrate Gill Man (Ben Chapman) with a rifle, looks ready to beat him into overdue extinction, as Richard Carlson and Julie Adams (embracing) react in shock. "Denning is a real stinker for a change," noted one *Black Lagoon* sneak preview audience member.

and quite challenging. For one thing, during their long straight-down descent, he and Stanley had to hold their breath and clear their ears multiple times (in order to prevent water pressure from bursting their eardrums) without letting the audience *see* that they were clearing their ears. Their long descent was shot twice, the first time right before lunch, Take #2 about two hours later.

The first unit spent Monday, October 26, on the Process Stage, their home for the next (and last) six days of production. Activity on the cave set began with the scene of Reed entering for the first time; he's getting an eyeful of his weird surroundings when Williams' hand suddenly enters the frame from the right and touches his shoulder. Next the Creature emerged from a pool of water with Kay in his arms. Just before lunch, the company filmed the shot of Kay awakening on the altar-like rock and Reed coming in from the foreground to embrace her. Notice that in this part of the grotto, a painted backdrop features a few white pillars with ornate bases. Whether they were meant to be spotted by audience members is open to conjecture but, if you *do* notice them, they add to the "storybook" look of the place; and they certainly make well-versed *Black Lagoon* fans think back to earlier script drafts that describe the grotto as cathedral-like.

After lunch, the rest of this climactic scene was shot amidst short breaks whenever the stage needed to be smoked up (for a mist effect) and whenever the smoke needed to be cleared. During Carlson's knife-to-claw tussle with the Gill Man, Carlson (rigged with wires attached to a crane) was grabbed by the waist and "lifted" into the air by Chapman; in all subsequent shots, Carlson has bloody claw wounds on his back and "claw thumb wounds" on his sides.

Part of October 27 was also spent on the cave set, doing a few bits of action a second time and shooting some new action, like Carlson ducking the swooping bat. Chapman was 22 minutes late getting to the set, having had trouble in the makeup department squeezing into "the #2 Gill Man suit" which was being used for the first time that day. After lunch, natives Luis and Tomas met their doom: On an interior tent set, actors Rodd Redwing and Perry Lopez were set upon by Gill Man Chapman.

At the Wednesday morning October 28 Studio Operating Committee meeting, it was mentioned that *Black Lagoon* was now approximately $19,000 over budget. That day on the Process Stage, the players enacted scenes on the deck of a duplicate *Rita,* including the one where Reed tells Kay that the Amazon is still exactly as it was when it was part of the Devonian era "150 million years ago." More *Rita* deck scenes were shot on the Process Stage on October 29 (Chapman's 25th birthday) and then the scene of Reed, Kay and Maia on the Morajo Bay barge.

At Wakulla, October 27 was a washout due to continuous heavy rain, muddy water and cold. On October 28, rain, cold and wind prevented shooting until almost noon, and then they had to stop at 4:12 due to "murky and dirty water." They finally got in a fairly full day on October 29, shooting from 9:29 a.m. to 3:32 p.m., including scenes of Reed repelling the Gill Man with sprays of rotenone. That day's production report reminds readers of the hazards of underwater work with its list of cast and crew members who, over the course of shooting, needed to visit Tallahassee physician Edson J. Andrews for ear and nose injuries, among them Welbourne, safety diver Fred Zendar, still photographer Bruce Mozert and more.

At Universal, October 30 was the last day for Carlson, Denning, Moreno, Paiva and Gozier. On the Process Stage, various night scenes on the *Rita* deck were shot, among them the Gill Man appearing out of the water and climbing a rope up the *Rita*'s side. In Florida, they shot from 9:56 a.m. to 4:25 p.m., and then the words "2nd Unit—Finished This Date" were written across the top page of the Daily Production Report. It had been over two weeks of nearly seven-days-a-week work, with much agita due to camera breakdowns and Mother Nature, plus plenty of breaks for medical attention. But the end results of their waterlogged labors were most of the best scenes from one of the best science fiction-horror-adventure films of the era.

October 31 (Halloween) was the final day of Universal shooting, with the cast's last Three Little Indians, Adams, Bissell and Chapman, on the Process Stage shooting a *Rita* deck scene (Thompson guards the tank containing the unconscious Gill Man, Kay comes up from below to join him, they talk, the Gill Man awakens and attacks). Prior to photographing the shot of the Gill Man unconscious in the tank, there was a 27-minute hold-up while his breathing apparatus was repaired; on the Daily Production Report was written the explanation "This was a very close shot—necessary for gills and throat to work." In the movie, the Gill Man's escape from the tank is off-camera, but a bust-out scene *was* shot: Crew members spent from 1:20 to 1:35 "[r]igging tank cover for special effect" and then, all in a single shot, the following action was shot: "[T]he GILL MAN leaps out of tank and THOMPSON pushes KAY out of way. THOMPSON picks up a lantern and scares the creature into backing up. The GILL MAN comes for THOMPSON then and claws his face." For interviewer Dennis Daniel, Adams reminisced, "When Whit Bissell came out from makeup with his face all bloodied up …, the guy who put the clapper in front of the camera asked, 'How are you fixed for blades?'" (a line made famous by Gillette shaving razor ads of that era).

Black Lagoon wrapped two days behind schedule and over-budget by approximately $14,000. The Florida underwater unit was three days behind schedule by the time they finished.

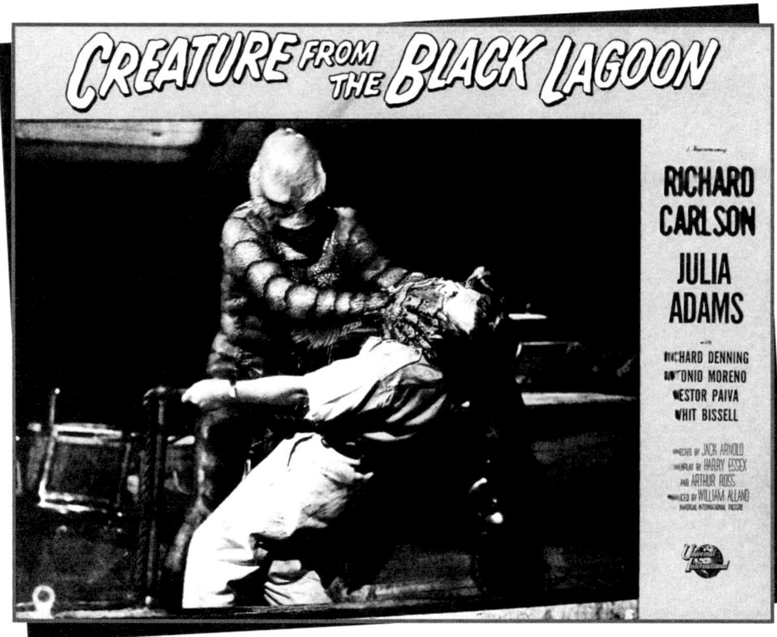

The Creature (Ben Chapman) gets its razor-fingered hands on Dr. Thompson (Whit Bissell). As the *New York Herald Tribune* reviewer put it, "After [the Gill Man's] diligent efforts, the cast of characters is much smaller at the end of the film than it was at the beginning."

On November 10, a week and a half after the movie completed production, part of the abovementioned Kay–Thompson–Creature deck scene was re-shot. Adams, Bissell and Chapman returned to the Process Stage, where Arnold directed Kay's entrance, her chat with Thompson and their reaction to the sound of the off-screen Gill Man bursting out of the tank. It's a safe bet that the conversation we see in the movie (Thompson advising Kay about her relationships with Reed and Williams) was what was shot on the 10th because their dialogue in the movie isn't in the script. What *is* in the script, and what was presumably filmed on October 31 and then discarded, is the short-and-simple exchange that follows:

KAY (*reacting to the sound of hunting calls in the jungle*): Some of them are cries of fear.... Like people who whistle in the dark.... The law of the jungle—survival of the fittest—of the strongest.

THOMPSON: Darwin only claimed that survival belonged to those who adapt best to new surroundings.

In the script, this is the point at which they're interrupted by the sounds of wood-snapping, cord-ripping and the gush of water, and Kay and Thompson whirl about to see the tank with its "cover torn open—the Gill Man standing on the deck, water receding around him."

Kay and Thompson's longer, more interesting conversation (about her career and love life) is a nice scene to have in the movie if only because, *finally*, Thompson gets to speak more than just a few words at a time; the rest of Bissell's performance consists almost entirely of one-liners, making it obvious that the character is in the movie only to give the Gill Man an extra victim.

Before and after shooting the Kay Thompson deck scene, the November 10 crew also photographed insert shots: the bat flying toward the camera, wet Gill Man footprints on the *Rita*'s deck, the harpoon hitting the *Rita*'s mast. After lunch, they moved to the Underwater Tank, adding some milk to the water to make it look a bit murky and then photographing a Gill Man dummy "as he is shot in back with spear" and "as he is shot in chest with spear" (shot descriptions from the Production Report). Then it was back to the Process Stage to get a shot of the Gill Man (Chapman's) hand "as it reaches out of water. There is a flash and the hand retreats, clawing the bank." (The flash was the flash of Dr. Maia's camera, photographing the fossil claw in the first scene at the geological camp; this shot wasn't used in the movie.) Then they got a few more insert shots: the photo of the fossilized claw, the photo taken by Reed underwater, etc.

During *Black Lagoon* pre-production, the name of the movie was up in the air: As early as September 1, publicity man Archie Herzoff was asking his colleagues to propose other titles. Staffers were told that the title needed to suggest "the shock and mystery value—and perhaps the prehistoric implications—of the story. However, we have been asked to stay away from words like 'monster' or 'beast' to avoid a title that might downgrade the picture." As of September 11, the list of offered-up titles included *The Amazon Man, The Being from the Dawn of Time, The Black Pool, The Chain of Life, Expedition Terror, The Fossil That Lived, Grotto of Fright, The Hand from the Past, Jungle Nights, Lost Age, The Man-Fish of Horror Lagoon, The Morajo Man Mystery, Man from the Amazon, The Stone Claw, Thundering Waters* and *Water Demon*.

Black Lagoon remained the title right up to the first day of production, and onward *through* production. On October 19 one of the matters under discussion at the Operating Committee meeting was the name of their new monster movie: Studio brass, not happy with the title *Black Lagoon*, decided to register the replacement title *River of a Million Years*. But on November 12, Universal's Sam Israel addressed the following memo to "THE STAFF": "Hereafter please refer to *Black Lagoon* as *The Creature from the Black Lagoon....*"

Creature from the Black Lagoon had its first sneak preview on January 7, 1954, at Los Angeles' United Artists Theatre, following a regularly scheduled showing of Universal's action drama *Forbidden. Assuming* that this preview was the only *Creature* preview, then it's the one Arthur Ross described to me. His main memory of that night involved Universal production chief Edward Muhl, and how "high" he was on *Black Lagoon*'s prospects:

Ed was a *very* bright man, highly intelligent, well-read. We got along well—we sort of liked each other. He sensed something in *Creature* that nobody else did, and they sort of laughed at him. But he said, "This is going to be an absolute *smash*." They used to have previews: They would take the main participants in the picture to dinner at, say, the Beachcombers or Chasen's or somewhere, and then they would go to the theater. Well, for the preview of *Creature*, there were three buses filled with people, they took us to dinner at the Beachcombers and then downtown for the preview. Ed made *every* executive, *every* contract producer, *every* contract director come watch *Creature* because, he said, "This is going to be the pattern and form and intent of our future films." At that point, Harry Essex and I looked at each other and said, "He must be crazy!" [*Laughs.*] But off it went!

One of *Black Lagoon*'s obvious plusses was a monster with pathos, but apparently Westmore thought otherwise because he was discouraged by preview audience members who had empathy for "the Creech." *So* discouraged, in fact, that he badmouthed the star attraction of Universal's as-yet-unreleased movie! Syndicated columnist Bob Thomas visited the U-I makeup department in February 1954, watched as some finishing touches were put on *This Island Earth*'s Metaluna Mutant, and talked to Westmore for his story "Bud Westmore Enjoys Doing Horror Makeup." And when the conversation turned to *Black Lagoon*, the department head came out with the surprising statement, "We sort of fell down on that one"!

"He wasn't frightening enough," Westmore continued. "The preview cards indicated that some people in the audience sympathized with him. The trouble was that they photographed the frog man in the bright sunlight. You can't do that with monsters. You have to keep them in the shadows." Apparently taking Westmore at his word that the Gill Man costume was a flop, Thomas adopted a better-luck-next-time tone for his closing comment, "Westmore needn't worry. [The Metaluna Mutant] will restore his reputation as a monstrosity-maker."

Westmore's unexpected "dissing" of the Gill Man suit couldn't have pleased whichever Universal honchos read Thomas' story. And then, for sheer swinishness, he outdid himself with what we'll euphemistically call "the Milicent Patrick incident."

Probably because Patrick was a knockout (a pretty brunette, statuesque, 40–25–38), *Black Lagoon* publicists proposed that she be sent to various cities where the movie was about to open, make appearances at theaters and give interviews about the creation of the Gill Man outfit.

But the mere suggestion that the movie be represented by this beauty brought out the beast in Westmore. When Clark Ramsay discussed with Westmore the idea of a Patrick tour, the makeup department bigwig made it plain that he resented the use of the tie-in phrase "The Beauty Who Created the Beast." Ramsay described their conversation in a memo to the Universal New York office's director of publicity and exploitation Charles Simonelli:

His point was that the eventual creation of the beast of the Black Lagoon was completely his own work. He pointed out that many people had been involved in the original sketches and thinking, but had all dropped out of the project when it became difficult and complex. As a result he spent four or five weeks, himself, developing the model which was eventually used.

Particularly because of these circumstances, I am afraid he would be a little upset if we credited his creation to someone else. ... Inasmuch as we depend upon Westmore for some rather close cooperation we felt it would be best if we tried to develop another tie-in line. We held a staff meeting and came up with a line we think will do as well. We will call Miss Patrick "The Beauty Who Lives with the Beasts."

It was felt that this would provide an opportunity to send her out, not only to discuss the Gill Man, but with some of the masks and photographs of the other horror creatures which our Makeup Department has turned out over the years. Her basic story could be that she is not only a creative designer of such creatures but another of her tasks is their care and preservation. In other words, "she lives with them." The newest in her colony of monsters is, of course, the Gill Man. We feel that this would not only provide excellent photographic material, but would certainly give her a good line for newspaper, TV and radio interviews.

Even when it appeared as though all of the bugs had been ironed out of the plan, things were still not All Quiet on the Westmore Front: Evidently Bud had come to realize that the Gill Man was one of the finest feathers in his department's cap and wanted all the credit. This black hole of need next stormed into the office of Sam Israel; Israel described their meeting in a January 26 letter to Eastern publicity manager Philip Gerard of Universal's 445 Park Avenue, New York, office:

[Westmore] made it very clear that he resented this whole project, although he denied it and put it on a different basis. He is perturbed, he says, by the fact that Milicent will claim credit for what he has achieved in putting these monsters together, and he would like us to make sure that as far as possible the interviews stress the fact that he is the one who supervises the creation of these creatures from start to finish. Milicent's job, he says, is merely to put his ideas in the form of sketches. It is a battle of credits, of

course, and I would suggest we be guided by his wishes if they do not get in our way. Frankly, I am getting a little fed up with these squawks from people who are paid to do a job, and from what I hear, Milicent's contribution in this work is very important.

Milicent Patrick, sketch artist and actress, has been engaged by U-I to aid in the coast-to-coast promotion campaign on *Creature from the Black Lagoon*, first 3-D production with extensive underwater sequences. Miss Patrick, working under the supervision of U-I makeup chief Bud Westmore, planes out Sunday for New York.

—*The Hollywood Reporter*, January 28, 1954

Patrick flew to New York on Sunday, January 31, and began thumping the tub for *Black Lagoon* in all media. On February 4, Gerard wrote Israel that Patrick had turned out to be an ideal personality for their promotional activities: "We have had excellent response from the press, radio and TV, and she comes off extremely well in all of these interviews." She then began touring with the movie itself, making appearances in numerous Michigan cities several days in advance of its first playdate there. By the 16th she was back in New York and supplementing her original press, radio and TV schedule. In total, according to Patrick's résumé, she "guest starred on 40 TV and radio shows" in New York and Michigan.

Even though Patrick had sallied forth with Westmore's imprimatur, and conducted herself strictly according to Hoyle, the kudos she received must have stirred the soup of his discontent and he continued to raise hell about it. On March 1, Ramsay wrote Simonelli that her tour "has apparently placed her in a rather awkward position here at the studio." He elaborated,

As I told you prior to the tour, Bud Westmore was very sensitive in the matter of credit for the designing of the Creature. Apparently under rather difficult circumstances he did it himself and Milicent Patrick's sketches were copied from the original design rather than the basis for the original design. You will recall that we had to switch our copy slant from "The Beauty Who Created the Beast," to "The Beauty Who Lives with Beasts."

Apparently Westmore went to the trouble of getting hold of newspapers from a number of the cities that Miss Patrick visited and discovered that she was being credited as the designer of the Creature with no mention of Westmore. He has let it be known in a general way that he is not going to use her as a sketch artist any more.

Even were the company to force Westmore to hire her the circumstances would be such that it would be impossible for her to do a satisfactory job for him. Somehow Westmore will have to be made to understand that she, herself, did everything possible to credit Westmore on radio and newspaper interviews. If there is any blame in the matter, I think we will have to take it ourselves or place it on the newspapers.

Whatever additional action was taken may not have been enough to get Westmore to stop lashing out from his hurt locker. Patrick's résumé reveals that she did makeup illustrations for Universal's *Captain Lightfoot* (1955), a movie whose production postdated the *Black Lagoon* controversy; her sketches might not have. Apart from that, she may never again have worked in a makeup or sketch artist capacity at Universal.

•••••••••••••••••••••••••

On the DVD audio commentary for *The Creature Walks Among Us*, Bob Burns said that he was a teenager in 1954 when he first saw *Black Lagoon,* back in the days when you could sit in a theater and watch a movie run "four or five" times if you wanted: "I did it for all four or five runs! The 3-D in it was amazing. The stuff they shot in Florida—the Creature looked like he was actually floating [in the air in the theater auditorium] in front of you. It was really something." As Dennis Saleh wrote in his book *Science Fiction Gold: Film Classics of the 50s*, "The darkened theater and shadowy waters of the Black Lagoon would join in mid-air, there where the creature swirled suspended above the audience."

Fabulist Jack Arnold told at least one interviewer that *Black Lagoon* saved Universal from bankruptcy. While the movie was certainly a moneymaker, it was not nearly in *that* class. At the beginning of 1955, *Variety* ran its list of 1954 movies that made $1,000,000 or more at the domestic (U.S. and Canada) box office, and Paramount's *White Christmas* headed the 124-title lineup with an estimated $12,000,000. In the sci-fi and horror categories, the top money-earner was Warners' *Them!* with $2,200,000, followed by the same studio's tri-dimensional *Phantom of the Rue Morgue* with $1,450,000. Batting cleanup monster-wise was *Black Lagoon* with its $1,300,000 domestic take. It's down near the bottom of the list in a tie with Lana Turner's *Flame and the Flesh*, Rosemary Clooney's *Red Garters*, Vera Ralston's *Jubilee Trail et al.*

The First Run, February to September 1954

Following ten days of print, radio and television publicity generated during the course of Milicent Patrick's promotional tour of Michigan and New York, the *Creature from the Black Lagoon* world premiere took place at Detroit's 3500-seat[1] Broadway-Capitol Theater on February 12, 1954, with Patrick and a 12-foot-tall "*papier mâché*" standee of the Gill Man in attendance. The Broadway-Capitol was the flagship venue of the Butterfield movie theater chain, and from February 13, *Black Lagoon* opened at other Butterfield theaters throughout Michigan, chiefly as a stand-alone attraction, though occasionally as the top half of a double-bill. For its February 19 opening at the State Theatre in Benton Harbor, for example, it played in 3-D on a double-bill with the "2-D co-hit" *Donovan's Brain*.

Although the majority of *Black Lagoon*'s February engagements took place in Michigan, the movie also had a limited number of openings as a 2-D stand-alone attraction in states including Colorado and Alabama in the days immediately following the world premiere. As early as February 17, *Variety* was able to report that "*Creature*, showing in 3-D in Detroit, is terrif in the Motor City and fine as 2-D'er in Denver." Some of the early Butterfield screenings, such as a three-day engagement as a stand-alone feature at the 506-seat Center Theater in Holland, Michigan, commencing on February 18, were likewise in 2-D.

From the beginning of March, *Black Lagoon*'s general release fanned out across the nation, with Universal undertaking "saturation openings" in 17 major cities[2] through to the end of April. On April 30, the movie had its New York City premiere as a 3-D stand-alone attraction at the 3664-seat Paramount Theatre in Times Square. This period represented the apex of *Black Lagoon*'s first-run commercial success: The April 14 *Variety* identified it as the eighth-best-performing feature nationwide, while the title appeared five times on *Boxoffice* magazine's "Boxoffice Barometer" (charting the most successful current releases in 20 key U.S. cities) between April 10 and May 15, with business reported to be between 23 and 34 percent above average.

Nevertheless, a look at newspaper listing columns shows the movie continuing to open as a first-run feature at neighborhood, small-town and rural theaters throughout the four subsequent months from June to September 1954 as well. With such venues regularly accounting for at least one-quarter of a feature's domestic gross, it is important to include these engagements within *Black Lagoon*'s first run, which may consequently be said to have extended roughly from the second week of February through to the end of September 1954.

3-D vs. Flat Screenings

Universal released *Black Lagoon* simultaneously in 3-D and 2-D versions, and as should already be evident, bookings in both formats were commonplace from the outset. Even in New York City, the feature played neighborhood theaters "flat" from May 20, initially in support of Warner Brothers' 3-D *Phantom of the Rue Morgue*, although by late June, a greater number of venues were showing both halves of the bill in 2-D.

Within a sample of 1200 first-run movie theaters across the U.S., 46 percent of openings of *Black Lagoon* between February and May were in 3-D; however, in the months from June to September, this figure dropped dramatically to just nine percent of openings. What this indicates is that 3-D bookings were restricted primarily to large downtown venues with heavy footfall during the saturation phase of the picture's release. As soon as first-run trade became focused on smaller theaters whose reduced customer base rendered them less likely to have undertaken the costly conversion to 3-D, Universal's Gill Man found himself effectively restricted to the shallow end, his potential for deep dives more or less dead in the water. A near-identical pattern would be attested during the first-run release of *Revenge of the Creature* the following year.

As a Stand-Alone Feature

Within the sample of 1200 first-run movie theaters, 62 percent of all *Black Lagoon* screenings took the form of a stand-alone presentation supported only by "selected shorts," making this the most common way to have originally experienced the movie. This form of presentation was equally prevalent for 3-D and 2-D engagements, and was attested in large cities, average-sized towns and rural communities alike throughout the entire period from February to September 1954. In a small number of instances, totaling around two percent of 3-D stand-alone screenings, the supporting short was identified as the 16-minute 3-D Three Stooges mad scientist horror comedy *Spooks!*, which had already done limited service at "depthie" engagements of Universal's *It Came from Outer Space* in 1953.

Regular Co-Feature

Within the sample of 1200 movie theaters across the U.S., 17 percent of all *Black Lagoon* screenings were supported by the Universal release *Project M-7* with Phyllis Calvert and Herbert Lom, a British-made sci-fi thriller that played in its homeland under the title *The Net*. Attested at 3-D and 2-D engagements in almost every state throughout the period from February to September 1954, this regular co-feature ensured Universal control of both halves of the bill at those venues which screened it.

Other Co-Features

The list of over 60 variant double-bill co-features below accounts collectively for the outstanding 21 percent of first-run *Black Lagoon* screenings within the sample of 1200 movie theaters. Even the most frequently employed among these co-features are indicative only of localized exhibition practices, with the use of *Killers from Space* as a supporting feature limited almost exclusively to neighborhood theaters in the Greater Los Angeles and Greater Chicago areas. "Double horror-show" openings with either the 3-D or 2-D versions of *Phantom of the Rue Morgue* were unique to New York City venues. The latter example is furthermore anomalous insofar as it represents just about the only example of *Black Lagoon* being employed as a supporting feature during its first run, rather than as the main attraction. The vast majority of these variant titles, by contrast, seem aimed at creating a so-called "balanced" program, a favored form of presentation among theater owners who maintained that a bill comprising works of two distinct genres had the potential to appeal to a wider audience than a genre-matched bill.

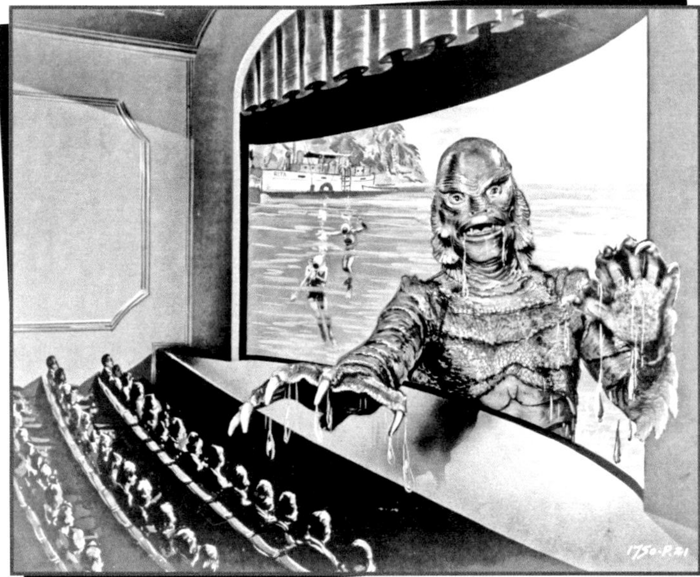

This great piece of vintage art emphasizes the movie's 3-D aspect. "Every inch of film in scenes underwater was superb not to mention the swimming fish within the theater," one sneak preview audience member wrote on a preview card. "I didn't, and couldn't relax."

The titles below are arranged alphabetically, with the month mentioned in each case being the earliest in which the pairing was attested within the sample of 1200 first-run movie theaters across the U.S. Only one in five of these titles was a Universal release, suggesting that the studio made little effort to control the entire bill at these venues.

(*) signifies a slightly more substantial number of playdates for the double-bill:

April 1954 *Apache Drums* (Stephen McNally)
August 1954 *Appointment in Honduras* (Glenn Ford)
May 1954 *Battle of Rogue River* (George Montgomery)
April 1954 *Border River* (Joel McCrea)
March 1954 *The Cruel Sea* (Jack Hawkins)
July 1954 *The Diamond Queen* (Arlene Dahl)
February 1954 *Donovan's Brain* (Lew Ayres)
August 1954 *Down Laredo Way* (Rex Allen)
August 1954 *Drums Across the River* (Audie Murphy)
February 1954 *Fangs of the Arctic* (Kirby Grant)
May 1954 *The Fighting Lawman* (Wayne Morris)
May 1954 *Fireman Save My Child* (Spike Jones)
April 1954 *Forbidden* (Tony Curtis)
March 1954 *Geraldine* (Mala Powers)
March 1954 *The Golden Idol* (Johnny Sheffield)
March 1954 (*) *The Great Diamond Robbery* (Red Skelton)
May 1954 *The Great Jesse James Raid* (Willard Parker)
April 1954 *Highway Dragnet* (Richard Conte)
April 1954 *Hot News* (Stanley Clements)
April 1954 (*) *The Iron Glove* (Robert Stack)
March 1954 *Jivaro* (Fernando Lamas)
May 1954 (*) *Jubilee Trail* (Vera Ralston)
May 1954 *The Kid from Left Field* (Dan Dailey)
May 1954 (*) *Killers from Space* (Peter Graves)
July 1954 *The Last Outpost* (Ronald Reagan)
April 1954 *The Last Posse* (Broderick Crawford)
March 1954 *The Long, Long Trailer* (Lucille Ball)
May 1954 *Lucky Me* (Doris Day)
April 1954 *Man in the Attic* (Jack Palance)
June 1954 *The Naked Jungle* (Eleanor Parker)
April 1954 *Outlaw Territory* (Macdonald Carey; Realart 2-D reissue of *Hannah Lee: An American Primitive*)
June 1954 *Overland Pacific* (Jock Mahoney)
April 1954 *Paris Playboys* (Bowery Boys)

May 1954 (*) *Phantom of the Rue Morgue* (Karl Malden; 3-D version)
June 1954 (*) *Phantom of the Rue Morgue* (Karl Malden; 2-D version)
September 1954 *Playgirl* (Shelley Winters)
August 1954 *Private Eyes* (Bowery Boys)
March 1954 *Project Moon Base* (Donna Martell)
April 1954 *Rachel and the Stranger* (Loretta Young; RKO reissue)
July 1954 *Racing Blood* (Bill Williams)
July 1954 *Rails into Laramie* (John Payne)
March 1954 (*) *Ride Clear of Diablo* (Audie Murphy)
May 1954 *Riding Shotgun* (Randolph Scott)
June 1954 *Saskatchewan* (Alan Ladd)
June 1954 *Siege at Red River* (Van Johnson)
August 1954 *Silver City* (Edmond O'Brien)
April 1954 *Sons of the Desert* (Laurel and Hardy; Film Classics reissue)
April 1954 *Spaceways* (Howard Duff)
July 1954 *Star of Texas* (Wayne Morris)
July 1954 *The Steel Lady* (Rod Cameron)
April 1954 (*) *Taza, Son of Cochise* (Rock Hudson; 2-D version)
April 1954 *Tennessee Champ* (Shelley Winters)
February 1954 *Texas Bad Man* (Wayne Morris)
March 1954 *Three Young Texans* (Jeffrey Hunter)
July 1954 *Thunder Over the Plains* (Randolph Scott)
May 1954 *Undercover Agent* (Dermot Walsh)
July 1954 *The Veils of Bagdad* (Victor Mature)
March 1954 *Who Killed Doc Robbin* (George Zucco; one theater only)
May 1954 *Wicked Woman* (Beverly Michaels)
April 1954 *Yankee Buccaneer* (Jeff Chandler)
June 1954 *Yankee Pasha* (Jeff Chandler)
June 1954 *The Yellow Tomahawk* (Rory Calhoun)

Triple-Bills

No examples were found of *Black Lagoon* playing on anything other than a single or double-bill during its first run. However, a lone theater, the 2061-seat Strand in Niagara Falls, New York, fashioned its own "triple shock and shudder program" in late April 1954 by augmenting a double-bill of the 2-D *Black Lagoon* and *Donovan's Brain* with Columbia's eight-minute animated adaptation of *The Tell-Tale Heart*, narrated by James Mason.

Beyond the First Run

Creature from the Black Lagoon continued to be booked regularly at second-run houses throughout 1955 and 1956, although it was solely the 2-D version that was seen at this time, shown more often than not as part of a "balanced" program alongside a Western, a comedy or a musical. More spook-worthy bookings were initially limited to special midnight screenings for Friday the 13th and Halloween, in which context the 2-D *Black Lagoon* was deployed throughout the years from 1955 to 1960. From 1957, the flat picture

Creature from the Black Lagoon, La Mujer y el Monstruo ("The Woman and the Monster")—what's in a title? Now and forever, it's the story of Beauty and the Beast.

also started to turn up on three- and four-feature monster movie bills at discount theaters and drive-ins, which united it not only with its own kin in the form of *Revenge of the Creature*, but also with other recent hits such as *The Beast of Hollow Mountain* (1956), in addition to a gaggle of low-rent horrors. The latter description might well be applied to the line-up at a series of "Spookarama" bills which played southwestern drive-ins during the second half of 1958, presenting the 2-D *Black Lagoon* together with the Herman Cohen-AIP double-bill of *Blood of Dracula* and *I Was a Teenage Frankenstein* (both 1957) and Bela Lugosi in *Bride of the Monster* (1956)!

During 1958 and 1959, there was also a limited reissue of 3-D prints of *It Came from Outer Space* and *Creature from the Black Lagoon* to first-run theaters. In the January 24, 1958, *Variety*, Leonard Kane of the Sullivan circuit in Wichita extolled the virtues of "revived 3-D" as a distinct novelty that permitted theaters "to recoup on once expensive equipment," but few others seem to have shared his optimism. At a meager number of engagements between February 1958 and December 1959, the reissue bill grossed an average of around $4000 to $5000 per week, which might have been acceptable for a discount theater, but represented rather slim pickings for the types of larger downtown venues that were actually screening the pictures. A nostalgic tagline—"Remember 3rd Dimension?"—may well have proved counterproductive too, at once making the reissue bill sound like a dusted-off relic and misguidedly attempting to awaken a sense of affection in patrons for a recently deceased, short-lived technological novelty.

Creature from the Black Lagoon was given a one-off television airing, in panned-and-scanned 2-D form, on Los Angeles-based KABC-TV on the afternoon of Saturday, April 15, 1961. Thereafter once again viewable only on discount theater and drive-in horror bills, the movie would finally begin to reach televiewers nationwide from March 1964, a full decade after its original theatrical opening.

Music from the Black Lagoon: The Music of *Creature from the Black Lagoon*

By David Schecter

Creature from the Black Lagoon had a score somewhere between the originality of *It Came from Outer Space* and the derivative approach of *Abbott and Costello Meet Dr. Jekyll and Mr. Hyde*. Fortunately, it was closer to the former, and much more creatively concocted and pieced together than the latter. The *Black Lagoon* scores is a mix of new and old cues not because horror pictures were taken less seriously by the studio; it was because it was the same musical treatment received by many other Universal movies of the period: *Bengal Brigade, Column South, Francis Covers the Big Town, The Kettles in the Ozarks*, etc. Despite *Creature from the Black Lagoon* not receiving the musical reverence it deserved, about two-thirds of the Gill Man score was original, which was probably reason enough for film music fans to celebrate.

The movie's score contained something only hinted at in *It Came from Outer Space*: an unforgettable monster theme. Herman Stein's three-note motif ***BAH-BAH-BAHHH!***, played on strident flutter-tongued brass, was used so frequently in the movie that it became a permanent part of viewers' memories. It was probably the most memorable monster theme heard in decades, and the connection between a monster and its musical signature wouldn't be equaled until John Williams' 1975 score for *Jaws*. The harsh flutter-tongue aspect of the motif was an approach that would be found in the themes of many 1950s movie monsters, including the creatures in *It Came from Beneath the Sea* (1955), *This Island Earth* (1955), *The Beast of Hollow Mountain* (1956), *The Incredible Shrinking Man* (1957) and *The Alligator People* (1959).

One reason *Black Lagoon*'s score works so well is because quite a bit of creative editing and rewriting went into the older music. Some of these pieces were flavored with newly written additions, including the incorporation of the monster motif, and much of the previously written material was reworked to closely match the new movie's visuals. Despite the borrowing of older sources, the film's soundtrack has an immediate freshness and appropriateness, largely because the first 18-plus minutes of the movie contain only newly written underscore. The musical chicanery in the picture was so well-done that many people have assumed the entire score was written specifically for the Gill Man film.

As was the custom, the only music credit went to Joseph Gershenson for "Musical Direction," that single credit belying the complexity of one of the more varied scores in 1950s sci-fi-horror. Of the movie's 44 cues, 29 were written specifically for *Black Lagoon*, while the remainder had been composed for prior Universal pictures. Hans J. Salter wrote 12 new cues, Henry Mancini ten and Stein seven, although Stein also composed some of the main thematic material that was reworked by Salter and Mancini. Of the 15 tracked cues, six had been composed by Milton Rosen, four by Stein, two by Mancini, two by Salter and one by Robert Emmett Dolan. There are actually only 36 different compositions in the film, as eight of the 44 were used more than once.

The movies contributing library music include *City Beneath the Sea* and *Mr. Peabody and the Mermaid*, both water-themed pictures and predictable choices for suitable-sounding music. Perhaps less obvious sources are the Westerns *Ride Clear of Diablo* and *The Redhead from Wyoming*, the crime drama *The Glass Web* and the exotic adventure *East of Sumatra*. Although *Black Lagoon* is a monster movie, only four pre-existing cues came from horror films, two from *It Came from Outer Space*, one from *The Ghost of Frankenstein* and one from *The Wolf Man*. These last two pieces were written by Salter in the early 1940s, but even a lot of Salter's "new" Creature music borrowed liberally from his previous scores, which implies that a rapidly approaching deadline was responsible for at least some of this self-appropriating.

Many of Universal's 1950s science fiction productions contained a healthy dose of music, but underscore played an amplified role in all three Gill Man movies. Although music covers less than half the running time of *It Came from Outer Space*, *Tarantula* and *The Monolith Monsters*, it's heard in 63 percent of *Black Lagoon*. Almost every one of the many underwater shots is musically enhanced, which should be a cinematic law because most aquatic scenes are slow-moving, and without music they can be ponderously dull.

The various composers' cues are distributed fairly evenly throughout the entire picture until Salter's music dominates the climax. This "scrambled egg" approach manages to lend a kind of haphazard uniformity to the musical proceedings, and the ubiquitous use of the Creature theme further ties everything together. Stein's Creature-advancing theme is also used quite a bit by Salter and occasionally by Mancini, but other than that, the three composers often went in their own directions. Universal's collaborative scores often contained a wider variety of thematic material than scores written by a single composer, and *Black Lagoon*—despite the omnipresent monster motif—has a wealth of musical ideas in it. The orchestrations for the new music and much of the earlier music were by David Tamkin, and all the music was recorded by Universal's orchestra in an 8½-hour session under Gershenson's baton on December 23, 1953. Along with the 36 contract players, tuba player Jack Barsby was once again added to the orchestra to supplement the brass.

Black Lagoon's Creature-advancing theme. (© 1954 Gilead Music Co.)

Stein's Creature theme serves as a very repetitive leitmotif (an identifying musical theme), and almost every time you see the Gill Man, or glimpse any part of his body, or even his wet footprints, you hear his theme. It blasts forth from the soundtrack approximately 130 times, which is why you might not be able to get it out of your head even a week after seeing the picture. Although the blaring motif is extremely effective when the Creature keeps mostly to the background, as he's seen more frequently over the film's duration, the theme loses some of its effectiveness. It eventually serves as more of a strident sound effect than a musical theme, especially since it was not adapted into many other forms beyond the initial creation, at least not in this first Gill Man movie.

The composers didn't like using this primitive style of scoring, which was common back in the '30s, because by the mid–50s it was considered passé to musically mimic something already visible on-screen. Given Gershenson's generally solid musical instincts, one would assume that producer William Alland or somebody else on the production side wanted to hear ***BAH-BAH-BAHHH!*** every time the Creature was seen, and it might have been felt that a musical signature would help cement the beast's "star status." It's unlikely that Universal had any idea how much the motif would become inseparable from the Creature, but along with his superbly designed rubber suit and unique aquatic style, the music helped forge a singular cinematic creation.

There are a lot of outstanding musical moments in *Black Lagoon*, courtesy of both the newly composed cues and the tracked sources. Stein's "Main Title" opens the film with a powerful brassy fanfare that plays during the Universal-International logo, and the remainder of the piece introduces the three-note theme playing on various instruments. This is followed by Hammond organ supplying an ominous melody while being accompanied by furtively trilling clarinets and strings, all of which add a sense of the unknown to the proceedings. Stein's "Prologue" is mostly hidden under the opening narration, with ethereal sounds from Hammond organ, vibraphone and string harmonics accompanying an image of the Earth forming from a nebula of cosmic dust. When the camera moves in on a fossilized claw protruding from a limestone deposit, a variation of the Creature theme plays, ending on a portentous trill.

"The Webbed Hand," also by Stein, begins after Dr. Maia tells his "boys" to wait in camp, and when the Creature's hand appears by the river bank, the "official version" of the Creature theme is heard for the first time, just in case

Herman Stein sketch of the *Black Lagoon* "Main Title." (© 1954 Gilead Music Co.)

you didn't notice the scaly, clawed appendage. Groaning brass plays the Creature-advancing theme until the hand vanishes from sight, this secondary motif being used throughout the film to connote the Gill Man's movement. Stein's related cue, "That Hand Again," reprises the same music, playing when the Gill Man kills the two natives. It's not known which piece was written first, as composers don't necessarily score their scenes in film order. The Creature theme blares forth 11 times in this cue, the two pieces helping to affix the Creature to his musical motifs. In case viewers weren't sure of the Gill Man's theme before, they certainly are after hearing these pieces!

Henry Mancini's "The Diver" displays the composer's lyrical skills, adding an evocative background as Kay (on the Morajo Bay barge) pulls on a depth marker rope to alert aqualung diver Reed to her presence above. When the scene cuts underwater, woodwinds, harp, celesta, vibraphone and strings add musical color to the shots of underwater life. Mancini's brief "Marine Life" offers a hypnotic riff on flutes and clarinets as Kay gazes at the institute's fish-filled aquarium. This is the kind of scene where a library cue could have easily worked, but thankfully wasn't used.

"Almost Caught" is Salter's first cue in the movie. He scored his scenes fairly close to the visuals, and the music follows every twist and turn of this sequence, which begins with a dissolve to a bloodied, gnarled hand. When Kay wanders near the water's edge and the Creature's claw reaches for her leg, *BAH-BAH-BAHHH!* cries out three times, and turbulent low brass and woodwinds bellow as the Gill Man swims away without his catch of the day. As the *Rita* navigates the Amazon tributary, Mancini's beautiful "Unknown River" augments the exotic surroundings; it also supplies appropriate background music for the romance between Reed and Kay, with French horns playing the melody while woodwinds provide accompaniment. A portion of "Unknown River" originated in the cue "Doctor's Diagnosis," a Mancini-composed piece from the 1953 Western *The Great Sioux Uprising*, where it complemented a budding romance. When the *Rita* approaches the Black Lagoon, a 59-second excerpt from Robert Emmett Dolan's gorgeous "Tale of the Mermaid" illustrates this sequence. It was written for the 1948 romantic-comedy *Mr. Peabody and the Mermaid*; only 17 of the 74 measures were used in *Black Lagoon*. Flutes, celesta and tremolo strings create a magical mood that provides one last moment of beauty and tranquility before the monster action that will soon follow.

Conductor's score of Hans Salter's "Almost Caught." (© 1954 Salter Publishing Co.)

Universal's 1953 adventure *City Beneath the Sea*, starring Robert Ryan and Anthony Quinn, is an enjoyable escapist yarn about romance and undersea treasure hunting off the coast of Kingston, Jamaica. Its score plays a prominent role in the Creature's musical legacy, with the film's cues appearing multiple times in *Black Lagoon* and *Revenge of the Creature*. Because a lot of the pieces were written for marine sequences, the music was ideal for inclusion in the Creature movies. Excerpts from Milton Rosen's *City Beneath the Sea* cue "Salvage of the Lady Luck" are heard thrice in *Black Lagoon*, with just over half of the four-minute, Novachord-laden composition dusted off when Reed and Williams leave the *Rita* to dive for rock samples. The cue can also be heard in *Abbott and Costello Go to Mars* when Bud and Lou land the spaceship in New Orleans. "Brad Rescues Tony," another Rosen cue from *City Beneath the Sea*, plays when Reed and Williams dive for rock samples. Mancini added the Creature theme when the Gill Man reaches out for Williams, as well as another brassy insert.

Kay's waterlogged ballet with the Gill Man is not only the most famous *Black Lagoon* setpiece, it's also the score's musical centerpiece. While the striking visuals and sexual imagery definitely help make it memorable, the music provides much of the dramatic impetus in this mostly dialogue-free sequence. Stein's "Kay and the Monster, Part 1" begins the sequence, and when Kay enters the water in her stunning white bathing suit, the glorious writing uses flutes, clarinets and swirling harp to emphasize her enjoyment; orchestra bells and vibraphone add a sparkle to Kay's aquatics. The first 18 measures of this piece derived from another *City Beneath the Sea* cue, Stein's playfully romantic "A Whale of a Catch." The composer's new writing for "Kay and the Monster, Part 1" begins when the Gill Man is glimpsed, whereupon darker music takes over, with the Creature-advancing theme sounding low on groaning clarinets, bass clarinets, bassoon, organ and string bass. Stein's "Kay and the Monster, Part 2" segues from the previous cue when the scene cuts back underwater, the music continuing the threatening mood. Low instruments play the Creature theme as the Gill Man swims around Kay's kicking legs, with brass crescendos and trilling woodwinds and strings accenting the three times the Creature reaches out to touch her. As Kay swims toward the *Rita* with the Gill Man following like a shadow, the orchestra plays a powerful reprise of the Creature-advancing theme, and the Creature theme sounds just before Kay climbs safely aboard, intensifying that last moment when we fear he will reach out and grab her. Another *City Beneath the Sea* cue by Stein, "Tony Visits Port Royale, Part 1" is heard when Reed and Williams, armed with camera and speargun, swim toward the audience for 3-D purposes. The music's propulsive quality creates a strong sense of motion lacking in the slow-moving visuals.

The film's fifth reel contains a lot of tracked music, both from other pictures as well as from within *Black Lagoon* itself, including Mancini's "Monster Gets Mark, Part 1." About a minute of this cue plays when Reed and Williams swim after the Creature. Mancini's complete "Monster Gets Mark, Part 1" was actually composed for *Black Lagoon*'s eighth reel, proving that the picture wasn't scored in sequence, as the whole composition would have been written first, with this excerpt later deriving from it. Most of Salter's contributions occur in the latter half of the picture. His writing is definitely weighted toward monster action, and therefore includes prominent use of Stein's Creature theme. "The Monster Strikes Back," which plays when the Gill Man kills Chico on deck, employs that motif and other aggressive brass.

"Henry's Trap" is a Milton Rosen cue that augments the scene of rotenone being dispersed on the water's surface to try to knock out the Creature. Harmonic tremolo strings create an unearthly atmosphere, and dissonant notes on harp and vibraphone add to the sense of uneasiness. Although the piece fits this scene very well, it was written for the engrossing 1953 crime melodrama *The Glass Web*. *Black Lagoon* used only nine of Rosen's 31 original measures, with one of the film's composers adding the newly written measures containing the Creature themes. The sixth reel begins with a lengthy excerpt from Rosen's atmospheric "Clay Meets a Badman," which plays as Reed and Williams drop rotenone packets to sink deeper into the lagoon. The cue, written for the 1954 Audie Murphy Western *Ride Clear of Diablo*, was also used in *Revenge of the Creature*.

Salter's three-part "Monster Attacks" sequence encompasses nearly six minutes of music, beginning as the *Rita* crew keeps watch while the Creature tries to climb aboard; it ends when the drugged Gill Man is captured. "Monster Attacks, Part 1" starts on pastoral English horn, but when the beast's head rises from the water, the Creature theme takes over and helps shatter the tranquility. "Monster Attacks, Part 2" plays when Reed and Williams swim after the Gill Man, with fast string writing being replaced at various times by alto flute, oboe and clarinet, all serving as the calms before the next storm. The Creature theme blares out to begin Salter's "Monster Attacks, Part 3," heard in the beach scene as the Gill Man gulps air before spotting his love interest sitting by the

Creature from the Black Lagoon's Gill Man themes. (© 1954 Gilead Music Co.)

water. Full-orchestral writing covers the sequence when he lifts Kay and tries to carry her off, helping to keep the dramatic level high despite Julie Adams almost needing to roll into the Creature's arms so he can pick her up. An excerpt from "Monster Attacks, Part 3" is reprised when the Gill Man mauls Dr. Thompson. This and other secondary uses of new music within the picture further imply that there was inadequate time to properly score it.

Henry Mancini's evocative "Monster Caught" uses bass clarinet and piano arpeggios to enhance the mysteriousness of the night as Dr. Thompson keeps watch over the caged Creature. A glimpse of Kay elicits a lovely (and rare) variation of the Creature theme on harp, this being an atypical instance of the motif playing during an image of someone other than the Creature—Mancini's clever way of linking the man-fish to the object of his scaly desires. "Minyora's Plan" sounds after Lucas pulls a colossal knife on Mark and then takes the *Rita* toward the lagoon exit, with vibraphone, harp and bass marimba beating time as the anxious crew heads toward a Creature-built barricade. This Mancini cue was composed for the previous year's *East of Sumatra*, where it enhanced a night-time scene when sexy Minyora (Suzan Ball) secretly visits he-man Duke (Jeff Chandler). The piece had much life thanks to Universal's music library, including appearances in *Drums Across the River, Gunpoint, Kitten with a Whip, Running Wild, Six Black Horses* and *The Thing That Couldn't Die.*

All of the cues in *Black Lagoon*'s seventh reel were tracked (including a repeat of "Monster Caught"), and although it wouldn't have taken more than a day for a single composer to score what little music was in that reel, it's likely that a looming deadline precluded anything new being composed and orchestrated. It's a safe bet that *Black Lagoon*'s entire score needed to be created fairly quickly, but probably because it was such an important movie for Universal, it was understood that the film still needed a healthy dose of new music to offset the older material.

Mancini's best *Black Lagoon* compositions are "Monster Gets Mark, Part 1" and "Monster Gets Mark, Part 2," which play during the lengthy sequence when Reed deals with the barricade while Williams fends off the Gill Man, the second cue ending after Williams' lifeless body floats to the surface. If you watch the underwater action with the sound off, you'll realize that a huge proportion of the dramatic impact is due to Mancini's splendid contributions. In one instance when Williams chases the Creature downward, the powerful music maintains the excitement despite some less-than-thrilling visuals, including an image of the Creature doing a backstroke more befitting a lazy Sunday afternoon at the lagoon. In the second part of the composition, eight bars originated in "Hot Fight," Mancini's climactic cue from *East of Sumatra.*

Eight of the last nine *Black Lagoon* cues were composed by Salter, many written in his furious monster mode idiom. But although the cue sheets list much of this music as being original, quite a bit quoted from Stein's themes, and Salter's cues were also peppered with passages Salter had written dating back to the early 1940s. Again, this was probably due to time constraints. "Monster Aboard" is heard when the Creature's arm reaches through the *Rita*'s porthole for the bandaged Dr. Thompson, with the beginning of the cue making use of material written by Stein. After "The Monster's Trial" from Salter's *The Ghost of Frankenstein* (1942) supplies a few tracked measures, Salter's "Doping the Monster" plays when the Gill Man is sprayed with rotenone, the cue appropriating 33 measures from the composer's climactic swordfight music in the 1952 Errol Flynn adventure *Against All Flags*, where it was titled "Rescue, Part 2." Salter's next *Black Lagoon* cue, "Kay's Last Peril," begins when the Gill Man climbs on deck after the barricade is cleared away. Salter reuses some material written in 1941 for *The Wolf Man*, and then a second cue, also named "Kay's Last Peril," plays when a motorized bat on a string apparently flew over to the Gill Man grotto from one of Universal's old vampire movies. Although it's credited as being newly written for *Black Lagoon*, this piece includes music Salter used in both the 1951 Van Heflin-Yvonne DeCarlo Western *Tomahawk* and the 1952 Joseph Cotten-Shelley Winters Western *Untamed Frontier.*

Composer Herman Stein. Behind him, a replica of an early version of a Gill Man head wears Stein's cap. (Photograph courtesy Monstrous Movie Music and Bob Burns.)

Salter's "End Title" bursts forth during *Black Lagoon*'s climax when the Gill Man rises from the Jacuzzi in his grotto and finds Reed and Kay snuggling when they should be high-tailing it out of there. The cue begins with a direct lift from "Monster Attacks, Part 3," and when a hail of bullets forces the beast to drop Reed and turn on his attackers, we hear a rousing and uncredited excerpt from "Miner's Fight," which was written for the classic 1952 James Stewart Western *Bend of the River*. If you close your eyes when watching this part of the Gill Man movie, you'll realize that Salter's creation is not "monster music," but rather just solid generic action music, as suitable for a Western, adventure or swashbuckler as it is for a horror picture. That's why the cue was reused by Universal in so many movies, including *Yankee Buccaneer*. *Bend of the River*'s score was one of the most popular sources in the studio's music library, donating cues to many subsequent films, among them *Column South, Dawn at Socorro, Gunsmoke, Lost in Alaska, Outside the Law* and even the next decade's *Taggart* (1964) and *Gunpoint* (1966). The final part of Salter's "End Title" adds some original music, with descending low brass and woodwinds playing while the beast tragically sinks to his sequel-laden doom. The piece concludes with a happy-ending fanfare originally written for the 1951 Genghis Khan picture *The Golden Horde*, which includes Salter's three-note signature tag—the composer's personal statement that he liked the music he wrote for a particular picture.

Herman Stein's "End Cast" closes *Creature from the Black Lagoon* on a bright note, which isn't surprising considering it was originally written to end the breezy Maureen O'Hara Western *The Redhead from Wyoming*. This same cue and a related one would be heard in the endings of both *Revenge of the Creature* and *Tarantula*.

Analysis
By Steve Kronenberg

Creature from the Black Lagoon is the watershed film of Universal's 1950s catalogue. It is the studio's first true horror film of the decade, the first to be filmed in 3-D (*It Came from Outer Space* belongs more to the science fiction genre) and the first to employ a full, head-to-toe monster suit to depict its title character, inspiring countless imitations that varied wildly in budget and quality.

But *Black Lagoon*'s greatest impact was cultural: The film unveiled a memorable monster that was immediately and forever associated with the 1950s. More importantly, the Creature became a horror icon even before the film was brought to television, joining the ranks of the great Golden Age monsters Dracula, the Frankenstein Monster, the Mummy, the Wolf Man and—the monster the Creature most resembles—King Kong.

> It's the idea of my picture. The Beast was a tough guy too. He could lick the world. But when he saw Beauty, she got him. He went soft. He forgot his wisdom and the little fellas licked him.
>
> —Carl Denham (Robert Armstrong) in *King Kong*

Like Kong, the Creature is not a product of mad science or myth, but a biological aberration and prehistoric holdover. The Creature rules his dark underwater domain in the Amazon the way Kong was master of the misty Skull Island—and neither of them takes kindly to strangers invading their space. Most of all, the Creature "apes" Kong's humanoid characteristics: Both are captivated and victimized by the desire for a beautiful woman, and both die amidst great audience sympathy. Indeed, producer William Alland specifically intended *Black Lagoon* to be an aquatic remake of *Kong*.

Aside from its tremendous importance to the horror genre, *Black Lagoon* is, in and of itself, a superb film. Reams of pages have been written about its flawlessly designed and executed monster suit. The film also boasts a fine cast of '50s genre stalwarts, and an imposing female presence in Julie Adams. But the real stars of *Black Lagoon* are its cinematographers William E. Snyder, who handled the topside photography, and the great "Scotty" Welbourne, who shot and co-directed the film's memorable underwater scenes.

The opening scene sets the film's tone: We see a series of explosions framing a lecture on the Earth's beginning and the process of evolution. We are then treated to a beautiful shot of the ocean and an adjoining beach—and an ominous shot of large webbed footprints leading from the water.

It's "Scotty" Welbourne's water imagery that dominates *Black Lagoon*. His mystic style gives the movie its panache as a horror film. His murky underwater photography makes the Creature's underwater kingdom as dark and ominous as *Dracula*'s Borgo Pass or *Kong*'s Skull Island. Initially, Welbourne, Snyder (and director Jack Arnold) "tease" us with mere hints of the Creature's presence: a footprint here, a shot of the Creature's slimy, webbed extremity there. But the first full shot of the merman is a joy to behold: In the depths of the lagoon, we get a startling close-up of the Creature lunging *upward* and past the camera! Welbourne's aptitude for mood and lighting is also exemplified by a fine medium shot of the Creature seen through a patch of seaweed, which filigrees the monster's face and further distorts his grotesque features. And it's Welbourne who deserves full credit for the justly celebrated scene in which the Creature sees and tracks Kay as she swims through the water.

He turns a standard "monster pursuing the girl" scene into a surreal and sexual water ballet. Welbourne's camera tracks with the Creature as he swims parallel to Kay beneath the water, contrasting her figure and form with the Creature's unnatural body as they move in unison. Welbourne also captures the scene's aesthetic beauty: Ricou Browning's Creature and Adams' underwater double, Ginger Stanley, swim and play off each other marvelously. And as Welbourne gives us a close-up of the Creature plucking at Kay's foot, the ballet's sexuality becomes even more explicit: Welbourne has presented us with the first example of underwater foreplay in horror film history! (Indeed, the scene resembles Kong's "foreplay" with Fay Wray both on the ceremonial altar and on Skull Mountain.) As Kay swims back to the boat, Welbourne follows the Creature's graceful yet ominous movements through the water in pursuit of his new love.

Welbourne tempers the beauty and grace of the scene with the appropriate mood: His camera captures the sheer isolation and darkness of the water, creating a classically scary and atmospheric scenario. The water ballet is *Black Lagoon*'s most famous and celebrated scene, and rightly so: Welbourne brilliantly blends beauty, grace, form and subtle lighting with the darkness that we expect and appreciate from any horror film.

Welbourne's aptitude for mood, light and shadow is prominent throughout the film. After Williams harpoons the Creature, Welbourne provides a magnificent, atmospheric long shot of the Creature swimming down, down to the entrance to its grotto in the depths of the Lagoon—a shot that also conveys the vastness of the Creature's underwater kingdom.

Yet this scene is merely a prelude for Welbourne's most unsettling underwater shot: the Creature seizing Williams and pulling him down to his death. Welbourne isolates the Creature and his struggling, hapless prey and follows their *every move* as the monster swims ever deeper. Welbourne's camera captures the furious, inhuman side of the Creature, while concentrating on Williams' claustrophobic peril: He is helplessly locked in the Creature's embrace and pulled to the darkest depths. Welbourne's remarkable penchant for contrasting lighting highlights the shot: As the Creature drags Williams ever deeper, Welbourne gradually and delicately dims the lighting, illuminating the murky grayness of the water with scattered shafts of light, creating a surreal tone as well as a sense of depth. In fact, it is the lighting that marks the sheer eeriness of this particular scene. The scene is, arguably, the most haunting and unnerving series of shots in any 1950s horror film.

Welbourne also shines in a similarly beautiful, although less startling underwater shot of the Creature, with the abducted Kay under his arm, taking her down to his underwater grotto: The scene is magnificently lit, an eerie *danse macabre*, as the Creature silently carries his still, unconscious "bride" to his bizarre, miasmic digs.

Welbourne's stunning underwater achievements are *Black Lagoon*'s highlights. But Snyder's topside photography succeeds in providing some subtle and not-so-subtle jolts. Snyder is especially adept at close-ups and point-of-view shots. In the several "teaser" shots that precede our full view of the Creature, Snyder delivers eerie, ominous close-ups of the Creature's scaly hand appearing on a bank of the Amazon and nearly grabbing an unknowing Kay. The best of these "teaser" shots has Snyder's camera segueing from Dr. Maia's discovery of the fossilized Creature hand to the *real* thing sliding up from the water and then down! Snyder also provides a menacing close-up of the Creature's legs as he shuffles along the deck of the boat.

Snyder gives us a memorably moody long shot in the night scene of the Creature standing near the shore as Reed (aboard the *Rita*) shines a searchlight onto him. Toward the end, we get fine medium shots of the Creature climbing onto the *Rita*, balanced with shifts to Kay, then to the Creature as he closes in. Much of the credit for this collage should go to the brilliance of editor Ted J. Kent, whose superb work graces such Golden Age masterpieces as *Frankenstein* (1931), *Bride of Frankenstein* (1935) and *The Invisible Man* (1933).

Particularly eerie is Snyder's close-up of the Creature after he is caught and caged on the boat, his distorted features and wide eyes made more grotesque by the water in which he is immersed. Snyder's lighting in this scene gives the Creature's face an unsettling glow, reminiscent of the way Karl Freund and Charles Stumar lit Boris Karloff's visage in *The Mummy* (1932). As the Creature tries to escape its cage, Snyder's camera tightly focuses on the monster's wide eyes and gasping mouth, augmenting the scene's nightmarish quality. And as the Creature breaks out of its cage, Snyder and editor Kent furiously shift from the monster to his mate, as Kay and Dr. Thompson casually converse on deck. Kent's editing work allows the tension to build as he blends Snyder's shots of the ready-to-make-his-move Creature with Kay and Thompson's oblivious socializing. Later, Snyder and Kent also combine to deliver another of the film's subtly suspenseful scenes: Snyder's camera focuses on the Creature's hand reaching through a porthole to menace a bandaged and bedridden Thompson, as Thompson mutely tries to alert everyone to the impending attack. *Black Lagoon* is a technical and artistic triumph, largely due to the haunting and imaginative camerawork of Snyder and Welbourne, and Kent's lean, fast and furious editing.

The final scenes in the Creature's caves and grotto contain the film's most atmospheric touches: subtle lighting, craggy, twisted sets, and a pervasive mist reminiscent of the most haunting Golden Age landscapes. A particular highlight is the way Snyder lights the water in the flooded grotto so that it reflects off the rocks, creating a surreal sense of distortion that adds to the spookery. Once the grotto scene is set, he then delivers a medium shot of the Creature rising from a shallow pool of mist-shrouded water—an homage both to the Golden Age Gothics, and to the scene in *King Kong* in which the brontosaurus ascends from the lake into the foggy, hellish marshland to chase Denham and his crew. Welbourne's camera consistently conveys and plays upon our fear of the unknown and what lies just below the surface of placid waters. His technique was not lost on the makers of *Jaws* and its sequels and innumerable rip-offs. (In fact, Steven Spielberg has repeatedly cited *Black Lagoon*'s influence on the making of his famous shark attack film.)

Black Lagoon's sound effects and music cannot be underestimated. The film's thunderous, ominous music score immediately commands audience attention. It was composed by three cinema stalwarts: Hans J. Salter (who created the memorable, haunting scores for Universal's Silver Age Classics *Son of Frankenstein* [1939], *The Wolf Man* [1941], *The Ghost of Frankenstein* [1942] *et al.*), Herman Stein and a young Henry Mancini. The score is pervaded by Stein's now-famous, crescendo-ing three-note Creature theme—which was used in the two sequels and which indelibly identifies the Creature with his audience. Salter, Stein and Mancini also furnish atmospheric music throughout the film's many eerie underwater scenes—and the Gill Man's three-note theme is used to heighten the suspense whenever the monster, or one of his webbed extremities, appears on screen. (For more on the score, see David Schecter's "Music from the Black Lagoon" essay.)

Black Lagoon's eeriness is equally dependent on sound effects. Especially prevalent are sinister jungle sounds: splashing waves, high-pitched bird calls and those throaty, unnerving Creature growls. The sound effects contribute much to the film's sense of suspense, the tense interludes between Creature scenes and the fear of the unknown that pervades *Black Lagoon*: an unmistakable influence on the way sound effects heightened underwater terror in countless *Black Lagoon* rip-offs and, later, in *Jaws*.

Though *Black Lagoon*'s greatness is marked by its technicians, the film is enhanced by the natural, believable acting of its solid cast. Richard Carlson, so stoic and natural in *It Came from Outer Space*, reprises the role of the serious scientific academic in his portrayal of David Reed. Reed gives us the Creature's evolutionary origins, providing us with the biologic linchpin of the monster's existence. Reed, like Carlson's John Putnam in *It Came from Outer Space*, is determined to solve the film's scientific mystery: What is this Creature, where did it come from and what are its human antecedents? Carlson's Reed is *Black Lagoon*'s scientific conscience—another echo of his performance in *It Came from Outer Space*. It's Reed who fights to preserve the Creature and prevent its exploitation (or destruction) at the hands of Richard Denning's greedy Mark Williams. Of course, the film implies that Reed and Williams are romantic rivals, vying for the affections of Julie Adams' Kay Lawrence. But the antagonism turns professional as each man has different designs on the Creature. This clash between Denning's flamboyant showman and Carlson's academician is, according to co-scripter Arthur Ross, the dramatic core of the film.

In addition, both actors convey this tension superbly. Williams' speech about capturing the Creature embodies his character's avarice: As he sits in the rowboat with harpoon gun at the ready, eyes darting and

The Gill Man, a horror that's haunted the world since before history began to walk, finally gets his chance to answer the call of booty. Pictured: Ben Chapman, Julie Adams.

lips pursing, he exclaims, "We must have the *proof*!" On the other hand, Reed is both a model of reserve and academic passion as he begs Williams to leave the Creature alone: "We didn't come here to fight monsters! We're not equipped for it!" In another scene, Reed chides Williams for harpooning the Creature. "Why did you shoot? You weren't attacked!" Carlson's calm, measured style counters Denning's greed and also provides the crucial sympathetic link between the Creature and the audience. Like his Putnam in *It Came from Outer Space*, Carlson's Reed is bent on protecting and preserving the alien in his midst. Yet, as Reed slowly realizes he must *indeed* fight a monster, his enthusiasm surfaces. Note Carlson's zeal as he develops his idea to stun the Creature with a spray gun full of rotenone. Reed finally develops into the film's stalwart but reluctant hero as he drives off the attacking Creature with the rotenone and, later, enters the Creature's grotto to rescue Kay.

Adams shines as the beautiful heroine, Kay Lawrence. She exudes a natural, relaxed quality, augmented by a sense of solidity and strength. She also seems to have more savvy than the average '50s horror heroine, even displaying some biological knowledge to complement Carlson's expertise. Adams carries herself with delicacy and poise, a lost art among today's leading ladies.

Finally, the two uncredited actors who play the Gill Man, Ricou Browning and Ben Chapman, are essential to the movie's iconography. Browning's wonderful balletic swimming makes this monster a thing of beauty, grace and yes, style. Indeed, the Creature's humanity—and the audience's sympathy—are invoked by the "water ballet" sequence with Adams and her double Ginger Stanley. This sense of sympathy is accentuated by Chapman, who conveys the Creature on land as somewhat clumsy, lumbering and lovesick.

In the summer of 2009, Universal raised the curtain on their new theme park stage show *Creature from the Black Lagoon—The Musical*, a pricey 30-minute production boasting Broadway-level production values. It floundered.

Below the surface of Wakulla Springs, two cameramen (on left) contend with the 3-D camera while one of Ricou "The Gill Man" Browning's safety men gives him a "drink" of air from a hose.

And Chapman's act of gasping for air while in the Creature suit is scientifically sound—but also augments the sense of pity we feel for him. The film's final scene, with Chapman gurgling as he lurches toward the water after being shot, is one of the most pathetic and touching images of 1950s horror. Again *King Kong* is invoked—both the scene in which Kong is stunned by a gas bomb and struggles for consciousness, and the moving finale atop the Empire State Building.

Much has been written about Milicent Patrick's brilliant and influential design contributions to the Creature's suit. But Browning and Chapman brought the suit to life, and gave us a monster both beautiful and terrifying to behold. At the same time, both men underscored the Creature's endearing pathos as a misfit and victim of man's inhumanity—a quality inherent in our greatest movie monsters.

From the memorable design of its monster to its brilliant underwater photography, *Creature from the Black Lagoon* is a triumph of technology. But the film ultimately stands as an example of how a moderate budget can still yield high adventure, a tight, no-nonsense storyline, and serious, believable performances from a carefully assembled cast. Audiences in 1954 heartily agreed—so much so that another cycle of Universal's sequelitis was born.

This Island Earth (1955)

Full Credit Information

CREDITS: Produced by William Alland; Directed by Joseph Newman; Screenplay: Franklin Coen and Edward G. O'Callaghan; Based on the Novel by Raymond F. Jones; Photography: Clifford Stine (Technicolor); Technicolor Color Consultant: William Fritzsche; Special Photography: David S. Horsley and Clifford Stine; Optical Printing: Roswell A. Hoffman; Art Directors: Alexander Golitzen and Richard H. Riedel; Set Decorators: Russell A. Gausman and Julia Heron; Sound: Leslie I. Carey and Robert Pritchard; Editor: Virgil Vogel; Gowns: Rosemary Odell; Hair Stylist: Joan St. Oegger; Makeup: Bud Westmore; Assistant Directors: Fred Frank; Music Supervisor: Joseph Gershenson; UNCREDITED: Original Music Composers: Herman Stein, Henry Mancini and Hans J. Salter; Orchestrator: David Tamkin; Conductor: Joseph Gershenson; Musicians: Emo Neufeld, Manuel Compinsky, Louis Pressman, Ambrose Russo, Lou Klass, Sam Fordis, Samuel Cytron, Sarah Kreindler, Leon Goldwasser, Howard Colf (Violin), Cecil Bonvalot, Harriet Payne (Viola), Victor Gottlieb, Stephen De'ak, Joseph Ullstein, Alec

Compinsky (Cello), Harold E. Brown (Bass), Arthur C. Smith, Ethmer Roten, Jr. (Flute), Norman Benno (Oboe), Blake Reynolds, Alan Harding, Karl Leaf (Clarinet), Lloyd Hildebrand (Bassoon), Arthur Frantz, Eugene Ober (Horn), Gene LaFreniere, Don Linder, Robert Goodrich (Trumpet), John Stanley, Bruce Squires, H.L. Menge (Trombone), Lyman Gandee (Piano), Joseph Quintile (Harp), John De Soto and Ralph Collier (Drums); Makeup: Nick Marcellino and Bob Dawn; Hair Stylist: Sweeney (Jo Sweeney?); Assistant Editor: Betty Carruth; Assistant Director: George Lollier; Second Assistant Directors: George Lollier and Cody; Production Manager: Gilbert Kurland; Unit Production Manager: Sergei Petschnikoff; Camera Operator: Bill Dodds; Assistant Cameramen: Swartz (Lew Swartz?) and Reisboard (William Reisbord?); Still Photographer: Lacey (Madison S. Lacy?); First Grip: Walter Woodworth; Second Grip: Carl Johnson; Gaffer: Tom Ouellette; Best Boy: Everett Lehman; First Prop Man: Harry Grundstrom; Assistant Prop Man: Laraby (Bud Laraby?); Wardrobe Man: Dave Preston; Wardrobe Woman: Bernice Pontrelli; Sketch Artist: Milicent Patrick; Sound Mixer: Jowett (Corson Jowett?); Sound Recordists: John Kemp and Condliff (Donald Cunliffe?); Mike Man: A.B. Robert; Cable Man: Everett Smith; Sound Technician-Panel Technician-Laboratory Technician: Wybrow; Sound Editors: Patrick McCormack and Ed Luckey; Lily Boy: Marlette; Script Clerk: Dorothy Hughes; Pilots: Larry Powell, Paul Franklin and Dianna Cyrus Bixby; Stand-ins: Joe Wall and Bill O'Driscoll; **Second Unit (February 5):** Jet Pilot: Larry Powell; Production Manager: Gilbert Kurland; Unit Manager: Sergei Petschnikoff; Photography: David S. Horsley; Camera Operator: Davis; Assistant Cameraman: King (James King?); First Grip: Thompson (Wes Thompson?); Radio Man: Buffinger; **Second Unit (February 22):** Director: Fred Frank; Unit Manager: Sergei Petschnikoff; Cameraman: David S. Horsley; Camera Operators: Meade (Kyme Meade?) and Hoffman; Assistant Cameramen: Marquette (Jacques Marquette?) and Thompson; Assistant Director: Welch (Jimmie Welch?); First Grip: Thompson (Wes Thompson?); Second Grip: Smith (Ken Smith?); First Prop Man: Neal (Roy Neel?); Wardrobe Woman: Pryor (Rose Pryor?); Wardrobe Man: Williams; Makeup: Holden (John Holden?); Script Clerk: Forrest (Robert Forrest?); Lily Boy: Vaughn; Technician: Wolfe (Harry Wolf?); **Per Joseph Newman:** Screenplay Contributor: Joseph Newman; ***Variety* "Assignments" List (February 2, 1954):** Technicolor Technicians: Roger Mace and Lew Swartz; Coordinator: Ray Gockel; **Per Robert Skotak's MagicImage book *This Island Earth*:** Mutant Head and Body Concepts: Jack Kevan, Beau Hickman and John Kraus; Miniatures Supervisor: Charles Baker; On-Set Special Effects: Fred Knoth; Animation Effects: Frank Tipper; 86 minutes.

Cast: Jeff Morrow (*Exeter*), Faith Domergue (*Dr. Ruth Adams*), Rex Reason (*Dr. Cal Meacham*), Lance Fuller (*Brack*), Russell Johnson (*Dr. Steve Carlson*), Douglas Spencer (*The Monitor*), Robert Nichols (*Joe Wilson*), Karl L. Lindt (*Dr. Adolph Engelborg*); **Uncredited:** Olan Soule, Guy Edward Hearn, Les Spears (*Reporters*), Edward Ingram, Jack Byron (*Photographers*), Robert B. Williams (*Webb*), Coleman Francis (*Railway Expressman*), Spencer Chan (*Dr. Hu Lin Tang*), Lizalotta Valesca (*Dr. Marie Pitchner*), Marc Hamilton (*Metalunan Man on Spaceship*), Richard Deacon (*Spaceship Pilot*), Regis Parton (*The Metaluna Mutants*), Larry Powell (*Cal Meacham in Jet*), Regis Parton, Louise Volding, Chuck Roberson, Louis Tomei (*Doubles*); **Per a Universal photo caption:** Mary Lovelace (*Metalunan Woman*), **Per Robert Skotak's MagicImage book *This Island Earth*:** Jay Brand (*Stellarscope Observer*), Charlotte Lander (*Converter Tubes Operator*), Fred Snyder (*Metalunan Man on Spaceship*).

Production History

By Tom Weaver

[You] are beginning a strange journey … a journey that no Earth people have ever undertaken before.

In *This Island Earth* (the title contains no comma, despite the poster on the previous page), Exeter, Master Physicist of the planet Metaluna, makes this portentous announcement to Cal and Ruth at the start of their spaceship voyage to his world. But Exeter might just as well have addressed the line to theater audience members seeing the movie for the first time in 1955. Never before had they been treated to an outer space action-adventure made in color and on such a scale. Sci-fi aficionados must have looked upon it as a dream come true at a time when some perhaps felt that the subgenre would seldom or never progress much beyond the production level of Flash Gordon, Buck Rogers, Commando Cody and the TV rocket jockeys. *This Island Earth* was the first *big* step up the ladder that led to the *Star Wars* and *Star Trek* movies and to the Hollywood of recent decades where, for better or worse, sci-fi action-adventures rule the box office roost. Scenes in which Exeter's spaceship blasts meteors out of its path even anticipated video games!

The seeds for *This Island Earth* were sown in 1949 when Raymond F. Jones' story "The Alien Machine" appeared in the June issue of *Thrilling Wonder Stories* magazine. Jones wrote two follow-ups featuring the same characters and con-

The February 1950 *Thrilling Wonder Stories* featured the third part of Raymond F. Jones' "Cal Meacham trilogy," "The Greater Conflict." A 1950 quarter (that'd be $2.49 today) also bought you same-issue yarns by Henry Kuttner, Leigh Brackett, Ray Bradbury and John D. MacDonald.

tinuing the storyline, "The Shroud of Secrecy" (December 1949) and "The Greater Conflict" (February 1950). In 1952, the trilogy was combined and issued by Shasta Publishers as a 220-page novel, *This Island Earth*.

This Island Earth (the novel): Synopsis

Chapter 1: Joe Wilson is the purchasing agent for Ryberg Instrument Corp., one of three industrial companies in a suburb called Mason. Looking out his office window at Ryberg's private landing field, he sees a silver test airplane piloted by engineer Cal Meacham flying at bullet speed before coming in for a landing.

Cal, a 35-year-old bachelor, soon appears in Wilson's office to ask about condensors he ordered from a company called Continental. Wilson shows him a mysterious letter he received from an A.G. Archmanter of Electronic Service—Unit 16, saying that those condensors are not carried by his company, and enclosing instead "the AB-619 model, a high-voltage oil-filled transmitting-type condensor." Enclosed with the letter: a box of glass beads like nothing the men have ever seen. A test on one shows that its capacity is amazing. The mystery deepens when Wilson tells Cal that Continental says they did not receive or fill a condensor order.

Additional condensors arrive along with an inch-thick manufacturer's catalogue. Printed on paper that can't be torn, it lists a myriad of other pieces of unheard-of electronic equipment. (Cal: "This thing reflects a whole electronic culture completely foreign to ours. If it had come from Mars it couldn't be more foreign.") When Cal's attention is caught by the announcement of the availability of a complete line of interocitor components, he asks, "Ever hear of an interocitor?"

> WILSON: Sounds like something a surgeon would use to remove gallstones.
>
> CAL (whimsically): Maybe we should order a kit of parts and build one up.

Chapter 2: At home in his apartment with the catalogue, Cal wonders how such amazing equipment could have been developed in secrecy, and why it's now being made available so prosaically. Upstairs neighbor Frank Staley, an engineer, and two other engineers, Edmunds and Larsen, appear at his door and soon a poker game is under way. Edmunds mentions having just received a far-out piece of equipment that could revolutionize the science of mechanical engineering; his anecdote sends "a wave of almost frightening recognition" through Cal. Eventually it becomes clear that three of Mason's industrial plants have been sent samples of product of an incredible technology.

Cal has Wilson place an order for an interocitor, and soon 14 crates arrive from the mysterious manufacturer. After three hours of unpacking, Cal finds himself amidst 4896 "unfamiliar gadgets of unknown purposes and characteristics. And he hoped to assemble them into a complete whole—of equally unknown purposes."

Chapter 3: Cal's project occupies all his nights for

months. He begins by figuring out which parts constitute a framework and gets an idea of the size and shape of the thing. One component is a large glass cube, one side coated as if it were a screen. He concludes that it will turn out to be a communication device—while Wilson worries that it might be a "Trojan Horse gadget." Cal accidentally breaks a tube and the mystery supplier won't replace it, so Cal brings in engineer Jerry Lanier to duplicate it.

Eventually the components have been assembled, and await only the arrival of Lanier's duplicate tube. When a delivery man arrives in the front hall with a package from Lanier, an excited Cal tears off all the wrappings on the way back to the lab.

Chapter 4: Cal installs the duplicate tube and plunges the power panel's master switch. Soon the image of a man comes into focus on the viewing screen. After saying that Cal has passed the aptitude test of building an interocitor,[1] he introduces himself as an employment representative of a group urgently in need of expert technologists. He continues,

> **It has undoubtedly occurred to you, as to all thinking people of your day, that the scientists have done a particularly abominable job of dispensing the tools they have devised. Like careless and indifferent workmen they have tossed the products of their craft to gibbering apes and baboons. The results have been disastrous....**

Cal and Joe (Rex Reason and Robert Nichols) order umpty-ump crates of interocitor parts, presumably on Ryberg Electronics' dime, and spend days (weeks?) tinkering together a ... well, they don't know *what* it's going to turn out to be. If it turns out to be *any*thing. As you watch these scenes, all you can think is that their boss must be very indulgent.

The man says that his group, the Peace Engineers, would more conservatively distribute these tools—but to do that, they need technicians of imagination and good will. Consumed by the desire to know more about their technology, Cal is prepared to join them. His interviewer says that a plane will land on the Ryberg airfield tomorrow at six p.m., wait 15 minutes and then take off with or without Cal. He then warns Cal to stand back, as the interocitor is about to self-destruct—which it does.

Although Cal knows he can't be sure that the Peace Engineers truly *are* altruists, the following day he resigns from Ryberg. While he's saying his goodbyes to Wilson, the Peace Engineers' propeller plane arrives. Wilson can see that the plane is pilotless, and knows that Cal must see that too, "but Cal's steps were steady as he walked towards it."

Chapter 5: The plane flies throughout the night, at one point skirting a vast thunderstorm, with Cal sitting in the cockpit—where there are no controls or instruments. He sees a desert city below as the plane heads for a valley beyond some mountains north of it. Soon a plant surrounded by hundreds of small houses is below. After the plane lands there, a polite young mechanic tells Cal that the nearby city is Phoenix and, regarding the ghostly plane, says, "I don't blame you for getting the willies out of a ride like that."

A slim, dark-haired girl introduces herself as Dr. Ruth Adams and offers her hand, which Cal notices is cold and trembles almost imperceptibly. A psychiatrist, Ruth is animated and talkative enough but he sees fear in her eyes.

Inside one of the plant's four buildings, Cal meets Dr. Warner, the man with whom he conversed via interocitor. Warner promises that the answers to Cal's many questions will come as he passes through a probationary period. Cal is surprised to learn that they intend to put him in charge of the interocitor assembly plant. "Eventually, you will meet Mr. Jorgasnovara, Engineer of the entire project," says Warner, "but it may be months. He's an elusive man."

Chapter 6: Touring the plant with Ruth, Cal learns that there are 500 engineers working on scores of projects, with everything they need "theirs for the whistling," as Ruth puts it—an engineer's paradise. Also employed there is Cal's pal from college days, big blond Ole Swenberg. Cal spends the afternoon settling into one of the company houses (two rooms and a kitchenette), where at eight his invited guests Ole and Ruth arrive with sandwiches and beer. Ole takes Cal aback by calling the Peace Engineers' stated goals "guff" and "phony window dressing." Ruth elaborates:

> **Peace Engineers! They knew that half the scientists of the country were sick at heart after the last war because of what had happened through the discoveries of science. It was the most obvious bait they could hold out. And the best brains in the nation bit on it. ...Ole and I and a dozen or so others of the engineers have become to put it mildly—suspicious of the whole set-up. And our suspicions have frightened us.**

Ole says that he fears that the cream of the nation's scientific brains are working for people who "aren't so peaceful in spite of their name"; he sets forth the possibility that our own military has corraled all these brains through this "Peace Engineers" deception. Ole and Ruth want Cal to use his high position to learn what's behind this false front. Cal balks. "You don't have to get sore," says Ole. "*Just try to find out.* You'll get curious sooner or later."

Chapter 7: After six months of study and work, it's a wonderful day for Cal as he watches the interocitor assembly line in full operation. To celebrate, he invites Ruth to dinner in town. He picks her up at eight and admires her evening dress; "It was utterly impossible to think of an M.D. and Ph.D. in that dress. He didn't try." Afterwards, in Cal's car at the outskirts of town, Ruth says that Ole is no longer at the plant, having been reduced to hysterics by some frightening occurrences: He said he saw some fearful thing in the sky; then on another occasion, while making some interocitor modifications, he said he found himself overhearing the *thoughts* of the Engineer.

The next day, Cal finally meets the Engineer, a.k.a. Jorgasnovara, a big man who appears to be about 60, and has a large, hairless head with a high-domed cranium. According to Jorgasnovara, the work of the Peace Engineers dates back to a seventeenth century Frenchman who fretted that in the distant future, "men of science could be bought like ancient mercenaries" and their discoveries put to destructive use. After his death, his philosophy was adopted by a number of learned men who held back a growing mass of scientific knowledge from the world. "Tungsten lamps were available 15 years before poor Tom Edison began his first carbon filaments. We knew the principles of high-tension power transmission and could have built electric generators as good as today." By withholding their technology, Jorgasnovara says they kept the atomic bomb from being used in the First World War instead of the second:

> **If it had not been so, the Second would perhaps have been the last, and you and I would even now be cowering in caves, snarling over a piece of rotten meat—provided we were alive at all.**

Chapter 8: Cal tells Ruth about his meeting with Jorgasnovara, admitting that the Engineer is "a strange egg"—

The novel's Jorgasnovara became the movie's Exeter; Jeff Morrow gives the role color and we end up likin' the guy, even if he does "spacenap" some Earth scientists (and kill others!). Alongside Klaatu from *The Day the Earth Stood Still*, he's one of the 1950s' more "down-to-earth" movie aliens. (Photograph courtesy John Antosiewicz.)

but a strange egg who's not trying to deceive anyone. Ruth asks Cal if he knows where the interocitors he manufactures *go*, and he doesn't. She says that yesterday there were 600 crated in the shipping department, today they're gone ... and she wonders if there'll be truck tracks outside the big doors of the shipping room. During his lunch break, Cal finds no truck tracks but does see a 20-foot-wide, saucer-like depression in the asphalt.

That night in Cal's lab, he is absorbed in his work while Ruth falls asleep with her head on a lab bench. As he activates an interocitor, an image of Jorgasnovara forms in his mind, and he can hear the big man's voice making an oral report about progress at the plant. After Jorgasnovara's image and voice disappear from Cal's mind, he sees that Ruth is awake. She also saw and heard Jorgasnovara in her mind.

Cal and Ruth hurry to the shipping department where, through the large open exterior doors, they see "a vast ellipsoid" with an open port; a gangplank runs between the shipping platform and the port. Over the space of several minutes, a chain of hundreds of crated interocitors follow the light of a flashlight-like instrument in Jorgasnovara's hands into the mystery freighter.

Rushing to the roof of the three-story building, Cal and Ruth see that the top of the ellipsoid looms ten feet above the edge of the roof. They hear the closing of doors, and then the freighter shoots straight up at incredible speed. Filled with awe, Cal realizes that the Peace Engineers are making interocitors for a market beyond the stars.[2]

Chapter 9: Cal and Ruth are in a car en route to L.A., Cal driving as Ruth sleeps beside him. He ruminates about his accomplishments of the past six months: putting the Peace Engineers' new plant into operation, seeing the first interocitor come off the assembly line—and placing an engagement diamond on Ruth's finger.

The two arrive at the Narcissus Radio Company where Ole now works. In the back of the shabby building they find Ole, who is friendly until Cal mentions the interocitor. Ole says he wants nothing more to do with the Peace Engineers and adds that if Cal and Ruth are still a part of it, he wants nothing to do with them either. As Cal and Ruth drive away, Cal reveals that he filched a box containing one of the company's car radios—and tells Ruth that in a room behind Ole, he spotted an interocitor. Pulling over on a residential street, Cal opens the box and finds that inside the "radio" are interocitor parts. Ruth says that if Ole is still working for the Engineers, that means that he's now under their "impressed influence"—i.e., he's their slave. She worries that this can also happen to them, and doesn't want to go back to Phoenix. But Cal *must* go back, now that he knows the Engineers have space flight; with their technology, they could make trips to the stars "with safety and regularity. And, Ruth—*I want to go to the stars*."

Chapter 10: A 400-mile drive later, Cal and Ruth are back at the plant. Cal is haunted by the question of why Ole, once so bitter about the Engineers, now runs a midget plant for them. In his locked laboratory, he turns on the interocitor hoping to do a bit more telepathic eavesdropping. Soon he can "hear" Jorgasnovara and another man talking back and forth. Cal "feels" Jorgasnovara's hatred for some enemy; hears Jorgasnovara mention "the death-struggle of a universe"; and gets glimpses of strange lands he thinks might be other planets, spaceships by the thousands consumed by flames in space, "fleets of ships and endless tons of material swallowed in the daily gorge of war."

Bathed in sweat, a shaken Cal phones Ruth and tells her to come over. He describes what he's heard and seen—adding that by getting the Earth involved, the Peace Engineers may have put all mankind at risk.

Chapter 11: Cal is now filled with hate for Jorgasnovara because he knows that the plant is producing war material ("And I was the guy who was so fed up with practicing science in the service of the warriors!"). Suddenly Ole contacts Cal and Ruth via interocitor: He says that as a result of spying on them via interocitor for days, he's overcome his fears that they are actually members of Jorgasnovara's secret police. According to Ole, he inadvertently found out about the outer space war the same way Cal did, via the interocitor, and it drove him nearly crazy ("Our little wars are like neighborhood kids brawling in the street compared to the way they fight"). Ole says he continues to work for the Peace Engineers while at the same time trying to figure out how to thwart them and get Earth out of this dangerous situation.

Ruth suggests to Cal that they take photos of the plant and samples of components to Army Intelligence—to the White House, if necessary—and make them aware of the situation. Cal tells her that's a direct route to a room in the booby hatch. Ruth also wonders if Ole is exactly what Ole said *he* feared *they* were: a spy for Jorgasnovara.

Chapter 12: Ole flies to the Phoenix plant in a pilotless plane to meet with Jorgasnovara. In his lab, Cal waits hours for the conference to end so that he can meet with Ole—but then he's told that Ole has already returned to L.A. Then Ruth phones him to say she's been reassigned to another plant and must leave immediately. Cal can tell that she's being forced to say these things and realizes that the Engineers now have Ole and Ruth. Seeing Ruth getting aboard a plane on the airfield, he chases after the rolling plane but can't catch up. Cal feels helpless knowing that "[w]ith their damned technology they could probe his brain and dissect every secret thought. There was no hiding. Why had he supposed for a moment that he and Ole and Ruth could operate in their midst without detection?"

Behind closed blinds in his lab, Cal fills briefcases with scores of small components foreign to our technology plus various booklets and textbooks, determined to deliver them to officials who will listen to him. After dark he goes to the airfield and asks for a manual plane with which to make a short trip. He waits, worried that the mechanic will call Jorgasnovara or Warner for instructions, until the ship is rolled out of the hangar. Incredulous at having outwitted the Engineers and gotten away, he heads in the direction of Washington and the challenge of getting someone to believe that the Peace Engineers have involved the Earth in an interstellar war.

Chapter 13: In the sky somewhere between Amarillo and Oklahoma City, Cal lets out a scream when one of the Engineers' vast spaceships comes between his plane and the moon. He tries to take evasive action and screams again when he realizes the spaceship is now silently flying right above him. The plane motor dies as a hatch in the base of the spaceship opens, and the spaceship descends around him. The hatch closes and the plane drops onto it. His boy-

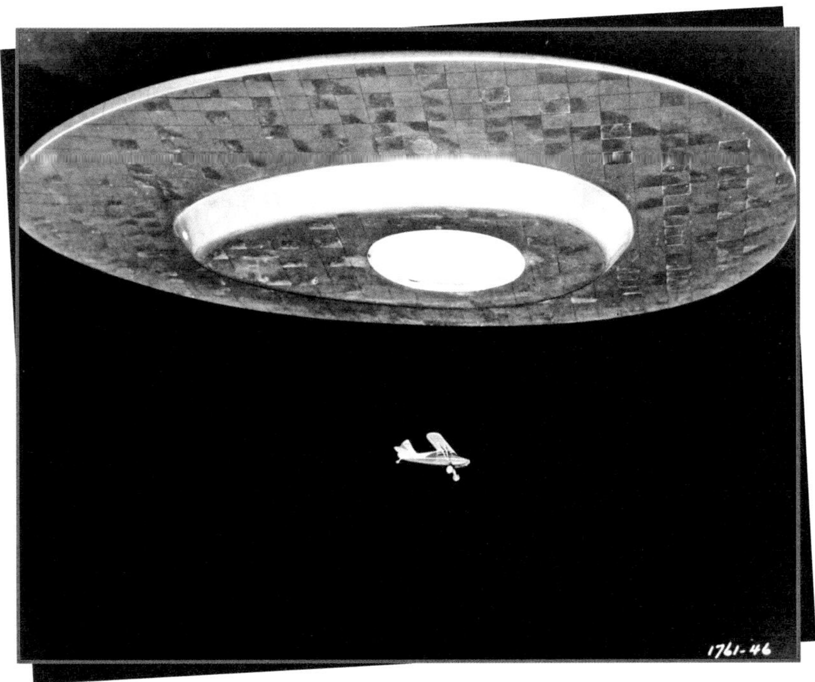

The Green Ray is about to emanate from the opening in the spaceship belly and "pull" the plane up and in; then, as if by magic, the opening will disappear. In the novel, there's no Green Ray: Cal is flying away from the Arizona plant when the spaceship positions itself above his plane and then descends onto it, his plane entering the spaceship through an open hatch in its underside. (Photograph courtesy C. Robert Rotter, *Glamour Girls of the Silver Screen* website.)

hood dreams of being aboard a spaceship have been fulfilled but there is no thrill to it, just "dull aching despair" within him.

Two men lead Cal down a corridor to his quarters. Looking out its ports, he sees the Earth seven or eight hundred miles below. He sleeps in a luxurious bed, then gets breakfast on a tray from his guides of the night before. Through the ports, he watches as the ship comes in for a landing amidst a group of one-story buildings on a plain on the dark side of the moon. The guides lead him through an airtight causeway from the ship to one of the buildings, where he's brought to a room where Ruth and Ole are seated at a table. Ruth and Ole have already met with Jorgasnovara, who has straightened them out on a few points. "Our mistake," says Ole, "was the assumption that the Engineers are Earthmen." Cal stares silently, trying to adjust to this undreamed-of development.

Chapter 14: Jorgasnovara apologizes to Cal for the "precipitate" way they had to overtake his plane. "You are at war," Cal says. "You let us overhear snatches of reports passing between you and others of your group. Why?" Jorgasnovara explains that it was necessary for him to know how much Cal, Ruth and Ole hated war—and now that he knows, he asks for their help. According to Jorgasnovara, the interstellar war has been going on for hundreds of generations.

To prove that the Peace Engineers are the ones with whom to side in the cosmic struggle, Jorgasnovara has Cal, Ruth and Ole don helmets. Wearing them fills their minds' eyes with the cozy sight of an Earth-like planet populated by Earth-like people—which is suddenly engulfed in blackness and left so burned that it can never again sustain life. This was the work of the Peace Engineers' enemies. Next they "see" a fleet of Peace Engineers warships imprisoned by the enemy "in webs of impenetrable time and space ... turning their crews into screaming things that would live forever."

Jorgasnovara tells Cal that his story of the Peace Engineers' seventeenth-century presence on Earth was true, and that because of the Engineers, our planet has been spared atomic war for many years. He then asks Cal to take charge of the Engineers' affairs on Earth for the rest of his life.

Cal, a man who has sworn never again to as much as *think* about any instrument of war, recalls the visions of evil and terror he saw via the helmet and slowly answers, "Yes. I'll help you."

Chapter 15: Two days later, via interocitor, Cal (back at the plant) gets from Jorgasnovara (still at the moon base) the full story of the war in space. Jorgasnovara belongs to the Llannan Council, an organization of worlds from 100+ galaxies combatting a vast enemy bent on conquering all life standing in its way.

> **The Llanna knew very little of the origin of the creatures they fought. There seemed to be an alliance somewhat like their own between wildly variant members of numerous galaxies. This alliance called itself the Guarra, and it was evident that no one had ever successfully halted its sweep of destruction except the Llannan Council.**

Llannan emissaries and technologists have setup manufacturing plants in a score of Earth nations and on thousands of other worlds whose inhabitants have also been kept clueless about the intergalactic battle. A tired Jorgasnovara admits that the war is currently going badly for "their" side, so production of weapons and equipment must be increased.

Cal is later visited by Ole, who says he's worried the plant workers will strike—not over money, but just out of restlessness and the "need" to strike periodically "to show things are still done the democratic way around here." Cal discusses this situation the next morning with Ruth and Dr.

In the novel, Cal and Ruth marry; amidst the pell-mell action of the movie, there wasn't much time for romance. But you'll find a bit in Rex Reason and Faith Domergue's publicity photos. (Photograph courtesy Alexander Rotter.)

Warner. Warner, a Llannan psychologist, says that Earthmen have an imagination and an inquisitiveness he's seldom encountered elsewhere, and "they make our dealing with you extremely difficult."

Chapter 16: Shortly after Cal becomes supervisor of all of Earth's Llannan projects, he marries Ruth. Two weeks later, a very tired Jorgasnovara makes an appearance, saying that interocitor production has to double and triple, and that they have to find other worlds where interocitors can be produced. Cal tells him about the labor unrest problem.

Jorgasnovara takes Cal on a tour of other Llannan plants throughout the world: Canada, England, France, Switzerland, Italy, Africa, Peru and more. The purpose of the items being made is sometimes unknown to the workers—and at least once, despite Jorgasnovara's best efforts at an explanation, even to Cal. Word reaches them that, at the Phoenix plant, the union workers have gone on strike and the place closed down. Returning to Phoenix, Cal learns that Ole had been forced to fire an incompetent assembly line worker and the union used this as an excuse to strike. Cal discusses the matter with Biggers, a union negotiator, and Cushman, a shop steward. No agreement can be reached.

Cal meets with Jorgasnovara, intending to tell him the bad news, but Jorgasnovara has worse news: Showing Cal a star chart that depicts the Guarra-Llanna battle lines, he says that the Guarran efforts have unexpectedly begun sweeping toward our galaxy.

Chapter 17: Cal and Jorgasnovara discuss the strike, and Jorgasnovara says that in light of the moving battle line, the Llannan work on Earth is "expendable." The word chills Cal, who thinks "of green jungle islands during the war, native villages smashed and people driven aside only to be ignored in pain and misery when the tide of battle swept past."

Cal is wakened by a four a.m. phone call from a watchman who just arrived and found the plant wrecked. Cal, Ruth and Ole tour the main assembly room and see that much of the nearly irreplaceable equipment is smashed, presumably by strikers. Biggers and Cushman react with surprise to the sight of all the damage and insist that their men had nothing to do with it. Cal tells them that in the future, assembly will be done cybernetically. After Biggers and Cushman leave, Ruth says she believes that the two men were genuinely surprised.

Cal goes on a desert picnic with Ruth and Ole. As they discuss the situation, they get a call (via a portable set in Cal's car) from Jorgasnovara, who has consulted with the Llannan Planning Committee: "[T]hey wish to know what your feelings are regarding the possibility of leaving Earth and taking up residence in the same work on a similar planet in another solar system."

Chapter 18: A meeting with Jorgasnovara covers much ground, including the Committee's insistence that the Phoenix plant be restored. Cal later ponders the fact that technologically the Llannans are supermen but psychologically "they didn't have sense enough to come in out of the rain"; after hundreds of years of interaction with Earth people, they were still unable to properly deal with them.

Ruth still doesn't think union goons wrecked the plant and gets Cal to agree to spend the night there with her in case the wreckers return. Just after midnight they hear something land on the roof. They don headpieces and tune in to an interocitor on the assembly floor, trying to catch the thoughts of the intruders; they detect "a flowing stream of sheer evil." Then they hear the sound of demolition. Cal hurries to the assembly floor, where he's nauseated by an odor like that of a jungle full of slimy, creeping things, and fetches a gun from a watchman's locker. Switching on his flashlight, he sees two monstrous aliens. As Cal raises the gun to shoot at them, he's struck from behind.

Chapter 19: Lying in bed in the plant dispensary, Cal

describes the intruders to Jorgasnovara, who pegs them as Suoinard—one of the species involved with the Guarra. Later, Ruth tells Cal she overheard his attackers' thoughts over the interocitor, and says that the one who struck him was Ole. Cal has known Ole since college ("We swapped ties and shirts and girl friends") and can't believe her.

A few days later, Cal visits the office of a now gaunt, almost cadaverous Jorgasnovara, who announces that the Peace Engineers are leaving the Earth because the Guarra are moving toward this solar system with Earth their specific objective. Ruth cries out that the Peace Engineers have drawn the Guarra here, and that she and Cal had been promised that Earth would be safe. Jorgasnovara says that Llannan war computers—to whom a world is not a world but merely a pinpoint in space—advised them against making any move in defense of Earth.

Jorgasnovara says that Cal and Ruth can be taken to one of the planets suitable for their habitation, his own home planet among them, but they have only a day to prepare. "Do you think we could ever live with ourselves knowing we had betrayed Earth and fled from the thing we had brought upon it?" demands Ruth. Jorgasnovara says he's surmised that this would be their attitude—but adds that if they change their minds, they are welcome to the very last moment.

Chapter 20: Jorgasnovara promises that the end of Earth will be easy and merciful: A Guarra fleet will encircle the planet, pushing a wave of fire ahead of it, and after a few hours of terrible panic, it will all be over.

Cal, still irritated by Ruth's insistence that Ole is working with the Guarra, insists on going to Ole's home to make sure he knows about this new development. Ole tells them he's evacuating along with the Peace Engineers, and urges them to do so. Cal and Ruth detect an odor—one that reminds Cal of the scaly creatures who confronted him at the plant. Realizing they know the truth, Ole holds them at gunpoint. He says he's really Martolan, chief Guarra agent for Earth. Out of a bedroom come the two creatures. "The boys are a little smelly," Ole cracks. "I knew you'd recognize it the moment you stepped in."[3]

Ole decides not to kill Cal and Ruth because he wants them to witness the end of the world, which they've brought about by their "meddling." He locks them in a bedroom closet and then leaves with his scaly sidekicks. Cal realizes that Ole fired the assembly line worker to provoke the union strike. Escaping from the closet, they don the headpieces of the interocitor in Ole's study and attempt to contact Jorgasnovara. Instead, they hear Jorgasnovara's desperate cry: "Cal, help me! Help me wherever you are!"

Chapter 21: Cal realizes that the interocitor is also a weapon by which one user—one mind—can reach out and twist or destroy another, and that the Guarrans are now trying to kill Jorgasnovara via the interocitor. He and Ruth join forces with Jorgasnovara, who directs their concerted efforts. With Ole on the other end, Cal must block from his mind the perception of Ole, college classmate and friend; the one desire of an interocitor operator has to be for the death of the enemy. Jorgasnovara gives Cal and Ruth a mental image of the Earth in flames—our planet as it would be after the Guarran attack—to intensify their desire for Ole's death. The battle between Cal, Ruth and Jorgasnovara vs. Ole and the two creatures ends with the latter's spaceship a molten ball of flame.

Cal and Ruth rush to Jorgasnovara's office and find the big man on the floor. When Ruth offers to get help, Jorgasnovara says, "There is no help for one who is the victor in such an interocitor contest as I am. One can fight but a single such battle. As in all war, he who wins is also the vanquished." Dying, he tells Cal and Ruth to go before the Llannan council and plead for Earth as he had intended to do. His last words are a request for his body to be brought home to his planet.

Cal and Ruth finish packing a half dozen suitcases by mid-afternoon and begin their wait for the midnight arrival of the spaceship. In Cal's mind, he's certain that life will soon be swept from the face of the Earth by the Guarra legions. Ruth is sure that the Guarran horde will be turned away.

Chapter 22: The spaceship picks up Cal and Ruth at midnight and they begin their 16-day voyage to the Llannan Council's center of government. On Jorgasnovara's home world, there are solemn rites accompanying the dissolution of his body and its dispersal into the seas.

The Llannan Council is made up of representatives of more than 100 races who "convene" via faster-than-light communication. Making his case before a sub-council, Cal condemns their abandonment of the Earth: "If you feel no obligation to defend this island Earth against the unexpected Guarran invasion you are not worthy to seek the goal you are fighting for." The matter is weighed on the many worlds of the Llannan Council, and then a group leader regretfully tells Cal that war can only be fought "by cold calculation which can predict accurately the outcome of any projected action." He offers Cal the opportunity to examine the military computers that make these decisions, and then announces, "All we can say is that your request cannot be granted, Cal Meacham of Earth."

Chapter 23: At Ruth's urging, Cal takes the group leader up on his offer to examine the military's decision-making computers. With the help of a young Llannan technician, Rakopt, he comes to realize that the purpose of the computer is chiefly that of prediction—and that the Peace Engineers never make a move without the computer predicting its chances of success or failure. At another meeting with the Council, he tells them that they are losing the war because the Guarra are better computermen: Guarran computers know what the Llannans' computers will advise them to do and then, knowing that the Llannans invariably follow the computers' advice, the Guarrans wait for them to do it. For the Llannans, the key to winning a battle with the Guarra is to do the opposite of what their computers suggest; for instance, send every ship they can spare to the defense of the Earth.

For Cal and Ruth, a few suspense-filled hours pass as the Council weighs the issues, and then Warner and Rakopt bring them the news that the Council has decided that Earth will be defended. Battleships are soon en route to the new battle zone, Cal and Ruth aboard one of them. Cal isn't sure that guerrilla fighting tactics will turn the tide of the war, but he's confident they will make the Llanna less vulnerable.

The novel's first four chapters are very much like the opening reels of the movie *This Island Earth*, but then Cal's mystery plane's destination turns out to be a Phoenix plant with 4000 workers instead of the movie's Georgia mansion; from then on, the movie keeps diverging from the novel until it reaches the point that the character names Cal Meacham and Ruth Adams are all you can find in both. Truth be told, after the divergence, the novel's plot is more interesting than the movie's. (The plot of the second half of the movie is so simplistic, it'd be difficult for the novel to be *less* interesting.) One reason the novel tops the movie is that, when it comes to the interplanetary war, we (Earth people) have skin in the game: If the Guarra continues to prevail in the space wars, Earth will get swept up in the conflict and destroyed. The movie gives viewers little or no reason to care which of the alien planets wins; a reader of the novel has a rooting interest in the Llannans.

Jones' "The Alien Machine" was reprinted in the 1981 book *They Came from Outer Space: 12 Classic Science Fiction Tales That Became Major Motion Pictures*; its editor Jim Wynorski wrote in an intro that Jones had recently said, "Though [Universal] made a few regrettable changes, I was still quite impressed with the remarkable effects. And although I was not consulted after the initial sale, the screenwriters did an admirable job of adapting my work."

Following this quote from Jones, Wynorski interjects, "One of the 'regrettable changes' obviously refers to the huge eight-foot-tall mutated monster that thankfully did not appear in the novel." I find it hard to believe that Jones was averse to alien monsters in the movie because *he* had alien monsters in his novel. More likely what struck Jones as a regrettable change was the filmmakers' elimination of his characterization of Cal as a fervent peacenik. Cal is haunted by World War II memories of the inhabitants of primitive islands being pressed into service by one side or the other (clearing jungles, laying airstrips, etc.); these islanders, who had little or no comprehension of the war "and no capacity for understanding the power and depth of the forces involved," were then decimated as "the tide of battle swept past." In the latter part of the novel, Cal realizes that by casting his lot with the Llannans, he's put his own planet, *our* planet, in the crosshairs: As a result of his actions, Earth is the primitive, backward "island" in the path of the Guarran wrecking ball. Twice the novel calls Earth an island, both times in connection with tales of the plight of the World War II islanders, so perhaps Jones gave the novel the title *This Island Earth* to underline the significance of this plot detail. One contemporary newspaper reviewer cited Jones' novel as "one of the truly memorable science fiction experiences of this or any other year" and summed it up nicely by calling it "a rare science fiction novel which combines a sense of social responsibility and thrilling action."

The son of a truck driver, Jones (1915–94) was born in "The City of the Saints," Salt Lake City, and was a lifelong Mormon. According to an autobiographical sketch he wrote for a 1951 issue of *Amazing Stories*, science fiction "inspired the course of my studies through high school and college." He attended the University of Utah and served a Mormon missionary stint in Galveston, Texas; several of the sermons he delivered at the Church of Jesus Christ of Latter-Day Saints were published in local newspapers that can now be found online. He worked as a radio operator, an installer of telephone exchange equipment and a Weather Bureau employee; then, during World War II, he returned to electronics via the engineering department of Bendix Radio in Baltimore. Jones had started, back in 1940, writing science fiction stories for fun; soon his tales were appearing in the pulp magazines *Astounding Science Fiction* and *Thrilling Wonder Stories*. Some time in the mid–1940s, a ten-year-old boy bought an *Astounding Science Fiction* in a neighborhood candy store, sat on a bench near the store, read his first modern sci-fi short story, Jones' "Pete Can Fix It," and got hooked on the genre. The boy was Carl Sagan, who described this life-changing interlude in his 1978 *New York Times Magazine* article "Growing Up with Science Fiction."

The transition of Jones' novel *This Island Earth* from page to screen may have begun with Hollywood director Joseph Newman. His nearly 100-year-long life began in 1909 in Logan, Utah, up the road a piece from Salt Lake City where Jones was born six years later. Newman got his first movie studio job at MGM during the silent era, filling the fountain pens of people like Louis B. Mayer and other chores on that level. During a stint as an MGM assistant director, he received two Oscar nominations in the now long-discarded Best Assistant Director category (for 1935's *David Copperfield* and 1936's *San Francisco*); his next step-up found him directing the studio's Pete Smith and *Crime Does Not Pay* shorts, and bringing a semi-documentary style to the latter.[4] Two of Newman's *Crime Does Not Pays*, *Don't Talk* (1942) and *The Luckiest Guy in the World* (1947), were Oscar nominees for Best Short Subject. By the late '40s he was regularly directing features; he spent the early '50s at 20th Century-Fox helming a number of movies, including *Love Nest* (1951) with up-and-comer Marilyn Monroe in one of her bigger Fox roles to date. Newman's Fox contract specified that he was free to do one outside movie a year, so late in 1952 he formed Joseph Newman Productions so that that once-a-year movie would be an indie of his own making. According to the Hollywood trades, he negotiated for the rights to the Ernest K. Gann novel *Island in the Sky* but apparently this came to naught. The next mention in the trades of Joseph Newman Productions may have been in the August 1953 *Variety* item "Joe Newman Schedules *This Island Earth*":

> **This Island Earth, science fiction novel by Raymond F. Jones, has been purchased by Joe Newman, who'll produce and direct it this fall under banner of Joseph Newman Productions.**
>
> **Newman, who recently ankled 20th-Fox pact to go into indie production, has already assigned George Callahan to write the screenplay.**

About a month later, when the industry again read of *This Island Earth,* the name of another Hollywood mover-and-shaker, much better-known than Newman, was part of the story.

Victor Orsatti (1905–1984) was the seventh and last child of Italian immigrants Morris and Mary Manze Orsatti, the former a bank vice-president and owner of the International Steamship and Railroad Agency.[5] In 1930, their son Frank, a former bootlegger, went into the agency business and brought in his brothers Al, Victor and Ernie. The Orsatti Agency represented actors, executives, producers, directors, writers and radio talent. By 1949 Frank and Al were dead of heart attacks (at 53 and 48, respectively) and Victor took charge. Tim Adler's book *Hollywood and the Mob* calls Victor "a gangster-cum-agent" which certainly has the ring of truth when you know about brother Frank's brushes with the law and their father's ties to organized crime; Dad spent time up the river in the 1920s.

On September 17, 1953, Orsatti went over to the moviemaking side of the biz, forming Sabre Productions and making Newman his vice-president and executive producer. The plan was to put out three features annually, two of them to be directed by Newman. Sabre's kickoff flick, according to *Variety*, would be the color-widescreen-stereophonic sound *This Island Earth*, scheduled to start in mid–November. In the *Variety* article, Orsatti claimed that financing for *This Island Earth* and their second film *Teheran*, an adventure drama with an Iran setting, "has already been completed and production will get underway as soon as cast is selected and shooting space secured."[6] Hedda Hopper told readers of her "In Hollywood" column (September 18) that cast-wise, Orsatti and Newman were "aiming high for the stars": "For *Earth*, the boys will try to get Richard Widmark, who wants a rest from Hollywood." (When Robert Skotak came across this Hopper column, he asked Newman about it, and the director said that Widmark was never under consideration. Perhaps Widmark was one of Hopper's pet favorites and she interjected his name into her column whenever the fancy struck her, truthfulness be damned.)

Scripter George Callahan, mentioned above, receives on-screen credit as Edward G. O'Callaghan on *This Island Earth* as well as on *Flight to Hong Kong* (1956), the latter a Sabre Production directed by Newman. He'd done a lot of writing for Monogram in the 1940s, penning entries in that Poverty Row studio's Charlie Chan and Shadow series; in the '50s he mostly worked in TV, including Orsatti's Western TV series *The Texan*. He and Newman co-wrote the *This Island Earth* screenplay according to a November 1953 column by Philip K. Scheuer, a statement not borne out by the on-screen credits (only O'Callaghan is listed). But Newman told *Fantastic Films* interviewer Al Taylor that he did have a hand in the writing: He said that he felt that the Jones novel "had the makings of a very exciting science fiction film [and] worked out a screen treatment," then hired Callahan to write the shooting script. He continued,

> **With this done we went ahead with all preparations to make the film independently. We even had a complete set of exciting sketches drawn up to illustrate the concept of the production. But, in 1953, it was just too hard for an independent film company to get good financing or adequate release for a picture.**

Republic and United Artists both showed a bit of interest, according to Robert Skotak's 1990 MagicImage book on the making of *This Island Earth*. Per Skotak, Saber Productions also contacted Universal about it, asking for a free hand in making the movie and profit participation. At that point, Universal's one "straight" (non-comedic) science fiction film of the 1950s, the 3-D *It Came from Outer Space*, was a recent hit and *Creature from the Black Lagoon* was in the works and looking promising.

> *This Island Earth* ... did a sudden switch yesterday from Sabre Productions to U-I, as did director Joe Newman.
>
> —*Variety*, November 12, 1953

As reported by *Variety*, Universal bought the project outright from Orsatti and Newman, and engaged Newman to direct. The item went on to say that, as part of the deal where Universal had acquired *This Island Earth* and Newman, Newman would also direct a second movie for the studio. (The second picture, *Kiss of Fire*, was shot in November-December 1954. Like *This Island Earth*, it co-starred Rex Reason.)

Selecting a producer for *This Island Earth* was a no-brainer for the Universal brass: The workhorse of the lot William Alland, who cooked up the basic ideas for *It Came from Outer Space* and *Black Lagoon* and produced those movies, was now their go-to guy for "scientifiction" subjects. Alland told me,

One day the studio called me in and said, "We've got a good one for you [*This Island Earth*]. Here, take this, we've just bought it." They didn't say, "Read it, we're *thinking* of buying it," they said, "We've *bought* it," which automatically puts you on the hook [*laughs*]! I couldn't go back in a week later and say, "I read this piece of shit, what are you talking about? You don't want *this*"—you couldn't say that. Well, actually you *could*, but I *didn't*. Maybe I *should* have, sometimes.

Alland had some qualms about the script, so O'Callaghan was engaged to make changes, additions and deletions. Still Alland was unhappy, and at last Universal acceded to his request to bring in another writer, Franklin Coen. *This Island Earth* was one of four movies that Coen wrote or co-wrote for Alland, the others being *Johnny Dark, Four Guns to the Border* (both 1954) and *Chief Crazy Horse* (1955); the writer was Oscar-nominated a decade later for *The Train* (1964).

Coen wrote in his introduction to Skotak's Magic-Image book,

I was awarded a bungalow to myself, assigned two secretaries, and I got the promise from Jim Pratt, executive in charge, of a case of the best available Scotch if I could deliver a viable new screenplay the day before yesterday, the old, old story. I was young and not too fazed. Besides, I had an ace in the hole in Bill Alland, a man with an agile and creative mind and a passion for science fiction.

Making the script acceptable, and keeping the budget manageable, was a process fraught with hurdles (fully described in Skotak's book), but soon *This Island Earth* was scheduled for a January 30 start date. Things were generally slow in Hollywood at that moment, so probably everyone involved was glad just to be working.[7]

The stars would shine bright on the movie's outer space backdrops, but not at the top of its castlist: When *This Island Earth* was shot (and right up 'til today), Jeff Morrow and Rex Reason were light years away from being household names. Veteran stage actor Morrow had recently made a good showing in a supporting role in his debut film *The Robe*, playing the black-bearded Centurion who sword-duels Richard Burton to a standstill in an exciting street fight. But since the release of that Biblical drama, Morrow had been seen in only one other movie, the dismal "foreign intrigue" drama *Flight to Tangier*, playing the nothing role of a local police official.

In *This Island Earth*, Morrow played the Jorgasnovara character, which was understandably renamed (Exeter) for the screen. He told me about his casting: "My [Universal] contract went into effect some time in February 1954, and just prior to that date Universal suddenly decided they wanted me to play the lead in [*This Island Earth*]. They sent me the script, I read it and went in to talk with the producer, Bill Alland, who is a very nice chap, quite able and talented, and the writer, Franklin Coen." Morrow said that in the script he'd read, Exeter was a two-dimensional heavy:

Prior to Jeff Morrow starring as Exeter in *This Island Earth* (above), most movie fans had seen him play only one part ... but *what* a part: the small but very memorable role of the Centurion in the 1953 Biblical drama *The Robe* (right). By year's end, it was challenging *Gone with the Wind*'s standing as the top money picture of all time.

You had no idea why Exeter was doing any of this stuff, except that he was an ornery character. I didn't have to do the picture because it was going to start ten days before my

contract went into effect, so this was one of the few instances in all the times I've signed for pictures that I had a little bit to say about it! I told them, "I'm interested in doing it, but he's such a heavy. Can't we do something about it—show that he is, let's say, the epitome of a true scientist, and really concerned about the effect of what he does upon the world?" So we talked for about an hour, and there was a sort of general agreement that it wasn't a bad idea. And when we walked down the street to the parking lot, Frank Coen said, "I'm so glad you were there, because I've been trying to sell them on that concept for a month!"

According to a March 28, 1954, *Brooklyn Eagle* interview with Morrow, the New Yorker was then living with wife Anna Karen and their daughter Lissa in a hotel in Westwood, California, a place like "a suburban college community"—so presumably that's where he was living when he made *This Island Earth* several weeks earlier. (The Morrows started in a one-bedroom apartment there, moved to a duplex in the same complex, and thence to what they called their "dream home" in Royal Oaks.)

Rex Reason had top-lined *his* first film, the stock footage-filled indie *Storm Over Tibet* (1952) with Diana Douglas, wife of Kirk. In Diana's 1999 autobiography *In the Wings: A Memoir* she indicated that, at the time, Rex had a ways to go as an actor: "I feel I did a credible job [in *Storm Over Tibet*] despite working with the very vain Rex Reason. He was inordinately fond of his profile, so it became difficult to get any eye contact with him." Quite Reason-ably, the actor himself felt there was room for improvement: After watching his *Storm Over Tibet* performance, he buckled down to another year of training.

Faith Domergue was in a dozen '50s films and she's dead at the end of half of them. In 1954 she told interviewer John L. Scott that her role in *This Island Earth* was a good one because "I stay alive all through the story." (Photograph courtesy Alexander Rotter.)

In late January 1954 when Reason started work on *This Island Earth,* he was a Universal contractee who had already played villainous roles in their *Taza, Son of Cochise* and *Yankee Pasha*; the former was just beginning its theatrical run, the latter was not yet released. He told me that he believed he was assigned the part of Cal as a result of being in a screen test that Piper Laurie had made for some upcoming Western. The scene was set inside a stagecoach, Reason was relaxed and casual, and when Universal production chief Ed Muhl screened the test, he liked it very much. "I think as a result of that, he thought of me for the role of Meacham in *This Island Earth.* I read the script and I found it very interesting. I started testing and the rest you know."

Faith Domergue, no stranger on the Universal lot (after the Westerns *The Duel at Silver Creek*, 1952, and *The Great Sioux Uprising*, 1953), was signed to play the role of Ruth. In 1955 when *This Island Earth* debuted, 29-year-old Domergue was its only recognizable name; it was her first sci-fi, but soon followed by more. Domergue and Reason did wardrobe, makeup and hair tests on January 27, and presumably all went smoothly. No such luck for Morrow, signed on January 28 to play the role of "Mr. High Dome" (as the *New York Herald Tribune* reviewer playfully renamed Morrow's "Exeter-restrial" character). Morrow told me that the makeup and hair people "gave me a slightly enlarged forehead, which had to be put on very, very carefully, and then a white wig over that. It was the kind of look where, if you walked down the street, people wouldn't notice you, but then 20 feet later they would suddenly stop, turn around and say, 'He looked a little odd, didn't he?'" Early in the proceedings, Morrow looked even odder on film:

The wigs we wore were so white that we were all very worried, especially the woman hairdresser, about how they would wind up looking on film. ... And, as we predicted, when we saw the dailies, we saw that my hair came out pure white—it looked like cotton candy. It was terrible! Well, after the producers and executives all went into a bit of shock, they decided, "We'll just print the film darker, and the hair won't look so white." So they printed it darker, but then my skin looked as though I had been out in the sun all my life! The consequence was that every day, little by little, the hairdresser would twist and comb so that there was a wave in the white hair—not for any cosmetic appearance, but simply so there'd be a little light and shade, and it wouldn't look this ghastly pure white. They also softened the lights on the hair, and after a short time I looked fairly human.[8]

Several mornings throughout the shoot, Morrow had to show up as early as 6:15 for the time-consuming process of having the forehead and wig applied.

Bud Westmore's makeup department had the task of designing and making the studio's newest ogre, the Metaluna Mutant. When it came to its head, the monster makers had a bit of a, pardon the pun, head start: Glob #2, the alien head that made an unsuccessful bid for *It Came from Outer Space* stardom, provided some inspiration for the Mutant head. (Read more about Glob #2 in the *Outer Space* chapter.)

Bob Thomas paid a visit to what he called "the monster factory" and "the freak works" (Westmore's makeup department) and in a February 1954 column wrote that he talked to Westmore's assistant Jack Gavin [*sic*—should have been Kevan] about the newest addition to Universal's family of monsters: "This fellow is called a mutant," Kevan told him. "They are half-man and half-ant, an interesting combination." Thomas reported that the Mutant cost $6500.[9] "Monsters Made to Order," a December 10, 1954, *Collier's* magazine article on the Universal monster mill, reported the cost of the Mutant as $6000, with Westmore telling writer Joseph Laitin that he originally envisioned the Mutant

> **in brown and yellow, which would add to his repulsiveness. But the sky ship was metal-colored, so a blue monster with red streaks was more photogenic. The blue suggests his environment, and the red streaks are for exterior blood vessels forced to the surface because of atmospheric pressures. Then we gave him an overall hard-shell effect, like a beetle.**

According to columnist Howard Heffernan, part of the reason Westmore wanted more "repulsiveness" was his recent disappointment over fan reaction to the Gill Man in *Creature from the Black Lagoon*:

> **In the case of the Gill Man, our preview audiences seem to be showing too much sympathy for him and regret seeing him killed off in the end. Now, we've got to see that "Mutant" doesn't double-cross us like that. That's why I'm putting in so much time roughing him up.**

Bud Westmore poses with a Mutant head and, in the foreground, a number of Mutant sculptures even more grotesque than the version that made it into the movie. "It was outrageous, to clutter the movie up with that ridiculous thing," said producer William Alland, who blamed the Mutants' inclusion on Universal and director Joseph Newman. (Photographs courtesy John Antosiewicz.)

Westmore being Westmore, he found his way into various makeup department shots of the Mutant-in-progress, in order to create the impression he did some of the work. During this time, he was probably grateful for any newspaper coverage that did *not* also mention singer-actress Rosemary Lane: The papers were regularly finding space for news of their wedded blitz and their equally bumpy trip to Splitsville. Late in 1952, the Associated Press reported that Lane was asking $1245.98 a month support for herself and their daughter, declaring that Bud needed only $400 a month. The article continued, "Westmore testified he has turned over his paychecks to his wife for the last ten years and that she gave him an allowance. 'Last year it was $15 a week,' he said." A month later it was revealed that Westmore was under court order to pay her $650 a month "and not molest or annoy her pending trial of her separate maintenance suit." According to Westmore, he was earning $1326.08 a month.[10]

News service photos of the Mutant, appearing in many newspapers, included in their captions the factoid "The Mutant's exposed brain pulsates with each heartbeat." It does not; Regis Parton, who played the monster, told Skotak that this macabre idea *was* considered, "but that became too big of a problem." A grossly misinformed Erskine Johnson told readers of his February 27, 1954, "Hollywood Today" column, "Faith Domergue, says U-I, will have love scenes with a creature from another world in *This Island Earth*. The guy's half human and half insect."

It's become *de rigeuer*, in Monster Kid circles, to complain about the Mutants. In screenwriter Coen's introduction to Skotak's *This Island Earth* book, he said he "hated" the concept of the Mutants:

> **I thought the intrusion of such a beast would cheapen the whole project which, of course, by this time was *my* baby. But Bill [Alland] loved his monsters—he had made his reputation with them—and the creature was already conceived and being built. Deeply proud of it, Bill kept bringing me to the lab to show it off and try to convince me. Well, I had to admit the damn thing was intimidating if not, within its own genre, superb. I gave in; I had no choice.**

Morrow also turned thumbs-down, telling me that Universal "felt they had to have the insurance of audience reaction on the part of the kids, and they wrote in a monster. That really could've been cut out of the script, but we lived with it." Rex Reason said in our interview that the Mutant scenes "definitely detracted" from the movie:

> **They didn't have the realism that the rest of the picture did—you could tell immediately that this was just a stuntman in a bug uniform, and that took away from the picture. If they had perhaps showed the monsters only in close-up, if they had kept the camera up around their heads, it might have had more impact, but the long shots spoiled the moment. For the small kids it was all right, but *This Island Earth* was in some ways a rather thouthtful story, and I felt it was just too bad that they had to have those in there.**

"I don't agree!" Faith Domergue enthused to *Fangoria* interviewer Mike Fitzgerald. "I thought the Mutants were wonderful." In her interview with Tom and Jim Goldrup, she called the Mutants "an absolute stroke of genius."

Synopsis

Alongside a jet on a Bolling Field (Washington, D.C.) runway, reporters pepper electronics expert Cal Meacham (Rex Reason) with questions about his recent meeting with the Committee on Atomic Power. As he climbs into his flight suit, the young and personable Meacham implies that there may soon be great advances in the industrial application of atomic energy.

Soaring high above a variety of stock footage shots, Meacham pilots the jet to his Los Angeles home base, Ryberg Electronics Corp. In the Ryberg airfield control tower, Cal's assistant Joe Wilson (Robert Nichols) and control tower operator Webb (Robert B. Williams) radio-converse with Cal via hand mike, then cower as mischievous Cal's jet makes a low pass over them. Cal proceeds to roll the jet—which, as a result of his hotdogging, flames out and loses power. With his controls immobilized, he is headed for a crash when the jet suddenly begins to pulsate with bright green light and emit a high-frequency howl and heartbeat-like thumping. Cal sits agape as the controls operate on their own. The jet pulls out of its death dive and makes a perfect runway landing. The green glow vanishes.

No Admittance is painted on the door of Cal's research laboratory, where Cal and Joe run a test on an atomic reactor. Peering into the reactor's interior, Cal lowers a large cylinder into its pile and watches until a small explosion indicates that a condenser has burned out. Joe says he recently placed an order for a replacement and received—not the large block-shaped condenser he expected—but an envelope containing tiny "bead condensers." Stranger still, Joe says the one he tested withstood a 33,000-volt charge. "If that were true," Cal mutters, "we could build a generator … one that would supply electric power to run an entire factory … and it would fit in a matchbox." Learning that the receiving department did not furnish the beads, Cal contrives to discover what the beads are made of—and finds that even a diamond drill can't scratch one.

The mystery deepens when an expressman (Coleman Francis) delivers a package which contains a catalogue whose cover reads

ELECTRONICS SERVICE
UNIT NO. 16

—the same outfit that supplied the beads. Eerie Novachord music makes the viewer aware, just slightly in advance of Cal and Joe, that the catalogue will list items undreamed of in the present world. The pages are not paper but a thin metal. The prize rose in Unit 16's garden of technological beauts is the interocitor, an electronic wonder with limitless capabilities. Deciding to take the DIY challenge, Cal tells Joe to order the complete line of interocitor parts. One dissolve later, the lab is filled with newly arrived packing cases containing 2486 parts; and after a montage of assembly activity, Cal and Joe are standing before an interocitor.

As the last part is installed and adjusted, the image of a man (Jeff Morrow) with a shock of snow-white hair appears on its triangular screen. The script directed that his voice be pleasant, that he have "a calm, deliberate manner" and conduct himself with "dignity and authority"; not since Klaatu had audiences been treated to a spaceman more courteous and companionable. However, the effect is slightly spoiled by his forehead; indented like a highway Jersey barrier and almost as tall as one, it makes him look like a 24-karat weirdo. After congratulating Cal on accomplishing "a feat of which few men are capable" (building an interocitor), he introduces himself as Exeter and says he is seeking scientists of exceptional ability. Then, banking on Cal's curiosity, he says that at five o'clock Wednesday morning a plane will land at the Ryberg field, wait five minutes and take off, with or without Cal. Red Rays emanate from the three corners of the screen, destroying the catalogue and interocitor blueprints. Then the interocitor itself explodes and burns, leaving only molten metal.

To quote Mary Shelley's *Frankenstein*, "None but those who have experienced them can conceive of the enticements of science": Come Wednesday morning, Cal is toting a single bag to the airfield alongside a worried Joe, who urges him to reconsider. Despite darkness and thick fog, a propeller plane makes a landing. It has covered cockpit windows, a lone passenger seat, an interocitor screen up front—and no pilot. The soothing voice of Exeter welcomes Cal aboard and the automatically closing door shuts out Joe and his shouted pleas for Cal not to go. The plane interior glows green and the high-frequency howl is heard as the plane lifts off.

Some time later, when the plane lands and the door opens, Cal finds himself on a dirt runway surrounded by green fields, not far from a hill crowned by a Southern mansion. (Cal's p.o.v., a neat matte shot, shows us the mansion, a lake and a small courier plane, a Stinson, giving us the lay of the land and setting the stage for a key scene later in the movie.) A Ford Super Deluxe Woodie Station Wagon, class of (circa) 1946, pulls up, the beautiful woman inside (Faith Domergue) telling Cal he's now in "*Jaw*-ja" (Georgia). "I kind of expected Neptune, or Mars," Cal quips, a cute foreshadowing of things to come.

Cal recognizes her as Ruth Adams, with whom he'd had a fling a few years back, but Ruth says—none too convincingly—that he's mistaken. She drives him to the mansion, which she calls "The Club," a posh and comfortable hideaway where an international mix of the scientific world's MVPs freely roam their velvet cage. Emerging from his office-study, Exeter cordially greets the newcomer. (From the script: "In the flesh [Exeter] is an imposing, striking man.") Exeter tells Cal that his goal is to gather men of vision and find a way to put an end to war—and startles him by knowing that the top-secret tidbit that Cal's on the threshold of discovering a means of creating limitless amounts of free nuclear energy (by converting lead into uranium).

Dinner is an out-of-this-world affair with fine cuisine, brandy, candles, Mozart on the turntable, Ruth rocking a white off-the-shoulder number ... and the tension between Cal, Ruth and scientist Steve Carlson (Russell Johnson) so thick, you could cut it with a service knife. In Cal's lab, they have a showdown that ends with Ruth and Carlson deciding to trust newcomer Cal and compare notes. All three of these little fish are uncomfortable in the Exeter think tank: They agree that Exeter, for all his talk of ending war, is only interested in new sources of atomic energy. Ruth and Carlson reveal that Exeter has a device that renders useless the areas of the brain that control the power of the will,[11] and that it's been used on some of the other scientists there. Exeter and his cold-as-ice assistant Brack (Lance Fuller) are eavesdropping via interocitor. Brack is all for subjecting them to the Thought Transformer; Exeter says the procedure would kill their initiative and make them useless to the project. Exeter later communicates via interocitor with yet another lofty-forehead chap, the Monitor (Douglas Spencer), supreme head of the government of the planet Metaluna, who orders that Cal and Ruth be brought there at once.

Faith Domergue's first day on the movie began with a scene (opposite Rex Reason) shot on a dirt runway in Thousand Oaks. She found Reason to be "fun, giving, charming. We got along, just like buddies."

Under cover of darkness, Cal, Ruth and Carlson go on the lam in the station wagon. Brack, manning Exeter's interocitor, begins firing Red Rays at them. Carlson, who's behind the wheel, suggests they stop the car, pile out and take cover. When he brakes, Cal and Ruth quit the car and run into a lake; Carlson drives away, obviously to give Cal and Ruth a better chance at survival. Red Rays continue to chase the car until Carlson zigs when he shoulda zagged and gets zapped, the car colorfully exploding into atoms. (*New York Times* reviewer Howard H. Thompson singled out the station wagon-death ray chase as "a dandy scene.") Fellow scientist Dr. Engelborg (Karl L. Lindt), out for one of his nightly rambles, appears on the scene and also gets blasted.

As a spaceship rises from behind a hillside, Cal and Ruth hotfoot it to the airfield and take off in the courier plane. In the distance, the mansion explodes with a thunderous roar and a mushroom of flames, the force of the blast rocking Cal and Ruth's plane. Then there's more mile-high mayhem as the spaceship positions itself over the plane, paralleling its flight, and projects down onto it a Green Ray. Like an invisible hand, the ray pulls the plane up through an opening in the spaceship's underside into a cavernous cargo hold.

The spaceship leaves the Earth in the (cosmic) dust as Cal and Ruth, escorted to a Control Room of palatial proportions, see that the extra-terrestrial in charge is, surprise (*not*!), Exeter. With Cal in a snit about the mass murder he's just witnessed (Carlson, Engelborg, all the scientists ... presumably even the orange tabby housecat), a conciliatory-sounding Exeter asks for a truce. He explains that they're bound for his planet Metaluna, far beyond our solar system. To avoid being crushed by Metaluna's atmospheric pressure, everyone aboard the spaceship, Metalunans and Earthlings alike, must undergo a metabolic alteration by standing in transparent Converter Tubes that descend from overhead and fill with vapor. As Cal and Ruth receive the treatment, we get a brief X-ray-like peek at their insides, veins, organs, bones and all, like something seen in mid-transformation in an Invisible Man movie.[12]

> Modern science is making the once-deadly six-gun resemble a harmless toy. In *This Island Earth* the baddies shoot guided meteors.
>
> —George E. Phair, "Retakes," *Variety*, June 17, 1955

With Cal and Ruth in Observer Chairs, gazing into a large Stellarscope Screen showing the immense interplanetary sea ahead of them, Exeter reveals that Metaluna is at war with the planet Zahgon. Even as he spins the tale, Zahgon spacecraft appear and guide meteors into collision courses with the spaceship; Red Rays fired by the spaceship destroy the meteors. During their approach to Metaluna, we see Zahgon-directed meteors hitting and exploding in the planet's "ionized layer," a Metalunan-made field of intense radiation. Exeter says that this layer requires enormous amounts of atomic energy—and that Metaluna's uranium deposits are exhausted (thus the need for help from outside, i.e., Earth scientists).

The blackened, battle-scarred surface of Metaluna could pass for a map of Hell: smoky ... cracked like a dry lakebed ... dotted with crags of rock ... pockmarked with large round openings that make it look like a slice of Swiss cheese used as an ashtray. The spaceship vertically drops through an opening and into the cavernous below-ground realm where the Metalunans have retreated. It lands in an area Exeter calls "the Prime Sector," a label which sounds like real estate agent lingo for a prize piece of property. But this neighborhood cries Bagdad, not Beverly Hills. There are fiery meteor strikes to right of them, fiery meteor strikes to left of them. There are no Wal-Marts on Metaluna 'cause there's a target on every corner.

Exeter, Cal and Ruth take a "travel car" shuttle ride through a tunnel to the Monitor's Structure,

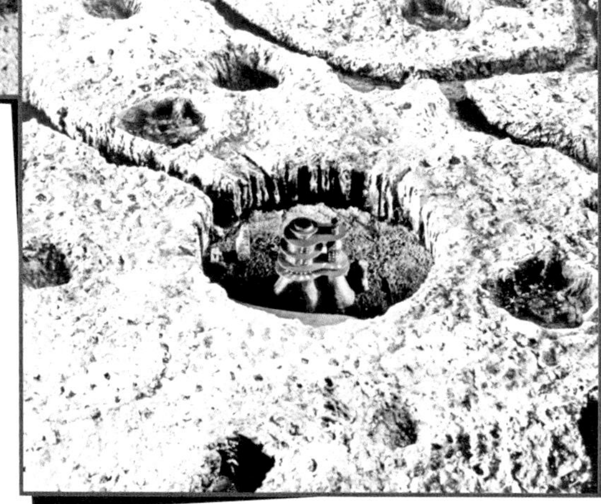

Exeter's spaceship skirts Metaluna's surface until it hovers above the opening over the subterranean Prime Sector. (Photographs courtesy C. Robert Rotter, *Glamour Girls of the Silver Screen* website.)

where the Monitor coolly greets Exeter and what he calls "Earth creatures." He announces that, with Zahgon about to launch an all-out attack, the people of Metulana must quickly begin their relocation to Earth. "A *peaceful* relocation," Exeter interjects for the benefit of a concerned-looking Cal. The Monitor, lacking Exeter's social graces, taunts Cal, uses the majestic plural ("You have wasted our time!") and orders Exeter to take the Earthlings to the Thought Transference Chamber.

Metaluna's ionization layer fails and the Zahgon fighters start making 9/11 look like a Macy's Fireworks show: Meteors explosively crash-land everywhere until the Prime Sector resembles "a giant pinball machine screaming 'Tilt!' in seven different colors" (*Time* magazine). As Exeter conducts Cal and Ruth through an open-view corridor, they are confronted by a large insect-man (Regis Parton). "This is a Mutant," Exeter explains. "We've been breeding them here for ages to do menial work." Then, sounding as if he's trying to get Cal and Ruth to like the Mutant better, he adds, "Well, actually they're similar to some of the insect life on your own planet. *Larger*, of course..." (The movie has as many clunker lines as the Zahgons have meteors.) When the structure is struck by a meteor, the corridor ceiling collapses and the Mutant is crushed. The camera makes a quick (two shots) return trip to the Monitor's Chamber to give us a glimpse at the body of the Monitor, looking a lot less high-and-mighty lying in the dark with huge hunks of rubble piled atop him, his forehead streaked with blood. It's the movie's first "feel-good" moment in many reels.

Exeter goes rogue, taking Cal and Ruth back to the spaceship. There they find the entrance blocked by a wounded Mutant (Parton again). It digs a pincer claw into Exeter before Cal clubs it into unconsciousness. With a gaping hole in his side, Exeter lifts off. Once in space, the ship's three passengers watch the Stellarscope as the intense heat of countless meteor strikes turns Exeter's planet into a blazing radioactive sun—"and yet still serving a useful purpose, I hope," says Exeter, looking at (pardon the pun) the bright side: "Yes, a sun, warming the surface of some *other* world."

While all three are in Converter Tubes, the battered, blood-covered Mutant staggers into the Control Room. Ruth's Converter Tube rises while Exeter and Cal are still trapped inside theirs, and the screaming woman, weak from the conversion, must run to escape the monster's clutches. The Henry Mancini music cue "Amorous Mutant," reminiscent of the Gill Man's *BAH-BAH-BAHHH!* theme, adds to the suspense. At last the tremendous pressure gets to the monster and he falls to the floor and dissipates into wisps of green vapor.

Millions of light years later, as the ship re-enters Earth's atmosphere, Exeter wistfully announces that he intends to explore the universe alone and "perhaps find another Metaluna"—but Cal knows that the sands of the hourglass are running out for the homeless (to say the least), injured alien. Despite Cal and Ruth's entreaties for him to join them on Earth, he directs them to return to their plane in the cargo hold.

The plane drops through the bottom of the ship and soars above an ocean coastline (America's, I hope!) as Cal and Ruth snuggle (Ruth: "Home!" Cal: "Thank God it's still here..."). Exeter puts the spaceship into a high-speed dive, air friction making the hull redden and flame. Exeter on the Pilot's Bench bravely awaits the end, the atom model to his side putting out less and less light and then going black. The ship crashes into the ocean with an explosive roar, raising a screen-filling cloud of steam.

Cast Biographies

> We felt that well-known stars would not be needed for the required cast of characters [of *This Island Earth*]. After all, science fiction, gorgeous Technicolor and special effects were going to be the real stars of our movie and we knew that from day one. Well-known stars probably would not have done the film anyway.
>
> —Joseph Newman to *Fantastic Films* magazine interviewer Al Taylor

Jeff Morrow as Exeter

In Raymond F. Jones' *This Island Earth*, the head alien is a chap who makes Cal Meacham feel as if he were in the presence of "an intellect that had seen the vast stretch of eons of time and light years of space." That character description was easier for Jones to write than it was for Universal to cast. But they rose to the challenge by selecting Jeff Morrow for the role.

A year earlier, in his first movie, Morrow had the kind of larger-than-life role at which he excelled: Paulus, the Roman tribune supervising Christ's crucifixion in 1953's biggest hit, *The Robe*. This was followed by a TV acting assignment that did much more, in terms of making people sit up and take notice: In a 1954 episode of *The United States Steel Hour*, "The Last Notch," shot in New York, he played a small-town storekeeper who gets drunk and shows off his prowess with a gun—an exhibition that makes him the target of a desperado (Richard Jaeckel) determined to be known as the fastest gun in the territory. A *Variety* reviewer called it "a tight, expertly fashioned show that had the punch and suspense of a top-rate Hollywood Western"; a subsequent *Variety* writeup laid it on even thicker, saying that it had

About 100 years ago, a knee-high Jeff Morrow loved cap guns and dressed up as both cowboys and Indians. (Photograph courtesy Lissa Morrow.)

"qualitative values on a par with the finest of the product emanating from the Hollywood pix studios or the Broadway show houses." Columnist Erskine Johnson's "In Hollywood" revealed (May 19, 1954)...

> **Jeff Morrow's gasping at the red carpet that's being rolled out for him at every studio in Hollywood since his smash performance in *U.S. Steel*'s TV show, "The Last Notch."**

...and said that Morrow "looks like James Mason and Cary Grant scrambled together."

In the mid–1950s, Morrow was under contract to Universal. The job might not have come along, said his daughter Lissa, if the studio decision-makers weren't under the misapprehension that he was much younger than he actually was (Morrow was born in 1907). And it appears that the Universal folks weren't the only people who were fooled: Fifty-two picture players were listed as candidates in the Most Promising Young Personality category in the 1955 COMPO National Audience Awards poll, and there amidst the names of scores of fresh-faced boys and girls, which included Rex Reason (and even pre-teens like Sandy Descher, the traumatized tyke from *Them!*) ... is *Jeff Morrow*! (The winner, announced at a December 1955 Beverly Hilton Grand Ballroom banquet: 24-year-old Tab Hunter.)

A Universal berth meant a relocation from their Peter Cooper Village apartment in Manhattan to California for Morrow, his actress-wife Anna Karen and little Lissa. Baseball-loving Morrow remained a fan of Dem Bums (the Brooklyn Dodgers) but, beyond that, Lissa can't say for sure that her parents missed New York. "Most people take well to California," she told me, continuing:

> **There's the occasional person who says, "No, no, I've got to be back in New York," but *they* didn't. In fact, in 1988 they came back to New York for a visit, my husband Darrell and I were driving them around the city, and my father was looking around, looking at the city. And he was going, "I don't remember New York being this *dirty*!"**
>
> **The hardest thing for my mom and dad was driving. And it never got better. This is true of almost anyone who comes from New York, especially if they're older. When you're not used to driving, and you start driving in your 30s or 40s, it's *hard*. They never were comfortable, either one of 'em, driving. Especially my father. When I used to go out to California to visit them, and I'd rent a car, or drive his car, he'd go, "Do you want to**

Native New Yorker Jeff Morrow came to the movies after decades of stage experience. In the 1930s, he trod the Broadway boards opposite some very heavy hitters. (Photograph courtesy Lissa Morrow.)

drive around a parking lot for a while before you go out on the streets?"

Watching a recent movie reminded Lissa of one of her father's fears during his acting heyday:

Darrell and I saw *Trumbo* [2015] a few months ago and Hedda Hopper is a prominent character. That made me remember that my father was terrified of her. And Hedda Hopper *liked* him! Louella Parsons did a couple of columns on him, but Hedda Hopper ... for at least four or five years, he was one of the people that she frequently wrote about. But she was just a *rabid* Republican, and he was terrified she would find out he was a Democrat!

Barbara Rush was one of the Universal contractees who went to Ireland to make the Rock Hudson starrer *Captain Lightfoot* (1955), and her memory of co-star Morrow was that he was "a *curious* man. He just loved Ireland and Dublin, and he and his wife were always out there touring. He was one of those people who likes to *learn* about things, so I liked him a lot." Faith Domergue reminisced about the *This Island Earth* star for *Fangoria* interviewer Mike Fitzgerald:

He was a man of the interior, very inside. Sweet, dear. He took his work seriously, and wouldn't budge on a point. He'd argue with the director because he thought he was right. He always stayed by himself—like a young Claude Rains.

What does Lissa think of *This Island Earth*, and her father's performance in it, today? "Gosh, it's hard to evaluate. By the standards of acting *then*, my dad was very good. But by the standards of acting *now*..." She paused, and then elaborated:

When Brando came on the scene, that changed everything. It didn't change overnight, but a change started, and by the time you got to the mid-1960s and the '70s and on, the actors were talking in a *whisper*. The men *and* the women. Very low. The acting change left my parents behind. The new type of acting was playing yourself, and the more natural you could be, the better. In my dad's day, in the theater, you didn't have any microphones. Coming from the theater, and then coming into films when [performances were] still a little more heavy-handed, made things tougher for him after the change.

As of about 1960, movie work got slow for Morrow, and some of the pictures he did make hardly added to his glories: the dirt-cheap *Harbor Lights*, shot in 1963 in Puerto Rico, and two 1971 genre flicks, the atrocious *Octaman* and the quirky horror-mystery *Legacy of Blood*, in which he and Merry Anders, cuddling in bed, die by electrocution. After TV work dropped almost to zero in the mid-1970s, he worked as an artist-commercial illustrator. Perhaps because Morrow now had a beard that gave him an Ernest Hemingway look, he was hired to do commercials for Japanese TV for Suntory Whiskey and became the "face" of the company. He told interviewers Tom and Jim Goldrup that the first commercial was shot in an elegant Malibu cliff house that faced the ocean. Only one of the six Japanese crew members spoke English—a little—and he insisted that Morrow drink the real stuff on-camera throughout the day. Morrow was blind drunk by 7:15 when they wrapped, and the Japanese weren't much concerned how he got home (35 miles away). Eventually he was driven two or three miles to a restaurant. There he spent an hour and a half sitting alone, drinking four cups of coffee, and then another hour and a half doing a lot of fast walking and deep breathing in the parking lot, before daring to undertake a 30 MPH drive home.

Jeff Morrow, right, on stage in *Jane Eyre* with (holding hands on the left) Katharine Hepburn as Jane and Dennis Hoey as Rochester.

Morrow died in 1993 at age 86. Lissa's husband Darrell Christian, managing editor of the Associated Press, brought the actor's passing to the AP's attention—and was rightly upset when the printed obit opened by making *This Island Earth*, Morrow's favorite film, sound like a career low point, with his role as "Exeter the friendly alien" characterized as "silly."

Read more about Morrow in the *Creature Walks Among Us* chapter of this book's companion volume *The Creature Chronicles*.

Faith Domergue as Dr. Ruth Adams

Faith Domergue's bio appears in the chapter on *Cult of the Cobra*.

Rex Reason as Dr. Cal Meacham

As *This Island Earth* opens, we see the first of the screenwriters' fantastic inventions: young scientist Cal Meacham. Standing beside his silver jet, this man of no known (to the audience) accomplishments nevertheless has a scrum of newspaper reporters and photographers gathered around him like paparazzi. Why? Because he was one of many scientists who just attended a Washington meeting. Yawn!

Having Cal unaccountably receive rock-star treatment may have been a story contribution by Universal's resident scaremaster William Alland, whose sci-fi flicks tended to have attractive, agreeable scientist-heroes. He said in a 1957 interview that it could be very important to "give the U.S. scientist some glamor. Make him appear dashing and important, so kids will want to be like him. … I believe films can help show how important and exciting science can be."

The actor playing Cal, big tall Rex Reason, filled the bill nicely. He was born in Germany because his parents were there on business and their return to the U.S. was delayed (a hurricane at sea was keeping all ships in port). By 15 he was 6'3" and had the basso voice we hear in his movies; at that age, these attributes made him painfully self-conscious. To remedy this, his mother had him start seeing a dramatic coach, and the coach encouraged him to go into the theater. Which, after a stint in the Army (from age 17 to 19), he did. Rex got the starring role in his very first movie, *Storm Over Tibet* (1952), because it would be filled with 1936 stock footage of a Himalayan expedition, and he resembled one of the climbers.

Listen to Reason! The actor's too-deep-to-be-true voice "stopped me from getting voiceovers, believe it or not," Reason told interviewer Marty Baumann. "They'd say, 'Too stentorian, Rex. You're not the average guy down the road.'" Pictured: Reason, left, and *Monstrous Movie Music* maestro David Schecter in November 2014, a year before the actor's death.

Signed by Universal, Reason played baddies in his first two movies there despite his Rock Hudson–like good looks. He told the *Pittsburgh Post-Gazette*'s Win Fanning that he got those "heavy" roles because his nose was curved the wrong way: "Heavies' noses usually curve outward; those of leading men generally have a slight inward curve just about at the level of the eyes." Fanning reported that he "underwent an operation to correct a deviated septum, and presto, his heavy days were behind him." According to Lucy Key Miller of the *Chicago Daily Tribune*, when Universal wanted Reason to tour the country plugging openings of *This Island Earth*, he argued with his bosses: "'Who ever heard of Rex Reason?' he demanded." At the time of the tour (yes, he went), he was 26, married, and had a 2½-year-old daughter and an adopted son.

Reason was starring in the Warners TV series *The Roaring 20's* (1960–61) when he chose to call it a day, acting-wise. In *The Creature Chronicles*, he told me he made that decision because "I realized that I did not want to live and die as an actor. Eleven years of working at breakneck speed suddenly began hitting me. I decided to bow out, to leave the business. … 'Fame and fortune' was not the answer to the quest in my life." Interviewed in the October 2016 issue of *Classic Images*, *Roaring 20's* co-star Donald May described the very moment Reason took the Show Biz Off-Ramp:

> **Toward the end of the first season of *20's*, Rex was told by a producer to wear a hat in his scenes. Rex said he did not wear a hat. The producer said all men wore some sort of soft hat in the 1920s. Rex repeated he did not wear a hat. The producer insisted, so Rex walked off the set, off the lot, and out of his contract with Warners. He never gave an explanation to me or his brother, Rhodes.**

Hatless Rex went into real estate. In his later years he hit the autograph show trail. Eventually he felt he was too old for the travel and toil, hung up his Sharpies and began turning down invitations. A bad fall in a local grocery store put a hurtin' on him, and this was soon followed by other medical problems including skin cancer, which he was told would spread if he didn't take care of it. He decided *not* to take care of it. Some time later, he made the same decision about bladder cancer; in November 2015, about a month after finding out he had it, he passed away from it in his Walnut, California, home at age 86. In a brochure handed out at his memorial service, his bio ends with, "Rex spent his life in discovery of beauty and truth. There is no doubt he rests within its arms."

Read much more about Reason in the *Creature Walks Among Us* chapter of this book's companion volume *The Creature Chronicles*.

Lance Fuller as Brack

Lance Fuller (real name: Ronald V. Johnson) was born in Somerset, Kentucky, on December 6, 1928. In a 1990s interview, he claimed that he came to Hollywood to compete for the role of 11-year-old Jody in MGM's *The Yearling* (a movie ultimately not shot until 1945–46, by which time Fuller would have been too old). He also said that he made his first screen appearances as an extra in early '40s movies, playing (for instance) a torch-wielding villager in *Frankenstein Meets the Wolf Man* (1943). I doubt that Universal hired 13-year-olds to play their torch-wielding villagers. His claim of working steadily in '40s movies is contradicted by a 1950s fan magazine article which says that during those years he was a ranch hand (until he was gored by a bull) and that he worked in the construction business and "made a small fortune." You now have your choice of deciding whether he was a 13-year-old movie torch-wielder or a wealthy teenage construction business mogul ... or disbelieving both.

In Lance Fuller's pre-movie days, he reportedly joined every little theater group within scouting distance of Hollywood. His motto was "Stardom or bust."

In 1950, *Variety* columnist Mike Connolly reported that "New Orleans blueblood" Fuller was being tested for a term contract at MGM. Two years later, Sheilah Graham wrote in *Variety*, "How downbeat dialogue can you get. Lance Fuller, discussing his career with Selene Walters (at the Cap'ns Table)—'Several things don't look so BAD for me.'" I don't know whether or not, at this point (1952), he'd ever appeared in a single movie, even as an extra, since we only have his word for it.

As a Universal contractee, he played uncredited parts in several 1953 movies, plus an 11th-billed role in *Taza, Son of Cochise*. The papers reported that on September 16, 1953, he filed a Federal Court petition in bankruptcy, listing assets of $283 and liabilities of $12,860. Included in the liabilities was $1200 in taxes due the federal government for 1949–50. The public humiliation continued when his actress-wife (since 1951) Joi Lansing sought a divorce, alleging that he gambled all their money away in Las Vegas and brought "all sorts of undesirable characters" into their home and embarrassed her in front of them. Fuller's longtime friend, actress Kathleen Hughes, told me that another reason the marriage ended was because he wanted to have sex once a year. (She got that "TMI" news flash directly from Fuller!) In the mid–1950s, gossip columnists regularly made Fuller and Hughes out to be lovebirds, but Hughes said that those stories were untrue publicity plants, and emphatically insisted that she and the asexual Fuller were "just friends—never romantic at *all*!"

Fuller played some of his best parts in producer Benedict Bogeaus' brightly Technicolored movies: In the Western *Cattle Queen of Montana* (1954) with Barbara Stanwyck, he was a university-educated, peace-craving Blackfoot Indian whose close friendship with Stanwyck, misconstrued, leads to strife. *Pearl of the South Pacific* (1955), a South Seas "goona-goona drama" (*New York Times*), found Fuller, the son of an uncharted island's high priest, locking lips with sarong-clad Virginia Mayo and fighting a lagoon-bottom octopus. Columnist Frank Morriss, a *Pearl* set visitor, poked fun at something recently written about Fuller (probably *by* Fuller): "[He's] the most classic masculine beauty since John Barrymore, perhaps even handsomer and with greater magnetism than Jack possessed."

Then Fuller's career went into a state of schlock as he began turning up in all kinds of off-brand pictures. In his first of several for producer Alex Gordon, *Apache Woman* (1955), he plays the title character's (Joan Taylor) college-

Jeff Morrow's Exeter had his softer side but not Fuller's born-to-be-bad Brack, who holds this island's Earthlings in contempt. (Photograph courtesy John Antosiewicz.)

educated, book-reading brother, a half-breed who's all-crazy.[13] Fuller played the hero in Gordon's Bridey Murphy-inspired *The She-Creature* (1956) but his too-intense, flashing-eyes performance instead made him look crazy and creepy. He added more rogues to his résumé via Gordon's *Girls in Prison*, *Runaway Daughters* (both 1956) and *Voodoo Woman* (1957). Returning to the horror-reincarnation genre, Fuller was the leading man in *The Bride and the Beast* (1958) as a big game hunter newly wed to Charlotte Austin, the reincarnation of a gorilla. Fuller is especially terrible in the movie, but surely the Ed Wood story and dialogue had a lot to do with it. At the end, when Austin deserts him to live in the jungle *with* gorillas, some viewers probably thought she was trading up. In Anthony Mann's *God's Little Acre* (1958), playing one of Robert Ryan's sons, he was yet another easy-to-hate scoundrel, which seemed to be the one type he played well.

Throughout Fuller's career, the Hollywood trades would regularly report that he had been signed to starring roles in various movies, some of them scheduled to be shot in exotic, far-off locales. No other cast members would ever be mentioned, you can't find these movie titles on IMDb or anywhere else, and the other people mentioned in these news items (writers, producers, etc.) also seem to be non-existent in the movie business. In other words, it looks as though Fuller and/or his publicist liked to write fictional publicity plants. In his 1990s interview, he also told the fairy tales that director Michael Curtiz wanted to remake some of his classic Errol Flynn movies with Fuller starring, that he was up for the male lead in Warner Brothers' deluxe *Helen of Troy* (1956), that he turned down starring parts in many Warners TV series, etc.

Kathleen Hughes couldn't remember Fuller ever having any job other than acting. If that's true, then time weighed heavy on his hands starting in 1960: After that point, he played in just a few TV episodes and movies, sometimes uncredited, and that was *it*. Circa 1968 he dropped in on Alex Gordon at 20th Century-Fox, wearing makeup on his eyes and face and acting strangely. Around Halloween of that year, Fuller walked down Beverly Glen Boulevard hitting parked cars with a three-foot iron pipe and announcing, "I am Jesus Christ! I am God!" Police officer Thomas Blaire arrived on the scene, satisfied himself that Fuller was neither the Father nor His son and moved in with his nightstick. Fuller used the pipe to knock it from his hand. As Blaire fell, he fired his gun and made it count: "Fuller was taken to UCLA Medical Center in critical condition with a gunshot wound in his right arm and chest," United Press reported. Kathleen Hughes said the incident came after Fuller, a migraine sufferer, had a three-day ordeal with lots of medicine and no shut-eye. The policeman's bullet went through both lungs, according to Hughes, who said Fuller was never the same after that. Hughes remembers another occasion when Fuller "overserved" himself meds-wise and sideswiped a number of cars. That time, Fuller's mother had Hughes accompany them to court.

Throughout the 1970s and into the 1980s, Mr. "Stardom or Bust" regularly took out stamp-sized *Variety* ads saying that he'd just completed work in this movie or that—movies in which I bet he was an extra, if he was in them at all—and was again available. In a 1971 ad, he called himself a "socialite actor." A 1978 ad proclaimed that he was "popular with today's Fitzgerald jet set."

Fuller lived in a house with his mother until she got sick and needed to move into a nursing home. He was eventually told that the house was going to be sold in order to pay for her nursing home care, so he had to vacate. Hughes, entering the house for the first time (along with other people) to help him remove his belongings, was confronted with "the most awful sight I'd ever seen":

> **It was shocking, disgusting, full of trash, dog poop everywhere, possibly no running water, the roof so leaky part of the ceiling had collapsed onto a couch. All that was salvageable out of the whole house, that I can remember, were a few clothes, a record player and a few records, things like that. The elements got most of the rest. It was beyond your wildest imagination, how terrible it was.**

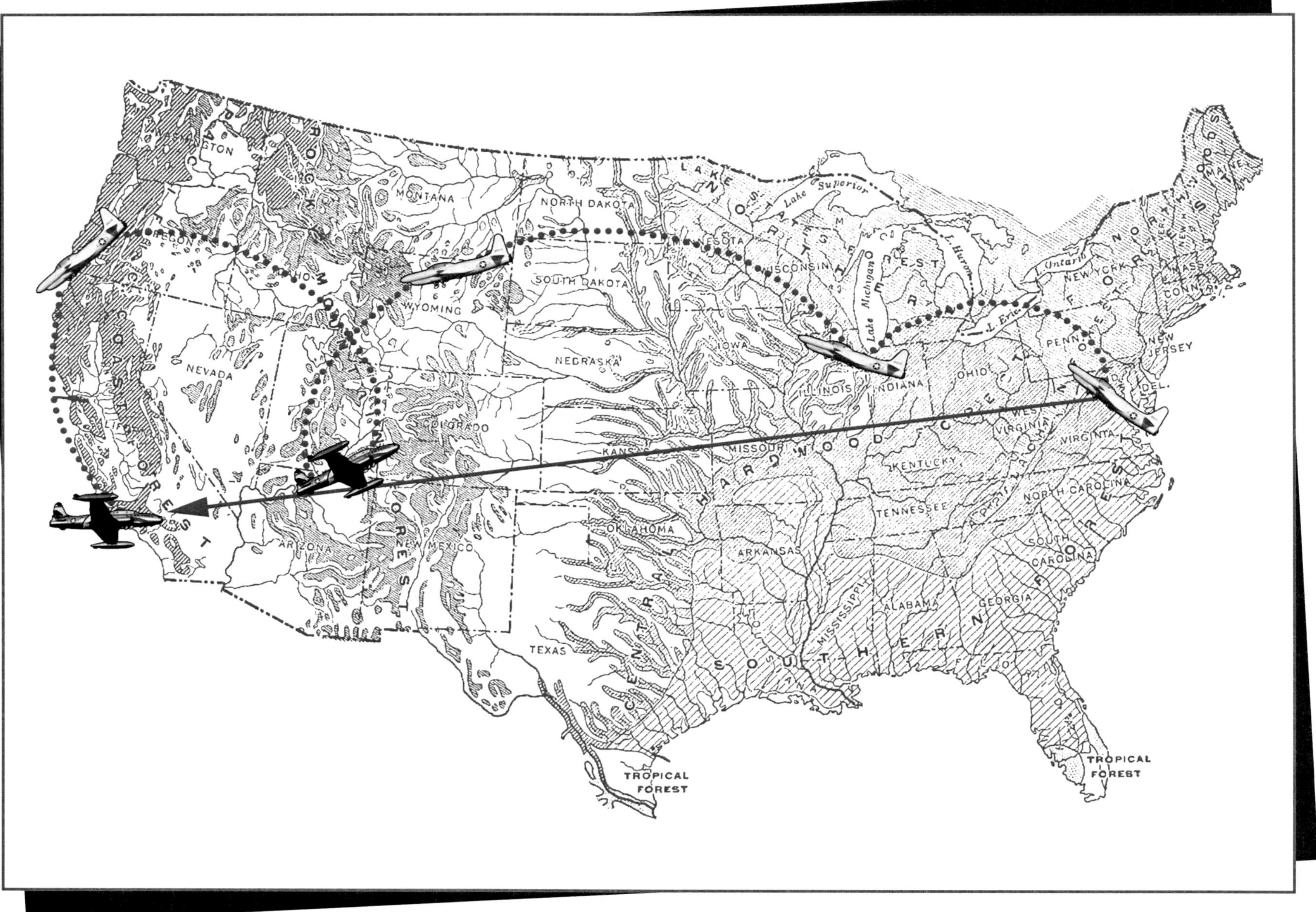

This Island Earth begins with Cal flying a jet from Washington, D.C., to Los Angeles, his cross-country progress indicated by stock footage shots of Chicago, the Rockies, the Grand Canyon and Mount Shasta. Look at the straight line he should have flown and, going by the stock footage, the route he did take. No wonder Joe Wilson, waiting for Cal in L.A., gripes, "That's my boss. The only guy in the world who can travel by jet and still be late." (Artwork courtesy Mary Runser.)

Through the Screen Actors Guild, he was put up in various motels and then in nursing homes and/or assisted living places. By this time his old Hollywood pals had either deserted him or shed their mortal coils, making Hughes his only friend. She visited him about once a month and helped him run his various errands (post office, bank, etc.) and paid for his haircuts. Sick and "kind of crazy" (per Kathleen), he ended up in Longwood Manor Convalescent Hospital; look up its online reviews for yourself, this bio is depressing enough already. Paralyzed on one side, one hand resembling a claw, he spent all his time in bed, joining in none of the facility's activities.

After multiple trips to a hospital, Fuller at last decided that he'd suffered enough and, the next time hospital care was required, he refused to go. He died a few days before Christmas 2001, at age 73. An Army vet (Korea), he's buried at Riverside National Cemetery.

Production

The shooting of *This Island Earth* got underway on Universal's Stage 16 on Saturday morning, January 30, 1954, scheduled for 23 days of first unit production and three days of second unit. The two actors working on opening day were Robert Nichols and "Bart Roberts"—the latter a name dreamed up by Universal because they thought the *real* name of their contractee Rex Reason was "too theatrical." In his previous Universals *Taza, Son of Cochise* and *Yankee Pasha*, Reason was billed as Roberts and then, according to a June 1955 Hedda Hopper column, the actor "blew up" at Universal and insisted on being billed under his own name in the future. The studio acceded *and*, wrote Hopper, even changed BART ROBERTS to REX REASON on the as-yet-unreleased *This Island Earth*.

The first two days of principal photography took place on Cal Meacham's Ryberg laboratory set. By 9:30 that a.m., they'd gotten their first shot: Cal and Joe entering the lab, with Cal beelining to the atomic reactor. Apparently one of the pieces of scientific equipment to be seen on screen still had manufacturers' logos on it because, per the Production Report, a half-hour was lost "Painting names off of mch. [machine]." You may recognize one large apparatus as a regular in Universal Horrors of the previous decade, including *Man Made Monster* (1941), *Frankenstein Meets the Wolf Man* (1943) and *House of Dracula* (1945). Most of this lab scene was in the can by quitting time, including Cal testing the bead condenser on the voltage rheostat and trying to pierce it with a diamond drill.

Day 2 began with a hallway shot of Cal and Joe approaching the lab door; then unbilled bit player Coleman Francis had his time in the spotlight, playing the expressman delivering the Unit 16 catalogue. Francis went on to become the triple-threat (accent on "threat") writer-producer-director of such trashterpieces as *The Beast of Yucca Flats* (1961) and *Night Train to Mundo Fine* (1966). On the lab set, Cal and Joe perused the catalogue, examined and began opening the Unit 16 packing cases, and conversed amidst the multitude of interocitor parts. At 5:20, after getting a few shots for the assembling-the-interocitor montage, the crew began preparing to shoot Faith Domergue's wardrobe test on that same stage: For ten minutes (5:55 to 6:05) she posed in two changes of clothes.

The next morning, February 2, Groundhog Day, *This Island Earth* crew members could see their long shadows at Metropolitan Airport (now Van Nuys Airport), where they photographed the Bolling Field and Ryberg airfield scenes.[14] One of their first orders of business was to get a shot of Cal's flamed-out jet safely landing on the Ryberg runway (the green glow would of course be added later). At 10:30, while preparing to shoot the movie's opening scene (Cal interacting with the Washington, D.C., reporters and photographers), there was a hold-up as the moviemakers scrambled to find a background that could pass for the flat-as-a-pancake area around our nation's capital. The solution was to park a large Air National Guard gas truck behind the actors, to hide the mountains on the horizon. When watching the movie's Ryberg airfield scenes, look at the distant mountains you *would* have seen in the Washington, D.C., scene had that truck not been there.

As the day progressed, there were minor delays caused by plane noise and the failure of a photographer's camera to flash. (Why do the photographers use flashbulbs in broad daylight anyway?) Truth be told, this scene, which establishes nothing but the fact that Cal is a scientist, gets the movie off to a shaky start. Even worse: Five times in this 75-second "Cal Meets the Press" scene, unfunny quips result in gales of phony-sounding laughter that get more irritating each time.

"Remember those opening shots, at the side of an airplane?" William Alland asked me. "That whole thing was so amateurishly shot, it was unbelievable. Go back and look at it."[15]

Metropolitan Airport was the home of the Air National Guard's 195th Fighter Squadron and, due to their proximity to Hollywood, they regularly heard from moviemakers preparing military pictures that required airplanes and flyers. Standing in for Rex Reason in *This Island Earth*'s jet scenes was Larry Powell, who had recently been promoted from Air National Guard captain to major. It's a small world (or, more appropriately, it's a small Island Earth) after all: At the airport, Powell recognized Rex and introduced himself and they had a reunion: When Powell was a teenager in the late 1930s and ran around with other kids his own age in Glendale, two others in their group were the several-years-younger Rex and his identical brother Rhodes Reason!

A veteran of World War II's 339th Fighter Group and an Air National Guardsman since 1946, Powell did his first "Hollywood flying" in 1948's *Fighter Squadron*: Eight Air National Guard B-51s were painted black and had German crosses put on them, and Powell and other airmen piloted them. In 1953, the 195th started changing to jets; Cal's jet in *This Island Earth* is a T-33, one of two that the 195th had in early 1954. "At the time that *This Island Earth* was being made, we were trying to get funds to build our Airmen's Officers' Club," Powell told me. "So I charged Universal $500 a day, and we worked with them for three days [February 2, 4 and 5]." In the movie, it's Powell at the controls in every scene of the jet in motion. When the jet buzzes the camera, "I probably wasn't doing more than 300, in order to keep it on film. If I'd gone much faster, Universal would have had to show it in slow motion." He also did a roll in the jet, "probably at about 150 feet. But I was pulling up, so there was no danger." According to a Universal report on this second unit work, Powell also did a loop-the-loop, but that footage didn't get into the movie. Powell said, "As I remember, I did a whole series of loops and Immelmans and things like that, that they could pick and choose from, and use what they wanted."[16]

On location in Thousand Oaks, Rex Reason is made to look muddy and wet for his out-of-the-lake, running-across-the-field scene. (Photograph courtesy Ronald V. Borst/Hollywood Movie Posters.)

As an aside: I bought Larry Powell a DVD of *This Island Earth*, thinking he'd enjoy seeing his jet scenes, conveniently (for him) all in the first few minutes. But he watched the whole movie. His verdict:

"It really wasn't much of a picture!"

February 3 again found the cast and crew on location, this time at Janss Airfield in Thousand Oaks, with Faith Domergue and Reason enacting the scene where Cal, arriving in Georgia via the mystery plane, is met by Ruth. The filmmakers spent the rest of the 3rd on the day-for-night scene where Cal and Ruth, escaping from Exeter's Mansion, run to the courier plane.

That day's Production Reports includes the names of pilots Paul Franklin and Dianna Bixby; presumably one flew Exeter's mystery plane (a C-47) and the other flew the courier plane (a Stinson), but the paperwork doesn't indicate who did what. However, Larry Powell told me that the C-47 was owned by Bixby so it's safe to assume that's the plane she flew, which makes Franklin the Stinson pilot. Aviation buffs with long memories may recall Dianna Cyrus Bixby from the publicity she regularly received back in the day. Her first husband John

The moving camera car gets a neat shot of Rex Reason and Faith Domergue sprinting across the airfield. Cal and Ruth's clothes have a bit of mud on them but look completely dry, which is strange since, in the movie, they were submerged in a lake just seconds earlier. (Photograph courtesy Ronald V. Borst/Hollywood Movie Posters.)

Cyrus taught her to fly; she was 22 when she was widowed by the Battle of the Bulge. In 1948, Dianna was newly remarried to Robert Bixby, an air freight line operator, when with great press fanfare she began to prepare for a solo round-the-world flight in her converted two-engine British Mosquito bomber. (She hoped to do it in 70 hours, to break the record of 73 and change.) Mechanical problems necessitated postponements, and by April 1950 when she finally took to the skies, the plan had changed: Husband Robert was at the controls, the pretty brunette (now the mother of their seven-month-old daughter) in the co-pilot's seat. The husband-and-wife flying team alternated piloting the plywood plane until a blown gasket stranded them in Calcutta. Next came three more years of bread-and-butter flying (their air freight service), and then the Bixbys announced their intention to enter the 12,207-mile England-to-New Zealand air race. This time it was financial problems that kept them earthbound: For the twin-engine Douglas DC-3 they intended to fly, gas alone would have cost $10,000-plus.

The interocitor gets loads of build-up, so when Cal and Joe (Robert Nichols, left, and Rex Reason) get to the end of the laborious process of building one and it's merely a color TV screen on a two-ton chassis, they ought to be as let-down as we in the audience are. (Photograph courtesy Ronald V. Borst/Hollywood Movie Posters.)

If at first you don't succeed, fly, fly again: In February 1954, just two days after diminutive (5'2") Dianna piloted a plane in *This Island Earth*, she again announced her intent to break the round-the-world record, this time solo and, with the Mosquito bomber newly souped-up, in just 60 hours ("It should be a cinch"). She attributed her dream of setting a global speed flight record to her lifelong admiration for Amelia Earhart. The need for modifications to the plane (plus some weather-related considerations) grounded her yet again.

One day in early January '55 the Bixbys left in separate planes for their ranch near La Paz, Mexico. Dianna, flying a twin-engine A-20 bomber, ran into some bad weather and radioed her husband that she was low on fuel and would attempt an emergency landing. Then she pulled an Amelia Earhart and went missing. After a search, the wreckage of her plane was sighted in shallow water near Loreto, Baja California Sur, and a Navy diver soon brought up the broken body of the 32-year-old mother of two. "If she'd had ten more gallons of gas," said a Coast Guard co-pilot, "she would have made it." It was later revealed that, just days earlier, she had ordered the plane's 230-gallon auxiliary fuel tank removed because she'd made several La Paz trips without ever using it.[17]

On February 4, the *This Island Earth* troupe was back at Metropolitan Airport, getting various shots of Cal in the jet cockpit plus footage of his instrument panel. After the lunch break, Robert Nichols got busy: His character Joe arrived at the airfield via Jeep; hustled up the control tower steps; and ran down them to get back to his Jeep.[18] In the late afternoon, Reason and Nichols returned to Stage 16 to get the shot of Cal and Joe putting the finishing touches on the interocitor and reacting to the voice that unexpectedly emanates from it. According to the Production Report, Jeff Morrow was on the set, his participation listed as "Voice Only." It seems strange that someone felt that the actor whose disembodied voice would be heard at that point in the finished film should be present on the set (presumably to deliver Exeter's dialogue), but it looks like that's what happened.

Morrow was again on the Stage 16 lab set the next day for the scene of Cal and Exeter conversing via interocitor. This time he is not listed as "Voice Only" but the Production Report shot descriptions make it clear that, again, he did not appear on camera at any point. As Exeter and Cal talk, Joe sneaks a photo or two of Exeter on the interocitor screen; Joe otherwise has little to do in this scene. But perhaps he passed some comments that landed on the cutting room floor. In the script, Joe occasionally makes his presence felt during the Exeter-Cal confab, giving Exeter "a mutinous look" (when Exeter comments on Joe's camera) and coming out with some snide remarks:

- When Exeter mentions his group's "superior technical knowledge," Joe wisecracks, "That's what I like about him—his modesty,"

- and when Exeter asks Cal to join his "team," Joe says, "Tell him where to get off, Cal."

Maybe Exeter, despite his pleasant and polite bearing, resents Joe's rudeness: He tells photo-snapping Joe that his camera will "pick up nothing but black fog ... images on the interocitor don't register on film," but when he zaps the catalogue and interocitor blueprints, he gratuitously zaps the camera. Payback?

In *Cult Movies* magazine, SF-fantasy novelist John De Chancie wrote of seeing *This Island Earth* as a kid at a Pittsburgh drive-in and described his memory of the interocitor in operation:

> **When this souped-up color television finally comes online, its screen gives forth with a veritable Crayola Super-Size crayon set of mauves and puces and magentas and cyans, enough to elicit a gasp of wonder from my mother.... It looked so ... modern, so gorgeously hi-tech. And so colorful. [The moviemakers] bathe our 1950s eyeballs in pastel light.**

For the shot where Cal tries to prevent the interocitor's destruction by pulling the power cable, Rex Reason does a nice job of pretending to get an electrical shock and takes a backwards fall against a wall. The movie's Cal, leaping into action to cut off the power, is—at this particular moment, anyway—brighter than the novel's Cal, who unsuccessfully tries to save *his* overheating, smoking interocitor with fire extinguishers.

At 6:30 the crew began preparing to shoot wardrobe, makeup and hair tests of Lance Fuller, who would play Brack. The actor was first photographed wearing his Metaluna outfit, then a suit. His refusal to bleach his eyebrows necessitated a makeup change, a second test *and*, one would assume, some head-scratching over the fact that this unheard-of actor had dug in his heels. At that moment in time, the former extra and bit player had been seen by audiences in exactly one movie where he did enough to be noticed, *Taza, Son of Cochise*, which had premiered just days earlier. Eleventh-billed, he played a craven, Indian-killing cavalry lieutenant; the redskins get their revenge during an attack on a fort, making Fuller a pincushion with their arrows and, yes, lances.

Returning on Saturday, February 6, to Stage 16's Ryberg lab set, Reason and Nichols enacted more of the scene in which their characters interact with Exeter on the interocitor. After lunch there was shooting on Stage 17, which was filled with fog for the eerie episode of Cal and Joe arriving in Joe's Jeep at the Ryberg airfield and reacting to the appearance of Exeter's plane. Keeping the amount of fog in the scene consistent was one of the moviemakers' challenges. The movie Cal seems to be rather an ingenuous soul, looking forward to the trip with keen anticipation, unlike the novel Cal who frets about the fact that he can't be sure that the Peace Engineers' motives truly are altruistic. From the novel: "With his past knowledge of human nature, [Cal] was more inclined to credit the possibility that he was being led into some Sax Rohmer melodrama."

Studio contractee Susan Cabot was on the Stage 17 set that day as well as on Monday, February 7, when more mystery plane footage was shot. Her participation is listed on the production paperwork as "Voice Only"; in the movie the voice of Exeter welcomes Cal aboard the plane but in the script it's a woman's voice, so Cabot must have been on hand to deliver those lines.[19]

More of the mystery plane interior scene was shot on the morning and early afternoon of the 8th plus, also on Stage 17, part of the scene of Ruth meeting Cal on Exeter's runway. After lunch, cast and crew reconvened on Stage 21 for the Ryberg airfield control tower scene with Robert Nichols as Joe and Robert B. Williams as Webb, awaiting Cal's arrival. It was Nichols' last day on the movie and Russell Johnson's first: On Stage 16, he, Reason and Domergue played the Exeter's Mansion basement scene of Cal, Ruth and Carlson making their way from the elevator to Cal's lab. Between 4:55 and 5:10, Jeff Morrow did a wardrobe, makeup and hair test.

Nearly all of February 9 was spent on the "Cal's Lab at Exeter's" set shooting the scene in which Ruth, Cal and

Cal (Rex Reason, middle) positions the lead slab in front of "the prying eyes of Exeter's interocitor" before his secret conversation with Steve (Russell Johnson) and Ruth (Faith Domergue). Just because the interocitor can't see them doesn't mean it can't *hear* them. Cal's "slick" trick wouldn't have thwarted eavesdropper Exeter; it wouldn't have thwarted Thomas Edison in 1878!

Carlson tensely feel each other out, then decide to work together. To the surprise of probably no one, the cat in the scene was somewhat less than a consummate actor, creating some brief delays. Toward the end of the day, they got a start on the scene where Exeter (on the interocitor screen) tries to put a scare into Cal by piercing the suspended lead slab with Red Rays. (Before the Red Rays are unleashed, notice the funky-looking round spot smack in the middle of the slab, exactly where the hole *will* appear.) It took most of the next day to finish that scene, and to shoot the other scenes set in this lab.

Early on the morning of February 11, brandy flowed on the *This Island Earth* set—or at least whatever passes for brandy in movies. Returning yet again to Stage 21 where they had shot the mystery plane and control tower scenes, they tackled the dining room scene with Exeter at the head of the table as he, Brack and the scientists finish a meal which Cal tells Exeter "was even more perfect than you promised." As Cal speaks that line, notice that the lady scientist across the table from him is putting her cup down onto a saucer with i-n-f-i-n-i-t-e slowness, obviously determined not to let the "clink" be heard on the soundtrack and perhaps spoil the take.

Exeter's office, a set you should recognize: It was Irving Thalberg's office in *Man of a Thousand Faces* (1957) and Dr. Jekyll's library in *Abbott and Costello Meet Dr. Jekyll and Mr. Hyde* (1953). In the latter, a bookcase revolves to provide access to Jekyll's lab; here it revolves to reveal an interocitor. From left: Jeff Morrow, Rex Reason, Faith Domergue. (Photograph courtesy Ronald V. Borst/ Hollywood Movie Posters.)

The lady in question, Lizalotta Valesca, cast as scientist Marie Pitchner, did spoil a take by blowing a line—one of just two that she has in the movie—and I'd like to know who *noticed* that she blew it, as she spoke it in Finnish. Universal's other movie of the decade with an outer space setting, *Abbott and Costello Go to Mars* (1953), had a cast loaded sky-high with beauty contest winners, and *This Island Earth* had one too, in Valesca. Unfortunately for girl-watcher Monster Kids, she was Miss Finland ... of 1930. (Wellll ... *she* said she was. With my limited Internet skills and my non-existent knowledge of the Finnish language, I couldn't verify that.) Valesca called herself a part-time movie actress even though her next-to-nothing part in *This Island Earth* appears to be her only credit. She also called herself an expert on preserving one's health and maintaining one's attractiveness, penning the 1961 book *More Than Beauty* and giving lectures and private lessons on the subject. Her beauty tips included such lulus as

> **Cover the face with honey. Pat it vigorously. Wash it off with cold water. A mask of honey and bran flour mixed with a few drops of water may be put on the face for 20 minutes [and] rinsed off with cold water for another beauty treatment.**

Washing her face in milk and pure cold rain water was also part of Valesca's routine. On at least one occasion, however, the old gal *did* make good sense, saying that the questions and requests for advice she received from oldtimers had led her to the conclusion that people encourage old age by doing nothing to prevent it.

After a change of clothes for some of the principal actors, the moviemakers did some shooting in the living room. Work resumed on that set on February 12, including the shot of Exeter stepping out of his office to greet the just-arrived Cal. In the movie, this is the first time we see Exeter in the flesh (i.e., not on the interocitor). In the script, the scene description calls for Exeter to wear "a grave smile" here but Jeff Morrow's eyes dance with fellowship as he stands beside his open office door with an air of invitation that'd be the envy of any customer-starved shopkeeper. Whenever possible, the actor gives viewers a glimpse of the human spirit behind the scientific mask, rather than playing the "ornery" Exeter with which he was initially presented. In the documentary *This Island Earth: 2½ Years in the Making* (2013), Robert Skotak says,

> **Both Bill Alland and Jeff Morrow wanted to push *that* aspect of it, to say, "[Exeter] has been on the Earth, he's lived with humans, he's *learned* something, he's learned some of our morality. Basically, he's found a soul."**

Morrow enriches just about every scene he's in, and his performance adds greatly to *This Island Earth*'s appeal.

In the afternoon on February 12, the company moved into Exeter's adjoining office, where they shot all the rest of that day, the whole of Saturday, February 13, and the morning of Monday, February 15. Activity on that set ended with the scene of Brack at the interocitor, directing Red Rays at Cal, Ruth and Carlson's fleeing station wagon. Also on the 15th, they completed the mystery plane interiors and got a start on shooting the Metaluna travel car scenes (the trip from the spaceship to the Monitor's HQ). Imperfect matte work (or whatever) gives Exeter, Cal and Ruth those dreaded blue outlines, which takes away from the scene. Their blowing hair enhances it.[20] Exeter points out a few ruined structures along the way ("Our educational complexes, now rubble ... over there was a recreation center."), Jeff Morrow letting his voice quaver just a bit, presumably because the script specifies that Exeter has "a haunted look in his eyes" as he surveys the ravaged landscape. In the script but not the movie, Exeter goes on to say:

EXETER
Even before I left for your earth they were standing—monuments to the greatness of our civilization.

CAL
What's happened to the people?—Where are they hiding?

EXETER
(a flash of anger)
We have but a few left, Meacham. And they're on duty—

When Morrow died in 1993, *Classic Images* columnist-obit writer Boyd Magers reached out to Faith Domergue for a quote, and she sang the actor's praises. She said that, despite the sometimes slow pace of shooting,

Jeff was quiet, never out of patience, and when our director would lose patience, Jeff never lost his concentration, nor his soft intenseness, nor raise his voice even if voices were raised all around him. He was a little hard to know, not having the usual lightness motion picture actors cultivate on the set. I would say his character was intense, highly intelligent, but he did have an inner glow that showed in his very black eyes. He had beautiful black hair also, but he wore in that film that yellowish-white wig, and had the raised forehead that all members of the "alien planet" had. The wig and forehead took an enormous amount of time to apply in the morning, and my hairdresser and makeup man would have been working on Jeff at least an hour in makeup before I arrived in the wee small hours of the morning. ... He gave the character a wonderful tragic, sad quality, almost Hamlet-like, and it was perfect for an alien of great spirit whose own planet and beings were doomed to total destruction. ... He was an actor who made an impression on me, and I enjoyed working with him, and did not mind his reserve.

"Jeff Morrow was, to me, *the* professional," Rex Reason told me. He continued,

He was very stimulating to watch and to work with. He was "in" his part, and he had a lot of respect for his fellow actors. And so as a result of this, I was better: He was "high," and this called forth every bit of my attention and involvement as an actor. His few remarks to me during the shooting helped me. He said, "You know, you have looks, Rex, but if you think that you do have looks, it's going to take away from your acting. You're the kind of person who's going to have to work a little harder." I did the best work I knew how on *This Island Earth*, and I think I held up my end of the picture to his satisfaction. He is to be categorized as an "actor's actor."

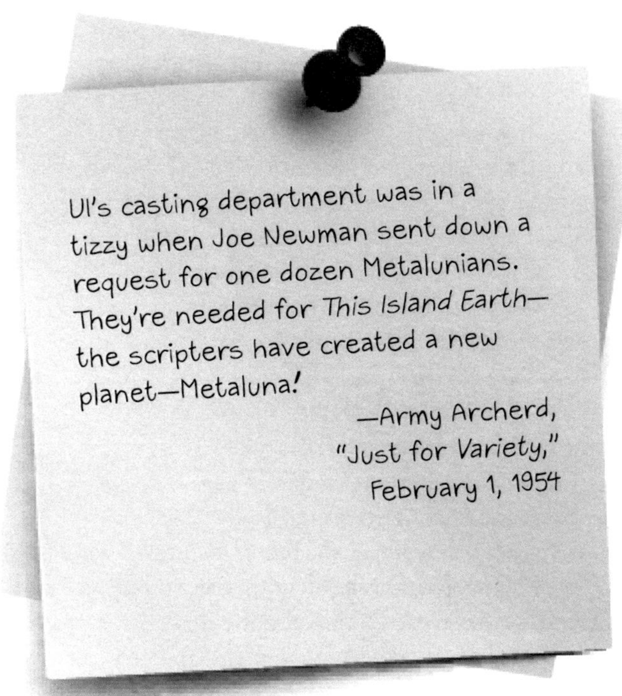

On Tuesday, February 16, 1954, the fifteenth day of production, just past the halfway point, the cast and crew left Earth behind: Shooting of Spaceship Control Room scenes on Stage 6 began with the Earth-to-Metaluna half of the journey. In the first shot of the day, Cal, Ruth and a Metalunan escort exit the elevator car, the two Earthlings getting their initial look at the Control Room and clashing with Exeter. When Exeter says that they're going "to a planet *we* call Metaluna," Cal responds, "Metaluna? There's no such planet in the solar system!," Cal unwilling to believe that another planet's inhabitants would give it a name different than the one we gave it on Earth. (This even after Exeter stressed the "we" in "a planet *we* call Metaluna"!)

A bit past noon, another important cast member set his insectoid foot on the set as test footage of stuntman Regis Parton in his Metaluna Mutant outfit was photographed. In the first of two shots, he wore a belt, in the other, no belt. (Two days later, February 18, on Stage 17, away from the first unit, more Parton-Mutant test footage was shot.)

Attack of the 50 Foot Faith? No, just the actress posing with a small replica of the spaceship Control Room set. (Photograph courtesy Ronald V. Borst/Hollywood Movie Posters.)

The 16th was also the first of four days of *This Island Earth* employment for Richard Deacon, later made famous via his TV role as Mel Cooley on *The Dick Van Dyke Show* (1961–66); he plays the spaceship pilot. (As musicologist David Schecter kiddingly points out, "He was probably hired for the role because he came with his own extended forehead.") When the spaceship is soaring through what Exeter calls Earth's "thermal barrier," outside its large windows we see clouds of steam lazily wafting straight up; but in intercut shots of the exterior of the hurtling, red-hot spaceship, all steam is being left in its wake at a jillion miles per hour.

From the "Don't believe everything you read" department: That same day, February 16, *Variety* ran the news item "Femme Flyer Lensing Jet *Island* Footage":

> **Dianna Cyrus Bixby, femme speed pilot who yesterday announced she will take a crack at global speed record, will helm a special jet camera plane for air sequences in *This Island Earth*, UI reported last night. Jet scenes will be shot at speeds exceeding 550 mph, and at an altitude of more than three miles.**

By announcing that Bixby would fly the jet, Universal was trading on her latest "15 minutes of fame" to get some publicity for *This Island Earth*; this was the sort of thing that Hollywood studios routinely did (and no doubt still *do*). The truth was that the movie's jet sequences had already been shot, with Larry Powell at the controls. As far as I can tell, Bixby's entire contribution to *This Island Earth* was to fly the mystery plane—and that footage, too, was already in the can. (Maybe she flew the plane that got the climactic coastline shots—but you wouldn't need a jet plane for *that*.)

February 17 and 18 were devoted to shooting the first Converter Tubes scene: With a female Metalunan operating the controls, Brack and two other Metalunans, and then Cal and Ruth, get the treatment. When this scene plays in the movie, it's the first time we're seeing Reason and Domergue in their Metalunan jumpsuits which, according to Hollywood columnist-set visitor Harrison Carroll, were made of blue wool.[21] The sweat we see on the faces of actors in the Converter Tubes may have been real: As Carroll wrote in a March 1954 column,

> **Most uncomfortable pair of actors on a Hollywood sound stage this week are Faith Domergue and Bart Roberts.**
>
> **I go out to the *This Island Earth* set at U-I and find the two of them trying to do a scene while encased in plastic tubes…**
>
> **The tubes are just big enough to contain their standing figures.**
>
> **To keep them from stifling, air is being pumped into the tubes from above, but a battery of arc lights is leveled on the hapless performers.**

Exeter's spaceship comes equipped with just three Converter Tubes so obviously the conversions can only be done three at a time, which means that for quite a long stretch of the space trip, passengers metabolically set for Earth co-mingle with passengers metabolically set for Metaluna. You'd think that would present a problem for one group or the other or both. But nobody beefs, so apparently that *is* Good Science. From left: Rex Reason, Faith Domergue, Jeff Morrow, unidentified actor.

When filming commenced, Carroll saw the actors' lips move but couldn't hear them. He learned from a set worker that there were microphones at the tops of the tubes. The actors wore tiny earplugs that were actually small receiving sets that allowed them to hear instructions spoken into a microphone. Carroll got a demonstration moments later:

> **[Joseph] Newman suddenly starts talking to the actors.**
> **"Look over to the left," he says. "You are watching the navigational screen in the spaceship. You see a comet approaching. It's coming very close. It looks as if it is going to hit the ship. No, it misses."**
> **… [A] creamy looking vapor starts to fill the tube in which Bart is standing. Then various colored lights hit it. The vapor takes on all the hues of a rainbow.**

After Newman cried "Cut!," the arc lights were shut off and the tubes rose, releasing the actors. Domergue made a beeline for a makeup woman who dabbed her forehead with a chamois. "It's awful in those tubes," she called out to Carroll. "You never felt such heat. I don't know what Bart is wearing under his suit, but I'm just wearing skin!"[22]

While making personal appearances with *This Island Earth* in June 1955, Reason talked to *Pittsburgh Post-Gazette* writer Win Fanning about playing scenes like the above: "It is terribly difficult to react to nothing more than the sound of the director's voice. You see, most of the 'effects' to which you are supposed to be reacting are added later in complicated laboratory work. However, it was good practice, and that's what I still need plenty of."

On the morning of Friday the 19th, Cal and Ruth reclined against the Stellarscope Observer Chairs and watched the approach of the Zahgon meteors. (The script describes the Observer Chairs in a Hollywood-friendly way: "[They] resemble the kind used on sets for actors to keep elaborate costumes from wrinkling.") Ruth may be a scientist but she's still a woman so, typically for sci-fi heroines of this era, her reaction is a panic-stricken "*They're going to hit us! They're going to hit us!*" while Cal merely braces himself a bit. Elsewhere in the movie,

- Cal and Ruth, inside the Converter Tubes, see the approaching baby-blue asteroid on the Stellarscope. Cal holds a brave face while Ruth gasps in horror and throws back her head.
- Running from Exeter's Mansion on foot, Ruth sometimes seems immobilized and needs to be dragged along by Cal.
- After escaping from the Monitor's Structure, she again becomes hysterical and says she'd rather be blown up then and there rather than get in the travel car.
- When Mutant #2 approaches the Converter Tubes, she lets rip with a series of screams while Exeter and Cal are stoic.[23]

Domergue also went from scientist to screamer in 1955's *It Came from Beneath the Sea*.

The rest of the 19th was spent getting shots of various characters watching the Stellarscope. Cast and crew came back to Earth on Saturday the 20th, specifically to the driveway of the back lot's Dabney House, built for Universal's Civil War tale *Tap Roots* (1948).[24] They shot the scene of Cal's arrival at Exeter's Mansion and then, day for night, the scene of his hasty departure with Ruth and Carlson. At the back lot's Upper Pollard Lake, footage was shot of Cal and Ruth piling out of the station wagon and running downhill into the lake and Carlson driving away.

Then, three different ways, the death of Dr. Engelborg was put on film. In the movie we see him in a long shot, turning to look behind him just before he's blasted by the Red Ray; that was the first take. If they'd used the second take, we would have seen Cal and Ruth in the lake in the foreground, Engelborg in the deep background, as he's hit; and if they'd used the third take, we'd have seen Engelborg run from the background into a close-up and then get hit. Reason and Domergue spent a good bit of the afternoon in the water, ducking under and coming up multiple times. The lake water, Domergue said, "was freezing cold and not clean. … The first time we had a take, I just couldn't bring myself to go under. Rex literally pushed me under that icy cold water. Universal's back lot, after dark, got extremely cold." (According to the production report, a bit before three o'clock, ten minutes were spent "warming up Miss Domergue.")

Five take five: Right to left, Jeff Morrow, Lance Fuller, Faith Domergue, Rex Reason and bit player Mary Lovelace relax against what Universal called a "specially built leaning board." (Photograph courtesy Ronald V. Borst/Hollywood Movie Posters.)

Reason told me he recalled dunking Domergue and dragging her in running scenes, "and she didn't ever complain. She never once played the 'Hollywood Queen' with me. She did a good job, she was a lovely lady and she was real nice. I'm sorry I didn't get to know her better."

In the late afternoon, the moviemakers returned to Stage 6 and prepared to resume work in the Spaceship Control Room, but the soaked-to-the-skin Domergue first required a wardrobe change plus hair and makeup sessions. When these took longer than expected, the company was dismissed.

A second unit was set loose on the back lot on the 22nd: In the Woodie, Chuck Roberson (Rex Reason's double), Louise Volding (Faith Domergue's) and Louis Tomei (Russell Johnson's) careened along a dirt road and the gully beside it, for the scene of the scientists trying to avoid Brack's Red Rays. Volding and Roberson also ran across the log bridge.[25] The first unit, meanwhile, was back on the Spaceship Control Room set, getting shots for the movie's Metaluna-to-Earth section: Exeter, Cal and Ruth proceeding from the elevator to the pilot's platform; making a lift-off despite the vibration from meteor strikes to the planet below; and getting into the Converter Tubes.

Holy cliffhanger!: In the day's last shot, the elevator door slid open and, on a far wall bathed in golden light, the shadow of Mutant #2's arm appeared; then the Mutant filled the doorway and, with the camera dollying back, walked toward the camera and *into* the camera. Only the first part of the shot—the shadow of the arm on the wall—is seen in the movie.[26]

The monster in *This Island Earth* is eight feet tall, with exposed brains, five mouths and claws. Director Joe Newman says: "We're taking the bull by the horns." You said it, buddy.—Army Archerd, "Just for *Variety*," *Variety*, February 24, 1954

The first shot on the 23rd: Mutant #2 again entering the Control Room, this time filmed from Ruth's point of view with the monster hazily visible through the front of her vapor-filled Converter Tube. Then its entrance was shot a third way: The camera started on Exeter and Cal in their Tubes; panned to Ruth as she begins to regain consciousness and open her eyes; then panned to the elevator door as it opens and the shadow of Mutant #2 is seen. Most of the rest of

The makeup department put pants on the Mutant to save themselves the job of making insect-like legs. The pantlegs, unfortunately, don't end, they "transition" into monstrous ankles and feet, so that the Mutant looks like he's wearing pants with insect-feet footies! The Mutant was played by stuntman Regis Parton, who got no screen credit but was included on the castlist in the pressbook.

the scene was done in bits and pieces. After the Mutant presses itself against Ruth's Converter Tube and falls to the floor, notice how much "blood" is now on the front of the tube—and also notice that, by the next shot of the tube, it's all gone. (The script called for this wounded Mutant to look as though it's "bathed in a green liquid." Its on-screen red blood—actually ketchup—is probably more effective.) The workday ended with the filming of an unused take in which Ruth, in close-up, struggles in the monster's arms.

The 24th began with a quick trip to the Phantom Stage, where Exeter, Cal and Ruth walked along a debris-strewn path from the spaceship elevator to the travel car tube (for the scene of their arrival on Metaluna). Once this was in the can, more debris, some of it burning, was added to the path and the three *ran* the other way, from the tube to the elevator (for the scene in which they flee *back* to the spaceship). Domergue sounded like she was exaggerating—but she was there and I wasn't, so what do I know?—when she told Tom and Jim Goldrup:

> **The entire stage was completely done over like a futuristic city in destruction. We had to run through that from the spaceship to the [travel car station]. There were explosions set up all around us. They're all mad, the special effects people. They are really all wonderful, marvelous, but completely crazy people. They have these wild ideas and they do crazy things. The man that did this was killed the following year on location with a bomb he set up for a war scene in North Carolina. Anyway, he set all these things up and we had to make our path very carefully through. It's like going through a mine field, so that we would miss the bomb or the flash.**

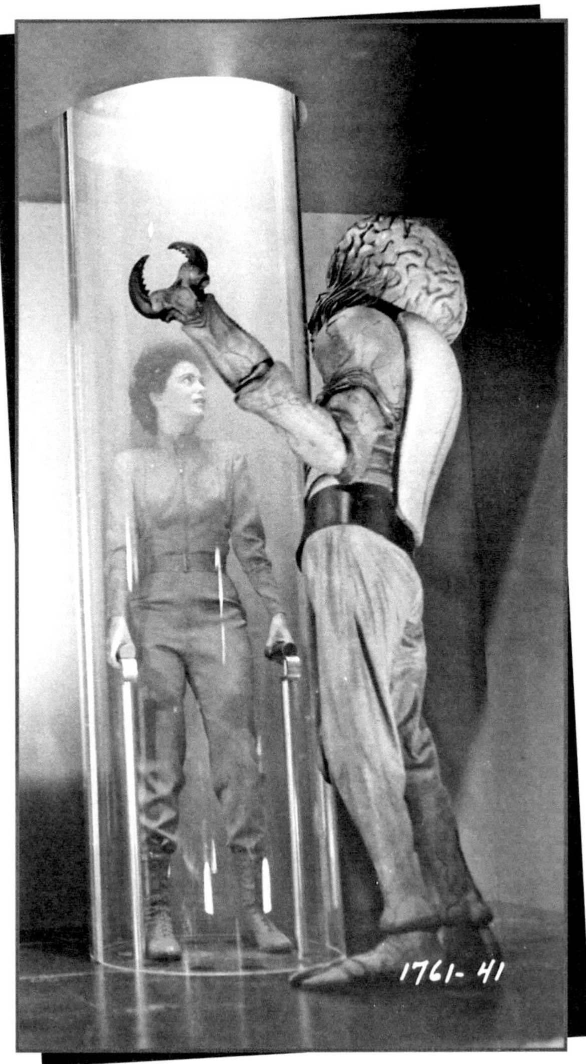

Ruth's (Faith Domergue) Converter Tube is about to rise, leaving her unprotected and stuck to the magnetized handrails, with the Mutant (Regis Parton) looming. It's the scariest and most exciting moment in the movie. (Photograph courtesy Ronald V. Borst/Hollywood Movie Posters.)

After this, it was back to the Stage 6 spaceship set for the scene of Mutant #2's last stand (and last fall) on the Control Room platform before its disintegration. Not used in the movie: footage in which the insect-man, in the last moments of its life, makes an additional "dash" for Ruth and an additional "grab" at her.

As mentioned above, some fans (and even screenwriter Coen) complain that the Mutants "cheapened" the movie, as though *This Island Earth* was some thought-provoking SF treatise rather than the gussied-up *Buck Rogers* yarn it is (more on that later). But the blood-splattered monster's invasion of the Control Room, while Our Heroes are trapped in the Converter Tubes, is arguably the best part of the movie—nicely enhanced by Henry Mancini's exciting music cue (later used to equally scary effect in *Tarantula*) and Faith Domergue's screams. Her screams apparently had the desired horrifying effect on the Australian censor, who made his wishes known to the staff in the cutting room: "Reduce the number of times the girl screams in terror and delete the attack upon her by the insect."

The first time Domergue saw *This Island Earth* was when it was screened on the Universal lot,

> **and I loved it! ... My children had seen Reggie [stuntman Regis Parton] in the monster outfit [on the set], without his monster head on. I assumed they would identify him when he was on the screen, but oh, no. Both were small, and they began screaming! I had to get up and take them out of the theater! I really shouldn't have let them see the film, because they became hysterical. But I really did think they'd recognize Reggie.**

The moviemakers next got a start on shooting the last-reel scene in which Exeter, Cal and Ruth watch the Stellarscope as the ship approaches Earth. Notice that we see darkness out the spaceship windows until Exeter announces that they're entering Earth's atmosphere, at which point the windows begin to lighten. The gravely injured Exeter bluffs

The Mutant (Regis Parton) gets rough ... or maybe romantic! ... with Ruth (Faith Domergue). In Domergue's interview with the Goldrups, she said that between takes, her monstrous mauler carried her kids around and fed them chocolate.

that he intends to explore the universe, "perhaps find another Metaluna," and Cal and Ruth don't buy it. The couple is now filled with respect and concern for their former enemy and abductor, and the scene is almost touching. Domergue told interviewer Boyd Magers, "I think [Morrow's] death scene in the end, when he takes his spaceship to its destruction in the sea, was splendid."

At one point on February 25, according to the Production Report, "Miss Domergue examined by insurance doctor—for injuries received in scenes—2/23/54." According to the actress (in her Goldrups interview), her fight scene with Mutant #2 included a lot of rough stuff that didn't reach the screen. "[Parton] was very powerful inside [the Mutant costume]; I don't think he realized. I was thrown all over the stage." She continued,

> **The violence of the scene and the terrible beating that I took—I was one mass of black and blue marks from my body to my toes for about three weeks afterwards and I could hardly walk. He was sorry; you see, inside the costume, he couldn't control himself. He picked me up and threw me down. I'd get up and try to run and he'd grab my leg, swing me around, grab my hair with those claws that he had. It actually was very exciting, but I was a wreck; I almost had broken bones.**

Fortunately for the filmmakers, the Metaluna outfit she wore exposed only her hands and feet, so her bruises were covered up. Despite having taken a thumpin', the actress put in a full day's work as Ruth: riding in the travel car with Exeter and Cal (on the Phantom Stage) and then alighting from the spaceship with Exeter and Cal (Stage 21). Then Parton worked again, playing Mutant #2 on the spaceship entrance set in two shots. There was more Mutant mayhem on Stage 21 on the 26th as the monster confronted Exeter, Cal and Ruth at the spaceship entrance and gouged Exeter with its lobster-like pincer claw. Let's hope that the Mutant head provided Parton complete protection from the blows that Rex Reason rains upon him with the plane's fire extinguisher; Reason doesn't appear to be holding back during this beatdown. Next came a move to Stage 14 and the shooting of the Monitor Structure corridor scene with Parton as Mutant #1 advancing on Cal and Ruth until a Zahgon explosion brings down the ceiling (actually debris dropped from a hopper).

Work started late the morning of February 27 because Domergue was being X-rayed at nine for her injuries of the 23rd. The moviemakers got that day's first shot on Stage 6 at 10:25: Exeter, Cal and Ruth striding into the chamber where the Monitor (played by Douglas Spencer), perched on a bench on his raised platform, imperiously presides. The atom model on the pedestal before him is heavy on the purple lights, giving the actors' faces an unbecoming grape hue throughout the scene. The combo of

In an interview with the Goldrup brothers, Rex Reason (wielding the fire extinguisher like a bat against bug-man Regis Parton) said he loved this movie's whole concept "because it was futuristic" and called it his favorite ... but referred to it as *"This Planet Earth"* throughout their chat.

purple faces and white hair make Exeter and the Monitor look like Smurfs. (*All* the Metaluna scenes look drab. According to Universal press materials, they were shot with a muted color palette, to differentiate Metaluna from Earth.)

Douglas Spencer is beloved by Monster Kids for his fine performance as *The Thing from Another World*'s resident Everyman, the hail-fellow-well-met reporter "Scotty." But Spencer may not have been particularly beloved on the *This Island Earth* set that February day. Getting one shot took 15 minutes because, according to the Production Report, Spencer was "n.g." (no good) four times. The next shot they tried to get, a medium close-up of the Monitor, he was "n.g." six times and it took a half-hour. After lunch, a shot took 20 minutes because he was "n.g." six *more* times. In addition to acting, Spencer also regularly worked as a stand-in for star Ray Milland and consequently had small parts in a number of Milland movies, most memorably in *The Lost Weekend* (1945) as an alcoholic ward inmate with the DTs, creating a middle-of-the-night ruckus by screaming and swatting at imagined beetles. The star of *The Thing*, Kenneth Tobey, told me that he'd heard tell that, post–*The Thing*, Spencer was working in a Western and tied the reins of a horse around his fingers—and when the horse lurched forward, it tore a finger right out of his hand. There's proof of this in the 1960 *The Rebel* episode "Explosion" which includes several close-ups of Spencer's right hand holding a bottle of nitroglycerin. Sure enough, he's missing half of his forefinger. By my math, that makes it a twofinger.

Douglas Spencer played his best-ever movie role in *The Thing from Another World*, helping bring the fight to James Arness' man from space. Amusingly, if you're easily amused, the actor's other sci-fi characters *were* men from space: a Martian in the 1961 *Twilight Zone* "Mr. Dingle, the Strong" and *This Island Earth*'s alien leader. (Photograph courtesy Ronald V. Borst/Hollywood Movie Posters.)

Even before the televising of that episode, Spencer, 50, was dead of a diabetic condition. According to his *Variety* obit his body was flown to Princeton, New Jersey, for services and interment. Right city name, wrong state: He hailed from Princeton, Illinois, and that's where he's buried, under a grave marker with his real name William H. Mesenkop.

The 27th ended on the Phantom Stage with the filming of various Spaceship Cargo Hold shots of Cal and Ruth getting in and out of the courier plane, etc. Not used in the movie: footage of the Mutant on the floor, rolling into the shot and under the plane's wing, then getting to its feet and staggering away.

The first day of March was the *last* day of principal photography, all of it spent on the Phantom Stage. First the moviemakers got some more cargo hold footage, starting with shots of the Mutant rolling on the floor and rising to its feet. Stuntman Parton was responsible for a few no-good takes, being off his marks two times, but that was understandable given that, with the Mutant head on, he could really only see straight ahead. Next Reason and Domergue got into the courier plane and did a number of shots, including ones where the plane is lit up by the Green Ray. In part of one shot, "RUTH and CAL … react to the moonlite being cut off," a recreation of the eerie moment in the novel when pilot Cal becomes aware that *something* flying above his plane has gotten between him and the moon.

> When I watched Faith Domergue and Bart Roberts "flying" in a plane on a soundstage against a painted backdrop for *This Island Earth*, [things] became all too realistic. A real plane flew over the studio and the scene had to be cut because the noise got on the soundtrack. The real sound will be dubbed in later under controlled conditions.
>
> —Hedda Hopper's column, March 4, 1954

Then process shots involving the station wagon were shot: Cal and Ruth outside the car near the mystery plane; Cal and Ruth *in* the car, driving to Exeter's Mansion; and Cal, Ruth and Carlson in the car, swerving around to avoid the Red Rays. Russell Johnson was recalled to again play Carlson in these shots. At around 7:30 that evening, in the last shot of the day, and the last shot of principal photography, Carlson, alone in the car, threw up his hands in horror in reaction to the death ray at last finding its mark (him!). Principal photography, which was supposed to take 23 days, had stretched to 26.

Next came two days of post-production. Nearly all of March 2 was spent getting the shots of Exeter that would be seen on interocitor screens. One take was spoiled when a fly landed on Morrow's white wig. Morrow was back the next day for more interocitor shots. Douglas Spencer returned as the Monitor, shooting the footage in which he's seen on Exeter's interocitor. A black velvet shot of Rex Reason as Cal, building his interocitor, was shot for use in the montage scene. They finished up by filming several shots of the Stellarscope, the camera shooting past the Operator seated in front of it. The company was dismissed at 6:30 p.m.

> How do you visualize interplanetary warfare? That's where Stanley [a.k.a. David S.] Horsley, special effects director for Universal-International, and his experts came in. For the answers they consulted Mt. Wilson astronomers, watched A-blast films and studied designs for planes to come.
> —*Popular Science* magazine, November 1954

The formidable task of providing *This Island Earth*'s special effects fell to Horsley, whose work was the subject of the short *Popular Science* article cited above. According to its writer Andrew R. Boone, Exeter's 18-pound spaceship sailed past a background of 1000 stars and, for some shots, was bathed in red light to make it look hot. He described how, on the stage where Metaluna effects footage was shot, "models of meteors and fighters slid down blackened piano wire and blew up, when trip wires set off tiny explosive charges within them. Multiple exposures brought together the saucer, fighters and Red Ray." He continued, "Staging special effects with miniatures is painstaking, costly business. Shooting the scenes took 26 days; matching bits of action on the frames, 15 weeks. The make-believe in this 16-minute bit of the film cost $100,000 to produce."

"I know they put a lot of money into the special effects," Rex Reason told me, "and day after day the more it progressed toward getting ready for the screen, there was a lot more talk about it. It seemed to be a very important project at the time—important enough for them to put the money into it and make it as first-class as possible." William Alland said in the documentary short *The Man Who Pursued Rosebud: William Alland on His Career in Theatre and Film* (2010),

> ***This Island Earth*** **could never have been made without the genius of Stanley Horsley, who is dead now. Brilliant, brilliant man. He labored at Universal for 25, 30 years. He was a sometime alcoholic, and I think that perhaps kept his career from becoming as great as [it] should have been.**

In the war between Metaluna and Zahgon, we ass-u-me that the Zahgon folks are the bad guys because ... because ... well, because at one point Exeter happens to mention that Metaluna has offered to make peace with Zahgon, to no avail. And because at least one of the movie's posters calls Zahgon an "outlaw planet." And because ... because ... well, because Zahgon starts with the reserved-for-bad-guys letter Z. That's all we know about them, and it wouldn't hold up at the Hague. We know more about the Metalunans because throughout the movie we have the displeasure of getting to know the icy, cruel Brack and then, mercifully more briefly, the icier, crueler Monitor, the blue-ribbon bad man in charge of the whole works. The Metalunans have bred the Mutants for slave labor and use their Thought Transformer to more or less do the same to some of the Earth scientists (and, who knows, maybe some of their fellow Metalunans too); "Take them to the Thought Transference Chamber" comes out of their mouths with the casualness of an Earthly "Got a match?" All I'm saying is that

Looking like Metalunan giants, special photographer David S. Horsley (standing) and miniatures supervisor Charles Baker (the whack-a-mole in the hole) are among the workers preparing the alien planet set. (Photograph courtesy Ronald V. Borst/Hollywood Movie Posters.)

the Zahgon folks could conceivably be getting a bad rap and that Metaluna's climactic transformation into a sun might possibly have been a Good Thing in more ways than one.

The real villain of *This Island Earth*? Well, that might have to be Jack Arnold. Starting in the mid–1970s, Monster Kid Fandom at last began to grow up and to seek interviews with favorite moviemakers; and Arnold, regularly profiled from that point on, proceeded to dish up enough whoppers to make Burger King look like a mom-and-pop operation. His most bastardly lie: The director of *It Came from Outer Space, Creature from the Black Lagoon, The Incredible Shrinking Man et al.* began boasting that he was also the uncredited director of the Metaluna scenes of *This Island Earth*!

Arnold may have debuted this lie in a *Cinefantastique* interview, telling Bill Kelley that, after principal photography was finished and *This Island Earth* cut together, "it lacked a lot of things. So they asked me if I would help them. I went in and re-shot about half of it, but I didn't take credit for it. Specifically, I re-shot most of the footage once they reached the dying planet." Kelley asked if he shot the Converter Tubes scenes and the Mutant scenes, and the director responded, "Yes, and also the escape, through the tunnel and back to the ship." Then Arnold slipped into semi-incoherence:

> ARNOLD: It could have been a hell of a better film right from the start, I thought. They didn't approach it the way I would have approached it. I think the whole atmosphere should have been explored. The whole idea of going back in a primeval time, into the depths of this planet and its ruins. It should have had an eerie, mystic kind of feeling, a whole tempo and atmosphere that contrasts the beginning of the film, when they begin their exploration. All the director was going for were the obvious tricks, and the obvious tricks aren't enough.
>
> KELLEY: Actually, they don't spend much time on Metaluna at all.
>
> ARNOLD: Which was a mistake. They really should have allowed more of an opportunity to get into the atmosphere of that planet and what was happening to it.

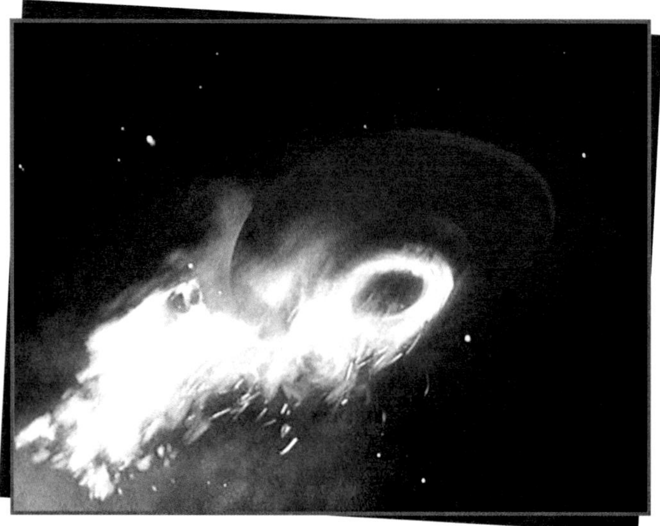

Science friction: Exeter's spaceship, passing through "the thermal barrier," spews flames even in airless outer space. In the movie's second half, the parade of eye-popping SFX sequences, decked out in Technicolor, were "a visual knockout for 1955." (DVD Savant Glenn Erickson.)

Perhaps Arnold biographer Dana M. Reemes smelled a rat, because in his book *Directed by Jack Arnold* he confined his coverage of *This Island Earth* to just a few lines: After calling Arnold someone who could be drafted at the last minute to save other directors' botched jobs, he writes, "Notable examples are his uncredited redirection of sequences in *The Land Unknown* and *This Island Earth*," and lets it go at that.

Unfortunately for Arnold's reputation, Monster Kid researchers *continued* to grow up, interviewing more and more filmland veterans and even poring over original production paperwork, and from *no* source came one ounce of proof of his *This Island Earth* claim. Over a ten-year period, Robert Skotak interviewed as many *This Island Earth* participants as he could find, and accessed probably *all* of the available, still-existent paperwork, without finding any Arnold connection.[27] Skotak told me that, when he at last broached the subject to Arnold, "he realized I knew a lot about the film and had access to records, and he backed *waaaay* off. He kind of clammed up, because I had kind of put him on the spot."

Consider *This Island Earth*'s Daily Production Reports: With **Director Joe Newman** atop every page, they document the filming of practically every non-effects shot, with descriptions of each shot perfectly matching the shots seen *in* the movie. Is it still possible for Arnold to have re-shot all the Metaluna scenes and even some Spaceship Control Room scenes (characters in the Converter Tubes)? *Wellll*, yes, but...

- only if every shot Arnold got was an exact duplicate of the shot Newman got;
- *and* only if every Daily Production Report filled out during the time that Arnold *was* in charge got lost over the years while every one of Newman's Daily Production Reports survived;
- *and* only if everyone who worked with Arnold on the re-shoots, cast and crew alike, made a pact among themselves to tell decades-later interviewers the lie that Arnold was never there.

Skotak even had Joseph Newman re-watch the movie in light of Arnold's bastardly (I may have used that word already) assertions, and Newman stated firmly that he had found no scene that may have been handled by anyone other than himself (with the obvious exception of second unit shots, etc., which had been planned right from the get-go and agreed upon by Newman). But adding these details is overkill: Skotak's confrontation of Arnold, with the director shamed into silence, is all that any fan needs to know about.

This Island Earth was sneak-previewed at the Picwood Theatre in Westwood, California. The Preview Comment Card question WHOM DID YOU LIKE BEST IN THE PICTURE? resulted in 80 votes for Jeff Morrow, 53 for Rex Reason, 14 for Faith Domergue—and four for "The Bug"! Here are some of the other questions and a few cherry-picked responses:

Which Scenes Did You Like Most?

The city on Metaluna.
Leaving Earth.
Thought all scenes in this picture were excellent. This is better than It Came from Outer Space.
The bug.
Flight to Metaluna.

Braced for out-of-this-world thrills on a distant planet gone mad: Rex Reason, left, Faith Domergue and Jeff Morrow. *This Island Earth* was none too heavy on marquee magnetism: Domergue was a recognizable name in 1954 but it was only Reason's second time as a movie lead, Morrow's first. (Photograph courtesy Alexander Rotter.)

Which Scenes, If Any, Did You Dislike?

I thought the mutants added little to the plot and could be omitted.
Leave out the mutants—they make an adult picture appear childish.
Too long at the beginning.

Were All The Story Points Clear To You?

No. Why did Exeter change from heavy to goodie and back and forth?
Why did advanced people need Earthmen's research?

Added Comments

I don't think English could be a language in other planets.
Moral: Beware of catalogs with metal pages.
I thought the acting was poor. I wouldn't blame it on the actors though. They didn't have anything to work with.

On May 26, 1955, *Variety* announced that Universal had assigned field exploitation men Mike Vogel, John McGrail, Bucky Harris, Ken Hoel, Ben Hill, David Polland, Julian Bowes, Jack Matlack, Bob Ungerfeld, Ben Katz, Harold Perlman, Bob Johnson, Dick Richman and Duke Hickey to cover 29 key cities in connection with *This Island Earth*'s upcoming 900-theater saturation launching. Film and theater critic Edith Lindeman of the *Richmond* (Virginia) *Times-Dispatch* wrote in the June 1955 article "Science Fiction Movies Fascinate Public and Tax Talents of Make-Up Men" that she could "hardly wait" to see it, and humorously passed along what she'd heard about the Mutant:

> **It is a giant monster, half human and half insect. Its arms are long enough to tie its shoelaces while it stands in an erect position, only, of course, it doesn't wear shoes. Its feet and hands are claws. Most startling of all, its head is five times normal size, and its cranial organs are external. In other words, its brain is showing.**
>
> **...It cost $24,000... You could make up eight "Draculas" for that money, but who wants eight Draculas.**

In 1955, as the release of *This Island Earth* loomed, a number of newspapers ran photos of the Mutant and reported that it had run up a $24,000 tab. The previous year, Bob Thomas wrote that it cost $6500 and Joseph Laitin of *Collier's* wrote $6000, and I have the feeling they were closer to the actual figure.

Some *This Island Earth* posters depicted Cal and Ruth on Metaluna in their street clothes rather than the Metaluna uniforms they wear in the movie, probably so that it wouldn't look like they were aliens themselves. In the background is colorful carnage worthy of the wooliest "Mars Attacks" trading card: exploding buildings (looking like futuristic Twin Towers!), a spaceship and a Zahgon fighter in flight, a falling meteor, Earth and Saturn in the distance and a posse of insect men, all obviously up to no good. It's not hard to picture 1955 auditoria packed with kids and *also* with grown-up Space Rangers watching through their Official Captain Video Space Helmets.

The movie's newspaper and magazine reviews were a mixed bag. A number of the favorable ones said many of the same things the same way, almost always including some variation on "The members of the special effects team are the real stars of this movie," which makes me think that these critics were doing a lot of copying from each other, or copying from Universal press materials. Thumbs-down reviewers included John McCarten of *The New Yorker*, who called Metaluna "duller than Canarsie." There were also critiques that gave the impression that it was a movie best-suited for small kids, and maybe some of Universal's marketing strategies put that idea in their heads. As Dr. Robert J. Kiss reveals in his essay "The Release" (below), invitees to the movie's New York City matinee preview would only be admitted if accompanied by children. Part of *Variety*'s June 16, 1955, "Hollywood Inside" column read:

In an attempt to entice adult patronage to a pic more heavily slanted to the moppet trade, UI's promotion for *This Island Earth* in Chicago is being tied in with the Salerno Biscuit Co. When pic opens June 24 at the McVickers Theatre in Chi, kids will be admitted free when accompanied by an adult and a Salerno cookie boxtop.

Reviewer W.K.Z. of the *New York Herald Tribune* got the feeling his nephews would be more "attuned" than he to *This Island Earth* so when he went to see it, he brought along little Bill, nine, and Dan, seven. Three times in his synopsis of the movie's first half, he interrupted himself with "'When are we going into space?' Dan asked," but once Cal and Ruth were Metaluna-bound, the kids and Uncle W.K.Z. finally started getting what they came for. He wrapped with: "Bill said he didn't like the way [Ruth] kept throwing herself into Cal's arms when things got tough. Dan fixed him with a look of scorn. 'If you were a girl,' he said, 'you'd do that, too.'"

One of *This Island Earth*'s toughest critics: its producer. In our 1995 interview, Alland mentioned time and again that he thought the acting (outside of Morrow), dialogue and direction were all "very poorly done," "wooden," "awkward," "subpar"—you get the idea. But he did wrap up on the subject by laughingly telling me that, over the years, his appreciation of the movie "has increased as the *audience's* appreciation has increased! *You* guys [sci-fi movie fans] are telling *me* how good it is, so, fine, I'll go along with you!" You'll find his full, uninterrupted take on the movie in my 1996 book *Monsters, Mutants and Heavenly Creatures*.

Serials-ly Speaking...

> To rabid science fiction fans, the initial half of [*This Island Earth*] is probably the best done thing in its line yet to come along. But from that point on, things in general deteriorate in a slaphappy and preposterously funny manner until the wind-up of the "epic" has you rolling in the aisles with laughter.
>
> This would be great, except the film is supposed to be dead serious.
>
> —from the *Kingsville* (Texas) *Record* newspaper review

Scratch off a bit of *This Island Earth*'s effects-laden Technicolor surface and hiding underneath you find a Flash Gordon adventure, complete with hokey dialogue, vague character motivation and monsters not too many rungs above Flash's Gocko and orangopoid. Pictured: Flash and Dale (Buster Crabbe and Jean Rogers) in *Flash Gordon*, Cal and Ruth (Rex Reason and Faith Domergue) in *This Island Earth*. (Photographs courtesy Ronald V. Borst/Hollywood Movie Posters.)

No Monster Kid ever wrote at length about *This Island Earth* without making mention of the way that, visually, the space and Metaluna scenes look to have leapt right off of the covers and out of the pages of the era's pulp comic books. Equally worthy of mention ... but rarely mentioned ... is the inconvenient truth that, once the story slips the surly bonds of Earth, it sinks to the level of a Saturday matinee kiddie serial. In fact, one particular serial, also made by Universal: *Buck Rogers* (1939). In *Buck Rogers* as in *This Island Earth*,

• a science fiction contrivance thrusts two 20th-century Earthlings into the thick of war. In *Buck Rogers* the heroes are Buck (Buster Crabbe) and his young sidekick Buddy (Jackie Moran), awakening from an unplanned suspended-animation siesta in the year 2440.

• *Buck Rogers*' Rip Van Winkles find that 25th-century Earth is ruled by "super-racketeer" Killer Kane (Anthony Warde) and that its remaining decent folk have retreated into an underground realm called the Hidden City. This is equivalent to Metaluna's war with Zahgon, with the Metalunans retreating into the underground Prime Sector.

• Both *Buck Rogers* and *This Island Earth* observe all the rules of film etiquette for the sci-fi-for-toddlers subgenre: There's fire and sound in space, aliens look exactly like us, they can breathe on our planet and we on theirs, and of course the aliens speak English. If *This Island Earth* had introduced us to a citizen of Zahgon, surely he too would capisce English. Even the *Mutant* understands English!

• You enter the Hidden City by spaceship by passing through a huge opening in the side of a rock formation. You enter the Prime Sector by spaceship through a huge opening in the rocky planet surface.

• Aware that they're destined for defeat, the Hidden City rulers reach out for help to the people of another planet, Saturn. The supreme head of the Metaluna government turns to Earth.

• Killer Kane has his own version of a Thought Transference Chamber: In his Dynamo Room, workers wear amnesia helmets that have robbed them of their will and made them slaves, the same way that Exeter's Mansion scientists have been lobotomized and put to work.

• The Hidden City folks and Killer Kane have interocitor-like two-way TV communicating devices. They have round screens rather than the Metalunan triangular screens.

• In *This Island Earth,* Cal is the man of the hour, every hour, often with his scientist-sweetie Ruth at his side. In *Buck Rogers,* Buck is the man of the hour, every 20-minute chapter, often with his navigator-sweetie Wilma (Constance Moore) at his side.

• In the first outer space scene of excitement in *This Island Earth,* Exeter's spaceship makes a super-heated passage through Earth's "thermal barrier." In *Buck Rogers*' first outer space scene of excitement, Buck's spaceship makes a super-heated passage through Saturn's atmosphere barrier.

• Both *Buck Rogers* and *This Island Earth* include dogfight-style encounters between futuristic airships.

• In *Buck Rogers*' Hidden City, characters regularly get into a cylindrical enclosure, and a special effects shot conveys that they're being teleported. In *This Island Earth*, characters regularly get into cylindrical tubes, and a special effects shot conveys that they're being metabolically altered.

• To get from their spaceships to the subterranean seat of government, *Buck Rogers* characters shuttle through a tunnel in a closed bullet car. To get from the spaceship to the subterranean seat of government, *This Island Earth* characters shuttle through a tunnel in an open travel car.

And so on, and so on. (DVD Savant Glenn Erickson chose to compare *This Island Earth* not to old serials but to 1950s kiddie fare: "In its dramatics, [it's] barely above the level of 'space cadet' television programming.") The point being, it seems like a real possibility that someone connected with the screenwriting of the second half of *This Island Earth*

Plot-wise, *This Island Earth*'s second half has a lot in common with Saturday matinee serials: The Monitor (Douglas Spencer, seated) is a Ming the Merciless sort, the perfect storm of tin-god superiority and evil ambition, squirrelled away in his cosmic Casbah dishing out dastardly orders. From left: Jeff Morrow, Spencer, Rex Reason, Faith Domergue.

had vivid recollections of *Buck Rogers* and/or kiddie-time space stories like it. Monster Kids who like to call *This Island Earth* Serious (with a capital S) Science Fiction ought to run all 12 kid-tested, mother-approved chapters of *Buck Rogers* past their eyeballs and see if they can bring themselves to call *that* Serious Science Fiction also.[28]

This Island Earth is highly regarded in many precincts of fandom, but story-wise there's just not a lot of *there* there—so little, in fact, that it isn't surprising that some at Universal felt that "moppets" would be its best audience. If you had to synopsize *This Island Earth* as simply as possible, a pretty good one would be: "An alien—a nice guy—brings two Earth scientists to his war-torn planet where he hopes they'll work for his side. But they arrive too late, the war's been lost, and after a few minutes the alien tells the Earthlings, in effect, 'Sorry about putting you to so much trouble. I guess I'd better get you kids home,' and he does." Have I omitted anything of particular importance or interest? After 75 minutes of build-up, it's almost immediately revealed that Exeter's entire mission has been a bust, and the movie begins madly rushing towards its final fadeout. The distraction provided by the Mutant scenes helps keep viewers from realizing, "I just watched a movie about *nothing*." In an interview with *Starlog*'s Kim Howard Johnson, Jim Mallon, director-producer-co-writer of 1996's *Mystery Science Theater 3000: The Movie* which spoofs *This Island Earth*, said the oldie had "a really dopey story" and pointed out that "hapless hero" Cal

> **pretty much just watches from start to finish—he never actively does anything to affect the direction of the film. In fact, the aliens are done in by other aliens on their home planet, and they're never going to come anyway! So, not much happens.**

The best thing about *This Island Earth*, to some fans: "It's like *Buck Rogers* ... on *steroids*!" The worst thing about *This Island Earth*, to other fans: "It's like *Buck Rogers* on steroids."

This Island Earth is also touted as a gaudy special effects-laden gala but this is somewhat misleading; you have to wait over half the running time for "the fireworks" (the special effects scenes) to begin. It was pretty spectacular eye candy in 1955, but some of it could have been better ... even in 1955. Setting aside a few bursts of Red Rays in the early going, the first SFX action is the destruction of Carlson in the station wagon, and it's Bert I. Gordon-level quality. Just before the Red Ray blast, we have plenty of time to see that the car (matted into the shot) is in mid-air, its tires *just* off the ground, and that the driver is on the wrong side, which means the shot was flipped; and then the car is replaced in the shot by a flamboyantly hued explosion that looks like a chrysanthemum fireworks effect. (As *Video Watchdog*'s Tim Lucas points out, "Things not only explode [in *This Island Earth*], they explode in rainbows.") A few moments later, the Red Ray reduces Dr. Engelborg to nothingness, an effect done just as *in*-effect-ively. The detonation of Exeter's hilltop mansion is another dud: An explosion is superimposed over the house, and for several moments you can easily see *through* this blast that the house is still intact. It's hard not to think about the fact that the use of a Lydecker-style scale model of the mansion, destroyed by fiery blasts, would have been a tremendous improvement. As for the car ... would it have busted the budget to actually blow up some $50 junker?

The second half of the movie is as improbable as a comic strip and done in the same style, skipping from panel to panel with a new emergency in every one; for instance, the escape from Metaluna, represented here by artwork. Unfortunately, the Metaluna buildings and backgrounds in the movie don't look much *better* than this Dr. Seuss storybook-level artwork.

When we see the Earth from space, it's the usual bone-dry blue ball with continents painted on it, a small replica of the way Earth must have looked on the day God made it but *before* He said to Himself, "Nope. No good. 'Needs clouds."

Shots of Exeter's ship in space, the asteroid and the guided meteors look good, Metaluna as seen from a distance looks *great*, and the spaceship's-eye views of the Metaluna surface, with smoke boiling in the various craters and openings, are also outstanding. But once the spaceship descends through an opening, preparing to dock in the Prime Sector, we're in the SFX bargain basement. Dark, bleak buildings and backgrounds look like cartoon artwork out of the Halloween episode of *The Jetsons*. Meteor-strike explosions and balls of fire and smoke are obviously superimposures. Zahgon fighters wobble in flight and you can't help notice that they're sometimes transparent. As various cartoony structures are hit with meteors and more superimposed flashes and fireballs appear, again we mourn the absence of scale models and on-set detonations. Shots of the spaceship soaring above the surface of an Earth ocean, spurting flames to the accompaniment of blowtorch-like sound effects, are breathtaking. But then the effect is spoiled by a shot of a fiery amorphous blob (meant to represent the spaceship) dropping out of the sky and hitting the surface of the water. This cues one last phony-looking superimposed explosion, and then a dissolve to a screen-full of yellow smoke.

"*None* of the old science fiction movies really hold up that well, mainly because of the special effects," Jeff Morrow's daughter Lissa told me. "If you go and see a *Star Wars*—not that I'm wild about *Star Wars*—but if you go and you see all the pyrotechnics and the blowing-up and the this and the that, then [*This Island Earth* and other oldies] are not so scary."

Withal, *This Island Earth*'s Technicolor special effects added a definite wow factor in 1955. It impressed many sci-fi aficionados in its day, and became a favorite of future generations who caught it on TV every time it ran. Jeff Morrow deemed it the best of all the sci-fi movies he did ... not that *The Creature Walks Among Us* and 1957's *The Giant Claw* and *Kronos* offered much competition. Morrow told Tom and Jim Goldrup that, partly as the result of script changes he suggested, Exeter became "a very strong three-dimensional heavy who ended almost as a tragic hero when you realized exactly why he was doing what he did. I never got fan mail in tens of thousands of letters a week, I wish I had, but I got quite a few, and I got more mail from that picture than any other picture I did."

The movie had only recently premiered when Morrow began hearing from its fans. Erskine Johnson wrote in his June 30, 1955, column:

Jeff Morrow received a fan letter from a teen-aged girl who saw his performance as a benevolent scientist from another planet in *This Island Earth* and is showing pals the closing paragraph in which she wrote:

"You reminded me of a Davy Crockett from outer space."

Other Script-to-Screen Changes

• The Jorgasnovara of the Raymond F. Jones novel became Exeter in the movie, but in early drafts of the script, he was called Warner. "Warner" was probably derived from the novel, where Jorgasnovara's associate was Dr. Warner. In early script drafts, the Monitor was called the Engineer, probably taken from the novel's Peace Engineers. During the procession of scripts, the name of his headquarters went from the Engineer's Palace to the Monitor's Dome. In the movie it's never called anything but the Monitor's Structure.

• In the script: At the Ryberg lab, Cal and Joe realize that the atomic reactor pile condenser has shorted out when the machine starts beeping and a pen recorder's reading drops to zero. In the movie, there's more excitement as the condenser failure results in an explosion within the reactor.

• In the script, Cal tests a bead condenser on a voltage rheostat, upping the voltage until the bead vanishes into thin air. In the movie, the test results in a small explosion, one that damages the apparatus.

• In the movie, when Cal receives a phone call from his jet's mechanic Sam, we only see and hear Cal's half of the conversation. The script calls for us to see both Cal and Sam, the latter using a wall phone in a hangar:

SAM
I've gone over every inch of it, Dr. Meacham, and it beats me.
(shakes his head)
I can't even find a loose rivet.

CAL (to Joe)
Sam can't find anything wrong.
(back to phone)
You double-checked the controls, Sam?

SAM
(he is very sincere)
Took each gizmo apart. Put it back together again.
(a small hesitant smile on his face)
Pardon me, boss—but you sure it wasn't the man at the controls ... you know what I mean—maybe a little too much of that Washington celebrating?

CAL
(quickly)
Of course not. I—
(then, grinning)
Now look here, Sam—

SAM
(shrugs; *he* knows the score)
Well, otherwise it just don't figure, boss.

CAL
Okay, Sam. You win. Maybe I did have just a couple. But—

SAM
Okay, boss. Okay. So what's wrong with that once in a while? Now you just go and get yourself a good night's sleep.

With that, Sam hangs up, "delighted with having solved his mystery."[29]

• In the script, the interocitor parts arrive in "weirdly shaped crates" instead of the conventional wooden boxes seen on screen.

• In the script, the mystery plane coming in for a Ryberg airfield landing is suffused in green light. Not only doesn't it have a pilot, it also doesn't have an instrument panel. Just before it lands on Exeter's Georgia runway, its interior lights up green and Cal's seat swivels around so that he is now facing the tail, then tilts forward in preparation for the bump of landing.

• Talking with Ruth and Carlson about the fishy set-up at Exeter's Mansion, Cal considers the possibility that Exeter is up to no good—and says that they could turn him in to the F.B.I. The line didn't make it into the movie. Perhaps if it had, DVD Savant Glenn Erickson wouldn't have written, "Politically, the film is a silly mess, with America's top scientists foolishly lending their talents to what looks like a blatant conspiracy of 'foreigners' to steal our top tech secrets—a 'brain drain.'"

• During the Exeter's Mansion getaway scene, the movie alternates shots of Cal, Ruth and Carlson's station wagon with cutaway shots of Brack at the interocitor, directing the lightning-like Red Rays at them. In the script, surprisingly, *Exeter's* in control of the interocitor during this passage, and responsible for the deaths of Carlson and Dr. Engelborg. This can also be found in the pressbook synopsis: "Exeter turns a red death-ray on several other laboratory aides seeking to flee." One sneak preview audience member thought Brack *was* Exeter, responding to the Preview Comment Card question "Were All the Story Points Clear to You?" with, "If Ruth and Cal were so valuable, why did Exeter try to kill them in car?" I guess to some people, all Metalunans look alike. Racists.

Russell Johnson began his stint as a Universal contractee in early 1952 with *Ma and Pa Kettle at Waikiki* and it looks like he ended it with *This Island Earth*. But because of a long delay in releasing the former, the two were double-billed in 1955! (Photograph courtesy John Antosiewicz.)

• In both the novel and the movie, the courier plane is instantly and easily trapped by the spaceship, but in the script, the scene is more exciting as Cal tries to take evasive action. When the Green Ray shoots downward toward the plane, Cal lunges at the controls and makes a bank turn. Despite Cal's frantic maneuvers, the Green Ray at last catches the propeller; for a moment it continues to spin, but then stops as the motor dies. Next the whole plane is bathed in green light, and the jig is up for Cal and Ruth.

• Standing in a spaceship Converter Tube in the movie, Cal says he feels like a new toothbrush. In the script, he compares himself to "a lonesome sardine."

• In the movie, Cal and Ruth are silent most of the first time they're in the Converter Tubes. In the script, they're both frightened and physically uncomfortable inside the Tubes and try to conceal this from each other by making small talk: Cal asks Ruth where she's from, she answers Alton, New Hampshire, he asks about Lake Winnipesaukee, she mentions fishing there with her dad, he asks when she decided to become a scientist, she answers, "When I was ten," Cal talks about the things *he* did at ten and about his dog, etc. It's the deep-space counterpart of the Dick Chasen-Eva hamburger drive-in date scene in *Indestructible Man* (1956).

But wait—it gets worse! Pages of script changes (dated February 8, 1954) omit all the childhood memories and replace them with banter about their three-years-ago Vermont flirtation!:

CAL
I keep remembering Vermont…
(smiles ruefully)
Meant to ask Exeter if he also had a machine that could take us back in time—

RUTH
It was a wonderful summer, Cal.
(pauses; a little laugh)
Only I can't forget how angry you were with me—especially at the end…

CAL
You were an egotistical little squirt—but nice.

RUTH
Hateful! Convinced that marriage wasn't for a budding physicist.

I didn't want to boil eggs. I wanted to split atoms!

(There is a silence. After a moment:)

RUTH

Cal, how do you like your eggs?

(Cal looks at her, laughs.)

CAL

Remember when we went on that picnic and got lost?

RUTH

Yes—

CAL

We weren't lost, Ruth. I just said that—I—

RUTH

I knew all the time we weren't lost, Cal. And I loved—

(But Ruth pauses, her ability to think coherently becoming affected.)

RUTH

—being lost with—I mean not lost with—

Fortunately for Cal and Ruth (and the audience), they pass out inside the vapor-filled Tubes at this point.

• In the movie, Cal and Ruth watch from their Observer Chairs as two Zahgon fighters appear on the Stellarscope, directing meteors at the spaceship in a frontal assault that's an almost comical waste of the Zahgon warriors' time and meteors because the Metalunans can't avoid seeing them coming and have plenty of time to fire their Red Rays. In the script, the encounter is more dramatic, almost dogfight-like. Four Zahgon fighters approach the spaceship, all steering meteors toward it. When one meteor is zapped, the debris destroys the fighter that guided it. A second Zahgon fighter makes a getaway, its meteor striking the spaceship a glancing blow and then exploding. The remaining two Zahgon ships come at the spaceship from different angles, safe from the forward-firing Red Rays. A Red Ray emanating from elsewhere on the spaceship destroys one of them. The fourth Zahgon meteor hurtles toward the spaceship, getting so close that it nearly fills the Stellarscope screen, before the spaceship banks sharply to avoid it.

• In the script, Exeter tells us more about the Metaluna-Zahgon war than we learn from the movie. He explains to Cal and Ruth that it's been going on for centuries and that the Metalunans consider the people of Zahgon barbarians, although far from unintelligent. "As a matter of fact, their ability to use meteors as projectiles is a feat we would be happy to understand ourselves."

• Not only can the Metalunans' Green Ray draw things *up* (for instance, the courier plane into the spaceship), in the script it can draw things down: When the spaceship gets to Metaluna, a Green Ray shoots upward from the planet surface and surrounds it, guiding it for a whisper-quiet landing.

• There are at least two lines of dialogue in the script's final draft that give the impression that, by the time of Exeter's return, there are *very* few Metalunans left, perhaps just the ones we see. Presumably these lines were deleted so that it seemed as though the Earth was being threatened with a world-changing mass migration. The writers could easily have upped the dramatic ante even more by floating the possibility that the relocation of Metalunans to Earth might also bring their Zahgon enemies here.

• The Monitor is more talkative in the script than in the movie, telling Cal and Ruth, "Intending to migrate to your earth we studied your history, your manners, your customs. Some are most noteworthy—others—[*shrugs*]—infantile. Particularly your gigantic ego." Cal has an extra line: After zinging the Monitor with "Our size is the size of our God," he tauntingly adds, "And I have a hunch He's a little bigger than you."

• The movie never shows us the inside of the Thought Transference Chamber, but in the script we spend rather a long time there. On its domed ceiling is a conical-shaped

Win, lose or claw: For the movie's still photographer, Rex Reason and Jeff Morrow put on a fight with the newest addition to the list of Universal's mascot monsters, the Mutant (Regis Parton). Notice that the bug-man is missing his eyes.

machine; in the center of the room, directly below it, are two chromium handrails, 24 inches apart, identical to the ones in the spaceship Converter Tubes. The rails, magnetized, hold a subject in position as the Thought Machine directs a beam down at them. Exeter explains that the effect is similar to a lobotomy operation, prompting Ruth to ask, "What happens to a subject when he is no longer useful to you…?" A shrug from Exeter causes Ruth to shudder and to say, "I withdraw the question."

Exeter departs, leaving a Mutant outside to guard the door. Cal devises a plan of escape, activating the Thought Machine, darkening the room and luring the Mutant inside. It spots Cal and Ruth and goes after them. Cal gets it to move toward the magnetized rails; one of the monster's claw arms touches a rail and is held fast. The Mutant rips the rail from the floor and it flies out into the corridor. Cal picks it up and, using it as a club, knocks the monster silly.

• The on-screen Mutants are silent but in the script, both are rather noisy. In the never-shot scene described above, Mutant #1 enters the Thought Transference Chamber "making strange threatening sounds," and does a lot of roaring when chasing Cal and Ruth and when stuck to the magnetized rail. When Mutant #2 idly wanders into the spaceship's otherwise unoccupied cargo hold, it roars with anger at nothing in particular. Coming through the elevator doorway into the control room, it's "roaring with pain."

• Another scripted scene not in the film: After the Monitor's Structure has been struck by a meteor, Exeter revisits the Monitor's Chamber and finds it mostly destroyed by fallen debris, the Monitor slumped across his bench. Though gravely injured, the Monitor asks whether Exeter has subjected Cal and Ruth to the Thought Machine. "Of what use can the Earth people be to you now?" Exeter asks quietly. The Monitor responds, "When we reach Earth they shall be our guides—our very docile guides." Exeter—finally—accepts the fact that the Monitor is a nasty piece of work, and defies him. Livid, the Monitor struggles to his feet and crosses to a control panel, frantically manipulating lights which glimmer momentarily but then die out. He collapses, apparently dead.

On the afternoon of February 27, 1954, a very abbreviated version of this scene was filmed…

> CL. [close-up] on elevator door as it opens and EXETER looks out [into the Monitor's Chamber], dolly in to close as he looks around the debris, to the dead Monitor, he closes the door.

…but it was not included in the movie.

• No More Mr. Nice Guy: In the script version of the scene of Cal and Ruth running away from the Monitor's Structure and Exeter, Cal is obviously "fed up to *here*" and warns the Metalunan, "Get away, Exeter, or I'll kill you right here."

• In the script, Cal and Ruth slip past Mutant #2 at the spaceship entrance, and then the monster digs a claw into Exeter; the script calls for an insert shot of the claw doing its damage. Then the Mutant releases Exeter, who pulls himself together and staggers away. The movie handles things more excitingly, with Cal rescuing Exeter by grabbing a courier plane fire extinguisher and treating the Mutant like a King (Rodney).

• After the courier plane drops through the bottom of Exeter's spaceship and Cal pulls it out of its dive, the first thing he does is turn on the radio! (According to the script, "From it comes a sudden burst of music. It is a typical American song, a lilting warm melody.") It's a conventional (read: corny) sweethearts-together ending.

• The script calls for Exeter's self-annihilation to play out in just four shots: He leans over the spaceship control unit to put it into a dive; the ship suddenly veers downward; Exeter smiles "a thin expectant smile"; and the camera follows closely behind the ship as it hits the ocean's surface, skips along, explodes and sinks, "a great cloud of steam obscuring camera." FADE OUT, THE END.

Marginalia

• No Monster Kid stumbling across Raymond F. Jones' story "The Children's Room" in the September 1947 issue of *Fantastic Adventures* would mentally compare it to *This Island Earth*; but I did, only because I discovered it while writing this chapter. This nutshell recap stresses the *This Island Earth* connections: An electronics engineer discovers that his ten-year-old son is reading children's books written in what looks like an alien language. By doing so, the boy has unknowingly passed an aptitude test given to him by a mysterious clan (Earthly, but diffusing a feeling of alienness) that now wants to permanently take him from his family. The clan knows that, because of a mutant trait, the boy will someday become super-intelligent, and they'll need his help to prevent an invasion of the Earth by another planet. Here it is again, with the nutshell even smaller: An electronics engineer's son passes an aptitude test (*à la* Cal being able to decipher the Unit 16 catalogue and build the interocitor) and is "kidnapped" by an alien-like race to help prevent a war between planets.

In 1952, "The Children's Room" was adapted for a *Tales of Tomorrow* TV episode with Claire Luce as the boy's mother and, kinda-sorta filling the Jorgasnovara-Exeter slot, Una O'Connor. (*Meta*luna O'Connor?)

• In *This Island Earth* the novel, the aliens have a plant on Earth, built and manned by unsuspecting locals. More Job Creators from Space arrived in Hammer's *Quatermass 2* (a.k.a. *Enemy from Space*, 1957), obliterating the isolated English town of Wynderden Flats and hiring locals to setup storage domes supposedly filled with "synthetic food."

• Jones' *This Island Earth* has probably never been categorized as anything other than sci-fi but it features more than a few effective dashes of horror. Some are like "Lovecraft in reverse": H.P. liked to hint at arcane terrors of the past, impossible to describe because they can only be called up as pseudo-memories "from deep cells and tissues whose retentive functions are wholly primal and awesomely ancestral" (from "The Shadow Over Innsmouth"). *This Island Earth* strums on the reader's inner sense of looming catastrophe by making us contemplate equally inconceivable terrors of our *future*, unleashed not by Lovecraft's eldritch gods but by the technologists of tomorrow. At one point in the novel, Ruth asks Cal, "Didn't you feel it—the sense that [Jorgasnovara] knows and has been aware of things of utter terror and frightfulness that a normal mind could scarcely endure?" When Cal nods in the affirmative, Ruth opines that it was when Ole learned some of those things that he lost his mind.

• When Universal began prepping *This Island Earth*, there were budget estimates for black-and-white and color. In black-and-white it was expected to cost $625,000, in Eastman Color $700,000. Ultimately the movie was made in Technicolor.

• In the opening reel, when Cal's jet is en route to L.A., the identification number **28546** on its tail fin is the mirror image of what it should look like; this footage of the jet was "flipped," either unintentionally or, more likely, intentionally (so that the jet would look like it was going west). Near the end of the movie, when the courier plane drops out the bottom of Exeter's spaceship, the identification number **N97422** painted atop one wing is backwards.

• The Metalunans' towering foreheads create the impression that they're brainy chaps; will we mental midgets of Earth ever boast such king-sized crania? Perhaps, if the forensic anthropologists of the University of Tennessee are to be believed. They studied about 1500 skulls, dating from the mid–1800s through the 1980s, and ascertained that they had gradually become bigger. According to a 2012 Huffington Post article on their findings, "[S]kull size in white men has grown by 200 cubic centimeters, which is about the volume of a tennis ball."

• Size matters—or does it? Giving slightly swollen foreheads to Exeter, Brack, etc., is a cheesy shorthand way of visually indicating that them thar Metaluna folks have big brains that make 'em right smart, smarter'n us Earth folks. But then what are we to make of the fact that the Mutants have even bigger brains?

• Many pieces of Metalunan machinery feature atom symbols, "which when I was a kid was a symbol of total terror, because we were led to believe that the atomic bomb was gonna obliterate us all at any moment," talking-head Joe Dante (born in 1946) says in *This Island Earth: 2½ Years in the Making*. "It was a very 'Cold War mentality' which I think you can see in the film. These movies ['50s sci-fis] *did* contribute to our healthy skepticism about atomic power, which continues today."

• Once you see *This Island Earth* and the name Exeter sticks in your head, it picks up added dignity as time passes and you learn that there are dukes and earls of Exeter, England, that England has an Exeter University, that *Exeter* is the name of several Royal Navy ships, etc. Brack, on the other hand, instantly makes you think of brackish (i.e., unappealing to the taste, repulsive).

Oh, and how appropriate is this?: Ten years after the release of *This Island Earth*, September 1965, there was a series of UFO sightings in the night skies near.... Exeter, New Hampshire. The strange events of that night came to be known as "the Exeter incident" and inspired the writing of *Incident at Exeter*, reportedly still one of *the* top-selling UFO books ever.

• Jeff Morrow with his white wig of course appears older than Rex Reason in *This Island Earth*, but watching them together in the subsequent *The Creature Walks Among Us* you might think they were of the same generation. Not by a long shot. When making *This Island Earth*, Reason was 25 and Morrow nearly twice his age, 47; Morrow was a grown man acting on stage before Reason was born.

Talking to *Classic Images* interviewer Mike Barnum about *This Island Earth*, Reason mentioned being 25 at the time, and continued, "The character I was playing was supposed to be around 35. The director would tell me, 'Rex, think 35. Think and act 35,' and I thought to myself, 'How do you think 35?' When I saw myself in this film I thought I seemed stiff. What was nice, though, was that I realized I was given the opportunity at 25 to do the lead in a picture..."

• To get viewers to consider the possibility that a Metaluna migration might eventually lead to our subjugation, (1) Exeter's mansion is in Georgia and looks like a plantation house you'd see in, say, *Gone with the Wind*; (2) Ruth refers to its laboratories as "slave quarters"; (3) a black maid waits on the scientists in the dinner scene; and (4) Exeter promises not to "start cracking the whip on Meacham" until the next day. I'm ass-u-me-ing that these touches were intentional (but who knows?). Except for *The Mole People* (1956), I can't think of many other '50s sci-fis with even *one* touch that might make viewers recall slave days, much less four.

• A shot of the spaceship en route to Metaluna is flipped and re-used when the spaceship returns to Earth. As the ship approaches Metaluna, we twice see (on the Stellarscope) meteors striking the planet's ionized layer; it's really the same shot played twice. A shot of the ship flying low over Metaluna's war-torn surface also does double-duty, when the ship arrives and when it leaves.

• The Metalunans' unisex outfits were later worn by the "dirty Clickers" in the stageplay-like cheapie *The Creation of the Humanoids* (1962).

• When Exeter says, "We are not all masters of our souls, Dr. Meacham," he becomes the second Universal space alien to mention souls. Glob George mentions the soul (twice, in fact) in *It Came from Outer Space*.

• On Exeter's spaceship (in front of the Pilot's bench) and in the Monitor's Chamber (in front of the Monitor's bench) are atom models on pedestal stands. They look more decorative (Christmassy, in fact) than functional, but both these characters intently gaze at them like they're waiting for something to happen, so maybe we *are* supposed to think they serve some purpose.

• As Cal and Ruth near the end of their Converter Tubes ordeal, get a gander at Brack as he enters the scene with what must be the largest forehead appliance seen in the movie. Or maybe his wig isn't correctly positioned. Whatever. You could fit a second Brack face (eyes, nose and mouth) on his forehead.

On the ... back side ... of this 8 × 10 photograph, Universal's caption begins with "OH MY BACK" and goes on to say that Faith Domergue is looking for a comfortable place to lean, because her spacesuit's so tight that sitting was impossible. Since she sits in the Metaluna travel car, we're calling b.s. on that ... but we're not complaining, mind you! (Photograph courtesy Ronald V. Borst/Hollywood Movie Posters.)

• When the spaceship pilot (Richard Deacon) and the Monitor (Douglas Spencer) have something to announce, they are able to make themselves sound like they're talking into a loudspeaker or microphone, without benefit of loudspeaker or microphone. The script doesn't explain how they do it, saying simply that it's as if they're speaking through "an unseen amplifying system."

• When the spaceship pilot makes his announcements, the booming, echoing voice that fills the Spaceship Control Room doesn't sound much like Richard Deacon. It does, however, sound a *lot* like Russell Johnson.

• As Exeter's spaceship passes through Metaluna's ionized layer, we see on the Stellarscope the dawn-of-Earth explosions from the beginning of the black-and-white *Creature from the Black Lagoon*, tinted brownish-yellow and complete with a black scratch.

• As Jeff Morrow's Exeter leads Cal and Ruth from the spaceship to the nearby travel car tube, he says that at one time, "these tubes covered the surface of our Earth." Ummm ... excuse me? ... "*Earth*"? The scripted line was "...the surface of our world." But it wasn't a slip on Morrow's part. Robert Skotak tells me that a notation in the script supervisor's copy of the script indicates that the actor made the conscious decision to say "our Earth" rather than "our world."

• The travel car was previously seen in *Abbott and Costello Go to Mars*, there with windshield, tail fin and rear-exhaust flames as beautiful Venusian guards skimmed across the Venus landscape.

• Exeter's planet, his whole *civilization* is on the brink of extinct, but at least he has a sense of humor about it: Twice in the script (but only once in the movie), he refers to the annihilators of Metaluna as "our Zahgon friends."

• There are a couple of dissolves during the Metaluna travel car scenes, but otherwise Cal and Ruth's entire adventure on that planet, from Exeter's spaceship landing to its departure, takes place in real time: about ten minutes. If Ruth had put a pot of white rice on the spaceship stove before they disembarked, it wouldn't have been half-ready when they got back. We spend nearly twice as much time with Cal and Joe at the Ryberg airfield and lab.

• Did Milicent Patrick, of Gill Man fame, design the Metaluna Mutant? In February 1954, while touring to promote *Creature from the Black Lagoon*, she must have given *Brooklyn Eagle* interviewer Jane Corby that impression during a *tête-à-tête* at Toots Shor's, 51 West 51st Street, Manhattan. Corby wrote that, beyond the Gill Man, Patrick's other creations include the ectoplasmic *It Came from Outer Space* aliens "and her recently completed giant bugs, known as Mutates, which will come from another planet to plague the earth people in the soon to be filmed *This Island Earth*.[30] A March 1954 column by Alice Hughes, "Hollywood Beauty Is Monsters' 'Mother,'" concentrates on Patrick's Gill Man work, but late in the piece Hughes adds that other Patrick-created monsters are the "giant bugs from Outer Space in the picture *This Island Earth*."

• During the return spaceship trip, Regis Parton's injured, bleeding Mutant drops to the floor on the Converter Tubes platform. As he gets up onto his pincers and knees, notice the sweat sloshing around in the large; protruding Mutant eyeballs.

• When Bob Burns learned that Parton would be at a Stuntmen's Association event that he (Bob) was attending, he brought along a replica Mutant head, took a photo of Parton holding it, and had his one conversation with the veteran stuntman:

> He told me that he couldn't see anything when the big eyes were in the Mutant head. They took the eyes out in some of the scenes where you didn't see him face-on.
>
> Also, when he's disintegrating on the floor of the spaceship, you suddenly see his foot move into position as it was out of the effect area. He could hardly hear in the big head when they told him to move the foot. He said that they had many other Mutant shots to do but they changed the script and never shot any more scenes with him.

• I told producer William Alland that I find *This Island Earth* very juvenile, and he blurted out, "Absolutely—no question about it. Including that ridiculous Mutant! I didn't want that in the movie, but they said, 'You gotta have a monster!' God Almighty!" This directly contradicts screenwriter Franklin Coen's claim, quoted earlier in this chapter, that at the time of the making of the movie, Alland "loved his monsters" and was "deeply proud" of the Mutant. Which man is remembering wrong? I vote Coen because I know that Alland wanted no on-screen aliens in *It Came from Outer Space* and a much less monstrous-looking Gill Man in *Creature from the Black Lagoon*; therefore, the idea of Alland *eager* to have Mutants in *This Island Earth* doesn't strike me as credible. That's my opinion. *We* report, *you* decide!

Regis Parton sees a familiar face at a Stuntmen's Association event. A product of Cambria, Pennsylvania, he was a lifeguard and swimming champion until devoting himself to a stunt career. Six-foot-one and 180 pounds, he regularly doubled Rory Calhoun and also stood in for many top stars. (Photograph courtesy Bob Burns.)

• Speaking from the deepest depths of ignorance, I have a feeling that a bunch of meteor strikes would *not* transform a planet (i.e., Metaluna) into a sun. But I bought it when I was knee-high to an astronomer and first instincts are usually right so, again, maybe this *is* Good Science.

• Cal and Ruth get into all kinds of fine messes, first on Earth and then on Metaluna, but who cares when the screenwriters are on your side? As too-often happens in juvenile movies, their escapes are all a little *too* hair's-breadth: Metaluna turns into a sun about 70 seconds after they lift off in Exeter's spaceship; and then, after zipping from one end of the universe to the other, they enter Earth's atmosphere and Cal and Ruth drop out of the spaceship's belly in their plane about 40 seconds before the spaceship power poops out. It's a good thing the last guy who gassed up the spaceship topped it off, or they wouldn't have made it.

• By the end of the movie, Exeter is okay in Cal and Ruth's book, and the average viewer probably would have preferred that he relocate to Earth rather than commit suicide by spaceship. But he chooses the latter, prompted by his *Man Without a Country* anguish and also, perhaps, the screenwriters' awareness of the Breen Office. Exeter was, after all, responsible for the lobotomizing of a flock of scientists and then for their deaths. In that era, the Breen Office could not have let him skate. Exeter dead in the ocean *is* a better finish than Exeter in the pokey, sentenced to life plus 50 years.

• William Alland told me that most of his movies had some message, "even *This Island Earth*. What's the theme of *This Island Earth*? That a man without a world is nothing. That's the whole point—that's why Exeter cannot come to our world after his world is destroyed, so he kills himself. ... The Earth people invited Exeter to come live on Earth and he said no, thank you, because *his* planet was gone. And as far as he was concerned, life was not worth living any more."

• In a "first" for Universal sci-fis of the '50s, there's no hand-on-the-shoulder scare moment in *This Island Earth*. The studio's next sci-fi more than made up for it: There are *three* in *Revenge of the Creature* (1955).

• *This Island Earth* posters proclaimed that it was "2½

Years in the Making!" Wellll ... not quite. Joseph Newman bought the rights to the Jones novel no later than August 1953 and the movie was sneak-previewed in January 1955, so even "1½ Years in the Making!" might have been an exaggeration. The tag line "The Supreme Excitement of Our Time" (also seen in the trailer, along with "Spectacular *Fantastic* Beyond Belief") is a bit hyperbolic for a movie whose first half is a polite mystery drama, peopled by technologists, with some sci-fi accouterments. Syndicated New York columnist Mel Heimer wrote in August 1955: "Am I aging? I sat through half of the science fiction film, *This Island Earth*, and then reluctantly got up and left the air-conditioned movie house for the hot streets outside."

• According to a July 12, 1955, Summary of Production Report, *This Island Earth* had total direct charges of $543,100 (with 26.75 percent studio overhead bringing its cost up to $688,379). Color plus the second-half special effects give it an expensive look, so Monster Kids who like to ass-u-me call it Universal's biggie of the decade, but $688K is less than the cost of *It Came from Outer Space* ($703,570) and *The Land Unknown* ($802,620). Also, for a movie whose fans like to think of it as deluxe, it's scarcely any longer running-time-wise than Universal's other sci-fis.

• On the night of December 15, 1955, *This Island Earth* was one of ten films nominated by Motion Picture Sound Editors for Best Sound-Edited Picture of the Year; *It Came from Beneath the Sea* was another. "The envelope, please...": Come March 1956, *This Island Earth* came out the winner, with plaques going to editors Patrick McCormack and Ed Luckey and producer Alland.

• Early in 1956, *Variety* ran a list of the 107 features of 1955 that had grossed a million or more in domestic rentals (U.S. and Canada). Probably for the first time ever, there was a science fiction movie near the top of that list (#4)—but it wasn't *This Island Earth*. It was Disney's *20,000 Leagues Under the Sea*, which had made $8,000,000, a total that earned it a spot not only on 1955's list of hits but also on the list of the top moneymakers of all time. The next sci-fis were more than 70 titles down: *It Came from Beneath the Sea* and *This Island Earth*, tied at $1.7 million. Then came *Revenge of the Creature* at #101 with $1.1 million and *Conquest of Space* squeaking in at #104 with $1 million.

• American pride took a beating in 1957 when we learned that the Soviet Union had launched the first satellite—but Hollywood took that lemon and made lemonade. By October 16, 12 days after Sputnik went into orbit, Disney's *Man in Space* (1955) had already been quickly booked into one theater and *This Island Earth*, *When Worlds Collide* (1951), *It Came from Outer Space* (1953), *Conquest of Space* (1955) and *Satellite in the Sky* (1956) were again making the exhibition rounds.

• In the late 1950s, Austrian-born Fred Gebhardt quit his theater manager job to become an indie producer, making the outer space adventures *12 to the Moon* (1960) and *The Phantom Planet* (1961), one as dull as the other. In the latter, an Earth astronaut (Dean Fredericks) is marooned on Rehton, a mysterious asteroid whose technologically advanced inhabitants (English speakers, natch) live underground in caves and dress like extras in *Cleopatra*. Suddenly, around the midpoint, it turns into the $1.98 version of *This Island Earth*: We learn that Rehton is at war with another alien bunch, the Solarites, who attack Rehton in ships engulfed in flames (and therefore resemble the Zahgon meteors).

An advanced alien civilization, living underground because they're at war with other aliens, watching on a Stellarscope-like viewscreen the approach of the meteor-like ships of their enemy—that right there is enough to make it pretty obvious that the *Phantom Planet* writer was familiar with *This Island Earth*. But the icing on the cosmic cake is the appearance of a poor man's Metaluna Mutant: 7'2" Richard Kiel as a Solarite. His costume appears to be a takeoff on the Mutant, except it came out looking like a cross between Disney's Goofy and a gargoyle. Like Mutant #2, the Solarite answers the call of booty (it grabs Dolores Faith and carries her around) and is disintegrated by gravity pressure.

• The test footage of the Metaluna Mutant, shot on the Spaceship Control Room set, must have landed in a stock footage library because it turns up in the witless sci-fi spoof *The Creature Wasn't Nice* (1983), in a scene in which Cindy Williams (aboard a spaceship in space) is watching a TV show called *Earth News*: A female newscaster says that Harvey Furman of Virginia has had "the first successful body transplant" as we see the Mutant, walking quickly and rather feyly, hotfoot it up onto the spaceship control platform and, in front of the Stellarscope, do a 360-degree turn like a model showing off a new dress. It's wearing a belt (but not the belt it wears in *This Island Earth*) and for some reason there's a little box hanging from the back of the belt.

• Talking about *This Island Earth* in *Fangoria*, Faith Domergue said, "Steven Spielberg must like our picture, because a few years ago I was watching *E.T.* [*E.T. the Extra-Terrestrial*, 1982] with my daughter in Santa Barbara. To my surprise, when E.T. turned on that television, there were Rex and I [in *This Island Earth*], being pulled up into that flying saucer! It was very exciting!" The moronic *The Incredible Shrinking Woman* (1981) also featured a *This Island Earth* clip seen on a TV: a shot of the Mutant outside the Converter Tubes.

• After Morrow and Reason were reteamed in *The Creature Walks Among Us*, they acted together a third and last time in the 1962 *Perry Mason* episode "The Case of the Ancient Romeo" with Jeff as the acid-tongued director of a down-

and-out repertory company, murdered on a darkened stage while playing Romeo to Reason's Paris in a production of *Romeo and Juliet.*

• At the end of the 1968 *Voyage to the Bottom of the Sea* "Nightmare," guest star Paul Mantee turns out to be an alien who, while dying, reverts to his true form. He wears an over-the-head Metaluna Mutant mask, maybe a Don Post one, this one with king-sized green "elf ears" and what looks like gold Christmas tree ornaments for eyes.

• One day in 1996 when I paid a visit to *Fangoria* editor Tony Timpone at the magazine's Manhattan offices, he told me he was going to a *Mystery Science Theater 3000: The Movie* press screening that night and invited me to tag along. Even though I was no fan of the recently cancelled *MST* TV series, I went because the movie marked for mockery was *This Island Earth.* I got the impression, sitting in the small theater just before showtime, that many in the audience were *MST*-friendly because there seemed to be an upbeat, anticipatory vibe. All it took to cool that enthusiasm was for the movie to start. During the opening scenes which featured the series' regulars saying and doing Stupid Stuff, there was near-total audience silence; *Variety*'s Todd McCarthy called these sections "mirthless and barely tolerable." My fellow moviegoers livened up a bit once these characters (now bottom-of-the-screen silhouettes) started screening *This Island Earth* and making their cracks. But the first time one of them used the kind of language impermissible on TV, there were a few audience gasps (and no laughs). Then, except for some forced laughter now and then, everybody pretty much fell silent for the loooong, depressing duration.

I rewatched *Mystery Science Theater 3000: The Movie* for this book, hoping I might find *one MST* peanut gallery quip worth quoting, and came away with nothing. It runs 73 minutes and I'd guess that *This Island Earth* was cut by about a half-hour for their use. The MSTies' jibes are often sophomoric and coarse, and by the midpoint they're so lame that some of them sound ad libbed (and this movie had a platoon of writers!). If this was a live performance, you would have smelled the flop sweat.

I ass-u-me-d that the other folks in attendance at this press screening were movie reviewers and, going by the fact that the laughter was sparse, I expected to see thumbs-down reviews in the New York newspapers once the movie opened. But all the reviews I saw were pretty positive, recommending *Mystery Science Theater 3000: The Movie* and heaping scorn on *This Island Earth*:

• Janet Maslin, *New York Times*: [Its] jokey soundtrack can be too freely confused with [*This Island Earth*'s] actual dialogue, which is sillier than most of what the "Mystery Science Theater" revisionists can imagine. ... Some of [*This Island Earth*] fails to achieve pure kitsch and remains quietly dull.

• Dave Kehr, *New York Daily News*: [*This Island Earth* has] enough bad makeup jobs, pretentious lines and coy sexual situations to give the chattering puppets plenty of fodder.

• Larry Worth, *New York Post*: [The MSTies'] series of in-jokes and bitchy asides is aimed at the 1955 disaster *This Island Earth.*

Then, on a national level:

• Susan Wloszczyna, *USA Today*: The subject of [the MSTies' mocking]—*This Island Earth*, a somnolent slice of '50s sci-fi—isn't exactly prime Limburger. It's more like cheddar that hasn't aged very well. ... There's plenty to trash even if *Earth*'s running time has been cut in half (no protest here)...

• *Entertainment Weekly*: Here, as in [the *MST* TV series], we watch as an unspeakably horrendous grade-Z movie—in this case *This Island Earth*—unspools in its entirety [*sic*]. Balsa-wood acting, no-tech special effects, aliens who look like Silly Putty thumbs in white televangelist pompadours—on its own, the film would be all but unendurable.

In the 1990s, I was phone pals with William Alland, and at one point I explained to him what *Mystery Science Theater 3000* was and warned him that *Mystery Science Theater 3000: The Movie,* deriding *This Island Earth*, was in the works. He expressed dismay—not so much at the idea that one of his movies would be ridiculed, but that a crude, demeaning show like *MST* was popular. Some time after the release of *MST—The Movie*, I told him I'd read that it had turned out to be quite the box office dud. He actually exclaimed, in an almost childlike voice, "*Goody goody*!"

• At the 1999 Monster Rally convention in Arlington, Virginia, I hosted an all-star panel of sci-fi movie vets, among them Rex Reason, who was asked by an audience member about *Mystery Science Theater 3000: The Movie.* He said he was invited to a preview at L.A.'s Pacific Design Center, watched it from the back and "had a good laugh." Next, he said, its producer-director Jim Mallon and actor Trace Beaulieu spoke for a bit, and then surprised the audience with the announcement that Reason was there. People applauded and stood as the actor made his way to the front of the auditorium, and he chatted with his hosts; but then, deciding to have a bit of fun at *their* expense, he pulled a piece of paper out of his pocket, presented it to them and said, "Here's your subpoena!"

A flyer for that night's presentation called *This Island Earth* "painfully bad."

• The Metaluna Mutant was one of several '50s movie monsters recreated for the Area 52 scene in Warners' *Looney Tunes: Back in Action* (2003). Tom Woodruff's special effects company Amalgamated Dynamics made the Mutant, and of course there was a lot more *to* it than there was to Universal's, a half-century earlier. On the *Looney Tunes* stage, *in* the Mutant outfit (minus the head), Woodruff told me that the eyes could move independently and even blink and dilate, the mouths could open and close, the head had a blad-

The Metaluna Mutant (with Tom Woodruff inside) on the *Looney Tunes: Back in Action* set (top) with director Joe Dante and (below) with mechanical effects technician Seth Hayes. "No matter how we tried," Dante said, "we couldn't figure out exactly how the Universal makeup guys from 1954 got the Mutant's eyes to shimmer like they do in the close-ups."

der system so that it could throb, etc. When wearing the head on-camera, Woodruff wore video goggles so that he could see.

My full report on that set visit includes more quotes from the Mutant (Woodruff) plus Robby the Robot (Robert Parigi), the Man from Planet X (John Munro Cameron) and Robot Monster (Mark Viniello): "Merrie Monstrosities & Looney Toons" in *Starlog* #317, December 2003.

• The back cover synopsis of one of Universal's old *This Island Earth* DVD releases doesn't bother to mention Exeter or the Zahgons. According to the synopsis writer, who either didn't watch the movie or (even worse) *did* watch it but didn't understand it, the conflict is between Earth and Metaluna. Cal and "the gorgeous Dr. Adams" are whisked by spaceship to Metaluna, "where they are blamed for the destruction" of Exeter's Mansion. Huh? "Will interstellar negotiation save the day, or will the scientists be forced to take part in a treacherous battle to the death?" Eeeek.

The Release

By Robert J. Kiss

Preview Screenings

Universal initially timetabled the general release of *This Island Earth* for mid–April 1955, with trade screenings correspondingly arranged to take place on the East and West Coast in late March. Despite the last-minute rescheduling of the general release date to June, these trade screenings went ahead as planned, with *Variety* consequently publishing its review on March 29 and other trade magazines following suit during the first week of April.

A matinee preview was held on April 9 at the Victoria Theatre on Broadway (a venue that had already been selected for the picture's New York City premiere), to which "children of the New York trade press, daily press, syndicate, magazine, television and radio contacts" were invited. Seeking to highlight the suitability of *This Island Earth* for all the family, Universal informed invitees that "adults will be admitted only if they are accompanied by children."

Further pre-release screenings took place at a number of Air Force Bases, with Sheppard Air Force Base in Texas, for example, showing *This Island Earth* on the evenings of April 13 and 15. Back when the movie was still scheduled to enter general release in April, Jeff Morrow had been lined up to make personal appearances at openings in several cities; the *Los Angeles Times* of April 26 now reported his having been flown in to attend at least one preview screening held at this time instead.

Some audiences may also have seen *This Island Earth* as a sneak preview during late May and early June, when the title appeared repeatedly on "teaser" lists of forthcoming major releases that *might* be presented at local theaters' one-off weekly sneak screenings, in particular in the state of Texas.

Premiere and Theatrical First-Run

By the time of these sneak previews, cinemagoers should have been well aware of *This Island Earth*. Its massive multimedia promotional campaign had commenced on May 2, with advance publicity stills starting to appear in daily newspapers from that date onward, together with announcements to watch out for a big double-page color spread on the movie that would feature in the issues of *Collier's* and *Look* that hit newsstands on June 9 and 14.[31] Adorned with a breathtaking piece of panoramic artwork by Reynold Brown that depicted action-packed highlights from the forthcoming feature, these double-page spreads listed the names of over 800 theaters in 46 states at which the movie would open within 30 days of entering general release on June 15.

In order to further promote this so-called "saturation release," Universal also launched a "saturation advertising campaign" on television, with small-screen ads for *This Island Earth* featuring on *Billboard* magazine's "*Billboard* Scoreboard"—detailing "The Top Ten New National Spot Commercial Campaigns on TV"—for three consecutive weeks, covering the period from May 29 through June 18.

With Jeff Morrow on the road in a stage tour of Herman Wouk's *The Caine Mutiny Court-Martial* (playing Barney Greenwald) and therefore unavailable to help publicize *This Island Earth*, as had been intended when the movie was set to open in April, Rex Reason was now drafted to undertake a three-week series of radio, television and personal appearances in ten major cities. Arriving in New York City on June 2, Reason assisted with advance publicity for *This Island Earth*'s June 10 "world premiere" at the 800-seat Victoria Theatre on Broadway, where the "matinee preview" of the picture for trade contacts had previously been held on April 9. Reason's promotional duties included helping to judge a tie-in beauty contest for the title of "Miss Island Earth." The winner, Janet Wilde, got to appear in a sash outside the Victoria Theatre, distributing novelty "space balloons" to passersby on the day of the premiere.

However, the "world premiere" of *This Island Earth* at the Victoria Theatre was in fact the movie's *second* opening with Rex Reason in attendance on June 10. The actual premiere, although not billed as such, had taken place at the Fulton Theatre in Pittsburgh, Pennsylvania, where Reason signed autographs between 2:30 p.m. and 4:30 p.m. before flying back for that evening's New York "world premiere."

The much-heralded and meticulously organized saturation release of *This Island Earth* followed, as announced, from June 15. The sheer scale of the enterprise immediately brought the picture to cinema screens from coast to coast, and the three-figure number of prints in circulation meant that many small-town theaters which were usually way down the distribution schedule got to see this first-run feature within days (or in some cases, mere hours) of its general release, a novelty that garnered the movie special attention and many additional column inches in these localities.

In Los Angeles, *This Island Earth* opened simultaneously at four hardtop theaters and seven drive-ins on the first day of its general release, June 15. Chicago wouldn't get to see

Janet Wilde, winner of Universal's "Most Beautiful Girl on This Island Earth" contest, distributes trick balloons in front of the Victoria Theatre in New York's Times Square on the movie's opening day there.

the film until June 24, with its opening at McVickers Theater accompanied by one of Rex Reason's final p.a.s in support of its first run. The McVickers opening was billed as the "Midwest Premiere" which, under ordinary circumstances, it might well have been; however, in the context of this saturation release, tens of other Midwestern theaters had beaten the McVickers to the punch, with the actual "Midwest Premiere"—likewise billed as such—almost certainly having taken place at the Uptown Theater in Racine, Wisconsin, on June 15.

As is typical of saturation releases, the substantial number of prints in circulation resulted in a markedly shortened first run, with theaters in towns and cities of all sizes already having played the movie by the end of August, and only small rural venues still opening it as a new picture during September. Thus, the domestic first run of *This Island Earth* may be considered to have lasted from mid–June to the end of September 1955 only. While the "saturation" approach allowed the movie to smash its way onto *Boxoffice* magazine's "*Boxoffice* Barometer" (charting the performance of first-run features in 20 different cities) some seven times between June 25 and August 20, 1955, averaging roughly 30 percent above "normal grosses" during that period, the conclusion of its reign at the box office came about equally swiftly, with *Variety* observing that trade was already "easing off" in some (well-saturated) locations as early as the first week of July. Reminiscent of several of the movie's scenes on Metaluna, the box office success of *This Island Earth* might be likened to a dazzling meteoric explosion.

As a Stand-Alone Feature

Within a sample of 1200 U.S. movie theaters during the period from June to September 1955, 39 percent of all *This Island Earth* screenings took the form of a stand-alone presentation supported only by selected cartoons, novelties and other shorts. This form of presentation was attested in towns and cities of all sizes; on occasion, this was because stand-alone screenings were already an established norm in given locations. However, in a far greater number of cases, this appears instead to have been based on cinema owners' confidence in the heavily advertised movie to stand on its own merits, even though their standard practice was to exhibit double-features. In Texas in particular, almost all first-run theaters showed *This Island Earth* as a stand-alone, a pattern also attested with other Universal sci-fi features (including the *Black Lagoon* trilogy) in the state during this period.

With Featurette Accompaniment

Within that sample of 1200 U.S. movie theaters, around one percent elected to play *This Island Earth* with accompaniment that was referred to in newspaper listings specifically as a "featurette"—meaning, in these instances, a movie with a running time of roughly a half-hour. This uncommon form of "lightweight double-bill" was attested mainly in small towns where no other competing venues were screening *This Island Earth*.

All of the attested "co-featurettes" are arranged alphabetically below. The month mentioned in each case is the earliest in which the pairing was encountered.

June 1955 *Black Fury* (Okeefenokee documentary, 32 minutes)

July 1955 *Devil Take Us* ("Theatre of Life" traffic safety docudrama, 21 minutes)

July 1955 *The Mighty Fortress* (Billy Graham documentary, 31 minutes)

June 1955 *The Missing Passenger* ('Calling Scotland Yard' mystery thriller, 27 minutes)

Double-Bills

Some 66 percent of all screenings of *This Island Earth* within the sample of 1200 U.S. movie theaters took the form of a double-bill, making this the most common way to have originally experienced the movie during its first run. Furthermore, in fully 92 percent of cases, *This Island Earth* was the top-billed picture.

Although Universal did not assign a regular co-feature to *This Island Earth*, the company clearly sought to control both halves of the bill whenever possible, with 49 percent of all double-bills comprising two Universal features. These included *This Island Earth*'s most frequently attested co-feature, *Abbott and Costello Meet the Mummy*, which accompanied it at 12 percent of twin-bill screenings, in addition to several other of the most commonly found pairings within the sample. Three percent of double-bill patrons nationwide even got to experience a double-dose of Rex Reason wherever *This Island Earth* was paired with the Universal Western *Smoke Signal*, in which Reason played in support of Dana Andrews.

Pretty much all of the different co-features listed below seem to have been selected with the aim of creating a so-called "balanced program" that paired the outer space spectacle of *This Island Earth* with the familiarly earthbound action of a Western, thriller, swashbuckler, drama or comedy. Genre-matched double-bills, coupling *This Island Earth* with either *Cat-Women of the Moon* or *Revenge of the Creature*, remained an exception, collectively accounting for barely 1.5 percent of double-bill showings in the sample.

One "matched" aspect of numerous double-bill pairings was stressed consistently in advertising, though: the fact that both features were in color. Indeed, 56 percent of all double-bill screenings in the sample comprised two color pictures, something that remained a relative novelty for cinemagoers, in particular where a top-billed sci-fi feature was involved.

All of the double-bill co-features attested within the sample are arranged alphabetically below. The month mentioned in each case is the earliest in which the pairing was encountered. No examples were found of *This Island Earth* playing on anything other than a single- or double-bill during its first run.

(*) signifies a slightly more substantial number of playdates.
(**) signifies a regular affiliation of the titles (between six percent and 12 percent of theaters).
bold titles are Universal releases.

June 1955 *5 Against the House* (Guy Madison)
June 1955 *Abbott and Costello Meet the Keystone Kops* (Abbott and Costello)
June 1955 (**) *Abbott and Costello Meet the Mummy* (Abbott and Costello)
June 1955 *The Adventures of Sadie* (Joan Collins)
July 1955 (*) *Ain't Misbehavin'* (Rory Calhoun)
June 1955 *Bengal Brigade* (Rock Hudson)
July 1955 *Big House, U.S.A.* (Broderick Crawford)
June 1955 *The Black Dakotas* (Gary Merrill)
August 1955 *The Black Shield of Falworth* (Tony Curtis)
August 1955 *Bowery to Bagdad* (Bowery Boys)
August 1955 *Canyon Crossroads* (Richard Basehart)
August 1955 *Cat-Women of the Moon* (Sonny Tufts)
June 1955 *Chicago Syndicate* (Dennis O'Keefe)
June 1955 *Code Two* (Ralph Meeker)
August 1955 *Davy Crockett: King of the Wild Frontier* (Fess Parker)
July 1955 *Dawn at Socorro* (Rory Calhoun)
July 1955 *Detour* (Tom Neal; Madison Pictures reissue)
August 1955 *East of Eden* (Julie Harris)
July 1955 *Escape to Burma* (Barbara Stanwyck)
June 1955 *The Eternal Sea* (Sterling Hayden)
July 1955 *The Far Horizons* (Charlton Heston)
June 1955 *The Fast and the Furious* (John Ireland)
August 1955 *Foxfire* (Jane Russell)
July 1955 *Frontiers of '49* (Wild Bill Elliott; Norman Distributing reissue)
June 1955 *The Glass Tomb* (John Ireland)
August 1955 *Hell Raiders of the Deep* (Eleonora Rossi Drago)
July 1955 *High Society* (Bowery Boys)
June 1955 *Hollywood Thrill-Makers* (James Gleason)
July 1955 *In Old Amarillo* (Roy Rogers)
July 1955 *Jalopy* (Bowery Boys)
September 1955 *Jamaica Run* (Ray Milland)
August 1955 *Jump into Hell* (Jack Sernas)
July 1955 *Jungle Moon Men* (Johnny Weissmuller)
August 1955 *Lady and the Tramp* (animated, Walt Disney)
July 1955 *Land of Fury* (Jack Hawkins)
August 1955 *The Little Kidnappers* (Duncan Macrae)
August 1955 *The Lone Gun* (George Montgomery)
August 1955 *Long John Silver* (Robert Newton)
June 1955 *Loophole* (Barry Sullivan)
June 1955 (**) *The Looters* (Rory Calhoun)
August 1955 *Lord of the Jungle* (Johnny Sheffield)
July 1955 (*) *Ma and Pa Kettle at Waikiki* (Marjorie Main and Percy Kilbride)
July 1955 *The Magnificent Matador* (Anthony Quinn)
June 1955 *Mambo* (Silvana Mangano)
June 1955 (**) *The Man from Bitter Ridge* (Lex Barker)
August 1955 *The Man from the Alamo* (Glenn Ford)
July 1955 *Man Without a Star* (Kirk Douglas)
June 1955 *The Marauders* (Dan Duryea)
July 1955 (*) *Moonfleet* (Stewart Granger)
July 1955 *Naked Alibi* (Sterling Hayden)
June 1955 *New Orleans Uncensored* (Arthur Franz)
September 1955 *New York Confidential* (Broderick Crawford)
June 1955 *Operation Manhunt* (Harry Townes)
August 1955 *Outlaw's Daughter* (Jim Davis)
July 1955 *Pirates of Tripoli* (Paul Henreid)
July 1955 *A Prize of Gold* (Richard Widmark)
July 1955 *The Prodigal* (Lana Turner)
June 1955 *Project M7* (Phyllis Calvert)
July 1955 *The Purple Mask* (Tony Curtis)
August 1955 *The Racers* (Kirk Douglas)
July 1955 *Rage at Dawn* (Randolph Scott)
September 1955 *Reap the Wild Wind* (Ray Milland; Paramount reissue)
July 1955 *Revenge of the Creature* (John Agar)
July 1955 *Ride Clear of Diablo* (Audie Murphy)
July 1955 *Run for Cover* (James Cagney)
August 1955 *Saskatchewan* (Alan Ladd)
July 1955 *Seminole Uprising* (George Montgomery)
June 1955 *Siege at Red River* (Van Johnson)
July 1955 *Sitting Bull* (Dale Robertson)
June 1955 (*) *Smoke Signal* (Dana Andrews)
August 1955 *Soldier of Fortune* (Clark Gable)
August 1955 *Spy Chasers* (Bowery Boys)
August 1955 *Strange Lady in Town* (Greer Garson)
June 1955 *The Stranger's Hand* (Richard Basehart)
August 1955 *Strategic Air Command* (James Stewart)
June 1955 (**) *Tall Man Riding* (Randolph Scott)
August 1955 *Tarzan's Hidden Jungle* (Gordon Scott)
July 1955 *They Rode West* (Robert Francis)
August 1955 *They Were So Young* (Scott Brady)
June 1955 *Top of the World* (Dale Robertson)
September 1955 *Track of the Cat* (Robert Mitchum)
July 1955 *Treasure of Ruby Hills* (Zachary Scott)
August 1955 *Tumbleweed* (Audie Murphy)
August 1955 *Untamed* (Tyrone Power)
August 1955 *Up Front* (David Wayne)
July 1955 *Violent Saturday* (Victor Mature)
July 1955 *War Arrow* (Jeff Chandler)
June 1955 *West of Zanzibar* (Anthony Steel)
July 1955 *The White Orchid* (William Lundigan)
September 1955 *The Window* (Arthur Kennedy; RKO reissue)
August 1955 *The Wizard of Oz* (Judy Garland; MGM reissue)

August 1955 *Wyoming Renegades* (Phil Carey)
July 1955 *Yellowneck* (Lin McCarthy)
June 1955 *You Know What Sailors Are* (Akim Tamiroff)

Theatrical Reissue

As a second-run feature, *This Island Earth* continued to do steady trade between 1956 and 1962, with *Variety* repeatedly noting weekly takings in the region of $4000 or $5000 at a single theater whenever the film was "reissued" to a limited number of venues during these years. In 1964, there was then a full national reissue of the picture on a double-bill with Universal's Lon Chaney biopic *Man of a Thousand Faces*, which according to *Variety* did "moderate" or "nice" trade. Eye-grabbing advertisements for the double-bill were adorned with oversized taglines in an angular font considerably larger and more striking than that employed for the titles of the two movies, promising *Blood Lust in Outer Space* and *A Chamber of Horrors*. It is perhaps unsurprising that a small number of theaters misconstrued these giant taglines as the names of the movies and ran newspaper listings for them under these unintended re-titlings.

Following this nationwide theatrical reissue, *This Island Earth* came to television—by way of a pan-and-scan version—in October 1965. Some residents of Bartlesville, Oklahoma, may have considered this old news, since *This Island Earth* had first played on the small screen there as early as February 1958, on the short-lived Telemovie subscription station operated in the town by Video Independent Theatres of Oklahoma City between the fall of 1957 and the summer of 1958. The number of subscribers to this early "Pay TV" station totaled between 500 and 2000 households, according to different contemporary estimates.

Although no one seems to have spotted it at the time, elements from Reynold Brown's original poster artwork for *This Island Earth* could also be found in pirated form between 1957 and 1960, in newspaper ads for Ron Ormond's release of the 18-minute featurette *Attack of the Flying Saucers*. Employed by Ormond to fill out underperforming double-bills (by questionably representing them as triple-bills!), this featurette was his redubbed version of a 1953 West German UFO documentary, originally titled *Fliegende Untertassen* ("Flying Saucers"), that contained dramatized sequences and animator Friedrich Wollangk's stop-motion depiction of a saucer attack. Despite the impression conveyed by the appropriated elements in its advertising campaign, Faith Domergue and Rex Reason were of course nowhere to be found in the movie.

The Critics' Corner

Film Bulletin: William Alland's production is top-drawer and Joseph Newman's direction conjures up a wealth of fascinating, eerie atmosphere, while maintaining a good pace.

Harrison's Reports: [T]he story is highly imaginative and frequently chilling and thrilling. ... It is all completely improbable, but those who accept the story for what it is should find it to their liking. The special effects are extraordinary...

Time: [*This Island Earth*] stays earthbound just a little too long...

Cue: The technical effects are excellent and the spatial color photography exciting. Thus this Captain Video kid stuff may just be the kind of escapist entertainment you're looking for.

The Hollywood Reporter: Richly invested, imaginatively conceived, and produced with class.... All performances are better than satisfactory, with Morrow, who has a special gift for bravura parts, dominating things...

The New York Times: [The movie's technical effects] are so superlatively bizarre and beautiful that some serious shortcomings can be excused, if not overlooked. ... [It] can also boast reasonable acting and plucky, even literate, writing. It sorely needs a pair of shears, a less conventional musical score and a director of considerably more drive and less awe toward his subject than Joseph Newman. ... [M]ost of the commotion is pretty wonderful, once the Universal art wizards take over, as the disk streaks toward its goal in a vast, brilliantly spangled, interplanetary void. One setting alone, a panoramic vista of the doomed planet "Metaluna," should leave anyone bug-eyed.

Motion Picture Daily (Al Steen): Take Buck Rogers, Space Cadets, Jules Verne and H.G. Wells, put them in a cocktail mixer, shake well and you have *This Island Earth*.

Boxoffice: By combining a suspenseful interplanetary drama with some of the most exciting technical effects to appear on the screen in recent years, *This Island Earth* will have appeal to young and old, sophisticated and unsophisticated alike.

Variety: Special effects of the most realistic type rival story and characterizations in capturing the interest of this exciting science fiction chiller, one of the most imaginative and cleverly conceived entries turned out to date in the outer-space field. ... [Interest] is of the edgeoftheseat variety during latter half of the film.

The Kingsville (Texas) *Record*: If U-I wants a fitting sequel, we suggest that for script writers they hire the inmates of an insane asylum, pass around a jug of tequila, and turn the boys loose. The resultant "story" should be even more absurd than the one presented here.

The weird planet in outer space in *This Island Earth* is named Metaluna. That's the tip-off to the title of the sequel. *Mad Metaluna*, featuring the Metalunatics.

St. Petersburg (Florida) *Times*: [This] is among Hollywood's best contributions to the science fiction field.

San Antonio (Texas) *Light*: Perhaps the producers have overdone it a bit by bringing in a giant monster, half human and half insect. But, after all, the general idea is to give the moviegoer some spine-tingling thrills. And he gets them.

The Summer Texan (Texas): Where so many pictures of this type have failed by insulting the intelligence of the audience, *This Island Earth* presents innovations which, though sometimes almost beyond comprehension, are believable. Science fiction enthusiasts will herald it as tops and it will set a standard which will not easily be surpassed by future attempts in the realm of fantasy.

San Rafael (California) *Independent-Journal*: [*This Island Earth*] is (for a change) top-drawer science fiction filmmaking, moved out of the hokum grade B class by some sound plotting and imaginative special effects. ... The panoramic vista of the doomed planet Metaluna is in itself enough to leave the viewer wide-eyed, for the Universal-International artists have had a field day: huge meteors bearing down on the space craft; the brilliantly spangled interplanetary void; flaming spaceships.

Los Angeles Times: *This Island Earth* is one of the most fascinating—and frightening—science fiction movies to come at us yet from outer space. We are told that it arrives from a place no farther away than the Universal-International studio in the San Fernando Valley; but this is patently an attempt to assuage the new alarm which the picture will inspire in us jittery mortals.

Clearly, the thing comes from Metaluna.

... To the camera and effects men must go the major laurels for making [the movie's] wonders visible and audible—in awesome Technicolor and a soundtrack that is as ear-wracking as it is eerie.

Cosmic Concerto: The Music of This Island Earth

By David Schecter

Of all the 1950s science fiction scores that have been unfairly neglected over the years—and there are quite a few of them—*This Island Earth*'s belongs near the top of the list. It's not only one of Universal's finest sci-fi scores, it's one of the studio's best soundtracks from any genre in any era. Its wealth of memorable themes and inventive approaches make it deserving of a place alongside such widely lauded works as Leith Stevens' *Destination Moon* (1950), Dimitri Tiomkin's *The Thing from Another World* (1951) and Bernard Herrmann's *The Day the Earth Stood Still* (1951). The only way to account for this oversight is that *This Island Earth* did not include a composer's film credit, which would have made talking and writing about the music a lot easier.

The job of writing the score went to staff composer Herman Stein, no stranger to science fiction and horror movies, as he had already contributed original material to *Abbott and Costello Go to Mars, It Came from Outer Space, Creature from the Black Lagoon* and even a bit to *Revenge of the Creature*. Stein wrote 21 *This Island Earth* cues but did not receive a screen credit because Universal's general policy was to omit a composing credit when more than one composer wrote music for the same picture. Therefore, because Hans Salter and Henry Mancini scored the movie's final six cues—lasting just under eight minutes—Stein didn't receive his credit.

This was unfortunate, because the studio's policy wasn't set in stone, and there were exceptions to this "rule" going all the way back to *The Invisible Man Returns* (1940) and *Pittsburgh* (1942), both co-credited to Hans J. Salter and Frank Skinner. Even in the Joseph Gershenson era, the 1956 Barbara Stanwyck film *There's Always Tomorrow* was co-credited to Herman Stein and Heinz Roemheld. In addition, *Sign of the Pagan* (1954) and *The Rawhide Years* (1956) were both co-credited to Salter and Skinner, although Stein wrote music for the former picture, and Eric Zeisl had some tracked music in the latter. In these last two films, Gershenson's credit for Music Supervision is wider—due to the length of his name—than Salter and Skinner's combined credits. And that's an amazing feat in *The Rawhide Years* because the two composers are credited on the same horizontal line! Both Salter and Skinner predated Gershenson's arrival at the studio and they had more clout than Stein, and that's probably one reason why Stein got stiffed on *This Island Earth*.

Another Universal policy stated that even when there were multiple composers on a film, if one of them wrote at least 80 percent of the score, that composer would get a screen credit along with Gershenson's. This rule didn't apply to all films; a few of the exemptions were *The Leech Woman, Let's Kill Uncle, The Monolith Monsters, No Name on the Bullet* and *The Saga of Hemp Brown*. On *Let's Kill Uncle*, Stein received one of his rare screen credits despite his name being on only 32 of that picture's 84 cues, and none of his cues were even composed for *Let's Kill Uncle*, as they had all been written for earlier movies. In *The Saga of Hemp Brown*, Stein composed 105 out of the 108 original and tracked cues in that feature, with the remaining three being public domain source cues. Even so, Stein didn't receive a screen credit on the picture. Go figure!

Regardless of studio policies, the reality is that almost every time more than one composer worked on the same movie, the only music credit went to Gershenson. As the head of the music department, he probably could have made sure that on certain assignments a given composer had enough time to write 80 percent of a score as opposed to just below that amount. But since that 80 percent number was fairly spurious anyway, it's doubtful anything could have altered the fact that so few Universal composers received screen credits during the 1950s. Far too many times, additional composers were brought in to add a few cues at the last minute, and in the case of *This Island Earth*, Stein ended up writing "only" about 75 percent of the score. Seeing as he composed over 23 minutes of music, while Mancini and Salter combined for less than eight—with some of Salter's writing being based on Stein's themes and ideas—there should have been some way to give Stein a screen credit.

Gershenson liked to keep his composers busy, and although he claimed that he "protected the composers from the directors," he actually dissuaded them from fraternizing with directors and producers on the lot. He tried to keep them isolated, such as wanting them to eat together at Universal's commissary. The composers were therefore a mostly anonymous bunch around Hollywood, where having your name in the credits meant everything. Although the composers were well-paid for their work (contract writers made at least $15,000 annually in the mid–50s), the lack of screen credits definitely affected some of them after the music department folded in the late '50s and they had to try to make it on their own. Even the chance meeting near Universal's barber shop that led to the remarkable partnership between Henry Mancini and director Blake Edwards occurred after Mancini had been fired by Universal and he just happened to be getting a haircut at his former studio.

In Universal's defense, it was a film factory, cranking out pictures at a rapid pace, and imminent scoring deadlines could be met by having a few composers simultaneously writing music for the same movie while others were adapting music from earlier pictures. This set-up allowed one composer to be taken off one film and moved to a more pressing assignment. However, when deadlines weren't looming, the only result of replacing one composer with another was that no composer received a screen credit, especially as one composer could pretty much compose just as fast as another. *This Island Earth* was in production for a long time, and although composing was one of the last things done to a film, Stein could write about three minutes of music a day, so he could have scored the end of the film in fewer than three days. Pre-release production notes credit Stein with scoring the picture by himself, and the composer remembered thinking the assignment was his alone, so it's certainly possible that outside assistance was needed because the picture was behind schedule when it was handed over to him. However, it would have taken Stein only about four hours to compose an additional 1:30 of music so he'd have written 80 percent of the score.

This Island Earth was one of the studio's most prestigious productions at the time, and it's just possible that the head of the music department didn't want to share such an important music credit with an actual composer, in which case he might have moved Stein onto another project prematurely; Stein couldn't recall whether that was the case or not. But other than producer William Alland and director Joseph Newman, the film's only other full-screen credit went to Gershenson. It's unfortunate that Stein never got the recognition he deserved for his marvelous contribution to the picture, because when the studio laid off its composing staff in 1958, he had trouble finding other movie work, partly because almost nobody in the industry was aware of all the masterful—but uncredited—work he did during his Universal tenure.

While it might seem obvious that a film of *This Island Earth*'s stature would rate an entirely original score, the fact that the classic *The Incredible Shrinking Man* didn't, and the not-exactly-classic *The Mole People* did, shows that things didn't always make logical musical sense at Universal. *This Island Earth* probably received an original score both because it was an important picture, and also because it was different enough from the studio's prior movies that little in the music library would have worked in many of the sequences. While some *It Came from Outer Space* cues might have been appropriate for certain *This Island Earth* scenes, much of the music from that earlier picture wouldn't have fit the tone or action of the new space opera. Still, viewers should probably be thankful that previous "love" music wasn't used to augment the romance between Cal and Ruth, as there were a lot of cues in the library that could have worked, although for certain scenes some of them would have needed to be affixed to more "fantastic" music.

One of the most noticeable characteristics of *This Island Earth*'s score is its brevity, as the movie contains only 31 minutes of original music and about a minute and a half of source music, which totals only about 37 percent of the running time. Although this percentage is similar to that of 20th Century-Fox's *The Day the Earth Stood Still*, Warner Brothers' *Them!* and RKO's *The Thing from Another World*, Universal usually favored much more musical accompaniment, as illustrated by *The Monolith Monsters*' 48 percent, *Tarantula*'s 49 percent, *The Mole People*'s 59 percent and all three Creature films, each of which contained over 60 percent of underscore. The limited amount of music in *This Island Earth* is because sound effects play an extremely large role in the picture. Substantial work went into the movie's many futuristic audio effects, some of which were created electronically. Stein didn't want music and sound effects battling each other in this film, so whether it's the futuristic hum of a flying saucer, a blast of Neutrino rays, or the roar of a conventional plane's engine, the sound effects rarely compete with score.

Besides the standard instrumentation, Stein and the other composers created celestial and futuristic-sounding music via the extensive use of keyboards and percussion, including piano, celesta, Novachord, marimba, xylophone, vibraphone and harp. Stein featured the Novachord prominently in the picture, and reverb was added to it so it could better blend with the acoustic orchestra. Reverb was seldom desired with conventional instruments, because echo was something to be avoided like the plague. Music needed to end with the footage it was written for, as opposed to having to snip it off prematurely when it lingered for an extra second after the film had already moved on to the next scene.

Because the Theremin had become a science fiction cliché in the two years since *It Came from Outer Space*, Stein and orchestrator David Tamkin decided to come up with a suitably "spacey" sound without using that electronic instrument: The Theremin-like sonorities heard in a number of *This Island Earth* cues were created by cellos and vibraphone playing together with a wide vibrato. The interference caused by the sound waves helped create the amazing musical effect, although how these two astonishing musicians came up with this idea is left for us lesser minds to ponder. Stein needed sufficient cellos to achieve this effect, but it's not known whether he had to specially request them for this picture, or whether they were already available to him.

The standard make-up of an orchestra's string section has many more violins than violas, more violas than cellos, and more cellos than string basses. Universal sometimes reversed their string proportion to favor cellos over violas, possibly because cellos have a more powerful sound, which would give more weight to the medium-sized ensemble. Of course, this altered string balance also resulted in a slightly deeper, mellower feel to the strings. *This Island Earth*'s string section was divided: five first violins, five second violins, two violas, four cellos and one bass. If Universal had scheduled more violas than cellos for *This Island Earth*, Stein probably wouldn't have been able to simply add more cellos to the orchestra as needed, because Universal was stingily reluctant to add additional players to its contract group. Instead, they might have taken away some violas or other instruments to keep the music budget where it was. Whether Universal already had the "flipped" string section planned for *This Island Earth*, or whether Stein convinced them to add some cellos and take away some violas, he had a sufficient number of cellists to create the effect he desired. Almost all the horror pictures made after *Creature from the Black Lagoon* used a string section proportion favoring cellos over violas. There were two recording sessions for *This Island Earth*, the first being a three-hour session on January 11, 1955, and the second being four hours on January 20, 1955. Gershenson conducted both, with the latter session including an hour devoted to the short film *The Dust Eaters*, which featured a tracked score conducted by Milton Rosen.

Another notable characteristic of *This Island Earth*'s score is that eight of the movie's last 15 cues were edited, meaning that cuts were made to the film after the score had already been recorded. These changes resulted in about five minutes of music being removed from the picture. As happened when *It Came from Outer Space* was edited late in the game, rather than rewriting *This Island Earth*'s cues and re-recording them after the last-minute film edits were done, the music tracks were edited, and you can hear some of the soundtrack cuts in the picture. What often occurred in cases like this was that the middles of these pieces would be removed, shortening them so the beginnings and endings re-

Conductor's score of Herman Stein's *This Island Earth* "Main Title." (© 1955 Gilead Music Co.)

Herman Stein sketch of *This Island Earth*'s "Main Title." (© 1955 Gilead Music Co.)

main married to the visuals they were written for, unless the part of the film that was excised came at the beginning or end of the composition, in which case the music edits would be made elsewhere.

Almost every musical sequence in *This Island Earth* is skillfully conceived and executed, starting with Stein's "Main Title." This cue begins as fairly conventional horror music under the Universal-International logo, but soon turns into something decidedly different, with Novachord playing the ethereal and haunting seven-note Metaluna theme used throughout the picture. When the film's title comes into focus, harsh trumpets foreshadow the horror aspects in the second half of the movie. The bulk of the piece uses Novachord to create a sense of mystery—one that will envelop much of the plot. Although it will be over 50 minutes before we glimpse a flying saucer or another outer space shot, the alien-sounding music prepares us for what lies ahead. The triumphant orchestral writing at the end brings us back to Earth, where most of the story will take place. Structurally, the piece resembles Stein's *Creature from the Black Lagoon* and *The Land Unknown* main titles, with their opening monster sounds being followed by long and mysterious keyboard-dominated sections.

"Jet West" introduces one of the last pieces of "conventional" music heard in the movie (apart from the picture's love theme), as the score will soon be colored by the presence of the extra-terrestrial Metalunans. This heroic Americana cue captures the freeness of flight as electronics expert-nuclear scientist-deep-throated heartthrob Cal Meacham jets across the U.S., with the music accenting scenic shots of the Grand Canyon and various mountain ranges. The upbeat piece was recycled for use in the Universal short subjects *Modern Minute Men* and *Cyclomania*.

After Cal's jet engine cuts out and his plane rolls safely to a stop at Ryberg Electronics Corporation, "Color Blind" begins with a dramatic orchestral punctuation. Film composers often begin their cues so the music's entrance doesn't call attention to itself, but Stein occasionally uses his *This Island Earth* cues to punctuate events that have just concluded, such as the musical exclamation point here. This illustrates how Stein wanted the sound effects and music to remain separate, as only the strange humming accompanies the eerie visual of the jet bathed in green light, and the music doesn't begin until the sound effect cuts out. This approach not only serves to underscore the aircraft's vulnerability, but it also helps the scene remain fixed in the viewer's mind long after the picture is over. "Color Blind" uses two flutes and an oboe to create a strange aural background, and when Joe tells Cal what he saw and heard, the Metaluna theme makes some subtle appearances. The portentous coda adds an uneasy touch as Cal tells Joe they should act blind by not revealing what they saw, hence the cue's clever title.

One of Stein's most interesting cues is the atmospheric "From Unit #16," which plays when Joe and Cal receive the futuristic catalogue from Electronics Service, Unit No. 16. Stein wanted the composition played "slow & mysterious," and the opening melody on bassoon hints that there's something odd about the unopened package. As the catalogue cover is glimpsed, Novachord offers a variation of the unearthly Metaluna theme, and when Cal places an order and receives more crates than there are at the end of *Citizen Kane*, Novachord again punctuates the bizarre visual. Stein requested the Novachord play "screwy." This was his way of requesting an organ setting with high partials (pure tones that are part of a complex tone), which adds strange sounds to the mix. He used a similar effect in the main titles of *Black Lagoon, The Mole People* and *The Land Unknown*. The chamber music approach of "From Unit #16" reveals Stein's ability to keep things interesting by offering a wide variety of instrumental touches to a cue that does not feature the entire orchestra. The piece was later used to lend an appropriately spooky touch to the lab sequence in *Tarantula* when Prof. Deemer fills a hypodermic needle with growth nutrient. It's equally effective in *Monster on the Campus* when Arthur Franz awakens on the school lawn after recovering from a stint as a rubber-faced ape-man.

As Cal points to the interocitor blueprint and decides how he and Joe will attempt to assemble the alien machine, "Interocitor Montage" begins. Stein's lively cue is propelled by staccato brass, pizzicato strings, trilling clarinets, xylophone and vibraphone, with the unique orchestration helping to convey the odd nature of the invention. After the interocitor is constructed, Novachord imparts an alien feeling that lets the viewer know the job has been successfully completed. As incongruous as it might seem, this cue was reused in Universal's *The Girl in the Kremlin* (1957), as well as in the studio shorts *Behind the Ticker Tape, Cyclomania* and *Modern Minute Men*.

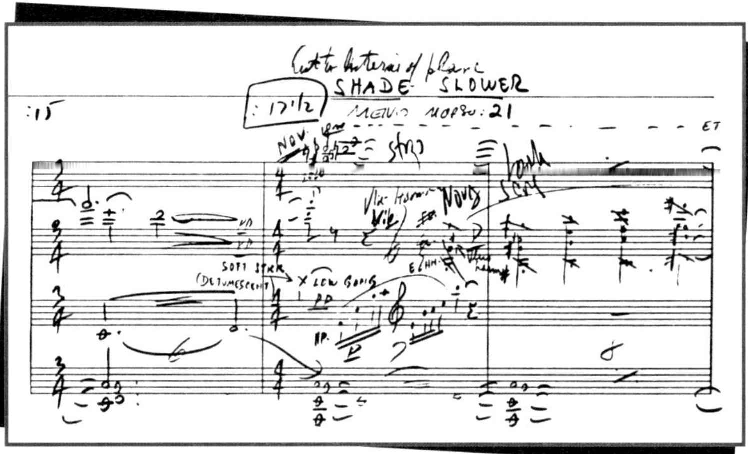

Excerpt from Herman Stein's sketch of "Robot Plane." (© 1955 Gilead Music Co.)

The title "*This Island Earth*" does not merely refer to the fact that the Earth is an island in the cosmos. Raymond F. Jones' novel mentions that even though the primitive islanders in World War couldn't understand the power of the forces involved in that confrontation, they still helped the advanced civilizations by doing menial labor such as clearing jungles to make airfields. Jones' Earthlings are being used to manufacture "pushbuttons" (interocitors), whose purpose they don't even comprehend, and Cal is merely a project engineer whose job is to get the Earthlings to build them. The screenplay transformed Cal and the other humans into more important characters, which made the film less believable, as it's doubtful that the intellectually advanced Metalunans—even with their scientists dead—would need the brainpower of puny Earthlings to help them develop nuclear energy sources.

"Eerie Remains" is heard after the scientists successfully build a working interocitor—a combination videophone and ray gun—which begs the question of whether your local department store would stock such a device in its electronics or weapons aisle. When Exeter destroys the machine, Stein refrains from scoring the actual destruction, which is replete with sound effects. Instead, he again uses the cue's opening to punctuate the action that just ended. Muted French horn, alto flute and bassoon comment on the weird events, as well as emphasize Cal's decision to visit Exeter in person. The movie's Exeter was a composite of two aliens in Jones' story, one named "Jorgasnovara," and the other with an even stranger name: "Warner." Warner was retained in early versions of the screenplay, and it makes one wonder whether Universal eventually changed it so audiences wouldn't associate their film with Warner Brothers. The interocitors in Jones' story are more powerful devices than the ones in the movie. They not only read people's thoughts, but instead of firing piddly little Neutrino rays, they convert the operator's very "life substance" into pure energy, which, while potent, makes it very difficult to reload.

The extraordinary "Robot Plane" sounds like almost no other cue in the annals of film music, and it begins after the unmanned mystery plane lands on the fog-shrouded airfield. Again, there's no musical accompaniment in this particular sequence, allowing us to hear the craft's engine emerge from the quiet misty distance. Clarinet and bassoon open the piece, and then harp, high Novachord, string harmonics and bass marimba underscore the emptiness of the pilotless aircraft, further accentuating the weirdness of the situation. When the cue ends, futuristic sound effects mix with the engine's whine as the plane takes off into the fog. Had Stein used music at this point, it probably would have undermined the sense of isolation felt when Joe stands alone at the airfield. In 1967, Stein used redressed versions of this cue in his music for "Cave of the Dead," a fourth-season episode of *Voyage to the Bottom of the Sea*.

After the plane lands in Georgia and its door opens, "Haven't We Met?" starts. Novachord and clarinet begin the composition, and then bass clarinet and alto flute enter, all

Herman Stein's *This Island Earth* love theme. (© 1955 Gilead Music Co.)

serving to perpetuate the mysterious mood via the Metaluna theme. These instruments are soon replaced by warm strings playing the love theme as Cal meets his old Vermont flame, Ruth Adams. When Ruth doesn't acknowledge their past relationship, solo clarinet replaces the strings to let us know something is awry. The love theme returns to add weight to Cal's belief, with the remainder of the cue underscoring the uneasiness of their meeting. Stein's writing is very subtle as it effortlessly provides a sense of the complexity of the various emotions felt during their conversation.

"Exeter's Mansion" portrays the Metalunans' living quarters in an almost paradise-like fashion, with harp, celesta and warm cellos highlighting the magical piece, its gentleness due in part to the absence of brass. Stein considered this to be an easy composition for him to write, and because it didn't offer him a real challenge, it wasn't one of his favorites. However, that doesn't lessen its immense beauty. The cue was reused in *Tarantula*, where it complemented Matt and Steve enjoying the magnificence of the desert by puffing on cigarettes; in this instance, the Metaluna theme emphasized some boulders being dislodged by the unseen spider. "Wrong Girl" is heard after Exeter gives Cal an interocitor's-eye view of his laboratory, with bass clarinet describing the uncomfortableness of Cal and Ruth's relationship. When Ruth warms up to him a little, the love theme from "Haven't We Met?" reprises.

The classical music that plays in the background while the Earth scientists and Metalunans eat dinner serves as one of Wolfgang Amadeus Mozart's rare contributions to pulp sci-fi cinema. Excerpts of both "Romance" and "Minuet" from "Eine Kleine Nachtmusik" are played by strings, although the screenplay had requested "the vibrant notes of a Mozart concerto." At least they got the composer right, if not the type of composition. The string arrangement was no doubt chosen because some of this music had already been prepared and used by Universal in the earlier films *The Black Castle* and *The Glass Web*, as well as because a string ensemble is cheaper to record than a full-orchestral concerto. These pieces were recorded using the studio's 17-member string section.

"This Way, Doctor" follows the meal, when Cal, Ruth and Carlson head to Cal's laboratory, with more "screwy" Novachord alerting us to the presence of Brack. Flute and oboe creates a disquieting mood, with insistent harp adding to the unspoken mystery. When they enter Cal's lab, they surprise pussycat Neutron, and if the furry feline looks familiar, that's because you no doubt remember him when he starred in Paramount's 1951 baseball comedy *Rhubarb*. Of all the scientific blunders in the screenplay, this scene has one of the more embarrassing ones, as Ruth informs us that the cat is named Neutron because he's so positive. Obviously, if he was positive he'd be named Proton. Maybe she meant that she was positive he'd been neutered?

"Secret Meeting" is listed as a "partial" cue on the cue sheets—being only 18 seconds long—when the complete 1:12 composition appears in the film. If this wasn't a clerical error, it could have been a rare occasion when footage or music was edited from the film, only to be reinserted after further consideration. Novachord is featured when Cal examines the hole that Exeter has put in his lead slab to demonstrate the power of Neutrino rays, the cue beginning shortly after the sound effects explosion has occurred. The composition serves as a transition between this scene and the following one where Cal, Ruth and Carlson compare sketches of Exeter and Brack, as if artwork were necessary to reveal that their foreheads extend so much that their heads resemble hairy footballs. The love theme appears when Cal mentions the good old days he spent with Ruth in Vermont.

"Neutronic Rays" is heard after deadly Neutrino rays blow up the station wagon. Again, the music doesn't begin until the futuristic sound effects have played out, with full-orchestral accompaniment punctuating the blast. Another orchestral surge occurs when Dr. Engelborg (the German scientist seemingly speaking Spanish in this scene) is blown into similar oblivion by another ray. The rest of the cue covers the action as Cal and Ruth decide to head for the airfield. This composition was shortened in the film, as music was originally supposed to be heard during the shot of the mansion at the end of the sequence. However, the saucer's hum was added to that shot, which might have been the reason that four bars were removed from the middle of the cue. This way, both the musical opening and closing were retained without the piece extending into the beginning of the sound effect.

Not a single note of score can be heard during the eight-and-a-half-minute stretch from when Cal and Ruth run for the courier plane, until long after the flying saucer abducts them and they're well on their way to Metaluna. Although it seems as if some of these action sequences cry out for music, there are non-stop futuristic sound effects during this span, which figured into Stein's plan of not mixing music and effects. However, some of the drama in this part of the movie probably would have benefited from the addition of underscore.

Music returns to *This Island Earth* courtesy of "Conversion Tube," which resembles a hybrid of sound effects and music. It plays when Cal and Ruth are prepared for Metaluna's gravity, thanks to some spooky Metalunan mist. Stein's composition begins with cluster chords on woodwinds, brass, xylophone and strings, with Novachord playing sustained chords. When the Converter Tubes descend, there's a long Novachord sustain, followed by the

Theremin-like sound that Stein and Tamkin created acoustically with cellos and vibraphone. They obviously succeeded in trying to duplicate the Theremin's sound without having to deal with that troublesome instrument, because in the rare instances when writers have described *This Island Earth*'s music, they almost invariably mention the presence of a Theremin. The score is sometimes referred to as being in large part "electronic," but there's really nothing electronic about it except for the Novachord, which was featured in thousands of other film scores, science fiction and otherwise. The only other thing even electric about the score is the motor on the vibraphone that creates vibrato, which helps differentiate it from other mallet instruments like xylophone or marimba. And again, vibraphone has been a common instrument used in film scores having nothing to do with sci-fi or horror, and it's popular in jazz, too. The musical trickery used to simulate the Theremin was so effective that it was featured at the beginning of *This Island Earth*'s trailer to create the proper extra-terrestrial ambience. A somewhat similar, albeit simpler, musical-sound effects combination was taken by composer Seitarô Ômori for the 1956 Japanese science fiction movie *Uchûjin Tôkyô ni arawaru* (U.S. title: *Warning from Space*), during a scene where a one-eyed starfish creature is transformed into a Japanese woman on board a spacecraft. Whether *This Island Earth*'s approach served as inspiration to Ômori can only be guessed.

"Vermont Memories" was supposed to play after the asteroid nearly hits the flying saucer, and it was to then segue into the next cue. It was written for a scene where Ruth discussed her New England upbringing, while Cal reminisced about a pet dog that died. However, neither the sequence nor its music exists in the released film. Although the entire 1:35-long composition was recorded, the cue sheets list "Vermont Memories" with a "partial" use of 1:06, meaning that the scene had already been shortened before the talky scene and its music were completely removed after this part of the picture wasn't well-received by members of a January 1955 preview audience. The piece was arranged for strings, clarinet and harp, and it offered an extended version of Stein's love theme heard in "Haven't We Met?," "Wrong Girl" and "Secret Meeting." There's nothing to set this pretty melody apart from other well-written love themes Stein penned over his career, which is not meant to belittle it, but rather to point out that romance seems to sound pretty much the same whether you're riding a horse, sailing on a pirate ship or traveling to another planet.

"Transformation" covers the scene when Cal and Ruth are X-rayed, Y-rayed and Z-rayed in the Converter Tubes, with harp, ponticello strings (bowed near the bridge) and "screwy" Novachord creating an unearthly sound to accompany various layers of their bodies being revealed. Harp glissandi and orchestra bells add some futuristic sparkle. This is another piece that was edited following the recording sessions. After some of the footage was excised from the film, a corresponding length of music was also removed from the middle of the cue so the beginning and ending would match the intended visuals. The composition can be heard in its entirety during its 1958 reuse in *The Thing That Couldn't Die* when Jessica grabs her dowsing fork and leads everyone to a coffin containing a live, headless body.

"Shooting Stars" begins after the flying saucer obliterates the Zahgons' attack-meteors, covering the visual of the ship approaching war-ravaged Metaluna. Novachord carries the melody for much of the cue's length, and when Exeter's home planet appears on the Stellarscope, vibraphone, orchestra bells and harp add percussive color. This is the first piece in the movie

Violin part from Herman Stein's unused "Vermont Memories." (© 1955 Gilead Music Co.)

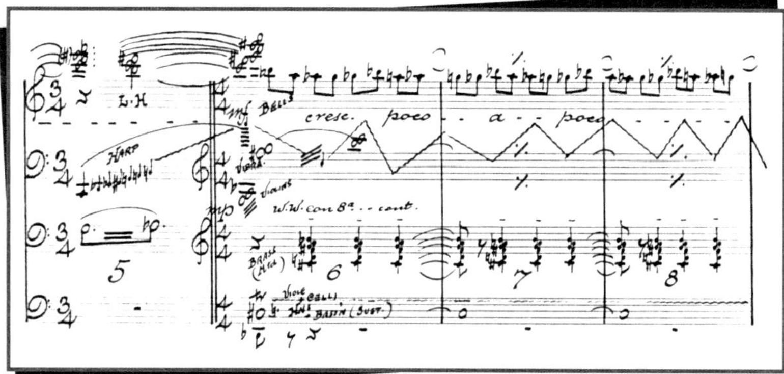

Musical sound effects from Herman Stein's "Transformation." (© 1955 Gilead Music Co.)

featuring simultaneous sound effects and music, as there was really no way around it at this point. Underscore was clearly needed to help suspend the viewers' disbelief so they'd actually think a spaceship was nearing a planet called Metaluna, and it would have been too noticeable if suddenly there were no sounds emanating from the saucer. Because of the need to musically enhance the experiences on the planet and the large number of sound effects associated with life on Metuluna, the movie's remaining cues are now heard alongside sound effects. It's interesting that Mancini and Salter handled much of this music, and they might not have been as insistent as Stein was in trying to keep the two different sound sources discrete. What's entirely coincidental is that when "Shooting Stars" was recorded by Dick Jacobs and His Orchestra for the 1959 record album "Themes from Horror Movies" (Coral Records CRL 57240), added to the music was a bizarre sound effect that resembled the flushing of an intergalactic toilet.

As the saucer approaches the planet's surface, Stein's "Meteor Battle" starts, reprising the "Theremin effect" heard in "Conversion Tube" as the mist-shrouded surface of the besieged world is observed. The composer requested that the cellos and vibraphone play as loud as possible to create the effect, as the weird sounds don't materialize unless the instruments are played at a substantial volume. Low brass and woodwinds propel the ship's descent, and as the saucer heads toward an opening in the planet's surface, descending, trilling strings and harp, along with flutter-tonguing piccolo and flute, emphasize the downward movement. After a meteor explodes near the ship, flute and piccolo (resembling Novachord) then introduce us to the underground world. There's a downbeat nature to this cue and the following one, which helps emphasize the dire situation facing Metaluna. "Meteor Battle" is an astounding and unearthly composition that makes one regret that Stein wasn't allowed to complete the score by himself.

"Metaluna Tunnel" sounds as Cal, Ruth and Exeter emerge from the saucer and enter the Space Age elevator, while Brack models an alien shower cap. Harp plods out the beat during this brief Stein composition that uses the Metaluna theme and features Novachord, alto flute and bass clarinet. It was written to segue to "Metaluna Transport," which is heard as the elevator descends to the planet's subsurface. Another "Theremin effect" highlights the walk to a travel car as meteorites explode spectacularly nearby. Alto flute and bassoon augment the travelers' underground trip in what looks like an amusement park ride. You almost expect a Metalunan to be standing nearby taking tickets.

"Metaluna Catastrophe, Part 1" is Stein's last cue in the film, with the remainder of the picture being scored by Henry Mancini and Hans Salter. Rather than have their brains rearranged by the Thought Transformer, Drs. Meacham and Adams decide to make a run for it, with shock chords crying out twice when the Earthlings are stopped by a half-human, half-insect Mutant (for some reason, pronounced *myoo-tant*). We're told this creature is similar to Earth's garden variety insects. Yeah, right. Can you imagine finding one of these critters outside in your garden, munching on the zucchini? Stein's violent musical onslaught also highlights meteorites reducing the planet's subsurface to rubble, as well as an image of the dead Monitor. Both the movie and its music were reduced by 24 seconds here, with one stretch of the missing music duplicated and heard near the opening of the piece. (It's likely that the deletion of the music was necessitated by the removal of a shot of Exeter returning to the Monitor's Chamber and seeing that the leader had been killed.) Part of this composition was used in the beginning of *The Incredible Shrinking Man*'s trailer.

The first *This Island Earth* cue by someone other than Stein is Mancini's "Metaluna Catastrophe, Part 2." It begins right after the shot of the dead Monitor, and you can immediately hear how the flavor of the music changes, as Mancini's writing style was very different from Stein's. When Cal and Ruth emerge from the travel car and make their way toward the elevator, a lively "telegraph" motif on trumpets and woodwinds calls out, soon repeated by woodwinds, piano, xylophone and upper strings. A flutter-tongued shock chord

Herman Stein's Metaluna theme. (© 1955 Gilead Music Co.)

Conductor's score of Henry Mancini's "Metaluna Catastrophe, Pt. 2." (© 1955 Northridge Music Co.)

sounds when they run into another Mutant, while stopped French horns (almost totally muted, thereby creating a nasal sound) accent Exeter ordering the big bug to "Stand back!" Suspended cymbal and forceful brass highlight the creature's attack. Some music and visuals were edited from this latter sequence, although whether that was done due to unacceptable special effects, bad pacing or something else isn't known. Parts of "Metaluna Catastrophe, Part 2" were reused in *Tarantula*, once after the giant spider causes a rock slide, and again when Matt and Steve drive from Prof. Deemer's house as the arachnid reduces it to rubble. This exciting cue became a popular Universal library piece, also appearing in the trailers of both *Tarantula* and *Monster on the Campus*.

"Flight from Metaluna" is Salter's first *This Island Earth* cue, heard as Zahgon meteorites bombard the planet. When Cal and Ruth approach the Converter Tubes, music begins that's more befitting a Western than a space fantasy, but as the tubes descend, Salter offers an inventive percussive effect on harp, Novachord and xylophone, also investing the piece with a bit of Stein's "Theremin effect." Trumpets call out at the end to help create a memorable image as the saucer flies through space. Salter employed four clarinets in two of his *This Island Earth* cues, whereas neither Stein nor Mancini used that many clarinets in any of their pieces. "Flight from Metaluna" was another cue that was altered when the picture was edited after the scoring sessions, the composition taking a beating in the process. A passage featuring woodwinds and low brass was deleted, along with accompanying shots of the Mutant in the cargo hold; another shot that was removed showed Ruth consoling Exeter because Metaluna had just been destroyed.

Although Salter was a superb film composer (Stein referred to him as "The Master of Terror and Violence"), he wasn't necessarily the best choice to contribute to this particular picture. While Stein and Mancini's American voices seem to fit the movie's futuristic flavor, some of Salter's music was more reminiscent of what he had written back in the 1940s. This same approach worked in *Creature from the Black Lagoon,* which was essentially a dressed-up '40s horror movie, but it wasn't as appropriate for the 1955 space fantasy. Certainly, some of his passages are every bit as imaginative as what Stein and Mancini contributed, but other sections sound like they belong in a period piece or some other non-futuristic drama. It's likely that other composers who occasionally worked for Universal like William Lava or Irving Gertz probably would have written more consistently "modernistic" music for this picture.

Hans J. Salter was born in Vienna, Austria, on January 14, 1896, got his education at the Vienna Academy of Music, and studied composition with Alban Berg, Franz Schreiker and others. He was music director of the State Opera in Berlin before being hired to compose music at UFA studios. Salter emigrated to America in 1937 and was soon under contract at Universal, where he worked for nearly 30 years, arranging, composing, conducting and serving as musical director. He also composed for other studios and for television, and was nominated for a number of Academy Awards, including *Christmas Holiday* and *This Love of Ours.* Some of his other film music was written for the 1966 *Beau Geste, Black Friday, Black Horse Canyon, Frenchie, The Ghost of Frankenstein, His Butler's Sister, If a Man Answers, Magnificent Doll, The Man in the Net, The Mole People, The Prince Who Was a Thief, Ride a Crooked Trail, Scarlet Street, The Spoilers* (both versions), *The Wolf Man, You Never Can Tell* and the television shows *Dick Powell Presents, Maya* and *Wichita Town.* Salter died in Studio City, California, on July 23,

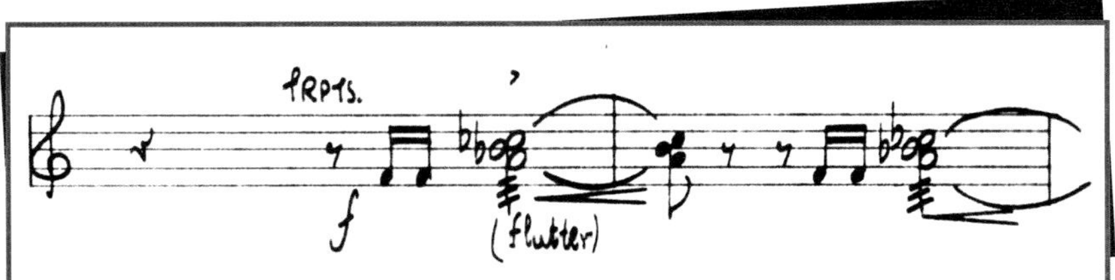

Henry Mancini's Mutant theme, "Amorous Mutant." (© 1955 Northridge Music Co.)

1994, at age 98, fortunately living long enough to finally hear new recordings of his music released on CD.

Mancini's second and last *This Island Earth* cue is "Amorous Mutant," one of his finest Universal monster compositions. It begins with an ethereal combination of vibraphone, harp, Novachord and violins playing harmonics, all of which augment the space travelers' semi-sleep in the Converter Tubes. As the wounded Mutant approaches, a deliberate rhythm on low brass, woodwinds and trilling strings makes the lumbering beast seem to be an unstoppable force. Mancini provides the bipedal bug with a three-note theme on flutter-tongued trumpets, an obvious variation of Stein's *Creature from the Black Lagoon* theme. It wouldn't be surprising to learn that somebody at the studio had asked Mancini to come up with something similar to the Creature motif, hoping it would help transform the interstellar insect into as big a star as the Gill Man. A reprise of Mancini's ethereal effect accompanies the space bug's disintegration at the end of the composition.

This sequence was also reduced in length after the music was recorded, and you can hear an obvious music edit as the Mutant hits its head just before it disintegrates. Mancini's powerful cue was as popular as his other *This Island Earth* composition, and excerpts from "Amorous Mutant" are reused four times in *Tarantula*, first during the end of the avalanche, then when the arachnid attacks the horses, again when the hairy menace begins razing Prof. Deemer's house, and near the climax when the spider approaches the dynamite boxes. The composition also makes a brief appearance in the all-tracked *Let's Kill Uncle*.

Salter's "Down to Earth" accompanies the sequence when Cal and Ruth bid a sad farewell to the wounded Exeter above the Earth. The piece creates a sense of impending doom, but when the courier plane departs, the composition cuts out to allow the plane's roar to dominate the soundtrack. Salter wrote music for this entire sequence, which was recorded but unfortunately not used in the film, including a quote from Stein's love theme. Salter's "End Title" was supposed to segue from the previous cue, but that doesn't happen because the ending of "Down to Earth" was removed. What's more, the "End Title" was also treated with the same lack of respect. As the saucer zooms above the ocean's surface, the music offers a brassy finale, but as soon as flames audibly dance from the ship, the music is muted from the soundtrack, only to reappear after the saucer explodes in the water. If the underscore in this and the previous cue was removed to prevent music and sound effects from being heard simultaneously, it was an appalling idea, as the silence seems totally out of place considering the amazing events that are unfolding. Unlike Stein's cues, which were conceived so they wouldn't conflict with the effects, just dialing the volume down and up from Salter's already-composed music was neither an artistic nor an intelligent approach to take, and the non-musical climax saps a lot of energy from some of the film's final shots.

Conductor's score of Hans Salter's *This Island Earth* "End Cast." (© 1955 Salter Publishing Co.)

The "End Title" is another composition that sounds like it belongs in a 1940s horror or adventure film rather than a futuristic sci-fi epic, with the end perfectly suitable for one of Salter's earlier Frankenstein or Wolf Man pictures. The original, complete "End Title" was mistakenly included at the end of a suite of Salter's music from *The Incredible Shrinking Man*, which was released on producer Tony Thomas' 1980 album *The Classic Horror Music of Hans J. Salter* and re-released on Intrada's 1994 *Creature from the Black Lagoon* CD.

Salter's "End Cast" manages to close *This Island Earth* with some sense of musical continuity, as it offers a full-orchestral version of Stein's love theme. It's a bit surprising that Stein wasn't credited with this piece rather than Salter, who merely adapted Stein's music. While a final musical statement more befitting the orchestration and harmonies of the bulk of *This Island Earth*'s score probably would have been more rewarding, Hollywood often took the generic "happy ending" approach Salter used here, using conventional feel-good music during the End Cast regardless of what happened right before it, in this case the sad death of the very appealing Exeter.

With or without the contributions by Salter and Mancini, Herman Stein's music for *This Island Earth* was possibly his high-water mark during his Universal tenure. It's lamentable that it wasn't until a few years before his 2007 death that people began to realize he was responsible for the majority of the score, and because of that, how responsible he was for much of the effectiveness of the film itself.

This Island Earth's memorable music was not reused in too many subsequent Universal pictures. But an exception was when two snatches of the movie's "Main Title" were appropriated along with bits of previously recorded tracks from *The Monolith Monsters, The Deadly Mantis* and *Man in the Shadow* and then ineptly edited together to create the main title for the Audie Murphy Western *Posse from Hell* (1961). Salter, either acting on his own or in tandem with somebody at Universal, licensed out recordings of some of his original music tracks for use in a host of independent movies, few of them memorable. These uses were probably not entirely on the up-and-up, as the master recordings were owned by the studio. The cues were renamed and assigned to new publishing companies in order to hide what was happening. This resulted in horror movie fans often being perplexed when they recognized some of their favorite monster and sci-fi music in these later productions. In the atrocious *Dracula vs. Frankenstein* (1971), Salter and Mancini's tracks from *This Island Earth* and *Creature From the Black Lagoon* were used. The equally abysmal *Women of the Prehistoric Planet* (1966) contains a healthy dose of Salter's tracks from *This Island Earth* and other Universal films, as does *First Spaceship on Venus* (1960) and *The Human Duplicators* (1965).

This Island Earth's "Main Title" and "Shooting Stars" are heard in director John Landis' *Amazon Women on the Moon* (1987) and Joe Dante's *Matinee* (1993), but these were the 1959 re-recordings made for Dick Jacobs' *Themes from Horror Movies* album, which was re-released decades later on LP and CD by the Varese Sarabande label under the title *Themes from Classic Science Fiction, Fantasy and Horror Films*. This low-budget, poorly arranged LP featured Jacobs conducting his minuscule orchestra through cheesy arrangements of mostly Universal sci-fi-horror film music of the 1940s and '50s with varying degrees of disappointment. The production included a roller rink organ substituting for harp, and a string section that probably didn't have enough players for bridge. *This Island Earth* was the only film that featured two cues on that album. These recordings also turned up on *Saturday Night Live* and other TV shows when outer space or spooky music was needed, not because they're good recordings, but because at the time they were rare examples of 1950s sci-fi music that was available for licensing. Herman Stein thought the recordings were appalling, but he kept copies of the album during his entire lifetime, as for over 35 years they were the only way his music could be heard outside of the films. This situation was remedied in 1996 when recordings of his music were released by this writer and his wife on the Monstrous Movie Music CD label, including the complete score for *This Island Earth*.

Analysis
By Steve Kronenberg

Flash back to 1955. Audiences are lined up to see Universal's latest science fiction thriller, *This Island Earth*. What brought them to the theater in the first place? Surely the poster graphics, replete with flying saucers and Metaluna Mutants, played a major role. But initially, the real attention-grabber was the film's title itself. It was the first truly thought-provoking science fiction movie title of the 1950s. Our Earth is anything but an island, and the film's Metalunans are ample proof of that concept. That Earth did not stand alone, that our universe was peopled by others, was illustrated by *This Island Earth*'s predecessors: *The Man from Planet X* (1951), *The Thing from Another World* (1951), *The Day the Earth Stood Still* (1951), *Invaders from Mars* (1953), *The War of the Worlds* (1953) and more. These films demonstrated to moviegoers that perhaps we were not at the top of the interplanetary food chain.

But *This Island Earth* was much more than its provocative title suggested. It was Universal's first sci-fi offering in Technicolor, and its rich collage of colors added immensely to its impact. *This Island Earth* was also the first '50s sci-fi to blend interplay among its characters with action scenes and scenes of interplanetary space travel, advancing upon the pioneering but static style of *Destination Moon* (1950) and the Earthbound action of *Day the Earth Stood Still*, *Invaders from Mars* and *War of the Worlds*. *This Island Earth*'s top-notch scenes of a saucer hurtling through space, dodging meteors, were indeed a precursor to George Lucas' efforts in *Star Wars* (1977).

But it is *This Island Earth*'s obsession with futurism and the technology of tomorrow that truly earns the film its status as a science fiction landmark. Today the film portrays a delightfully "retro" look at flying saucers, space travel and alien landscapes. But back in 1955, audiences probably gazed at the film in unbridled wonder. Indeed, nearly every Technicolor-splashed set-piece in *This Island Earth* would qualify for the cover of any science fiction pulp, trading card or comic book. *This Island Earth* is perhaps the first and best sci-fi film to exploit our paranoia about, and our optimism over, the technology rampant in postwar America. The superb script by Franklin Coen and Edward G. O'Callaghan is loaded with scientific double-talk and technological jargon. Equally important are the film's props, a treasure trove of arcane machinery that illustrates the film's emphasis on the wondrous technology of the future: interocitors, AB-619s, a catherimine tube with an endiom complex of plus four, intensifier disks, etc. The Coen-O'Callaghan script capitalizes on America's burgeoning postwar obsession with science and machinery—and the country's cautious attitude toward the developing Red Scare. The interocitor built by Rex Reason's Cal at the behest of Jeff Morrow's Exeter exemplifies the film's futuristic approach. The machine has the kind of '50s futuristic look so prevalent in the pulps and comics of its day, complete with curves, angles and a television screen that portrays the early influence of television and pictophones. Significantly, the interocitor also displays a "nuclear fission"-type logo, a not-so-subtle reference to the Atomic Age influences that mark *This Island Earth*. Note, too, how the lights on the interocitor blink in unison with Exeter's voice when his image appears on the machine's monitor.

This same "retro-futuristic" look suffuses Exeter's mystery plane which transports Cal to his rendezvous with Exeter. Its interior features arched ceiling panels, accompanied by automated controls that require no pilot. The craft's interior lighting is a collage of muted pastel colors, creating an eerie, glowing effect when combined with the rich Technicolor photography of Universal veteran Clifford Stine.

Exeter's machinations provide another backdrop to '50s science and paranoia: At Exeter's Mansion, Ruth and Carlson reveal to Cal that Exeter may be using a machine to lobotomize other scientists so he can compel them to develop new forms of atomic energy. *This Island Earth*'s first action scene also underscores the important dichotomy between technologic wonder and technophobia: As Cal, Ruth and Carlson try to escape from Exeter's Mansion, their car is bombarded with bolts of red lightning from the interocitor, culminating in Carlson's destruction after he brakes to heroically let Cal and Ruth run to safety.

Much of *This Island Earth*'s groundbreaking look and attitude are the work of its superb technicians: cinematographers Stine and David S. Horsley, art directors Alexander Golitzen and Richard H. Riedel and the aptly named optical printer Roswell A. Hoffman. One of its iconic scenes is a long shot of Exeter's saucer cruising through green-glowing skies, a classic '50s image. The saucer itself is equally impressive, its rounded deco-like body an obvious influence on films such as *Forbidden Planet* and *Earth vs. the Flying Saucers* (both 1956). Watch for the scene in which the saucer hovers above the courier plane: The flying disk captures it in a beautifully rendered beam of light that literally lifts it into the belly of the gigantic spaceship!

The saucer's interior design is a visual highlight. The eye is immediately drawn to a huge, globular flashing red light and a smaller, illuminated "nuclear fission" logo. We see the saucer bathed in a fiery red glow as it travels through the thermal barrier, emitting flames that stand out against the blackness of space—a memorable image. Inside the ship, Stine delivers a superb shot blending the ship's interior colors and flashing lights with the thick smoke outside, viewed through the saucer's windows.

The set design again dominates as we first view the Converter Tubes housing the eerie-looking, white-haired Metalunans emerging from sleep. Indeed, the scene in which Cal and Ruth are housed in the tubes seems straight out of a science fiction pulp or the cover of E.C. Comics' *Weird Science*. There's also a fine medium shot of the Earthlings' metabolism changing: Reminiscent of John Fulton's special effects in Universal's Invisible Man movies, and John Carradine's resuscitation in *House of Frankenstein* (1944), we see Cal and Ruth's internal organs, then their skeletons before they return to normal. Yet, the meteor scene is perhaps Stine and Horsley's best work in the film—and arguably the film's most influential segment. Up until *This Island Earth*, every other film depicting interplanetary space travel featured static, relatively uninvolving effects and photography. But Stine and Horsley show Exeter's ship speeding through space, turning and dodging meteors, while under attack from the planet Zahgon. In addition, they give us beautiful shots of Exeter's ship destroying the meteors with a series of powerful rays—an unprecedented example of *This Island Earth*'s technical achievement, and an obvious influence on *Star Wars* and its progeny.

As the spaceship descends through an opening in Metaluna's surface, we are treated to a fine long shot of a stray Zahgon meteor narrowly missing the ship, followed by a long shot of Metaluna's underground: a swirl of gray lines, colors and weird geometric objects, blended with sporadic meteor explosions. After the ship lands, there's a wonderful long shot of the ship on the right side of the screen, with Exeter, Cal and Ruth walking out amidst the wreckage of meteor attacks. And our characters' ride through Metaluna is a vision from Hell, highlighted by the planet's eerie landscape and dark sky.

The film's climax seems lifted from a Saturday matinee dream, infused with fire and explosions as we watch the destruction of Metaluna. The camera captures the carnage in unparalleled style. The movie culminates with the memorable shot of the fiery saucer crashing and exploding in the ocean. *This Island Earth* excels on all levels, but it is the set design of Golitzen and Riedel, in tandem with the photographic effects, that lift it to iconic heights. The influence of *This Island Earth*'s pioneering depictions of space travel and interplanetary conflict should not be underestimated; it's the blueprint for every space opera that followed.

This Island Earth is marked by a typically fine performance from Jeff Morrow as Exeter. His style lent a sense of earnestness to all of his genre work, even the laughable *The Giant Claw* (1957). In *This Island Earth*, Morrow adopts a cultured, reasoned tone as Exeter, tempered by a sense of superiority. Exeter is reasonable and even-tempered, not a shape-shifting, man-eating monster. But Morrow plays Exeter as a being who is aware of both his superiority to Earthlings—and his need for their help in saving his planet. And he impudently assumes that Cal Meacham, as a fellow scientist, will join Team Exeter. Morrow also affects a sinister persona as he delivers his cryptic invitation to Cal. via interocitor, to board the mystery plane and meet him. In another menacing moment, Exeter delivers an unsettling warning to Cal: "Meacham, I must ask you to have faith in our ultimate aims. I must also ask you to refrain from meeting with your co-workers."

The words seem harmless enough, but Morrow imbues them with a threatening, unnerving inflection. Yet, Morrow can modulate from sinister to sincere: After the Metalunans kill Carlson and the rest of the Exeter's Mansion scientists, an angry Cal confronts a subdued Exeter, who skillfully blends a sense of contrition with a sense of conviction:

EXETER: What happened was not in my control.
CAL: What happened was mass murder!
EXETER: We are not all masters of our souls, Dr. Meacham.
CAL: That's a nice little phrase coming from you!
EXETER: I learned it on Earth.

Morrow is also adept at blending Exeter's somewhat "human" side (his look, mannerisms and sensitivity to his planet's plight) with an otherworldly, intellectual demeanor. And his performance belies a touch of obsession and fanaticism beneath the cultured veneer—a quality he would later display in *The Creature Walks Among Us*. Yet Morrow's performance as Exeter is also limned with a strong sense of pathos. In the Exeter's Mansion scene in which the Monitor (seen on the interocitor) questions Exeter's effectiveness, Morrow looks imploringly into the interocitor, requesting the audience of his planet's high council, before being further berated.

Throughout the first half of *This Island Earth*, we wonder whether Exeter will turn out to be friend or foe to his Earthling colleagues—a tribute to the subtlety of Morrow's playing. As the film progresses, we see Morrow's facial expressions gradually soften as the pathos begins to emerge. Referring to the deaths of Carlson and the other scientists, he tells Cal and Ruth, "I'm not asking you to condone what we've done. All I ask is that when you understand the plight of my people, you try to have more sympathy for our deeds."

Morrow's sensitivity is contrasted with the lordly, mer-

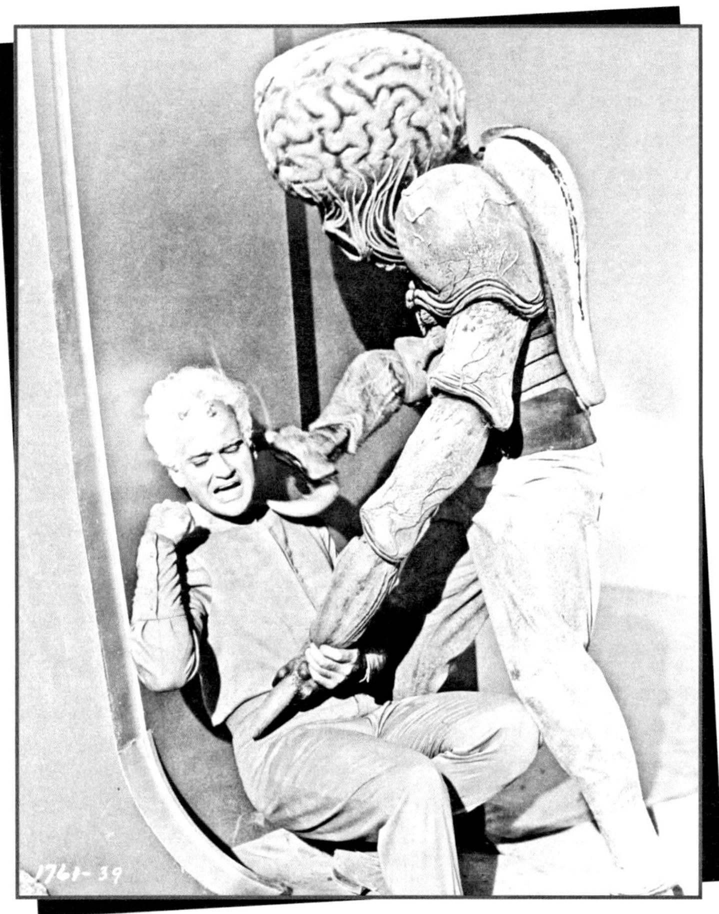

"The mutant is a blue-green horror with vivid red veins lashed around its body," columnist Bob Thomas wrote after a visit to the Universal makeup department. "It has a two-foot-high head that appears to be an exposed, oversize brain. The arms, with vise-like pincers, dangle down to his ankles and he has a shell-like back. He's a doll, all right." Notice the length of the Mutant's (Regis Parton) extension arms as he fatally gouges Exeter (Jeff Morrow).

ciless persona of Spencer's Monitor, who plans a migration to Earth—and perhaps conquest. When the Monitor asks Exeter if he still feels Earthlings can have free minds, the reply is sincere and heartfelt: "I do. I know them. I've lived with them." Morrow's eyes and soulful facial expressions augment the sincerity of those words. When the Monitor tells Cal and Ruth that the Metalunans plan to relocate to Earth, Exeter quickly and humanly interjects, "A *peaceful* relocation. We hope to live in harmony with the citizens of your Earth." Morrow conveys unmistakable earnestness in this scene, enough to erase our doubts about his desire to peacefully coexist with us. And note the look of concern on Exeter's face as Cal asks him whether his saucer has enough power to escape the doomed Metaluna: "Our ionization layer has failed completely. If we have to ward off any heavy Zahgon attacks.... *I don't know...*"

But it is at the conclusion of *This Island Earth* that we truly appreciate the range and modulation of Morrow's performance. We have seen Exeter evolve from a cryptic, sometimes sinister invader to a zealous champion of his planet, to a sensitive advocate of his Earthling prisoners and, finally, to a weary, beaten and pathetic shell. When asked by Ruth where he will go now that his planet is destroyed, he bluffs, "Our universe is vast, full of wonders. I'll explore, perhaps find another Metaluna. You see, I'm more adventurous that you imagined me."

When Exeter says, "I'm afraid my wounds can never be healed," we know that his death is inevitable—and his downturned eyes and mouth, just before his ship crashes, show that he is resigned to his fate. Morrow's work in *This Island Earth* is one of the most subtle and modulated performances of the 1950s, blending arrogance, menace and pathos in a style reminiscent of the best mad doctors of the Golden Age. He gives us a portrait of the space alien as true believer—an earnest, believable performance that augments the film's equally serious theme and technical achievements.

Morrow's work may be the film's thespic highlight, but Rex Reason's natural, relaxed style blends well with Morrow's intensity. As scientific colleagues with opposing personalities and motives, both men effect a fine chemistry that would be replicated one year later in *The Creature Walks Among Us*: Reason as the stolid, conscientious academic, Morrow the fervent, goal-oriented zealot. Reason also interacts believably and naturally with Faith Domergue's Dr. Ruth Adams, but he's at his best when he adopts the persona of a dedicated, persevering academic: "I want to know [what an interocitor is] and what it does." His determination to unravel the mystery of Metaluna is really the core of the film's theme. Faith Domergue provided solid backup as Ruth.

Two supporting players really stand out. Russell Johnson as Steve Carlson is as believable, natural and poised as Morrow and Reason. Carlson interacts well with Cal and Ruth as they try and solve the mystery of Exeter and his goals. And Douglas Spencer as the Monitor conveys the right touch of haughtiness and coldness to counter Morrow's increasingly sympathetic portrayal. To truly gauge Spencer's range, contrast his malevolent *This Island Earth* performance with his affable "Scotty" in *The Thing from Another World*. Watch for the scene in which the Monitor treats Cal and Ruth as inferiors who are unable to see beyond the confines of their own planet: "It is indeed typical that you Earth people refuse to believe in the superiority of any planet but your own. Children looking into a magnifying glass, imagining the image you see is the image of your true size."

Once Morrow reveals himself as the film's most sensitive, misunderstood character, Spencer still provides us with a performance that personified the classically merciless aliens that the 1950s embraced.

Kudos must also go to the sound effects department. *This Island Earth* is infused with the sounds of flying saucer engines, meteor attacks, death rays and explosions. Sound effects like these were pioneered by Universal's Flash Gordon serials and refined by films like *The Day the Earth Stood Still*, *Invaders from Mars* and *The War of the Worlds*. In *This Island Earth*, they're used with an intensity and frequency not previously heard in any film.

Finally, honorable mention to the beleaguered Metaluna Mutant. Many fans have criticized the inclusion of a monster in what they otherwise perceive as a pure science fiction film. But the Mutants lend *This Island Earth* a welcome touch of horror—while maintaining the BEM (bug-eyed monster), brain-exposed alien tradition of science fiction pulps and comics. The Mutant suit itself, while not in the same league as the Gill Man suit, is still superbly and seamlessly designed, its parts integrated into the whole. In its Control Room scene, Mutant #2 is presented in the same manner as the Creature: First we see only its shadow, then a shot of its shuffling feet, then just a peek at its pincer reaching for Ruth. While the Metalunans are human in appearance and attitude, the Mutant provides a nice blast of unearthly terror—and yet another classic creature to add to Universal's beloved pantheon of monsters.

Much more than a good genre piece, *This Island Earth* represents a tremendously important step in the evolution of science fiction and fantasy filmmaking. Its technically advanced depiction of interstellar transport and spaceship action, as well as its exotic set design, influenced subsequent science fiction films. In addition, it was the first serious film to combine its moral lessons and the dramatic conflicts among its characters with the interplanetary action created by its technicians. It is a landmark science fiction film—and one of the purest examples of the fear and wonder that gripped America in the 1950s.

Revenge of the Creature (1955)

Full Credit Information

CREDITS: Produced by William Alland; Directed by Jack Arnold; Screenplay: Martin Berkeley; Story: William Alland; Photography: Charles S. Welbourne [a.k.a. "Scotty" Welbourne]; Editor: Paul Weatherwax; Art Directors: Alexander Golitzen and Alfred Sweeney; Set Decorators: Russell A. Gausman and Julia Heron; Sound: Leslie I. Carey and Jack Bolger; Music Supervisor: Joseph Gershenson; Gowns: Jay A. Morley, Jr.; Makeup: Bud Westmore; Hair Stylist: Joan St. Oegger; Assistant Director: Fred Frank; UNCREDITED: Original Music Composers: William Lava, Herman Stein and Henry Mancini; Tracked Music Composers: Hans J. Salter, Herman Stein, Henry Mancini, Milton Rosen, Frank Skinner, Nick Nuzzi, Milton Rosen, Everett Carter, Don Raye, Gene de Paul and Pat Johnson; Conductor: Joseph Gershenson; Musicians: Emo Neufeld, Manuel Compinsky, Louis Pressman, Ambrose Russo, Lou Klass, Sam Fordis, Samuel Cytron, Sarah Kreindler, Leon Goldwasser, Howard Colf (Violin), Cecil Bonvalot, Harriet Payne (Viola), Victor Gottlieb, Stephen De'ak, Joseph Ullstein, Alec Compinsky

(Cello), Harold E. Brown (Bass), Arthur C. Smith, Ethmer Roten, Jr. (Flute), Norman Benno (Oboe), Blake Reynolds, Alan Harding, Karl Leaf (Clarinet), Lloyd Hildebrand (Bassoon), Arthur Frantz, Eugene Ober (Horn), Gene LaFreniere, Don Linder, Robert Goodrich (Trumpet), John Stanley, Bruce Squires, H.L. Menge (Trombone), John De Soto, Ralph Collier (Drums), Lyman Gandee (Piano), Joseph Quintile (Harp), Jack Barsby (Tuba); Unit Production Managers: Russ Haverick and Edward Dodds; Second Assistant Director: Dolph Zimmer; Script Clerks: Dixie McCoy and Hughes (Dorothy Hughes?); Assistant Cameramen: Walter Bluemel and Mellatt/Melott? (Mark Marlatt?); Camera Operator: L. Ward (Lloyd Ward?); Extra Camera: Ted Saizis and Blache (Irwin Blache?); Extra Assistant Cameraman: Vincent Saizis; Process Crew Cameraman: Stine (Clifford Stine?); Still Photographers: Glenn Kirkpatrick and Sherman Clark; Camera Mechanic: F. McConihay; Sound Editors: Al Kennedy and Ben Hendricks; Key Grip: Jack Flesher; Grips: E. Jones (Ed Jones?) and S. Vanzanten/Van Zanten?; Gaffer: T. Bellah (Tex Bellah?); Best Boy: L. Hopton (Lyman Hopton?); Electrician: H. Honn; Generator Operator: H. Spear; First Prop Man: Solly Martino; Prop Shop Man: D. Wolz; Wardrobe Man: M. Tierney (Michael Tierney?); Wardrobe Woman: M. Bunch (Martha Bunch?); Hair Stylist: Lillian Burkhart; Body Makeup Woman: B. Craven (Beverly Cravens?); Cashier: M. Epstein; Propmaker: Frank Brendel; First Aid Men: R.A. Guyer and Jerry Parker; Technician: Ledge Haddow; Assistant Prop Man: Bud Laraby; Sound Recordist: Donald Cunliffe; Mike Man: F. Wilkinson (Frank H. Wilkinson?); Cable Man: Moran (Harry Moran?); Publicist: Robert Sill; Coordinator: Ray Gockel; Safety Divers: Charles McNabb and Shirley Woolery; Stand-in for John Agar: Joe Walls; Stand-in for Lori Nelson: Barbara Jones; Photo Double for Lori Nelson: Edna Ryan; Stand-in: Paul Mathews; Florida Extras Casting: Maude Hecht and Charlotte Kaye; Dog Provider: Henry East; **September 28 Added Scenes:** Director: Joseph Pevney; Writer: *probably* Richard Alan Simmons; Photography: Glassberg (Irving Glassberg?); Art Director: Smith (Robert E. Smith?); Set Dresser: Austin (John Austin?); Editor: Paul Weatherwax; Camera Operator: Dodds (William Dodds?); Assistant Cameramen: Walter Bluemel, Williams (Walter Williams?); Unit Manager: Dodds (Edward Dodds?); Assistant Director: G. McLean (Gordon McLean?); Second Assistant Director: J. Cunningham (Jack Cunningham?); Script Clerk: Hughes (Dorothy Hughes?); First Grip: Brown (Everett Brown?); Second Grip: Jones (Ed Jones?); Gaffer: Kurland (Norton Kurland?); Best Boy: Harris; First Prop Man: Solly Martino; Assistant Prop Man: Gunstrom (Harry Grundstrum?); Makeup: F. Prehoda (Frank Prehoda?); Mixer: Jowett (Corson Jowett?); Sound Recorder: Swartz (James Swartz?); Mike Man: Gorback (Frank Gorback?); Cable Man: Perry; **Per Tom Hennesy:** Creature Costume: Jack Kevan, Tom Case and Beau Hickman; 82 minutes.

CAST: John Agar (*Prof. Clete Ferguson*), Lori Nelson (*Helen Dobson*), John Bromfield (*Joe Hayes*), Nestor Paiva (*Lucas*), Grandon Rhodes (*Jackson Foster*), Dave Willock (*Lou Gibson*), Robert B. Williams (*George Johnson*), Charles R. Cane (*Captain of Police*), Flippy the "Educated" Porpoise (*Himself*); UNCREDITED: Tom Hennesy (*The Gill Man/Oceanarium Diver*), Ricou Browning (*The Gill Man/Laboratory Assistant*), Robert Nelson (*Dr. McCuller*), Diane De Laire (*Miss Abbott*), Clint Eastwood (*Jennings*), Betty Jane Howarth (*Screaming Oceanarium Onlooker*), Don C. Harvey (*Mac—Group Leader*), Robert Wehling (*Joe—Searchlight Operator*), Sydney Mason (*Police Radio Announcer*), Jack Gargan (*Police Launch Skipper*), Charles Victor (*Police Launch Helmsman*), Ned Le Fevre (*Radio Newscaster*), Brett Halsey (*Pete*), Robert Hoy (*Charlie*), Charles Gibb, Mike Doyle (*Cops on Beach*), Bill Baldwin (*Voice of Police Dispatcher*), Ken Peters (*WNTV Announcer*), Wallace Mussallem (Rita II *Crew Member*), James Fisher (*Radio Announcer-Interviewer on Receiving Tank Promenade*), Jere Beery, Sr. (*Photographer on Receiving Tank Promenade*), Steve Wehking (*Reporter on Receiving Tank Promenade*), Gloria Selph (*Ocean Harbor Patron*), Richard O. Watson (*Ocean Harbor Patron Who Knocks Over the Creature Standee*), John Carcaba, Mildred Baskin, Mary Blackmer (*Running Patrons at Ocean Harbor*), Sally Baskin (*Running Child at Ocean Harbor*), Judeena Blackmer (*Child at Ocean Harbor*), Julian Fant, Pat Powers (*Smoochers in Convertible*), Bill Young (*Policeman Who Interrupts Smoochers*), Loretta Agar (*Screaming Woman on Boat*), Don House, Maria Gardner (*Bits*), Robert Lee Tinney (*John Agar's Double*), Ginger Stanley (*Lori Nelson's Double*); **Per Universal publicity blurbs:** Jack Brandon, Harry Neill (*Photographers*), Faye Weathersby, Melissa Butcher (*Girls on Beach*); **Per Universal Weekly Layoff Reports:** Clint Eastwood, David Janssen, Race Gentry, John Saxon, William Reynolds (*Voices*); **Per Tom Hennesy:** John Lamb (*Diver*); **Per Lovin' Spooful bassist Steve Boone's memoir *Hotter Than a Match Head: Life on the Run with the Lovin' Spoonful*:** Steve Boone (*Child at Ocean Harbor*); **In footage that may not have made the final cut:** John Lamb (*The Gill Man*).

Production History

By Tom Weaver

In *Creature from the Black Lagoon*, the Gill Man got a measure of payback against the humans who arrived uninvited in his edenic Black Lagoon and disrupted his solitary but satisfactory existence. And that was just a warm-up…

> **Since *Creature from the Black Lagoon* will probably be a $2,000,000 grosser, Universal-International has already started Martin Berkeley on a script for a follow-up feature and re-engaged director Jack Arnold, who made the other film, besides assigning William Alland to produce. Studio feels it has another Frankenstein monster, Dracula, Wolf Man potential in the new horror manifestation.**

So wrote Edwin Schallert, drama editor of *The Los Angeles Times*, in his April 15, 1954, column—but the idea that the web-footed wonder was sequel-worthy had occurred to producer Alland long before the successful 1954 release of *Creature from the Black Lagoon*. In fact, long before the *production* of *Creature from the Black Lagoon*. In fact, before the first word of the first *Creature from the Black Lagoon* screenplay had been written!

By December 1952, when the ink was still wet on Maurice Zimm's *Black Lagoon* treatment, Alland had already decided that one of the things that had to change was Zimm's ending in which the Gill Man is devoured by piranha. Alland foresaw the advisability of keeping the frog-like fellow alive, or at least leaving his fate in doubt, in order to have the freedom to let him swim on into sequels.

On February 25, 1954, around the time of *Black Lagoon*'s first playdates, the hiring of Berkeley as sequel-writer was discussed at the meeting of Universal's Operating Committee. According to the minutes, "We have an agreement employing him to write a treatment of not less than 40 pages on '*Black Lagoon* Sequel.' Treatment is to be delivered within 4 weeks from February 24, 1954, and compensation will be payable at the rate of 1/3 upon execution of agreement, 1/3 at the end of two weeks and 1/3 upon delivery of treatment." Berkeley earned his money early: His treatment is dated March 19. Location shooting at Marineland, Florida's, Marine Studios, "The World's First Oceanarium," was obviously already under consideration, because that's where much of this treatment (and his eventual script, and the eventual movie) is set. In April, *Black Lagoon* director Jack Arnold (who had left Universal) was invited back to direct the movie then being called "*Black Lagoon* Sequel." At about that same time, "Scotty" Welbourne, photographer (and, some would say, director) of *Black Lagoon*'s Wakulla Springs location footage, received from Universal general production manager Gilbert Kurland a letter asking if he would be available to shoot the sequel.

Kurland next reached out to the Creature himself, Ricou Browning—but not to offer him the opportunity to reprise his role. In a May 13 letter to Browning (then residing at 401 Roosevelt Drive in Tallahassee) he wrote,

> **At this time we are planning to make a sequel of [*sic*] the picture *Creature from the Black Lagoon* starting about the 15th of June at St. Augustine, Florida. We are going to use a man who is six foot six tall [*sic*] and weighs about 220 pounds, as, in this picture, the creature has more work above water and it is necessary for him to appear larger.**
>
> **I am writing you to see if you might be interested in working with us at St. Augustine helping with the creature and doing odd and end jobs [*sic*] underwater. Therefore, if you are interested, write me by return mail giving me your telephone number and I will discuss what I have in mind more fully with you at that time.**

In 2013 I showed a copy of this letter to Browning, who said he has no memory of ever receiving it. He distinctly remembered that the movie was already in production at Marine Studios when he was telephoned and offered the Creature role; we'll get to that story in a bit.

On May 11, Kurland reported to the Operating Committee that he had "engaged one man and lined up a second to portray the Gill Man" in the sequel, and that their full-

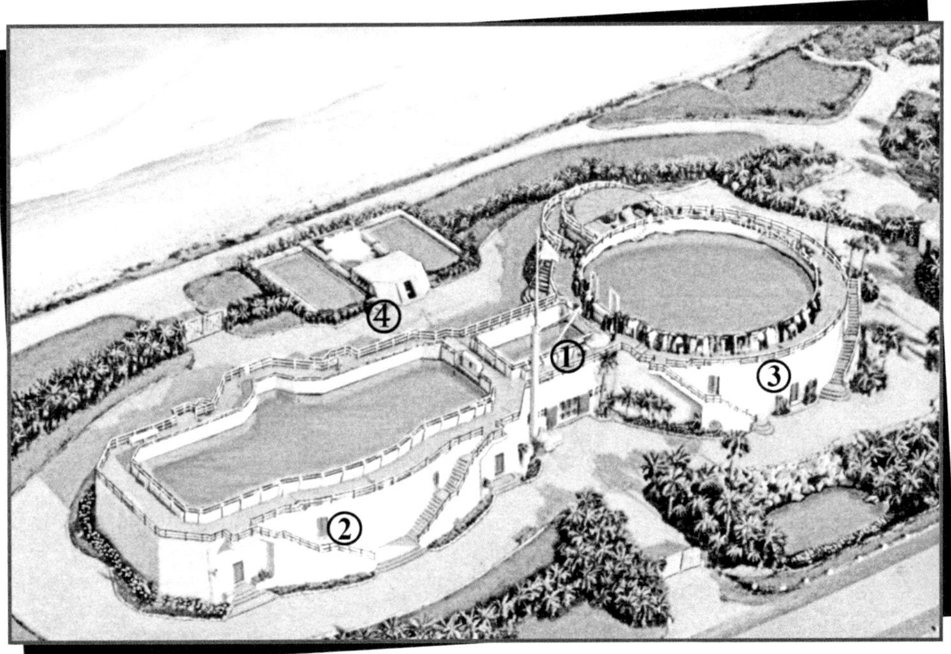

A God's-eye view of Marine Studios: (1) the flume where the knocked-out Gill Man was "walked"; (2) the tank that became his permanent (*not*!) home; (3) Flippy the "Educated" Porpoise's tank; (4) the filter house where sand and shells were cleaned out of ocean water before it went into the tanks.

body costumes were currently being designed and built. Presumably the two unnamed men were the two men who *had* the jobs at the start of shooting, diver John Lamb and stuntman Tom Hennesy. A bit later in *Revenge*'s production history, a memo indicated that $300 a week would be the salary of both Lamb ("Gill Man #1"), scheduled to work from May 5 to August 2, and Hennesy ("Gill Man #2"), working from June 5 to August 2.

"I was called out to Universal for an interview with the producer, Bill Alland," Hennesy said in our 1994 interview:

> **I had a *couple* of interviews with him—I had to wear a swimsuit and so forth, so that he could determine how I would look in the Creature suit. I was hired on the basis of those interviews, apparently, and on the basis of my experience as a stuntman and actor. I then started to work [on the Creature costume] with the fellows in the makeup department, like Bud Westmore, who I knew very well. Bud and Jack Kevan and Tom Case and Beau Hickman were the ones who I worked with, mostly.**

According to Bob Burns, the Gill Man suits for this movie were made very differently than the *Black Lagoon* suits: Full-body casts, front and back, were made of Hennesy and Lamb, from the neck clear down to the ankles. Using the resultant molds, front-and-back Gill Man suit halves were created and put together. Burns said, "Doing it that way was a lot easier and a lot faster than doing it piecemeal, which was how they did it for the first movie. *That* took forever."

On May 17 or 18 (sources differ), Alland, Arnold and unit production manager Edward Dodds departed for Florida to scout locations. Within days, they had completed arrangements with representatives of Marine Studios, located on the ocean shore in north Flagler County, and received a promise of cooperation in shooting the new Creature movie there. (In *Revenge*, the seaquarium where the story takes place is called Ocean Harbor.) At that time, this deep-sea zoo was one of the state's top tourist destinations, drawing as many as 500,000 visitors annually. Throughout the 1950s, Marineland was *home* to Sally Baskin, the daughter of Tom and Mildred Baskin who operated Marine Studios' motel, the Marine Village Court, which was a few hundred feet south of Marine Studios on Ocean Boulevard. The Marine Village Court was the Universal troupe's headquarters during their Marineland shooting. "I was the only child raised at Marineland—I was there from 1947 until 1960," said Sally, who was 12 years old when the Gill Man came a-calling. She not only got to watch a lot of the filming, she even makes a fleeting appearance in the movie.

> Doesn't look like Dick Long will accompany [his actress wife] Suzan Ball on location for *Crazy Horse*. He's pencilled in for the sequel to *Creature from the Black Lagoon*.
> —Army Archerd, *Variety*, June 1, 1954

(A year earlier, Long was under consideration for the top role in the *first* Creature movie.) Long did not join the cast of this 3-D sequel; the top male spots went to John Agar and John Bromfield. On June 12, Jack Arnold made tri-dimensional underwater tests of Agar, Bromfield and Gill Man John Lamb in the studio tank, with "Scotty" Welbourne manning the cameras. *Revenge* was Agar's first Universal assignment under a new contract, and it was female lead Lori Nelson's *last* under *hers*. When Alland first ideated a man-fish movie back in 1952 and wrote his *King Kong–like* story treatment "The Sea Monster," he called for a blonde (as in *Kong*, with Fay Wray in blonde wig as Ann Darrow); now, with champagne blonde Nelson in this sequel, he got one.

Amidst all the pre-production activity on the new Gill Man movie, the vital matter of its title was also being considered. For rather a long time, it was internally called "*Black Lagoon* Sequel," "*Creature* Sequel," "Sequel to *Black Lagoon,*" "Sequel to *Creature from the Black Lagoon*" and *Return of the Creature from the Black Lagoon* as the titling can was endlessly kicked down the road. On June 4, publicity man Archie Herzoff wrote in a memo to members of his staff,

Chains await the Gill Man (Tom Hennesy) after his arrival in our civilized world, as they did for King Kong a generation before.

A new title is being sought for our forthcoming sequel to *Creature from the Black Lagoon*. Inasmuch as the picture is scheduled to go into production shortly, the studio would like to resolve the question of a title as quickly as possible. The problem with a new title is that while it is of extreme importance to capitalize on the identification benefits of the previous picture, the new title must also convey the feeling that the sequel is completely new, and not a reissue of the first picture.

On June 22, a memo revealed that the movie would be called *Return of the Creature*; that title hung on throughout production, but fell by the wayside soon after.

Synopsis

Putt-putt-putting its way along the torrid Upper Amazon is the *Rita II*, captained by Lucas (Nestor Paiva) and carrying two passengers, husky he-man Joe Hayes (John Bromfield) and middle-aged George Johnson (Robert B. Williams). Employees of Ocean Harbor, a Florida oceanarium, Joe and Johnson have come to capture the Gill Man and bring him back alive, for scientific study and public exhibition. When Joe catches sight of a crocodile and mistakes it for the man-fish, Lucas reacts with amusement: "You think maybe that eez eet? Ho ho, *no*! The thing you are looking for can break that in two, pfffft!"

Creature from the Black Lagoon is almost up to the 25-minute mark before our first good look at the Gill Man, but in *Revenge* we get Creature action right out of the box. Just short of the eight-minute mark, during a shot of a large bird (perhaps a white stork) perched on a floating log, he surges up out of the water to grab it; seconds later, in an underwater shot, he swims toward camera and pokes his head above the surface to watch as more two-legged snakes (aboard the *Rita II*) enter his primordial Garden of Eden. Joe dons old-fashioned "John Brown" diving equipment and goes underwater to seal off the lagoon entrance with a net; he and Johnson talk back and forth via an intercom. No doubt remembering the last time he had "guests," an unprovoked Gill Man attacks the submerged Joe from behind. Joe's attempts to escape the Creature's clutches fail, but the men on the boat are able to drive the monster away with rifle fire.

Joe and Johnson decide to take the easy way out and kayo the Gill Man by doing some "dynamite fishing" (a.k.a. "blast fishing," a real-life, usually illegal practice). Multiple metal cans of explosives dot the lagoon surface as, using a plunger, Johnson detonates them all simultaneously. Fish float to the surface, then a lifeless-looking Gill Man. We next see a telephoto of that image, in the hand of a TV newscaster who tells his audience that the Creature, still numbed by the dynamite blast, is now being flown to Ocean Harbor. The scene switches to a university setting as Prof. Clete Ferguson (John Agar), director of the Department of Animal Psychology, hears from his assistant Dr. McCuller (Robert Nelson) about the Gill Man's capture. McCuller excitedly urges Clete to get in on the Ocean Harbor action, and Clete rushes off to arrange a leave of absence.

The Gill Man arrives at Ocean Harbor aboard the seaquarium's *Porpoise III*. Joe tells park manager Foster (Grandon Rhodes) and press agent Lou (Dave Willock) that their newly arrived "big attraction" is still comatose and may not survive. A stretcher hoist is used to get the man-fish from the boat to Ocean Harbor's shallow "receiving tank" (also known as "the flume"); the top deck of the tank is aswarm with reporters, still photographers and newsreel cameramen watching the procedure. Joe glides the face-down Gill Man back and forth across the surface in hopes that the water moving past his gills will revive him. A radio announcer (James Fisher) with a portable mike describes the (in)action and gets a quick interview with Helen Dobson, a Belmont University science major visiting Ocean Harbor to gather material for her master's thesis on ichthyology. After about two hours of being "walked" by Joe, the Creature wakes up ornery, roaring and attacking attendants until being netted and roped. Joe is again in charge of operations when the Gill Man, still struggling against the net and ropes, is moved by divers from the receiving tank through an underwater gateway to the park's enormous oceanarium. On the bottom, a long chain runs from a ring in a steel plate to a manacle that is snapped closed around the monster's left ankle before the net is removed.

Bubble trouble: *Revenge* was made more quickly and economically than *Creature from the Black Lagoon* and the moviemakers had to take a few shortcuts, like not sweating the fact that air bubbles constantly seep out of the top of the Gill Man's (Ricou Browning) foam rubber head.

There's excitement in the salt air on the day that Ocean Harbor officially debuts its newest attraction, the Gill Man; the circus-type music heard in different parts of the "Creature Opening Day" scene helps create a bit of a Ringling Brothers–Gargantua the Gorilla atmosphere. Helen is part of the horde of gaping patrons scrutinizing the Gill Man from corridors on the dry side of the oceanarium's large sub-waterline portholes. The man-fish is soon spending a lot of time giving Helen the glad eye. Also attracted to Helen are both Clete and Joe.

To test the Gill Man's capacity to learn, Clete and Helen begin a regular routine of donning skin diver gear and joining him in his tank. The first time, Helen brings a metal basket full of food, puts it down in front of the Gill Man and, as he approaches, sternly says "Stop!" into her throat microphone; via an underwater amplifier, she can be loudly heard. As the uncomprehending Gill Man opens the cage, Clete pokes him with an electrified bull prod. To avoid further tastes of the bull prod, the Gill Man quickly learns that "Stop!" means stop, and does just that. Working together brings on romance for Clete and Helen.

One day in the oceanarium, when Helen gets too close, her scaly-armored admirer grabs her. Clete comes to her rescue with the bull prod but quickly finds himself disarmed and engaged in a life-and-death struggle. (The Gill Man tears off Clete's diving mask and air supply to give himself the upper claw, just as he did when fighting Mark Williams in *Black Lagoon.*) Helen's shouts of "Stop!" get the now-conditioned Creature to release Clete, who swims to safety with Helen. The Creature proceeds to run amok (well, to *swim* amok), breaking the chain on his ankle manacle. When he tries to climb out of the oceanarium, Joe pushes him back in with a boat hook. But in the process, Joe loses his balance and topples into the water, where the Creature throttles him and pounds his head face-first on the tank bottom. He then spectacularly springs from the oceanarium bottom to the top of the wall. Scores of screaming spectators flee as the Gill Man grapples with an attendant on the promenade and then, bellowing with rage, walks out on his show biz career. He ambles

Decisions, decisions! In June-July 1954, Marine Studios visitors had their pick of watching the making of *Revenge* (notice the Gill Man on bottom left) or the porpoise show (notice the leaping porpoise at the top).

through the park, out an exit, overturns a parked car, then makes his way down the beach and into the Atlantic. Standing on the promenade over the body of the fished-out Joe, Clete shakes his head to signify to Helen that he's a goner.

Several days after the Gill Man's escape, he makes a dead-of-night appearance from out of the river near the Star Motel where Helen has a room. From outside, the aqueous ogre watches through a screen door as she undresses and goes into the bathroom to take a shower. When the Gill Man enters the living room, Helen's snarling German Shepherd Chris takes a flying leap at him. Clete, also staying at the motel, hears Chris' dying howl and hurries to the scene. The Gill Man is gone, and Helen (just stepping out of the shower) heard nothing. The Gill Man spies on them behind a patch of palmetto, the dead dog at his feet.

When Clete and Helen decide to go on a leisurely cruise to Jacksonville aboard the *Porpoise III*, the Gill Man shows up at the wharf at departure time and begins to trail the boat up the river. The lovers dance to slow music and kiss on deck, and then when the boat develops motor trouble that necessitates a stop, they go for a swim. This leads to a reprise of another scene from *Black Lagoon*, "the underwater ballet," with the Gill Man spying on them, playfully touching her foot and even swimming directly below the unsuspecting couple. At one point, Clete and Helen are underwater when they go into a tight embrace and smooch and sink to the shallow river's bottom; as the camera tilts down with them, it reveals that the Gill Man is standing just feet away, watching. After Clete and Helen go back aboard the boat, the monster tries to climb a rope hanging from the transom. When the motor starts and the boat lurches forward, he falls back into the water.

That night in Jacksonville, Clete and Helen dance at a river's-edge Southbank restaurant, "The Lobster House," and make honeyed conversation about love. Jazz musicians are performing a hot number when the Gill Man strides in, lets out a bellow, grabs Helen and dives into the river with her. Search operations begin immediately but, even with an unconscious girl under one arm, the Gill Man manages to elude them. From their moving car, two young men (Brett Halsey and Robert Hoy) see a motionless Helen lying on a moonlit beach; they pull over and rush to her side. The Creature, who had waded off-shore for a breath of fresh water, resents their intrusion and ragdolls the Good Samaritans.

Once the men's bodies are found, a cavalry of cops and civil defense men converge on the area. Men with a mobile searchlight find on the beach the unconscious Helen, again unattended as the Gill Man has had to make another brief return to the water. When he reappears in time to prevent her rescue, one searcher fires his Very pistol. Helen awakens and begins screaming as the Gill Man (dripping wet and therefore looking like he's peeing on her) picks her up and carries her away. Arriving with reinforcements, Clete repeatedly shouts "Stop!" into a loudspeaker as the Gill Man wades into the river. At last the amphibious man obediently comes to a halt and, turning to face his pursuers, sets Helen down (in the script's words) "as though she were a delicate Dresden doll." Tension fills the air as Helen inches away from the Gill Man toward Clete—and as soon as she's clear of the monster's claws, the many gathered policemen open fire. Bellowing, he turns and dives into the water as the fusillade continues. An underwater shot of the man-beast stock-still and sinking into the darkness caps the movie.

Cast Biographies

John Agar as Prof. Clete Ferguson

Biographical entries on John Agar can be found in *The Creature Chronicles* (McFarland, 2014) and in this book's chapter on *Tarantula*.

Lori Nelson as Helen Dobson

Only child Dixie Kay Nelson was born in Santa Fe, New Mexico. At two and a half, the blue-eyed moppet danced in a home town show. Later voted Santa Fe's most talented and beautiful child, she toured the state billed as Santa Fe's Shirley Temple. When she was still a tyke, the family moved to Hollywood where she worked as a photographic model (children's clothes), appeared in USO shows at veterans' hospitals, acted in little theater productions, etc. She had her first shot at a movie job when she tested for the role of Cassandra Tower in Warners' *Kings Row* (1942); she lost out because she looked too young. Her parents allowed her to continue to model and act right through her teenage years as long as it didn't interfere with her schoolwork.

The Nelson family's neighbors knew of Dixie Kay's ambitions and introduced her to producer Arthur Landau, self-proclaimed discoverer of Jean Harlow, who expressed interest in casting her as Harlow in a movie account of the platinum bombshell's life and times. This went nowhere. The same neighbors brought her to the attention of agent Milo Frank, who saw possibilities in her, but Mom didn't want Dixie Kay making the studio rounds instead of having a normal high school life. Finally the mother agreed to allow Frank to take her on a Saturday to MGM, to meet one of the casting people—but on the big day, they learned that the casting man had suffered an attack of appendicitis. Undeterred, Frank instead took her to Universal where a casting exec showed interest. After Universal dramatic coach Sophie Rosenstein tutored Nelson for several weekends, an audition resulted in a seven-year contract.

In the early 1950s, Lori Nelson was one of scores of young hopefuls training at Universal and appearing in their movies, from a Francis the Talking Mule and Ma and Pa Kettles to the college football drama *The All American* (1953). From left: *All American* stars Tony Curtis, Lori, Mamie Van Doren, Richard Long. (Photograph courtesy Alexander Rotter.)

Renamed Lori Nelson, the $75-a-week contractee debuted in *Bend of the River* (1952), the Technicolor tale of a wagon train of Missouri farmers seeking to form a settlement in Oregon (where much of the movie was shot). Julie Adams and Lori played the daughters of settler Jay C. Flippen, Julie clinching at the fadeout with star James Stewart and Lori with a pre-stardom Rock Hudson. Next she played the oldest of the 15 Kettle children in two Ma and Pa Kettle comedies, *Ma and Pa Kettle at the Fair* (released in 1952) and *Ma and Pa Kettle at Waikiki* (not released until more than three years later, in 1955). The Ma and Pa Kettle movies were money magnets for Universal, not one of them making less than $2,000,000 domestically (U.S. and Canada).[1]

For a long spell, Nelson was on loanout to RKO for the deep-sea diving adventure *Underwater!* (1955), returning to Universal to find that some shuffling-of-personnel had gone on in her absence: "When I came back," she told me, "I knew practically no one and practically no one knew me!" She left after two more pictures, *Destry* and *Revenge of the Creature*. In 1956 she told interviewer Bob Thomas that the split with Universal was her idea "because I knew I was getting nowhere playing the girlfriend of Tony Curtis and Audie Murphy."

Freelancer Nelson alternated between major-studio movies (*I Died a Thousand Times* and *Sincerely Yours*, both 1955, and Paramount's *Pardners*, 1956) and low-budgeters like *Day the World Ended* (1956) and *Hot Rod Girl* (1956). There was also lots of TV work, including her own series *How to Marry a Millionaire*, co-starring with Merry Anders and Barbara Eden as sexy New York bachelorettes looking to trap wealthy husbands. Away from the studios, she was still living at home with her parents on Bellaire Avenue in North Hollywood.

Around the same time as a 1960 interview in which the never-been-married beauty said she'd never wed an actor ("I don't like actors"), there was romance and a little-publicized engagement to Burt Reynolds, then beginning his career. Six months after Reynolds' manic depressive behavior resulted in a breakup, Nelson married Johnny Mann of the Johnny Mann Singers. Daughter Lori Susan was born the following year (1962), and then Jennifer Lee three years later. After a series of separations and reconciliations, Nelson and Mann untied the knot in 1971. In 1979 she began acting again on little theater stages. Then acting was crowded out of her life by her duties as owner of Lori Facials and Cosmetics, a business operating out of a beauty shop near her home.

In 1983 she wed LAPD Detective Sgt. Joe Reiner and subsequently kept busy by buying and selling antiques and even playing a few additional movie roles. She also guested at a number of autograph shows, where the average fan coming to her table was mainly interested in Guess Who. "I played opposite Rock Hudson, Tony Curtis, Jimmy Stewart, Dean Martin and Audie Murphy," she told me, "but who's the leading man *everybody* wants to ask me about? The Gill Man! ... It's so funny, Universal had to twist my arm a little to be in a monster movie. But if I knew then how popular they would remain, I would have twisted *their* arm to be in a couple more!"

This book's companion volume The Creature Chronicles *includes biographies for* Revenge of the Creature *co-stars John Bromfield, Nestor Paiva, Flippy the "Educated" Porpoise and Tom Hennesy.*

Production

In 1953, the first unit and second unit scenes of *Creature from the Black Lagoon* had been shot simultaneously, Jack

Arnold working on the former at Universal and James Havens and "Scotty" Welbourne handling the latter in Florida. On *Revenge*, Arnold was the director of both units. The second unit work came first: Arnold and members of the key crew departed on the morning of June 18 for St. Augustine to confirm all the location arrangements. The schedule called for pre-production shooting to begin on June 25 and continue for ten days without sound, lights or cast.

In the days leading up to the scheduled start of production, the balance of Arnold's second unit crew arrived in Florida, and shooting began right on schedule on June 25. According to that day's production report, and those of June 26 and June 28, John Lamb and Ricou Browning were both present bright and early on each of three days. The paperwork doesn't specifically say what they *did* on June 25 and 26, just that both of 'em were *there*. Memorize that tidbit of info, because we'll be returning to it.

Right away the *Revenge* team ran into hard luck: As they tried to get some of their first underwater shots in the oceanarium, they twice had to contend with a camera in need of repair, plus park personnel who, in order to feed the fish, regularly made them leave the oceanarium. Many of the crew members had arrived by 7:30 a.m. that June 25 but there was no filming until over eight hours later, at 3:35 p.m. They didn't expose much footage that day, just part of the scene where the bound-in-a-net Gill Man is brought into the oceanarium by divers and chained to the floor. (The 30-foot chain and shackle were made of aluminum.)

Who played the Creature on that first day (and on the second and on the start of the third)? Lamb was hired to play the monster underwater, and at Universal a Creature suit was made for him; but as many fans already know, his "performance" failed to impress director Arnold, who then had Browning assume the role. But Lamb had to have played the Gill Man at *some* early stage of production, in order for Arnold to *be* unimpressed—yes? On Day Three of second unit work (June 28), the Daily Production Report includes the notation "LAMB COULD NOT DO SCENE—PUT RICKY [RICOU BROWNING] INTO SUIT," which *to me* indicates that in all Gill Man footage shot prior to that Day Three notation, Lamb is in the suit. But Browning flatly insists, "I did *all* the underwater scenes"—and Tom Hennesy told me in 1994 that in the scenes featuring the bound-in-a-net Gill Man (shot on Days One and Two), the Gill Man was Browning.

Day Two, a Saturday, went much better than the first, with a crew call of 7:30, a first shot at 9:08, and the only problems minor ones (repairs to the camera and to the Gill Man suit). The morning was spent in the receiving tank getting underwater shots of the kayoed Gill Man being "walked" by Joe; reviving and swimming around; and fighting with Joe. In the afternoon, after work moved back to the oceanarium, there were retakes of the shots of three divers bringing the netted-up Gill Man to the bottom and securing the anklet chain, plus shots of the net being removed and the Gill Man doing his first bit of oceanarium swimming. As mentioned above, *according to the Daily Production Reports* the Gill Man casting switch (from Lamb to Browning) wasn't made until Monday, so it should still be Lamb on Saturday. But Hennesy, who played one of the three divers, told me,

> **I remember the sequence where Ricou played the Creature in a cargo net, being transported into the Marine Studios oceanarium. They had an air hose in there for him so that he could get air when needed; they incorporated it into the scene in such a way that it looked like a line. John Lamb, myself and one or two underwater attendants [played the men who] introduced the Creature into the oceanarium.**

And Ricou Browning recalls *being* the Gill Man in that scene, in an email to me adding the detail, "In long shots it was a dummy Creature, in close shots it was me."

Moviemakers—including a modest-looking Jack Arnold—setup in the receiving tank under the gaze of swarms of Marine Studios guests. Where are the thousands of photographs and the home movie footage these people must have shot?

Monday, June 28, began comically, although surely no one there at the time was amused: First thing in the a.m., a loaded camera went down into the oceanarium and a shot was lined up … and then the camera had to be brought up and *re*loaded, because it was accidentally running throughout that entire process! Lamb *was* in the Gill Man suit that morning, the production paperwork unmistakably says it was him: In the first shot of the day, a bit after 9:30, he swam around in the oceanarium, trying to convey anger. And at 10:30, script supervisor Dixie McCoy made the abovementioned Production Report notation "LAMB COULD NOT DO SCENE—PUT RICKY INTO SUIT." Elsewhere on that report, someone else (different handwriting) wrote, "50 minute delay due to John Lamb being unable to do required underwater swimming—necessitating changing to Ricou Browning."

Now you know how the surviving production paperwork … very sloppily handwritten, some of it indecipherable, with many misspellings, … describes the initial shooting of Gill Man scenes on Friday, June 25, Saturday, June 26, and the morning of Monday, June 28. According to the paperwork, Lamb and Browning were both there on those three days (but the paperwork does *not* say what they did on the first two days); Day Three began with Lamb floundering in the Gill Man suit and Browning replacing him.

Browning has an unshakable memory of playing the Gill Man right from *the very first moment* he stepped foot on the Marineland location—not only in the net scene but also being "walked" in the flume. He told me,

> **I got a call from Jack Arnold asking me, "How would you like to work on a new Creature film?" I said sure and asked, "You want me to come to L.A. and get fitted for the costume?" He said, "No, we are already at Marine Studios in Florida and we need you to come down and work as the Creature. Can you get down here as soon as possible?" I said, "Okay, I can leave tonight," and I did—I drove down to Marine Studios. Once I arrived, Jack Kevan started cutting the John Lamb suits down to fit me so that I could begin to work immediately.**

There's a natural inclination to place more trust in original production paperwork than on someone's (Browning's) memory of 60-year-old events … but when he's as emphatic as Ricou is, and when Hennesy backs him up (saying that it was Ricou as the Creature in a scene shot on Day One and/or Day Two), that "trust" in the paperwork begins to waver. There has to be a simple explanation that would make both the production paperwork *and* Ricou's memory correct, but probably too many years have passed to figure out what it is.

"John Lamb was a 'water man,' and they had hired him to do part of the [Creature swimming scenes]," Hennesy told me. "They did makeup tests and built a suit for John; he spent quite a bit of time in the [makeup department] before he went to Florida. But he ended up doing very little. I guess they shot a couple of things with John as the Creature, and the director became disenchanted with the way that John looked in the water; he said he looked like a man in a suit! So, unfortunately for John, they decided to terminate his employment [as the Creature]."

Sally Baskin remembers being told at the time that "the Hollywood stuntman" (Lamb) had to be replaced by Browning. Keep in mind that these are second-hand stories relayed to me by someone who was 12 when *she* heard them: Sally told me, "[Lamb] was there playing the Gill Man, but then the next thing I knew, it was Ricou Browning. I asked why, and they said that the first guy finally said, 'I can't *do* this!' The suit made him real nervous, claustrophobic, and he didn't like the sharks and other big fish all around."

Is John Lamb seen in the movie, even in a single shot, as the Creature? I don't know.

While Lamb did remain with the unit, from that morning on, only Browning played the Gill Man in underwater shots. But the switch created an annoying distraction: Browning's suits in *Black Lagoon,* made specifically for him, were form-fitting, whereas the Lamb suits that he had to wear in *Revenge* were big on him. Ricou said they were cut down a little, in order to make them fit better, but apparently there wasn't much they could do about the too-big head. Consequently, as the submerged Browning did his between-takes breathing, air would collect inside it—and, as cameras rolled, it seeped out through the foam rubber top via a stream of bubbles.

"Just before I'd do a shot, I'd push down on the top of my head, trying to get some of the air out," Browning told me. "But that head was so much bigger than the original [*Black Lagoon*] head, so much looser on me, that it held a lot more air." Equally unfortunate: The Creature heads worn in this movie by Browning *and* Hennesy have eyes that look like tanning bed goggles. Also, because the Marine Studios tank was filled with saltwater that made Browning's Gill Man suit more buoyant, he had to have more weights strapped to his body in order to be able to stay below the surface.

With Ricou in the Lamb suit, Monday's shooting resumed with the scene of Joe bringing the Gill Man a mesh cage full of fish, and the Gill Man sitting on the bottom-of-the-oceanarium anchor eating them. In the afternoon, $200-a-week underwater swimmers Ginger Stanley and Robert Lee Tinney joined the underwater cast of players: Stanley played Helen and Tinney played Clete in the scene where they begin to teach the Gill Man the meaning of "Stop!"

Florida rain became a problem for the *Revenge* team for the first time that day: It clouded up at 3:25 and began

For this Ginger Stanley photo, picture-snapper Bruce Mozert was at a depth of 50 feet, just inside the Silver Springs cave whence the waters of this artesian spring flow. In the mouth of the cave, Stanley got air from a hose originating on a sightseeing boat above—and clung to the bottom for dear life, so that the water pouring out of the cave wouldn't push her up to the surface.

raining ten minutes later, and it was still raining when they called it quits at 4:25. It didn't pay to get out of bed on the 29th, a day when practically nothing got on film because of heavy overcast skies, Marine Studios' regular fish-feedings, multiple camera jams, director Arnold needing to meet with the oceanarium manager, etc.

The next day (June 30) there was a different location, Silver Springs, but the same headaches (camera trouble, poor light, etc.). On this, the first of three days of Silver Springs production, the camera went down into that underwater fairyland for a Gill Man's-eye view of swimming lovers Clete and Helen (Tinney and Stanley) taking their *Porpoise III* dip, hardhat diver Joe's descent into the Black Lagoon, part of the Black Lagoon fight between the Gill Man and Joe, and a shot of the Gill Man swimming as "bullets" strike the surface and course downward. That last bit of footage was used in both the Black Lagoon scene when it's Johnson firing, and in the Florida beach finale when it's the police firing. A forgotten prop at Silver Springs: the Ocean Harbor manacle for the Gill Man's left ankle. He should be wearing it as he trails the *Porpoise III,* as he swims under Clete and Helen, and as he swims away from the rifle-firing policemen, but in all of those second-half-of-the-movie underwater scenes, his leg is bare.

On July 1 at Silver Springs, the moviemakers again alternated between shooting underwater scenes of the Gill Man fighting Joe, and the Gill Man voyeuristically watching Clete and Helen. Browning told me he can't remember who doubled for John Bromfield as Joe in their fight scene: "He was just a hardhat diver who I think they hired out of Jacksonville. I have no idea who he was." The July 1 production paperwork doesn't mention the participation of an additional local diver, and *does* say that John Lamb and Browning's safety diver Charles McNabb *were* there; but Browning said that Joe's double was neither of them.

Around midday, the glass on the blimp of the underwater camera broke and the camera flooded, ruining all the film inside. Welbourne drove to Palatka, almost 50 miles north, to fetch his own camera and he returned with it a little after two o'clock. Shooting resumed around three but then ended for the day at 3:35 when a thunderstorm came in. At this point, the production was a bit over budget and a day behind schedule. Welbourne's mobile underwater camera was again used on July 2, the company's last day in Silver Springs, as they concentrated on finishing the Clete–Helen–Gill Man scene.

Ginger Stanley underwater-doubled Julie Adams in the first Gill Man movie and Lori Nelson in the second. Her "day job" was with Silver Springs' publicity department, enacting unusual scenes for newsreel cameras and/or photographs. In this shot taken by Bruce Mozert, she cooks a Thanksgiving dinner underwater.

They wrapped things up at 2:40, loaded their trucks and got back to Marineland at just past six.

Saturday, July 3, was a long, productive day at Marine Studios (lots of underwater oceanarium footage of Clete and Helen working with the Gill Man). Following the Fourth of July, they made up for Saturday's success with a lousy day on Monday, July 5: The scene of the Gill Man dragging Joe to the oceanarium bottom was all they had "in the can" by ten o'clock, when the light got bad and *stayed* bad. When a rainstorm set in at 3:30, they called it a day. By now they were two days behind schedule and $5000 over budget. July 6 got off to a bad start light-wise, but once things improved they got back into the oceanarium and shot more Clete–Helen–Gill Man byplay plus the monster's fight with Clete.

Shooting on July 7 went well, other than the fact that a member of Ricou's safety team, his sister Shirley Woolery, "became ill from water infection from tank," according to the Production Report. One of the scenes shot that day: Clete and Joe attaching wires to the Gill Man (doped and unconscious on the floor of the oceanarium) in order to measure his brain's electrical impulses.

Thursday, July 8, was the twelfth and last day of second unit work (which was supposed to take only ten days). The morning began with irritation and a lost hour as Flippy the "Educated" Porpoise refused to perform for the moviemakers who had setup cameras at his pool. Retreating in defeat, the crew moved to the area near the Marine Studios box office—where, unlike Flippy, residents of St. Augustine were ready, willing and *eager* to perform. According to Universal publicity, during the *Revenge* team's several weeks at Marineland, they used 300 extras, all townsfolk of St. Augustine, the sleepy Florida city of approximately 14,000 located 18 miles away. Many of them were members of the St. Augustine Little Theater ... not surprising, since the extras casting was done by Maude Hecht and Charlotte Kaye, the Little Theater's leading lights. Another local present at Marine Studios for the filming: ten-year-old Steve Boone, who grew up to become the bassist for the Lovin' Spoonful.

"All right, Mr. Arnold, I'm ready for my closeup": The 3-D camera gets in close on the Gill Man (Ricou Browning) at the bottom of the Marine Studios tank.

"It was like the circus coming to town!" Judeena Blackmer excitedly recalled for me; she was five and a half when she played the child who trips and falls in the path of the Gill Man. "When the *Revenge* people arrived and made it known that they needed extras, it was a big deal for the people there, and I think everybody in St. Augustine showed up [*laughs*]! I'm *serious*! I know all my mom's friends went, and all their kids went. I wish you could talk to my mom, she's gone, but she always told of the story of how, when the Creature escaped from the oceanarium and everybody ran, the people literally mowed down one of the chain link fences. When they ran, *they ran* [*laughs*]!"

Working for the first time with the St. Augustine locals, Arnold and Co. got the shot where the camera focuses on a life-sized cutout of the Gill Man, then pulls back to show a pretty girl getting her picture taken standing next to it. On the left is the box office, which is doing a brisk business. The movie camera then pans right to follow the girl and her photographer and, beyond them, we see the oceanarium.

The filmmakers then got the adrenaline of the extras going by shooting various shots of folks fleeing the wrath of the Gill Man. Seventy-three people earned $10 a head that day, before rain put an end to all activity in the mid-afternoon. In one memorable moment, especially for fans seeing a tri-dimensional print, a pair of young men vault over a railing near the box office, the second one (Richard O. Watson) bumping the Creature standee which topples toward the camera.

Extra Gloria Selph told me that even though there was no sound equipment there, "everybody—*everybody* who was running and waving their arms and acting like terrified people—we all *screamed*. Rewatching the movie the other day, I did not see my son, a little boy at that time, running beside me, but he did and he had a wonderful time yelling, 'cause he had to be so quiet other times!"

Like many Hollywood movies, *Revenge* was planned with the precision of troop movements: Overlapping with the completion of the second unit work was the arrival from California of cast members plus behind-the-scenes folks (makeup, wardrobe, sound, electricians, etc.) whose services hadn't been needed during all the no-actors, no-lights, no-sound shooting done to date. The *Revenge* troupe's sleeping accommodations (61 beds) were provided by the Marine Village Court.

On July 9, the words "Start of Principal Photography" were written across the front of the Daily Production Report. And on Day One of first unit production, Florida weather being what it is, they had to play everything by ear: At 8:45 a.m. when they were ready to shoot outdoors, the sky *wasn't* ready (insufficient light), so they moved to a porthole corridor and shot the first scene of Clete and Helen (now played by Agar and Nelson) watching the Gill Man through portholes. But even this scene, an *interior*, was affected by the weather: As the actors rehearsed, a bad storm broke out and the oceanarium water became so dark that little could be seen through the portholes! A change in the camera setup enabled Arnold to shoot close-ups of the two actors delivering their dialogue with the viewing window less prominently featured. The rain stopped at 12:20 but the heavy storm clouds lingered and continued to put a crimp in the activities. In the mid-afternoon, the cameras went back into the oceanarium for inside-looking-out panning shots of the faces of gawkers (including Agar and Nelson) at the portholes. Since the light conditions had been extremely poor all day and might be just as bad the *next* day, Arnold and a few crew members adjourned to Marine Studios' research lab and discussed the possibility of having to spend July 10 shooting in there.

Sure enough, there was no sun in that part of the Sunshine State on Saturday, July 10, so into the lab Agar, Nelson and the crew went, getting lots of shots of Agar putting a crab in a small fish tank and putting drops in a beaker, Nelson using a microscope and handling test tubes, etc. (Some of these shots aren't in the movie.) Browning even makes a cameo appearance here. This was one of just three interiors shot in Florida, the other locations being the porthole corridor and Jacksonville's Lobster House. After lunch, all equipment was moved back to the porthole corridor and more of that Clete-Helen scene was shot. At the day's end, rather than simply dismissing the corridor's many extras, the moviemakers instructed them to *run* out—footage that could eventually be added to the Gill Man's Ocean Harbor rampage scene.

A day of rest (Sunday, July 11) and then back in the oceanarium on Monday for shots of the Gill Man looking out a porthole at Helen; and then back to the corridor for shots of Helen looking *in* the porthole at the Gill Man. Here for the first of *three* times in *Revenge*, Arnold fell back on his tried-and-true hand-on-the-shoulder trick: Nelson is at the porthole, tensely staring through the tempered glass into the face of Browning's Gill Man inches away, when Agar suddenly reaches in and touches her. But surprise-wise it's a complete bust, because Agar's stationary shadow is clearly visible on the wall beside her throughout the buildup.

Newly arrived in Florida, actors Grandon Rhodes, Dave Willock and Robert B. Williams did their first work on July 13 as scenes in and around the Marine Studios receiving tank were shot: the stretcher bearing the Gill Man (Hennesy) being lowered into the tank, Joe "walking" the Gill Man, and onlooker Helen being interviewed by a microphone-wielding radio announcer (played by James Fisher, in real life a radio announcer on WFOY, the oldest radio station in St. Augustine). Hennesy remembered the stretcher hoist well in our interview:

> **When they first brought the Creature into the small receiving tank, I did that part of it.... [T]he operator of the hoist said that it was very ancient and rickety and noisy, and he said that he hoped that it worked better than it did the last time. When asked what he meant by that, he said that they had been hoisting a shark or a porpoise into the tank and the thing unwound and collapsed, and the fish was dropped onto the pavement below, and killed, evidently.**

According to Universal paperwork, it was decided early in *Revenge*'s planning that for the scene of the Gill Man arriving at Ocean Harbor, "we will use the identical methods employed at Marine Studios for the transference and handling of large fish, since they are colorful and extremely visual." And Sally Baskin confirms that they did just that:

> **The Gill Man arrives on the boat *Porpoise III*, which was an actual Marine Studios boat that would go out and capture porpoise, dolphin, shark, whatever [which would then be kept in a "live well" inside the boat]. The boat would come in to the dock, just as you see in the movie, and they would take the porpoise, dolphin, shark, whatever, out through the side hatchway and onto that canvas stretcher and bring it to the receiving tank—the whole procedure you see in the movie. Then the sharks had to be walked, to get their gill systems working. The dolphins would be walked, too, but it was pretty much to calm them down. Smaller fish—barracudas and all—would be put directly into the oceanarium, but the sharks and dolphins had to be walked before they could be let loose.**

On July 14, the receiving tank battle between the Gill Man and his captors was filmed. Except for a few mid-afternoon minutes spent waiting for the light to improve, the weather apparently cooperated, making it a good day for the still-behind-schedule, still-over-budget production. But it wasn't a good day for the beleaguered Gill Man Tom Hennesy, who told me:

> **I was fighting at least three people there, Bromfield and two local Florida stuntmen. It was very difficult, and I had to fight to keep from being drowned. They weren't accomplished Hollywood stuntmen, *any* of 'em, so I had a hell of a fight with all three of them. I got frustrated, 'cause these guys were choking me, and if they had gotten me under-**

water, they would have held me down and drowned me! I could tell immediately that this was no game—maybe these guys thought I *was* a creature! Maybe they thought they were fighting for *their* lives, but I felt that I was fighting for *mine*. So I finally said, "The heck with it," it was do or die, so I did what I had to do, and it became a knock-down, drag-out brawl!

In 2003, Hennesy told this anecdote to the World 3-D Film Expo audience, this time specifying that Bromfield was *not* one of the guys fighting as though Hennesy was an actual monster. He now classified the others as local musclemen rather than stuntmen and, perhaps playing to the audience, came up with an even better punchline:

I finally got so exasperated with these guys.... I picked up one guy and threw him into the wall [*audience laughter*]. I was told that he got three fractured ribs out of it [*audience gasps and groans*]. And the rest of 'em kinda backed off a little bit [*audience laughter*].

On July 15, Hennesy's Creature was back in the oceanarium, struggling to climb out past a boat hook–wielding Joe, and pulling Joe into the water. The accent remained on action on July 16 with more takes of the abovementioned battle, plus the memorable down-shot of Browning's Gill Man rocketing head-first out of the tank toward the tridimensional camera. Browning told me that, in preparation for that shot, "they put a strap around my waist that also went over my shoulders, and the straps all came together in a big ring at the back of my neck. Once that was all secure, I got into the Creature suit. They hooked a cable into that ring, and then they had the cable go up into a pulley. Then they had men with ropes that were tied to the cable, and they all just yanked it, and yanked me right outta there!" He recalled being jerked up too high on the first attempt, and everything going well on the second. The book *Directed by Jack Arnold* includes storyboard artwork of this scene, and it shows the Creature standing on the oceanarium bottom on one end of a seesaw; Browning said no such contraption was used.

July 17 found cast and crew in Porpoise Stadium getting shots of Clete, Helen and Joe in the audience of a Flippy performance. They were joined there by the newest member of the cast, a six-year-old male German Shepherd playing Chris, Helen's "one true love and favorite boyfriend." After lunch, operations moved to the Marineland wharf and the scene of the *Porpoise III* arriving with its Creature cargo. As noted above, the *Porpoise III* was the actual "collection boat" or "catch boat" on which Marine Studios' specimen hunters went out to sea to get new recruits for exhibition at the marine mammal park. The body of water in the wharf scenes is a lagoon off of the Intracoastal Waterway.

Perhaps because *Revenge* was now behind schedule and $12,500 over budget, Florida shooting became seven days a week. The first Sunday of work (July 18) began back in Porpoise Stadium with Flippy again failing to do his tricks for the cameras. Thinking on their feet, the filmmakers moved their equipment to the beach near the Marine Village Court in preparation for the shooting of Clete and Helen's love scene, then returned to Flippy's tank, setup a camera and filmed part of the "Educated" Porpoise's regular 9:30 performance (Flippy jumping through the suspended paper hoop). They then headed *back* to the beach and shot the romantic scene with Agar, Nelson and Chris the dog. Then it was back to Porpoise Stadium to photograph *two* more regularly scheduled Flippy performances. An unhappy Arnold had to burn up a lot of film photographing most or all of the Flippy shows newsreel-style because he didn't know what Flippy would do next or when he'd do it: Arnold went through over 6680 feet of raw stock that day, 2460 of it wasted. Clete and Helen's love-on-a-beach-blanket scene was also shot that day.

Agar and Nelson, the only two actors to work that Sunday, got the next two days off as the rest of the *Revenge* company trekked to Palatka, Florida, to shoot the topside parts of the Black Lagoon opener. On Monday they traveled to the

On a stretcher hoist, the knocked-out Creature (Tom Hennesy) is taken from a boat to the receiving tank at his new home, Ocean Harbor. This photograph was taken by a member of the Baskin family who ran the Marine Village Court, a motel a few hundred feet south of Marine Studios on Ocean Boulevard.

location from 6 a.m. to 7:15, spent 45 minutes loading their belongings onto a barge, and then at eight o'clock they proceeded several miles up Rice Creek, a St. Johns River tributary. Repeating his Lucas role from *Black Lagoon*, Nestor Paiva joined the cast that morning, sharing scenes with Bromfield and Robert B. Williams as Ocean Harbor's Creature hunters. Shot this first day at Palatka were the action scenes: the *Rita II* arriving and dropping anchor; Joe climbing down the ladder into the water; Johnson, Lucas and the two native crew members on deck trying to save the underwater Joe from the Creature.

Cast and crew got back to Marineland at 6:40 p.m. The next day (Tuesday, July 20), the second half of the Palatka shooting was done. Universal publicity mentions that these Black Lagoon scenes were shot under a fierce sun and in stifling atmosphere, and this time, it was no flack's fabrication: At 9:15 a.m., Wallace Mussallem, a Florida local playing one of Lucas' native crewmen, fell unconscious as a result of the steamy, jungle-like heat. At another point in the day, script clerk Dixie McCoy became the second casualty of the subtropical climate. Browning added a detail *not* supplied by the publicity department: Not only was Rice Creek hot and the air thick with humidity, but they were shooting about a mile from a paper mill, and the stench was overpowering! "The paper mill, just down the way, discharged their waste water [chemicals, etc.] in Rice Creek," he ruefully recalled.

Spotting intruders in the Black Lagoon, the Gill Man lays out the un-welcome mat—and Johnson (Robert B. Williams) reacts with rifle fire. Topside Lagoon scenes were shot in Rice Creek, Florida, over the space of two blistering-hot days, in water so polluted that Ricou Browning compared it to "swimming in your toilet."

Sally Baskin didn't accompany the gang to Rice Creek but she saw them when they returned:

They were transported back and forth by bus, and I'd be around when they returned to Marineland and I can remember how bad they smelled. Rice Creek was very smelly, very odorous, very slimy, and when they would come out of the water there, they'd have slime coming off of their suits and off of their bodies. When they got back to Marineland, the first place they headed was to the beach. Nobody went straight to their rooms, they went straight to the beach and jumped into the ocean, clothes and all, trying to get that smell off of 'em. There's no other smell like a paper mill!

On that second day of Rice Creek shooting, the blast that (storyline-wise) concusses the Gill Man was set off a little before three, sending water sky-high. You'll notice that, after the detonation, the cans that supposedly contained the explosives drop from the sky and bob around undamaged; that's because no explosives were used. According to Browning, the large upheaval of water was created by a great "eruption of air," as he calls it. "I don't know exactly how they set the charge, but it wasn't dynamite or anything like that." The fish on the surface in the next scene were dead fish that had been bought and brought to the location. "Some would float and some wouldn't," Browning continued, "so air was pumped into the ones that wouldn't, to make them stay on the surface."

July 21 was a never-to-be-forgotten day for many St. Augustinians as Arnold and Co. resumed shooting at Marineland with more shots of the stampede that follows the Gill Man's escape. Seventy-five extras got $10 each for joining in this mass exodus. First they shot, twice, the vignette where a mother and her little girl (Judeena Blackmer) are trying to outpace the Gill Man, the latter falling onto a cargo net while the mother obliviously continues on alone. Then the filmmakers moved their cameras back to the top deck of the oceanarium and photographed Gill Man Tom Hennesy clambering out over the wall, with hysteria breaking out all about him.

More escape scene footage was shot in the afternoon. In order for Gill Man Hennesy to flip the Pontiac sedan, cables ran from the vehicle to a tow truck which pulled it over. (It was Hennesy's memory that a tow truck was used, and there *is* a tow truck on the July 21 production report's "Special Equipment" list. But onlooker Sally Baskin remembers men on the beach pulling the cables on the car, which she described as "stripped until all it *was* was a shell.") Many extras formed a large off-camera audience as the action was shot twice: once with the camera shooting up from the beach at the car and Creature with Marine Studios in the background, the other time shooting the car and Creature with the Atlantic Ocean in the background. *Both* times, Hennesy was a bit concerned: "It was a dangerous thing for people working around there," he said in our interview, "because if a cable had broken and whipped back, it could have killed *every*one." (In an early script, it's not an empty car but a stalled car filled with sightseers that gets overturned.) The camera-on-the-beach take was used even though the rolling car very noticeably clips the camera.

On the morning of Thursday, July 22, Agar and Nelson bid farewell to Marineland ... on film, anyway. That was the day they went to the wharf and shot the scene of Clete and Helen leaving on the *Porpoise III*, with Johnson (played by Robert B. Williams) on hand to see them off. Then the filmmakers proceeded in boats up the St. Johns River to shoot Clete and Helen's romantic cruise. Ricou Browning and Tom Hennesy came along on the excursion but neither worked on camera until after 6 p.m. when one of them was in the shot where the Gill Man reaches out of the water for the boat's dangling stern rope, and has it pulled from his hand when the boat begins moving. Browning guesses that it was Hennesy because he doesn't remember doing it himself.

The last day of Marine Studios photography, Friday, July 23, began late because the company planned to shoot night-for-night scenes well past the witching hour. The first stop was the receiving tank, to shoot retakes of the fight (the Gill Man vs. Joe and the Ocean Harbor attendants). There was a crew call for one p.m. but because of poor light and off-and-on rain, nothing was shot until 3:20—and even then, they were shooting in the rain. This was the last scene, and the last day on the movie, for actors Bromfield and Williams. That night they shot the motel scene of Clete and Helen looking for Helen's dog, unaware that the Gill Man has killed it and is watching them from hiding. Eleven days earlier in the shooting, in a porthole corridor scene, director Arnold pulled the old "hand on the shoulder" gag out of his bag of fright tricks and had Clete scare Helen; at the motel, Helen returns the favor, unexpectedly coming up behind Clete during their search for the dog. Agar and Nelson finished the scene and were dismissed at 11:42.

At that point, on that same site (near the water's edge by the motel), more St. Augustinians joined the cast: Pat Powers and Julian Fant as lovebirds in a Ford convertible. Here again, Arnold uses the hand-on-the-shoulder trick: As we watch the boy (driver's seat) and girl (passenger seat) kissing, a hand enters the shot from camera left and touches the girl, who lets out a horrified cry. But it's not the Gill Man, it's a policeman (played by local cop Bill Young) who tells the kids to break it up and go home. The hand-on-shoulder gag worked well in *It Came from Outer Space* and *Creature from the Black Lagoon* but not one of the three in *Revenge* (Clete to Helen, Helen to Clete, policeman to smooching girl) is effective at all.

Most of the Universal people involved with the late-night shooting probably slept late the next day (July 24), and then at four in the afternoon, the crew and what remained of the cast (Agar, Nelson, Creatures Browning and Hennesy, Nelson's water double Ginger Stanley) made the one-hour, 45-minute hike north to Jacksonville, where the balance of the Florida shooting would take place. Again they would be shooting night-for-night on July 25 (the second and last Sunday that the company worked), this time at Jacksonville's river's-edge Lobster House restaurant. Universal paid $250 a night to use it as a location.

Cameras rolled for the first time that night at 8:50 with an out-the-restaurant-window shot of downtown Jacksonville's skyline on the other side of the St. Johns River; the camera pulls back across the

"No tank town tank can hold me!": The Creature (Tom Hennesy) storms out of the seaquarium. Notice that, for *now* anyway, there's someone in the car (top middle) that the Creature is about to overturn.

dance floor to show bartenders, band members and dancers, including Agar and Nelson. Forty-one extras were used plus three bartenders. And a long night it was, as many parts of the Lobster House scene, some featuring the Gill Man, were photographed, including (between three and four a.m.) footage of the carried-away drummer and his priceless expression when he first sees the party-crashing man-fish. (In the script, the music makers are described as a small Dixieland band, their music "hot, orgiastic, passionate," with the faces of their listeners "reflecting the jungle beat." An earlier draft specifies that they're "colored musicians.")

Browning was napping on the Lobster House roof when he heard the screaming start—and these were no play-acting screams:

> **They used people from the insurance building next door as extras, and these people all came with their husbands, wives, girlfriends, whatever, all dressed in formal wear.... I was sitting on top of the roof when suddenly I heard all this commotion. What had happened was, they had moved the arc lights up into the ceilings, and set off the automatic sprinkler system. The entire bunch of people were just full of water and rust—the sprinkler system probably was never used, and was full of rusty water.**

It was circa 4 a.m. when the heat from the lights activated the sprinklers. The extras' all-nighter had ended with a shower of dirty water, and some of them went home with ruined clothes; there was no begrudging *any* of them their $10 paychecks. ("But they were all good sports about it," Browning told me.) The extras were dismissed at 4:10, in the midst of a 50-minute clean-up. In the one and only shot taken afterwards, a Creature-clobbered Clete fell to the restaurant floor, woozily picked himself up and ran out the door.

Mayhem was on the Lobster House menu again the following night (Monday, July 26), another long one for all concerned. Forty-eight extras worked, plus Agar, Nelson, Hennesy and (their last day of employment on the picture) Browning and Ginger Stanley. Shooting began with the scene of the Gill Man (Hennesy) carrying Helen (Stanley) toward the Lobster House railing and diving with her into the St. Johns River, with Clete (Agar) in hot pursuit. Later they shot footage of Clete in the water with the gong buoy and the police boat, and then spent an hour lining up, rehearsing and trying to shoot a scene in which man-and-woman boaters (played by locals) react to the sight of the Gill Man and Helen by the buoy. The time was wasted; according to the script clerk's notes, "2 PEOPLE COULD NOT DO SCENE." With dawn approaching, they went back to the Lobster House and shot the exterior scene of Clete and Helen talking and kissing, plus a dolly shot of the Gill Man coming into a big close-up. Then the moviemakers took another stab at the man-and-woman-in-a-boat scene ... but on this go-round, the woman was Loretta Agar, John's wife, who did it at director Arnold's request. By now, it was after 5 a.m. the next morning. Agar, Nelson and Hennesy were finally dismissed while the cameras went back inside the Lobster House for shots of the jammin' musicians; and then they shot a process plate of the Jacksonville skyline. The sun had risen by the time the last of the members of the company were free to leave.

With the Florida shooting complete (two days behind schedule and $20,000 over budget), cast and crew headed back to California. A Universal publicity item pointed out that they had worked a month in Florida where it was sweltering hot not only by day but also at night—and then returned to California where, during some of the nighttime outdoor work, chilly cast members swathed themselves in coats, wraps and blankets as soon as the cameras stopped grinding.

On July 29, on Universal's Stage 14, the Star Motel interiors were photographed. Work began with a shot of Nelson removing a stocking and combing her hair as the Gill Man (Hennesy) stands gaping outside her window. That shot, plus others with the Creature watching through the room's screen doors as Helen disrobes, reached the screen even though, in a June 1954 letter to Universal, the Production Code Administration's Joseph Breen emphatically stated that the "entire sequence of the Creature peeking through a window to watch Helen undress is not acceptable as written. In any rewrite of this material we feel it important that care be exercised to avoid any sexual emphasis that might suggest bestiality." Universal did suggest bestiality by filming and using the shots of a gaga Gill Man ogling Helen; and when *Revenge of the Creature* was ready for release, they did much *more* than just suggest it in their radio spots:

> **When the Black Lagoon surrendered this monster from the dawn of time—all civilization shuddered! When a woman's beauty tempted him—a million dead years of wild desire was aroused!**

And in a different radio ad:

> **Be startled by the dangerous desires that enflame him ... as he seizes a beautiful woman, holding her captive for his distant Amazon lair!**

Additionally, in the *Revenge of the Creature* trailer, narrator Marvin Miller proclaims in awestruck tones, "They dared to [tempt the Gill Man] with the lure of a woman's beauty, thinking that mere chains could hold in check the primeval forces that surged and roiled within this strange being from the dawn of time!"

Howard H. Thompson of *The New York Times* wrote in his May 14, 1955, *Revenge* review, "Yesterday's audience was convulsed when Gill, let's call him, spying on Miss Nelson's preparations to retire, gives a tremendous adenoidal gulp." One man's trash is another man's treasure: A *Castle of Frankenstein* reviewer called the Gill Man's gulping an example of the picture's "strong thread of period eroticism"!

If a Gill Man fan could travel back in time and visit the sets of *Revenge of the Creature* for one day, probably no one would pick Friday, July 30, because nothing but dud scenes were shot on that date. But they'd all miss out on witnessing a historic Hollywood event: the on-camera debut of Universal contractee Clint Eastwood, playing the role of a student on the movie's Animal Psychology Lab set. The 24-year-old actor arrived on Stage 16 on time for his 8:30 set call and waited while the comedy relief scenes of laboratory assistant Miss Abbott (played by Diane De Laire), Clete (Agar) and Neal the chimpanzee were shot. Of course the chimp ruined a bunch of takes, not to mention the one spoiled when his trainer showed up in the shot.

Then, before and after lunch, Eastwood (in a white lab coat) did his first movie acting as Jennings, a student who announces to Clete his suspicion that a missing white mouse must have been eaten by its cage-mate, a cat—but then Jennings finds the mouse in his own lab coat pocket. Goofy music from *Francis Joins the Wacs* (1954) plays throughout the scene, which couldn't be un-funnier. Scrutinizing the Daily Production Report, it appears that on his first day acting in a movie, Eastwood may have blown as many takes as the chimpanzee!

On the afternoon of July 30, the rest of the Animal Psychology Lab scene was shot, including the entrance of Dr. McCuller (Robert Nelson), who brings Clete a copy of a newspaper featuring a story on the Creature's capture. Nelson blew a line, but apparently no one noticed or cared because the take is in the movie: He was supposed to say that Devonian critters like the Gill Man should have died out a quarter of a *billion* years ago, but instead he says "quarter of a million." What's funny about this is that, in *Creature from the Black Lagoon*, Dr. Reed says that the Devonian period (which lasted from 400 million years ago until 350 million years ago) was just *150* million years ago, an unforgivable boner coming from scientist Reed. Now in *Revenge*, Dr. McCuller is "off" by an *additional* 149,750,000 years. Funnily enough, in the whole Creature trilogy, the only character who *isn't* incorrect when he puts an approximate date on the Devonian period ("millions of centuries [ago]")—is Lucas!

After the lab sequence was done, two more mundane interior scenes were tackled, the first featuring a police radio announcer talking into a microphone. The minuscule role was played by Sydney Mason, who you'll find funny-looking in a bushy black toupee if you recognize him as the bald Dr. Matos of *Creature from the Black Lagoon*. Then longtime radio actor Ned Le Fevre played his scenes as a radio newscaster reporting on the Gill Manhunt; in his three appearances, spaced throughout the closing reels, the one thing he tells us which we wouldn't otherwise know is that Clete is Helen's fiancé.

July 30 was also the day that Universal's Archie Herzoff notified his staff via a memo that a *second* search for a title was being instituted, the present title *Return of the Creature* having been deemed unacceptable. Herzoff wrote, "This time—please note—the new title should *not* use the word *Return* or any other word that might suggest that this is a return of the original feature. Please forward your suggestions to me by noon Wednesday, August 4."

Lori Nelson screams and struggles in the grip of Tom Hennesy's Creature. *Bottom right:* Nearly a decade later, her image was turned into artwork and employed on the poster of another movie company's *The Day of the Triffids*!

On Saturday, July 31, Hennesy had an 8 a.m. set call but arrived late following a car breakdown en route to the studio. Then it was right to work alongside Lori Nelson as they got into the Process Stage's pool and enacted the scene where Helen climbs onto the clanging gong buoy and then is pulled back into the water by the Gill Man. With footage of the nocturnal Jacksonville skyline on the process screen, this action was repeated several times before they moved on to shots of Clete swimming around, riding with cops in the police launch, etc.

The day ended with actor Brett Halsey and actor-stuntman Robert Hoy in a roadster in front of the process screen playing Pete and Charlie, young men debating the wisdom of going to college. On Monday, August 2, Halsey and Hoy completed the scene, no longer on the Process Stage but now on the back lot—in fact, on the edge of Park Lake, the body of water that "played" the Black Lagoon in the first *Creature* movie. (Park Lake shows up a third time in *The Creature Walks Among Us*, there "playing" the Florida Everglades waterway where the scientists in the dinghy search for the Gill Man.) Again it was night-for-night work with a shooting call of 8:15, with much of the initial activity involving shots of Pete and Charlie spotting Helen unconscious on the beach and rushing to her side. There was a midnight dinner, and then in the wee small hours of the night the fun started with a shot of Hennesy's Creature attacking the men, making short work of them, then picking up and carrying off Helen. Between 4 and 5 a.m., they got the attention-getting shot of the Gill Man holding Charlie (Hoy) overhead and flinging him through the air into a palm tree. Hoy told me that he was wearing a harness, with piano wire running from the harness to a crane boom high above. The crane had him at a point where he was horizontally positioned right above Hennesy's head, and then Hennesy pretended to throw him and he swung away at the end of the wires. Late in his flight, Hoy must be right under the boom because he *regains* a little bit of altitude before reaching the tree, but despite this mini-blooper, it's still quite a striking moment.

Revenge served to give John Agar (pictured, with Lori Nelson) a boost along the Universal Sci-Fi Hero path first blazed by Richard Carlson. After the additional sci-fi assignments *Tarantula* and *The Mole People*, Agar felt sure that, career-wise, it was a path to nowhere.

Again cast and crew were dismissed by morning twilight and the next couple nights would be more of the same. They assembled on the back lot on the evening of August 3 for scenes of the police captain (Charles R. Cane) and Clete at the mobilization point, addressing the searchers; group leader Mac (Don C. Harvey) and spotlight operator Joe (Robert Wehling) spotting Helen supine on the beach but also encountering the Creature; Clete, the police captain and others arriving on the scene, etc. *Castle of Frankenstein*'s *Revenge* reviewer liked the look of these climactic scenes, calling it a "strikingly photographed floodlit climax."

The company was dismissed at 5:50 a.m. on the morning of the 4th but they were back late that afternoon, in daylight, filming Agar and Nelson swimming in Park Lake—retakes of the above-water half of the river cruise scene where Clete and Helen swim and cavort, unaware that the Creature is beneath them. When the dinner break was over and darkness had fallen, the company shot the movie's closing sequence: the Gill Man carrying Helen toward the water with Clete yelling "Stop!," multiple takes of the Gill Man putting Helen down in the water, being shot by the cops, etc. What a way for Hennesy to spend his (31st) birthday. Following a midnight dinner, parts of earlier beach scenes were also shot. The company was dismissed at 4:55 a.m.

Thursday, August 5, was the last day of principal photography and the cast was down to just Lori Nelson and Tom Hennesy. The latter arrived first for some late-afternoon Park Lake shots of the Gill Man standing in water amidst floating flowers; these were for use in the Black Lagoon scene of the Gill Man looking at the *Rita II*, but they didn't make it into the movie. There were also retakes of the scene of the knocked-out Gill Man rising to the dead-fish-covered lagoon surface; Hennesy rose face-up the first time and face-down the second. Following dinner, various beach scenes were tackled, among them a shot of the Very pistol flare lighting up the sky. Nearly a dozen duds rocketed upward before one finally worked and they got the shot.

This bit of aggravation was followed by yet another delay when one of Hennesy's toenails somehow got torn off(!), a mishap that cost the company 25 minutes. From then until almost 11:30, more Creature, Helen and Creature-

and-Helen beach shots were taken, and then a midnight lunch was served for those who wanted it. The picture was now finished (wellll ... sorta), two days behind schedule and approximately $22,000 over budget. When Lori Nelson was dismissed at 11:15 that night, her required services in connection with *Revenge of the Creature* were completed and her employment at Universal expired.

Throughout pre-production and production, the movie was alternately called *Return of the Creature from the Black Lagoon, Return of the Creature* and *The Return of the Creature*; I suspect that all three were "placeholders" while the publicity department tried to dream up something better. On September 7, a Universal memo advised that a title had been selected from the lists submitted by their publicists: *Revenge of the Creature,* which had been suggested by both Harry Ormiston and Herman Levy. A promised $75 prize was split three ways, between Ormiston, Levy and Bob Holt, whose submissions had included the close-enough *The Creature's Revenge* and *Vengeance of the Creature.*

Apparently *some*one at Universal got the idea that the beginning of *Revenge* seemed rushed, or that the movie was too short, or that it didn't quite make sense, or *some*thing, because many weeks after *Revenge* wrapped, added scenes were filmed. Screenwriter Richard Alan Simmons was assigned to the picture from September 20 to 27, so presumably everything shot on September 28 flowed from his pen (or typewriter). By now Jack Arnold had moved on to his next directing assignment, the Western *The Man from Bitter Ridge* (1955), so Joseph Pevney helmed the shooting of these additional scenes. There was an 8:30 shooting call on Stage 6 and the first order of business was the *Rita II* cabin scene with John Bromfield, Nestor Paiva and Robert B. Williams as Joe, Lucas and Johnson, respectively. After a 25-minute delay caused by the need to apply a makeup beard to Paiva (so that he'd look like he did in the exterior scenes shot in Palatka), the three cigarette-puffing actors played the scene, which runs three and a half minutes in the picture. After lunch, John Agar came in to stand in close-up, hold two test tubes and spout a bit of scientific double-talk ("Red corpuscle content only ten percent less than human blood ... un-nucleated structure!"), a 20-something-second tag for the Ocean Harbor research lab scene. Last came the 30-something-second scene of an on-the-air TV newsman (Ken Peters) at his desk, holding up a photo of the newly captured Gill Man and describing its transport to Ocean Harbor. This extra day of shooting caused a budget revision from $502,625 to $509,000.

The addition of the cabin and TV newsman scenes (both featured in *Revenge*'s first quarter-hour) do improve the movie; without them, there'd be no recap of the events of *Black Lagoon*, no upfront mention of the Gill Man's Missing Link status, no indication why Ocean Harbor is interested in the aquatic humanoid, no reminder of his inability to exist out of water for more than a few minutes, etc. (Also, Lucas' new, solemnly delivered spiel about the "man-feesh" having an inner demon driving it through "millions of centuries" nicely sets a mood.) Realizing how much these scenes add to the movie also makes you realize how sloppy Berkeley's script is, and how anxious he was to get to the action: In his final screenplay, we get our first Gill Man sighting (seizing the bird on the log) in the second paragraph of page one, his underwater fight with Joe on page six, and he's knocked out by the explosion on page ten. By page 14 we're already at Ocean Harbor! After the Gill Man is chained to the oceanarium floor, however, the pace gets quite

Revenge of the Creature patrons suffering from shock had the option of going from bad to nurse.

slack: The whole middle of the movie is strictly dullsville, and an editor could clip out 15 minutes or more with no viewer ever knowing the difference.

The Release
By Robert J. Kiss

Theatrical First Run, March to October 1955

Creature from the Black Lagoon had premiered at Detroit's 3500-seat Broadway-Capitol Theater on February 12, 1954, and in January 1955, Universal announced that the "world premiere" of *Revenge of the Creature* would likewise take place at the same venue. Thereafter, the movie was to receive "a nationwide, simultaneous release" in both 3-D and flat versions. At midnight on March 29, 1955, *Revenge* duly opened in 3-D at the Broadway-Capitol, supported by its regular 2-D co-feature *Cult of the Cobra*, for a series of round-the-clock screenings that ads also described as a "24-hour shriek preview." The Gill Man resurfaced in the Motor City aloft a tidal wave of ballyhoo, with three local television shows featuring promotional appearances by someone costumed as the Creature. An usher in a Creature suit paraded back and forth outside the theater, and posed for snapshots with patrons; multiple eight-foot-tall cutouts adorned nearby streets and shop windows, along with a further six inside the theater; and a nurse on duty in the lobby offered to "restore strength" to anyone feeling faint at the sight of the amphibious humanoid on the big (and deep and wide) screen. As far as this gimmicky publicity was concerned, the Gill Man constituted the entire show, with neither his human co-stars nor *Cult of the Cobra* meriting any mention whatsoever.

Later the same day, the *Revenge-Cult* double bill opened for regular business (without being referred to as a premiere of any kind) at another flagship venue, the 3005-seat Loew's Poli in New Haven, Connecticut, prior to being unleashed at three Los Angeles theaters on March 30. On April 1, *Revenge* had its "flat" premiere at Loew's Majestic in Bridgeport, Connecticut. Ballyhoo-laden engagements at first-run downtown houses in major cities were subsequently just as likely to be in 3-D or flat. For example, the April 7 opening at Chicago's RKO Grand Theatre, with a nurse in attendance in the lobby, was in 2-D; while the following day's big launch at Philadelphia's Stanton Theatre offered female patrons (or "girls," as newspaper ads put it) the chance to have a Polaroid photo snapped with the Creature before experiencing the movie in 3-D. (The Stanton's Creature was another usher squeezed into a Gill Man suit, most likely the same suit that had done service in Detroit. Temperatures east of the Mississippi mercifully remained cool to chilly, thus minimizing the odor potential for each new wearer of the rubbery hand-me-down.)

Although not quite receiving the "saturation release" hinted at in Universal's initial trade announcements, *Revenge* nevertheless swiftly reached many tens of cities from coast to coast. It had even played theaters at U.S. military bases in the Far East ahead of its May 13 (Friday the 13th) opening at New York City's Globe Theatre (today the Lunt-Fontanne). It thereafter continued to do significant new trade at neighborhood houses and in smaller towns and rural communities, achieving full national penetration by late October 1955, which may accordingly be considered the end of the first run.

Somebody wearing a Gill Man head mugs for the camera at Detroit's WXYZ-TV, an early ABC affiliate.

3-D vs. Flat Screenings

Erskine Johnson, in his syndicated *Hollywood Today!* column of April 23, 1955, observed: "Revival of 3-D by U-I for its *The Return of the Creature* [*sic*] is a 50 per cent success. Half of the theaters booking the picture, in both wide screen and 3-D, are playing it as a depthie." This statement seems to be roughly accurate for the point in time when it was published: Within a sample of 900 first-run movie theaters across the U.S., 44 percent of *Revenge* openings during March and April were in 3-D. However, in the months from May to October, this figure slumps to just nine percent of bookings. A markedly similar pattern had been attested during the first run of *Creature from the Black Lagoon*, with 46 percent of openings between February and May 1954 in 3-D, before likewise dropping off to nine percent during the period from June to September 1954. In *Revenge*'s case, though, this sharp decline had set in far more quickly, after only five weeks of exhibition rather than the three and a half months it had taken with *Black Lagoon*.

As a Stand-Alone Feature

Within the sample of 900 first-run movie theaters across the U.S., 38 percent of *Revenge* screenings took the form of a stand-alone presentation supported only by selected shorts. This too marks a decided downward plunge when compared with *Creature from the Black Lagoon*, which had played as a stand-alone at 62 percent of first-run engagements.

Stand-alone presentation was common in three types of locations: (i) higher-rung theaters showing the movie in 3-D in large cities; (ii) theaters in small towns where single bills were generally the norm anyway, typically showing the movie "flat"; and (iii) hardtops and drive-ins throughout Texas, in line with the standard exhibition practice for first-run Universal horror and sci-fi features attested in the territory since *The Black Castle* in 1952–53. Furthermore, while 43 percent of stand-alone screenings nationwide were in 3-D, in Texas this figure rises to 84 percent. The distinct treatment of the film in Texas was picked up on by contemporary commentators, with Frank Morriss commenting in his May 5, 1955, *Here, There and Hollywood* column: "So successful was Universal-International with *Revenge of the Creature* that it is considering several more 3-D movies. Although 3-D is dead in most quarters, it is still popular in Texas, and there are plenty of movie houses there."

Regular Co-Feature

Universal's suggested co-feature for *Revenge of the Creature* was *Cult of the Cobra*, with the two movies regularly employed together as a "special double horror show" throughout the entire period from March to October 1955. Within the sample of 900 U.S. movie theaters, 44 percent of

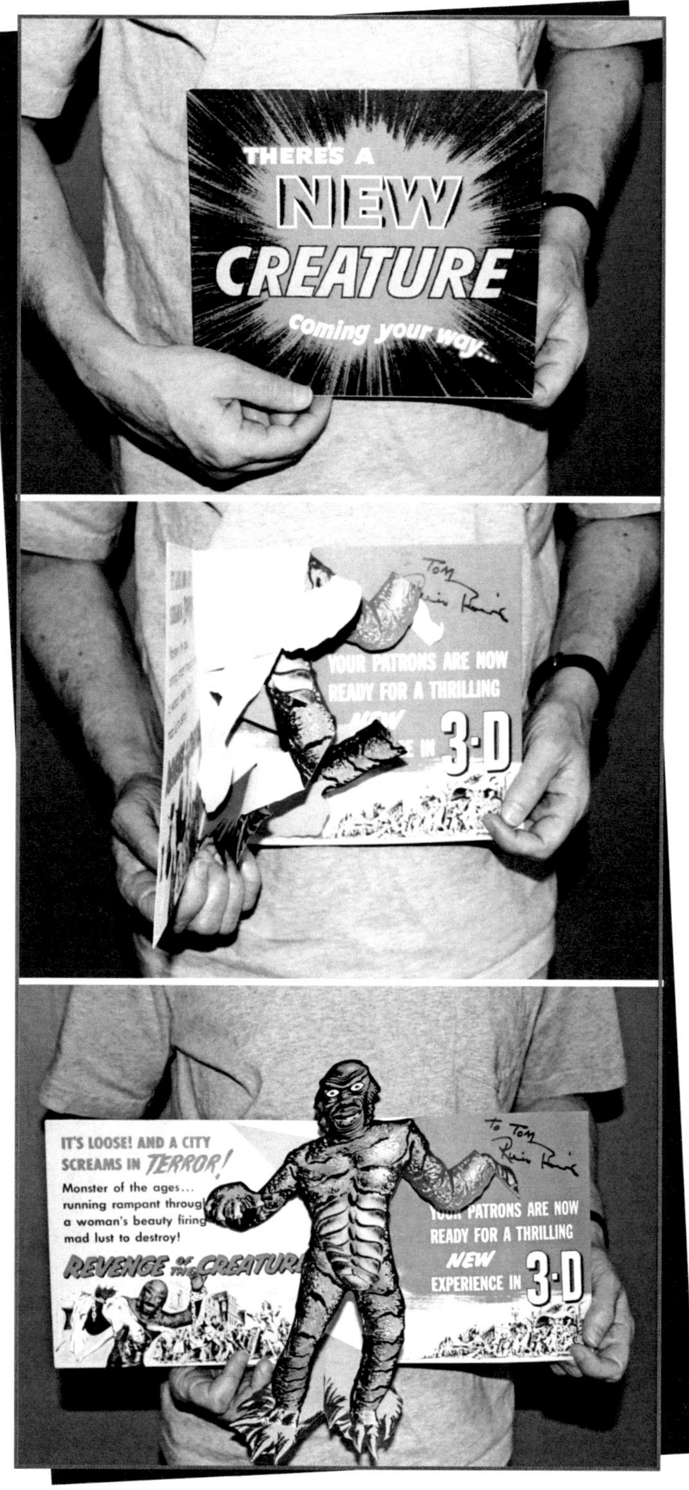

Even some of *Revenge*'s advertising material was in 3-D, for instance this pop-up book: Open it and a folded cut-out of the Gill Man starts comin' at ya. (Photographs courtesy Mary Runser.)

all *Revenge* screenings were indeed double-billed with *Cult*, making this the most common way to have encountered the Black Lagoon sequel during its first run. Just one in five of these screenings showed *Revenge* in 3-D, while *Cult* was the lower-billed title in every instance without exception, indicative of its status as lesser-but-necessary companion to a "major release" deemed not quite strong enough—*in particular when exhibited flat*—to be able to carry the bill on its own.

Other Co-Features

Eighteen percent of screenings in the sample of 900 first-run movie theaters took the form of a variant double-bill pairing *Revenge of the Creature* with a co-feature other than *Cult of the Cobra*. The overwhelming majority of these screenings were at lower-rung neighborhood and small-town venues that generally presented a so-called "balanced" program which sought to appeal to a broader audience by offering works of two distinct genres. In other words, the decision of these theater owners not to book Universal's suggested genre-matched co-feature represented a standard business practice. Likewise, the fact that just five percent of these engagements showed *Revenge* in 3-D was completely normal for this sector of the market, whose premises lacked the scale and footfall to readily amortize the costs of conversion to 3-D.

All of the variant double-bill co-features attested within the sample are arranged alphabetically below; the month mentioned in each case is the earliest in which the pairing was encountered. Universal appears to have been keen to retain control over the entire bill at these venues also, with 40 percent of bookings comprising a second Universal title. *Revenge* served as the top-billed feature in all instances, with the lone exception of its use at a handful of East Coast engagements where it played as support for the more recent release *This Island Earth*. This extremely limited usage was furthermore anomalous insofar as it constituted a genre-matched bill.

(*) signifies a more substantial number of playdates for the double-bill (at between seven percent and ten percent of venues).
bold titles are Universal releases.

October 1955 (*) *Abbott and Costello Meet the Mummy* (Abbott and Costello)
July 1955 *The Barefoot Contessa* (Humphrey Bogart)
August 1955 *Captain Lightfoot* (Rock Hudson)
May 1955 *Crashout* (William Bendix)
September 1955 *Deep in My Heart* (Jose Ferrer)
August 1955 *Destry* (Audie Murphy)
October 1955 *The Far Horizons* (Fred MacMurray)
July 1955 *Four Guns to the Border* (Rory Calhoun)
May 1955 *High Society* (Bowery Boys)
May 1955 *Island in the Sky* (John Wayne)
July 1955 *Ma and Pa Kettle at Waikiki* (Marjorie Main and Percy Kilbride)
May 1955 *Meet Me at the Fair* (Dan Dailey)
May 1955 *New York Confidential* (Broderick Crawford)
June 1955 *Playgirl* (Shelley Winters)
September 1955 *Port of Hell* (Dane Clark)
June 1955 (*) *Rage at Dawn* (Randolph Scott)
April 1955 *Rails into Laramie* (John Payne)
August 1955 *Run for Cover* (James Cagney)
August 1955 *Siege at Red River* (Van Johnson)
July 1955 *Smoke Signal* (Dana Andrews)
September 1955 *Southwest Passage* (Rod Cameron)
April 1955 *The Square Ring* (Jack Warner)
July 1955 *This Island Earth* (Jeff Morrow)
May 1955 *Underwater!* (Jane Russell)
May 1955 *You Know What Sailors Are* (Akim Tamiroff)

Beyond the First Run, and Back to Detroit

As with *It Came from Outer Space* and *Creature from the Black Lagoon*, only the 2-D version of *Revenge of the Creature* went on to circulate at second-run and repertory theaters. It initially continued to be booked together with its regular co-feature, *Cult of the Cobra*, for a limited number of engagements including midnight special shows on Friday the 13th, which in 1957 fell both in April and July. After that point, bookings fell off dramatically, although *Revenge* did secure a small amount of playdates on discount theater and drive-in bills pairing it with either *Creature from the Black Lagoon* or *The Creature Walks Among Us*. Triple-bills comprising the complete Black Lagoon trilogy were organized too in the early 1960s, but remained exceptionally uncommon, likely striking all but the most determined Devonian devotees as overkill. *Revenge*'s final pre-television appearances in 1963 and 1964 took the form of support at a few second-run screenings of *Reptilicus* and *Twice Told Tales*.

For its small-screen debut, *Revenge* returned to Detroit. In the run-up to the theatrical premiere on March 29, 1955, a fellow wearing a Gill Man head had mugged for cameras at the city's WXYZ-TV studios to help promote the picture. A sliver less than nine years later, the station's viewers finally got to eyeball the Creature in his entirety—or as much of him as a pan-and-scan print would allow—when *Revenge of the Creature* was broadcast in WXYZ's "Big Movie" slot at five p.m. on March 23, 1964. It was repeated on April 3. Televiewers in other parts of the nation wouldn't begin to see *Revenge* until the end of August, with the picture gradually airing from coast to coast between fall 1964 and spring 1965. Thereafter, it turned up with only reasonable regularity in TV schedules during the late 1960s and 1970s.

Lucky Cleveland moviegoers got to have their picture taken with the Gill Man when *Revenge of the Creature* and *Cult of the Cobra* played in "The Mistake by the Lake."

Revenge of the Music: The Music of Revenge of the Creature

By David Schecter

Because the Gill Man was already a celebrity by the time his sequel went into production, it was obvious that part of his star image was his musical theme from *Creature from the Black Lagoon*. Not surprisingly, Herman Stein's three-note *BAH-BAH-BAHHH!* motif figures prominently in *Revenge of the Creature*, as does a lot of other music heard in the original Gill Man movie. The sequel's score borrows liberally from cues composed for the first film as well as from older compositions that were tracked into the original Creature picture, as some of those library pieces had now become inextricably associated with the monster. There's much less original music in *Revenge of the Creature* due to all the borrowing from the earlier picture, and there is only limited new music from Stein and Henry Mancini, and no new music by Hans Salter. Almost all the new compositions were courtesy of William Lava, who was not involved in the first Gill Man movie. His eight original compositions provide most of the musical highlights in the webbed sequel.

Revenge of the Creature's soundtrack contains a dizzying 72 cues, with 53 having already appeared in *Black Lagoon*. Although there were only 44 cues in the first film, multiple uses of many of those pieces were incorporated into the sequel. Additional tracked cues came from *Francis Joins the Wacs* and *You Can't Cheat an Honest Man*, as well as some songs that were used as source music. Another difference from the first Creature film is that while its score contained only 21 cues under a minute long, *Revenge of the Creature*'s score features 49 cues of that length, resulting in the sequel's score sounding much more disjointed.

There's more than 59 minutes of music in *Revenge of the Creature*'s 82-minute running time, a whopping 72 percent of its length. The high percentage of musical accompaniment shows that somebody at Universal knew how important music was to a Gill Man movie. However, new music was obviously not deemed quite so important, because only about 14 minutes of original underscore can

William Lava with daughters Charmaine, left, and Rochelle. (Photograph courtesy William Lava family.)

be found in the picture. Needless to say, the movie's only music credit for this concoction was Joseph Gershenson's for "Music Supervision." Other than Lava's original compositions, there were only three additional pieces specifically written for the movie. Stein was asked to add six measures to the middle of his *Black Lagoon* "Main Title," with this amended opening musical statement being used to fill up the longer credits needed to thank Florida's Marineland. This partial reuse of the previous film's musical opening helped re-immerse the audience in the Gill Man's world while also offering a hint that there would be some new surprises.

Lava's "Jungle Boat" is heard after the "Main Title," but unfortunately, this atmospheric composition is mixed so quietly in the film's soundtrack that it's easier to hear animal and bird cries than Lava's evocative creation. *Revenge of the Creature*'s first two reels contain a potpourri of older cues, with eight written for *Black Lagoon*. It's likely that all this familiar music was used near the opening of the picture to immediately refresh memories of the first film. The third original piece of music occurs a full 13:30 into the picture, with Stein's inconsequential five-second "Stunning Captive" being heard after the crew spots the unconscious Creature floating on the lagoon's surface. It's hard to understand why anyone felt that a new composition should be used here, as a note or two from any other previously written cue would have equally sufficed.

After the story moves to Clete Ferguson's Department of Animal Psychology, two lightweight Frank Skinner cues from *Francis Joins the Wacs* are used in the laboratory scene featuring Clint Eastwood and a chimpanzee. Lava or another composer certainly could have provided more suitable original material that would have kept the Eastwood sequence light without totally losing the mood of the horror picture, which the comedic *Francis* music unfortunately does.

Amidst some Mancini, Rosen, Salter and Stein cues previously used in *Black Lagoon*, the film is invigorated by the inclusion of two original Lava compositions. As the Gill Man is fastened to the bottom of Ocean Harbor's permanent tank, "Chained" offers a number of novel orchestrations of the Creature theme that are markedly different from the flutter-tongued trumpet approach taken in the original man-fish movie. "Exhibit of the Prehistoric" is heard on the Gill Man's opening day at Ocean Harbor, and after a playful beginning highlighting fish being fed to eager porpoises, the composition becomes moodily effective, with stopped horns, piano and vibraphone imparting an appropriate sense of mystery to shots of the Creature. It's a welcome relief that not all of the sequel's Gill Man images are accentuated with Stein's blaring Creature theme. In addition to helping prevent the motif from becoming as stale as it did in the first movie, this subtler approach works well because the sequel sometimes presents a quieter and more intelligent monster than what's seen in the original.

Previously written music takes over until the laboratory scene where Clete's team analyzes the Gill Man's biology, with Lava's "Physical" providing mysterious sounds from harp, celesta and vibraphone. "Romance Disturbed" highlights Clete and Helen relaxing at the beach with her dog, Chris. Strings, clarinets, harp and vibraphone provide the humorous "hit" at the end of the pretty composition when the dog shakes his wet fur on the couple. Fortunately, Lava was given the opportunity to provide an original love theme for this first romantic scene between the two characters, although it's unfortunate he couldn't use this music elsewhere in the film to provide some musical continuity.

The lengthy sequence when the Gill Man breaks loose from his chain, kills Joe and escapes into the ocean was scored with excerpts from *Black Lagoon*'s "Monster Attacks, Part 2" and "Monster Attacks, Part 3" by Salter, and "Monster Gets Mark, Part 2" by Mancini. Over eight minutes after Lava's previous cue, the composer's anything-but-subtle "Newspaper Montage" is a brief, cacophonous and enjoyably outlandish original piece that uses Stein's Creature theme five times in clever fashion, highlighting newspaper headlines announcing the monster's escape. Another Lava original, "Gillman on the Prowl" is heard when the Creature spots a **VACANCY** sign at Helen's motel and decides to check in on her. Although Lava accentuates the Creature theme with flutter-tongued trumpets, he does it quite different from Stein's original incarnation, muting the brass to maintain the scene's quiet ambiance. The theme reverts to its snarling past when the amphibious visitor is attacked by canine Chris.

"Where Is Chris?," Lava's last original composition in the picture, builds a suitably suspenseful atmosphere using tremolo and

Variations of the Creature theme in William Lava's "Chained." (© 1955 RABB Trust Publishing/Willenora Publishing Co.)

Conductor's score of William Lava's "Gillman on the Prowl." (© 1955 RABB Trust Publishing/Willenora Publishing Co.)

pizzicato strings, harp and other orchestral coloring as Clete and Helen search outside for the dog, with a gong signaling the pet's demise. Lava's music is perfectly appropriate for the visuals and allows filmgoers to remain ensconced in the drama, which is what you'd expect from original underscore.

Of the last 19 cues in the movie, 18 were either originally written for *Black Lagoon*, older pieces that were tracked into that film, or songs. In the midst of the musical drudgery that covers *Revenge of the Creature*'s last act, there is one final original composition. Henry Mancini's sole new contribution is a jazz combo instrumental heard at the river's-edge restaurant. Titled "The Gillman Stomp," it's the type of piece Mancini was already associated with at this point in his film music career. It begins as Clete and Helen talk about love outside the Lobster House. Climbing from the river and entering the restaurant, the Gill Man is seen without his theme being heard, a rare occurrence in the first movie and throughout much of this sequel. Mancini's peppy number appeared in other Universal movies, including *Running Wild* (1955) and *Live Fast, Die Young* (1958), and it was also used in a beach scene in *Imitation of Life* (1959).

Revenge of the Creature's ending offers a virtual repeat of *Creature from the Black Lagoon*'s musical finale, using bits and pieces of Salter's "Doping the Monster," "The Monster's Trial," "Kay's Last Peril" and "End Title." Not surprisingly, Universal didn't want to mess with the musical coda used in the original Gill Man picture, so Herman Stein's same "End Cast" (originally written for *The Redhead from Wyoming*) was again recorded for *Revenge of the Creature.*

As appropriate as the tracked music dominating *Revenge of the Creature* might have been, the freshness of William Lava's contributions demonstrates that a completely original score would have noticeably improved the movie while still keeping it close to its musical roots. But it's obvious that Universal wasn't interested in offering too novel a perspective on the Gill Man at this point in his cinema career. That approach would have to wait until the final film of the "Gillogy," still another year off. Even though Lava wrote more than 80 percent of *Revenge of the Creature*'s original music, he didn't receive a screen credit because, due to the wealth of tracked cues that were used, he was only responsible for about 19 percent of the film's score. But given how important his music was to the movie, it's unfortunate that there couldn't have been a credit acknowledging his significant contribution.

Analysis
By Steve Kronenberg

The popularity, quality and impact of *Creature from the Black Lagoon* made a sequel inevitable. But *Revenge of the Creature* was also a hastily made sequel; it represents the quickest turnaround time for any Universal horror follow-up. And perhaps it's this haste which makes *Revenge* so inferior to its glorious progenitor. Coincidentally, the only other genre sequel that was just as speedily produced was 1933's *The Son of Kong*—the inferior follow-up to the classic that *Black Lagoon* most resembled! Researcher Robert J. Kiss points out that *Revenge* followed so hard on the heels of *Black Lagoon* that the latter was still playing widely throughout Florida during June and July 1954 (when *Revenge* was being filmed there), both as a regular feature and also by way of special midnight screenings.

Above: Joe (John Bromfield) drops headfirst into horror: the oceanarium prison of the Gill Man. *Revenge*'s script makes occasional mention of the Gill Man's hatred for Joe but it isn't conveyed in the movie. *Wellll,* other than the Gill Man killing him.

Clete and Helen (John Agar and Lori Nelson) look on helplessly as resuscitation efforts fail and Joe (John Bromfield, bottom) becomes the Gill Man's first *Revenge* victim.

It's not as though *Revenge* doesn't try to be a worthy sequel. The familiar and beloved three-note *Creature* theme music opens the film and is pervasive throughout. William Alland reprises his role as producer, Jack Arnold again directs and, most importantly, Charles "Scotty" Welbourne lenses the *entire* film—both underwater and topside.

The film's beginning also resembles *Black Lagoon*. There is an evolutionary-biological prologue that serves as a build-up to the Gill Man—delivered by another returning *Creature* vet, Nestor Paiva, again playing Lucas. Lucas' opening segment is one of *Revenge*'s highlights, as he warns Joe and Johnson about the size and strength of the monster they are seeking:

> **It doesn't *belong* in our world.... This beast exists because it is stronger than this thing that you call "evolution." In it is some force of life ... a demon! ... driving it through millions of centuries. And it does not surrender so easily to weaklings like you and me. This is the thing that you hunt for. Think on it.**

Lucas then laughs ominously—a fine teaser for an audience nervously awaiting the Gill Man's appearance.

Fortunately, the audience doesn't have long to wait: We see Ricou Browning's Creature almost immediately, accompanied by his theme music, swiping at a bird on a log on the Black Lagoon surface. Welbourne's camera then captures the Gill Man gliding gracefully through the water filigreed by sunlight—a reprise of the arresting photographic style Welbourne brought to the original *Black Lagoon*.

Indeed, whatever style *Revenge* possesses is almost entirely a function of Welbourne's camera. *Revenge* proves that Welbourne's aptitude for underwater photography is peerless. All of *Revenge*'s sub-aquatic scenes are highlighted by Welbourne's murky, spooky lighting technique. The Creature's memorable Black Lagoon attack on Joe Hayes is shot as a chaotic crazy quilt of bubbles and thrashing bodies. (Still, the excitement of the scene doesn't approach Welbourne's unsettling shot of Mark Williams being dragged to the depths of the lagoon in the original film.) After the attack on Joe, Welbourne shoots the Creature swimming off into gray and murky waters amidst furious gunfire—an example of how Welbourne can precisely capture mood and tone.

Later, in the receiving tank scene, Welbourne delivers an eerie shot of the Gill Man silently floating face down in the water, just waiting to strike as Joe attempts to revive him. Welbourne beautifully captures the heightened anticipation conveyed by this silent tableau. We continue to see Joe quietly gliding the Creature through the water; as Welbourne shoots the Creature from *below* the water, we are the first to see him regain consciousness. He then moves his limbs, stands up and roars at the curious crowd surrounding him, before the battle royal ensues. Welbourne's camera (and Arnold's direction) allow the initially subdued scene to build to a crescendo, and it represents one of *Revenge*'s most exciting segments.

After this action-packed scene, Welbourne delivers an excellent, atmospheric shot of the Creature brought to the oceanarium bottom in ropes and netting. Welbourne shoots the Gill Man as a squirming, thrashing prisoner of "civilization." Credit Welbourne *and* Ricou Browning for again evoking our sympathy for this monster, as we see him chained and swimming desperately.

Welbourne is equally adept at capturing the Creature's ominous qualities: We get an excellent, arresting close-up of the monster staring at Helen for the first time through a porthole of the oceanarium in which he is imprisoned. Yet, the Creature's mystery, menace—and style—are diluted by these

Joe (John Bromfield) takes a hands-on approach to keeping the Gill Man (Tom Hennesy) in the receiving tank.

scenes, as we watch him receiving a basket of fish food in his aquatic prison. This ferocious monster of *Black Lagoon* almost resembles a domesticated lab rat as he eats a drugged fish and pathetically sinks to the bottom, asleep.

When the Creature finally escapes his captors and rampages through Ocean Harbor, Welbourne captures the chaos of the crowds in medium and close-up shots reminiscent of King Kong's wild walk through the streets of New York. We also get a fine long shot of the Gill Man heading for the ocean after his escape, a shot which accentuates his loneliness and solitude. And as the Creature heads toward Helen's motel room, Welbourne delivers a haunting, sinister medium shot of the monster enveloped in darkness, advancing toward his new bride-to-be. This moody scene is immediately followed by an equally unnerving shot of the Creature peering at Helen through the motel window, backed by the black night landscape, again reminiscent of Kong peeping in at Fay Wray through the New York hotel window. As the Gill Man enters Helen's room, the action is effectively punctuated by the loud, crescendo-ing Creature theme music. Helen later takes a river swim with Clete. Welbourne then sets up an abridged "water ballet" sequence, similar to the memorable scene in *Black Lagoon*, as Helen and the Gill Man swim parallel to each other in a series of shots. Welbourne's underwater photography in *Revenge* is typically beautiful but, sad to say, the surreal lighting and editing in the original *Black Lagoon* are absent here.

After the Gill Man abducts Helen, Welbourne's aptitude for atmosphere is again displayed as the Creature advances on the pair of boys who discover her unconscious on a dark, lonely stretch of beach. After dispatching them, the Creature sweeps Helen in his arms in classic 1950s style and walks with her into the darkness—a superbly moody long shot. Immediately, Welbourne delivers a disturbing close-up of the Creature dripping wet, gills pulsating, carrying Helen as both are enveloped in the darkness. Likewise, during the film's climax, we get a startling medium shot of the monster advancing toward Helen, lit by a police spotlight.

Clearly, Welbourne is responsible for whatever panache *Revenge* possesses. His penchant for crisp underwater photography and his ability to capture mood and action are all that make *Revenge* worth savoring. Unfortunately, the cast—and especially the script—do not do justice to Welbourne's work. John Agar, always a stock 1950s hero, delivered solid if uninspiring performances in several genre films. But in *Revenge*, his stolid stiffness is not helped by Martin Berkeley's second-rate script. Agar is hopelessly caught in a series of silly interludes with Lori Nelson and, at the beginning of the film, a particularly annoying scene with a chimp and a young Clint Eastwood. In addition, Agar's stock leading man is devoid of the complexity and credibility of Richard Carlson's

David Reed in the 1954 original. Lori Nelson is an attractive leading lady, but she has none of the strength and natural acting ability of Julie Adams. In addition, Berkeley's script only hints at some possible tension between Clete and Joe over Helen's affections. The kind of dynamism that existed between Reed and Williams in the original never surfaces here, robbing the film of a potentially interesting subplot. In addition, Berkeley wastes too much time "explaining" the biology of the Creature, his evolutionary origins, blood type and sleeping patterns. The script delivers plenty of boring "science" but not enough interesting "fiction."

Further, Berkeley's screenplay focuses far too much on the romantic byplay between Clete and Helen in a series of annoyingly saccharine scenes. When Agar clumsily tries to exude manly charm with the sylph-like, flirtatious Nelson, their lack of chemistry is only accentuated. Audience time is also wasted by a series of boring romantic scenes between the two lovers—obvious, time-consuming "filler" when contrasted with the supercharged action of *Black Lagoon*. And Berkeley's dialogue for these scenes is as insipid as 1950s Hollywood could get. During Clete and Helen's beach scene she muses, "Sometimes I wonder how I ever got started in all this ... science, fish, ichthyology. Where will it all lead me? As a *person*, I mean." Later, Berkeley saddles Nelson with even more banality: "[Love] makes the word go 'round, but what do we know about it? Is it a fact? Is it chemistry, electricity?" (Not that there is any to be had here!) No wonder *Revenge*'s *Time* magazine reviewer wrote, "Between screams, Lori Nelson unfortunately has enough breath left to engage John Agar in just about the limpest dialogue since the invention of talking pictures."

While the film takes too much time building the Clete-Helen romance, we see far too little of the always-delightful Nestor Paiva, a memorable player in *Black Lagoon*. Paiva's role is almost a token cameo, though Berkeley gives him the film's funniest line: "I hope you ain't going to blow up my boat, Mr. Johnson. Like my wife, she's not much, but she's all I have!"

Berkeley is also guilty of wasted character potential. Dave Willock's Lou Gibson is the film's exploitative huckster—seemingly willing to endanger hundreds of people for the chance to cash in on the Creature's captivity. Yet, this mini–Carl Denham is given nothing to do and very little to say. John Bromfield and Robert B. Williams would have been equally interesting as exploiters—the yin to John Agar's scientific yang. Unfortunately, that tension never develops: Agar is not allowed to display any academic conscience over the Creature's plight, and Bromfield does little before the Creature kills him off.

What Berkeley *tries* to get right is the Creature's pathos—a concept which, as in *King Kong*, is underscored when the Gill Man is forcibly moved from his Amazon home to "civilization." We see this ferocious monster subdued by ropes, nets, chains and drugs—a Kong-like freak for the world to gape at. In one scene, Clete tells Helen how he plans to shock the Creature with an electric bull prod to condition his behavior. Notably, he says he "hates" to use the bull prod, but he uses it frequently all the same! Helen is the only character to express any *real* sympathy for the man-fish: "Y'know, I ... I *pity* him sometimes. He's so *alone*," she tells Clete. "The only one of his kind in the world. Well, he's like an orphan in time." This is *Revenge*'s most evocative line of dialogue—and the only one that concedes the Creature's pathos.

It almost seems as though Jack Arnold *knew* that *Revenge* could not live up to *Black Lagoon* in any meaningful way. While Welbourne acquits himself well, Arnold was left without the supremely effective cast and screenwriters of the original film. What he *did* have was a hack screenwriter in Martin Berkeley and an uninteresting cast. Worse, our Gill

Blacky LaGoon mixes with his fans. *Revenge* wasn't as much of a moneymaker as its predecessor but, clawing in $1.1 million in domestic rentals, it came in at #101 on *Variety*'s list of 1955's top grossers.

Man hero, while more pathetic than ever, seems surprisingly subdued by Berkeley's script and Arnold's direction. The exotic mystery and style with which he was imbued in *Creature from the Black Lagoon* is sadly diluted here. In the Amazon River of the original, the Gill Man's environs were just as ominous and terrifying as he was. In *Revenge*, imprisonment seems to tame him: There's little menace, explicit or implicit. We may *see* more of the Creature in this sequel, but his confined, sterile surroundings rob him of his mystique. When he escapes, he is just another '50s monster on the loose: more interesting, but still not much different than the Beast from 20,000 Fathoms or Godzilla.

Still, *Revenge of the Creature* was popular enough to inspire yet a second sequel. *Revenge of the Creature* represented the last time Jack Arnold and the Gill Man would work together. Arnold would go on to bigger (*Tarantula*), smaller (*The Incredible Shrinking Man*) and *better* things.

Cult of the Cobra (1955)

Full Credit Information

CREDITS: Produced by Howard Pine; Directed by Francis D. Lyon; Screenplay: Jerry Davis, Cecil Maiden and Richard Collins; Story: Jerry Davis; Photography: Russell Metty; Editor: Milton Carruth; Art Directors: Alexander Golitzen and John Meehan; Set Decorators: Russell A. Gausman and Ray Jeffers; Sound: Leslie I. Carey and Joe Lapis; Gowns: Bill Thomas; Hair Stylist: Joan St. Oegger; Makeup: Bud Westmore; Assistant Director: George Lollier; Music Supervisor: Joseph Gershenson; UNCREDITED: Original Music Composers: William Lava, Irving Gertz, Stanley Wilson and Lou Maury; Tracked Music Composers: Larry Russell, Milton Rosen, Everett Carter, Harold Adamson, Jimmy McHugh, Frederick Herbert and Arnold Hughes; Conductor: Joseph Gershenson; Musicians: Emo Neufeld, Manuel Compinsky, Louis Pressman, Ambrose Russo, Lou Klass, Sam Fordis, Samuel Cytron, Sarah Kreindler, Leon Goldwasser, Howard Colf (Violin), Cecil Bonvalot, Harriet

Payne (Viola), Victor Gottlieb, Stephen De'ak, Joseph Ullstein, Alec Compinsky (Cello), Harold E. Brown (Bass), Arthur C. Smith, Ethmer Roten, Jr. (Flute), Norman Benno (Oboe), Blake Reynolds, Alan Harding, Karl Leaf (Clarinet), Lloyd Hildebrand (Bassoon), Arthur Frantz, Eugene Ober (Horn), Gene LaFreniere, Don Linder, Robert Goodrich (Trumpet), John Stanley, Bruce Squires, H.L. Menge (Trombone), John De Soto, Ralph Collier (Drums), Lyman Gandee (Piano), Joseph Quintile (Harp); Production Manager: Gilbert Kurland; Unit Manager: Tom Andre; Second Assistant Director: Willard Kirkham; Dialogue Director: Harold Goodwin; Coordinator: Charles Baqueta; Camera Operator: Phil Lathrop; Assistant Cameramen: Robison, Hager, Ranaldi (William John Ranaldi?), Williams and Ledge Haddow; Still Photographer: Madison Lacy; Key Grip: Dean Paup; Second Grip: Ken Smith; Gaffer: Max Nippel; Best Boys: Al Todd and Hobson (Edward Hobson?); First Prop Man: C.H. Barrett Jr.; Assistant Prop Man: Martino (Solly Martino?); Sound Recorder: James Swartz; Mike Man: Frank Gorbach; Cable Man: Harry Moran; Wardrobe Man: Sol Rous; Wardrobe Woman: Bernice Pontrelli; Makeup: Nick Marcellino and Perell (Sid Perell?); Hair Stylist: Merle Reeves; Assistant Editor: Eddie Broussard; Dance Director: Betty Curtis; Script Clerks: Fred Applegate, Betty Abbott and Gibson (Winnie Gibson?); Stand-ins: Harold Lockwood and Tina Menard; Monkey Provided by Chester Hayes; Wrangler: Draw Stanfeld; **Added Scenes (January 15, 17 and 21, 1955):** Directed by Francis D. Lyon; Photography: Guthrie (Carl Guthrie?); Editors: Carruth (Milton Carruth?) and Eddie Broussard; Set Decorator: Austin (John P. Austin?); Production Manager: Gilbert Kurland; Unit Manager: Norman Deming; Assistant Director: George Lollier; Second Assistant Director: T. Nelson (Terence Nelson?); Script Clerk: Forrest (Bob Forrest?); Camera Operator: Mead (Kyme Meade?); Assistant Cameramen: Norton (William Norton?) and Reisbord (William Reisbord?); First Grip: Gulliver (Stanley Gulliver?); Second Grip: Hilbert (Jim Hilbert?); Gaffer: Monroe; Best Boy: Todd (Al Todd?); First Prop Men: Barrett (C.H. Barrett Jr.?) and Martino (Solly Martino?); Assistant Prop Man: Martino (Solly Martino?) and Maier; Wardrobe Woman: Demetropolis (Rosamond Demetropolis?); Wardrobe Man: Loschak (Rydo Loshak?); Makeup: Case (Tom Case?); Hair Stylist: House (Edith House?); Sound Mixer: Wilkinson (Frank H. Wilkinson?); Sound Recorder: Kemp (John Kemp?); Mike Man: Anderson Jr. (Glenn Anderson?); Cable Men: Wilson and Rogers; Coordinator: Baqueta (Charles Baqueta?); **Per William Alland:** Story Idea: William Alland; 80 minutes.

CAST: Faith Domergue (*Lisa Moya*), Richard Long (*Paul Able*), Marshall Thompson (*Tom Markel*), Kathleen Hughes (*Julia Thompson*), William Reynolds (*Pete Norton*), Jack Kelly (*Carl Turner*), Myrna Hansen (*Marian Sheehan*), David Janssen (*Rico Nardi*), Leonard Strong (*Daru*), James Dobson (*Corp. Nick Hommel*), Walter Coy (*Police Inspector*), Ruth Carlsson [as The Carlssons] (*Snake Woman in Lamian Ceremony*), Carl Carlsson [as The Carlssons] (*Warrior in Lamian Ceremony*), Olan Soule (*Major Martin Fielding*), Helen Wallace (*Mrs. Weber*), Mary Alan Hokanson (*Army Nurse*), John Halloran (*High Lamian Priest*), Alan Reynolds (*Capt. Steve Williams*); UNCREDITED: Harry Mendoza (*Man at Bazaar*), Jose Ferran (*Sower in Lamian Ceremony*), John Daheim (*Richard Long's Stunt Double*), Dale Van Sickel (*Jack Kelly's Stunt Double*), Loren Janes (*James Dobson's Stunt Double*), Leroy Johnson, Richard Farnsworth, Paul Baxley, Louis Tomei, Roger Creed, Allen Pinson, Jack Williams, Erwin Neal (*Lamians*), Edward Platt (*High Lamian Priest*), Ben Frommer (*Hot Dog Stand Proprietor*), George Sowards (*Cart Driver*), Don Dillaway, Larry Williams (*Gawkers Looking at Carl's Body*), Jack Rutherford (*Policeman at Carl's Death Scene*), Jarl Victor (*Lab Worker*), Bing Russell (*Laundryman*), William Vedder (*Joe—Theater Doorman*).

Production History

By Tom Weaver

La'mi-a (la'mi-a) *Class. Myth.*
The head and breast of a woman…
the body of a serpent.

In 1935, Universal's original (frat) house of horrors went coed when they produced and released *Bride of Frankenstein* while at the same time preparing the following year's *Dracula's Daughter*. A generation later, when Universal-*International* rebooted the genre, the first "deadlier than the male" addition to its roster was Lisa Moya the Cobra Goddess, who compiles a travelogue rap sheet from Southeast Asia to Lower Manhattan in *Cult of the Cobra*.

Fourth in the batting order on Team Universal Terrors[1] (after the Globs, the Gill Man and the Metaluna Mutants), the Cobra Goddess goes down swinging; her story may be far-out but it's hardly original. And, needless to say, a prop cobra doesn't even rise to the level of the studio's second-fiddle '50s monsters (the Mole People, the Monster on the Campus, etc.). What *is* notable about the movie is Faith Domergue's performance and the fact that all of its top male players went on to TV stardom: Richard Long most memorably on either *77 Sunset Strip* or *The Big Valley* (choose one), Marshall Thompson on *Daktari*, William Reynolds on *The*

F.B.I., Jack Kelly on *Maverick* and David Janssen on *The Fugitive*. In 1955 when *Cult* was released, it was none too heavy on marquee magnetism, Domergue being its most recognizable name. By the 1960s when it was playing on TV, the guys were the cream of the cast, the stars of some of TV's top shows, while *Domergue* was well on her way to "Who??"ville! Perhaps *Cult of the Cobra* was the start of her slide: In its *Cult* review, Bridgeport, Connecticut's, *Sunday Herald* referred to the movie's star as "Faith Domergue, who once seemed to be getting somewhere."

What makes the movie interesting ... but at the same time, disappointingly derivative ... is the fact that whoever cooked up the idea had to have been quite familiar with producer Val Lewton's *Cat People* (1942), one of *the* genre milestones of the 1940s. In a Manhattan brownstone lives a foreign girl (Irena in *Cat People*, Lisa in *Cult*), new and friendless in the big city. A clean-cut all-American boy (Oliver in *Cat People*, Tom in *Cult*) takes her under his protective wing and falls in love with her. Both gals reciprocate ... up to a point. Irena can't go all the way with Ollie because, descended from an ancient Serbian race, she knows she can turn into a panther. Lisa, also hailing from a land of exotic mystery, can't get serious with Tom because she turns into a cobra, and Tom is on her hit list. Even though these gals won't let their guys get past first base, they still resent competition: Irena has her panther claws out for Ollie's gal pal Alice, Lisa sharpens her cobra fangs for Tom's ex-girlfriend Julia.

For much of *Cult of the Cobra*'s running time, the seasoned genre fan will think of *Cat People* only occasionally, but in the homestretch it gets to the point where thwarted interspecies romance, Lisa's angst and Tom's confusion and frustration are the film's focus, which means that now it's mirroring *Cat People* exactly, and now *Cat People* is *all* that the seasoned genre fan can think about. Things become almost ridiculous toward the end: In *Cat People*, Irena becomes a panther and kills her psychiatrist, but not before he stabs her with his sword cane; back in human form, she keeps her hand to her left shoulder where the broken-off end of the cane is embedded. In *Cult*, Carl hits the cobra with a china statue, with the result that Lisa spends the subsequent scene rubbing *her* upper left arm. *Cult of the Cobra* really *is* quite a, pardon the pun, copycat, from the inscrutable written foreword that begins both movies, to the almost identical endings: in *Cat People*, a screech of police car brakes, a dead panther under its front bumper and a disconsolate Ollie shuffling off into the night; in *Cult of the Cobra*, a screech of police car brakes, a dead cobra-turned-Lisa under its front bumper and a disconsolate Tom takin' a walk down Lonely Street.[2]

Compounding the feline-y (felony) is the fact that *Cult* also reuses some of Lewton's famous scare tactics, including variations on the legendary "Lewton walk" and even the "Lewton bus." But *Cult*'s scripters screw things up, not realizing that in these scenes it's Julia and other innocent characters who need to appear to be in danger, not Lisa who *is* the danger!

Snakes, of course, have been up to no good since Garden of Eden days when a certain serpent was in*sssssss*trumental in Adam and Eve receiving their eviction notice; tales of snake women go back as far as the Gorgons. *Cult of the Cobra*'s other plot hook, the business about a curse following "infidels" back to civilization, was also hoary, even in 1955.[3]

Moya sestras? It's probably too late to ever know for certain, but it sure appears that *Cat People*'s Irena (Simone Simon, above) was the inspiration for *Cult of the Cobra*'s Lisa (Faith Domergue, right). (Photographs courtesy Ronald V. Borst/Hollywood Movie Posters.)

UI Coils Serpent Onto Alland's Slate

The Cult of the Serpent, a horror yarn, has been assigned producer William Alland at Universal-International. Jerry Davis will screenplay. No shooting date has been set.
—*Variety*, April 14, 1954

In one of my interviews with Alland, I raised the topic of *Cult of the Cobra* even though, ultimately, he was *not* the producer. His first comment was an exasperated "Oh, for Christ's sake!" From that mood-setting takeoff point, he continued:

Let me tell you what that was all about: I had an idea to do a story in which a woman, when possessed with passion, becomes a cobra. I was going to develop a story but, more importantly, I had an idea of how to photograph the scenes in which she's a snake. I was going to get a camera and have the lens *right* on the floor. Since a camera is not flat like that, to get that effect I would have had to either use mirrors or actually dig a trench on a stage, to get that camera right down to the level of where a snake would be. But right at this point, because I hadn't taken a vacation in the four years or so that I'd been under contract, I decided to go to Europe for a month and a half. While I was in Europe, [production department head] Jim Pratt sent me a very terse telegram: DEAR BILL—WE HAVE TO START PRODUCTION ON CULT OF THE COBRA. UNLESS YOU CAN GET BACK, WE WILL DO IT WITHOUT YOU. We had only been away less than two *weeks*, we were in London, I think, when this happened. It made me so mad, I sent him a message back: DEAR JIM—BE MY GUEST! [*Laughs*] But, remember now, I didn't even have a screenplay, I had a [story] idea and the idea of how to do it from a technical point of view and that's *all*—in fact, it may have been something I would never even have *done*. Is my name mentioned at all in the credits? [*Tom Weaver: No.*] Not even in connection with the screenplay? [*Tom Weaver: Nope.*] Thank God!

After doing some light research on *Cult*'s writers Jerry Davis, Cecil Maiden and Richard Collins, my hunch was that the person responsible for the movie's "Lewton-esque" qualities was Collins: He worked at RKO in the early 1940s, should have been aware of the Lewton movies and might even have crossed paths with Lewton. I called him in 2004 when he was 90, and discovered that the *Cult* writing job was vague in his memory and he couldn't say yea or nay regarding the touches in question. I *was* correct, however, about Collins and Lewton having met: "We weren't great friends or anything, but I did know him, yes. He was a pleasant man and he was obviously pretty bright. Seemed like a nice guy. I remember him fondly." Collins' opinion of *Cult of the Cobra*: "I thought it was pretty good."

"Richard Collins was a very famous person," Alland told me. "He was one of the upper mucky-mucks in the Hollywood [branch of the Communist] party. He was the secretary of some big wheel. When the Committee [HUAC] came to Hollywood and started to hand out subpoenas, he got terrified and he went to the FBI and volunteered to give them every name of everybody in Hollywood who had been in the party. And he did! He had been married to Dorothy Comingore, the actress [famous for playing *Citizen Kane*'s wannabe-opera-singer wife]. After all that happened, I got to know him, and we became very friendly." One of the names that Collins tossed into the HUAC hopper was screenwriter Martin Berkeley; Berkeley in turn became the "gift that keeps on giving" for the Committee, providing them with more names than the Tokyo phone book.[4]

Jerry Davis, mentioned in the *Variety* squib above, appears to have been the first writer attached to *The Cult of the Serpent*. Like Collins, he was a screenwriter who later had greater success in television. His TV producing career started in the late 1950s at Warners (where he would have run into *Cult* veterans Richard Long, Jack Kelly and William Reynolds, contract players there). After Warners, he produced a few small-screen favorites, including *Bewitched, That Girl* and *The Odd Couple*, and picked up several Emmy nominations along the way. In 1954 when Davis wrote *Cult*, he was dating sexy singer-actress Marilyn Maxwell (even though he lived next door to her ex!); he married her in New York later that year. Omnipresent at the Davis-Maxwell home: Rock Hudson, of all people. Davis once said of the situation, "I felt a little like Woody Allen—'Hi, honey, I'm home.' She would get quite defensive. 'Are you paranoid? Do you actually think this man has any interest in me?'" The Davis-Maxwell marriage lasted until 1960, the Hudson-Maxwell friendship (or was it more than a friendship?) lasted until the end of her life: Maxwell suffered a fatal heart attack in 1972 and it was Rock who discovered her body.

When it came to the casting of *Cult of the Cobra*, many names were run up the flagpole. The earliest casting-related memo I've seen, from late June 1954 when it was still *Cult of the Serpent*, has RKO contractee Ursula Thiess as Lisa, Mala Powers as Julia and, as the six G.I.s, Richard Long (as Paul), John Agar (as Tom), Brett Halsey (as Pete), Rex Reason (as Carl), William Reynolds or John Saxon (as "Frank," according to this memo; none of the G.I.s ended up with that name) and David Janssen as Nick.

Ursula Thiess retiring to be just Mrs. Bob Taylor [MGM star Robert Taylor]? Not this season, chillun.

The bride ... stays at Universal-International [where she'd recently finished *Bengal Brigade*, 1954] to star in *The Cult of the Serpent*, which is just what it sounds like—a horror thriller, only more so.

It's about a high priestess of a modern cult with the power to turn herself into a serpent—a cobra—and her trek to the USA to do in some local infidels for their sacrilege against her "faith."

William Alland, who has produced a lot of moneymakers of this type for U-I, handles the Thiess film.—Columnist Dorothy Manners, July 1954

Thiess was born in 1924, not a good year to be born if the place you picked to be born was Hamburg, Germany. Once Hitler started shaking things up, Thiess had a number of harrowing experiences, perhaps most memorably giving birth to a baby daughter in a Hamburg hospital and still being there a few days later when Allied air raids created a firestorm in that city. Then 20 months later she was carrying two buckets of water to her vegetable garden, her tiny daughter in tow, when an Allied fighter plane started firing machine-gun bullets at her! After the war she became a model and then migrated to Hollywood. *Modern Screen* magazine dubbed Thiess and Marilyn Monroe the Most Promising Stars of 1952 as she was getting her movie career started with the made-in-India *Monsoon*. While in India, she almost got an eye-ful of a religious rite she was not meant to see (holy *Cult of the Cobra*!), as a party at a penthouse "turned into a chilling experience for me":

[Others at the party] seemed to be totally oblivious to the eerie screeching of some mysterious flock of birds somewhere very near.

RKO contractee Ursula Thiess (Mrs. Robert Taylor), briefly in the running—in the slithering?—to play the Cobra Goddess.

While looking for a door to the roof to still my curiosity about those lamenting birds, I was stopped and strongly advised by one of the British guests to remain inside. "You see, Miss Thiess, the mother of our host passed away a few days ago and her body has been laid out for the birds on the Tower of Silence, not far from here," he explained rather calmly. When he realized my shock, he added, "They are Parsee, you understand."

I didn't even come close to comprehending this information about one of their religious customs, but was to learn later that once the vultures had performed their gruesome task on the body, the bones of the deceased would fall through a grill in the Tower of Silence, and then be collected for burial by the relatives.—from Thiess' autobiography *... but I have promises to keep.*[5]

Universal's plan to borrow Thiess from RKO and make her their Cobra Goddess was short-lived, an early hint of difficulties coming in Army Archerd's July 28, 1954, *Variety* column: "Bob Taylor and Ursula Thiess up at Cheyenne, Wyo., to inspect some of his oil wells.... If UI's waiting for Ursula to do *Cult of the Serpent*, they may have a long, long wait."

An October 18 casting memo calls the movie *Cult of the Cobra* and—Universal having dropped the idea of Mrs. Robert Taylor as the cobra woman—it lists Patricia Medina as Lisa (at a cost of $12,500), with **Blanchard** handwritten in pencil nearby. Other names: Marshall Thompson as Tom (with a pencilled-in **Danton** nearby), Earl Holliman as Carl and Race Gentry as Rico. An October 22 memo includes all the actors who ended up playing the top roles with one exception: Danny Dayton is listed as playing Carl, but Jack Kelly got the part.

Between the first casting memo mentioned above, and the last, there were at least four days of Francis D. Lyon-directed screen tests, the first September 28, 1954: On Stage 9, Martha Hyer and David Janssen rehearsed and then played Lisa and Tom in tests that took a couple of hours. Just before quitting time, Hyer was photographed in a black wig. On the morning of September 30, again on Stage 9, Karen Kadler and Liam Sullivan were Lisa and Tom. October 5 found Kadler and Richard Long on those Stage 9 sets, Kadler again as Lisa and Long as Tom. (In the movie, Long played Paul, ever-suspicious of Lisa, but in this test he played Lisa's beau.) On what might have been the last day of tests, October 19, the place was Stage 7 and the actors were Mari Blanchard, Ray Danton and 20-year-old Miss USA winner (and Miss Universe runner-up) Myrna Hansen. At different parts of the day, Danton played Paul *and* Tom; Blanchard was Lisa and Hansen was Julia. Hansen did end up in the movie, but not as Julia; she played the comic relief role of Pete's giggly date at Carl's party. *Cult* and *The Purple Mask*, in which Hansen played a featured role, were made at the same time, and she bicycled between the two Universal movies.

She's a must to avoid. A serpentine monstrosity. The Big Apple murder rate rises once Lisa (Faith Domergue) arrives to give the airmen their comeuppance via deadly snake bite. Lisa's got the coroner's office working nights and yet by movie's end she comes off as a pitiable, semi-sympathetic character. (Photograph courtesy C. Robert Rotter, *Glamour Girls of the Silver Screen* website.)

On October 25, *Variety* reported that Faith Domergue had been signed "to replace previously announced Ursula Thiess in the star role of *Cult of the Cobra*. Film, which rolls this week, originally was to have gone before the camera some weeks ago, at which time Miss Thiess was to have been loaned by RKO for stint. Picture also draws a producer switch. With William Alland now on a vacation in Europe, Howard Pine will produce."[6]

This *Variety* item ends by announcing that over the October 23–24 weekend, Universal had signed art director John Meehan to a term pact and put him right to work on *Cult*. One wonders what Meehan, a three-time Oscar winner (*The Heiress*, 1949, *Sunset Blvd.*, 1950, *20,000 Leagues Under the Sea*, 1954), thought of the caliber of his first assignment at Monster Central!

Synopsis

> Slender hangs illusion, fragile the thread to reality. Always the question: Is it true? Truth is in the mind and the mind of man varies with the time and place.
> The time is 1945.
> The place is Asia.[7]

Yes, the place is Asia—but *where* in Asia? We never find out. (The script offers up the clue that it's an area "served by the 10th Air Force in World War II in the C.B.I. [China-Burma-India] Zone." *That* narrows it down.) In an open-air bazaar, six American Air Force men on the eve of discharge snap pictures and visit vendors' stalls amidst a throng of natives and tourists. As Paul (Richard Long), Tom (Marshall Thompson), Pete (William Reynolds), Carl (Jack Kelly), Rico (David Janssen) and Nick (James Dobson) watch snake charmer Daru (Leonard Strong) hold his cobra, Paul mentions having once heard about a secret snake-worshipping society: "Lamians." As Paul says the word, the soundtrack lets out with a musical squawk and Daru looks up sharply. Paul explains to his friends that the Lamians believe that men and women can change into snakes and back again.

With a new intensity about him, Daru confides that *he* is a Lamian—a member of the Cult of the Cobra—and says that, for $100, he will smuggle them into tonight's meeting so that they can see "she who is a snake, and yet ... a *woman*." At eight that evening, Daru meets the men at a café and they ride in a Jeep to a temple where, Daru promises, they will see a ceremony "that recreates the first time the Cobra Goddess came to the aid of the Lamian people." He warns them that, if they're discovered, a Lamian with the power to transform into a snake will kill them all. "Either this guy is crazy, and I don't like it," Pete deadpans, "or he's tellin' the truth. And I like it *less*!"

In hooded robes, the G.I.s make their way into a large, torchlit central space within the temple. Here they become the first outsiders ever to see the weird ritual: As ceremonial music plays, a dancing man (pantomiming sowing seeds from a wooden bowl) is set upon by a performer dressed as a warrior. Near a shrine to the Cobra Goddess, a basket pops open and out come the hands of a woman, her fingers held in the shape of a cobra's head. The snake woman continues to sinuously rise out of the basket and we see that she's

Poor James Dobson (indicated by arrow): Not only did he get stuck with the role of the Cobra Goddess' first victim, he was the only one of the movie's male stars who didn't go on to TV stardom. The "TV stars in training" are, left to right, William Reynolds, Marshall Thompson, Richard Long, Jack Kelly and David Janssen. (Photograph courtesy Ronald V. Borst/Hollywood Movie Posters.)

dressed (a spotted and striped costume) and made-up to resemble a snake. She slides on her belly across the polished floor toward the warrior, "biting" and "killing" him. She's about to disappear back into the basket when Nick, drunk, snaps a flash photo. He is instantly beset by Lamians, and soon all the snake worshippers and the temple invaders are brawling. Nick grabs the basket (which now has a *cobra* inside) and escapes on foot as a high priest (Edward Platt), explosively angry, shouts, "The Cobra Goddess will avenge herself! One by one you will die!" Daru becomes the first "one" in that "one by one" death sentence when the warrior runs him through with his scimitar.

The five remaining airmen fend off the cultists with their fists and torches and Tom sets the drapes afire, giving them time to get away in their Jeep. Soon their headlights illuminate Nick lying in the street; beside him is the empty basket and a black-clad, veiled woman (Faith Domergue) who silently scurries into a nearby alley. On Nick's neck are snakebite marks. Later that night, in a military hospital room, Nick is recovering nicely when, under cover of darkness and a rainstorm, a hooded cobra enters his room through the open window. The camera becomes the eyes of the cobra[8] as it slithers up onto the bed; a crash of thunder drowns out Nick's scream as the snake lunges for his throat. "One by one," two are dead. The next morning, Nick's body tells a forensic story of cobra venom causing paralysis of the heart. "Only a snake with a brain coulda got into that room last night and singled out that same kid," babbles a mystified Major Fielding (Olan Soule). "It's almost as if … he were *meant* to go that way!" Already Paul is associating Nick's death with the high priest's curse.

The five G.I.s return to civilian life in New York, where Paul and Tom share an apartment. Paul's first order of business is to get engaged to Julia (Kathleen Hughes), a pretty blonde preparing to appear in a stage show. Tom is sweet on her too; at Rico's Bowling Alley on Charles Street in Greenwich Village, she tells Tom that she and Paul are to be married. Fiancée it ain't so!: Tom is bitter and angry ("You'll have to work. Paul will be a research assistant all his life. Sixty bucks a week!"). Getting hold of

"For hundreds of years, there have been those in every generation who have the power to change from humans into snakes," Daru (Leonard Strong, third from left) warns the airmen (Marshall Thompson, William Reynolds, David Janssen, Jack Kelly, James Dobson, Richard Long). "These are used as the instruments of the cult's vengeance!"

himself, he congratulates the happy couple. After Tom returns home and goes to bed, a woman's screams are heard. Tom puts his shoulder to the door of the apartment across the hall and finds nightgown-clad Lisa Moya (Domergue again) tearfully insisting that a man broke in. (Holy Kitty Genovese: Lisa screamed loud enough to scare every cat in the neighborhood, and Tom smashed his way in, but no other tenants appear.) As Tom searches her rooms, she regards him coldly, the look on her face (and the music) getting across the point that there *was* no man, and that she is the Cobra Goddess. (The name Lisa Moya doesn't sound Asian and Faith Domergue certainly doesn't look Asian. But if she can turn herself into a snake, I guess she can also turn herself into someone who doesn't look Asian. I wonder if the name Moya came from the famous *Cat People* line "Moya sestra?") Lisa talks to Tom about being a newcomer to the city, and finding it cold and unfriendly, so—as though she had planned it, which she did—Tom offers to show her the town.

Tom takes Lisa to the Staten Island Ferry, the Statue of Liberty, Wall Street and the Fulton Fish Market—but we don't get to see these things, we just hear Tom recap them as they munch at a sit-down hot dog stand. Tom brings Lisa back to the apartment house and gives her a kiss, but her reaction makes it clear he's struck out.[9] He then introduces her to Paul; at the sight of Lisa, the men's dog Corky whimpers and backs into a corner. Whenever Lisa reacts in a strange way to things the men say, the music score gets all dissonant. By the end of the scene, Paul looks like he's already picking up a strange vibe from her.

Lisa heads for Greenwich Village, where Rico is alone in his closed-for-the-night bowling alley. We don't see the cobra but we know it's there because it slithers through a bowling pin rack and knocks over the head pin. By the time Rico leaves, the cobra is in the back seat of his car. He sees it in his rear view mirror just before it goes in for the kill. The car jumps the curb, takes out a lamp post and flips onto its side. Rico's body protrudes from the wreck and a crowd gathers as Lisa clip-clops away in her high heels. "One by one," three are dead.

At a party at Carl's apartment, Tom has a few drinks and then serves Carl a knuckle sandwich for getting too friendly with Lisa. By now Paul is certain that Lisa is connected with the high priest's curse, which is kind of a stretch but it keeps the story moving.

Lisa starts to fall for Tom and asks him questions about love, as if it's something she's never experienced. And she doesn't seem to like the idea that he was once in love with Julia. Later that night she steals back to Carl's apartment where he's alone doing after-party clean-up. Carl acts like he thinks he's going to get lucky and pours some drinks while Lisa puts on a face that conveys a sense of dark purpose. Soon the cobra is going after Carl, who throws a small china statue at it and backs out onto his terrace. The snake grabs a quick bite before Carl goes over the side. Four down. *Waaay* down. In a crowd gathered around Carl's body on the sidewalk, Pete sees Lisa rubbing her arm—the result of being hit by the statue. (What part of the cobra did the statue strike that, back in human form, became her *arm*?)

Julia is alone in Paul and Tom's apartment when Lisa unexpectedly walks in. Julia mentions Paul's suspicion that there are people who can turn into snakes, which gives Lisa cause for concern. A "snakey look comes into [Lisa's] eye" (according to *Cult*'s Continuity & Dialogue), cuing ominous music, and she takes several steps toward Julia, who registers alarm. But Julia is saved by the bell—the doorbell, rung by a laundryman (Bing Russell) making a delivery. Julia hightails it out of there.

Investigating Carl's death, a suit-and-tie police inspector (Walter Coy) interrogates Paul and Tom. Paul's suspicions of foul play are running so high that he tells the inspector about the Lamian death curse—and shares his hunch that Lisa is the agent of the curse. At the same time, Pete, also leery of

When Lisa (Faith Domergue) seems to take a fancy to someone, it's the prelude to sudden death. Here's the snake woman giving a come-slither look to Carl (Jack Kelly), her penultimate victim. (Photograph courtesy C. Robert Rotter, *Glamour Girls of the Silver Screen* website.)

Lisa, is confronting her in her apartment and threatening to holler cop. This time we see Lisa's shadow, cast on a bedroom wall, transform into a cobra's shadow. Five down. Lisa crosses the hall, sees Tom with his back to her fiddling with a radio, and twice looks like she's preparing to switch to cobra form and put the bite on him—but she can't do it. "Tom, *nothing* can happen to you. It just *can't*," she says emotionally. "If anything did happen to you, I'd die!"

For the police inspector, the case goes around an unexpected bend when a coroner's report on Rico and Carl ("Venom from a large cobra!") forces him to accept Paul's story. They rush to Lisa's apartment, where they find Pete's body. Meanwhile, Lisa in evening gown and Tom in his best bib and tucker are at the opening of Julia's new stage show. Paul phones the theater, gets through to Tom and makes him aware of Pete's death—proof of Lisa's guilt. As they talk, Lisa sneaks up to Julia's dressing room, looking for Paul. After Julia enters, the cobra goes after her. Tom bursts in, throws a chair to shatter a window, and uses a coat tree to push the cobra toward the window. When he scoops it up and out of the window, it lands on a walkway outside; through the window, Tom jabs at it with the coat tree hooks until it slips over the edge. The cobra falls into the path of the inspector's police car, which screeches to a stop in the alley below. As Paul and the inspector stand over the dead cobra, and Tom and Julia watch from above, it morphs into the body of Lisa. Tom pushes his way through a crowd of onlookers and kneels at her side, holds his head in his hands for a few moments and then rises and walks off in a daze.

Cast Biographies

Faith Domergue as Lisa Moya

Howard Hughes famously discovered Jean Harlow and Jane Russell, so when he began grooming Faith Domergue, there was a feeling she might be the Next Big Thing. She wasn't. By 1955 she'd been in the movie biz for 15 years and yet *Cult of the Cobra* was only the second movie in which she was top-billed. In fact, she fared better *away* from Hughes than she did *with* him: During the 12-month stretch (1954–55) during which she made *Cult of the Cobra*, she was in more features than in all previous years combined!

Born in the French Quarter of New Orleans, Domergue was six when her family moved to Hollywood in the early 1930s. At seven she got her first look inside a movie studio: She and a girlfriend scaled a Fox fence and strolled around until a studio cop escorted them out. She told interviewers Tom and Jim Goldrup that, in school, "I was a very poor student; all I wanted to do was get up in front of people and act."

At 15, Domergue was screen-tested and signed by Warners, where she was renamed Faith Dorn. On a life-changing day in 1941, she was part of a covey of Warners starlets serving as eye candy and arm candy at an industry party on industrialist Howard Hughes' yacht, the *Southern Cross*. Aboard the floating palace, Hughes, 36 (a year younger than Faith's father), was attracted to the raven-tressed teen. The story of the mutual obsession that ensued could fill a book, and *did*: Faith's memoir *My Life with Howard Hughes,* which was being shopped around circa 1972 (while the tycoon was still with us). Then, suddenly, it stopped being shopped, and was never published, and fans surmised that some money had changed hands. The manuscript was unearthed in the 1990s by Pat H. Broeske, and with Domergue's blessings the story of her years with Hughes was encapsulated and incorporated into Broeske's book *Howard Hughes: The Untold Story*, co-authored by Peter Harry Brown.

According to Domergue (as relayed in *Untold Story*), their starry-eyed romance quickly hit a high point when, on a moonlit terrace, he gave her a diamond engagement ring

Common sense says ... no, common sense *shouts* that the relationship between Howard Hughes and protégée Faith Domergue was physical, but sex goes unmentioned in her memoir; and with that notorious "collector of women" Hughes, crazy as a pet coon, who knows what did and didn't happen in that department. (Photograph courtesy C. Robert Rotter, *Glamour Girls of the Silver Screen* website.)

to slip onto her finger and told her, "You are the child I should have had." (Eek!) Once he purchased her Warners contract, Faith began a new life under his all-seeing eye. At Hughes' Hollywood HQ, a sterile building in an industrial neighborhood, she finished high school and took drama lessons from tutors. The tycoon and the teen also shacked up, if by "shack" you mean the vast expanses of his elegant mansions. In addition to the child-woman he called Little Baby, Hughes publicly dallied with other dolls, including sex goddesses Lana Turner, Rita Hayworth and Ava Gardner. This displeased Faith, but her contract was owned by Hughes and by now both her father *and* grandfather were Hughes employees: "I felt like a butterfly on a pin—beautiful, vibrant and utterly trapped." One night while driving, she spotted Hughes and Ava in his Cadillac and gave chase. In the Farmer's Market parking lot where Hughes pulled over, Little Baby repeatedly crashed her roadster into his passenger side door, bouncing a screaming Ava up and down.

In 1945, Faith appeared in her first feature: Hughes loaned Jane Russell and Faith to producer Hunt Stromberg for *Young Widow*. Russell played the title role, a war widow, and Faith had a small part as a Russell co-worker who asks her how to *avoid* becoming a war widow(!). By 1946, Domergue and Hughes had closed the chapter on their relationship, and she married band leader Teddy Stauffer. But by the end of their first month as man and wife, they'd already separated.

That same year, Domergue began work on her first starring vehicle *Vendetta*, based on Prosper Mérimée's novel of bloody family feuds in 19th-century Corsica. Preston Sturges, Hughes' partner in California Pictures, wrote the screenplay and Max Ophüls began directing. When the picture fell behind schedule, Hughes insisted that Ophüls get the boot and that Sturges take the reins.[10] Then Hughes dumped Sturges and hired Stuart Heisler. In the month between Sturges' ouster and Heisler's takeover, nearly the entire production crew was replaced and new screenwriters hired to increase the importance of Faith's character. After Heisler's inevitable eviction, Mel Ferrer inherited the director's chair. Hughes may have directed the finale himself. The millions spent on the prolonged production represented a new high in investment in a picture starring unknowns (Faith, George Dolenz and Donald Buka). During the umpteen-month shoot, one kid actor grew up so fast that at the end of production he had to stand in a hole in order to appear to be the same size as in other scenes.

In October 1947, while Domergue was in Juarez, Mexico, shooting scenes for *Vendetta*, she and MGM director Hugo Fregonese were secretly married; they had two children, Diana (born in 1949) and John (born 1951). By late 1949 her Hughes contract had expired and she signed a deal with Hughes' RKO and starred in *Where Danger Lives*. In this film noir, mentally ill Faith's weapon of choice is a pillow of death with which she smothers her dominating husband (Claude Rains) and then attempts to snuff out lover Robert Mitchum. Her marquee moment came in 1950 when audiences got a double-dose of Domergue in this murder yarn and then *Vendetta*. The latter is set on the Island of Revenge (Corsica) where a murdered man must be buried in the very spot where he falls, and can't be removed to hallowed ground until his death has been avenged. After Faith's father (Fritz Leiber) is killed, we get the superimposure THE ONLY THING THAT SUSTAINS HER IN THIS HOUR OF GRIEF IS HER HEART'S VOW FOR ... **VENGEANCE**. Faith is at her most beautiful in *Vendetta* and *Where Danger Lives* but playing back-to-back bloodthirsty characters in a pair of morbid yarns may not have been the optimum start to a starring movie career.

On loanout from RKO, Domergue played fancy filly Opal Lacy in Universal's *The Duel at Silver Creek* (1952) and it looked as though she was getting a break from her run of homicidal characters—until Opal is left alone with an unconscious miner injured by claim jumpers, and she garrotes him with his own neckerchief! Nearly *all* of her early movies were obsessed with murder, starting with the above three and progressing with more kill-crazy roles in *Cult of the Cobra* and *Soho Incident* (1956), the third and last time she got top billing. In one of her few early movies in which she does *not* commit a murder, *This Is My Love* (1954), she's suspected of one! On her first movie as a "good girl," the Oregon-made *The Great Sioux Uprising* (1953), an ambulance stood by because the local Yumatilla Indians were wheat harvesters who knew nothing of horses and kept falling off.

Talking to interviewer Mike Fitzgerald about switching from movies to TV, Domergue explained, "I took what came along—I had two children, no support from my ex-husband [Fregonese], and there were bills to pay." In her interview with the Goldrups, she added, "Live television is what gave me the ulcer." There was a "reunion" of sorts for Domergue and Fregonese in 1970 when Faith, living in Rome with Husband #3 Paolo Cossa, and Fregonese, also residing in Europe, rushed to counsel their son John, a Loyola student who made them aware that he was smoking marijuana and slipping into a state of mental confusion. In the 1960s and '70s there was no telling where Faith would next show up to make a movie (or how awful it would be): *L'amore breve* (1969) in Italy, *The Gamblers* (1970) in Yugoslavia, *L'uomo dagli occhi di ghiaccio* (1971) in New Mexico [*sic*], *The House of Seven Corpses* (1974) in the Governors Mansion in Utah, etc. Her career ended when Cossa told her he didn't really want her to work in films any more. Given the quality of her final films, 1974's *So Evil, My Sister* for instance, probably her fans didn't want her working any more either!

"I did what he wanted," Domergue told the Goldrups.

I missed it, but the jewelry business [Cossa's profession] is very, very exciting and I enjoyed that. It wasn't my business, but I enjoyed all the accouterments, all the glamour and all the life around it. Monte Carlo, St. Moritz, Paris and Geneva, I liked all that. The exhibitions and parties, the international set; that was a great deal of fun. We moved to Geneva in the spring of 1977 and I was there for 17 years.

Cossa, whom she called "the great love of my life," died in 1992 and Faith died of cancer in Santa Barbara on Easter Sunday, 1999. She made a 2004 return to the screen in director Martin Scorsese's *The Aviator*—not in the flesh, of course, but as a character (played by Kelli Garner) in this biopic of Howard Hughes (Leonardo DiCaprio). The Hughes-Domergue section of the movie depicts their first meeting where she "auditions" for him and tells him she's 15 (Hughes: "Holy Mother of God…!"); a nightclub scene; and the incident described in Faith's memoir and in *Howard Hughes: The Untold Story*: Domergue crashing her car into Hughes and Ava's. Actress Sara Shane told *Classic Images* interviewer Mike Barnum that she was disgusted with *The Aviator*: "Faith Domergue was a very close friend of mine so I knew the story between the two of them. It was nothing like it is portrayed in this movie."

Richard Long as Paul Able

> Paul [Richard Long] and Tom [Marshall Thompson] are both in their early thirties, better educated than the [four other G.I.s] and accustomed to a somewhat higher social level of living. Paul is a little less "physical" looking than the others. He is a student of philosophy and his face has a sensitive, intellectual charm about it that is very disarming. Even in his uniform, that of a Sergeant, he has the look of a scholar.
> —script description of Long's *Cult of the Cobra* character

One of the frustrating things about writing about the oldies, and wanting to get things right, is that so much of what was written in the past falls somewhere between half-wrong and dead-wrong. Take for example the story of Richard Long's "big show biz break." It begins in 1945 when casting director Jack Murton gave a lift to a couple of hitchhiking Hollywood High School kids, who piqued Murton's interest by saying that fellow student Long, preparing to tackle the lead in a school play, was wow-ing his drama instructors. In other published accounts, Long's leading lady was the hitchhiker. Then there's the version where Murton gives a lift to high school girls, not boys, and *they* tell him how attractive Long is, not what a good actor he is. In other versions, Murton was the hitchhiker and the kids had the car(!). Murton either went to see the play or simply told the boys (or was it the girls?) to have Long call him. Murton worked for International Pictures in some accounts, Universal in others. And so on and so on, for every detail in the story. What really happened? At this late date, who knows?

The upshot was that 17-year-old Long went from appearing in his first play to testing for the featured role of the son of Claudette Colbert and Orson Welles in International's upcoming *Tomorrow Is Forever* (1946), a part they'd been trying to cast for months. He got the job *and* an International contract, with *Tomorrow* producer William Goetz calling the newcomer "the most remarkable find since Lew Ayres in *All Quiet on the Western Front.*" Soon Paramount, MGM and Fox wanted to borrow him, but he continued working for International in *The Stranger,* again with Welles, and *The Dark Mirror* (both 1946). After the Universal-International merger, he played the eldest son of Ma and Pa Kettle in *The Egg and I* (1947) and reprised the character in *Ma and Pa Kettle* (1949) and two of its follow-ups. When he went into the Army in December 1950 as a buck private, he was accepting a demotion: He'd played a lieutenant in his last picture. During his army service he was stationed in Japan, where at one point he was given permission to co-star in Universal's *Back at the Front* (1952), being filmed there on location!

Chicago-born, the son of a commercial artist, Richard Long (seen here with Suzan Ball) grew up in Illinois until the family's 1944 move to Hollywood. Entering movies while still in school, he began by playing boy-next-door types. He was 26 in *Cult of the Cobra.* (Photograph courtesy C. Robert Rotter, *Glamour Girls of the Silver Screen* website.)

Following his discharge, there was a return to Universal and a romance with teenage contractee Suzan Ball. Shortly after their courtship began, Ball learned that she had bone cancer in her knee. The knee then got some unhelpful jolts in an auto crash and when Ball fell in her apartment kitchen. *Hollywood Reporter* columnist Mike Connolly, by all accounts a Grade-A rat, heard the rumor that she had cancer and called Long to get the story. Long refuted it and implored Connolly not to write about it because it would break Suzan's heart. Connolly wrote it, Suzan's heart broke, and Connolly got shoved up against a wall, grabbed by the throat and knocked out cold by Long.

To stop the spread of malignancy, Suzan's leg was amputated above the knee on January 12, 1954, a month before her twentieth birthday. Three months later, Long walked and Ball limped down the aisle, Ball on an artificial leg, with*out* her crutches, clutching the arm of her father. It was 100 feet from the door of El Montecito Presbyterian Church's Spanish-style chapel to the altar but she made it, as she'd vowed she would. Outside were 1200 fans; inside attending the candlelit ceremony were guests including Jeff Chandler, Barbara Rush, Mala Powers, Julie Adams and Hugh O'Brian.

The Longs acted together in an episode of TV's *Lux Video Theatre* with Ball a wheelchair-bound accident victim and Richard as her doctor; they also began doing a nitery act in different cities. Ball even got to co-star in another Universal movie: She played an Indian maiden in *Chief Crazy Horse* (1955), made in the Black Hills of the Dakotas where the historical events depicted took place. In scenes that required walking, she had a double. Universal footed (sorry!) all her medical bills; by the end of July 1955, they were up to $70,000. Long knew from her doctors that she still had cancer, and Ball didn't.

Long was at the Columbia Ranch making the Western *Fury at Gunsight Pass* (1956) when the sad day came. The movie's female lead was Lisa Davis, 19 at the time; in 2008 she told me:

> **One night [Ball] was extremely ill, and Richard was in a terrible state the next day. And that was the day that another actor, Marshall Thompson [the husband of Long's twin sister Barbara], came to the set to tell Richard that she had passed away.**
>
> **One of our sets there at the Columbia Ranch was a Western-style mortuary, with coffins, and on the day that she died, I held him while he was sobbing, crying, standing there on that set, surrounded by all those wooden coffins—it was very grim.**

Ball died in their Beverly Hills home. She was buried in her wedding gown. The next movie for her grief-stricken young husband, who some say never got over her death, was mockingly titled *He Died Laughing* (released as *He Laughed Last*, 1956).

On TV, Long made a good impression playing the slippery Gentleman Jack Darby in several episodes of Warners' *Maverick*, and the studio signed him to a long-term contract. His first series was *Bourbon Street Beat*, in which he played New Orleans sleuth Rex Randolph. *Bourbon Street* got beat in the ratings badly enough that it lasted just a year but Long as Rex Randolph resurfaced as a regular on *77 Sunset Strip*. When Long wasn't fighting crime at Warners, he was at home fighting wife #2, actress Mara Corday. Lisa Davis told me with a gasp, "They fought and fought and fought, and she'd throw all his stuff out on the front lawn and turn on the sprinklers. They had a really tempestuous relationship!"

"He still wants to be a playboy, a sort of marital wanderer," Mara said in 1959, "even though he's the father of two children." Long and Corday had a third child in 1960. One is reminded of the old quip, "No matter how much cats fight, there always seem to be plenty of kittens."

Their marital mess reached critical mass in April 1961 when Long came home drunk to his missus and opened up

Post-Universal, Richard Long was more often seen on the small screen than the big one. Movie-wise, his platinum credential (for us Monster Kids, anyway) was *House on Haunted Hill* (1958) with Carolyn Craig.

a can of whoop-ass, grabbing her by the throat, throwing her on a couch and trying to strangle her. (She gave me a blow-by-blow you can read in my book *It Came from Horrorwood.*) The actor was tossed in the Van Nuys clink, then (sources differ) released when brother-in-law Marshall Thompson arrived with bail, or released when Mara refused to sign a complaint. Their divorce case was slated to come up in court just a few days later, but instead of being in a Burbank courtroom, 33-year-old heart attack victim Long was in a North Hollywood hospital. "Miss Corday expressed sympathy over Long's illness," the Associated Press reported, "but indicated there would be no reconciliation." Reconcile they did, while *77 Sunset Strip*'s parking lot attendant "Kookie" (Edd Byrnes) was promoted to full-fledged detective to fill the void left by Long. According to *Cult* co-star William Reynolds, Long knew his heart would be the end of him: "Not that he talked about it particularly, but.... I mean, I understand that he prepared his own funeral. That's a little macabre, at least fatalistic, but he was aware that he had limited time."

In 1962, Long, who obviously considered himself an *ac*-tor, groused, "I hope I've had it with [TV] series," but fine words butter no parsnips and for the next ten years he did almost nothing else *but*: the Western *The Big Valley* and the sitcoms *Nanny and the Professor* and *Thicker Than Water*. He even did a bit of directing, starting with the first Finnish-American co-production *Make Like a Thief* (1964), in which he started, and then two *Big Valley* episodes in which he did *not* appear. In 1969, he and Mara plus Mike Connors, Shelley Berman and *their* wives were the jovial celebs on the premiere episode of the game show *It Takes Two.* Meanwhile, at home, the beat went on: Suing for divorce in 1969, Mara alleged that

1. Richard uses the family house as a "boarder" would and comes home at odd and unusual hours, usually in a belligerent and unruly mood.
2. He frequently erupts into hostile, abusive and angry moods, displaying a strong and uncontrollable temper.
3. On January 22, 1969, he pushed her violently to the floor, injuring her, and threatened to throw a glass at her—although he ended up merely dousing her with water.
4. Richard gambles frequently, losing large sums of money, making it advisable to restrain him from selling, transferring or disposing of community assets, except in the ordinary course of business.

And then there was this:

On another occasion the defendant (Richard) grabbed plaintiff's (Mara) hand violently, causing injury to her hand and breaking the only long fingernail she had....

The above excerpts are from James Crenshaw's *Inside TV* magazine article "Happy 12th Anniversary? 'I Want a Divorce'" (the article title alluding to the fact that they'd separated on January 26, 1969, their anniversary). Corday told *Inside TV*,

When I first met him he was very depressed and I thought that was just because of his wife [Suzan Ball], but now—when I look back and talk to his mother and people he knew in the army—I realize he's *always* been this kind of fellow. So life is bad, as far as he's concerend.

Why should life be taken away from a beautiful girl like that [Suzan]? We have talked to doctors about it and they can't figure out why one should live—for instance, a drunk—while another—perhaps a baby—should die. So there are no answers—and that bugs Richard a lot.

But you've got to forget that and get out of your depression. We're all here and we've got to live and enjoy what we've got. But he just can't seem to do it.

Long, wife Mara Corday and their daughter Valerie at a Little League baseball game. News of the Longs' tussles was regularly relayed by the press, a 1959 item revealing that they were separated 16 times in the two years since their 1957 Las Vegas wedding. *TV Guide* reported in 1968, "They squabbled, fought, separated and sued for divorce so many times that it began to play like comedy." (Photograph courtesy C. Robert Rotter, *Glamour Girls of the Silver Screen* website.)

Yet again those two crazy kids got back together. Then in 1974 Long's heart troubles landed him in Tarzana Medical Center where he spent more than a month before dying a few days after his 47th birthday. As Mara Corday put it, "He died December 21, 1974, at Tarzana Hospital, at 20 minutes of two. Just before the bars closed." His funeral service was held at Pepperdine College in Malibu; *Variety* reported that the body would be cremated and buried at sea.[11] He's made just one reappearance since: Corday told *Western Clippings* magazine writer Mike Fitzgerald that after Long's death, she consulted a psychic,

> **a Mexican woman, she could barely speak English. A friend said she wasn't a phony, she was legitimate. She also didn't charge me any money! I asked her to ask Richard if he and Suzan Ball, his first wife…, were together and happy. The psychic told me Richard expected me to say something dumb like that. "He also wants you to forgive him for all the bad times in the marriage." That was just like Richard—how could this woman know? I've lost touch with this medium. She went back to South America. But I would love to contact her again.**

Marshall Thompson as Tom Markel

> Tom [Marshall Thompson], a commercial artist in private life, is dark, well-built and interesting looking. There is a touch of boyish high spirits about him which shows itself in quick gestures and confident responses.
>
> —script description of Thompson's *Cult of the Cobra* character

Executive producer Richard Gordon, who cast Marshall Thompson in his English-made horror-sci-fis *Fiend Without a Face* (1958) and *First Man into Space* (1959), remembered him as very religious and a family man, "conservative and withdrawn. Perfectly professional, but kept pretty much to himself." Presumably Gordon did not yet know all this about the actor the day that co-producer Ronald Kinnoch suggested to Gordon that, since Thompson hadn't brought his wife along to England, they should try to keep their far-from-home headliner happy by taking him out one night and "fixing him up" (getting him a girl). Once Thompson figured out what they were up to, not only did he decline, now he wouldn't even go out for a drink with the two men! "He wouldn't be led astray!" Gordon laughed.

Thompson has a formidable list of genre titles—those two Gordon movies, *Cult of the Cobra, It! The Terror from Beyond Space* (1958) and more, and (alongside Richard Carlson) he was uber-fan Robert Skotak's favorite sci-fi hero. Skotak tracked Thompson down to Santa Monica and was perhaps the only person ever to ask him to talk about his genre credits. But Skotak hit a brick wall: "He simply didn't want to talk about himself," Skotak told me. "Nice, but … well, he never pursued publicity or sought much attention, unless it was for a cause." Thompson's modest, business-like monster-movie heroes may just have been Thompson kinda playing himself.

The actor was born in Peoria, Illinois; his father was a dentist, his mother a concert singer. The father's health woes later prompted a move to California. Marshall's performance in the high school play *Our Town* resulted in a screen test that led to nothing. While he was in college, Universal offered him $350 a week to appear in the Gloria Jean musical *Reckless Age* (1944) so he dropped out of school to give the movies a try. Actor Richard Whorf thought enough of the 18-year-old's *Reckless Age* performance to cast him in his (Whorf's) first feature as director, MGM's *Blonde Fever* (1944). Gloria Grahame and Thompson got "And Introducing" billing on its posters and even on-screen in the opening credits, above their side-by-side cameos.

By the fall of 1944, Thompson had a term acting pact at MGM, where for years he played many bland, boyish supporting roles. Toward the end of the decade there was some improvement, with *Variety*'s reviewer saying that in the World War II tale *Battleground* (1949) Thompson "gets his best break as a mama's boy who becomes a man." *Dial 1119*

Whether playing the boy next door, a protector of jungle animals, even military men (as in *Fiend Without a Face*, pictured), Marshall Thompson usually exuded "Mr. Nice Guy" charm. But he could also play sourpusses, like *Cult of the Cobra*'s cast-aside boyfriend.

(1950) starred Thompson as an escapee from a hospital for the criminally insane, repeatedly scratching his homicidal itch while holding hostages in a neighborhood bar, and the Civil War era suspenser *The Tall Target* (1951), set on a southbound train, cast him as a Dixie-accented West Pointer intent on assassinating Abraham Lincoln. During the making of *Roseanna McCoy* (1949), about the Hatfield-McCoy feud, Thompson (playing a McCoy) took time off from hatin' on the Hatfields to marry Barbara Long, sister of Universal contractee (and future *Cult of the Cobra* star) Richard Long. Their daughter Janet was born in 1951.

"It's a tie between Audie Murphy and Marshall Thompson for *Red Badge of Courage*, with [writer-director] John Huston holding out for Murphy," a *Variety* columnist reported in 1951; Murphy got the part in the Metro movie and, soon after, Thompson began freelancing. There was plenty of work for him: more movies, some stage (including a Broadway play) and lots of TV.[12]

Tall (6'2"), lean (175 lbs.) and serious-looking, Thompson turned out to be a top monster fighter in *Fiend Without a Face* and *First Man into Space* and, best of all, *It! The Terror from Beyond Space*, in which he and other spaceship crew members, returning from Mars, discover that they have an armor-scaled, ape-like stowaway (Ray Corrigan). Thompson again ventured into sci-fi in 1958 when he starred in the Ziv pilot *Little Man*, which became the teleseries *World of Giants*. Obviously *Incredible Shrinking Man*-inspired, it featured Thompson as Mel Hunter, a six-inch-tall U.S. government secret agent. In the first episode we learn his backstory: Mel, infiltrating a behind-the-Iron-Curtain missile launching site, was exposed to a new type of rocket fuel; an unknown ingredient affected his molecular structure and caused him to shrink to tiny proportions, but also gave him manual dexterity, agility and reflexes "somewhere between a hummingbird and a mongoose" (presumably that's a good thing). Traveling from place to place in a tiny chair inside his full-sized colleague Bill's (Arthur Franz) attaché case, Mini-Mel now continues to do the work of Uncle Sam.[13] Thompson's next series, the sitcom *Angel* (1960–61), lasted just a single season; the actor wrote at least one episode.

In 1962 Thompson trekked to the Philippines for the World War II drama *No Man Is an Island* starring Jeffrey Hunter (Thompson's character is beheaded) and to Vietnam for *A Yank in Viet-Nam*. In the latter, he starred and also directed; "In both departments his talent proved depressing" (*New York Herald Tribune*). According to daughter Janet, Thompson had a price put on his head by the Viet Cong and was shot by one of his crew members—the bullet deflecting off a sterling silver lighter in his pocket. For Ivan Tors Productions' *Clarence, the Cross-Eyed Lion* (1965), set at an East African veterinary hospital, Thompson co-wrote the story

Animal lover Marshall Thompson's obituaries unsurprisingly ended with, "The family has asked that any memorial contributions be sent to the William Holden Wildlife Foundation."

and starred as Dr. Marsh Tracy; he reprised Tracy in the TV series *Daktari* (1966–69), filmed at an L.A.-area wild animal park. In the Tors feature *Around the World Under the Sea* (1966), Thompson and other familiar TV faces (Lloyd Bridges, Brian Kelly and David McCallum) saved the world from earthquakes, seaquakes and tidal waves.

Movie and TV roles got scarcer in the 1970s, and by the 1980s wildlife enthusiast Thompson was spending most of his time in Africa, where he produced, directed and starred in the syndicated documentary series *Orphans of the Wild*. He was 66 when he died of congestive heart failure in Royal Oak, Michigan, in 1992.

Kathleen Hughes as Julia Thompson

I don't have many inhibitions, I'm afraid. It's my revolt against my Boston upbringing. Against all the narrow-minded codes that vilify happiness!

Yes, Kathleen Hughes said that. But in a movie. Her breakthrough movie *For Men Only* (1952), star-director-co-producer Paul Henreid's "social problem picture" that put college fraternity hazing on trial. In white shorts and sweaters that stick to her like the label on a perfume bottle, Hughes' blonde and busty Tracy Norman brings new meaning to "student body," and she's got a schoolgirl crush on science teacher Henreid, who's trying to abolish hazing. When the married man won't give her a tumble, she frames him for sexual assault. In *For Men Only*, Hughes proved that she was very good at being bad, and soon found herself typecast as meanies. This came as a surprise to Hughes, who started her career picturing herself playing "innocent" parts.

The niece of screenwriter F. Hugh Herbert, Hughes (*nee* Betty von Gerkan) had designs on an acting career right from childhood. At about age 17, during a performance of a play called *Night Over Taos* at the Geller Workshop, she did a terrible acting job, felt ill, and even passed out between acts one and two—and yet a Fox talent scout in the audience thought enough of her performance (or maybe just her look) that he wanted her to screen-test. Uncle F. Hugh, then at Fox, wrote and directed her in a cute "personality test" that got her a contract there. Fox gave her the new moniker Kathleen Hughes and started her off with an uncredited role in the film noir *Road House*, as a teenager hanging around the title locale. (In 2016 she told me what she did in *Road House* and recited some of her dialogue, then busted out laughing at herself: "Isn't it ridiculous that I can remember lines from a movie in 1948?!") During her time at Fox she received on-screen billing for her supporting performances in other movies, played additional uncredited roles, acted in several movies that she was cut out of, and was The Girl in Fox's screen tests of various young wannabe actors, including Rock Hudson, Peter Graves and Robert Horton. At the time, the future femme fatale "wanted to be another Jeanne Crain," one of the goody-two-shoes stars of that era.

Teenager Betty von Gerkan as she appeared in the Geller Workshop stage production *Night Over Taos*, circa 1948. This led to a contract at Fox, where she was rechristened Kathleen Hughes.

At the end of her third year at Fox, the studio dropped her option. For her *For Men Only* role as the brainy and unbridled Tracy, Hughes went to a beauty shop and had her long brown hair dyed blonde (and it's been blonde ever since). In the screen credits she got special "Introducing …" billing, along with Russell Johnson, Vera Miles and Robert Sherman, and many thought she was the best thing in the picture. (In 1953 when distributor Lippert retagged it *The Tall Lie* and prepared to put it back into release, Hughes was elevated to co-star billing with Henreid in revised ads.)

Impressed with Hughes in *For Men Only*, Universal signed her to a long-term pact on January 3, 1952, and put her right to work in the lightweight *Sally and Saint Anne*. Over the next few years she appeared in a half-dozen movies on the Valley lot, including *It Came from Outer Space* (1953) as Jane, girlfriend of telephone linesman Russell Johnson. (Johnson *also* got his foot in Universal's door via *For Men Only*.)

In her one short hip-flipping scene in *Outer Space*, Kathleen's 3-D curves caused a tempest in a c-cup and Universal elevated her to star status (well, third-billed) in the 3-D crime drama *The Glass Web* (1953). It starts off with a bang (actually three bangs): Hughes argues with a man (Sydney Mason) in the desert and, as she walks away, he pumps two bullets into her back, then a third once she's on the ground dawdling toward death. But what we're really seeing is the filming of part of an episode of the *Crime of the Week* TV series in which actress Paula Ranier (Hughes) has just played a death scene. Soon life imitates art: Paula, a hard-boiled, gold-digging blackmailer, is strangled by the show's writer (Edward G. Robinson)—and this unsolved murder becomes the subject of a *Crime of the Week* episode!

Again Kathleen excelled in a venomous vixen role, and critics noticed. *The New York Times* called her "a dainty dish of poison" and preferred her performance to those of stars Robinson and John Forsythe. *Harrison's Reports* also gave her top acting honors over the two men "as the heartless, designing beauty," and *The Hollywood Reporter* called her "tantalizing performance … one of the film's top delights." In actuality, the screen's newest wicked woman may, at that point, have still been living at home with her mom. (Her dad died when she was a teenager.)

In a 1950 Hollywood Bowl production of *Faust*, the New York Metropolitan Opera's renowned Jerome Hines (6'6"!) was Mephistopheles and Kathleen Hughes, left, was one of his two apprentices. Hines and Hughes dated at the time. Attendance topped 35,000. Every night, as soon as Kathleen finished her last scene, she rushed out into the audience, found a seat and watched the rest of her favorite opera ("It was a wonderful production!"). The actress on right is unidentified.

In early 1954 Hughes was in New York promoting *The Glass Web* when producer Sam Spiegel asked her to read for a part in a picture he was about to shoot there. At the same time she was ordered by Universal to report back to the studio pronto to appear in one of their pictures. She dutifully told Spiegel no and returned to Universal to play the supporting role of a dance hall girl in the Western *Dawn at Socorro*, thereby passing up a chance to vie for the femme lead in Spiegel's picture: *On the Waterfront* with Marlon Brando ("I blew it!").

By July of '54 she didn't care whether Universal picked up her option or not (according to Army Archerd in *Variety*) because she was so happy about her forthcoming marriage to writer-producer Stanley Rubin. They wed at the home of Uncle F. Hugh, in what she called "a beautiful setting." The following month, the new Mrs. Rubin made her professional stage debut as "The Girl" in a La Jolla production of *The Seven Year Itch*. Her last Universal picture *Cult of the Cobra* was no fun for her because she was sick at the time and had no use for director Francis D. Lyon, who would grouse at her in front of cast and crew, "You're being too coy!"

The reason I was coy in *Cult of the Cobra* is that I was so totally miscast that I had no idea how to play it! It was easy to be *bad* and *evil*—but it was hard to be sort of an ingenue.

After she left Universal, audiences saw less of Hughes in the movies (although she did unforgettably horsewhip Marla English in *Three Bad Sisters*, 1956) and more of her on TV, including the *Alfred Hitchcock Presents* episode "Vicious Circle" that was like a *For Men Only* reunion with Hughes and Russell Johnson in the cast and Paul Henreid directing. She became the mother of John, born in 1956,[14] Chris, born in 1958, Angie, born in 1964, and Michael, born in 1966. Acting got to be a family affair with the Rubins: In Stanley's *Peyton Place* TV series, their infant Michael played Dorothy Malone's baby and Kathleen was his nurse; in Stanley's *The President's Analyst* (1967) Kathleen and sons John and Chris played White House tourists; and in Stanley's *Promise Her Anything* (1965) John, Chris and Angie *and* Kathleen appeared.

Hughes had semi-regular stints on the Rubin-produced series *The Ghost and Mrs. Muir* (as Mrs. Coburn, one of Mrs. Muir's neighbors) and *Bracken's World* (as Mitch, Peter Haskell's secretary). She also had parts in several of her husband's movies, telemovies and TV episodes. Fifty-one-year-old Kathleen signed to play a small role (including a topless scene) in *Battle Creek Brawl* (1980), Hong Kong martial arts star Jackie Chan's first American movie. "There I was in a nightgown, with nothing under it," she told me. "And at the very last minute the director said, 'I've been thinking about it. We're not going to be able to use this scene, so I'm not going to shoot it.' I was relieved!"

In the early 1950s, Kathleen Hughes had a neighbor who enjoyed photography. Who *wouldn't*, with Kathleen up the street and happy to pose? "He never saw me nude!" she quickly adds.

The Rubins' son Chris, a writer, died in 2008, and Kathleen was widowed in 2014. Showing no signs of slowdown, she continues to attend film festival screenings and autograph shows—and even auditions for roles.

Production

Cult of the Cobra represents several unusual "firsts" in the Universal Monsters pantheon; for instance, surely it's the first Universal Horror to begin production in a bowling alley. The movie started shooting on October 26, 1954, at Airway Bowling Lanes, 221 East Ventura, Burbank. There was a crew call for six in the morning, long before sun-up; Kathleen Hughes was there at 5:45, Richard Long, Marshall Thompson, William Reynolds, Jack Kelly and David Janssen arriving an hour later. In addition to cast and crew, a local policeman and a fire warden were on hand. The moviemakers got the ball rolling by getting various shots of Janssen's Rico alone in the place, closing up for the night. After the noon-to-one lunch, Long, Thompson, Reynolds and Kelly played their characters for the first time as the remainder of the bowling alley scenes were shot. Thompson looks dorky rockin' a butch haircut but he'd come to consider it a good career move: According to a United Press article, he got it for the Korean War movie *Battle Taxi*, made over the summer, and said it was "sort of a shock to see how this lawn-mower effect changed my appearance." While making *Battle Taxi*, his next job offer came along, one that called for him to retain that hair style, and then another and another, until he'd done five movies in a row with no days off in between, and began feeling that his crew cut look was keeping him in demand. For the fifth of the five, *Cult of the Cobra*, "Universal didn't tell me to report with the flat top, but I decided to play it safe." (Of course, if Thompson had no days off between his previous movie and *Cult*, as he claims, then it's not like he had a decision to *make*!)

October 26's Daily Production Report ends with a shot description that makes you think about shots we take for granted when we see them in movies: The bowling alley scene begins with a shot of a bowling pin rack, a ball rolling in and scoring a strike. Easier conceived and written in a script than done:

5:06–5:16	Setting up	
5:16–5:17	Sc. 84	
	[Shot] 72–06" [feet of film used]	no strike
	[Shot] 73–06" [feet of film used]	"
5:24–5:29	[Shot] 74–06" [feet of film used]	"
	[Shot] 75–06" [feet of film used]	"
	[Shot] 76–06" [feet of film used]	"
	[Shot] 77–06" [feet of film used]	"
	[Shot] 78–06" [feet of film used]	Print

The company was dismissed at 5:29, leaving just a few fellows behind to, yes, *strike* the set.

The rest of the movie was shot at Universal, starting the next morning on Stage 20. The first order of business: scenes set in the police inspector's office. The inspector was played by Walter Coy, one of those instantly recognizable actors whose name no one knows, because he never came within shouting distance of the top of any movie castlist. Several months later, he had a typically small but key role as John Wayne's brother Aaron in *The Searchers*: Aaron and his wife are killed, and their daughters kidnapped, by "the Comanch," setting the story in motion.

After the Inspector's Office scenes were shot, there was concern that the film might not be usable. The Daily Production Report reveals:

Four scenes in the Inspector's Office were shot on Tri X, the new fast type negative, by accident as the marks identifying the film were not conspicuous. It is possible it may be necessary to retake these scenes. However, steps have been taken to correct the identification of the film so that this will not happen again in the future.

Following lunch, the moviemakers tackled the Doctor's Headquarters scene in which Paul, Major Fielding and Capt. Williams discuss the overnight hospital death of Nick, and then on Stage 7 the first of many scenes in Paul and Tom's apartment. Most of the 28th was spent on the Process Stage in front of the process screen: the airmen homeward bound in the belly of an airplane; the airmen driving away from the temple in their Jeep; Paul and Julia in the back of a taxi; and, from the "What the hell is *this*?" department, a scene of "Rico, Carl & boy with abacus"! From 3:21 to 6:13, back on Stage 20, the previous day's Inspector's Office scenes were indeed reshot, this time on the right kind of film.

Friday, October 29, found actors and crew again on the Paul and Tom's Apartment set. They began with the late-night scene of Tom comforting their scared dog, Corky, just prior to hearing Lisa screaming from the across-the-hall apartment. In one shot the dog *is* shivering, as if in great fear, but an item on that day's Special Equipment list is EFFECTS—FAN—WIND, so probably we're just seeing its hair blow.

Later came the filming of the kitchen table scene with Paul, Tom and Julia (Kathleen Hughes). On Daily Production Reports, next to each unacceptable take is the reason it was "N.G." (no good); on this date, and for this scene, ten times the reason is "Julia N.G.," which may indicate that Hughes was having an off day. Now and then the shooting of scenes was interrupted for the shooting of silent Faith Domergue wardrobe tests. The actress sported a series of outfits, the first (shot in the morning) a black suit with mantilla, gloves, black purse and a gold wrist chain, the last (shot at the end of the day) a negligee plus "light green silk brocade robe with heliotrope lining."

The movie doesn't make it clear whether the Cobra Goddess (Faith Domergue with book) would like to put the bite on Julia (Kathleen Hughes)—but it's not hard to imagine that she would. Jealousy could trigger Irena's *Cat People* transformations. (Photographs courtesy C. Robert Rotter, *Glamour Girls of the Silver Screen* website.)

In *Cult of the Cobra* you'll see the woman of fatal beauty—whose kiss is irresistible—whose caress is deadly—whose mystic, menacing occult power transforms her into a hissing monster—who destroys men with love!

—from *Cult of the Cobra*'s 60-second radio spot

Add *Cult of the Cobra* to the list of Universal Horrors partly shot on Halloween: On Saturday, October 30, as kids prepared for their trick-or-treating, Domergue did her first acting in the movie. She began with the Paul and Tom's Kitchen scene where Domergue's Lisa and Hughes' Julia meet for the first time, and Lisa menacingly approaches Julia. With 11 "Julia N.G."s on the Daily Production Report, Kathleen Hughes topped the previous day's ten. Done very differently, the scene could have had a bit of the flavor of the suggestive Countess Zaleska-Lili sequence in *Dracula's Daughter* (1936), which would have been interesting. Incidentally, notice the titles as Julia digs through Paul's stack of door-stopper books: *A History of Cults, Metamorphosis—Fact or Fiction?, Snakes in Religious Ceremonies,* etc. Who knew that McFarland was around way back then?!

As indicated in the Domergue bio above, late 1954 was a busy time for the actress as she rushed from one picture to another. Reminiscing about *Cult* with Mike Fitzgerald in *Fangoria*, she began with,

> **I had been on location in St. George, Utah, shooting *Santa Fe Passage* [1955] with John Payne for Republic. We were there over a month, and that picture turned out to be my favorite of the features I did, with *This Island Earth* coming in second. Anyway, we were back at Republic, doing the interior shots, when I got a call from Universal telling me I had to report immediately for *Cult of the Cobra*. I told [Universal] I wasn't finished with *Santa Fe Passage*, but since I had signed that two-pictures-per-year pact, they told me to report on my noon hour for costume fittings! Luckily, Republic and Universal were near each other in the Valley, so that wasn't as much of a problem as it could have been. This kept up, and then the day after I finished at Republic, I was to report to Universal. Well [*laughs*], I showed up for work the next day—at Republic, where they told me, "Miss Domergue, you finished the picture yesterday." I couldn't believe it, but going back and forth so much confused me! I hurried over to Universal, and it was the only time in my life that I was late for work. They were very nice and understood the predicament.**

Scenes set in Paul and Tom's Apartment featuring Lisa and Tom took up the rest of the day and most of Monday, November 1. This included the movie's last apartment scene with Lisa and Tom, both dressed to go to the theater, talking about Paul's suspicions and then getting lovey-dovey. Watching this scene in the finished film, we realize why (in the first part of the movie) Domergue's Lisa is aloof and deadpan: because there needed to be a contrast between instrument-of-the-cult's-vengeance Lisa and the defrosted, very-much-in-love Lisa in the story's final lap. By the end, even Lisa's slight foreign accent has been dropped.[15]

The kissing part of the scene had to be done a couple times, and Marshall Thompson presumably didn't complain. He presumably did complain later, when doing the hallway scene where he puts his shoulder to Lisa's apartment door and busts in; he somehow managed to injure his hand in the process, and received hospital treatment. Then the filmmakers moved to the Phantom Stage, seen here as the theater where Julia's show is opening. Filmed that day: Tom searching for Lisa, and Lisa making her way down the corridor to Julia's dressing room door.

Tuesday, November 2, was Election Day—the U.S. Senate election of 1954. *Cult*'s cast and crew returned to the Phantom Stage for palaver between Tom and the harried theater doorman (William Vedder), Tom looking for Lisa, etc. Two of my favorite moments in the movie were put on film that day, the first in the morning: a neat shot of Tom on the phone in the doorman's glass-walled office, coping with the news of Pete's death and Lisa's obvious guilt, while through the glass behind him we see Lisa, murder on her mind, mounting a circular staircase, en route to Julia's dressing room.

My other favorite moment was filmed in the afternoon: the boom shot of Lisa, still on her way to Julia's dressing room, reaching the top of the staircase, walking into a shadowy medium shot—and then hesitating as though she might forsake her mission of murder and go back to Tom. The look on her face, suggesting the inner struggle, is worth 1000 words; Lisa is conflicted and, if *you* feel her pain, then Faith Domergue has actually managed to achieve a small measure of sympathy as a character who doesn't invite much. Probably the best review *Cult of the Cobra* ever got in a mainstream newspaper (the *New York Daily News*) was the Phantom of the Movies' column on its 1994 VHS release, titled "Serpent's Tale Tips Scales as Tragic '50s Cult Classic," in

"It seems to me that if you play the leading lady, you kind of get the same part over and over again," Faith Domergue told the interviewing Goldrup brothers. "But if you play a heavy or if you play a villainess, then you get something juicy." In this tense scene, William Reynolds is on the verge of getting a juicy snakebite. (Photograph courtesy Ronald V. Borst/Hollywood Movie Posters.)

which he wrote: "There's a legit tragic quality to the melancholy Thompson and the self-doubting Domergue's impossible attraction."

Next on the schedule: getting a start on the climactic theater exterior scene, shot near Universal's Editorial Building (the police car bobbing to a stop with Lisa's body in front of it, Tom and Julia descending the fire escape and Tom kneeling by the body, etc.). In a nice attention-to-detail touch, the police car has a 1946 license plate. This exterior was shot night for night, after dinner, and the company was dismissed at 9:55. At one point during Election Day 1954, Universal had to give all the extras who hadn't yet voted 90 minutes off to do so.

Because the company had worked late, the next day's crew call was for 9:24 a.m., and they didn't get their first shot until 10:44. On Stage 7, Lisa's Apartment scenes were shot, starting with the policemen and Paul finding Pete's snakebit body. For the rest of the morning and part of the afternoon, Domergue and William Reynolds enacted the showdown between Lisa and Pete. "I only really had one big scene with [Domergue], confronting her with my suspicions that she is the killer," Reynolds told me, "and I don't think that it was paid off very well. I don't know whether it was *my* fault or the cutter's fault or *whoever*, but my character's reason for being suspicious wasn't particularly well articulated by the movie. I wasn't terribly pleased with what I was doing when I saw *Cult of the Cobra* the first time—and [after rewatching the movie in 2007] I see now why I wasn't!" (As for the movie itself, however, Reynolds admits that it "was a pretty good product, for what it was at the time.") In the afternoon, the moviemakers got a start on the Lisa's Apartment scenes between Lisa and Tom, and then after dark it was back to the Editorial Building for shots of the cobra getting poked off the balcony with the coat tree, and of Tom and Julia at the window and coming down the fire escape.

That day, November 3, the United Press column "Hollywood Film Shop" included a brief interview with Richard Long's starlet wife Suzan Ball. According to Ball, playing "bad" or "mean" girls was one of the best ways to graduate to better parts. "When I say 'go bad,' I mean [actresses] should try and snag heavy roles with meat in them."[16] It might have been interesting to get Faith Domergue's take on Ball's advice. Domergue came onto the movie scene with much fanfare in *Vendetta* and *Where Danger Lives*, *two* movies that showcased her as heavies of a kind; a less-than-stellar career followed, and now here she was, playing a Cobra Goddess!

During the making of *Cult of the Cobra*, Richard Long was contending with a "death sentence" on the sound stages at work (in the storyline, the high priest's curse) ... and with a real-life one at home. Suzan Ball *thought* that she had licked the cancer that in January 1954 had cost her a leg but, circa July 1954, her doctors told Long that the cancer had returned. Long was advised *not* to let her know, in order to keep up her mental attitude, and so he kept her in the dark for about nine months, a stretch that included the making of *Cult of the Cobra*. "When Suzan did have some trouble," he said later, "we managed to camouflage the symptoms as something else." Presumably Long trusted his sister Barbara with the secret; if so, then probably her husband Marshall Thompson—Long's *Cult of the Cobra* co-star—was also in on the merciful deception. (*Cult* was Long's first picture since marrying Ball more than half a year earlier.)

> Ed Muhl, head man at U.I., personally chose Dick for one of the leads in *Cult of the Cobra*, and it's interesting that Dick's brother-in-law, Marshall Thompson, who was best man at his wedding, also has a top role in the same picture.
> —Hollywood columnist Louella O. Parsons

For Suzan Ball's courage in the face of the ravages of cancer, she had won America's sympathy, and she refused to abandon her career: The "film star amputee" (*Variety* actually called her that) appeared with Long on TV, co-starred in *Chief Crazy Horse* and, according to Army Archerd in *Variety* (November 5, 1954), would again don Indian

With a well-timed scream, Lisa (Faith Domergue) brings Tom (Marshall Thompson) into her apartment—and into her clutches. *Variety* called Domergue "a standout in an exotic role" and said that Thompson "lends conviction to his part in a well-enacted characterization." (Photograph courtesy Ronald V. Borst/Hollywood Movie Posters.)

pigtails in the upcoming *The Long Hunters* with James Stewart.[17] Perhaps the most exciting project on the horizon for Ball was the "song-and-laugh act" that she and Long planned to debut at the Chi Chi in Palm Springs. Ball was a trouper, bravely determined to die with her boot on—but was purposely being made *un*-aware how soon that would happen.

On November 4, the day columnist Earl Wilson told readers that Suzan Ball "will dance with husband Dick Long in their night club act, debuting November 25," more Lisa's Apartment scenes were shot on Stage 7, starting with Tom bursting in, seeing Lisa for the first time and searching for the Intruder Who Never Was. Put on film a bit before the lunch break: a silent shot of Lisa "looking after Tom—light fades away from all but eyes." As mentioned above, Domergue speaks with a trace of a foreign accent in early scenes but not afterwards—presumably part of the actress' plan (or *some*body's plan) to make Lisa seem "more normal" as the picture progresses and as Tom's influence humanizes her.

Work on November 5 took place on Stage 20, starting with the Carl's Apartment party scene where Carl gets too friendly with Lisa and eats a punch from Tom. In the afternoon came the shooting of the scene in which Lisa returns to Carl's and goes cobra on him; the camera becomes the cobra as Carl, with the shadow of the cobra on his body, throws the statue and backs out onto the terrace. There's a skittish handheld p.o.v. shot as the camera goes for Carl's throat. In the movie, as Carl topples over the railing, the scream we hear sure sounds like the scream of Karloff's Frankenstein Monster as he plummets into the sulphur in the *Son of Frankenstein* (1939) finale. Photographed but not used: a shot of Carl on the terrace with the head of the cobra in the right frame-line, and another shot (a tight close-up) of Carl as the cobra strikes him in the throat.

November 5's Daily Production Report reveals that Carl Carlsson—part of the yet-to-be-shot Lamian ceremonial dance—cut his left ear on a spangle on the costume of the cobra woman, and was sent to the hospital. Presumably this was while they were rehearsing somewhere other than *Cult*'s sets, because no part of the temple scene was shot on November 5. Also that day, there was drama for Kathleen Hughes, who didn't want to *do Cult of the Cobra* because she felt she was miscast, was hated by director Lyon, returned the favor, and found *Cult* "a very, very unpleasant experience." She told me,

I really thought [Lyon] was a bad director because he would give me direction, that was kind of embarrassing direction, in a loud, clear voice, so that ev-er-y-bod-y on the set would hear. He'd say, "You're being too coy!" and he'd say this so the whole set heard it. I don't think that's very nice. A good director would have taken me aside and told me quietly how he wanted the scene played.[18]

Hughes came down with an intestinal flu a few days after the start of production and on November 5 stayed home in bed until she got a call saying she was needed. On the set she happened to pass the assistant director's desk and

The same curiosity that killed the cat makes short work of the ex-G.I.s. Here Jack Kelly is about to learn the hard way that he shoulda respected the mysteries of the East. (Photographs courtesy John Antosiewicz.)

I saw that there were notes to the front office or the production office that said I had held up production by coming in late [that day]. They had phoned me and told me to get in as fast as I could, and I said, "Well, I can be there at such-and-such a time, that's the best I can do." And then when I got there, I saw [a production report] that said I had come in *many* hours late and screwed up *every*thing for them. I was outraged, because I was *so* sick, and I came back before I was totally recovered.

Hughes said she made the assistant director scribble out that part of his report—and sure enough, decades later, when I got a-hold of that day's paperwork, the notation about Hughes' lateness *was* scribbled over but still readable. The following exchange is from my 2000 interview with Hughes:

TOM WEAVER: The production report you talked about—
HUGHES: I wish I could remember exactly what it said.
WEAVER: You ready to hear it?
HUGHES: Yes!!
WEAVER: Daily Production Report, November 5, 1954—"Unable to get hold of Kathleen Hughes, who promised to be home all day waiting for her call—"
HUGHES: That's such bullshit, I was in bed.
WEAVER: "Casting unable to get hold of her at noon when she was needed. She called at 2:05."
HUGHES: I was home in bed, *and they didn't call me.* They wrote that in the report to cover up their own mistake. I had been in bed for days! ... That's so rotten, and *that* just made it a really, really bad experience. Really the only bad experience I *had*!

William Reynolds told me he didn't recall much interaction with director Lyon:

[H]e was kind of a herder more than a director. When you've got a cast this size doing things, you didn't really have much of a relationship with the director. But under the studio system, most directors had limited authority. There were some who did have authority, for instance, Douglas Sirk, a very important director. At Universal, he may have been one of the very few who really had much autonomy in terms of what he could do, and a final cut, which most other directors did not have. I'm not sure that Lyon had a final cut on *Cult of the Cobra.* Directors were primarily responsible for getting the words and action on film on time. They exercised control by cutting in the camera—in other words, selective coverage. They could do *that*, they weren't totally impotent [*laughs*]. They could do *that* much before the cutters got it.[19]

Presumably Hughes' Julia would have been at Carl's party in the movie, if Hughes hadn't been sick and/or if the above-described mix-up hadn't occurred. Julia's absence from the party scene doesn't make an ounce of difference movie-wise, although it *is* strange that she's nowhere to be seen at the party but *is* in a taxi with Paul going home *from* the party.

Kathleen Hughes looks happy enough in this shot (with Richard Long) but she's still rankled by some of the things that happened on the *Cult* set. And *off* the set: "Up till then I'd always had the big star's dressing room. Well, this was my last Universal film ... and so I had this crummy little canvas dressing room on the set, and it was freezing ... and there were all these holes in the canvas. I was just treated so badly!"

Nearly the entire cast, including the presumably still-ailing Hughes, was on hand the next day, Saturday, November 6, which started on Circle Drive with the shooting of an exterior: Lisa, Paul, Tom, Pete and Carl outside the church after Rico's funeral service. Lisa, Paul and Tom walk along the street toward a horse-drawn cart and the horse whinnies and rears—upset by Lisa's approach. This too is taken from Lewton's meow-sterpiece *Cat People*: In one scene, a kitten sees Irena and gets its back up (Irena to Oliver: "Cats just don't like me"), and in another, Irena gets all the critters in Miss Plunkett's Pet Shoppe in an uproar just by coming through the door.[20] (Miss Plunkett: "Animals are ever so psychic. There are some people who just can't come *in* here.") The rearing horse had been rehearsed the day before and yet the scene did not go smoothly: According to the Production Report, wires were used to make the horse rear, and in the process the wires cut the hand of wrangler Draw Stanfeld, who soon found himself in the studio hospital.

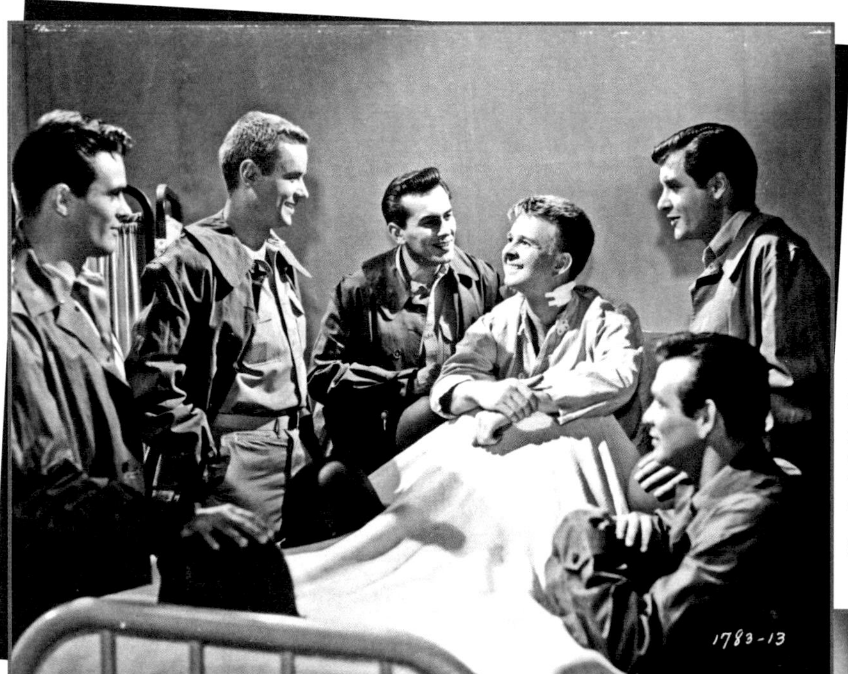

The hospitalized Nick (James Dobson) is all smiles when visited by his buddies (from left, William Reynolds, Marshall Thompson, Jack Kelly, David Janssen [kneeling] and Richard Long). He doesn't know that once they leave, he'll have about two minutes to live. His murder is the curtain-raising work of the Lamian snake woman. (Photographs courtesy Ronald V. Borst/Hollywood Movie Posters.)

In the afternoon, Nick's hospital room scene was shot, starting with the visit by his fellow G.I.s. As with Carl's death scene, and with Rico's to come, Nick's death scene was shot twice, from the point of view of the cobra and also with the prop cobra on-camera. In the movie, there's a storm raging outside during this scene, nature yet again conspiring to bring together lightning, thunder and Universal monsters. That day's last order of business: an unused scene of Julia, in a Philadelphia hotel room, talking on the phone (with Paul supposedly on the other end). Since the movie is set in 1945, it's funny that the assistant director had a dyslexic moment and put 11/6/45 (shoulda been 11/6/54) on the Production Report.

The loopy premise of *Cult of the Cobra* brought out the wannabe comedian in some folks. On November 5, *Variety*'s Army Archerd split his readers' sides with, "Out at UI, *Cult of the Cobra* cast member suggested this new title: *Rebecca of Sunnybrook Fang*." And around the time of the movie's release, Albert D. Ricketts of *Pacific Stars and Stripes* reported that William Reynolds said that "in keeping with the publicity gimmick used to publicize the rollicking comedy *Phffft*, U-I is considering changing the title of *Cult of the Cobra* ... to *Ssssst!*—'Don't say it—slay it!'"[21]

The final week of shooting *Cult* was tough for Domergue: Over the November 6–7 weekend, her director husband Hugo Fregonese returned home from Europe where he'd spent nine weeks scouting locations and prepping for his next movie. Divorce proceedings were in the works—even though, according to "Here There and Hollywood" columnist Frank Morriss, "They say that Faith is carrying quite a hefty torch for her husband, Hugo Fregonese, who is divorcing her"—and his reappearance apparently made the situation tense. Domergue told the Goldrups:

> **The ending of *Cult of the Cobra* was difficult for me because [Fregonese] and I decided to separate; we were getting along very poorly before the film was over, so I was upset. I think the ending was disturbed by that emotional disturbance in my life. But up until that time I was enjoying [making *Cult of the Cobra*] very much.**

Production on Monday, November 8, commenced on a Stage 7 café set with the beer-swilling G.I.s awaiting the arrival of Daru. The scene opens with a shot of a monkey perched in a phonograph horn; the monkey is seen in the background for much of the rest of the scene, a soldier at the bar playing with it for the amusement of a few onlookers. (Filmed but not used: shots of the monkey on the soldier's shoulder, "smoking cigarette in Mae West position"!) At the G.I.s' table, Paul talks earnestly about ancient man-into-animal folklore, prompting Tom to indicate the monkey and derisively quip, "Hey, maybe the professor [Paul] can change that monkey into a beautiful blonde!" According to Army Archerd in *Variety*, the monkey belonged to Kathleen Hughes and it was named Shalimar. Hughes told me that around that time she was *briefly* the custodian of a spider monkey, but doesn't remember its name and doesn't remember letting it appear in *Cult of the Cobra*. A Production Service Memo says the monkey was rented for $25 from Chester Hayes, a monkey trainer-actor-stuntman and, his claim to fame, the guy inside the walking tree Tabanga in *From Hell It Came* (1957).

After lunch the filmmakers returned to the Process Stage and shot Lisa and Tom's hot dog stand scene. (I hesitate to write this without checking more thoroughly, but I believe Cobra Goddess Lisa was the first Universal monster ever to be seen eating a hot dog.) The cook dishing up the wieners is small-time actor and part-time publicist Ben Frommer; in the book *Ed Wood's* Bride of the Monster (BearManor, 2015), Dr. Robert J. Kiss explores his colorful career at some length. Monster Kids may remember Frommer from his small *Bride* role as the belligerent drunk at police headquarters, snarling dialogue at Kelton the Cop ("No tank town jail can hold *me*!"). Apparently *Cult*'s hot dog stand scene was originally meant to be set somewhere other than a New York City street: The *Variety* item "Ballyhooligan Frommer Handing Out Baloney" announced Frommer's casting in *Cult* and added that he "will portray a hot dog vendor in the baseball park sequence." Next came Rico's Car interior shots for the scene in which the ex-G.I. falls victim to the cobra. Again it was done two ways, from the cobra's p.o.v. and with the on-camera prop cobra on the attack.

With about an hour left before the end of the work day, cast and crew moved to Stage 19 and got a start on the Lamian temple scene: Daru and the six airmen, robed and hooded, huddling in the temple entrance as the snake charmer gives them a final briefing on all the (Hin)du's and don't's of crashing a sacred ritual. Daru emphasizes that if they are discovered, they'll be killed, prompting Rico to exclaim, "They'll have to catch me first!"—a funny line to hear coming from future TV *Fugitive* David Janssen.

In the same way that it's fun to see future movie icon Clint Eastwood serving time in *Revenge of the Creature* and *Tarantula*, it's also a kick to find one of 1960s TV's hottest stars, David Janssen, bringing up the rear in *Cult of the Cobra*. For Janssen's Rico, a profaner of the Lamian temple, death comes, not on swift wings but in snakeskin.

> Rico Nardi is a warm-eyed Italian boy with a bland and cheerful outlook. He is full of an eager-beaver naivete, and has a closeness to old-world superstition and tradition which stems from his Italian stock.
>
> —*Cult of the Cobra* script description of Rico

Universal contractee Janssen played minor parts in a number of the studio's movies starting in 1951, until a two-year Army hitch interrupted his fun. Upon his discharge he came right back to Universal and *Chief Crazy Horse*, *To*

Hell and Back (1955) and *Cult.*[22] As Rico, he's fairly natural and likable and gets off a few funny lines, but some still thought there was plenty of room for improvement in the 23-year-old's acting, among them the *Variety* critic who reviewed a 1955 *Lux Video Theatre* episode in which he appeared:

> **David Janssen, who may have the ambitions but not the dimensions of Clark Gable, conjures up a likeness both in voice and general bearing, but the deep breathing must be his own idea to build up for a big scene. He seemed unduly nervous and awkward in his movements. He needs more training.**

William Reynolds told Chris Soldo of the website The David Janssen Archive, "[*Cult*] was actually one of the first good parts that Davey Janssen got at Universal. He was very good in the film, better I think than any of us, which was kind of funny because I don't think anyone expected that from him at that time. Davey was the least experienced of all of the cast, but was probably the most memorable person in the film."

If as a viewer, you expected the sinister Lamian snake ceremony to be performed in a third-world den of shadows, think again...

With just one exception it was boys-only on Stage 19 (the temple set) the next day: the airmen, Daru, the Lamian high priest (John Halloran), dozens of worshippers and the ritual dancers. The snake woman was played by Ruth Carlsson, the Warrior by her husband Carl Carlsson and the shirtless Lamian dancer by Jose Ferran. *Cult of the Cobra*'s Continuity & Dialogue says that Ferran's character represents a sower because he "pantomimes sowing seeds from a wooden bowl," so "the sower" he shall be in this chapter. Presumably they did their routine to music because on the list of Special Equipment is an item you don't see every day, Cobra Dance Records.

The morning was devoted to getting medium shots and long shots of Daru and the G.I.s entering and sitting (or, in Nick's case, standing by a pillar), etc. After lunch, the shooting of the dance began, the camera shooting from the points of view of Paul, Nick and the high priest plus various other angles. In the movie, the Sower and the Warrior are grappling on the floor when the sound of a gong is heard and we cut to a shot of the basket popping open and the cobra woman emerging hands and arms first; she waves her arms like they're snakes and her hands their heads. Filmed but not used: a medium close-up of the high priest watching the fight, turning toward the basket and clapping his hands, and then a whip pan to the basket opening. This was just one of several shots of the high priest destined for the dustbin. Also put on film on the 9th were shots of the high priest kneeling, salaaming and chanting, watching the dance in close-up, reacting to Nick's camera flash in close-up, etc. When a retake of one part of this scene was shot in January 1955, Edward Platt instead of John Halloran played the high priest, so perhaps the number of shots of Halloran was reduced so that audiences wouldn't notice the switch in actors.

John Halloran (1902–68) led an interesting life in which few movie fans have taken any interest. In 1943 when he was LAPD officer Jack Sergel (his real name), a *Popular Mechanics* article revealed that he

> **has made a hobby of personal combat, everything from boxing and wrestling to the knife-throwing of Latin America and "la savate" of France. He knows how the Chinese use the fists, fingertips, knees and elbows in the "sick kung foo" combat drill, and he is one of the few Causasians who have attained the rank of second degree black belt in Japanese judo.**

In 1944, Sergel's status as the nation's top judo expert was mentioned in a newspaper story that caught the eye of producer William Cagney, then casting his brother James' movie *Blood on the Sun*, set in 1929 Tokyo. William contacted Sergel, who changed his name to John Halloran for the movies and played the egg-bald man-mountain baddie Sgt. Oshima of the Imperial Secret Police. Halloran also taught Cagney judo for their climactic battle to the death, a blood-spattered three-minute slobberknocker that's gone down in

The place is clean, brightly fire-lit and richly draped, with tiered seating that makes "every seat a good seat," like they promise you at the ballpark. (Photographs courtesy Ronald V. Borst/Hollywood Movie Posters.)

the books as one of *the* great movie fights. Even *The New York Times*' Grade-A grouch Bosley Crowther dubbed the room-wrecking brawl "a beauty."

Halloran appeared in a number of William Cagney productions and also in several James Cagney starrers, and even in the one movie James directed, *Short Cut to Hell* (1957). Funnily enough, Halloran, who probably had his choice of seven different ways to kill you with his thumb, had his best movie role (after *Blood on the Sun*) in *Angel and the Badman* (1947), playing Gail Russell's *Quaker*(!) father. According to a 1949 press clipping, Halloran taught judo to U.S. Marines during the war and gave Edmond O'Brien judo instruction for a fight scene in Cagney's *White Heat* (1949). A 1950 article called him Cagney's bodyguard and described the wild judo battle that broke out in the star's home when Cagney's former butler Kenneth Kuniyuki, a judo instructor himself, reportedly struck his estranged wife, a domestic there. Halloran "went into action … and soon restrained Kuniyuki." To see Halloran in action without the heavy Japanese makeup of *Blood on the Sun,* catch the *Abbott and Costello Show* episode "Police Rookies": An unbilled Halloran demonstrates judo to police recruits, calling out the name to each move as he mops the floor with an opponent. Prof. Melonhead (Sid Fields) tells Bud and Lou, "This is Jack Halloran, one of the world's foremost judo experts"—and then Halloran mops the floor with Lou.[23]

On November 10, cast and crew shot *Cult*'s opening scene on California Street, which was decked out to look like a bazaar. The set would have been an embarrassment if seen in the opening shot of, say, *Casablanca* but for a movie on the level of *Cult of the Cobra* it was fairly elaborate, with (according to the production paperwork) 77 extras, dogs, burros, goats, chickens, our six G.I.s plus Leonard Strong back in diaper and turban as the snake charmer Daru. The California skies over California Street were heavily overcast throughout the entire day but the moviemakers got their first shot at 9:25 and forged ahead anyway.[24] Listed as a bit player on the Production Report is Harry Mendoza; since he was an actor-illusionist, I'd wager that he's the native with the Chinese linking rings. William Reynolds shared with me a funny memory of the bazaar scene:

I had done *Son of Ali Baba* with Tony Curtis in 1951—in fact, when Tony said his famous line, "Yonda lies the castle of my fodder," the four of us, Tony, me, Piper Laurie and Susan Cabot were on top of a hill on the back lot. Anyway, when we were doing that big opening scene in *Cult of the Cobra*, one of the extras walked by me in this red vest, and I recognized it as my outfit from *Son of Ali Baba*!

On the 11th there was a noon crew call and a return to Stage 19 to shoot the balance of the interior temple footage. A total of 31 extras were on hand, plus a clutch of stuntmen, a few doubling for the stars and others playing Lamians in the fight scene. Carl Carlsson made a second trip to the studio hospital (no reason given in the paperwork) and returned a half-hour later; actor-stuntman Erwin Neal, injured in the fight, later paid the medicos a call. In the movie, as we watch the G.I.s exiting the temple, we hear a man shouting, "Fools! They'll kill you! They'll follow you to—" and a gurgling cry; and then we cut to a crowded long shot that includes the Warrior pulling his sword out of the belly of Daru, who is being held by the Sower and other Lamians. It's so abrupt that it's hard to tell what just happened, and to who. More footage than that *was* shot, but perhaps it was a bit too gruesome for inclusion:

Med [medium] into Stands as Daru stands up and yells to Paul who runs out. Daru follows him but the Lamians grab him. He calls after exiting G.I.s but Warrior runs him thru with his sword.

Leonard Strong, who plays Daru, did his first movies during World War II, often playing Japanese characters at a time when all of Hollywood's Japanese actors, and all of Hollywood's Japanese everything-elses, were "enjoying" the scenic splendor of Montana and Idaho. I don't think Strong *was* Asian, or anything close, but even after the internment camp gates swung open for the Japanese, he continued to play guys with names like Lee Quong, Ming Tang and Hijikata—the latter in *Blood on the Sun* where he and John Halloran provided tag team villainy. *Twilight Zone* fans will remember Strong as the "shabby, silly-looking scarecrow man," trying to thumb a ride with Inger Stevens as she drives ghost to ghost in "The Hitch-Hiker" ("I believe you're going ... *my* way?").

The shooting of the temple scene wrapped at 9:45 p.m. and the moviemakers shifted to the Phantom Stage and got a start on filming the Julia's Dressing Room scene (Julia sees the cobra emerging from her closet and screams). The company wrapped at 11:40 after getting an insert shot of the cobra swaying back and forth.

Cast and crew again shot night-for-night on November 12, this time on the back lot's Tower of London set; with a matte painting of an Asiatic temple obscuring most of it, the Tower "played" the Lamian temple. In one shot, the legs of sandal-wearing Lamians passed the camera as they climbed the stairs—and then the legs of the Americans, all of them wearing G.I. boots. This shot, designed to make audiences worry that the boots will give them away, wasn't used. We find in the script another suspense-building moment that never reached the screen (probably wasn't filmed): As the Air Force men shuffle into the temple, whispering the password to a Lamian "doorman,"

CAMERA TILTS DOWN and we see that the Lamians wear sandals or are barefoot. Suddenly a G.I. boot comes into shot, followed by another.

MED. SHOT—THE HIGH PRIEST

He looks closely at the men as they enter. He looks at Nick, then his eyes start to look down but, at that moment, a Lamian passes close by the priest and, bending close to him whispers in his ear. The G.I.s move quickly toward the interior.

One stuntman, Allen Pinson, is on the list of players, so presumably he's the Lamian brawling with Carl on the colonnade. Starting at about 8:30 p.m., the moviemakers photographed silent shots of Lisa, caught in the Jeep's headlights, hurrying away from the fallen body of Nick, then shots of Tom searching an alley for Lisa as she hides behind a large box. It was after midnight when the troupe moved to Brownstone Street, where a building on one side of the street represented Paul and Tom's apartment house and a building on the *other* side of the street represented Carl's.[25] In the wee hours, Domergue and Thompson did one scene on each of the two locations. The scene shot in front of Carl's apartment is yet another that didn't survive into the movie; it obviously would have followed the party scene where Tom plastered Carl:

LMS [Long Medium Shot] Tom & Lisa come to MCU [Medium Close-up]—dolly them as he tells her that he's angry because she's his girl—she denies it & tells him he's acting like a child, but he insists he's crazy about her.

The company was dismissed at 1:59 a.m. Again on Saturday, November 13, the 17th and last day of production, there was a late crew call (1:54 p.m.), with filming beginning on the Phantom Stage's Julia's Dressing Room set with a cobra p.o.v. shot of "Julia's frightened feet" as she tries without success to open a window and then cowers in a corner. *More* shots not in the movie: "MS Julia as cobra rises into f.g. follow cobra closer thru above action until close on Julia" and "Julia thru above action, but with cobra's shadow on her." Arriving in the nick of cinema time is Tom, tossing a stole over the cobra and heaving a chair at the window. (Notice that the chair breaks only a few panes, but in the next shot that shows the window, all the glass and even the muntin are gone, as though someone had shoved a king-sized air conditioner clean through it.) Next they got shots from the other side of the window (Tom using the coat tree to push the cobra out the window and off the balcony, Tom and Julia looking down from the balcony). They were of course working with a prop cobra, but Kathleen Hughes said she'd have worked with a real McCoy if need be: "I wouldn't have minded, I'm not really afraid of snakes. I once helped somebody feed a boa constrictor—I held onto part of it as it was force-fed."

Then it was back to Brownstone Street, where Lisa ducks into hiding as she sees Carl and Marian exiting Carl's apartment house. Next came the shot of Carl's fallen body at the foot of his apartment house steps; it's a nice touch that the entrance canopy is obviously damaged, indicating that he fell through it. Amidst the many gawking extras, one spectator (played by Larry Williams) tells Pete, "Some guy jumped." The Daily Production Report indicates that Pete notices fang marks on Carl's neck, but this doesn't happen in the movie. Brownstone Street then became the site of Rico's Bowling Alley, with a high medium long shot (booming in) of Rico loading a case of beer into the back of his car. Here we get Universal's required-by-law "hand on the shoulder" moment, as Mrs. Weber (Helen Wallace) the Salvation Army woman appears behind Rico, tapping him on the back and then hitting him up for a donation. As the clock neared midnight, the filmmakers got the eerie insert shot of the nearly closed bowling alley front door opening wider "as if some sinuous body were working its way through below the frameline." The

Julie (Kathleen Hughes) stands clear as Tom (Marshall Thompson) contends with the reptilian dressing room invader. Surely the Cobra Goddess was the first Universal Monster to be dispatched with a coat tree.

first of the movie's two *completely* ineffectual "Lewton busses" came as Carl, walking along the sidewalk, stops as a noisy street sweeper passes. Principal photography ended at two a.m. Sunday morning with a shot of Rico's car on its side on Brownstone Street, the camera dollying in on Rico's half-in half-out body. (In the movie the shot is run in reverse.)

"Production completed this date" is written on the bottom of the November 13 production report. Days later, gossip queen Louella O. Parsons told her readers:

> **Faith Domergue is an unhappy girl now that she feels there's no chance for her and Hugo Fregonese to get back together. She'll file for divorce in Santa Monica within the next 10 days—and then she's off on a two months trip to forget it all.**
>
> **She completes *The Cult of the Cobra* at U-I this weekend and takes a few days rest before the ordeal of getting her divorce.**
>
> **I hear Faith has already booked passage for the Bahamas, Haiti and Puerto Rico.**

Life went on for *Cult* co-star Richard Long. Five days after the end of principal photography, November 18, *Variety*'s Army Archerd wrote that Long and Suzan Ball had postponed the Chi Chi debut of their act until January, *Cult of the Cobra* having curtailed Long's rehearsal time. On December 20, a few days after Long's 27th birthday, gossip guru Louella Parsons revealed that

> **[v]ery quietly, Suzan Ball and Dick Long have gone to Phoenix where they will open their night club act at the Westward Ho.**
>
> **A few months ago, Suzan and Dick arranged to open at the Chi Chi in Palm Springs but I can tell you now that it was impossible at that time for Suzan to perfect the muscular movements necessary to their act.**
>
> **Now she is so much better and has learned to manage her artificial limb so efficiently that they will go from Phoenix to the Chi Chi and eventually to the Pot of Gold in Las Vegas.**

In mid-January 1955, two months after *Cult of the Cobra* wrapped, cast members returned for three days of retakes, added scenes and inserts. During principal photography, the interior temple set was on Stage 19 but on Saturday, January 15, a shot of the high priest being driven back by a torch-wielding Rico and pronouncing the curse on the temple defilers was shot on the Phantom Stage. In the role of the priest, previously played by John Halloran, was day player Edward Platt. Platt was on the set on time at 11 a.m., enacted the short scene several times and was dismissed at one p.m. If you're enough of a Baby Boomer TV-holic, it's funny that in the movie, the first to die after being cursed by Platt (*Get Smart*'s Chief of CONTROL) is Daru, played by Leonard Strong (*Get Smart*'s KAOS villain "The Claw"). Platt looks and sounds off the dial in fury as he delivers the movie's key lines but it's John Halloran, seen only in distant long shots where he's practically lost in the crowd, who gets on-screen billing for playing the high priest. A few months later, Platt played his best early movie role as the police juvenile officer who "connects" with troubled teen James Dean in *Rebel Without a Cause* (1955). When Platt returned to the fantasy genre five years later, it was in George Pal's *Atlantis, the Lost Continent*—playing *another* high priest.

The moviemakers remained on the Phantom Stage for other shots: Lisa in her apartment; Paul, the inspector and two cops in Lisa's apartment; Lisa in Carl's apartment. After the dinner break they again shot outside the Editorial Building: the police car arriving on the scene and Lisa lying on the pavement in front of the car. One interesting additional shot (not used): "MED. FULL SHOT … GIRL in snake dancer's costume … lying on street in front of Police Car." The best action that night happened behind the scenes: During a dolly shot of the police car, the camera dolly was tied *to* the moving car until it came loose and crashed into a railing, breaking off a wheel. This created a 20-minute delay. The rest of the night was spent getting up-from-the-street shots of the cobra being pushed off the balcony edge (right into the camera, 3-D-style, in the shot used in the movie), the cobra in various positions in front of the police car, etc.

On Monday the 17th, the camera first rolled on Stage 7 in the mid-afternoon, getting Lisa's Bedroom shots of Lisa, her shadow on the wall and the cobra's shadow on the wall. Additional Paul and Tom's Apartment footage followed. There was a 6:30-to-7:00 meal break and then the troupe reconvened on Brownstone Street for a not-in-the-movie cobra's-p.o.v. shot in which the reptile approaches a window of Lisa's apartment house. Then they re-shot part of the scene where Pete finds a crowd gathered around Carl's body on the street. This time uncredited bit player Don Dillaway played the onlooker who delivers the line, "Some guy just jumped," and it's Dillaway (rather than Larry Williams, who did it the first time around) who wound up in the movie. The next scene to be redone: Rico, loading the case of beer into the back of his car, being half-scared to death by a tap on the back from Mrs. Weber.

Once that scene was re-shot and Janssen was dismissed at 12:40 a.m., it was all Faith Domergue: various shots in which Lisa walks down the street, into an alley, reacts to a scared, yowling cat on a brownstone stoop, etc. Because of several "N.G." shots of the cat, filming that short scene took over an hour. Domergue's last shot of the night (and, presumably, her last shot of the movie) was *Cult*'s second unsuccessful "Lewton bus": Lisa is walking along the sidewalk, headed for Carl's, when a police car, its brakes squealing, rolls into the foreground, a policeman climbing out and making a beeline for a phone box. In the 21st century, Lewton busses still "work" but (Francis D.) Lyon busses are still dull enough for sleeping. In fact, Lyon's *Cult of the Cobra* busses are so *in*effective that probably most viewers don't realize they were meant to startle.[26]

Friday, January 21, the third and last day of post-production shooting, was a short one, with just two performers: James Dobson and the prop cobra. First, on Stage 7, with the camera on a special rig, the filmmakers got a subjective (cobra's-eye) shot as it approaches the window of Rico's Bowling Alley. Next they got more footage for Nick's hospital room death scene:

MED. SHOT ... EXT. HOSPITAL GROUNDS Cobra slides thru brush and is disclosed by brief flash of lightning.

CLOSER SHOT ... Cobra slides thru brush and is disclosed by brief flash of lightning.

INT. HOSPITAL ROOM—CLOSE SHOT ... toward open window ... as Snake Head appears outside ... enters thru open window ... and starts down to floor.

LOW ANGLE—Camera starts moving thru bushes toward window. Moves up wall to open window ... to see Nick lying in hospital bed.

CAMERA MOVES down from window ... crosses floor to bed.... MOVES UP toward NICK, who is lying in the bed ... as Camera moves in toward him, Snake Shadow appears.... Nick reacts.

INSERT—Nick's neck ... showing two fang marks.

In the movie, we *do* get to see the cobra on the ground outside Nick's room, but not inside.

Richard Long appeared in retakes on January 15 and 17, and on the 19th he and Suzan Ball opened their act at the Chi Chi in Palm Springs. On February 4, the day after Suzan's 21st birthday, it was off to New York for the lovebirds: They did two weeks of public appearances, thumping the tub for Suzan's *Chief Crazy Horse*. On the 13th they were on Ed Sullivan's *Toast of the Town*, and there was talk that they'd again reteam for TV in an episode of *Climax!* This New

The coroner's report on Carl's death says, "Death from asphyxiation due to snake venom." That's some mighty fast-acting venom if it killed him between the time he fell off the terrace and hit the sidewalk. (Photograph courtesy Ronald V. Borst/Hollywood Movie Posters.)

York trip was also their delayed honeymoon. At some point Ball and Long took their song-and-dance act to Ball's native Buffalo, New York. Comeback kid Suzan must have thought that things were going good, all things considered—and, of course, without the knowledge that she still had cancer and the end was on the horizon.[27]

Eventually it was decided that the awful truth couldn't be kept from her any longer. Long was at her bedside continuously, and refused to talk with newsmen, so the papers included conflicting reports. Some made it sound as though Ball was coping bravely, but others were less rosy, and eventually readers learned that she was in a sanitarium, often in an oxygen tent, and on the brink of death from lung cancer. She was now less than 100 pounds and had special nurses around the clock. According to Kirk Crivello's book *Fallen Angels*' chapter on Ball, Long "slid into an affair with Suzan's nurse Kay Biddle. The relationship became something of a bond among the three but ended with Suzan's death." The sanitarium mentioned above has to be City of Hope Medical Center where Ball underwent 25 days of diagnostic study before leaving in an ambulance for a "secret hideout" to continue her cancer fight.

Right at that same time, probably out of financial necessity, Long (now no longer a contractee at his alma mater, Universal) began playing a co-starring role in the Western *Fury at Gunsight Pass* at the Columbia Ranch. Marshall Thompson came to that set to deliver heartbreak to Long on August 5, 1955.[28]

• •

> [*Cult of the Cobra* director] Francis D. Lyon is no Jacques Tourneur. ... Ultimately it's the inescapably galumphing U-I grade B obviousness that does in what must have seemed at the time like an attempt at a slightly classier horror pic. ... Overall, nothing to be ashamed of, but nothing special either.
>
> —Joe Dante on the Classic Horror Film Board

That about sums it up. The big problem with *Cult of the Cobra* is that the average viewer isn't much inclined to *like* any of the airmen. The first thing these extremely Ugly Americans do is invade a religious ceremony, half in the bag (or in Nick's case, blind drunk). In order to escape, they beat up worshippers and set the place on fire. Snake charmer Daru, who warned them time and again that they mustn't be detected, is seized by Lamians thanks to the recklessness of Nick, the #1 G.I. Jerk. As Paul, Tom, Pete and Carl fight their way out as a unit, not one shows any interest in the plight of helpless Daru. Not even subsequently do the airmen show an ounce of remorse over getting the old guy slaughtered; his body probably isn't yet cold when the boys are in Nick's hospital room yukking it up over the night's hijinks.

In Manhattan, Tom shows himself up to be a rather nasty sore loser when Julia opts for Paul. Carl comes across as a bit sleazy (but he doesn't deserve it when Tetchy Tom hangs one on him). We don't see enough of Pete or Rico to know if they're okay guys or not, but the fact that they're unfazed (as far as we can tell) after causing Daru's death may indicate "not." Once the Cobra Goddess makes the scene, it becomes obvious that most or all of the boys will die, and the viewer is mildly curious and *perhaps* mildly sorry, but that's all. The movie has suspense aspirations but because the people getting killed have heavy-duty misdeeds to thank for their troubles, the movie is a lightweight in the scare department; terrible things happen in the service of very little terror or discomfort. It might have squeaked by if it was done with some style; but it isn't.

Cult of the Cobra is the one Universal genre flick of the '50s to employ scare tactics scavenged from Lewton's plate and one of the few that tries to deliver a light tap or two on the anvil of human emotions. The scenes devoted to Lisa and Tom's Futile Attraction are refreshingly "different" and it's commendable that the moviemakers at least *tried*. But as far as getting audience members to empathize, it couldn't have the full desired effect since one of the lovers is a petulant sorehead, the other a snake woman on a world tour of death.

William Reynolds told me, "The story was kinda preposterous, but the acting paid it off and made it more believable. *Unlike*, say, *The Land Unknown* [Reynolds' next monster movie], whose premise was logical ... interesting ... and the body of it became preposterous!"

Marginalia

• The first paragraph of this chapter says that the Bride of Frankenstein and Dracula's Daughter were the Universal Horrors cycle's first femme monsters. I wrote that because I know the value of name recognition, and in the sure and certain hope that most readers would not recall the brides of Dracula, very briefly seen in the opening reels of the cycle's kick-off movie *Dracula* (1931). In fact, in *Dracula*, and even in the Spanish *Dracula*, we see one of the brides before we see Dracula, so *the very first Universal Monster ever seen* was a woman.

In more breaking news from the "full disclosure" front, some might say that Universal's first '50s femme fiend was Glob Ellen from *It Came from Outer Space*. But since we're given no clue as to the gender of that particular shapeshifting Xenomorph, Glob Ellen has been scratched from the competition.

• In *Cult of the Cobra*'s main titles, director of photography Russell Metty gets a card of his own, making *Cult* Universal's only '50s monster-horror flick where the d.p. credit fills the screen. In the good ol' days of the studio system, guys like Metty built up filmographies on which you can find wonderful tripe (*Cult of the Cobra*, 1958's *Monster on the Campus*, etc.) commingled with Hall of Fame titles like *Bringing Up Baby* (1938), *Touch of Evil* (1958), *Spartacus* (1960), for which he won an Oscar, and more. Francis D. Lyon wrote in his autobiography *Twists of Fate*, "*Cult of the Cobra* went along smoothly with a good cast and a crew headed by Russell Metty, a very good cinematographer."

• A Universal Weekly Layoff Report says that Susan Cabot did "wardrobe" for *Cult of the Serpent* on August 2, 1954. Was she up for a part? Did she sew on buttons? Your guess is as good as mine. But it's fun to entertain the notion that the Wasp Woman may have been in the running to play the Cobra Woman.

• On October 21, 1954, the eve of the start of production, Sylvia Blumberg from the office of Universal's director of public relations William Gordon notified *Cult* producer Howard Pine via a memo that a dialogue reference to a Coke and the use of a Coke machine as a prop should be dropped; that there could be no dialogue reference to Manhattan's Stork Club "since it is contrary to studio policy to use actual names of clubs, restaurants and hotels"; and that Universal was reaching out to stage star Mary Martin to see if she'd allow the use of her name in the dialogue of one scene. Did Universal fail to contact her, or did she opt out of being name-dropped in a snake woman flick? Inquiring minds want to know!

• Universal didn't want to specify the native country of the snake worshippers, perhaps to avoid offense to that country so that *Cult of the Cobra* could someday play there. But according to *The AFI Catalog*, an October 1954 *Hollywood Reporter* news item identifies the locale as Burma. In his October 23, 1954, *Los Angeles Times* column, Philip K. Scheuer announced Faith Domergue's casting as "a native Burma beaut." Around that same time, columnist Louella O. Parsons summarized the movie as "the story of a Burmese girl who can turn herself into a cobra at will."

• Probably because the bazaar scene is the opening scene, at least one version of the script called for the main titles and credits to be "overlaid on a SCENE over the shabby awning-and-gunnysack roofs of the stands of an open-air Bazaar. The DOWN ANGLE SHOT REVEALS, in the strong sunlight, intriguing glimpses of seething activity in the cracks and alleyways between the awnings. There is sufficient solidity in the tawdry coverings to make a good b.g. for titles and credits." Under the accompanying music, we were to have heard the voices of merchants and customers, barking dogs, clucking hens, etc. Behind the credits in the movie as released is a stone slab bearing symbolic carvings of cobras and the cobra goddess. We later see it in the Lamian temple, behind the Cobra Goddess' basket.

• (T)urban renewal! *Abbott and Costello Meet the Mummy* (1955) was made in October-November 1954, right alongside *Cult of the Cobra*, and Universal saved a few shekels by having them share a couple of sets. *Cult*'s Lamian temple interior is also Klaris' subterranean crypt room, which looks much bigger in the Abbott and Costello movie without the curtains and seats we see in *Cult*. The same set is seen again at the end of *Meet the Mummy*, redressed as the swanky Klub Klaris, with the Cobra Goddess' shrine now a bandstand for musicians in mummy wrappings. *Cult* and *Meet the Mummy* both shot their bazaar scenes on California Street, probably with a lot of the same booths and extras and everything else. At one point in that bazaar scene, Costello plays a flute and a cobra rises out of a basket behind him—and it sure looks like Daru's cobra. The two movies undoubtedly also used a lot of the same turbans, robes, props and more. Perhaps for this reason, they do not appear to have ever been double-billed.

• Even though the G.I.s are told that they'll be risking their lives by entering the temple, they're awfully casual about it: They show up after a night of drinking, don't do much to hide their white faces, their G.I. boots poke out of the bottoms of their robes, and Paul speaks English within earshot of Lamians. Pete appears to be chewing gum as he gawks at the ceremony; or maybe in his robe he has a bag of popcorn. And as they make their escape, we see that they couldn't have parked their Jeep a foot closer to the temple without driving up the stairs!

• Notice that in the temple scene, the Lamian cultists keep their faces hidden inside their hoods more carefully than the infidel intruders do. I'll betcha this was because most or all of these extras and stuntmen were as Caucasian as the actors playing the G.I.s. A sea of white-bread faces, combined with the robes, hoods and torches, would have made this look more like a Klan shindig than an Asian religious ceremony. One of the Lamians is stuntman Richard Farnsworth; as an actor, he later received Oscar nominations for *Comes a Horseman* (1978) and *The Straight Story* (1999).

• A sign of the changing times: Today there'd be a sentence of death—*career* death—to any moviemaker who shot a scene set in an Asian temple full of worshippers, high priests and dancers and used nothing but crackers!

• After the snake woman emerges from the basket, she lies on her back on the floor, puts her feet against the basket, pushes off hard and slides away—and the basket doesn't budge. But later we see that it's an ordinary, nearly weightless fiber basket. As she slides on her belly across the floor toward the feet of the Warrior, and then up the side of the Warrior, she is doing nothing to locomote herself. These little touches, once you notice them, give her a supernatural quality.

• The first time Jack Kelly's name appeared in the credits of a movie, and the first time he had a decent-sized part, it was *Where Danger Lives* (1950), which opens with Kelly as a hospital doctor attending a girl who's just attempted suicide. The girl: Faith Domergue in *her* first starring movie. (*Where Danger Lives* preceded *Vendetta* into release.)

• In the movie as released, Rico, closing his bowling alley for the night, goes into a small room behind the lanes, bolts the back door and turns out the light; in the background, the curtain on a window is moving slightly in the breeze. This is the only time we see this room. But the original plan was to draw out the tension a bit more, and the necessary footage *was* shot. If all of it had been used, this is what we would have seen: Rico goes into the back room, bolts the door, turns out the light and *closes the window*. A bit later, in an insert shot, we would have seen the window slowly opening. After the tenpin mysteriously falls, Rico puts it back in place, and then hears a noise from the back room. Investigating, he finds the window open and closes it again.

• *Cult*'s Marshall Thompson, Jack Kelly and David Janssen were also in Universal's *To Hell and Back* that same year. In *Cult*, Lisa kills two out of three, giving her a better batting average than the whole German Army did against them.

• Hey, maybe there *is* something to this curse business: With the exception of William Reynolds, *still* in the land of the living at the time of this writing, not one of the actors playing the G.I.s got to be old men. Marshall Thompson, Jack Kelly and James Dobson all died in their mid-60s, David Janssen at 48, Richard Long at 47.

• Cobra bites aren't instantly fatal, not even close, so the deaths of Nick and Pete don't make serpentine sense; even though snakebit, both coulda-shoulda hotfooted it away from the incident to seek medical help. Okay, let's say for Universal Monsters' sake that the venom of a Cobra Goddess *is* industrial strength and gets the job done in jig time ... but if that's the case, why did Nick survive his first cobra bite?

• Paul and Julia's taxi scene is preceded by a stock footage nighttime shot of a taxi zipping along Broadway in Times Square. *Cult of the Cobra* is set in the mid-1940s but in the stock shot you can't fail to notice that one movie theater is playing *Wagon Master* and another *Bright Leaf*, both 1950 releases. Run the shot in slo-mo and squint like crazy and you'll see that a third theater, the Gotham, is playing director Jack Arnold's *With These Hands*, also 1950. There's a photo of the Gotham in this book's *It Came from Outer Space* chapter.

• *Way* too much of *Cult of the Cobra* takes place at the apartment house where Lisa, Paul and Tom live: We first see it at around the 24-minute mark and then spend more than half of the rest of the running time there, a half-hour-plus. By the time the picture's over, you feel like you ought to chip in a few bucks toward the rent!

• The U-I scare tactic "The shadow isn't what it appears to be" is employed in *Cult* when Tom is sleeping on Lisa's couch and what looks like the shadow of the cobra falls on him—but it turns out to be Lisa. The script called for a second such scene: Lisa and Tom return to his apartment after Carl's party; Tom goes into the darkened kitchen and struggles to get an ice cube tray out of the refrigerator. As he does so, what looks like the cobra shadow, weaving and swaying, appears on his back. Eventually he pulls the tray free—and we see that the shadow was cast by part of a tropical plant on a nearby ledge. This vignette was in the "Fooled ya!" tradition of the Joshua tree silhouette mistaken for a monster in *It Came from Outer Space* and the monkey shadow mistaken for the giant spider in *Tarantula*.

Faith Domergue lies dead in the alley as Walter Coy and Richard Long look up in *Cult*'s imitation *Cat People* finish. Reviewer Mark Clark wrote in *Filmfax*, "There are so many similarities [that the *Cult* scripter] should have shared his story credit with Lewton!" (Photograph courtesy Ronald V. Borst/Hollywood Movie Posters.)

Cult's co-feature *Revenge of the Creature* also had a "Fooled ya!" shadow moment in the script but not the movie: On the grounds of Clete and Helen's motel where the Gill Man is on the prowl, "a weird, crouching shadow" frightens Clete until he realizes it's the shadow of a tree.

• Investigating Carl's death, the New York police take blood from suspects Pete, Paul and Tom and compare it to the blood on the statue. You'd think that New York's Finest would have noticed that the statue blood was snake blood and wouldn't have felt the need to try to find a suspect whose blood matched.

• In the kitchen scene where Lisa eerily invades Julia's space, the tension is broken by a knock on the door—a laundry man is making a delivery. The laundry man is unbilled actor Bing Russell, the father of a three-year-old who'd grow up to be a movie star, Kurt Russell.

• The cobra appears to be an average-sized specimen so in the cobra p.o.v. shot where it goes after Carl, we should be looking way up at him. But Carl is obviously gaping at something as tall as he is.

• As usually happens in movies of this sort, you can count on deaths occurring in roughly the reverse order of the actors' billing. Killed in rapid succession on the same night, the first casualties are Leonard Strong and James Dobson (ninth- and tenth-billed, respectively), followed by David Janssen (eighth), Jack Kelly (sixth) and William Reynolds (fifth). The movie ends with the death of top-billed Faith Domergue.

• I love the modern-day *Cult of the Cobra* reviewers who mockingly point out that in the climactic theater alley scene, when the dead cobra morphs into the body of Lisa, she's in the evening gown she wore before her snakesformation. Supernatural magic changing woman into snake, snake into woman, over and over, apparently these fans found this perfectly believable throughout, but when the gown materializes—*now* the fans feel they've caught the movie in a mistake, something that couldn't possibly happen, and they call the moviemakers to account on it.

Fandumb. It gets fandumber every year.

• In the movie's final reel, Tom hears Julia's screaming in her theater dressing room, barges in, sees the cobra and goes right into hero mode. But in the script there's a moment of hesitation because Tom "is sharply and terrifyingly aware that the snake beneath him is indeed Lisa. For a tense second he holds the chair motionless." Then, however, he turns pest exterminator, using the coat tree to push the beast out the window and then over the edge of the ledge. By the time Tom and Julia look down, the body of Lisa is under the front bumper of the police car.

Tom and Julia come down into the alley, Julia hurrying into the protective arms of Paul while Tom, overcome with emotion, kneels beside Lisa's body. From the script:

> The sight of Julia with Paul and the sudden shocked realization that this is the end of Lisa's life is too much for [Tom]. Still looking at Julia [off-screen], Tom starts to cry—at first slightly; then with utter disregard of those around him. He lowers his face and at the same time turns away, rising to his feet again.

He then starts walking away from Lisa:

> As if the crowd senses that this is something that they must not interfere in, they begin to part for him and [the moving camera halts and holds on Tom] as he goes through the crowd and alone towards the shaft of light coming from the stage door. He lurches drunkenly towards this light and passes through it into the darkness beyond.

In the movie Tom does not cry, and he walks not toward the stage door but toward the street—but probably most viewers still sympathize with him a bit, even if he *is* a boor. In the horror movie world, it's the most downbeat ending for the leading man since Robert Paige in *Son of Dracula* (1943), a movie whose ending approaches the dignity of authentic tragedy.[29]

Dracula's Daughter (Gloria Holden, top) is a vampire and Lisa Moya's (Faith Domergue) a cobra but, to paraphrase Cyndi Lauper, each wants to be the one to walk in the sun 'cause "Ghouls Just Want to Have Fun."

• Plot-wise, *Cult of the Cobra* is so clearly modeled after *Cat People* that you'd think the writers would have called it quits after showing us Lisa's effect on the freaked-out dog and horse and spared us the scene with ... the *cat*. And maybe they shouldn't have hired a director named Lyon! Another potentially homicidal half-human (or is she?): the amusement park "mermaid" (Linda Lawson) in the Val Lewton-inspired *Night Tide* (1963).

• Every Monster Kid and his brother has noticed *Cult*'s indebtedness to *Cat People* but there are also definite echoes of *Dracula's Daughter* (1936). Like Lisa Moya, Dracula's daughter, Countess Zaleska (Gloria Holden), wants to leave her supernatural past behind; wants to be "[f]ree to live as a woman, free to take my place in the bright world of the living. ... I can live a normal life now, *think* normal things." When she's attracted to a mortal man, psychiatrist Jeffrey Garth (Otto Kruger), who doesn't know she's a vampire, she doubles down on achieving that goal. These two *femmes fatale* are both globe-trotters (Lisa: Asia to New York; the countess: Transylvania to London), both aspire to normalcy, both are perhaps emboldened now that they're far from their haunted homelands and evil influences (Lisa: the Lamians; the countess: dear old Dad). And both dislike having other women interested in their man, with Lisa stalking Julia and the countess targeting Garth's assistant (Marguerite Churchill). Even the twin bite marks on their victims' throats are identical. The reluctant, conflicted Lisa is the countess' sister under the (snake)skin.

• The moviemakers shot the death scenes of Nick, Rico and Carl two ways, with and without the cobra on camera, and opted for the latter. Eighteen minutes into the movie we see the cobra in the shrubbery outside Nick's hospital room and then we don't see it again until it slithers out of Julia's dressing room closet at the 77-minute mark...

• ...which raises a question. What if *Cult of the Cobra* had gone 100-percent hifaLewton, and for most of the footage, we never saw the snake? Just subjective shots of each of the temple desecrators as they're scratched off the Lamians' death ledger. Until the last reel, we wouldn't know if the killer was Lisa or Snake Lisa. We wouldn't know if there *was* a Snake Lisa. We wouldn't know for sure if the killer *was* Lisa. To create this alternate version of the movie, all they'd have had to do was delete the shot of the snake in the hospital shrubbery (and shots featuring the snake's shadow) and eliminate the superimposures of the snake eye. This new approach would physically change the movie very little—the loss of a few shots and a few superimposures—but psychologically it would have changed it completely. Would that have made *Cult of the Cobra* better or worse?

• "CAN A WOMAN'S **Beauty** BE TRANSFORMED INTO A THING OF TERROR TO FULFILL THE CURSE OF THE COBRA WORSHIPPERS?"—this long-winded question is posed in the trailer, much of which is scored with rootin'-tootin' music that sounds like it came from one of Universal's 1940s cowboy B-movies. The trailer gives us an alternate take of the high priest cursing the G.I.s plus not-in-the-movie shots of Pete and Carl holding off temple Lamians with torches (in the background, Daru is being restrained by the Sower and men in temple shrouds); the G.I.s high-tailing it out of the temple; and Tom armed with the wooden chair in Julia's dressing room.

• When the movie ends ... is it really over? The Lamians' homicidal box score is incomplete with Paul and Tom still among the living. It might have been fun to have the movie end with an indication that another exotic young woman, with beauty enough to give her access to Paul and Tom's world, lies in their future.

• Universal's May 11, 1955, Summary of Production Budget reveals that *Cult* had total direct charges of $364,900, with 26.75 percent studio overhead boosting that figure to $462,511. Outside talent Faith Domergue got $10,000, Marshall Thompson $3500, Jack Kelly $2000, Leonard Strong $1167, Walter Coy $875 and James Dobson $600. Director Francis D. Lyon made $6000. This summary also reveals that writer Jerry Davis worked on the movie first, starting on April 12, 1954, followed by Cecil Maiden, who started July 30, and then Richard Collins, who started October 7.

• This is faint praise, but on the short list of vintage woman-into-reptile movies, *Cult of the Cobra* is by far the best. The other contenders, both English-made, are:

• *The Snake Woman* (1961), the first directing credit for Sidney J. Furie, is so junky that it should have left the up-and-comer down and out, and yet Furie went on to a lengthy mainstream career. In 1890 Northumberland, a doctor gives his pregnant wife snake venom to cure her insanity. It works, but the baby grows up into a pretty gal (Susan Travers) who lives in the woods and, in snake form, puts a dent in the population of the nearby village. Even if a Monster Kid has prepared for *The Snake Woman* by setting his brain on "low," the story is still annoyingly senseless, and some of the hisstrionics are hiss-terical ("I have *chaaaarms* to ward off *eee*-ville!"). At least *Cult of the Cobra*'s Lisa doesn't shed her skin and leave it lying around in the woods for the hero to find and talk to, before he realizes what it *is*!

• Hammer's *The Reptile* (1966) is set in Clagmoor, Cornwall, where a half-human creature, dimly seen but obviously of the female persuasion, attacks several bit players, who wear blackface and froth at the mouth to show that they're dead. Ray Barrett, the brother of a victim, arrives with wife Jennifer Daniel to investigate. A local theologian (Noel Willman) has a shrinking-violet daughter (Jacqueline Pearce) whose status as the only other female in the story makes it impossible not to guess that she's the monster. The minutes pass like hours before we learn that, years ago in Burma, Willman antagonized some snake worshippers and they've taken revenge by making Pearce a part-time snake woman. Who saw *that* coming? The "mystery" is so transparent that one flatters the movie by calling it a mystery. Scripter Anthony Hinds used a pseudonym, and the reason for *that* shouldn't be a mystery either.

The Reptile is a flat-out bore *but*—Roy Ashton did a bang-up makeup job; surely I wasn't the only knee-high Monster Kid who stared long and hard at shots of the face of the ferocious-looking Reptile in the old monster mags. Which makes me idly wonder if the reputation of *Cult of the Cobra* would be better or worse if Lisa had morphed, *not* into a cobra, but into a half-human female fiend like the Reptile, the Jungle Woman, the Wasp Woman, etc. Faith Domergue was glad it didn't happen that way, telling *Fangoria*, "I didn't transform into a snake like, say, Lon Chaney Jr. changed into the Wolf Man, so I was lucky in that way."

• A production company called Stampede Entertainment, responsible for the *Tremors* movies and the Sci-Fi Channel's short-lived *Tremors* series, approached Universal Home Video about doing sequels and/or remakes of some of their monster oldies. The only titles Universal was willing to discuss were *Cult of the Cobra, Tarantula, The Mole People, The Deadly Mantis* and *The Leech Woman.* The one that got developed was *Cult of the Cobra*; Stampede's Greg Stevens wrote the script, which got him into the Writers Guild. But then the Home Video people lost interest, and it all came to nothing.

• Think of *Cult of the Cobra* as a consolation prize for every Baby Boomer Monster Kid who ever tuned in to his local *Creature Features* the week they ran Universal's strictly off-the-cob *Cobra Woman* (1944) and found himself with egg on his face after 90 minutes of Maria Montez South Seas adventure-nonsense-mush, and nary a cobra woman in sight.

The Release
By Robert J. Kiss

Although many Monster Kids maintain a sense of nostalgic affection for *Cult of the Cobra*, the history of its first run at theaters is that of a picture in which Universal appears to have lost confidence prior to release. It was rather spontaneously attached as a supporting feature to the studio's *Creature from the Black Lagoon* sequel *Revenge of the Creature*, so that it could turn some profit by piggybacking on that movie's box office appeal. Beyond that, it was effectively relegated to the status of low-rent second-feature fare. Newspaper movie critics paid scant attention to *Cult*, usually mentioning it at the tail end of their *Revenge of the Creature* reviews, and for the most part glossing over it in a throwaway sentence that commenced with the words "Also on the bill is...," "On the same program is..." or "The co-feature is...." Though *Cult* made it onto *Boxoffice* magazine's "*Boxoffice* Barometer"—charting the performance of first-run features in major U.S. cities—some five times between April 23 and June 4, 1955, this was never on the strength of its own merits, but solely as a "piggybacker" on the relative commercial success of *Revenge of the Creature*, just as Universal had envisaged.

Television critic Rob Word, in his "Focus on Entertainment" column of April 11, 1976, was probably the first to characterize *Cult of the Cobra* as a picture that had come to possess greater appeal retrospectively than it had enjoyed during its original release. Under the headline "Old star-studded horror film not big success but is now more interesting than ever before," he expounded:

> **Major new movies have a tendency to cast every lead part with a big "name" star. [*The*] *Towering Inferno* featured Steve McQueen, Paul Newman, Richard Chamberlain and William Holden while George C. Scott, Anne Bancroft, Roy Thinnes and Gig Young cavorted endlessly aboard *The Hindenburg*. Two giant box office successes. Two tense films filled with shocks and superstars.**
>
> **The stars mentioned above have worked often on television and all except Holden, Newman and Bancroft have started [sic] in their own series.**
>
> **What if a horror film were made starring other successful television actors? Would it too be a hit? Well, a star-studded horror film was made. It was called *Cult of the Cobra* and starred Richard "*Big Valley*" Long, David "*Harry O*" Janssen, Jack "*Maverick*" Kelly, Marshall "*Daktari*" Thompson, William "*The F.B.I.*" Reynolds and Edward "*Get Smart*" Platt. It was extremely well done but only marginally successful.**
>
> **...Today *Cult of the Cobra* is more fun to watch than ever before. With every showing, the film gains new admirers. Not very special when it first came out, *Cult of the Cobra*, due to the abundance of TV stars, becomes more popular every year.**

As the Regular First-Run Supporting Feature for Revenge of the Creature

As noted, the theatrical first run of *Cult of the Cobra* was to a large extent bound up with that of *Revenge of the Creature*, and the most common way for audiences to have originally encountered both movies at theaters was as a double-bill. The two movies premiered together in Detroit, Michigan, and New Haven, Connecticut, on March 29, 1955, and opened at three theaters in Los Angeles the following day. During April, the double-bill reached more than a dozen other states from Florida to Alaska and from Nevada to Ohio, with particularly heavy coverage attested throughout the Midwest. By the end of May, the *Revenge-Cult* combo had hit theaters in all states from coast to coast.

However, although the March 29 opening of *Revenge of the Creature* had already been announced by Universal in January 1955, the decision to employ *Cult of the Cobra* as its supporting feature seems to have been reached only at the last minute, with the March 1955 editions of every trade publication without exception still identifying *Cult* as a forthcoming May release, as per Universal's original schedule.

Since the two movies never constituted a fixed double-bill, their release histories also diverge at various points, in particular during the period from May 1955 onwards. For example, numerous theater owners chose to exhibit the pictures as stand-alone attractions, or to pair them with a different co-feature. Furthermore, it took slightly longer for *Cult* to fully penetrate small-town and rural communities, with the first run of *Revenge* effectively completed by October. *Cult* continued to open as a first-run feature at small-scale venues throughout November.

Within a sample of 900 U.S. movie theaters that screened *Cult of the Cobra* as a first-run picture between March and November 1955, fully 56 percent of screenings took the form of a double-bill with *Revenge*. Yet within a sample of 900 U.S. movie theaters that screened *Revenge of the Creature* as a first-run picture, a markedly lower percentage of screenings, 44 percent, took the form of a double-bill with *Cult*. This indicates that *Revenge* was more frequently employed in alternate contexts than *Cult*. In large part, this was surely due to the (justified) perception of *Revenge* as the "bigger" of the two, which made it appear better suited for stand-alone exhibition. Within both samples, the hierarchical relationship of the two movies remained evident, with every single double-bill screening of *Revenge* and *Cult* employing *Revenge* as the top of the bill and *Cult* as the supporting picture.

As a Stand-Alone Feature

Within the sample of 900 theaters that exhibited *Revenge of the Creature* as a first-run feature, some 38 percent of screenings took the form of a stand-alone presentation

During the 1950s "Red probe," screenwriter Richard Collins fingered fellow writer Martin Berkeley; this led to Berkeley famously becoming HUAC's jackpot witness, naming 150 names. Four years later, Collins' *Cult of the Cobra* was twin-billed with Berkeley's *Revenge of the Creature*.

supported only by "selected shorts." In the case of *Cult of the Cobra*, meanwhile, just 18 percent of first-run screenings were as a stand-alone presentation, implying a considerably lower level of confidence in the picture's ability to perform on its own merits. Moreover, while many of *Revenge*'s stand-alone engagements were at higher-rung theaters in large cities, this was almost never the case with *Cult*, whose stand-alone screenings were predominantly at small town venues where single bills were generally the norm anyway. In other words, the employment of *Cult* as a stand-alone feature fell within the realm of standard exhibition practice, in marked contrast to *Revenge*, which major venues went out of their way to secure as a stand-alone.

In the state of Texas, the use of *Revenge* as a stand-alone feature was more widespread than anywhere else in the nation, and as a consequence, *Cult* also picked up a slightly greater number of stand-alone bookings there; however, the majority of Texan exhibitors still appear to have felt uncertain about *Cult*'s ability to perform without support and elected to pair it with a different co-feature instead, rather than risk running it on its own.

With Featurette Accompaniment

Within the sample of 900 first-run theaters screening *Cult of the Cobra*, around one percent played the picture with accompaniment that was referred to in newspaper listings specifically as a featurette. In fact, this form of "lightweight double-bill" was attested exclusively in Texas, with four-fifths of such engagements employing Universal's Technicolor novelty short about the 1955 Miss Universe contest, *A World of Beauty*, as the featurette. This activity again points toward exhibitors' apparent lack of confidence in *Cult* to perform as a stand-alone feature, with the bill accordingly augmented with a second element whose presence was heavily promoted (if not outright overemphasized) in advertising.

Both of the attested "co-featurettes" are listed alphabetically below. The month mentioned in each case is the earliest in which the pairing was encountered.

July 1955 *The Mighty Fortress* (Billy Graham documentary, 31 minutes)

April 1955 *A World of Beauty* (Universal novelty about the 1955 Miss Universe contest, 17 minutes)

Other Double-Bills

Some 25 percent of all screenings of *Cult of the Cobra* within the sample of 900 first-run movie theaters paired the picture with a co-feature other than *Revenge of the Creature*. However, just as *Cult* always served as the supporting feature when co-billed with *Revenge*, so it also played as the lower half of the bill at 83 percent of these alternate double-bill engagements. With the lone exception of *20,000 Leagues Under the Sea*, none of the other co-features listed below was a horror or sci-fi picture; this suggests a desire on the part of certain theater owners to adhere to their usual practice of showing a so-called "balanced program" rather than a genre-matched one, meaning that they may very well have actively avoided booking the standard *Revenge-Cult* package.

Most of the alternate double-bill features listed below constitute uncommon examples of disparate local usage. However, the nine Universal pictures on the list account collectively for one-quarter of all alternate double-bill screenings, implying that Universal was still eager to control both halves of the bill whenever possible.

All of the double-bill co-features attested within the sample are arranged alphabetically below. The month mentioned in each case is the earliest in which the pairing was encountered.

(*) signifies a more substantial number of playdates (at between five and eight percent of theaters).
bold titles are Universal releases.

June 1955 *Along the Navajo Trail* (Roy Rogers; Republic reissue)
July 1955 *Bad Day at Black Rock* (Spencer Tracy)
October 1955 *Bedevilled* (Anne Baxter)
September 1955 *Beyond the Pecos* (Rod Cameron; Realart reissue)
August 1955 *The Black Knight* (Alan Ladd)
June 1955 *Black Tuesday* (Edward G. Robinson)
June 1955 *Blackboard Jungle* (Glenn Ford)
June 1955 *Canyon Crossroads* (Richard Basehart)
September 1955 *Captain Lightfoot* (Rock Hudson)
July 1955 (*) *Chief Crazy Horse* (Victor Mature)
September 1955 *Cowboy and the Senorita* (Roy Rogers; Republic reissue)
June 1955 *Crashout* (William Bendix)
May 1955 *Crime Wave* (Gene Nelson)
August 1955 *Double Jeopardy* (Rod Cameron)
May 1955 *Dragnet* (Jack Webb)
September 1955 *Drum Beat* (Alan Ladd)
May 1955 *The Far Country* (James Stewart)
October 1955 *Fort Ti* (George Montgomery)
September 1955 *The Green Buddha* (Wayne Morris)
August 1955 *Hell's Island* (John Payne)
May 1955 *High Society* (Bowery Boys)
June 1955 *Hit the Deck* (Jane Powell)
September 1955 *How to Marry a Millionaire* (Marilyn Monroe)
October 1955 *Interrupted Melody* (Glenn Ford)
September 1955 *Jump into Hell* (Jacques Sernas)
August 1955 *Land of Fury* (Jack Hawkins)
June 1955 *The Looters* (Rory Calhoun)

June 1955 *Mambo* (Silvana Mangano)
August 1955 (*) *The Man from Bitter Ridge* (Lex Barker)
September 1955 *Man from Texas* (James Craig; United Artists reissue)
May 1955 *Man Without a Star* (Kirk Douglas)
August 1955 *The Marauders* (Dan Duryea)
September 1955 *Mister Roberts* (Henry Fonda)
May 1955 *New York Confidential* (Broderick Crawford)
May 1955 *The Noose Hangs High* (Abbott and Costello; United Artists reissue)
May 1955 *The Purple Plain* (Gregory Peck)
August 1955 *Quest for the Lost City* (Dana and Ginger Lamb)
May 1955 *Rage at Dawn* (Randolph Scott)
June 1955 *Run for Cover* (James Cagney)
July 1955 *Seminole Uprising* (George Montgomery)
July 1955 *Seven Brides for Seven Brothers* (Howard Keel)
July 1955 *The Seven Year Itch* (Marilyn Monroe)
October 1955 *Shotgun* (Sterling Hayden)
November 1955 *The Shrike* (Jose Ferrer)
September 1955 *Sign of the Pagan* (Jeff Chandler)
August 1955 *Smoke Signal* (Dana Andrews)
October 1955 *Soldier of Fortune* (Clark Gable)
June 1955 *The Stooge* (Martin and Lewis)
June 1955 *Strange Lady in Town* (Greer Garson)
October 1955 *The Stranger from Texas* (Charles Starrett; Columbia reissue)
September 1955 *Topeka* (Wild Bill Elliott)
July 1955 *20,000 Leagues Under the Sea* (Kirk Douglas)
May 1955 *White Feather* (Robert Wagner)
July 1955 *Yellowneck* (Lin McCarthy)

Beyond the First Run

As a second-run feature, *Cult of the Cobra* continued to be booked for a limited amount of engagements during 1956 and early 1957, most frequently playing in support of its regular first-run co-feature, *Revenge of the Creature*. However, from mid–1957, *Cult*'s second-run bookings fell off dramatically, with the picture having all but disappeared from cinema screens during the years 1960 to 1963, aside from an extremely meager number of engagements at low-end hardtops and drive-ins.

Cult's television debut took place to little fanfare at 6 p.m. on August 16, 1964, on Los Angeles' KABC-TV. Small-screen showings on stations from coast to coast followed during October and November 1964, after which the movie became something of a TV staple, with the cavalcade of then-current TV stars in its cast arguably setting it on course for the retrospective revival outlined by Rob Word in his April 1976 review.

For further details on the first-run release of *Revenge of the Creature*, see Robert J. Kiss, "The Release," in this book's companion volume *The Creature Chronicles* (pages 203–05).

The Critics' Corner

Many newspapers gave the *Revenge of the Creature-Cult of the Cobra* double-feature two-in-one reviews, devoting most of the space to the top-of-the-bill Gill Man feature. A writer for the *Fitchburg* (Massachusetts) *Sentinel* called *Cult* "[p]erhaps not as adventurous [as *Revenge*], but more spine-chilling in its creepy insidious way..." The *Los Angeles Times* review didn't get to *Cult* until the final few lines, dismissing it as "some nonsense about cobra women and a curse. Plot-wise, *Cobra* comes out on top of *Revenge of the Creature*, but when you see a horror picture who looks for plot? You're out to be scared, and you'll certainly be that." Other reviewers who weighed in:

Film Daily: [*Cult* is] an absorbing melodrama which should send goose bumps up and down many a spine. Francis D. Lyon's direction is imaginative and delivers a full complement of strange and mystifying devices...

Motion Picture Exhibitor: There's enough horror, mysterious atmosphere, etc., to give some audiences thrills and chills.

Motion Picture Daily: The picture ... is overloaded with dialogue and the thrills are too few and far between. The result is a mildly diverting picture. ... One interesting departure in the film is the various murders being seen through the eyes of the cobra. It adds a needed eerie quality to the proceedings.

Variety: Francis D. Lyon's direction is responsible for good suspense, heightened by interesting optical effects as the camera becomes the eye of the striking cobra...

Harrison's Reports: The atmosphere is appropriately eerie and the action holds one in pretty tense suspense.

Film Bulletin: The first horror melodrama in some time, this Universal offering should give fans of the eerie a mild thrill. ... [I]t never quite reaches a pinnacle of suspense or great excitement, but manages to be moderately interesting and fast-moving.

The Hollywood Reporter: The screenplay proves that almost any idea can be dramatized with taste and interest if the writers are clever enough. The film is not the cheap horror story that the title implies. It is an intelligent treatment of the werewolf theme ... and, while the treatment is geared for box office and the popular trade, it is done in a manner that shows a good understanding of the fascinating oriental mystic cults that have been engaging the serious attention of scholars and students of psychic phenomena here and abroad for 50 years past.[30]

Reptilian Rhapsody: The Music of Cult of the Cobra

By David Schecter

A brilliant film doesn't guarantee that a brilliant musical score will be written for it, nor does a lesser film guarantee that a lesser score will be composed. *Cult of the Cobra* is by no means one of Universal's best horror movies, but it received an excellent score which, if you pay attention to it, can provide much listening pleasure. Other than a few source music songs tracked in from previous films, *Cult of the Cobra* contains an entirely original score co-written by William Lava, Irving Gertz, Stanley Wilson and Lou Maury. While Maury was given a number of less dramatic scenes that might not have been as inspirational as they could have been, Wilson does a solid job in one of his early Universal assignments, and Lava and Gertz are in their usual superb form of contributing consistently appropriate, effective and enjoyable music.

There are 44 cues in the movie totaling about 47 minutes, a clue that the music was written specially for the picture, as original cues are generally much longer than tracked ones. About 58 percent of *Cult of the Cobra* contains music, which makes it one of Universal's more musically enhanced 1950s horror films. This percentage is very similar to the following year's *The Mole People,* whose score also used a lot of ethnic touches to create the impression of foreign influences. Lava wrote eight *Cult of the Cobra* cues for a total of 11 minutes, Wilson wrote 12 for ten minutes, Maury wrote eight for ten minutes, and Gertz wrote eight for nine minutes. The remaining seven minutes of source music cues include songs, whistling and the sound of an orchestra tuning up.

The score was recorded on February 10, 1955, with the session lasting from 7¾ to 8½ hours depending upon the instrument. Extra time was devoted to the players who performed the ethnic dance music heard at the beginning of the movie. A rehearsal pianist was also used for one week, probably to aid in the staging of the snake dance. Added to the budget at one point was $840 for the use of 12 voices for a single day, but this idea was later discarded, saving some money. This singing would have been heard during the opening temple scene, where the screenplay describes "a strange and monotonous chanting, rather 'tenor voice' in character. A deeper voice, that of the High Priest, is rising and falling in serpentine counterpoint through the melody." The movie's total music budget exceeded $25,000, quite a bit more than a tracked score would have cost.

What sets *Cult of the Cobra*'s score apart from many other Universal collaborative efforts of the '50s is that all the composers included the same motif (a seven-note ethnic-sounding snake theme) in the majority of their cues, which lent a consistency to the soundtrack missing from some of the studio's other multi-composered creations. When Irving Gertz, Henry Mancini and Herman Stein scored *It Came from Outer Space*, they used similar themes when they could, but as those themes were written for specific visuals, if those visuals weren't in a particular scene, the composers didn't employ them. And even though *Creature from the Black Lagoon*'s composers used Stein's Creature theme from start to finish in that picture, it was treated as more of a recurring musical sound effect than a melodic phrase that could be altered or adapted into other forms. *Cult of the Cobra*'s composers incorporated the snake theme into their cues with a lot of instrumental and compositional creativity, with the length of the motif aiding in their ability to write so many variations of it. The use of the theme helps the score hold together admirably well despite the four writers' stylistic differences. Although it isn't known who concocted the motif, it sounds like something Lava might have come up with, and it plays an important role in most of the cues he composed. Occasionally, a trill (back-and-forth alternation of two notes) was added to the theme's last note, which helps make the motif even more threatening.

Although both Mancini and Stein were quoted as saying that Universal's composers were given their own reels to score in these collaborative efforts, this didn't happen all that much. Usually, these scores contained more than one composer's music within a reel. *Cult of the Cobra* is a good example of how successfully this approach worked, as the blend of styles lent an overall unity to the score. For whatever reason, Lava's cues were weighted toward the first half of the picture, while the others contributed more or less consistently throughout the movie. Four of *Cult of the Cobra*'s cues were edited, with some of the music being removed from the film, but whether these edits were done to both the movie and the music, or just to the music, is a mystery.

Lava's "Main Title" begins the show with a *grandioso* fanfare on potent brass that plays during the Universal-International logo. Unlike Alfred Newman's 20th Century-Fox fanfare, Max Steiner's fanfare for Warner Brothers or even Jimmy McHugh's Universal Pictures fanfare heard during the 1930s and '40s—all of which were heard in countless movies—many of Universal's 1950s films featured an individual fanfare written to play during the logo of that one particular film. This approach helped get the various adventures off in their own new directions rather than remind the audiences of previous Universal motion pictures they had seen.

After the fanfare, piccolo and woodwinds play the cobra theme, accentuating that we're in Asia. The remainder of the exciting "Main Title" is a mixture of mostly brass, winds and percussion, with strings not accentuated. The brass voicings (which instruments play what notes) are similar to some of the monstrous sounds Lava would create for *The Deadly Mantis* two years down the line. There's not much structure to the piece, and the snake theme is pretty much what holds it all together, but that doesn't make it any less enjoyable. Vibraphone, finger cymbals, celesta and alto flute underscore the opening legend that follows the title sequence, the exotic touches reinforcing the idea that we're in a faraway place.

William Ben Lava was born on March 18, 1911, in St. Paul, Minnesota. He started piano lessons when he was seven, but eventually quit his studies. As a youth he supposedly could play any melody after hearing it, and he soon became proficient on many instruments. Although he studied conducting with Albert Coates, he considered himself a "composer without formal musical education," and he attended Northwestern University as a journalism major. Lava sold stories to the magazines *Argosy* and *The Literary Digest*, but when he had trouble finding enough work as an author, he got a job as an assistant to a claims agent at a railway, and then sold automobiles and bedsprings. He learned to arrange music from an old friend who was an arranger for Wayne King's orchestra, and before long Lava sold his first arrangement and was working for radio programs and theater engagements. Arriving in Hollywood in 1936, he arranged for the musical radio shows *Camel Caravan* and Fred Astaire's *The Packard Hour*, with John Green.

Lava signed a contract with Republic in 1937, his first background score being for the serial *The Painted Stallion*, and three years later he signed with Warner Brothers. He also scored short subjects and a lot of series television, with some of his best-known work done for *Zorro* and *F Troop*. His music can be heard in an incredible number of productions, including *Abbott and Costello Meet the Keystone Kops, Cattle Town, Chamber of Horrors, Chubasco, Dracula vs. Frankenstein, House of Dracula, The Littlest Outlaw, Moonrise, Phantom from Space, Red River Range, Smoke Signal, Stormy the Thoroughbred* and a slew of Looney Tunes, Merrie Melodies, and Pink Panther cartoons. Lava is also reputed to have contributed to the landmark scores of *Since You Went Away, Saratoga Trunk* and *Destination Tokyo*. The composer passed away on February 20, 1971, in Los Angeles.

Stanley Wilson's *Cult of the Cobra* "Flute Sequence" uses alto flute and English horn to subtly add to the atmosphere as the G.I.s notice the bazaar snake charmer. Requiring more air than a regular flute, the alto flute's breathy tones evoke a sense of strangeness and mystery, and that's why this particular instrument was called on time and again in the movies to create such a mood. Wilson's "Snake Charmer" is a quiet piece heard when the G.I.s meet Daru at the bazaar. Muted French horns alert us that the idea of snakes turning into people might not be as ridiculous as one might think, but the cue's effectiveness is limited because it was mixed too quietly in the soundtrack.

Born in New York City in 1915, Wilson began as a jazz trumpeter, arranged for Freddie Martin's band and spent eight years at Republic Pictures, orchestrating and composing for an endless stream of films and serials. He eventually wound up as the head of Universal's new television music division, composing for a wide variety of series, including *Adam-12, The Alfred Hitchcock Hour, Cimarron City, Laramie, The Munsters, The Name of the Game, Tales of Wells Fargo, Thriller, The Virginian* and *Wagon Train*. He was nominated for a Grammy for an album of music from *M Squad*, and he recorded a highly regarded exotica album called "Pagan Love." Wilson died of a heart attack in 1970 in Aspen, Colorado, right after addressing the Aspen Music Festival on composing for films and television.

That the Universal musical goulash could work so flawlessly is manifested after Larry Russell's "Tia Juana Tea Party," from the 1943 film *Moonlight in Vermont*, plays in the café where the G.I.s wait for Daru. When Daru cautions them just before they enter the temple, Lou Maury's "Dire Warning" begins, offering some subtle variations on the snake theme amidst a variety of other quiet devices, this approach being suitable for the secret mission they're on. As the men enter the sanctuary, Gertz's "Ceremonial #1" takes over for about a minute, with brass fanfares and a large gong that Gertz wanted to "let ring." As the final gong rings outs, Lava's "Ceremonial Snake Dance, Part 1" begins even before a cut to the shirtless male dancer, which serves to offer a new composer and a new composition with almost nobody being able to detect a change. Lava's excellent cue musically describes "the dance that should not be observed," with temple blocks (quite appropriate for a temple), finger cymbals and harp contributing ethnic-sounding percussion. The continuous and seamless succession of cues was due to gifted composers who could not only write well by themselves, but who could also function in an environment requiring teamwork.

Lava's "Ceremonial Snake Dance, Part 2" starts just before the basket lid pops open and the hand-snake dance begins. The composer adds marimba, gong and celesta, with the cue building and receding in orchestration as the choreography changes. Rapid runs on flute and other woodwinds, robust string passages and the snake theme in various guises—some threatening and full-orchestral, others delicately played on solo instruments—result in a spectacular composition that highlights Lava's tremendous talent. Of all the "palace dance music" that's been written for untold movies, Lava's creation for this sequence stands out.

Lava uses more conventional orchestration in "Hunting the Snake Girl," which provides action music as the Americans flee the temple and find Nick, and Tom searches for the cobra woman. Fast string and brass writing highlights the opening, and there are some nice touches from stopped horns and muted trumpets about halfway through the piece, which musically describe the fact that the snake woman is hiding, the way a mute somewhat "hides" the sound of a brass instrument. During a close-up of Lisa's veiled face, there's a memorably spooky Novachord effect with trilling cluster chords that approximates some notes of the snake theme. This was not written in Lava's score, and it was probably ad-libbed at the recording session when an emphasis was requested for this image. There's also the possibility that it was overdubbed after the session, but in either case, it was similarly added "after the fact" to similar visuals in other composers' cues. This probably occurred after all the music had been written and it became evident that these similar shots of Lisa's face could be enhanced by a musical motif. The Novachord effect seems to have derived from one of a number of Wilson cues in which he included that device in his written scores.

When Lisa kills Nick, Lava's "Visiting Cobra" offers ethnic touches like alto flute, gong and marimba, along with variations on material heard in his "Main Title," with flutter-tongued brass signaling Nick's demise in this composition. It's always difficult figuring out which cue a particular motif or passage might have been initially written for, as films are often composed out of sequence. Therefore, while one piece might have inspired another, it might also have been the other way around. Main titles were often written last, since this way a composer would have all the other cues at his disposal to best inspire him. Gertz's "Deadly Prowler" announces that the mysterious events in Asia have now spread to the United States, starting with a version of the snake theme on alto flute and clarinet. The composer uses the motif to further tie the overseas events to Lisa, who pretends that an intruder has broken into her apartment. Gertz colors his sinewy writing with a number of effective devices, including flutter-tongued brass, Novachord and an undercurrent of vibraphone and marimba, providing both a mysterious ambiance and some shocks. As Gertz would later show with his superb giant spider music for *The Incredible Shrinking Man* (1957) and his excellent score for *The Alligator People* (1959), flutter-tonguing creates a raspy sound that is befitting to monsters of all types! Part of this cue was not used in the picture, and during a shot of Lisa's lit-up face, there's another instance of the Novachord effect heard earlier in "Hunting the Snake Girl," again something that wasn't initially composed for this piece, but which was added during the recording session or overdubbed later.

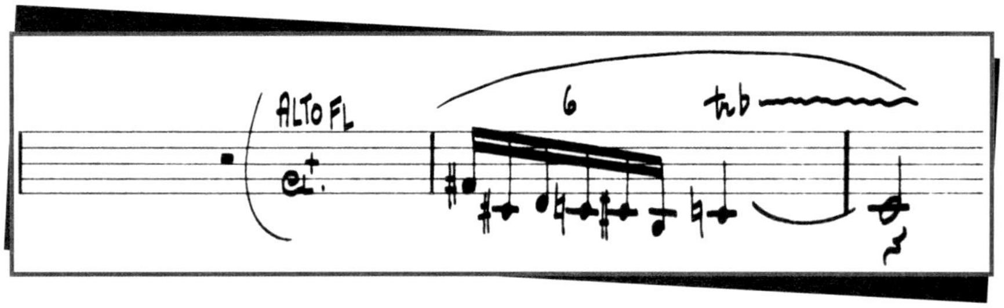

Wilson's "I'll Show You the Town" is indicative of the lighter scenes this composer was given on *Cult of the Cobra*, and the corresponding easygoing approach he took in his writing for the picture. While Gertz or Lava might have done a better job with this and similar cues, Wilson makes good use of the cobra theme, offering hints of it on strings to maintain the flirty mood. When Lisa's lit-up face is again shown, Wilson uses the Novachord effect with trilling cluster chords, which plays alongside woodwinds. Since he was the only composer who wrote that motif in his manuscripts, that suggests that he created it, and it was later added to some of the other composers' cues. The repeated use of this motif further helps tie his different style to that of the other writers. Strings and woodwinds predominate in Wilson's "Cold Liza," a romantic cue heard when Tom and Lisa end their lunch in front of a rear-projected shot of a bustling city. After Tom fails in his attempt to kiss the serpentine siren, the composer incorporates the snake theme in a less threatening manner.

Maury's "Liza and the Boys" is an almost three-minute piece that plays when Lisa learns about the surviving G.I.s from Tom, and while the cue is gentle throughout—flavored by woodwinds, strings and quiet percussion—it offers some ominous sounds courtesy of the Novachord effect, while it also makes subtle use of the snake theme. It's not known whether Maury chose to keep this sequence as light as he did, or whether it was requested of him, because this cue could have easily been scored with a more menacing tone, which might have been more suitable to the story. Regardless, it's a well-conceived composition, even if the dramatic undertones could have been amplified a bit.

Lou Maury (Henry Lowndes Maury, Jr.) was born on July 7, 1911, in Butte, Montana. He learned piano from his mother, and in 1931 he graduated from the Univer-

The snake theme from Irving Gertz's "Deadly Prowler." (© 1955 Accolade Music Publishing Co.)

Lou Maury in 1945. (Photograph courtesy Elizabeth Maury.)

sity of Montana–Missoula. He also studied piano and composition at the Chicago Musical College, and with Arnold Schoenberg at the Malkin Conservatory in Boston. His Hollywood career began in the 1930s, where he served as a pianist, organist, arranger, composer and conductor, doing extensive work for radio, including Eddie Cantor and Jack Haley shows, *Life with Father* and *The Life of Riley*. He composed music for UPA's Mr. Magoo cartoons, wrote for U.S. Air Force training films, and he was a contract pianist for 20th Century-Fox. Some of his work for Universal included *Abbott and Costello Meet the Mummy* and *To Hell and Back*. Maury wrote concert works including cantatas, concertos, an opera, a violin sonata and a rhapsody for alto flute and string orchestra, and in later years he established the Lou Maury Piano School in North Hollywood. He also helped develop a new approach to music notation, and in 1974 he wrote four volumes of piano teaching books entitled *Magic Lines and Spaces*. Maury was awarded an honorary Doctor of Letters by the University of Montana. He passed away in Encino, California, on December 11, 1975.

While some of the lighter moments in *Cult of the Cobra*'s score could have easily been tracked with pre-existing source music cues playing over a radio in the background, Maury and Wilson were able to bolster these scenes' dramatic intentions with their original compositions. Tracked cues would have introduced entirely different thematic material that would have been detrimental to the all-encompassing presence of the snake cult, which the four composers were able to maintain by the melodic and instrumental touches they imparted to their pieces. The use of the snake theme by Maury and Wilson and the Novachord effect definitely prevented their disparate compositional styles from jumping out as much as they might have otherwise. For whatever reason, Lava's and Gertz's music—although extremely different in style from the other's—always seemed to work well t ogether, possibly because Lava had a tight and forceful sound, while Gertz's looser compositional approach had many moments of "breath" that offered a nice respite from that. Their sublime musical partnership can also be heard in *Smoke Signal, Francis in the Navy* and *The Deadly Mantis*.

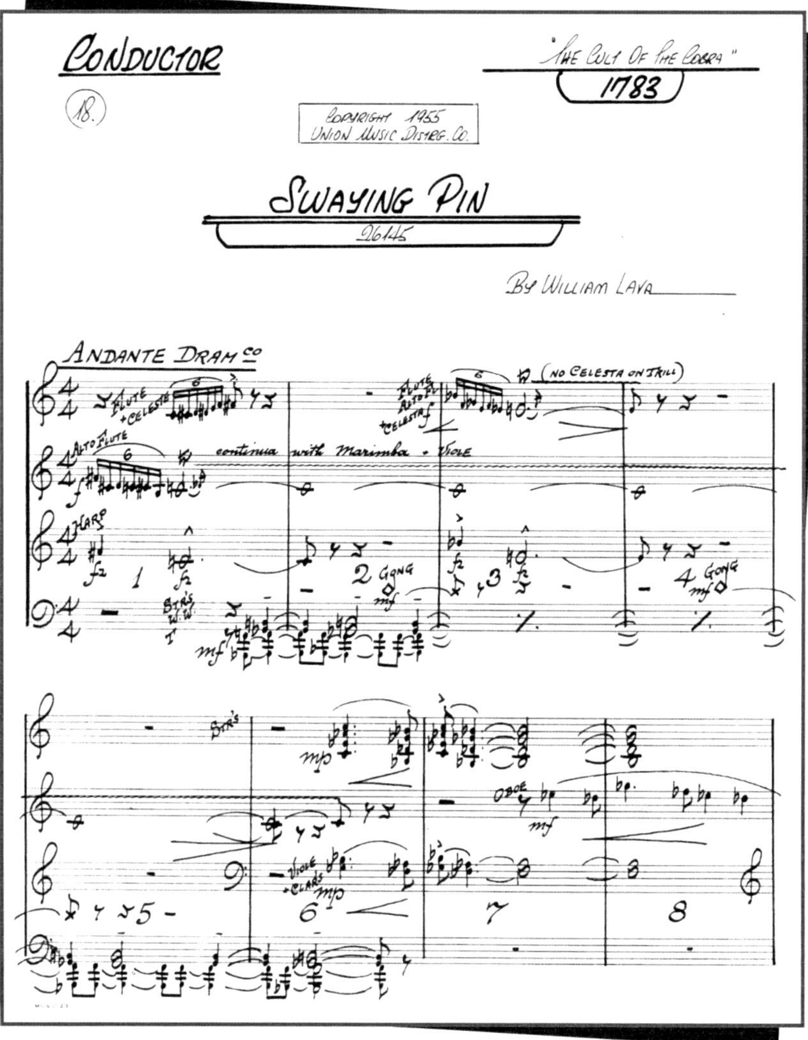

Conductor's score showing deleted music from William Lava's "Swaying Pin." (© 1955 RABB Trust Publishing/Willenora Publishing Co.)

Snake theme played by (funeral) chimes in Irving Gertz's "Cobra Gets Rico." (© 1955 Accolade Music Publishing Co.)

Cue sheets are supposed to contain every bit of music used in a motion picture, regardless of the source, and that's why after Maury's brief Novachord-laden "Sneaking Out" cue, in which Lisa encounters an upset cat, a piece named "Whistling Ad Lib" is listed on the cue sheets. Although it's not credited to anybody, the cue was included so there'd be no confusion as to whether Rico was whistling a copyrighted song that would have required clearance (and payment) to be used in synchronous fashion within the movie.

Lava's "Swaying Pin" is an atmospheric cue heard when Rico is alone in the bowling alley. It features marimba, stopped horns and vibraphone in addition to the rest of the orchestra *sans* brass; you can hear the beginning of the music being dialed up in the soundtrack, as the opening five bars were removed from the picture. This missing music contained some exotic touches like celesta, alto flute and gong, as well as the snake theme. When the bowling pin falls on its own, the composition contains a particularly nice instrumental moment courtesy of trilling flutes, marimba and celesta.

"Cobra Gets Rico" is an excellent shock cue by Gertz, with trilling woodwinds and short ascending string runs anticipating the brass-laden car accident. Even the ringing church bells (played by chimes) mimic part of the cobra theme at Rico's funeral, a really clever touch. The opening measures of this cue were deleted from the soundtrack, but whether the footage accompanying it was also cut remains a slithering mystery.

Opening with a Gershwinesque flourish to accentuate the city nightlife, "Girl Assistant" is a two-minute Wilson-composed piece that underlies Paul and Julia's conversation in the cab. While it's an above-average cue, it's not up to the compositional subtlety of Gertz or Lava, but to be fair to Wilson, it's not the easiest thing to try to stay out of the way of so much dialogue so viewers can understand what's being spoken. Touches of alto flute and vibraphone offer a few ominous touches amidst the lighter moments, and the snake theme works very well played quietly on clarinet.

The three-part "Tom Loves Cobra" offers over four minutes of continuous music from Maury, the first section beginning when Tom goes to fetch some ice from Lisa's apartment. A clarinet melody highlights the string-emphasized piece, but the melody seems unrelated to anything else in the picture, and the music doesn't always have the effect it should, as it's more middling when it should be decisive. It comes across more as "filler" when it could have offered some emotional insight into Lisa's mind so we'd know whether she's starting to think about things other than murder. "Tom Loves Cobra, Pt. 2" starts when Tom returns to his apartment, and again the music seems to be painting a traditional romantic setting instead of offering some dramatic subtext, especially because G.I.s have been dropping like flies.

As for the cutesy woodwind flourishes that accompany the shot of Tom with his dog, they have no place in a horror movie. One is reminded of the comedic music in *Revenge of the Creature*'s lab scene with Clint Eastwood, but at least that

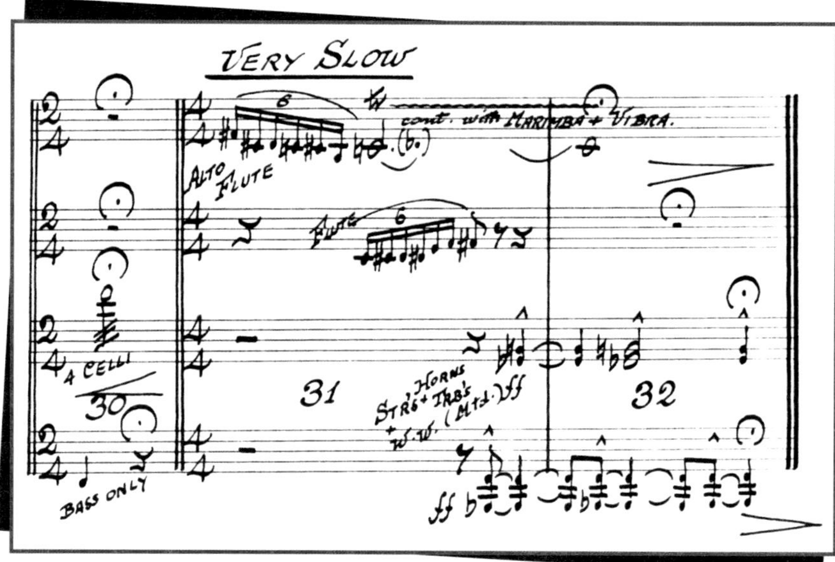

The snake theme from the end of Lou Maury's "Tom Loves Cobra, Part 3." (© 1955 Mauryworks.)

was due to a poor choice of library music from a Talking Mule picture, whereas the music in *Cult of the Cobra* was written specifically for the movie. Of course, you never know if Maury might have been asked by someone to add some "comic relief" to a picture with almost no humor whatsoever. It's only in "Tom Loves Cobra, Pt. 3," when Tom picks up Lisa's gloves and goes to her apartment, that the music has more depth to it, with Novachord and bassoon imparting a slightly darker edge. Overall, these three compositions don't achieve what one would have hoped for until the final shot of the open window, when alto flute plays the snake theme alongside some truly exciting brass-powered writing. This entire part of the movie needed to be scored more in keeping with the picture's serious tone, and Universal might have been better off had *Cult of the Cobra* only used Lava and Gertz. However, the use of four composers implies that Joseph Gershenson needed the score churned out as quickly as possible.

Novachord effects used in *Cult of the Cobra*. (© 1955 Union Music Distributing Co.)

Gertz scored four consecutive cues in *Cult of the Cobra*, starting with "Carl Gets It," where vibraphone, marimba and Novachord sustains announce from the outset that foul events are imminent. On a close-up of Lisa's eyes, the Novachord effect was again incorporated after Gertz wrote the piece without it. As Lisa heads toward her apartment building after the murder, the vibraphone-heavy "Tom Waits for Cobra" adds marimba and muted brass to create a mysterious atmosphere that wisely doesn't tip off the eventual outcome of their meeting. The two-part "Snake Loves Tom" plays after Lisa finds Tom sleeping in her apartment. Opening with a gentle version of the snake theme on alto flute, the music is warm without becoming sappy, and vibraphone, a variety of woodwinds and harp don't allow the cue to ever become excessively melodic for too long. Tender strings are present, but they aren't allowed to get overly romantic, since Lisa is caught between her love for Tom and her desire to bite and kill all of his friends. Just as Gertz's "Star Gazing" from *It Came from Outer Space* complemented a troubled relationship, the "Snake Loves Tom" cues also perfectly capture the uneasy relationship between Tom and his viper vixen. Dorothy Gertz, Irving's wife of more than 60 years, has noted, "It's impossible to hum Irving's music," her comment referring to her husband's writing approach that seldom favored traditional melodies. Regardless, Gertz's often circuitous composing style was a very effective one for the movies, proving that unforgettable tunes aren't a prerequisite for great dramatic underscore.

"Julia Has a Hunch" when Lisa visits her, and runs on flutes and strings are emphasized in this Wilson cue that could have been written by Gertz, whose compositional perambulations can almost be detected here. As Lisa advances threateningly toward Julia, trilling cluster chords on Novachord provide the effect that Wilson wrote in a number of his cues, as well as in the next two pieces, the brief "Julia Escapes" and "Girl Into Snake." The latter is heard after Pete threatens to call the police on Lisa and she turns into a reptile. Some fresh instrumental effects including honky woodwinds and fluttering flute, along with timpani, augment the transformation.

The sequence when Lisa visits Tom's apartment and their romance blossoms into a kiss could have used a better aural background than the one chosen. The source music song "Spell of the Moon," written by Milton Rosen and Everett Carter for *Pardon My Rhythm* (1944), plays when Lisa plies Tom for answers regarding Paul's suspicions. Two

Lou Maury compositions follow, but they're rather nondescript. Both "Radio Sequence" and "Tame Cobra" don't sound much more appropriate than library music. Given the subtext of the scene, some more fitting dramatic musical support was called for, especially when the acting fails to convince anyone that these two characters have actually fallen in love. Why a song was used here is a mystery, since the opening shot when an undetected Lisa enters the apartment could have benefited from some furtive underscore. As was often the case with source music, the appropriateness of a given song came in second to who wrote or (especially) published the tune, as monetary considerations were always in the forefront when you had a chance of getting a tune placed in a film, even if it was an older song. "Poor Pete Is Dead" is a brief cue by Wilson that uses the snake theme to augment the bite marks on Pete's neck.

Songs from previous Universal movies were used during the theater scenes after 19 seconds of the cue "Orchestra Tuning Up" plays, which wasn't credited to anyone on the cue sheets. It's too bad nobody ever copyrighted the sound of a symphony tuning, because he or she would have made millions in royalties over the years! "Oh! Oh! Oklahoma" from *You're a Sweetheart* (1937), written by Harold Adamson and Jimmy McHugh, is heard in the theater first, followed by "If You Can Can-Can" from *Destry* (1954), by Frederick Herbert and Arnold Hughes; all four songwriters were Universal stalwarts. Originally, the song "Don't Go Making Speeches" by Milton Rosen and Everett Carter from *Under Western Skies* (1945) was to be used in the theater sequence, but either the scene it was meant for was cut, or else the song was replaced by another. Two of their other songs appear in *Cult of the Cobra*: the previously mentioned "Spell of the Moon," plus "Nice to Know You" from *Playgirl* (1954), which is heard at Carl's party about 40 minutes into the picture.

Why Rosen had so many songs in Universal's movies might have had something to do with him being Joseph Gershenson's assistant, although to be fair, Rosen was a capable

Conductor's score of William Lava's *Cult of the Cobra* "Main Title." (© 1955 RABB Trust Publishing/Willenora Publishing Co.)

composer as well. In an interesting aside, Universal's 1946 Abbott and Costello film *The Time of Their Lives* featured a score conducted and composed by Rosen, who received screen credit for both of his jobs. However, Arthur Lange, who did not receive a screen credit, wrote a few cues, including the frothy "Main Title," which contains a pronounced brassy musical "hit" to acknowledge Joe Gershenson, the film's "Executive Producer," a role he sometimes filled before he took over the studio's music department. One wonders if Lange thought that giving his boss a musical emphasis might have resulted in a screen credit?

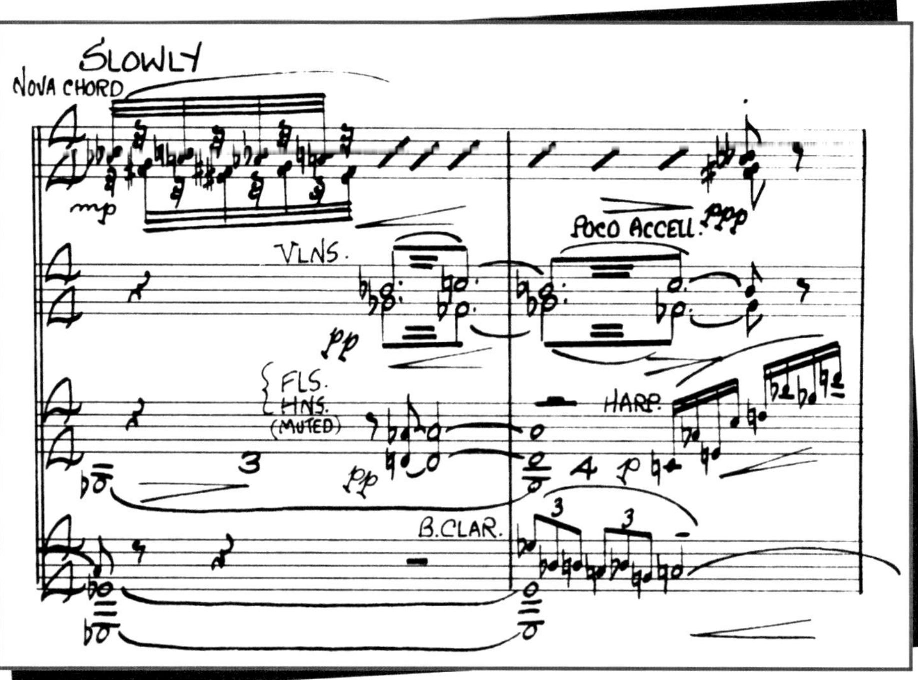

Snake-into-woman transformation music from Stanley Wilson's "End Title." (© 1955 Union Music Distributing Co.)

The songwriting team of Frederick Herbert and Arnold Hughes had a lot of their tunes placed in Universal motion pictures after they joined the studio in the early 1950s. Herbert was born Herbert Stahlberg on June 4, 1909, in New York. The son of Frederick "Fritz" Stahlberg, a Pittsburgh Philharmonic violinist, Herbert later changed his first name to his last name to match that of operetta king Victor Herbert (his godfather and a close friend of his father), and then he took his father's first name. Professional reasons were also behind his name change, as he felt that his German surname was holding him back in the strong Jewish presence of postwar Hollywood. Frederick "Herbie" Herbert studied piano and music theory with L. Leslie Loth, and was a cub reporter for *The New York Times* in the late 1920s. In the '30s he collaborated with Richard Whiting ("Hooray for Hollywood," "Ain't We Got Fun?," "On the Good Ship Lollipop"); Whiting's premature death at age 46 was a setback to Frederick's goal of becoming a lyricist. He worked as a music editor, mixer, music supervisor and lyricist in Hollywood, spending time with 20th Century-Fox, MGM, Universal and Revue Productions. At Universal, Herbert was one of their main lyricists when he wasn't the studio's head music editor. He contributed to such films as *Abbott and Costello Meet Dr. Jekyll and Mr. Hyde, The Far Country, Magnificent Obsession, Meet Me at the Fair, A Stranger in My Arms* and *The World in His Arms*, plus TV's *The Virginian* and *Wagon Train*. His favorite songs were "Man Without a Star," co-written with Arnold Schwarzwald, and "Tomorrow," co-written with John Williams. As music editor, Herbert would spot the pictures with the composers to determine what scenes would and wouldn't have music written for them. He also came up with a lot of Universal's cue titles, many of which were quite witty, employing puns and other knowing references. He passed away in Encino, California, on September 2, 1966.

Another writer who changed his name, composer Arnold Hughes was born Arnold Schwarzwald in Chicago on September 10, 1918. He was the son of Milton Schwarzwald, a musical director, producer, writer and director on many Universal features and shorts in the 1930s and '40s. Arnold studied piano with Lawrence Bernhardt, and composition with Konstantin Schedov, Otto Cesana and Mario Castelnuovo-Tedesco. After writing for Republic Studios, he became a music editor for Universal. Besides writing concert works, he composed for a wide variety of pictures, including *Back to God's Country, City Beneath the Sea, Destry, Man Without a Star, Quantez, The Rawhide Years, Remember Pearl Harbor* and *The Spoilers*.

"Tom Slays Serpent" is Lava's first cue in *Cult of the Cobra* for almost 40 minutes, and this exhilarating action piece reminds the listener what's been missing due to this composer's absence from the soundtrack. From beginning to end, the composition uses the snake theme via many different instruments, with piatti and gong percussively highlighting the mostly conventional orchestration, which also features fluttering brass, trilling woodwinds and rapid-fire string figures. The final descending version of the snake theme ably sums up the cobra's plunge off the ledge. Some of the commanding brass near the end would have also been quite at home in Lava's contributions to *The Deadly Mantis*.

Wilson handles the "End Title" sequence, which begins just before Lisa de-reptiles back into a woman, the Novachord effect sounding one final time during her transfiguration, this time harp coloring it to accentuate her human aspect. Instead of ominous versions of the snake theme, sad and longing renditions are heard—mostly on strings and pretty woodwinds—which was a solid decision. Although the solo violin steers it toward sappiness, it avoids crossing the line. But after all, she *was* the sexiest snake most of us have ever seen! The cue builds to a tutti (full-orchestral) ending that is strong, but not triumphant, nor should it have been given the film's sad resolution. With Lisa dead, all exotic instrumentation has vanished as well, a clever creative choice that Gertz echoes in his outstanding "End Cast." His closing musical statement recaps the snake theme with fresh variations of it, while harp glissandos are almost continuous in the background. The composer deftly sends us on our merry-but-sad way, probably unaware that we have just heard one of Universal's most undeservedly overlooked horror scores of the decade.[31]

Analysis
By Steve Kronenberg

Cult of the Cobra is, at first blush, a paradox. It represents a major shift from the Technicolor-drenched opulence and special effects of *This Island Earth* and the elaborate monster suits of the Gill Man trilogy. Indeed, *Cult* more resembles the first of Universal's 1950s horrors, the uncluttered black-and-white *The Strange Door* and *The Black Castle*. Yet *Cult* is a landmark among Universal's '50s offerings: It marks a return to supernatural rather than scientific horror, and a portent of things to come.

Unlike many of Universal's offerings in the '50s, *Cult* is not a technician's showcase. It's made watchable by Faith Domergue's memorable performance as Lisa, the shape-shifting snake woman and agent of the curse that befalls the hapless G.I.s. Lisa emerges as vampiric, a female Bela Lugosi who, remarkably, is lit and photographed in a style similar to that used by Karl Freund in *Dracula* (1931). We get our first full view of Domergue as she eyes Tom, using her large, sultry eyes, honey-hewed voice and excellent diction to full advantage. Her reply to Paul's offer of an alcoholic drink—"I don't drink"—is a subtle throwback to Lugosi's time-honored quote "I never drink ... wine." And Domergue, dressed in black throughout *Cult*, is most adept at adopting an air of menace. Watch her eyes sparkle with grim intensity as she gazes at a photo of the G.I.s she is in the process of victimizing! Note the ominous aura that hangs over the film each time she appears. This sense of imminent doom is exemplified by scenes in which various animals become agitated at the sight of Domergue—reminiscent of scenes from *Were-Wolf of London* (1935), *The Wolf Man* (1941), *House of Dracula* (1945) and others. Domergue augments *Cult*'s sense of doom with her own acting style, a combination of furtive glances and downturned, sorrowful eyes that belie her monstrous persona. No weird or elaborate makeup is needed here. The dread that infuses *Cult* is carried by Domergue's voice, facial expressions and lithe, reptilian body language.

Domergue's cold, steely, snake-like style is best illustrated in her chilling confrontation with Kathleen Hughes' Julia. Note how Domergue eyes Hughes with malignant intent as she spots Hughes clutching a book about cults. Domergue furtively asks Hughes, "What are you reading?"—but the line is coated with a patina of evil intent. Then, with cat-like grace and speed, she takes the book from Hughes' hands and eyes Hughes with unbridled malevolence. Domergue's beauty and undeniable evil seem inspired not only by Lugosi's Dracula, but Disney's wicked queen in *Snow White and the Seven Dwarfs* (1937)!

Cult also displays Domergue's range as an actress. Her Lisa combines remorseless evil with a sense of vulnerability and sadness. As Lisa begins to fall in love with Tom (Marshall Thompson), her face takes on a subtly distressed, sympathetic quality. She knows that she must fulfill the curse and kill Tom and his friends. The conflict between Lisa's emotions and her unholy mission is underscored in Domergue's facial expressions, which are limned by sadness and confusion in some of the scenes she shares with Thompson. Her confused, sad and almost childlike expressions are a startling contrast to the evil she exudes with the film's other characters. Watch how she torturously struggles with her feelings as she tells Thompson she loves him—and begs him to leave before her transformation begins: "I've said everything that I *can* say. Now, please go!" After Tom has fallen in love with Lisa, Paul attempts to convince him that the doe-eyed beauty is really an angel of death. When Tom broaches the subject with Lisa, she protests her innocence. We know she is lying but Domergue's beautiful, expressive eyes and downturned mouth evoke our sympathy anyway. And Domergue's ability to express an uneasy, tentative tenderness toward Thompson only serves to compound our feelings for her. In fact, by the time Domergue's Lisa is preparing to go after Paul, her sad-eyed look has nearly won us over: She clearly does not want to continue killing, but delivering death is her destiny. Domergue's ability to combine sorrow with the inevitability of her fate is also reminiscent of yet another classic horror icon: Simone Simon's Irena from *Cat People* (1942).

Domergue made two other genre films in 1955, *This Island Earth* and *It Came from Beneath the Sea*. In both, she provided solid if unspectacular support. Neither of those films permitted her to display her talent and range the way *Cult of the Cobra* did. Her Lisa emerges as a study in contrasts: insidious, monstrous evil tempered by vulnerability, sorrow and, as Lugosi once said, "the taint of human emotions." These same contrasts, along with Domergue's body language and natural beauty, also make her "monster" one of the sexiest and most sensual characters of the 1950s. Quite simply, *Cult* is Domergue's show, and she delivers a beautifully nuanced performance, superior to that of every other leading lady in Universal's 1950s catalogue.

Marshall Thompson is equally believable and natural as Lisa's victim *and* paramour. His scenes with Domergue are surprisingly tender and revealing as he expresses his love for her. Thompson also displays palpable anger when roommate Richard Long accuses Domergue's Lisa of murder. The film's final, arresting shot, of a distraught and shocked Thompson reacting to Domergue's death—and the truth about her—marks one of the most memorably downbeat conclusions to any of Universal's '50s entries. Thompson's chops in the genre are unquestionable, with 1958 being an especially productive year for him: *It! The Terror from Beyond Space* and *Fiend Without a Face*. In each of these films, Thompson's approach was always serious and credible. His work in *Cult* was no exception: His portrayal of a man refusing to accept the incredible truth about the woman he loves is a strong counterpoint to Domergue's cold, serpentine yet vulnerable persona. Their unusual chemistry is one of *Cult*'s most arresting qualities.

The serious undertone conveyed by Domergue and Thompson is countered by Richard Long's breezy, relaxed style. *Cult* sometimes teeters toward the downbeat, especially considering the somewhat somber approach of Domergue and Thompson. But Long's easygoing attitude does much to leaven what could have been leaden. His character is the first of the G.I.s to believe in the legend of the shape-shifting Lamians. As the others, including Thompson, scoff, Long conveys his true belief in the legend (and also invokes the werewolf and vampire tales of classic Universal lore). Long performs these scenes with a delicate blend of darkness and light—serious, but just shy of being *too* intense. Throughout *Cult*, Long remains a believer in the Lamian cult and its supernatural powers, marking him as the essential counterpoint in the relations between Domergue and Thompson. Long consistently and convincingly conveys to us the frustration he feels when his best friend refuses to believe that the woman he loves is a monster. Watch Long interact with Kathleen Hughes as he attempts to convince her of Domergue's evil intent: "Julia, meet her. Meet this girl. And I feel certain that you'll sense something ... something *strange*." In this scene, Long's versatility comes to the forefront as he subtly shifts from his usual tone to one of deadly earnest, without overplaying to the point of intensity. Long's natural style was later displayed in 1958's *House on Haunted Hill*. Not just another pretty-boy, he ranks as one the most underrated actors of the 1950s and early 1960s.

Admittedly, *Cult* is more a showcase for its actors than its technicians. Yet Russell Metty's camerawork aids in conveying a sense of dread and mood. The film opens with a fine torchlit shot of the Lamian temple's stone slab with its weird carvings. This sets the proper tone with a nod to Karl Freund's opening shot in *The Mummy* (1932). And in a throwback to *It Came from Outer Space*, Metty deftly employs the p.o.v. camera as, during a raging thunderstorm, the cobra slithers through the hospital window and ap-

Cult of the Cobra had a few chilling moments (James Dobson's Nick, pictured, would agree) but it apparently made no flurries at the box office: After its release, Universal U-turned away from supernatural horror and back to sci-fi monsters.

proaches Nick's bed. Just as the snake strikes and Nick wails, there's a cut to the open hospital window lit by lightning. It's one of *Cult*'s most effective moments.

The film's dark mood is also augmented by the Asian street scene in which Tom sees and pursues a veiled Lisa. Metty bathes the scene with shadows, blending the darkly dressed Lisa with the long, dark alley. His lens captures Lisa in long shot as if her black, serpentine figure disappears into the night. Metty also underscores the film's sense of dread with an effective scene in Rico's bowling alley. The camera floats onto an open window in the bowling alley, focusing on windblown curtains and accentuating the eerie, anxiety-laden tone. We fully expect the cobra to slither through the window and murder Rico. But the future *Fugitive* meets his fate outside, in his car. Metty waits until Rico is behind the wheel before showing us the ominous shadow of Cobra Lisa on the back of the driver's seat, looming up and ready for the attack. After the car crashes, Metty shows us Lisa, fully dressed, walking quickly from the accident and the murder. Metty's camera perfectly captures her slithering, serpentine menace.

An open window and blowing curtains also mark another example of Metty's ominous camerawork. As Tom enters Lisa's apartment to return her gloves, the camera pans to an open window, curtains billowing in the breeze—signaling Lisa's exit into the night. Metty also delivers an excellent shot of Lisa's shadow on a wall, which gradually transforms into that of the hooded cobra.

In *Cult*'s final scene, after Tom contends with the cobra and pushes it off the building ledge, Metty's camera shoots the snake from *above* as it slowly transforms into Lisa lying dead on the pavement. It's a fine coda to the film. *Cult*'s dearth of special effects transformations is reminiscent of *Cat People* and proof that elaborate makeup and special effects are no substitute for the chilling simplicity of imagination and dread.

Metty is also adept at lighting and shooting Domergue's face. He focuses on her beautiful eyes, lighting only the upper half of her face in a manner similar to Karl Freund's lighting of Lugosi in *Dracula*. Each time she is preparing to morph and dispatch her next victim, Metty's lens concentrates on her cold, dark eyes. Our ability to *believe* in Domergue as a monster is crucial to this film—and that belief is a function of Metty's camera and Domergue's multi-layered performance.

Amidst the fan furor over *It Came from Outer Space*, *Creature from the Black Lagoon*, *This Island Earth* and *The Incredible Shrinking Man*, *Cult of the Cobra* is perhaps Universal's most sadly underrated genre film of the 1950s. It was the studio's first truly supernatural horror entry of that decade—a form to which Universal would later return with a passion. *Cult* is also the first '50s film to seriously explore the effects of a deadly curse, invoking such classics as *The Mummy*, *The Wolf Man*, *Cat People*—even *Gunga Din* (1939), but also paving the way for *Curse of the Demon* (1958). And, like *Invasion of the Body Snatchers* (1956), the film can be viewed as a Cold War allegory: Even those we love and trust can turn out to be deadly enemies in disguise.

Universal announced in November 2015 that it would revive its monsters in movies with modern settings, tied to contemporary themes; writer-producer Chris Morgan said they would explore questions of, "Where do I belong in the world?" Sixty years earlier, Universal's Cobra Goddess (Faith Domergue) dealt with that dilemma in *Cult of the Cobra* with Marshall Thompson. (Photograph courtesy C. Robert Rotter, *Glamour Girls of the Silver Screen* website.)

But *Cult's* true calling card, like *Invasion* and *Cat People*, is its sinister subtlety: Eschewing expensive effects and makeup, Universal chilled us simply with subtle, moody camerawork and fine, modulated performances from a solid cast.

Tarantula (1955)

Full Credit Information

CREDITS: Produced by William Alland; Directed by Jack Arnold; Screenplay: Robert M. Fresco and Martin Berkeley; Story: Jack Arnold and Robert M. Fresco; Photography: George Robinson; Special Photography: Clifford Stine; Editor: William M. Morgan; Art Directors: Alexander Golitzen and Alfred Sweeney; Set Decorators: Russell A. Gausman and Ruby R. Levitt; Sound: Leslie I. Carey and Frank Wilkinson; Music Supervisor: Joseph Gershenson; Hair Stylist: Joan St. Oegger; Makeup: Bud Westmore; Assistant Director:

Frank Shaw; UNCREDITED: Based on the *Science Fiction Theatre* TV episode "No Food for Thought" by Robert M. Fresco; Original Music Composers: Herman Stein and Henry Mancini; Tracked Music Composers: Herman Stein and Henry Mancini; Music Conductor: Milton Rosen; Musicians: Emo Neufeld, Manuel Compinsky, Louis Pressman, Ambrose Russo, Lou Klass, Sam Fordis, Samuel Cytron, Sarah Kreindler, Leon Goldwasser, Howard Colf (Violin), Cecil Bonvalot, Harriet Payne (Viola), Victor Gottlieb, Stephen Deak, Joseph Ullstein, Alec Compinsky (Cello), Harold E. Brown (Bass), Roger Stevens, Ethmer Roten, Jr. (Flute), Norman Benno (Oboe), Blake Reynolds, Alan Harding, Karl Leaf (Clarinet), Lloyd Hildebrand (Bassoon), Eugene Ober, Gene Sherry (Horn), Gene LaFreniere, Don Linder, Robert Goodrich (Trumpet), John Stanley, Bruce Squires, H.L. Menge (Trombone), John De Soto and Ralph Collier (Drums), Lyman Gandee (Piano), Joseph Quintile (Harp); Special Photography: David S. Horsley; Camera Operator: Kyme Meade; Assistant Cameraman: Marvin Gunter; Still Photographer: Madison Lacey; First Prop Man: Hoyle Barrett, Jr.; Assistant Prop Man: Ed Case; Sound Recorders: William Sosteleo, Shwartz/Schwartz? and Kempt (John Kemp?); Mike Man: Glenn Anderson, Jr.; Cable Men: Thomas, Janssen and Hogue; Assistant Directors: Cliff Reid and Frank (Fred Frank?); Unit Manager: Norman Deming; Production Manager: Gilbert Kurland; Coordinator: Al Trosin; Makeup: Jack Kevan and Jim House; Special Appliances: Jack Kevan; Hair Stylist: Edith House; Wardrobe Man: Saul Rous; Wardrobe Woman: Nevada Penn; Dialogue Directors: Jack Daniels and Irvin Berwick; Script Clerk: Luanna Sherman; First Grip: Charles Cowie; Second Grip: Sherman Allison; Gaffer: Warren Munroe; Best Boy: Al Todd; Livestock Man: Phillips (Jimmy Phillips?); Welfare Worker: Gladys Hoene; Publicity Man: Banker (Fred Banker?); Laborer: Breyfogle; Stand-in: Benjie Bancroft; May 1955: Care and Feeding of Tarantulas: Jim Dannaldson; Second Unit (June 7, 1955): Director: Frank Shaw; Unit Manager: Norman Deming; Assistant Director: Fred Frank; Photography: C. Stine (Clifford Stine?); Camera Operator: Mehl (John Mehl?); Still Photographer: Thomas; First Grip: Losey (Art Losey?); Post-Production (June 16, 1955): Director: Jack Arnold; Unit Manager: Norman Deming; Assistant Director: Frank (Fred Frank?); Script Clerk: Luanna Sherman; Photography: Stein (Clifford Stine?); Camera Operator: Kyme Meade; Assistant Cameraman: Marvin Gunter; First Grip: Charles Cowie; Second Grip: Sherman Allison; Gaffer: Warren Munroe; First Prop Man: Ed Case; Assistant Prop Man: Todd; *Tarantula* Pressbook: Costumer: Jay A. Morley Jr.; American Film Institute: Sound Editors: Joe Sikorski and Ed Sandlin; *Variety* "Assignments" List (June 6, 1955): Sound Technician: Dolph Thomas; Assistant Editor: Bill Dornish; Special Effects: Frank Brendel; 80 minutes.

CAST: John Agar (*Dr. Matt Hastings*), Mara Corday (*Stephanie "Steve" Clayton*), Leo G. Carroll (*Prof. Gerald Deemer*), Nestor Paiva (*Sheriff Jack Andrews*), Ross Elliott (*Joe Burch*), Edwin Rand (*Lt. John Nolan*), Raymond Bailey (*Dr. Townsend*), Hank Patterson (*Josh*), Bert Holland (*Barney E. Russell*), Steve Darrell (*Andy Andersen*); UNCREDITED: Ed Parker (*Prof. Eric Jacobs/Attendant at Airport/Paul Lund*), Bud Wolfe (*Bus Driver*), Vernon Rich (*Ridley—Photographer*), Don Dillaway (*Jim Bagny—Hardware Store Owner*), Wendy Berwick (*Little Girl*), Norman Papson (*Mike Andersen*), Rusty Wescoatt (*Pickup Truck Driver*), Jack Stoney (*Driver's Helper*), James J. Hyland (*State Trooper Grayson*), Betty Jane Howarth (*Jean—Co-ed Secretary*), Dee Carroll (*Telephone Operator*), Tom London (*Jeb—Miner*), Edgar Dearing (*Ed—Miner*), Billy Wayne (*Mr. Murphy*), Robert R. Stephenson (*Warehouse Man*), Bing Russell (*Deputy*), Bob Nelson, Ray Quinn (*State Troopers with Submachine Guns*), Clint Eastwood (*Jet Pilot*), Jack Sterling (*Stunt Double*), Doris Barton (*Mara Corday's Photo Double*); Scene Deleted: Stuart Wade (*Major*).

Production History

By Tom Weaver

Seeing the great Leo G. Carroll in the trailer for *Tarantula* resulted in *weeks* of begging my father to take me to see it at the local theater. To keep the peace, he finally relented—and watched most of it by himself once I got too scared and hid out in the lobby. I'll never forget how burned up he must have been to find himself sitting alone, watching a giant spider movie!

—Joe Dante

Some of the makeup on the mortals in [*Tarantula*] would put Frankenstein to shame. If you have many kids in to see this, they'll be in the lobby during most of it.

—a Spring Valley, Illinois, theater manager commenting in *Boxoffice* magazine[1]

Universal contributed to the Big Bug boomlet in 1955 with *Tarantula*, the first such movie made after the gi-ant success of Warners' *Them!* (1954). *Tarantula* rates on the high end of the Big Bug movie scale, one of the few that almost lives up to its model. It even has the added spice of human monsters, three of them, each more horrific than the last. The first rears his very ugly head before the opening credits.

Part of the reason the movie works so well is the use of real tarantulas, photographically enlarged. *Them!* represents '50s sci-fi moviemaking at its most muscular, but you have to suspend disbelief in order to see its giant ants (actually huge puppets) as anything but what they are. As Monster Kids watch the various monsters in action in *The Black Scorpion* (1957), they think "Stop-motion animator Willis O'Brien was da *man*!," not that they're seeing any kind of living critters. And on and on through the catalogue of oldies. But the title role in *Tarantula* is played by real McCoys, and this enhancement helped to put the movie in the top tier of *Them!* follow-ups. This is the Big Bug movie with the best Big Bug; outside of the Gill Man, it's Universal's best '50s monster. Certainly their biggest.

Between the August 1954 wrap of *Revenge of the Creature* and *Tarantula*'s June 1, 1955, start date, Jack Arnold directed just one movie, the Universal Western *The Man from Bitter Ridge* (1955). During that interim, Universal's "scientific-tion" director got his foot in the door at Ziv Television, helming four Season One episodes of producer Ivan Tors' *Science Fiction Theatre*. Believe it or not, the seeds for the super-scarer *Tarantula* were sown on the set of that staid series.

Science Fiction Theatre's third episode "No Food for Thought," shot on February 22 and 23, 1955, was written by "a baby screenwriter," 24-year-old Robert M. Fresco; his original title was "The Hothouse People." John Howard starred as an Arizona county health officer whose curiosity is piqued after his examination of the body of a 52-year-old man dead from viral pneumonia: It has the muscle tone of a 20- or 30-year-old. The dead man had been working with reclusive Nobel Prize-winning nutrient biologist Otto Kruger in a house out in the desert. Gaining entry to the house with a sheriff's writ, Howard learns that Kruger, his assistant Vera Miles (daughter of the dead man) and Chinese research biologist Clarence Lung have developed an artificial nutrient and, now that they're on it, it has rejuvenated them. The down side: Their bodies now reject food, and they're highly susceptible to disease. Through transfusions of whole blood, Howard is able to restore the researchers to normalcy.[2]

Tarantula was a neat combination of the old and the new: Its bestial mutants were updated versions of the acromegalic Ralph Morgan in 1944's *The Monster Maker*, its mega-spider as up-to-the-minute as the latest Atom Age developments. Pictured: Morgan in *The Monster Maker* and Eddie Parker in *Tarantula*. (Photographs courtesy Ronald V. Borst/Hollywood Movie Posters.)

Any card-carrying Monster Kid who watches "No Food for Thought" will think of *Tarantula* a half-dozen times. Take the scene where Kruger talks about overpopulation, world hunger and his nutrient. Compare Kruger describing his work to John Howard…

> **[T]his Earth has gotten to the point where it cannot produce enough food to feed the people that live on it. This is gonna be an overcrowded world, doctor. Which means, not enough to eat. *Now* think what an inexpensive synthetic like our nutrient would *mean*.**

…to Leo G. Carroll's speech to John Agar and Mara Corday:

> **An overcrowded world … that means, not enough to eat. … The world may not be able to produce enough food to feed all these people. Now perhaps you'll understand what an inexpensive nutrient will *mean*.**

A desert setting; a "country doctor" protagonist; a funeral parlor scene with the doctor certain that a corpse can't be the man it's supposed to be; scientists working on a nutrient in a house far afield of civilization; an oversized rabbit in a lab cage; some nearly identical dialogue ... when Monster Kids familiar with *Tarantula* watch "No Food for Thought," they will hear the *déjà vu* bells jingling regularly. Needless to say, the big *difference* between the two is that "No Food" features no walloping spider, no mutants, no kind of excitement whatsoever. If one had to very briefly synopsize "No Food for Thought," it wouldn't even sound like sci-fi: A doctor learns that some researchers, experimenting on themselves, have made a mess of it and now he must find a cure.[3] And yet something about this plot appealed to its director: "[Jack Arnold] liked the script and he liked the quality of the dialogue," Fresco told me. "And one day he said, 'You know, there may be a *movie* in this.' I said, 'Okay with me.' Then he added, 'But you gotta put a *monster* in it.'"

Tarantula screenwriter Robert M. Fresco in a late-in-life shot. He joined the Screen Writers Guild in 1951 when he was 20, and from sci-fi movie beginnings (*Tarantula, The Monolith Monsters, The Alligator People,* more) he went on to become a documentarian. In 1970, he and filmmaking partner Denis Sanders won an Oscar for one of their films. (Photograph courtesy Judy Fresco.)

According to Fresco, he and Arnold re-convened a few times and talked about the possible movie, and then Fresco penned a seven-page story. Fresco said he came up with the idea of a giant spider ... but Arnold tried glomming the credit in the book *Directed by Jack Arnold*:

> **[My wife and I] were about to have a kid, and I was broke. I knew [Universal] needed something. At a certain time of the year my driveway used to be covered with tarantulas. They won't hurt you—I've picked up plenty of them—but I knew a lot of people were afraid of them. That's where I got the idea for *Tarantula*....**

So according to Jack, spiders in his driveway were his inspiration for *Tarantula* ... except when interviewed on-camera in 1983 for a German TV station preparing to show some of his movies. At that time, he said he got the idea from one of his own past projects, the 1948 documentary *The Chicken of Tomorrow*, which

> **dealt with a chemical preparation to produce huge chicken breasts. "That's an idea," I said. "Let's see what we can do with it. We'll combine that with something extremely horrifying." Most people are deadly scared of spiders. I took an empty page of paper and wrote *Tarantula*. "That will catch their attention," I thought. And then I developed the story of a scientist ... experimenting with a chemical nutrient which enlarges creatures, but the attempt goes awry. A spider escapes, and when [the scientist is injected with] the drug, he is afflicted with acromegaly.... It turned out to be a very good and successful horror movie. That's how I got to *Tarantula*.**

What the flock? Instead of spiders in his driveway, now *chickens* hatched *Tarantula*? A biological miracle! Okay, now it's chickens ... at least until you get to the interview Arnold did with *Cinefantastique*: He testi-lied to the magazine's Bill Kelley:

> **I tried to use the scientific discoveries the botanists were making in growing larger vegetables, the work of [Luther] Burbank, just taking it one or two steps further, using it on living animals.**

The only thing Arnold was consistent about was omitting Fresco from the history of *Tarantula*, even though Fresco wrote the *Science Fiction Theatre* that provided the backbone of the story, *and* (according to Fresco) was the one who thought of making the monster a spider, *and* wrote the script. The screen credits say "Story by Jack Arnold and Robert M. Fresco"—but to hear Fresco tell the tale, that's a lie. Fresco said that, in order to land the job of writing his first movie, he had to give Arnold an undeserved co-credit *and* a hunk of the money. "[Arnold] never wrote a word," Fresco told me. "Universal liked Jack—he'd already done *It Came from Outer Space* and *Creature from the Black Lagoon*, so he was 'hot' in that strata."

A 21st-century Fresco looked back on his decision to let Arnold steal story credit and part of the pay as "the price of admission" (admission to the ranks of screenwriter). "I remember discussing the situation with my agent Milt [Rosner]. He shrugged and he said, 'You wanna do the screenplay at Universal?' I said yes. He said, 'Okay, put Jack's name on it.' So I did. And that was it."

Things came together quickly: "No Food for Thought" wrapped on February 23, and 13 days later, *Hollywood Re-*

porter readers learned that "*Tarantula*, an original by TV writer Robert M. Fresco, has been packaged for production at U-I, with Fresco doing the screenplay, Jack Arnold directing and William Alland producing." Arnold's return to the studio to direct it was a one-picture deal which, at $750 a week, paid him $9500.

Fresco recalled having "a very good time" doing the actual writing of *Tarantula*. But the good times dried up when it was time for him to meet producer Alland:

Oh, I'll tell you about Bill Alland. With displeasure [*laughs*]! I was 24 years old and I had my eyes on the stars. I'd been raised as a clean kid in a dirty world. I mean, I wasn't a *baby*—I joined the United States Army the day I was 18 and I went to Ranger School. So I wasn't a fool or a virgin, but I *was* an optimist. One day early on, Jack says to me, "Well, now you're gonna meet Bill Alland," and he takes me to Alland's office and introduces me. Then Jack gives me a *look*—I realized later it was a warning look, but I didn't know it at the time. Then he turns on his heel and exits, and I'm surprised that he left. Well, he's left me in the lion's den: I find myself in this oversized office with this man who starts telling me how terrible the story is. How unhappy he is that he has to be involved with it. Who doesn't really have any confidence in my ability to write it. It was a pure "I'm gonna fuck with his head" kind of meeting. I was completely taken aback, because it was so surprising and so upsetting. I held my own, but I couldn't understand what was goin' on. Well, what was goin' on was, Alland was saying "I'm the boss and you better believe it" and a *nyah nyah nyah* and a scowl and a this and a that.

I can't believe, looking back, how vulnerable I was. I mean, the Robert M. Fresco who's got the Academy Award and the Cannes Film Festival and all the documentary festivals and the Guggenheim Fellowship is *not* the same guy who stood in Alland's office and listened to him give me shit. *I* didn't realize he wanted me to walk out so he could put [screenwriter Martin] Berkeley on the script. So he was stuck until I was done and fulfilled my contract and left with a smile on my face—and the next thing I know, Jack tells me, "Marty Berkeley's on it." I ask, "Why?" He says, "Well ... because." I ask, "What do you mean, 'Because'?" and he says, "Well ... he and Alland are buddies."

Berkeley, past writer of Alland's *Revenge of the Creature*, and future writer of Alland's *The Deadly Mantis* (1957), was brought onto *Tarantula* "to get a credit and make some money," said Fresco. He continued,

[Berkeley] paraphrased my scenes. He didn't change a single character, he didn't change a single name. It was a joke. He just sort of ... rewrote lines. He did just enough to get the credit. (Somewhere I have the original and the final script, and there's really no tangible difference.) And I realized the fix was in from the beginning: Alland was just waiting for me to walk out so he could bring in Berkeley. But I was learning the ways of [*singing*] *Hol*-ly-wooood, and that was part of my upbringing.

Fresco described to me the Screw Job he got from Arnold (taking co-credit and part of the pay) and the Screw Job Part Deux from Alland (bringing in Berkeley). Then it was *déjà screw* all over again when I made him aware that Arnold typically made himself out to be the one and *only* writer of *Tarantula*.[4] "Well, take my word for it—not a word [did he write]," Fresco repeated. "Not a word. He didn't even invent the spider, we just talked out the idea of what kind of a *thing* to have that could grow, what could we possibly have as a lab animal that could get big and frighten somebody."

Who needs Nutrient Type 3Y? If lies were cheese sandwiches, Jack Arnold could cure world hunger.

Topcast in the movie, John Agar fills the prescription as **MATTHEW HASTINGS, M.D.** (the name on his office door). Agar had become a Universal contract player on June 1, 1954, and was in the studio's Underwater Tank doing 3-D tests for his first assignment, *Revenge of the Creature*, 11 days later. He was in no more Universal movies the whole of his first year,[5] but Universal lifted his option for another year on May 25, 1955. He began working in *Tarantula* a week later, June 1, his first "anniversary" there.

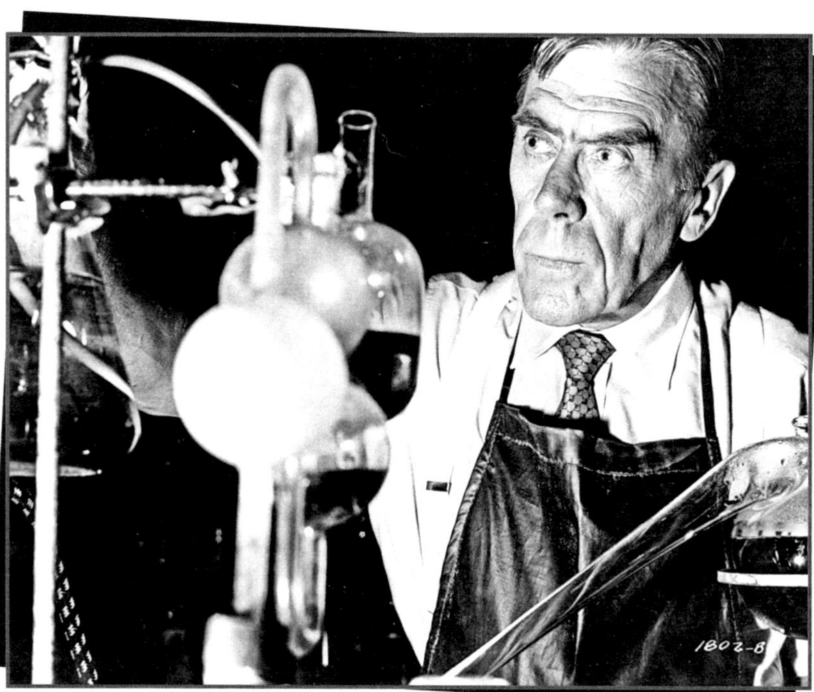

According to the *Hollywood Reporter*'s *Tarantula* reviewer, Deemer's (Leo G. Carroll) "sugar-free atom mixture is supposed to make everything get better (unfortunately, none of it spills on the dialogue)." (Photograph courtesy John Antosiewicz.)

For the role of "Steve" Clayton, Universal called Mara Corday up from their bullpen. And for Prof. Deemer, a soldier of science on the battlefield of disease (the "disease" of world hunger), Universal gave their monster movie a touch of class by signing Leo G. Carroll, a character actor with a résumé filled with top-flight movies and a few Broadway hits; he had just recently finished playing the general store proprietor in Paramount's *We're No Angels.* When Carroll's commitment to *Tarantula* was announced in the trades, he was in England attending his son William's graduation from Oxford. If Britisher Carroll as an American giant-monster movie's resident scientist strikes you as odd casting, remember that he followed in the Oxfordsteps of Cecil Kellaway in *The Beast from 20,000 Fathoms* (1953) and Edmund Gwenn in *Them!* (1954).

Fresco's involvement with the movie did not end when he finished his script. At Arnold's invitation, he accompanied the director to Apple Valley to look at possible locations, and was often on the set. Regarding the location scouting, he told me,

> **Jack had been a pilot in the war, and he found out that I was a civilian pilot. So, prior to production, we flew ourselves to Apple Valley to scout locations. He got Universal to pop for a day's rental of a Cessna 170, a four-seater, and the two of us flew all the way out there, we had lunch in Palm Springs and flew ourselves *back*! He was the pilot, I was the co-pilot. It was fun. My one location flight, and I helped fly the plane [*laughs*]!**

"By the way," Fresco added, "I gotta tell you that the lawyer who did my contract for *Tarantula*—do you know the first question he asked me? 'Are you a Communist?'"

Based on a final screenplay dated May 18, 1955, Universal estimated that *Tarantula* would have total direct charges of $265,900.

Synopsis

> By George, you just can't predict what's liable to come galloping out of the American desert next.
>
> In *It Came from Outer Space*, a hair-covered blob of Jell-O hid out among the cactus and terrorized everybody in sight.
>
> Ants the size of race horses descended upon Los Angeles and chewed up the local populace in the spine-tingling thriller, *Them!*
>
> Now comes Tarantula, a spider with thyroid trouble....
>
> —Al Ricketts, *Pacific Stars and Stripes*, January 16, 1956

In a pre-credits sequence, we see a patch of Arizona desert, an otherworldly landscape marked by scrub and bizarre rock formations. The only sound is the wind. A man in pajamas (Eddie Parker) wanders into view, weaving and lurching like a puppet on strings, until he finally flops to the ground with a thud. In a closer shot, we see him struggle to his feet and face the camera. His features are distorted, halfway bestial. He looks like Mr. Hyde in *Abbott and Costello Meet Dr. Jekyll and Mr. Hyde*, right down to the little moustache (i.e., it might be the same mask). A few more unsteady steps. Another face-first flop. Buzzards—death's patient sentinels—circle. His fingers claw at the sand until his hand goes limp in death. The camera tilts up up up to again take in the landscape and sky and with great musical fanfare the title *Tarantula* appears on screen.

In nearby Desert Rock, Puma County Sheriff Jack Andrews (Nestor Paiva) consults with Dr. Matt Hastings (John Agar) about the body. The sheriff thinks it's biologist Eric Jacobs ... "but maybe he ain't." At the undertaker's, Matt lifts the sheet and announces that it isn't the body of Jacobs ("This man has had the disease for *years*"). In walks Jacobs' colleague Prof. Deemer (Leo G. Carroll), who takes a peek and says that it is indeed Jacobs' mortal coil. According to Deemer, Jacobs fell victim to acromegalia, a rare glandular condition that distorts the face, neck, hands and feet; his first symptoms showed four days ago. Matt's not buying it.

Deemer returns to his home, set back from the highway in the middle of desert nowhere, and makes a beeline for his lab full of animal cages. Reaching through gloves into a dry box, he fills a syringe with liquid (Nutrient Type 3Y) from a vial and then crosses to cages containing a white rat eight times normal size and a guinea pig as big as a sheep. In a large glass cage is the prize nightmare in this mutant menagerie, a tarantula several feet in diameter. Apparently Nutient 3Y is like steroids ... on *steroids*! (In the pressbook, Deemer's nutrient is called "the 'horror' drug.")

While Deemer prepares to inject a monkey, another acromegalic man, Paul Lund (Eddie Parker again, with Hyde-type face and giant swollen forehead, clad in pajamas and robe), lurches into the lab and attacks Deemer. Lund swings a lab stool at Deemer, accidentally shattering the tarantula cage glass. Deemer throws a jar that misses Lund and hits an electric panel, and soon the lab is ablaze. As the tarantula exits through an open exterior door, Lund chokes Deemer into unconsciousness and sticks him with the nutrient syringe. Lund collapses and dies as the lab continues to burn. At last Deemer comes to, and rushes to get a fire extinguisher. Later, by lantern light, he digs a desert grave for Lund. He doesn't know that he's been injected with the atom juice—or that Tarantula took to the hills.

At the Palace Hotel where Matt has his office, he meets head-turner Stephanie "Steve" Clayton (Mara Corday), a new arrival in town, in need of a ride to Deemer's. En route to the professor's in Matt's convertible,[6] Steve, an Owens Uni-

Like many sci-fi movie scientists, Prof. Deemer (Leo G. Carroll) had good intentions but left behind an earthquake of damage—including to himself. *Variety*'s reviewer said, "Carroll is excellent in his scientist role." (Photograph courtesy Robert Skotak.)

versity student doing graduate work in biology, says she's taken a summer job with Deemer and Jacobs. Matt breaks the news that Jacobs has died. Tarantula, making a quick cameo, appears on the highway after the car has passed; it's now the size of a tank.

Matt and Steve arrive at Deemer's in time to "save" the old gent from nosy, pushy newspaperman Joe Burch (Ross Elliott). Matt introduces Steve to the professor; she asks if her fellow student Paul Lund still works there. "He's not with us any more," Deemer replies with double meaning. He shows them around his burned lab and talks about his goal of producing a nutrient that will prevent hunger in the world of tomorrow, when a multiplying population and a finite food supply may add up to lots of rumbling bellies. This being a sci-fi thriller, once the words "radioactive isotope" and "the atom" pass his lips, we in the audience know that it's now permissible for *any*thing to happen.

Days later, when Matt and Steve run into each other in town, he offers her a lift back to Deemer's. She's falling under the spell of the desert, and asks him to pull over near a rock formation called Devil's Rock. They're sitting at its base when boulders start tumbling from the top; Matt and Steve scamper for their lives. After they drive away, we see what started the rockfall: Tarantula, now vastly larger, looms over the crest.

At Deemer's, Steve brings Matt into the lab where she's shocked to see that a rabbit and a baby rat injected with Nutrient 3Y that very morning have already increased in size. After Matt leaves, an uncharacteristically choleric Deemer lights into Steve for bringing Matt into a lab where confidential experiment research is in progress. She hears every word he says but mostly she fixates on his face, now starting to show signs of acromegalia distortion. A peek in a mirror makes Deemer aware at last that he was on the receiving end (from Lund) of his own nutrient syringe.

The sheriff brings Matt to the ranch of Andy Andersen (Steve Darrell), who last night owned cattle but today only piles of their bones, "stripped clean, like peeling a banana." Nearby is a pool of white goo, several feet across and a few inches deep. That night, the horses in Andy's corral sense danger and start running in circles. Tarantula appears atop a nearby hill, temporarily roosts there like an unhurried Grim Reaper, and then starts down toward the corral, "making more noise shaking its claws than a regiment of Latin maraca players" (from the *Cleveland Plain Dealer* review). We get a Tarantula's-eye view as the roaring monster closes in on a rearing horse. Shotgun in hand, Andy runs into the corral and into a nightmare: He gets off one rifle shot and several screams as the super-spider descends upon him. Next we see a pickup truck with sheep in the back, rolling through the night—and toward Tarantula. It throws the truck sky-high and then advances toward the wreckage.

Converging on the truck crash scene the next day, Matt, the sheriff, Burch and State Trooper Lt. Nolan (Edwin Rand) bleakly eyeball the skeletons of the driver, his helper and the sheep. Nearby are more pools of goo. Matt takes a Thermos-full back to his office and determines that it's related to insect venom. Deciding to ask Deemer to verify his findings, he phones the professor's house, and Steve answers. While they're talking, Deemer (just off-camera) accosts Steve, who screams. Matt rushes to Deemer's, where we see that the professor's face is now even more malformed. Although suffering from acromegalia's suffocating effect, he gasps out the story of how his co-workers Jacobs and Lund injected themselves with the nutrient. When Deemer mentions that one of his test subjects was a tarantula, a light bulb comes on over Matt's head.

In his private plane, Matt flies to the Arizona Agricultural Institute and meets with Dr. Townsend (Raymond Bailey) of the Zoology Department's Entomology Laboratory. Townsend says that the goo is tarantula venom and projects for Matt a 16mm film that shows tarantulas in action. Meanwhile, back at the ranch, Tarantula, now many storeys tall, knocks down telephone poles as it crosses a highway. On the menu for dinner: two old miners (Tom London, Edgar Dearing) sipping coffee outside their mine.

Home sweet home: Tarantula returns to its old stamping grounds, the Deemer place, creeping up on it by night as Steve is preparing for bed. It sees her through her windows and begins wrecking the house to get at her. Deemer, wakened by the noise, sits up in bed and gives us a great look at his mutant face, which now appears half-melted (his right eye has traveled south, *à la* Karloff in *The Raven*). When Tarantula comes crashing into his bedroom, acromegalia suddenly becomes the least of Deemer's headaches. Nightgown-clad, Steve goes tearing out the front door just as Matt's car comes to a skidding stop in the drive. They zip away and Tarantula starts after them. Deemer's house, formerly a two-storey showplace, is now a one-storey fixer-upper.

Claws for alarm! Mara Corday cowers beneath "Science's Deadliest Accident," Tarantula. (Photograph courtesy Ronald V. Borst/Hollywood Movie Posters.)

On the highway, Matt and Steve stop as they see the sheriff's car and several state trooper cars headed in their direction. Tarantula crests a hill in the distance, eliciting a "Jumpin' Jupiter!" from the sheriff. They head for Desert Rock in the cop cars, leaving two troopers (Bob Nelson, Ray Quinn) with submachine guns behind to slow Tarantula down. The men's bullets have no effect, and they can't get away when Matt's car fails to start. The troopers *do* slow Tarantula down (**CRUNCH CRUNCH**), just not the way they intended.

Come the dawn, Matt, Steve and Burch are on hand as a deputy supervises the placement of boxes of dynamite on the highway near Devil's Rock. Tarantula appears, crawling toward them until it's right over the boxes and they're detonated. After a few tense moments with the smoke from the blast concealing Tarantula from view, it emerges unharmed and continues to advance.

Everyone hightails it back to Desert Rock and stands in the middle of the street in the evacuated town as Tarantula, now roughly the size of Flagstaff, creeps across the sea of desert toward them, chattering deafeningly. Suddenly four jets appear in the sky: Sands Air Base jets, requested by Nolan. The head pilot (Clint Eastwood) and the others fire rockets at Tarantula, but the monster doesn't seem to notice, and now it's towering over the town. Then the flyboys start dropping napalm, and keep dropping it, until the Mighty Tarantula looks like the Great Chicago Fire.

Cast Biographies

John Agar as Dr. Matt Hastings

> DR. MATT HASTINGS—a small-town M.D., but there is nothing of the hick about him. In his early thirties, lean, bright, with an almost Southern charm and indolence of manner, he loves his work—and the ever-changing desert. He has a bulldog tenacity and plays his hunches.
>
> —character description from the *Tarantula* script

The son of an Illinois meat packer, John Agar was 24 in September 1945 when he left private life behind and married former child star Shirley Temple (then 17) at Wilshire Methodist Church in Los Angeles. The thousands of traffic-blocking fans outside the church that night made the event look more like a movie mob scene. Three years later, Temple and Agar met and, egged on by John Wayne, courted again—this time on screen in the cavalry Western *Fort Apache*, Agar's movie debut. He went on to appear in the Wayne war movie *Sands of Iwo Jima* (1949) plus a second Wayne Western, *She Wore a Yellow Ribbon* (1949), where the *She* of the title (Joanne Dru) wears that symbolic ribbon for cavalry lieutenant Agar.

A lot of gossip ink was splashed on the Agars' 1949 split, with Temple hauling into court all the usual beefs (drunkenness, staying out late, lipstick on his collar). This, and Agar's well-publicized inability to separate the bottle and the throttle, killed his career momentum.[7] In August 1951, a judge branded habitual drunk driver Agar a potential killer and he soon found himself in durance vile; for a while, the only elbow-bending he did was with a chain gang pick and shovel. After he shed the sheriff's honor farm hospitality, he and new wife Loretta Barnett Combs perched at his mother's Brentwood home while seeking a nest of their own. (Agar had married model–movie extra Loretta in Las Vegas in May 1951 over the objections of the district judge performing the ceremony, who thought Agar was drunk.)

Washed-up movie-wise by the early 1950s, Agar took work and got exposure wherever he could: He sang in vaudeville (he had hopes of becoming a film musical star), guested on a middle-of-the-night radio show, helped judge a beauty contest, showed up at a theater opening, etc. He also exercised his still underdeveloped acting muscles in his TV debut on the series *The Unexpected* ("Agar is stiff and lacks warmth"—*Variety*) and in the straw hatters *The Gramercy Ghost* with Sally Forrest and *Peg o' My Heart* with Joan Evans. Playing a British nobleman in the latter, he was "inclined to be a trifle wooden" (*Variety*).

Momentarily fast-forwarding ahead a decade: In 1962, 22-year-old June Wilkinson co-starred on stage with Agar in *Pajama Tops*, a sex farce she described to me as "silly, but an audience pleaser." They did it first at the Seattle World's Fair, where it was such a tremendous success that it went on the road and then landed on Broadway. For Wilkinson, Agar was "a real pain in the ass in the beginning. There was a scene where he sat on a couch and I had to jump on him, and my makeup would get on his suit—I couldn't *help* it. He was always very fussy about the way he looked, and when a little makeup would get on his lapel, he'd gripe. I said, 'What do you want me to do, not wear makeup?'" (As if a single drooler in the show's male audiences was looking at Agar's lapel. Or looking at Agar, period!) Wilkinson went on:

He hadn't done many stage shows, I'm sure, so he wasn't used to all that sort of thing, he wasn't casual about it, everything was a major issue. I didn't think he was that comfortable on stage. When you're doing a show, occasionally you'll want to make a suggestion, "Why don't we try this or that?," or other actors will suggest something and you'll say "Sure!" You couldn't *do* that with John. He had to do it exactly the way he learned it. He never wanted to try anything new.

According to Harry and Michael Medved's book *The Golden Turkey Awards*, the bust-up of the John Agar–Shirley Temple marriage, "fortunately for bad-film buffs ... pushed him down that Glory Road toward the roles in low-grade Westerns and horrendous science fiction films for which he is best known." And we bad-film buffs are very glad it did.

Back to the '50s: After a few years of catch-as-catch-can acting gigs on TV and for indie movie producers, Agar was signed by Universal in 1954 and put right to work in *Revenge of the Creature*. A berth at a major studio coulda-shoulda meant smooth sailing, but...

> Bill Alland, producer of *Tarantula*, is importing real [spiders] to make the picture more realistic. If you were a film actor, how would you like to play opposite a tarantula?
>
> —*Variety* columnist George E. Phair, May 12, 1954

...Agar wasn't wild about the fact that the Gill Man movie was followed by *Tarantula* and then *The Mole People* (1956). According to one newspaper writer, "Agar has had a good deal of experience out-acting monsters. He is convinced that every time U-I producers get a brainstorm about a creature from another world they think of Agar for its co-star." On April 16, 1956, a day when Agar was on a *Mole People* set with a cloth bag over his head, being manhandled by one of the Beasts of the Dark, *Variety*'s Army Archerd wrote, "John Agar, now in *Mole Men* [*sic*], after *Tarantula* and *Creature*, hopes he soon gets to work with people again."[8] Tired of the creature feature grind, the Universal contractee wanted out. Decades later, he told *VideoScope* magazine interviewer Raymond Alvin,

William Alland was the producer [of all these monster movies]. Seemed like any time one would come up, he'd come and get me. …So when my contract came to a close, I went over to [Universal v-p James Pratt] and I said, "I'd kinda like to be doing other things besides science fiction films." At that time, they were grooming Tony Curtis, George Nader, Rock Hudson. And he said to me, "We can't make you any guarantees." … I said, "Okay, no hard feelings, but I think I'd just rather go on my own, be a freelancer." So I left. Doggone it, I went right back into science fiction.

Well, not "right back"; his first post–Universal was AIP's Western *Flesh and the Spur* (1956) with Marla English, and then he was off to Japan for a small part in Universal's *Joe Butterfly* (1957). *Then* the monsters reinfested his movie career, starting with *Daughter of Dr. Jekyll* and *The Brain from Planet Arous* (both 1957).

In the interim between those two bargain-basement thrillers, he made another movie abroad: *Day of the Trumpet*, shot in the Philippines. While there, Agar continued to grasp the grape of happiness, as co-star William Phipps remembered well:

John Agar was an alcoholic. I mean, a *raaaging* alcoholic. To get the picture finished, I had to baby-sit him, because a couple of times they had to stop shooting, and shoot stuff over, because he was too drunk, or he was still recovering and his eyes were obviously glazed over. So I would sit with him in his hotel room night after night, drinking Cokes and coffee and watching TV, and keeping him engaged in conversation, just to keep him sober and out of trouble. … If I hadn't done that, we wouldn't have been able to finish the picture.

It was amazing: He was the worst abuser of the booze but he never got belligerent, he never got cross, he never insulted anybody.

Perhaps not, but there *were* Agar's periodic strolls down Crazy Street; for instance, the day that Phipps and Agar went to a bullfight:

There was a female bullfighter with blonde hair from the United States, and she was *awful*. Agar and I were in the stands together, and he was drunk, and he was *booing* her at the top of his lungs: "Booooo! *Booooo!*" John got everybody *else* to booing too. It must have been very embarrassing for her, but she *was* terrible. Then, later on, he ran down and got into the fucking bullring [*laughs*]—can you believe that? They had to get him out of there before he got killed!

Sometimes his drinking was not much more than an inconvenience to his co-workers but, at least once, Agar had a sodden impact upon others. In the late '50s, actor-stuntman Robert Hinkle had aspirations of becoming a TV producer, and along came a golden opportunity to start his own series, *Test Pilot*. Using investors' money, he shot a pilot episode with Agar in the lead. But after Pontiac semi-committed to sponsor it for NBC, Agar fell off the wagon with one of his louder thuds. Hinkle wrote in his 2009 memoir *Call Me Lucky: A Texan in Hollywood* that on New Year's Eve 1959, Agar

came to my house for a small get-together, then left for another party. He didn't drink at my house, but I guess he couldn't resist the temptation at his later stop. I picked up the paper the next morning to stare blankly at a headline announcing that he had been

John Agar was initially reluctant to become an actor, saying in a latter-day interview, "I was scared for the first 25 years I was in the business!" Well, with co-stars like Tarantula, who can blame him? (Photograph courtesy Alexander Rotter.)

arrested for drunk driving. ... Back then, drunk driving was sometimes swept under the rug or buried by publicists, but unfortunately for John, he was a repeat offender. To make matters worse, he had been driving with a suspended license.

Hinkle told his investors to be ready for the worst because he knew that Pontiac probably would not sponsor a show starring a serial drunk driver. When the car company backed out, Hinkle had lots of 'splaining to do to his investors who had been left high and dry. And Hinkle's chance at a new career as a TV producer, which was in the bag, was over before it began, because Agar was in the bag.

The abovementioned *Pajama Tops* came to the Great White Way (the Winter Garden Theater on West 50th) in 1963—but without Agar. "Unfortunately, John didn't *get* to Broadway because he had his drinking problem," June Wilkinson revealed. "When he first got the job, he was good ... but then one day he showed up drunk, there was no way he could go on. So they replaced him with Richard Vath. Richard was the director, but he had done the play as an actor a lot of times and he knew it backwards and forwards so he just went in and took over."

Wilkinson added,

But I really liked John years later, when we started doing memorabilia shows. He had obviously been off alcohol for a long time, he was now "in a good place," and he was the sweetest man then. I really liked him at the end of his life, he was a very, very nice human being. His whole big problem was alcohol.

June Wilkinson and John Agar did *Pajama Tops* for nine weeks on a Seattle stage before it went on the road: Miami, Pittsburgh, Jamaica, even the U.S. Naval base at Guantanamo Bay, Cuba! (Photograph courtesy June Wilkinson.)

Continue reading about Agar in the *Revenge of the Creature* chapter of this book's companion volume *The Creature Chronicles.* And there'll be yet more on him in *Universal Terrors, 1956–1960.*

Mara Corday as Stephanie "Steve" Clayton

STEPHANIE (STEVE) CLAYTON is working for her doctorate at a nearby University. She is an attractive bit of fluff, but don't let externals fool you. Behind that pretty forehead is a brain.

—character description from the *Tarantula* script

That's how *Tarantula* viewers were supposed to perceive "Steve" Clayton. With drop-dead-gorgeous Mara Corday in the role, some reviewers didn't buy it, *The Philadelphia Inquirer*'s Mildred Martin quipping that Corday "looks as though she wouldn't recognize a test tube if she fell over one." Okay, maybe Mara *didn't* quite look the part, but except for the Mildred Martins of the world, probably not one viewer of *Tarantula* has ever complained.

Welsh-French-English, a child of the Depression, she was born Marilyn Joanne Watts in Santa Monica in 1930. At age three she drew a crowd by dancing the hula on a beach. "I just loved the applause," she told *Fangoria*'s Steve Swires. "I guess it was always in me to be a performer." As a teenager she began working as an usherette in the legit theaters the Belasco and the Mayan, learning about live stage presentations in the process.

At the age of 15 it became apparent that her 36-inch bust, 24-inch waist and 35-inch hips would look much better in a photographer's lens that they did in schoolgirl's rompers.

—"Biography of Mara Corday (Appearing in the Hal Wallis Production, *Money from Home*)," 1953

With her mother's encouragement, she became a showgirl (even though just 17, underage) at renowned showman Earl Carroll's Hollywood theater-restaurant. Dropping her real name in favor of Mara Corday provided an extra touch of exotica. She quickly advanced from the ensemble line to principal showgirl, and then to appearing in skits with comic Pinky Lee. Corday tells the story of this part of her life in words and pictures on her website maracorday.com, whence came some of the information in this paragraph.

Carroll's 1948 death in a no-survivors airliner crash closed his theater, and Mara went on to other venues. She also did photographic modeling[9] and acted in a little theater production where she was spotted and signed by a talent agent. This led to roles on some shoestring TV series and screen tests at various studios. At MGM and Fox she was told she didn't photograph well, a judgment that mystified Corday who had been voted *the* most photogenic West Coast model by several picture magazines. In the summer of '53, inked to a contract at Universal, the auburn-haired knockout was an eager-beaver pupil in its development program: diction, singing, dancing, fencing, riding a horse, etc. And Universal found spots for her in their movies, initially in bitty parts: *Yankee Pasha, Playgirl, Francis Joins the Wacs, So This Is Paris.* After that, she spent most of the rest of her on-camera time in the studio's Westerns.[10]

Mara Corday thought that she and husband Richard Long would make a great show biz team but instead he resented her working at *all,* throwing monkey wrenches into the cogs of her career whenever he could. (Photograph courtesy C. Robert Rotter, *Glamour Girls of the Silver Screen* website.)

At one point during her Universal years, Mara and low-on-the-totem-pole contractee Clint Eastwood had to do a scene from Noël Coward's *Private Lives* in acting class, with studio brass observing and then deciding if the two players' options would be picked up. She said in her *Fangoria* interview that she told Eastwood, "We are so *wrong* for this scene that I need a drink to get me through it"; but with all the local bars closed for some holiday, they had to search the studio for a fellow guzzler who could provide them with some liquid courage (it turned out to be Edgar Buchanan).

"I liked Mara, she and I just hit it off great," Mamie Van Doren told me. She continued,

> **She was a lot like I was, we both sort of marched to the beat of a different drum. … I was always "different," Universal didn't know what the hell to do with me. And Mara was the same way, she was kind of promiscuous and … she had a little problem with alcohol. They had to doctor her up quite a bit in the mornings—it starts to show if you drink, it starts to show in the eyes and on the face, I don't care *how* old you are.**

Mara came *thisclose* to being in both of Universal's Big Bug movies: She was assigned to *The Deadly Mantis,* but was so unhappy about it that she betook to a nearby bar (with a *Deadly Mantis* script in hand and pal David Janssen in tow), moaned to him about it, got to drinking, and began tearing out script pages, making them into paper airplanes and sending them sailing. Her Universal bosses weren't happy about her antics and a short time later, when a number of the contract players were pink-slipped, so was she.[11]

The first thing she did post–Universal was the cheapie Western *The Naked Gun* (1956); she told interviewer Mike Fitzgerald, "I knew I was in trouble when they asked what I wanted to play—the heavy or the ingénue." In 1957 she added more giant monsters to her list of co-stars, the bus-sized bugs of *The Black Scorpion*[12] and the astro-buzzard of *The Giant Claw.* By the time she made them, the man in her life was actor Richard Long; they married in 1957 and by 1960 they were the parents of three. The middle one was born in September 1958 while Long was starring in *House on Haunted Hill*; he handed out cigars on the set. He could also have shown off the new issue of *Playboy* in which Mara was the centerfold. (The photos weren't taken for *Playboy* but for an *Esquire* magazine layout, years earlier.)

The Corday-Long marriage was marked by frequent fights and a slew of separations. A co-star of popular teleseries

(*77 Sunset Strip*, *The Big Valley*), Long had ongoing heart problems that would cut short his life in 1974; according to Mara, while he was dying, "[he] chose to be in bars with strangers instead of with me and the kids" (Fitzgerald interview). When Long had multiple toes in the grave, Lex Barker, Mara's former co-star and romantic partner, reappeared in her life, wanting to get back together with her. With Long dying, she couldn't bring herself to do it. Then 54-year-old Barker cashed in *his* chips—an out-of-nowhere heart attack that laid him out on a Lexington Avenue (Manhattan) sidewalk—ahead of Long.

When Long's first wife, actress Suzan Ball, died at age 21 in 1955, she left $10,000 to her younger brother Howard; but Howard had disappeared, couldn't be found and didn't get the money. At Long's 1974 funeral service, Suzan's father appeared out of the past and walked up to Mara to tell her that Howard had been located and wanted his dough!

After Long's passing, Corday hoped for a comeback but couldn't get an agent ("They didn't want to know me"), so the "comeback" began and ended with one episode of TV's *Joe Forrester*. Her old Universal crony Clint Eastwood made her day by giving her minor parts in *The Gauntlet* (1977), *Sudden Impact* (1983), *Pink Cadillac* (1989) and *The Rookie* (1990). For years she talked about having production deals in the works, putting together (with her older son Carey) a *Big Valley* reunion show for NBC, etc., but it all seemed to come to naught. And by 1995, when she gave her *Fangoria* interview, she'd even given up the idea of pursuing additional acting jobs:

> **I've put on weight, and I don't like the way I look in [the Clint Eastwood] films. I would like to look better than I do now. … I know that I'll never look the way I used to, but my contemporaries all look better than I do. I'm afraid I'm beginning to look like a bag lady. I had better do something about it, so my fans don't throw up.**

Leo G. Carroll as Prof. Gerald Deemer

> Prof. Gerald Deemer—a world-famous nutritional expert and physician, is in his late sixties. He is a kindly, cultured gentleman, slightly vague, with the look of the future in his eyes.
>
> —character description from the *Tarantula* script

Many of the stateside articles and mini-bios on Leo G. Carroll make a point of his Englishness, and the fact that years over here had not put a dent in it. The actor was indeed brought up in Yorkshire and London, and talked as though he had a mouthful of monocles, but he once pointed out, "[T]hat doesn't mean I'm English. My father was a wild Irishman who read *The Freeman* [*The Freeman's Journal*, "Ireland's National Newspaper"] every week and my mother was as Irish as himself."

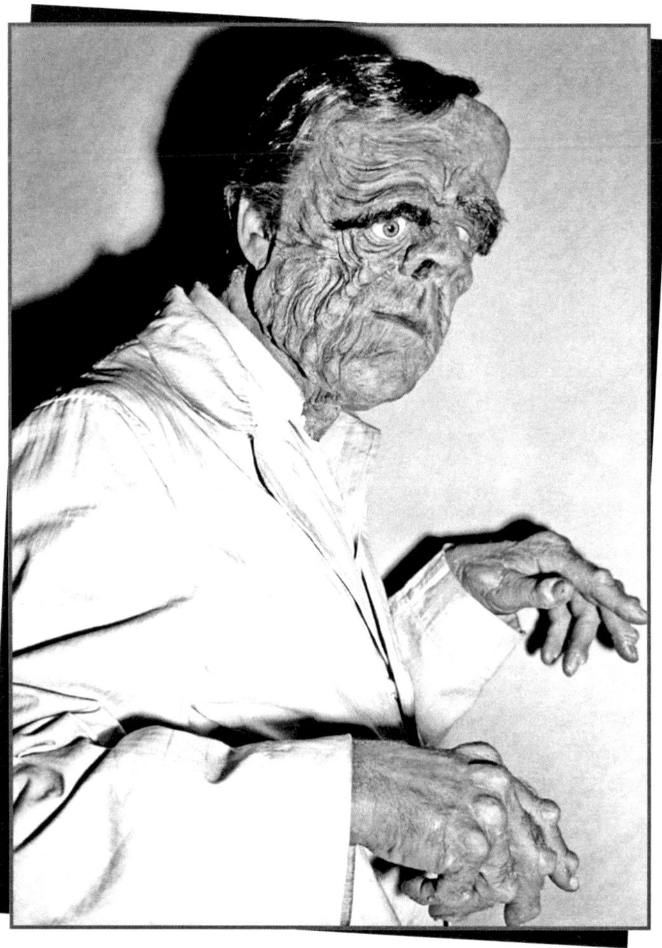

The *Tarantula* pressbook says that Leo G. Carroll wears "the most frightening makeup seen on a human being since the days of Lon Chaney."

The youngest of six children of a British army officer, Leo Grattan Carroll was born in Weedon, Northamptonshire, in 1892. Probably there was an expectation that he would go into the army,[13] "but someone chucked a play at me one day. I read it. And I read others. As I grew up I realized that some of the plays I was reading were being performed in the West End. In the end I was steeping myself in theater. When a reckless director assigned me a part in an amateur production, really, the mischief was done. I had to become an actor." According to an interview he gave around the time of *Tarantula*, he was 16 when he played the oldest character he had so far (1955) *ever* played, a white-haired attorney in a London production. In 1911 he made his professional debut on the London stage via *The Prisoner of Zenda*; the following year, he made his first appearance before Broadway footlights.

Soon the curtain went up on World War I and Carroll joined the Artists Rifles, a regiment consisting largely of performers, musicians, artists and civil servants. During a 1916 battle, a bullet went through both his lungs (he called it "a very clean drilling") and it took him two years to get out of the hospital.

In the mid–1920s, Carroll made the U.S. his home and began dividing his time between New York and London (and later Hollywood). In 1934, he told *The San Francisco Chronicle* with a sigh that probably he'd never get the chance, "but what I have always really wanted is to be a real old-fashioned knockabout clown!" That was the same year he appeared in his first movies, Metro's *Sadie McKee,* playing a butler, and *The Barretts of Wimpole Street,* as bedridden Elizabeth Barrett's (Norma Shearer) doctor. Soon he could be found in occasional movies of tangential Monster Kid interest, among them *London by Night* (1937), *A Christmas Carol* (1938, as Marley's Ghost), *Bulldog Drummond's Secret Police*, *Wuthering Heights* and *Tower of London* (all 1939). On Broadway in the 1940s he added several portraits to his stage gallery, among them Scotland Yard's Inspector Rough in the psychological melodrama *Angel Street* (with Vincent Price and Judith Evelyn) and the title character in *The Late George Apley*, the latter based on a Pulitzer Prize-winning novel.

He also kept racking up movie credits, among them a half-dozen Hitchcocks starting with *Rebecca* (1940), Hitch's first Hollywood directing gig. Carroll's sixth and last for the Master of Suspense was *North by Northwest* (1959) in which he memorably played the Professor, a droll, tweedy U.S. Intelligence Agency bigwig. Despite his lugubrious countenance, lined face and shaggy brows ... or maybe *because* of them.... Carroll was a hit as the title character in TV's *Topper* (1953–55), a stuffy banker whose house is haunted by two fun-loving ghosts (Anne Jeffreys, Robert Sterling) determined to get him to loosen up. Other TV credits included a *Matinee Theater* version of *Angel Street* that re-teamed him with Price and Evelyn, an episode of Boris Karloff's *Thriller* and a regular berth on Gene Kelly's short-lived sitcom *Going My Way*.

For Baby Boomer couch potatoes, Leo G. hit the heights with his casting as Alexander Waverly, head of the secret Manhattan headquarters of the United Network Command for Law and Enforcement, in the hit spy-fi adventure series *The Man from U,.N.C.L.E.* A character very much like *North by Northwest*'s Professor, Mr. Waverly dispatched his enforcement agents Napoleon and Illya (series stars Robert Vaughn and David McCallum) on their various missions. While Napoleon and Illya globe-trotted and battled evil THRUSH operatives, "I'm stuck sitting at that bloody table all the bloody time," Carroll half-seriously told *TV Guide*. Apparently he *did* want to get in on the action: Jon Heitland's *The Man from U.N.C.L.E. Book* reveals that he requested more action scenes because his grandchildren were wondering why Mr. Waverly sat around all the time. "So a script was changed to allow him to administer a karate chop. Because of his age, several takes were necessary, but when he did get it right the entire crew erupted in spontaneous applause." When the spin-off series *The Girl from U.N.C.L.E.* with Stefanie Powers and Noel Harrison came along, Carroll played their boss as well.

At the time, he lived in a large Hollywood home with his wife (since 1927), Nancy, tending to his roses and tinkering with clocks and old cars. In 1972, after a long illness, Carroll died at Presbyterian Hospital, survived by Nancy (who died later that same year), their son and the grandchildren.

From left, Leo G. Carroll, Robert Vaughn and David McCallum, the stars of TV's *The Man from U.N.C.L.E.* For his performance as Mr. Waverly, Carroll was twice Emmy-nominated (Outstanding Performance by an Actor in a Supporting Role in a Drama), and twice he lost. Open Channel D ... jection!

Of his career, he once said, "It's brought me much pleasure of the mind and heart. I owe the theater a great deal. It owes me nothing."

Ross Elliott as Joe Burch

> JOE BURCH ... runs the local newspaper and wields considerable influence. He likes the facts, sir, and he doesn't like to be horsed around.
>
> —character description from the *Tarantula* script

A product of New York City, Ross Elliott (real name: Elliott Blum) did his first acting in plays at summer camp and in high school. While at the City College of New York, he entertained thoughts of becoming a lawyer, but he also went into the dramatic society. Their production of *The Last Mile* "was done in the Stanislavsky method of acting," he told me, "and I got into it." He enjoyed acting so much "that it led up to the point where, I guess in my senior year, I was sitting there cracking the books for my final exams and finally I was 'over-studied' and I just threw the books away and said, 'Oh, the hell with this, I'm gonna be an actor anyway!'"[14]

After doing some summer stock, Elliott, then 20-ish, became part of Orson Welles' Mercury Theatre, playing minuscule parts on Broadway in their modern-dress *Julius Caesar*, *The Shoemaker's Holiday* and *Danton's Death*. On Welles' *Mercury Theatre on the Air* radio series, he performed on the infamous Halloween 1938 *War of the Worlds* broadcast ("That was one joke that backfired," Elliott told an interviewer on the set of a 1955 *Navy Log*). He described his Mercury days to me as "an exciting time, it was a helluva good thing for a guy to be tied up with." Another young Mercury Player was William Alland, and perhaps because of their association in Mercury days, Elliott was in three Alland movies, including *Tarantula*.

Edwin Rand, left, Ross Elliott, John Agar and Nestor Paiva can't imagine how men and livestock are being reduced to bones—"stripped clean, like peeling a banana"—leaving behind puddles of insect venom.

Elliott went into the army on August 4, 1941, pre–Pearl Harbor. Thanks to an old summer stock chum, Ezra Stone, he was soon part of the soldier-casts of various touring shows, including the biggie, Irving Berlin's morale-builder *This Is the Army*. "We went overseas with it and we played *every*where in the world where there were American troops," Elliott said. "That was quite a saga." Alongside many other *This Is the Army* players, he also acted in Warner Brothers' 1943 film version of the play.

Back in civilian life, Elliott returned to the stage; he hoped that touring in *Apple of His Eye* with Walter Huston would get him out to Hollywood, but the tour ended early in Detroit when Huston left to appear in his director son John's *The Treasure of the Sierra Madre* (1948). "One day while we were touring, he read us the [*Sierra Madre*] script," said Elliott. "'I'm gonna do this with my boy' was the way he put it. Every day during that tour, he reserved time that no one could get near him, and he worked on that script and worked out that wonderful characterization. One day he showed us that dance that he did in it." Soon Elliott made his way out to the movie capital where his first job was in the hard-hitting, but now all but forgotten *The Burning Cross* (1947), an exposé of the Ku Klux Klan. "[It's] smash material for dynamiting exploitation and film is thrilling enough to live up to sensational bally," *Variety* raved. (In 1951's *Storm Warning*, Elliott, *sans* hairpiece, was a Klansman himself.)

In 1950 he appeared in the indie *Woman on the Run* which should have been titled *Man on the Run*: Elliott, sole eyewitness to a gangland-related killing, goes on the lam because he knows it won't be healthy to testify. His estranged wife Ann Sheridan must find him herself, to give him the prescription medicine he can't go without. Elliott appears only in the first and last reel and yet this was seen as a good opportunity for him; trade papers reported that *Woman* was the "Broadway newcomer's" first film, even though by 1950 he'd done a passel of them. *Variety* columnist Mike Connolly called Elliott "a dead ringer for Sexy Rexy [Rex Harrison]. Difference is, Elliott likes it here."

Apparently he did: In his 40-year Hollywood career, he amassed a list of hundreds of movie and TV credits. He had his biggest movie roles early on; at that time, he was helped by the fact that he was known to be a New York actor. "Then I started losing jobs three years later to New York actors," he told interviewers Tom and Jim Goldrup. "I don't know when I lost my citizenship." Movie-wise the closest he ever came to starring roles was in the unremembered programmers *Woman in the Dark* (1952), *Problem Girls* (1953) and *Carolina Cannonball* (1955). For some reason he played a corpse, uncredited, in the Rita Hayward-Glenn Ford *Affair in Trinidad* (1952). Now and then there was also a return to the stage, including a Hollywood production of *Joan of Lorraine* with Luise Rainer, who was attempting a comeback. "What I liked about the stage," he told the Goldrups,

> **was that you put your two feet on the ground, and you feel it through your feet and sense an audience out there. Having to project; project excitement, but at the same time project vocally. I have a hunch that maybe I lost something when I was conscious of the camera. It would look right into your head, through your eyes and down your throat. I begin to work a little lower and I became a character actor.**

Some of his credits are of special interest to Monster Kids:

- He enjoyed pretending to be caught in an Arctic blizzard in *The Beast from 20,000 Fathoms* (1953) even though he broiled in furry winter wear on the "North Pole" soundstage during a midsummer hot spell.
- He found Lon Chaney to be "really a fascinating guy" as they worked together several times, including on *Indestructible Man* (1956), with Elliott as the crooked lawyer who puts Chaney's "Butcher" Benton on his fast-track trip to the death house.
- He was a suit-and-tie cop in *Monster on the Campus* (1958), falling victim to the title beast.

He was also on TV's *Science Fiction Theatre, One Step Beyond, Twilight Zone, Thriller, Voyage to the Bottom of the Sea, The Invaders* and more. Twice he appeared on *The Time Tunnel*; he told me, "The first one I did, [producer] Irwin Allen was crazy about, and he brought me back for a second one." That's when the fun ended:

> **I got in trouble with the Master [Allen] on that second one, because of my predilection for saying "I can't say this line": My character referred to creatures from another world as "supernatural," which to me meant ghostly, and I brought this up to the director. Irwin the next day was very, very upset. He walked up to the director and said, very firmly, looking at me without saying my name, "Don't let these actors change my dialogue." I think I lost some work doing that.[15]**

On one episode of TV's *I Love Lucy*, Elliott played Ross Elliott [*sic*], director of Lucy's Vitameatavegamin commercial; in other *Lucys* he played Ricky's publicity agent. The actor who never got on a horse until 1950 when he did the Sam Katzman serial *Cody of the Pony Express* played Wyatt Earp's brother Virgil in several episodes of *The Life and Legend of Wyatt Earp* and Sheriff Abbott in scores of episodes of *The Virginian*. Talking to *Western Clippings* magazine's Boyd Magers, the Virginian himself, James Drury, described Elliott as "always a shining light of reason on a set when emotions flared and people got overworked and overtired and nasty to each other. He'd come in, tell a joke and everybody'd relax and laugh."

The career that began in the rarefied atmosphere of the Mercury Theatre ended in 1986 with a supporting role in the tenth-rate *Scorpion* starring former karate champ Tonny Tulleners, "[who] makes Chuck Norris look like Laurence Olivier" (*Variety*). Like many actors, Elliott didn't retire, he got "phased out":

Ross Elliott said that in his career, he made "a few wrong turns, [including one or two] that I won't go into. If I hadn't made them, my career would have had more lasting up-turns. I think I might not have had the fade-out. But by and large, [my career] was exciting, there were quite a lot of exciting things." He's pictured here with wife Sue, shortly after their 1954 marriage.

It happened to a whole generation. Pretty soon you went on interviews and—I might sound a little bitter at this point—"What have you done lately?" Finally once I came out with the answer that we *all*, in joking, said we *would* give: I walked in somewhere and I looked at someone and I *knew* he grew up watching me, and he said, "Well, tell me about yourself. What have you done?" And I said, "About *what*?" [*Laughs*] And out I went!

My career petered out. I sold real estate for a while, and I kept working what jobs came along in between. I didn't really retire as much as I *got* retired. Occasionally the phone would ring and it would be somebody who remembered me or heard about me. Then all of a sudden it just wasn't there any more.

It was a good run. I'll be honest with you, I made some wrong turns. I made some career decisions and did some dumb things that cost me and sent me off-track. I was in a soap opera, *General Hospital*, they wanted me to stay, but I got mad about something, so when I got a chance to go back into *The Virginian,* I got out of *General Hospital*. Going back to *The Virginian* gave me the security to tell *General Hospital* to go screw themselves. But who I was screwing was me, because that *General Hospital* character went on and on and on [now played by Peter Hansen] for decades and it grew to an hour show from a half-hour show. That would have made me quite secure.

A cancer victim, Elliott died at the Motion Picture and Television Fund residence facility in 1999. He was survived by his second wife Sue.

Production

Tarantula went into production in Universal Studios' Gausman Gulch on Wednesday, June 1, 1955, scheduled for 14 days of first-unit work and three days of second unit. The actors on hand were John Agar, Ross Elliott, Nestor Paiva, Edwin Rand[16] and, working their one and only day on the movie, Steve Darrell and James J. Hyland. Things began with a bang: the day-for-night shot of Darrell as rancher Andy Andersen seeing (the off-camera) Tarantula in his corral and firing his rifle. Next came the Tarantula point-of-view shot as the camera dollies in and booms down on the shrieking Darrell. Rehearsing the actor and the camera and getting the needed footage required 45 minutes and a dozen takes.

With one of the movie's most frightening moments (Tarantula claiming its first human victim) already in the can, the company moved to Dabney Road for the post-truck crash scene of Matt, the sheriff, Burch, Lt. Nolan *et al.* surveying the truck wreckage, human and ovine bones and pools of venom. The scene features one of the movie's unintended laughs (or groans) as Matt eyeballs the venom pool, sticks a middle finger in it, sniffs it—and then *tastes* it. Mara Corday told me that that was the one scene in *Tarantula* she found "disgusting": "When I saw it with an audience, they all went *eeeewwww*!"

Needing to wait for good light caused a few delays during the Dabney Road shoot and also in Lawton Canyon where they reconvened after lunch for the scene of Matt and the sheriff arriving at Andy's to inspect the cattle bones and venom pool. The busy afternoon continued with a move to Stage 16's Sheriff's Office set, where scenes for different parts of the picture were shot until quitting time.

By the start of Day Two, what was originally projected as a 14-day shoot had been revised to 13. The whole of the second day was spent on Universal's familiar Courthouse Square, with more than two dozen extras moseying about, plus quite a number of vehicles (at various times, Matt's convertible, Burch's station wagon, the sheriff's car, police cars, a half-ton dynamite truck and three "atmosphere trucks"). Mara Corday was due on the set at 9:30; a wardrobe fitting delayed her until ten, but traffic-stopper Corday was worth the wait. For the actress, *Tarantula* was the start of three

Mara Corday behind the scenes with *Tarantula* director of photography George Robinson. (Photograph courtesy Robert Skotak.)

years of giant monster flicks: *Tarantula* in 1955, the indie *The Black Scorpion* which began filming around Thanksgiving 1956, and the one that *should* have been made on Turkey Day, Sam Katzman's *The Giant Claw*, in 1957. Being assigned to *Tarantula* was fine with Mara because, she told me, it was a Jack Arnold picture

> **and I got along great with Jack [who'd already directed her in *The Man from Bitter Ridge*]. He was a prankster, and I happen to like a very fun set. I like to tell jokes and kid around and that's what he did. ... He would tell dirty jokes, and then all of a sudden he'd break into a little dance. He used to be a chorus boy in New York, a little dancer, so he'd do steps. He'd fix your chair so that when you sat on it, you'd almost fall, things like that. [*Tom Weaver: Was he a good director?*] He was not the kind of director that gives you a lot, but then, in this kind of a film, what's there to do? There's not much plot. You're at the mercy of the "fright," the "horror," or whatever. You're at the mercy of the special effects people [*laughs*], 'cause if they don't do a good job, then the whole picture goes in the toilet. For instance, *The Giant Claw*!**

Before and after lunch, Agar, Corday, Elliott, Paiva and Rand clustered in the middle of the otherwise unpopulated street, enacting the last scene of the movie: reacting to the approach of Tarantula and cheering the appearance of the Air Force jets. Of course, as in all movies of this sort, no gargantuan spider was approaching (*duh*!) and there *were* no jets. Talking to Dennis Daniel in *Psychotronic*, Agar said that playing *Tarantula* scenes of this sort "was like being a kid all over again. We had to pretend that there was this big tarantula out in the desert with us. We were looking up and reacting to something that wasn't there! It was fun to use our imagination like that."

Throughout the last quarter-hour of the movie, Corday's Steve is dressed for bed, because that's how she was dressed when Tarantula attacked the Deemer house. Corday—who didn't like her *Tarantula* wardrobe to begin with ("really conservative")—told me,

> **I thought maybe I could at least wear a negligee for the ending—the whole last part of that show was me running away from this tarantula in a night outfit. But they said, "Oh, no, not on your life"—I had to wear pajamas, and even a light cover over *that*! So there was no sex appeal there [*laughs*]!**

Alland told me that Edward Muhl, Universal's head of production, "was ten years behind everybody else" and wouldn't allow actresses to show too much skin, so probably he was responsible for a no-sex-appeal Steve.

Among the actors playing bits on Courthouse Square throughout the day were Bud Wolfe (he was the Frankenstein Monster, plummeting into the sulfur pit in 1939's *Son of Frankenstein*) as the driver of Steve's bus, Billy Wayne as Mr. Murphy who provides the dynamite ("Don't forget to prime 'em!") and Don Dillaway as the hardware store owner chatting with Matt ("Say, when are you and me flyin' out for some more fishin'?"). Movie-wise, Dillaway was now playing nothing but uncredited bits after having starred or co-starred in a clutch of Poverty Row movies in the '30s. In *Pack Up Your Troubles* (1932), he and Laurel and Hardy were World War I doughboys, Dillaway a single father, and his death makes Stan and Ollie "responsible" for his little daughter.

On June 3 there was a return to Stage 16 to shoot a scene that ended up on the cutting room floor: In a briefing room, a skeptical Air Force major assigns two pilots to check out the report of a giant spider approaching Desert Rock. From the script:

INT. BRIEFING ROOM—CLOSE SHOT—WALL MAP—DAWN

(showing the outline of Desert Rock. A finger is tracing the outline. As CAMERA PULLS BACK:)

MAJOR'S VOICE

Well, there you are, gentlemen—

(The ANGLE is wide enough now to REVEAL a sleepy Major and a couple of weary young pilots in flying togs.)

MAJOR

The State Police're having nightmares—

(bitterly)

They want you flyboys to help 'em get back to sleep.

In a scene shot but not included in the movie, an Air Force major (Stuart Wade, with pointer) assigns pilots (Clint Eastwood and an extra) to a Tarantula "search and destroy" mission.

FIRST PILOT
(disgusted)

Not flying saucers again?

MAJOR

This is even better—they've got themselves a giant tarantula!

FIRST PILOT

A what?

MAJOR
(sarcastically)

St. George and the Tarantula. Get going!

Putting the briefing room scene on film took only 18 minutes, from lining up and lighting the stand-ins, to rehearsing with the actors, to getting it in the can; it appears to have been filmed exactly as described above. The skeptical major was played by Stuart Wade, past star of *Monster from the Ocean Floor* (1954) and future star of *Teenage Monster* (1958), picking up $125 for a quick morning's work. Dismissed at 9:05, he was probably home in time for breakfast. The weary young pilot who does all the talking, as you've probably assumed by now, was played by Universal stock player Clint Eastwood, then three days past his 25th birthday.

The rest of the morning was spent filming Sheriff's Office scenes. Nestor Paiva's Lucas, in the Gill Man movies, has always been a hit with fans, but I get more of a kick out of his Sheriff Jack. He's a far cry from Charles Drake's dour *It Came from Outer Space* desert lawman; he's got a sense of humor (and a few funny lines) and a back-slapping disposition, and it's fun to watch him ride Matt after Matt appears to bungle the Jacobs case. Sheriff Jack's more entertaining than the lawman characters in other movies of this sort, and when he runs for re-election, he gets my vote as Favorite Nestor Paiva genre character.

After lunch, in front of a Stage 22 process screen, various car scenes were shot: Matt, Steve, the sheriff and Nolan in the sheriff's car, speeding away from Tarantula; Matt and Steve in Matt's convertible, as they're being chased by Tarantula; Matt and Steve in the convertible en route to Deemer's, etc. This movie doesn't make the mistake some other '50s monster movies make: In *Tarantula*, as soon as the authorities set eyes on the giant spider, they're on the police radio asking for military help. This is in contrast to *The Monster That Challenged the World*, *The Monolith Monsters* (both 1957) and other flicks where communities risk the safety of all mankind by electing to battle gargantuan creatures on their own, as if outside help was not an option.

On Saturday, June 4, all the Palace Hotel interiors were done on Stage 16. There were two takes of Matt standing in his office, talking on the phone with the sheriff, the one we see in the movie and the other with Hank Patterson's nosy old codger of a hotel clerk visible in the distance through Matt's open office door, eavesdropping on *his* phone. Under the Preview Comment Card heading "Which Scenes Did You Like Most?," one member of the audience at an October 4 *Tarantula* preview wrote, "The hotel manager was good and had a good voice."[17]

> Apple Valley, on the vast Mojave Desert, is approximately 100 miles from Hollywood. It offers ideal situations for moviemaking. The weather is favorable for outdoor shooting, the desert scenery is beautiful for color filming, or even plain old black-and-white. This, plus the fact that the Apple Valley Inn offers complete facilities for housing a large movie company, makes it a favorite location site for all studios.
>
> —*Variety* ad for the Apple Valley Inn, 1956

Lots of alarm clocks were set to ring early on Monday, June 6: Cast and crew converged at the studio and then left at 5:45 for "the Golden Land of Apple Valley" to shoot most of *Tarantula*'s desert scenes. A seven-passenger car, a bus and a stretchout, all on that day's Special Equipment list, were presumably among the vehicles used to get the people there; others must have traveled in the cars needed on-camera (Matt's convertible, the sheriff's car, Burch's car, etc.). The first order of business: the highway shot of Matt and Steve in the convertible (driving away from the pursuing Tarantula) stopping when they see the procession of cars (the sheriff, Nolan and his state troopers) coming the other way. This shot and other parts of this scene, which in the movie takes place in the darkness before dawn, were photographed in the morning and early afternoon. For the Tarantula's-eye view of the two troopers scrambling to get out of Matt's car, the camera was high on a platform, zooming in on them.

After a 2:15-to-2:45 move to another stretch of highway, they tackled the scene of the dynamite truck being unloaded, wire strung, etc. The supervising deputy is played by Bing Russell. One scripted line in this scene hit a roadblock and didn't make it to the screen: Presumably to sidestep censor trouble, Universal's William Gordon advised producer Alland, "It is recommended that Nolan's line 'I'll *shoot* the first man that runs' [directed at the dynamite planters who start to flee, their work undone, when Tarantula appears] be modified to indicate equal firmness with less drastic severity."

Also on the to-do list: getting shots of various players' bug-eyed (bad pun) reactions to the sight of the approaching Tarantula. Doing these shots in the late afternoon was a challenge for Ross Elliott, who told me:

> **In that key scene, we were all standing in the road, and off in the distance we were supposed to see the tarantula. But it was late in the day, and between the sun and the reflectors, there was *nothin'* you could do to [make yourself]**

During World War II, America unsheathed her atomic sword. A decade later, movie theater screens were crawling with A-bombinations like Tarantula.

> **open your eyes wide at the sight. You were just frozen by the tremendous light! I guess all of us resorted to doing the same thing, which was all you *could* do: Drop your jaw and *try* to open your eyes [*laughs*]!**

A few shots later, with Tarantula still bearing down on them, suddenly Elliott is wearing sunglasses which I'd bet were his own, put on between takes; and then, when the camera rolled again, he forgot to remove them. An "ohnosecond" is the fraction of time in which you realize you've just made a big mistake, and there's an unmistakable ohnosecond vibe as sunglasses-wearing Elliott freezes up, does a lightning-fast turn away from the camera, whips off the glasses, then gets back into character.

For Alland and Arnold, *Tarantula* marked a return to an evocative desert setting, after their *It Came from Outer Space*. (In fact, the *same* desert—the Mojave near Apple Valley.) "Ranches" and "desert" don't seem like they should go together but they do in real life (weather permitting!) and in *Tarantula*, which is attractive among the Big Bug movies because it sometimes has the feel of a Western: It features a good bit of music originally written for Westerns (including its main title cue); we visit Andy's cattle and horse ranch; some actors and extras are dressed in "modern cowboy" clothes; Nestor Paiva plays a sheriff in double-pocket cowboy shirt, froufrou string tie, garish belt buckle, etc. The Western-garbed players, all clean as a new dime, look more like dude ranch cowboys, but it gets across the Western vibe, to the movie's benefit.

Cast and crew stayed overnight in what Mara Corday calls "a lovely lodge," presumably the Apple Valley Inn. You can see the place as it looked in 1953 in the movie *Highway Dragnet*; according to one of the inn's 1955 ads, it rented "Luxurious Rooms from $8." The next day, the *Tarantula* troupe filmed on more local sites, including the scene of Matt and Steve smoking and talking at Devil's Rock and coming *thisclose* to being pulverized by the falling boulders. Devil's Rock was "played" by a rock formation actually called Dead Man's Point, located at the eastern edge of the town of Apple Valley. Why it's called Dead Man's Point isn't known, but it's had that name for a while; it's referred to as Dead Man's Point in some 19th-century newspapers. Monster movie fans saw this location two years earlier in the *It Came from Outer Space* roadblock scene where the sheriff and his posse shoot at Glob Frank's approaching truck.

Universal didn't know it when they signed Mara Corday but she had a gap between two of her front teeth; to remedy the situation, a dentist gave her a dental veneer. By the time of *Tarantula* she could no longer wear the veneer, so instead she was melting wax and sticking it in the space. "That's what I did and it worked great—*until* we hit Apple Valley, which was 120 degrees!" she told me. "I would be standing there talking and then my teeth would melt [*laughs*]! We could barely get any of these shots, especially the ones where John Agar and I are standing by the rocks. That's when it fell out, and I had to keep getting my little Sterno going to melt more wax! One hundred twenty degrees, it was awful. When I wasn't working, I was in a bathing suit."

This being an Alland-Arnold Universal, "by law" there had to be a hand-on-the-shoulder scare moment, and this was put on film in the afternoon, with the sheriff coming up behind Matt at Devil's Rock and giving him a start. The script called for Matt to jump like a jackrabbit, whirl and bring his hands up as though to fight an attacker, but on-camera Agar's reaction is less extreme.[18]

A bit later, also at Dead Man's Point, Eddie Parker played his first of *three* characters in the movie: the mutant Prof. Jacobs, lolloping around like a drunken Indian, then dying face down on the ground. In this, the movie's curtain-raising sequence, he wears what might be the same Mr. Hyde mask he donned to double Boris Karloff in *Abbott and Costello Meet Dr. Jekyll and Mr. Hyde* in 1953, plus shoulder pads (or somesuch) to give his upper body a grotesquely swollen look. One wonders if anyone on the crew was at Universal a decade earlier, during real-life acromegalic Rondo

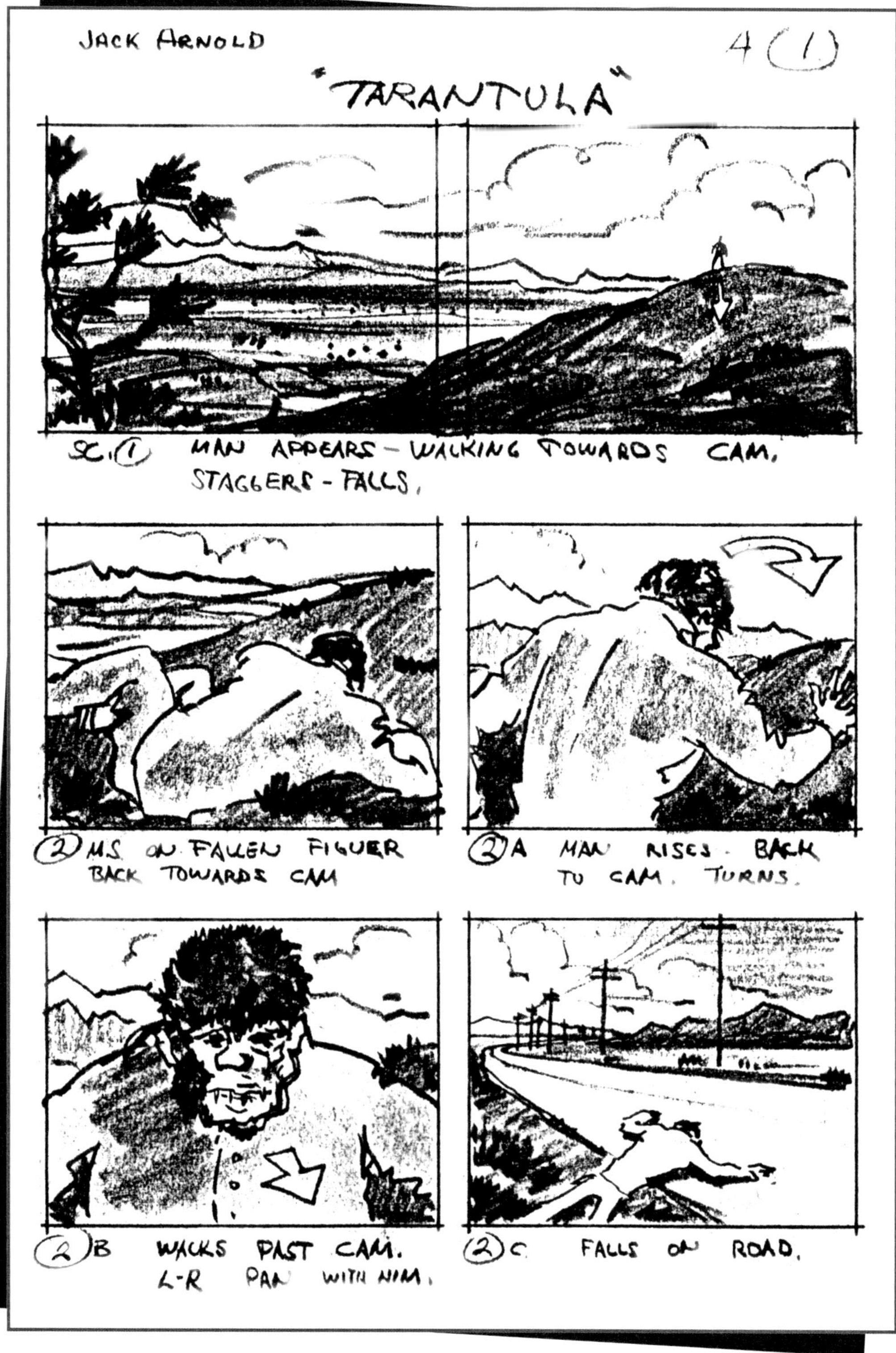

Page one of Jack Arnold's *Tarantula* storyboards. The acromegalic Jacobs looks even more like an ape man here than he does in the movie. (Storyboard courtesy Robert Skotak.)

keep upping the horror ante. In his day, Hatton had a face that launched a thousand shits, but that wasn't good (bad?) enough by 1955.

As Hatton fans know, the disease is acromegaly and *Tarantula* changed it to acromegalia. I asked Robert M. Fresco why this happened, and with his usual candor he said,

'Cause I probably fucked up [*laughs*]! Listen, let me tell you my standard operating procedure when I got to Universal. Every time. I would call the library and I would say, "Please send me a copy of *Merck's Manual of Medicine*." And I would sit there, drinking coffee and leafing through every hideous disease that could afflict the human race. And I came up with acromegaly. *I* don't know why I called it acromegalia, I have no idea. But I'm sure I'm quite capable of having screwed it up!

The sick notion of giving someone the disease via injection was the centerpiece of the Poverty Row horror flick *The Monster Maker* (1944) with J. Carrol Naish as the mad doctor on the syringe plunger end and Ralph Morgan on the sharp end.

Now that the moviemakers had shot their pre-credits sequence, it was off to a nearby airport for the first post-credits scene, Matt arriving by plane and chatting with an attendant. (The airport *has* to be Apple Valley Airport, just 300 yards from the Apple Valley Inn; around this same time, it was regularly seen in the *Sky King* TV series.) The attendant is again Eddie Parker, playing his second *Tarantula* character an hour after he finished playing his first. The rest of the af-

Hatton's horror heyday. The way Hatton looks is, obviously, the way a sufferer of that disease *really* looks, not like the two angry-looking ape men Parker plays in *Tarantula*. But as audiences started becoming scareproof, studios had to

ternoon was spent filming the plane taking off and landing. This same day, a second unit headed by director Frank Shaw shot run-bys (with Doris Barton, photo double for Mara Corday, in the car; I don't know who Agar's double was), plates, etc.

The first *and* second unit folks were all back at Universal by 10:20 that night. Ross Elliott, who made the trip alone, came back with a four-legged friend: He told me,

> **A puppy, more like a jackrabbit than a dog, was hanging around the set, and I brought it home. But ... poor little Joe, I should have left him in the desert. He had a pretty good life with me for a while, and then the night that my wife Susie and I moved from Hollywood to the Valley, into our first house, which we *still* live in, I took Joe out early one morning and he got away from me and ran into a car.... [*Elliott paused, still pained by the 40-year-old memory.*] That hurt. I kinda apologized to the little guy.... I should have left him out there.**

Most of the 8th found cast and crew again on Stage 16 for the scene of Matt consulting with the Agricultural Institute's Dr. Townsend. Without a toupee, Raymond Bailey, who played Townsend for a $250 payday, isn't instantly recognizable as the same actor who portrayed the spectacularly stingy banker Mr. Drysdale in the TV sitcom *The Beverly Hillbillies*. Jean, the co-ed secretary who sets up Townsend's 16mm projector, was Universal stock player Betty Jane Howarth, whom you might recognize as the woman who screams when the Gill Man shoots up out of the Ocean Harbor tank in *Revenge of the Creature*. The scene where Townsend shows Matt the 16mm nature film about tarantulas calls to mind the passage in *Them!* where Dr. Medford (Edmund Gwenn) projects a film on ants for the Washington bigwigs.

The first of *Tarantula*'s terrors appears in the pre-credits sequence: Eddie Parker as Prof. Jacobs, victim of acromegalia, here posing amidst the inhospitable rocks of the Apple Valley desert. Fifteen months earlier, some of Alland-Arnold's *It Came from Outer Space* exteriors were shot here. (Photograph courtesy Robert Skotak.)

After finishing the Dr. Townsend scene, Arnold & Co. moved to a part of the lot known as Southwest Property for the scene of the two miners (Tom London and Edgar Dearing), yukking it up over their desert campfire until Tarantula noisily surmounts the hill behind them. Edgar Dearing had played Sam, the desert rat-miner Globbed by the Xenomorph in *It Came from Outer Space*, but apparently he learned nothing from that experience because here he is, mining out on the desert again, and this time getting chased by the spider. The day ended with a high full shot (Tarantula's p.o.v.) of London and Dearing lying on the ground in "the spoon position," about to become spider chow. Two burros were brought to the location for use in the scene but they don't show up on camera, perhaps because someone felt it would look silly for Tarantula to bypass a thousand pounds of good eatin' for a shot at the two old coots.

Trade paper news blurbs indicated that Leo G. Carroll would be arriving home from England on June 8, and at eight a.m. on the morning of the 9th he began work on *Tarantula*. Carroll's first scene, appropriately, was Deemer's first scene in the movie, the professor's appearance at the funeral parlor (a Stage 20 set). In the afternoon, operations shifted to Stage 19 which housed Deemer's lab set. There Deemer filled his syringe with nutrient and crossed to the animal cages to give his giant white rat and guinea pig the once-over. Behind the cages was a process screen on which footage of the white rat and guinea pig was being projected, so a visitor to the set would have seen in person exactly what we see in the movie. Eddie Parker once again got in front of the camera playing his third *Tarantula* character, the mutant Lund.

The fight between Deemer and Lund was shot the next morning, with two cameras recording the action. To a set visitor it would have appeared as though there *was* a giant tarantula in the glass cage, as footage of a tarantula was being projected onto a process screen behind the glass. According to the Daily Production Report, the first take in which Lund shatters the glass was "n.g." so the glass was replaced and they had a second go at it. A shorter delay that same morning: "Cleaning monkeys cage."

A stuntman named Jack Sterling was on hand but presumably stuntman Parker took care of all of his own action, and it looks like Carroll throughout the scene; so *if* Sterling got in front of the cameras, the footage may not have made it into the movie. The lab fire is, disappointingly, more smoke than fire, perhaps to reduce the risk to Carroll, who was sometimes in the thick of it. After lunch they shot the scene of Deemer, on the now-wrecked lab set, contending with Burch and his photographer Ridley. The whole of the next day, Saturday, June 11, was spent on that lab set: in the morning and early afternoon, Matt and Steve's first visit with Deemer, who talks about his work; from mid-afternoon to quittin' time, Steve and Deemer working in the lab with the dry box, etc. The latter is a too-long, unrewarding scene whose sole purpose may have been to beef up the running time.[19]

Most of Monday, June 13, was devoted to getting some of the other scenes set on the Deemer house ground floor, including the moment where the professor, slaving over a hot microscope, rubs his upper right arm—the spot where Lund acro-punctured him. Courtesy of the makeup man, his left hand has a bit of the same look as the mutated hands of Jacobs and Lund.

When we see Deemer's hand and instantly realize that he now has acromegalia, we also realize why, in prior scenes, the camera lingered on the hands of Jacobs and Lund:

- As the mutant Jacobs lies dying in the pre-credits sequence, for several moments our attention is drawn to his hand, lumpy, and with bulging veins, clawing at the ground. (The script indicated that there should be a second long look at Jacobs' hand when his body is in the funeral parlor workroom, but the moviemakers didn't oblige.)
- And as the acromegalic Lund prepares to creep into Deemer's lab, for several moments our attention is focussed on his similarly horrid hand, reaching around the edge of a louvered door.

The moviemakers wanted us to know what acromegalic hands looked like, so that when we later saw Deemer's distorted hand, we'd know at once that Lund's attempt to give Deemer the disease via the syringe was a jab well done. Later they shot the tense hallway encounter between Deemer and Steve ("My laboratory is not open to the *public*, Miss Clayton!") where the audience—and Steve—see that acromegalia is now starting to show on Deemer's face. There was a mid-afternoon move to Stage 22 where, in front of a process screen, more Matt-Steve car scenes were filmed. Then on a small, dark "desert" set, Deemer sprinkled the last shovel-full of sand onto Lund's grave—and was nearly scared to death himself by the surprise reappearance of his screeching lab monkey. In the take that was shot on this date, the monkey jumped on Deemer's back; it would be shot again a few days later, this time with the monkey jumping into Deemer's arms. The latter take is in the movie.

In this behind-the-scenes photograph of Deemer's lab, Tarantula's cage has no back (and you can see people through it). That's because a process screen is going to be put behind it, and close-up footage of a spider projected onto it. Voila! Instant giant spider. (Photograph courtesy Robert Skotak.)

Yet more lab scenes were shot on the 14th, including the last one, where the mutated Deemer, in a state of near-collapse, comes clean about the deaths of Jacobs and Lund and describes his oversized lab animals ("Burned … all burned!"). In the afternoon, with footage of Tarantula projected on a process screen beyond Steve's bedroom window, Steve prepares for bed until she notices the venomous voyeur and screams, as debris and dust start to drop from above. A number of fans have opined that the Tarantula-at-the-window scene is hilarious because they've somehow reached the bizarre conclusion that Tarantula is "lusting" after Steve. If Tarantula instead came to Deemer's window in exactly the same way, would these fans assume Tarantula was lusting after *him*? Fandumb. It gets fandumber every year.

The Giant Monster at the Window already had a bit of a genre history. The granddaddy of all such scenes was in *The Lost World* (1925), with the loose-in-London Brontosaurus sticking its head through a building window and startling a group of card players. Perhaps the best-known Peeping Tom was Kong, excitedly peering through Ann Darrow's Manhattan hotel room window in *King Kong* (1933). *Tarantula* may be the '50s film with the best such scene, but there were a number of other contenders. Nineteen fifty-seven was a banner year for Giant Monster at the Window movies: Universal's mantis gaped at Marge at the polar base in *The Deadly Mantis*; one of Bert I. Gordon's locusts eyeballed a woman combing her hair in *Beginning of the End* (1957); and Glenn Manning (Glenn Langan) ogled a woman in her bathtub in *The Amazing Colossal Man* (1957), another Mr. B.I.G. opus. That same year there was also a not-so-giant at a very *small* window: the housecat clawing at dollhouse dweller Grant Williams, the Incredible Shrinking Man.

Mask hysteria! Mara Corday recalled of Leo G. Carroll, "He had a terrible time with that makeup; he had to have everything sipped through a straw 'cause it was like a mask that he had to wear. It took forever to get it on, so you don't take that off for lunch [*laughs*]!" *Tarantula*'s acromegalia appliances set Universal back $1675. (Photograph courtesy Alexander Rotter.)

On Deemer's bedroom set, amidst a shower of dust and ceiling plaster, two cameras recorded Deemer's death scene: The old professor contended with a giant claw forcing him to stagger backwards toward the mouth of the spider, positioned where his large bedroom window *was*, before Tarantula knocked it down (a breakaway window and cork bricks). The Daily Production Report makes no mention of any injury to Leo G. Carroll, but both director Arnold and writer Fresco recalled that the player was bloodied. Arnold's version of events, told to *Fangoria*'s Al Taylor: "[E]verything is falling down as the house crumbles, and Leo got caught in some of the debris. He cut his hands very badly and it gave me quite a turn. When finished, the scene was very real: that was real pain and agony on Leo's face and his reactions were too real for comfort." The "pain and agony on Leo's face" is a neat punchline to the story, except for readers who remember that Leo was wearing an acromegalia mask and therefore neither Arnold, nor anybody else, could see his face.

Also in *Fangoria*, Fresco told me:

There's a scene where the tarantula is attacking the house and the claw of the tarantula hits Leo G. Carroll.... Of course it was a fake claw and it was cushioned and all that, but they dropped it as they were shooting the scene, and they really hurt Mr. Carroll, they cut his forehead. Nothing *serious*, no stitches, but he had to go to the infirmary. That happened in the morning. He and Mara Corday and Jack were having lunch afterwards, when I was also in the commissary. I left the writers' table ... and I walked over to Mr. Carroll and I apologized for my spider having hurt him [*laughs*]. And he "responded in kind," he was funny as hell. He was very nice.[20]

Two reports of a bloody Carroll injury make it likely that the actor *did* do some leaking but, as noted above, it went unrecorded on the Daily Production Report.

Wednesday, June 15, was the thirteenth and last day of production. It began on Stage 19 with Steve dodging falling debris on both the lower and upper levels of the shaking-to-pieces Deemer home. The dirt on her was applied by a (lucky) makeup man. Next, after a move to Stage 22, came a re-do of the shot in which Deemer, just finishing his chore of burying Lund, is startled by the sudden reappearance of his chattering lab monkey. The Daily Production Report mentions a fake monkey, which must be what flies through the air into Deemer's arms.

Next they shot the scene where Matt phones the sheriff from the airport ("Round up every available man! Arm 'em, and..."). In the script, Matt calls from a telephone booth but in the movie he's in what appears to be an office. The big window behind him looks enough like Steve's bedroom window that it seems safe to assume that the moviemakers made things easy for themselves by doing this scene on the Steve's Bedroom set with Venetian blinds added. In 1955, audience members who knew that Agar's career had long-suffered from the wages of too much merry-making (his battle with the bottle) probably remembered it when Paiva's incredulous sheriff growled, "You must be drunk!"

Lunch, and then Clint Eastwood worked his second day on the movie, again playing the pilot: He did the cockpit close-ups that, in the movie, are intercut with footage of Tarantula on the wrong end of rocket fire and napalm bombs. All of the Eastwood footage this day was shot silent, the actor looping his lines at a later date (September 9)—and without the nuisance of trying to match lip movements, as the pilot wears an oxygen mask. He appears in a total of four shots. In the BBC documentary *The Man with No Name* (1977) the actor referred to *Tarantula* as "another biggie that I was in":

> **In that I played the part of the jet pilot who came in and bombed this giant tarantula at the end. I was enthusiastic when I read the part because I was enthusiastic about doing *any*thing that would increase my experience. But I have goggles on and a mask on and a helmet on, so it could have been just [anybody].**

Tarantula isn't the champeen Big Bug movie, that's *Them!*, but it has a leg up (sorry) on *Them!* and others by dint of its excellent use of real spiders.

After Clint was in the can, a break in the weather allowed the filmmakers to head out to the back lot where the Dabney House was used as Prof. Deemer's house. Various arrivals and departures were photographed, including (day for night) Steve running from Tarantula into Matt's arms.

The movie was in the can but, as always, there was still plenty to shoot. So, with Jack Arnold in charge, a post-production silent unit was at work the very next day, June 16. They started on the same location where principal photography got under way, Gausman Gulch. Two cameras recorded the horses stampeding around the corral; the neighboring hill was photographed, so that the special effects folks could later add Tarantula to that footage; and they got a "boom down" shot of a rearing horse—the giant tarantula's p.o.v. as it hunkers down for its next meal. The cold stare of the camera captures the gripping scene perhaps *too* well for animal lovers, as the horses sense danger in the air, start acting spooky but, penned in, can only run in circles and cry out as death on eight legs descends upon them.

A year after Universal's Dabney House was seen as Exeter's Georgia hilltop mansion in *This Island Earth*, a year *before* it was seen as Dr. Barton's lakeside home in *The Creature Walks Among Us*, the studio's special effects department placed it in a desert setting for *Tarantula*.

Then it was off to Southwest Property, where two cameras followed the action as the pickup truck became the *picked*-up truck, sailing through the air and crashing to earth. The thrown truck had to have been some old junker, not the truck we see in the footage leading up to that shot, because that lead-up (the truck tooling down the road, the sheep baaa-ing in the baaack) was the next thing filmed, in Killer

Canyon. On Stage 22, Arnold grabbed a process shot of the two men in the doomed pickup truck (Rusty Wescoatt and Jack Stoney), with "camera whirl[ing] at end as truck crashes" (the production report's shot description). The company was dismissed at 5:40.

Still at this point, the movie's title character had spent very little time before the cameras. Then on May 12, *Variety* columnist George E. Phair reported, "Bill Alland, producer of *Tarantula*, is importing real ones to make the picture more realistic." In July 19's *Variety*, as part of the article "10 Pix in Prod'n This Week at UI—Busiest in Months," it was revealed that "[s]everal days of special effects shooting with a giant tarantula are scheduled for *Tarantula*." A July 27 *Variety* item referred in the present tense to the shooting of the spider scenes.[21]

Eleven-year-old Susan Alland, producer William's daughter, saw some of this work being done:

Dad took me to the set where the special effects men were working. There were little miniature buildings that couldn't have been more than two or three inches tall, little tiny buildings, like a girl's dollhouse set kind of thing. One of the special effects men had a tarantula in his hand, and he had some paint, and he was painting the hairs on the body of this critter so it looked more grotesque than it is by nature. Then they'd kind of tickle the hind legs of the tarantula to make it crawl over these buildings, maybe with a little feather or something.

Perhaps Tarantula was goosed a time or two with a feather, but in *Fangoria* Jack Arnold recalled a different means of getting his hairy star from place to place:

We controlled the spider in *Tarantula* with air jets. We matched the rocks in the studio to the actual rocks out there in the desert, then shot them in perspective. We'd push the spider about with air jets until I got the shot I wanted. I would want, say, a leg to appear over the top of the hill first, then the mandibles, etc. Usually after about ten minutes we got the shot I wanted. [It was later superimposed] into the scenes with live actors.

Special effects wiz Robert Skotak gave me a more technical description of the process:

Out of white plaster, they sculpted a tiny terrain that matched the live action plate, at least as best as could be done from a non-three-dimensional image. The spider was lit and photographed walking on the small contoured landscape, casting its own natural shadow, which conformed fairly well with the location ground contours. They pulled mattes from the tarantula which also contained its shadow and composited the image. There's more steps as to how the tarantula shots were actually composited (percentage matte needed, roto work, etc.) in order to properly retain the shadow—which, of course, had to be somewhat transparent in order to look like a shadow, meaning *some* degree of ground detail had to still be seen, though darkened. But this is the very basic idea of what was done.

In a few shots of Tarantula standing on the horizon, the bottoms of some of its legs disappear in midair, the best (worst?) example being when it looms up over a hill at about the 55-minute mark. In some night scenes, and in the finale as Tarantula approaches Desert Rock, the monster is just a black-as-ink traveling matte; it's easy to tell, because we can no longer see the lighter patches of hair at its joints. In some last-reel shots of Tarantula outside town, you can't help noticing that it's transparent. But even if *Tarantula* isn't quite state-of-the-art even by '50s standards, its arachnid looks far more "real" than *Them!*'s puppets and *Black Scorpion*'s stop-motion models, simply because it *is* real. And the use of slow motion makes the monster even more loathsome, its unhurried, ponderous approach extending the agony of the prey that knows that, out in these wide open spaces, there *is* no escape. With sky backgrounds, Tarantula pauses on the hill overlooking the horse corral, and on a hill looking at Matt, Steve, the sheriff and the troopers, both times patiently, as the cat waits for the mouse, as if contemplating the situation before beginning its inexorable march. Columnist Jimmie Fidler rightly pegged *Tarantula* "a pure-blood horror picture."

> The outstanding factor in *Tarantula* is its excellent photography. The overgrown insect is a frightening looking thing. It appears as something pretty real and threatening.
>
> The overall atmosphere of the picture is one of supreme tension. From start to finish there is an air of mystery and suspense.
>
> —reviewer R.L.S., *Syracuse* (New York) *Herald-Journal*

Like *The Black Scorpion*, *Tarantula* includes insert shots of the monster's face. The spider puppet used in these situations is seen four times: as Tarantula is descending on the corraled horses, a few seconds later when it's attacking Andy, as it's descending on the miners and when it peers in Steve's window. At least Tarantula has the presence of mind not to drool when it's on-camera, the way the Black Scorpion does. The mechanical spider head was made at a cost of $930. The mammoth claw, seen in other scenes, set Universal back $750.

When we see things from Tarantula's point of view, its mandibles hang into the shots (on both sides) and we see the victims between them. The p.o.v. footage of its victims (one of Andy's horses, Andy, the two miners, the two state troopers) is always blurry. Tarantula must need glasses. *Tarantula* follows in the tradition of p.o.v. shots for Universal's '50s monsters; *It Came from Outer Space* and *Creature from the Black Lagoon* preceded it, and there were more to come.

This Tarantula puppet was made for close-up insert shots of the monster's face, as it descends on victims. It's also seen at Steve's bedroom window.

Poor Robert Fresco, who began his *Tarantula* adventure with a run-in with William Alland, ended it with another one, this time at the preview:

There was a line of dialogue that [during production] I realized was no good and I said, "Jesus, don't shoot that, Jack." And he said, "No, no. I'll shoot it and we'll cut it later." But he didn't, it was still in there. There is this moment where our hero John Agar is about to do something completely stupid, he's gonna go where he shouldn't go, and the girl looks at him and she says ... "Be careful." [*Laughs*] I did what *you* just did—I laughed at the preview. I was sitting behind Alland and I laughed. He turned and he *spit* at me, practically. (He didn't spit, but he went, "*Hey*! Be *quiet*, for God's *sake*!" He was just *furious*.) He didn't have enough sense to realize that it was a shit line and that it shouldn't be in the movie.

[*Tom Weaver: And the line stayed in?*] Jack didn't have any courage. That was one of the reasons Jack never [made it]. Jack didn't take chances. He wouldn't stand up to Bill Alland and say, "That's a terrible line. The writer said it's a terrible line, I agree with him, let's cut it."[22] But he was a *good director*. He had a profound sense of movement, he had an understanding of lighting, he was a good director. But he didn't have the balls. That's why, I guess, he had to lie and boast. I don't want to speak ill of the dead, but I'm telling it straight.

Special effects men also worked their magic on non-Tarantula shots, putting a desert on the horizon beyond Universal's Courthouse Square, adding desert around the Dabney House, etc., so that this studio-made movie's exteriors looked as though they were actually shot in those barren expanses.

Miniatures made for the movie, according to Universal paperwork, included an exterior desert miniature, miniature cages (for the shot of Tarantula crawling down out of its cage) and miniature telephone poles. The top of Devil's Rock, whence boulders rain down on Steve and Matt, was presumably also a miniature.

Tarantula was previewed at L.A.'s Orpheum Theatre on October 4, 1955, following a regular showing of *The Night of the Hunter*. Audience members filling out Preview Comment Cards were asked about the scenes they liked best; the answers included scenes featuring the spider, the transformation of Deemer and (again!) the hand-on-the-shoulder moment. Among the scenes that were *dis*liked:

Some scenes of magnified spider looked quite phony.
Scenes showing excessive closeup of the Tarantula.
Tasting of spider venom by Agar.

Other comments included:

This picture was so horrible I'm sorry I paid money to see it.
Who cares about the story—Mara was enough.
Mr. Agar has to loosen up a bit more, then he will be all right.
Best picture I've seen this year.
What's Mara's phone number?

If ever a Universal Terror deserved an exclamation point at the end of its title, it was *Tarantula*. Unfortunately, it didn't get one, though the title *is Tarantula!* on the various posters. The reports of *Tarantula*'s box office reception should also have included a few exclamation points. It began playing in late October, and by December 9, *Variety* was announcing that Universal's newest monsterpiece was "doing tremendous business throughout the country." When the show biz bible wrote about the reaction$ to the movie in various cities, they used words like "robust," "big," "tall," "nifty," "hefty," "wow" and "hotsy"(!). Universal coulda-shoulda created a trade paper ad with Tarantula wearing a Santa Claus hat, as the movie truly was an early Christmas present to exhibitors during that season when attendance traditionally slumped. Overseas the spider movie also had legs, with its London box office take described by *Variety* as "boffo" and "socko."

Tarantula, aided by a giant sidewalk spider display, is big at [Detroit's] Broadway-Capitol and top showing in city.
—*Variety*, November 23, 1955

Bruce Dettman, co-author of 1976's *The Horror Factory*, saw the spider movie as a moppet and recalled for me:

I first saw—but didn't hear—this film at the drive-in with my parents. They were watching some mainstream movie while *Tarantula* was playing across the highway at another

outdoor theater. Fortunately, I knew this in advance and brought my binoculars with me. Even without the sound I was thrilled by it!

On January 11, 1956, a *Variety* article listed *Tarantula* as December 1955's #4 movie, outpaced only by the biggies *Guys and Dolls* and *The Tender Trap*, both with Frank Sinatra, and *Cinerama Holiday*. *Variety* went on to say that *Tarantula*, which was paired with Universal's *Running Wild*, was "one of the few new films to get far in December. Thrill subject combined with the one on juvenile delinquents [*Running Wild*] apparently was sufficient in appeal to tear Xmas shoppers away from their store prowling." Theater marquees reading **TARANTULA RUNNING WILD** were not only advertising their current double-bill but also accurately describing the spider movie's popularity. John Agar told me that *he* was once told that *Tarantula* "was a top moneymaker in terms of what it cost and what it brought in.... I had heard that it was Number 5 in 1955." Mara Corday also got word of its success: "Shortly after it was released, I ran into my agent and he said, 'My God, Mara, it's number one in France.' I couldn't believe it, I was *thrilled*."

Variety's 109-title list of the year's top-money pictures (in terms of domestic market rentals) led off with the abovementioned *Guys and Dolls* and *The King and I* with $9,000,000 and $8,500,000 respectively. The Universal title highest on that list, #25, was *Away All Boats* with $3,500,000. With its $1,600,000 take, *Forbidden Planet* was the science fictioner that made the best showing (#62). It was followed by *Earth vs. the Flying Saucers* (#85, with $1,250,000) and *Invasion of the Body Snatchers* (#89, with $1,200,000). The list was in triple-digits by the time it got to *Tarantula* at #100, with $1,100,000. As always, Universal's ever-popular Ma and Pa Kettle and Francis the Talking Mule movies outdid its monsters at the box office: *The Kettles in the Ozarks* pulled in $1,300,000, *Francis in the Haunted House* (the last in that series) $1,200,000. "Francis and Ma and Pa Kettle were the two series from which you'd run for the hills," said *Filmfax* interviewee Mamie Van Doren, speaking for herself and the other Universal contract players. "As a performer, you just didn't want to do those movies. But those movies allowed Universal to do all of their other movies. They were their top-grossing films."

Tarantula paid for itself and much, *much* more. As Robert M. Fresco told me:

Ed Muhl was running the studio in those days, and he believed in these smaller films. He was a very interesting guy, very dour-faced guy, always well-dressed, blue suit, dark hair—he looked like Ed Murrow. I remember.... God, I must have been callow and raw in those days.... I remember, we'd just come out of a screening of something, I think it was a screening of one of George Zuckerman's films, *Written on the Wind* [1956] or something really nice. And, half-ashamed, I said, "It's no *Tarantula*," or something like that. He said, "Don't put it down. That little movie of yours, it cost a couple hundred thousand and it's made four, five million. This studio keeps its doors open on movies like yours. Those are the things that pay the bills around here." I always remembered that.

Other Script-to-Screen Changes

• In early drafts of the script, Prof. Deemer was Prof. Mitchell and Paul Lund was Paul Sanders. Steve was a student of Owens University in the movie, Midlands University in the script. "No Food for Thought" also name-dropped the fictional Midlands University (Otto Kruger's character was associated with it).

• The script called for the undertaker's workroom to include several sample caskets and coffins on tables and a cabinet stocked with embalming materials and instruments. And—the old cliché—the body of Eric Jacobs lies sheet-covered on a table but his arm has dropped off the table edge so that his hand can be seen "dangling weirdly." The camera closes in on this "gnarled and twisted and clawlike" hand.

Mara Corday: "I thought [*Tarantula*] was very good, for what it was—very, very good—and I'm very proud to be in it, to tell you the truth." (Photograph courtesy Alexander Rotter.)

• In the first Deemer lab scene, his other humongous test subjects are a white rat and a guinea pig. In the script, they're a prairie dog about five times normal size and a rooster the size of an eagle.

Evidently Deemer never read H.G. Wells' *The Food of the Gods*: That 1904 novel's oddball scientists are developing a substance to increase the growth of various critters and contemplate trying it first on tadpoles; "One always does try this sort of thing upon tadpoles to begin with; this being what tadpoles are for."

Reynold Brown artwork for one of *Tarantula*'s posters. Here as on others, the mega-spider is in town, carrying in its fangs a beautiful woman. At Tarantula's feet we see a flee-for-all, a panicked throng scattering as a gust scatters dead leaves.

• When talking about the desert, Matt never becomes as "poetic" (i.e., creepy) as *It Came from Outer Space*'s John Putnam, but maybe he *would* have, if all his dialogue in the script had made it to the screen. For instance, the first time he's en route to Deemer's with Steve, he rhapsodizes, "To me, it's like the sea ... filled with the past and the present and, who knows?—the future."

• When Matt and Steve are sitting at the base of Devil's Rock, the script called for some "down shots" (from the top of the mammoth mound) of them and, in the foreground, a boulder moving closer and closer to the edge; "We cannot see what is propelling it." After the avalanche, the script indicated that they should be covered in dirt and dust.

• In the movie, Steve knits her brow and looks nonplussed when she sees the first acromegalia changes to Deemer's face, and shows concern. In the script, she backs away from him in terror and races upstairs.

• On-screen, the pools of tarantula venom are chalk-white and look like oatmeal. The script describes them as looking like liquid; the sheriff says the pool at Andy's is probably just water, and a state trooper at the truck crash site thinks it's gasoline or liquid fertilizer. Maybe the moviemakers made it a thicker substance simply because they knew that audiences would know that there wouldn't still *be* a puddle of liquid many hours after a tarantula attack, because it would evaporate and/or soak into the ground. (In two scenes we see a total of four pools; cost to Universal, $100.)

In his office, Matt examines the stuff and says it's related to insect venom, prompting Joe Burch to blurt out, "I'll play ball with you, Matt, but there's a limit to what I'll swallow." In the script but not in the movie is Matt's funny comeback line: Indicating the Thermos and test tubes full of venom, he dryly quips, "I wouldn't recommend swallowing any of this."

• In Deemer's last scene, his acromegalic face looks melted; the musical score, presumably as shocked at the sight as we are, lets out a blast. The script didn't indicate that he should look any worse than when we last saw him, downstairs in the lab.

• When Steve, Matt, the sheriff, Nolan and the state troopers see Tarantula eyeballing them from its hilltop perch, Nolan orders two of his men to slow it down with submachine guns. In the script, the sheriff enthuses, "That'll stop it!" In the movie, the line he delivers is a hopeless-sounding "*That* won't stop it!"

• During the finale with the jets, the script indicated that there should be two pilot's-point-of-view shots of Tarantula skittering toward town. With no disrespect to the Universal effects crew intended, it's hard to imagine that in a God's-eye-view shot like that, the spider would look like anything but what it really was. Maybe that's why they didn't include that shot.

• In the movie, the jet pilot radios the other flyers, "Dropping napalm! Follow in order!"; in the script, the line is, "Let's hit it with the hot stuff!"

• At the end of *Them!*, Dr. Medford (Edmund Gwenn) offers up a sobering observation about Man having entered the Atomic Age and "opened a door into a new world. What we eventually *find* in that new world, nobody can predict." It's atomic food for thought. Perhaps because *Tarantula* follows many of the plot beats of its progenitor, there's also a Thoughtful Closing Comment in the script—but, mercifully, not the movie. As Tarantula burns, Matt pontificates, "Evil is goodness turned upside down. Someone else will go on from where [Deemer] left off—and it'll work next time."

Marginalia

• *Tarantula* is skeery and "No Food for Thought" stodgy, but believe it or not there was more excitement on the set of the latter. According to writer Eve Starr, who visited American National Studios (formerly PRC) while the episode was being filmed, "unscheduled bedlam broke loose" when all the lab scene rats, white mice, rabbits and guinea pigs escaped from their cages. Everybody on the set "sought altitude," the ladies climbing on tables and chairs. "When one works in science fiction," Jack Arnold told her, "all sorts of things can happen—and do!" It appears that, characteristically, Arnold gave Starr the impression he was the show's big kahuna even though he wasn't: "He went on to tell us about his new *Science Fiction Theatre* series."

• Conventional wisdom has it that the monster-movie cinemilestone *Them!* laid the tracks for all the Big Bug movies that followed. Can we be sure that *Tarantula* was made as a result of *Them!*'s popularity? I'd wager that it was ... but no one seems to have gotten any of the *Tarantula* folks to 'fess up. I asked writer Robert M. Fresco if, when he had to pick a giant monster to add to his expansion of "No Food for Thought," the success of *Them!* influenced him, if it steered him toward making the giant monster an insect. Too many years had passed for Fresco to remember why he made that decision, but he nevertheless told me, "Oh, I'm *sure* that [*Them!*] was the inspiration."

On the other hand, Jack Arnold told interviewers that, story-wise, *Tarantula* originated with him, with *Them!* playing no part in it whatsoever.[23] And William Alland made the same claim for himself. From Arnold it isn't surprising, since he thought the sun came up every morning just to hear him crow; he *had* to have remembered that the basis for *Tarantula* was his friend Fresco's "No Food for Thought." But for me, it was surprising to hear the same sort of thing from Alland, who was my idea of a "credit where credit is due" kind of guy, never a credit-poacher. After our marathon interview, I fact-checked everything he told me as thoroughly as I could, and in all the hours we talked, "*Tarantula* came from an idea of my own" was his one and only statement that seemed like it had to be incorrect. Since he does get story credit on *The Deadly Mantis* (written very soon after *Tarantula*) and may have mixed up the two Big Bug movies in his head, *I* consider his undoubtedly incorrect *Tarantula* claim a case of misremembering. *We* report; *you* decide.

In any event, it seems safe to ass-u-me that the Universal brass was aware of *Them!*'s success when they green-lit *Tarantula* so yes, I'd opine that *Them!* begat *Tarantula*.

• With no disrespect to Robert M. Fresco, his first screenplay (*Tarantula*) occasionally "reads" like a first screenplay, i.e., the 24-year-old liked his exclamation points. In nearly all the Hollywood scripts I've read, the action, regardless of how exciting or surprising it is, is described matter-of-factly, but Fresco uses exclamation points in an attempt to quicken the reader's pulse: "INTO SHOT, coming over the second hill, is the Tarantula!," "The tarantula is moving on the house!," "[Steve] sees the huge eye of the tarantula at the window!," "From above comes the ROAR of JETS!"

• *Tarantula* is done in a completely different style than *Them!*: Except for the idea of an atomically enlarged bug and

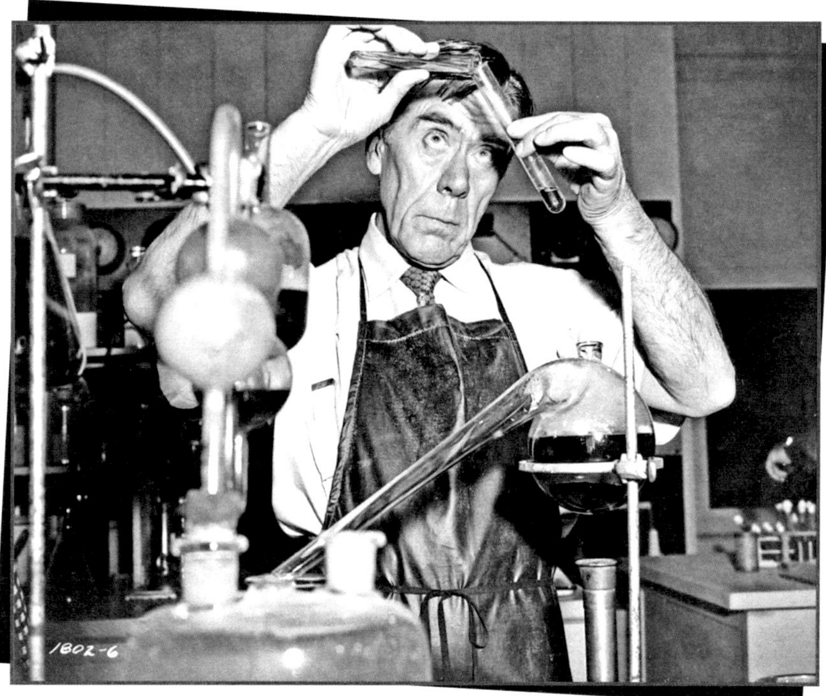

The citizens of Desert Rock are unaware of the caliber of disaster indicated by the presence of a mad scientist in their community: In his scientific playground, Leo G. Carroll mixes up a batch of (a)tomfoolery in *Tarantula*. (Photograph courtesy John Antosiewicz.)

(for the first part of *Them!*, anyway) a shared desert setting, they don't have much in common. This is in sharp contrast to the way that the cliché-a-thons *The Monster That Challenged the World, The Deadly Mantis* and *The Black Scorpion* take pains to hit every note in the *Them!* playbook.

• Would there have *been* a Big Bug subgenre if *Them!* hadn't started the ball rolling? I vote yes, partly because there almost *was* a Big Bug movie *before Them!*: A *Variety* columnist announced on April 23, 1953, that producer-director Andrew Stone "is coming up with *Tarantula*, the tale of a huge man-eating spider in three dimensions and color. … The modern 3-D horror film makes old Dracula look as tame as the little doggie in the window." Other *Variety* items reveal that the script was written by Stone and wife Virginia; that the cast would include Margia Dean (in the female lead), Jane Wooster and UCLA theater arts department teacher Ruth Swanson; that Dimitri Tiomkin had signed up to score it; and—wait for it—that Stone had "offered Robert Donat, currently in Britain, on a participation basis, the starring role of Dr. Alfred Beigen, scientist-explorer."

Louella O. Parsons wrote in her February 25, 1953, column, "According to Andrew, the Tarantulas will appear on the screen the size of elephants. He'll show how their bodies can be slashed with a knife and the parts live on independently. Ugh! He plans to film the picture in Honduras…." Hedda Hopper chimed in on April 1 that Stone's pick for the lead, Donat, was "leery of coming to Hollywood because of an asthmatic condition which the climate doesn't help. But since the picture is to be made in Honduras, Andy thinks he can lure him there." On April 7, Hopper revealed that Stone was bringing Kane Richmond out of retirement for a featured role and that Alix Talton would play "a fat part." According to Edith Gwynn (July 23), "Jean Peters will be the femme lead in *Tarantula* if Eddie Small [*sic*—where'd *he* come from?] can borrow her from 20th-Fox for the film he's making with all those super-spiders."

The October 19 *Film Bulletin* reported that *Tarantula* would be distributed by United Artists. According to *Film Bulletin*'s November 30 issue, Stone had been filming background scenes in Honduras for several weeks—and actorwise, "only Grady Sutton has been cast"!

Somebody needs to do more research on this, and find out if a script still exists. Somebody who isn't me.

If you have arachnophobia (a word we now all know; thanks, Steven Spielberg), if real-life spiders press your panic button, *Tarantula* may be Universal's scariest '50s monster film. (Poster courtesy Ted Bohus.)

• There have been a lot of fan scribblings about Universal's sci-fis' "preferred" or "usual" desert settings when actually the number of their films set in the desert adds up to a grand total of three, *It Came from Outer Space*, *Tarantula* and *The Monolith Monsters*. An equal number of their movies—*The Mole People, The Land Unknown* and *The Deadly Mantis*—are set in lands of cold and ice.

• According to Universal production notes, maybe bogus, maybe not, three dozen spiders—assorted types and sizes—were procured from Mexico, Arizona, Panama and South America. Camera tests were made, and a different spider was used for each important sequence. Ultimately a total of five tarantulas were utilized. "We had a wonderful tarantula guy who brought 'em in," producer William Alland told me. "They're very harmless, you know, they don't bite unless you bother them a lot. I remember being in a publicity photo where I had live tarantulas crawling all up and down me!"

• From the deepest vaults of trivia: On *Tarantula*'s budget sheets, under "Hairdressing Miscellaneous," you'll find "Dye job for J. Agar," a $35 expense.

• "Please Don't Talk About Me '*Til* I'm Gone": At the funeral parlor, Matt tells the sheriff that the dead man can't be Eric Jacobs—and then Prof. Deemer waltzes in and announces that it *is* Jacobs. After Deemer says his goodbyes and exits the frame, Matt instantly starts scoffing and mocking him to the sheriff. Not until several seconds later do we hear a door open and close, signifying Deemer's exit from the room!

• One of Deemer's lab animals, a monkey, figures in three scenes. This is probably just publicity department horse crap (or monkey crap), but according to *Variety*'s June 22, 1955, "Hollywood Inside" column, the *Tarantula* troupe borrowed this monkey, Fuzzy, from the set of the World War II movie *Away All Boats* (1956) where it was playing Jeff Chandler's shipboard pet. It was reported that Fuzzy would bicycle between the two sets for five days; "It's believed the first time production skeds have ever been juggled to suit an animal actor."

• Nutrient injections cause some of Deemer's test animals to die and cause others to double, triple, quadruple, octuple (*ad infinitum*) in size. No other result is ever mentioned. In umpty-ump years of watching *Tarantula*, I still haven't figured out which of those two outcomes Jacobs and Lund hoped for, when they injected themselves … or why anybody would hope for *either*! Did they wish to become amazing colossal men? (In Steve and Matt's park bench scene, Steve describes the growth rate of Deemer's animals and, in a line found in the script but not the movie, Matt thoughtfully says, "If he ever uses it on humans, it could create a race of giants!")

In the script, there's an explanation for the actions of Jacobs and Lund: The acromegalic Deemer, woozily seated at the lab table stam-mam-mering out his story to Matt and Steve, says,

> Eric was certain our nutrient would save the future and our results *were* encouraging. Nine times out of ten, the test animals grew strong and healthy—but ten percent of the time we never knew what to expect—the animals either died—or they were mutants of monstrous size and strength.

A one-in-ten chance of dying or becoming a mutant? I don't care for those Russian Roulette odds.

• Speaking of odds makes one realize how lucky we monster movie fans are: There was only a one-in-three chance that Paul Lund's wild swing with the lab stool would free the mutated tarantula, a two-out-of-three chance it would free the white rat or guinea pig. I don't think the movie we mathematically "should" have gotten, either *White Rat* or *Guinea Pig*, would have been as exciting.

• Many movies, including sci-fis, trot out the strictly off-the-cob comic schtick where a lady doctor or scientist with a man's first name arrives (somewhere), the people there were expecting a guy, and "hilarity" ("But—but you're a *woman*!") ensues. Mara Corday is Steve in *Tarantula* and, before *her*, Joan Weldon was Pat in *Them!* and Faith Domergue was Lesley in *It Came from Beneath the Sea*. But in all three instances, mercifully, the movies spare us the scene of "comic" confusion.

• Talking to Matt and Steve about the ballooning world population, Deemer says that in 1975 there'll be three billion people; in actuality, the world hit three billion in 1959 and by 1975 there were nearly 4.1 billion. Deemer goes on to say that in 2000 there'll be 3.625 billion; in 2000 there were actually more than six billion.

The reason Deemer's estimates were "off" is because the poor old geezer didn't know how many people were in the world *currently*, in *1955*, his own present day: He says that there are now two billion people in the world (there were really almost 2.8 billion) and that that number was growing by 25 million a year (it was then growing by 45 or 50 million a year). In 2017, we hit 7.6 billion.

Even though it's Deemer's life's work and one passion, when talking about the stats he gets *ab-so-lute-ly noth-ing* right; in fact, he low-balls everything which makes his work seem less urgent. Well, I guess that's why they're called *mad* scientists.

• It might be fun to be a fly on the wall during a scientific conclave between Messrs. Deemer, Jacobs and Lund and *The Devil-Doll*'s Marcel (Henry B. Walthall). In that 1936 sci-fi flick, Marcel was similarly het-up over population vs. the food supply (he even blamed the extinction of dinosaurs on a food shortage), but *his* solution was not to make factory-farmed animals bigger but to make people smaller ("Think of it ... every living creature reduced to one-sixth its size, one-sixth its physical need! Food for *six times all of us*!"). *The Devil-Doll* was Walthall's last movie: Later that same year, the actor eased the problem of overpopulation by one.

In the *Voyage to the Bottom of the Sea* episode "The Village of Guilt" (1964), set in Norway, a pair of scientists, concerned about food in the world of tomorrow, cross-breed sea life so that the entire world can be fed at an infinitesimal cost. Giant catfish and a king-sized octopus are the resultant critters that we see. This is all to the mustard until one of the scientists (Richard Carlson with singsong accent) becomes more interested in chasing scientific glory than in humanitarianism, starts calling the giant octopus "my child" (never a good sign) and gets to like the idea of people in the octopus' belly better than the other way around.

• You can tell by the fixed, troubled look Prof. Deemer wears throughout the movie that he loses sleep over the "Overpopulation = Starvation" crisis. Too bad he didn't have a lab gizmo to give him a peek into the future, 21st-century America, where not only is there enough food, thank you very much, but nearly two-thirds of adults are overweight or obese!

• While driving Steve to Deemer's, and while sitting with her at Devil's Rock, Matt explains why he finds the desert so beautiful:

> Everything that ever walked or crawled on the face of the Earth ... swum the depths of the ocean ... or soared through the sky, has left its imprint here. ... You can still find seashells if you keep your eyes open.[24]

He *does* later admit that, from the air, the desert can look "strangely evil," but overall he does a good job of explaining why he loves it there. Contrast this with John Putnam's couldn't-be-creepier *It Came from Outer Space* spiel about the desert ("A thousand ways the desert can kill...") to see why Desert Rock thinks Matt's a good guy and Sand Rock thinks Putnam's kind of an asshole.

• Given a choice between being killed by a spider the size of a pony and a spider the size of a Walgreens, it might be smarter to opt for the latter, only because it'd all be over quicker. Nineteen-fifties sci-fi-wise, the giant spiders that preceded *Tarantula* were "small giants": the beasties in *Mesa of Lost Women* and *Cat-Women of the Moon* (both 1953). It's hard to imagine a major studio like Universal using a prop from a trashy movie like *Mesa of Lost Women*, but except for the face, the two *do* look a lot alike and maybe it's possible.

Yet another "small giant" spider appeared in the Jungle Jim adventure *Fury of the Congo* (1951): In a scene where Jim (Johnny Weissmuller) and a few other characters were pinned down by a desert sandstorm, along came a hairy prop spider, four-legged and very phony-looking. Even for kids, the scene must have seemed funny rather than suspenseful: The spider looks like it's being dragged along the ground, Weissmuller has to "cooperate" in order to get into its clutches, and when he uses his knife to chop and slash at it, he seems to be stabbing himself more often than he stabs the spider! After the spider is dead and the sandstorm passes, Jim rather casually asks one of his companions what this monster *is*, she just as casually says it's a "desert spider," and they go on their merry way.

• As we watch Tarantula crawl around the desert, it's sometimes hard to know how big it's getting, because there's nothing to compare it to; yes, it's as big as that hill, but how big's that hill? Wisely the moviemakers occasionally give it some perspective (showing it behind Matt's car, with telephone poles, etc.) so that you can't help noticing that it's still growing. Unfortunately, things don't seem like

"Poor John [Agar]," Mara Corday said of her *Tarantula* teammate. "He was like a brother to me, he was very quiet, very respectful, but he couldn't drink, you could *not* give this man a drink of alcohol. He'd *turn* into ... something else. Luckily, I did not see that (except maybe once), because he was straight-arrow on that set, he did a fine little job for us and we got along great." (Photograph courtesy Ted Bohus.)

they're always consistent: Tarantula dwarfs the telephone poles, but it's later dwarfed by the electric transmission towers. The spider's size also alternated in Universal's publicity materials, with the pressbook synopsis calling it "bigger than a barn," one pressbook article estimating it as "over 60 feet tall and 50 feet wide" and the posters calling it "100 Feet High!"

• For the first time in a '50s Universal fright flick, the leads aren't in love. Steve and Matt "meet cute" and they look like they'd make a handsome couple, and as the story progresses we perhaps subconsciously *assume* that affection is blooming ... but never once is there any on-screen sign of it. In the script, after Matt and Steve see the jackrabbit at Devil's Rock, "[t]hey look intently at one another. Each is terribly conscious of the other." But don't look for that interlude in the movie. Perhaps somebody made the decision, "This time, let's skip the mush."

• Tarantula lets out a roar or two, even though probably no real-life tarantula ever managed that feat. (Even deaf and hard-of-hearing Monster Kids should know this: On the *Tarantula* DVD, several of the giant spider's appearances come with the subtitle **ROARING**.) When threatened, tarantulas *can* rub their hind legs together and make a hissing or rasping noise. Speaking of hind legs, something else that tarantulas do, that perhaps the one in the movie should have done, is rear up. Who knows if the special effects fellows could have pulled off a shot of this type, but it sure would have been jaw-dropping if, say during the jets' attack, Tarantula *had* reared up mile-high and knocked one of them out of the sky, the way King Kong manages to take one of the biplanes out of the game. The *Tarantula* finale in which the monster is killed by the jets "was right out of *King Kong*," William Alland told me. Alland had already dipped into *King Kong* for his *Creature from the Black Lagoon* storyline.

• Deemer says that he and Prof. Jacobs once worked together at Oak Ridge. The line would have made 1955 audiences mentally associate them with the Manhattan Project.

Between its atomic spider and mutant men (including Leo G. Carroll, flanked here by John Agar and Mara Corday), *Tarantula* scored a hit with 1955–56 audiences. Rodda Harvey, Jr., of the Grove Theatre in Lindsay, California, played it for three days (January 15–17, 1956) and wrote for *Motion Picture Herald*'s "What the Picture Did For Me" column, "Excellent business which broke house record. Topped all candy counter income for a Sunday. Had SRO out for first time in three years."

• We in the audience see plenty of Tarantula, right from the time when it's a little shaver, but for seven-eighths of the movie, not one of the main characters do. Like *Them!* and several other *Them!* imitators, *Tarantula* is a "whatdunnit" where *we* know that a giant (fill in the blank) is on the prowl but, for a while at least, all the main characters are in the dark.

Poor Prof. Deemer! In just seconds, he goes from being asleep in bed to being in Tarantula's maw, so who knows whether or not he had an "ohnosecond" where he figured out that he was being attacked by his own tarantula. In all the many movies where the monster destroys its maker, Deemer might be the only monster maker who died without ever knowing he'd *made* a monster!

• It's difficult to accurately predict what one would do when chased by a giant tarantula. If I was a miner like Jeb and Ed, sitting outside my mine when a tarantula the size of a building came moseying along, I predict that I'd want to hotfoot it *into* the mine. Jeb and Ed instead head for the hills. Given the outcome, I'm tempted to call that a bad move, but what do I know about mining?

Jeb falls right off the bat, then gets up, runs and falls a second time; Ed turns around, runs back and helps him up. Away they go again, Jeb falls a third time, and again Ed runs back to help. God bless Ed. I don't think I'd have gone back for my friend after his third fall. In fact, with a giant tarantula breathing down my neck, I'm sure I wouldn't have gone back for my friend after his *first* fall.

• Before the start of the Dr. Townsend scene, we see an outdoor sign that reads ARIZONA AGRICULTURAL INSTITUTE. This was filmed in front of Universal's executive offices, which are visible in the background.

• It's daylight when Matt consults with Dr. Townsend; they have to pull down the window shades to watch the spider movie. Then in a mad rush, Matt flies back to Desert Rock (200 miles, maybe an hour) and drives right to Deemer's (20 miles outside town) … and suddenly it's almost dawn of the next day. How'd *that* happen??

• It looks like the night sky is wrinkled in the highway scene where Tarantula, patiently pausing on a hilltop, is eying Matt, Steve and the lawmen. The road, soaking wet at the beginning of this short scene, is dry seconds later.

• Like the explosions seen in *This Island Earth*, many (all?) of the *Tarantula* explosions are separate, overlaid elements. Some "work," others … not so much. After the boxes of dynamite explode right under Tarantula on the highway, notice that the boxes are still intact.

• At least one of the shots of the USAF jets over Desert Rock is flipped (it's made obvious by the **ꟻASU** on the underside of a wing). As Tarantula advances on the town, there are frequent cutaways to a long shot where we see (from the back) Our Heroes in the street, watching. Once you notice that one of the men is shifting his weight from one foot to the other and adjusting his hat, it becomes annoyingly apparent that it's the same shot again and again.

• Artwork of a fallen, nightgown-clad Mara Corday is prominently featured on *Tarantula* posters. Fallen, nightgown-clad Mara was seen again on posters three years later, this time on Universal's posters for *Horror of Dracula*!

• *Tarantula*'s October 1, 1955, Total Cost Report shows that it had total direct charges of $267,337. Add the 25 percent studio overhead and the tab comes to $334,171.

• In October 1955, the month *Tarantula* had its first playdates, John Agar was up to his old tricks—according to *Whisper* magazine, anyway. It reported that Agar and a pal dropped in on a pair of starlets for a night of drinking (etc.)—and then Agar's wife Loretta and Agar's *mother*(!) arrived on the scene. As Loretta wept in the car, the mother came up to the front door and Agar bolted out the back. *Whisper* writer Sam Schaeffer continued,

> As is often the case when a guy is carrying a 100-proof load, John's exit did not achieve the ultimate in silence. … John's mama did a quick end run of her own, and emerged into the drizzling night just in time to see the cornered youth dive headlong under the house next door. … John peered out and saw two feminine feet advancing inexorably. … When a guy has hidden himself under a house on a moonless night, and there stands his mama, there isn't much point in further resistance—it's just one of those nights a guy can't win.

Schaeffer went on to report that Agar and his friend did eventually return to spend the rest of the night with the starlets. In boldface he announced, "Now Wifey Knows!"

• The *Syracuse* (New York) *Herald-Journal*, and probably many other papers, ran an article on Jack Arnold, called him an expert on monster movie matters and identified him as the maker of *Creature from the Black Lagoon* and *Revenge of the Creature*, both featuring the Gill Man, a monster that committed dastardly crimes but was not responsible for what he did. According to Arnold, "People invaded its domain, made its life miserable and it had no recourse but to fight back. The same thing happens with the tarantula. Man creates in it a six-legged [*sic*] Frankenstein's monster." The article writer continued,

> Arnold pointed to this theme as being responsible for the success of all horror films. People have to hate the monster, animal or human, for what he does, Arnold stated, but they must also realize that fate has forced the action on him. This is what builds up emotion.
>
> Arnold pointed to other classic monster examples such as *King Kong*. [Tarantula] dwarfs King Kong and is a record-breaking misfit in the history of horror films, but old Kong had the same problem. The giant gorilla did not belong in Manhattan and he was a little sore about the matter so he tried to tear the city apart.

• My German pen pal Harald Gruenberger tells me that the actor who dubbed John Agar in the German version of *Tarantula* was "Gert Günther Hoffmann, soon to become one of Germany's top voice artists. He was, amongst many others, the regular voice for Sean Connery, William Shatner,

According to *Missile to the Moon* (1958) director Richard E. Cunha, he found a prop spider "in terrible disrepair" at Universal and patched it together for use in his movie. It *had* to have been a *Tarantula* leftover … but that sure isn't the Tarantula face. What say you?

Michel Piccoli, Paul Newman, Lex Barker and Rock Hudson, and also served as a narrator for the Pink Panther cartoons (which had no narrator in the originals). His ability to broadcast warmth and intelligence no matter what nonsensical lines he had to speak served him well. He was also able to rise to the occasion and play evil and crazed characters just as well. I wish he'd dubbed Agar in *The Brain from Planet Arous* [1957]."

• *Tarantula* was one of the Universal '50s films shot in 1.33 but framed to be projected in 1.85 with the top and bottom of the frame cut off in projection. (This hybrid framing continued throughout the decade, as many theaters had yet to widen their screens.) Still today we frequently see *Tarantula* in 1.33 and the extra headroom in some dialogue scenes makes it seem as though comic-book word balloons were supposed to be added.

• One wonders what the running time of *Tarantula* ended up being in Australia, where cutters must have been knee-deep in footage the censor ordered deleted. The bossy Aussie decreed:

> Delete stranglehold just before the professor collapses to the floor. Only sufficient of the many shots of Tarantula to establish its presence will be allowed. Delete shots of Tarantula before and after truck is thrown off the road. Allow one brief shot only of Tarantula approaching two men. Allow start of long shot of Tarantula approaching house. Allow brief first shot of Tarantula through window. Delete various shots of Tarantula outside house. Allow a short view of professor's distorted face. Delete most of Tarantula after girl escapes from house. ... Delete repeat shots of Tarantula escaping from dynamite. Reduce shots of air rockets on Tarantula.

• Just as Alland knew, long before the release of *Creature from the Black Lagoon*, that it would be popular enough to rate a sequel, he must have sensed the same about *Tarantula*: Already on the drawing board in November 1955, or perhaps sooner, was his follow-up *The Giant Mantis*, ultimately released as *The Deadly Mantis*.

• It seems like a safe bet that writer-producer-director-SFX wiz Bert I. Gordon was aware of the success of *Tarantula*. He subsequently made 1958's *Earth vs the Spider* ('nuff sed) plus 1957's *Beginning of the End*, a movie more indebted than *Earth vs the Spider* to the plot of *Tarantula*—even with*out* a spider. *Beginning of the End*'s locusts become giant not through nutrient injections but by eating the Department of Agriculture's radioactive plant food, and then go on the march through the Illinois countryside. It's full of scenes and "moments" taken from *Tarantula* or *Them!* or both: a scientist projecting a 16mm nature documentary, monster p.o.v. shots as locusts close in on victims, even a locust spying on a pretty girl through her window.

• *Tarantula*, "Science-Fiction's Most Terrifying Thrill" (according to the trailer), became comedy fodder when stock footage of the king-sized brute was used in the Three Stooges' *Have Rocket, Will Travel* (1959). The slapstick trio, newly arrived on Venus in *Destination Moon* spacesuits, are panic-stricken when they see the spider via the *Tarantula* clip where it looms over the top of Devil's Rock; in *Have Rocket* the shot runs longer than it does in *Tarantula* and we get to watch the spider crawl down the front of the rock formation. Courtesy of *Have Rocket, Will Travel*'s special effects folks, the mega-spider is now new and improved: While chasing the Stooges, it occasionally stops stock-still and breathes fire blowtorch-style at them (and always aiming at their asses). The music playing during the first of the spider's two scenes is the *It Came from Beneath the Sea* (1955) octopus theme.

Coogan's Bluff (1968) features a trippy scene where Arizona deputy sheriff Coogan (Clint Eastwood) crosses a New York City nightclub's crowded dance floor (complete with flashing colored lights and wall projections)—and there's a cutaway to a split-second *Tarantula* clip of the spider ambling across the desert. The shot seen in *Coogan's Bluff* wasn't used in *Tarantula*.

We dare you to watch producer-director Bert I. Gordon's *Earth vs the Spider* (1958) without thinking of *Tarantula*. We double-dog-dare you to watch it without thinking of *Tarantula* when the spider's loose on the Universal back lot!

• Zacherley, the cadaverous, comic "horror host" of New York TV station WPIX's *Chiller Theatre* in the mid–1960s, made a historic one-night return on Saturday, October 25,

2008, emceeing a new prime-time Halloween special—and the featured fright flick was *Tarantula*. "The Cool Ghoul" did not break into the movie itself with irreverent comments and sight gags as in years past, but in various "bumpers" he revealed that *Tarantula* was referenced in the *Rocky Horror Picture Show* (1975) song "Science Fiction Double Feature"; pointed out that the movie's spider was a real one, propelled by air jets; dispelled the notion that the sting of a tarantula was deadly; and called attention to Clint Eastwood as the flyboy.

Tarantula fans, skip ahead; Zacherley fans, stick around; if I don't write about this now, I never *will*: Zacherley (real name: John Zacherle), then 90, initially turned down WPIX's offer to make a Halloween comeback, but then on October 6 he told them he'd do it. And on October 7 (the next morning!), with me in tow, he walked onto a small, "spooky" set in WPIX's newsroom in the News Building (220 East 42nd Street). The two very nice ladies in charge, both born long after his heyday, didn't know Zach from Shaq from Monterey Jack and tried to get him to stick to a script written by someone equally unfamiliar with the Zacherley persona. His lines appeared one at a time on a teleprompter, a take would begin and Zach, mad-libber that he was, would "do his thing": He used the lines as a springboard for half-demented, rambling spiels. At the end of every take, the ladies would "laugh" politely, tell him he was great, and then remind him that the take could last only x-number of seconds and ask him to try it again. They made him do it over and over, Zach adding less each time, until they got him down to pretty much just the scripted lines. The ordeal lasted about an hour. He and I then had lunch in the Main Concourse in nearby Grand Central Station, where with resignation he called what he'd just done "a waste of time."[25] I got the feeling he was sorry he did it; I didn't say it, but I was too. About a week later, a message from Zach's friend and biographer Richard Scrivani was posted on the Creepy Classics website:

> [When Zacherley] got there and found out they only wanted him to do an intro and a few bumpers, he almost walked out. He did them though, being the professional that he is, but told me to let everyone know that he wasn't given any real stuff to do, and what he *did* do was scripted.... I can't tell you how disappointed I am; I guess it's just been too many years since anyone in the TV business has seen what he used to do.

"It *was* good to see Zach back in harness," posted Craig Wichman of the Classic Horror Film Board, "for what was, most likely, his swan song as TV host." It was.

• According to "Agar the Horrible," a newspaper article in the October 30–31, 1999, *Burbank Leader*, Agar's sci-fi star status had earned him a spot as a judge on that year's West Hollywood Halloween Contest Carnaval. The article ended on this note:

> [Loretta Agar] has seen many of her husband's movies. Of those in the sci-fi category, she said, "I thought they were kind of crazy, and so did he."
>
> But Loretta does have a favorite—*Tarantula*, the 1955 film in which a super-growth formula turns an arachnid into a man-eating giant.
>
> "It was a cute movie," she said.

• The Alland-Arnold team won another feather for their cap with *Tarantula*. Unfortunately, it was the final feather. Their subsequent collaborations were the dullsville *The Space Children* (1958) and the poor comedies *The Lady Takes a Flyer* (1958) and *The Lively Set* (1964).

The Release

By Robert J. Kiss

As the Top Half of a "Double Shock Show" with *Running Wild*

For the theatrical first run of *Tarantula*, Universal issued both a standard eight-page pressbook and a six-page "special pressbook," the latter composed entirely of promotional texts and ad mats for showing the movie on a double-bill with their juvenile delinquency crime thriller *Running Wild* starring William Campbell. Billing it as the "Greatest Double Shock Show of All!," this was Universal's preferred mode for theaters to exhibit *Tarantula*.

The double-bill's first openings took the form of a "pre-Halloween midnight show" at selected small town theaters in the Midwest on the night of Saturday, October 29, 1955, with the actual premiere (not billed as such) taking place at the 700-seat State Theatre in Dubuque, Iowa, which started its midnight show an hour early(!) at 11 p.m.

The first "regular" opening of the movie, with five screenings a day, followed at the Stanton Theatre in Philadelphia, Pennsylvania, on November 4. John Agar, who was already in the midst of an East Coast personal appearance tour with Cleo Moore to promote the Hugo Haas-directed Universal release *Hold Back Tomorrow*, took a brief detour to attend the Philly opening of the *Tarantula*-*Running Wild* double-bill. Although the November 4 event was described in the trade press as *Tarantula*'s "world premiere," no use was made of this term in local newspaper listings, which likewise neglected to mention Agar's presence at some of the screenings that day. Nevertheless, the picture grossed a hefty $7500 during its first four days at the 1450-seat venue, and

$7000 during its second week. While still playing at the Stanton, the *Tarantula-Running Wild* double-bill also opened throughout Michigan, as well as in a limited number of cities around the nation, including Billings, Montana, and Portland, Oregon.

The double-bill's ten-theater Los Angeles opening (November 23) grossed what *Variety* referred to as a "socko 87G" during its first week, with the trade publication's November 30 edition further expounding, "Universal is pairing *Tarantula* and *Running Wild* with some considerable success. Combo is smash in Detroit, torrid in Portland and rousing in L.A."

From the beginning of December, a three-figure number of *Tarantula* prints was placed into circulation at theaters nationwide, with *Variety*'s December 9 issue reporting that the movie "now is doing tremendous business throughout the country." The *Tarantula-Running Wild* opening at San Francisco's 2400-seat Golden Gate Theatre that week was judged to be "the best b.o. [box office] bet among the new entries on Market Street," where it bankrolled a colossal $14,000 during its first seven days.

With a considerable number of prints in circulation, *Tarantula*'s swift penetration of venues from coast to coast was slowed only a little due to the movie being repeatedly held over in multiple locations. The title appeared on *Boxoffice*'s "Boxoffice Barometer"—charting the performance of first-run features in 20 major U.S. cities—some seven times between Christmas Eve 1955 and February 11, 1956, with initial trade that was around one-quarter above the national average leveling off to roughly one-eighth above average by the end of this period. In broad terms, *Tarantula*'s first run may be considered to have lasted from the end of October 1955 to mid–March 1956, by which time it had reached even the smallest rural towns. This equates to around three and a half months of prolific nationwide play, preceded by a month of (limited but profitable) early engagements.

Within a sample of 900 U.S. movie theaters that screened *Tarantula* as a first-run picture between October 1955 and March 1956, 75 percent of screenings took Universal's preferred form of a double-bill with *Running Wild*, making this by far the most common way to have originally experienced the movie. In every instance without exception, *Tarantula* represented the top of the bill, with *Running Wild* playing as support, just as Universal had intended.

As a Stand-alone Feature

Nevertheless, some 18 percent of first-run screenings within the sample of 900 theaters took the form of a stand-alone presentation supported only by "selected shorts." Throughout the vast majority of the nation, these stand-alone screenings took place almost exclusively at small town venues where single bills were generally the norm anyway.

The lone exception was Texas, where stand-alone presentations accounted for 59 percent of all first-run *Tarantula* screenings.[26] The same phenomenon is attested

The reviewer for the *Sunday Herald* of Bridgeport, Connecticut, gave *Tarantula* three stars and wrote, "Top credit goes to both cameramen and makeup men who turned this one into an excellent spook show." Its excellence translated into "tall coin" at theater ticket windows, according to this full-page *Boxoffice* ad (November 26, 1955).

with regard to other Universal monster movies of the period, including the Black Lagoon trilogy and *This Island Earth*, and should therefore be construed in terms of divergent standard practice among Texan exhibitors at this time.

Other Double-Bills

Within the sample of 900 U.S. movie theaters that screened *Tarantula* as a first-run picture between October 1955 and March 1956, just seven percent elected to pair it with a co-feature other than *Running Wild*. In the case of big city and neighborhood theaters, the motivation behind such substitutions was evidently a desire to distinguish their product from that of immediate competitors who were already screening the standard *Tarantula-Running Wild* double-bill. In other instances, the reasons for substitutions remain less clear; for example, it is difficult to discern precisely what might have motivated a handful of New England exhibitors to exchange one juvenile delinquency crime thriller for another, by replacing *Running Wild* with the Columbia release *Teen-Age Crime Wave*.

Jack Silverthorn, manager of Cleveland's Hippodrome Theatre, with the striking lobby display he created.

The alternate double-bill features listed below all represent examples of limited disparate local usage. The only common factor is that 84 percent of such screenings continued to employ *Tarantula* as the top of the bill. A limited number of theatergoers in Wisconsin during December 1955 and January 1956 were the only ones within the sample who got to experience a John Agar double-bill comprising *Tarantula* and *Hold Back Tomorrow*, with the two movies equally weighted insofar as each topped the bill at precisely half of all Wisconsin venues that paired them.

All of the double-bill co-features attested within the sample are arranged alphabetically below. The month mentioned in each case is the earliest in which the pairing was encountered.

February 1956 *Boys' Ranch* (Jackie "Butch" Jenkins)
March 1956 *The Bridges at Toko-Ri* (William Holden)
February 1956 *Count Three and Pray* (Van Heflin)
January 1956 *Double Jeopardy* (Rod Cameron)
January 1956 *Duel on the Mississippi* (Lex Barker)
February 1956 *Fury at Gunsight Pass* (David Brian)
December 1955 *Hold Back Tomorrow* (John Agar)
February 1956 *Jail Busters* (The Bowery Boys)
December 1955 *A Lawless Street* (Randolph Scott)
February 1956 *Lord of the Jungle* (Johnny Sheffield)
January 1956 *Mad at the World* (Frank Lovejoy)
January 1956 *Man with the Gun* (Robert Mitchum)
March 1956 *The Mississippi Gambler* (Tyrone Power)
November 1955 *My Sister Eileen* (Janet Leigh)
February 1956 *The Naked Dawn* (Arthur Kennedy)
January 1956 *The Road to Denver* (John Payne)
January 1956 *Seven Cities of Gold* (Richard Egan)
January 1956 *Special Delivery* (Joseph Cotten)
December 1955 *Svengali* (Donald Wolfit)
February 1956 *Teen-Age Crime Wave* (Tommy Cook)
January 1956 *Two-Gun Lady* (Peggie Castle)
February 1956 *Yankee Buccaneer* (Jeff Chandler)

Beyond the First Run

Tarantula's career as a second-run feature commenced while its first-run engagements were coming to a close: From late March 1956 through to the end of 1957, it continued to receive a markedly greater-than-average number of bookings at second-run houses, most frequently alongside its original regular co-feature, *Running Wild*. Theatrical screenings between 1958 and 1961 grew gradually lesser in number, and increasingly frequently took place on triple and quadruple bills.

Even within the context of such multiple bills, *Tarantula* experienced a final spurt of heavy theatrical engagement at Southeast and Midwest drive-ins during 1962 and 1963, when it became the oldest regular screen fixture at ballyhoo-laden BUG-A-THON shows. (The show name was also given as BUGATHON and BUG-O-THON.) Organizers provided ticket buyers with themed premiums such as fly-swatters and offered prizes to those who brought along the largest, smallest or ugliest bugs (*in jars*, as drive-in owners were keen to emphasize!), in addition to showing three or four "big, buggy features." *Tarantula* was coupled variously with *The Deadly Mantis, Earth vs the Spider, The Fly* (1958), *The Wasp Woman* (1959), *The Leech Woman* (1960) and *Mothra* (1962).

Tarantula was thereafter released to television in a pan-and-scan version, making its small-screen debut on stations from coast to coast during the course of September and October 1965.

The Critics' Corner

Motion Picture Exhibitor: This one should scare the daylights out of many a viewer and with a little exploitation could give a good account of itself for the type of entry it is.

Harrison's Reports: [I]t is so fantastic that most moviegoers probably will find it more laughable than frightening.

The Hollywood Reporter: [Tarantula] goes around stepping on houses and peeking at pretty girls through bedroom windows until you darned near wish nobody had ever invented the process shot. ... All in all, it's a great children's picture—particularly for bad children—as it should scare hell out of the little monsters. And it's a pretty fair horror film.

Variety: Quite credibly staged and played....

Los Angeles Mirror News (by a reviewer with the unfortunate name Viola Hegyi Swisher): [T]he monster's not a bit scary, except to the people in the cast.... One reasonably representative audience, composed largely of kids, giggled and groaned moderately through it all without missing a single mouthful of popcorn.

Schenectady Gazette: Teenagers and the rest of the Sunday afternoon crowd at the Plaza Theater had a lot of fun screaming and shuddering at [*Tarantula*]. ... Most of the footage concentrates on the giant spider crawling, crawling, which occasioned wild reaction from the excited audience. ... [T]he audience seemed so keyed up that there were shrieks punctuating most of the plot developments.

Los Angeles Examiner: The special photographic effects used to depict this monster are fairly impressive; but if they failed to scare me it was because the script had reduced me to a state of lethargy.

Cleveland Plain Dealer: [*Tarantula*] made some weak-hearted youngsters scream at the matinee performance. I also heard snickers, probably coming from teenage cynics weaned by the *Creature from the Black Lagoon* and *Beast from 20,000 Fathoms*. Those monsters were more impressive but this eight-legged beast also puts on a lively, fairly eerie show. ... [Even in his grotesque makeup,] poor old Leo G. can't compete with Lon Chaney, Jr., as a bogeyman. ... Clifford Stine's tricky camera effects in magnifying the spider to fantastic size are more amazing than the yarn.

The Daily Texan (Austin): Well, the State Theater is right in the swing of the Christmas season. It's now giving us two movies for the price of one; so let's open this package deal and see what we've got. [Snarky descriptions of *Running Wild* and *Tarantula* follow.] Now, the audience loved both of these, understand. In fact, there were moments when the laughter, catcalls and general cacophony drowned out everything. So for those who like to laugh at the wrong places (there are plenty of wrong places), this package at the State is for them. but personally this is one little gift I think I'll exchange, thank you.

Motion Picture Daily: [T]he process photography used for the giant spider is not as convincing as it might be.

Fangoria magazine (1993): While *Them!*'s approach to its giant-ant story was sober, "adult" and credible, *Tarantula* unambitiously panders to kids of all ages by squeezing every last ounce of lurid menace out of its more juvenile storyline.

Spidey Sounds: The Music of Tarantula

By David Schecter

While few film music aficionados know who wrote the music for many of Universal's 1950s films, there appears to be more of a consensus that Henry Mancini composed the score for *Tarantula*. In addition, it seems well-known that it was one of his earliest pictures, and his work on it attracted the attention of Hollywood and helped propel the composer to a lifetime of fame, fortune and multitudinous awards.

The only problem with this scenario is that none of it is true, as Mancini's immense career accomplishments were somehow achieved without any help from this giant spider film. Yet no matter how often these misstatements are corrected, the legend survives, so perhaps there's some need for people to believe it. Maybe it makes them feel that this elevates the movie's pop culture status beyond merely being an enjoyable colossal critter film? Or maybe people just have a hard time un-learning false information?

Mancini already had three years of film scoring experience with Universal when *Tarantula* crept into his life, as he had written cues for dozens of pictures, including *Abbott and Costello Go to Mars, City Beneath the Sea, Creature from the Black Lagoon, Drums Across the River, Four Guns to the Border, Horizons West, It Came from Outer Space, Johnny Dark, Lost in Alaska, Naked Alibi, The Raiders, Tanganyika, This Island Earth* and *The Veils of Bagdad*. And *Tarantula* wasn't a particularly difficult assignment for Mancini, as he

Joseph Gershenson (left) and Henry Mancini (third from left), others unidentified. (Photograph courtesy Henry Mancini Estate.)

wrote only 38 seconds of original music for the film, with the rest of his contributions being tracked in from movies he had worked on earlier in his career. The majority of music heard in *Tarantula*, as well as the majority of new music composed for the picture, was written by Herman Stein.

The misconceptions about Mancini's role in *Tarantula* can probably be traced back to 1959, when the Dick Jacobs-conducted "Themes from Horror Movies" record album offered a "theme" from *Tarantula*. In reality, that track was a combination of excerpts from four Mancini cues that were used in *Tarantula*, one being the ten-second "Squeeze Play, Pt. 2," which was one of the two original pieces he specifically wrote for the picture. The other musical snippets in that "theme" came from *East of Sumatra* ("Hot Fight") and *This Island Earth* ("Amorous Mutant" and "Metaluna Catastrophe, Part 2"). The reason these passages happened to be lumped together is because one of *Tarantula*'s conductor's scores had them arranged this way when the music was being recorded for the film, and that particular score was what Dick Jacobs recorded for his album. When the Varese Sarabande label re-released the record on LP in 1978 and on CD in 1993 under the title "Themes from Classic Science Fiction, Fantasy and Horror Films," the liner notes mistakenly claimed this track was *Tarantula*'s "Main Title," which it definitely wasn't. There was no mention that Herman Stein figured prominently in *Tarantula*'s soundtrack, which helped create the impression that Mancini was solely responsible for its score. While the liner notes stated that the composition's sense of motion in the brass and interesting flute notes suggested the menace of the eight-legged monster, those brass and flute notes were actually written for an *East of Sumatra* scene where a half-naked island king battles a mining engineer. This demonstrates why so much music tracking went on at Universal and other studios, as a piece of music composed for one scene would often work just as effectively in a completely different context in another picture. It also shows why people who write about film music shouldn't read into things too much, this author included!

As for *Tarantula* helping Mancini's career, at this early point when his career might have needed help, there weren't many people who even knew he had anything to do with the picture, because as usual, Joseph Gershenson's "Music Supervision" credit was the only music credit on the film. However, in this particular case, the score was conducted by Gershenson's assistant Milton Rosen on September 22, 1955, in a mere six hours, which was right on the cusp of being enough time to record all the music in the picture. It's possible that some of the music heard in the movie might have come from older recordings used in previous Universal productions, although this is just speculation, as the entire score sounds newly recorded.

Herman Stein in the late 1940s. (Photograph courtesy Monstrous Movie Music.)

Excerpt from Henry Mancini's "Hot Fight" from *East of Sumatra*, reused in *Tarantula*. (© 1953 Northridge Music Co.)

Tarantula's mostly tracked score contains an astonishing 90 cues, 52 by Stein and 38 by Mancini, but there were really more pieces than that, as new intros and outros were often added to help the various pieces fit together better. Many of the cues are brief, with 39 of them being 20 seconds or less, and only seven are longer than a minute. There's 39:10 of music in the picture, 23:33 coming from the pen of Stein, with the remaining 15:37 from Mancini. Of the new music composed specifically for *Tarantula*, Stein contributed 22 cues totaling 6:30, with Mancini adding two new pieces totaling 38 seconds. While the score was more of an old creation than a new one, almost all the new touches were courtesy of Stein. The composer recalled that he would be told by either Gershenson or Rosen whether his present assignment would require new music, reused music or a combination of both, and in the last two cases, he'd often be responsible for choosing the tracked selections. This mix of new and old was certainly not limited to monster movies; other Universal films of the period featuring this approach included *Has Anybody Seen My Gal, Here Come the Nelsons, Horizons West* and *Son of Ali Baba*. There were also many Universal movies whose old music was limited to source music cues and songs, with all of the dramatic underscore being new.

The films and cues supplying most of the music to *Tarantula* were among those that had already been endlessly recycled in other Universal pictures. The picture was tracked from 20 different movies made in the early to mid–1950s, the majority being other science fiction films and Westerns. The most cues were donated by *It Came from Outer Space* (23), *This Island Earth* (eight), *Six Bridges to Cross* (seven), *Dawn at Socorro* (four), *Four Guns to the Border* (four) and *Smoke Signal* (three), with further entries coming from *East of Sumatra, Girls in the Night, The Man from Bitter Ridge*, three Audie Murphy Westerns (*Drums Across the River, The Duel at Silver Creek, Ride Clear of Diablo*) and other pictures. Additional Universal productions that used some of the same cues that were tracked into *Tarantula* include *Monster on the Campus, Running Wild, The Saga of Hemp Brown, Showdown at Abilene* and *The Thing That Couldn't Die*.

Despite the preponderance of musical snippets, *Tarantula*'s score flows fairly seamlessly, and this is because Stein wrote original music transitions and short cues to bridge his previously written cues. Another trick Stein used to make the new and old music co-exist so well was to add instrumental and compositional touches to his new writing that matched aspects of the library cues around it. For some reason, Mancini's sections were handled differently, with many of his cues lacking transitions, or else there were simple sustains or extremely quick bridges. Whether Mancini, Stein or somebody else handled "the Mancini aspect" of the soundtrack is lost to history.

Because only two composers contributed music to *Tarantula*—rather than the truckload of writers Universal often used—when the score was newly performed and recorded by the studio's orchestra under Rosen's baton, it sounds fairly unified. Unless you're familiar with the previous films' music, you'd be hard-pressed to guess that it's such a patchwork affair. While there weren't any new musical motifs pertaining to the characters, events or even to the spider, the preponderance of music originating in *It Came from Outer Space* and the occasional flutter-tongued brass during the monster sequences managed to create the impression of some thematic unity related to the titular character.

Tarantula opens with the horror fanfare Stein wrote for *Creature from the Black Lagoon* and reused in *Revenge of the Creature*. In *Tarantula*, the piece is performed at a much faster tempo, which was a good way of freshening it up a bit; it's over before you even know it was stolen! It also provides early evidence that, while Universal was willing to add some new musical touches to *Tarantula*, they wouldn't be going all-out. The music serving as *Tarantula*'s main title perfectly conjures the terror of a giant, rampaging spider, as well as many other exciting images, and that's why this electrifying cue was used on more than one occasion when an explosive musical statement was needed. The piece is part of the "Main Title" Stein composed for *The Lawless Breed* (1952), a superb Western about outlaw John Wesley Hardin (Rock Hudson). For its *Tarantula* reuse, Stein removed the opening nine measures and the closing 20 he wrote for *The Lawless Breed*, replaced them with a timpani roll to begin the picture, added high strings to the end, and *voilà!*—goodbye Western music, hello monster music! The timpani nicely builds from the sound of the wind as the camera tilts up on the desert boulders, while the strings ease us into the drama, especially as nothing too monstrous is going to happen until the second reel, when we glimpse some way-too-big white rats in Prof. Deemer's lab. In 1956, *The Lawless Breed*'s "Main Title" was slowed down considerably, where it served as the main title for *Showdown at Abilene*. A truncated version became the main title for *Monster on the Campus*, and another shortened rendition was used as part of the main title of the 1967 oater *Ride to Hangman's Tree*. The piece also appears in the trailer for the excellent psychological Western *No Name on the Bullet* (1959).

The Lawless Breed features 17 original cues by Stein, including the last nine in the picture, which is rather odd considering the ends of pictures were more prone to tracking than the beginnings. The climaxes probably suffered a lack of musical respect for a couple of reasons. First, the closing reels were the last ones scored more often than not, when encroaching deadlines might have necessitated a last-minute switch to using already-written music. In other instances, it appears as if some musical freshness was more important in the beginning of a picture (e.g., *Creature from the Black Lagoon*), because near the end, the audience might

Full score of Herman Stein's "Main Title" from *The Lawless Breed*, reused in *Tarantula*. (© 1952 Gilead Music Co.)

be so caught up in the drama they'd be less likely to notice they were hearing music familiar from other contexts. In addition to Stein's contributions, *The Lawless Breed* contains a few short original cues by Hans Salter and Milton Rosen. The tracked music in the picture comes from Frank Skinner (*The Black Angel, The Naked City, The Raging Tide, Smash-Up: The Story of a Woman, Swell Guy, Tap Roots*), Hans Salter (*Bend of the River, Frenchie, The Michigan Kid, Scarlet Street, Thunder on the Hill, Tomahawk, Untamed Frontier*), Arthur Lange (*Belle of the Yukon*, made for International Pictures before they joined with Universal), Miklós Rózsa (*Secret Beyond the Door...*), Walter Scharf (*Red Canyon*) and William Lava (*She-Wolf of London*). There were a few older songs in *The Lawless Breed* as well, and the conglomeration of 55 cues was a fairly typical Universal-International concoction of the era.

In *Tarantula*'s opening 38:45 of running time, Stein wrote 26 of the first 27 cues, his pieces consisting of originals as well as tracked cues that had been composed for *Dawn at Socorro, It Came from Outer Space, Six Bridges to Cross, Naked Alibi, Tanganyika* and *This Island Earth.* The first three films in that list provide nine cues to the opening two reels of *Tarantula,* and hearing similar themes more than once in such a short span serves to create a sense of musical continuity to this mélange of a score. So perfect are the musical choices that it's hard to imagine any of this music not having been composed specifically for this movie. In the laboratory sequence when Jacobs attacks Deemer, Stein wrote new connective material (some of it titled "Havoc in Lab") to tie together eight tracked cues, but unfortunately, too much of the fight music was either not recorded or else was recorded and then removed, to the detriment of the film, where the silences during the battle are deafening. Even if you want the audience to hear monkey chirps and spider chatter, once the music starts, it needs to continue until the end of the fight, not be turned on and off like a spigot. One of the cues in this sequence is "Visitors from Space" from *It Came from Outer Space,* which appears five times in *Tarantula,* and which was originally intended to be used even more than that. The piece rears its Xenomorphic head the first two times Prof. Deemer stands in front of the glass-encased spider, although a bad edit in the film or cue—possibly due to an unacceptable special effect—slightly spoils the intended musical impact.

The only non–Stein cue in the first few reels of the picture is Mancini's "Stealing the Car" from *Johnny Dark,* heard when Deemer inspects his humongous rodents. Only the end of the original composition was used, and it was re-arranged for woodwinds, strings and harp. This was an odd musical choice for a couple of reasons. First, it's a single Mancini cue in the middle of non-stop Stein, and while the moody passage is definitely appropriate, Stein no doubt worked on this part of the movie, and he had a wealth of similar cues that would have worked just as well. But what's really peculiar is that it's the only piece in *Johnny Dark* remotely suitable for a horror movie, and it's strange that anyone even considered this film as a source for a cue of this flavor, especially as the car-stealing scene it ac-

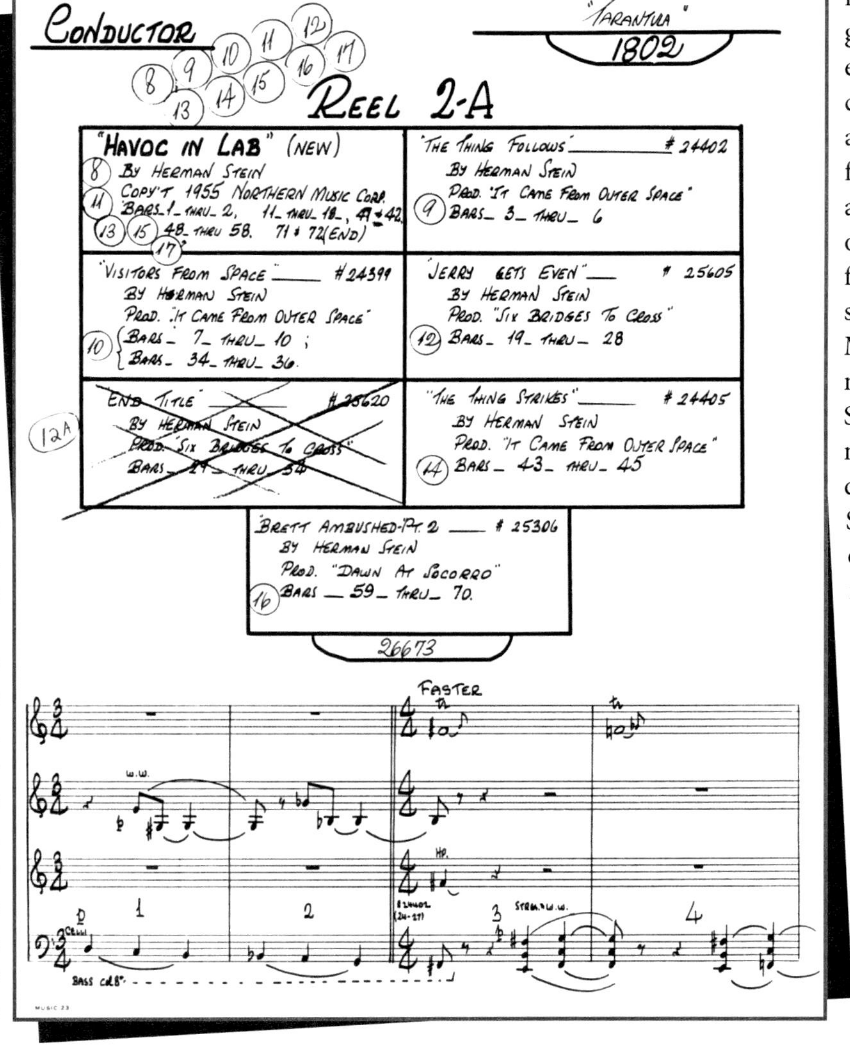

Conductor's score showing a plethora of old and new cues used in *Tarantula*'s "Havoc in Lab" sequence. (© 1955 Gilead Music Co./USI A Music Publishing.)

companied was a humorous one. Whether Mancini recalled it being appropriate and suggested it to Stein is anybody's guess. The jaunty 1954 Tony Curtis-Piper Laurie racing car picture contained a mostly original Hans Salter score with some new cues by William Lava, Mancini and Stein, and some tracked cues and source music pieces as well. Interestingly, there were some musical changes made to the picture atypical for a Universal film of this era, with Stein having to rewrite his "Main Title" into something completely different, Salter doing the same thing with his "End Title," and other music that was written for the movie being removed so certain sections could play without underscore. One wonders what was going on during production that resulted in so many musical anomalies.

An eerie sequence in *Tarantula* occurs when Deemer surveys what's left of his destroyed lab, Stein's music originating in "The Great Truck Robbery, Part 2" from *Six Bridges to Cross*. This 1955 Tony Curtis crime picture featured a fine original score by Stein and Frank Skinner. Mancini and actor Jeff Chandler collaborated on the song "Six Bridges to Cross," heard throughout the film and sung during the main title by Sammy Davis, Jr. This was the song where Davis Jr., couldn't make the original recording session because he was in a car accident that cost him his left eye. When the *Tarantula* lab scene dissolves to the desert burial sequence, Stein's "Coffee Stop" from *Dawn at Socorro* makes an ominously lit scene even spookier until it's drowned out by a screaming monkey being launched into Deemer's chest by some off-screen factotum. Universal sometimes tracked its cues into subsequent films in similar combinations, and the previous two pieces were also reused in the same order in *Step Down to Terror* (1958).

Dawn at Socorro is a dark but satisfying 1954 Western starring Rory Calhoun and Piper Laurie. The score was composed fairly equally by Skinner and Stein, a combination that Gershenson seldom used, but the result is a solid affair, with the string-dominated work helping to create an appropriately pessimistic mood throughout. There were a handful of older Western cues reused in the picture that were composed by Stein, Mancini and Salter, but these were mainly employed as source music, as much of the film takes place in gambling halls, where background music was supposedly a constant in the Old West. However, the bulk of this source music comes from instrumental versions of past Universal Western songs composed by Everett Carter and Milton Rosen, Frederick Herbert and Arnold Hughes, and other songwriting teams. One of Universal's finest Western scores of the era, it supplied a wealth of cues to a wide variety of subsequent pictures, with many of the most popular pieces being Stein compositions such as the three-part "Stockyard Fight," the two-part "Brett Ambushed" and the two-part "Duel at Socorro."

An example of a new cue that Stein wrote for the Jack Arnold monster movie is the 15-second "Tarantula on the Way," which plays when Matt drives Steve to Deemer's house and a spider the size of a truck follows in a marvelous composite shot. Part of the composition was not used in the picture, the remainder being a brass-and-timpani heavy hit with trilling woodwinds, as good as any way to musically depict an arachnid this big. Short cues like this one add sparkle to *Tarantula*'s score amidst all the library pieces. Outside of the monster sequences, much of the music used in the movie are quiet pieces favoring chamber instrumentation, including most of Stein's new compositions. These cues help add a layer of mystery and unease to the picture during some of the non-action sequences. An example of this is when Stein's "Merrion Killed" from *Tanganyika* sounds as Deemer and Steve work together in the lab, about 31 minutes into *Tarantula*, with flute and strings predominating. Because Stein's new pieces had similar orchestrations as some of the tracked cues in the movie, his original compositions sounded like they "belonged" with the other pieces. When louder or faster music was needed, library cues were usually chosen, probably because Stein didn't have the time to write more complex or involved pieces.

The well-executed mixture of old and new can be appreciated in the scene when Deemer notices he's suffering from an injection he received at the hands of his mad assistant, with Stein's original "First Symptom" adding subtle accompaniment to the scene when the professor rubs his arm, carrying over into the scene when Steve leaves to get her hair done. When a close-up reveals Deemer's mutated hand, eight seconds of the composer's "Duel at Socorro, Part 1" from *Dawn at Socorro* applies the moderate aural shock. While one might have thought that the scene change would be where one cue ended and another began, the use of the same cue to bridge scenes as well as using a snippet of a tracked piece to apply a tag to another composition further creates the impression that all the music in *Tarantula* was expressly written for the picture. Although the movie might have benefited from additional underscore during some of the dialogue-heavy scenes, it doesn't suffer from that absence, in large part because the monster sequences—when they arrive—hold up so well both visually and musically.

Another visitation of music from *It Came from Outer Space* occurs in *Tarantula* when Matt and Steve drive out and enjoy the scenic beauty of the desert landscape, with Stein's "Sand Rock" and "End Cast" playing. By using two cues that share the same melody in back-to-back fashion, this enables the music to build with the drama as we go from the chamber sounds of the first piece to the full-orchestral rendition of the second. And then, as if the desert can't sound any lovelier, the sequence is capped off by an excerpt from

Stein's glittering "Exeter's Mansion" from *This Island Earth*, which flows perfectly due to a short transition Stein wrote to link the compositions.

Mancini makes his presence felt when the spider causes an avalanche near Matt and Steve, with a reuse of his *It Came from Outer Space* "End Title." This is quickly followed by a mishmash of other cues from *This Island Earth* ("Amorous Mutant," "Metaluna Catastrophe, Part 2") and more *It Came from Outer Space* entries ("Zombie George" and "George's Double"), but the sequence feels like it was hastily thrown together, resulting in disjointed musical accompaniment. It also doesn't help that the "End Title" was not the most appropriate composition for the avalanche. Stein scored the "giant rabbit" sequence with mostly new material, and then pre-existing Mancini cues take over for the next eight minutes.

Mancini's "Robbery on Schedule" and "Home at Last" from *Four Guns to the Border* accompany Steve noticing Deemer's face is undergoing some unpleasant changes; then there's an interesting use of tracked music in the form of the composer's "Down River," written for the 1955 Dana Andrews-Piper Laurie Western *Smoke Signal*. The cue augments Matt's investigation of the avalanche, and the piano motif has that Mancini "feel" to it, the cue's Western origin revealed by the "Indian" sound played on French horns. The little-known Western is not only a very rewarding movie, but it contains one of the finer Western scores of the decade, co-composed by Mancini, Irving Gertz and William Lava, with Lava's main theme—heard at both the beginning and end—being a particularly majestic composition. The high quality of that collaborative score makes it appear as if all three composers were suitably motivated by this inspiring motion picture. *Smoke Signal* provided a wealth of cues to later Universal movies, and "Down River" can be heard just before the main title of the crime drama *Outside the Law*, where it paradoxically highlights a title card stating "Berlin 1946." How this cue was chosen for such a use is a mystery, unless the cue's title reminded somebody of Germany's Spree River.

Some wonderful Mancini cues enhance the memorable sequence when the now-colossal spider attacks the horse corral. *The Far Country*'s "Claim Jumpers Stopped" creates a sense of unrest as the horses begin to get agitated, while "Deadly Ore, Part 2" from *The Yellow Mountain* does a masterful job of further raising the tension. This two-part cue was written for the climactic gunfight in the 1954 Lex Barker Western, and Mancini's distinctive low four-note phrase on stopped horns and muted trombones was used in both parts—making these extremely popular Universal music library pieces. These cues appeared in swarms of later films, including *Showdown at Abilene* (1956), and even as far into the future as *Taggart* (1964) and *Ride to Hangman's Tree* (1967). The motif is one of the most memorable in *Tarantula*'s entire score, as it was perfect in capturing the presence of the eight-legged behemoth.

When the spider's silhouette appears from behind the hill, "Zombie George" from *It Came from Outer Space* supplies the monstrous impact. "Amorous Mutant" from *This Island Earth* supplements the tarantula's walk down the hill

Conductor's score of Henry Mancini's "Robbery on Schedule" from *Four Guns to the Border*, reused in *Tarantula*. (© 1954 Northridge Music Co.)

Excerpt from Henry Mancini's "Deadly Ore, Pt. 2" from *The Yellow Mountain*, reused in *Tarantula*. (© 1954 Northridge Music Co.)

and rancher Andy's death, as the spider somehow manages to roar like a lion. "Tomahawk Stage" from *The Man from Bitter Ridge* mysteriously underlines the pickup truck as it approaches the super-spider, and then the first of six *Tarantula* uses of *It Came from Outer Space*'s "The Thing Strikes" covers the action as the truck is destroyed. Although "The Thing Strikes" is a suitably monstrous cue to enhance various shots of the giant creepy-crawler, it's unfortunate that a newly composed attack motif couldn't have been composed by either Stein or Mancini to be used in some or all of those instances, especially considering that neither composer ever seemed to run out of excellent creature themes. As usual, time and money were probably standing in the way of that happening.

In 1990, Mancini recorded a short suite from *Tarantula* (titled "Terror Strikes") for his enjoyable "Mancini in Surround" CD, and this re-orchestrated and re-edited composition consisted of some of his cues in this particular part of the movie, although he didn't record all of them, and he also altered instrumentation and tempos. The album's track title "Terror Strikes" has nothing to do with any of the cues in *Tarantula*—it's just a name that somebody thought would be exciting for the album release.

Stein and Mancini's compositions are mixed together throughout most of *Tarantula*'s last three reels, with some outstanding moments despite many being library cues. If the music that accompanies Matt pouring spider venom into a Thermos sounds familiar, that's because it's the alien glitter trail music Stein wrote for *It Came from Outer Space*'s "Visitors from Space." About six minutes earlier, when a pool of venom is first spotted, Mancini had used a similar theme he had written for the same movie's "John's Discovery, Part 2," thereby creating a recurring motif in *Tarantula*, even though the motif originated in a prior film. When Steve phones Matt, who then races to Deemer's, Stein used a number of short original compositions (all titled "Growing Wild") to link together some of his own tracked cues from Westerns and another reuse of Mancini's "The Thing Strikes." This *It Came from Outer Space* piece is heard when Tarantula is seen scuttling behind a rocky hill, backing up when it apparently realizes it has crossed an annoying matte line.

While the colossal critter searches for food and happens upon two hapless miners, an original Stein cue called "Fatal Fall" uses solo bassoon to create an ominous mood, and when the old men notice the approaching monster, "Visitors from Space" does an excellent job of capturing the event, the piece being orchestrated slightly different from its *It Came from Outer Space* use. At the end of the attack, there's another instance of Mancini's ubiquitous "The Thing Strikes." As the abominable arachnid stealthily approaches Deemer's house, 2:21 of Stein's "The Great Truck Robbery, Part 1" from *Six Bridges to Cross* (as opposed to "Part 2," heard earlier in *Tarantula*) enhances the action via two excerpts, with the second being by far the longest single cue in the entire picture. The second excerpt begins on piano notes that accompany the eye-catching shot of the spider on the horizon behind Deemer's house. This tracked music is combined with three newly penned Stein snippets called "Squeeze Play, Part 1," which emphasize the spider touching electrical wires, Matt driving down the road, and Deemer's house beginning to collapse around the professor.

The original use of "The Great Truck Robbery, Part 1" in *Six Bridges to Cross* serves as a masterful example of the dramatic potency of film music, playing during a dialogue-free sequence when robbers furtively ascend a stairwell to the Trans-Continental Armored Car Service Building. The piece builds deliberately in intensity by virtue of its thematic development, increasing orchestration and heightened dynamics, which is why it was perfect for many situations when the drama needed to increase slowly, but steadily. Stein slightly rearranged the cue for *Tarantula*, and it works so well it somehow manages to convince us that a house-sized spider can actually sneak up without anyone noticing until they're undressing for bed! "The Great Truck Robbery, Part 1" became a fixture in Universal's music library, being dusted off for *The Saga of Hemp Brown*, *Showdown at Abilene* and *Running Wild*, this latter appearance occurring when William Campbell hides from a police car that pulls into a gas station. The cue also found its way into the 1959 *Westinghouse Desilu Playhouse* episode "The Hanging Judge" and the 1960 *Pony Express* episode "Trial by Fury."

After Mancini's "Amorous Mutant" from *This Island*

Earth and "Hot Fight" from *East of Sumatra* accentuate Tarantula destroying Deemer's house, the composer's "Metaluna Catastrophe, Part 2" from *This Island Earth* plays a notable role when Matt and Steve drive away. You can hear Mancini's two original cues in *Tarantula* (both named "Squeeze Play, Part 2") just before the above sequence starts, and then when Steve spots the hairy beast following them on the highway. *The Yellow Mountain*'s "Deadly Ore, Part 1" ("Part 2" was used earlier in the movie) is heard when the silhouetted multi-legger stops to pose on a distant hill while Our Heroes watch from the road, making for a stunning audio-visual combination.

Along with some original Stein music titled "Dynamite Didn't," the spider's assault on the highway is scored with further uses of Mancini's "The Thing Strikes" and "Amorous Mutant" and Stein's "Visitors from Space." There are also a couple of tracked snippets that you can tell were personally chosen by Stein. Long after the composer retired, his favorite film cues remained three long contiguous pieces he wrote for one of his earliest pictures, the Jack Arnold-directed *Girls in the Night* (1953), and that's why he reused parts of "Interrupted Murder, Part 1" and "Interrupted Murder, Part 3." They play from when Matt tells the truck to "Hold it!" so that the dynamite's detonator can be wired, continuing until the spider emerges from the explosion. Stein also reused all three of the "Interrupted Murder" cues in *The Saga of Hemp Brown*, a score he assembled with 105 fragments of his new and old music. "Interrupted Murder, Part 1" also made an appearance in the 1953 Barbara Stanwyck drama *All I Desire*, and the two pieces heard in *Tarantula* also featured prominently in *Tarantula*'s trailer.

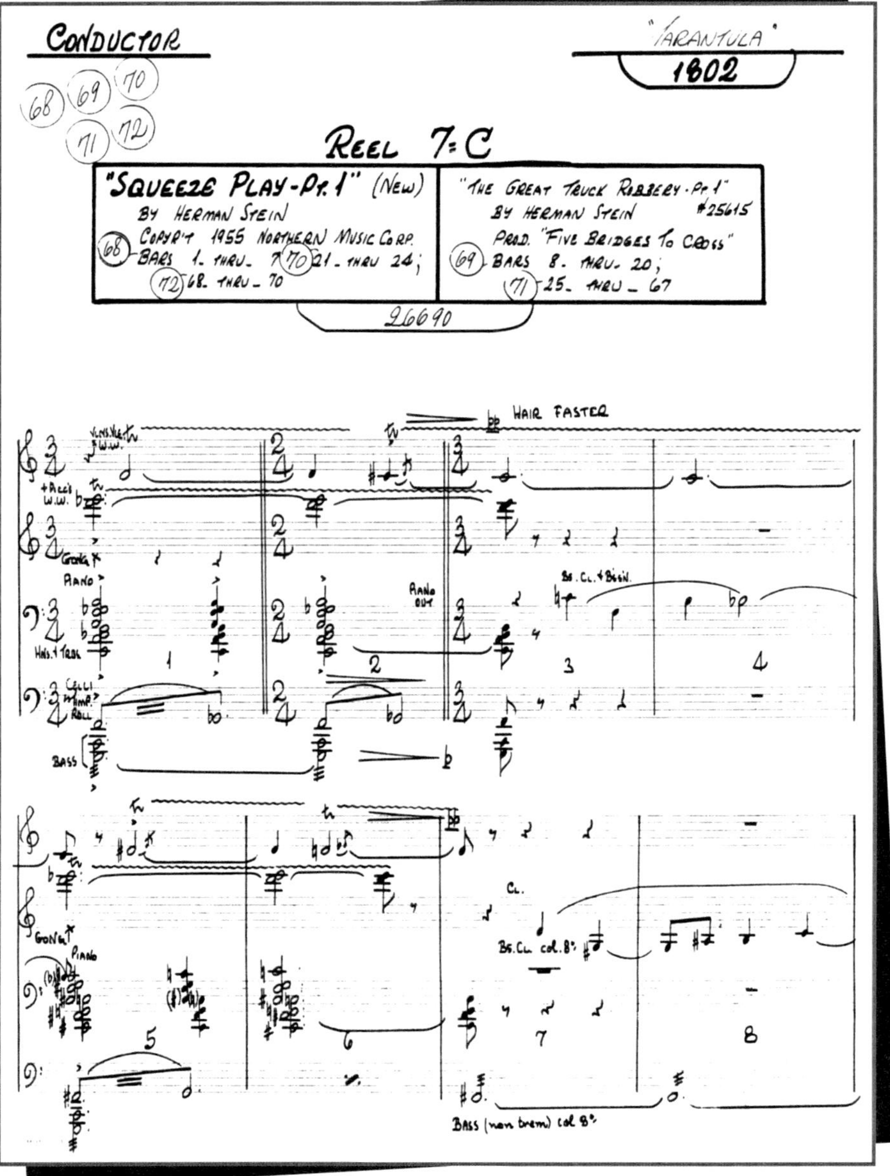

Conductor's score showing a combination of new and old Herman Stein music in *Tarantula*. (© 1955 Gilead Music Co./USI A Music Publishing.)

For some odd reason, almost two minutes of *Tarantula*'s climax have no musical accompaniment, including the Air Force bombing sequence. This omission manages to sap almost all the excitement from the movie, which is a shame considering music played such an important role in the picture up until that point. Why this part wasn't scored is anybody's guess, but perhaps Stein was totally exhausted from helping to piece together this incredibly complex score and he needed a nap. As a result, we get to hear pilot Clint Eastwood utter a series of terse Eastwoodisms like, "Dump 'em all," without music to take our attention off the mundane dialogue.

As Tarantula turns into a massive, hairy fireball, Stein's full-orchestral "End Title" sounds. Although it's listed as an original composition on the film's cue sheets, it's actually an extended version of part of the "End Title" written for *Six Bridges to Cross*. Stein's End Cast music in *Tarantula* is correctly notated on the cue sheets as being the *Redhead from Wyoming* "End Title." This last cue added some Western closure to a horror film whose main title also came from a Western, and as a number of Universal Westerns and sci-fi thrillers were filmed in the same desert setting, it's only appropriate they would share a great deal of the same music.

The Redhead from Wyoming, an easygoing 1953 Maureen O'Hara Western, also contributed its "End Cast" (thematically related to its "End Title") to *Creature from the Black Lagoon* and *Revenge of the Creature*, where it served as both of those films' End Casts. *The Redhead from Wyoming* contained seven new pieces by Stein, a short cue by Milton Rosen and a plethora of tracked music, most from other Westerns. Stein obviously had little time to score *The Redhead from Wyoming*, as he copied the "End Cast" from *Redhead*'s "End Title" to create it, and that "End Title" had already been copied in part from Stein's "Fireside Chat," written for *The Duel at Silver Creek* (1952). What the origin of "Fireside Chat" might have been should probably be filed away in an immense drawer labeled "Universal's Music Mysteries." Two excerpts from *The Redhead from Wyoming*'s "End Title" and one from "Fireside Chat" helped wind up the climax of the 1955 juvenile delinquent flick *Running Wild*, with the musical similarities helping one cue to flow seamlessly into the next.

While almost any film would benefit from a half-decent original score as opposed to a tracked effort, *Tarantula*'s soundtrack was extremely well put together from previously existing sources. It was not merely successful due to the particular library cues that were selected, but also in the professional and creative way the music was adapted into such a sonorous gumbo, not to mention how it was then integrated into the picture. Because of that, it's hard to complain too much that so little original music was composed for *Tarantula*. But even though it was a superb job, it's fortunate that Universal offered mostly original science fiction scores for the next two years. And that was probably good news for Stein, who wasn't crazy about all the work involved in piecing together such a complicated score without the creative satisfaction he would derive from writing new music. Based on the musical stitch-jobs he and some of the other Universal composers were asked to crank out on occasion, had these artists not gotten into the movie business, it's possible they might have become first-rate surgeons!

John Agar and Mara Corday recoil from some sky-high horror—but famed columnist Walter Winchell was unaffected by the movie: "*Tarantula* strives to be a shocker. It is more Sandman than Bogeyman." (Photograph courtesy Alexander Rotter.)

At first glance, it's tempting to consider *Tarantula* nothing more than Universal's knock-off of *Them!* (1954), the first Atomic Age Big Bug movie and an equally big success for Warner Brothers. But given a closer look, *Tarantula* is much more. It's the first film to *center* around a giant spider (though previous movies such as the 1940 *The Thief of Bagdad* and the legendary lost footage in the 1933 *King Kong* incorporated huge arachnids into their plotlines). *Tarantula's* concentration on the spider was the first of numerous giant arachnid encounters, culminating in the retro *Eight Legged Freaks* (2002). *Tarantula*, like *Them!*, benefits from its moody desert locale, director Jack Arnold replicating his previous success with desert environs in 1953's *It Came from Outer Space*.

Tarantula works some old-fashioned mad science into its monster spider story by making Leo G. Carroll's Prof. Deemer responsible for the outsize brute. The film also delivers a unique touch: the pre-credits sequence in which Deemer's colleague Eric Jacobs (Eddie Parker), mutated by the radioactive growth nutrient, turns into a man-monster and is seen staggering through the desert. (Prior to *Tarantula*, was there another horror film with a similarly eerie pre-credits sequence?) This early scene is startling, adding a dose of pure horror to what was billed as a Big Bug science fiction opus. It also commands audience attention immediately, even before the film's credits roll. Later, the mutating effects of Nutrient Type 3Y are weaved into the film as a horror subplot when another of Deemer's now-monstrous colleagues, Paul Lund (also played by Parker), attacks him and injects him with the monster-making serum. Deemer's gradual, disfiguring transformation is yet another horror subplot to the spider attacks—a one-of-a-kind variation on the standard Big Bug films of the '50s.

And it is Leo G. Carroll's Deemer who carries the show. The story immediately establishes him as a weird recluse with a secretive agenda—and Carroll's off-kilter style contributes immeasurably to the characterization. Carroll always lent dignity and grace to his film roles. In *Tarantula*, his excellent diction and sonorous voice are equally capable of dignity, warmth and coldness. Perhaps Carroll's best quality was his ability to convey a cold, cryptic quality while expressing that dignity and warmth. In such films as *Spellbound* (1945) and the obscure *London by Night* (1937), Carroll expertly conveyed a dignified veneer masking a heartless psychopath. In *Tarantula*, he successfully tempers his avuncular qualities with that same secretive, sinister persona—especially as we watch his slow disfigurement.

Carroll perfectly expresses concern and sympathy in the funeral parlor scene as he talks about the death of Jacobs:

> **Sheriff, have you ever watched a friend dying before your eyes and not been able to help? ... It's particularly tough when you're a physician and you know what's wrong with him, and there isn't a single, solitary thing you or anyone else can do.**

As Carroll speaks these words, his downcast eyes and mouth expressions convey sadness. Carroll immediately sounds a sinister note as he discusses how his colleague developed acromegaly so quickly: "The next morning, he began to ... *change*." Carroll accentuates the word "change" with a note of menace and foreboding, giving this Big Bug film a welcome undertone of pure horror. His words also resonate after Carroll himself is injected with the nutrient—and we wait for his gradual, inevitably monstrous transformation.

When Carroll begins morphing, he also begins modulating his avuncular quality with a coldness and irritability that parallels his physical change. Carroll gives *Tarantula* its element of mad science, making the film a full-tilt work of horror rather than just an Atom Age "monster-on-the-loose" yarn. Initially, Carroll's interaction with Mara Corday's "Steve" Clayton is that of a kindly mentor to the young, comely assistant. After Lund's vengeful assault, Carroll subtly signals his metamorphosis by rubbing his right shoulder and arm, accompanied by ominous Herman Stein music. Carroll's physical cues keep us on edge waiting for the ultimate morphing of man to monster. As the change progresses, so does Deemer's increasingly cold demeanor towards Steve. He angrily confronts her after she permits Matt (John Agar) to tour his laboratory, and we are unnerved both by his facial disfigurement and his sudden, uncharacteristically angry tone: "My laboratory is not open to the *public*, Miss Clayton!" Carroll's ability to modulate between warmth and coldness is best displayed in this scene—and it combines with his already-evident disfigurement to unnerving effect.

Yet when Deemer finally explains the cause of his monstrous morphing to Matt and Steve, he reverts to a pathos that captures our sympathy: "The isotope triggered our nutrient into a *nightmare*." He then begins deliriously reminiscing about his "guinea pig ... big as a police dog"—and his escaped tarantula, whose size he can articulate only by

Deemer (Leo G. Carroll) strays off the beaten path of science and must pay a steep price. His colleague Lund (Eddie Parker) is the debt collector. Lund has the Mr. Hyde look, plus a lofty forehead perhaps handed down from one of *This Island Earth*'s big-brow aliens. (Photograph courtesy Alexander Rotter.)

spreading his arms wide. By now, Deemer's facial transformation has progressed, and the film has successfully worked its horror subplot into the giant spider framework.

Like all victims of mad science (Henry Frankenstein, Dr. Moreau, Dr. Jekyll, Jack Griffin), Carroll's Deemer is obsessed with his experimentation—and Carroll delivers that obsession calmly, rationally and effectively.

Thus, Deemer shares the same altruistic quality that possesses many Golden Age mad doctors: a desire to do good that eventually mutates into disaster. Deemer embodies *Tarantula's* Golden Age, Gothic roots. In the end, we witness Deemer's full, monstrous transformation just before the giant spider he created destroys him. Deemer is a monster too—a victim of mad science who "meddled in things man must leave alone." Like the greatest mad doctors of the '30s and '40s, Leo G. Carroll brings to *Tarantula* a performance marked by multifaceted moods that veer from the avuncular, to the cold, to the monstrous. *Tarantula* is memorable largely for Carroll's characterization and its importance to the film's horror subplot.

The rest of *Tarantula's* cast pales alongside Carroll's subtle, layered and menacing performance. John Agar is his usual competent, stolid self as Dr. Matt Hastings. But he is more relaxed and natural here than in *Revenge of the Creature*. Agar shows genuine righteous indignation when he questions the sudden transformation of Jacobs. Watch how slyly Agar eyes Nestor Paiva's sheriff as he (Agar) questions the motives of Deemer and Jacobs: "I'd say they might be working on something they're not too anxious to talk about." And Agar projects a reasoned, believable tone as he warns newspaperman Joe Burch (Ross Elliott) not to spread the distressing news about men, cattle and sheep reduced to skeletons: "If you print anything as vague as what we've got, you'll scare half the state to death."

One of Universal's most charming leading ladies, Mara Corday, as usual, looks beautiful, elegant and poised. Like Julie Adams in *Creature from the Black Lagoon* (1954), she displays both scientific knowledge and a degree of independence.

Other than Carroll, the real stars of *Tarantula* are its technicians, particularly its cameraman George Robinson. We get our first view of the huge spider as Deemer views it in its glass prison. A real tarantula was used in footage that was projected on a screen inside the cage; it's a truly creepy scene as we hear the spider squealing and its claws scratching the glass. The use of a real spider lends a touch of realism to the fantastic plot whenever we see the creature loping speedily through the lonely desert landscape. Watch for the scene in which Matt and Steve sit at the base of Devil's Rock. Their intimate moments are intercut with ominous shots of boulders, just before one of the big rocks mysteriously falls toward the young couple. The scene is an effective, spooky prelude to the shot of the spider's huge black legs appearing over the boulders. It's reminiscent of *Creature from the Black Lagoon's* scattered shots of the Gill Man's webbed hand sliding onto the shore and into and out of the water.

Perhaps *Tarantula's* best photographic effect is the Arach Attack on a corral full of horses. After an ominous night shot of the open desert landscape, the spider's enormous, pitch black outline suddenly appears atop a hill and it stands motionless against the twilit sky. For anyone with arachnophobia, the image is truly unsettling. The camera follows the creature down to the horses before giving us an aerial view of the attack. The camera becomes the spider's jaws as the audience literally rides the spider's mouth down to meet an equine victim—and a hapless rancher who happens to be in the way! The terror and ferocity of this monster is never better conveyed than in this scene.

We are also treated to an excellent long shot of the spider slowly advancing toward two prospectors in the desert. They shoot the spider as if it were filling the entire desert by night—and the monster's creepiness is augmented when its enormous black outline is juxtaposed against the dark desert sky. As the spider crawls its way toward Deemer's house, its massive form is contrasted with the night sky. We also get a shot of the spider peeping through Steve's bedroom window, a surreal, frightening moment reminiscent of King Kong peering at Fay Wray through her hotel window!

The scene in which the spider destroys Carroll's home is equally unnerving. We see a long shot of the monster's furious attack, its legs writhing and wiggling intensely as it throws its body onto the house. Ultimately we see only the massive spider enveloping the house and then the screen itself.

Scenes of the spider alternate with interplay among the human characters, making *Tarantula* one of the best-paced Universal horrors of the '50s. In one scene, an entomologist (Raymond Bailey) lectures Matt on how furious and fearless tarantulas really are. When Matt asks what to expect from a *giant* tarantula, the entomologist stuns him into a long silence by telling him to "expect something that's fiercer, more cruel and deadly than anything that ever walked the Earth." Now there's a cut to a long shot of the giant creature crawling through the desert, accompanied by ominous music. Later we get an unsettling shot of the spider perched silently on a hill by night, as Matt, Steve, the sheriff and others look on in horror. There's also an excellent long shot of the spider's surviving a dynamite blast; through the cloud of smoke, the thing looks even larger and more menacing than before. And before its destruction, the massive spider is seen advancing toward Desert Rock, looming over the comparatively diminutive town and its frightened human inhabitants.

The model ants used in *Them!* make that film's attack scenes more effective and startling than those in *Tarantula*. But *Tarantula* conveys the *size* of its monster more effectively than cinematographer Sid Hickox did in *Them!* In addition, the dark, sinister desert world of *Tarantula* augments the creepiness of its arachnoid terror. Subjective shots of the spider's attacks lend a furious, stylish panache that was missing from *Them*'s straightforward approach. Even in a Big Bug movie, Universal's time-honored sense of style carried the day.

Universal camera veteran George Robinson adds much to *Tarantula's* creepy style with his interior shots. He is especially adept at lensing and lighting Deemer's gradual facial disfigurement. Once Deemer begins to deteriorate, Robinson shows him in low-key lighting, which heightens the tension. When Deemer angrily scolds Steve for bringing Matt to the lab, Robinson gives us a good look at the subtle but noticeable changes in the scientist's face: the first hints of swelling and wrinkling, which Robinson photographs in half-shadow As Steve phones Matt to tell him about his disfigurement, Robinson shows us only the lower half of Deemer's body as he silently descends the staircase behind her, then his hand as he takes the receiver from Steve. The scene abruptly ends with Steve looking at the off-camera Deemer and screaming—but we *don't* see what she does. And when Tarantula attacks the Deemer house, Robinson delivers an excellent medium shot of Deemer's fully distorted face, with drooping Quasimodo eye, as he awakens from sleep—an unusual "horror upon a horror."

In the 1950s, a hand unexpectedly reaching into a shot was a frequently used Universal scare tactic. Here, Mara Corday's receiver hand is on the receiving end. *The Hollywood Reporter* called *Tarantula* "a great children's picture—particularly for bad children—as it should scare hell out of the little monsters." (Photograph courtesy Ted Bohus.)

Robinson was Universal's most prolific horror cinematographer. He began his tenure in horror films with the Spanish *Dracula* (1931) and continued through the Golden and Silver Ages, adeptly working with shadow and fog in *Dracula's Daughter* (1936), *The Invisible Ray* (1936), *Son of Frankenstein* (1939), *Frankenstein Meets the Wolf Man* (1943), *House of Frankenstein* (1944) and *House of Dracula* (1945). His vast experience in these atmospheric Universal favorites adds to *Tarantula*'s dark mood.

In addition to the camerawork, the makeup effects are invaluable to the film. Deemer's transformation is developed ever so subtly until we see the full-throttle finish near the film's end—an effect which makes it seem as if one side of Carroll's face has completely melted!

Some of *Tarantula*'s most unnerving touches can be credited to the crescendoing, threatening music score, and to the sound effects department. The spider emits an eerie sound akin to high-pitched radio static, while creeping along—and an unsettling roar, when it's about to attack.

The film's only weak link might be its script, co-authored by Robert M. Fresco and the infamous Martin Berkeley, the latter responsible for the dumbed-down dialogue in *Revenge of the Creature* and *The Deadly Mantis*. *Tarantula* has a little more "science" added to its "fiction" than previous Universal efforts, but the exchanges between Agar and Corday can sometimes be painful:

> STEVE: Are you sure your patients can spare you?
> MATT: I'm such a good doctor, they never get sick!

As the first *real* giant spider film, *Tarantula* spawned innumerable imitators, and comparisons are inevitable. But, aside from more current CGI-driven films, the movie that comes to mind is Bert I. Gordon's *Earth vs the Spider* (1958). Gordon's film was clearly made on a lower budget than *Tarantula*, but it's arguably more fun to watch: It has a better leading man in Ed Kemmer and has the huge arachnid dwelling in a dark cave, spinning a huge web and actually attacking a small town. Despite Reynold Brown's superb poster art, the spider in *Tarantula* only gets as far as the edge of town.

Still, *Tarantula* is highlighted by its moody photography and atmospheric desert locale. The film was especially enhanced by its then-unique horror-within-a-horror subplot and Leo G. Carroll's poised performance. It's one of the '50s' most enjoyable Big Bug films, in the grand tradition of Universal's classic combinations of camerawork, music, makeup and mad science.

Notes

The Strange Door

1. As an aside to this plot comparison: In 1938 when Universal was preparing to get back into the business of making horror flicks, one of the first ideas floated was a remake of *The Raven*, again pairing Boris and Bela but with "a fresh angle" (*The Hollywood Reporter*, September 17, 1938). This is nothing but sheer speculation, but could the "fresh angle" have been the incorporation of Stevenson's story? Could *The Strange Door be* the 1938 *The Raven*, finally coming to the screen more than a decade later? Could Jerry Sackheim have been its writer? He *was* then Universal's scenario editor. It's food for thought for allegiant Universal Horrors fans, who may enjoy idly envisioning what *The Strange Door* might have been like if made at Hollywood's Horror Factory in the '30s. (Imagine an in-his-prime Lugosi in the role of the mad nobleman!)

2. Pevney's subsequent Universals include the Joan Crawford starrer *Female on the Beach* (1955), the war story *Away All Boats* (1956) and the Lon Chaney biopic *Man of a Thousand Faces* (1957); in later years he became a prolific TV director via *Ben Casey, Wagon Train, The Alfred Hitchcock Hour, The Munsters, Star Trek* (including "The Trouble with Tribbles"), *Adam-12, Bonanza, The Incredible Hulk, The Paper Chase* and many others. He retired in 1985 and passed away in his Palm Desert home in May 2008, a few months shy of his 97th birthday.

3. Laughton was "a child at heart," according to William Phipps—but sometimes the child refused to come out and play. This Phipps anecdote adds nothing to the store of useful accumulated knowledge about Laughton, and is included only because it's fun to picture the proceedings:

> One night Shelley Winters talked Laughton and me into going with her to Ciro's, the three of us. Martin and Lewis were appearing there. Laughton didn't really want to go, but she insisted and so we went. They were playing "Shine On, Harvest Moon" and Jerry Lewis was circulating in the crowd, there were a lot of celebrities there, and he'd put the microphone in their faces and try and get them to sing a verse of "Shine On, Harvest Moon." And they all complied, including Shelley. Then he put the microphone in Laughton's face. Laughton didn't get belligerent or irritated, he just shook his head very slowly, indicating that he didn't want to do it. And Laughton could sing, too! For instance, on one show he and Elsa did "Baby, It's Cold Outside," a duet.
>
> Well, Jerry Lewis *insisted*—and Jerry Lewis being Jerry Lewis, he thought that he would win out. He kept insisting and insisting, and Laughton was adamant, he was stone-faced about it. Well [*laughs*], guess who won! After an interminable length of time, where everybody was getting a little bored and restless with it, Lewis gave up.

4. In 1994 at the Hollywood Roosevelt Cinegrill, there were productions of *Swanson on Sunset*, a musical based on Swanson, Stapley and Hughes' experiences while working on *Starring Norma Desmond.* Laurie Franks played an over-the-top Swanson, Richard Liebell was Stapley—and Hughes played himself! Called "a musical in progress" by a *Hollywood Reporter* columnist-reviewer, it too failed to take off.

5. After Laughton's 1962 passing, his *Arch of Triumph* (1948) director Lewis Milestone said, "A director couldn't hope to direct a Laughton picture. The best he could hope for was to referee." Even Alfred Hitchcock may not have been able to rein

What genius thought backstage photographs like this were a good idea? *Strange Door* director Joseph Pevney dangles a dead fish as Charles Laughton holds his nose.

him in. In *The New York Times*' lukewarm review of *Jamaica Inn* (1939), Frank S. Nugent wrote that it "will not be remembered as a Hitchcock picture, but as a Charles Laughton picture. It bears the Laughton stamp.... Perhaps that is the root of the evil, if it is an evil."

Laughton makes himself the whole show in *The Strange Door* and if that turns you off, be fair, don't blame the director. If Milestone and Hitchcock couldn't control Laughton, what chance did newbie Joseph Pevney have?

6. Some extra information on William Cottrell: Raised on the Rogue River and a graduate of the University of Oregon, he stayed on in those environs for six years to act in and direct the Oregon Shakespeare Festivals. He later got some of his stage and film breaks through Laughton, not because Laughton had a high opinion of Cottrell's talents (he didn't) but because Laughton may have had an attack of conscience. According to William Phipps,

> I was at the Actors Lab with Bill Cottrell and we were both in a play there, and we were also both in *Galileo* [Laughton's 1947 stage production of Bertold Brecht's play]. Cottrell conned a lot of young people into thinking that he was kind of a guru and a teacher, because young people who are aspiring to act are pretty easy to con. Cottrell and his acting group operated in the Hollywood area at the same time that Laughton had an acting group. And one day Laughton visited Cottrell's group and took it over! Laughton went in and started talking to the people, and before he knew it, he was in charge of the place [*laughs*]! Bill Cottrell was put completely in the background! So Laughton, I think, felt kind of an obligation to Cottrell after having done that.

In addition to appearing in *Galileo*, Cottrell played a small part in the made-in-Paris *The Man on the Eiffel Tower* (1949) with Laughton, worked with Laughton's Shakespeare company, and was associated with Laughton and Paul Gregory in their stage productions *Don Juan in Hell*, *John Brown's Body*, *The Caine Mutiny Court Martial* and *The Cherry Orchard*. His other film credits include *Donovan's Brain* (1953, as Lew Ayres' hospital doctor) and several of the bargain-basement adventure films from the writer-producer team of Aubrey Wisberg and Jack Pollexfen.

7. De Maletroit later confirms this, telling Blanche that Armand "was too saintly for this wicked world. I sent him to Paradise!" De Maletroit keeps Armand's ring in a hollowed-out book. In 1952's *The Black Castle*, also scripted by Jerry Sackheim, mad count Stephen McNally keeps the rings of two of *his* victims.

8. Shed no tears for Dear Boris: His horror movie heyday was behind him, but in other media he was still a great success. In fact, he came a-knockin' on *The Strange Door* directly from the dual roles of the fussy Mr. Darling and Captain Hook in *Peter Pan*. The show had opened at Broadway's Imperial Theatre on April 24, 1950, with Jean Arthur flying high as James M. Barrie's immortal creation and songs by Leonard Bernstein. (Karloff sang "The Pirate Song" and "The Plank.") Venerable *New York Times* critic Brooks Atkinson called *Peter Pan* Karloff's "day of triumph" and the show ran for 321 performances. (How interesting and inspiring to know that a man who was in a wheelchair in the summer of 1944—Karloff—could play Captain Hook eight times a week in Broadway's *Peter Pan* in 1950!)

Karloff romped through *Peter Pan*, but there was Hook vs. Pan enmity in the company: Jean Arthur's quirky personality, demands for an early vacation, and lapses in professional behavior exasperated the stoical Boris. (On opening night, the curtain came up for another bow, only to reveal Karloff literally dragging Arthur out of the wings to accept the ovation!) Arthur and Karloff headlined the 1951 touring company; Arthur eventually dropped out and Joan McCracken replaced her. *Peter Pan* closed in Minneapolis on April 29 and Karloff, ever the workhorse, made a beeline for his old Universal City haunts and *The Strange Door*.

9. I have to assume, now that it's too late to ask Pate to elaborate (he died in 2008), that by "your boys" he was referring to Cottrell and Farley. William Phipps, one of the members of the Laughton acting group who was not gay, recalled Farley as "*very*, very swishy" and Cottrell as "a sober, prim, proper guy ... but drunk he was wild, going after all the boys."

10. Richard Stapley told me that he, too, had "*crashing* headaches" at the end of each day as a result of the way hair stylist Joan St. Oegger secured *his* fall (wig).

11. *Strange Door* was made at a time when Napier's movie career was slowing because of the speed bump known as the Hollywood blacklist (or, in Napier's case, the graylist). The year before *Strange Door*, 1950, he had trekked to Colorado as part of the cast of MGM's *Across the Wide Missouri* and there he found himself regularly sharing a limo with Adolphe Menjou, one of the witch-hunt era's more predatory hunters. Napier wrote in *Not Just Batman's Butler* that one day Menjou was ranting that the Hollywood Ten should be stood up in front of a wall and shot, and Napier—who knew better than to talk politics with him—couldn't resist asking, "Isn't that rather un-American, Adolphe?" Even though the two actors liked each other, Menjou dutifully reported this comment to the proper authorities, and for Napier, "work in Hollywood became very scarce for the next few years." In 1951 and '52, Napier played supporting parts in three movies featuring Laughton in starring or prominent roles; perhaps Laughton pulled a few strings to help an old stage colleague.

12. Originally it was Karloff, not Hardwicke, who was signed to go on that tour; Hardwicke was in hot water with the tax man and couldn't leave the country. Then on June 6, the day after *The Strange Door* wrapped, *Variety* announced that Hardwicke and the tax man had straightened things out, and that Karloff's *Don Juan* contract was cancelled by mutual agreement.

The Black Castle

1. This column states that Karloff was trying to get away from playing movie villains but according to the 1954 book *The Laughton Story* by Kurt Singer, Karloff told Laughton, "I'm perfectly content to be the villain. It means that I always know what is expected of me. Once in a while I've played straight parts in pictures, but they did not turn out well. The audience kept expecting me to do something terrible. I think they were deeply disappointed when I didn't. That's what happens when you get typed." Holy about-face—assuming that both quotes are legit.

2. *The Black Castle*'s Otto Waldis is also in *The Exile* in a supporting role as Corday's abusive cousin—coincidentally, pretty much the same role he plays in *Black Castle*.

3. Chaney fans put his casting in *High Noon* high on their lists of Reasons He Deserved More Respect. According to Michael F. Blake, author of the book *Code of Honor: The Making of Three Great American Westerns*, it represented a mere two days' work: Friday, September 7, the interior of Mart Howe's (Chaney) home, where marshal Gary Cooper seeks his help and advice, and Saturday, September 8, 1951, Cooper and Grace Kelly's wedding scene.

In *The Black Castle,* Von Bruno (with eye patch) plunges his finger into Stieken's swordfight wound and makes him howl with pain. In a take not used, he grabbed Stieken's arm and dashed caustic ointment on it to elicit the yowl. From left: Boris Karloff, Stephen McNally, John Hoyt, Michael Pate. Notice Hoyt's gym-dandy physique.

4. In 1985, octogenarian Hoyt told *Fangoria* interviewer Tony Timpone, "Four years ago, a guy I knew told me he was putting together a nude calendar of men over 50 and asked me to pose for it. I said, 'Sure,' since I had no objections and I have a good body. … Then the calendar came out and made a mild sensation and *TV Guide* mentioned it. The bishop from my diocese wrote me a letter and practically excommunicated me!"

5. There's so much good stuff that's easy to miss in this short scene:

- The light from the flames in the walk-in fireplace chase shadows up and down a far wall, and faintly flicker upon the men.
- Mounted animal heads, and what look like ugly death masks, underline the Von Bruno-Count Zaroff connection.
- Meissen, ordered to leave the room, does—but his stationary shadow remains, indicating that he's paused outside to eavesdrop.
- Von Melcher picks up the bottle of poisoned wine and brings it to his lips, to take a pull on it—and then Meissen's line "He's dead" stays his hand at the last instant and he puts it down.
- And, best of all, poisoner Meissen's parting line to Von Melcher, delivered eagerly, hopefully: "If *you* would like some wine, I could…"

Much of this is captured in the previously mentioned low-angle shot that shows us the room's high walls, plenty of heavy shadows—and at the bottom of the frame, the eyes-open-wide corpse of Stieken and the mouth-open-wide head of a tiger skin rug. Hear, hear: "Irving Glassberg's photography is excellent, as are the settings of Bernard Herzbrun and Alfred Sweeney" (from *Hollywood Reporter*'s October 22, 1952, review).

6. On the subject of an actor who could play the role, Chaney opined to Johnson that Paul Muni in his heyday would have been perfect. In *Filmfax* magazine, Chaney's wife Patsy told interviewer Jack Gourlay that Muni was his favorite actor.

7. Like *The Black Castle*'s Sir Ronald, Inn was also once mistaken for dead: In the '30s, he was hit by a car and pronounced dead, but was saved when an embalming student noticed a heartbeat! In addition to Benji, Inn's other four-legged friends included the MGM lion, *Green Acres*' Arnold the Pig and the *My Three Sons* dog Tramp. When Inn died for real in 2002, he wanted the cremains of Benji, Arnold, Tramp *et al.* placed in his coffin. Suddenly dueling pistols placed in a coffin doesn't sound quite as strange.

8. On Karloff's last day on *A&C Meet J&H*, he and a small crew shot two of that movie's transformation scenes, and then the actor left a Universal Horrors set for the last time. A black day for Monster Kids, it was a Friday the 13th (of February 1953).

It Came from Outer Space

1. Universal took instant advantage of the publicity surrounding the *War of the Worlds* panic broadcast: Just *three days later*, they ran a double-page *Hollywood Reporter* ad to promote their newest feature release *Mars Attacks the World.* The ad is mostly comprised of newspaper headlines describing the commotion caused by the Mercury broadcast—but eagle-eyed readers might have caught the fine print in a tiny box in a corner, indicating that *Mars Attacks the World*'s "70 MINUTES OF BLOOD-CHILLING EXCITEMENT" were based on the comic strip *Flash Gordon* (i.e., this was a feature version of the studio's then-newish serial *Flash Gordon's Trip to Mars*). *Mars Attacks the World* was shown to New York circuit bookers on November 1 and it was now being advertised in the November 2 *Reporter*. Universal patted its own back in the ad, calling the "Amazing! Unbelievable! Stupendous! Awe-Inspiring" new release the "Most Timely Attraction in Motion Picture History!"

Given a death-in-life drug by the helpful Dr. Meissen (Boris Karloff, right), Elga (Paula Corday) and Burton (Richard Greene) now lie in their respective "tombs of the flesh," the clay of their bodies the prisons for their still-active minds as they await premature burial. Doc ... next time, please: *Don't help us*!

2. Bradbury liked to talk about his two treatments as though they were worlds apart, but that was either a case of an extremely faulty memory or it was a lie. Except for the finale, they're exactly the same story, one told in short form, the other in long form. If most of the Alland ideas used in the "vulgar obvious" treatment are indeed vulgar and obvious, then so are the ones in the treatment that Bradbury prefers, and in the movie itself.

Another indication that "The Turkey That Attacked New York" may have been nothing more a nasty piece of fiction: Bradbury wrote about preliminary talks with the "vulgar obvious" producer *and director*, disparaging Alland *and Jack Arnold*. The truth is that Arnold wasn't assigned to *It Came from Outer Space* until the second half of January 1953, by which time Bradbury had written his treatments and was long gone from the Universal lot. (Arnold to interviewer Bill Kelley in *Cinefantastique*: "When I was assigned the script to direct, it was already in final draft.") Bradbury may have thought that his "Turkey" essay would be more "entertaining" if he ripped the director as well as the producer.

3. A good bit of the dialogue in Bradbury's treatments is similarly "not ready for prime time." As Rod Serling once said of Bradbury (talking not about *Outer Space* but just generally), "[He's] a very difficult guy to dramatize, because that which reads so beautifully on the printed page doesn't fit in the mouth—it fits in the head. And you find characters saying the things that Bradbury's saying and you say, 'Wait a minute, people don't *say* that.'" As an aside: Rod Serling criticizing any other writer's un-lifelike dialogue may be the very definition of "the pot and the kettle"!

4. The reason that Adams was suddenly yanked was because Universal liked the idea of reteaming Glenn Ford and Adams, stars of *The Man from the Alamo* (1953), in their upcoming *Wings of the Hawk* (1953). But then Van Heflin instead of Ford starred with Adams in *Wings of the Hawk*!

5. Young actor Ray Walston saw Arnold in the Fredric March-starring Broadway production *A Bell for Adano* (1944) and remembered his performance well: "He was the type of actor who attracted your attention because he was full of deliberate gestures," Walston told me. "That is to say, when he had a line, he would extend his arm and point his finger *right* at the person he was speaking to. At that particular time, I thought that was rather attractive; I don't any more, of course [*laughs*]!" Walston continued:

> In 1946, we were in a revival of *The Front Page*; then he was cutting film somewhere on Seventh Avenue, just around the corner from Broadway, and learning his trade as a director then and there. Later, of course, he came out here [Hollywood] and started directing pictures. Then I saw him many years later at the Universal commissary, with a couple of crutches propped up against the wall near his table. He had had a leg removed. From then on, he just went right down—his health disappeared and so forth. He was a very likable guy and I liked him very much.

6. Stephen Strimpell, star of producer-director Arnold's superhero-comedy TV series *Mr. Terrific* (1967), greatly disliked what he called Arnold's satyriasis and saw red whenever he observed the director's antics; he once confronted Arnold in the Universal commissary after watching him paw a young starlet. Strimpell told interviewer Mark Phillips:

> Mr. Arnold was in the grip of a sickness which manifested itself in disgustingly overt and unrelenting sexual advances to women. Very skilled and worldly women had no trouble with Jack whatsoever. Luciana Paluzzi simply smiled when he hit on her and said, "You are so naughty and so handsome." He knew he had been put in his place, but brilliantly. Luciana came from Italy and was raised in an atmosphere of blatant flirting and womanizing. She told me some stories about filming there, and laughed Jack off as a sort of ladies' man in training compared to the Italian men, who were really good at it, according to her. Whatever the approach, it is always an ugly and degrading thing to see, and were it to happen now, Jack Arnold's behavior would be ripe for condemnation. However, in the Hollywood of the late '60s it was considered being "just one of the guys."
>
> One day, after he had made a particularly nasty crack followed by a "love" or "sweetie," I knocked his arm off my shoulder and reverted, I am afraid, to my Brooklyn street behavior by leaning close to his ear and whispering, "Keep your fuckin' hands off me, you double-crossin,' skirt-chasin' scumbag!" He kept his distance pretty much after that, which was jim-dandy as much for him as for me, I am sure.
>
> I tried to figure out why a man such as Jack Arnold would let himself grow so hard and cold. I never have succeeded in doing so, but I think it's safe to conclude that the nature of his riches and fame (in this case, an empty vessel, unless you consider *Gilligan's Island* the key to 15 Warholian minutes of glory) never were what he had hoped for.

7. "Into every Broadway season, a little total insanity must fall, and this season's quotient has just fallen, with a thud," reads the opening paragraph of Frank Rich's *New York Times* review. He continued,

> In this amateur theatricale … Miss Rush spends over two hours reciting letters attributed to a fictional Texas matriarch named Bess Steed Garner. Bess is a selfish but persevering woman whose life extends from 1899 to 1977. … At one point, Bess almost goes broke—but it is the evening's principal tragedy that she is never so impoverished that she must forgo postage stamps.

8. Also in *Career*: the *Gateway to Hollywood* contestant who beat him, John Archer, making *his* debut in a much bigger part.

9. Johnson and Phipps' teacher at the Actors' Lab, Phoebe Brand, was also the director of *Men in White*, and 70 years later Phipps still recalls a comment she made about them and the show: "Too bad Bill Phipps has all the talent but Russell Johnson is better looking"!

10. Thanks to Harald Gruenberger of the Classic Horror Film Board for the above translation—and all other translations of Arnold's German TV appearance throughout this book.

11. Alland was one of four witnesses that November 23. (Another was radio and TV actor John Brown, *The Life of Riley*'s "Digger" O'Dell, who digger o'dug his career grave by taking the Fifth.) In a transcript of Alland's testimony, available on the Internet, he said he hired Virginia Mullen as an actress once after his withdrawal from the Communist Party, when it was actually three times; but since they were all microscopic parts, who knows if he was fibbing or forgetting. He said he hired her

> for two reasons—but I was sort of led to believe, I heard that she would, if she were called [by the Committee], be cooperative, and then she had two children and she was—how shall I put it—she appealed to my sympathy on that ground, that she needed the work. So I gave her a day's work. … [S]he appealed to me on the basis of needing a job, and I, having known her and having known she had two kids, I did give her one.

12. In the September 1952 Bradbury treatment that he himself thought of as the *good* one, Putnam *thoroughly* tarnishes his movie-hero halo, killing both Glob Ellen *and Glob Putnam* even though he is in no clear danger from either. As mentioned above, Putnam later makes the wholly accurate statement, "It all would have gone better if I'd kept my mouth shut."

13. By the time news of this mishap reached *Variety*, Lawrence's injuries had been reduced to "severe cuts about the

head." Two years later, *Variety* reported that a judgment of $50,000 had been handed down in L.A. Superior Court in favor of Lawrence against Kern Copters, Inc., of Bakersfield, and that "in the accident, Lawrence lost one eye." Fifty thousand dollars in 1955 would be $467,307 in 2017.

In 1981, director Boris Sagal again demonstrated that the Helicopter Always Wins: At a Mount Hood, Oregon, resort, Sagal—notorious for his temper tantrums—got into an argument during a copter flight and, upon landing, angrily stormed *out* and right *into* the tail rotor of the...chopper. Five hours later, with wife Marge Champion at his bedside, he died of head and shoulder injuries at a Portland hospital.

14. Alland, Arnold and Boyle weren't the only ones who went on record in later years with their disapproval of the decision to add on-screen monsters. Ray Bradbury once wrote, "I warned them not to bring the monster out in the light—ever. They ignored my advice. The bad moments in the film come when the monster does just that—stops being mysterious, steps out, and becomes a laugh riot." In a *Take One* interview, he conceded that it might have been all right to show the monster for just half a second, long enough for the audience to see it but not long enough for them to tell exactly what it looked like. The way the film was made, he said, "The camera is held on it for three, four, five seconds, and that's plenty of time to see all the makeup dripping off." He told an interviewer for the magazine *The Perfect Vision*, "I learned all my lessons from Val Lewton. Use darkness, use suggestion. Well, [Universal] thought they had to bring the monster up in the light and they did, stupidly. The film can be improved by cutting 20 seconds out of it."

When I told Russell Johnson about the divergence of opinion, he weighed in: "Probably I would agree with leaving out [the Globs], and letting people picture in their minds their own monster." Barbara Rush also thought the executive edict to add on-camera monsters was unfortunate; she told me,

> You have people in high places making decisions that make you think, "*Arrrgghh*. Why don't they let us *alone*?" So now the movie has several shots of the giant eye, and the [superimposed Glob p.o.v. shots] of the eye fibrillating. The movie would have been much better without them. A monster wasn't necessary. The unknown is always more mysterious. When they make it real, then you *know* what it looks like! It's one thing to open the closet door and see where a mysterious noise is coming from; but to open a closet door and it's dark and you *can't* tell where the noise is coming from ... now *that's* scary!

Maybe nobody kept the *Outer Space* poster artist in the loop by telling him that the movie would have an on-screen monster: Alien-wise, the ads show nothing but a large, fairly human-looking (and sometimes a *very* human-looking) eyeball, usually dripping some kind of ooze, or perhaps a tear. Kathleen Hughes, George Eldredge and even Brad Jackson are prominent on some posters even though they were barely in the movie.

15. In the same column, Richard Carlson enthused,

> At last Hollywood is really, truly exciting again. Imaginations are running wild and everyone is having a ball. It looks like sure-fire stuff, too. All you have to do is look at the statistics. There are 40,000,000 science fiction fans now who are reading almost 100 [*sic*] different science fiction magazines. They have their own clubs, even their own slang.
>
> Clubhouses are slanshacks, fan magazines are fanzines, male members are fens and the women are called fennes. They don't mind a split infinitive once in a while, but they scream if the atom is split incorrectly in a story.

The above quote sounds more like something whipped up by a publicist than something spouted by an actor, but Carlson supposedly *was* a science fiction fan so who knows?

Creature from the Black Lagoon

1. Previous accounts of the *Black Lagoon* premiere have referred to the Broadway-Capitol as a 2700-seat venue. From its opening in 1922 through to 1960, it in fact seated 3500. Following refurbishment in 1960 through to a fire in 1985, it seated 3367. Only after extensive renovation to transform it into the Detroit Opera House in 1988 has it had a seating capacity of 2700.

2. *Motion Picture Daily* (March 3, 1954) lists the 17 localities in which saturation openings were planned as Boston, Chicago, Des Moines, Indianapolis, Minneapolis, Omaha, Kansas City, San Francisco, Milwaukee, Seattle, Atlanta, Birmingham, Dallas, Houston, San Antonio, Austin and Amarillo.

This Island Earth

1. In Chapter 6 we learn that Cal may have been the first and only person whose aptitude test *was* an interocitor.

2. I can't help but wonder how this "vast ellipsoid" can regularly land at the plant to pick up interocitors without being seen by some, most and eventually *all* of the nearly 4000 people who work and live around there.

3. I laugh on the inside at the "highbrow" Monstuh Kids who tsk-tsk at the presence of the two Mutants in Universal's *This Island Earth*, feeling that monsters dumbed-down the movie. As readers of the novel know, Ole's two Suoinard "henchmen" were monsters. ("They were green and minutely scaly and spoke of alien swamp lands. Tiny puffs of greenish atmosphere with the overpowering odor exuded from the vents in [their] suits.") When I come to parts of the novel in which these alien bruisers are featured, I get mind's-eye images of the fish-faced alien soldiers in the 1964 *Outer Limits* TV episode "Keeper of the Purple Twilight."

4. *The New York Times'* Dave Kehr wrote in 2006 that he can see a bit of that style in *This Island Earth*, calling it "cool, precise [and] emotionally uninvolved." He continued, "Mr. Newman, in this case, becomes a kind of accidental Luis Buñuel, who knew well that the most outrageous situations were best served by a neutral, naturalistic mise-en-scène."

5. The first of the Orsatti kids to stick a toe in the movie business may have been Victor's brother Ernie, who got his start as a prop man and went on to do stunts in Buster Keaton movies. He may even have doubled for Keaton in *The Navigator* (1924) and *Seven Chances* (1925). Playing first base on Keaton's baseball team was a harbinger of things to come for Ernie, who later played nine seasons for the St. Louis Cardinals. With Ernie part of their lineup, the Gashouse Gang made four trips to the World Series.

6. It looks like Orsatti was fibbing when he announced that the financing for *This Island Earth* was in place. According to a June 1955 *Motion Picture Daily* article on Sabre Productions, "Orsatti said their first venture would have been *This Island Earth*, a screenplay which they developed ... but sold to Universal when they felt it might require too much capital to make as independents."

7. A *Variety* story with a February 9,

1954, dateline revealed that just 13 movies were currently in production on the major lots, *five* of them at Universal: *This Island Earth, Sign of the Pagan, Dawn at Socorro, The Matchmakers* (later retitled *Ricochet Romance*) and *Bengal Rifles* (retitled *Bengal Brigade*). And Jeff Morrow was in *two* of 'em, *This Island Earth* and *Sign of the Pagan*—the latter returning Morrow to ancient Rome, the setting of his first film *The Robe* (1953).

8. After the release of *This Island Earth*, Hollywood gossip columnist Sheilah Graham wrote that "Jeff Morrow's fans hated the weird white hair he wore" in the movie—and she added, "In U-I's *The Creature Walks Among Us* [1956], the script first called for another odd makeup. But this will now be normal." I think I've seen all drafts of the *Creature Walks* script and I can't recall one with Morrow's character having an odd look, but who am I to argue with Sheilah Graham?

9. Thomas ended the article by mentioning that the makeup department's most expensive job "was for no monster at all. It was making Ann Blyth's [mermaid] tail in *Mr. Peabody and the Mermaid* [1948]. Bud and his staff spent three months on that job, making tail after tail until the studio bosses decided on one they liked. The cost: $22,000."

10. On March 25, 1954, not long after *This Island Earth* wrapped, Lane won a divorce after testifying that Westmore was indifferent to her charms, stayed away from home without explanation and, the missus averred, was "rude to my friends and family, told me he didn't love me and wanted out." The blonde Lane's equally beauteous brunette sister Lola corroborated Rosemary's claims. A full five *years* later, Rosemary and Bud again made the papers: According to Rosemary, for 29 weeks she had allowed him to reduce his weekly alimony payments from $110 to $70 because he claimed he was short of cash—and then she came to find out he was building a swimming pool. (According to Rosemary, Westmore told her, "The swimming pool didn't cost a dime.") She wanted $1160 in back alimony. During a hearing, Westmore's lawyer said the makeup maestro was doing his best, considering that he was remarried, had two children and a third in the oven. The fortyish Westmore's new missus was Jeanne Shores, teenage winner of the 1952 Miss California contest.

11. We never see the thing, which Ruth and Carlson describe as looking like a sunlamp. In the novel, scrambling brains is yet another function of the all-purpose, "But *wait*—there's *more*!" interocitor.

12. If the script had been adhered to, the Converter Tubes would have vibrated violently ("By Special Vibrator Mounted On Camera") and Cal and Ruth would have turned into black silhouettes (going from positive to negative film, and then back again). *This Island Earth* might have been the first movie to concern itself with whether aliens could exist in our atmospheric pressure, and vice versa.

13. Book-smart half-breeds somehow became Fuller's regular sideline: He again put his best heel forward in *Secret of Treasure Mountain* (1956), playing one who murders at the drop of a headdress.

14. One of the many other movies partly shot at the Metropolitan Airport was the 1942 hall of famer *Casablanca*; at the airport, they got a shot of Major Strasser (Conrad Veidt) arriving by plane.

15. I have the feeling that horror-sci-fi producer Alland liked attention-grabbing action right off the bat: *The Black Castle* begins with the hero about to be buried alive, *It Came from Outer Space* features the pre-credits in-your-face 3-D spaceship crash, *Creature from the Black Lagoon* has the Creation of the World sequence (complete with 3-D explosions) followed immediately by the high-excitement discovery of the Creature claw, and *Tarantula* features the eerie and mysterious pre-credits scene of the ape-like chap wandering in the desert. *This Island Earth*'s opener with Cal and the fawning reporters is as dull and useless as openers get.

16. The aforementioned Universal report offers this chronological rundown of the Air National Guard's contributions to *This Island Earth*: On February 2, "T-33 jet trainer Major Larry Powell flew two takeoffs and landings plus several taxi shots." On February 4, "the company completed shots inside the National Guard hangar using the jet airplane and a power unit to work dashboard instruments for inserts." On February 5, "Larry Powell flew the jet so that we could photograph aerial shots between San Fernando Valley Airport and Palmdale. He also flew the jet at the Palmdale Airport for ground-to-air shots in which he buzzed the camera, fishtailed at low altitude and also looped-the-loop in spirals going away from camera."

17. A haunting postscript: Dianna's doomed bomber was the same type of craft her war casualty husband Cyrus was flying the day *he* was shot down and killed—and she died on the ten-year anniversary of his death.

18. In the first act of *This Island Earth*, Joe is the movie's Everyman, funny, likable and admirably protective of his boss Cal. Characters like Joe lighten the mood in several of Universal's early sci-fis: Lucas (Nestor Paiva) in the first two Gill Man movies, Pete the helicopter pilot (Dave Willock) in *It Came from Outer Space* and Lou the press agent (Willock again) in *Revenge of the Creature*.

19. The script called for the woman's voice to be mechanical, telling Cal, "Please lean back and make yourself comfortable, doctor." When he gropes for a seat belt that's not there: "A seat belt is not required."

20. "When we did [the Metaluna scenes], we obviously weren't up there on Metaluna, and the huge set in the background wasn't there; it was painted in with special effects brought later," Rex Reason told interviewers Tom and Jim Goldrup. "But they were explaining this was over here and that over there; so we had to relate within our mind to the fact that we were on this monorail traveling through Metaluna with bombs exploding all over."

21. Harrison Carroll was there and *This Island Earth* super-fan Robert Skotak wasn't, but I tend to believe Robert that the Metaluna costumes were *not* blue wool. "I owned one of the suits," he told me, "and they had a very light, faint magenta-gray cast, nearly pink, and very pale. This type of tint was used so that the uniforms appeared to be gray on film. They were lined with a cotton cloth material. I couldn't tell you exactly what the outer material was, but it was not particularly heavy and not woolen in nature. They had a tiny bit of a sheen, a slight suggestion of 'metal' which barely shows as such in the movie. Any difficulty with the costumes being hot to wear probably came from the cotton lining and the fact that the sets, in general, especially the saucer control room, were extremely hot due to the light levels needed to get proper exposure on the very, very slow film stock."

22. Regis Parton, who played the Mutant, had to have gotten just as hot, or hotter, in his outfit. Occasionally an eye would be removed from the head and some fresh air blown in at Parton with a hair dryer. On a personal note I'll mention that, as a frequent visitor to the set of *Looney Tunes: Back in Action* (2003) during the shooting of the monster-filled Area 52 scenes, I got

friendly with Bill Malone, owner of the *Forbidden Planet* Robby the Robot suit, and Robert Parigi, who wore it in *Looney Tunes*, and I gave myself the job of using a blower to shoot air through an opening into the suit whenever Parigi wanted it.

23. The script also called for Ruth to scream in the courier plane when the spaceship shoots the Green Ray towards it, to cry out when the green light fills the cabin, and to scream in horror when she sees the first Mutant.

24. Monster Kids know that Universal "famously" placed some of its better '50s sci-fi movies in desert settings, so it's funny to find that their adaptation of the novel *This Island Earth* (mostly set in the desert near Phoenix) was relocated to the grassy hills of Georgia.

25. Roberson's Monster Kid claim to fame: In 1955, the stuntman played the Creature in a *Creature Walks Among Us* scene. It was shot in post-production so Roberson was the last actor to play the Creature. That same year, 1955, Tomei was part of a fight scene on a boat in San Francisco Bay for the movie *Hell on Frisco Bay* (1956) when he hit his head on a bulwark. The 45-year-old stuntman, a former Indianapolis Speedway race contender, lingered for about three weeks before he died from this injury.

26. On a 1966 episode of *Green Acres*, Oliver (Eddie Albert) suffers a "Sprained Ankle, Country Style" and, laid up in bed, watches (or, rather, *tries* to watch) that day's "Multi-Million Dollar Movie Matinee," an English mystery titled *Frankenstein Meets Mary Poppins*. Every time we get a glimpse of the TV screen, we see a black-and-white clip from a different horror oldie, among them the Mutant arm shadow shot.

27. On a much smaller scale, I had the same experience: Whenever I talked about *This Island Earth* with a participant, I'd ask if they recalled Arnold being part of the movie, and the answer always landed somewhere in the gulf between "Not that I recall" to "No way!" William Alland had the most colorful answer when I asked about Arnold's claim of being the real director of *This Island Earth*: He laughed and then said, "That's shit, although I'm sure he could have done as good a job as the guy who *did* direct it." (Alland felt that Newman's direction of *This Island Earth* was "pretty poor.")

28. On the Classic Horror Film Board, I once posted that the novel *This Island Earth* could have been brought to the screen as a 12-chapter Sam Katzman-Columbia serial, if its writers had made the same changes to it that the writers of the feature did:

> Plot-wise, there isn't a lot that would seem out of place in a serial, except the ending, where the aliens we've gotten to know *lose* the war, and Exeter rides his plummeting spaceship Slim Pickens-style right down into the drink. And all the cliffhangers are there: Cal's jet nearly crashing, death rays directed at Cal and Ruth's car, meteors on a collision course with the spaceship, etc. "Will Cal and Ruth ever leave this benighted planet? What diabolical plans does the Monitor *have* for them? You'll learn the thrilling answers next week in 'Menaced by the Metaluna Mutant,' Chapter 11 of *This Island Earth*, here in this theater!"

The movie's #1 fan Robert Skotak says he's always thought of it "as more of a science fantasy, like *Star Wars*," rather than real SF.

29. On February 10, 1954, actor Sid Clute was engaged by Universal to play Sam, but his name appears nowhere in the movie's Production Reports so presumably his half of the above-described scene was never filmed. Clute played scores of minor movie and television roles and had a bit of late-in-life success in the 1980s when he became a regular on TV's *Cagney and Lacey*. He died smack in the middle of the series' run.

30. Perhaps filled with liquid courage (the first line of the article has "tall, languorous Milicent" sipping a Scotch and soda), Patrick happily glommed the credit for the look of the Gill Man in this interview, saying that these monsters "grow on a sketchboard in front of me." Corby, who had to be reporting what Patrick told her, added that Bud Westmore and his staff then "handle the actual mechanics of making a monster to fit Miss Patrick's lurid imaginings."

31. The issue of *Collier's* that hit newsstands on June 9 bears the cover date June 24, 1955, while the *Look* that reached stands on June 14 is dated June 28, 1955. See in particular "U Promotion Men to Field for *Earth*" in *Motion Picture Daily*, May 24, 1955.

Revenge of the Creature

1. In July 1953, with the newish *Ma and Pa Kettle on Vacation* (the fifth in the series) on track to make $2,150,000 in domestic distribution, *Variety* called the ongoing popularity of the Kettle series "one of the strangest phenomena of the film industry, if not all of show business. … Universal, it is hinted, has been suspecting upon the release of each new *Kettle* picture that series might suddenly falter, but so far there's been no indication as expressed by the public."

Cult of the Cobra

1. The good ol' sexist '50s: Universal's first female monster has to bat *clean-up*!

2. *Cult* is even set back in the mid-1940s, so clothes and cars are as they would have been if *Cult had* been made in the Lewton era.

3. *Cult*'s writers were all probably about the right age to lap up newspapers accounts of the deaths of the men who invaded King Tut's cursed tomb. In Monogram's *House of Mystery* (1934), a 1913 archaeologist (Clay Clement) kills an Indian temple monkey, whacks everybody in sight (including a priest) with his stick and steals their treasure. Then the story jumps ahead 20 years as the curse of Kali makes his American home a haunted house, with ghostly tom-toms heard as a gaggle of his guests are stalked by a killer ape. In 1942, Kharis the Mummy kept the party going in *The Mummy's Tomb*, following the desecrators of an Egyptian princess' resting place to the U.S. of A. with murderous intent. Rex Reason, who was briefly in the running for a *Cult of the Cobra* role, film-debuted in *Storm Over Tibet* (1952) as a U.S. Army captain who steals from a Tibetan temple the skull mask of the God of Death and returns home convinced he's on the Death God's hit list.

4. Collins got in Red-hot water with HUAC in 1947, when he was subpoenaed and became one of the Hollywood 19 (19 unfriendly witnesses). Ten of them went to jail while Collins' professional dance card suddenly went blank and stayed blank. Subpoenaed again in 1951, this time he named more than a score of names. His now-ex-wife Comingore heard him "singing" on the radio and, highly distressed, cut off her hair. Collins started working again, including some uncredited writing on *Invasion of the Body Snatchers* (1956), but sometimes felt like "a son of a bitch, a miserable little bastard" (Collins in an interview with author Victor Navasky). He later became a TV producer, churning out episodes of *Bonanza* and *Matlock* (more than 100 each) and other series. He

was approaching the century mark when he died in 2013. In the 1991 movie *Guilty by Suspicion*, one character, Dorothy (Patricia Wettig), an overwrought, hard-drinking actress, was reportedly inspired by Comingore; if so, then her name-dropperpalooza husband (played by Chris Cooper) must be modeled on Collins.

5. Thiess had an equally "charming" experience the day her *Monsoon* role called for her to float in the waters of a pond-like pool created and filled with cloudy water by the crew. During the two hours or so she spent there, she occasionally felt herself being touched underwater even though it hadn't been stocked with fish; with her imagination working overtime, she was more than happy to get out when the scene was finished. Once the pool was drained the next day, crew members found in the murk a specimen of one of India's deadliest water snakes, its bite fatal within three minutes. Holy *Cult of the Cobra* Part Deux!

6. In the 1940s and early '50s, the Tinseltown tag team of William H. Pine and William C. Thomas produced so many low-budget movies that they became infamous as the Two Dollar Bills. William Pine's son Howard worked as an assistant director and production manager for Pine-Thomas Productions for several years before joining Universal as a producer in January 1954; his four movies there were 1955's *The Man from Bitter Ridge, Cult of the Cobra, The Private War of Major Benson* and *Running Wild.* A few weeks after the April 1955 death of his father, he requested a release from his Universal producing contract and returned to Pine-Thomas, where I guess *he* was now the Pine-. Eventually he went back to his old unit production manager job.

7. The written foreword is different in the Final Screenplay, dated October 14, 1954, and titled ***The** Cult of the Cobra*: "There is a part of the world where the impossible sometimes happens. It is a land where illusion can become reality, and reality illusion. This tale of the possible impossible began one day in 1945."

8. When Nick, Rico and Carl are killed, we get cobra point-of-view shots, a weird, watery, screen-filling "eye" superimposed over them. This eye-dea (idea) had to have been inspired by the Xenomorph point-of-view shots in *It Came from Outer Space* (1953), which are nearly identical.

9. Romantically, Tom never gets any further with Lisa than Parker (Richard Arlen) does with Lota (Kathleen Burke) in *Island of Lost Souls* (1933), than Oliver (Kent Smith) does with Irena (Simone Simon) in *Cat People*, than Fred (Milburn Stone) does with Paula (Acquanetta) in *Captive Wild Woman* (1943). I don't think "Keep your penis in your genus" was on the Production Code's list of regulations but the old-time moviemakers adhered to that unwritten law.

10. That's the official version of why Ophüls left. Faith, talking to the Goldrups, remembered it differently: "Preston, once we started the film, never let poor Max direct. Preston just took right over. Max would say, 'Action,' and Preston would have him taken off the set. Max was just a figurehead."

11. In 1978 *Variety*'s Army Archerd noted that Corday was just back from Rockland, Maine, where Richard's brother Phil "christened his $1,500,000 ketch the *Whitehawk*, dedicated to Richard—and with some of Dick's ashes buried in the mainmast."

12. In 1955 he starred in *The United States Steel Hour*'s "The Rack," scripted by Rod Serling and made in New York. When MGM bought the movie rights, they interviewed him about reprising his role but then rejected him as too young and gave the part to the same-age Paul Newman. Other small-screen credits included a *20th Century-Fox Hour* remake of 1939's *Young Mr. Lincoln*, a *Hallmark Hall of Fame* in which he played George Washington, and about six of *the* dullest *Science Fiction Theatre* episodes. Reportedly Thompson made around $25,000 in TV in 1954 *and* worked in five movies (including *Cult of the Cobra*) besides. He told *Variety* in 1955, "In pictures I was typed; I was the all-American boy next door. My first part in TV was that of a 45-year-old man, and I've had far more variety of roles in TV than I ever had in pictures."

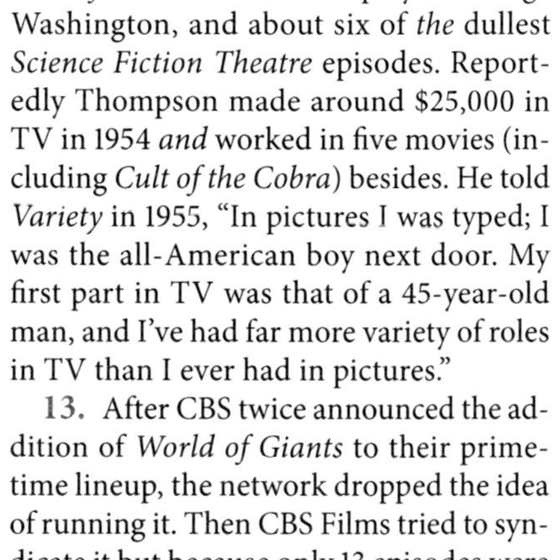

13. After CBS twice announced the addition of *World of Giants* to their prime-time lineup, the network dropped the idea of running it. Then CBS Films tried to syndicate it but because only 13 episodes were made, nobody wanted it. Not until 1961 was it sold into its first TV markets; it wasn't seen in Los Angeles until 1964, and there were probably lots of markets in which it was *never* seen. In the decades since, it seems to have vanished almost completely.

14. The June 6, 1956, *Variety* revealed, "Kathleen Hughes (Mrs. Stanley Rubin) spent 16 hours sans drugs, etc., in attempting to welcome her first child via natural childbirth, then UCLA medics took over."

15. William Reynolds, after watching *Cult of the Cobra* in preparation for our interview, told me that he had more respect for Domergue now (2007) "because I think she did very well with what she had to work with. The role was very limiting in terms of what she could do emotionally. She had a much harder job than I gave her credit for when we were doing it."

16. Ball got special "Introducing..." billing two years prior in Universal's *Untamed Frontier*. Contrary to her contention that heavy roles were good career springboards, *Variety* called her *Untamed Frontier* appearance as a treacherous dance hall girl "hardly an auspicious debut."

17. Universal never did make *The Long Hunters*, which according to *Variety* was to have been "backgrounded against the War of 1812."

18. Truth be told, Hughes *is* a bit too wide-eyed and chipper as Julia. She knew herself that she wasn't cut out to play a sweet ingénue, and now thanks to *Cult of the Cobra*, *we* know it too!

19. As a kid, Francis D. Lyon *so* wanted to be part of the movie business that he'd beg his parents to move from Min-

A behind-the-scenes *Cult of the Cobra* shot of the opening bazaar scene: the first encounter between the airmen and the Lamian snake charmer.

neapolis to Hollywood, which they eventually did. He worked odd jobs in silent movie days and then got his foot in the cutting room door during the transition from silents to sound. He was employed by Mack Sennett, cutting shorts starring comics like Andy Clyde, when London Film Productions got busy and suddenly needed lots of experienced editors (and lots of experienced everything-elses), he was unexpectedly recruited. Quite a turnaround, going from Mack Sennett to working in England on movies like *Things to Come, Rembrandt* (both 1936) and *Knight Without Armour* (1937) and rubbing shoulders with René Clair, H.G. Wells, etc. Back in Hollywood he edited big pictures like *Intermezzo: A Love Story* (1939) and *Body and Soul* (1947), winning an Oscar for the latter, plus a lot of lesser ones. His movie directing career began with the sports pictures *Crazylegs* (1953) and *The Bob Mathias Story* (1954). He also directed some early TV, including episodes of Ralph Bellamy's *Man Against Crime*; each was shot in three days at the Bronx's historic Bedford Park Studios where the 1910 *Frankenstein* was made. Starting in the 1960s, most of Lyon's directing was done for TV. He died in 1996.

20. In fairness, Universal did it pre-Lewton. To name just one: Before Dr. Glendon's (Henry Hull) first transformation begins in *WereWolf of London* (1935), his cat senses danger, lays back its ears, snarls and repeatedly swipes a claw at empty air in feline fright.

21. Corny, yes—but in 1973, on the posters for Universal's *Sssssss*, the sibilant title had the parenthetical instruction "Don't say it, hiss it" right underneath! In this early effort from the producing team of Zanuck-Brown (*The Sting, Jaws*), serpent specialist Strother Martin is convinced that Man must evolve if he is to survive the inevitable nuclear holocaust. Like a mad scientist from a Herman Cohen movie, he secretly gives his young lab assistant Dirk Benedict injections that start him on the road to snakedom.

22. Once Janssen got his honorable discharge, he thought he was done with the service—but then Universal put him in uniform in one movie after another: *Cult of the Cobra*, the abovementioned *Chief Crazy Horse* and *To Hell and Back*, plus *The Private War of Major Benson, Francis in the Navy* (both 1955) and *Never Say Goodbye* (1956). In four of them he wore the *same* khaki uniform!

23. Assuming that John Halloran is also the Jack Sergel of North Hollywood who has a letter in *Black Belt* magazine's May 1967 issue, this should also be of interest to anyone who's read this far: Sergel writes,

> I started out as a child with a hostility toward all of mankind. Many hours were spent in punching the bag and neighbor boys, running not less than a mile each day to improve my wind and endurance, doing a hundred or more pushups daily so that I might hit harder and so making a pest of myself in school and on the street.
>
> Each time anyone came to town purporting to teach a method of mayhem or fighting method, I would somehow wrangle the tuition fee. I learned a lot, even from some of the phonies under whom I studied. It was more a matter of good fortune than good management that they did not lock me up and throw away the key, for I felt the need to demonstrate my powers at the least provocation.

Sergel goes on to say that at that point he joined the class of judo expert Sego Murakami, and that Murakami's "benign influence" made him "a very changed man."

24. Shot but not used in the movie: footage of Daru on his feet, talking to a group of native boys. Any reader of *Cult*'s Daily Production Reports can't help but notice the number of scenes plus scenes-within-scenes that were photographed but ended up on the cutting room floor; *Cult* might have reached (or topped) 90 minutes had they all been included. At 90-plus minutes, *Cult* would have been one of the longest Universal Horrors.

25. Even though *Cult* was entirely shot on the Universal lot and at that Burbank bowling alley, the Phantom of the Movies (a New Yorker himself, mind you) wrote that it "exhibits a strong eye for subtle period details and ... presents a credible portrait of 1945 Manhattan that ranges from the Village to Broadway."

26. Another "Did they really think that would be scary?" moment: Julia is in the kitchen browsing through Paul's books when a loud noise is heard. She very casually turns, and there's a cut to a close-up of a pressure pot on the stove, steam hissing out of the top.

27. In New York, Ball vented to an interviewer about the situation with her amputation: "The minute you don't walk like a Powers model, with an absolutely glass walk, people think of your leg. That does make me kind of mad sometimes." One wonders if she saw Army Archerd's *Variety* column the day it included just one line about the movie *War Arrow*: "[It] reveals Suzan Ball's obvious limp."

28. *Fallen Angels* offers a different version of the Suzan Ball's Dying Day story: Here Richard is at the bedside of the semi-conscious Ball when she slips away with the name of the Love of Her Life on her lips. Upsettingly for him, that name was not Richard but Tony—Ball's one-time costar (in *City Beneath the Sea* and *East of Sumatra*) and lover, Anthony Quinn! "Richard Long suffered a tremendous emotional blow because of Suzan's final word in reference to Anthony Quinn," Crivello wrote. "This unfortunate incident was to haunt him for many years." Bullshit or not? You decide.

29. In the closing seconds of *The Mummy's Ghost* (1944), hero Robert Lowery sees his girl (Ramsay Ames) die. But throughout the movie, Lowery has been such a lout that even though Ames is a complete innocent (not a vampire like Paige's girl, not a cobra woman like Thompson's), the Sympathy Meter needle doesn't budge.

Snake woman Lisa (Faith Domergue, flanked by Marshall Thompson and Richard Long) frightens animals who sense the therianthropic (look it up!) truth.

30. In Francis D. Lyon's autobiography *Twists of Fate: An Oscar Winner's International Career*, he writes that the following comment by Jack Moffitt appeared in *The Hollywood Reporter*. It's *not* part of Moffitt's *Cult of the Cobra* review, quoted above, but let's take Lyon's word for it that this Moffitt quote did run in the *Reporter*:

> When a director makes a good picture out of good material, he, of course, deserves a lot of credit. But when a director makes a good picture out of material that most good directors would pass up, he deserves some sort of special award—even though he'll probably never get it. High on the list of such unsung meggers should be the name of Francis "Pete" Lyon. In *The [Bob] Mathias Story*, Pete took three cans of Olympic Games stock shots and two amateurs (Mr. and Mrs. Bob Mathias) and turned out a heart-warming little film whose human appeal and good taste have been warmly commented upon even by the slick magazines, which usually ignore low-budget efforts. In *Cult of the Cobra*, he has taken the sort of yarn that frequently is seen on Saturday afternoon in a small-town grind house and produced an intelligent horror-suspense story that should advance the careers of everyone in it. A former film cutter, he has but one rule—"Make every character act like someone you might meet in everyday life."

31. Around the same time as *Cult of the Cobra*, Gertz and Maury also worked together on the all-original score for *Abbott and Costello Meet the Mummy*, which contained 55 minutes of music consisting of 41 cues. Maury contributed 40 percent of the music, Gertz wrote 29 percent, Henry Mancini added 15 percent, and Hans Salter wrote 14 percent. The remaining music consisted of the song "You've Come a Long Way from St. Louis" by Bob Russell and John B. Brooks. It wasn't one of the best Abbott and Costello scores, but neither was it one of the best Abbott and Costello movies. As was common in the comedy duo's 1950s films, it included an unrelenting series of comedic musical touches, often in the form of muted trumpet *"wah-wahs,"* a sort-of musical version of a laugh track, letting you know what you were supposed to find amusing. Despite occasional atmospheric and horror sounds, the reliance upon these outdated comedic devices managed to make the picture more juvenile than it already was, assuming that was even possible. Mancini's extremely light "Main Title" for the movie was well below his usual standard, and it didn't sound as if any of the composers were stimulated by the material they were asked to enhance. Everything that was done musically right in *Abbott and Costello Meet Frankenstein* was done wrong in *Abbott and Costello Meet the Mummy*. Of course, the monsters were treated seriously in the former movie, so Frank Skinner's straight musical approach in that picture was the correct course to take. But Klaris, this movie's bandaged clown of a mummy, was such a hopeless buffoon that it's hard to know whether an effective score could have been written. One of *Meet the Mummy*'s few musical highlights occurs during the climax, with Gertz's "Blow Up, Part 1" and "Blow Up, Part 2" augmenting the explosion in the temple.

In *Cult of the Cobra*'s temple scene, the Cobra Goddess and the Warrior were played by Ruth Carlsson and Carl Carlsson. The Swedish couple appeared in niteries and in movies and on TV, mostly as jugglers. One of their routines was a "mouth-juggling act" in which they juggled small white balls with their tongues and breath. Pictured: James Dobson, William Reynolds, David Janssen, Marshall Thompson, Richard Long and, in their arms, Ruth Carlsson. (Photograph courtesy John Antosiewicz.)

Tarantula

1. And what happens when kids too scared to watch a movie spend extra time in the lobby? According to Ed Johnson of the Washington Theatre in Bay City, Michigan, quoted in a *Tarantula* ad in *Boxoffice* magazine, the spider movie "[b]roke all-time popcorn record."

2. According to dialogue found in Fresco's script but not in the episode, the nutrient enabled the researchers not only to live without food but also without sleep; Vera Miles' character says, "In the three years we've been on this nutrient, there isn't a one of us that's slept even an hour." *Variety* reviewer Daku wrote that the episode "maintains a fast and suspenseful pace. Jack Arnold's direction is a big plus; as is Robert M. Fresco's teleplay, well-constructed and original in its conception."

3. Funnily enough, Fresco penned one of *Science Fiction Theatre*'s "least sci-fi" stories, "No Food," plus two of its most far-out, "The Other Side of the Moon" and "Stranger in the Desert," the latter even featuring an alien visitor. In 2002 I sent him copies of all three and his reaction to watching them was: "I wish I could have rewritten them! The last line of 'No Food for Thought,' where Vera Miles looks at John Howard and says, 'Thank you for coming here and opening the windows,' I *yelled*—I said, 'Oh, *shit*! I wanted to *cut* that line!' I had wanted to cut that line out, and Ivan Tors said, 'No, no, no, no, it's okay, it's all right.' Well, it *wasn't* all right!"

4. The one interview I found where Arnold didn't glom all the writing credit was in *Fangoria*, with the director telling Al Taylor, "Universal was having a problem and they were looking for some exploitation films; they didn't want to spend much money. So I sat down and wrote a story called *Tarantula* and submitted it." Then, according to this version of events, along came Fresco and Martin Berkeley to develop a screenplay from his story.

5. During that time, the studio did let Agar do two movies on loanout. The first, Hugo Haas' *Hold Back Tomorrow* (1955), was ultimately bought outright by Universal, who spent approximately $4000 shooting extra scenes and released it themselves. The

other was the Lippert Western *The Lonesome Trail,* which looks like it was made dirt cheap (flying insects swarm the actors in exterior scenes!) but had a neat twist: Agar, wounded in his shootin' shoulder by dry-gulchers, becomes a Robin Hood-level marksman with bow and arrow to even the score. Agar played the movie's best and biggest part but, presumably because Wayne Morris had more of a name, Morris got top billing even though his part as a cigar-chewing bartender was small and unimportant.

6. The *Syracuse* (New York) *Herald-Journal*'s reviewer R.L.S. liked *Tarantula* but had two small beefs with the movie; one was that, for a small town doctor, Matt "drives a very fancy convertible." For the record, it's a showroom-new 1955 Ford Fairlane Sunliner with panorama windshield.

7. In Agar's autobiography *On the Good Ship Hollywood,* published years after his 2002 death, he said that during the making of his first movies, John Wayne and other hard-drinking actors had set the bar, so to speak, for him as a juicer. Elsewhere he said that he drank to excess because of the pressures of living with wife Temple in a cottage on the Temple family grounds, a stone's throw from her parents' home; "Basically, it was like having to live in the same house with them." But both times, he followed up by accepting all the ultimate responsibility for his giggle-water ways: "It was my fault that I began, and it's been my fault every time I've fallen off the wagon."

8. After *Tarantula,* Agar did have a one-movie respite from monsters: the starring role in the Western *Star in the Dust.* Co-star Leif Erickson told Tom and Jim Goldrup that in his fight scene with Agar, "he starts slugging and he knocked me galley-west. He stopped and said 'I'm sorry' and I said, 'Don't say you're sorry, keep going or we'll have to do it again.' We had to do it again and he hit me again. He couldn't control his punches."

9. In 2014, Mara's name was unexpectedly blown back into the news by Hurricane Sandy: An Alberto Vargas painting titled "Mara Corday" (a.k.a. "Pin-Up Girl") was one of three Vargas paintings improperly kept in a Brooklyn storage facility's ground-floor staging area and then ruined by storm-related flood waters, according to the art dealer who shipped the paintings there. He filed a $12 million suit.

10. A run-down of Corday's Universal Westerns, for the cowgirl movie fans in this book's audience:

- There were no drums in *Drums Across the River* (1954), and the river looked more like a stream, but there was plenty of compensation in seeing Mara in low-cut blouses and bling, as a seductive saloon girl in cahoots with her baddie boyfriend Lyle Bettger. The star was Audie Murphy. (Mara to interviewer Mike Fitzgerald: "Audie was psychotic—insane!")
- *Dawn at Socorro* (1954), a dud with Rory Calhoun, gave her an almost identical "window dressing" role, this time in a barroom-casino. After her character is established as an old flame of Calhoun's, she recedes into the background, watching men roll dice and play cards.
- In *Man Without a Star* (1955) she played Moccasin Mary, one of the girls in a Wyoming bordello, and described as "a rough exterior with a heart of stone." Star Kirk Douglas got sore at her one day and, while getting a publicity photo where he's grabbing her by her necklace, he halfway choked her and told her he didn't like her attitude. She had the fun of telling him, "Go screw yourself, I just got renewed!"
- *The Man from Bitter Ridge* (1955) was the same ol' hackneyed yarn of cattlemen vs. sheepmen but Mara, playing a tomboy aligned with the latter, enjoyed working with director Jack Arnold for the first time, experienced her first taste of stardom (she was second-billed, after Lex Barker)—and got romantically involved with Barker, then estranged from wife Lana Turner.
- In 1842 Oregon, the land of 1000 men for every woman, there's a barbaric custom where a widow belongs to the first man who claims her. That's the premise of *Raw Edge* (1956) with Corday third-billed as an Indian girl whose husband (John Gavin) is wrongly hanged. Almost before he's finished dancing, a passel of horny cowboys descends upon the shrieking widow! Sorry, ladies, but the scene is hilarious.
- Corday might have had her best movie role in the offbeat *A Day of Fury* (1956), a Western that should be of mild Monster Kid interest. Just by showing up in a frontier town, silver-tongued, manipulative desperado Dale Robertson makes its thin veneer of "civilization" vanish: Reformed troublemakers go back to their old ways, upright citizens turn vigilante, etc. He's called a "creature from Hell" and other, similar invectives enough times that you realize that the moviemakers are trying to convey that he may not be a man but an irresistible force of evil—maybe even sent by the Devil. At the end, the sound of a church bell rattles him and he loses a gun duel with marshal Jock Mahoney. Corday is Mahoney's fiancée, a one-time dance hall girl who, after Robertson's evil influence pervades the town, goes back to her old profession.

Is that really the sound of *Drums Across the River*—or the fast-beating hearts of Mara Corday's male fans?

11. Another sci-fi movie which *almost* had Mara in its cast: the soap-suds shocker *The Unknown Terror* (1957). It appears that she was briefly set to play the movie's mad doctor's native wife.

12. In 1994, when *Black Scorpion* was a hard-to-find movie, I mailed her a VHS tape and she promptly wrote to thank me and to tell me she thought it held up fairly well—then added, "But I had forgotten how unskilled the Mexican actors were. Dreadful!"

13. Carroll rolled far from his military roots and his son William rolled a far piece farther: In 1956, when the 25-year-old student-draft dodger arrived in New York on the liner *Saxonia* after a five-year stay in Europe, he was welcomed with open arms—the long arms of the law. When he agreed to induction into the armed forces, the charges were dropped.

14. He went from Elliott Blum, his real name, to Ross Elliott while in college: "In '36 or '37 we were doing a recording of *Macbeth* for the American Foundation for the Blind, which was just starting. I looked at a list of the actors and the characters they'd be playing, and there was a character called the Thane of Ross. So there was R-o-s-s. And then across from it was Elliott, the name of the guy who was gonna play it. And that's how I got to be Ross Elliott. That was a different era, an era in which you had to have a good-sounding stage name. Or you *thought* you did."

15. Elliott was lined up to play Jor-El, father of Superman, in the first *Adventures of Superman* episode, "but then I couldn't play the part. A girl named Karen Steele was supposed to play his mother and I was gonna play his father, and then something else came up that I had previously committed to." Aline Towne ended up playing the mother and Robert Rockwell played Jor-El and yet Elliott's name, not Rockwell's, appeared in the end credits.

16. Agar and Mara Corday were Universal contractees, the rest of the cast outside talent. Leo G. Carroll made $3250 for his one week's work. Nestor Paiva's rate was $1000 a week, Ross Elliott $750 and Edwin Rand $500.

17. A few months before *Tarantula* was made, Patterson appeared as a rural mailman in *Tarantula*'s "inspiration," *Science Fiction Theatre*'s "No Food for Thought." Then, three years *after Tarantula*, he played a high school janitor in the very *Tarantula*-like *Earth vs the Spider* (1958), and even fell victim to that movie's monster.

18. Perhaps *Tarantula* was meant to have a second hand-on-the-shoulder scene: In the script, Steve gives Matt a tour of Deemer's lab, she sees him to the door, he leaves, she starts walking toward the camera, and: "As she nears the stairway, [Deemer] stops her with his hand. She lets out a shocked SCREAM." In the movie, she doesn't see Deemer on the stairway as she approaches it but viewers do, so there's no startling moment for us.

19. In the 19 minutes between Deemer's speech about overpopulation and world hunger, and the Andy Andersen ranch scene with the cattle bones, nothing happens story-wise, and the only action is the Devil's Rock rockfall. Later in the movie, Matt's visit with Dr. Townsend at the Agricultural Institute is another show-stopper (but not in a *good* way). Delete those two stretches of footage and *Tarantula* would be the greatest 56-minute Big Bug movie on Earth.

20. Contrary to Fresco's anecdote, the Deemer-Tarantula scene wasn't shot in the morning but in the late afternoon; Fresco could not have seen Carroll in the commissary that day, but the next day at the earliest. A minor point.

21. A long October 19 article in the *Pasadena* (California) *Independent*, "Anybody Want a Giant Spider? Studio Won't Pick Up His Option," reads more like a publicist's batch of nonsense than anything that really happened, but it's amusing enough to mention here. It says of the casting of the movie's spiders:

> Cables were dispatched to tarantula agents (not to be confused with the Hollywood variety, who just act like tarantulas) in Panama, Mexico, Texas and various countries in South America. To [Russell A.] Gausman's great surprise the biggest spiders did not come from Texas, but from the tropical fastnesses of Argentina.
>
> "My real headache started," said Gausman, "when I received word from my various sources that some 60-odd of the furry killers were on their way to Hollywood. Suddenly I had to ask myself, 'If you were a tarantula, where would you want to live in the film capital?'"
>
> Gausman admitted later that what he really asked himself was, "Who would be foolish enough to board five dozen hairy poisoners and how much would he charge?"
>
> Jim Dannaldson, a naturalist of repute who lives in the San Fernando Valley happily surrounded by pythons, cobras and Gila monsters, answered Gausman's cry with the remark, "There's nothing foolish about it. Tarantulas are lovable when you understand them. That'll be $100 a week."

22. Apparently the line *was* eventually cut; it isn't in the movie.

23. Arnold in a 1983 German TV interview: "[*Them!*] had nothing to do with scientific experiments to enlarge living beings. It was about a colony of ants in the sewers of Los Angeles, and that surely had nothing to do with our movie."

24. In his German TV interview, Jack Arnold sounded like he was reading out of the *Tarantula* script when he said he favored shooting in the desert "because everything which ever lived and died left something in the desert. Because one time it was the bottom of the sea. Out there in the Mojave Desert, you can find shells." He went on,

> The desert is full of mysteries, it has an atmosphere and it has a strange feeling. And I felt that is great background for a story in which the audience is required to believe in against their better knowledge. It helps to put them in an environment which is bizarre in the beginning. The same is true for the movies I shot near water, including rock formations and the sea. I've always been careful with the locations I pick, because they are an integral part of storytelling, especially if the story is bizarre.

25. Now, to say a few words in defense of the ladies in charge: They had certain expectations of what a 90-year-old would be able to do—and then in walked the spry, ever-youthful Zach, who wanted to open the show by lying on the floor on top of a six-foot poster of himself from the old days, so that as he sat up, he'd reveal the "young" Zach beneath. His idea was accepted, the camera guys re-adjusted, Zach got down on the floor atop the poster—and one lady whispered to the other, "We *shoulda* got the coffin! We *shoulda* got the coffin!"—apparently they'd had some grand ideas but didn't know if a 90-year-old would be "up" to doing the things they concocted. Because my middle name is Fairness, I have to say that half the reason the show was less than it coulda been was that Zach didn't finally agree to do it 'til the day before it had to be shot. The special ran on Saturday night, October 25, 2008; eight years later, almost to the day, Zach died at age 98.

26. When *Tarantula* crawled into Texas, Roy Ragsdale of *The Brady Standard and Heart of Texas News* wrote, "The picture has proven to be a big success in the larger cities and has all the earmarks of being the best horror movie in years."

Index

Page numbers in ***bold italics*** indicate pages with illustrations

Abbott and Costello Go to Mars (1953) 119, 151, 152, 161, 237, 256
Abbott and Costello in the Foreign Legion (1950) 80
Abbott and Costello Meet Dr. Jekyll and Mr. Hyde (1953) 20, 28, 69, 90, 161, 179, 364, 378, 413
Abbott and Costello Meet Frankenstein (1948) 37, 48, 62, 80
Abbott and Costello Meet the Invisible Man (1951) 80
Abbott and Costello Meet the Keystone Kops (1955) 38, 152, 349
Abbott and Costello Meet the Killer, Boris Karloff (1949) 20, 80
Abbott and Costello Meet the Mummy (1955) 262, 340, 420
The Abbott and Costello Show (TV) 335
Across the Wide Missouri (1951) 412
An Act of Murder (1948) 82, 83
Adams, Julie 70, 99, 130, 174, ***177***, 178, 180, ***182***, 183–85, ***184***, ***185***, ***186***, ***188***, 190, ***191***, 192, 193, 204, 206, ***206***, 207, 307, 320, 409, 414
Adler, Tim 219
The Adventures of Rin-Tin-Tin (TV) 121
The Adventures of Robin Hood (TV) 59
Adventures of Superman (TV) 422
Affair in Trinidad (1952) 374
Against All Flags (1952) 47, 179, 203
Agar, John 282, 291, 292, 294, 295, 296, ***297***, 298, ***305***, 306–07, 312, 363, 366–69, ***367***, ***368***, ***369***, ***373***, 375, 376, 378, 383, 385, 386, ***391***, ***392***, 393, 395, ***407***, 409, 410, 420–21, 422
Agar, Loretta 295, 367, 393, 395
The Alfred Hitchcock Hour (TV) 140
Alfred Hitchcock Presents (TV) 138, 325
"The Alien Machine" (story) 210, 218
Alien Trespass (2009) 143–44
The All American (1953) ***286***
Alland, Susan 384
Alland, William v, 54, 64, 69, 87, 90–91, 92, 97, 98, 99, 115, 117–18, 125, 126, 129, 132, 134, 161, 166, 167, 168, 169, 171, 173, 174, 177, 178, 185, 187, 188, 200, 204, 220, 223, 229, 233, 237, 245, 248, 257, 258, 259, 281, 282, 312, 313, 363, 367, 368, 373, 377, 378, 384, 385, 388, 390, 392, 394, 395, 413, 414, 415, 416, 417
Allen, Irwin 71, 374
The Alligator People (1959) 53, 350
Alvin, Raymond 368
The Amazing Colossal Man (1957) 382
Amazing Stories (TV) 218
Amazon Women on the Moon (1987) 275
America's Got Talent (TV) 15
Amfitheatrof, Daniele 36, 82–83, ***82***, 83
Anders, Merry 228, 286
Anderson, Andy 123
Anderson, James 30
Andrews, Edson J. 192
Angel (TV) 323
Angel and the Badman (1947) 335
Angel Street (stage) 372
Apache Drums (1951) 60
Apache Woman (1955) 230–31
Arabian Nights (1942) 46
Arch of Triumph (1948) 411
Archer, John 414
Archerd, Army 141, 142, 238, 241, 282, 313, 325, 329, 332, 333, 337, 367, 418, 419
Arlen, Richard ***50***
Arnold, Jack 90, 92, 99–100, ***100***, 112, 113, 114–15, 117, 119, 121, 123, 124, 125, 126, 127, 129, 130, 142, 144, 150, 161, 163, 169, 176, 177, 178, 185, 193, 195, 204, 246, 281, 282, 286–87, ***287***, 288, 289, 290, 291, 292, 294, 295, 298, 306, 307, 308, 361, 362, 363, 364, 376, 378, 382, 383, 384, 388, 393, 395, 407, 414, 415, 417, 420, 421, 422
Arnold, Kenneth 134
Arnold, Susan 129
Arnold the Pig 413
Around the World Under the Sea (1966) 323
Arsenic and Old Lace (stage) 55
Arthur, Jean 412
Ashton, Roy 344
Asso, Raymond 43
Astounding Science Fiction (book) 218
Atkinson, Brooks 412
Atlantis, the Lost Continent (1961) 337
Attack of the Crab Monsters (1957) 111
Atwill, Lionel 86
The Aviator (2004) 319
Away All Boats (1956) 390
Ayres, Lew 60

Back at the Front (1952) 319
Back Street (1941) 48
Back to God's Country (1953) 99, 107
Back to the Black Lagoon (2000) 190
Bailey, Raymond 380
Baird, Jenni 143
Baker, Charles ***245***
Ball, Edward 175
Ball, Suzan 282, ***319***, 320, 321, 322, 329–30, 337, 338, 339, 371, 418, 419
Barker, Lex 371, 421
Barnum, Mike 255, 319
The Barretts of Wimpole Street (1934) 25, ***49***
Barrie, Wendy ***59***
Barrymore, John 68
Barsby, Jack 153, 200
Barton, Doris 380
Basehart, Richard 142
Baskin, Sally 282, 288, 291 293
Batman (TV) 108
The Battle at Apache Pass (1952) 48
Battle Creek Brawl (1980) 325
Battle Taxi (1955) 326
Battleground (1949) 322
Bawden, James 27
Baxley, Paul 14
Baxter, Frank C. 105, 135
Beach, James 110
The Beast from 20,000 Fathoms (1953) 145, 364, 374
Beaulieu, Trace 259
Beginning of the End (1957) 382, 394
Bela Lugosi Meets a Brooklyn Gorilla (1952) 74, 76
A Bell for Adano (stage) 414
Ben-Hur (1925) 174
Bend of the River (1952) 36, 185, 204, 286
Benedict, Dirk 419
Bengal Brigade (1954) 416
Benji 69
Benno, Norman ***47***
Benny, Jack 122
Berkeley, Martin 281, 306, 307, 308, 312, 345, 363, 410, 420
Bern, Paul 12
Bernstein, Leonard 412
Betz, Jack 187, 191
The Beverly Hillbillies (TV) 380
The Big Valley (TV) 321, 371
Bissell, Whit ***182***, 185, ***185***, 192, 193, ***193***
Bixby, Dianna Cyrus 234–35, 239, 416
The Black Castle (1952) 20, 22, 28, 34, 48, 52–87, ***52***, ***54***, ***55***, ***56***, ***57***, ***58***, ***61***, ***63***, ***64***, ***65***, ***66***, ***67***, ***68***, ***70***, ***71***, ***72***, ***73***, ***74***, ***75***, ***77***, ***81***, ***85***, ***86***, ***87***, 161, 270, 356, 412–13, ***413***, 416
The Black Cat (1934) 141
The Black Cat (1941) 64
Black Friday (1940) 64, 82
The Black Room (1935) ***9***, 73
Black Saddle (TV) 111
The Black Scorpion (1957) 361, 370, 376, 384, 389, 421
The Black Sleep (1956) 53
Blackmer, Judeena 290, 293
Blackstone, Harry, Sr. 34
Blake, Michael F. 412
Blanchard, Mari 313
Bloch, Ernest 45
Blonde Fever (1944) 322
Blood on the Sun (1945) 334, 336
Blumberg, Sylvia 340
The Bob Mathias Story (1954) 420
Boccherini, Luigi 48
Bodeen, DeWitt 75
Body and Soul (1947) 6
The Body Snatcher (1945) 28, 61, ***61***, 62
Boetticher, Budd 151
Bogeaus, Benedict 230
Boone, Steve 290
Bourbon Street Beat (TV) 320
Bow, Clara 175

The Boy and the Pirates (1960) 6
Boyer, Charles 25
Boyette, Patsy 187
Boyle, Robert 125, 126, 127, 415
Bracken's World (TV) 325
Bradbury, Ray 90, 91–92, ***91***, 94, 97, 98, 99, 123, 129, 130, 134, 135, 136, 137, 138, 139, 141, 142, 143, 144, 169, 413–14, 415
The Bradbury Chronicles (book) 91
The Brain from Planet Arous (1957) 143
Brand, Phoebe 414
Brando, Marlon 108
Breen, Joseph I. 100, 174, 295
The Bride and the Beast (1958) 231
Bride of Frankenstein (1935) 51, 120, 310
Bride of the Gorilla (1951) 29, 31
Bride of the Monster (1956) 333
Briggs, Colin 61, 62
Bright Victory (1951) 68, 184
Broadway (1929) 120
Broder, Jack 76
Broeske, Pat H. 317
Broken Arrow (1950) 68
Bromfield, John 282, 292, 293, 294, 298, ***305***, ***306***, 307
Brown, James 121
Brown, John 414
Brown, Peter Harry 317
Brown, Reynold 261, 264, 410
Brown, Vanessa 12
Browning, "Buddy" 176
Browning, Ricou ***175***, 175–77, ***176***, ***177***, 178, ***178***, ***179***, 180, ***180***, 181, ***181***, ***184***, 185, 186–87, 188–89, 190, 191, 192, 205, 207, ***207***, 208, 283, 281, ***283***, 287, 288, 289, 290, ***290***, 291, 292, 293, 294, 295, 305, 306
Browning, Ricou, Jr. 176
Brunas, John 1
Brunas, Michael 1
Bryant, Bob 71
Buchanan, Edgar 370
Buck Rogers (1939) 249–50
Buka, Donald 318
Burbank, Luther 362
The Burning Cross (1947) 373
"The Burning Man" (story) 142–43
Burns, Bob 127, 130, 137, 177–78, 179, 190, 195, 282
Burson, Polly 70, 71, 190
The Bushwhackers (1952) 62
... but I have promises to keep (book) 313
Bwana Devil (1952) 101, 120
Byrnes, Edd 321

Cabot, Susan 130, 236, 340
Cagney, James 334
Cagney, William 334
Cahoon, Richard 126
The Caine Mutiny Court-Martial (stage) 261
Call Me Lucky: A Texan in Hollywood (book) 368
Callahan, George *see* Callahan, Edward G
Callow, Simon 11, 16, 27
Cameron, John Munro 260
The Canterville Ghost (1944) 10
Captain Lightfoot (1955) 195, 228
Captive Wild Woman (1943) 418
Career (1959) 109, 414
Carlson, Mona 106
Carlson, Richard ***93***, ***98***, 100, 101, ***101***, ***103***, 104–06, ***105***, ***106***, 112, 113, ***113***, 114, 115, ***115***, 116, ***116***, 117, ***117***, 118, ***118***, 119–20, ***119***, 122–23, ***123***, 124, ***124***, 127, 128, 129, ***129***, 130, ***133***, 135, 137, 138, ***139***, 141, 150, ***161***, 162–63, ***162***, 181, ***182***, 185, ***185***, 186, ***186***, ***188***, 190, ***191***, 192, 206, 207, 306–07, 391, 415
Carlsson, Carl 330, 334, 335
Carlsson, Ruth 334, ***420***
Carmilla (book) 74–75, 120–21
Carmilla (unmade movie) 74–75
Carpenter, John 144
Carpenter, Sandy King 144
Carr, Lawrence 14
Carrasco, Jonathan ***143***
Carroll, Earl 369, 370
Carroll, Harrison 239, 240, 416
Carroll, Leo G. 360, 361, ***363***, 364, ***365***, 371–73, ***371***, ***372***, 380, 381, 382, ***382***, ***388***, ***392***, 408, ***408***, 409, 421, 422
Carson, Robert 114
Carter, Everett 353, 354, 403
Casablanca (1942) 416
Case, Tom 282
Castelnuovo-Tedesco, Mario 152, 154, 155
Castle of Frankenstein (magazine) 296, 297
Cat People (1942) 71, 311, ***311***, 316, 331, 343, 356, 358, 418
Cat-Women of the Moon (1953) 391
Cattle Queen of Montana (1954) 230
Cavalry Command (1963) 368
Cavanagh, Paul ***8***, 23, 27, 29, 174
Cave of Outlaws (1951) 44
Cavens, Albert 63
Cavens, Fred 63
Chambers, Wheaton 65
Champion, Marge 415
Chandler, Helen 27
Chandler, Jeff 144, 320
Chaney, Lon 62, 67, 68, 72, 91, 113, 413
Chaney, Lon, Jr. 27, 53, 55, 56, ***56***, ***58***, 62–63, ***63***, 64, 65, 67, 69, 70, 71, 72–73, 74, ***75***, 82, 86, 87, 374, 412, 413
Chaney, Patsy 413
Chapman, Ben 177, 184, 185, 186, 187, 188, 189, ***189***, 190, 191, ***191***, 192, 193, ***193***, ***206***, 207, 208
Charles Laughton: A Difficult Actor (book) 11
Charles Laughton: An Intimate Biography (book) 27
The Cherry Orchard (stage) 22
The Chicken of Tomorrow (1948) 100, 362
Chief Crazy Horse (1955) 282, 320, 329, 338
"The Children's Room" (story) 254
Christian, Darrell 228
Cinefantastique (magazine) 144, 246, 362, 414
Citizen Kane (1941) 68, 166, 312
City Beneath the Sea (1953) 200, 202
Clarence, the Cross-Eyed Lion (1965) 323
"The Classic Horror Music of Hans J. Salter" (record album) 275
Classic Images (magazine) 229, 238, 255, 319
Clatterbaugh, Marian ***184***
Clift, Montgomery 13
The Climax (1944) 44
Close Encounters of the Third Kind (1977) 144, 163
Clute, Sid 417
Code of Honor: The Making of Three Great American Westerns (book) 412
Cody of the Pony Express (1950 serial) 374
Coen, Franklin 220, 221, 223, 242, 257, 276
Cohen, Albert J. 23–24
Collier's (magazine) 91, 222, 247, 417
Collins, Richard 312, 343, 345, 417–18
Colton, David 35
Comingore, Dorothy 312, 417, 418
Comstock, Ned v
Conan Doyle, Arthur 165
Connolly, Mike 320, 374
Conquest of Space (1955) 134, 258
Conrad, Robert 140
Coogan's Bluff (1968) 394
Corday, Mara 320–22, ***321***, 364, ***366***, 369–71, ***370***, 375, ***375***, 378, 380, 382, ***382***, 386, ***386***, 390, ***391***, ***392***, 393, ***407***, 409, 410, ***410***, 418, 421, ***421***, 422
Corday, Paula 55, 61–62, ***61***, ***62***, ***63***, ***67***, ***68***, 69, 70, ***70***, 71, ***72***, ***73***, ***74***, ***75***, ***77***, 86, 87, ***413***
Corday, Rita *see* Corday, Paula
Corden, Henry 63, 67–68, 69, ***70***, 74
Cording, Harry 22
Cornthwaite, Robert 162, 163
The Corsican Brothers (1941) 73
Cossa, Paolo 318–19
Costello, Lou 335, 340
Cotten, Joseph 60, 68
Cottrell, William 7, ***7***, 14, 15, 16, 17, ***17***, ***26***, 29, ***50***, 412
The Court Jester (1956) 63
Cousins, Kay 111, 112
Cousteau, Jacques 169
Cowan, Claudia 108
Cowan, Warren 108
Coy, Walter 326, ***341***, 343
Crabbe, Buster ***248***, 249
Craig, Carolyn ***320***
Craig, Helen 60
Crawford, Joan 107
The Crawling Eye (1958) ***142***
The Creation of the Humanoids (1962) 256
The Creature Chronicles (book) 1, 2, 98, 117
Creature from the Black Lagoon (1954) 22, 38, 39, 47–48, 70, 97, 105, 121, 134, 137, 139, 142, ***147***, 150, 151, 154, 156, 163, 164–208, ***164***, ***177***, ***178***, ***179***, ***180***, ***181***, ***182***, ***185***, ***186***, ***188***, ***189***, ***191***, ***193***, ***197***, ***198***, ***206***, ***207***, 219, 220, 222, 256, 257, 268, 273, 274, 275, 280, 281, 282, 283, 286–87, 293, 294, 296, 297, 298, 299, 300, 301, 302, 303, 304, 305, 306–07, 308, 348, 362, 384, 392, 400, 401, 409, 416
Creature from the Black Lagoon—The Musical (stage) ***207***
The Creature Walks Among Us (1956) 39, 139, 255, 258, 277, 278, 297, 301, 416, 417
The Creature Wasn't Nice (1983) 258
Cregar, Laird 153
Crenshaw, James 321
Crews, Stanley 187
Criss Cross (1949) 82
Crivello, Kirk 339
Croset, Paule *see* Corday, Paula
Crossett, Raymond 24
Crosswinds (1951) 176
Cult Movies (magazine) 236
Cult of the Cobra (1955) 38, 299, 300, 301, 309–58, ***309***, ***311***, ***314***, ***315***, ***316***, ***327***, ***328***, ***329***, ***330***, ***331***, ***332***, ***333***, ***334***, ***335***, ***337***, ***338***, ***341***, ***342***, ***345***, ***357***, ***358***, 417–20, ***418***, ***419***, ***420***
Curse of the Demon (1958) 358
Curse of the Faceless Man (1958) 71
Curse of the Undead (1959) 38, 41, 50, 63
The Curse of the Werewolf (1961) 24
Curtis, Tony ***286***, 335
Cushing, Peter 87

D'Agostino, Mack 100
Daktari (TV) 323
The Dalton Gang (1949) 184
Daniel, Dennis 184, 192, 376
Dannaldson, Jim 422
Dante, Joe 255, ***260***, 339, 360
Danton, Mitchell 184, 185
Danton, Ray 184, 313
Danton, Steven 184, 185
Darrell, Steve 375
Da Silva, Howard 68
Davis, Bette 109
Davis, Jerry 312, 343
Davis, Lisa 320
Dawn at Socorro (1954) 325, 400, 402, 403, 421
Day, Richard 55
A Day of Fury (1956) 421
The Day of the Triffids (1963) ***296***
Day of the Trumpet see *Cavalry Command*
The Day the Earth Stood Still (1951) 90, 134, 139, 142, 152, 163, 265, 266, 276
Dayton, Danny 313
Deacon, Richard 239, 256
Dead Man's Eyes (1944) 85
The Deadly Mantis (1957) 38, 349, 355, 363, 370, 382, 388, 389, 390, 394, 398, 410
Dean, Margia 389
Dearing, Edgar ***96***, ***119***, ***127***, 157, 380
De Chancie, John 236
De Laire, Diane 296
DeLisa, Jolene 108, 110
del Rio, Dolores 166
Denning, Richard 174, ***182***, 185, ***185***, 186, 187, ***188***, 190, ***191***, 192, 206, 207
Descher, Sandy 227
Dessau, Paul 44, 46, 81, 82, 83
Destination Moon (1950) 101, 265, 276, 394
Destry (1954) 354
Dettman, Bruce 385–86
Devil and the Deep (1932) 10
The Devil-Doll (1936) 390–91
Devil's Canyon (1953) 171
Dexter, Alan 113, ***162***
Dial 1119 (1950) 322
DiCaprio, Leonardo 319
Did They Mention the Music? (book) 155
Dietrich, Marlene 75
Dillaway, Don 338, 376
Directed by Jack Arnold (book) 115, 144, 246, 292, 362

Dobson, James **315**, **332**, 338, 341, 343, **357**, **420**
Dodds, Edward 282
Dolan, Robert Emmett 199, 201
Dolenz, George 318
Domergue, Faith **216**, 221, **221**, 223, **224**, 228, 233, 234, **234**, 236, **236**, **237**, 238, 239, **239**, 240, 241, **241**, 242, **242**, 243, **243**, 244, 247, **247**, **248**, **249**, **256**, 258, 278, 310, 311, **311**, 314, **314**, 316, **316**, 317–19, **317**, 327, **327**, 328, **328**, 329, **329**, 332, 337, 338, 341, **341**, **342**, 343, 344, 356, 357, 358, **358**, 390, 418, **419**
Don Juan in Hell (stage) 19, 25, 30, 412
Donat, Robert 389
Donovan's Brain (1953) 412
Doorway to Life (radio) 117
Douglas, Diana 221
Douglas, Kirk 108, 221, 421
Douglas, Melvyn 27
Douglas, Robert 15
Dow, Peggy **21**
Dow, Tony 143
Dracula (1931) 5, 30, 161, 120, 339, 356, 358
Dracula (1931 Spanish-language version) 339, 410
Dracula vs. Frankenstein (1971) 275
Dracula's Daughter (1936) 310, 327–28, **342**, 343, 410
Drake, Charles 100, 101, 108–10, **109**, 113, 115, 116, **116**, **117**, **118**, 120, 122, 124, 128, 132, 141, 150, **162**, 163
Dreyfuss, Richard 144
Drums Across the River (1954) 400, 421, **421**
Drury, James 374
The Duel at Silver Creek (1952) 318, 400
du Pont, Alfred I. 175
DuPont Show of the Month (TV) 28
The Dybbuk (opera) 45

Earth vs. the Flying Saucers (1956) 276, 386
Earth vs the Spider (1958) 394, **394**, 398, 410, 422
East of Sumatra (1953) 200, 203, 399, 400, 406
Eastwood, Clint 296, 303, 306, 370, 371, **376**, 377, 383, 394, 395, 406
Ed Wood's Bride of the Monster (book) 333
Edeson, Arthur 4
Edwards, Blake 266
Edwards, Colin 73
The Egg and I (1947) 319
"Eine Kleine Nachtmusik" (musical composition) 83, 270
Eldredge, George 118, **119**, 415
Electric Man (unmade movie) 142
Elliott, Ross 373–75, **373**, **374**, 377–78, 380, 422
Elsa Lanchester Herself (book) 11, 18, 30, 35
Endore, Guy 24
Enemy from Space see *Quatermass 2*
Engel, Roy **66**
English, Marla 325
Erickson, Glenn 252
Erickson, Leif 421
Escalante, Henry 186
Escape (radio) 27
Esquire (magazine) 91, 370
Essex, Harry 97–98, 129, 132, 138, 141, 142, 143, 168, 169, 171, 173, 174, 194
E.T. the Extra-Terrestrial (1982) 123, 163, 258
Evelyn, Judith 372
Everson, William K. 148
The Exile (1947) 61–62, 82, 412

Fairbanks, Douglas, Jr. 13, 62, 73
Fairchild, Edgar 40
Fallen Angels (book) 339, 419
Fangoria (magazine) 35, 74, 79, 223, 228, 258, 259, 328, 344, 369, 370, 371, 382, 384, 413, 420
Fant, Julian 294
Fantastic Adventures (magazine) 254
Fantastic Films (magazine) 219, 226
The Far Country (1955) 404
Farley, Morgan **7**, 14, 16, 17, **17**, 412
Farnsworth, Richard 340
The Fatal Witness (1945) 6
Faust (stage) **325**
Feature Players: The Stories Behind the Faces (book) 21
Ferguson, Perry 55
Ferran, Jose 334
Ferrer, Mel 318
Fidler, Jimmie 109, 384
Fiedler, Arthur 85
Fields, Sid 335
Fiend Without a Face (1958) 322, **322**, 323
Figueroa, Gabriel 166, **166**, 177
Filmfax (magazine) 413
Films in Review (magazine) 148
Films of the Golden Age (magazine) 12, 61, 62
Finders Keepers (1951) 36
Finley, Larry 144
The First Legion (1951) 107
The First Legion (stage) 107
First Man into Space (1959) 322, 323
First Spaceship on Venus (1960) 275
Fisher, James 291
Fitzgerald, Mike 223, 228, 318, 322, 328, 370, 421
Flaherty, Robert J. 100
Flame of Araby (1951) 27
Flaming Feather (1952) 107
Flash Gordon (comic strip) 413
Flash Gordon (1936) **248**
Flash Gordon's Trip to Mars (1938) 413
The Fleischmann's Yeast Hour (radio) 27
Flight to Tangier (1953) 220
Flippy the "Educated" Porpoise 290, 292
The Fly (1958) 398
Fontanne, Lynn 13
The Food of the Gods (book) 387
For Men Only (1952) 111, 117, 323–24, 325
Forbidden Planet (1956) 276, 386
Ford, Glenn 414
Ford, John 55, 59
Ford, Tennessee Ernie 11
Forrest, Sally 7, **9**, 11–13, **12**, **13**, 17, **17**, 18, **18**, 19, **19**, 20, 21, **23**, **26**, 27, **49**, 50, 86
Forsythe, John 324
Fort Apache (1948) 366
Forty Carats (stage) 108
Forward the Heart (stage) 28
Four Guns to the Border (1954) 400, 404
Four Men and a Prayer (1938) 58–59
Francis, Coleman 233
Francis in the Haunted House (1956) 87
Francis Joins the Wacs (1954) 302, 303
Franciscus, James 143
Frank, Milo 12–13, 285
Frankenstein (1910) 419
Frankenstein (1931) 4, 29, 50, 75, 86, 120, 163
Frankenstein (unmade color 3-D movie) 75
Frankenstein Meets the Wolf Man (1943) 44, 81, 84, 86, 230, 233, 410
Franklin, Paul 234
Franks, Laurie 411
Franz, Arthur 323
Fredericks, Dean 258
Freeman, Leonard **100**
Fregonese, Hugo 318, 332, 337
French Without Tears (stage) 58, 59
Fresco, Robert M. 361, 362, **362**, 363, 364, 379, 382, 385, 386, 388, 410, 420, 422
Freund, Karl 86, 161, 162, 205, 356, 357, 358
Friese-Greene, William 59
From Hell It Came (1957) 333
Frommer, Ben 333
The Front Page (stage) 414
Frye, Dwight 5
Fryer, Robert 14
Fuller, Lance 230–33, **230**, **231**, 236, **241**, 416
Furie, Sidney J. 343
Furmanek, Bob 75, 131, 141, 149–51, **149**
Fury at Gunsight Pass (1956) 320, 339
Fury of the Congo (1951) 390
Future Tense (unmade movie) 14

Gable, Clark 71
Galileo (stage) 110, 412
Gardiner, Reginald 22
Gardner, Ava 318, 319
Garner, Kelli 319
Gateway to Hollywood (radio) 109, 414
Gausman, Russell A. 86, 422
Gebhardt, Fred 258
General Hospital (TV) 375
Gentry, Race 313
Gerard, Philip 194, 195
Gershenson, Joseph **37**, 39, 40–41, 42, 43, 81, 152, 154, 160, 199, 200, 265, 276, 277, 303, 353, 354, 355, 399, **399**, 400, 403
Gershenson, Louis **37**
Gertz, Irving 39, **39**, 41, 152, 154, 156, 157, 158, 159, **160**, 163, 348, 349, 350, 351, 352, 353, 356, 420
Get Smart (TV) 337
The Ghost and Mrs. Muir (TV) 325
The Ghost of Frankenstein (1942) 81, 84, 86, 200, 203
The Giant Claw (1957) 277, 370, 376
The Giant Gila Monster (1959) 153
Gilbert, Herschel Burke 152
Gilligan's Island (TV) 414
The Girl from U.N.C.L.E. (TV) 372
The Girl in the Kremlin (1957) 269
Girls in the Night (1953) 100, **100**, 113, 142, 158, 400, 406
The Glass Web (1953) 107, 117, 142, 150, 151, 200, 270, 324, 325
Glassberg, Irving 51, 68, 86, 87, 127, 413
God's Little Acre (1958) 231
Goetz, William 90, 97, 125, 141–42, 319
The Goldbergs (1950) 107
The Goldbergs (TV) 107
The Golden Horde (1951) 204
The Golden Turkey Awards (book) 367
Goldrup, Jim 21, 223, 228, 242, 243, 251, 317, 318, 332, 374, 416, 418, 421
Goldrup, Tom 21, 223, 228, 242, 243, 251, 317, 318, 332, 374, 416, 418, 421
Goldsmith, Jerry 45
Goldstein, Leonard 54
Golitzen, Alexander 276, 277
Goodwin, R.W. 143–44
Gordon, Alex 60, 230, 231
Gordon, Bert I. 394, 410
Gordon, Richard 322
Gordon, William 54, 174, 340, 377
Gorgeous George 26
Gorss, Sol 14, 16, 22
Gould, Harvey 123
Gourlay, Jack 413
Gozier, Bernie 191, 192
Graham, Sheilah 230, 416
Grahame, Gloria 322
Grant, Lee 143
Graves, Peter 324
Gray, Coleen 27
The Great Sioux Uprising (1953) 318
"The Greater Conflict" (story) 211
Green, Johnny 36
Green, Mitzi 6
Green Acres (TV) 417
Greene, Richard 27, 54, 55, **55**, **57**, **58**, 58–60, **59**, **64**, **68**, 69, 70, 71, **71**, **74**, **75**, 86, 87, **413**
Gregory, Paul 11, 30
Grofé, Ferde 152
Gruenberger, Harald 393–94, 414
Guilty by Suspicion (1991) 418
Gwenn, Edmund 364, 388

Haines, Chauncey 43
Hajos, Karl 36
Hall, Charles D. 51
Halloran, John 334–35, 336, 337, 419
Halsey, Brett 297, 312
Hamilton, Kim 28
Hangover Square (1945) 153
Hansen, Myrna 313
Hansen, Peter 375
Hard, Fast and Beautiful (1951) 20
Harding, Al **47**
Hardwicke, Cedric 25, 412
Hardy, Patricia **100**
Harlow, Jean 12, 13, 285, 317
Harvey (1950) 109
Hatton, Rondo 378–79
Haupt, Whitey 123
Have Rocket, Will Travel (1959) 394
Havens, James C. 180, 181, 185, 188–89, 287
Hayes, Chester 333
Hayes, Seth **260**
Hayward, Lillie 6

Hayworth, Rita 61
He Laughed Last (1956) 320
Hecht, Maude 290
Heffernan, Howard 131
Heflin, Van 414
Heisler, Stuart 318
Heitland, Jon 372
Hell on Frisco Bay (1956) 417
Henderson, Marcia 99
Hennesy, Tom 282, ***282***, ***284***, 287, 288, 291–92, ***292***, 293, 294, ***294***, 295, ***296***, 297, ***306***
Henreid, Paul 111, 117, 323, 324, 325
Henry, Thomas B. 106
Hepburn, Katharine ***228***
Herbert, F. Hugh 116, 324, 325
Herbert, Frederick 72, 83, ***83***, 161, 355
Here Come the Nelsons (1952) 152
Here on Gilligan's Isle (book) 111–12
Herrmann, Bernard 152, 163, 265
Herzbrun, Bernard 28, 50, 86, 413
Herzoff, Archie 193, 282, 296
Hickman, Beau 282
Hickox, Sid 410
High Noon (1952) 62, 412
Higham, Charles 27
Highway Dragnet (1954) 378
Hildebrand, Lloyd ***47***
Hill, Lloyd 119
Hilsberg, Ignace 153
Hinds, Anthony 344
Hines, Jerome ***325***
Hinkle, Robert 368–69
Hitchcock, Alfred 28, 140, 162, 372, 411–12
Hitler's Children (1943) 61
Hoey, Dennis ***228***
Hoffman, Roswell A. 276
Hoffman, Samuel 152, 156
Hoffmann, Gert Günther 393–94
Hold Back Tomorrow (1955) 395, 420
Holden, Gloria ***342***, 343
Holden, Joyce ***100***
Holland, William 55
Holliman, Earl 313
Hollywood and the Mob (book) 219
Hollywood Story (1951) 45–46, 82
Hopper, Hedda 105, 112, 181, 219, 228, 233, 244, 389
Hopper, Jerry 106
Hopper, Wes 14
The Horror Factory (book) 385
Horror of Dracula (1958) 393
Horsley, David S. 130, 131, 245, ***245***, 276
Horton, Robert 324
Horvath, Charles 14, 15, 22, ***22***, 29
The Hound of the Baskervilles (1939) ***59***
House of Dracula (1945) 44, 84, 86, 233, 356, 410
House of Frankenstein (1944) 44, 45, 46, 50, 51, 67, 72, 80, 81, 82, 85, 86, 410
House of Horrors (1946) 44, 45
House of Mystery (1934) 417
The House of the Seven Gables (1940) 82, 85
House of Wax (1953) 99, 105, 120, 127
House on Haunted Hill (1958) ***320***, 370
How Green Was My Valley (1941) 55
How to Marry a Millionaire (TV) 286
Howard, John 361
Howard Hughes: The Untold Story (book) 317, 319
The Howards of Virginia (1940) 105
Howarth, Betty Jane 380
Hoy, Robert 297
Hoyt, John 64, 65, 72, 74, 87, 413, ***413***
Hudson, Rock 312, 324
Hughes, Arnold ***83***, 161, 354, 355
Hughes, Dickson 14, 411
Hughes, Howard 12, 317–18, 319
Hughes, Kathleen 111, 116–17, ***117***, 118, 128, 129, 130, 150, 151, 230, 231, 233, 323–26, ***324***, ***325***, ***326***, 327, ***327***, 330–31, ***331***, 333, 336, ***337***, 356, 357, 415, 418
The Human Duplicators (1965) 275
The Hunchback of Notre Dame (1939) 10, 25, 109
Hunt, Marsha 106
Hunter, Jeffrey 107, 130
Hunter, Ross 74, 121
Hunter, Tab 227
Huston, John 323
Huston, Walter 373
Hyer, Martha 313

I Led 3 Lives (TV) 105
I Love Lucy (TV) 374
I Married a Monster from Outer Space (1958) 143
I, the Jury (1953) 171
The Illustrated Man (book) 91, 98
In the Wings—A Memoir (book) 221
Incident at Exeter (book) 255
The Incredible Shrinking Man (1957) 38, 39, 141, 163, 266, 272, 275, 323, 350, 382
The Incredible Shrinking Woman (1981) 258
Indestructible Man (1956) 53
Inferno (1953) 149
Inn, Frank 69, 413
The Invaders (TV) 109
Invaders from Mars (1953) 276
Invasion of the Body Snatchers (1956) 161, 162, 163, 358, 386, 417
Invisible Agent (1942) 44
The Invisible Man (1933) 5
The Invisible Man Returns (1940) 22, 265
The Invisible Man's Revenge (1944) 44, 45, 46, 84
The Invisible Ray (1936) 50, 410
Irma La Douce (1963) 11
Iron Man (1951) 7, 85
Isherwood, Christopher 11
Island of Lost Souls (1932) 10, 25, 49, ***50***, 418
Island of the Lost (1967) 105
Israel, Sam 101, 193, 194–95
It (1927) 175
It Came from Beneath the Sea (1955) 240, 258, 390, 394
It Came from Horrorwood (book) 22, 321
It Came from Outer Space (1953) 38, 39, 88–163, ***88***, ***93***, ***95***, ***96***, ***98***, ***101***, ***102***, ***103***, ***105***, ***111***, ***113***, ***115***, ***116***, ***117***, ***118***, ***119***, ***120***, ***121***, ***122***, ***123***, ***124***, ***125***, ***127***, ***128***, ***129***, ***130***, ***133***, ***135***, ***137***, ***139***, ***140***, ***141***, ***142***, ***145***, ***147***, ***153***, ***154***, ***156***, ***157***, ***158***, ***159***, ***161***, ***162***, 169, 171, 179, 181, 199, 206, 207, 219, 220, 222, 256–57, 258, 267, 294, 324, 339, 341, 348, 353, 357, 362, 378, 380, 384, 387, 390, 391, 400, 402, 403, 404, 405, 407, 413–15, 416, 418
It Came from Outer Space (2004 book) 92, 134
It Came from Outer Space II (1996) 143, ***143***
It Conquered the World (1956) 163
It Grows on Trees (1952) 81
It Takes Two (TV) 321
It! The Terror from Beyond Space (1958) 142, 323
Ivy (1947) 82, 83

Jackson, Brad 118–19, ***119***, 415
Jacobs, Dick 155, 272, 275, 399
Jamaica Inn (1939) 28, 412
Jane Eyre (stage) ***228***
Janssen, David 311, 312, 313, ***315***, 326, ***332***, ***333***, 333–34, 338, 341, 370, 419, ***420***
Jaws (1975) 199, 206
Joan of Lorraine (stage) 374
Johnny Belinda (1948) 60
Johnny Belinda (stage) 60
Johnny Dark (1954) 402–03
Johnny Stool Pigeon (1949) 109
Johnson, Erskine 67, 131, 223, 227, 251, 300
Johnson, Russell 100, 101, ***103***, 110–12, ***111***, 114, 115, 116, 119, ***119***, 120, 121, ***122***, 123, 126, 127, ***127***, 130, ***137***, 144, 163, 236, ***236***, 241, 244, ***252***, 256, 278, 324, 325, 414, 415
Jones, Raymond F. 210–11, 218, 219, 226, 251, 254, 255, 258, 269
Jordon, Claudia 14
Jungle Woman (1944) 44
Juran, Nathan 28, 54–55, ***55***, 67, 68, 69, 71

Kadler, Karen 313
Kane, Joe 121
Karen, Anna 221, 227, 228
Karloff, Boris 4, ***4***, 5, 6, 7, ***9***, 10, 11, 16, 20, 21, ***21***, 22, ***22***, 23, 24, 27, 28, ***28***, 29, ***29***, 30, ***31***, 48, 50, 53, ***54***, 55, ***55***, ***56***, 62, 64, 65, 66, 67, ***68***, 69, 72–73, 74, 80, 86, 87, 90, 205, 411, 412, 413, ***413***
Karloff, Evelyn 55
Kaye, Charlotte 290
Kaye, Danny 63
Keaton, Buster 415
Kehr, Dave 259, 415
Kellaway, Cecil 364
Kelley, Bill 246, 362, 414
Kelly, Jack 311, 313, ***315***, ***316***, 326, ***330***, ***332***, 341, 343
Kemmer, Ed 410
Kennedy, Arthur 68
Kenny, Joseph E. 100, 113, 114, 115, 124
Kent, Ted J. 205
Kerry, Norman 113
Kerwin, Brian 143
Kevan, Jack 178, 180–81, 222, 282, 288
Kiel, Richard 258
The Killers (1946) 47
Killers from Space (1954) 141
King Kong (1933) 165, 167, 169, 204, 205, 206, 207, 304, 306, 307, 382, 393, 407, 409
King Solomon's Mines (1950) 105
King Tut *see* Tutankhamun
Kings Row (1942) 285
Kinnoch, Ronald 322
Kintz, Greg 135, 137, 149–61, ***149***
Kirby, George 19
Kiss of Fire (1955) 220
Klum, Heidi 15
Koontz, Mel 71
Krenek, Ernst 155
Kruger, Otto 361, 386
Kurland, Gilbert 179, 281

Lady on a Train (1945) 47
The Lady Takes a Flyer (1958) 395
Laid Back in Hollywood: Remembering (book) 60
Laitin, Joseph 222, 247
Lamb, John 282, 287, 288, 289
L'Amour, Louis 105
Lamparski, Richard 110
Lanchester, Elsa 10, ***10***, 11, 18, 30, 35, 411
The Land Unknown (1957) 38, 141, 268, 339, 390
Landau, Arthur 285
Landis, John 99
Lane, Lola 416
Lane, Rosemary 222, 416
Lang, Fritz 12
Lange, Arthur 37, 355
Lansing, Joi 230
Lardner, Ring, Jr. 59
The Late George Apley (stage) 372
Laughton, Charles 6, ***6***, 7, ***7***, ***9***, 10–11, ***10***, ***11***, ***12***, 14, ***14***, 15, 16, 17, ***17***, 18–19, ***18***, 20–21, ***21***, 22, ***23***, 24, ***24***, 25, ***26***, 27–28, 29, 30, 48–50, ***49***, ***50***, ***51***, 66, 86, 110, 411–12, ***419***
The Laughton Story (book) 412
Laurie, Piper 221
Lava, William 39, 41, 44, ***44***, 45, 46, 83, 84, 152, 302, ***302***, 303–04, 348, 349, 350, 351, 352, 353, 355
Law and Order (1953) 111
The Lawless Breed (1952) 38, 401, 402
Lawrence, Carl 124, 414–15
Lawson, Bob 123
Le Fanu, Sheridan 74, 75, 121
Le Fevre, Ned 296
Leaf, Karl ***47***
Lee, Pinky 370
The Leech Woman (1960) 38, 41, 398
Lees, Paul 106
Legacy of Blood (1973) 228
Lembeck, Harvey ***100***
Leps, Wassili 154
Let's Kill Uncle (1966) 265, 274
Levy, Benn 10
Lewis, Jerry 411
Lewis, Milton 106
Lewton, Val 28, 60, 74, 311, 312, 331, 343, 415
Lieberman, Leo 169, 170
The Life and Legend of Wyatt Earp (TV) 374
The Life of Riley (TV) 414
Lincoln, Elmo 71
The Lively Set (1964) 395
Loan Shark (1952) 110
Loftin, Carey 14, 26
London, Tom 380
London by Night (1937) 408
The Lonesome Trail (1955) 421
Long, Barbara 320, 323, 329
Long, Richard 130, 174, 282, ***286***, 310, 312, 313, ***315***, ***319***, 319–22, ***320***, ***321***, 323, 326, 329, ***331***, ***332***,

337, 338, 339, 341, ***341***, 357, 370–71, ***370***, 418, 419, ***419***, ***420***
Looney Tunes: Back in Action (2003) 259–60, ***260***, 416–17
The Looters (1955) 184
Lopez, Perry 190, 191, 192
Lost in Space (TV) 153
The Lost Weekend (1945) 152, 244
The Lost World (book) 165
The Lost World (1925) 165, 382
Lovejoy, Frank 107, 174, 181
Lovelace, Mary ***241***
The Lovin' Spoonful 290
Lucas, Tim 250
Luce, Claire 254
Luce, Greg 17
The Lucky Southern Star: Reflections from the Black Lagoon (book) 183, 184, 190
Lugosi, Bela 6, 20, 29, 64, 74, 356, 357, 358, 411
Lunt, Alfred 13
Lupino, Ida 12, 18, 20
Lux Video Theatre (TV) 27, 59, 107, 320, 334
Lyon, Francis D. 313, 325, 330, 331, 338, 339, 340, 343, 418–19, 420
Lyons, Cliff 186

M (1931) 62
M (1951) 62
Ma and Pa Kettle (1949) 319
Ma and Pa Kettle at the Fair (1952) 286
Ma and Pa Kettle at Waikiki (1955) 111, 286
Ma and Pa Kettle on Vacation (1953) 417
Mack, Al 43
Mackenzie's Raiders (TV) 106
Magers, Boyd 238, 243, 374
The Magic Flute (opera) 48
The Magnetic Monster (1953) 104, 105, 119, 135, 141
Magnificent Obsession (1954) 107
Mahoney, Jock 421
Maiden, Cecil 312, 343
Make Like a Thief (1964) 321
Mallon, Jim 259
Malone, William 140, 417
Man Against Crime (TV) 419
Man and Superman (stage) 19
The Man from Bitter Ridge (1955) 298, 361, 376, 400, 405, 421
Man from Interpol (TV) 14
The Man from Planet X (1951) 90, 101, 134, 139, 162, 163
The Man from the Alamo (1953) 36, 414
The Man from U.N.C.L.E. (TV) 372, ***372***
The Man from U.N.C.L.E. Book (book) 372
Man in Space (1955) 258
Man in the Dark (1953) 141
Man in the Shadow (1957) 160
Man Made Monster (1941) 97, 142, 233
Man of a Thousand Faces (1957) 264
The Man Who Killed Lincoln (stage) 60
The Man Who Pursued Rosebud: William Alland on His Career in Theatre and Film (2010) 187, 245
The Man with No Name (1977) 383
Man Without a Star (1955) 421
Mancini, Henry ***37***, 39, 40, 41, 42, 45, 116, 151, 152, 155, 156, 157, 158, 159, 160, 161, 163, 199, 200, 201, 202, 203, 206, 242, 265, 266, 272, 273, 274, 303, 304, 348, 398, ***399***, 400, 402, 403, 404, 405, 406, 420
"Mancini in Surround" (CD) 405
Mandel, Howie 15
Mandell, Paul 130
Mann, Johnny 286
Manners, Dorothy 312–13
Mantee, Paul 259
Marconi, Guglielmo 136
Mars Attacks the World (1938) 413
Marsh, Marian ***9***
Marsh, Tani ***189***
The Martian Chronicles (book) 91, 98
Martin, Mary 340
Martin, Strother 419
Mason, James 108
Mason, Sydney 296, 324
Massey, Raymond 27–28
Mathias, Bob 420
Matinee (1993) 275
Matinee Theater (TV) 372
"A Matter of Taste" (short story) 134, 141
Mature, Victor 71
Maury, Lou 348, 349, 350–51, ***351***, 352, 353, 354, 420
Maverick (TV) 320
Maxwell, Charles 41
Maxwell, Marilyn 312
May, Donald 229
Mayer, Louis B. 13
Mayne, Kathleen ***108***
The Maze (1953) 104
McCallum, David ***372***
McCarthy, Todd 259
McCormack, Eric 143
McCoy, Dixie 288, 293
McCracken, Joan 412
McGee, Mark 101, 105
McGraw, Charles 142
McGregor, Warren ***96***, ***119***, ***127***
McLeod, Clyde 69
McNabb, Charles 187, 289
McNally, Stephen 60–61, ***61***, ***62***, 64, 65–66, ***65***, ***66***, ***67***, 68, 69, 71, ***71***, ***74***, ***75***, 86, 87, ***87***, ***413***
Medina, Patricia 59, 60, 313
Medved, Harry 367
Medved, Michael 367
Meehan, John 314
Mel B 15
Men in White (stage) 110, 414
Men of the Fighting Lady (1954) 181
Mendelssohn, Felix 48
Mendoza, Harry 335
Menjou, Adolphe 412
Merck's Manual of Medicine (book) 379
The Mercury Theater on the Air (radio) 90, 138, 373
Mesa of Lost Women (1953) 391
Messuri, Anthony 110
Metty, Russell 340, 357, 358
Miles, Vera 324, 361
Milestone, Lewis 411, 412
Milland, Ray 244
Miller, Edwin 43
Miller, Kenny 119
Miller, Marvin 295
Missile to the Moon (1958) ***393***
Mr. Peabody and the Mermaid (1948) 200, 201, 416
Mister Roberts (stage) 105
Mr. Sardonicus (1961) 73
Mr. Terrific (1967) 414
Mistress Mine (stage) 13
Moffitt, Jack 420
The Mole People (1956) 38, 135, 255, 266, 268, 348, 367, 390
Molly see *The Goldbergs*
Monnot, Marguerite 43
The Monolith Monsters (1957) 142, 266, 377, 390
Monsoon (1952) 313
Monster from the Ocean Floor (1954) 114
The Monster Maker (1944) ***361***, 379
Monster on the Campus (1958) 41, 159, 269, 273
The Monster That Challenged the World (1957) 377, 389
Monsters from the Vault (magazine) 91
Monsters, Mutants and Heavenly Creatures (book) 248
Moonlight in Vermont (1943) 349
Moore, Cleo 395
Moore, Constance 249
Moorehead, Agnes 25
Moran, Jackie 249
More Than Beauty (book) 237
Moreno, Antonio 174–75, ***182***, 185, ***185***, ***188***, 192
Morgan, Ralph ***361***, 379
Morris, Howard 143
Morris, Wayne 421
Morrow, Jeff ***213***, 220–22, ***220***, 223, 226–28, ***227***, ***228***, 235, 236, 237, ***237***, 238, ***239***, ***241***, 245, 247, ***247***, 251, ***253***, 255, 256, 258–59, 260, 261, 277, ***277***, 278, 416
Morrow, Lissa 221, 227–28, 251
Mothra (1962) 398
Mozart, Wolfgang Amadeus 48, 83, 270
Mozert, Bruce 192
Mueller, Chris 177–78, 179
Muhl, Edward 118, 178, 194, 221, 329, 376, 386
Mullen, Virginia 117–18, ***117***, 414
The Mummy (1932) 5, 50, 205, 357
The Mummy's Ghost (1944) 419
The Mummy's Hand (1940) 82, 84
The Mummy's Tomb (1942) 417
Muni, Paul 413
Murphy, Audie 111, 323, 421
Murton, Jack 319
Mussallem, Wallace 293
Mutiny on the Bounty (1935) 10, 25
My Favorite Martian (TV) 153
My Life with Howard Hughes (book) 317, 319
Mystery Science Theater 3000 (TV) 259
Mystery Science Theater 3000: The Movie (1996) 259
Mystery Submarine (1950) 15

Naish, J. Carrol 379
Naked Alibi (1954) 402
The Naked Gun (1956) 370
Napier, Alan 22, 26, 412
Nash, Mike 175, 187
Nat "King" Cole and Russ Morgan and His Orchestra (1953) 146
Navasky, Victor 417
Neal, Erwin 335
Neal, Tom 109
Nebenzal, Harold 62
Nebenzal, Seymour 62
Negulesco, Jean 60
Nelson, Lori 130, 282, 285–86, ***286***, 291, 292, 294, 295, ***296***, ***297***, 297, 298, ***305***, 306, 307
Nelson, Robert 296
The Net see *Project M-7*
Neufeld, Erno 81
Never Fear (1950) 12
Newman, Joseph 218–19, 220, 226, 240, 241, 246–47, 255, 258, 415, 417
Newman, Kim 15
Newman, Paul 418
Nichols, Robert 158, ***212***, 233, 235, ***235***, 236
Night Gallery (TV) 107–08
Night Monster (1942) 64
Night of the Demon see *Curse of the Demon*
The Night of the Hunter (1955) 10, 11
Night Slaves (book) 143
Night Slaves (1970) 65, 143
Night Tide (1963) 343
Nims, Ernest 98–99, 126, 134, 173
1980 (unmade movie) 142
No Man Is an Island (1962) 323
Nocturne (1946) 6
North by Northwest (1959) 372
Not Just Batman's Butler (book) 22, 412
Not Wanted (1949) 12
Novak, Kim 162
Novarro, Ramon 174
Now Is the Time (1951) 146
Now, Voyager (1942) 109
Nuzzi, Nick ***37***

O'Brian, Hugh 100, 130, 320
O'Brien, Edmond 335
O'Brien, Margaret 10
O'Brien, Willis 361
O'Callaghan, Edward G. 219, 276
O'Connor, Una 254
Of Mice and Men (1939) 62, 67
The Old Dark House (1932) 4–5, 10, 27
Ômori, Seitarô 271
On the Good Ship Hollywood (book) 421
On the Waterfront (1954) 325
Ophüls, Max 61, 318, 418
Orbom, Eric 28, 51
Orphans of the Wild (TV) 323
Orsatti, Al 219
Orsatti, Ernie 219, 415
Orsatti, Frank 219
Orsatti, Victor 219, 415
The Outer Limits (TV) 107
Outside the Law (1956) 39
Owen, Tudor ***57***, 59, 69

Pace, Terry 91
Pack Up Your Troubles (1932) 376
Paget, Debra 68
Paiva, Nestor 174, ***182***, 185, ***185***, ***188***, 192, 293, 298, 305, 307, ***373***, 377, 378, 422
Pajama Tops (stage) 367, 369, ***369***
Pal, George 107, 134
Palmer, Gregg 174
Paluzzi, Luciana 414
Paranoiac (1963) 79
Pardon My Rhythm (1944) 353
Parigi, Robert 417
Parker, Eddie 14, 22, ***22***, ***361***, 378, 379, 380, ***380***, 407, 408, ***408***
Parsons, Louella O. 60, 75, 228, 329, 337, 340, 389
Parton, Regis 222–23, ***222***, 238,

240, ***241***, 242, ***242***, 243, ***243***, 244, ***253***, 257, ***257***, ***277***, 416
Pate, Michael 11–12, 16, ***17***, 19–22, ***19***, 27, ***29***, 50, 60, 62, 63, 64, ***64***, 66, ***66***, 71, 74, ***86***, 87, ***87***, 412, ***413***
Patrick, Milicent 137, 179, 194, 195, 196, 208, 256, 417
Patterson, Hank 377, 422
Payne, John 176
The Pearl of Death (1944) 44, 46, 84
Pearl of the South Pacific (1955) 230
Peege (1973) 108
The Perfect Vision (magazine) 415
Perry, Newton 175, 176
Perry Mason (TV) 258
"Pete Can Fix It" (story) 218
Peter Pan (stage) 55, 412
Peters, Jean 389
Peters, Ken 298
Petschnikoff, Sergei 179–80
Pevney, Joseph 6–7, 16, 17, 18, 19, 20, 21, 23, 25, 54, 298, 411, ***411***, 412
Peyton Place (TV) 107, 325
Phair, George E. 53, 90, 121, 175
Phantom from Space (1953) 139, 141, 147, 152
The Phantom of the Opera (1925) 56, 91
The Phantom of the Opera (1962) 79
Phantom of the Rue Morgue (1954) 195, 196, 197
The Phantom Planet (1961) 258
Philbin, Mary 113
Phillips, Mark 414
Phipps, William 10, 16, 27–28, 30, 110, 368, 411, 412, 414
Photon (magazine) 101, 105, 119
Piaf, Édith 43
Piccadilly (1929) 16
Pillow of Death (1945) 44, 45, 47, 82, 84
Pine, Howard 314, 340, 418
Pine, William H. 418
Pinner, Dick 114
Pinson, Allen 70, 71, 186, 336
Pittsburgh (1942) 265
Platt, Edward 334, 337
Playboy (magazine) 370
Playgirl (1954) 354
Poe, Edgar Allan 73
Popular Science (magazine) 245
Porchon, Tao 15, ***15***
Posse from Hell (1961) 275
Powell, Larry 233–34, 239, 416
Powell, Will 134
Power, Tyrone 59
Powers, Mala 312, 320
Powers, Pat 294
Pratt, James T. 178, 220, 312, 368
The President's Analyst (1967) 325
Presley, Elvis 11
Previn, Charles 40, 44, 81, 84
Price, Vincent 12, 30, 372
Prine, Andrew 143
The Private Life of Henry VIII (1933) 10, 16, 49, 66
Project Moon Base (1953) 152
Promise Her Anything (1965) 325
Psychic Killer (1975) 184
Psychotronic Video (magazine) 184, 376
The Purple Mask (1955) 29, 313

Quatermass 2 (1957) 143, 254–55
Quebec (1951) 107
Quinn, Anthony 419
The Raging Tide (1951) 82
The Raiders (1952) 54, 78, 118
Rainer, Luise 374
Rains, Claude 5
Ramsay, Clark 194, 195
Rancho Notorious (1952) 111
Rand, Edwin ***373***, 422
Randolph, Donald 174
Rapp, Max ***37***, 81
Rathbone, Basil 63
The Raven (1935) 6, 24, 29, 366, 411
The Raven (unmade 1938 movie) 411
Raw Edge (1956) 421
The Rawhide Years (1956) 265
The Razor's Edge (1946) 55
Readick, Frank 138
Reason, Rex 174, ***212***, ***216***, 220, 221, 223, ***224***, 227, 229–30, ***229***, 233–34, ***234***, 235, ***235***, 236, ***236***, ***237***, 238, 239, ***239***, 240, 241, ***241***, 243, ***243***, 244, 247, ***247***, ***248***, ***249***, ***253***, 255, 258–59, 261, 262, 278, 312, 416, 417
Reason, Rhodes 229, 234
The Rebel (TV) 244
Rebel Without a Cause (1955) 337
Rebello, Stephen 144
Reckless Age (1944) 322
The Red Badge of Courage (1951) 323
The Red House (1947) 152
The Redhead from Wyoming (1953) 200, 304, 406–07
Redwing, Rodd 190, 191, 192
Reemes, Dana M. 115, 144, 246
Reiner, Joe 286
The Reptile (1966) 343–44
Requiem for a Gunfighter (1965) 60
Respighi, Ottorino 45
Revenge of the Creature (1955) 39, 154, 163, 187, 202, 257, 258, 279–308, ***279***, ***282***, ***283***, ***284***, ***287***, ***290***, ***292***, ***293***, ***294***, ***296***, ***297***, ***298***, ***299***, ***300***, ***302***, ***305***, ***306***, ***307***, 342, 344, 345, ***345***, 346, 347, 352–53, 361, 363, 367, 380, 400, 409, 410
Reynolds, Blake ***47***
Reynolds, Burt 286
Reynolds, William 310–11, 312, ***315***, 321, 326, ***328***, 329, 331, 332, ***332***, 334, 335, 339, 341, 418, ***420***
Rhodes, Gary D. 75
Rhubarb (1951) 270
Rice, Grantland 176
Richmond, Kane 389
Richmond, Ted 13, 19
Richter, Francis 45
Ride Clear of Diablo (1954) 200, 400
Riders to the Stars (1954) 104
Riedel, Richard H. 276, 277
Riley, Bruce 25
Road House (1948) 324
The Road to Mandalay (1926) 68
The Roaring 20s (TV) 229
Robby the Robot 417
The Robe (1953) 131, 220, ***220***, 226, 416
Roberson, Chuck 241, 417
Robert Montgomery Presents (TV) 110
Roberts, Glen *see* Freeman, Leonard
Robertson, Dale 12, 421
Robinson, Edward G. 130, ***130***, 324
Robinson, George ***375***, 409, 410
Rocketship X-M (1950) 101, 152
Rockwell, Robert 422
The Rocky Horror Picture Show (1975) 395
Rocky Marciano, Champion vs. Jersey Joe Walcott, Challenger (1953) 146
Roemheld, Heinz 39, 41, 265
Rogers, Jean ***248***
Rogues' Regiment (1948) 82, 83
Rolfe, Guy 73
Rolfe, Sam 91
Romeo and Juliet (1936) 55
Roseanna McCoy (1949) 323
Rosen, Milton 37, ***37***, 39, 42, 81, 85, 151, 199, 202, 303, 353, 354–55, 399, 400
Rosenberg, Aaron 134, 142
Rosenstein, Sophie 285
Rosner, Milt 362
Ross, Arthur 97, 168, 169, 170, 171, 194, 206
Roten, Ethmer ***46***, ***47***
Rózsa, Miklós 36, 47, 82
Rubin, Angie 325
Rubin, Stanley 325
Rubio, Eduardo 135
Running Wild (1955) 386, 395, 396, 397
Rush, Barbara ***98***, 99, 100, 101, ***101***, 106–09, ***107***, ***108***, 113, ***113***, 114–16, ***115***, ***117***, ***118***, 119, 120, 123, ***123***, 124, ***124***, 127, 128, 129, ***129***, 130, ***131***, ***133***, ***135***, 138, 158, 162, ***162***, 163, 228, 320, 414, 415
Russell, Bing 342, 377
Russell, Gail 107
Russell, Jane 317, 318
Russell, Kurt 342

Sackheim, Jerry 6, 53, 64, 411, 412
The Saga of Hemp Brown (1958) 265
The Saga of the Viking Women and Their Voyage to the Waters of the Great Sea Serpent (1957) 119
Sagal, Boris 415
Sagan, Carl 218
St. Oegger, Joan 412
Saleh, Dennis 195
Sally and Saint Anne (1952) 74, 116, 158, 324
Salter, Hans J. 36, 39, 40, 44, ***44***, 45, 46, 47, 48, 81–82, 83, 84, 85, 199, 200, 201, 202, 203, 204, 206, 265, 266, 272, 273–74, 274, 275, 303, 304, 420
Sands of Iwo Jima (1949) 366–67
Sanford, Joseph G. *see* Gershenson, Joseph
Santa Fe Passage (1955) 328
Satellite in the Sky (1956) 258
The Saturday Evening Post (magazine) 91
Sauers, Patty 122
Sawtell, Paul 36, 39, 40, 44, 46, 84, 85, 154
Sawyer, Joe ***93***, 101, ***103***, 114, 116, ***121***, 121–22, ***122***, 123, 124, 127, ***137***, 144, 163
Saxon, John 312
Sayer, Jay 119
The Scarlet Claw (1944) 44
Scarlet Street (1945) 45
Schallert, Edwin 99, 119, 281
Schallert, William 162
Scharf, Walter 36
Scheuer Philip K. 219, 340
Schwartz, Sid 97
Schwarzwald, Milton 40, 355
Science Fiction Gold: Film Classics of the 50s (book) 195
Science Fiction Theatre (TV) 361–62, 386, 388, 418, 422
Scorpion (1986) 374
Screem (magazine) 149
Scripts from the Crypt: Dracula's Daughter (book) 75
Scrivani, Rich 395
The Search for Bridey Murphy (1956) 119
The Searchers (1956) 326
Secret Beyond the Door... (1947) 47
Secret of the Chateau (1934) 73
Secret of Treasure Mountain (1956) 416
Selk, George ***119***
Selph, Gloria 290
Sennett, Mack 419
Serling, Rod 414, 418
The Seven Year Itch (stage) 12
77 Sunset Strip (TV) 320, 321
Shadow of a Doubt (1943) 107, 109
Shakedown (1950) 7
Shane, Sara 319
Shaw, Frank 380
Shaw, George Bernard 19
The She-Creature (1956) 231
She-Wolf of London (1946) 44–45
She Wore a Yellow Ribbon (1949) 367
Shearer, Norma ***49***
"The Shroud of Secrecy" (story) 211
The Sign of the Cross (1932) 23, 25
Sign of the Pagan (1954) 179, 265, 416
The Silent World (book) 169
Simmons, Richard Alan 298
Simon, Simone ***311***, 356
Simonelli, Charles 194, 195
Sinatra, Frank 108
Singer, Kurt 412
"The Sire de Malétroit's Door" (story) 5–6, 28, 59, 411
Sirk, Douglas 54, 107, 151, 331
Six Bridges to Cross (1955) 400, 402, 403, 405, 406
Skal, David J. 130
Skinner, Frank 36, 37, 39, 40, 44, 45, 46, 47, 48, 80, 81, 82, 83, 84, 265, 303
Skotak, Robert 219, 220, 220, 223, 237, 243, 246, 247, 256, 322, 384, 416, 417
Sky King (TV) 379
The Sleeping City (1950) 82
Smith, Art ***47***
Smoke Signal (1955) 262, 400, 404
Smuggler's Island (1951) 85
The Snake Woman (1961) 343
The Snow Creature (1954) 141
Snow White and the Seven Dwarfs (1937) 356
Snyder, William E. 204, 205, 206
Sohl, Jerry 143
Soho Incident (1956) 318
Soldo, Chris 334
Something for Nothing (stage) 97
Son of Ali Baba (1952) 335
The Son of Dr. Jekyll (1951) 29, 31, 32, 33
Son of Dracula (1943) 81, 342
Son of Frankenstein (1939) 50, 330, 376, 410
The Son of Kong (1933) 304

Son of Sinbad (1955) 12, ***13***
Southwest Passage (1954) 171
The Space Children (1958) 395
Space Island (unmade movie) 134
Spaceways (1953) 147
Spartacus (1960) ***11***
Spellbound (1945) 152, 408
Spencer, Douglas 244, ***244***, 245, ***249***, 256, 278
Spiegel, Sam 325
Spielberg, Steven 144, 206, 258
Spooks! (1953) 146, 197
Springfield Rifle (1952) 67
Sssssss (1973) 419
The Stand at Apache River (1953) 99
Stanfeld, Draw 331
Stanley, Ginger ***176***, 184, 190, 192, 205, 207, 288, 289, ***289***, 294, 295
Stapley, Richard 7, ***12***, 13–14, ***14***, 15, ***15***, 16, 18, ***18***, 19, 20, 22, ***22***, 24, 26, ***26***, 27, 28, 29, ***35***, 50, 87, 411, 412
Star in the Dust (1956) 421
Star Trek (TV) 13, 111
Star Wars (1977) 276
Starlog (magazine) 54, 67, 91, 130, 260
Starring Norma Desmond (stage) 14, 411
Stauffer, Teddy 318
Steele, Karen 422
Steele, Tom 26
Stein, Herman 38, 39, ***39***, 40, 41, 45, 48, 152, 153, 154, 155, 156, 157, 158, 160, 161, 163, 199, 200, 201, 202, 203, ***203***, 204, 206, 265, 266, 267, 268, 269, 270, 271, 272, 273, 274, 275, 302, 303, 304, 348, 399, ***399***, 400, 401, 402, 403, 404, 405, 406, 407, 408
Step Down to Terror (1958) 41, 109
Sterling, Jack 381
Stern, Howard 15
The Steve Allen Show (TV) 14
Stevens, Greg 344
Stevens, Leith 265
Stevenson, Robert Louis 5, ***5***, 20, 27, 28, 30, 32, 33, 48, 411
Stine, Clifford 150, 162, 276
Stoll, Frieda 69
Stone, Andrew L. 389
Stone, Ezra 373
Stone, Virginia 389
Storm Over Tibet (1952) 221, 229, 417
Storm Warning (1950) 373
The Story of Molly X (1949) 109
Strange, Glenn 63
The Strange Door (1951) 3–51, ***3***, ***4***, ***6***, ***7***, ***8***, ***9***, ***12***, ***14***, ***15***, ***17***, ***18***, ***19***, ***21***, ***22***, ***23***, ***24***, ***26***, ***28***, ***29***, ***31***, ***35***, ***49***, ***50***, ***51***, 53, 54, 55, 57, 59, 63, 64, 66, 67, 68, 71, 72, 73, 74, 75, 76, 78, 79, 80, 81, 82, 85, 86, 87, 161, 356, 411–12, ***411***
A Stranger in My Arms (1959) 39
Strimpell, Stephen 414
"String Quintet in E" 48
Strong, Susan 13, 19
Strong, Leonard ***315***, 335–36, 337, 343
Stumar, Charles 205
Sturges, Preston 318, 418
"The Suicide Club" (story) 28
"The Suicide Club" (unmade movie) 28
Sullivan, Liam 313
Sunset Blvd. (1950) 14
Sutton, Grady 389
Svengali (1931) 68
Swanson, Gloria 14, 411
Swanson, Ruth 389
Swanson on Sunset (stage) 411
Sweeney, Alfred 86, 413
Swires, Steve 51, 67, 369
Swisher, Viola 48
Sword of Sherwood Forest (1960) 59
Szalay, Jeff 91
Szold, Bernard 70

Take One (magazine) 415
A Tale of Two Cities (1935) 73
Tales from the Crypt (1972) 60
Tales of Tomorrow (TV) 254
The Tall Lie see *For Men Only*
The Tall Target (1951) 323
Talton, Alix 389
Tamkin, Alex 45
Tamkin, David ***37***, 41, 45, ***45***, 82, 200, 267, 271
Tanganyika (1954) 402, 403
Tangier (1946) 85
Tanner, Paul 153
Tap Roots (1948) 240
Tarantula (1955) 114, 139, 154, 157, 242, 266, 269, 270, 273, 274, 341, 359–410, ***359***, ***361***, ***363***, ***365***, ***366***, ***367***, ***368***, ***371***, ***373***, ***375***, ***376***, ***378***, ***379***, ***380***, ***381***, ***382***, ***383***, ***385***, ***386***, ***387***, ***388***, ***389***, ***391***, ***392***, ***396***, ***397***, ***407***, ***408***, ***410***, 416, 420–22
Tarantula (unmade Andrew Stone movie) 389
Target: The Corruptors (TV) 60
Tarzan's Magic Fountain (1949) 109
Tarzan's Secret Treasure (1941) 175
Taylor, Al 219, 226, 382, 420
Taylor, Robert 312, 313
Taza, Son of Cochise (1954) 107, 151, 221, 233, 236
Teen-Age Crime Wave (1955) 397
Temple, Shirley 366, 367, 421
Ten Tall Men (1951) 21
Tesla, Nikola 136
Test Pilot (TV pilot) 368–69
Tewes, Lauren 143
Theatre '59 (TV) 109
Them! (1954) 195, 266, 360–61, 364, 380, 384, 388–89, 390, 392, 394, 407, 409–10, 422
"Themes from Horror Movies" (record album) 155, 272, 275, 399
There's Always Tomorrow (1956) 265
They Came from Outer Space: 12 Classic Science Fiction Tales That Became Major Motion Pictures (book) 92, 218
They Live by Night (1948) 68
The Thief of Bagdad (1940) 407
Thiess, Ursula 312, 313, ***313***, 314, 418
The Thing from Another World (1951) 11, 90, 101, 139, 152, 161, 162, 163, 244, 265, 266, 278
The Thing That Couldn't Die (1958) 157, 271
This Is My Love (1954) 318
This Is the Army (1943) 373
This Is the Army (stage) 373
This Island Earth (MagicImage book) 219, 220, 223
This Island Earth (1955) 38, 83, 111, 126, 139, 142, 194, 209–78, ***209***, ***212***, ***213***, ***215***, ***216***, ***220***, ***221***, ***222***, ***224***, ***225***, ***231***, ***234***, ***235***, ***236***, ***237***, ***239***, ***241***, ***242***, ***243***, ***244***, ***245***, ***246***, ***247***, ***248***, ***249***, ***250***, ***252***, ***253***, ***256***, ***261***, ***277***, 301, 328, 393, 399, 400, 402, 404, 405–06
This Island Earth (Raymond F. Jones book) 211–18, 219, 226, 251, 252, 254, 255, 258, 269, 415–17
This Island Earth: 2 1/2 Years in the Making (2013) 237, 255
This Love of Ours (1945) 47, 81
Thomas, Bob 55, 90, 101, 104, 105, 117, 194, 222, 247, 286, 416
Thomas, Tony 275
Thomas, William C. 418
Thompson, Marshall 310, 313, ***315***, 320, 321, 322–23, ***322***, ***323***, 326, 328, 329, ***329***, ***332***, ***337***, 339, 341, 343, 357, ***358***, ***419***, ***420***
Three Bad Sisters (1956) 325
The Three Stooges 394
Thriller (TV) 50, 65, 106
Thrilling Wonder Stories (magazine) 210, ***211***, 218
Thunder Bay (1953) 131
Thunder on the Hill (1951) 47, 48, 82
The Time of Their Lives (1946) 37, 355
The Time Tunnel (TV) 71, 374
Timpone, Tony 74, 259, 413
Tinney, Robert Lee "Sonny" 288, 289
Tiomkin, Dimitri 45, 152, 163, 265, 389
To Hell and Back (1955) 341
Toast of the Town (TV) 338
Tobey, Kenneth 244
Tobor the Great (1954) 109, ***109***
Toch, Ernst 154
Tom Corbett, Space Cadet (TV) 123
Tomahawk (1951) 203
Tomei, Louis 241, 417
Tomorrow Is Forever (1946) 319
Topper (TV) 372
Tormented (1960) ***106***
Tors, Ivan 105, 420
"Touched with Fire" (short story) 138
Towne, Aline 422
Tramp (dog) 413
The Treasure of Lost Canyon (1952) 33, 118
The Treasure of the Sierra Madre (1948) 373
Trouble for Two (1936) 28
Trumbo (2015) 228
Tucker, Forrest 176
Turner, Don 14, 16, 22, 24, 26, 29
Turner, Lana 421
Tutankhamun 417
12 to the Moon (1960) 258
20,000 Leagues Under the Sea (1954) 258
The Twilight Zone (TV) 87, 336
Twists of Fate—An Oscar Winner's International Career (book) 340, 420

Underwater! (1955) 286
The Unexpected (TV) 367
The United States Steel Hour (TV) 226–27, 418
Universal Horrors (book) 1
The Universe According to Universal (2002) 130, 131
The Unknown Terror (1957) 421
Unmasked: A Memoir (book) 108
Untamed Frontier (1952) 203, 418

Valentine, Nancy 65, ***65***, 87
Valenca, Lizalotta 237
Valley of the Dolls (1967) 109
Van Doren, Mamie 130, ***286***, 370, 386
Van Sickel, Dale 115
van Vogt, A.E. 13
Vargas, Alberto 421
Vath, Richard 369
Vaughn, James T. 178
Vaughn, Robert ***372***
Vendetta (1950) 318, 329
Vertigo (1958) 162
Video Watchdog (magazine) 15, 250
VideoScope (magazine) 368
Vincent, Sailor 24–25
Viniello, Mark 260
The Virginian (TV) 374, 375
Voight, Jon 14
Volding, Louise 241
Voyage to the Bottom of the Sea (TV) 142, 259, 269, 391

Wade, Russell ***61***
Wade, Stuart ***376***, 377
Waldis, Otto ***66***, 412
The Walking Dead (1936) 121
Wallis, Hal B. 13
Walston, Ray 414
Walthall, Henry B. 390–91
War Arrow (1953) 419
The War of the Worlds (book) 90
The War of the Worlds (1953) 134, 163, 276
"The War of the Worlds" (radio episode) 90, 115, 138, 373, 413
Ward, Edward 36, 40, 44
Warde, Anthony 249
The Wasp Woman (1959) 398
Watson, Richard O. 290
Waxman, Stanley 118
Wayne, John 366–67, 421
Weatherwax, Paul 126
The Web (1947) 45, 81, 82
"Wedding March" (music) 48
Weinberg, Roger J. 177
Weiner, M.W. 112
Weird Tales (magazine) 91
Weissmuller, Johnny 175, 390
Welbourne, "Scotty" 176–77, 178, 180, 181, 185, 186, 187, 188, 189, 204, 205, 206, 281, 282, 287, 289, 306, 307
Weldon, Joan 390
Weller, Sam 91
Welles, Orson 61, 90, 115, 166, 177, 373
Wells, Dawn 112
Wells, H.G. 90, 387
WereWolf of London (1935) 356, 419
The Werewolf of Paris (book) 24
The Werewolf of Paris (unmade movie) 24
West, Mae 71
Western Clippings (magazine) 60, 322, 374
Westmore, Bud 177, 179, 194, 195, 222, ***222***, 416, 417
Westmore, Frank 177
The Westmores of Hollywood (book) 177
Whale, James 27

What a Picnic! (1945) 176
Whatever Became of...? (book) 110
When Worlds Collide (1951) 99, 107, 258
Where Danger Lives (1950) 318, 329, 341
While the City Sleeps (1956) 12
Whisper (magazine) 393
White Cargo (1942) 105
White Heat (1949) 335
White Woman (1933) 25
Whitsell, Bob 153
Whorf, Richard 322
Whyte, Patrick 19
Wichman, Craig 395
Widmark, Richard 219
The Wild Wild West (TV) 140
Wilde, Janet 261, ***261***
Wilder, Billy 11
Wilder, W. Lee 141
Wilkinson, June 367, 369, ***369***
Williams, Cindy 258
Williams, John 199
Williams, Larry 336, 338
Williams, Robert B. 236, 293, ***293***, 294, 298, 307
Willock, Dave 113, ***162***, 307
Wilson, Earl 330
Wilson, Stanley 348, 349, 350, 351, 352, 354, 356
Winchester '73 (1950) 60
Wings of the Hawk (1953) 145, 150, 151, 414
Winters, Shelley 119, 411
With These Hands (1950) **99**, 100
Witness for the Prosecution (1957) 11
The Wolf Man (1941) 81, 120, 141, 200, 203, 356
Wolfe, Bud 376
Wolfe, Thomas 19
A Woman of Independent Means (stage) 108, 414
Woman on the Run (1950) 373
Women of the Prehistoric Planet (1966) 275
The Wonders of Wakulla Springs (19??) 176
Wood, Ed 231
Wood, Jeane 121
Wood, Sam 121
Woodruff, Tom 259–60, ***260***
Woodworth, William 123
Woolery, Shirley 290
Wooster, Jane 389
The World in His Arms (1952) 36, 179
World of Giants (TV) 323, 418
Wray, Fay 205
Wyatt, Al 115
Wyler, Richard *see* Stapley, Richard
Wyman, Jane 60, 108
Wynorski, Jim 218
Wynter, Dana 162

A Yank in Viet-Nam (1964) 323
Yankee Buccaneer (1952) 48
Yankee Pasha (1954) 221
The Yearling (1946) 230
The Yellow Mountain (1954) 404, 406
You Can't Cheat an Honest Man (1939) 302
You Never Can Tell (1951) 109
Young, Collier 12
Young Widow (1946) 318
Your Show Time (TV) 27
You're a Sweetheart (1937) 354

Zacherle, John 394–95, 422
Zacherley *see* Zacherle, John
Zanuck, Darryl F. 58
Zeisl, Eric 36, 45, 265
Zendar, Fred 192
Zimm, Maurice 167, 168–69, 170, 177, 281
Zombies of the Stratosphere (1952) 118